forgiving
yourself

FORGIVING YOURSELF

Why You Must, How You Can

Robert H. Lauer & Jeanette C. Lauer

THE PILGRIM PRESS

CLEVELAND

TO

Jon, Kathy, Julie, Jeffrey,

Kate, Jeff, Krista, Benjamin, David,

and John Robert

AS ALWAYS

The Pilgrim Press, 700 Prospect Avenue, Cleveland, Ohio 44115
thepilgrimpress.com
© 2010 by Robert H. Lauer

Scripture quotations, unless otherwise noted, are from the New Revised
Standard Version of the Bible, © 1989 by the Division of Christian
Education of the National Council of Churches of Christ in the United
States of America, and are used by permission. Changes have been made
for inclusivity.

Printed in the United States of America on acid-free paper

14   13   12   11   10   5   4   3   2   1

Library of Congress Cataloging-in-Publication Data

Lauer, Robert H.
    Forgiving yourself : why you must, how you can / Robert H. Lauer
and Jeanette C. Lauer.
      p. cm.
    ISBN 978-0-8298-1841-3 (alk. paper)
    1. Forgiveness—Religious aspects—Christianity.   2. Self-acceptance
—Religious aspects—Christianity.   I. Lauer, Jeanette C.   II. Title.
BV4647.F55L39 2010
241'.4—dc22   2009035090

CONTENTS

Preface

We love the old tale about the hound dog that took up residence in Slim Jones's country store. The dog howled continuously with that wailing sound unique to hounds. A man traveling through town stopped by the store and was unsettled by the howling dog. He asked the clerk what was the matter with the dog. "Oh," said the clerk, "he's all right. He's just sitting on a cocklebur." "So why doesn't he get off?" asked the stranger. The clerk shrugged, "He'd rather holler."

Stories are designed to make a point about people. In this case, the point is that many people deal with a painful situation in a counterproductive way—like when you need to forgive yourself. Indeed, we have known people who sat on a cocklebur of guilt and self-deprecation for years because of something they once did or failed to do. Some tried to forgive themselves but stopped trying when they didn't achieve immediate results. Some simply didn't know where to begin and so did nothing. Others believed that they deserved to keep on suffering and so did nothing. Still others assumed that the passage of time would heal their pain and were still waiting for the elusive healing to occur. But, happily, we have also worked with those who have undertaken the work of self-forgiveness and have stuck with it until they were free.

It is the frequency with which we have encountered such experiences that led us to write this book. It is our prayer that it will enable that surprisingly large number of people who find it harder to forgive themselves than to forgive others to engage successfully in the process of self-forgiveness and to experience the resulting emotional and spiritual healing that God intends for all of us.

We are grateful to all those who shared their stories with us or who invited us to help them as they undertook the journey of self-forgiveness. We have changed the names and details of the stories in order to protect their anonymity. But they can know that they are now a part of helping others to engage in that same liberating process of self-forgiveness.

PART I

why you must

*"You shall love your
neighbor as yourself"*

—Matthew 22:39

Introduction

Forgiving Yourself—
The Myths and the Reality

She was clearly distressed. "I want to sign up for your seminar on forgiveness," she told us. "But I'm not sure it will help me." We assured her that we've worked with many people who believed that they couldn't forgive another person for some deep hurt. However, with a better understanding of what it means to forgive along with determined effort, they finally experienced the healing freedom of forgiveness. "Oh," she responded, "I don't have trouble forgiving someone who has hurt me. What I can't do is forgive myself for some of the things I've done. Past mistakes keep eating at me. They torment me. And I don't know what to do."

We've heard it over and again: Forgiving yourself can be the most difficult kind of forgiveness to practice. Yet, *not* forgiving yourself can be corrosive to your well-being. In fact, self-forgiveness is the natural corollary to God's forgiveness. Both, as we discuss in the next chapter, are essential to your personal health as well as the health of your relationships.

You begin with God's forgiveness, which comes to all of us freely through confession. "If we confess our sins, he who is faithful and just will forgive us our sins and cleanse us from all unrighteousness" (1 John 1:9). For some Christians, however, even God's forgiveness doesn't clear the path to self-forgiveness. As a man struggling with an act of infidelity told us: "I *do* believe that God has forgiven me. But I still can't forgive myself. I would do anything in the world if I hadn't been unfaithful to my wife. But I was. And I can't stop feeling guilty." Why is it so hard to practice self-forgiveness?

I HATE WHAT I'VE DONE

We all say and do things that we regret. Sometimes it goes beyond that. Sometimes the very thought of what you have done causes you anguish or even revulsion. It haunts you. And you hate yourself for what you have done. This is the way our friend Maggie put it: "Until I angrily blurted out to my mother that she was interfering with my life, I never thought I could be so cruel. The hurt look on her face will stay with me as long as I live. I just hate what I did to her." Maggie still struggles to forgive herself for her hurtful words.

In our experience, such an intense reaction is especially likely in three situations. First, it can happen when you've hurt someone close to you. For Mark, it was an incident with his wife. "Sandi and I have been married for thirteen years, and it's a good marriage. She is the most considerate and sensitive and loving person I've ever known." He paused, then, told us:

It happened about six years ago. Her parents had a fourth of July party. I didn't want to go. It was mostly her parents' friends who were coming. I thought we should stay home with our son, maybe have a few friends over for a cookout, and shoot off some fireworks. But she convinced our son that several of his cousins would be there, so he wanted to go too. This really made me mad. I steamed all the way there. I knew she thought I'd be okay once we arrived. But I was determined this wasn't going to happen. I stalked around the yard in an obvious snit while she chatted with an old school chum. She caught my eye, and I just made an ugly face at her. It was my way of telling her off. She knew it. I saw her mumble something to her friend, drop her head, and walk quickly into the house. I found her inside, crying. How could I have done that to her? She'd never treated me that way. I felt terrible and apologized for my behavior. But I still fret about the way I treated her.

Sandi forgave Mark quickly and may not, by this point, even remember the incident. For Mark, however, it lives on as a painful memory, a blemish on his efforts to be a loving husband.

A second situation is when you fall short of your own ideals. Mark, of course, illustrates this point; in fact, whenever you hurt someone else, you fall short of your ideal as a Christian. Yet you can even fall short when you haven't hurt another person. Perhaps your ideal involved being an effective leader in your church, but you found yourself frustratingly ineffective when you accepted a position of responsibility. Perhaps your ideal involved teaching and being a model for young people, but your tendency to be caustic in what you say greatly diminished the impact you had on their lives. Or perhaps you've had an experience like Sharon—forty-five years old and self-employed. Much of Sharon's work is done at the computer and, because she's a "night owl," she frequently works late at night when the rest of the family is in bed. One night, out of curiosity, she entered a chat room to see what kinds of things people talked about. Here's her account:

I found a lot of the stuff to be boring. I was about to sign off when I noticed an intriguing comment from a man. I thought he made a good point, so I responded. Well, we began to correspond. We went from the chat room to instant messaging, and from harmless comments to increasingly personal matters. I started to feel uncomfortable, but I was hooked. As we revealed more about ourselves, he started flirting with me. I was flattered. He knew my age and the fact that I had children, but he seemed quite taken with me. Our messages became more and more erotic, and I felt more and more like I was having something close to an affair!

I love my husband. I would never cheat on him. But I found my cyber lover strangely exciting. Until I woke up one morning after a hot correspondence, looked at my husband, and remembered him telling me just a few hours earlier how much he loved me. I thought to myself: "I've betrayed you in my words and my thoughts. God help me. How did it happen?" That was a year ago, and I still haven't come to terms with it. I'm ashamed to tell my husband what I was doing. I've asked God to forgive me. But I still feel guilty. What can I do?

The third situation in which people find it hard to forgive themselves is when they've been severely hurt and didn't take the necessary steps more quickly to stop the hurt. This can happen, for example, to someone in an abusive relationship. It's not uncommon for a victim to look back and say, in effect, "I hate the fact that I let it go on so long. I was beaten physically, emotionally, and spiritually. And now I'm beating myself up for not getting out of it sooner."

It can also happen in other kinds of situations. Carrie, in her thirties, worked nine years for a man who tyrannized his employees. Every employee who had worked for him for any length of time had been, or had seen someone be, publicly humiliated and berated. It happened to employees who made mistakes. Or to those who weren't as productive as the boss thought they should be. Or to those who didn't produce the kind of work that the boss considered high quality. Or even to those who said something that the boss found (often for reasons unfathomable to everyone else) irritating.

Carrie endured the situation for nine years before giving notice. It bothered her to be the victim, but it also bothered her to see her colleagues get the boss's tongue-lashing. She was stressed to the point where she became ill. Her doctor diagnosed her problem as "a clear case of too much stress." She must, he told her, do something about her job situation. Carrie took the only option she could—she found another job. She got a final tongue-lashing when she told her boss she was leaving in two weeks. After six months at her new job, she is relieved and happy—except for one thing. She periodically accuses herself of being "too weak" to make the change sooner. "I'm basically happy now, but sometimes I despise myself for letting that man abuse me for so many years. How do I get over that?"

Mark, Sharon, and Carrie illustrate the kinds of situations that give birth to long-term anguish. And they raise the questions that we have heard repeatedly. How do you get over it? How do you deal with it? What can you do? Beginning with chapter 2, we will discuss in detail the answer to these questions. Here we want to make two points. First, we know by experience that you *can* find satisfactory answers to the questions; you *can* experience the liberation of forgiving yourself. Second, before looking at specific techniques, you need to be free of some common myths about self-forgiveness.

WHAT FORGIVING YOURSELF IS, AND WHAT IT ISN'T

Self-forgiveness often isn't easy. If you accept any of the false notions about self-forgiveness (what we call the myths), it becomes even more difficult or even impossible. It becomes the spiritual equivalent of doing a one-arm handstand. So let's begin by being clear about what self-forgiveness is not, as well as what it is.

What Self-Forgiveness Isn't: The Myths

There are three common but wrong ideas, or myths, about the meaning of self-forgiveness. The first is that self-forgiveness is mainly a way to let yourself off the hook. Mark accepted this myth. As he put it:

> How can I forgive myself? That wasn't the only time I upset Sandi or made her cry with my anger. I have more control now than I did then, so it happens less frequently.

But it did happen. And it happened more than once. I can't just pretend it never happened by forgiving myself. I was wrong to act that way. I'm not going to make it worse by easily letting myself off the hook.

Mark had fallen into the common trap of thinking about his behavior in terms of the following sequence:

1. I behaved badly, in a way unworthy of a Christian.
2. I deserve to be punished for such behavior.
3. I must, therefore, continue to punish myself with guilt and regret.

In Mark's thinking, practicing self-forgiveness would mean changing this sequence by substituting a different kind of behavior in step 3:

1. I behaved badly, in a way unworthy of a Christian.
2. I deserve to be punished for such behavior.
3. But I will let myself off the hook by forgiving myself and moving on.

But this is not the meaning of self-forgiveness. It is not simply a matter of declaring yourself pardoned and thinking no more about the offense. It doesn't let you off the hook. For one thing, as we will discuss in chapter 2, self-forgiveness requires you to make amends whenever possible. For another, forgiving yourself involves a good deal of work. You can't make the guilt vanish merely by stating your intention to forgive yourself.

As Mark came to realize, the sequence is more complex than the three steps just listed:

1. I behaved badly, in a way unworthy of a Christian.
2. I deserve to be punished for such behavior.
3. But I will ask for God's forgiveness.
4. And I will strive to forgive myself, taking all the steps necessary to be free of guilt.

We believe that you let yourself off the hook when you *don't* work at forgiving yourself. To be blunt, some Christians act as if it's easier to live with the guilt than to put forth the time and energy it takes to forgive themselves. Note that we say "act as if." We haven't met anyone who would actually admit to it. But we have met people who are reluctant or even unwilling to do the work of self-forgiveness. They opt to continue beating themselves up with regrets and guilt—which, as we discuss in chapter 1, is contrary to biblical teachings and examples.

A second myth is that you can't forgive yourself when you've hurt someone unless that person forgives you. Sharon had this notion:

> How can I forgive myself when I feel that I've betrayed my husband? I have a friend who told me that I was making too much of it. That it didn't lead to anything and it didn't hurt my marriage. But I can't think of it that way. It's not like I just forgot to kiss my husband good night. I wronged him. I betrayed his trust in me. I desperately need for him to forgive me. But I still can't bring myself to tell him about it. What will he think of me? How will it affect our marriage? I feel like no matter what I do, I'm doomed. If I don't tell him, I'll keep feeling guilty and unworthy. If I do tell him, it could wreck our marriage and our family, and I'd feel guilty about that.

You might ask two questions about Sharon's dilemma. One is: *Can* she forgive herself without first receiving her husband's forgiveness? The answer is yes. Being forgiven by someone you have hurt is a great help, but not an indispensable step, in forgiving yourself. But another question demands a response: *Should* she forgive herself without first receiving her husband's forgiveness? For some, the answer is clear: Of course not. Sharon, they would argue, must confess her behavior to her husband and seek his forgiveness. As we shall discuss in more detail in chapter 2, however, the answer to the second question is not always clear. Sharon is actually right in thinking that she is in the midst of a painful dilemma. Confessing to her husband could result in his forgiveness, might require a time of readjustment, and hopefully would result in the eventual resumption of their happy marriage. Her confession, however, could also leave a long-term or even permanent scar on their relationship and on their family.

In other words, if you face this kind of situation you should not quickly decide either to confess or not confess. It's a complex issue. It requires careful thought and prayer before you make a decision. Whatever you decide, and whatever happens, you can forgive yourself whether or not the other person has forgiven you.

The third myth is that forgiving yourself means that you trivialize your offense—that you minimize the seriousness of what you have done. Carrie, who let herself be tyrannized by her boss, struggles with this myth:

> To be honest, I can't forgive myself because what I did— or I guess I should say what I didn't do for so long—was so stupid and weak. I mean, I don't have any trouble forgiving myself for minor things like being late sending someone a birthday card or missing church once in a while. But this experience taught me that I have a major character flaw. I'm too willing to let others take advantage of me and abuse me. This could get me into really serious trouble again. I don't want to be that kind of person, but I guess I am. And I can't pretend it isn't important by just forgiving myself and forgetting all about it.

Carrie, incidentally, illustrates another problem with not forgiving yourself. She suffers from a lowered sense of her own worth and capability. She no longer regards herself as someone who is empowered by God's Spirit to deal effectively with any situation. She no longer lives as someone whose faith is the victory that overcomes the world. Carrie bears in her spirit the emotional and spiritual scars of failing to forgive herself.

She has failed to forgive herself because she believes that self-forgiveness would somehow lessen the seriousness of enduring the abuse for so many years. She thinks about her behavior in a different way from Mark and Sharon. Her sequence of thinking is:

1. I allowed someone to abuse me.

2. I am a weak, submissive person.

3. I will always be susceptible to others taking advantage of me.

If asked to practice self-forgiveness, her sequence adds an element:

1. I allowed someone to abuse me.

2. I am a weak, submissive person.

3. Self-forgiveness won't help, because this is a serious character flaw, not a minor problem.

4. Therefore, I will always be susceptible to others taking advantage of me.

Carrie needs to revise her notion of self-forgiveness and practice a different sequence, one that will free her from her lowered sense of worth:

1. I allowed someone to abuse me.

2. This was a serious wrong and should not be tolerated.

3. I am God's child, and God will enable me to resist abuse in the future.

4. I will strive to forgive myself for my lapse so that I can be free of self-hatred and be open to God's empowering presence in my life.

What Self-Forgiveness Is: The Reality

If self-forgiveness is not letting yourself off the hook or trivializing what you have done, what exactly is it? In brief, it is an act of love toward yourself. As such, it rids you of destructive and unwarranted anger and guilt and restores your sense of self-worth as a child of God. Perhaps the best way to describe it is in the terms shared with us by Joe:

> When you've lived as long as I have, believe me, there have been plenty of times when I've needed to forgive myself. It's hard to describe how important self-forgiveness is, and what it does for a person. Let me try to explain with an analogy. A few years ago, I was having problems with some of my joints. Every day was a struggle, dealing with the aches and pains and limitations on what I could and couldn't do.
>
> Then my doctor prescribed a new medication that he thought would help. I was hoping for instant healing. That didn't happen. But over a period of time, the aches and pains subsided. And one day, I suddenly realized that I was free of them. I could move without hurting. I could do things I hadn't been able to do for years. I was free! It was exhilarating! When I had my next visit with the doctor, he asked me whether the medication had helped. "Help?" I said. "It more than helped. I feel like I have a whole new life."
>
> What happened to me physically is what happens spiritually when I forgive myself. Of course I ask for God's forgiveness first. But then I go to work on affirming God's forgiveness by forgiving myself. It doesn't happen instantly. It takes a little time. But eventually I am free of the remorse I felt. It's like getting rid of the spiritual pain in your soul and enjoying the freedom of God's life. It really is exhilarating.

Joe's words should make you *want* to practice self-forgiveness. The next chapter will show you why you *must* practice it. In the remaining chapters, we'll show you *how* to practice it effectively.

The Imperative of Love

One of the delightful discoveries we've made in our Christian journey is a fuller understanding of John's observation: "And his commandments are not burdensome, for whatever is born of God conquers the world" (1 John 5:3–4). There have been times when we've thought otherwise. That loving an enemy was not as enjoyable as fantasizing about the enemy coming to grief. That forgiving others was not as soul satisfying as making them pay for their offenses. But we've come to realize that none of God's commands are burdensome, because they come not from a stern father laying down the rules but from a loving Father guiding us to an abundant life.

This is why we call this chapter the "imperative" of love. It's not an imperative in the sense that a scowling God demands it of us. It's an imperative because every cell in our being hungers for fulfillment—fulfillment that cries out for us to walk the path of love. For this is the way God has made us—we cannot be whole until we love and are loved.

A CONVERSATION WITH GOD

Let's go back to Mark, who can't forgive himself for mistreating his wife, Sandi. Imagine this conversation between Mark and God:

MARK: God, I can't forgive myself for what I've done to Sandi.

GOD: (Sigh)

MARK: It makes me squirm to hear you sigh, God. I, too, have sighed with regret. That's why I can't forgive myself. I don't deserve it.

GOD: Mark, you misinterpret my sigh. I do not groan for what you did, but for what you are now failing to do.

MARK: But how can I forgive myself? I simply don't deserve it.

GOD: (Sigh) And tell me, Mark, which of my blessings have you deserved? Have you merited everything I have done for you?

MARK: Uh, well, I guess not.

GOD: (Silence)

MARK: Oh, I get it. You forgive me even though I don't strictly deserve it.

GOD: And?

MARK: And . . . I'm supposed to do the same. But, God, I do that for others. That's different from doing it for myself.

GOD: So you can forgive others even though they don't deserve it, but you can only forgive yourself if you do deserve it?

MARK: I . . . I . . . don't think I understand. I sort of thought I was being a better Christian by not forgiving myself for what I've done.

GOD: Tell me, Mark. Would you willingly abuse a child?

MARK: (Relieved to apparently be off the subject of self-forgiveness). Of course not, God.

GOD: Why not?

MARK: Because I'm called to love people, not abuse them.

GOD: Good! Now spend some time thinking about why it's wrong to abuse someone else but okay to abuse yourself by not forgiving yourself, and why it's okay for you to keep on condemning that which I have forgiven.

If Mark had this conversation with God, it hopefully would be an "aha!" moment for him. For this imaginary conversation contains the biblical bases for self-forgiveness, which are rooted in the fact that love is an imperative of the Christian life. The two greatest commandments, as Jesus reminds us, are to love God and to love others as ourselves. And forgiveness—whether of others or of oneself—is an act of love.

The Greek word for "forgive" in the teachings of Jesus means to let go, give up, cancel, or pardon. In essence, then, to forgive is to let go of anger and resentment and to change the way you think about and behave towards the offender. This is what we do when we forgive others. We refuse to hang on to anger and resentment. We give up the desire to retaliate. We relinquish the right to punish the person for the offense. We are open to reconciliation. Clearly, such forgiveness is an act of love. And what we do when forgiving others is what we must do when we forgive ourselves—let go of negative thoughts and feelings about ourselves and accept ourselves for who we are, the beloved children of God. This is also an act of love.

Thus, if you refuse to forgive yourself because you don't believe you deserve it or because you don't think you can do it, you violate the imperative of love. Instead of loving yourself, you abuse yourself by nursing your anger, suffering from nagging guilt, and continually debasing yourself.

The imperative of love also means to accept God's love. One way in which God loves us is the offer to forgive us. When we are forgiven, it means that God wipes the slate clean. As Paul put it: "There is therefore now no condemnation for those who are in Christ Jesus" (Rom. 8:1). This raises a disturbing question for those who do not forgive themselves: How can you not forgive what God has forgiven? How can you continue to condemn that which God declares to be free of condemnation? If you do not forgive yourself, you reject God's loving forgiveness. If you do not forgive yourself, you are, in essence, attempting to overrule God by continuing to punish yourself.

Finally, the imperative of God's love is seen in the offer of abundant life. Jesus said that he came so that we might have abundant life (John 10:10). "Abundant" may even be too tame a translation of the Greek word. We think that Eugene Peterson captures the meaning well in *The Message*: "more and better life" than you ever dreamed of having. As we will show below, those who are unforgiving, whether of self or others or both, have a lower quality of life. In other words, when you don't forgive yourself, you are rejecting the abundance of life that God wills to give you. You thwart the imperative of God's love.

We don't mean to sound harsh here. Our purpose is not to punish those who don't forgive themselves. They're already sufficiently punishing themselves. Our purpose is to convince them that self-forgiveness is not only compatible with, but is required by, biblical teachings. It is, therefore, an essential element of the Christian life.

Of course, even if you accept this intellectually, you may struggle emotionally to forgive yourself. Or you may be perplexed as to how to go about forgiving yourself. The chapters that follow address these issues. In the remainder of this chapter, we look first at studies that show the troubling emotional and physical consequences of not forgiving yourself. Then we give two biblical examples and one contemporary case that illustrate how self-forgiveness brings healing, power, and fulfillment to God's children.

A CONVERSATION WITH A THERAPIST

As pointed out above, in addition to the detrimental spiritual consequences of not forgiving yourself, there are serious physical and emotional consequences. Some of these consequences emerged in a conversation we (L) had with a therapist friend (T):

L: Have you dealt with people who struggle because they can't seem to forgive themselves?

T: Oh, yes. I've had many clients who struggle with this problem, including a number of pastors and other church leaders.

L: What happens to people physically and emotionally when they don't forgive themselves?

T: It varies. But it's always detrimental. I've seen everything from gastrointestinal problems to chronic fatigue. Emotionally, the most common problems are anger, persistent guilt, and self-condemnation. And, for a lot of people, it also leads to depression.

L: What about the old idea that time heals all things? Won't some of these problems eventually subside or disappear?

T: Well, anything is possible. But you need to keep two things in mind. First, for some people the problem is not a particular incident that continues to vex them. It's a pattern of life—they keep doing things for which they condemn themselves, and every new thing only reinforces their notion that they're bad people. And second, for some when the problem is a particular incident, no amount of time seems to bring healing.

L: Even after many years?

T: Yes. Let me tell you about a patient I had some years ago. She was a middle-aged woman who was emotionally abused by her husband for the twenty-one years she was married to him. He also emotionally abused their two sons. She told me that she had only stayed in the marriage because her church taught that a woman should be submissive to her husband and wait on God to change his hurtful behavior.

So she tried to tough it out. But she kept having severe headaches, for which her doctors could find no physical cause. She also struggled with feelings of worthlessness and depression. She got to the point where she no longer cared if she lived or died. She prayed, in fact, for God to end her life. It wasn't until her two sons were away at college that she finally took the drastic step of divorcing her husband.

She came to me six years after the divorce. She was still having both physical and emotional struggles. She couldn't forgive her husband, but she also couldn't forgive herself. And her lack of self-forgiveness was hurting her as much as her unwillingness to forgive her husband.

L: We can understand why she had difficulty forgiving her husband, but why did she even need to forgive herself?

T: Well, as she put it, she couldn't forgive herself for two things. One was for making the blunder of marrying him in the first place, and the other was for allowing him to deprive her and her sons of a normal and happy life. She felt particularly guilty about her sons. She said that, as their mother, she should have protected them from her husband's abuse.

L: Were you able to help her?

T: We were making progress, but her ex-husband began harassing her and things got nasty. So she moved out of the city. I don't know what's happened to her, but I truly believe that if she didn't get help, the abuse from her past will continue to dominate her and deprive her of the kind of life she craves.

Pastors and other therapists confirm the observation of our therapist friend that not forgiving yourself is likely to lead to physical and emotional as well as spiritual problems. In fact, forgiveness is no longer a concern only in the Christian community. In recent years, clinicians and researchers have studied the role of forgiveness in people's well-being and have concluded that there are strong positive effects to being a forgiving person and equally strong negative effects for those who are not forgiving.

With regard to emotional problems, those who do not forgive others or themselves are likely to struggle with one or more of the following:

- Anger
- Guilt
- Anxiety
- Depression
- Nervousness and restlessness
- Feeling of being stressed
- Frustration and resentment
- Chronic thoughts of vengeance

As you would expect, such emotional struggles tend to result in various physical problems. In particular, the unforgiving may develop one or more of the following:

- Recurring aches and pains, including headaches
- A depressed immune system
- More frequent colds and flu
- Chronic fatigue
- Cardiovascular problems, including elevated blood pressure

And if all that weren't enough, the unforgiving are also likely to have more problems relating in a meaningful way to others. Family counselors agree that the practice of forgiveness is one of the crucial elements in a satisfying intimate relationship. The unforgiving, therefore, are not likely to maintain a long-term relationship that fulfills their intimacy needs. And even more casual relationships can be affected. Terry, in her thirties, has had a life-long struggle with forgiving herself. Raised by fundamentalist Christian parents who etched into her mind her tendency to fall prey to "wicked" behavior, Terry cannot forgive herself for falling short of what she believes she should be. She continually berates herself even for such small slights as forgetting to thank someone. Her fear of falling short is so strong that she holds back from forming close attachments. People who meet her for the first time think of her as cold and withdrawn. They do not see what her counselor sees: a young woman whose inability to forgive herself for being a normal rather than a flawless human being chokes her every relationship.

GOD'S CHILDREN FORGIVING THEMSELVES

The social scientific findings on forgiveness underscore the wisdom of the biblical teachings. And the Scriptures help us understand self-forgiveness by case studies as well as by teachings. In the Hebrew Scriptures, David provides us with an instructive example of a child of God practicing self-forgiveness. Recall that David committed adultery with Bathsheba, then compounded the matter by having her husband, Uriah, slain in battle. For a time, David tried to keep his sins secret. But after the prophet Nathan confronted him and condemned what he had done, David plunged into a tailspin of remorse and self-condemnation.

David's unconfessed sins had physical and emotional consequences—consequences captured dramatically in Psalm 32: "While I kept silence, my body wasted away through my groaning all day long. For day and night your hand was heavy upon me; my strength was dried up as by the heat of summer" (Psa. 32:3–4).

When he finally did confess, he experienced the joyous freedom of God's forgiveness, as proclaimed in the opening verses of the Psalm: "Happy are those whose transgression is forgiven, whose sin is covered. Happy are those to whom the LORD imputes no iniquity, and in whose spirit there is no deceit" (Psa. 32:1–2).

Clearly, David was able to forgive himself after he realized that God had forgiven him. Note the interesting phrase "you forgave the guilt of my sin" (Psa. 32:5). God forgave the *guilt* of his sin. It was as if God said to him, "David, I forgive your sin and your guilt, so you need no longer feel guilty about what you have done." And David was able to forgive himself. The psalm ends on a note of joy: "Be glad in the LORD and rejoice, O you righteous, and shout for joy, all you upright in heart" (Psa. 32:11). The guilty soul does not rejoice. The guilty soul does not break forth in song. David was free of God's condemnation and free of his self-condemnation as well.

For another biblical example, consider the apostle Peter. There were a lot of incidents in Peter's life that could have haunted him and made self-forgiveness difficult. He could have obsessed about the times he put his foot in his mouth, blurting out things for which Jesus had to reprove him. He could have beat himself up emotionally and spiritually for the times he was slow to understand the teachings and mission of his Lord. And, of course, he could have been haunted by the three times he denied Jesus.

But Peter must have known God's forgiveness and he must have practiced self-forgiveness, for he emerges in the pages of Scripture not as a self-condemning, impotent disciple, but as a joyous, spiritually powerful apostle. He was a leader in the early church. He was mentor to Christians like John and Mark. And he wrote words of gratitude and encouragement that ring with freedom and life:

> Blessed be the God and Father of our Lord Jesus Christ! By his great mercy he has given us a new birth into a living hope through the resurrection of Jesus Christ from the dead, and into an inheritance that is imperishable, undefiled, and unfading, kept in heaven for you." (1 Pet. 1:3–4)

He said that those who believe "rejoice with an indescribable and glorious joy" (1 Pet. 1:8). Again, such expressions do not flow from one who is mired in self-condemnation. They erupt from the mouth of the person who knows the joyous freedom of God's forgiveness and the self-forgiveness that follows.

Nor are the examples confined to biblical figures. Lest you think that what happened with David and with Peter is beyond the reach of the average Christian today, consider the story of Susan, a thirty-two-year-old housewife and mother. Susan had been an active member of her small, suburban church for a number of years when she asked her pastor if she could meet with him. Because she looked so troubled, the pastor set the meeting for the next afternoon. What, he wondered, did she need? She had a strong marriage, a husband with a good income, and two healthy children. She taught a children's class in Sunday school. The pastor knew of no health issues or financial problems in the family.

When Susan met with the pastor, she struggled nervously with her words. She admitted that she didn't even know if she had the courage to tell him why she had requested the meeting. But with his reassurances calming her, she shared with him an issue that had been vexing her for years:

> Everyone thinks I'm such a good Christian. But I feel like a fraud. When I was a teenager—and I was a Christian at the time—I went through a . . . a rebellious stage. My parents would have been horrified if they knew what I did —because I still went to church and I pretended to be as religious as they were. But I wasn't.

Susan hesitated. "That seems pretty normal for a lot of teenagers," the pastor said, hoping to encourage her to continue and still puzzled by her concern. She bit her lip for a moment, then went on with her story:

> Yeah, teenagers do rebel. But not the way I did. And especially not if they're Christians. You see, I grew up in a small town. And there wasn't much for the kids to do. Some of them found ways to get beer, and we did a lot of drinking. But that wasn't the worst thing. When we were seniors, someone came up with the idea . . . I hate to even talk about it now . . . the idea of a sex club. Everyone in the club was free to have sex with anyone else if they both wanted it. The idea was that by the time we graduated no one would be a virgin, and the one who had the most sex with the most other kids would be the champion.

Susan hesitated again. "And you participated?" the pastor asked. "Yes," she mumbled. "And no one ever knew?" he asked. She sighed deeply:

Only the kids in the club. Well, two of the families found out a little when their daughters got pregnant. But even those girls didn't give all the details. They only identified the last guy they had sex with as the father. I'm grateful that I didn't get pregnant. But I did have sex with a number of the guys. I've never told anyone about it until today. But I just can't keep quiet anymore. I feel so ashamed, so guilty. Even my husband doesn't know. So you see why I feel like a fraud? What can I do?

After further discussion, the pastor led Susan in a ritual of confession that assured her of God's forgiveness. They talked about whether she should tell her husband but decided to postpone a decision on the matter. Finally, they agreed to meet regularly while Susan worked through the difficult process of forgiving herself. She had to forgive herself not only for the sex, but also for waiting so long before asking for God's forgiveness and for hiding her past from everyone.

Eventually, using some of the techniques we will describe in subsequent chapters, Susan forgave herself. At the last session with the pastor, he asked her to describe how she felt. Her response was both grateful and joyous:

> I have my life back. It's more than just a weight lifted, it's like I'm finally untied after being knotted up for so many years. I think I understand in a way I never could before how amazing God's forgiveness is, and why we need to accept that forgiveness by forgiving ourselves. It's just awesome!

Indeed, forgiveness is one of God's true gifts. To accept God's forgiveness, to forgive others, and to forgive yourself are essential elements in experiencing that "more and better life."

PART II
how you can

For it is God who is at work in you, enabling you both to will and to work for his good pleasure.

—Philippians 2:13

Make Whatever Amends You Can

Whe call it the messy room syndrome, in honor of a woman who put the struggle with self-forgiveness in these terms: "Have you ever faced the job of cleaning up the messiest room you've ever seen in your life? You just stand there for a while and wonder where in the world to start. Well, that's what it's like for me when I need to forgive myself. I know that I should, but where do I begin? What can I actually do?"

If you've been caught up in the messy room syndrome, if you're perplexed about how to go about forgiving yourself and getting your life back in order, here is the place to begin: make whatever amends you can. What does this involve?

WHAT IT MEANS TO MAKE AMENDS

Let's begin with what it *doesn't* mean. Unfortunately many Christians are hampered in their efforts to forgive themselves because they feel like they have to erase their hurtful actions. They want to make amends by turning back the clock on their behavior and rewriting history. Because this is impossible, they never feel worthy of self-forgiveness. At the very least, they believe that they have to make everything right by completely undoing whatever damage they have caused. This isn't realistic.

For example, suppose that you have hurt an acquaintance by spreading gossip about the person. While we all would welcome the power to do so, your words can't be recalled—you can neither erase them nor completely recant them. Can you track down everyone who heard the gossip and assure them that it wasn't true? Unlikely, if not impossible. Even if you located everyone who heard your damaging words, would they believe you? Probably not. Some would likely conclude that your words must be partially true: "Where there's smoke, there's fire, you know." And even if you had the power to recant your hurtful words, would this wipe out your own memory of the remark?

In addition to being unrealistic, the idea that you have to make everything right is contrary to the very notion of forgiveness. Recall Peter's denial of Jesus. Was Peter forgiven? Clearly, he was. And just as clearly, it would have been unrealistic for Peter to round up everyone who heard his denial and retract what he said. Happily, forgiveness—whether of others or of yourself—means you no longer have to strive to undo all the damage.

What, then, do we mean by making amends? In essence, you make amends when you acknowledge the hurt that you have caused and take some kind of action that both eases the hurt and demonstrates that you are sorry.

ACKNOWLEDGE

There are two aspects of acknowledging an offense: confession and apology. Let's look first at confession.

Confess

You need to confess the offense both to God and to another person—and each is essential to self-forgiveness. In both cases, it is important to confess the specific offense. In other words, when you confess to God, it isn't enough to offer a generalized confession and request for forgiveness such as "God, I have sinned and ask for your forgiveness." Rather, be specific: "God, I hurt Phil today when I spoke harshly to him. Forgive me."

"Why?" you may wonder. "Why should I confess to God about specific things I've done? God knows them already. So why can't I just ask for forgiveness for all my sins?" It's true that you're not informing God of something that God doesn't know when you confess. *But the point of confession is not that God needs to hear, but that you need to articulate what you have done.* Otherwise, you may find yourself trying to suppress the incident or denying the seriousness of the offense. There is a little of the Pharisee in all of us—we all want to think of ourselves, and to be thought of by others, as good people, as those who are morally above average, if not superior. It's difficult to maintain an image of moral superiority when you confess the specific ways in which you have fallen short. And that's the point! When you confess a specific sin, you are forcing yourself to deal with it in an open, unpretentious manner. And you are doing what is necessary to begin the healing process of forgiving yourself.

Here's our friend Jim's observation about the importance of confessing a specific offense:

At our church, we have a general confession of sin at each worship service. I always thought that was enough. It covered my mistakes of the past week and left me feeling pretty good about myself. But one day I broke the trust of a colleague—I took partial credit for a departmental reorganization plan that was mainly his idea. I realized quickly that I'd messed up big time. I let our department head know that I had taken more credit for the plan than I deserved and told him that it was mainly Tom's work. Then, I apologized to Tom and told him of my efforts to set the record straight. But he was still really angry.

I decided there was nothing more I could do, so I just had to put the whole affair out of my mind. Easier said than done. I saw Tom every day at work, and each time I felt a pang of regret. I reminded myself that time heals everything, but time didn't seem to make any difference.

Finally, I was praying one day and just told God what I had done and asked for forgiveness and healing. I was surprised to see that I immediately felt a sense of relief. For the first time, I really felt forgiven by God. And that was the beginning of two more things I had to do: I had to forgive myself, and I had to do something more to try and mend my relationship with Tom.

As Jim's experience illustrates, confession is more than "good for the soul." It is an effective, practical way to start the process of self-forgiveness and deal with the consequences of your hurtful action in a constructive way.

However, your confession shouldn't stop there. We are also told to confess our sins to one another (James 5:16). While this isn't necessary in order to secure God's forgiveness, it may be necessary in order to forgive yourself. We'll discuss the matter of confessing to another person—why it works and how to do it—in the next chapter when we explore the task of talking about the situation with someone you trust. Here, we simply want to stress the fact that confession needs to be both to God and to another person. We have known individuals who confess to God and hope this alone will enable them to forgive themselves, only to discover that their guilt continues to torment them.

Apologize

In addition to confession, you need to acknowledge your offense with an apology to the person you have hurt. Be careful how you phrase your apology. Too many so-called apologies are, in part, self-justfications: they go beyond an expression of regret and include an explanation or rationale for your harmful action, including what the other person said or did that elicited the hurtful behavior.

When you apologize, don't try to justify what you did. Simply acknowledge your offense and say that you are sorry for behaving in a hurtful way. If you try to throw part of the blame on the other person, you neutralize the effectiveness of your apology. Consider, for instance, a situation where a couple is running late for a din-ner engagement, in large part, because he got home late from work. The situation only worsens when the zipper of her dress gets hopelessly jammed. He shouts: "You're so stupid. You can't even get yourself dressed. " She is angry and hurt and, as a result, the evening is a strained affair. Later, he attempts an apology.

Which of the following apologies would you expect to be ef-fective?

- "I'm sorry I hollered at you. But you know I say things I don't mean when I'm irritated. And you've got to admit, you really do dumb things at times."

- "I'm sorry I shouted and called you stupid. There's no excuse for what I said. I don't think of you that way, and I don't want to ever say it again. I hope you'll forgive me."

The second one, of course, wins hands down.

In addition to conveying a sense of regret, an apology has the added benefit of giving you a better sense of how hurt the other person is. You may discover that your behavior didn't offend the other person as much as you thought, or even as much as it now offends you. In such a case, it is easier to forgive yourself. The op-posite may be true—the other person may be more offended than you realized. In any case, you need to understand the extent to which the he or she has been hurt so that you can gauge the ex-tent to which you need to make amends.

Act

A frequent question from those struggling to forgive themselves is "What can I do?" Actually, it's a good question to ask. Because you need to do *something* in order to get on with the process of forgiv-ing yourself. In particular, you need to do something that attempts to communicate two things to the person you have offended: you are truly sorry and you are trying to ease the hurt. Note that we say "attempts" to communicate that you are sorry and "trying" to ease the hurt. Your attempt may be rejected by the person. But as with all things in the Christian life, your responsibility is with what *you* do and not with the effectiveness of the results. There is no action you take that will guarantee a positive outcome.

Many churches have a Stephen Ministry—a group of trained lay people who provide a one-on-one care ministry for those who are struggling in some way. The Stephen Ministry has a mantra: "We are the caregivers, God is the curegiver." In other words, Stephen Ministers strive to relate to others in a Christian way. Sometimes this brings about the results they would like to see and sometimes it doesn't. Yet as long as they have been caring Christians, they cannot fault themselves if the hoped-for cure doesn't happen.

Actually, this same notion is found in the Hebrew Scriptures. God told Ezekiel that he was to be a watchman for Israel, warning the people of consequences of their sin (Ezek. 33:7–9). Many of the Israelites would ignore the warning. But Ezekiel was only responsible for caring for them by being a faithful watchman, not for being so persuasive that they would all turn away from their sins. Ezekiel was the caregiver. God was the curegiver. The people were responsible for choosing whether to accept the care and the cure or to persist in their evil ways.

So think of yourself as a caregiver. True, you were responsible for the hurt. But now you've turned away from being an offender and are striving to be a caregiver. This means that you are opening the way for God to be a curegiver. Hopefully, the person you hurt will accept your care and God's curing work. Yet even if this doesn't happen, you've fulfilled your responsibility as a Christian and can get on with the task of forgiving yourself.

So what kinds of things can you do? When you apologize, you have already taken the first and most important step. Here are a few more actions that people have found useful:

1. *Compensate.* We once had some friends over for dinner. We were relieved that for once our rambunctious Brittany spaniel puppy was quiet and unobtrusive. Our relief came to an end when

the dinner was completed. Hidden from view by the tablecloth, one of the women had slipped off her shoes and our puppy had amused herself by teething on them. We discovered her mischief after the shoes were damaged beyond repair. We were embarrassed, and the woman was clearly distressed. We apologized for our misbehaving puppy and, of course, bought her a new pair of shoes. She accepted both and the friendship continues.

Compensation takes many forms other than monetary. A man with a turbulent relationship with his adult daughter told us he came to realize that most of the strain between them resulted from years of neglect while she was growing up and he was growing his business. By the time she left for college, they were barely speaking. With his daughter away at school, he realized how much he had missed of her life. He wanted to know her better and have her know him. He decided that he needed to show her his love and spend time with her. So whenever she came home from college, he planned time with her—lunch out, a visit to the art museum, a walk on the beach. At first, she reluctantly went along on these adventures. But when they were together he gave her his full attention, initially as she talked about trivial matters and, later, as she talked about her dreams and goals for the future. It took a while before she trusted that he wasn't going to fade from her life as he had so often done in the past. As her trust grew, she was able to talk about how his absence had affected her. He, in turn, was able to tell her how sorry he was for the pain he had caused as well as for how much he had cheated himself of her presence. For him, this was the beginning of his self-forgiveness.

2. *Give a gift.* A small gift can often break down the walls of animosity and begin the process of forgiveness and reconciliation. Listen to Emily's experience. For nearly three years she had been alienated from her neighbor. The problem began when she blew up after her neighbor's dog shredded Emily's newspaper for five consecutive days:

In my frustration, I overreacted and said things that I shouldn't have. I apologized but my neighbor wanted nothing to do with me. If we happened to be working in our yards at the same time or saw each other at the grocery store, we avoided each other like the plague. This ongoing cold war began to really weigh on me. She had once been a friend, and now we didn't even acknowledge each other's existence. I knew I had to try something more than an apology. So one day I left a vase of peonies I'd picked from my flower garden on her front porch. That gesture broke the ice.

The next day she saw me working in the yard and hesitantly thanked me for the flowers. She told me she loved peonies and asked how difficult it was to grow them. After a few minutes of gardening talk, I decided the time was right to apologize again. I told her I was sorry for reaming her out for her dog's behavior and that I missed being with her. Well, we wound up with some healing tears, a shared pot of coffee, and a renewed friendship—all because of a gift of flowers.

One caveat here: we all dislike gifts that we think are attempts to buy our affection or loyalty or, for that matter, forgiveness. Don't use gift-giving as a delete button for the hurt you have inflicted. Rather use it to express your regret for the offense and desire for reconciliation. Certainly, never use gift-giving as an attempt to buy forgiveness. Rather use it as a way to break down what seemingly has become an impenetrable wall of unforgiveness.

In the quest for self-forgiveness, you can also give a gift to yourself. Does this idea startle you? We have found various reactions to the suggestion, none of which fall into the category of "what a great idea." Rather, people are more likely to react with: "Wait a minute. I'm the offender. I've tried to make amends, but I still feel more like punishing myself than giving myself a gift." Precisely. But that's exactly what you want to stop doing. You want to escape the punishing mode, accept God's forgiveness, and forgive yourself so that you can get on with the abundant life God wills for you.

Giving yourself a gift (after, of course, you have tried to make amends with the person you offended) is a way of affirming that you are not a wicked, evil person; you are a human who, like all other humans, falls short at times but who is striving to walk the righteous path. So a gift is a way of making amends for continuing to punish yourself even after God has forgiven you. And it is a way to celebrate the fact that you are a grace-touched human who, though fallible, lives in the freedom of forgiveness.

What kind of gift? Maybe a bouquet of fresh flowers. Each time you look at them, think of them as a symbol of God's forgiveness and your journey to self-forgiveness. Or how about a nice bottle of wine? As you savor it, remind yourself that it symbolizes forgiveness. Whatever the gift, link it up with God's forgiveness and your self-forgiveness.

3. *Change your behavior.* Nothing communicates sorrow over an offense better than changed behavior. A woman who publicly humiliated her husband by making fun of his athletic ability claimed she was just "teasing" him. When she realized how hurt he was by her repeated efforts to poke fun at him, she not only apologized but changed her behavior. She determined never again to say anything negative about him to others. Instead, she talked about his qualities that she admired and praised him for his achievements. Her changed behavior helped her to forgive herself for the embarrassment and hurt she had caused him.

In some cases, it helps to tell the person you offended about your intention to change your behavior. You may even want to enlist his or her help in doing this. Consider saying something like this: "I'm sorry I cut you short when you were speaking. I know I tend to do that, and I want to stop it. I'm going to try and hear you out from now on rather than cutting you off. And I'd like for you to help me. Instead of letting me get away with it, interrupt and tell me to wait a minute until you have finished what you wanted to say."

4. *Repeat.* Rarely is a single act sufficient to change behavior— particularly if it's an ingrained behavior. The woman who had "teased" her husband about his athletic ability realized that a single instance of praise would not wipe out years of humiliation she had caused him. She knew that she had to change her behavior, refrain from the teasing, and replace it with some kind of positive behavior. When people are hurt and feel betrayed, a single act may not convince them that you are sincerely regretful. If needed, therefore, go the second mile.

BUT WHAT IF . . . ?

Two "what if's" come up when we talk about making amends. First, what if the person you hurt is not accessible, because he or she has moved away or has died? And second, what if the other person is unaware of the hurt (for example, a secret affair) or unaware that you are the source of the hurt (for instance, the person doesn't know that it was you who gave the information that led to a job loss)? Each of these situations requires imagination and caution on your part.

Consider first the case of someone who is inaccessible. If the person has simply moved away, you can always write or e-mail or call or send a gift. It is more difficult to make amends when you can't deal with the person face to face, but it can be done. However, when someone has died, making amends is more troublesome. Yet it still may be important for you to take some sort if action in order to forgive yourself.

How can you make amends to a person who has died? Here are two examples of how people have answered this question. One occurred at a memorial service we attended. During the course of the service, the pastor announced that he had a brief letter he wanted to read. It was from the aunt of the young man who had died and it was addressed to him. In her letter, the aunt wrote of her love and admiration for her nephew and told of her nephew's empathy and care for others. She closed her letter with these words: "My deepest regret is that I never told you how much I love and admire you while you were with us."

The other example is a technique used by some therapists. You can do this alone or in the presence of someone else. Place two chairs facing each other. Sit in one. Imagine the person who has died sitting in the other. Then tell the person what is on your heart. You can do the same thing without the chairs, of course. Sam, a successful San Francisco attorney, told us how he resolved long-standing issues with his mother several years after her death:

> The longer I live, the more I realize that my mother was not the harsh and arbitrary woman I believed her to be when I was younger. The Lord knows I spent years bitter and angry about her, but I finally came to the realization that she did the best she knew how to do in mothering me. And that she really did love me as much as she was able to love anyone. I was thinking about these things one day as I walked the labyrinth in my church. And I just quietly started telling her how I felt and asked her to forgive me for misjudging her. After that, I felt at peace with her and also with myself.

Consider next how you should deal with a situation where the person is unaware that you have done something hurtful. At first, it might seem that the Christian way is to be open and honest with the person and confess what you have done. In some cases, this is true. But we urge caution. Sometimes a confession may be good for your soul but hurtful to the relationship.

This really hit us in a marriage support group we were leading for young married couples. The topic for the day was the role of honesty in a satisfying marriage. Everyone in the group seemed to agree that honesty is essential and that dishonesty impairs the intimacy of a Christian marriage. This is when Jenny spoke up. Three couples who had been married for twenty years or more, including Jenny and her husband, Dan, were our panel of "experts" for the day. Jenny and Dan, a college teacher, had been married for twenty-four years. "Too much honesty early in our marriage," she said firmly, "nearly wrecked our relationship." The startled group quieted down and listened to her story:

> When Dan finished his PhD, he accepted a position at a small college in the Midwest. I wasn't too thrilled about moving to a small town where we didn't know anyone. But I was happy for Dan and wanted to be a supportive wife. When we got there, we didn't meet any other couples our age. And Dan's responsibilities at the college took all his time. I quickly felt lonely and isolated. The only person I talked to all day was our two-year-old son. I suddenly found myself with a totally different life, and I was struggling. I had given up my own work on a master's degree, and I could find no comparable program in nearby colleges. So I had to temporarily put the preparations for my own future career on hold. But Dan was riding high. He loved his work, and he got lots of attention. The young female students were attracted to him. And worse, he was attracted to one of them. He was in his "honesty" phase and decided to tell me all about it.

The incident she was relating had happened eighteen years earlier. But both the tone of her voice and the expression on her face made it clear that she still found it painful:

> Well, I was devastated. I felt that not only had my life been radically changed by the move. Now my marriage was threatened as well. It turned out that Dan's feelings about the coed didn't amount to much and passed quickly. But since I was already feeling depressed about our situation, it was a crisis for us. He kept telling me that he only wanted to be honest so that we could stay close to each other. Well, I can tell you that his confession did *not* help us stay close to each other. It just drove us farther apart.

Dan had remained silent so far. A bit abashed, he said:

> I really was trying to be the kind of husband I thought I
> ought to be as a Christian. I really did think that by telling
> Jenny we would continue to have the honest relationship
> that we both wanted. Instead, for a long time Jenny didn't
> trust me to be around other women, especially if she
> wasn't there.

Dan and Jenny now have a strong, long-lasting marriage. Did
that bit of honesty on his part actually help in the long run? Was
it the right thing to do even though it was very painful at the time?
Jenny doesn't think so: "At that point in my life, honesty wasn't
what I needed. I needed support and understanding and reassur-
ance. Dan's so-called honesty really hurt our marriage for a while."

Our point in sharing this story is to issue a *caution*, not a *direc-
tive*. In some cases, the person you hurt *should* be told. In other
cases, it will be better to confess to someone else and made amends
in other ways than by confessing and apologizing. Each case has to
be decided on its own. And we recommend that the decision be
made in consultation with another person whose support and wisdom you trust. Because when you try to make amends with someone who doesn't know that you are the offender, you have to confront both the demands of honesty and the possibility of inflicting
unnecessary hurt. It's not an easy road to travel.

Talk with Someone You Trust

Let's begin with a quiz:

1. You have just won your dream vacation in a drawing. Which of the following are you most likely to do?

   a. Share the news with friends and family.

   b. Keep the news to yourself.

   c. Notify the local newspaper.

2. You have yielded to temptation and watched a porno site during a lull at work. Which of the following are you likely to do?

   a. Keep what you've done a secret.

   b. Share the site with your boss.

   c. Tell your friends and family what you have done.

We suspect that you answered "a" to both questions. Most of us want to share the news when something good happens to us; it's a way to enhance and extend our pleasure. By the same token, most of us would rather hide our shortcomings in the closet of our minds. There's no pleasure in reliving those things you regard as a moral failure. Yet, in your search for self-forgiveness, you need to get beyond the normal tendency to resist telling another person what you have done.

For most of us, that's not easy. We are reluctant to share our failings with another person because we fear that they will be shocked by our revelations or think less highly of us. Also many of us believe that we *should* solve our own problems. We think it's a sign of strength and virtue to say, "I can handle this myself. God has forgiven me; that's all the help I need." But when the guilt continues to nag and self-forgiveness eludes us, we clearly need help. And talking to another person can be a significant source of help in forgiving one's self. Both the reason we say this and the way to go about it will be clear as we look at the "why," the "what," and the "who" of talking with someone.

WHY?

Josh put it this way: "I'm embarrassed enough about what I've done; I don't want to share my embarrassment with another person. I'm an adult and should be able to figure out how to handle this on my own. I certainly don't need someone else telling me what to do." We frequently hear comments like this from people who resist talking to another person when they're struggling. They're often surprised when we agree with them. "That's not the point of talking with someone," we tell them. "It isn't for advice or directives." Why, then, the need to talk? There are two basic reasons. One is negative: you need to confess so that you don't feel like a fraud. The other is positive: you need to talk because it's an inherently healing activity when done appropriately. Let's look first at the matter of fraud.

Confession and Fraud

Confessing to God may bring about a refreshing sense of liberation. But if you only confess to God, you may feel that you are presenting a front to the world that is better than you deserve. This was at the heart of Josh's difficulties in forgiving himself. When he was a young financial adviser, Josh had given some faulty investment advice to a couple who were close family friends. While the advice was well-meaning and seemed sound at the time, the friends lost a part of their retirement funds in the investment. The friends never blamed Josh for his advice, but he certainly blamed himself. He told us:

> My friends, who looked on me as a son, let me off the hook, but I've never been able to do the same—even after all these years. I loved these people and felt that I had let them down. Recently I received a civic award for "providing sage investment advice" when our city was experiencing a financial crisis. As I accepted the award, my friends' faces flashed before my eyes. And, once again, I felt like a fraud.

No one but Josh and his friends (and they had passed away by this time) knew of his mistake. But he knew. And as long as he told no other person, he had trouble erasing the notion of "fraud" and, thus, forgiving himself.

The point is, when no one else knows, you may feel doubly guilty—guilty for what you have done or failed to do and also guilty for hiding the offense behind a facade of goodness. A middle-aged, professional woman expressed her own struggle this way:

> I'm in management and have the reputation of being concerned for the well-being of those who work for me. In fact, I often tell my employees that my main job is to represent their interests to the higher-ups and to protect them from unfair rules. And that's generally true. But for a long time now, whenever one of my subordinates praises me for being such a thoughtful boss, I feel a twinge of pain. Because once I did something—or, really, I didn't do something that I should have done—and I've struggled with it ever since. I've had a hard time forgiving myself for letting a young woman in my department get fired because she was frequently late for work. She was a single

mother and really needed the job. I could have covered for her until she got her life in order, but I didn't. I've not told anyone that I didn't intervene on her behalf until now. But I'm tired of feeling guilty about not helping her, and I'm tired of feeling guilty because I've never admitted to anyone that I failed her.

Talking and Healing

It was one of his patients who characterized what Freud did as the "talking cure." The phrase is an apt one and has been used ever since to describe the therapeutic power of talking through one's struggles with a sympathetic listener. Talking about something like your difficulty in forgiving yourself will not, of course, bring instant cure. But talking with a good listener is a powerful way to help you along the rocky path to healing.

Why? Why does talking to someone have a healing effect on you? There are at least three reasons. One is that talking about your struggle helps clarify it in your own mind. Have you had the experience of feeling out of sorts, having your spouse or a friend ask you what's wrong, and realizing that you're not even sure why you feel that way? Then when you try to explain it you begin to see various possibilities. You help clarify the source of your feelings for yourself as well as for the other person.

When dealing with self-forgiveness, one of the roadblocks you may encounter is your seeming helplessness in the face of your guilt. Nothing you do seems to make much difference in the way you feel. You don't understand why guilt continues to vex you. And you may not understand until you talk it out with someone. For example, Frank took money from a joint savings account for speculative investments without telling his wife, Louise. He invested poorly as it turns out, so he lost most of their money. Louise left all the financial matters to him, so she suspected nothing until she decided that they needed to remodel their kitchen. When she brought up the matter to Frank, he quickly said they couldn't afford it. "We'll just have to take it out of our savings," she replied.

"No," he told her, "we can't. It's in CDs and we can only with-draw it once a year." "Well," she wanted to know, "when is the year up so we can get started on the kitchen?"

Frank kept trying to deflect her questions and convince her that the kitchen did not need remodeling. But she persisted and eventually he had to confess what he had done. Louise was en-raged. She felt betrayed. For a time, she even thought of leaving him. Eventually, they worked through the matter. They estab-lished some new rules about their financial affairs, which hence-forth would be carried on jointly or not at all. Then Frank ran into the wall of his guilt: He could not forgive himself for hav-ing betrayed Louise and causing her so much pain: "I know that God has forgiven me. And I know that Louise has forgiven me. But I just can't forgive myself, and I don't know why or what to do about it."

It was only after several counseling sessions with his pastor that Frank began to understand his struggle. He felt that he deserved to be punished for his appalling behavior. Neither God nor Louise, in the grace of forgiveness, would punish him, so he did it to himself. Eventually, he was able to let go of his anger against himself and to experience the liberation of self-forgiveness.

A second reason that talking with a sympathetic listener has such healing power is that it puts you in a close relationship with someone who cares about you. And such relationships are inher-ently healing. Social scientists call it your support group. But the importance of social support is not a modern discovery. The an-cient preacher put it this way: "woe to one who is alone and falls and does not have another to help" (Eccl. 4:10). And Paul urged us: "Bear one another's burdens, and in this way you will fulfill the law of Christ" (Gal. 6:2). The wisdom of these biblical teachings is seen in the results of modern research into the effects of social sup-port. In brief, those who have a social support network also have higher rates of emotional, physical, and spiritual well-being.

A third reason that talking is healing is that you gain new in-sights and new perspectives. In part, this happens as you share your

pain with another person and, in the process, gain greater understanding of your actions and struggles. Your listener's reactions and
comments can also be helpful. Consider the following examples:

- You are having trouble forgiving yourself because you betrayed a friend's confidence and you believe there's no way to
  redeem the situation. But your confidant seems hopeful and
  suggests ways that you can repair the damage. Perhaps, you
  think, there may be a way to turn this around after all.

- Having been unfaithful to your spouse, self-forgiveness is out
  of the question. You have not only been unfaithful to your
  spouse, but to God and to your own principles. The failure is
  shocking. Yet, the person with whom you talk doesn't seem
  shocked, only concerned about you and your marriage. You
  begin to feel that not only forgiveness but perhaps reconciliation is also possible.

- You cannot forgive yourself for having neglected your father
  for years before his death. Your behavior was shameful. But as
  you confess your failure, the other person does not react with
  disgust or even disapproval. She nods and says she understands
  how much it hurts you. She doesn't react with moral indigna-
  tion. She doesn't evict you from the human race. She clearly
  only wants to help. It's your first hint that you need not be
  shackled by painful guilt for the rest of your life.

So, yes, the talking cure really works.

WHAT?

The answer to this question may seem obvious. Clearly, talking
about the weather or sports or politics, as interesting and important as these might be to you, won't enable you to forgive yourself.
Clearly, you must talk about your struggle to gain self-forgiveness.
But there are two important aspects of the "what" to keep in
mind: you need to talk about both what you've done and what
you now can do.

What You've Done

Again, this sounds obvious. We say it, however, to underscore the point that *you must talk with someone with whom you can be totally honest; a selective account won't suffice.* To be selective in what you say is like telling your doctor only some of the symptoms you are having. With only partial information, the doctor is not likely to give you the help you need. Nor are you likely to find talking with a confidant helpful if you withhold information. Of course, you probably won't tell your confidant everything the first time you are together. It may take time to build trust and rapport. Over time, as you talk with someone—especially someone you don't know or don't know very well—you will either become more or less confident that you can divulge anything and everything. If you're not comfortable being totally honest, you need to find a different confidant.

Why would you be selective in talking about your struggles? Why would you withhold any information or any of your feelings? There are several seasons. One is illustrated by Susan, whom we discussed in chapter 1. She had a hard time confessing her past even to her pastor. She told him: "I really had to work up my courage just to come and see you. I'm so embarrassed by what I've done. I really admire you, and I want you to respect me and value what I do here at the church. I was afraid you'd have a bad opinion of me once you heard about my past. And that would really hurt."

In other words, one reason for being selective is that you don't want to reveal anything that will diminish you as a person or a spouse or a friend or a Christian in the eyes of others. A second reason is closely related: you don't want to diminish yourself in your own mind. That is, you don't want to think of yourself as the kind of person who easily or routinely does the kind of things for which you need to forgive yourself. As Susan put it: "I'm not that kind of person anymore. In fact, I don't feel that what I did was ever the kind of person I really am. I still don't understand why I got caught up in it. But I know that wasn't the real me then and it isn't the real me now."

Because she felt this way, she was reluctant to fully divulge her past to her pastor. She had hoped that she could just tell him that she was a rebel or that she violated her ideal of chastity. The more details she shared, she thought, the more likely he was to see her in negative terms. And if he thought less of her, how could she think anything else about herself? Fortunately, she came to realize that she had to be open or she would continue to feel like a fraud.

A third reason why you may want to be selective is to avoid the pain of reliving the past. You may feel diminished and anguished as you once again wend your way through the details. We once heard of a writer who kept all his rejection slips, posting them on a bulletin board above his desk. All writers get rejection slips, but we suspect that most are like us—they throw them away rather than keep them displayed as a macabre gallery of past failures. Who wants to relive all those painful moments? Most of us prefer to follow Paul's advice and dwell on those matters in the past that are honorable, just, pure, pleasing, and commendable (Phil. 4:8).

Thus, it's tempting to forego the details. You'll discover that the more you withhold the less value you'll get from talking about your past error. So avoid a selective account even though it is painful to relive the experience.

What You Now Can Do

The other important aspect of the "what" of talking relates to the actions you take as you go about forgiving yourself. You may not find it easy to determine what actions to take, particularly as you address a number of questions: What exactly can you do that will convey the message that you are sorry? When have you done enough to make amends? Or is there more that you should do? How do you handle the situation where the person you offended is unaware of what you have done or where the person you offended is no longer accessible?

You realize, for example, that you need to try to make amends but don't where to begin. A confidant can help you come up with some useful possibilities. A man struggling with how to approach a friend he had offended told his confidant: "I'm afraid I won't say the right thing, and that he'll just get angry and then I'll get angry and we'll be worse off than we are now." "Why don't you just write him a letter first?" the confidant asked. The confidant went on to point out that by writing a letter the man could craft his words carefully so that he would say just what he wanted. Then, when the two of them talked the matter over, they might both start off on a better footing. The idea of a letter hadn't occurred to the man. But he liked the idea and it turned out to be a useful first step in resolving the problem.

Another difficult situation is when the person you offended doesn't seem satisfied with what you have done to make amends. It's easy to fall into one of three traps: you conclude that you haven't done the right thing, or that you haven't done enough, or that you've done all you can and that you can do nothing more to make amends. Any of these may be true, but they also may be wrong. If you find yourself in such a situation, talking with your confidant can help you make a decision about what, if anything, more you should do. Whatever your decision, you will feel better about it for having discussed it with someone else and having that person's understanding and support.

Finally, it is helpful if not imperative to talk to someone when the person you offended is no longer accessible for some reason. This is a vexing situation, particularly when the person has died. Jane, a middle-aged realtor, felt torment for years until she shared her struggle with a coworker, Kelly, who was known around the office as someone with a sympathetic ear. Jane confessed to Kelly that she had spoken harshly to her mother and rushed out of the house in a huff. However, her mother died suddenly a few weeks later without Jane telling her mother how sorry she was for her unkind words. Kelly listened as Jane talked about the relationship she had with her mother. There had been times of tension, but generally the relationship was a good one. And Jane never doubted her mother's love for her.

Jane repeatedly told Kelly how much she agonized over what she had done. Then Kelly said to her, "Jane, may I do something? Would you let me talk to you like I believe your mother would? I'm a mother, and you've helped me get to know your mother. And I really think I know what she would like to say to you now. Is that all right?"

Jane agreed, and Kelly continued, "Jane, honey, you know how much I love you. So it hurts me to see you suffer like this. I don't blame you. I want you to know that I forgive you. I, too, have said things to you that were hurtful. We all do that at times. But the important thing is that I love you. I want you to remember how proud I am of you and that I only want you to be happy and have the good life you deserve."

Kelly paused a moment, then said: "That's what I would want to say to my kids. And I'm sure it's what your mother would say to you."

Jane's struggle didn't come to an immediate halt. But the perspective she gained by talking with Kelly was a huge first step in helping her to forgive herself .

WHO?

We share the story of Jane and Kelly for two reasons. First, it illustrates how helpful a confidant can be as you engage in the various tasks involved in self-forgiveness. Second, it illustrates the importance of *who* you choose to be your confidant. Clearly, Jane made a good choice in Kelly. And just as clearly, not everyone would be a good choice. We've heard more than one horror story of people who've tried to talk to someone only to come away worse off than they were because the person reacted with disgust or disapproval or indifference or with simplistic advice or platitudes.

So how do you choose someone to be a confidant? A wide range of people are possibilities. It could be your spouse or a family member. It could be a friend. It could be a coworker. It could be a pastor or a therapist. Whomever you choose, he or she needs to be someone you can *trust*. In order to make the best choice, ask yourself the following questions.

Is This Person a Good Listener?

That is, is this the kind of person who hears others out and tries to understand their struggles, or is he or she a "bottom-line" person who wants to get quickly to the nub of the problem and then tell you how to fix it? We all know "I can fix it for you" people. They're often well-intentioned, usually self-confident, and generally ready to tell you exactly what to do. You might have someone like that who is a close friend. Enjoy your friendship, but do *not* make that person your confidant when you're struggling with self-forgiveness. What you need is not someone's quick fix, but someone who, in biblical terms, is "quick to listen" and "slow to speak" (James 1:19). You need someone to whom you can confess and then fully explore such things as how you feel and what steps you can take to bring about self-forgiveness. Only then will your talking be the healing process that we discussed earlier in this chapter.

Can I Trust This Person to Keep a Confidence?

We have known people who didn't mind sharing their confession and their struggle with anyone and everyone willing to listen. If you fall into this category, you can skip this question. But if you are like most of us, and prefer to maintain your struggle as a private matter rather than as public information, confidentiality is of the utmost importance.

Many people misunderstand confidentiality. They believe they are keeping your confidence when they don't tell anyone except their spouse or another person who's very close to them. Let's say, for example, you choose Howie as a confidant. Howie doesn't tell another soul about your difficulties—that is, except for his wife, Marian, who is curious and concerned about you. But Marian confides your troubles to her best friend, Toni, who is also her prayer partner. She reasons that they can pray together for you, and your confidence will go no further. She's wrong. Toni tells her mother, who shares all of Toni's secrets. And so it spreads.

We hold confidentiality to be a sacred responsibility. It's so important that even if you believe you can trust the person to maintain whatever you say in confidence, we recommend that you make your expectation explicit. Say something like: "I would like for you to keep this just between the two of us. Please don't tell anyone else, not even . . ." In the case of Howie, the "not even" would have been his wife. Make it clear that you expect your discussions to go no further than the two of you.

Is This Person Nonjudgmental?

Be careful with this question. A person can be nonjudgmental without approving what you did. After all, even you don't approve of what you did. Rather, a nonjudgmental person is one who is there to help you rather than to evaluate you. There is nothing worse than to unburden yourself to someone, only to have that person react to you with shock or disgust or condemnation. Beth, a church secretary, shared with us just such a painful experience:

> When my husband left me for another woman, I bounced back and forth between intense anger and deep depression. When I was angry, I would fantasize about doing things that would inflict as much pain on my husband as he had inflicted on me. When I was depressed, I would fantasize about killing myself and leaving my husband so guilty and grief-stricken that he wouldn't be able to work or enjoy life. I knew I had to do something about it, but the senior pastor, whom I was close to, was on vacation at the time. So I went to one of the associate pastors. I began by telling him about some of my fantasies when I was angry. He interrupted me after a bit, and told me I needed to learn how to control my anger. I could tell by the look on his face that he strongly disapproved of me. Clearly, in his mind, no Christian should have such feelings.
>
> Of course, I hadn't told him everything yet. But I wasn't about to get more of his disapproval. I just thanked him for his advice, told him I would work on it, and left. I

guess the only thing I learned from him is how unfeeling and how lacking in sympathy some people can be.

Beth already felt badly about herself before talking to the associate pastor. Afterward she felt even worse. Fortunately, she went to her pastor when he returned and he worked with her as someone in need rather than as an evil person worthy of condemnation.

Does This Person Resort to Platitudes?

A colleague told us of the time when one of his children was hospitalized with a life-threatening illness. His pastor visited him in an effort to bring him some comfort. Our friend said, "I know he only wanted to console me. But he offered up every spiritual platitude I've ever heard. I thanked him, but inside I was screaming in anger: 'That doesn't help. That doesn't help me.'"

Similarly, when you're struggling with forgiving yourself, you don't want someone to respond with a simplistic solution such as "Just turn it over to Jesus." Such platitudes do one or more of the following:

- They trivialize your struggle.

- They cut short your need to talk.

- They increase your guilt (if you can deal with it just by turning it over to Jesus, what's wrong with you that you haven't already done this?).

- They prolong your struggle.

Those who resort to platitudes may be well-meaning. However, as the list above illustrates, platitudes are dangerous to your well-being. And they are clearly no substitute for wisdom and compassion.

Having addressed the questions of why, what, and who, perhaps we should add one more: when? The answer is simple. ASAP. The sooner you find a trustworthy confidant, the sooner you begin your journey of healing.

Don't Let "Should" and "Shouldn't" Cripple Your Efforts

There's an old story about a man who played the cello, but he only played a single note over and over again. When asked why, he replied with a satisfied smile, "Some people are looking for the note. But I've found it." The endless repetition of one note may have pleased him, but it was a source of misery for everyone else.

Now think of that man and his relentless single note as a thought that keeps playing in your head. The thought takes the form of "I should have . . ." or "I shouldn't have . . ." Those may not be the exact words whirling around in your head. Instead, the words that trouble you most often may be:

- "Why do I do such things?"

- "I wish I could erase that time and start over."

- "I'm a bad person."

- "I screwed up royally."

Or they may take other forms. They all amount to the same thing: an obsession with what you did or failed to do that makes you feel guilty and hampers your efforts to forgive yourself.

It's what we call a toxic form of thinking. And it's making you miserable.

Those around the cellist would not find peace unless they could change his pattern of playing. And you will not find peace until you change your pattern of thinking.

TOXIC THINKING AND LEARNED HELPLESSNESS

The notion of learned helplessness emerged from the work of experimental psychologists. In essence, it refers to the belief that you are unable to cope with a particular challenge or adverse situation because you have learned that you are powerless to do so. Even though an outsider can see a clear way to cope, the person afflicted with learned helplessness doesn't even try, believing that any and all efforts are pointless.

Early experiments about learned helplessness were done on animals. For example, the experimenter can put lab rats in a situation where they are periodically shocked. Initially, they will try to escape the shock. However, the experiment is set up in a way that does not allow them to escape. Subsequently, when they are put in a situation where they actually can escape the shock, they no longer try to do so. They have learned that they are helpless and they act accordingly.

The circus elephant is another example of learned helplessness. A circus elephant tethered to a large post with a heavy chain will try to pull away from the post. When it realizes that it cannot do so, it stops trying. Subsequently the elephant can be effectively tethered with a smaller chain or a rope that it could easily break. But it won't try to do so. It has learned to be helpless.

Learned helplessness also applies to people. It may be a factor in depression. An individual may face very difficult circumstances, try a variety of ways to get out of the difficulty, make little or no progress in doing so, and conclude that he or she is helpless. Being helpless in difficult circumstances, in turn, results in depression. It also results in something else—the person stops trying to deal with the difficulty. Learned helplessness deals a lethal blow to motivation.

HOW TOXIC THINKING CREATES LEARNED HELPLESSNESS

You may have put forth a few efforts to forgive yourself, failed, and concluded that you can't do it. But the more likely source of the learned helplessness that cripples efforts at self-forgiveness is toxic thinking. It is thinking that gets mired in "I should have . . ." or "I shouldn't have . . ." Consider the following situation. A man has a long-standing dispute with his sister and, as a result, has little contact with her. He is getting married, is excited about his new phase of life, and would like to be reconciled with his sister. But he isn't sure how she'll react to an invitation to the wedding. He doesn't want to deal with an angry sibling in the midst of the hectic preparations, so he decides against an invitation. Sometime after the wedding, he learns that his sister is very hurt that she was left out. He keeps berating himself, and his thinking about the matter includes the following, recurring ideas:

1. I should have tried to patch things up with my sister by telling her about my engagement and inviting her to my wedding.

2. That was a terrible thing to do to her.

3. I didn't mean to hurt her, but that doesn't make the hurt any less.

4. There's no way I can undo the hurt.

By regularly chewing on the thought that he didn't do what he should have done, he arrives at the point where he feels helpless to do anything. And he does so for two reasons. First, his toxic thinking has diverted him from more productive thinking about how to make amends and repair the relationship. And second, his toxic thinking includes the notion that he must "undo" the hurt, which would mean changing the past. And that, clearly, is impossible. In short, his own thinking pattern has taught him that he is helpless to do anything about the situation.

HOW LEARNED HELPLESSNESS CRIPPLES
SELF-FORGIVENESS EFFORTS

The final ideas in the man's toxic thinking flow easily from the four just listed:

5. I'll just have to live with what I've done.

6. Even if she forgives me some day, I can't forgive myself for hurting her so.

Other ideas can enter people's toxic thinking once they get mired in "I should have . . ." or "I shouldn't have . . ." For example: "I should have done that, and I didn't, so I'm not a good Christian"; or "I shouldn't have done that and I did, so I don't deserve forgiveness." But whatever the ideas, the basic sequence is to move from should or shouldn't to being helpless to undo the harm to the conclusion that forgiveness is not possible. And this means, of course, that the person stops trying.

Such toxic thinking is common in people who cannot forgive themselves. For example, in the early years of her marriage Karen felt uncertain about her husband's love for her. And they had their share of arguments and stresses. But she did not like confrontations, so she never felt comfortable bringing up the subject of his love. Then someone told her that her husband was having an affair. It happened at a point in the relationship where she believed it was true. She came to the conclusion that her marriage was over. She confided in a male friend and that led to a one-night affair with him. She felt miserable, but she wasn't sure she wanted to end her marriage. Eventually, she decided she could no longer tolerate the tension, that she and her husband would have to face up to their situation. For the first time, she talked openly and honestly with him. To her horror, she found out that he had been faithful to her all along. And although he was extremely distraught when he learned about her own unfaithfulness, he eventually forgave her and worked with her to rebuild the marriage. The major problem now is, as she says, "I can't forgive myself. I don't deserve his love. I have to live with this for the rest of my life." She continues to condemn herself.

BUT I SHOULDN'T HAVE . . .

There it is again. Even when we explain the dangers of toxic thinking, people may slip back into the should and shouldn't mode of thinking. That's why it's toxic. It tends to cling to your mind and divert you from the work of forgiving yourself. Why is it so difficult to break the pattern of toxic thinking? A pastoral counselor told us:

> One of the things that bothers people is their belief that their sin is a particularly grievous one. They might think of it as grievous because it hurt someone deeply. Or because they really missed the mark as a Christian. But in any case they take the matter very seriously. And they think that if they stop reminding themselves that they shouldn't have sinned, it means that they are turning something serious into something trivial, or that they aren't taking responsibility for what they did. The irony is that it's the obsession with their sin that keeps them from taking the responsibility they need to take—to face up to the sin, deal with it, and use it as a growth experience.

Let's reflect on a couple of these points.

It's Serious

Yes, it is. Whatever it is, we would never tell you that what bothers you is only a trivial matter.

Consider the following list:

- Having an extramarital affair
- Speaking harshly and hurtfully to my spouse

- Spreading gossip

- Forgetting to call a sick friend

- Putting the blame on someone else for something I did

- Laughing at my boss's racist jokes to advance my career

- Not being with my father when he died

Are some of the above more serious than others? Would you be able to forgive yourself easily for some of them? If so, keep in mind that there are others who would not easily forgive themselves, for the list is only a small sampling of the kinds of things with which people have struggled for self-forgiveness.

The point is, if you're struggling to forgive yourself for something, it *is* a serious matter. And nothing we say in this book should be taken to mean that your struggle involves something trivial.

I Need to Take Responsibility for My Actions

Yes, you do. And that brings up the very important point that the counselor made. You don't take responsibility by beating yourself up emotionally and spiritually. You don't take responsibility by giving the nagging guilt a home in your mind. In fact, these are traps that divert you from your true responsibility—to deal with the matter in a healthy way. Hear a parable:

> A man who made a meager living by cutting and delivering firewood to homes had three teen-aged boys. One morning he said to them: "Boys, I need you to come home right after school today and help me. I have a big order from one of my best customers. And he insists on having it delivered today. I'll start cutting this morning, but I can't get it finished unless you're all here to help."
>
> The boys all said they would and they went off to school. But all three returned home two hours late to find a distraught father. He looked at them angrily and said, "You made me lose one of my best customers. Why didn't you come home when I told you to?"

The youngest son said: "Father, you are right to be angry. I did say that I would be home. But my girlfriend said she needed help with her homework, so I worked with her." The youngest son went to his room and thought no more about the matter.

The oldest son said: "Yes, father, you should be angry. I, too, told you I would come home. But a couple of the guys had a pickup game of basketball. You know how much I want to make the team, so I need to play as much as I can. I'm really sorry." The oldest son went to his room, but he felt badly about hurting his father for a long time.

The middle son said: "Father, I understand why you are angry. I'm so sorry I didn't keep my promise to you. I, too, got into a game with my friends. But that's no excuse, and I want to somehow make it up to you." The middle son and his father spent time talking about what, if anything, could be done to salvage the situation.

Which of these three sons took responsibility for his behavior?

How would you answer the question? What *does* it mean to take responsibility for your actions? Is it simply a matter of owning up to what you have done? The youngest son did that, but it didn't help anyone. Is it, then, a matter of both owning up to your behavior and also expressing remorse for it? The oldest son did that, but it didn't help anyone either. In fact, it only made the oldest son feel guilty for a long time. Neither response is adequate. To take responsibility, then, means to do as the middle son: own up to what you have done, express remorse for it, and take some kind of action to redeem the situation.

Note that all three sons agreed that they shouldn't have broken their promise. The youngest son did not get mired in the "shouldn't have," but he is hardly a model for us. He seemed oblivious to his father's hurt. The oldest son did get mired in the "shouldn't have," and illustrates the consequences: personal suffer-

ing but no action to rectify the situation. Only the middle son reacted in a healthy way, acknowledging the "shouldn't have" but
moving on to doing something that would not only rectify the situation but enable him to forgive himself.

BREAKING FREE

Let's be honest. You're right. You shouldn't have, or should have, as
the case may be. We're not denying the validity of the charge.
We're simply saying that it's unhealthy to keep repeating the
charge. Imagine a courtroom where a man is charged with theft.
About every five minutes, the judge interrupts the proceedings,
looks sternly at the man, and says: "You shouldn't have stolen those
goods." Clearly, the judge is right. But what profit is that to anyone
in the courtroom or to the criminal justice system? The repetitious
charging simply delays justice. Similarly, repetitious self-condemnation simply prevents or delays the process of self-forgiveness.

Now you may agree with all that we have said so far. But you
still have a problem: "It keeps haunting me. It just pops into my
mind. How can I stop it?" Actually, if you've come that far, you're
in good shape. At least you've gotten beyond the notion that you're
trivializing the offense if you stop thinking about the fact that you
offended. To break the final link in the chain that has bound you
to this toxic thinking, counter any thoughts about "I shouldn't
have" or "I should have" by replacing them with healthy thoughts.
In particular, whenever a toxic thought enters your mind, replace
it with three thoughts that are healthy and more realistic: I am
human; I cannot, and I do not have to, totally undo the hurt; and
I can do what is needed to rectify the situation and forgive myself.

I Am Human

How many flawless people do you know? If you name anyone at
all, we would say that you don't really know that person well
enough. Because as the Scriptures remind us, we all have sinned
and fallen short of the glory of God (Rom. 3:23). That means that
every single person has hurt someone else, has fallen short of his

or her ideals, has violated some Christian principles, and so on. Only God is flawless.

"But," as one man objected to us, "I don't know anyone who cheated on their wife the way I did." His problem was that he did what a good many American Christians tend to do: establish a hierarchy of sins, with sexual sins right at the top of the list. Such a hierarchy does not exist in the Bible. In the same passage in which Paul lists sexual sins, he includes such things as jealousy, anger, quarrels, and envy (Gal. 5:19–20). Some sins may be more noticeable than others, but, again, we all have sinned.

So if our first reaction to "I shouldn't have" is "you're right, you shouldn't have," our second reaction is: "welcome to the human race." We all have done things that we shouldn't have done and failed to do things that we should have done. That's the reality of being human. And the appropriate and healthy reaction is not to embark on a time of mental self-flagellation, but to glory in and accept God's forgiveness and to forgive yourself. Karen, whom we discussed earlier, said: "Nothing can change what I've done." That's only partly true. There is one thing that can change it, that can stop it from corroding her life—forgiveness, including God's forgiveness (which she has received), her husband's forgiveness (which she has received), and self-forgiveness (with which she still struggles). When she finally forgives herself, she'll be able to say: "Nothing can change what I've done, but I thank God that through forgiveness I am no longer a prisoner of my own past."

So the next time the shouldn't or should pops into your mind, push it out and replace it with, "But I'm human; only God is flawless."

I Cannot, and I Do Not Have to, Totally Undo the Hurt

A second thought to replace the toxic thoughts that come to your mind is that you simply can't, nor do you need to, completely erase the hurt. We discussed this briefly in chapter 2. Of course, it's a natural reaction to want to undo the offense and its consequences. We once observed a university class in which a student make a remark that the professor regarded as naive. The professor blurted out a sarcastic response, then stopped. He knew immediately that he his remark was inappropriate and hurtful. Sheepishly, he looked at the class and said, "I'm sorry. Did you ever wish that life was a video recorder, so that when you mess up you could just put your life on rewind and go over that part again? That's the way I feel right now. And I do apologize."

His statement eased the tension and the hurt inflicted on the student. But did it completely undo the hurt? No. The student was hesitant to speak up in that or any other class for some time, not wanting to be humiliated again.

So of course you would like to completely undo the damage. And of course that's impossible. That's the point at which Karen is stuck. As she put it:

> Every day, I wish I could go back and do it over. I wish I would have been more open with my husband and less willing to cry on someone else's shoulder. And I desperately wish I hadn't cheated on my husband. He says he's over it and we need to move on. But I can't get rid of the feeling that there's anger or disappointment in his eyes whenever he looks at me.

In point of fact, there may well be a measure of anger or disappointment in him. If so, it will subside and even disappear in time. But he's doing the best he can for now. What Karen needs to recognize is that her continual self-loathing over not being able to remove all traces of anger and disappointment is part of the problem. It affects the way she relates to him. It constantly reminds him of what she did. It prevents her from moving on to self-forgiveness. And the net effect is corrosive to their relationship.

I Can, and I Must, Do What Is Needed to Rectify the Situation and Forgive Myself

Toxic thinking teaches you to feel helpless. But you are not helpless. You are, after all, a child of God. You are one of those of whom it is said that God "is at work in you, enabling you both to will and to work for his good pleasure" (Phil. 2:13). You are one of those who are called to "be strong in the Lord and in the strength of his power" (Eph. 6:10). So replace the toxic thoughts with the thought that you can, and indeed you must, act in a way to redeem a bad situation and you can, and you must, forgive yourself.

We say it again. You can and you must. Because if it's destructive and therefore wrong to punish others with unforgiveness, it's destructive and wrong to do it to yourself as well. If it's an act of love to forgive another person, it's also an act of love to forgive yourself. And if we are called by God to be forgiving people, God will give us the power we need to obey.

Indeed, Christian history is filled with remarkable instances of forgiveness. Jesus asked God to forgive those who crucified him. Stephen asked God to forgive those who stoned him to death. In more recent times, Holocaust survivors have learned to forgive the Nazis, and people caught up in genocide or religious or civil wars have been able to forgive those who perpetrated the violence against them. And we recall the incident in 2006, when a man walked into a one-room Amish schoolhouse in Nickel Mines, Pennsylvania, and, for no apparent reason, shot ten young girls, killing five of them. He then killed himself. The grieving Amish community soon expressed forgiveness for the man and his family. They buttressed the reality of their forgiveness by donating money to the killer's widow and her three children. And a number of them attended the killer's burial service.

Was this easy for them? Not at all. Did they struggle to express forgiveness? Of course. Have they recovered quickly from the tragedy? Of course not. It is never easy to forgive someone who wants to kill you. It is painfully difficult to forgive someone who has killed your child. The point is not that it is easy, but that it can be done.

And this is true for self-forgiveness. We know people who get discouraged because it doesn't come quickly or easily to them.

They fall into the trap of thinking it simply can't be done. But it can be done. It has been done. If it's possible to forgive the killer of your child, it is possible to forgive yourself for whatever you have done or failed to do. We know. We have seen people do it. But it won't happen as long as you allow toxic thoughts to dominate your mind. So rebuke them and replace them with the kind of healthy, appropriate thoughts we have suggested.

Don't Turn a Part into the Whole

Have you heard the ancient Hindu tale of the six blind men who were asked to feel an elephant and describe what the animal was like? One of the blind men touched the elephant on the side and said that the animal was like a wall. Another ran his hand along a tusk and declared the elephant to be like a spear. The third took hold of the elephant's wiggling trunk and thought the elephant was like a snake.

The fourth cried out that they were all wrong. He had his arms around one of the legs and was certain the elephant was like a tree. But the fifth blind man, feeling the elephant's waving ear, said the animal was like a fan. And the sixth, who had taken hold of the tail, confidently told the others that the elephant was truly like a rope.

We have a saying that the whole is greater than the sum of its parts. What the blind men were doing was to make the whole equal to one of its parts. And this is what we want to explore in this chapter—the tendency of those who are finding it painful to forgive themselves to turn what is a part—their own offense—into the whole—their character.

TOXIC THINKING REVISITED: I AM A BAD PERSON

The kind of thinking we discussed in the last chapter—getting stuck on "should" and "shouldn't"—is not the only kind that is toxic. Turning an act or a series of acts into a metaphor for who you are often follows from "I should have . . ." or "I shouldn't have . . ." It is equally toxic.

We have found that when it comes to self-forgiveness many people tend to think not just of a particular act but of their whole character. It isn't just "I said something hurtful to Marla," but "I'm a bad person who says hurtful things." We call this process toxic generalization. You take something specific and turn it into a general characterization of who you are. And it can begin with "should" or "shouldn't" thinking. The sequence of thinking goes like this:

1. I shouldn't have said those hurtful things to Marla.

2. Good people don't talk like that.

3. But I did it and I'm without excuse.

4. Therefore I am clearly a bad person.

Recall Sharon, whose story we told in the introductory chapter. Her online dalliance with a man she met in a chat room haunts her not only because she believes she has betrayed her husband, but also because it says something about the kind of person she is:

> I used to think of myself as a pretty good woman. Not perfect. But you read about all the sexual stuff that goes on in Hollywood and among politicians, and you think, "Wow, at least I haven't gotten into any of that. At least I'm faithful to my husband." And then I go and do the same kind of thing. I don't personally know anyone else who's done what I have. So suddenly I don't feel so good about myself anymore. I'm just like those movie actors and actresses and the politicians who cheat on their partners. I look in the mirror and I say to my reflection,

"You're not the good woman I thought you were. I can't tell you how disappointed I am in you."

Before commenting on Sharon's self-condemnation, we'd like to tell you about another woman, Fran, a forty-five-year-old who has a very fragile sense of her own worth. If you spent time with Fran, you would find her attractive and intelligent. She has achieved a great deal in her life—raising two children, working as a librarian, and volunteering at her church and a local hospital. But Fran doesn't think of herself as a success:

> I get so weary of always falling short. I never can seem to do enough. At times, I feel like I've wasted a good part of my life. In my mind, I know this isn't true. But emotionally I'm stuck with my failures. I guess it goes back to my childhood. My father expected so much from me. I remember bringing home a report card from high school with five A's and one B+. The only thing my father said was "What happened in the class with the B grade?" And I can remember the first meal I cooked for my parents— my mother worked full time so I tried to help out. I worked for hours on the meal. I could tell my mother liked it. But my father only had one comment: "You didn't cook the potatoes long enough." That's the kind of thing he would say over and over. I just couldn't seem to measure up to what he expected me to be.
>
> My father is dead now. But not to me. His demanding spirit is always with me. It's like I feel his displeasure every time I fall short of perfection. And even when I don't, I still wonder if I've done enough.

What would you say about such a father? Most people react negatively when they hear Fran's story. They believe, and we agree, that it was the father and not the daughter who fell short— way short! He turned what was a part of her—her inability to be perfect in everything she did—into the whole of her—a person who can never do enough or be enough. Tragically, an intelligent, capable woman can only see herself as one who will invariably mess things up in some way. And now she faces the vexing problem of not only forgiving her father for what he did, but also of forgiving herself for letting it happen.

We tell Fran's story for a particular reason. What her father did to Fran, people often do to themselves. This, in fact, is what Sharon has done. She has turned a part of herself—her lapse in the chat room—into the whole of herself—she is an evil person. Ironically, even Sharon is appalled by what Fran's father did to his daughter. We hope that Sharon can come to the point where she stops doing the same thing to herself that she finds so offensive in Fran's father. Whether imposed on someone else or on oneself, this kind of toxic thinking is destructive.

THE MAZE WITHOUT AN END

When you turn a part of you into the whole of you, you enter a maze without an end. You're trapped, wandering from one dead end to another. Your only hope is to escape the maze and find a better path to take.

Dead End Number 1: Affirming the Unrealistic

As we pointed out in the last chapter, toxic thinking is unrealistic because it assumes that you can live a flawless life. Toxic thinking is also unrealistic because it affirms a distorted view of who you are, namely that the offense for which you feel guilty represents the whole of you rather than a part of you.

We love a story told by a priest. He said to his five-year-old niece one day to think about a world in which all the good people were painted blue and all the bad people were painted yellow. Then he asked her which of those colors she would be. She thought about it for a moment, then said: "I'd be streaky." She knew that at times she behaved well and at other times she misbehaved. But she refused to let either of those kinds of behavior be the whole description of who she was.

So the message we'd like Sharon and all who think like her to accept is: you're not evil, you're just streaky like all the rest of us. Reject the toxic generalization that turns a part of you into the whole of you because it puts you in a dead end that goes something like this:

1. I have done something bad.

2. I did it because I am an evil person.

3. If I forgive myself, I'm not facing up to the kind of person I am.

4. Therefore I cannot forgive myself.

Dead End Number 2: Raising Unanswerable Questions

Another dead end is when you seek an answer to questions such as: Why am I an evil person who does bad things? What's wrong with me? What happened to make me the way I am? These are questions for which there are no answers and that shouldn't be raised in the first place.

These questions can't be answered because they're based on false assumptions—that you *are* an evil person and that something *is* wrong with you. In chapter 1, we discussed Susan and her sexual experimentation when she was a teenager. During her counseling sessions Susan often raised an unanswerable question:

> I look back on what I did, and I try over and over to figure out why. I know all of the stock answers. It was teenage rebellion. It was peer pressure. It was a reaction against the strict religious training of my parents. Maybe so. But none of that helps me now. I still can't get over the feeling that I'm missing something that I ought to have as a Christian. Why didn't I refuse to be drawn into it? And I sometimes wonder—was that the real me? Is the person I am today not the real me?

In effect, Susan wondered if she was an evil person who only pretended to be righteous—the proverbial wolf in sheep's clothing. Susan started making progress toward forgiving herself only when she realized that her questions could not be answered because they were based on a false assumption.

Dead End Number 3: Focusing on the Wrong Thing

Focusing on the wrong thing cannot only be a dead end; it can be deadly to your well-being. We once read about a high-wire artist who, after decades of successful performances, fell from the tightrope. Although he was not killed, he did suffer severe injuries. He was interviewed while recovering and asked what had happened. He could only think of one thing. Throughout his career, he said, his focus had been on stepping on the tightrope. For some reason, on the day he fell he shifted his attention to not falling off the tightrope. He focused on the wrong thing. And by shifting his focus from what he needed to do to what he didn't want to do, he essentially set himself up to fail.

We've seen the same sort of self-defeating focus in people who struggle to forgive themselves. Instead of focusing on what they need to do—forgive themselves—they focus on self-deprecating thoughts. Stuck on the notion that they are evil people, they give no thought to the matter of self-forgiveness. We've not only seen this happen, we've seen it literally torment some people for decades. They are in a dead end that turns out to be deadly for their emotional and spiritual health.

FROM TOXIC TO HEALTHY

As we pointed out in the last chapter, toxic thinking needs to be replaced with healthy thoughts. If you have fallen into the trap of confusing a part of yourself with your whole self, there are healthy ways to defeat this toxic generalization.

That Isn't Me

Whenever the thought that you are a bad or evil person enters your mind, you can counter it by telling yourself "That isn't me." There are two reasons why it really isn't you. One has to do with intent and the other has to do with your reaction.

Let's think about intent first. Consider the following scenario. Pam is married, the mother of two children, and a part-time salesperson in a department store. She helps out at her children's school and with their soccer teams. Like many mothers today, she typically feels time-pressured and caught up in a whirlwind of activities. She also finds herself frequently impatient and short-tempered. As a result, she may snap at someone or say something hurtful as she struggles to cope with the pressures.

One day, a colleague neglected to tell Pam about a special sale that had started in their department. When Pam charged the regular price on a necklace, the customer became irate and accused Pam of incompetence. After the customer left, Pam vented her frustration by complaining to her colleague: "You're supposed to alert me to all the sales. You're full-time here. If you don't do your job, I can't do mine. I'm sick of taking the blame for your screw-ups." Flushed with anger, her colleague struck back at Pam, accusing her of being arrogant, rude, and irresponsible.

It wasn't the first time that Pam and her colleague had exchanged angry words. So here's our question. Is Pam an evil person? Her colleague might say, "Yes." And if Pam believes that her impatience and temper define the whole of who she is, she might also say, "Yes." But of course Pam is more than that. Her children know her as a sometimes irritable but loving mother. Her husband knows her as an oftentimes harried but loving wife. Her friends know her as a concerned woman who doesn't tolerate incompetence well but who contributes a good deal to her community.

The point is this: to say that someone is an evil person requires that the person *intends* to do evil. In the first chapter of Romans Paul describes the evil people upon whom the wrath of God is poured. In addition to a long list of sins, he says that they are "inventors of evil" and that they not only practice varied sins themselves but "even applaud others who practice them" (Rom. 1:30, 32). An inventor of evil is someone who intends to engage in evil acts and who looks for ever more varied ways of committing those acts. Since the intent is to justify and spread the evil, the evil person rejoices in other people who do the same things.

And that is precisely what differentiates Pam from those who are evil. In fact, in all of our dealings with people struggling to forgive themselves for some offense, we have not yet encountered one who set out with the *intent* of committing a sin. Pam angered and hurt her colleague, but she did not set out that day intending to do so. Nor does she approve this kind of behavior nor admire and applaud others who anger and hurt people by their words. Similarly, the woman who feels guilty about neglecting her aged parents did not decide one morning that she would no longer look after them, nor does she approve of people neglecting their parents. The man who committed adultery did not decide one morning that he would initiate an affair that day nor does he approve of infidelity. The young woman who broke her "abstinence only" vow did not decide one morning that this would be the day she'd lose her virginity, nor does she approve of those who break such vows.

If you're struggling to forgive yourself for some act, we have two questions for you. Did you intend to do it? Do you applaud other people who do it? If your answer is "no" to both those questions, you are not an evil person.

The other reason you are not an evil person has to do with your reaction to your offense. You feel guilty. That's why you're struggling with self-forgiveness. If you were an evil person, forgiving yourself wouldn't be an issue. You wouldn't feel guilty. As a man put it:

> I didn't become a Christian until I was an adult. So I have a different perspective on things than a lot of people. I see Christians who try to convert others by convincing them that they are sinners who need a Savior. That's true, but it didn't work with me. I never had a sense of sin until *after* I became a Christian. I became a Christian because I heard about God's promise of abundant life and that's what I wanted. It was only afterwards when I started

learning about what it means to be a Christian, what it means to be righteous, the kinds of things that offend God, only then did I have a sense of my own sins.

Having neither the intent nor the reaction of those who are evil, then, you can dismiss the thought that you are an evil person. Replace it with: "I don't need to forgive myself for being the kind of person I am. I need to forgive myself for an action that I, as an individual striving to grow more like Christ, regret and don't want to repeat."

Forgiveness Is Always for the Offense, Not the Offender

A second way to counter toxic generalization is to remind yourself that forgiveness is always for the offense and not for the offender. In the first chapter, we dwelt at some length on your need to love both others and yourself, and on the fact that forgiveness is an act of love. Think for a moment about what it means to forgive another person. Let's say the person has said some hurtful things about you. Just what is it that you are forgiving? You might say, "I forgive you," but what you are really forgiving is the offense and not the person. That is, you are saying that you forgive the person for having said the hurtful things, not that you are forgiving the person for being the kind of person that he or she is.

Take Ken, for example. Ken told us that he has no trouble forgiving others but has a difficult time forgiving himself. When asked to give us an example of how he has forgiven someone he told this story:

> When I told my brother that I was getting married, he got really upset. He didn't think that Betsy was right for me. Actually, he didn't think that she was good enough for me. Her family wasn't as well off financially as ours, and she didn't have a college education. I could overlook him saying that, but then he suggested that she had been in an awful lot of relationships. He said she had no doubt slept with more guys than anyone I had ever dated.

Well, that really angered me. We got into a big argument and didn't talk to each other for months. But the more he got to know Betsy, the more he realized how wrong he was about her. So he apologized. And I forgave him. I know he was only concerned about me. He didn't want me to get hurt by Betsy.

Note that Ken did not use toxic generalization in referring to his brother. He did not take the hurtful things his brother said and use them to turn his brother into a generally hurtful person. In fact, he acknowledged that his brother is a generally caring, supportive person who happened to say some very hurtful things. Thus, when he forgave his brother he was forgiving the specific offense —the hurtful things his brother had said.

Ken needs to apply the same insight to himself. When he struggles with forgiving himself, he needs to focus on his behavior rather than on who he is as a person. He needs to treat himself with the same respect and understanding that he gave to his brother.

When, in short, you find yourself thinking what an evil person you are for having done or failed to do something, push that thought aside. In its place, remind yourself that your task is to do for yourself what you do to others—focus on forgiving the offense rather than condemning the self.

Use Your Spiritual Resources

Hear another parable:

A man and his wife purchased a place in the country where they could raise horses. They decided to spend their weekends getting the house and the grounds ready before they moved in. On the first weekend, the husband said he'd start digging postholes because the entire tract needed to be fenced. He went out to work, while his wife began cleaning up the house.

At noon, the man returned to the house for lunch. "How many holes did you dig?" his wife asked.

"Four," he replied.

"Four?" the wife asked, calculating that at this rate he would be digging postholes for months. "What happened? Is the ground really hard?"

"No," he said. "Fortunately, it's quite workable."

"Did you get tired and have to rest?" she asked.

"It was very tiring," he said. "In fact, I think I'm going to take the rest of the day off."

"I thought the posthole digger would make it easier," she said.

"The what?" he asked.

"The posthole digger I bought for you last month and put in the trunk of the car so we wouldn't forget to bring it," she replied.

He looked abashed. "Oh dear," he said, "I completely forgot about it. So I looked for a shovel in the shed. But there wasn't one there. So I used the only thing available—a trowel. It takes a long time to dig a posthole with a trowel."

The exasperated couple sat down to lunch. No more holes were dug that day.

We call this the parable of the foolish hole-digger. The man was foolish for trying to dig holes with a trowel. He was foolish for forgetting about the posthole digger. In short, he didn't make use of a readily available resource that would have enabled him to efficiently complete his task.

In the same way, we've seen people struggling with self-forgiveness make the same mistake. They forget about or neglect using one of the most powerful tools they have—spiritual resources. What do these spiritual resources include?

TALK WITH GOD

Our pastor does not say, "Let us pray." He says, "Let's talk with God." We like that. It reminds us that prayer is not just a ritual, not just a repetition of standard phrases, but a conversation with God. Time-honored prayers have value for their familiarity and for the way in which they beautifully express the comfort and hope we have in our faith. But for many purposes, including forgiving yourself, you need to have a personal conversation with God.

When you talk with God, you talk as you would with a trusted confidant. You use your own words. You begin, as we noted in chapter 2, with your confession. You go beyond that, however, with an honest disclosure of your thoughts and feelings and a willingness to be quiet and listen.

Honest Disclosure

The Psalms model for us what it means to honestly share our thoughts and feelings with God. Among other things, the psalmist freely pours out to God his:

- Despair: "My tears have been my food day and night, while people say to me continually, 'Where is your God?'" (Psa. 42:3).

- Frustration with vexing problems: "Have mercy upon us, O Lord, have mercy upon us, for we have had more than enough of contempt" (Psa. 123:3).

- Experience of God's lack of response: "How long, O Lord? Will you forget me forever? How long will you hide your face from me?" (Psa. 13:1).

Similarly, the prophets spoke bluntly with God. Like the psalmist, Habakkuk complained about God's lack of response: "O Lord, how long shall I cry for help, and you will not listen? Or cry to you, 'Violence!' and you will not save?" (Hab. 1:2). And perhaps no one ever complained more bitterly to God or argued more with God than did the prophet Jeremiah. At one particularly low point in his life, he charged God with overpowering him and calling him to a task that made him "a laughingstock all day long" (Jer. 20:7). So great was his distress that he cried out: "Cursed be the day on which I was born! . . . Why did I come forth from the womb to see toil and sorrow, and spend my days in shame?" (Jer. 20:14, 18).

These expressions of vexation do not sound like the prayers we hear in church. They probably do not sound like the prayers people typically utter in private. But they are honest expressions of thoughts and feelings. That's what talking with God is all about. It's sharing your joys and your griefs, your hopes and your disappointments, your beliefs and your doubts, your thanksgivings and your complaints. In other words, it's like talking with your confidant. You freely express what you are thinking and feeling in order to confront and deal with the challenges and opportunities of your life.

For example, consider the prayer of a woman who cannot forgive herself for verbally abusing her hyperactive son when he was small:

> Dear God, I just can't stand myself when I remember how I talked to him. I'd give anything to go back and do it over. Every time I think about the look on his face when I would holler at him, I could cry. Why couldn't I just accept him as he was? Why did I have to hurt him that way? Why did you let me do it? Why didn't you help me be a better mother? I prayed for help, but I don't feel I got it. Now I feel like such a failure. You say you forgive me. But I don't know how I'll ever be able to forgive myself. I'm trying. But I'm not getting anywhere. Where are you, God?

Is this an appropriate prayer? Absolutely! Because it is an honest prayer. Like the psalmist and the prophets, the woman pours out her heart to God. And whatever you may think about her blaming herself and blaming God, the important thing is that she is being open with God. And that's a crucial step in the healing process.

Quiet Listening

Talking *with* God, as opposed to talking *to* God, implies a conversation rather than a monologue. In other words, your prayer does not end when you stop speaking and say, "amen." A time of quietness and listening is an important component when talking with God. We're not suggesting meditation, in which you focus your mind on a word or a Scripture verse. Meditation is very useful for many purposes. However, when struggling with self-forgiveness we suggest that, after you honestly disclose your thoughts and your feelings to God, you quietly wait and allow thoughts and images to flow freely through you. If your mind drifts off to something totally removed from your struggle (such as some task awaiting you), briefly recall what you have told God and try again.

What will happen while you quietly listen? You may have a thought pop into your mind that, as you reflect on it, is a word from God to you. Or you may have an image run through your mind that brings you a message from God. A man who struggled to be free of guilt about what he regarded as a deficient spiritual life told us about the following experience when he was in the midst of his struggle:

> I read a psalm before taking a walk through the park. I can't even remember which psalm it was. But I thought about it as I walked. I was impressed with how much spiritual insight there is in the Psalms. Which only reminded me of how defective my own spiritual life was. I came to an empty bench and sat down. No one else was around. I prayed briefly: "God, I so want to feel closer to you. Why can't I? What's wrong with me?"
>
> Then I just sat there and tried to think about nothing except the beauty of the scenery. After a few moments, an image came into my mind. I don't know what triggered it. It just came. It was a picture of Jesus coming up and sitting beside me. He put his arm around me. He didn't say a word. He just sat with me for a moment with his arm around me. It was as if he was saying to me, "I love you, I'm with you, and I'll always be with you." I believe God was speaking to me in that image. He was reminding me that he loves me as I am. And that he'll keep loving me and stay with me as I strive to grow as a Christian. I don't have to be perfect. I just have to keep trying.

RECALL THE ACTS AND TEACHINGS OF GOD

Remember. Again and again we are told in the Scriptures to remember what God has said and done. When the Israelites crossed the Jordan into the promised land, they set up twelve stones as a memorial to God's deliverance of the twelve tribes from the land of Egypt (Josh. 4:1–9). The Passover celebration is also a call to remember that deliverance. Holy Communion is a reminder of the death of Jesus and of our own deliverance from death to life.

These are examples of positive remembering. (We say "positive remembering" because clearly one can also engage in negative remembering of failures and painful times and sink into apprehension and fear about new challenges.) The wisdom of positive remembering is easily seen in everyday experiences. The father who reminds his little league son of how well he hit the ball in the last game, the manager who reminds her team of the superb work they did on their last assignment, and the physician who reminds a patient of how quickly he or she recovered from surgery are all tapping into the wisdom and power of positive remembering. By using positive remembering, they are acting as encouragers and motivators.

Two kinds of positive remembering can help you as you work to forgive yourself. One is your own life experiences. The other involves the experiences of biblical characters along with biblical passages that offer guidance, comfort, and hope.

Your Own Life

Do the following exercise. On a blank piece of paper draw a line from top to bottom maybe half way across the page. Then, starting at the top with your earliest event, make a vertical time line—listing as many significant events in your life as you can remember and marking the age at which they occurred. These events can include relationships, experiences, decisions, or anything else you consider a significant point in your life. They should include both positive and negative kinds of events. For example, your life line might begin something like this:

SIGNIFICANT EVENT	AGE
Role in 6th grade play	11
First love	14
College acceptance	18
Changed major	21
Lost first job	25

And so on. Depending on your age and how packed your life has been, you may need several sheets of paper.

Once you have listed the events, go back over them and ask yourself a question: In what way was God at work in my life at this point? It doesn't matter if you didn't feel God at work at the time. In retrospect, you should be able to see the hand of God at work in some way in the major events of your life. This doesn't mean that God manipulated you so that the event had to happen. It only means that whatever happened, God was—as promised— at work for your good (Rom. 8:28).

People who do this exercise often find patterns in their lives of which they were unaware (such as significant events at regular intervals or similar kinds of events that turn out to be significant). But whether or not you find a pattern, you will gain a greater appreciation for the many ways in which God has been at work in your life. A woman put it this way:

> When I look at my life line, I'm struck by a number of things. One is that I've really been blessed by so many good things. Another is that the bad times—those times when I felt like God had taken a vacation and left me on my own—look different to me now. For example, going through my divorce was horrible. But now I can see how I've grown by struggling through it. And although I didn't always feel it, I also recognize that God was with me through those difficult days. I keep my time line handy as a reminder of God's action in my life and as a help when I go through rough periods.

That's the point. Remember what God has done in your life so far. Remember that God has been with you throughout. And now that you're striving to forgive yourself, know that God is with you in your struggle. God, who has blessed you in numberless ways, God, who has been with you in your difficulties, will continue to bless you and be with you in your struggle to forgive yourself. You are not alone.

Biblical Experiences and Teachings

In chapter 1 we reminded you of the experiences of David and Peter. They both illustrate the point—as do others in the Scriptures—that we are all human, that we all have sinned against each other and against God. And they both illustrate the point that God will forgive you and that you can forgive yourself no matter how serious the offense or offenses may be. Recall David's mental and physical agony over his sins as he expressed them in Psalm 32 and Psalm 51. Yet David experienced the forgiveness of God, and he was able to forgive himself. Thus, the psalm that describes his torment ends on a note of joy: "Be glad in the Lord and rejoice, O righteous, and shout for joy, all you upright in heart" (Psa. 32:11).

Many biblical passages also offer guidance and encouragement as you strive to forgive yourself. They don't deal directly with self-forgiveness, but they stress such things as the forgiveness, mercy, and grace of God. They also stress your responsibility to deal in a forgiving and gracious way with others. And remember, if this is the way you are to act with others, it's also the way you're to act with yourself. The following list represents a sampling of biblical passages that people have found helpful. You may want to memorize one or more of them:

- "Call on me in the day of trouble; I will deliver you, and you shall glorify me" (Psa. 50:15).

- "Cast all your anxiety on him, because he cares for you" (1 Pet. 5:7).

- "The Lord upholds all who are falling, and raises up all who are bowed down" (Psa. 145:14).

- "If we confess our sins, he who is faithful and just will forgive us our sins and cleanse us from all unrighteousness" (1 John 1:9).

- "He does not deal with us according to our sins, nor repay us according to our iniquities. For as the heavens are high above the earth, so great is his steadfast love toward those who fear him; as far as the east is from the west, so far he removes our transgressions from us" (Psa. 103:10–11).

- "Then I acknowledged my sin to you, and I did not hide my iniquity; I said, 'I will confess my transgressions to the Lord,' and you forgave the guilt of my sin" (Psa. 32:5).

- "[A]nd be kind to one another, tenderhearted, forgiving one another, as God in Christ has forgiven you" (Eph. 4:32).

- "For you, O Lord, are good and forgiving, abounding in steadfast love to all who call on you" (Psa. 86:5).

- "And when you were dead in trespasses and the uncircumcision of your flesh, God made you alive together with him, when he forgave us all our trespasses" (Col. 2:13).

- "For I am convinced that neither death, nor life, nor angels, nor rulers, nor things present, nor things to come, nor powers, nor height, nor depth, nor anything else in all creation, will be able to separate us from the love of God in Christ Jesus our Lord" (Rom. 8:38–39).

The preceding passages are useful substitutes for the toxic thoughts we have discussed. You might find it helpful to meditate on them when you talk with God. The more you saturate your mind with thoughts of grace and forgiveness, the easier it will be for you to reach your goal of forgiving yourself.

OTHER RESOURCES

Talking with God and using the Scriptures are the more obvious spiritual resources available to you. There are, however, a number of other resources that people have found helpful. Keep in mind that none of these resources works effectively for everyone. Nevertheless, we still encourage you to give one or more of them a try.

Seek Absolution

Many churches, including the Roman Catholic and a number of Orthodox and Protestant denominations, have a long tradition of including absolution—the declaration of forgiveness of your sins by a priest or minister—as a regular part of worship. If you find it more comforting and meaningful to hear someone other than yourself declare that you are forgiven, you may want to attend a worship service that includes the act of confession and absolution.

You may find it even more comforting and meaningful to hear someone assert that you are forgiven in a one-on-one rather than a group situation. If so, seek absolution from a pastor who is willing to hear your confession and declare you forgiven. We noted in chapter 2 that many churches have a Stephen Ministry. A part of the training of Stephen Ministers involves ways to provide spiritual care, including listening to a confession and giving assurance of God's pardon. If your church does not have a Stephen Ministry, find one that does and ask for a Stephen Minister to contact you.

Use Music

Because we view all creative activity as a result of God-given talent, we include music of any kind as a spiritual resource. The music you find useful may be nothing more than an annoyance to someone else. The point is to use the music that lifts your spirits and gives you a greater sense of God's presence in the world and in your life. For the greater your sense of God's presence, the easier it will be for you to forgive yourself. You cannot bask in the presence of a loving, forgiving God and continue to berate and degrade yourself. For example, a woman told us:

> It was at a time when I was alone and feeling stressed. I decided to go to a concert. They were performing Beethoven's Ninth Symphony. When they came to the Ode to Joy, I was transported into another realm. It was as though God reached down and lifted me up high into the heavenly places. I went home feeling unburdened, happy, and better prepared to deal with the problems I was facing. To this day, I still regard that as one of the spiritual highlights of my life.

Or you may find hymns helpful. We have heard of Christian leaders who sing a hymn every day as a part of their devotions.

Singing—aloud or to yourself (there are those among us who should always confine our singing to ourselves)—is healing both because music really can soothe the savage (as well as the struggling) soul and because the words themselves can be healing. Darrel, at midlife, wrestled with the question of whether he should quit his career in the automotive business and prepare for the ministry. He felt led to do so. But he also felt a serious constraint, namely, his indulgence with on-line pornography some years earlier. How could he think of becoming a minister, particularly in an era when sexual scandals were causing turmoil in the church? It was a hymn that gave him the courage to proceed with his career change:

> I went to church one Sunday when my insides were still in turmoil over the matter. I have to admit that I didn't expect anything at the service would help me resolve the issue. But it so happened that a young woman sang a solo during the offertory. She sang an old hymn called "Grace Greater Than Our Sin." And the last line hit me right between the eyes. God's grace really is greater than all our sin. I don't have to be perfect to be a minister. I just have to accept the grace of God that forgives and cleanses me. I left that service knowing what I was going to do.

Attend a Healing Service

For many people the term "healing service" conjures up an image of a ranting preacher who smacks the sick on their foreheads and tells them they are healed of their various physical illnesses. There are numerous healing services throughout the nation, however, that do not involve a showy spectacle and are not limited to dealing with physical illness. You can attend such healing services when your inability to forgive yourself has put you in need of emotional and spiritual healing.

Many Episcopal churches, for example, have a chapter of the International Order of St. Luke the Physician, which is an ecumenical, healing ministry. These churches have regular healing services. At such a service, there may be a healing prayer, the laying on of hands, or an anointing with oil. You won't be asked to do anything that would be uncomfortable for you. Instead, what you will discover is a group of people who believe in God's healing, who care about each other, and who work together in their quest for healing.

Search the Media

Both the print and the electronic media are good resources. The fact that you are reading this book means that you are already using the print media. In addition, browse your church library, your public library, or your local bookstore to find other books that deal with forgiveness. Some of them will have at least a short section on self-forgiveness. You can also use your local library to search for articles in magazines.

Also take advantage of the electronic media, particularly the Internet. Use a search engine to explore the topic "forgiving yourself." We tried it and came up with hundreds of thousands of hits. (It occurred to us that someone might get so weary going through such a glut of sites that he or she would exercise self-forgiveness simply to get relief from the seemingly endless number of possibilities.) You'll find some stories of people who have struggled with self-forgiveness as well as numerous suggestions on how you can learn to forgive yourself.

Of course, as you go through the media, you'll encounter many repetitious ideas. That's okay. Your mind has been assaulted by repetitious toxic thinking. Now let it be inundated with ideas that bring healing.

Use Visualization

Have you ever looked up at the night sky and tried to comprehend the enormity of the universe? When David did, he was struck with a sense of wonder: "When I look at your heavens, the work of your fingers, the moon and the stars that you have established, what are human beings that you are mindful of them, mortals that you care for them?" (Psa. 8:3–4).

David felt small, even trivial, as he pondered God's creation. And the universe with which he compared humans was minuscule compared to what we know today. It is composed not just of the thousands of stars that awed David, but of a hundred billion or more galaxies that are composed of, on the average, around 150 billion stars.

Still, someone once said that the mind that encompasses the universe is greater than the universe than encompasses the mind. We agree. David suggested the possibility when he went on to say about humans: "Yet you have made them a little lower than God, and crowned them with glory and honor" (Psa. 8:5). Humans, made in the image of God, have minds that are incredibly powerful. Of course, the universe is staggering in its immensity. But the mind is awesome in its capabilities, in doing that which not even the universe can do. For the mind can observe and strive to understand the universe, but the universe cannot probe into the mind.

The power of the mind is seen in the ways that it can influence your body and your emotions. Among other things, researchers have discovered how you can use your mind to:

- Lower your blood pressure.
- Reduce your tension level.
- Create a more optimistic outlook on life.
- Induce healing processes in your body.

One activity of this powerful mind that helps many people, including those struggling with self-forgiveness, is visualization. All it requires of you is a little imagination and a little time.

WHAT VISUALIZATION IS

Visualization is the technique of using your imagination to create a mental and/or emotional picture of what you want to happen or that allows you to achieve a desired emotional state. Actually, it's likely you are already using visualization but in negative rather than positive ways. For it is common among those who struggle with self-forgiveness to have images from the past that continue to trouble them. This negative visualization is seen in such statements as:

- "I can still see the hurt look on his face."
- "The thought of my mother dying in that room with no one around to hold her hand or comfort her just haunts me."
- "I wish I could erase that image of her breaking down and crying because of what I did."
- "I just stood there. I didn't say a word. I could have really helped him. But I just stood there like a dummy."
- "When I looked in the mirror the next morning, I said, 'You're a fraud.' And I've done the same thing almost every morning since then."

These kinds of negative visualization are symptoms of an unforgiving attitude toward yourself. They reflect ongoing guilt. If they have any value at all, it is only to illustrate for you how to visualize and how visualization can affect your feelings and your behavior.

Although many psychologists use visualization as an effective, modern tool for dealing with the challenges of life, it is an ancient technique. For example, the prophet Isaiah used visualization to portray the kind of social order that would replace the sin-laced society in which he lived. He used the imagery of animals to fashion of picture of peace and righteousness:

> The wolf shall live with the lamb, the leopard shall lie down with the kid, the calf and the lion and the fatling together, and a little child shall lead them. The cow and the bear shall graze, their young shall lie down together, and the lion shall eat straw like the ox. The nursing child shall play over the hole of the asp, and the weaned child shall put its hand on the adder's den. They will not hurt or destroy on all my holy mountain, for the earth will be full of the knowledge of the Lord, as the waters cover the sea. (Isa. 11:6–9)

Isaiah's portrait represents his dream for the future, the kind of society he would like to see. Creating an image of what you want to happen in the future is one way to use visualization, and we'll discuss it below.

The other way to use visualization is as a technique for getting free of negative emotions and creating a desired emotional state. You do this by visualizing something positive. For example, let's say you are distressed about offending someone, and your distress impedes your efforts to forgive yourself. You can use visualization to create a positive image that will foster a sense of peace.

In fact, we'd like you to practice it, preferably now, or as soon as you can. Don't put it off until you "have enough time." That may never happen, and besides the exercise requires very little time. To begin, you need to be as relaxed and quiet as possible. So sit in a comfortable chair. Do not cross your arms or legs. Let your hands rest in your lap. You may close your eyes or keep them open, whichever works best for you. Begin with a series of slow, deep breaths. Breathe slowly in, hold it for a moment, then breathe slowly out. After two or three deep breaths, you will likely feel more relaxed. If not, continue breathing slowly until you do. Once you are relaxed, visualize something or someone that makes you feel good (continue to breath slowly and deeply as you visualize). It can be a happy experience: a joyous birthday party, the day you knew you were in love, your wedding day, the first time you saw your new baby, the time your boss praised your work, or any other experience that created a sense of joy or well-being. You could also imagine a peaceful scene such as mountains or the beach or a garden. For some people, visualizing the smiling face of someone they love is most effective.

Hold the image in your mind long enough to experience the positive emotions associated with it. The whole process may take no more than a few minutes. Of course, this kind of visualization doesn't solve your problem of forgiving yourself. But it does give you sufficient freedom from negative emotions so that you can work effectively on your problem with self-forgiveness.

WHY VISUALIZATION WORKS

We have just given one reason that visualization works: it creates the positive emotional state that is necessary for the work of self-forgiveness. Yet it does much more, as illustrated by the career of Martin Luther King Jr. Think about the various options that faced King when he began his ministry. As an African-American growing up in the South, he knew how racial prejudice can destroy the human spirit. He tasted the bitter fruit of discrimination. He knew the frustrations of a society that proclaims freedom and justice for all but only practices freedom and justice for certain groups. How could he have responded?

First, he could have responded with an agenda of accommodation. He could have accepted the given role for African Americans in the nation and focused on ministering to the hurts and advocated patience in the face of injustice. Second, he could have become embittered and responded with an agenda of condemnation and separation from the larger society (in a manner similar to some of the early Black Muslims). Or third, he could have followed an agenda of "I have a dream." In other words, he could have focused on what the nation would be like if freedom and justice were truly accorded to all the citizenry. That, of course, is what he did.

However, think about these three options. The first two would have been driven by the past. The history of prejudice and discrimination would color and drive accommodation, condemnation, and separation. The third option, however, was driven by the future—his vision of a truly free and just America. In short, King helped transform the nation because he was pulled into the future by his vision rather than pushed into the future by his past.

That's what visualization is all about—being pulled into the future by something better rather than being pushed into it by the worst of the past. This is what makes visualization an effective and powerful tool. To be sure, it has been misused by some. For example, there are those who advocate such things as visualizing yourself as rich. Do so, they claim, and you will become rich. Such people are rich themselves only because so many people buy their books or pay to attend their lectures. Visualization was never meant to be used in such a crass and unrealistic fashion.

On the other hand, people have found visualization to be a powerful tool for enhancing performance, changing emotional states, and guiding behavior. For example, athletes use visualization to enhance their efforts. A runner may visualize an entire race beforehand, including seeing himself or herself running each step of the way. A golfer may visualize each shot at a particular hole, including how he or she will hit the ball and where it will land. People also use visualization to do such things as reduce anger, cope with illness, become more effective parents, boost self-esteem, and forgive those who have hurt them. And it's a powerful tool for bringing about self-forgiveness.

Consider a woman whose addiction to alcohol led to the disruption of her marriage and the loss of her children. In trying to reconstruct her life, she struggles with severe self-condemnation. She particularly grieves over the way she hurt her children. What are her options? She could allow herself to be pushed into the future by her self-condemnation and the undying images of her failure. This could mean nothing more than eking out a daily existence that focuses on survival rather than satisfaction. Or it could mean continuing bitterness and anger over the way she ruined her life. Fortunately, she has another option. She can replace the painful images of the past with positive visualization and be pulled by the new images into a meaningful future. This brings us to the important topic of what you visualize.

WHAT TO VISUALIZE

As we noted earlier, for purposes of getting rid of negative emotions as you deal with self-forgiveness, you can visualize anything that makes you feel good. However, when you create an image of what you want to happen in the future, you need to visualize both the person you hurt and also yourself. Further, you need to visualize each of you separately as well as the two of you together. For each of these, we recommend a couple of visualizations that could work for you. If they do, use them as often as needed. If they don't, use your imagination and your understanding of your own situation and needs to visualize something else. Visualization is an effective tool, but no single visualization works for everyone. So don't get discouraged. If your first effort doesn't seem to help, find the visualization that does work for you.

Visualize the Person You Hurt

You have probably already engaged in a good deal of negative visualization of the person you hurt. Now it's time to use positive visualization. Reject whatever images you have of the person's hurt or anger or disappointment. Instead, picture the person forgiving you and telling you that he or she has grown through the experience. No, this is not an exercise in justifying what you did or in minimizing the hurt that you caused. Forgiveness, whether of others or of yourself, is *never* meant to trivialize hurtful behavior. Rather, forgiving yourself is the only way to get beyond the point where the offense keeps on vexing you.

So visualize the person you hurt forgiving you. If the person has done so, recapture the scene. If the person hasn't, picture him or her doing it anyway. Some people wonder if that is appropriate. Or even if it is realistic. After many attempts at reconciliation with parents who had rejected him, a gay man wrote an angry letter to his father questioning the reality of the father's Christian faith. The father responded with an angry letter of his own, asserting that as long as the son lived a sinful life he would not be welcome in their home. This left the gay man feeling guilty for having done something that further upset his father and deepened the rift between them:

> So how could I possibly picture him as forgiving me? Besides, you don't know my father. He never forgives anyone for anything. He got mad at my cousin once because when we visited her home she talked a lot with her aunt—my mother—but said very little to him. He felt slighted, and for the next fifteen years—until my cousin died—would have nothing to do with her. Nothing my mother said made him change his mind about my cousin.
>
> So if he is that unforgiving about being slighted, what makes you think he will ever forgive me for writing the letter? To him, it's just more evidence that I'm what he calls a "perverse sinner bound for hell." He won't talk to me about it. He won't speak to me on the phone when I call. He does write me letters, but they are just about my being condemned. As far as he is concerned, there is nothing to say and nothing to do except for me to repent and abandon my evil ways. I can still see the shock on his face when I told him I was gay. And I can imagine the snarl on his face

as he writes the letters. What I can't imagine is him looking at me in a loving way and saying "I forgive you."

In spite of this bleak picture, our response to the gay man is
still yes, it is perfectly appropriate to imagine him forgiving you.
No matter the situation, the principle still holds: just as it's important to your physical, emotional, and spiritual well-being to forgive others, it's also important to the person you hurt to forgive
you. It is therefore appropriate to visualize the person as forgiving
even when the person has not or will not do it. Think of it as the
person doing what he or she needs to do for the well-being of
both of you.

In addition to visualizing the person forgiving you, visualize
him or her expressing overtly or implicitly that the experience has
been one of growth. This, too, is appropriate. It is, after all, through
meeting and overcoming various challenges and adversities that
we are most likely to grow. If the person you hurt acknowledges
the growth, it means that the person has not merely gotten beyond
the hurt but has used it to reach a more mature level of life.

Thus, we suggest that the gay man visualize something like the
following:

> Picture your father welcoming you home. Imagine him
> saying to you that though he does not understand and
> cannot approve of you being gay, he does forgive you for
> the angry letter. He understands your anger and hopes you
> can understand his. But now he wants to move beyond the
> anger. He wants you to know that he still loves you as his
> son. He wants to be able to talk with you without anger
> or disappointment.

Visualizing the other person in this way has a couple of benefits for you. First, it provides you with your own "I have a dream"
image that pulls you into a better future. You have a goal to strive
for, a goal that will enhance your own and the other person's well-
being. Second, it focuses your mind on what is or what could be.

If the person has forgiven you, visualizing that forgiveness will make it easier for you to forgive yourself. And if the person has not forgiven you, your visualization will remind you that such forgiveness is possible and that ultimately the other person must take responsibility for forgiving or failing to forgive. This is important, because sometimes those who struggle to forgive themselves engage in the toxic thought that the unwillingness of the other to forgive is justified: "No, he hasn't forgiven me. And I don't blame him. No one could forgive what I have done." If that were true, of course, then obviously you could not forgive yourself. Your positive visualization of the other person, then, reminds you that the other person *ought* to forgive you and that you *can* forgive yourself.

Visualize Yourself

One of the ways we suggest you visualize yourself involves your feelings. The other relates to your behavior. With regard to the first, try to experience what it will feel like when you are free of guilt, how you will react when you have fully forgiven yourself. In the process, keep reminding yourself that it is *when* you have forgiven yourself, not *if* you forgive yourself.

What could you visualize to capture the feelings? Among other things, you could picture yourself at some point in the past when you felt good about your life. Or you could visualize yourself feeling happy and at ease, even in the presence of the person you hurt. As you do the visualization, try to experience your feelings. Note what you are feeling in your body. Note your mood. Breathe deeply and slowly, and create the happy, relaxed state that you will achieve when you have forgiven yourself. To experience even a little of such an emotional state is a strong incentive to complete the work of self-forgiveness.

The other visualization involves your behavior. Visualize yourself in a similar situation to the one where you offended. Only this time, you will act in a way that imparts grace rather than hurt. Or you will act in a way that lives up to, rather than falls short of, your ideals. Steve, an engineer, describes how this helped him:

For a long time, I struggled with my self-esteem. Because whenever I was with people at work or I would meet new people, I did my best to say things that would impress them. I wanted to come away with the feeling that they admired and respected me. The sad thing is, I didn't even realize what I was doing until I was assigned to a task group at work. There were five of us. Immediately, in my typical fashion, I set out to impress the others with how lucky they were to have me in the group. But I was stopped cold when one of the men, Gene, said to another: "Bill, how are things going with you?"

I thought that was an unusual question. But it turned out that Bill was struggling with massive medical bills because of a chronically sick child. And he also had responsibility for his aged father. The poor guy was really stressed out. The rest of us wouldn't have known about Bill's situation if Gene hadn't brought it up.

Gene's concern for Bill was eye-opening to me. It was also gut-wrenching. Here I am, a Christian man, a man who is supposed to be a follower of the most compassionate person ever to live on this earth. But I was more concerned with impressing people than helping them. I wondered how many other struggling people I had ignored over the years because I was all wrapped up in myself.

Anyway, I found visualization a real help in dealing with my guilt. I started visualizing myself in various kinds of social situations. Instead of talking about myself or thinking of clever or intelligent things to say, I visualized myself asking people about themselves. How they were doing. How their families were. How things were going at work. That kind of stuff. And you know what? I still don't do it every time, but I'm much better now at focusing on the people I'm with instead of focusing on the kind of impression I'm making on those people. I have to tell you, it really makes you feel good—in fact it makes you feel a whole lot better—when you walk away from people who look grateful for your concern rather than impressed with your good qualities.

Steve had discovered the power of visualization to affect his subsequent behavior. So if you've fallen short of your ideals, visualize yourself as behaving in accord with those ideals and you will be more likely to do so in the future. If you've hurt someone, visualize yourself as being helpful in a similar situation and you will be more likely to act accordingly in the future.

Plus there's one more benefit. As you behave differently, it will be easier to accept the offense as an unwanted incident in someone who is trying to follow Christ rather than as an expression of an evil person.

Visualize Yourself and the Person You Hurt Together

A final kind of visualization that can help is to bring yourself and the person you hurt together. For one thing, you can imagine yourself and the person in the situation where the hurt occurred, except this time you will behave with more grace than you did before. For another, you can picture the two of you as reconciled. Imagine the two of you sitting together, having coffee or lunch, chatting about various matters in an amiable way. The hurt is behind you, and you relate as two close friends who simply enjoy being together.

This kind of visualization can affect the way you relate to someone you've hurt. Listen to a woman who struggled with an aged aunt:

> She lives near me, and she's alone. So I'm responsible for watching out for her. But we're on opposite sides of the political spectrum, and we're both passionate about it. It's really tough in election years. A few years ago, we got into a heated debate and I told her she was just acting like a senile old idiot. I regretted the words as soon as I uttered them. They really hurt her, and I could tell that she still

felt hurt. I apologized on several occasions, and every time she said that she'd forgiven me. But she still seemed uncomfortable and a bit chilly around me.

I got to the point where I dreaded going to see her. I would get tense at the prospect of going over to her house. And I knew this wasn't helping matters. I'm certain she picked up on the fact that I was uncomfortable. But neither of us wanted to bring up the hurtful argument again. I decided that things might never be the same between us.

Then a friend told me about visualization. I tried it. I visualized the two of us drinking a glass of wine, sitting in her living room and enjoying family tales from the past. I wasn't convinced this would do much good, but it really did! Eventually, I could go to her house and not feel tense by bringing to mind that image of us being comfortable and laughing together.

I don't know if we'll ever be as comfortable as I visualize. I don't know if she'll ever truly forgive me and feel warm toward me again. But at least I've forgiven myself and can visit her without that dread.

It may be that eventually the woman and her aunt will be fully reconciled. Certainly, that is what the woman wants, and it is far more likely now than it was before the visualization. But even if the reconciliation never occurs, the visualization represented the woman's "I have a dream" and made it easier to forgive herself.

This, of course, is the real value and power of visualization. It changes *you*. It gives you a goal. It facilitates positive emotions. It affects your behavior in constructive ways. And it may even facilitate reconciliation with the person you hurt. Whether or not reconciliation occurs, visualization can make it easier for you to forgive yourself.

Practice Healthy Spinning

You're no doubt familiar with "spin doctors." This term was first used in the 1980s to refer to those advisers whose political assignment is to influence the way the press interprets situations. The goal of "spin doctors" is to cast what their candidates say and do in the best possible light.

While many people have little use for the work of spin doctors, their efforts underscore an important point: there is always more than one way to view matters and legitimately interpret a situation. All of us, at one time or another, engage in spinning when we look at the same situation and see it differently. Consider, for example, the varying explanations for a recent natural disaster. When hurricane Katrina devastated New Orleans in 2005, there were those who saw it primarily as a calamity of nature. Others saw it as a calamity of nature but also as a massive failure of government. Others proclaimed it as an opportunity to rebuild and to demonstrate resilience and hope in the face of calamity. Still others saw it as God's judgment upon the sins of the city.

In short, you can put different kinds of spin on any situation. You can also change the spin that you previously put on something. We have worked with many people whose initial spin on a personal crisis was one of dread and foreboding. However, they eventually changed the spin and viewed the crisis as an opportunity to become stronger individuals and to grow closer to God. In the process, this new spin greatly facilitated their ability to deal with the crisis. That's what we mean by "healthy" spinning. It's putting a spin on a situation that enables you to deal with it in a constructive way.

As you struggle to forgive yourself, then, we urge you to engage in healthy spinning. This means to put a Christian spin on your situation. What does this involve?

CHRISTIAN SPINNING

We define Christian spinning both in terms of what it isn't, and what it is. First, look at what it isn't. When you think of the political spin doctors, you are likely to think of people who deny or distort the truth for political gain. Sometimes that's true; sometimes it isn't. Let's say that unemployment rises in an election year. Many people blame the President. But the spin doctors in the President's party point out alternative explanations. They note that Congress is controlled by the other party, and they're to blame. Or they assert that unemployment reflects problems in the global economy that have nothing to do with the President's policies. Or they assure people that the increased unemployment is only temporary and will soon reverse through presidential action. Any of these could be legitimate perspectives on the situation. They don't necessarily deny or distort truth.

Of course, there could also be a deliberate denial or distortion of truth. Consider a situation in which Bud has offended his wife, Rachel, by teasing her at a party for being "plump." There are a number of ways he could spin the incident:

- "She wasn't really hurt. She just pretended to get angry for the benefit of the other wives there."

- "She got a little perturbed with me, but she was okay. We tease each other all the time."

- "I know she didn't like me saying it. But if she doesn't want people to comment on it, she shouldn't keep gaining weight. Maybe this will help her to start watching her weight like she's always promising to do."

The first of these is denial. Bud insists that his comment really didn't bother Rachel. The second is trivialization. He asserts that the offense wasn't as hurtful as it appeared, and that it's a common experience for both of them. The third is blaming the victim. Bud acknowledges the hurt, but points out that it is really Rachel's fault.

None of these is a healthy way to spin the situation. At some point, the incident either will come back to haunt Bud, or he will find himself diminished as a person because he has not faced up to and dealt with his offense.

In short, if you spin a situation in such a way—denying the offense or the hurt it caused, distorting your role in the hurt, or minimizing the offense and the hurt, you have not engaged in Christian spinning. You have fallen into self-deception.

Hopefully, by now, it goes without saying that spinning the situation in terms of your failure and your deserved guilt is also unhealthy. When you continue to obsess about offending someone, you have fallen into self-denigration.

What, then, is a Christian way to spin a situation? In brief, it means to look at the matter in the light of God's gracious love. The word most commonly translated as "love" in the Christian Scriptures is *agape*. There are other Greek words that also mean love, but agape has a specific meaning that makes it the most appropriate word to define both God's love and the love practiced by God's children. Agape means that you believe that other people are God's creation and, thus, you act in behalf of their well-being. In other words, agape emphasizes more what you do to others than how you feel about them. In simplest terms, it means you *choose* to do what is good for someone independently of that person's merit or even of your own feelings of affection.

Now apply that understanding of love to the situation where you have offended someone and are having problems forgiving

yourself. What would it mean to see your situation in the light of
God's love? Let's use an analogy at the human level. Clearly, agape
is the kind of love often exercised by a parent whose primary concern is the well-being of the child. If you are a parent, think about
how you would want the situation resolved if it was your child
rather than you who had offended someone.

We are parents and know how we hope we'd react. First, we'd
be sorry that our child had offended someone. Second, we'd want
our child to acknowledge the hurt and desire to make amends.
Third, we would not want our child to continue to feel guilty and
unworthy. Fourth, we'd want our child to take action in accord
with both his or her well-being and the well-being of the person
who was offended. Fifth, we'd be available to do whatever we
could to make such a resolution come about.

Can you imagine God wanting anything less? So when you
look at your situation from the perspective of God's gracious love,
think of it this way:

- I regret my offense, but I will do what I can to make amends.

- In spite of the hurt I caused, God will help me to turn this into
  something good both for myself and for the person I hurt.

- I will therefore focus my thoughts and energies on what I
  now can do to act in accord with God's love for me and for
  the person I hurt.

This is the general outline of a healthy spin on your offense. Let's
look at it in more detail. For there are two aspects to which you
should attend: the spin you put on the consequences of the offense
and the spin you put on yourself as an offender.

SPINNING THE CONSEQUENCES OF THE OFFENSE

If you can't yet forgive yourself, it means that you've been spinning
the consequences of the offense in an unhealthy way. Perhaps you
have defined the offense as a moral failure that inflicted hurt on
someone and, thus, is unforgivable. This can happen when you set
unrealistically high standards. Katy is a professional woman who is

also a wife and mother. As such she typically feels pressured for time and often has little patience for people who are not fulfilling their responsibilities. One day she telephoned her best friend, Chris, who had shared her marital problems with Katy in confidence. The husband answered and curtly said that Chris wasn't at home. After a few more tense exchanges, a frustrated Katy blurted out that she could see why Chris was so unhappy with her marriage. She regretted the words as soon as she had said them. He hung up. Obviously, he confronted Chris when she returned home about what Katy had said. The incident led to a disruption of friendship:

> I know that I'm not the only woman who has betrayed a friend's trust. But Chris was my best friend. And now she won't even talk to me. I understand that. I'd probably do the same to her if she had betrayed me. In any case, as you can see I'm not just talking about some little failure. I'm talking about doing something that is totally contrary to everything I value. If you told me a year ago that I'd ever do something like that, I'd have told you that you're very much mistaken. That I could never sink to that level. But I did. And I can't forgive myself.

Katy reminds us of the apostle Peter. He, too, thought that there was one thing he'd never do. He'd never desert or deny Jesus whatever the circumstances:

> Peter said to him, "Though all become deserters because of you, I will never desert you." Jesus said to him, "Truly I tell you, this very night, before the cock crows, you will deny me three times." Peter said to him, "Even though I must die with you, I will not deny you." (Matt. 26:32–35)

Peter did desert and deny Jesus. Like Katy, Peter trod that road of dangerous self-confidence that is called "I would never . . ."

When you set such high standards and fall short, it becomes even more difficult to forgive yourself. Your unrealistic expectations are a spin on the situation that makes self-forgiveness itself seem like a betrayal of your standards. You need, therefore, to spin the situation as one of those painful experiences that can (and will) turn out to benefit you in three ways. First, it can help you be more realistic about yourself. Second, it can help you be less judgmental of others. And third, it provides you with an opportunity to grow. Think of each of these as a part of your healthy spin, as assertions of what is going to happen to you as you deal with your offense in a constructive way.

I Will Become More Realistic About Myself

To be more realistic means that you will regard yourself as a person who, like every other human, is capable of both good and evil. This realization is good for your humility as well as for shedding any unrealistic notions you have about whether Christians ever do such things as you have done. In addition, it will make it easier for you to practice self-forgiveness.

Are we advocating that you lower your standards? Actually, we are if your standards have been unrealistically high. We have known people who expected themselves to be what only God can be. God never created us to be God: "Yet you have made them a little lower than God . . ." (Psa. 8:5). But God did create us to be godly. To be realistic, then, you can strive to be more than you are while recognizing that you are not God and are not, therefore, beyond the capacity to engage in evil.

A father put it this way:

I know that I messed up in various ways with my kids. This really used to bother me. I felt guilty about not treating them fairly. Or about not spending enough time with them. Or when I was frustrated about something and took it out on them. And I fought forgiving myself for doing those things because I thought it might only encourage me to do them again.

But then I realized that no matter how much I wanted to be a perfect dad, it wasn't going to happen. No father is perfect. You can only do your best and pray that your love will trump your mistakes. Thankfully, it's worked for me and my sons.

This father has gained a more realistic perspective about himself. It's a perspective that is as Christian as it is realistic. For if we were not going to fall short, we would not have been told to continue confessing our sins throughout our lives. And if you think "But why did I do *that*?" you can console yourself with the thought that if you hadn't done *that*, you would have messed up in some other way and would be asking the same question. So learn to be realistic. "If we say that we have no sin, we deceive ourselves, and the truth is not in us" (1 John 1:8). And the way we are called to respond to that disconcerting realization is not self-condemnation, but confession and forgiveness.

I Will Become Less Judgmental

"Do not judge, so that you may not be judged" (Matt. 7:1). The word translated "judge" can mean to criticize unjustly or to condemn, and that is its meaning here. To be judgmental is to practice regularly the unjust criticism or condemnation of others. There are two good reasons why this is a harmful practice when it comes to forgiveness.

First, judgments are always made on the basis of partial information. When Daniel Inouye was first elected as a United States senator from Hawaii, a picture of all the new senators taking the oath of office appeared in our local paper. A reader wrote in that the new senator from Hawaii obviously didn't know his right hand from his left, for his left hand was clearly raised as he took the oath.

The reader was right about Senator Inouye taking the oath with his left rather than his right hand. Senator Inouye grew up in a poor Japanese-American family. When the Japanese bombed Pearl Harbor, he enlisted in the army. He fought in Italy as a teenager and was seriously wounded four times, winning a number of medals for his valor. Daniel Inouye risked his life for his country. So the reason that Daniel Inouye raised his left hand to take the oath of office was not his ignorance. It was because he lost his right arm fighting for his country in the Second World War.

Those who are judgmental repeatedly put their foot in their mouths because they never know everything about those they are judging. To be sure, we all tend to be judgmental. But we all can strive to be less judgmental, and this will enhance our ability both to forgive others and to forgive ourselves. For when you are judgmental, whether of others or of yourself, you are focused on the offense and the punishment of the offender. When you emphasize loving rather than judging, you focus on how to ease the hurt and bring about forgiveness.

How then can you become less judgmental? Go back to the first potential benefit—becoming more realistic—and work on it until you have made progress. As you become more realistic you will find it easier to become less judgmental. After all, if it is the common lot of humankind to fall short of the glory of God, then it is not our task to condemn each other but to help each other. To help is to be godly: "Indeed, God did not send the Son into the world to condemn the world, but in order that the world might be saved through him" (John 3:17).

These ideas are also expressed in Paul's admonition: "My friends, if anyone is detected in a transgression, you who have received the Spirit should restore such a one in a spirit of gentleness. Take care that you yourselves are not tempted" (Gal. 6:1). Rather than criticizing or condemning those who have transgressed, we are called to help them. And note the warning to take care that you are not tempted. This means to be realistic, to recognize that you could fall prey to the same transgression. Such a recognition makes it easier to help rather than to condemn the transgressor. It also makes it easier to forgive, including the forgiveness of yourself, because you too are a member of the human family.

I Will Use My Failure as an Opportunity to Grow as a Christian

We are told to "grow in the grace and knowledge of our Lord and Savior Jesus Christ" (2 Pet. 3:18). Growing in knowledge implies that you increase your understanding of spiritual truths and your grasp of what it means to walk in the paths of righteousness. Growing in grace implies that you increasingly behave in ways that are loving, that is, in ways that enhance the well-being of other people.

There are many ways to grow, including Bible study, prayer, meditation, worship, and ministering to others. There is another way that is not as pleasant—confronting and dealing constructively with the varied challenges of life, including temptations, adversity, and suffering. Among these challenges, we also include self-forgiveness because it requires you to face up to your failures and to do the difficult work of turning something disagreeable into something positive in your life.

Self-forgiveness, then, facilitates growth in two ways. First, when you forgive yourself you have successfully dealt with a most vexing challenge. And every success at confronting and dealing constructively with challenges is a growth experience. Having dealt well with one challenge, you will feel better able to deal with others.

Second, self-forgiveness makes you feel better about yourself and your world. Moreover, your enhanced mood makes you more likely to be helpful to others. That's one of the findings of psychological research: people in a good mood are more likely to help others in need than are people in a bad mood. Listen to what one person told us:

> When you claimed that forgiving ourselves would be liberating, I thought you were just overstating the case to make us listen and accept what you would say. But you're right. I didn't realize how much energy my guilt was taking, and how much it was distracting me from taking advantage of opportunities to serve, until I experienced the freedom of self-forgiveness. You know, intense guilt can dull your eyes and your ears to all the needs of the world.

The point is, if you do not forgive yourself, you miss an opportunity to grow. If you do forgive yourself, you become a stronger, more mature Christian.

SPINNING YOURSELF AS AN OFFENDER

Let's go back to Katy, who unintentionally betrayed her best friend. How would you spin her as an offender? We know how she spins herself: she has done the unpardonable and must somehow learn to live with that fact. Do you agree? Most people we know are easier on Katy than she is on herself. After all, she did not intentionally hurt her friend. She herself was horrified by what she said to the husband. Even if Katy's friend eventually forgives her, Katy may find it difficult to forgive herself because of the way she now thinks of herself. In fact, in our experience those who have trouble forgiving themselves are typically more severe on themselves than are others.

So let's begin at that point. As you think about how to spin yourself as an offender, remind yourself that the person you offended may be more forgiving of you than you are of yourself. You are not, therefore, adding insult to injury by engaging in the process of self-forgiveness.

On the other hand, you may be like Katy—her offense remains unforgiven by the person she hurt. This may make it harder to put a healthy spin on yourself. But it's still not beyond your capacity to do so. Katy did try to make amends with her friend. Eventually, this may bring about forgiveness and reconciliation, but it hasn't yet. In the meantime, Katy should move on with the work of forgiving herself. She must not allow herself to be diminished because her friend still expresses hurt.

So whether you are either more severe on yourself than the one you hurt or struggling because the one you hurt won't forgive you, it's time to put a healthy spin on yourself as the offender. We suggest two components to that spin—how you stand in God's sight and where you stand in your Christian walk. And again, we will state them as affirmations of what *is* true rather than as ideals that you would like to be true.

I Am God's Beloved Child

First, think of yourself as God's beloved child in spite of your offense. When Paul wrote his letter to the Romans, he addressed it,

"To all God's beloved in Rome, who are called to be saints" (Rom. 1:7). Note the "beloved" of God that Paul applies to all the Christians. (And keep in mind that this is the same letter in which he reminds us more than once that all have sinned and come short of the glory of God.) The word "beloved" is the same word used when Jesus was baptized: "And a voice from heaven said, 'This is my Son, the Beloved, with whom I am well pleased'" (Matt. 3:17). In other words, God loves each of us with the same love that God bestowed upon Jesus Christ.

That's a rather staggering thought. It can also be a transforming thought in your life if you keep it in mind. Our friend Mike discovered this for himself:

> Every so often I meet somebody who puts me off from our first encounter. I remember reacting negatively to a young person with piercings all over his body. And to a man who reminded me of an old uncle who used to tease me all the time. And to a person who seemed arrogant and rude and totally wrapped up in himself. I knew that I was being judgmental and struggled with how I should try to relate to these people as a Christian. One day I decided to try a new approach. Now, whenever I meet somebody who turns me off, I remind myself that God loves that person. And it works! You can't feel the same way about someone when you're aware of how much God loves that person.

Indeed, to see anyone else as beloved of God is to be more kindly disposed to the person. This doesn't mean you approve of whatever the person does or says, but it does mean that you can't treat someone the same once you're convinced that he or she is God's beloved.

And this includes yourself. Reminding yourself that you are God's beloved will make it harder to keep berating and condemning yourself for your offenses. Or put in positive terms, it will make it easier for you to forgive yourself.

I Am Growing in Godliness

There's an old story about a poorly educated man who attended a small, rural church that regularly gave time for members to give their testimonies. When the time came for people to give their testimonies, the man stood and said: "Well, I ain't what I ought to be. And I ain't what I'm going to be. But at least I ain't what I was."

Whatever else the man was or wasn't, he was clearly insightful into the nature of the Christian life. It is not a life that takes place in the realm of the flawless. It is a life that is wending its way toward ever increasing godliness—a journey punctuated by fits and starts, advances and regressions, failures and successes.

Yet how can you think of yourself as growing in godliness when you are mired in guilt over some offense? We have two pieces of evidence. First, the very fact that you are reading this book shows that you are growing in godliness because you are striving to complete the godly act of forgiving yourself. Second, the fact that you feel guilty over your offense indicates that it is the kind of behavior that distresses you and that you don't want to repeat. Therefore, you are less likely to repeat it, and that translates into growing in godliness.

One final point. When you spin your situation as one of growing in godliness, you make it easier to forgive yourself. We heard of a man who was frustrated with his five-year-old daughter because her room was a mess and it was time for her to go to bed. Even though she was young, her parents had given her the responsibility for straightening up her room before she went to bed. "Why haven't you finished cleaning up your room?" he demanded of her. "Why can't you be a good girl and do your job?" She thought about it for a moment, then said: "I don't know. I try. Doesn't it count for something if you try?"

Yes, the father agreed. It does count if you try. It counts even if you don't always succeed. So he decided to cut her some slack and forgive her lapses as long as she was trying. In essence, that's what we're asking you to do for yourself. You're trying. This means you're growing in godliness. So cut yourself some slack. Forgive the relapses. And keep on growing.

Use Self-Talk

Paula was a delight. She was a coworker on a church staff where we served for a time. During our years with Paula, we found her to be a constant source of inspiration and good humor. At the appreciation luncheon for her when she retired, we mentioned how much we valued the way she listened carefully to our ideas and our concerns, the creative input she made to our responsibilities, and the ready smile she had for everyone. We even enjoyed her quirky habit of mumbling to herself as she went about her work. "Yes," said a pastor in response, "she does talk to herself all day long. But that's only because she really enjoys an intelligent conversation."

This, we suppose, is one good reason for talking to yourself—the opportunity to have an intelligent conversation. Another good reason is that talking to yourself—or self-talk, as we refer to it here—is a crucial part of determining the quality of your life, including your ability to forgive yourself.

WHAT IS SELF-TALK?

Self-talk is simply the conversation that you carry on with yourself throughout the day. We all do it, and it can be fairly continuous. It can, as with Paula, be aloud or it can be in your mind. And it can be positive or negative. You've already experienced the negative in your struggle to forgive yourself. Like others who share your struggle, you have said to yourself something like the following:

- "I wish I had never said that."
- "If only I could take it back."
- "Why did I do that kind of thing?"
- "I've ruined the relationship for good."
- "I wish I could have it to do over."
- "I'm just no good at this sort of thing."
- "I don't deserve to be forgiven."

And so on. You may not have used those exact words, but you have undoubtedly expressed similar thoughts to yourself.

Persistent negative self-talk reflects regret, guilt, and self-degradation. Unfortunately, it also tends to perpetuate and even intensify the regret, guilt, and self-degradation. Think of it this way. Let's say you have fallen into a deep hole. There is a ladder and a shovel in the hole. For some reason, you choose the shovel and try to dig yourself out of the hole. But all you do is to get yourself in deeper. The hole represents the guilt and self-degradation that is marring your well-being. The shovel is negative self-talk. As long as you persist in negative self-talk, you are simply digging a deeper hole for yourself.

The ladder, on the other hand, represents positive self-talk and provides a way out of the hole. It has been practiced since biblical times. Consider, for example, David's expression of gratitude for God's blessings:

> Bless the Lord, O my soul, and all that is within me, bless his holy name. Bless the Lord, O my soul, and do not forget all his benefits—who forgives all your iniquity, who heals all your diseases, who redeems your life from the Pit,

who crowns you with steadfast love and mercy, who satisfies you with good as long as you live so that your youth is renewed like the eagle's (Psa. 103:1–5).

To whom is David speaking? Clearly, he is speaking to himself ("O my soul"), telling himself not to forget the manifold ways in which God had blessed him.

Positive self-talk leads to positive outcomes for your well-being and can be used in all kinds of endeavors. For example, we know many coaches who teach their athletes to use positive self-talk in preparation for a performance. They know that negative self-talk (for example, "I've never been able to hit this pitcher") will depress performance, while positive self-talk (such as "I can hit this guy if I concentrate") will enhance performance.

The same principle holds true for self-forgiveness. The more you engage in negative self-talk the less likely you are to forgive yourself, while the more you engage in positive self-talk, the more quickly you will forgive yourself. That is, you can talk yourself into a deeper hole of remorse and guilt, just as you can talk yourself into the freedom of self-forgiveness.

What happens is that your conversations become a self-fulfilling prophecy. Your self-talk tends to find expression in your feelings and your behavior. For instance, if you regularly tell yourself that you are clumsy, you will frequently act in a clumsy way. If you regularly tell yourself that you are not very good at something, you never will be good at it. On the other hand, if you regularly tell yourself that you have the capacity to do something well, you are more likely to do so. If you regularly tell yourself that you are fundamentally a good person, you will increasingly act like a good person. And if you regularly tell yourself that you will forgive yourself, you are more likely to do so.

In fact, we would take this a step further. *Unless* you regularly tell yourself that you can and will practice self-forgiveness, you won't do it. Positive self-talk is a powerful tool for forgiving yourself. Don't neglect it.

WHAT SELF-TALK DOES

There are a number of things that positive self-talk does that you need in order to forgive yourself. First, when you substitute positive self-talk for negative self-talk, you cease digging a deeper hole of guilt and remorse for yourself. In addition, positive self-talk helps you to control your feelings, motivates you, consoles you, and builds your confidence.

Self-Talk Helps Control Your Feelings

Try an experiment to test the truth of this assertion. Think of a situation that irritates or frustrates or angers you. The next time you find yourself in that situation, try some positive self-talk and see if it doesn't help turn your negative feelings into more positive ones.

For example, we know many couples who experience frequent tension because one spouse is always late while the other feels compelled to be on time. Let's say that you're the one who wants to be on time and your partner is always late. You are going to a party one evening and your partner is running late as usual. What kind of self-talk do you use? One possibility is something like the following: "Late again. I just hate it when we don't get there on time. We'll miss out on some of the fun. And our friends will be wondering where we are. This could ruin the whole evening." This, of course, is the kind of negative self-talk that guarantees feelings of frustration or anger.

However, you could also use a different kind of self-talk: "Late again. But it's not the end of the world. I'd prefer to be on time. But I won't let this ruin my mood or spoil my fun. It isn't worth it. I'll just think of it as being fashionably late and getting to the party when things are already warmed up." This is positive self-talk, and it will ease or even erase your irritation and substitute feelings of anticipation for an evening of fun.

Try the experiment. It works. It works for self-forgiveness as well. Take the feeling of guilt that people typically have before they forgive themselves. Whenever a pang of guilt strikes you, try something like the following, which incorporates prayer into your self-talk: "Why do I feel guilty? I have tried to make amends. God has forgiven me. I'll try to forgive myself. After all, this guilt doesn't help me or the person I hurt in any way. So, God, I thank you for forgiving me. I thank you that you forgive the guilt of my sin. Now help me to forgive myself."

Note that we include that phrase from the Psalm 32, "the guilt of my sin." As we explained in chapter 1, David used the phrase to indicate that God's message to us is that we need no longer feel guilt when God has forgiven us. It's a phrase that we suggest you keep in mind and regularly repeat to yourself. As you do, the feelings of guilt should subside and open the way for you to begin experiencing the freedom of forgiveness.

Now be realistic. We are not claiming that you will find instant and permanent relief by repeating one positive statement to yourself. As we will discuss in more detail in the next chapter, you must give yourself time to heal. This means you will frequently need to use positive self-talk. Don't get discouraged if you seem to be progressing more slowly than you had hoped. Like every other kind of healing, self-forgiveness is a process and not an event.

Self-Talk Motivates You

Have you heard the story of the man who started his career at the bottom and liked it so much that he stayed there? This apocryphal tale is meant to spoof those who lack motivation. No one really likes being at the bottom, just as no one really enjoys being hounded by guilt.

Still, there are people who, for whatever reason, stay at the bottom in their field of work. And, for whatever reason, there are people who continue to struggle with guilt. Sometimes the problem is a lack of motivation. It isn't that they don't want to be free of their guilt or that they're unwilling to work at forgiving themselves. Rather, we hear such things as:

- "I tried, but I just couldn't do it."
- "I don't even know where to begin."
- "Until she forgives me, I can't forgive myself."
- "I said I would forgive myself, but nothing happened so I gave up."

In such cases, the person acknowledges the continuing guilt and self-deprecation but feels helpless to move beyond it. Of course, if you're truly helpless, it makes no sense to even expend the time and energy to move beyond your guilt and self-loathing. Yet as we pointed out in chapter 4, helplessness is primarily learned behavior, and one of the more effective ways for moving beyond it is to motivate yourself with positive self-talk.

Consider the difference it would make if you replaced each of the preceding four forms of negative self-talk with:

- "I've been trying, and I'm going to keep on trying until I'm successful."
- "I not sure of where to begin, but I'm going to do something."
- "Even though she hasn't forgiven me, I must and I can forgive myself."
- "It hasn't happened yet, but it will happen if I keep working on it."

As noted earlier, you can combine self-talk and prayer. In fact, we urge you to frequently include prayer in your self-talk. Many Christians repeat to themselves the cry of the man who came to Jesus and asked him to heal his son: "I believe; help my unbelief" (Mark 9:24). "I believe" is their self-talk. "Help my unbelief" is their prayer that their self-talk will be real. This combination of self-talk and prayer can be most effective, as illustrated by the experience of Todd:

> Although I'm a very conservative Christian, I have a friend who is liberal in his beliefs. Bryan has had a lot of struggles

in his life. When he lost his job, I discovered something about myself that I didn't like. I should have felt really sorry. But I didn't. In fact—and I hate to admit this—I secretly felt a little pleased by Bryan's loss. I never let him know that I felt this way. Instead, I sympathized with him and encouraged him. But I was disappointed with myself as I thought about my pleasure in his misfortune.

Shortly after losing his job, Bryan and his oldest son began quarreling a lot. And again, I realized that I was—on some level—enjoying his difficulties. I started really feeling guilty. What kind of person was I to take satisfaction from a friend's misfortune. I started trying to figure out what was wrong with me. I finally decided that it was because his troubles were like a sign to me that his liberal faith was wrong and that his problems somehow vindicated my beliefs.

But this explanation only made me feel worse. I admitted to myself that Bryan is a faithful Christian and began to doubt the quality of my own faith. I felt both judgmental and hypocritical. After months of struggling with guilt and feelings of inadequacy, I told myself: "I'm going to get over these terrible feelings." I began by reminding myself that I'm not perfect—that I'm a sinner like everyone else. And I told myself that I was going to get past my guilt. I asked God to forgive me and help me. And now, whenever I feel a little pleased because something bad has happened to someone else, I immediately tell myself I don't want to feel that way, I pray for forgiveness, and I pray for God to help and bless the person.

Self-Talk Consoles You

Consolation? Do you need to be consoled? Probably. The reason is illustrated by Todd: "When you recognize a dark side in yourself that you didn't realize you had, you feel guilty. But you feel more than that; you grieve the loss of the person you once thought you were. I wanted to be the kind of person who cared for others—who rejoiced with my friends when things were going well and struggled alongside them when things weren't going so well."

Todd experienced what many of us do when we find it hard to forgive ourselves—a sense of loss. It's a loss of innocence. It's the loss of the person you thought you were as you face up to what you have done.

If you are feeling this sense of loss, you can console yourself with self-talk. Todd has done this by reminding himself that all humans, not he alone, have sinned and come short of God's glory. But there are additional things to say that are consoling:

- "God has forgiven me; I must not continue to condemn what God has forgiven."

- "God loves me as I am, not as I think I ought to be."

- "It's better and healthier to be realistic about myself."

- "When I get rid of the delusions I can grow into the kind of person that God wants me to be."

In short, rather than continuing to grieve the loss of the kind of person you thought you were, use self-talk to remind yourself that you are now free to become the kind of person you want to be.

Self-Talk Builds Your Confidence

Athletes use self-talk as a confidence-building tool. They remind themselves that they are trained, competent, and can reach their goals. You can use self-talk to build your confidence in your ability to reach your goal of self-forgiveness. If you lack the confidence, you sabotage any efforts you make. If you have the confidence, you are already a step further toward your goal.

Todd built his confidence when he said such things as "I'm going to get over these terrible feelings." Note that he did not say "I want to" or "I hope to" but "I'm going to." Similarly, your self-talk should express confidence even if you lack it. Talk to yourself as though self-forgiveness is going to happen, not as though you wish it would happen. Thus, you might try one or more of the following:

- "I'm going to forgive myself because God has forgiven me and expects me to forgive myself."

- "I can forgive myself because God is at work within me to fulfill God's purpose."

- "The same power that brought about the resurrection of Jesus from the dead is at work in me and will enable me to fulfill God's will for my life."

THE THEMES OF YOUR SELF-TALK

In the course of discussing what self-talk achieves, we suggested a number of things you can say. Those suggestions can be incorporated into four themes that should comprise the content of your self-talk:

- Focus on forgiveness rather than failure so that your thinking and your energy are not consumed by the hurtful incident.

- Remind yourself of the physical, emotional, and spiritual consequences of forgiving.

- Rehearse the way that self-forgiveness helps you become a stronger, more effective Christian.

- Keep in mind the fact that forgiving yourself transforms you from a victim into a victor.

Focusing on Forgiveness Rather than Failure

If you're like most people we know who struggle to forgive themselves, the uninvited thoughts that break into your mind are more likely to be about your failure than your effort to forgive. You can't keep such thoughts from barging in, but you can learn to deal with them in a constructive way.

For example, Stacy told us about the way she had mistreated her ex-husband after their divorce. She tried to make the children believe that he was primarily to blame for the breakup and, every chance she got, sabotaged his efforts to spend any time with them. As her anger subsided, she realized the harm she was doing to both her children and her ex-husband and deeply regretted her behavior. She apologized to both her ex-husband and her children but still felt guilty. Thoughts about what she had done continued to haunt her.

Eventually, Stacy learned to use self-talk to cope with these intrusive thoughts of failure:

> I expected my apologies to make everything okay, but they were only a first step. I couldn't stop thinking about the hurt I had caused my ex and my children. I knew that they had forgiven me. That God had forgiven me. Why couldn't I forgive myself? Why did I keep on thinking about the way I failed them?
>
> I read somewhere about a technique for dealing with unwanted thoughts, so I decided to try it. Whenever the thought came, I just said: "Stop. This isn't a productive way to think. Remember instead the forgiveness they gave you. I am forgiven. How blessed I am. I now forgive myself. Thank you, God, for the gift of forgiveness." And then I sometimes pictured myself getting on with my daily tasks and feeling really comfortable and good about myself.

The "technique" that Stacy used is both simple and effective. When an unwanted thought pops into your mind, don't let it settle in. Rather, say to yourself, "Stop!" and turn your thoughts to something positive. There are other ways to stop the unwanted thoughts, such as putting a rubber band around your wrist and snapping it as soon as the thoughts come. But we prefer to avoid even a small amount of pain if there are other ways that work. And saying "stop" works for us.

Note something else. Stacy illustrates a very important principle, namely that the techniques we have discussed are not alternatives that are used independently of each other. You can profitably combine them. We suggested this already when we talked about combining the spiritual resource of prayer with self-talk. Stacy found it effective to use self-talk, prayer, and visualization together, each of them focusing on forgiveness rather than her failure.

Remembering the Consequences of Forgiving Yourself

As we pointed out, there are physical, emotional, and spiritual consequences when you practice, or fail to practice, self-forgiveness. We listed many of the negative consequences of not forgiving yourself in chapter 1. In your self-talk, however, you'll want to take a positive approach and remind yourself of the many desirable consequences that flow from forgiving yourself.

In essence, self-forgiveness liberates you from the destructive feelings, vexing thoughts, physical ailments, and spiritual malaise surrounding your offense. Your self-talk might include such things as:

- "I'm going to live as one who is forgiven."
- "When this is over, I'll be free of guilt, anxiety, and depression."
- "I'm a child of God and God has forgiven me."
- "To forgive myself is to become a better Christian."
- "Forgiving myself is not a cop-out; it's a way to improve my emotional, physical, and spiritual health."
- "When I forgive myself, I am a more obedient and happier child of God."

So far, we have been treating self-talk as something that just goes on your mind. Some people find it even more meaningful if they write down their self-talk. Subsequently, they can read and reread it. Listen to this account:

> I tried self-talk one day, and it seemed to help. But a few days later, I was feeling bad again. I tried to remember

what I had said that helped, but I couldn't quite recall it. So I decided in the future to write down whatever I said that helped. This way, I could refer to it later. In fact, I decided to write a letter to myself just as I would write to a friend who is having trouble forgiving herself.

In my letter, I said I was sorry for what I had done and I put down all the good things that I could expect when I was able to forgive myself. I told myself to keep working at it, because the results would be worth the effort.

If writing is more effective for you, write such a letter to yourself. Or write a letter to God. You can acknowledge your offense and your struggle, but keep the tone of the letter positive.

Becoming a Stronger, More Effective Christian

We grow through struggle. The struggle can be the exhausting efforts of the student to earn a degree. It can be the mind-boggling number of hours of training of the professional athlete or musician. It can be the unsettling conflict that challenges every married couple. Whatever the worthwhile goal for which you strive, you are going to have to struggle.

James noted the role of struggle in the Christian life: "My brothers and sisters, whenever you face trials of any kind, consider it nothing but joy, because you know that the testing of your faith produces endurance; and let endurance have its full effect, so that you may be mature and complete, lacking in nothing" (James 1:2–4). Perhaps, like us, you feel like saying: "But, God, isn't there another way? An easier way? Can't we grow without all the pain of struggle?" The answer is no.

Included in the long list of those struggles that bring about maturity we would include the struggle to forgive yourself. You already know that self-forgiveness does not come easily. Guilt and self-degradation do not disappear simply because you declare you have forgiven yourself. Sometimes the struggle even takes a perverse turn, as you not only deal with the guilt of your offense but with guilt over the effort to get rid of your guilt. This happens if you believe that you don't deserve to be forgiven. Hopefully, by this point you are beyond that belief.

Still, you continue to struggle. Well cheer up. This struggle is making you a stronger and more effective Christian because you are learning how to deal with difficult spiritual challenges and you are practicing Christian love. Use self-talk to remind yourself of this fact. Todd tells how he did it:

> I got discouraged when I tried to forgive myself. At times, I thought I wasn't making any progress at all. I kept feeling guilty. And I kept getting down on myself. One of the things I started doing that really helped was to remind myself that even though what I was going through was unpleasant, God was going to use it for my good. Romans 8:28 has always been my favorite verse: "We know that all things work together for good for those who love God, who are called according to his purpose."
>
> So I'd repeat that verse. And then I'd tell myself: "This is good for me. God is going to use it to make me a better Christian." That got me through some of the more discouraging times and helped me keep working on forgiving myself. Because I knew that there was going to be a good outcome.

Going From Victim to Victor

You probably don't think of yourself as a victim. You think of the person you hurt as a victim and you as the victimizer. But you are both—a victimizer and a victim. For until you forgive yourself, you are victimizing yourself, inflicting upon yourself the pain of guilt and self-degradation.

God has called us to be victors, "for whatever is born of God conquers the world. And this is the victory that conquers the world, our faith" (1 John 5:4). Therefore, let your self-talk include something similar to that suggested by a man who faced up to the challenge of self-forgiveness and emerged a victor: "I am God's child. I have faith. If I am willing, if I cooperate with God, nothing can keep me from conquering whatever challenge comes my way. I will face each day with a smile and with confidence, knowing that nothing will happen to me during the day that God and I can't handle."

Give Yourself Time

Which of the following appeal to you?

- Quick and easy ways to relieve your stress
- A short-cut to obtaining your dream job
- Selling your home quickly and easily
- A guaranteed fast and painless diet for losing weight
- An effective way to speed up your computer
- Getting relief from pain in minutes
- Recipes for quick, tasty meals

We have seen recently all of the above and countless other appealing ideas in books, in ads in magazines, and on the Internet. Did you notice the common theme in this list? Not only are they appealing, but they all promise *quick* results. We are a nation of time-conscious people. Most people feel pressured for time. Most people wished they had "more time" to do the things they want to do. And all of us would like to get the desired things in life as quickly as possible. "Wait for the Lord" (Psa. 27:14) is not one of the biblical injunctions that we like to think about. When we want something or want to get rid of something, we prefer to do it as quickly and easily as possible.

Living in a culture where the ads constantly tap into the desire for fast and effortless results, it's not surprising that when you are struggling with something like forgiving yourself you want to do it quickly and easily. It could happen. But it isn't likely. Our final tool for self-forgiveness is, therefore, a most important one: give yourself time because, in our experience, most people find self-forgiveness a journey for which there are no short cuts.

A PROCESS, NOT A QUICK FIX

The terms we prefer to use are "process" and "quick fix." The quick fix is what we'd all like. The process is what we must settle for. There's no forgiveness pill to take for instant relief and a quick cure. You can't highlight your guilt, press a delete button, and automatically achieve self-forgiveness. Rather, forgiving yourself takes place only as you work at it over a period of time.

WHY PROCESS?

Your first efforts to forgive yourself may seem to yield little or no progress. Eventually, you reach a point where the guilt has subsided and you feel that you are finally on the verge of being free. However, you still may find the guilt returning and troubling you once again. This is normal. Think about it in terms of habitual behavior. Have you ever tried to break a habit? Or create a new habit? Rarely does anyone make an instant change in habitual behavior. A woman told us of her efforts:

> I used to have this habit of interrupting people when they were talking to me. I would finish their sentences or complete what I believed was their line of thinking. One day a friend interrupted my interruption! She told me to wait until she had finished. That I didn't understand yet what she was going to say. And she was right. It turned out that what I said when I interrupted her was totally inappro-

priate after I heard her out. I decided right then that I
needed to listen more carefully and fully to people. But I
had been interrupting for decades, and I want to tell you
it was a real struggle to change. I kept relapsing. I needed
something to remind me, so I started pressing my thumb
and forefinger together whenever I talked with someone.
This helped. I still catch myself starting to interrupt at
times, but I'm pretty good at listening now. It sure took a
long time though.

It's much the same with self-forgiveness. One reason that it is
difficult to forgive yourself is that guilt and self-degradation tend
to become habitual. And like any habitual behavior, you are likely
to find yourself relapsing from time to time even after you have
made progress.

In addition, feelings are much harder to change and control
than is behavior. It takes time for your feelings to catch up with
your decision to forgive yourself and your efforts to do so. But
here's the crucial thing to remember: you don't have to be tyrannized by your feelings. In time, you can use your behavior (including such things as self-talk and the way you think about the
matter) to change your feelings. So when the guilt returns, don't
think you are a lost cause and that you must endure your guilt till
death do you part. Keep the process going.

PROCESS INCLUDES ACTION

"Keep the process going" means that you must take action. Don't
be seduced by the old notion that time heals all things. That all
you have to do is wait it out and eventually you'll be okay. When
people suggest to us that they're hoping for time to be their healer,
we have two responses. Our first response is, even if it is true that
time will eventually heal you, why wait? Why spend weeks or
months or years agonizing when you could experience the freedom of self-forgiveness? Our second response is that time alone is
not an automatic healer. We have worked with people who liter-

ally spent decades waiting for their guilt to subside, and it still hadn't happened. In fact, they felt no better about their offense or about themselves than they did when the offense occurred.

Daniel is nearly eighty years old. In his fifties, he escaped from a high-stress work situation by drinking heavily. When he drank too much, he became abusive toward his wife. The abuse was mostly verbal, but it became physical on one occasion and it nearly broke up the marriage. Counseling enabled them to survive as a couple. They are still together and generally happy in their marriage. Only one thing, as Daniel explains, continues to taint their lives:

> I know that God has forgiven me for what I did to myself and to Dora. And Dora has forgiven me. Yet I just can't forgive myself. It's like every time Dora does something extra nice for me I feel guilty all over again. How could I have abused such a caring woman? And I want to apologize again. But I've apologized so many times that Dora told me she doesn't want to hear it any more. She says she's gotten over it and I need to get over it too. So I don't apologize, but I still feel like a heel. I just can't seem to get over it.

Daniel says he had expected to feel better in time. Unfortunately, he took no more action beyond confessing and making amends with his wife. He just waited for time to heal him. But that didn't happen. Instead, his offense has vexed him for nearly three decades. Finally, he's ready to take on the work of forgiving himself. Yet think of the years he's wasted by not being able to enjoy the freedom and contentment of self-forgiveness.

MAKING THE MOST OF THE TIME

We are advised to make "the most of the time, because the days are evil" (Eph. 5:16). It is excellent advice. In terms of self-forgiveness, it suggests that you engage in a planned rather than a haphazard course of action. That is, some people decide to use the tools we have suggested whenever it occurs to them or whenever they are particularly harassed by their guilt and self-deprecating thoughts. This is better than doing nothing. Yet it's not the most efficient way to proceed. It isn't making the most of your time. You need to develop a plan of action. After all, no matter how helpful you may think some of the materials in this book are, they will do you no good if you don't regularly put them into practice.

The Content of Your Plan of Action

In order for you to develop an effective plan, let's review the steps involved in the process of self-forgiveness. These steps form the outline of your plan:

1. Ask for God's forgiveness.

2. Apologize and ask for forgiveness from the person you hurt.

3. Make whatever amends you can to the person you hurt.

4. Elicit the help of someone you trust, to whom you can confess and who will listen to and support you.

5. Practice healthy patterns of thinking; don't allow "should" and "shouldn't" to hamper your efforts and don't turn a part of you—your offense—into your whole character.

6. Use a variety of tools and techniques, including:
   a. Visualization
   b. Healthy spinning
   c. Self-talk

7. Give yourself time—accept the fact that there are no quick fixes because self-forgiveness is a process.

Take Action

Use the preceding list to devise a plan of action for forgiving yourself. You may need to do some of the items only once (for instance, asking and receiving God's forgiveness). You may need to repeat others several times, and some may require regular use.

The important thing is to act—to move beyond good intentions and get to the job of changing how you think and behave.

Otherwise you may be like the son who, when his father asked him to work in the vineyard, said that he would (Matt. 21:30). But he didn't. There is no reason to assume that the son lied to his father. He may well have intended to do the work. Perhaps other matters caught his attention and he never got around to fulfilling his intention. This is what happens to many people who intend to forgive themselves. They agree that self-forgiveness is necessary. They agree that the steps we outlined above are a good way to proceed. But they continue to languish in their guilt for a time because they don't put the principles for self-forgiveness into action.

We'd like for you to schedule your action plan now. Construct a "to-do" list. If you haven't asked for God's forgiveness, which is the first step, stop and do it now. If you hurt someone and haven't yet apologized, set a time tomorrow or as soon as possible to do so. Write down what you intend to say and when you will do it. If you haven't yet tried to make amends, write down what you will do and when you will do it. If you haven't yet elicited the help of someone you trust, identify the person and write down a time to contact that person.

Then decide how and when you are going to incorporate the tools and techniques we have suggested into your daily life. You may want to try them each separately for a period of time or try them as a whole. It's important that they become a part of your mind-set. Thus, whenever you lapse into your old pattern of self-flagellation and guilt, you can replace it with your new way of thinking. This may sound like too much work. Or it may sound a bit threatening. Change always makes people uncomfortable. Thus, even if you're miserable in your lack of self-forgiveness, it's at least a known quantity.

So recognize that you're likely to find excuses to avoid changing your way of thinking and behaving in this matter. Or that you are likely to postpone tackling the matter until a more convenient time. Resist the excuses and say "no" to the postponement. Dive right into the healing process—knowing that nothing is more important than being what God has called you to be—a forgiven child.

HOW LONG?

How long will it take to forgive yourself? We don't know. People differ. It may take weeks or months or years. It depends on such things as how much time and effort you put into the process. It also depends on your conceptions of God and of humans. For example, if you are part of a church that places great stress on your sinfulness and God's holiness, you may have an ongoing struggle with feelings of inadequacy and even worthlessness. You may feel that you can't possibly measure up to God's demands or your own ideals. You feel guilty so often that it seems to be an essential part of your life. Self-forgiveness, thus, seems to violate the essence of your being.

To the extent that this description fits you, you will have a difficult time forgiving yourself. Self-forgiveness will be more of a struggle for you than for others and will probably take more time. You will need to shift your image of God from that of the Great Disciplinarian to that of the Giver of Grace.

In contrast, self-forgiveness may come more easily if you are part of a church that places stress on the call to be Christ-like, on your status as God's child, and on God's love and grace. If so, God's grace, love, and forgiveness are elemental components of your life. Forgiving yourself will require less of a struggle and less time than for those whose image of God is that of the Great Disciplinarian.

We once read an account by a Catholic priest that illustrates the two approaches. As a child, he regularly attended a church with a large sanctuary. In the center part of the high ceiling was an enormous eye in the middle of a triangle from which rays of light spread out over the pews. The priest said that he always found the eye intimidating. As a young man, he stopped in the church one day and stood next to an elderly woman who was praying. She apparently noticed him staring at the eye, which continued to unsettle him even as an adult. She interrupted his reverie and told him that some people thought of the eye as God watching them, watching to spot any sins that needed to be punished. But, the woman assured the future priest, that this wasn't true. What the eye really meant is that God loves us so much that God can't take his eyes off us.

That's the way we like to think about God: God's eyes are always on us because God loves us so much. If you think in those terms, forgiving yourself will come sooner and with less struggle.

WHAT CAN YOU EXPECT?

We raise this final question because we find that people tend to hold on to unrealistic expectations. These unrealistic expectations reflect common, but wrong, notions about forgiveness. We've already dealt with one of them—the expectation that forgiving yourself can happen quickly. Such an expectation reflects the idea that self-forgiveness is a quick fix rather than a process. Another unrealistic expectation is based on the old saw, "forgive and forget." Some people take that too literally. They believe that when they forgive themselves they will come to a point where they can't even remember the incident. Conversely, they assume that as long as they can remember the offense, they haven't really forgiven themselves. But whether you're talking about forgiving yourself or someone else, the "forget" part should be banned from your thinking. You can't erase an experience from your memory—nor do you need to in order to forgive.

One other unrealistic expectation is that whenever you do remember the offense you will not feel any pang of regret or remorse. This expectation reflects the idea that forgiveness eliminates all negative emotions. To feel any such emotions, therefore, means you haven't fully forgiven yourself. Such a thought should also be banned from your thinking. Of course you can remember painful incidents. And of course they can still cause you a moment of grief. There isn't a person alive who can't recall an incident or experience that he or she regrets and would like to erase from his or her memory.

So if forgiving yourself does not mean that you can't recall the incident and doesn't mean that any recollection carries with it a bit of pain, what can you expect as you work through the process? In brief, you can expect that your sense of guilt and self-denigration over the offense will abate and come to an end. Being liberated from such nagging negative ideas and emotions, you can expect to feel better about yourself and about your life. And you can expect to feel closer to God and to others.

All of these expectations are well captured by Janet's account of her experience. Janet works full time as the director of senior ministries in her church. Some twenty years ago, she divorced her cheating husband. As a Christian, she felt badly about her marriage breaking up and even worse about the fact that she was the one who initiated the divorce. She experienced guilt and self-blame both about the divorce and about her own part in allowing the marriage to deteriorate. This is her story:

> I was bitter. I was bitter because I had failed. I was bitter because I thought that God had failed to help us. I was bitter that my husband had gotten involved with another woman and married again soon after the divorce. I couldn't forgive him, and I couldn't forgive myself for letting it happen.
>
> This went on for about five years. I finally realized that I was becoming an emotional and physical wreck. The only thing my bitterness was doing was destroying me. So I went to work on forgiving my ex-husband. This was really tough. Then I went to work on forgiving myself. This was even tougher. But I did it. And it transformed my life. I felt good about myself again. I felt good about my relationship with God. I felt good about life.
>
> Do I ever feel badly about the divorce? I really don't think about it much. On occasion, when we have a family gathering and he is there with our children I still think about what might have been. I regret the fact that we didn't do more to keep our family together. But the feeling passes. I don't feel guilty about it any more. I just regret that we had to go through something like that.

If I had it to do over, I'm sure there are things I could have done and things my ex could have done to keep our marriage intact. But you know what? We've all messed up in one way or another. So I don't live in the past. Life is good. God is good. And I'm just gratefully enjoying it all.

And that's what you can expect. As you go through the process of forgiving yourself, you can be confident that you will come to the point where you no longer live in the past, where you know that life is good and God is good. And you will enjoy your forgiven life with gratitude.

Other books from THE PILGRIM PRESS

HEALING WORSHIP
Purpose and Practice
BRUCE G. EPPERLY
ISBN 978-0-8298-1742-3/paper/144 pages/$18.00
A resource to enable pastors and other church leaders to integrate
healing services into the total life of the church using a wholistic approach
that connects healing liturgies with the theology, pastoral care, and social
concerns of the church.

HEALTH MINISTRIES
A Primer for Clergy and Congregations
DEBORAH L. PATTERSON
ISBN 978-0-8298-1791-1/paper/128 pages/$12.00
Patterson tackles the unique questions and concerns clergy have about
starting and maintaining a health ministry program within their congregations.
She believes clergy can best learn about and understand the importance of
congregational health ministries by listening to the stories and experiences
of parish nurses from within the United States and around the world.

THE ESSENTIAL PARISH NURSE
ABCs for Congregational Health Ministry
DEBORAH L. PATTERSON, ET AL.
ISBN 0-8298-1571-6/paper/160 pages/$20.00
This resource is a practical and useful tool for churches that are interested
in developing a parish nurse program. Covering a broad range, it discusses
the need for such ministry, a brief history of parish nursing, the role of the
parish nurse, and other details of interest to those wishing to establish such
a ministry. Valuable sample materials are included.

THE HEALING CHURCH
Practical Programs for Health Ministries
ABIGAIL RIAN EVANS
ISBN 0-8298-1309-8/paper/260 pages/$24.00
What role can churches and religious organizations play in health care
today? Abigail Rian Evans answers this question and others in this valuable
guide to practical programs for health ministries. It includes a vast list of
existing ministries that can be used as models.

MEDICINE AS MINISTRY
Reflections on Suffering, Ethics, and Hope
Margaret E. Mohrmann, M.D.
ISBN 0-8298-1073-0/paper/120 pages/$15.00

How does one begin to reconcile faith in a merciful God with the crushing reality of human suffering? Over twenty years, Mohrmann has sought to heal children racked by disease and dysfunction, helping many to recover— and watching some die. This book is her moving story of the implications of a theological understanding of health, illness, and hope.

To order these or any other books from The Pilgrim Press call or write to:

The Pilgrim Press
700 Prospect Avenue East
Cleveland, Ohio 44115-1100

Phone orders: 1-800-537-3394 ▪ Fax orders: 216-736-2206

Please include shipping charges of $6.00 for the first book and $1.00 for each additional book.

Or order from our web sites at www.pilgrimpress.com and www.ucpress.com.

Prices subject to change without notice.

The
Promise
of Power

VER

rs' Dialogue
rlos Castaneda

Studios Inc. for an anonymous author

of this book may be used or reproduced in any form
ssion in writing from the publisher, except for brief
ritical articles or reviews.

blishing Company

HAMPTONROADS
PUBLISHINGCOMPANY, INC.

A 22902

navailable from your local bookseller, it may be obtained
he publisher. Call toll-free (800) 766-8009 (Orders only).

57174-024-4

by Dizzy Fish Studios Inc.

0 9 8 7 6 5 4 3 2 1

Printed on acid-free paper in Canada

Fk

THE PROMISE OF POW

Reflections on the Toltec Warrio
From the Collected Works of Ca

For information, write

Hampton Roads P
134 Burgess Lane
Charlottesville, V

If this book is
directly from

ISBN 1-

Design

Cov

1

HAMPTONROADS
PUBLISHING COMPANY, INC.

For the warrior who rests
and the warrior who waits.

CONTENTS

FOREWORD

We are artists by trade, and as is the case with many of our professional colleagues, we have often found ourselves involved in situations that challenged our creativity in unexpected ways.

Four years ago, when we moved our small design studio to a coastal state, we began an association with a man who led us into such a creative endeavor, an undertaking that defied even our well-developed sense of the unexpected. This adventure involved a series of events that seem unbelievable in the retelling; a tale of power that led us to the day of this writing.

We have been privileged to edit and prepare this manuscript on behalf of a special friend of ours, a man we have come to know only as "Tomas." This delightful older gentleman was one of the first friends we made in our new seaside home, and for some unnamed reason we hit it off with him right away. Over the years we have spent many wonderful evenings discussing art and life with this captivating man, and even though we feel we know him well, circumstances have forced us to realize that we really don't know him at all.

Tomas is of Latin descent, an artist and writer by profession (although he has been reluctant to share a great deal of his other work with us). As near as we can tell, Tomas is in his sixties, even though he is much more vital than the average sexagenarian. Lean and dark-skinned, he is blessed with a very engaging smile .

Even though he has alluded to being a grandparent like us, Tomas has an impish, child-like quality which we find endearing in a most inexplicable way. So much so in fact, that my wife now calls this older man "Tommy" as an expression of her affection for his irrepressibly youthful qualities.

Our sporadic relationship with Tomas has been characterized by a series of inconsistencies. On one hand, he has been very open and friendly with us, but at the same time he has avoided revealing much of anything about himself or his family. He has been a frequent guest in our home, but he has never invited us to his house or even told us where he lives. He seems to be relatively well-fixed, but as far as we can tell, he has no telephone or car.

Beyond these superficial discrepancies, we have realized that Tomas' entire way of being is strangely contradictory. He appears to be old and young at the same time; innocent and playful in the midst of his obvious wisdom and sophistication. There is also an infectious dynamism about this man, and yet he is calm and at peace in a way we have never experienced before.

Tomas is like no one we have known, and my wife and I have come to treasure his friendship dearly. In many ways we know Tomas' companionship was instrumental in helping us make the difficult adjustment to a new town, and yet for more than a year we took our pleasant relationship with him more or less for granted. Then one night everything changed.

During one of our occasional weekend chats, we happened to discover that Tomas had compiled a personal reference guide to the collected works of a well known new-age author. We learned about the existence of this "catalog" when the name of Carlos Castaneda came up in the course of conversation.

As a casual student of various spiritual writers, my wife was familiar with Castaneda's work, and that evening we happened to be discussing how she had introduced me to passages from *The Fire From Within* on our honeymoon. I told Tomas how I became intrigued with the story of a man who had jumped off a cliff and survived to tell about it, and how my interest had led me to read several more of Carlos' books.

I was forced to admit, however, that despite my early enthusiasm, I had become frustrated with the Castaneda material. Although I enjoyed the lyrical narrative quality of the books, I found it difficult to get a handle on their underlying spiritual content. After reading three of them, I just couldn't seem to "get it," even though I had a clear intuitive sense that something tantalizing was mirrored in the pages of Carlos' work.

I commented that despite this vague intuition, my inability to connect with the essence of don Juan's teachings led me to abandon Castaneda's work for other more pressing matters. My wife agreed that she too had experienced difficulty distilling anything substantive from the numerous Carlos books which she had read. In her opinion, the essential themes of many other new age writings were much more accessible to the average reader.

Tomas took us off guard when he responded to our frustrations concerning the Castaneda books. He said he knew exactly what we were talking about because he had been a devoted student of Carlos Castaneda's writings for many years, having read his entire collection of work countless times.

My wife and I were both a little surprised by Tomas' revelation. He had never impressed us as the studious type, much less as the kind of person who would dedicate himself to the writings of a controversial new-age guru. But our surprise became astonishment when Tomas went on to tell us that his personal study of Castaneda's work had led him to compile a complex series of notes and references on the material.

We were actually somewhat skeptical as Tomas explained how, over of period of many years, he had assembled a massive reference guide to the Toltec warriors' dialogue; a catalog of sorts that allowed him to cross-reference and easily access thousands of isolated references scattered throughout the eight Castaneda books in print. He told us he had prepared his reference guide as a personal exercise designed to help him access the underlying essence of what he called "nagualism".

Once we determined that Tomas wasn't joking with us about his catalog, my wife and I immediately became interested in finding out more about it. Months later, when we finally convinced him to share some small portions of it with us, we were amazed at the intuitive and organizational clarity he had brought to the Castaneda material. It only took a brief review of his work for us to realize that Tomas was much more of a scholar than we had ever suspected.

It was very clear that our casual friend had accomplished something remarkable. He had created a reference work that rendered an intimidating body of very abstract material much more understandable. To our minds, his efforts paralleled those of Marianne Williamson, (an insightful author who had distilled concepts from an underground treatise called *A Course In Miracles* and published them as a national bestseller titled *A Return to Love*).

After studying his notes in depth, we prevailed upon Tomas to consider publishing his work as well. My wife and I guessed (based on our own experience) that many casual Castaneda readers would find Tomas' work of interest and that a book based on his catalog would be received with great enthusiasm.

It occurred to us that perhaps the Castaneda material would benefit from the same kind of distillation as *A Course in Miracles* . We felt that many people must have been tantalized by the same unspoken something that we had encountered in the Carlos books, and we were sure that our friend's catalog would make this intriguing core much more accessible .

Our theory led us to become keenly focused on the inspirational potential of Tomas' work. We came to believe his catalog was a diamond in the rough; that once polished and presented, it would bring great additional clarity to a body of knowledge that had intrigued (and probably somewhat frustrated) millions of readers all around the world.

But despite our enthusiasm for publishing his reference guide, we quickly learned Tomas had a very different opinion of our idea. He vehemently disagreed with our well-intentioned suggestion and refused to even consider publishing his notes, arguing that his catalog had been prepared as a personal task of learning, and not as a project for publication.

For months, Tomas remained adamant that creating a book from his notes would taint the very personal nature of his work and produce a most undesirable series of "first attention" consequences. He simply refused to involve himself and his catalog in the contractual, financial, and ego-related issues of new age book authorship.

But much to our own surprise, my wife and I would not take no for an answer. We are normally not pushy people, but our intuition kept nagging us about this project, and so we kept pestering Tomas, hoping that he might eventually change his mind. Finally, after months of additional coaxing, we were able to break through and convince our friend that a book based on his notes could be published without the first attention consequences that so concerned him.

The solution we proposed was simple. It called for us to act as Tomas' personal representatives on the project. We would handle everything in his behalf, including all necessary dealings with attorneys, agents and publishers. We also assured Tomas that we would gladly do all the design, editing and mechanical assembly work on the manuscript, since this was something we already did as part of our professional repertoire.

This suggestion eventually turned the tide in our favor, and months later, Tomas finally gave us his enthusiastic go-ahead with one all-important condition. He insisted that we coordinate all aspects of the publishing process without his direct involvement, and above all else, that we keep his identity secret.

Remaining anonymous has always been of paramount importance to Tomas. As he explained it to us, without his anonymity, he would be unable to his maintain his "equilibrium" with respect to the catalog he had created. He said that in order to preserve the spirit of his efforts, the private nature of his learning task had to be preserved.

We never fully understood what Tomas meant by all this, but we respected his point of view just the same. Since the day we first became his representatives, my wife and I have done everything in our power to honor our friend's wish for anonymity. This has not been difficult, since even we know precious little about Tomas in the first place.

And now, years later, the day has come when our dreams for Tomas' catalog have been realized. As caretakers of this unique manuscript, we believe in both its power and its promise. We have spent years and literally thousands of hours doing our best to edit, design and prepare this book as impeccably as possible, and we are honored to have played some small part in bringing this powerful work to light.

As you proceed from here, please remember that *The Promise Of Power* is designed to be read and re-read in conjunction with the collected works of Carlos Castaneda. As relative newcomers to this material ourselves, we strongly echo the author's recommendation that this book not be used alone, but rather as a kind of informational and intuitive "directory" to the Castaneda books themselves.

As Tomas has pointed out to us so often, *The Promise Of Power* can only find its true meaning within the larger context of the Toltec warriors' dialogue. This manuscript is not intended to stand alone; it is rather, as our agent so aptly put it, "a kind of concordance," a reference guide which is meaningless without the collected works on which it is based.

If you don't already have copies of the nine Castaneda books, we suggest you acquire them all before going any further. (You'll find a list of titles and information regarding the specific editions on which the concordance is based in the editor's note on page 71.) With the complete Castaneda library at your side, *The Promise Of Power* can function as it should, to lead you back again and again to the dialogue of the eloquent men and women who were don Juan's companions on the road to power.

As we put the finishing touches on this manuscript we are saddened by the fact that Tomas is no longer here with us. In spite of his absence, our magical experience with this book's author has left us convinced that he is a true warrior in the Toltec sense, even though he never once referred to himself as such.

We believe Tomas to be a simple and selfless man whose quiet power is beyond our limited comprehension. Our intuition tells us we were meant to be touched by him and by his work, just as we believe in turn that Tomas was meant to share his insights on the Toltec warriors' dialogue as an impeccable deposit to the account of the spirit of man.

D.F.S. - 1993

PART I

PRELUDE

PRELUDE

A FOOL'S TALE

I am a fool, but a fortunate fool indeed. Good fortune has smiled on me and woven a thread of magic in my life. I sit today among my friends the trees who spin tales of the unimaginable and reflect with me on how the mystery of existence makes fools of us all. I have been resting and waiting for many years, and now, when I least expect it, the hour of the moth has at last arrived. Once again magic sweeps over me like a wave and leaves me breathless. A fool and his humble task have been transformed!

My personal history is long since lost, a tale of power moving. This is as it should be, because I am a simple man with only a simple story to tell. I have lived and learned as all men do. In fact, my life has been uneventful with the exception of the magical thread that has invisibly woven itself through the fabric of my days.

My gift of magic has been silent and unobtrusive, it never revealed itself in a dramatic way. It did not distinguish me as a scholar or great talent, nor did it lead me to riches and fame. I was never especially lucky, or charming, or charismatic; whatever my magical gift, it chose to remain out of sight for a great many years. And yet it was there at my fingertips every moment of my life, a noiseless and faithful companion that I was too foolish to fully appreciate.

My stupidity led me to scorn my gift of magic, even curse it. As my life unfolded, some part of me always knew I had a gift, but that bequest was never validated by my waking experience. I could not understand why magic would not manifest itself in the concrete ways that mattered to me. If my intuition was correct and I truly had a gift, why hadn't it aided

3

me in realizing my goals of recognition, wealth and personal happiness?

It took many long years of frustration and self-pity before I finally realized that my life was not going to unfold in accordance with my self-involved agendas. Decades of unrewarded struggle at my chosen profession culminated in a devastating blow which crushed my last hopes for wealth and professional acclaim. I was left with no choice but to accept the fact that my life was playing itself out in keeping with some other kind of plan, a blueprint which had clearly eluded me throughout more than fifty years of living!

As a result of my overwhelming professional set-backs, I lost almost all the material things I had worked for my entire life. I was publicly humiliated and financially ruined. Thirty years of professional expectations lay shattered at my feet, and my overwhelming disappointment drove me to the brink of suicide. I didn't know it at the time, but I was caught in the midst of a cataclysmic clash of agendas; a conflict between a personal timetable that reflected my own selfish desires and one that mirrored an impersonal outside order beyond my comprehension.

Late one night, I finally decided not to take the pills, and in that critical moment I chose to empower my life rather than destroy it. As sorry as I felt for myself, I ultimately refused to accept the notion that I was a pathetic individual being punished by the cosmos for the all-too-human mistakes I had made along the way. I simply wasn't ready to believe that everything was lost, and instead of giving up, I forced myself to take a painful look at the real resources and options in my life.

It was this soul-searching that eventually brought me back to an awareness of my magical thread. On the deepest intuitive level, I had never completely lost sight of my gift as something constant and real. Even during those most terrible days, magic remained part of my awareness, and even in spite of my overwhelming despair, my intuition kept reminding me of its presence.

These unwavering feelings eventually led me to the possibility that maybe I was too much of a fool to fully appreciate my own gifts. Perhaps I wasn't being punished at all, perhaps my problem centered around the fact that I was just incredibly stubborn and short-sighted. This thought comforted me, and in some way I sensed that it was true.

One day an odd analogy popped into my head out of nowhere. Perhaps I was like a poor fool with an overpowering intuition he was going to find some money at his feet. This terribly frustrated man would spend years searching the busy streets in vain, unaware all the while that he had a thousand dollar bill stuck to the bottom of his shoe.

I reasoned that if this analogy was true, then my intuition about my magical gift could have always been correct, despite my many years of "searching the streets" in vain. Perhaps my gift had indeed been with me all the time; perhaps I just hadn't considered all the unlikely possibilities as to where it might be waiting for me to discover it.

Somehow this strange analogy sparked a new and very subtle receptivity in me. Consciously, I was still much too involved with my own self-pity to recognize any change in attitude, but in retrospect, I now realize this peculiar insight into my unrealized possibilities prepared me on some deep level for the events of a day that was yet to come.

Just a few weeks later, on an otherwise ordinary afternoon, I finally began a true appreciation of the elusive and magical thread that had been an integral part of my life since the day I was born. In an unguarded and unexpected moment, power caught me by surprise and finally coaxed me to stop and take a look at the bottom of my shoe.

A CHANCE ENCOUNTER WITH MY DOUBLE

It was a sharp day in late autumn, with a cutting edge that unknowingly severed the ties that bound me to the life I had always known. The spirit knocked on my door that day and my life was never the same again.

It had been less than a month since the turning point in my suicidal feelings, and even though I had chosen to continue my life, I was still in a very black mood on this crisp and windy afternoon. My despondency sprang from the failure of a personal creative project that had consumed me for more than fifteen years of my life. I had been absolutely convinced this undertaking would finally earn me the recognition so long overdue me. When it failed miserably I was overcome with despair, convinced that my credibility and career could never recover.

And yet I struggled to be philosophical about it all so that I could begin the task of putting my life back together. On this particular day I was trying my best to distract myself by running some mindless errands in a metropolitan shopping district near where I lived at the time. My strategy wasn't working though, and all I did was mope about from shop to shop, completely lost in my own self-pity. Then, as I turned a busy corner, I was startled by the sound of an abrupt whisper behind my right ear.

"You know, it really ticks me off when my friends ignore me in the street!"

I spun around to face a beautiful blond haired woman whom I had never met before. As she looked into my eyes I could see her embarrassment, realizing at that moment she had mistaken me for someone else. The woman apologized profusely and told me that I looked just like her friend Escobar who worked at the sandwich shop around the corner.

As she frantically explained herself, I was totally enchanted! To my amazement, her effervescence and charming good looks instantly dispelled some of my dark mood. I immediately managed a smile and surprised myself with the thought that I hoped she was trying to pick me up. Summoning all the enthusiasm I could muster, I told her I was delighted she had mistaken me for a friend.

The woman apologized again and continued to insist her mistake was quite understandable because I was an exact double of her friend Escobar. I felt very comfortable with her as we chatted casually for a moment about the eerie concept that we might all have doubles roaming the streets, living lives that were somehow parallel to, but separate from, our own.

I was surprised to realize that even our brief conversation had lifted my spirits tremendously. Something about this woman was having a very positive effect on me and I knew I didn't want our exchange to end. So when I sensed she was ready to excuse herself and say good-by, I took a chance and asked her if she would join me for a cup of coffee at the deli where her friend Escobar worked. I told her that I was intrigued to meet my double, (but what I really wanted was to get to know her a little better).

Much to my delight, she accepted my offer with great enthusiasm. She grasped my hand in both of hers and said "Oh, let's do!". We quickly rounded the corner to the coffee shop and ducked into the old fashioned revolving door. Conversation continued to come easily between us, and after we had ordered coffee, my companion asked our waitress if Escobar was working in the kitchen. Our server gave us an affirmative nod and said she would send him out to our table when time allowed.

After the waitress left, I continued to make small talk with my lovely new acquaintance. We chatted freely about that particular neighborhood and how a number of wonderful old buildings in the area had been saved from the wrecking ball by historically minded investors. As we conversed, I could not get over how quickly her presence was dissipating the feelings of despair that had been plaguing me for long. She was like a breath of fresh air and I gladly filled my lungs with her soothing energy.

And then, quite abruptly, Escobar appeared at our table. I was amazed to find that he really did look a lot like me, although slightly heavier perhaps, with a bit more of a chin. He seemed sensitive and quite refined as he leaned over our table to kiss the blond woman on the cheek.

With a slight Mexican accent, Escobar addressed my female companion as Marie and told her he was enchanted to see her. Marie then playfully introduced me as his "daily double," apologizing to both of us as she realized we had talked all this time without exchanging names.

I told them that my friends called me Tomas, and we all laughed as Marie described our accidental meeting in the street. The Mexican and I looked each other over as Marie commented on the remarkable resemblance between us. Then Escobar jokingly asked if I would be willing to stand in for him the next time he needed to visit the Immigration office.

The outspoken cook remained at our table for a few more moments making animated conversation and regaling us with the details of his day in the kitchen. When he reached a convenient stopping point he politely excused himself, shaking my hand and giving Marie another peck on the cheek. Then as he walked away from the table, Escobar suddenly turned and pulled something out of his apron pocket.

"Oh, by the way Marie," he said. "Here's your Carlos book. I finally finished it but I'm afraid it wasn't my cup of tea. Maybe I need to read his other one before I'll really understand what he's driving at."

Marie took the book from him and thanked him for returning it so promptly. As Escobar walked back to the kitchen she called after him and said she'd be happy to loan him *A Separate Reality* any time he'd care to stop by her place and pick it up. Escobar answered that he'd call first as he disappeared behind the swinging kitchen doors.

After he'd left, Marie and I continued talking about my resemblance to her friend. But as our discussion progressed, I found myself increasingly curious about the well-worn paperback she was turning over and over in her hands. I finally asked her about it and she told me it was a fascinating book on spirituality by a new California author. I told her that I didn't have much use for books on religion, but she insisted that this one was different and asked if I would like to borrow her copy of *The Teachings of Don Juan*.

To this day its unbelievable to me that I accepted the loan of that book, because at the time it was very unlike me to have any interest whatsoever in religious writing. But I borrowed the book just the same and today I know it was no accident that I met that beautiful blond haired woman and the man who was my double.

Several days later, when I called the phone number Marie had given me, her girlfriend told me she had left town with a boyfriend for Colorado. She never returned, but the innocent gift of the book she loaned me changed my life forever.

THE TEACHINGS OF DON JUAN

There is no rational way to describe the effect that the works of Carlos Castaneda have had on me. These books have changed me in a subtle yet dramatic way. I realize now that the essence of the Toltec warrior' dialogue crept up on me gradually and caught me unaware, and yet it took me with a power so overwhelming that to this day I have never encountered anything else like it.

At first, I read the books about don Juan with only casual interest, but somehow I found myself being drawn back to them again and again. Over a period of time, I eventually read them all, and one day I awoke to realize, much to my own surprise, that the abstract essence of Carlos' work had engaged me on a very deep level.

For me, the spirit of the Castaneda books is as real as anything I have ever known. Many people have tried to discredit Carlos' work for various reasons, but this controversy is of absolutely no concern to me. I have banished all doubts from my mind and allowed magic to overtake me instead. I "know" the principles of nagualism are true, not because of what my reason tells me, but because power has led me to my own indescribable experience of those truths.

My encounter with this material has helped me transform myself in ways I never would have dreamed possible. The Toltec warriors' dialogue has brought forth the thread of magic in my life to a point where I can not only *see* it clearly, but I am now able to manipulate it as well. There is nothing I can say about my experience with these books, other than that it has been "real" to the greatest degree imaginable. So "real" in fact, that it has even led me to redefine the term "reality" for myself.

The warriors' dialogue that changed my life so completely is contained within a series of nine books written by Carlos Castaneda between 1968 and 1993. These penetrating works of non-fiction chronicle Carlos' staggering experiences with the knowledge of "nagualism" and a magnificent warrior-sorcerer named don Juan Matus. Together these books comprise an awesome body of work that has engaged the attention of millions of readers like myself.

The Works of Carlos Castaneda

The Teachings of Don Juan
A Separate Reality
Journey To Ixtlan
Tales of Power
The Second Ring of Power
The Eagle's Gift

The Fire From Within
The Power of Silence
The Art of Dreaming

There is no way for anyone to comment adequately on the spirit and content of these books. They must be read, and reread and reread again; absorbed and internalized by the individual with an intuitive taste for knowing.

The essence of the Toltec warriors' dialogue does not give itself up easily because it is not superficially accessible to the rational mind. The essence of nagualism's written record is something much more elusive, an indefinable abstract which must be accessed and channeled into practice on a very personal level.

There is no holy scripture contained in the warriors' dialogue; no dogma to be memorized, propounded or defended. There is only an unfathomable reality that gleams in the eyes of Toltec warriors, a promise that hovers between the lines of an epic tale of power.

A FOOL'S TASK

As I have said, I came to the warriors' dialogue innocently and with no expectations. I was not a student of religion or spirituality, nor did I have any interest in shamanism or American Indian cultures. Nevertheless, the writings of Carlos Castaneda gathered my attention over a period of years and engaged my being in a way that made it impossible for me to ever be the same.

Over time I read and reread the Castaneda books as they were released, and in so doing, I began to feel a connection with the essence of don Juan's teachings. This emerging link continued to grow until I felt that I had undergone the beginnings of some sort of informal "apprenticeship" to the knowledge of nagualism.

I realize now that this was a fool's assumption, because any novice in the face of power cannot begin to imagine the nature of the forces he is tapping. In spite of my foolishness however, I felt compelled to further define my relationship with the warriors' dialogue. The only resources I had at my disposal were my sincere desire to learn and the Carlos books themselves, so I proceeded with these simple tools and the focus of my fool's intent.

I immersed myself in Castaneda's work, reading and studying all the books as much as I could. I had grown to feel these editions had been published as a special deposit to the account of the spirit of man, and I was determined to make the most of the books' magical availability.

I am not particularly organizationally minded, but as I proceeded with my studies, I became increasingly intrigued with the idea of creating some sort of reference guide that would help me organize some of the various concepts presented within the warriors' dialogue.

This idea fascinated me because as I reread the books I became increasingly interested in particular passages that seemed of special importance to me. The problem I ran into was my inability to remember the precise location of these special references when I wanted to access them for study.

I addressed this difficulty by first beginning to mark my copies of the books with little scraps of paper and by making informal notes to myself. I realize now that it was these early exercises that really set the mechanics of my reference guide in motion.

As the number of my hand-scribbled notes grew to rather unwieldy proportions, I surprised myself one day by formally deciding to set myself a fool's task. I didn't know exactly how I was going to do it, but I decided to prepare an impeccable catalog of references to the Toltec warriors' dialogue.

I had no qualifications for such an endeavor, I was not an apprentice in sorcery or a gifted scholar. I actually began the project without much thought by simply buying a large three ring binder and several reams of notebook paper. From there I just played it by ear, working diligently on my special catalog whenever I could find the time. The task was a monumental one, and soon consumed me to an alarming degree. But I worked joyfully, never thinking twice about the demands that the project made on my time.

As I proceeded, the thing I noticed most about the cataloging process was that the more I read and reread the Carlos books, the more I seemed to get from them. I was amazed to find that the personal significance of the material actually seemed to change before my eyes from month to month and from year to year.

Continuing my studies, it became increasingly apparent to me that the amount of information I was able to assimilate from the books at any given moment was directly dependent on a personal variable over which I had no control. This was a frustrating realization because I had to accept the fact that every time I reread one of the books my comprehension level was dictated by an energy level that was beyond my conscious control.

And so, as I progressed with my fool's task, I came face to face with a basic contradictory premise of don Juan's knowledge. I was forced to realize there would be no closure for my foolish cataloging task, because my ability to comprehend and organize the material at hand was destined to shift with the fluctuations of my own personal power. This contradiction put my efforts in a strange and pointless new light, but being a fool, I continued them just the same.

THE CONTRADICTIONS OF KNOWLEDGE

I remained focused on my cataloging efforts for many years, tremendously enjoying the time I spent studying and cross-referencing various topics of the warriors' dialogue. As my perspective on the material continued to evolve, certain things began to become clear to me.

I slowly began to understand that the path of knowledge only reveals itself as part of power's unfathomable design. It does not unfold in conjunction with any individual's first attention agenda. I realized that in and of itself, my conscious desire to learn would never be enough to open the door to silent knowledge. I believe that anyone who comes to the warriors' dialogue with a similar thirst for knowledge must accept this basic premise before proceeding.

It is imperative to remember that Carlos Castaneda's books do not represent pure knowledge. At best, they are a marvelous sorcery story, an elaborate abstract core that reflects the silent knowledge of nagualism. This direct knowledge flows straight from power itself; a spiritual thread that remains beyond the control of any conscious process or agenda. Don

Juan reminds us often that this silent knowledge is an abstract which exists independent of language all together; an abstract which can only be claimed by warriors with sufficient personal power to do so.

In light of these truths, I realized that the acquisition of knowledge must be treated as a magical and incomprehensible process. Knowledge cannot be chased down at the whim of the individual, it cannot be rationally catalogued and arbitrarily confined. Knowledge must be stalked with the patience, sobriety and humility of the warrior. Those who believe they can assimilate the essence of don Juan's teachings through a simple formula or classroom exercise, will never find what they seek, because true knowledge does not make itself available to us in this kind of rational way.

From don Juan's Toltec perspective, knowledge is a much more elusive creature. It hovers around us and beckons to those of us impeccable enough to internalize it as part of our own experience. I realized on some level many years ago that I was never going to access knowledge through a meticulously cross-referenced catalog of the warriors' dialogue. Even so, I continued joyfully with my pointless task because my intuition kept coaxing me to do so.

The contradictions of knowledge are an impenetrable mystery for the workings of the rational mind. Even though I found myself caught between two opposing perspectives, I realized that living this strange contradiction was part of the road I was meant to follow. This strange realization made me even more certain that I was no more than a fool; only now I was a joyful fool walking his path with heart.

THE CONTRADICTIONS OF KNOWLEDGE
COME FULL CIRCLE

After several years of additional work, I was able to shed some additional light on my cataloging task by realizing that I could incorporate the Toltec perspective on "the true pair" into my continuing efforts. This involved creating a balance between the "doing" and "not-doing" of the task I had undertaken.

One day it occurred to me that since my cataloguing efforts had begun, I had focused almost exclusively on informational references to the warriors' dialogue. This realization disturbed me because at that point I knew there was much more to nagualism than a series of reasoned explanations for the conscious mind. Combined with my perspective on the essential futility of my catalog, this insight led me to foolishly expand the scope of my already pointless task.

The expansion of my work took the form of supplementing the informational "doing" of my catalog, with an intuitive and parallel "not-doing" of the same fool's task. I decided to combine a subset of intuitive references to the warriors' dialogue with the group of informational references I had already been busy cataloging for so long. This decision greatly broadened the scope of my task, and helped me realize even more how elusive the acquisition of knowledge really is.

The focus of my new intuitive initiative was the group of abstract cores and sorcery stories that are presented as part of the Castaneda books. The intriguing thing about these special teaching tools is that they are intended for an awareness beyond reason and rationality altogether.

Don Juan makes it clear that the sorcery stories are designed to communicate an abstract message independent of the any plot or narrative content. No one can ever "reason out" when or how these abstract cores will reveal themselves to a person; that unfolding remains in the hands of power.

As students of don Juan's teachings we can read and reread the sorcery stories to our heart's content, scanning between the lines for an intuitive essence which we can never access directly. But this is the most we can do of our own volition, because the internalization of the abstract cores functions independent of the students' conscious desire to learn. All any of us can hope to do is to remain impeccable and wait for the spirit to descend on us.

And perhaps after years of reading and thinking and intuiting, one day the fool's world will change and he or she will come to know the abstract directly, without the intervention of language at all. Perhaps on an average day, when least expected, power will move in accordance with its own design and touch the fool in a way that is beyond description.

What a preposterous notion! As fools we can only laugh in the face of such an overwhelming contradiction, because somehow it all makes sense to us!

THE EVOLUTION OF A FOOL'S TASK

I have now arrived at a point in my story where I can begin to discuss this book and how it evolved into its present form. As I have mentioned previously, the catalog which forms the core of this manuscript was begun many years ago as an intimate task of learning. During the years of its assembly, I never for a moment considered it to be anything but a private exercise. In fact, no part of this book (with the exception of this introduction) was ever created with publication in mind. My intent for the materials collected here has always centered solely around my personal desire to reconnect myself with the abstract order of the Toltec warriors' dialogue.

I began my study of the works of Carlos Castaneda in 1972 and started cataloging references from those books early in 1974. I continued my cataloging efforts until the late 80's when my involvement with nagualism eventually led me to the doorway of the sorcerer's world. At that time I began a new set of experiences that led me away from the cataloging work which had occupied me for so long. As part of this transition in my life, I moved to a rural locale where I could live more simply and accommodate my dreaming practices with greater facility.

I struggled for several years on the verge of insanity, trying desperately to assimilate the overpowering events which had suddenly overtaken my life. One morning, however, at the end of a particularly harrowing experience, I finally resolved that I did not have the makings of a sorcerer, and retreated to a more familiar urban setting where I could distance myself from sorcery and the intensities of my dreaming practice.

It was then that the story of this book really began. I chanced to meet one day, a man and his wife who had just recently moved to the seaside community where I had taken up residence. They were both creative people like myself, and we immediately became fast friends. During the following year we spent many wonderful evenings discussing life, the arts and the magic of the world. I became particularly fond of both of them and greatly enjoyed the time we spent together.

One night, most abruptly, the name of Carlos Castaneda came up in the course of one of our after-hours conversations. At that time, I had purposely distanced myself from my cataloging work, and was very surprised to be so suddenly reminded of the books that had consumed me for so many years.

Before I even had time to think about what I was saying, I blurted out to my artist friends that I had created a reference catalog for the warriors' dialogue (even though I had never mentioned this very personal endeavor to another living soul before that night). At the time I couldn't believe I was capable of such an indiscretion, but now I understand that this unwitting disclosure was meant to be.

My friends seemed fascinated with my reference work, and eventually convinced me to share some of my hand-written notes with them. That's where the trouble really began, because both husband and wife became insistent that we work together to publish my catalog as a comprehensive reference for students of don Juan's teachings.

I was stunned by their suggestion and absolutely refused to even consider such a possibility. I tried to explain to them the intimate and personal nature of the work I had done, and that it was never intended to be a project in print. It simply would not be appropriate for my fool's task to become the basis for a book!

But my friends were relentless. Even though I remained completely closed to their ludicrous proposal, they kept after me to reconsider. Their insistence was based in part on the fact that I had already collaborated with them on a screenplay, and they felt they knew me well enough to aggressively suggest a second collaboration. I must say that their persistence put a real strain on our relationship, but before things got to the breaking point, they finally got me to discuss the matter with them further.

In the weeks that followed they argued passionately, telling me over and over how much the book would be appreciated by thousands of people like themselves, people who had had difficulty in distilling the essence of nagualism from the Castaneda books alone. In return, I kept reminding them about the contradictions of knowledge and the fact that just publishing my notes was not going to further the cause of knowledge in the slightest. I also tried to explain to them that if my notes were published, the intimate process at the heart of my efforts would be overshadowed by the flurry of first attention distractions which would unavoidably surround the publishing of such a book.

I had some experience with publishing, and knew of which I spoke. I simply could not imagine associating my fools task were the "doings" of contracts, editors, publicity tours and money. I knew in my heart that I wanted nothing to do with any of those things, not to mention whatever social attention my authorship of the book might generate. I was absolutely clear in my resolve to keep my fool's task private.

But my friends countered with what eventually became a series of deciding arguments. Their suggestion revolved around the idea that my catalog could be published anonymously, and that no one would ever have to know who I was. They reasoned that this would permit me to remain detached from my first attention concerns, thereby allowing me to keep the intimate nature of my catalog intact. They also reminded me that if I was not interested in the money that the book might generate, my portion of the proceeds could go into an account for the benefit of those in need.

My last mechanical reservations were addressed when my friends volunteered to take on the horrific task of transcribing all my hand-written notes and preparing the catalog electronically for publication. They agreed to this daunting task willingly, having designed and prepared numerous book of various kinds before. I knew from my experience with them that they were more than capable of handling the job, and so I was left with no rational objections to their publishing proposal.

The only thing I had yet to decide was an intuitive question; whether or not the publishing of the catalog was in keeping with my path with heart. Part of me didn't want to consider that the course of my fool's task might take such an unexpected turn. Yet I knew from personal experience that the designs of power are beyond the grasp of any man.

And so in humbleness, I looked to the south for an answer to my questions. I knew then that this book was meant to be, even if its "doing" only proved to be a stalking exercise for the individuals involved. Once my intuitive concerns had been resolved in silence, my entire outlook on the project changed and a new enthusiasm possessed me.

From that point forward I developed a very positive perspective on this book, and came to view it as a deposit to the account of the spirit of man. My new outlook cleared the way for a publishing initiative to begin, and so early in 1992 we began a collective effort to assemble this book under the title, *The Promise of Power*.

THE PROMISE

I chose the title of this book because it epitomizes for me the hopes and struggles of the human condition and the magical realization of the promise which power holds for each of us as luminous beings.

The promise of power is the promise always kept.
The shadow of the bird of freedom
glides over an unsuspecting shoulder,
And the warrior bids for power.

The promise of power is made to the warrior who rests.
All things come to the warrior who rests,
And all things become nothing for the warrior who waits.
The promise of power is the promise always kept.

Since deciding to proceed with this project, my direct involvement with it has been relatively minimal. It was my artist friends who actualized this manuscript by organizing and transcribing the mountain of hand-scribbled notes and references which I had accumulated over the years. For over a year, they worked to assemble a presentable first draft of my reference catalog for the Toltec warriors' dialogue.

At the same time as these transcription and editing efforts began, my friends also started to search for a suitable literary agent to represent the project. I must admit that I remained skeptical they would find anyone interested in the manuscript at all. I was tremendously surprised when after only a few short weeks, they reported back to me with remarkable news.

Not only had they managed to locate and engage the enthusiastic services of a very established literary agent, but the man they found was a professional acquaintance of Carlos Castaneda himself, having been involved in negotiations for paperback rights to several of his first books. I considered this a very positive omen, and I felt more reassured than ever that *The Promise of Power* was meant to be.

My friends worked diligently in their spare time to assemble the first draft of our manuscript. It was based almost exactly on the organizational structure of my original catalog and included a great many quotes from the various Carlos books. When it was finally complete, we were all very enthusiastic about it and sent it off with great anticipation to our agent. He liked the draft very much but had several significant concerns which gave us reason to stop and reflect.

Our agent's first worry revolved around a legal issue called "fair usage." He informed us that in terms of publishing legality and protocol, it was not considered permissible to publish a book with such a large number of direct quotes from previously published material. The rights to those quotes properly belong to the original author (in this case, Carlos Castaneda) and therefore, it would not be possible for us to publish a book of that kind without Carlos' direct consent.

I was very concerned about this disturbing development, but my friends were hardly fazed. As professionals with some experience in creative problem solving, they suggested that we had two options. The first was to try and contact Carlos himself and see if we could get his permission to use quotes from his books. The second option would involve the creation of a complete revision of the manuscript.

We decided to pursue the first option before thinking too seriously about revising the book. We also agreed that if Carlos reviewed the manuscript and did not want it published, we would honor his wishes without question. This meant that we would either try to correct any objections he had with the book, or we would drop the project all together if Carlos personally asked us to.

Our agent immediately contacted Carlos' own literary representative to discuss the matter. Much to our dismay, the young man at Toltec Artists offered us little encouragement. The teachings of don Juan, the agent said, could be discovered only as presented in the context of the Castaneda books themselves. He also made it clear that Carlos had been approached many times by authors who wanted to write commentaries about his work, and that he had always refused permission for the use of extensive quotations in any book of that type.

But our agent explained that *The Promise of Power* was not intended as a substitute for the original books - it was, rather, a kind of concordance - and sent a sample of the text for the agent to read and forward to Carlos Castaneda for his opinion.

As we waited for a reply we decided to explore the theoretical possibility of our second option. We talked about various ways of reworking the original manuscript so that the fair usage issue would not come into play. At first I found it impossible to generate enthusiasm for any of these possibilities.

My concerns centered around the original intent of my catalog. I was not sure at first how it could be formatted without using a large number of direct quotes. After all, the entire point of the project was to provide some kind of further insight into the warriors' dialogue, and those insights seemed to be dependent on the ability to quote passages from the original Castaneda materials. But again my friends intervened with some realistic solutions.

I talked with them at length about ways we could preserve the essence of the original catalog without the use of extensive quotes. After a great deal of thought and intuitive review, it became clear to me that such a revision was possible, but that it would require reworking the manuscript from the ground up.

Knowing the months and perhaps years of additional work that would be necessary to revise the catalog, I was ready to drop the whole project at this point. Things seemed to be getting much too complicated and I simply didn't care if the catalog was ever published or not.

But my friends were relentless in their sincere desire to bring the manuscript to print. They reminded me repeatedly that they had developed a true love for the project and could not imagine letting it drop without conscientiously exploring all its possibilities. They also reminded me that they would gladly be the ones to complete the enormous amount of work required to produce a revised manuscript.

We continued to review our options and discuss possible revisions while we waited for a response from Carlos. After almost six months with no word, we all agreed that it was unlikely we would ever get a reaction from Mr. Castaneda, either positive or negative. In fact we guessed it was unlikely Carlos would ever even see the material at all.

This turn of events forced us to make our own decision about *The Promise of Power*. As we examined the situation again, we reaffirmed our collective belief in the spirit of the project and decided that it was well worth a continuation of our efforts.

We then began a major revision of the book, based on the discussions we had had previously. Soon after we started, however, we also heard from the elusive Mr. Castaneda, but not in the way we had always hoped. Carlos did not contact us directly about *The Promise of Power,* but after more than six years of silence, he did publish a new book called *The Art of Dreaming.*

Each of us read this new release with great interest and concluded after completing it that we were more interested than ever in getting *The Promise of Power* published. We also agreed that we should take the extra time necessary to add all pertinent references from *The Art of Dreaming* to the existing concordance so that the final manuscript would cover all nine Castaneda books.

And this is where things stand as I complete this prelude for *The Promise of Power*. I have coordinated the revisions and additions to my catalog and have supplemented them with some personal reflections on warriorship. The editing and final cross-checks of the manuscript are all in progress and within a matter of months the revised version of the book will be complete.

I am leaving this introductory piece for my friends to find because I am departing from this place soon, never to return. They will not read it until after I have gone, and so I don't know if this prelude or its attendant manuscript will ever be printed or not.

Either way, I wish to express my gratitude to my friends for their diligence and consideration in my behalf. This project is now truly theirs, and what ever happens with it from here forward is up to them. My work with *The Promise of Power* (and the catalog which inspired it) is complete. The details of this fool's tale have transformed themselves into a memory of power moving.

Now things lie in the hands of the warriors who rest.

T.W.W. - 1993

PART II

REFLECTIONS ON WARRIORSHIP

THE WARRIOR AND THE PROMISE

During the course of my life, I have developed an affinity for the term "warrior" as it is defined in the Toltec tradition. For me, this word embodies the spirit of those individuals committed to the intent, actualization and realization of power's promise.

THE PROMISE OF POWER

"One day each and every human being
will return to the abstract in a state of total awareness."

This simple statement is the promise of power, a covenant which binds us as luminous beings to the unknowable abstract. This promise is a quiet reflection of the unalterable essence of the universe. It is not an imagined or theoretical contract, it is a verifiable aspect of *seeing*. The promise of power is an incomprehensible absolute that always finds fulfillment in the timeless and unconditional world of power.

Warriors of the Toltec tradition live for the fulfillment of power's promise, and have demonstrated that it is possible to accomplish this miraculous journey of return to the abstract. But the Toltecs have also shown us that the attainment of total awareness is cloaked in contradiction; that the recovery of our silent knowledge is within our grasp, yet beyond our conscious control.

Through their example we *see* that if we are to reconnect ourselves with power, we must live a staggering contradiction. We must assume responsibility for an empowering way of life, while simultaneously abandoning ourselves to the indescribable forces that define the universe.

It is impossible for any human being to fully understand this contradiction. It is based on the incomprehensible designs of power or how they manifest themselves in our world of solid objects. All we can know from the Toltec perspective is that we must accept this contradiction and hope to one day wriggle in between its polarities in order to find ourselves.

For the fact remains that the equilibrium of our personal creative victory lies hidden in the contradictory aspects of our lives. Freedom waits for us in the balance of the true pair, and regardless of the conditional circumstances which characterize the life we know, each of us remains poised to fulfill the promise which power always keeps.

This unfathomable state of affairs is the preamble to the magical circumstance of the warrior. Through a process beyond reason or volition, some men and women are tricked (or invited) by the spirit into pursuing the promise which power holds for them. These individuals are not volunteers, they have not arbitrarily decided to return to power. They are soldiers of the third attention, recruited through the mysterious auspices of intent.

These men and women are true warriors in the Toltec sense of the word, unwitting individuals who wake one day to find themselves totally committed to the intent, actualization and realization of power's promise in the moment of now. These warriors have not consciously chosen warriorship, they have had warriorship thrust upon them through an incomprehensible set of circumstances unique to each of their lives.

The practitioners of don Juan's tradition define a warrior as anyone who is in direct contact with the spirit. This clear link with intent is predicated on the fact that warriors have shifted the base of their perception from a foundation of mechanical solidity and rationality to a perspective predicated on the unalterable abstract.

This simple shift of emphasis is the key in the lock to a magical door to power, a new perspective that establishes an awareness of an energetic absolute and promotes the active conservation of the unlimited resources hidden within ourselves. This fresh outlook on the universe is the beacon of nagualism, a minimal chance for mankind to recognize the awesome ramifications of power's promise.

There is no doubt that in the flurry of the modern world, most human beings turn a blind eye to the mysterious realm of intent and to the promise that power always keeps. The bias of the first attention focuses them so completely on a single familiar expression of the abstract that they remain powerless to recognize, much less realize, their inconceivable potential. In their ignorance, all they perceive are the boundaries of a world which they themselves have created, a world of solid objects and reactive circumstance.

Man's all-consuming self-absorption depletes his natural energy to the point that he pays no attention to the indications of power beyond the mirror of his own self-reflection. The promise of his most magical opportunities dance before him every day, but he is too involved with his own self-reflection to respond.

But not so the warriors of the Toltec tradition. We commit ourselves to the realization of power's promise by gathering our energetic resources and declaring war on that portion of ourselves which deprives us of our power. We conserve ourselves and summon the courage to emerge from our self-reflective tunnels into the expanse of the mysterious world of the unknown and the unknowable.

And in so doing, we expand our vision to include that which waits beyond our conditional assumptions and expectations. We train ourselves to release the things that held us prisoner in the world of solid objects, and we open ourselves instead to the magic of power's promise.

This manuscript has been prepared with an intentional bias towards the empowering struggle of the warrior, because warriorship is the first hinge in the multi-faceted door to power's promise.

The remaining pages of this section contain a series of personal reflections on warriorship. These thoughts are drawn from my own experience and from the experience of those who have shown me the tonal and the nagual.

AN AFFIRMATION FOR
THE WARRIOR WHO RESTS

Dreaming has directed me to focus this book on two specific things. One is *the promise of power* and the other is *warriorship.*

The promise of power is the promise always kept, a promise of return to the abstract in a state of total awareness.

Warriorship is the first hinge of power, the initial pivot point of the doorway to the unalterable. It is a universal path of empowerment that opens us to the miracle of our unlimited potential.

The road to knowledge links *warriorship* and *the promise of power* through the quest for what the Toltecs call *impeccability.*

Impeccability is defined as the most efficient utilization of one's energy. Therefore, an *impeccable* individual is simply someone who has learned to channel and conserve his or her energetic resources in the most strategic way possible.

Dreaming has led me to equate the Toltec concept of *impeccability* with the term *rest.* For the purposes of this book, the reader may assume that *impeccability* and *rest* are used synonymously; i.e., the warrior *impeccable* is the warrior who *rests.*

Some years ago, my teachers assisted me in discovering *An Affirmation for the Warrior Who Rests.* When repeated often, this simple verse serves as an important reminder of how *rest* (or the warriors' *impeccability*) relates to the realization of *power's promise.*

29

AN AFFIRMATION FOR
THE WARRIOR WHO RESTS

The promise of power
is the promise always kept.

The promise of power
is made to the warrior who rests.

All things come
to the warrior who rests.

******

I am the warrior who rests.
I am the warrior impeccable.

I am the warrior who rests.
I am the warrior empowered.

I am the warrior who rests.
I am the warrior proactive.

***

I am the warrior who rests.
I have learned to protect myself.

I am the warrior who rests.
I have learned to nurture myself.

I am the warrior who rests.
I have learned to love myself.

***

I am the warrior who rests.
I am the warrior who breathes deeply.

I am the warrior who rests.
I am the warrior who *sees* clearly.

I am the warrior who rests.
I am the warrior who chooses well.

***

***

I am the warrior who rests.
I have learned to conserve my own energy.

I am the warrior who rests.
I have learned to be in touch with my own strength.

I am the warrior who rests.
I have learned to direct my life with my intuition and my intent.

***

I am the warrior who rests.
I have balanced sobriety and abandon.

I am the warrior who rests.
I have shattered the mirror of my own self-reflection.

I am the warrior who rests.
I have transformed my own facade.

***

I am the warrior who rests.
I have prepared myself for dreaming.

I am the warrior who rests.
I have joyfully walked my personal path with heart.

I am the warrior who rests.
I have found peace in my creative victory,
a victory without glory or reward.

***

I am the warrior who rests.
I have learned the gentle art of letting go.

I am the warrior who rests.
I have learned there is no substitute for resting.

I am the warrior who rests.
I have learned that resting is the key to my unlimited potential.

******

*All things come
to the warrior who rests.*

*And all things become nothing
for the warrior who waits.*

*The promise of power
is the promise always kept.*

100 THOUGHTS ON WARRIORSHIP

The following are a series of reflections on how the warrior perceives the world. Some of these thoughts are a product of my own experience, while others were passed on to me by my teachers.

ACTIONS

The actions of warriors are clear and decisive because once we act, we must immediately prepare ourselves to act again.

ADAPTABILITY

As warriors we adapt ourselves easily to any situation because we have no other agenda than to flow with power.

ADDICTIONS

Warriors must be free of all addictions because we know there is no such thing as an impeccable addict.

ADVANTAGE

Awareness is the only advantage which warriors possess.

AGENDA

As warriors we learn to exchange the agendas of the individual self for the unfathomable agenda of power.

ANALYSIS

Warriors do not rely on analysis alone for answers because we are humble in the face of forces which we know we cannot analyze.

ASSUMPTION

As warriors we make no assumptions other than that the spirit will surely move in our lives everyday.

ATTENTION

Attention defines the limits of the everyday world. As warriors, we respect this fact, even as we go about the business of expanding ourselves beyond those very boundaries.

AWARENESS

The warriors' awareness is constantly expanding. This is the design of power, not the conscious choice of man.

BENEVOLENCE

The benevolence of warriors flows directly from power and from power alone, otherwise our benevolent gestures are merely acts of pointless self-indulgence.

CAPABILITY

The true capability of warriors is not measured by our illusion of control, it is measured instead by the strength of our link with intent.

CHALLENGE

The greatest challenge of warriors is our impeccable bid for power.

CHANGE

Warriors do not fear change because we understand that change is simply the result of the abstract moving around us.

CHOICE

The choice of warriors is simple, we will choose impeccability and freedom!

CLARITY

Warriors are not concerned with the clarity of the first attention. We are interested instead in a clarity beyond imagination, the silent and crystalline knowledge that flows to us directly from power itself.

COMFORT

The warriors' comfort is knowing that only impeccability matters.

CONNECTION

As warriors we must learn to execute a critical shift in our connection to the world. Ties to the first attention give way to a dynamic link with intent.

CONSCIENCE

The conscience of warriors is clear because we no longer have any pity for ourselves.

CONTROL

As warriors we never allow our impeccability to foster feelings of "being in control." Even though we may stalk ourselves successfully to some degree, we always remember that power is stalking us as well, in ways we can never imagine or predict.

COURAGE

Our courage as warriors must focus on our struggle to perceive things differently. We are faced with the frightening task of exchanging the cozy world of solid objects for the terrifying vastness of an incalculable abstract mystery.

COURTESY

Our courtesy as warriors flows from our respect for the spirit and the way it is reflected in the faces of all men.

DEEDS

The deeds of the warrior are not the well-thought acts of the average man, they are reflections of the shine of the spirit.

DEFENSE

Warriors require no defense because in the end there is nothing to defend about a luminous being.

DETACHMENT

As warriors we must learn to cultivate a detachment which transforms us from reactive objects in a world of circumstance to proactive beings in a world of power.

DISCIPLINE

The discipline of warriors is fluid and free, it is as unpredictable as the agenda of power itself. We refuse to believe that ego-driven rigidity and contrived routines could ever replace impeccability.

EMPHASIS

As warriors our critical emphasis is all we have, so we struggle to breathe deeply, see clearly and choose well.

ENERGY

Energy is every warriors' responsibility, we must claim it and conserve it for ourselves.

EXPECTATION

What expectations can warriors have, power does not reveal its designs in advance.

EXPLANATION

The warriors' explanation is like dust in the wind, we know it cannot be articulated for the edification of others. We can only choke on the inadequacy of our words and intuit the essence of something we know is beyond explanation.

FEROCITY

The ferocity of warriors is never evident to those around us because our fierceness is focused solely on the struggle to curtail our own self-importance.

FIRST ATTENTION

Warriors understand that the despots of the first attention are like frightened children left to run the kingdom, they know no better than to indulge in their limited view of the world. Warriors learn to parent these frightened children and gently remove them from the throne of awareness.

FLUIDITY

As warriors we remain fluid in the world of solid objects because we do not attach ourselves to mechanical things and circumstances. Instead of clinging to everything, we empower ourselves to flow with intent through the magical situation of our lives.

FOCUS

The focus of warriors remains fixed on the mystery that lies beyond our eyes.

FORBEARANCE

As warriors our forbearance flows from our humility in the face of power, our clear perception that we must continually stalk ourselves.

FORGIVENESS

The forgiveness of warriors is a by-product of our impeccable vision. We are aware of the true insignificance of the acts of men.

FREEDOM

Freedom is the Eagle's gift, the ultimate realization of our creative victory.

GOAL

Warriors have only one goal, to realize the promise of power!

GRATITUDE

The warriors' gratitude is not a personal response to the things that appear to be our blessings. Warriors gives thanks, but only for the opportunity to make an impeccable bid for power.

GRIP

The unwavering grip of warriors is no more than our intuitive connection with intent, it allows us to hold fast in the act of letting go.

HISTORY

The history of the warrior is a chronicle of power moving, beyond that there is nothing more to tell.

HUMILITY

As warriors our humility is a natural state of being which reflects the correctness of our relationship with the abstract.

HUMOR

It is our sense of humor that sustains our lives of warriors. If we cannot laugh at ourselves we are doomed to wallow in the quagmire of our own self-reflection.

IMPECCABILITY

As warriors, our impeccability is everything, for without it there can be no journey of return.

INSPIRATION

Inspiration is the voice of the nagual whispering in the warriors' ear. Through it the designs of power are revealed.

INTENT

As warriors we spend a lifetime clearing our link with intent and preparing to make our journey of return to the abstract.

INTERVENTION

Warriors do not intervene unless power beckons us to do so. We watch for our omens and respond to the indications of the spirit. When we act, it is not intervention as the average man defines it. As warriors, we do not presume to know what is best, we remain humble in the incomprehensible face of power.

INVENTORY

As human beings, we have no choice but to take our inventory; as warriors, we have no choice but to cast that inventory aside.

IRREVERENCE

The warriors' irreverence springs from our ability to see the world clearly. We will not worship the things which drain us of our energy.

JOURNEY

Our journey as warriors is a definitive journey with power, the intent, actualization and realization of the four hinges of power.

JOY

Joy is the warriors' ultimate accomplishment. It is an expression of our unconditional ability to reconnect ourselves with the overwhelming beauty of a mysterious universe.

KINDNESS

The warriors' acts of kindness are free from emotion and analysis. They are simply our way of showing respect for the incomprehensible designs of the abstract.

KNOWLEDGE

The warriors' knowledge comes silently, without conscious manipulation. It washes over us like a wave, and then it is gone.

LIFE

The life of warriors unfolds one day at a time in accordance with the designs of power.

LIGHTNESS

Our lightness as warriors is a direct result of our fluid nature, because we are unencumbered by the weight of self-reflection.

LOVE

For warriors, love is a bridge between contradictions, it is never an excuse for self indulgent behavior.

MAGIC

The magic of the warrior is the shine of a spotless mirror. We have banished all doubts from our minds and opened ourselves to reflect the brilliance of power itself.

MASTERY

As warriors we do not concern ourselves with thoughts of mastery and achievement. These are only petty indulgences that detract from an impeccable life.

MEMORY

The warriors' memory is the sorcerers' recollection, the reliving of actual events through the manipulation of the assemblage point.

MIRACLES

The warriors who rest are living miracles. We have expanded our attention beyond its own limits!

OBJECTIVITY

Our warriors' objectivity is grounded in our mysterious journey with power. We objectify all things because we have seen that everything is the same.

OBSESSION

Warriors have no obsessions. We have learned the gentle art of letting go and allow that which does not matter to pass us by.

OMEN

Power manifests itself at every turn, revealing itself to all men with equal consistency. But only warriors are attuned to the edifices of intent.

OPENNESS

Openness is the warriors' state of mind because it is the first prerequisite for the expansion of our awareness.

PATIENCE

Patience is more than a virtue for warriors, it is the key to the way we face the oncoming time.

PERCEPTION

Above all else, warriors are perceivers.

PETTY TYRANT

As warriors we give thanks for our petty tyrants, the guides who show us where to find peace in the midst of chaos.

POSSIBILITIES

Warriors redefine the scope of human possibilities. We know without a doubt that we are limitless.

RINGS OF POWER

There are two rings of power co-existing in eternity. As warriors we rediscover ourselves by bridging the gap between them.

PREDICTABILITY

The predictability of the warrior is at once absolute and non existent.

PRESENTATION

The warriors' presentation is flawless, not by virtue of our reason, but because we flow impeccably with power.

PRIDE

Warriors are fluid and free. We have left our false pride behind with the rest of the things that weigh us down.

PROACTIVE

As warriors we are in tune with the spirit, we have risen above the world of reactive circumstance to become proactive beings in a world of power.

REALITY

As warriors we know that reality is simply an interpretation that we make.

REALIZATION

As warriors our moment of realization is never tearful or emotional. It is a quiet affair which reconnects us with the abstract.

REASONABLE

As warriors we are reasonable but we do not live our lives chained to reason. We are free because we understand the strengths and limitations of the rational mind.

REGRET

Warriors do not regret anything because we know the only way to empower our decisions is to abandon all regrets.

RESOLVE

As warriors, we have only one resolve, we will make an impeccable bid for power.

RESPECT

Warriors respect all things because we have "seen" that the mystery of the universe permeates all things.

SELF RESTRAINT

Self restraint is the voice of sobriety ringing in our ears and urging us as warriors to make each day more impeccable than the last.

SLOPPINESS

There is no room for sloppiness in the tight life of an impeccable warrior.

SOBRIETY

Our warriors' sobriety sustains us on the avenue of power because it is the essence of our quiet internal strength.

SPIRIT

As warriors we listen for the knock of the spirit, and when it calls we do our best to answer impeccably.

STORY

The story of the warrior is not a tale of people, places and events. The story of the warrior is an abstract tale of power.

STRATEGY

The strategy of warriors is simple, we must learn to live our lives impeccably!

STRENGTH

Our strength as warriors flows directly from our impeccable link with intent, not from the first attention circumstances that appear to prop us up.

STRUGGLE

The struggle of the warrior is not a battle with personalities and physical circumstance. It is a war with the part of the individual self that deprives us of our power.

TALENT

Whatever talent we possess as warriors is simply a guide that power bestows upon us. It is not an excuse to indulge in self-importance.

TIMING

Our timing as warriors is impeccable because we flow with the indications of the spirit.

TRICKERY

At some point warriors realize that we have been caught by the trickery of the spirit. We are grateful for this sublime entrapment and marvel at our magical good fortune.

TRUTH

The warriors' truth is universal and constant. We "see" it everywhere and in everything.

UNDERSTANDING

The warriors' understanding is a personal trophy, hard won on a very private battleground.

UNEXPECTED

As warriors, we are always prepared for the unexpected, because we know the designs of the spirit are beyond anything we could ever anticipate.

VICTORY

The warriors' victory is not recognized in the world of solid objects because it brings with it no glory or reward.

VIGILANCE

Our vigilance as warriors is based on our knowledge that we are at once "predator" and "prey." As we stalk ourselves and the challenges of our world, we must always remember that there are forces which can overwhelm us in the blink of an eye if we are not forever on our guard.

VISION

Our vision as warriors becomes clear only when we train ourselves not to look.

WARRIORS' TONAL

The warriors' tonal is fluid and free, it welcomes the existence of the nagual.

WARRIORSHIP

It is not possible for us to choose warriorship, we wake one day to find that power has lead us to it.

WEALTH

Our wealth as warriors is not measured by our conditional holdings, but by the unconditional energy that we have gathered for ourselves.

WONDER

The warriors' life is filled with wonder. We stand in awe in the face of our own staggering possibilities.

WORK

Warriors know there is no important work, there is only an endless series of opportunities for the practice of our impeccability.

******

THE RIDDLE OF THE HEART

The art of stalking is the riddle of the heart; the puzzlement sorcerers feel upon becoming aware of two things: first that the world appears to us to be unalterably objective and factual, because of peculiarities of our awareness and perception; second, that if different peculiarities of perception come into play, the very things about the world that seem so unalterably objective and factual change.

The Power of Silence - Page xv

Power is and power moves and the mystery of power is beyond all comprehension. On the path of knowledge this is all that warriors know for sure. Yet full in the face of this incomprehensible mystery, we struggle against all odds to reestablish our connection with power; to flow with it and lay bare its secrets. ***And as we struggle we ponder the riddle of the heart, the mystery of our unalterable description of the world and the way that description somehow changes.***

There is no question that warriors have a unique view of day-to-day "reality." We perceive it as an alterable perceptual condition based on an unalterable energetic absolute. Warriors *see* that the essence of the universe produces a condition of alignment which is commonly accepted as an unshakable reality, (even though it is merely the result of social convention and a habitual position of the assemblage point).

Even though the first attention may perceive this familiar reality as something "unalterable," warriors know that this is certainly not the case. Whatever unalterable reality is, it must be defined by what is truly unalterable in the universe, and not by what the first attention foolishly believes its unalterable reality to be.

Warriors begin to understand the true nature of what is real by corroborating what we intuit through direct experience. We eventually come to glimpse the unalterable and *see* that power is and that power moves. We also *see* that man is a direct extension of power and that he has the capacity to alter his perception through the movement of the assemblage point.

The warriors' concept of unalterable reality extends far beyond the limits of the first attention. It is based on *seeing* and includes all the alterable possibilities of perception which luminous beings are capable of assembling. We know that we are an awareness and that something out there is affecting our senses. For warriors, the existence and the movement of these incomprehensible forces is the essence of what is "unalterably real."

Everything else in the realm of man's perceptual experience must be characterized as "alterably real." The total world which most human beings experience is no more than a variable perceptual condition which is based upon a specific position of the assemblage point. Although this alterable reality seems real to the greatest degree imaginable, it actually represents only a minute reflection of the unalterable reality which defines the fundamental basis of the energetic universe.

This is the essence of how the warriors' perspective on reality diverges from the commonly accepted view. For the average man, one familiar alterable reality is all there is to the universe. The assemblage points of nearly the entire race of men are fixated on a single habitual position which produces the commonly accepted world of solid objects. Mankind's total commitment to that single position of assemblage is so total and unshakable that it does not allow for the existence of anything else beyond it.

Warriors, on the other hand, know that the unshakable reality of the average man is only one of many alterable realities which warrior-sorcerers are capable of assembling. We clearly understand that the total world before us at any given moment is no more than a product of the position of the assemblage point, and however real that world may seem, it cannot be equated with the unalterable reality which defines the essence of the energetic universe.

As warriors we keep this contradictory sense of "reality" in perspective by remembering that the objective and factual world of men is not what it appears to be. We understand this alterable reality for what it is, a complex description of the world that has been taught to each and every human being from the moment of birth.

Warriors know that this total yet alterable description of the world is undeniably useful for what it is, since it makes possible our passage on this earth. The problem begins when we forget that this familiar description of the world is only a superficial sampling of the unlimited possibilities open to all luminous beings.

Warriors never worship any single alterable reality because we know that to trap our totality within any world of our own assembly is a very grave mistake. Rather than imprison ourselves within apparently solid confines, we struggle to tap the unalterable forces of the universe by gathering our own personal power.

This empowerment enables us to establish "perception" and "reality" as alterable, dynamic conditions which change with the position of the assemblage point. As a consequence of our impeccability, we clear our link with the unalterable and empower ourselves to move between alterable realities in a way the average man can not possibly conceive.

As warriors we master the riddle of the heart by learning to stalk ourselves. First and foremost we know we are perceivers, and as such we are clear about the nature of our perceptions. We know that we are not really objects in a world of conditional solidity, even though our first attention senses tell us so. Our description of the world makes our time on earth convenient, but it does not define the scope of the mysterious universe. It is our challenge as warriors to keep the nature of our description in perspective.

Instead of being confined by the limitations of any single alterable reality, we chose to remain focused on the incomprehensible totality of ourselves and how it reflects the essence of the unalterable. We then actualize that focus by struggling to realize an awareness of our totality through the conservation of our hidden energetic resources. And as we reclaim that precious energy, we empower ourselves to alter the most inviolable aspects of our self-reflective description of the world.

THE RIDDLE OF THE SPIRIT

The mastery of intent is the riddle of the spirit, or the paradox of the abstract - sorcerers' thoughts and actions projected beyond our human condition.

The Power of Silence - Page xv

Power is and power moves and the mystery of power is beyond all comprehension. On the path of knowledge this is all that warriors know for sure. Yet full in the face of this incomprehensible mystery, we struggle against all odds to reestablish our connection with power; to flow with it and lay bare its secrets. **And as we struggle we ponder the riddle of the spirit, the mystery which allows us to extend ourselves beyond our own limits by transforming the commands of the Eagle into our own commands.**

Our aim as warriors is to accomplish a return to the abstract by clearing our living link with intent. The revival of this unalterable connection with power is an elusive quest because it exists beyond all limits of reason and conscious understanding.

And yet as warriors, we stalk the promise of power with fierce and unbending purpose, waging a war with our individual sense of self for the energetic resources on which the realization of freedom depend. We actualize our bid for power by stalking ourselves through a lifelong battle for impeccability, sobriety, and humility. We struggle without expectation or worry, and patiently wait for will to be magically transformed into intent.

The riddle of the spirit is the riddle of how the warriors' command becomes the Eagle's command; the riddle of how the impersonal force of alignment transforms itself into a personalized force at the service of the warrior. As we explore this mystery, we accept completely that it can never be explained, simply because we know there is no way to describe intent. The most we can hope for is to come to know intent directly by experiencing it with our energetic being.

And so as warriors we wait and ponder the riddle of the

spirit, and in the process we learn to rest and listen for the whispers of the nagual. The shadow of the bird of freedom has glanced across our shoulder and we revel in our great good fortune, the opportunity to bid for power's promise.

THE RIDDLE OF THE DREAMER
AND THE DREAMED

"What is the warrior's feat don Juan?"
"I told you that Genaro came to show you
something, the mystery of the luminous beings as
dreamers. You wanted to know about the double.
It begins in dreams. But then you asked, 'What is
the double?' and I said the double is the self. The
self dreams the double. That should be simple,
except that there is nothing simple about us.
Perhaps the ordinary dreams of the self are simple,
but that doesn't mean that the self is simple. Once
it has learned to dream the double, the self arrives
at this weird crossroad and a moment comes when
one realizes that it is the double that dreams the
self."

Tales of Power - Page 76, 77

Power is and power moves and the mystery of power is beyond all comprehension. On the path of knowledge this is all that warriors know for sure. Yet full in the face of this incomprehensible mystery, we struggle against all odds to reestablish our connection with power; to flow with it and lay bare its secrets. **And as we struggle we ponder the riddle of the dreamer and the dreamed, the mystery of the dreaming body and the third point of perception.**

As warriors, we struggle to conserve our personal power through a lifetime of impeccable acts. And as we rest, we empower ourselves to make possible the movement of the assemblage point. This realization of this incomprehensible energetic activity eventually leads us to the reality of the dreaming body.

Through the practice of dreaming, warriors solve the riddle of the dreamer and the dreamed by reaching out for the third point, an awareness of the "here and here." The third point is the warriors' freedom of perception, an operational awareness of the functioning of the true pair.

This unique position of the assemblage point somersaults warriors into the miraculous, allowing us to be in the place of reason and the place of silent knowledge at the same time. From this magical, tri-dimensional perspective, we experience an incomprehensible facet of our totality; the silent knowledge that the self dreams the double while the double dreams the self.

The riddle of the third point is the riddle of the indescribable tonal and the indescribable nagual. By experiencing this mystery ourselves, we *see* that both members of the true pair reflect an unfathomable outside order and that both are completely beyond any explanation or conscious understanding.

As warriors we must accept that the mystery of the world is all-inclusive, that our unalterable reality extends far beyond the world of solid objects and the realm of rational understanding. We know that the essence of our waking bodies is no less mysterious or inexplicable than the essence of our dreaming bodies, and that both the dreamer and the dreamed coexist within an energetic context far beyond the familiar description of the world.

THE WARRIORS' PATH TO KNOWLEDGE AND POWER

THE WARRIORS' JOURNEY WITH POWER

A friend of mine has a minivan and one of the most charming small dogs I have ever encountered. The dog is irresistibly cute and shaggy and possesses an amazing capacity to melt your heart from the moment you first meet him. He is just beyond puppy hood, and epitomizes all the energy and enthusiasm that endears us to dogs so easily. The dog's name is Steve, and whenever he greets anyone he fairly bursts with affection and excitement, wiggling his little rear end and whimpering with pure joy as he offers his puppy kisses and unconditional puppy love.

This little black dog is generally well behaved and occasionally takes a ride with his master into the small town near their home. One day I rode with them on just such an excursion. Steve was very excited about the ride in the van and did not hesitate an instant as he hopped onto the passenger seat with me.

As we pulled out of the driveway though, the dog became increasingly agitated. He ran back and forth inside the van, pressing his nose to all the windows and squealing with anticipation. We hadn't traveled half a block when he spotted an Irish setter out for a walk with it's owner. The sight of this strange dog was enough to drive Steve nearly hysterical. He quivered up against the window of the van and barked with all his might.

We pulled past the setter as Steve continued his

obsessive focus on the larger dog, running to the back window and howling until we finally turned a corner and the setter dropped out of sight. Then the little fellow returned at full speed to a position on my lap, totally agitated and out of breath.

Steve continued to whimper uncontrollably, scanning the landscape for any other distractions. Not a minute had gone by before he saw two young boys on skateboards and the entire frenzied exercise began all over again. By the time we arrived in town the poor dog was exhausted from the ten or twelve encounters we'd had with pets, pedestrians, and bicyclists on the way.

As soon as we parked at the market, little Stevie finally calmed down. He behaved normally as we walked between stores doing our errands, happily greeting every man, woman and child on the sidewalk with an enthusiastic wiggle of his fluffy tail. When we finished our shopping, we returned to the car and prepared for the drive home. As we left the market parking lot I braced myself for a hysterical repeat performance.

My friend retraced the route towards home, but to my amazement, Steve remained completely calm and collected. Instead of racing frantically around the car barking his head off, he just sat alert on my lap, quietly watching all the shoppers and the kids on bikes. For some reason he was now content to just let the world go by and simply twitch his floppy ears as we passed the very distractions that had driven him into a frenzy only half an hour before. To my astonishment, little Stevie remained at peace the whole way home, never uttering a sound as he calmly observed everything out the passenger side window.

Later I commented to my friend about his dog's behavior. He said that our ride had been typical and that Steve just seemed to have a much harder time of things when he wasn't sure where he was going. Any trip away from his house spurred the dog into a manic state, while the return journey was always the same calm affair. The little fellow knew when he was going home and that knowledge seemed to somehow comfort him.

Power is and power moves and the mystery of power is beyond all comprehension. On the path of knowledge this is all that warriors know for sure. Yet full in the face of this incomprehensible mystery, we struggle against all odds to reestablish our connection with power; to flow with it and lay bare its secrets. **And as we struggle we accept that we are captives of power; that power will take us on a journey with or without the cooperation of our reason, emotions and conscious minds.**

On our journey with power, the only thing that matters is impeccability, the ability to conserve ourselves and flow with power within the context of our personal life circumstance. And as we travel the road to knowledge, the Eagle commands that we take our inventory, that we witness the details of the world we have assembled. Human beings have no choice with regard to this command, so the warriors' bid for impeccability must begin with the disposition of that inventory once it has been taken. The story of the little dog's journey to town captures the essence of the warriors' options in this all-important matter.

On the way to town my friend's dog was, to use don Juan's words, a complete nincompoop! He agitated himself to the point of exhaustion with the details of a moving landscape that inevitably passed him by. He focused on those fleeting specifics so completely that he remained totally unconcerned with the essence of his journey and the spirit of the force that was carrying him along. Instead of remaining calmly aware of the essence of his trip, the little dog's awareness was consumed with an obsessive attachment to the details surrounding the mechanical conditions of his travels.

But on his way home the dog remained impeccable! He conserved his energy and chose to quietly observe the passing landscape with an appropriate sobriety and detachment. On his journey of return, the pup's focus remained more on the essence of his travels than on the details of the passing scenery.

Warriors share a great deal with the travels of my friend's dog. Like little Stevie, we journey with forces we do not understand on an avenue of power which only reveals itself to us from minute to minute. And on that road, we must pass the moving landscape of our first attention inventory, an inventory which the Eagle commands each of us to take. This inventory beckons to us and demands our energy, but as little Stevie so aptly illustrated, warriors have an option when responding to those demands.

Will we press our figurative noses to the windows of our lives and exhaust ourselves with our first attention attachments, or will we choose to observe the passing scenery with the sobriety of the warrior? Will we cling in desperation to the items of our inventory, or empower ourselves by releasing that inventory the instant it has been taken? Will we drive ourselves to distraction because we refuse to trust in the incomprehensible designs of the spirit, or will we humbly accept the unexpected developments that present themselves on our unfathomable journey with power?

The warriors' choice is simple. We will always choose the impeccable path to freedom.

THE WARRIORS' RING OF POWER

He paused. The silence around us was frightening. The wind hissed softly and then I heard the distant barking of a lone dog.

"Listen to that barking," don Juan went on. "That is the way my beloved earth is helping me now to bring this last point to you. That barking is the saddest thing one can hear."

We were quiet for a moment. The barking of that lone dog was so sad and the stillness around us so intense that I experienced a numbing anguish. It made me think of my own life, my sadness, my not knowing where to go, what to do.

"That dog's barking is the nocturnal voice of a man," don Juan said. "It comes from a house in that valley towards the south. A man is shouting through his dog, since they are companion slaves for life, his sadness, his boredom. He's begging his death to come and release him from the dull and dreary chains of his life."

Don Juan's words had caught a most disturbing line in me. I felt he was speaking directly to me.

"That barking, and the loneliness it creates, speaks of the feelings of men," he went on. "Men for whom an entire life was like one Sunday afternoon, an afternoon which was not altogether miserable, but rather hot and dull and uncomfortable. They sweated and fussed a great deal. They didn't know where to go, or what to do. That afternoon left them only with the memory of petty annoyances and tedium, and then suddenly it was over; it was already night."

Tales of Power - Page 293

Power is and power moves and the mystery of power is beyond all comprehension. On the path of knowledge this is all that warriors *know for sure. Yet full in the face of this incomprehensible mystery, we struggle against all odds to reestablish our connection with power; to flow with it and lay bare its secrets. **And as we struggle we accept the fact that power is within us and around us and forever at our fingertips in an unimaginable way.***

From the moment of birth, awareness begins to focus in on itself in an unimaginable way. And as it solidifies, it acts to define its own limits by crystallizing into a magical ring which the Toltecs call the first ring of power. Power lies within this ring and power lies beyond it, and even though the boundaries of our sanity and our solid world are defined by its familiar curves, a part of us always longs for an awareness of the unimaginable that hovers beyond those limits.

The life of the average man is defined by the confines of the first attention, the attention of the first ring of power. The agendas and conditions of this attention are the agendas and conditions of the known. They define the limits of what our eyes can see and direct us to expend our energy on the details of the total world we have assembled. Within the confines of the world of the first ring of power, we remain safe and sane, unchallenged and immortal.

But the security of a warm and cozy prison is simply not enough to sustain the warriors for total freedom. We will not be satisfied with the illusion of our immortality or even the socially accepted description of our sanity. In a daring bid for power, we challenge ourselves to step beyond the confines of the very world we have assembled, because the narrow limits of the first ring of power are simply not enough to hold us.

As warriors we intuit and experience the world from a different point of view. We know firsthand that there is a second ring of power, a second attention that beckons to us from beyond the everyday description of the world. We sense its presence hovering about and we are not content to merely pine for it from the confines of a prison of our own making.

As warriors, we act to realize the second ring of power in our lives by committing ourselves to warriorship and the struggle for impeccability. We assume the responsibility to expand and empower ourselves on our own behalf, to claim a magical second attention as our warrior's ring of power.

We know without thinking that power's promise waits for us, and so we struggle to extend ourselves to reach it. In order to accomplish this indescribable feat, it is necessary for us to coax our first attention beyond its own narrow limits, so that it might harmonize itself with the attention of the nagual.

We find the courage to pursue this inconceivable course because as warriors we recognize that it is not necessary to hold ourselves prisoner in a boring and sterile realm of our own creation. We dare instead to direct ourselves into the arms of an unalterable mystery, for when all is said and done, there is nothing more terrifying than the prospect that the poignant barking of a distant dog and the melancholy of a tedious Sunday afternoon might one day engulf us unaware.

THE WARRIORS' TRANSFORMATION

The collected writings of Carlos Castaneda are an epic tale of power. They chronicle the struggles of a warrior for a period spanning more than thirty years. But these books represent more than just a collection of weird tales about sorcery in the desert; they are a single interconnected tale of one warrior's journey with power; a story of transformation from student, to apprentice, to warrior, to sorcerer, to seer.

Anyone who cares to read this compelling warriors' dialogue can easily do so, the beautifully written narrative is readily available. But the crux of the warriors' transformation cannot be accessed by just picking up some books. It is an intensely personal process, directly linked to the our individual impeccability and intent.

And even though Carlos' tale of transformation cannot be superficially imitated, it still fascinates us and holds us spellbound; if for no other reason than it touches a glimmer of the truth within us. For on some long forgotten level, the warrior within us knows that the potential of every human being is unlimited, and that we each possess the awesome capacity to reach beyond ourselves in a magical act of impeccable transformation.

Power is and power moves and the mystery of power is beyond all comprehension. On the path of knowledge this is all that warriors know for sure. Yet full in the face of this incomprehensible mystery, we struggle against all odds to reestablish our connection with power; to flow with it and lay bare its secrets. **And as we struggle we dare to transform ourselves by bridging the contradictions of our expanding awareness.**

As warriors on the road to power, we know we must someday build an unimaginable bridge, a bridge which will connect the first and second rings of power and return us to the unalterable limitlessness of the abstract. The blueprint for our magical bridge is elusive and invisible, we cannot read or study it with the resources of our minds. Instead we must trust that we will access it directly through a process beyond our conscious control. For the warriors' blueprint of power lies hidden in the immensity of the unknowable, far beyond the conditional capacities of reason, language and deliberate action.

Yet in spite of its incomprehensible qualities, we wait for the minimal chance that this magical blueprint may materialize within our lifetimes. And while we wait, we practice the art of resting. Our impeccable demeanor empowers and nurtures us. Our cleansing breaths clear our vision and enable us to choose well. The conservation of our precious energy empowers us to direct our lives with our intuition and our intent. Our warriors' facade is rearranged as we shatter the mirror of our own self-reflection.

And as we rest, our warriors' transformation begins. We reorder ourselves and find peace in a creative victory without reward. We free ourselves by abandoning the agendas of the first attention for the unfathomable agenda of power. As warriors transformed we joyfully walk our personal path with heart, and as we travel, the petty things we once clung to are now released in an impeccable act of letting go.

Our magical transformation changes us from reactive objects in a world of circumstance to proactive beings in a world of power. Instead of being drained by the demands of the first attention, we empower ourselves through an ever-strengthening link with intent. Instead of remaining victims, we reconnect with our own strength and hidden resources. Instead of being pinned down within the boundaries of the tonal, we dare to dream and break the barrier of our own perception.

And if one day we wake to find that the magical blueprint of power has found its way to us, then we will become magical warrior architects poised to complete an impossible bridge across forever. The bridge we build with the power at our service will vault our attention beyond its limits into the arms of an incomprehensible victory where all contradictions are reconciled. All things will now have come to us but in our humility and our detachment, they will seem as nothing.

And then, at the appointed time, we will stand ready, ready to bravely cross the magical bridge of our own construction. At that moment we will stand poised on the very brink of eternity, ready to burn with an inner flame that will bring our time on earth to an end. In an instant we will be gone, and like true warriors we will leave behind hardly a trace. Only the trees will speak of us and the impeccability of our warriors' spirit.

THE PROMISE ALWAYS KEPT

"If, on the other hand, your impeccability and personal power are such that you are capable of fulfilling your tasks, you will then achieve the promise of power. And what's that promise? you may ask. It is a promise that power makes to men as luminous beings. Each warrior has a different fate, so there is no way of telling what the promise will be for either of you."

Tales of Power - Page 287

Power is and power moves and the mystery of power is beyond all comprehension. On the path of knowledge this is all that warriors know for sure. Yet full in the face of this incomprehensible mystery, we struggle against all odds to reestablish our connection with power; to flow with it and lay bare its secrets. **And as we struggle we come to realize one last thing, the promise of power is the promise always kept.**

All men and women in the world, are the same in one respect; each of us is a luminous being with unlimited potential, existing in a universe of unimaginable mystery. The implications of this unalterable reality are staggering, but for the most part, they pass by unrecognized. Yet for warriors, these implications are paramount; we spend a lifetime struggling to claim them as knowledge.

But whether we are warriors or not, our unalterable reality remains the same, each of us is a luminous being, a bubble of perception intimately connected to an endless sea of power. And there can be no doubt that our link to the abstract brings with it a magical promise.

This is the promise of power itself, a universal promise articulated by the four hinges of power. It is a promise always kept; a promise whose individual realization depends upon intent, impeccability and the intricacies of power's unfathomable design; a promise that carries us from warriorship and sorcery to the joyous equilibrium of our ultimate creative victory.

***

The promise of power is the promise always kept.
The shadow of the bird of freedom
glides over an unsuspecting shoulder,
And the warrior bids for power.

The promise of power is made to the warrior who rests.
All things come to the warrior who rests,
And all things become nothing for the warrior who waits.
The promise of power is the promise always kept.

***

PART III

A CATALOG OF ONE THOUSAND SECRETS

A FOREWORD TO THE CATALOG

A FOOL'S TASK AND A FOOL'S INTENT

I cannot deny the improbable premise of this catalog. It was begun as a personal task of learning many years ago by a fool with no other qualifications than a sincere desire to learn. And even though he had no one to validate his efforts, that fool prepared his catalog faithfully with only the humblest of intentions.

I of course am that fool, and since I began my task I have watched it evolve in power's hands in a most unexpected way. This catalog was originally prepared for very private reasons, with no thought whatsoever that it might one day be published and read by others.

Now, to my complete surprise, I find that power had something else in store. I can only believe that this is as it should be, because the designs of power are beyond the comprehension of any man. I stand and marvel at the way my work has been transformed, but despite that transformation, I know in the private recesses of my heart that a fool's task and a fool's intent remain the same.

THE WARRIORS' DIALOGUE

After years of studying Carlos Castaneda's work, I became intrigued with the idea of consolidating references to the written record of nagualism into a more accessible reference guide. That idea eventually evolved into this *Catalog of One Thousand Secrets,* a two-part index of references designed to serve as an informational and intuitive concordance to the warriors' dialogue presented within these compelling books.

The Works of Carlos Castaneda:

The Teachings of Don Juan
A Separate Reality
Journey To Ixtlan
Tales of Power
The Second Ring of Power
The Eagle's Gift
The Fire From Within
The Power of Silence
The Art of Dreaming

I remind the reader in the strongest possible terms that the sole purpose of this manuscript is to guide the reader back to these nine books, a body of work which is the source of the purest available record of the Toltec warriors' dialogue (see page 71 for information regarding the specific Castaneda editions on which this book's concordance is based.)

If you are just discovering the Castaneda material, *The Promise of Power* will help you coordinate your exploration of these magical texts. If you are already familiar with Carlos' books and the teachings of don Juan, then the use of this concordance will be self-evident.

Either way, it is important that you utilize this book in the way that it was intended; as an informational and intuitive directory to the previously written record of Toltec knowledge. Please don't be tempted to use this book as some kind of condensed replacement for the books on which it is based. As the fool who prepared *The Promise of Power*, I know this was never my intent. If you truly seek to expand yourself, then search for your insights where you have the best chance to find them, in the empowered dialogue of the warriors for total freedom.

AN ORGANIZATIONAL NOTE

At the beginning of this book I explained how this catalog evolved as two distinct subsets of entries. The first and largest of these subsets is a collection of informational references for the right side awareness. For reasons outlined in *The Warrior and the Promise*, I have presented these analytical entries with an emphasis on warriorship and the warriors' life perspective.

The second smaller subset in this catalog is a collection of intuitive references for the left side awareness. I have identified these entries as individual <u>T</u>ales <u>O</u>f <u>P</u>ower (TOP) because through their retelling, they illustrate and convey the abstract order of knowledge. By definition, these entries are not analytical at all, they focus on something unspoken and unexplainable.

At the end of the intuitive reference subset, the reader will also find a brief organizational outline. This outline represents an overview of many of the significant references contained within *A Catalog of One Thousand Secrets*. Please remember that the organizational scheme of this outline is based on my own perspective of the warriors' dialogue, and as such, it should not interfere with the reader's personal interpretation of the teachings of don Juan.

A CATALOG
OF ONE THOUSAND SECRETS

Editor's Note: As the author has outlined in the introduction to this catalog, there are two groups of references presented here. Part I is a group of *Informational References* while Part II is a group of *Intuitive References* which the author refers to as Tales Of Power (TOP). The informational portion of this catalog begins here, and continues in alphabetical sequence through the letter "Z." Following these informational references, the reader will find the much smaller alphabetical listing of intuitive references.

With the author's permission, and in hopes of providing the reader with the most comprehensive reference guide possible, we have cross-indexed the intuitive Tales of Power entries and included them as part of this informational subset. Consequently, Part I of this catalog can be used to search for any given reference, either intuitive or informational. When the reader encounters an entry with a (TOP) designation within the informational portion of this catalog, it simply means that a complete reference to that term will be found in the intuitive listing which follows. In addition, we have used an asterisk to mark each informational reference which has a concurrent listing in the intuitive subset.

It is important for the reader to know that this catalog is keyed to very specific editions of the Carlos Castaneda books. References from the first eight books (*The Teachings Of Don Juan, A Separate Reality, Journey To Ixtlan, Tales Of Power, The Second Ring Of Power, The Eagle's Gift, The Fire From Within and The Power of Silence*) are all drawn from the Washington Square Press paperbacks (either the small pocket size mass market editions or the larger trade paperback editions). References to *The Art Of Dreaming* are keyed to the Harper Collins publications (either the hard cover or trade paperback editions).

The numerical designations that accompany each reference denote the page number and position on the page where the reference will be found. Since many of the references begin and end in the midst of other unrelated material, the author has used a system to aid the reader in finding the beginning and end of each reference. He has divided each page into nine imaginary segments. and used a decimal value after each page number to indicate where the reader should look on any given page for the reference sited.

For example, the very first reference in the catalog will be found in

The Teachings Of Don Juan. It begins on page 86 in the bottom ninth of the page with the words "No, that is not true." The reference continues from that point to the top of page 87 where it ends in the first ninth of the page with the words "have really abandoned himself to it." The illustration below shows exactly how the author has designed this locating system to work.

The entry begins here in the ninth of nine imaginary segments on page 86.

The entry ends here in the first of nine imaginary segments of page 87.

SUBSET I
INFORMATIONAL REFERENCES

A

ABANDON-[ABANDON]: (Warriors know they must live their lives with impeccable abandon; the warriors' ability to create a gesture for the spirit; the warriors' ability to let go of first attention agendas and concerns.)
SELECTED REFERENCES: **The Teachings of Don Juan - Page [86.9-87.1]** ("No, that is not true...have really abandoned himself to it.") **A Separate Reality - Page [142.7-142.9]** ("It is up to us as...hunger and pain will destroy him.") **A Separate Reality - Page [151.1-151.3]** ("Only the idea of death makes...tries, without craving, all of everything.) **A Separate Reality - Page [211.8-211.9]** (I was dumbounded. I could not...when I had tried to pierce her.) **Journey to Ixtlan - Page [111.1-111.2]** ("Self-pity doesn't jibe with...time it calls for abandoning himself.) **Journey to Ixtlan - Page [120.2]** ("A warrior, on the other hand...He lets go. That's abandon.") **Tales of Power - Page [290.3]** (All of them laughed with abandon...sublime situations to utterly ludicrous ones.) **Tales of Power - Page [294.2]** ("Only the love for this splendorous being...in the face of any odds.") **The Eagle's Gift - Page [14.1]** (The Nagual said that if the man...have been any fear in him.") **The Eagle's Gift - Page [280.3-281.5]** ("I've told you how the principles...Warriors don't waste an instant.") **The Fire From Within - Page [30.5]** ("What happens after warriors are defeated...join the ranks of the petty tyrants for life.") **The Power of Silence - Page [95.1-95.3]** (As their temporary protector it was...be with minimal help from him.) **The Power of Silence - Page [105.7-105.8]** (He said that if I had to...we faced it with ultimate abandon.) **The Power of Silence - Page [241.2-241.3]** (Don Juan said that the nagual...silently offer it to the abstract.) **The Art of Dreaming - Page [48.6-48.7]** ("With organic beings, the secret is...to be of power and abandon.) **The Art of Dreaming - Page [143.6-143.7]** ("Don't say anything. At the third...irrational abandon to counteract that insistence.")
SEE ALSO: *LETTING-GO, SPIRIT-GESTURE-FOR, WARRIOR-CONTROLLED-ABANDON, ATTENTION-FIRST-INTENT-ABANDON*

ABANDON-CONTROLLED-WARRIOR-[THE WARRIORS' CONTROLLED ABANDON]: SEE: WARRIOR-ABANDON-CONTROLLED-[THE WARRIORS' CONTROLLED ABANDON]

ABANDON-REFUSAL-[THE REFUSAL TO ABANDON ONESELF]: (Warriors know they must refuse to give up or abandon themselves to anything but power itself; the warriors' determination to struggle against all odds; an aspect of the warriors' control, a reflection of the warriors' spirit.)
SELECTED REFERENCES: **The Teachings of Don Juan - Page [86.8-87.1]** ("A man is defeated only when...have really abandoned himself to it.") **A Separate Reality - Page [151.1]** ("A hermit is not detached, for...incapable of abandoning himself to anything.") **A Separate Reality - Page [179.6-179.8]** ("I think you must be aware by now...You're willing to abandon yourself.") **A Separate Reality - Page [180.4-180.6]** ("You abandoned yourself. You willed to abandon...to anything, not even his death.) **A Separate Reality - Page [181.5-181.7]** ("Life for a warrior is an...He would be battling to the end.")
SEE ALSO: *WARRIOR-STRUGGLE*

ABERRATION-MORBIDITY-[ABERRATION AND MORBIDITY]: (Warriors know that aberration and morbidity are the inherent pitfalls of the path of knowledge; the misdirection of knowledge and power resulting from an individual's inability to resolve the issues of self-importance and self-indulgence; aberration and morbidity are the results of being caught up in the intricacies of knowledge, of being waylaid by the high adventure of the unknown, of getting caught up in one's own indolence and laziness; an aberrant fixation on the first face of the second attention; a fixation of the second attention on items of this world.)

SELECTED REFERENCES: **Tales of Power - Page [14.1]** ("Now you can understand why a teacher…would only breed obsession and morbidity.") **Tales of Power - Page [50.9-51.2]** (He casually remarked that I was somber…sorcerers' world was to laugh at it.) **Tales of Power - Page [239.6-239.8]** (He asserted that because of his decoy…plunge him into aberration and morbidity.) **Tales of Power - Page [242.6]** (Don Juan said that once all…as a joke or an aberration.) **The Eagle's Gift - Page [19.1-19.3]** ("The Nagual said that there is…we walk into one of those pyramids.) **The Eagle's Gift - Page [19.9-20.2]** ("The Nagual said that the fixation…like money and power over people.") **The Eagle's Gift - Page [204.3-204.5]** (Don Juan advised me that I should…a performance staged by someone else.) **The Fire From Within - Page [102.4-102.5]** ("You'd be surprised what men are…to the depths they found marvels.") **The Fire From Within - Page [125.1-125.3]** ("The mystery is outside us,"…but what makes us perceive.) **The Fire From Within - Page [137.7]** ("If you think about scary things,"…woman seer, run for the hills!") **The Fire From Within - Page [147.1-147.3]** ("All I can say is that…hope that we won't follow them.") **The Fire From Within - Page [148.3-148.4]** ("To be given a chance to…into the unknown and love it.") **The Fire From Within - Page [157.6-157.7]** (He then told me that we were…was rescued by the new seers.) **The Fire From Within - Page [166.2-166.4]** ("They taxed their awareness to the limit…had to become trees to do that.") **The Fire From Within - Page [167.5-167.9]** (As we walked, don Juan told…scorn and reject their own tradition.") **The Fire From Within - Page [204.7-204.8]** ("It was the old seers who…knowing what they had accomplished.") **The Fire From Within - Page [210.3]** ("You're coming of age," don Juan…Julian, except that he was brilliant.") **The Fire From Within - Page [235.7-235.9]** ("The nagual Sebastian found out marvels…both show you the same sample.") **The Power of Silence - Page [10.4-10.5]** ("The fact that you're still too…you don't become morbidly obsessed.") **The Power of Silence - Page [58.4-58.5]** (Don Juan had explained that sorcerers of…a classic example of an aberration.) **The Power of Silence - Page [262.9-263.2]** (He said he had *seen* that…attaching it to man's dark side.) **The Power of Silence - Page [263.7-263.9]** (After a moment's pause, don Juan explained…abstract, free of liens and mortgages.) **The Power of Silence - Page [264.1-264.3]** ("Ritual can trap our attention better…liens and mortgages on our awareness.") **The Power of Silence - Page [264.5-264.7]** (Morbidity was the antithesis of the surge…being coached by the spirit itself.") **The Art of Dreaming - Page [2.8]** ("Do you mean, don Juan, that…I like the immensity of thought.) **The Art of Dreaming - Page [13.1-13.8]** ("In what way was it unusual…pinned down by their own machinations.) **The Art of Dreaming - Page [47.7-47.9]** ("Yes, but for a perfect result…is unnecessary, to say the least.") **The Art of Dreaming - Page [203.3-203.9]** ("For years now, I have been…or like the new ones.") he said.

SEE ALSO: *OBSESSION, SEER-OLD, TENANT, TOLTECS, POWER-OBJECTS, KNOWN-OBSESSIVE-MANIPULATION, SORCERY-FUTILITY-PITFALLS, KNOWLEDGE-INTRICACIES, ATTENTION-SECOND-FACES-TWO, INDOLENCE, REASON-ABERRATION, AWARENESS-DEATH-STOPS*

*ABSTRACT-THE-[THE ABSTRACT]: (Warriors define the abstract as the force which sustains the universe; the spirit; the nagual; intent; the indescribable; the element that propels the warrior; the idea of the abstract is the only residue that is important to the warrior.)

SELECTED REFERENCES: **The Power of Silence - Page [xv.5]** (The mastery of intent is the…projected beyond the human condition.) **The Power of Silence - Page [11.3-11.5]** ("Can you explain *intent* to me?…it the spirit, *intent*, the abstract.") **The Power of Silence - Page [31.2]** ("Meanwhile, lets continue with the element…any warriors in search of knowledge.") **The Power of Silence - Page [32.1-32.2]** ("Are you saying, don Juan, that…the self becomes abstract and impersonal.") **The Power of Silence - Page [37.1-37.3]** ("The nagual Elias used to tell…can exist independent of each other.") **The Power of Silence - Page [38.1-39.3]** ("Your problem." he said, is that…touching it or feeling its presence.") **The Power of Silence - Page [218.9-219.2]** ("That is not the residue I am…the spirit by being aware of it.") **The Art of Dreaming - Page [2.3-2.7]** (During one of our conversations, don…seers or the sorcerers in residence.")

SEE ALSO: *INTENT, SPIRIT, NAGUAL*

ABSTRACT-TO-[TO ABSTRACT]: (Warriors know they must abstract themselves by making themselves accessible to power, by becoming aware of intent; warriors overcome their feelings of self-importance, and as a result their sense of self becomes abstract and impersonal; warriors must take every available opportunity to abstract themselves; the warriors' journey is a journey of return to the abstract.)

SELECTED REFERENCES: The Power of Silence - Page [32.1-32.2] ("Are you saying, don Juan, that...the self becomes abstract and impersonal.) **The Power of Silence** - Page [218.9-219.2] ("That is not the residue I...spirit by being aware of it.")

SEE ALSO: *WARRIOR-ACCESSIBILITY, ABSTRACT-RETURN, SELF-IMPORTANCE-LOSING, WARRIOR-JOURNEY-RETURN*

ABSTRACT-ALLEGIANCE-[SEALING ONE'S PERMANENT ALLEGIANCE TO THE ABSTRACT]: (Warriors know that their permanent allegiance to the abstract is sealed the moment the spirit descends on them.)

SELECTED REFERENCES: The Power of Silence - Page [89.1-89.6] (He asked me if I remembered...best to forget all about it.)

SEE ALSO: *ABSTRACT, THRESHOLD-NO-RETREAT, SPIRIT-DESCENT, ABSTRACT-CORE-FOURTH*

ABSTRACT-ARRANGEMENT-ULTERIOR-[THE ULTERIOR ARRANGEMENT OF THE ABSTRACT]: (Warriors know that the ulterior arrangement of the abstract is another term for the abstract cores of the sorcery stories.)

SELECTED REFERENCES: The Power of Silence - Page [29.9-30.1] (Obviously, what sorcerers recognize as an...the ulterior arrangement of the abstract.")

SEE ALSO: *ABSTRACT-CORES*

ABSTRACT-CORE-FIFTH-[THE FIFTH ABSTRACT CORE]: (Warriors know that the fifth abstract core is called the requirements of intent.)

SELECTED REFERENCES: The Power of Silence - Page [155-195] (We spent a night at a spot... I've kept mine in mint condition.")

SEE ALSO: *INTENT-EDIFICE, ABSTRACT-CORES, ABSTRACT-CORE-(ALL), ABSTRACT-CORES-(ALL), INTENT-REQUIREMENTS-(TOP)*

*ABSTRACT-CORE-FIRST-[THE FIRST ABSTRACT CORE]: (Warriors know that the first abstract core is called the manifestations of the spirit.)

SELECTED REFERENCES: The Power of Silence - Page [1-24] (Don Juan, whenever it was pertinent...Her name was Talia.") **The Power of Silence** - Page [40.7-40.8] ("The second abstract core of the...invited - or rather force - to enter.)

SEE ALSO: *INTENT-THE EDIFICE OF, ABSTRACT CORES, SPIRIT-MANIFESTATIONS, ABSTRACT-TRAGI-COMEDY, ABSTRACT-CORE-(ALL), ABSTRACT-CORES-(ALL), SPIRIT-MANIFESTATIONS-(TOP)*

ABSTRACT-CORE-FOURTH-[THE FOURTH ABSTRACT CORE]: (Warriors know that the fourth abstract core is called the descent of the spirit.)

SELECTED REFERENCES: The Power of Silence - Page [88.5-89.9] ("Before we leave for the cave...for nobody wants to be free.") **The Power of Silence** - Page [118.3-118.6] ("As I have already told you...way, the first principle of sorcery.)

SEE ALSO: *INTENT-EDIFICE, ABSTRACT-CORES, SPIRIT-DESCENT, ABSTRACT-CORE-(ALL), ABSTRACT-CORES-(ALL), SPIRIT-DESCENT-(TOP)*

ABSTRACT-CORE-SECOND-[THE SECOND ABSTRACT CORE]: (Warriors know that the second abstract core is called the knock of the spirit.)

SELECTED REFERENCES: The Power of Silence - Page [25-51] (We returned to don Juan's house...that is determining our fate.")

SEE ALSO: *INTENT-EDIFICE, ABSTRACT-CORES, SPIRIT-KNOCK, ABSTRACT-CORE-(ALL), ABSTRACT-CORES-(ALL), SPIRIT-KNOCK-(TOP)*

ABSTRACT-CORE-SIXTH-[THE SIXTH ABSTRACT CORE]: (Warriors know that the sixth abstract core is called the handling of intent.)

SELECTED REFERENCES: **The Power of Silence - Page [196-265]** (Don Juan often took me and the rest...reach the place of silent knowledge.")
SEE ALSO: *INTENT-EDIFICE, ABSTRACT-CORES, INTENT-HANDLING, ABSTRACT-CORE-(ALL), ABSTRACT-CORES-(ALL), INTENT-HANDLING-(TOP)*

ABSTRACT-CORE-THIRD-[THE THIRD ABSTRACT CORE]: *(Warriors know that the third abstract core is called the trickery of the spirit; the trickery of the abstract; stalking oneself; dusting the link with the spirit.)*
SELECTED REFERENCES: **The Power of Silence - Page [52-86]** (The sun had not yet risen...return me to a normal state of awareness.)
SEE ALSO: *INTENT-EDIFICE, ABSTRACT-CORES, SPIRIT-TRICKERY, STALKING-ONESELF, SPIRIT-DUSTING-LINK-(TOP'), ABSTRACT-CORE-(ALL), ABSTRACT-CORES-(ALL), SPIRIT-TRICKERY-(TOP)*

ABSTRACT-CORES-[THE ABSTRACT CORES]: *(Warriors know that the abstract cores are the abstract order of knowledge; the ulterior arrangement of the abstract; the edifice of intent; degrees of the warriors' awareness of intent; the silent voice of the spirit; the not-doing of the sorcery stories; the abstract cores reveal themselves extremely slowly, erratically advancing and retreating.)*
SELECTED REFERENCES: **The Power of Silence - Page [xviii.4-xix.2]** (Until now it has been impossible...requirements of *intent*, and handling *intent*.) **The Power of Silence - Page [2.7-3.2]** ("Perhaps, don Juan, things would be...them - relive them, so to speak.") **The Power of Silence - Page [6.4-6.5]** (Don Juan explained that sorcerers understood...blueprints of complete chains of events.) **The Power of Silence - Page [7.1-7.5]** ("If any warrior is aware of...that caps and seals a pyramid.") **The Power of Silence - Page [29.7-30.7]** (I told him I had been thinking...directly, without the intervention of language.") **The Power of Silence - Page [105.2-105.3]** (Examined in this way, sorcery became...degrees of our being aware of intent.) **The Power of Silence - Page [107.3-107.9]** ("It doesn't take a genius to...may make perfect sense to you.") **The Power of Silence - Page [248.5-249.3]** (He changed the subject then and...extremely slowly, erratically advancing and retreating.)
SEE ALSO: *INTENT-EDIFICE, KNOWLEDGE-SILENT, SORCERY-STORIES, ABSTRACT-ARRANGEMENT-ULTERIOR, ABSTRACT-CORE-(ALL), SPIRIT-DECISIONS, SPIRIT-VOICE-SILENT, ABSTRACT-CORES-(ALL)*

ABSTRACT-CORES-CONFORMATION-WARRIOR-[THE WARRIORS' CONFORMATION TO THE PATTERNS OF THE ABSTRACT CORES]: SEE: WARRIOR-ABSTRACT-CORES-CONFORMATION-[THE WARRIORS' CONFORMATION TO THE PATTERNS OF THE ABSTRACT CORES]

ABSTRACT-CORES-UNDERSTANDING-[UNDERSTANDING THE ABSTRACT CORES]: *(Warriors know that understanding the abstract cores means understanding the abstract directly.)*
SELECTED REFERENCES: **The Power of Silence - Page [30.3-33.8]** ("If the abstract cores are beyond...the explanations about the abstract cores.)
SEE ALSO: *ABSTRACT-CORES, SORCERY-STORIES, ABSTRACT-THE, ABSTRACT-CORE-(ALL), ABSTRACT-CORES-(ALL)*

*ABSTRACT-MEETING-[MEETING THE ABSTRACT]: *(Warriors know that they meet the abstract without thinking about it or seeing it or touching it or feeling its presence.)*
SELECTED REFERENCES: **The Power of Silence - Page [39.1-39.3]** ("Consider this," he said. "It was...touching it or feeling its presence.")
SEE ALSO: *ABSTRACT, SPIRIT, INTENT, NAGUAL, NAGUAL-FACING*

ABSTRACT-PURPOSE-WARRIOR-[THE WARRIORS' ABSTRACT PURPOSE]: SEE: WARRIOR-ABSTRACT-PURPOSE-[THE WARRIORS' ABSTRACT PURPOSE]

ABSTRACT-RETURN-[A RETURN TO THE ABSTRACT]: *(Warriors know they must strive to return to the abstract; the definitive journey of the warrior; the return to silent knowledge; the return to intent; the return to the beginning; the return to paradise; the warriors' victorious return to the spirit; the warriors' journey of return to the abstract.)*
    SELECTED REFERENCES: The Power of Silence - Page [37.1-37.4] ("The nagual Elias used to tell...without words or even without thoughts.) The Power of Silence - Page [103.3-103.5] (Don Juan had stated his belief...the beginning, a return to paradise.) The Power of Silence - Page [159.9-160.1] ("As I have said to you...Understanding is one of our trophies.") The Art of Dreaming - Page [2.3-2.4] (During one of our conversations...away from concreteness towards the abstract.)
    SEE ALSO: *GARDEN-EDEN, WARRIOR-JOURNEY-DEFINITIVE, WARRIOR-JOURNEY-RETURN, KNOWLEDGE-SILENT, VICTORY-(ALL)*

ABSTRACT-SEEKING-[SEEKING THE ABSTRACT]: *(Warriors know they must seek the abstract because the abstract lies at the heart of the quest for freedom; warriors seek to perceive all that is humanly possible; warriors seek total freedom and total awareness.)*
    SELECTED REFERENCES: The Art of Dreaming - Page [2.5-2.7] ("And what do you call the abstract...have no interest in concrete gains.)
    SEE ALSO: *ABSTRACT, WARRIOR-FREEDOM-TOTAL, AWARENESS-TOTAL, HUMAN-ALTERNATIVES-POSSIBILITIES-POTENTIAL*

ABSTRACT-SILENCE-[THE SILENCE OF THE ABSTRACT]: *(Warriors know that silence is the essence of the abstract because the abstract exists as silent knowledge.)*
    SELECTED REFERENCES: The Power of Silence - Page [41.4-41.6] ("I can say that this is an...you and make you feel secure.")
    SEE ALSO: *ABSTRACT, KNOWLEDGE-SILENT*

ABSTRACT-TRAGI-COMEDY-[THE ABSTRACT TRAGI-COMEDY]: *(Warriors know that the first abstract core represents a script for an abstract tragi-comedy with three players; one of the players, intent, is abstract; the two other players are the nagual and his apprentice.)*
    SELECTED REFERENCES: The Power of Silence - Page [53.7-54.2] (We sat there and don Juan...into words I found myself babbling.)
    SEE ALSO: *ABSTRACT-CORE-FIRST, INTENT, SPIRIT-KNOCK, NAGUAL-MAN-WOMAN, APPRENTICESHIP-NAGUALISM*

ACCEPTANCE-WARRIOR-[THE WARRIORS' ACCEPTANCE]: SEE: WARRIOR-ACCEPTANCE-[THE WARRIORS' ACCEPTANCE]

ACCESSIBILITY-WARRIOR-[THE WARRIORS' ACCESSIBILITY]: SEE: WARRIOR-ACCESSIBILITY-[THE WARRIORS' ACCESSIBILITY]

ACCOMPLISHMENT-SUPREME-[THE WARRIORS' SUPREME ACCOMPLISHMENT]: SEE: WARRIOR-ACCOMPLISHMENT-SUPREME-[THE WARRIORS' SUPREME ACCOMPLISHMENT]

ACCOMPLISHMENTS-TRANSCENDENTAL-WARRIOR-[THE WARRIORS' TRANSCENDENTAL ACCOMPLISHMENTS]: SEE: WARRIOR-ACCOMPLISHMENTS-TRANSCENDENTAL-[THE WARRIORS' TRANSCENDENTAL ACCOMPLISHMENTS]

ACCOMPLISHMENTS-WARRIOR-[THE WARRIORS' ACCOMPLISHMENTS]: SEE: WARRIOR-ACCOMPLISHMENTS-[THE WARRIORS' ACCOMPLISHMENTS]

ACCOUNT-SPIRIT-MAN-[PAYING BACK TO THE ACCOUNT OF THE SPIRIT OF MAN]: SEE: MAN-SPIRIT-ACCOUNT-[PAYING BACK TO THE ACCOUNT OF THE SPIRIT OF MAN]

ACQUIESCENCE-WARRIOR-[THE WARRIORS' ACQUIESCENCE]: SEE: WARRIOR-ACQUIESCENCE-[THE WARRIORS' ACQUIESCENCE]

ACT-ACTOR-[THE ACTS OF AN ACTOR]: (Warriors know that when they practice controlled folly, their acts are sincere, but at the same time they also know they are the acts of an actor.)
    SELECTED REFERENCES: A Separate Reality - [79.4-80.3] (I felt I needed to recapitulate at that...men is folly, because nothing matters.")
    SEE ALSO: *WARRIOR-CONTROLLED-FOLLY*

ACT-AMUSE-THEMSELVES-WARRIOR-[WARRIORS NEVER ACT TO AMUSE THEMSELVES]: SEE: WARRIOR-ACT-AMUSE-THEMSELVES-[WARRIORS NEVER ACT TO AMUSE THEMSELVES]

ACT-IRREVOCABLE-WARRIOR-[THE IRREVOCABILITY OF THE WARRIORS' ACTS]: SEE: WARRIOR-ACT-IRREVOCABLE-[THE IRREVOCABILITY OF THE WARRIORS' ACTS]

ACT-LEARNING-[LEARNING TO ACT]: (Warriors know they must learn to act in keeping with the warriors' way, the way of the impeccable action; to act for the spirit; the exercise of controlled folly; to act without believing; to act without expecting rewards or anything else in return; to act just for the hell of it.)
    SELECTED REFERENCES: A Separate Reality - Page [79.3-79.5] ("With whom do you exercise controlled...only the acts of an actor.") **A Separate Reality - Page** [81.2-81.3] (He paused for a moment and...learned to think they are important.") **A Separate Reality** [85.3] (You should know by now that...think when he has finished acting.) **A Separate Reality - Page** [85.7-86.2] (Nothing being more important than anything...what one does is important. Nothing!) **A Separate Reality - Page** [144.4-144.5] ("You must act like a warrior,"...warrior by acting, not by talking.") **A Separate Reality - Page** [251.3] ("Hey! Hey! Wait a minute!" don Genaro...ask what can a warrior do?") **Journey to Ixtlan - Page** [39.3-39.4] (He replied that was the reason...was action, acting instead of talking.) **Journey to Ixtlan - Page** [80.9-81.2] ("We're not talking about the same...for witnessing all the marvels of it.") **Journey to Ixtlan - Page** [84.8-85.1] ("Use it. Focus your attention on...the acts of a timid man.") **Journey to Ixtlan - Page** [120.3] ("A warrior, on the other hand,...his calculations are over, he acts.) **Journey to Ixtlan - Page** [157.8-157.9] (I felt obliged to assure him...be done. You have just begun.") **Journey to Ixtlan - Page** [168.4-168.5] (Don Juan put his hand over...whether it is small or enormous.") **Journey to Ixtlan - Page** [191.7-191.9] (It is here that a warrior...*not-doing*. See what I mean?") **Journey to Ixtlan - Page** [227.6] ("A warrior never indulges in thoughts...that doing there are only actions.") **Tales of Power - Page** [23.6-23.7] ("All of us go through the same...at a given moment everything changed.") **Tales of Power - Page** [24.3-24.5] ("That's the flaw with words,"...where new acts have new reflections.") **Tales of Power - Page** [237.4-237.5] ("Together with the right way of walking,...acting just for the hell of it.") **Tales of Power - Page** [287.6] ("You have learned that the backbone...without expecting anything in return.") **The Fire From Within - Page** [176.8-176.9] (All that is required is impeccability, energy...the warrior realizes his full potential.) **The Power of Silence - Page** [79.4-79.6] ("Malicious acts are performed by people...for profit but for the spirit.") **The Power of Silence - Page** [194.1-194.2] (He reminded me that he had taught...and let the spirit decide the outcome.)
    SEE ALSO: *WARRIOR-WAY, WARRIOR-CONTROLLED-FOLLY, WARRIOR-IMPECCABILITY, WARRIOR-DECISIONS, WARRIOR-CHOICE, ABANDON, ACTING-SPIRIT, ACTING-(ALL)*

ACT-LEARNING-BELIEVE-IMPORTANT-[LEARNING TO BELIEVE THAT THE ACTS OF MEN ARE IMPORTANT]: (Warriors know that the acts of the average man appear to be important to him because he has learned to think that they are important; it is the process of "thinking" that leads man to his own self-importance, but once man learns to "see", he realizes that he can no longer think about the things he looks at and therefore the things he looks at become unimportant.)

SELECTED REFERENCES: **A Separate Reality - Page [80.8-81.5]** (I was bewildered. Never would I...what he looks at everything becomes unimportant.")

SEE ALSO: *THINKING-LOOKING, SEEING, EQUAL-UNIMPORTANT, SELF-IMPORTANCE*

ACT-ONLY-WARRIOR-[THE WARRIORS' ONLY ACT]: SEE: WARRIOR-ACT-ONLY-[THE WARRIORS' ONLY]

ACT-POWER-[ACTS HAVE POWER]: (Warriors know that acts have power, especially when warriors behave as if those acts are their last battle on earth; the happiness of warriors is to act with the full knowledge that they do not have any time.)

SELECTED REFERENCES: **Journey to Ixtlan - Page [83.6-83.9]** ("There are some people who are...bring your acts into that light.") **Journey to Ixtlan - Page [84.4-85.1]** ("Your continuity only makes you timid...the acts of a timid man.")

SEE ALSO: *WARRIOR-LAST-STAND, WARRIOR-HAPPINESS, DEATH-ADVISER*

ACTING-HELL-[ACTING FOR THE HELL OF IT]: (Warriors know they must learn to act just for the hell of it, they must act for the spirit alone.)

SELECTED REFERENCES: **Journey to Ixtlan - Page [35.4-35.5]** (We remained quiet for more than...attaching any intellectual purpose to it.) **Tales of Power - Page [237.4-238.2]** ("Together with the right way of walking...without really expecting anything in return.) **The Eagle's Gift - Page [161.5-161.7]** (After we became extremely proficient in...act impeccably without any thought of reward.) **The Power of Silence - Page [20.9-21.3]** (Don Juan commented that it took incidents...mattered, and there he stopped dying.)

SEE ALSO: *ACTION-VS-TALKING, ACTING-SPIRIT*

ACTING-SORCERY-[ACTING AND SORCERY]: (Warriors know there is nothing to understand about the actions of sorcerers, their extraordinary feats are performed from the center of the will, not from the center of understanding or reason.)

SELECTED REFERENCES: **A Separate Reality - Page [261.8-262.1]** (He said that there was nothing...yet you know what it is.")

SEE ALSO: *WILL, ASSEMBLAGE-CENTERS, SORCERY, REASON*

ACTING-SPIRIT-[ACTING FOR THE SPIRIT]: (Warriors know they do not act for profit or reward; it is impeccability that dictates the warriors' acts because warriors act only for the spirit.)

SELECTED REFERENCES: **The Power of Silence - Page [78.9-79.9]** (He stressed repeatedly that teaching...be angry or disillusioned with you.")

SEE ALSO: *WARRIOR-BEHAVIOR, ACTING-HELL, WARRIOR-IMPECCABILITY, WARRIOR-DESIRE, WARRIOR-WANTS, VICTORY-WITHOUT-GLORY-REWARD*

ACTING-VS-TALKING-[ACTING VS TALKING]: (Warriors know that the difference between acting and talking is the difference between the worlds of the tonal and the nagual; in the world of the tonal the warrior talks; in the world of the nagual the warrior acts.)

SELECTED REFERENCES: **A Separate Reality - Page [90.1-90.3]** (At a certain moment today I...I won't talk about this any more.") **Journey to Ixtlan - Page [39.3-39.4]** (I told him that his explanation...really wanted to learn about plants.) **Journey to Ixtlan - Page [177.3]** ("There is only one way to...it you must tackle everything yourself.) **Tales of Power - Page [24.4-24.6]** ("That's the flaw with words," he...where new acts have new reflections.") **Tales of Power - Page [151.5-151.6]** (He criticized, without getting angry, my...about it I was dissipating it.) **Tales of Power - Page [175.5-175.6]** (In these matters one can either...to work with your *tonal*.)

The Second Ring of Power - Page [269.5-269.9] (There was an abyss between our...you talk, in the other you act.") **The Fire From Within - Page [297.4-297.6]** (A couple of days later, all...in a state of total war.) **The Power of Silence - Page [37.7]** ("I told you there is no way...spirit can only be experienced.)
    SEE ALSO: *ACT-LEARNING, TALKING, LANGUAGE-VS-KNOWLEDGE, TONAL, NAGUAL, WORDS-(ALL), ACTING-(ALL)*

ACTING-VS-THINKING-[ACTING VS THINKING]: *(Warriors learn to act instead of thinking too much about acting, or thinking about their actions once they have acted; warriors only have problems understanding the spirit when they think about it; when they act, the spirit easily reveals itself to them.)*
    SELECTED REFERENCES: **The Power of Silence - Page [27.1-27.4]** ("I took you to that cave...heavily toward the aberrations of reason.") **The Power of Silence - Page [87.8-88.5]** ("As I see you in greater detail...My benefactor was that way.)
    SEE ALSO: *ACTING-VS-TALKING, ACT-LEARNING, ACTING-(ALL), THINKING-(ALL)*

ACTING-THINKING-ABOUT-[THINKING ABOUT ACTING]: *(Warriors know that if a man thinks about his acts then he has to believe that his acts are important, when in reality nothing really matters in the life of the warrior, least of all his thoughts about his acts.)*
    SELECTED REFERENCES: **A Separate Reality - Page [86.1-86.4]** ("You think about your acts," he...it is something you cannot think about.")
    SEE ALSO: *THINKING, ACT-LEARNING, ACTING-VS-TALKING, ACTING-VS-THINKING, ACT-LEARNING-BELIEVE-IMPORTANT*

ACTING-WARRIOR-[ACTING AS A WARRIOR]: SEE: WARRIOR-ACTING -[ACTING AS A WARRIOR]

ACTING-WILL-[ACTING FROM THE WILL]: *(Warriors know there is nothing to understand about the actions of warrior-sorcerers because their extraordinary feats are performed from the center of the will, not the center of understanding or reason.)*
    SELECTED REFERENCES: **A Separate Reality - Page [80.5-80.6]** ("Perhaps it is not possible to explain...will controls the folly of my life.") **A Separate Reality - Page [261.9-262.1]** (He said that there was nothing...yet you know what it is.")
    SEE ALSO: *WILL, ASSEMBLAGE-CENTERS*

ACTION-COURSE-ONLY-WORTHWHILE-[THE ONLY WORTHWHILE COURSE OF ACTION]: *(Warriors know that the only worthwhile course of action for warrior-sorcerers or average men is to restrict their involvement with the self-image.)*
    SELECTED REFERENCES: **The Power of Silence - Page [158.2]** ("I've been trying to make clear to...with our self-image," he continued.)
    SEE ALSO: *SELF-IMAGE, SELF-REFLECTION-MIRROR, SELF-IMPORTANCE-LOSING*

ACTION-DEPTH-[THE DEPTH OF THE WARRIORS' ACTIONS]: SEE: DEPTH-ACTION-[THE DEPTH OF THE WARRIORS' ACTIONS]

ACTION-WITHOUT-KNOWLEDGE-[ACTION WITHOUT KNOWLEDGE]: *(Warriors know that those who have been schooled by "doers" rather than "explainers" know what they can do with their awareness and their will, but they don't care to know how they do it.)*
    SELECTED REFERENCES: **The Fire From Within - Page [69.3-69.5]** ("Genaro is the master of awareness...the weird confines of the unknown.)
    SEE ALSO: *DOER-EXPLAINER, LANGUAGE-VS-KNOWLEDGE*

ADOPTING-ANIMAL-FORMS-[ADOPTING ANIMAL FORMS]: SEE: ANIMAL-FORMS-ADOPTING-[ADOPTING ANIMAL FORMS]

ADVANTAGE-WARRIOR-[THE WARRIORS' ADVANTAGE]: SEE: WARRIOR-ADVANTAGE-[THE WARRIORS' ADVANTAGE]

AFFECTION-REAL-[REAL AFFECTION]: (*Warriors know that real affection cannot be an investment.*)
> SELECTED REFERENCES: The Fire From Within - Page [268.9] (I thought that I understood then...real affection cannot be an investment.)
> SEE ALSO: *WARRIOR-LOVE, WARRIOR-AFFECTION*

AFFECTION-WARRIOR-[THE WARRIORS' AFFECTION]: SEE: WARRIOR-AFFECTION-[THE WARRIORS' AFFECTION]

AGE-OLD-[OLD AGE]: SEE: OLD-AGE-[OLD AGE]

AGITATION-[AGITATION]: (*Warriors know that agitation is the tendency of self-absorbed individuals to turn the impulses of the emanations at large into a force which stirs the trapped emanations inside their cocoons; this agitation acts to shorten the life of the individual.*)
> SELECTED REFERENCES: The Fire From Within - Page [75.4-75.7] (He asserted that the awareness...create more agitation, shorten their lives.)
> SEE ALSO: *SELF-ABSORPTION, REASON, EAGLE-EMANATIONS, EAGLE-EMANATIONS-LARGE-AT*

AGREEMENT-OMENS-[OMENS VS AGREEMENTS]: SEE: OMEN-AGREEMENT-[OMENS VS AGREEMENTS]

AIRBORNE-WARRIOR-[AIRBORNE WARRIORS]: SEE: WARRIOR-AIRBORNE-[AIRBORNE WARRIORS]

AIRLINE-OFFICE-DOORWAY-[THE DOORWAY OF THE AIRLINE OFFICE]-(TOP)

ALAMEDA-PARK-[DEATH FINDS A MAN IN ALAMEDA PARK]-(TOP): SEE: DEATH-ALAMEDA-PARK-[DEATH FINDS A MAN IN ALAMEDA PARK]-(TOP)

ALCOHOL-[ALCOHOLIC BEVERAGES]: SEE: BOOZE-[BOOZE]

ALERTNESS-WARRIOR-[THE WARRIORS' ALERTNESS]: SEE: WARRIOR-ALERTNESS-[THE WARRIORS' ALERTNESS]

ALIEN-ENERGY-[ALIEN ENERGY THAT HAS CONSCIOUSNESS]: SEE: DREAMING-EMISSARY-[THE DREAMING EMISSARY]

ALIGNMENT-[ALIGNMENT]: (*Warriors know that alignment is the phenomenon which allows awareness to be cultivated by living creatures; the force that leads to perception; the unique force that either keeps the assemblage point stationary or helps make it shift; the secret passageway to other worlds; the force which selects a small number of the millions of Eagle's emanations passing through the luminous cocoon at the site of the assemblage point; alignment has to be a very peaceful, unnoticeable act.*)
> SELECTED REFERENCES: The Fire From Within - Page [49.6] ("They say that perception is a condition...be cultivated by every living creature.") The Fire From Within - Page [54.5-54.8] ("What is *seeing*, then I asked...When such an alignment occurs one *sees*.) The Fire From Within - Page [108.5-108.6] ("The next truth is that perception...point is located on our cocoon.") The Fire From Within - Page [164.5-164.8] (He said that a true change...and

consequently we perceive other worlds.") **The Fire From Within - Page [170.5-171.4]** (They began by *seeing* how the...of *will*, the energy of alignment.) **The Fire From Within - Page [172.8-173.1]** (Because *dreaming* is so dangerous and...that suddenly become aligned in *dreaming*.") **The Fire From Within - Page [181.4]** (I asked him how intent helps...the movement of the assemblage point.) **The Fire From Within - Page [206.1-206.3]** (Since both the earth and man...allows them to enter unimaginable worlds.) **The Fire From Within - Page [214.5-214.6]** ("We living beings are perceivers,"...the earth's boost is the key.") **The Fire From Within - Page [215.9-216.1]** ("Genaro just helped you align your...No flying away, no great fuss.") **The Fire From Within - Page [216.9-217.2]** ("This is the marvel that the...makes us perceive another total world.") **The Fire From Within - Page [218.6-218.9]** (He repeated, as if he were...at the service of each individual.) **The Fire From Within - Page [294.7-294.8]** (He said that for warriors the...of getting stranded in that inconceivable aloneness.) **The Fire From Within - Page [299.5-299.6]** ("The new seers burn with the force...that total freedom means total awareness.") **The Power of Silence - Page [102.2-102.7]** (On another occasion don Juan had...them was definitely an independent force.) **The Art of Dreaming - Page [6.5-6.7]** ("What did the old sorcerers *see*...filaments passing directly through that glow.)

SEE ALSO: *PERCEPTION, ALIGNMENT-MYSTERY, EAGLE-EMANATIONS, ASSEMBLAGE-POINT, PERCEPTION, AWARENESS, AWARENESS-TRUTH-FIFTH, AWARENESS-GLOW, AWARENESS-ALIGNMENT, ALIGNMENT-(ALL)*

ALIGNMENT-CANCELING-[CANCELING ALIGNMENT]: (Warriors know that the only force that can cancel alignment is alignment itself; warriors must intend a new position of their assemblage point in addition to intending to keep that point fixed at its new position.)

SELECTED REFERENCES: **The Fire From Within - Page [289.2-289.4]** ("The only force that can temporarily cancel...another world and escape this one.)

SEE ALSO: *ALIGNMENT-FORCE, WORLD-OTHER, ASSEMBLAGE-POINT-MOVE*

ALIGNMENT-FORCE-[THE FORCE OF ALIGNMENT]: (Warriors know that will is the energy or the force of alignment; the force of the emanations at large makes the warriors' assemblage point select certain emanations for alignment and perception; the force of alignment is crushing and the warrior must have sufficient energy to sustain the pressure of alignments which never take place under normal circumstances; the force of alignment hooks onto another of the great bands of emanations provided that warriors have stored sufficient energy so that they can use the force of alignment of those bands to perceive other worlds; intent is the purposeful guiding of will, the energy of alignment; will is the impersonal force of alignment that keeps the assemblage point stationary; intent is the personalized force of alignment which makes the assemblage point move; warriors know that the force of alignment is all there is to the apparent stability of the perceivable world; the fixation of the assemblage point on one specific spot is all there is to the everyday world; warriors know that if they succeed on the path of knowledge they will one day burn with the force of alignment, with the force of will which he has transformed into the force of intent through a lifetime of impeccability.)

SELECTED REFERENCES: **The Fire From Within - Page [133.4-133.5]** ("The force of the emanations at...our command, our gift of magic.") **The Fire From Within - Page [145.8-145.9]** ("Without enough energy, the force of...never take place under ordinary circumstances.") **The Fire From Within - Page [164.5-164.8]** (He said that a true change...and consequently we perceive other worlds.") **The Fire From Within - Page [170.2-170.5]** (Don Juan said next that the...energy of alignment is that force.) **The Fire From Within - Page [218.7-218.9]** (He repeated, as if he were...at the service of each individual.) **The Fire From Within - Page [258.3-258.5]** (Don Juan had told me then...what makes the assemblage point move.) **The Fire From Within - Page [283.5-283.9]** (He said that now I needed...all there is to our world.) **The Fire From Within - Page [299.5-299.6]** ("The new seers burn with the...that total freedom means total awareness.")

SEE ALSO: *ALIGNMENT, EAGLE-EMANATIONS-PRESSURE, ASSEMBLAGE-POINT-THRESHOLD, WORLD-OTHER, WILL, INTENT*

ALIGNMENT-HUMAN-FORM-[ALIGNMENT AND THE HUMAN FORM]: *(Warriors know that the human form is the compelling force of alignment of the emanations lit by the glow of awareness on the precise spot where man's assemblage point is normally located; to be a person is to be affiliated with that force of alignment.)*
SELECTED REFERENCES: The Fire From Within - Page [222.8-223.4] (I asked him to explain to me,...force that makes us persons.)
SEE ALSO: *ALIGNMENT, HUMAN-FORM, AWARENESS-GLOW, ASSEMBLAGE-POINT-POSITION-NORMAL*

ALIGNMENT-MASTERY-[THE MASTERY OF ALIGNMENT]: (Warriors know that a complex series of techniques has been developed by seers to "master" or handle the alignment of the Eagle's emanations; this term was abandoned because seers realized that those techniques dealt with much more than alignment, they dealt with the energy that comes out of alignment, and that energy is will; the mastery of alignment is therefore now more properly referred to as the mastery of will or intent.)
SELECTED REFERENCES: The Fire From Within - Page [170.5-170.8] (They began by *seeing* how the...They called that energy *will.*)
SEE ALSO: *INTENT-MASTERY, WILL, INTENT, INTENT-HANDLING*

ALIGNMENT-MOMENT-WITNESSING-[WITNESSING THE MOMENT OF ALIGNMENT]-(TOP)

ALIGNMENT-MYSTERY-[THE MYSTERY OF ALIGNMENT]: (Warriors know that the mystery of alignment is the mystery of the luminous beings; the mystery of the warriors' ability to align other worlds.)
SELECTED REFERENCES: The Fire From Within - Page [289.5-289.8] ("What will happen if I succeed...you won't be in this world.") The Fire From Within - Page [295.7-295.8] (He smiled and pointed to a street...It's time. Go now! Go!")
SEE ALSO: *LUMINOUS-BEINGS-MYSTERY, AWARENESS-TRUTH-SEVENTH, WORLDS-OTHER-ASSEMBLE-TOTAL*

ALIGNMENT-PASSAGEWAY-SECRET-[ALIGNMENT IS THE SECRET PASSAGEWAY TO ASSEMBLING OTHER WORLDS]: (Warriors know that alignment is the secret passageway to assembling other worlds with other great bands of awareness; warriors also know that the earth's boost is the key to using the passageway of alignment.)
SELECTED REFERENCES: The Fire From Within - Page [214.5-214.6] ("We living beings are perceivers," he said...the earth's boost is the key.)
SEE ALSO: *ALIGNMENT, EAGLE-EMANATIONS-BANDS-GREAT, WORLD-OTHER, EARTH-BOOST*

ALIGNMENT-PERCEPTION-[PERCEPTION IS ALIGNMENT]: SEE: PERCEPTION-ALIGNMENT-[PERCEPTION IS ALIGNMENT]

ALIGNMENT-RENEWING-[RENEWING ALIGNMENT]: (Warriors know that alignment is ceaselessly renewed in order to give normal perception its continuity; the energy that comes from the alignments themselves is automatically rerouted to reinforce some of those alignments.)
SELECTED REFERENCES: The Fire From Within - Page [171.1-171.3] (Don Juan said that the new...rerouted to reinforce some choice alignments.)
SEE ALSO: *ALIGNMENT-FORCE, ALIGNMENT, PERCEPTION, CONTINUITY*

ALIGNMENT-WILL-INTENT-[ALIGNMENT, WILL AND INTENT]: *(Warriors know that will is the aspect of alignment that keeps the assemblage point stationary and intent is the aspect of alignment that makes it shift; will is the impersonal force of alignment and somehow it changes into intent, the personalized force of alignment which is at the service of the individual; warriors also know that alignment alone does not fully explain the process that lights up the emanations within man's cocoon because the emanations do not need to be aligned to be lit up; the force that energizes them is an independent force; it is not awareness per se, because awareness is the glow of the emanations being lit up; warriors came to call this independent force will, or intent.)*

SELECTED REFERENCES: **The Fire From Within - Page [218.7-218.9]** (He repeated, as if he were...at the service of each individual.) **The Power of Silence - Page [102.2-103.2]** (On another occasion don Juan had...has with everything in the universe.)

SEE ALSO: *WILL, INTENT, ALIGNMENT-FORCE, ASSEMBLAGE-POINT-MOVE, AWARENESS-GLOW*

ALIVE-MEANING-[THE MEANING OF BEING ALIVE]: *(Warriors know that to be alive is to be aware, that the emanations that cause awareness are encased inside a receptacle or luminous cocoon; the average man thinks that to be alive is to be an organism.)*

SELECTED REFERENCES: **The Fire From Within - Page [81.9-82.1]** ("For seers, to be alive means...awareness are encased inside a receptacle.) **The Art of Dreaming - Page [45.8-45.9]** ("For sorcerers, having life means having...as the precondition of being alive.")

SEE ALSO: *EXISTENCE-REASON, EAGLE-EMANATIONS, LUMINOUS-COCOON*

ALIVE-PRECONDITION-[THE PRECONDITION OF BEING ALIVE]: SEE: PERCEPTION-[PERCEPTION]

ALIVE-PROCESS-BEING-[THE PROCESS OF BEING ALIVE]: SEE: AWARENESS-ENHANCEMENT-[THE ENHANCEMENT OF AWARENESS]

ALLIES-[THE ALLIES]: *(Warriors know that allies are inorganic beings characterized as a force or tension; entities with awareness but no life as we understand it; forces that are neither good nor bad; givers of secrets; creatures that populate the earth together with organic beings; the allies are living creatures because they are aware, not because they can reproduce and metabolize; the allies possess emotions such as emotional dependency, sadness, joy and an indescribable kind of love; the allies make themselves known to man all the time, but we do not usually perceive them because the energy necessary to recognize them is consumed by the first attention; an ally is a power a man can bring into his life to further his knowledge and give him the strength to perform acts, big or small, right or wrong; allies are an aspect of the nagual.)*

SELECTED REFERENCES: **The Teachings of Don Juan - Page [51.7-53.4]** (An "ally" he said, is a power...takes you out to give you power.") **A Separate Reality - Page [38.1-38.7]** ("They were not people? What were they?"...allies of a man of knowledge.") **A Separate Reality - Page [39.4]** (Don Juan said that the three...were in reality don Vicente's allies.) **A Separate Reality Page [40.3-40.6]** ("How does an ally look to you,...never fooled, neither is a crow.") **A Separate Reality - Page [43.7-43.8]** (Then he explained that the allies...out the worst in a person.) **A Separate Reality - Page [233.6]** (Don Juan said that the third type...places, places which were almost inaccessible.) **Journey to Ixtlan -Page [256.2-256.5]** ("Power plants are only an aid...is the way of the sorcerer.") **Journey to Ixtlan - Page [172.1]** (I felt relieved and asked him...he said in a whisper.) **Tales of Power - Page [83.3-83.6]** ("But what actually is an ally...To meet ally is no different.") **Tales of Power - Page [244.5-244.8]** ("If they are used only to...the ally as sorcerers

usually do.) **The Second Ring of Power - Page [52.1-52.5]** ("How did the girls manage to stop...Gorda changed more than anyone else.) **The Second Ring of Power - Page [151.3-154.9]** ("What do you know about the allies...see them as heavy ugly creatures.") **The Fire From Within - Page [81.4-82.6]** ("The counterpart of the earth was...there is no possible interaction.") **The Fire From Within - Page [98.4-105.2]** (Don Juan said that as he...that immensity that is the Eagles' emanations.") **The Fire From Within - Page [162.1-163.1]** ("Those emanations, under certain circumstances," he...produced as many organisms as possible.) **The Fire From Within - Page [191.6-192.2]** (Don Juan said that when he...made a deal with the creature.") **The Power of Silence - Page [104.3-104.5]** (So in a judicious mood, sorcerers...but no life as we understand life.) **The Power of Silence - Page [183.2-183.7]** ("But we told you the monster...Your fear made it into a monstrosity.") **The Art of Dreaming - Page [48.4-49.4]** ("What do sorcerers do with inorganic...to worlds beyond the human domain.") **The Art of Dreaming - Page [67.4-67.9]** ("The problem with the old sorcerers...bent is to teach, to guide.")
SEE ALSO: *INORGANIC-BEINGS, SPIRITS, ATTENTION-FIRST, NAGUAL, ALLIES-(ALL)*

ALLIES-ANIMALS-[ALLIES AND ANIMALS]: (Warriors know that animals are capable of "seeing" allies; a dog or a crow is never fooled by an ally's disguise; animals are usually afraid of allies; if they are accustomed to "seeing" them, then they normally leave them alone.)
SELECTED REFERENCES: **A Separate Reality - Page [40.3-42.2]** ("Real people look like luminous eggs...at things, we don't notice them.")
SEE ALSO: *ALLIES, ALLIES-SEEING*

ALLIES-ANTITHETICAL-[THE ALLIES ARE ANTITHETICAL TO THE WARRIOR]: (Warriors know that the allies are antithetical to the warrior for total freedom; the allies love slavery while the warrior loves freedom.)
SELECTED REFERENCES: **The Second Ring of Power - Page [152.6-152.9]** ("What are you supposed to do...choose whether or not to keep them.") **The Art of Dreaming - Page [58.6-58.7]** ("Do you fear them now, don...to buy, and don't sell.")
SEE ALSO: *ALLIES, WARRIOR-FREEDOM-TOTAL, FREEDOM, WARRIORSHIP-VS-SORCERY, INORGANIC-BEINGS-REFUSING*

ALLIES-APPOINTMENT-[THE APPOINTMENT WITH THE ALLIES]-(TOP)

ALLIES-AWARENESS-RIGHT-SIDE-BARRED-[THE ALLIES ARE BARRED FROM THE WORLD OF RIGHT-SIDE AWARENESS]: (Warriors know that any emanations an ally may share with man are on the left-side awareness; for this reason allies are barred completely from the world of right-side awareness, from the world of rationality.)
SELECTED REFERENCES: **The Fire From Within - Page [101.3-101.7]** (The new seers also found out...awareness, or the side of rationality.")
SEE ALSO: *ALLIES, AWARENESS-LEFT, AWARENESS-RIGHT, REASON-RATIONALITY*

ALLIES-BONDAGE-TOLTECS-[THE TOLTECS HELD THE ALLIES IN BONDAGE]: SEE: ALLIES-EMOTIONS-ATTRACT-[THE ALLIES ARE ATTRACTED BY EMOTIONS]

ALLIES-CALLING-[CALLING THE ALLIES]-(TOP)

ALLIES-CHOOSING-[THE WARRIOR DOES NOT CHOOSE THE ALLIES]: SEE: ALLIES-ANTITHETICAL-[THE ALLIES ARE ANTITHETICAL TO THE WARRIOR]

ALLIES-COMMANDING-VS-SEEING-[COMMANDING AN ALLY VS SEEING]: **(Warriors know they do not need to command an ally in order to "see".)**

SELECTED REFERENCES: **A Separate Reality - Page [167.5-167.7]** (He spoke about "seeing" as a...other hand, had no effect on men.)
SEE ALSO: *ALLIES, SEEING*

ALLIES-COMMUNICATE-[COMMUNICATING WITH THE ALLIES]: **(Warriors know that normally it is the organic beings that initiate any communication with the inorganic beings; the inorganic beings then proceed with a subtle and sophisticated follow-up; once the barrier of awareness is broken, inorganic beings become what seers refer to as allies; allies are sensitive to the seer's most subtle thoughts, moods and fears.)**

SELECTED REFERENCES: **The Fire From Within - Page [161.9-162.3]** (Don Juan said that the only...subtle thoughts or moods or fears.)
SEE ALSO: *ALLIES, INORGANIC-BEINGS*

ALLIES-CONTACT-[CONTACT WITH THE ALLIES]: **(Warriors know that direct contact with the allies produces a most injurious perspiration that must be washed off immediately; the warriors' clothes must also be washed and left in the sun to dry before they can be worn again; contact with the allies is debilitating; coming in contact with an ally is dangerous because the ally is capable of bringing out the worst in a person.)**

SELECTED REFERENCES: **A Separate Reality - Page [43.7-43.8]** (Then he explained that the allies...bringing out the worst in a person.) **The Second Ring of Power - Page [167.3-167.8]** (It was a short drive to the...and got another one for herself.) **The Second Ring of Power - Page [175.1-175.2]** (La Gorda returned around noon...that she felt very weak herself.)
SEE ALSO: *ALLIES, SUNNING-CLOTHES*

ALLIES-DEATH-MERGE-[THE ALLIES TRY TO MERGE WITH THE WARRIORS' DEATH]-(TOP)

ALLIES-EMOTIONS-ATTRACTED-[THE ALLIES ARE ATTRACTED BY EMOTIONS]: **(Warriors know that the allies are attracted by emotions; the emanations inside them are rallied by animal fear more than anything else, although the energy released by other emotions such as love, hatred, or sadness are also equally effective; the old seers actually learned to parcel out their fear and thereby keep their allies in a form of bondage.)**

SELECTED REFERENCES: **The Fire From Within - Page [102.9-103.6]** ("But why did it chase you for...actually held the allies in bondage.)
SEE ALSO: *ALLIES, TOLTECS, FEAR, ALLIES-LOVE, FEAR-PARCELING-OUT, ALLIES-FEAR-FEED, MIRROR-STREAM-(TOP)*

ALLIES-ENCOUNTER-[ENCOUNTER WITH THE ALLIES]-(TOP)

ALLIES-ENERGY-[THE ALLIES' ENERGY]: **(Warriors know that the allies don't really have enough energy to be aggressive; allies have a different kind of energy which is more like an electric current.)**

SELECTED REFERENCES: **The Fire From Within - Page [102.7-102.8]** (I told don Juan that from...beings are more like heat waves.")
SEE ALSO: *ALLIES, ENERGY, ALLIES-SEEING-DREAMING-(TOP)*

ALLIES-ENERGY-EXCHANGE-[THE ALLIES EXCHANGE OF ENERGY WITH THE WARRIOR]: **(Warriors know that an exchange of energy is possible with certain types of allies, those that share occasional emanations with man.)**

SELECTED REFERENCES: The Fire From Within - Page [101.3-102.2] (The new seers also found out the...I had *seen* in the mirror.) The Fire From Within - Page [106.9-107.3] (Don Juan then made a strange gesture...I felt an even greater jolt.)
SEE ALSO: *ALLIES-POWER-SURRENDER*

ALLIES-FACING-[FACING THE ALLIES]-(TOP)

ALLIES-FEAR-FEED-[THE ALLIES FEED ON FEAR]: *(Warriors know that the allies feed on raw human emotions, particularly on animal fear.)*

SELECTED REFERENCES: The Fire From Within - Page [102.9-103.6] ("But why did they chase you...actually held the allies in bondage.) The Fire From Within - Page [191.6-192.2] (Don Juan said that when he...made a deal with the creature.") The Fire From Within - Page [246.3-246.4] ("How do you know I had...was attracted by your animal terror.")
SEE ALSO: *FEAR-PARCELING-OUT, ALLIES-EMOTIONS-ATTRACTED, FEELINGS, MIRROR-STREAM-(TOP)*

ALLIES-GAP-[THE ALLIES' GAP]: SEE: LUMINOUS-COCOON-INORGANIC-BEINGS-[THE LUMINOUS COCOON OF THE INORGANIC BEINGS]

ALLIES-GRAPPLE-HOW-TO-[HOW TO GRAPPLE WITH AN ALLY]-(TOP)

ALLIES-HURLED-AWAY-[HURLED AWAY BY THE ALLIES]-(TOP)

ALLIES-JUAN-BOUT-[DON JUAN'S BOUT WITH THE ALLY]-(TOP)

ALLIES-LOVE-[THE LOVE OF THE ALLIES]: *(Warriors know that the allies are capable of love, a kind of love which the average man can't even conceive.)*

SELECTED REFERENCES: The Fire From Within - Page [82.1-82.3] ("Organic living beings have a cocoon...of love man can't even conceive.") The Fire From Within - Page [102.9-103.6] ("But why did it chase you for...actually held the allies in bondage.) The Fire From Within - Page [104.9-105.2] ("Are your allies useful to you...immensity that is the Eagle's emanations.")
SEE ALSO: *INORGANIC-BEINGS, WARRIOR-COMPANIONS-UNKNOWN*

ALLIES-LUMINOUS-COCOON-[THE ALLIES' LUMINOUS COCOON]: SEE: LUMINOUS-COCOON-INORGANIC-BEINGS-[THE LUMINOUS COCOON OF THE INORGANIC BEINGS]

ALLIES-MATERIALIZE-THEMSELVES-[THE ALLIES CAN MATERIALIZE THEMSELVES AS PART OF THEIR ENERGY EXCHANGE WITH MAN]: *(Warriors know that allies seek the greater energy field of man, and with it they can even materialize themselves.)*

SELECTED REFERENCES: The Fire From Within - Page [101.8-101.9] (He said that the matching emanations give...with it they can even materialize themselves.) The Fire From Within - Page [104.2-104.4] ("As you know, I have my...even take a grotesque human form.")
SEE ALSO: *ALLIES-SHAPE-SHIFTING, ALLIES-ENERGY-EXCHANGE*

ALLIES-MESSAGE-DREAMER-[THE DREAMER'S MESSAGE FOR THE ALLIES]-(TOP)

ALLIES-OMENS-[THE ALLIES AS OMENS]: *Warrior recognize that the presence of allies can represent a gesture of the spirit, especially when more than one of them is "seen" at the same time.)*

SELECTED REFERENCES: A Separate Reality - Page [42.8-43.3] ("Did it have a special significance...my experience was even more unusual.)
SEE ALSO: *ALLIES, OMENS, SPIRIT-GESTURE-OF*

ALLIES-PATTERN-ADOPTING-[ADOPTING THE ALLIES' PATTERN]:
(Warriors know that some of the old seers chose to adopt an ally-like pattern, a particular configuration of their luminous cocoon; this luminous configuration was a fixed position in one of the seven bands of inorganic awareness; the old seers sought it out as a haven but found instead only a terrible dead-end; the death defiers were able to render dormant all the emanations within their cocoons except those that matched the emanations of the allies; in this way they were able to imitate the allies in some form; for all the death defiers except the tenant, this patterning of emanations prevented them from returning their assemblage point to its normal position so that they could interact with people again.)
SELECTED REFERENCES: **The Fire From Within** - **Page [232.7-233.9]** ("As Genaro told you, the old...an apparent state of deep sleep.) **The Fire From Within** - **Page [247.8-248.2]** ("You claim that they are alive...perception set by the assemblage point.) **The Fire From Within** - **Page [253.7-254.1]** (Don Juan explained that the death...as if nothing had ever happened.) **The Fire From Within** - **Page [255.2-255.4]** ("My opinion is that he's caught...as long as he possibly can.")
SEE ALSO: *DEATH-DEFIER, ALLIES, WORLDS-SEVEN, EAGLE-EMANATIONS-BANDS-AWARENESS-EIGHT, INTENDING-DEATH-AWAY, TENANT, ASSEMBLAGE-POINT-POSITION-NORMAL-RETURN*

ALLIES-POWER-[THE ALLIES' POWER]: SEE: ALLIES-WRESTLING-[WRESTLING WITH THE ALLIES]

ALLIES-POWER-SURRENDER-[THE ALLIES SURRENDER THEIR POWER]: (Warriors know that when wrestling an ally, the ally's energy wanes, and it is at that moment that the ally surrenders its power; that power in and of itself is of little or no consequence to warriors; the only thing that matters at that moment of surrender is the warriors' impeccability, which is what permits a fair exchange of energy with the ally; allies have power only if the seer who "sees" them is impeccable.)
SELECTED REFERENCES: **The Fire From Within** - **Page [100.8-101.9]** ("The ancient seers believed that at...it they can even materialize themselves.) **The Fire From Within** - **Page [162.3-162.5]** ("The old seers became mesmerized by...and those old seers just weren't")
SEE ALSO: *ALLIES-WRESTLING, POWER, WARRIOR-IMPECCABILITY, ALLIES-ENERGY-EXCHANGE, ALLIES-FACING-(TOP)*

ALLIES-RETURN-LEVEL-[THE ALLIES' RETURN TO THEIR LEVEL]:
(Warriors know that once the allies get out of their level, it is very difficult for them to go back; the reverse is also true, if a man ventures into the realm of the inorganic beings with his entire body, it is not likely that he will be heard from again.)
SELECTED REFERENCES: **The Fire From Within** - **Page [98.7-98.9]** (His benefactor knew what kind of...they are never heard from again.)
SEE ALSO: *INORGANIC-BEINGS-REALM, TOLTEC-LEVELS, MIRROR-STREAM-(TOP)*

ALLIES-RUMBLE-[THE ALLIES' RUMBLE]: (Warriors know that a characteristic roar or rumbling noise often heralds the presence of the allies.)
SELECTED REFERENCES: **Journey to Ixtlan** - **Page [202.3-202.8]** (I again squinted my eyes and...which an ally heralded its presence.) **Journey to Ixtlan** - **Page [250.2-250.4]** (I heard a particular roar at that...the vibration of an electrical current.) **Journey to Ixtlan** - **Page [255.2-255.3]** ("You have seen the lines of the...I will take you to myself.") **Tales of Power** - **Page [221.4-221.7]** (Nestor and Pablito huddled against me...had turned, flew up towards us.)
SEE ALSO: *ALLIES, MESCALITO, ALLIES-SEEING*

ALLIES-SEEING-[SEEING THE ALLIES]: (Warriors know that the energetic essence of the allies cannot be "seen" by the warrior in the everyday world; instead of "seeing" energy, warriors will only "see" that which the ally is pretending to be; animals are capable of "seeing" the allies insofar as they can distinguish them from what they are pretending to be; the way warriors perceive an ally depends on their energetic level and whether or not they have lost their human form; reason does not put the ally together, the ally is perceived by the body; every time warriors perceive an ally to whatever degree, those perceptions are stored in the body; allies can only be witnessed at the center of will at times when the warriors' ordinary view has stopped; for this reason, the allies are properly considered the nagual.)

SELECTED REFERENCES: **A Separate Reality - Page [39.4-39.6]** (I reminded him that he had...stemmed from my insistence on talking.) **A Separate Reality - Page [40.3-42.8]** ("How does an ally look to you...life I have ever seen two together.") **Journey to Ixtlan -Page [256.2-256.5]** ("Power plants are only an aid...is the way of a sorcerer.") **Journey to Ixtlan - Page [258.7-259.1]** (His movement was so sudden that...assured him that I had "seen" it.) **Tales of Power - Page [83.5-83.9]** ("Just like in the case of...any other way of describing it.") **Tales of Power - Page [244.5-244.8]** ("If they are used only to...the ally as sorcerers usually do.) **The Second Ring of Power - Page [153.1-155.1]** (I told her that I personally liked...to do is lose your human forms.")

SEE ALSO: *ALLIES, SEEING, ALLIES-SHAPE-SHIFTING, ALLIES-ENERGY, HUMAN-FORM-LOSING, FISH-FACED-MAN-(TOP), FORCES-FOUR-(TOP)*

ALLIES-SEEING-DREAMING-[SEEING THE ALLIES IN DREAMING]-(TOP)

ALLIES-SHAPE-SHIFTING-[THE ALLIES' SHAPE-SHIFTING CAPABILITIES]: (Warriors know the allies possess the capability to take on any shape they please; the only way warriors can change the true shape of those creatures is to lose their human form.)

SELECTED REFERENCES : **A Separate Reality - Page [41.7-41.9]** ("How does an ally look to...like a pebble or a mountain.") **The Second Ring of Power - Page [154.9-155.1]** ("Is there something we can do to...to do is lose your human forms.")

SEE ALSO : *ALLIES, HUMAN-FORM-LOSING*

ALLIES-SMOKING-[SMOKING AN ALLY]-(TOP)

ALLIES-SORCERER-EXCHANGE-ENERGY-[THE SORCERER'S EXCHANGE OF ENERGY WITH THE ALLIES]-(TOP)

ALLIES-SPINNING-[SPINNING WITH THE ALLIES]: (Warriors know that spinning with the allies is another term for the movement of the warriors' assemblage point under the influence of an ally's power.)

SELECTED REFERENCES: **Journey to Ixtlan - Page [259.8-260.2]** ("What happened when you grabbed your...feeling! What a feeling it was!) **Journey to Ixtlan - Page [266.1-266.5]** ("No. Your ally will spin you,...that changes, the world itself changes.") **The Second Ring of Power - Page [213.7-213.9]** ("Dona Soledad told me that Eligio...them, so they let him go.)

SEE ALSO: *ALLIES, ASSEMBLAGE-POINT-MOVE, NAGUAL-WIND, ATTENTION-SECOND-SPINNING, ALLIES-HURLED-AWAY-(TOP)*

ALLIES-SPIRIT-CATCHER-[THE ALLY AND THE SPIRIT CATCHER]-(TOP)

ALLIES-VS-SPIRIT-HELPERS-[ALLIES VS SPIRIT HELPERS]: (Warriors know allies and spirit helpers are two different types of inorganic beings which can be attached to the sorcerers' world.)

SELECTED REFERENCES: The Teachings of Don Juan - Page [184.5-184.6] ("How about the woman who took...a helper on the other side.")
SEE ALSO: *ALLIES-TYPES, SPIRIT-HELPER, SPIRITS-TYPES-THREE, INORGANIC-BEINGS-TYPES*

ALLIES-SUMMONING-*[SUMMONING THE ALLIES]-(TOP)*

ALLIES-TALES-*[TALES OF THE ALLIES]-(TOP)*

ALLIES-TOLTEC-GHOULS-*[ALLIES OF THE TOLTEC GHOULS]-(TOP)*

ALLIES-TRANSPORT-DREAMER-*[THE ALLIES TRANSPORT THE DREAMER]-(TOP)*

ALLIES-TYPES-*[THE TYPES OF ALLIES]*: *(Warriors know there are allies of several types; some share no emanations with man and others have occasional emanations which do match those of man; those which do not share emanations with us are so totally foreign to us that we cannot connect with them; the allies which do share emanations with man are remarkably few in number, and are capable of conducting a fair exchange of energy with a man based on their shared emanations; with familiarity, a deeper link is established between a sorcerer and his ally, a relationship which allows both forms of life to profit within a certain restrictive context.)*

SELECTED REFERENCES: A Separate Reality - Page [232.5-233.9] ("There are three kinds of beings...of a branch breaking off.) The Fire From Within - Page [101.3-102.2] (The new seers also found out the...I had *seen* in the mirror.)
SEE ALSO: *SPIRITS-TYPES, ALLIES, INORGANIC-BEINGS-TYPES*

ALLIES-UNDERSTANDING-*[UNDERSTANDING THE ALLIES]*: *(Warriors know that understanding the allies is a personal matter; allies are different for every man, the way we perceive them depends on the bent of our nature.)*

SELECTED REFERENCES: A Separate Reality - Page [227.3-227.5] ("What do they look like...for me is something very precise.) Tales of Power - Page [85.4-85.6] ("Is the ally a moth for you...it's up to your personal power.")
SEE ALSO: *ALLIES, UNDERSTANDING, ALLIES-SEEING*

ALLIES-USELESS-USABLE-*[USELESS AND USABLE ALLIES]*: SEE: ALLIES-TYPES-*[THE TYPES OF ALLIES]*

ALLIES-VISITS-*[VISITS WITH THE ALLIES]-(TOP)*

ALLIES-WAIT-*[THE ALLIES WAIT]*: *(Warriors know the allies wait for them, just like death waits for them, everywhere and nowhere.)*

SELECTED REFERENCES: Tales of Power - Page [84.5-84.8] ("Those are ways of talking about mysteries...that the ally is a moth.)
SEE ALSO: *ALLIES*

ALLIES-WHISTLE-*[THE WHISTLE TO DISPERSE THE ALLIES]-(TOP)*

ALLIES-WRESTLING-[WRESTLING WITH THE ALLIES]*: *(Warriors know that once an ally comes in contact with them, they either have a heart attack and die or they wrestle with the ally; after a moment of sham ferocity, the ally's energy wanes because there is really nothing an ally can do to the warrior or vice versa; warriors know that they are separated from the allies by an abyss; allies cannot push at all, but they can scare human beings and make them fall; once on the ground, they can hold anybody down; in order to meet an ally, individuals must be spotless warriors, otherwise the ally may turn on them and destroy them.)*

SELECTED REFERENCES: **A Separate Reality - Page [43.7-43.8]** (Then he explained that the allies...bringing out the worst in a person.) **A Separate Reality - Page [192.3-192.5]** ("What about the face I saw...turn against him and destroy him.") **A Separate Reality - Page [217.5-217.8]** (" A warrior encounters these inexplicable...your gap and make you solid.) **A Separate Reality - Page [232.5-235.2]** ("There are three kinds of beings...like anything one has ever touched.") **A Separate Reality - Page [251.1-251.9]** ("The ally will come to you regardless...is the master at all times.") **The Fire From Within - Page [100.6-100.8]** ("What would have happened if the...We are separated by an abyss.) **The Fire From Within - Page [243.4-243.6]** (Don Juan, as nimbly as an athlete...had nearly cost me my life.)

SEE ALSO: *ALLIES, ALLIES-CONTACT, ALLIES-POWER-SURRENDER, WARRIOR-STANCE, ALLIES-ENERGY, ALLIES-GRAPPLE-HOW-TO-(TOP)*

ALOOFNESS-WARRIOR-[THE WARRIORS' ALOOFNESS]: SEE: WARRIOR-ALOOFNESS-[THE WARRIORS' ALOOFNESS]

ALTERNATIVES-HUMAN-[HUMAN ALTERNATIVES, POSSIBILITIES AND POTENTIAL]: SEE: HUMAN-ALTERNATIVES-POSSIBILITIES-POTENTIAL-[HUMAN ALTERNATIVES, POSSIBILITIES AND POTENTIAL]

AMBITION-WARRIOR-[THE WARRIORS' AMBITION]: SEE: WARRIOR-AMBITION-[THE WARRIORS' AMBITION]

ANALYSIS-STRUCTURAL-[THE STRUCTURAL ANALYSIS]: SEE: STRUCTURAL-ANALYSIS-[THE STRUCTURAL ANALYSIS]

ANCIENT-MAN-[ANCIENT MAN]: SEE: MAN-ANCIENT-[ANCIENT MAN]

AND-YET-["AND YET"]: (Warriors know they must cultivate an attitude that will allow them to keep going, even in the face of disaster or impossible odds; warriors live exclusively in the twilight of a feeling best described by the words 'and yet'; this attitude keeps them focused on doing their best without any remorse or regrets, and when their acts are complete, it is this understanding which allows them to relax and let the spirit decide the outcome, without any wasted energy on their part; when everything is crumbling around them, warriors accept that the situation is terrible and immediately escape to the twilight of 'and yet'.)

SELECTED REFERENCES: **The Power of Silence - Page [193.7-193.8]** ("I missed the children and I consoled...escape to the twilight of 'and yet...')

SEE ALSO: *WARRIOR-SPIRIT, WARRIOR-ATTITUDE, WARRIOR-STRUGGLE, WARRIOR-IMPECCABILITY, WARRIOR-ACTING, WARRIOR-REGRETS, ACT-LEARNING, WARRIOR-DECISIONS, SPIRIT-DESIGNS*

ANGER-WARRIOR-[THE WARRIORS' ANGER]: SEE: WARRIOR-ANGER-[THE WARRIORS' ANGER]

ANGUISH-WARRIOR-[THE WARRIORS' ANGUISH]: SEE: WARRIOR-ANGUISH-[THE WARRIORS' ANGUISH]

ANIMAL-CRY-WARRIOR-[THE WARRIORS' ANIMAL CRY]: SEE: WARRIOR-ANIMAL-CRY-[THE WARRIORS' ANIMAL CRY]

ANIMAL-FORMS-ADOPTING-[ADOPTING ANIMAL FORMS]: (Warriors know that the aberrant practice of moving the assemblage point to the immeasurable area below allows a sorcerer to become expert at adopting animal forms; these practices convince warriors that those animal forms are their nagual and result in transformations that are horrifying and complete.)

SELECTED REFERENCES: The Teachings of Don Juan - Page [14.9-17.5] (In describing his teacher, don Juan...secret to one of his kin.") The Teachings of Don Juan - Page [66.8-66.9] ("It was different when there were...For what? To frighten the Indians?) The Teachings of Don Juan - Page [67.8-68.3] ("Why did you let her in...that's something we'll take up later.") The Teachings of Don Juan - Page [164.1-164.5] (Don Juan did not talk about my...to the ground, wherever you fall.") The Teachings of Don Juan - Page [168.3-176.3] ("You must tell me all that...lose fear to understand what I mean.") A Separate Reality - Page [199.6-200.1] ("Watch what I do," he said...to the best of my judgment.) A Separate Reality - Page [201.9] (He explained that he had an...who had attempted to kill him.) The Second Ring of Power - Page [211.5-212.2] (In order to calm myself down...nothing else for me to do.) The Second Ring of Power - Page [296.4-296.8] ("The Nagual said that with his...Gorda's explanation somehow had simplified everything.) The Fire From Within - Page [135.7-136.5] (Don Juan also said that among...is to us at man's level.) The Fire From Within - Page [137.5-137.8] (Women give the impulse to cross...woman seer, run for the hills!") The Fire From Within - Page [150.3-152.5] (I did not have time to get...down and put on my clothes.) The Fire From Within - Page [155.4-156.5] ("La Catalina came to us as...great band of the Eagle's emanations.) The Art of Dreaming - Page [78.3-78.7] (He explained that the cohesiveness of...another person, a bird, or anything.) The Art of Dreaming - Page [217.2-217.4] (He took himself as an example...to work a very complex machine.)
SEE ALSO: *ABERRATION-MORBIDITY, SHIFT-BELOW, SORCERY-FUTILITY-PITFALLS, WORM-CAVORTING-WITH-(TOP), CROW-TRANSFORMATION-CARLOS-(TOP)*

ANIMAL-THOUGHTS-READ-[ANIMALS CAN READ OUR THOUGHTS AND FEELINGS]: (Warriors know that certain big animals are not encumbered by reason and are capable of reading a man's thoughts.)
SELECTED REFERENCES: The Power of Silence - Page [200.9-201.3] ("It's not so easy," he said...jaguar to read us," he replied.) The Power of Silence - Page [204.6] ("Both the jaguar and I can read thoughts...get the maximum effect from them.") The Power of Silence - Page [209.4-209.6] (Don Juan explained that human feelings...create a vacuum in the receiver.)
SEE ALSO: *REASON, JAGUAR-CHOICES-MATCHING-(TOP)*

ANNIHILATION-FACES-WARRIOR-[THE WARRIOR FACES IMMINENT ANNIHILATION]: SEE: WARRIOR-ANNIHILATION-FACES-[THE WARRIOR FACES IMMINENT ANNIHILATION]

ANSWERS-VERBALIZED-[ANSWERS MUST BE VERBALIZED]: (Warriors know that the answers to their questions must be verbalized to be of any value.)
SELECTED REFERENCES: The Power of Silence - Page [223.3-223.4] (There were a lot of questions I...verbalized to be of any value.)
SEE ALSO: *KNOWLEDGE-SILENT, KNOWLEDGE-VS-LANGUAGE, WORDS*

ANXIETY-WARRIOR-[THE WARRIORS' ANXIETY]: SEE: WARRIOR-ANXIETY-[THE WARRIORS' ANXIETY]

APLOMB-WARRIOR-[THE WARRIORS' APLOMB]: SEE: WARRIOR-SOBRIETY-[THE WARRIORS' SOBRIETY]

APOLOGY-WARRIOR-[THE WARRIORS' APOLOGY]: SEE: WARRIOR-APOLOGY-[THE WARRIORS' APOLOGY]

APPARITIONS-WORLD-[THE WORLD OF APPARITIONS]: SEE: HEAVEN-[HEAVEN]

**APPEARANCES-INTENDING-[INTENDING APPEARANCES]: (Warriors know that appearances are the essence of controlled folly; stalkers create appearances by intending them, rather than by producing them with props; props create artificial appearances that look false to the eye; intending*

appearances is exclusively an exercise for stalkers; appearances are asked for or forcefully called on, they are never invented rationally.)
    SELECTED REFERENCES: **The Power of Silence - Page [260. 8-261.2]** (Don Juan asked Tuliuno about Tulio's...on; they were never invented rationally.)
    SEE ALSO: *INTENDING, FOLLY-CONTROLLED, STALKING-ART, TULIOS-FOUR-(TOP)*

APPRENTICE-[THE APPRENTICE TO KNOWLEDGE]: SEE: APPRENTICESHIP-NAGUALISM-[AN APPRENTICESHIP TO NAGUALISM], APPRENTICE-(ALL)

APPRENTICE-BEGINNER-[THE BEGINNER APPRENTICE]: *(Warriors know first-hand the particular problems of an apprentice who is still a beginner in sorcery and warriorship.)*
    SELECTED REFERENCES: **The Teachings of Don Juan - Page [20.2-20.5]** (My inability to arrive at an...my own terms would be futile.) **The Teachings of Don Juan - Page [83.9-84.2]** ("When a man starts to learn...His purpose becomes a battlefield.)
    SEE ALSO: *APPRENTICESHIP-NAGUALISM, INTENT-VAGUE, SORCERY-WARRIORSHIP*

APPRENTICE-DECISION-[THE DECISION OF THE APPRENTICE]: *(Warriors know first-hand that the apprentice must make a decision regarding the continuation of his apprenticeship; in actuality, this "decision" is more an act of acquiescence to power than it is a conscious choice.)*
    SELECTED REFERENCES: **Tales of Power - Page [248.1-249.4]** (I left his house and drove...all we do is to acquiesce.)
    SEE ALSO: *WARRIOR-DECISIONS, WARRIOR-ACQUIESCENCE, WARRIOR-CHOICE*

APPRENTICE-GRATITUDE-[THE GRATITUDE OF THE APPRENTICE]: *(Warriors know first-hand the overwhelming feeling of gratitude that the apprentice feels for his teacher and benefactor.)*
    SELECTED REFERENCES: **The Power of Silence - Page [10.7]** ("Calling a nagual a benefactor is...and guides them through unimaginable areas.")
    SEE ALSO : *NAGUAL-MAN-WOMAN,*

APPRENTICE-IMPASSE-[THE IMPASSE OF THE APPRENTICE]: *(Warriors know first-hand the unavoidable impasse reached by every apprentice; the apprentice retreats from the world of sorcery after his internal dialogue has been stopped.)*
    SELECTED REFERENCES: **Tales of Power - Page [246.2-246.5]** (Don Juan said that after the...most artful trap, the worthy opponent.)
    SEE ALSO: *INTERNAL-DIALOGUE-STOPPING, WORTHY-OPPONENT, NAGUAL-TRICKS-APPRENTICE*

APPRENTICE-INDIVIDUALITY-RELINQUISH-[THE APPRENTICE MUST RELINQUISH HIS INDIVIDUALITY]: *(Warriors know that one of the most challenging things for the apprentice to accomplish is to relinquish his individuality as his connection with the spirit is revived.)*
    SELECTED REFERENCES: **The Power of Silence - Page [42.7-42.8]** ("An apprentice is someone who is...his individuality. That's the difficult part.")
    SEE ALSO: *WARRIOR-WAR, VOLUNTEERS, LETTING-GO*

APPRENTICE-MEETING-NAGUAL-[THE INITIAL MEETING BETWEEN A PROSPECTIVE APPRENTICE AND A NAGUAL]: *(Warriors know that the initial meeting between a prospective apprentice and a nagual is an incomprehensible event from the warrior-sorcerers' point of view; it is*

nonsensical to try and explain that the nagual, by virtue of his lifelong experience, focuses his second attention on his invisible connection with some indefinable abstract; he does this to emphasize and clarify someone else's invisible connection with that same indefinable abstract.)

SELECTED REFERENCES: **The Power of Silence - Page [47.6-47.9]** (Don Juan said that, for instance...invisible connection with that indefinable abstract.)

SEE ALSO: *APPRENTICE, NAGUAL-MAN-WOMAN, SPIRIT-CONDUIT, JUAN-CARLOS-MEET-(TOP), JUAN-JULIAN-FINDING-(TOP)*

APPRENTICE-NAGUAL-[THE APPRENTICE NAGUAL]: *(Warriors know that a candidate must be suited to become an apprentice nagual by virtue of being a double man or woman; the first thing the nagual does to his prospective apprentice is to trick him or her by delivering a jolt to his connecting link to the spirit.)*

SELECTED REFERENCES: **The Power of Silence - Page [13.5]** (The nagual Julian immediately evaluated the...candidate to be his apprentice nagual.) **The Power of Silence - Page [54.5-54.6]** (The first thing a nagual does...which my benefactor used on me.)

SEE ALSO: *DOUBLE-BEINGS, LUMINOUS-COCOON, NAGUAL-MAN-WOMAN, NAGUAL-TRICKS-APPRENTICE, SPIRIT-TRICKERY, INTENT-INTERVENTION*

APPRENTICE-REWARD-[THE APPRENTICES' REWARD]: *(Warriors know that the only reward that apprentices receive from their apprenticeship to nagualism is the way the apprenticeship serves to attack their self-reflection.)*

SELECTED REFERENCES: **The Power of Silence - Page [158.4-158.8]** ("Each of us has a different degree...real help you've gotten from me.")

SEE ALSO: *WARRIOR-REWARD, SELF-REFLECTION-MIRROR-SHATTERING, APPRENTICESHIP-NAGUALISM, SELF-IMPORTANCE-LOSING, MAN-NEEDS*

APPRENTICE-SECOND-GROUP-[THE SECOND GROUP OF APPRENTICES]: *(As a three-pronged nagual, Carlos Castaneda was unable to lead the party of warriors which don Juan originally assembled for him; instead, don Juan subsequently assembled a second more compact group of apprentices for Carlos; this nagual's party of warriors consisted of a dreamer named Florinda, a stalker named Taisha and Carol the nagual woman.)*

SELECTED REFERENCES: **The Art of Dreaming - Page [ix.5-xi.1]** (I have already described all this...as an energetic configuration of awareness.) **The Art of Dreaming - Page [200.1-200.2]** ("My time on this earth is...It's all up to the spirit.) **The Art of Dreaming - Page [221.5-221.8]** (For a moment, I seemed to...to do with what they knew.)

SEE ALSO: *NAGUAL-PARTY-WARRIORS, NAGUAL-THREE-PRONGED, FLORINDA-(TOP), NAGUAL-WOMAN-(TOP)*

APPRENTICE-SORCERY-WARRIORSHIP-[AN APPRENTICE TO SORCERY AND WARRIORSHIP]: SEE: APPRENTICESHIP-NAGUALISM-[AN APPRENTICESHIP TO NAGUALISM]

APPRENTICE-SORCERY-WORLD-OPPORTUNITY-[THE APPRENTICES' OPPORTUNITY TO JOIN THE SORCERERS' WORLD]: *(Warriors know that power provides them with a magical opportunity to join the world of sorcerers and begin a journey on the path of knowledge.)*

SELECTED REFERENCES: **The Power of Silence - Page [22.7-23.2]** (When the time came for the...sorcerers along or leave them behind.)

SEE ALSO: *BIRD-FREEDOM, APPRENTICESHIP-CARLOS-(TOP), JUAN-CARLOS-MEET-(TOP)*

APPRENTICE-TASK-[THE APPRENTICES' TASK]: (Warriors know that the apprentices' task is a pragmatic chore which must be fulfilled in the course of daily life; this task is usually some sort of farfetched life situation.)
SELECTED REFERENCES: **Tales of Power - Page [249.5-249.8]** (Don Juan said that after the...had to be earnest about it.)
SEE ALSO: *APPRENTICESHIP-NAGUALISM, WARRIOR-TASK*

APPRENTICE-VIEW-THEMSELVES-CHANGE-[APPRENTICES CHANGE THEIR VIEW OF THEMSELVES AND THE WORLD]: (Warriors know first-hand that after novices decide to become apprentices to knowledge, they change their view about themselves and the world; the product of the first of the four steps on the path of knowledge.)
SELECTED REFERENCES: **The Fire From Within - Page [23.6-23.9]** (Don Juan said that his benefactor...fourth step and have become seers.)
SEE ALSO: *KNOWLEDGE-PATH-STEPS-FOUR, WARRIOR-VIEW*

APPRENTICE-WARRIOR-[FROM APPRENTICE TO WARRIOR]: (Warriors experience first-hand the process through which the individual evolves from an apprentice into a warrior; once the apprentice has been assigned the task of apprenticeship, that individual is ready for another type of instruction; the apprentice has become a warrior then; an apprentice is simply someone striving to clear their link with intent; once that link is revived, the individual is no longer an apprentice.)
SELECTED REFERENCES: **Tales of Power - Page [249.5-249.8]** (Don Juan said that after the..."He is a warrior then.) **The Power of Silence - Page [42.6-42.8]** ("An apprentice is someone who is...his individuality. That's the difficult part.")
SEE ALSO: *APPRENTICE-TASK, APPRENTICESHIP-NAGUALISM, INTENT-LINK-CLEANING, WARRIOR-INSTRUCTION*

APPRENTICESHIP-CARLOS-[HOW DON JUAN ENGAGED CARLOS FOR HIS APPRENTICESHIP]-(TOP)

APPRENTICESHIP-NAGUALISM-[AN APPRENTICESHIP TO NAGUALISM]: (The personal apprenticeship of Carlos Castaneda to his teacher don Juan Matus and his benefactor don Genaro Flores; an apprenticeship in nagualism, sorcery and warriorship.)
SELECTED REFERENCES: **The Teachings of Don Juan - Page [13.1-26.1]** (In the summer of 1960,...order of the phenomena he had experienced.) **A Separate Reality - Page [1.3-15.6]** (Ten years ago I had the fortune...recording I endeavored to suspend judgment.) **Journey to Ixtlan - Page [vii.3-xiv.5]** (On Saturday, May 22, 1971,...don Juan's words to speak for themselves.) **Tales of Power - Page [176.4]** ("When an ordinary man is ready,...benefactor, and he becomes a sorcerer.") **Tales of Power - Page [234.1-234.6]** ("Let me begin by telling you...I had become obsessed with that look.) **The Second Ring of Power - Page [1.3-2.8]** (A flat barren mountaintop on the western...being in the world as sorcerers.) **The Eagle's Gift - Page [1.4-5.2]** (Although I am an anthropologist,...still into the art of sorcery.) **The Fire From Within - Page [ix.4-xii.7]** (I have written extensive descriptive accounts...free, as if they had never existed.) **The Power of Silence - Page [vii.6-vii.9]** (My books are a true account...knowledge is as, or perhaps more, complex.) **The Power of Silence - Page [ix.6-xix.2]** (At various times don Juan attempted...requirements of intent, and handling intent.) **The Power of Silence - Page [42.5-43.6]** (He stressed that in order to...the disciple turns out to be.") **The Power of Silence - Page [47.6-47.9]** (Don Juan said that, for instance...invisible connection with that indefinable abstract.)
SEE ALSO: *TEACHERS-TEACHING, LEARNING, SORCERY, WARRIORSHIP, PROTEGIDO, ESCOGIDO*

ARGUMENTS-CLINGING-[CLINGING TO ONE'S ARGUMENTS]: SEE: REASON-FLAW-[THE FLAW OF REASON]

*ARRANGEMENTS-WARRIOR-[THE WARRIORS' ARRANGEMENTS]:
SEE: WARRIOR-ARRANGEMENTS-[THE WARRIORS'
ARRANGEMENTS]*

*ART-BRIDGE-[ART AS A BRIDGE]: SEE: WARRIOR-BRIDGE-[THE
WARRIORS' BRIDGE]*

*ART-WARRIOR-[THE WARRIORS' ARTS]: SEE WARRIOR-ART-[THE
WARRIORS' ARTS]*

*ARTIFICE-SPIRIT-LAST-[THE SPIRIT'S LAST ARTIFICE]: (Warriors
know that the sorcery stories are the spirit's last artifice.)*
    SELECTED REFERENCES: **The Power of Silence** - Page [7.4-7.6] ("You must forgive
me, don Juan...that caps and seals a pyramid.") **The Power of Silence** - Page [40.9-41.2] ("This
second abstract core could be...the spirit knocked on the door.)
    SEE ALSO: *SPIRIT-TRICKERY, ARTIFICE-SUBTERFUGE*

*ARTIFICE-SUBTERFUGE-[ARTIFICE AND SUBTERFUGE]: (Warriors
know that artifice and subterfuge lie at the core of the teaching method of
nagualism; the subterfuge and trickery of the spirit)*
    SELECTED REFERENCES: **Tales of Power** - Page [236.9] (He said that the right way
of walking was a subterfuge.) **The Power of Silence** - Page [7.4-7.6] ("You must forgive me, don
Juan...that caps and seals a pyramid.") **The Power of Silence** - Page [40.9-41.2] ("This second
abstract core could be...the spirit knocked on the door.) **The Power of Silence** - Page [52.8-53.5]
('We are going to talk now...and subterfuge in order to teach.) **The Art of Dreaming** - Page
[27.2-27.4] (When I told don Juan about...is looking at in a dream.") **The Art of Dreaming** - Page
[35.8-35.9] (His subterfuge was to say that...examine the elements of one's dreams.)
    SEE ALSO: *TEACHERS-TEACHING, NAGUAL-MAN-WOMAN, SPIRIT-
TRICKERY*

*ARTS-IMPORTANCE-WARRIOR-[THE IMPORTANCE OF THE
WARRIORS' ARTS]: SEE: WARRIOR-ARTS-IMPORTANCE-[THE
IMPORTANCE OF THE WARRIORS' ARTS]*

*ARTS-WARRIOR-[THE WARRIORS' ARTS]: SEE: WARRIOR-ARTS-
[THE WARRIORS' ARTS]*

*ASSEMBLAGE-CENTERS-[THE CENTERS OF ASSEMBLAGE]: (Warriors
know that there are two primary centers for the assemblage of perception;
one is the reason and the other is the will; reason assembles our view of the
everyday world of the tonal, while will assembles our view of the nagual.)*
    SELECTED REFERENCES: **Tales of Power** - Page [244.5-244.9] ("That's a difficult
point to explain...enlarging their views of the world.) **Tales of Power** - Page [273.3] ("There is no
way to refer...*nagual* can be witnessed, the *will*.) **Tales of Power** - Page [276.2-276.4] ("Those
leaps were only the beginning...although one can never explain it.) **Tales of Power** - Page
[277.5-277.6] ("Sorcerers do the same thing with...it is that we are witnessing.) **The Eagle's Gift** -
Page [196.3-196.4] (The most important of those points...Juan Tuma, I forgot my anger.) **The
Eagle's Gift** - Page [252.7-253.4] (I disregarded Zuleica's order to enter...thought I could feel a
dent.)
    SEE ALSO: *REASON, WILL, PERCEPTION, TONAL, NAGUAL-FACING,
REASON-VS-WILL*

**ASSEMBLAGE-POINT-[THE ASSEMBLAGE POINT]: (Warriors know
that the assemblage point is the place where perception is assembled within
the structure of man's luminous cocoon; the assemblage point is the crucial
feature of human beings as luminous entities; a round spot of intense
brilliance about the size of a tennis ball; the discovery of the assemblage
point was the decisive finding of the sorcerers of antiquity; an invisible*

point where perception is assembled; the assemblage point is also sometimes referred to as the glow of awareness.)
    SELECTED REFERENCES: The Fire From Within - Page [108.5-108.6] ("The next truth is that perception...assemblage point is located on our cocoon.") The Fire From Within - Page [110.9] (He also said that the old seers...luminous shell, the cocoon itself.) The Fire From Within - Page [199.5-199.6] ("What I am trying to do...we behave and how we feel.") The Fire From Within - Page [216.2-216.4] (We were coming closer to the main...leave room for anything except realness.) The Fire From Within - Page [258.6] ("After all, there is really very...point fixed at a certain position.") The Fire From Within - Page [283.5-283.7] (He said that now I needed...cease to be what it is to us.) The Power of Silence - Page [xvi.2-xvi.3] (5. Perception occurs when the energy fields...assembled" or simply "the assemblage point.") The Power of Silence - Page [Page 56.9-57.1] (Don Juan said that perception is...location of the assemblage point.) The Power of Silence - Page [219.3-219.6] (It was stupidity that forced us to...to entertaining the thought of its existence.") The Power of Silence - Page [264.9-265.1] ("Freedom," he said. "He wanted their...that it can be accomplished." The Art of Dreaming - Page [6.8-7.1] (Finally, they *saw* two things...are perceiving in an unfamiliar manner.) The Art of Dreaming - Page [7.9-8.3] (Don Juan stated that, *seeing* that...and the glow that surrounds it.) The Art of Dreaming - Page [11.4-11.5] (In his teachings he put a...egg, which is our energy self.)
    SEE ALSO: *AWARENESS-TRUTH-SIXTH, PERCEPTION, ALIGNMENT, REALITY-INTERPRETATION, AWARENESS-GLOW, EAGLE-EMANATIONS, ASSEMBLAGE-POINT-(ALL)*

ASSEMBLAGE-POINT-ALIGNMENT-[THE ASSEMBLAGE POINT AND ALIGNMENT]: *(Warriors know that perception takes place because the assemblage point selects internal and external emanations for alignment.)*
    SELECTED REFERENCES: The Fire From Within - Page [108.5-108.6] ("The next truth is that perception...point is located on our cocoon.")
    SEE ALSO: *ASSEMBLAGE-POINT, ALIGNMENT, PERCEPTION, EAGLE-EMANATIONS*

ASSEMBLAGE-POINT-ATTENTION-FIRST-[THE ASSEMBLAGE POINT AND THE FIRST ATTENTION]: *(Warriors know that in order for the first attention to bring the world we perceive into focus, it has to emphasize certain emanations from man's band of emanations; these emphasized emanations are known as the first attention, the known, the tonal, reality, rationality, right-side awareness.)*
    SELECTED REFERENCES: The Fire From Within - Page [109.2-109.8] (He told me that in order to discuss...calls it reality, rationality, common sense.)
    SEE ALSO: *EAGLE-EMANATIONS-EMPHASIZED, ASSEMBLAGE-POINT, ATTENTION-FIRST, TONAL, KNOWN, AWARENESS-RIGHT-SIDE, REALITY-INTERPRETATION, REASON*

ASSEMBLAGE-POINT-COMMANDING-[COMMANDING THE ASSEMBLAGE POINT]: SEE: SPIRIT-COMMANDING-[COMMANDING THE SPIRIT]

ASSEMBLAGE-POINT-CONCEPTION-EXISTENCE-MOVEMENT-[THE CONCEPTION OF THE EXISTENCE OF THE ASSEMBLAGE POINT AND ITS MOVEMENT]: *(Warriors know that they must train themselves to do two transcendental things: first, to conceive the existence of the assemblage point, and second, to make that assemblage point move.)*
    SELECTED REFERENCES: The Power of Silence - Page [144.8-145.1] (I mentioned to don Juan that I...to make that assemblage point move.)
    SEE ALSO: *ASSEMBLAGE-POINT, ASSEMBLAGE-POINT-MOVING, AWARENESS-TRUTHS*

ASSEMBLAGE-POINT-DISLODGE-[DISLODGING THE ASSEMBLAGE POINT]: *(Warriors know that their assemblage points become dislodged from their original positions through confrontations with the nagual.)*

SELECTED REFERENCES: The Fire From Within - Page [194.3-194.4] (Don Juan said that when the...ideal for dislodging the assemblage point.) **The Fire From Within - Page [258.3-258.5]** (Don Juan had told me then...what makes the assemblage point move.) **The Fire From Within - Page [266.5-266.9]** (Don Juan explained that he had...if nothing has happened to us.)

SEE ALSO: *ASSEMBLAGE-POINT-MOVING, ASSEMBLAGE-POINT-SHIFT, NAGUAL-FACING*

ASSEMBLAGE-POINT-DISPLACEMENT-[MOVING OR DISPLACING THE ASSEMBLAGE POINT]: SEE: ASSEMBLAGE-POINT-MOVING-[MOVING THE ASSEMBLAGE POINT]

ASSEMBLAGE-POINT-DISPLACEMENT-DREAMS-[DREAMS AND THE DISPLACEMENT OF THE ASSEMBLAGE POINT]: *(Warriors know that the movement of the assemblage point is totally associated with the unusual character of one's dreams; the more unusual the dream, the greater the displacement of the assemblage point.)*

SELECTED REFERENCES: The Art of Dreaming - Page [18.7-19.1] (Another monumental breakthrough that the old...even knowing it, they created dreaming.)
SEE ALSO: *ASSEMBLAGE-POINT-MOVING, DREAMING-VS-DREAMS*

ASSEMBLAGE-POINT-DISPLACEMENT-TYPES-[THE TWO TYPES OF DISPLACEMENT OF THE ASSEMBLAGE POINT]: *(Warriors know there are two distinguishable types of assemblage point displacement; one is a "shift" of the assemblage point and the other is a "movement" of the assemblage point.)*

SELECTED REFERENCES: The Art of Dreaming - Page [9.1-9.3] (Don Juan explained that the old...nature of the perception each allows.)
SEE ALSO: *ASSEMBLAGE-POINT-SHIFT-VS-MOVEMENT*

*ASSEMBLAGE-POINT-FIXATION-[THE FIXATION OF THE ASSEMBLAGE POINT]: *(Warriors know that the fixation of the assemblage point is responsible for the uniformity and cohesion of the energy body; the internal dialogue is what keeps the assemblage point fixed on its normal position; the first attention is the fixation of the assemblage point on its habitual position; the second attention is the fixation of the assemblage point on each of an enormous number of new positions; to fixate the assemblage point on any new spot means to acquire cohesion; the art of stalking deals with the fixation of the assemblage point once it has been displaced; the fixation of the assemblage point is extremely important because if the assemblage point does not become stationary, there is no way to perceive coherently and the warrior only experiences a kaleidoscope of disassociated images; the fixation of the assemblage point on one specific spot is all there is to the apparent solidity of the everyday world or any of the other worlds which the warrior is capable of assembling.)*

SELECTED REFERENCES: The Fire From Within - Page [119.5-119.8] ("I've mentioned to you that sorcery...keeps your assemblage point rigidly fixed.) **The Fire From Within - Page [131.3-131.5]** (While we were having lunch the...point fixed in its original position.) **The Fire From Within - Page [132.9-133.2]** ("But would it be possible to encourage...being caught in the clutches of rationality.") **The Fire From Within - Page [283.5-284.2]** (He said that now I needed...a mirage as the old fixation.) **The Art of Dreaming - Page [14.5-14.6]** ("How are uniformity and cohesion acquired...of the assemblage point," he said.) **The Art of Dreaming - Page [16.7-17.1]** (Don Juan then gave me a...an enormous number of new positions.) **The Art of Dreaming - Page [69.4-69.9]** (Don Juan expressed his bewilderment...on a number of dreaming positions.") **The Art of Dreaming - Page [70.1-70.3]** ("How do we fixate the assemblage...any particular dream you are having.") **The Art of Dreaming - Page [75.8-77.9]**

(Don Juan changed the subject and...which the old sorcerers were involved.) **The Art of Dreaming - Page [77.5-77.9]** ("The art of stalking," he continued...which the old sorcerers were involved.) **The Art of Dreaming - Page [103.9-104.1]** ("We are energy that is kept...of that energy will change accordingly.)
SEE ALSO: *ENERGY-BODY, AWARENESS-FIXATION, ASSEMBLAGE-POINT, AWARENESS-FIXATION, ATTENTION-FIRST, ATTENTION-SECOND, ENERGETIC-UNIFORMITY-COHESION, STALKING-ART, DREAMING-VS-STALKING, ASSEMBLAGE-POINT-MOVING, WORLDS-OTHER-ASSEMBLE-TOTAL*

ASSEMBLAGE-POINT-FIXATION-DREAMER-DIRECTS-[DREAMERS DIRECT THE FIXATION OF THE ASSEMBLAGE POINT]: *(Warriors know that dreamers cannot command their dreams other than to direct the fixation of their assemblage points; dreamers are like fishermen equipped with a line that casts itself wherever it may; all dreamers can do is keep the line anchored in whatever place it sinks.)*
SELECTED REFERENCES: The Fire From Within - Page [174.1-175.1] (After observing *dreamers* while they slept...at the place where it sinks.)
SEE ALSO: *ASSEMBLAGE-POINT-FIXATION, DREAMING-ART, DREAMING-COMMAND*

ASSEMBLAGE-POINT-FIXATION-SELF-IMPORTANCE-[SELF-IMPORTANCE AND THE FIXATION OF THE ASSEMBLAGE POINT]: *(Warriors know that self-importance is the force which keeps the assemblage point fixed in its habitual position.)*
SELECTED REFERENCES: The Power of Silence - Page [150.8-151.1] (Don Juan described self-importance as...self-pity masquerading as something else.) **The Power of Silence - Page [159.6-159.7]** (He explained that the specific sequence...without premeditation, into an inconceivable journey.)
SEE ALSO: *ASSEMBLAGE-POINT-FIXATION, SELF-IMPORTANCE*

ASSEMBLAGE-POINT-FLUIDITY-[THE ASSEMBLAGE POINT'S MARGIN OF FLUIDITY]: *(Warriors know they must develop a margin of flexibility and fluidity for the assemblage point; without it they are doomed to remain imprisoned by the peculiarities which are characteristic of the habitual position of their assemblage point; every human being has a natural hidden capacity for the fluidity of the assemblage point; the problem is that the average man never uses it except in the midst of life or death struggles.)*
SELECTED REFERENCES: The Power of Silence - Page [238.7-239.2] (He said that don Juan's assemblage point...as a life-or death struggle.) **The Art of Dreaming - Page [75.4-75.7]** (I asked don Juan about this...be like them: righteous and hysterical.")
SEE ALSO: *ASSEMBLAGE-POINT-RIGIDITY, POWER-HIDDEN, DOUBLE-MORTAL-COMBAT-(TOP), JUAN-RIVER-BOUT-(TOP)*

ASSEMBLAGE-POINT-IMMOBILIZING-[IMMOBILIZING THE ASSEMBLAGE POINT]: *(Warriors know that locking the assemblage point into its habitual position is the greatest single accomplishment of our human upbringing; once it has been immobilized there, the assemblage point can be guided to interpret what we perceive.)*
SELECTED REFERENCES: The Art of Dreaming - Page [76.4-76.6] (Don Juan expressed wonder at what...are fixed on the same spot.)
SEE ALSO: *INFANTS-INTERNAL-DIALOGUE, ASSEMBLAGE-POINT-FIXATION, AWARENESS-FIXATION, HABITUATION, ASSEMBLAGE-POINT-IMMOVABLE*

ASSEMBLAGE-POINT-IMMOVABLE-[WHEN THE ASSEMBLAGE POINT IS IMMOVABLE]: *(Warriors know that to remain "healthy and sane" in the terms of the average man means that the assemblage point must remain immovable; the warriors' quest for knowledge is predicated on the ability to*

move the assemblage point, so warriors know that in a sense they must "lose their minds"; in reality, however, warriors know that all they lose is the self-reflection of their inventory.)
    SELECTED REFERENCES: **The Fire From Within - Page [120.1-121.3]** ("What happens to the persons whose...than if you had kept it.")
    SEE ALSO: *ASSEMBLAGE-POINT-FIXATION, MIND, INVENTORY, SANITY, INSANITY, ASSEMBLAGE-POINT-IMMOBILIZING, SELF-REFLECTION*

ASSEMBLAGE-POINT-INORGANIC-BEINGS-[THE ASSEMBLAGE POINT OF THE INORGANIC BEINGS]: *(Warriors know that the assemblage point of inorganic beings can be on either the lower part or upper part of their cocoons; those with low assemblage points are alien to man but akin to plants; those with it up higher on the cocoon are closer to man and other organic creatures.)*
    SELECTED REFERENCES: **The Fire From Within - Page [165.6-165.7]** ("What about the inorganic beings...to man and other organic creatures.")
    SEE ALSO: *ASSEMBLAGE-POINT, INORGANIC-BEINGS-TYPES*

ASSEMBLAGE-POINT-JOURNEY-RETRACING-[RETRACING THE JOURNEY OF THE ASSEMBLAGE POINT]: SEE: WARRIOR-TEST-GRAND-[THE WARRIORS' GRAND TEST]

ASSEMBLAGE-POINT-LIGHT-CHANGE-[THE LIGHT SHIFT WHICH MARKS THE MOVEMENT OF THE ASSEMBLAGE POINT]: *(Warriors experience first-hand the characteristic change in light which marks some lateral shifts of the assemblage point; in the daytime light becomes very dark and at night, darkness becomes twilight.)*
    SELECTED REFERENCES: **A Separate Reality - Page [166.6-166.7]** (At one point I noticed that the...word don Juan had taught me.) **Journey to Ixtlan - Page [202.3-202.7]** (I again squinted my eyes and...and did not let me move.) **Tales of Power - Page [221.8]** (The shape first hovered over us,...all of a sudden it had become twilight.) **The Fire From Within - Page [239.4-239.5]** (I wanted to turn tail and run...sky was definitely lighter toward the east.) **The Fire From Within - Page [245.3-245.5]** (I heard everything he said with...before that it was already dawn.) **The Fire From Within - Page [246.1-246.3]** (Don Juan commented on how well...that warriors have nothing to fear.)
    SEE ALSO: *ASSEMBLAGE-POINT-MOVING*

ASSEMBLAGE-POINT-LUMINOUS-COCOON-[THE ASSEMBLAGE POINT IS LOCATED IN THE LUMINOUS COCOON]: *(Warriors know that the assemblage point is not located in the physical body, rather, it is located in the luminous shell, in the luminous cocoon itself.)*
    SELECTED REFERENCES: **The Fire From Within - Page [110.8-110.9]** (He also said that the old...pushes it, rather than striking it.)
    SEE ALSO: *ASSEMBLAGE-POINT, LUMINOUS-COCOON, ASSEMBLAGE-POINT-PHYSICAL-BODY-NOT, ENERGY BODY*

ASSEMBLAGE-POINT-MANIPULATING-[MANIPULATING THE ASSEMBLAGE POINT]: SEE: AWARENESS-MANIPULATING-[MANIPULATING AWARENESS]

ASSEMBLAGE-POINT-MOVEMENT-CREATURES-OTHER-[THE MOVEMENT OF THE ASSEMBLAGE POINT IN OTHER CREATURES]: *(Warriors know that the assemblage point in other creatures can move, but that it is not a voluntary thing with them.)*
    SELECTED REFERENCES: **The Fire From Within - Page [137.8-137.9]** (I asked him whether other organisms...not a voluntary thing with them.")
    SEE ALSO: *ASSEMBLAGE-POINT-MOVING*

ASSEMBLAGE-POINT-MOVEMENT-DYING-[ANY MOVEMENT OF THE ASSEMBLAGE POINT IS LIKE DYING]: (Warriors know that any movement of the assemblage point is like dying, because everything in us gets disconnected and then reconnected again to a source of much greater power; that amplification of energy is felt as a killing anxiety.)

SELECTED REFERENCES: The Power of Silence - Page [149.2-149.3] ("Any movement of the assemblage point...is felt as a killing anxiety.")

SEE ALSO: WARRIOR-WORLD-COLLAPSES-REASSEMBLES, ASSEMBLAGE-POINT-MOVING

ASSEMBLAGE-POINT-MOVEMENT-ENERGY-[THE MOVEMENT OF THE ASSEMBLAGE POINT DEPENDS ON ENERGY]: (Warriors know that the movement of the assemblage point depends on an increased energy level, and not on instruction.)

SELECTED REFERENCES: The Power of Silence - Page [158.7-159.1] ("The only concrete help you get from me...increased energy and not on instruction.")

SEE ALSO: ASSEMBLAGE-POINT-MOVING, ENERGY, WARRIOR-IMPECCABILITY, WARRIOR-INSTRUCTION

ASSEMBLAGE-POINT-MOVEMENT-ENERGY-AMPLIFICATION-[THE MOVEMENT OF THE ASSEMBLAGE POINT AND THE AMPLIFICATION OF ENERGY]: SEE: ENERGY-AMPLIFICATION-[THE AMPLIFICATION OF ENERGY]

*ASSEMBLAGE-POINT-MOVEMENT-FREE-[THE FREE MOVEMENT OF THE ASSEMBLAGE POINT]: (Warriors know that the free movement of the assemblage point is the warriors' attainment of "the third point"; split perception.)

SELECTED REFERENCES: The Fire From Within - Page [133.9] ("I used to give you power...that can have a similar effect.) The Power of Silence - Page [161.7-161.8] ("I have insisted to the point...that happens all by itself.") The Power of Silence - Page [224.1-224.3] (Split perception, if accomplished by one's...reaching out for the third point.") The Power of Silence - Page [233.7-233.9] (Don Juan contended that that simple...felt himself running along the riverbank.) The Power of Silence - Page [250.5-251.2] ("But didn't your benefactor tell you...a free movement of his assemblage point.)

SEE ALSO: PERCEPTION-SPLIT, POINT-THIRD, WARRIOR-SPLIT-TWO

ASSEMBLAGE-POINT-MOVEMENT-HUMAN-FORM-LOSING-[THE MOVEMENT OF THE ASSEMBLAGE POINT AND LOSING THE HUMAN FORM]: (Warriors know that by reason of their activities with the warriors' way, at a given moment the assemblage point begins to drift toward the left; this displacement is the beginning of a series of greater shifts and is a permanent move; this initial shift of the assemblage point is called losing the human form and marks the irreversible loss of the warriors' affiliation to the force that makes us persons.)

SELECTED REFERENCES: The Fire From Within - Page [223.2-223.4] (By reason of their activities, at...the force that makes us persons.)

SEE ALSO: ASSEMBLAGE-POINT-MOVING, HUMAN-FORM-LOSING, SHIFT-LEFT

ASSEMBLAGE-POINT-MOVEMENT-IMPECCABILITY-[IMPECCABILITY AND THE MOVEMENT OF THE ASSEMBLAGE POINT]: (Warriors know that in order to command the spirit, or command the movement of the assemblage point, they must have energy; the only thing that stores energy for warriors is impeccability.)

SELECTED REFERENCES: The Power of Silence - Page [228.2-228.3] ("Sorcerers say that in order to...energy for us is our impeccability.")

SEE ALSO: *WARRIOR-IMPECCABILITY, SPIRIT-COMMANDING, ENERGY*

ASSEMBLAGE-POINT-MOVEMENT-INTENDING-[INTENDING THE MOVEMENT OF THE ASSEMBLAGE POINT]: *(Warriors know that they stop their thinking or "stop the world" by intending the movement of the assemblage point; intending the movement of the assemblage point is the warriors' greatest accomplishment.)*

SELECTED REFERENCES: The Fire From Within - Page [117.8-117.9] ("Your assemblage point moved away from...the new seers strive to elucidate.") The Power of Silence - Page [123.9-124.1] ("But how do I stop thinking..."*Intent* is beckoned with the eyes.") The Power of Silence - Page [218.5-218.6] ("*Intending* the movement of your assemblage...the residue sorcerers look forward to.") The Power of Silence - Page [228.2-228.3] ("Sorcerers say that in order to...energy for us is our impeccability.")

SEE ALSO: *INTENDING, ASSEMBLAGE-POINT-MOVING, ASSEMBLAGE-POINT-MOVING-WILL, ASSEMBLAGE-POINT-MOVING-WITHIN, STOPPING-WORLD, WARRIOR-ACCOMPLISHMENT-SUPREME*

ASSEMBLAGE-POINT-MOVEMENT-INTENT-UNBENDING- [UNBENDING INTENT AND THE MOVEMENT OF THE ASSEMBLAGE POINT]: *(Warriors know that moving the assemblage point with unbending intent is the method preferred by warriors.)*

SELECTED REFERENCES: The Power of Silence - Page [220.1-220.2] ("It is," he assured me. "This is...is the preferred method of sorcerers.")

SEE ALSO: *ASSEMBLAGE-POINT-MOVING, INTENT-UNBENDING*

ASSEMBLAGE-POINT-MOVEMENT-INVOLUNTARY-[THE INVOLUNTARY MOVEMENT OF THE ASSEMBLAGE POINT]: *(Warriors know that stresses of various kinds can contribute to an involuntary movement of the assemblage point; the dangerous part about these involuntary movements is that they open warriors to the rolling force, which then cracks the luminous cocoon and opens the warriors' gap; if the shift of the assemblage point is minor, the crack will be very small and will quickly repair itself, leaving warriors "seeing stars" even when their eyes are closed; if the shift is larger, then the crack will also be more extensive and the cocoon will take time to repair itself, leaving warriors feeling numb and somewhat frozen inside; if the shift of the assemblage point is drastic, the rolling force produces a crack the entire length of the cocoon and warriors die as a result.)*

SELECTED REFERENCES: The Fire From Within - Page [225.8-226.7] (He said that a shift of the...on itself, and the individual dies.)

SEE ALSO: *ASSEMBLAGE-POINT-MOVING-STRESS, ROLLING-FORCE, LUMINOUS-COCOON, WARRIOR-SOLIDITY, GAP, ROLLING-FORCE-HANDLING, ASSEMBLAGE-POINT-SHIFT, ASSEMBLAGE-POINT-MOVING, WARRIOR-MOTOR-CONTROL-LOSS-OF*

ASSEMBLAGE-POINT-MOVEMENT-REALITY-[THE REALITY OF THE MOVEMENT OF THE ASSEMBLAGE POINT]: *(Warriors know that they must overcome one of the average man's great flaws, which is to think that the movements of the assemblage point are purely mental occurrences instead of being real energetic events.)*

SELECTED REFERENCES: The Fire From Within - Page [133.8-134.1] ("I used to give you power...It isn't, as you yourself can attest.")

SEE ALSO: *ASSEMBLAGE-POINT-MOVING, MAN-FLAW*

ASSEMBLAGE-POINT-MOVEMENT-SOBRIETY-[SOBRIETY AND THE MOVEMENT OF THE ASSEMBLAGE POINT]: (*Warriors know that sobriety is crucial to dealing with the movement of the assemblage point.*)
SELECTED REFERENCES:: The Power of Silence - Page [58.6-58.8] (Don Juan used to repeat every chance...the moving of the assemblage point.)
SEE ALSO: *WARRIOR-SOBRIETY, ASSEMBLAGE-POINT-MOVING*

ASSEMBLAGE-POINT-MOVEMENT-SORCERER-[THE MOVEMENT OF THE ASSEMBLAGE POINT MAKES ONE A SORCERER]: SEE: SORCERER-ASSEMBLAGE-POINT-MOVEMENT-[THE MOVEMENT OF ASSEMBLAGE POINT MAKES ONE A SORCERER]

ASSEMBLAGE-POINT-MOVEMENT-SORCERY-[ALL SORCERY ACTIVITY IS A CONSEQUENCE OF A MOVEMENT OF THE ASSEMBLAGE-POINT]: (*Warriors know that everything sorcerers do is a consequence of the movement of the assemblage point.*)
SELECTED REFERENCES: The Power of Silence - Page [144.6-144.7] (He then said something which I already...energy sorcerers had at their command.)
SEE ALSO: *SORCERY, ASSEMBLAGE-POINT-MOVING*

ASSEMBLAGE-POINT-MOVEMENT-VOLITIONAL-[THE VOLITIONAL MOVEMENT OF THE ASSEMBLAGE POINT]-(TOP)

ASSEMBLAGE-POINT-MOVEMENT-VOLUNTARY-[THE VOLUNTARY OR VOLITIONAL MOVEMENT OF THE ASSEMBLAGE POINT]: SEE: ASSEMBLAGE-POINT-MOVEMENT-INTENDING-[INTENDING THE MOVEMENT OF THE ASSEMBLAGE POINT]

ASSEMBLAGE-POINT-MOVEMENT-VOLUNTARY-GAP-[THE VOLUNTARY MOVEMENT OF THE ASSEMBLAGE POINT]: (*Warriors know that sometimes even the voluntary movement of the assemblage point can produce a dangerous opening in the gap.*)
SELECTED REFERENCES: The Fire From Within - Page [226.7-226.9] ("Can a voluntary shift of the...it open and makes it collapse.")
SEE ALSO: *ASSEMBLAGE-POINT-MOVING, ASSEMBLAGE-POINT-MOVEMENT-INVOLUNTARY, GAP*

*ASSEMBLAGE-POINT-MOVING-[MOVING THE ASSEMBLAGE POINT]: (*Warriors know that it is possible for the assemblage point to move; the warriors' ability to allow the spirit to move the assemblage point from its usual position on the surface of the luminous cocoon to another position, either on the surface of the cocoon or into the luminous interior; moving the assemblage point is also referred to as "commanding the spirit"; the art of dreaming is concerned with moving the assemblage point; the presence of the nagual induces a movement or shift of the assemblage point.*)
SELECTED REFERENCES: The Fire From Within - Page [118.5-118.9] ("But what is a matter of ...as a consequence of new habits.") The Fire From Within - Page [133.7-133.9] (The explanation behind all these complex...that can have a similar effect.) The Fire From Within - Page [195.4-195.5] (He repeated that in the warrior's way...position which determined what they perceived.) The Fire From Within - Page [283.6-283.7] (He said that now I needed...cease to be what it is to us.) The Power of Silence - Page [xvi.3-xvi.5] (6. The assemblage point can be moved...new energy fields, making them perceivable.) The Power of Silence - Page [xvi.9-xvii.1] (On that practical level don Juan...and stalking, the control of behavior.) The Power of Silence - Page [72.3] (He stressed, over and over, that...or continued moving on into infinity.) The Power of Silence - Page [119.4-119.8] (He replied firmly that my confusion...It is as simple as that.") The Power of Silence - Page [122.1-122.3] (I had asked don Juan how...which had moved those assemblage points.) The Power of Silence - Page [161.7-161.8] ("I have insisted to

the point of exhaustion...an effect that happens all by itself.") **The Power of Silence - Page [219.4]** (It was stupidity that forced us...the fact that it could move.) **The Power of Silence - Page [223.5-223.7]** (I voiced the first question that...spirit which moves their assemblage points.) **The Power of Silence - Page [228.2]** ("Sorcerers say that in order to...the assemblage point, one needs energy.") **The Power of Silence - Page [265.6-265.7]** (Moving the assemblage point is everything...reach the place of silent knowledge.") **The Art of Dreaming - Page [6.8-7.1]** (Finally, they *saw* two things...are perceiving in an unfamiliar manner.) **The Art of Dreaming - Page [8.7-9.5]** (The effect of the assemblage point's...trace of human antecedents in them.) **The Art of Dreaming - Page [11.6-11.7]** ("How is it displaced?" I asked...currents that obey the sorcerer's intent.") **The Art of Dreaming - Page [18.9-19.1]** (Don Juan said that this observation...even knowing it, they created dreaming.) **The Art of Dreaming - Page [21.1-21.3]** (Don Juan told me that what...awareness of the assemblage point's displacement.) **The Art of Dreaming - Page [28.5-28.7]** (When I made your assemblage point shift...to do that at this time.") **The Art of Dreaming - Page [143.9-144.3]** (Yet all this wealth of experience...of the assemblage point ." he said.) **The Art of Dreaming - Page [175.2-175.3]** ("What is going on with me...a fraction of an inch leeway.")

SEE ALSO: *AWARENESS-TRUTH-SEVENTH, DREAMING-ART, DREAMING-VS-STALKING, ASSEMBLAGE-POINT-FIXATION, SPIRIT-COMMANDING, LUMINOUS-COCOON, ASSEMBLAGE-POINT-MOVEMENT-(ALL), ASSEMBLAGE-POINT-MOVING-(ALL)*

ASSEMBLAGE-POINT-MOVING-CONTRADICTION-[THE CONTRADICTION OF MOVING THE ASSEMBLAGE POINT]: *(Warriors know that moving the assemblage point is tremendously difficult and at the same time the easiest thing in the world.; only the spirit can move the assemblage point, but the warriors' feelings, processed into intent can also move the assemblage point.)*

SELECTED REFERENCES: **The Power of Silence - Page [219.9-220.2]** ("But you yourself told me that...is the preferred method of sorcerers.") **The Power of Silence - Page [222.8-222.9]** ("That big cat came out of nowhere...elation, no lesson, no realizations.") **The Power of Silence - Page [223.3-223.9]** (There were a lot of questions I...feature shared by everything there is.")

SEE ALSO: *WARRIOR-CONTRADICTION-KNOWLEDGE, ASSEMBLAGE-POINT-MOVING*

ASSEMBLAGE-POINT-MOVING-DISPLACING-[MOVING OR DISPLACING THE ASSEMBLAGE POINT]-(TOP)

ASSEMBLAGE-POINT-MOVING-DREAMING-[DREAMING MOVES THE ASSEMBLAGE POINT]: *(Warriors know that under normal conditions, dreaming acts to move the assemblage point even more effectively that stalking.)*

SELECTED REFERENCES: **The Fire From Within - Page [172.4-172.6]** (The new seers deemed it imperative to...way to move the assemblage point.) **The Fire From Within - Page [173.4-173.5]** (He remarked that there is hardly...help them move their assemblage points.) **The Power of Silence - Page [35.4-35.6]** ("I've taught you *dreaming* the same...point erratically and lose their minds.")

SEE ALSO: *DREAMING-ART, ASSEMBLAGE-POINT-MOVING, STALKING-ART*

ASSEMBLAGE-POINT-MOVING-EYES-SHINE-[THE SHINE OF THE WARRIORS' EYES MOVES HIS ASSEMBLAGE POINT]: *(Warriors know that they can use the shine of the eyes to intend the movement of the assemblage point.)*

SELECTED REFERENCES: **The Power of Silence - Page [126.1-126.9]** (Ruthlessness makes sorcerers' eyes shine...eyes to move their assemblage points.") **The Power of Silence - Page [130.4-131.4]** (Don Juan began to explain what...is especially true for the naguals.")

SEE ALSO: *WARRIOR-INTENT-BECKON-EYES, EYES-SHINE, ASSEMBLAGE-POINT-MOVEMENT-INTENDING*

ASSEMBLAGE-POINT-MOVING-FURTHER-[THE ASSEMBLAGE POINT CAN ALWAYS MOVE FURTHER]: (Warriors know that no matter how far the assemblage point has moved, it can always move further; this is the only reason that warriors need a teacher, to spur them on mercilessly.)
  SELECTED REFERENCES: **The Power of Silence - Page [249.3-249.5]** ("I can't repeat often enough that...he was, had not spared him.)
  SEE ALSO: *SELF-CONGRATULATING, ASSEMBLAGE-POINT-MOVING, TEACHERS-TEACHING*

ASSEMBLAGE-POINT-MOVING-HABITS-[MOVING THE ASSEMBLAGE POINT THROUGH NEW HABITS]: SEE: ASSEMBLAGE POINT-

MOVING-WILL-[MOVING THE ASSEMBLAGE POINT THROUGH WILL]

ASSEMBLAGE-POINT-MOVING-INTENT-[IT IS INTENT THAT MAKES THE ASSEMBLAGE POINT MOVE]: (Warriors know that since alignment is the force involved with everything, intent is what makes the assemblage point move.)
  SELECTED REFERENCES: **The Fire From Within - Page [258.3-258.5]** (Don Juan had told me then...what makes the assemblage point move.)
  SEE ALSO: *ASSEMBLAGE-POINT-MOVING, INTENT, ALIGNMENT*

ASSEMBLAGE-POINT-MOVING-NORMAL-INSTEAD-HEIGHTENED-AWARENESS-[MAKING THE ASSEMBLAGE POINT MOVE FROM NORMAL AWARENESS INSTEAD OF HEIGHTENED AWARENESS]: SEE: DREAMING-BODY-DEMONSTRATIONS-PURPOSE-[THE PURPOSE OF THE DEMONSTRATIONS OF THE DREAMING BODY]

ASSEMBLAGE-POINT-MOVING-POWER-OBTAINED-[THE POWER OBTAINED BY MOVING THE ASSEMBLAGE POINT]: (Warriors know that the sorcerers of antiquity knew through silent knowledge about the power to be obtained through the movement of the assemblage point; on a reduced scale, warriors of today recapture that power; with a movement of their assemblage points they manipulate their feelings and change things.)
  SELECTED REFERENCES: **The Power of Silence - Page [210.1-210.3]** (He said that men of antiquity became...in that fashion were called *intent*.)
  SEE ALSO: *ASSEMBLAGE-POINT-MOVING, INTENT, KNOWLEDGE-SILENT*

ASSEMBLAGE-POINT-MOVING-SPIRIT-[THE SPIRIT MOVES THE ASSEMBLAGE POINT BY ITSELF]: (Warriors know that when the spirit descends on an individual, its presence alone moves the assemblage point; no procedure can cause the movement of the assemblage point, it is something that happens all by itself; the nagual, being a conduit for the abstract, is allowed to express the spirit and move the assemblage point through his actions; the spirit expresses itself in accordance with the nagual's impeccability; the spirit can move the assemblage point with the mere presence of an impeccable nagual.)
  SELECTED REFERENCES: **The Power of Silence - Page [118.3-118.5]** ("As I have already told you...way, the first principle of sorcery.) **The Power of Silence - Page [119.3-120.3]** (I remarked that his statements that...the spirit move my assemblage point.) **The Power of Silence - Page [122.1-122.5]** (I had asked don Juan how the...the realm where miracles are commonplace.") **The Power of Silence - Page [161.1-161.8]** ("The nagual's presence is enough to...effect that happens all by itself.") **The Power of Silence - Page [162.5-162.9]** (He stated that what seemed a...mere presence of an impeccable nagual.")
  SEE ALSO: *SPIRIT-DESCENT, SPIRIT-CONTACT, SPIRIT, SPIRIT-CONDUIT, NAGUAL-MAN-WOMAN, ASSEMBLAGE-POINT-MOVING*

ASSEMBLAGE-POINT-MOVING-STALKING-[STALKING MOVES THE ASSEMBLAGE POINT]: *(Warriors know that the art of stalking has the effect of moving the stalker's assemblage point in a steady, mild, harmonious, barely noticeable fashion.]*
SELECTED REFERENCES: **The Fire From Within - Page [168.8-169.4]** (Don Juan stopped talking and stared at...made their assemblage points move steadily.) **The Fire From Within - Page [172.1-172.3]** (As soon as the women left...them out became an unbearable burden.) **The Fire From Within - Page [185.7-185.9]** ("By not teaching it in normal awareness...that may be offensive to reason.)
SEE ALSO: *STALKING-ART, ASSEMBLAGE-POINT-MOVING, STALKING-PURPOSE*

ASSEMBLAGE-POINT-MOVING-STRESS-[THE ASSEMBLAGE-POINT MOVES UNDER STRESS]: *(Warriors know that a variety of stressful conditions can contribute to the movement of the assemblage point from its normal position; those conditions include hunger, a moment of tiredness, fever, fright, ill health, anger, grief, mysticism, or the ingestion of power plants.)*
SELECTED REFERENCES: **The Fire From Within - Page [133.8-133.9]** ("I used to give you power...that can have a similar effect.) **The Fire From Within - Page [225.8-226.1]** (He said that a shift of the...as being frightened or being drunk.) **The Power of Silence - Page [210.4-210.7]** (He said that possibly every human being...the prescribed position of normal living.) **The Power of Silence - Page [220.1-220.2]** ("It is," he assured me. "This is...is the preferred method of sorcerers.") **The Power of Silence - Page [228.3-228.5]** (Don Juan remarked that we do...circumstances: craving the return to normalcy.)
SEE ALSO: *ASSEMBLAGE-POINT-SHIFT-MOVEMENT, POWER-PLANTS, CONVENTIONS-BREAKING, ASSEMBLAGE-POINT-MOVEMENT-INVOLUNTARY, ASSEMBLAGE-POINT-MOVING*

ASSEMBLAGE-POINT-MOVING-TECHNIQUES-[THE THREE SETS OF TECHNIQUES FOR MOVING THE ASSEMBLAGE POINT]: *(Warriors know that there are three sets of techniques for moving the assemblage point; these sets of techniques are the three masteries of the warrior and spring from the arrangement of the truths about awareness; these three masteries are the mastery of stalking, the mastery of intent, and the mastery of dreaming; with these three sets of techniques the new seers succeed in accomplishing the extraordinary feat of systematically making the assemblage point shift away from its customary position; the old seers also accomplished this feat but by means of capricious, idiosyncratic maneuvers.)*
SELECTED REFERENCES: **The Fire From Within - Page [167.9-168.5]** ("The most important thing the new seers...the very first day we met.)
SEE ALSO: *WARRIOR-MASTERIES, SEER-NEW, SEER-OLD, ASSEMBLAGE-POINT-MOVING, STALKING-ART, DREAMING-ART, INTENT-MASTERY*

ASSEMBLAGE-POINT-MOVING-VOLITIONAL-[THE VOLITIONAL MOVEMENT OF THE ASSEMBLAGE POINT]-(TOP)

ASSEMBLAGE-POINT-MOVING-WILL-[MOVING THE ASSEMBLAGE POINT AT WILL]: *(Warriors know that only when they learn to intend can they move the assemblage point at will; warriors know that the way to move the assemblage point is to establish new habits; warriors must will their assemblage points to move.)*
SELECTED REFERENCES: **The Fire From Within - Page [199.6-199.8]** ("My great flaw at that time...so that one can celebrate them unbiasedly.") **The Power of Silence - Page [80.5-80.7]** (In a very low voice don Juan...could they move their assemblage point at will.)

SEE ALSO: *ASSEMBLAGE-POINT, WILL, HABITS-UNNECESSARY, ASSEMBLAGE-POINT-MOVING, INTENDING, ASSEMBLAGE-POINT-MOVEMENT-INTENDING*

ASSEMBLAGE-POINT-MOVING-WITHIN-[MOVING THE ASSEMBLAGE POINT FROM WITHIN]: *(Warriors know that it is possible for an impeccable man to move his assemblage point from within.)*

SELECTED REFERENCES: **The Fire From Within - Page [176.3-176.5]** ("The conviction that the new seers have...the possibilities that seers have unraveled.") **The Fire From Within - Page [238.3-238.5]** (I felt a shiver run through my...situation dictate where it should move.) **The Fire From Within - Page [277.1-277.2]** (I realized why he was acting...my assemblage point move by itself.) **The Power of Silence - Page [216.1-216.3]** (I told him everything made sense...to the place of silent knowledge.)

SEE ALSO: *ASSEMBLAGE-POINT-MOVING, IMPECCABILITY-SOBRIETY-ASSEMBLAGE-POINT-MOVE, ASSEMBLAGE-POINT-INTENDING*

ASSEMBLAGE-POINT-MYSTERY-[THE MYSTERY OF THE ASSEMBLAGE POINT: SEE: SORCERY-HINGE-[THE HINGE OF SORCERY]

ASSEMBLAGE-POINT-PHYSICAL-BODY-NOT-[THE ASSEMBLAGE POINT IS NOT PART OF THE PHYSICAL BODY]: *(Warriors know that the assemblage point has nothing to do with what we normally perceive as the physical body; the assemblage point is part of the luminous energy body.)*

SELECTED REFERENCES: **The Art of Dreaming - Page [11.4-11.5]** (In his teachings, he put a...egg, which is our energy self.")

SEE ALSO: *BODY-PHYSICAL, ASSEMBLAGE-POINT, ENERGY-BODY, ASSEMBLAGE-POINT-LUMINOUS-COCOON*

ASSEMBLAGE-POINT-PLANTS-[THE ASSEMBLAGE POINT OF PLANTS]: *(Warriors know that the assemblage points of plants are on the lower part of their luminous cocoons; this low position of the assemblage point makes it easier for them to break the barrier of perception.)*

SELECTED REFERENCES: **The Fire From Within - Page [165.5-166.4]** ("But the real difference between plants...to become trees to do that.")

SEE ALSO: *PLANTS, ASSEMBLAGE-POINT*

ASSEMBLAGE-POINT-POSITION-[THE POSITION OF THE ASSEMBLAGE POINT]-(TOP)

ASSEMBLAGE-POINT-POSITION-ADJUST-[THE NATURAL TENDENCY OF THE ASSEMBLAGE POINT TO ADJUST ITS POSITION TO FIT THOSE AROUND US]: *(Warriors know that the assemblage point naturally adjusts its position to conform with the positions of the assemblage points of those around us; this happens on the right side awareness during ordinary perception and it also happens on the left side during dreaming together.)*

SELECTED REFERENCES: **The Fire From Within - Page [181.9-182.2]** (He added that in *dreaming together,* something...the left side, while *dreaming together.)*

SEE ALSO: *ASSEMBLAGE-POINT-POSITION, AWARENESS-RIGHT, AWARENESS-LEFT, DREAMING-TOGETHER, BLACK MAGICIANS, ASSEMBLAGE-POINT-POSITION-TRAINED-ALL-CREATURES*

ASSEMBLAGE-POINT-POSITION-VS-BEHAVIOR-[THE POSITION OF THE ASSEMBLAGE POINT VS BEHAVIOR]: *(Warriors know that an individual's behavior and perception is directly related to the position of the assemblage point; when the assemblage point is in its habitual position, the behavior of that person appears to be normal; when the position of the*

assemblage point moves, unusual behavior always results from the fact that the individual is then perceiving in an unfamiliar manner.)

    SELECTED REFERENCES: **The Fire From Within** - Page [199.5-199.6] ("What I am trying to do with...how we behave and how we feel.) **The Art of Dreaming** - Page [6.8-7.2] (Finally, they *saw* two things...evidently, the consequent awareness and perception.)

    SEE ALSO: *ASSEMBLAGE-POINT, PERCEPTION, ASSEMBLAGE-POINT-MOVING, AWARENESS-NORMAL, ASSEMBLAGE-POINT-POSITION-NORMAL*

ASSEMBLAGE-POINT-POSITION-DREAMING-BODY-[THE POSITION OF THE ASSEMBLAGE POINT WHERE THE DREAMING BODY APPEARS]: (Warriors know that the dreaming body is a position of the assemblage point.)

    SELECTED REFERENCES: **The Fire From Within** - Page [271.9-272.3] (He repeated over and over that...he said with tremendous urgency.) **The Fire From Within** - Page [275.2-275.7] ("That night, as he had done...in a *dreaming position*," he said.)

    SEE ALSO: *ASSEMBLAGE-POINT-POSITION, DREAMING-BODY*

ASSEMBLAGE-POINT-POSITION-EVERYTHING-[THE POSITION OF THE ASSEMBLAGE POINT IS EVERYTHING]: (Warriors know that the position of the assemblage point is everything and that the world it makes us perceive is so real that it does not leave any room for anything except its realness.)

    SELECTED REFERENCES: **The Fire From Within** - Page [216.2-216.4] (We were coming closer to the main...leave room for anything except realness.)

    SEE ALSO: *ASSEMBLAGE-POINT-POSITION, WORLD-OTHER, REALITY-INTERPRETATION*

ASSEMBLAGE-POINT-POSITION-FOUR-[FOUR POSITIONS OF THE ASSEMBLAGE POINT]: SEE: STALKING-MOODS-FOUR-[THE FOUR MOODS OF STALKING]

ASSEMBLAGE-POINT-POSITION-INFINITE-LEFT-SIDE-[THE INFINITE POSITIONS OF THE ASSEMBLAGE POINT]: (Warriors know that one of the difficulties in remembering what takes place in the left side awareness is the infinite number of positions which the assemblage point can adopt once it has been loosened from its normal position.)

    SELECTED REFERENCES: **The Fire From Within** - Page [184.6-184.7] (Don Juan began his elucidation by...being loosened from its normal setting.)

    SEE ALSO: *ASSEMBLAGE-POINT-POSITION, REMEMBERING-BODY*

ASSEMBLAGE-POINT-POSITION-INTENDING-[INTENDING A NEW POSITION OF THE ASSEMBLAGE POINT]: (Warriors know that in order to assemble another world, they must intend a new position of the assemblage point and intend to keep it in its new position; warriors know that such intending begins with a command given to the self.)

    SELECTED REFERENCES: **The Fire From Within** - Page [289.2-289.4] ("The only force that can temporarily cancel...another world and escape this one.) **The Fire From Within** - Page [297.8-298.2] ("In a moment, you're going to...the moment warriors reach inner silence.)

    SEE ALSO: *INTENDING, WORLD-OTHER, ASSEMBLAGE-POINT-THRESHOLD, WARRIOR-COMMAND, SPIRIT-COMMANDING, ASSEMBLAGE-POINT-POSITION*

ASSEMBLAGE-POINT-POSITION-MAINTENANCE-[THE MAINTENANCE OF THE POSITION OF THE ASSEMBLAGE POINT]: (Warriors know that the position of the assemblage point is maintained by the internal dialogue, and that is why this normal position is flimsy at best.)

SELECTED REFERENCES: **The Fire From Within - Page [154.6-154.7]** ("The position of the assemblage point on...repetitious, boring and without any depth.)
SEE ALSO: *INTERNAL-DIALOGUE, ASSEMBLAGE-POINT-POSITION-NORMAL*

ASSEMBLAGE-POINT-POSITION-MOLD-MAN-[THE POSITION OF THE ASSEMBLAGE-POINT WHERE THE MOLD OF MAN APPEARS]:
(Warriors know that the reason why the new seers recommend that the mold of man be "seen" and understood is because the position of the assemblage point where one "sees" the mold of man is very close to the position where the dreaming body and the barrier of perception appear.)
SELECTED REFERENCES: **The Fire From Within - Page [269.5-269.6]** (He said that the position where one...of man be *seen* and understood.) **The Fire From Within - Page [271.9-272.4]** (He repeated over and over that...in order to assemble another world.)
SEE ALSO: *MOLD-MAN, DREAMING-BODY, PERCEPTION-BARRIER, ASSEMBLAGE-POINT-POSITION*

ASSEMBLAGE-POINT-POSITION-NEW-[THE ASSEMBLAGE POINT'S NEW POSITION]: *(Warriors know that when they store enough energy to catch a glimpse of the unknown, that increased level of energy will create a new spot to house the assemblage point.)*
SELECTED REFERENCES: **The Fire From Within - Page [153.7-153.8]** ("It's all very simple," don Juan...together will solidify that new position.")
SEE ALSO: *ASSEMBLAGE-POINT-POSITION, ENERGY, WARRIOR-IMPECCABILITY, WARRIOR-EVICTION-NOTICE*

ASSEMBLAGE-POINT-POSITION-NORMAL-[THE NORMAL POSITION OF THE ASSEMBLAGE POINT]: *(Warriors know that the assemblage point remains fixed in its normal position during the entire life of most human beings.)*
SELECTED REFERENCES: **The Art of Dreaming - Page [5.9-6.1]** (In the course of his teachings...of a person's right shoulder blade.) **The Art of Dreaming - Page [6.8-6.9]** (Finally, they *saw* two things...behavior of the subjects being observed.) **The Art of Dreaming - Page [75.8-76.6]** (Don Juan changed the subject and...are fixed on the same spot.) **The Art of Dreaming - Page [211.2-211.4]** ("I understand all that," he said...the total value you're talking about.)
SEE ALSO: *ASSEMBLAGE-POINT, AWARENESS-NORMAL, ATTENTION-FIRST, ASSEMBLAGE-POINT-POSITION*

ASSEMBLAGE-POINT-POSITION-NORMAL-ARBITRARY-[THE NORMAL POSITION OF THE ASSEMBLAGE POINT IS AN ARBITRARY ONE THAT REQUIRES STEADY REINFORCEMENT]: *(Warriors know that the normal position of the assemblage point is an arbitrary one which requires steady and constant reinforcement; the exact position of the assemblage point was chosen for us by our ancestors, but warriors know that the assemblage point can move from that spot with relatively little effort.)*
SELECTED REFERENCES: **The Fire From Within - Page [132.7-133.8]** (The internal dialogue is a process that...alignments of emanations, thus new perceptions.)
SEE ALSO: *ASSEMBLAGE-POINT-POSITION-NORMAL, POINT-FIRST, POINT-THIRD, POINT-THIRD-INVERSION, HABITUATION, ASSEMBLAGE-POINT-MOVING, MAN-ANCIENT, ASSEMBLAGE-POINT-POSITION-NOT-PERMANENT, ASSEMBLAGE-POINT-POSITION*

ASSEMBLAGE-POINT-POSITION-NORMAL-LOCATION-[THE LOCATION OF THE ASSEMBLAGE POINT]: *(Warriors know that the assemblage point is normally lodged permanently inside the luminous cocoon, flush with its surface, about two feet back from the crest of the right*

shoulder blade; this normal position allows for the alignment of emanations which are perceived as the first attention, the world of men; the assemblage point is located high up, three-fourths of the way toward the top of the luminous egg on the surface of the luminous cocoon.)

SELECTED REFERENCES: The Fire From Within - Page [122.2] ("The assemblage point of man is located...on the surface of the cocoon.)

SEE ALSO: *ASSEMBLAGE-POINT, ASSEMBLAGE-POINT-POSITION-NORMAL, ASSEMBLAGE-POINT-POSITION*

ASSEMBLAGE-POINT-POSITION-NORMAL-NOT-PERMANENT-[THE HABITUAL LOCATION OF THE ASSEMBLAGE POINT IS NOT A PERMANENT FEATURE]: *(Warriors know that one of the most important breakthroughs of the new seers was finding out that the habitual location of the assemblage point is not a permanent feature, but that it is established on that specific spot by habit.)*

SELECTED REFERENCES: The Fire From Within - Page [118.3-118.4] (He affirmed that one of the most...arrive at new usages, new habits.) The Fire From Within - Page [154.5-154.9] ("The position of the assemblage point...lose anything, they lose their dimple.")

SEE ALSO: *ASSEMBLAGE-POINT-POSITION-NORMAL, ASSEMBLAGE-POINT-MOVING, ASSEMBLAGE-POINT-POSITION-NORMAL-ARBITRARY*

ASSEMBLAGE-POINT-POSITION-NORMAL-RETURN-[THE ASSEMBLAGE POINT RETURNS TO ITS NORMAL POSITION]: *(Warriors know that under normal circumstances the assemblage point always returns to its original position; if it doesn't, individuals are then either incurably crazy [because they can never again assemble the world as we know it], or they become peerless seers who have begun an inexorable movement towards the unknown; when the assemblage point moves through stress, it is our academic, religious and social backgrounds that come into play; they assure our safe return to the flock by returning the assemblage point to the prescribed position of normal living.)*

SELECTED REFERENCES: The Fire From Within - Page [120.3-120.8] (He said that two options are...with their friends or with strangers.") The Power of Silence - Page [210.5-210.8] (He said that possibly every human...the prescribed position of normal living.) The Power of Silence - Page [259.3-259.5] (Don Juan understood with perfect clarity...would return to its point of departure.)

SEE ALSO: *ASSEMBLAGE-POINT-MOVING, INSANITY, SEER, UNKNOWN, CONVENTIONS-BREAKING, ASSEMBLAGE-POINT-POSITION, MAN-EVOLUTION*

ASSEMBLAGE-POINT-POSITION-OPTIMUM-[THE OPTIMUM POSITION OF THE ASSEMBLAGE POINT]: *(Warriors know that the position of the assemblage point which allows them to move the energy body is the optimum position of the assemblage point.)*

SELECTED REFERENCES: The Art of Dreaming - Page [161.3-163.7] (He explained that since everything related...body curtailed its obsession with detail.")

SEE ALSO: *ENERGY-BODY-MOVING, ASSEMBLAGE-POINT, DREAMING-BODY, ASSEMBLAGE-POINT-POSITION, ASSEMBLAGE-POINT-SHIFT-PERMANENT*

ASSEMBLAGE-POINT-POSITION-PERCEPTION-[PERCEPTION AND THE POSITION OF THE ASSEMBLAGE POINT]: *(Warriors know that they must come to the irrational but coherent realization that everything in the world they have learned to perceive is inextricably tied to the position of the assemblage point; perception is the hinge for everything that man is or does and perception is ruled by the position of the assemblage point; the*

most sophisticated knowledge that warriors possess is that the content of perception depends on the position of the assemblage point.)

SELECTED REFERENCES: **The Fire From Within** - Page [283.5-283.7] (He said that now I needed...cease to be what it is to us.) **The Power of Silence** - Page [56.9-57.2] ("I don't quite understand what you're...assemblage point could become anything he wanted.) **The Power of Silence** - Page [145.2-145.3] (He emphasized over and over that...the position of the assemblage point.)

SEE ALSO: *PERCEPTION, ASSEMBLAGE-POINT-POSITION*

ASSEMBLAGE-POINT-POSITION-PERCEPTION-BARRIER-[THE POSITION OF THE ASSEMBLAGE POINT WHERE THE BARRIER OF PERCEPTION APPEARS]: (Warriors know that the barrier of perception is a position of the assemblage point.)

SELECTED REFERENCES: **The Fire From Within** - Page [271.9-272.4] (He repeated over and over that...in order to assemble another world.)

SEE ALSO: *ASSEMBLAGE-POINT-POSITION, PERCEPTION-BARRIER*

ASSEMBLAGE-POINT-POSITION-RATIONALITY-[THE POSITION OF THE ASSEMBLAGE POINT WHERE RATIONALITY APPEARS]: (Warriors know that rationality is a condition of alignment, a result of a position of the assemblage point.)

SELECTED REFERENCES: **The Fire From Within** - Page [282.3-282.6] (He explained that I had to...as long as the emotion lasts.)

SEE ALSO: *ASSEMBLAGE-POINT-POSITION, REASON*

ASSEMBLAGE-POINT-POSITION-RECOIL-[THE RECOIL OF THE POSITION OF THE ASSEMBLAGE POINT]: (Warriors know that they must be alert for the recoil of the assemblage point; once the assemblage point has begun to solidify itself into its new position it has a tendency to periodically return to its old position; this recoil is a drawback which warriors must be prepared for.)

SELECTED REFERENCES: **The Fire From Within** - Page [153.7-155.1] ("It's all very simple," don Juan...added, of them again howled with laughter.)

SEE ALSO: *ASSEMBLAGE-POINT-POSITION-NEW, ASSEMBLAGE-POINT-POSITION-RETURN-NORMAL, ASSEMBLAGE-POINT-POSITION*

ASSEMBLAGE-POINT-POSITION-STABILITY-[THE STABILITY OF THE ASSEMBLAGE POINT]: SEE: ASSEMBLAGE-POINT-STABILITY-[THE STABILITY OF THE ASSEMBLAGE POINT]

ASSEMBLAGE-POINT-POSITION-TRAINED-ALL-CREATURES-[THE ASSEMBLAGE POINT IS TRAINED TO APPEAR IN THE POSITION THAT IT DOES IN ALL CREATURES]: (Warriors know that the assemblage point in all creatures, including man, is trained to appear where it does; every newborn organism is trained and coaxed to do what its own kind does; the presence of adults acts to fasten the shifting assemblage point of a newborn to a single spot.)

SELECTED REFERENCES: **The Fire From Within** - Page [137.9-138.3] ("Is the assemblage point of other organisms...same happens to every other organism.)

SEE ALSO: *SEE-CHILDREN, INFANTS-INTERNAL-DIALOGUE, ASSEMBLAGE-POINT-POSITION-ADJUST*

ASSEMBLAGE-POINT-POSITION-SORCERER-TRANSFORMATION-[THE ASSEMBLAGE POINT AND THE SORCERERS' TRANSFORMATIONS]: SEE: SORCERER-TRANSFORMATION-[THE SORCERERS' TRANSFORMATION]

ASSEMBLAGE-POINT-POSITIONS-[POSITIONS OF THE ASSEMBLAGE POINT]: SEE: SORCERER-OPTIONS-[THE SORCERERS' OPTIONS]

ASSEMBLAGE-POINT-PUSHING-[PUSHING THE ASSEMBLAGE POINT]: (*Warriors know that pushing the assemblage point is another term for the way one warrior can move the assemblage point of another more deeply into the left side, once it has been jolted out of its position by the nagual's blow; if the assemblage point is pushed by someone who can "see" it and has enough energy to move it, it slides within the cocoon to whatever position the pusher directs.*)

SELECTED REFERENCES: The Fire From Within - Page (110.8-111.1) (He also said that the old...the air out of the lungs.) The Fire From Within - Page [115.6-115.8] ("Genaro has something to tell you...it had been a bit dangerous.) The Fire From Within - Page [117.7-117.9] ("Genaro again pushed your assemblage point...the new seers strive to elucidate.") The Fire From Within - Page [122.2-123.2] ("The assemblage point of man is located...ends up is always virgin ground.) The Fire From Within - Page [131.3-131.5] (While we were having lunch the...point fixed to its original position.) The Fire From Within - Page [145.5-145.6] (Genaro turned to me and assured me...and let them fend for themselves.) The Fire From Within - Page [165.7-166.4] (He added that the old seers were...to become trees to do that.") The Fire From Within - Page [275.2-275.7] ("That night, as he had done...in a *dreaming position*," he said.) The Power of Silence - Page [58.1-58.8] (Don Juan used to repeat every chance...the moving of the assemblage point.) The Power of Silence - Page [68.1-68.2] ("Of course," he replied with a grin...but are very difficult to arrange.") The Power of Silence - Page [72.3-72.5] (He said that heightened awareness was...from which there is no return.")

SEE ALSO: NAGUAL-BLOW, ASSEMBLAGE-POINT-MOVING, WARRIOR-SHOVE

ASSEMBLAGE-POINT-REALITY-[THE ASSEMBLAGE POINT AND REALITY]: SEE: REALITY-INTERPRETATION-[REALITY IS AN INTERPRETATION WE MAKE]

ASSEMBLAGE-POINT-RECORDS-[RECORDS OF THE ASSEMBLAGE POINT]: (*Warriors know that sorcerers are capable of leaving accurate records in the position of the assemblage point; these records are complete and can be relived instead of being simply read.*)

SELECTED REFERENCES: The Art of Dreaming - Page [145.5-146.2] (My discomfort was so great that...an accomplishment of the highest magnitude.)

SEE ALSO: INFORMATION-EXPERIENCE-STORAGE, RECOLLECTION-SORCERER

ASSEMBLAGE-POINT-RIGIDITY-[THE RIGIDITY OF THE ASSEMBLAGE POINT]: (*Warriors know that the power of reason and self-absorption tend to keep the assemblage point rigid; when warriors' assemblage points begin to lose their rigidity, warriors think they are losing their minds, but in reality they know that all they are really losing is the self-reflection of their inventory; the inability of the assemblage point to have a minimal margin of flexibility; the flexibility of the assemblage point is essential to the survival of sorcerers, so they must overcome whatever conditioning has resulted in the assemblage point's rigidity; warriors overcomes this rigidity with sheer understanding.*)

SELECTED REFERENCES: The Fire From Within - Page [119.6-121.3] ("The new seers realized the true...than if you had kept it.") The Fire From Within - Page [123.4-123.6] (He went on to say that the...point shift is a genuine triumph.) The Art of Dreaming - Page [75.4-75.8] (I asked don Juan about this...know, to discover, to be bewildered.")

SEE ALSO: ASSEMBLAGE-POINT-FIXATION, ASSEMBLAGE-POINT-FLUIDITY, UNDERSTANDING-SHEER, INSANITY, INVENTORY, REASON, SELF-ABSORPTION

ASSEMBLAGE-POINT-SECRETS-*[THE SECRETS OF THE ASSEMBLAGE-POINT]*: *(Warriors know that now, more than ever, man needs to be taught the secrets of the assemblage point.)*
    SELECTED REFERENCES: The Power of Silence - Page [228.9-229.2] (He said that man needs now...the secrets of the assemblage point.)
    SEE ALSO: *AWARENESS-TRUTHS, ASSEMBLAGE-POINT, MAN-NEEDS*

ASSEMBLAGE-POINT-SHIFT-*[THE SHIFT OF THE ASSEMBLAGE POINT]*: *SEE: ASSEMBLAGE-POINT-MOVING-[MOVING THE ASSEMBLAGE POINT], ASSEMBLAGE-POINT-SHIFT (ALL)*

ASSEMBLAGE-POINT-SHIFT-ERRATIC-*[THE ERRATIC SHIFT OF THE ASSEMBLAGE POINT]*: *SEE: SEX-ENERGY-CONSERVING [CONSERVING SEXUAL ENERGY]*

ASSEMBLAGE-POINT-SHIFT-GRAND-*[A GRAND SHIFT OF THE ASSEMBLAGE POINT]*: *SEE: ASSEMBLAGE-POINT-SHIFT-MOVEMENT-[A SHIFT VS A MOVEMENT OF THE ASSEMBLAGE POINT]*

ASSEMBLAGE-POINT-SHIFT-IMPERCEPTIBLE-*[THE IMPERCEPTIBLE SHIFTS OF THE ASSEMBLAGE POINT]*: *(Warriors know that the assemblage point is always shifting to imperceptible degrees and that in order for it to shift to precise spots, warriors must engage intent.)*
    SELECTED REFERENCES: **The Power of Silence - Page [125.4-125.5]** ("Our assemblage points are constantly shifting...sorcerers let their eyes beckon it.") **The Art of Dreaming - Page [70.9-71.2]** (My nervousness made it impossible for...was so simple it was ridiculous.)
    SEE ALSO: *ASSEMBLAGE-POINT, ASSEMBLAGE-POINT-MOVING, INTENDING*

ASSEMBLAGE-POINT-SHIFT-LATERAL-*[LATERAL SHIFTS OF THE ASSEMBLAGE POINT]*: *(Warriors know that lateral shifts of the assemblage point are superficial shifts of that point along one or both edges of man's band of emanations [the human junk pile]; a minimal shift of the assemblage point which is experienced as a fantasy or a hallucination; interim or "lateral" alignments which the assemblage point makes as it approaches a crucial position of total reassembly; the preamble of the unknown; what makes the assemblage point move laterally is a nearly unavoidable desire to render the incomprehensible in terms of what is familiar to us.)*
    SELECTED REFERENCES: **The Fire From Within - Page [134.3-134.8]** ("Those visions are the product of...considerable, the results are called hallucinations.") **The Fire From Within - Page [293.2-293.3]** ("The wall of fog, the plain...as they approach a crucial position.") **The Fire From Within - Page [248.7-248.8]** (Don Juan explained that since he...and their allies as they are.) **The Fire From Within - Page [250.6-250.9]** (Don Juan left me alone in the...be a bit dizzy, even drunk.") **The Fire From Within - Page [267.8-268.2]** (I asked him why it was...see the mold as a woman.)
    SEE ALSO: *ASSEMBLAGE-POINT, ASSEMBLAGE-POINT-MOVING, PARALLEL-LINES-LAND, HUMAN-JUNKPILE, MOLD-MAN, WORLD-APPARITIONS, UNKNOWN-PREAMBLE, SLEEP, WARRIOR-DIALOGUE*

ASSEMBLAGE-POINT-SHIFT-LATERAL-BYPASSING-*[BYPASSING ALL LATERAL SHIFTS OF THE ASSEMBLAGE POINT]*: *(Warriors know that in order to assemble another total world they must bypass all lateral shifts of the assemblage point and move beyond a certain threshold at the midline of the luminous cocoon.)*

SELECTED REFERENCES: The Fire From Within - Page [295.2-295.3] ("I want you to bypass all...it in order to escape death.")
SEE ALSO: *ASSEMBLAGE-POINT-SHIFT-LATERAL, WORLD-OTHER-ASSEMBLING, ASSEMBLAGE-POINT-THRESHOLD, EAGLE-EMANATIONS-MAN-BAND-MIDSECTION*

ASSEMBLAGE-POINT-SHIFT-LEFT-[THE SHIFT TO THE LEFT]: SEE: SHIFT-LEFT-[THE SHIFT TO THE LEFT]

ASSEMBLAGE-POINT-SHIFT-MINUTE-VS-GROSS-[MINUTE SHIFTS VS GROSS SHIFTS OF THE ASSEMBLAGE POINT]: *(Warriors know that the subtle transformations of sorcerers require magnificent control of the assemblage point and the keenest knowledge of human nature; more gross shifts of the assemblage point to the positions of animals, for instance, do not require the same subtlety and finesse on the sorcerer's part.)*

SELECTED REFERENCES: The Power of Silence - Page [57.2-57.4] ("The nagual Julian's proficiency in moving...the keenest knowledge of human nature.")
SEE ALSO: *ANIMAL-FORMS-ADOPTING, SORCERER-TRANSFORMATION, WARRIOR-FINESSE, ASSEMBLAGE-POINT-MOVING*

ASSEMBLAGE-POINT-SHIFT-VS-MOVEMENT-[A SHIFT VS A MOVEMENT OF THE ASSEMBLAGE POINT]: *(Warriors know the significant difference between a "shift" and a "movement" of the assemblage point; a "shift" is a minimal movement of the assemblage point within man's band of emanations, and a "movement" is a profound change of position so extreme that the assemblage point might even reach one of the other great bands of emanations; a shift of the assemblage point is a displacement to any position on the surface or into the interior of the luminous ball; a movement of the assemblage point is a displacement to a position outside the luminous ball; the difference between these two kinds of displacements lies in the nature of the perception that each allows; the worlds engendered by shifts of the assemblage point remain part of the human domain, no matter how bizarre or unbelievable they may be; the worlds engendered by movements of the assemblage point are completely beyond the human realm and include the seven totally alien worlds which man is capable of assembling.)*

SELECTED REFERENCES: The Power of Silence - Page [220.4-220.7] (Don Juan then made a meaningful...perceived as the world of everyday life.) The Art of Dreaming - Page [9.1-9.5] (Don Juan explained that the old...trace of human antecedents in them.) The Art of Dreaming - Page [70.3-70.5] ("Do I really maintain a new...all of them is a triumph.") The Art of Dreaming - Page [217.4-218.5] (Don Juan further explained that most...closer to the old sorcerers' mood.)
SEE ALSO: *ASSEMBLAGE-POINT-MOVING, ASSEMBLAGE-POINT-SHIFT-LATERAL, SHIFT-LEFT, WORLDS-OTHER-ASSEMBLE-TOTAL*

ASSEMBLAGE-POINT-SHIFT-NEED-IMPERATIVE-[THE IMPERATIVE NEED TO SHIFT THE ASSEMBLAGE POINT]: *(Warriors know that at some hidden level, they have an imperative need to shift the assemblage point, a need which will eventually serve as a launcher into the unknown.)*

SELECTED REFERENCES: The Fire From Within - Page [290.2-290.3] (He said that I could not as...to serve me as a launcher.)
SEE ALSO: *DREAMING-TRAVELING-GUIDE, IMPECCABLE-MAN-NO GUIDE, ASSEMBLAGE-POINT-MOVING*

ASSEMBLAGE-POINT-SHIFT-PERMANENT-[THE PERMANENT SHIFT OF THE ASSEMBLAGE POINT]: (*Warriors know the importance of not allowing the assemblage point to shift permanently to any position other than that of heightened awareness.*)
    SELECTED REFERENCES: The Fire From Within - Page [298.5-299.2] (He explained that the old seers...but to choose total consciousness, total freedom.)
    SEE ALSO: *AWARENESS-HEIGHTENED, ASSEMBLAGE-POINT-POSITION-OPTIMUM*

ASSEMBLAGE-POINT-SHIFT-ROLLING-FORCE-[THE SHIFT OF THE ASSEMBLAGE POINT AND OPENING ONESELF TO THE ROLLING FORCE]: SEE: ROLLING-FORCE-HANDLING-[HANDLING THE ROLLING FORCE]

ASSEMBLAGE-POINT-SHIFT-SUDDEN-[A SUDDEN SHIFT OF THE ASSEMBLAGE POINT]: SEE: AWARENESS-GLOW-SHIFT-SUDDEN-[A SUDDEN SHIFT IN THE GLOW OF AWARENESS]

ASSEMBLAGE-POINT-SPRINGBOARD-[THE SPRINGBOARD OF THE ASSEMBLAGE POINT]: (*Warriors know that the energy which they conserve through the curtailment of self-reflection is the springboard that launches the assemblage point on an inconceivable journey.*)
    SELECTED REFERENCES: The Power of Silence - Page [159.6-159.7] (He explained that the specific sequence...without premeditation, into an inconceivable journey.)
    SEE ALSO: *ENERGY, SELF-REFLECTION, THOUGHT-SOMERSAULT, ASSEMBLAGE-POINT-SHIFT-NEED-IMPERATIVE, WARRIOR-IMPECCABILITY*

ASSEMBLAGE-POINT-STABILITY-[THE STABILITY OF THE ASSEMBLAGE POINT]: (*Warriors know that one of the primary purposes of the new seers' teachings is to enable the apprentice's assemblage point to move and then reinforce its stability in that new position.*)
    SELECTED REFERENCES: The Fire From Within - Page [266.9-267.9] (He remarked that the value of...and shifted laterally in man's band.)
    SEE ALSO: *ASSEMBLAGE-POINT-RIGIDITY, DREAMING-ART, STALKING-ART, WARRIOR-EQUILIBRIUM*

ASSEMBLAGE-POINT-THRESHOLD-[THE THRESHOLD OF THE ASSEMBLAGE POINT]: (*Warriors know that there is a threshold of the assemblage point beyond which a seer is able to assemble entirely new worlds; this threshold is reached when enough energy is stored for the assemblage point to move deep enough into man's band to use another of the great bands of emanations; this threshold is associated with the midline of the luminous cocoon; the threshold of the assemblage point is at the limit of the known.*)
    SELECTED REFERENCES: The Fire From Within - Page [164.5-164.8] (He said that a true change...and consequently we perceive other worlds.") The Fire From Within - Page [283.5-283.9] (He said that now I needed...all there is to our world.) The Fire From Within - Page [293.1-293.3] ("It's the easiest world to assemble...as they approach a crucial position.") The Fire From Within - Page [298.5-298.7] (He explained that the old seers...or perhaps they never wanted to.) The Fire From Within - Page [299.3-299.4] (He explained that the new seers...emanations inside the cocoon at once.)
    SEE ALSO: *EAGLE-EMANATIONS-MAN-BAND, ASSEMBLAGE-POINT-MOVING, WORLD-OTHER, THRESHOLD-NO-RETREAT, WORLDS-OTHER-ASSEMBLE-TOTAL, ASSEMBLAGE-POINT-SHIFT-VS-MOVEMENT*

ASSEMBLAGE-POINT-WALKING-[WALKING THE ASSEMBLAGE POINT]: *(Warriors know that walking the assemblage point is simply the lateral shifting of the assemblage point triggered by the gait of power and the disconnecting effects of inner silence; hooking the force of alignment on the edges of man's band of emanations [the human junk pile] or on one of the other great bands of emanations available to the warrior.)*

SELECTED REFERENCES: **The Fire From Within - Page [133.5-133.7]** (He said that in the light...walk away with one's assemblage point.) **The Fire From Within - Page [134.7-135.2]** ("One of the easiest things one can...so as to give a complete view of that human junk pile.") **The Fire From Within - Page [207.4-209.4]** (Genaro stood up and started doing...I had comprehended a great truth.) **The Fire From Within - Page [275.2-275.7]** ("That night, as he had done...in a *dreaming position*," he said.)

SEE ALSO: *ASSEMBLAGE-POINT-SHIFT-LATERAL, HUMAN-JUNKPILE, GAIT-POWER, INNER-SILENCE*

ASSISTANT-STALKER-CLASSIFICATION-ONE-[THE ASSISTANT CLASSIFICATION OF PERSONALITY]: SEE: PEOPLE-TYPES-[THE STALKERS' CLASSIFICATIONS OF PERSONALITY TYPES

ASSUMPTIONS-RATIONAL-[RATIONAL ASSUMPTIONS]: SEE: IMPECCABILITY-STATE-OF-BEING-[AN IMPECCABLE STATE OF BEING]

ASSURANCE-WARRIOR-[THE WARRIORS' ASSURANCE]: SEE: WARRIOR-ASSURANCE-[THE WARRIORS' ASSURANCE]

ASSUREDNESS-WARRIOR-[THE WARRIORS' ASSUREDNESS]: SEE: WARRIOR-ASSUREDNESS-[THE WARRIORS' ASSUREDNESS]

ATLANTEANS-[THE ATLANTEANS]: *(Warriors know that the Atlanteans are a row of four colossal column-like figures of stone which stand on the flat top of a pyramid in the midst of some archaeological ruins in the city of Tula, Hidalgo, Mexico; for warriors these ruins represent a colossal example of the aberrant fixation of the second attention.)*

SELECTED REFERENCES: **The Eagle's Gift - Page [9.8-10.5]** (They wanted to know what I...going to that town scares me.")

SEE ALSO: *PYRAMIDS, TOLTECS, ABERRATION-MORBIDITY, ATTENTION-SECOND-FACES-TWO, ATLANTEANS-(ALL)*

ATLANTEANS-EXPLANATION-CARLOS-[AN EXPLANATION OF THE ATLANTEANS]: *(Carlos Castaneda's explanation of the Atlanteans walking at night.)*

SELECTED REFERENCES: **The Eagle's Gift - Page [26.6-27.4]** (I explained to them at great length...then the Atlanteans would walk at night.)

SEE ALSO: *PYRAMIDS, TOLTECS, ATTENTION-SECOND-FACES-TWO*

ATLANTEANS-TALES-[TALES OF THE ATLANTEANS]-(TOP)

ATTAINMENTS-WARRIOR-[THE WARRIORS' ATTAINMENTS]: SEE: WARRIOR-ATTAINMENTS-[THE WARRIORS' ATTAINMENTS]

ATTENTION-[ATTENTION]: *(Warriors know that attention is that with which we hold our images of the world; attention is the harnessing and enhancing of awareness through the process of being alive; the end product of maturation, refined from the raw material of awareness; attention has three levels of attainment, three independent domains [the first, second and third attentions]; perception and awareness are a single, functional, inextricable unit that is also called attention.)*

SELECTED REFERENCES: **The Second Ring of Power** - Page [247.1-247.7] (Her laughter was clear and contagious...or by gazing at the clouds.) **The Second Ring of Power** - Page [306.5-306.7] (Don Juan had asserted time and...disengaging the attention of the tonal.) **The Eagle's Gift** - Page [18.4-18.7] (In order to explain these concepts,...physical and the luminous bodies.) **The Eagle's Gift** - Page [141.1-141.2] (The Nagual said that attention is...He had reasons to say that.) **The Fire From Within** - Page [63.9-64.1] (Suddenly, don Juan began his explanation...and complex, which seers call attention.) **The Fire From Within** - Page [64.4-64.7] (Seers, witnessing an enhancement of this...the whole scope of human possibilities.) **The Fire From Within** - Page [65.3-65.4] ("Seers say that there are three...an independent domain, compete in itself.)

SEE ALSO: *ATTENTION-FIRST, ATTENTION-SECOND, ATTENTION-THIRD, ATTENTION-(ALL)*

ATTENTION-ART-[THE ART OF ATTENTION]: *(Warriors know that the art of attention is the art of the dreamer.)*

SELECTED REFERENCES: **The Second Ring of Power** - Page [274.3-274.4] ("The Nagual told us to show...dreamer is the art of attention.") **The Second Ring of Power** - Page [275.8-276.2] (What don Juan struggled to vanquish...hold the images of any dream.")

SEE ALSO: *DREAMER-ART, ATTENTION, DREAMER-GLANCE*

ATTENTION-AWARENESS-ENHANCEMENT-[ATTENTION IS THE ENHANCEMENT OF AWARENESS]: *(Warriors know that attention is the enhancement and harnessing of awareness through the process of being alive.)*

SELECTED REFERENCES: **The Fire From Within** - Page [64.4-64.5] ("How do seers describe attention...process of being alive," he replied.)

SEE ALSO: *ATTENTION, AWARENESS, SKIMMINGS*

ATTENTION-BECKONING-POWER-[THE BECKONING POWER OF ATTENTION]: *(Warriors know that attention in general [and the second attention in particular] has the power to beckon things to us; this is an unnoticed property so taken for granted in daily life that its results are often referred to as accidents or coincidences.)*

SELECTED REFERENCES: **The Eagle's Gift** - Page [139.3-139.5] (Don Juan also told us that... our attention having beckoned the event.)

SEE ALSO: *OMENS, INDICATIONS-SPIRIT, WARRIOR-INTENT-BECKONS-EYES, ATTENTION-SECOND-BECKONER*

ATTENTION-DOMAINS-TWO-[THE TWO DOMAINS OF ATTENTION]: *(Warriors know that perception and awareness are a single, functional, inextricable unit that is also called attention; attention has two domains, the attention of the tonal and the attention of the nagual.)*

SELECTED REFERENCES: **The Second Ring of Power** - Page [274.8-278.2] (Don Juan said that the core of...and that pathway is through "dreaming.") **The Second Ring of Power** - Page [306.5-306.7] (Don Juan had asserted time and...disengaging the attention of the tonal.)

SEE ALSO: *ATTENTION-TONAL, ATTENTION-NAGUAL, ATTENTION, PERCEPTION, AWARENESS, POWER-RING-FIRST, POWER-RING-SECOND, ATTENTION-FIRST, ATTENTION-SECOND, ATTENTION-THIRD*

ATTENTION-DOUBLE-[THE ATTENTION OF THE DOUBLE]: SEE: DOUBLE-ATTENTION-[THE ATTENTION OF THE DOUBLE]

ATTENTION-DREAMING-[THE DREAMING ATTENTION]: *(Warriors know that the dreaming attention is the door to the second attention; the second attention is like an ocean and the dreaming attention is like a river feeding into it; the second attention is the condition of being aware of total*

worlds, while the dreaming attention is the condition of being aware of the items of one's dreams; the warriors' ability to fixate the assemblage point on any new position to which it has been displaced in dreaming; an incomprehensible facet of awareness that exists by itself, waiting for the warrior to entice it and give it purpose; the dreaming attention is the door to the second attention, and is the key to every movement in the sorcerers' world; the mastery of the dreaming attention is an awakening, something dormant in the warrior suddenly becomes functional; the dreaming attention comes from an area behind the roof of the mouth.)

SELECTED REFERENCES: **The Eagle's Gift - Page [138.9-139.1]** (Don Juan explained to us...turn an ordinary dream into *dreaming*.) **The Art of Dreaming - Page [16.7-17.1]** (Don Juan then gave me a...an enormous number of new positions.) **The Art of Dreaming - Page [22.3-22.5]** (Don Juan described the dreaming attention...opportunity to use in everyday life.) **The Art of Dreaming - Page [28.7-29.1]** ("And how! Dreaming is a very sober...every movement in the sorcerers' world.) **The Art of Dreaming - Page [34.4-34.6]** (Don Juan stated that as we tighten...awakening. Something dormant suddenly becomes functional.) **The Art of Dreaming - Page [35.9-36.2]** (I realized, almost as soon as...impact, and the dreaming attention blooms.) **The Art of Dreaming - Page [37.2-37.4]** (Every time he had an opportunity...existing energy, by any means available.) **The Art of Dreaming - Page [95.5-95.7]** (The most vital piece of information...normal attention to the daily world.) **The Art of Dreaming - Page [169.8-170.3]** ("You want to know where your...that it resembles an ordinary dream.)

SEE ALSO: *DREAMING-ART, ATTENTION-SECOND, ATTENTION-DREAMING-(ALL)*

ATTENTION-DREAMING-NEEDED-[THE ATTENTION NEEDED FOR DREAMING]: *(Warriors know that in men, the attention needed for dreaming stems from the area at the tip of the sternum, at the top of the belly; in women that attention originates from the womb.)*

SELECTED REFERENCES: **The Eagle's Gift - Page [136.2-136.4]** (Later on, when I had succeeded...for dreaming originate from the womb.) **The Eagle's Gift - Page [138.9-139.1]** (Don Juan explained to us...turn an ordinary dream into *dreaming*.)

SEE ALSO: *ATTENTION-DREAMING, ATTENTION, WOMB*

ATTENTION-DREAMING-SELF-IMPORTANCE-[SELF-IMPORTANCE AND THE DREAMING ATTENTION]: *(Warriors know that the emergence of the dreaming attention is directly proportional to the extent to which warriors redeploy their energetic resources; the best means of oiling the wheels of this redeployment is the process of losing self-importance.)*

SELECTED REFERENCES: **The Art of Dreaming - Page [37.2-37.9]** (Every time he had an opportunity...the actual grandeur of the universe.)

SEE ALSO: *SELF-IMPORTANCE-LOSING, ATTENTION-DREAMING, ENERGY, WARRIOR-IMPECCABILITY*

ATTENTION-DREAMING-WORLDS-[THE WORLDS OF THE DREAMING ATTENTION]: *(Warriors know that the worlds of the dreaming attention are worlds that sorcerers conjure up exclusively in the realm of their dreaming; the images of those worlds have no life beyond the dreamers' dreaming attention.)*

SELECTED REFERENCES: **The Art of Dreaming - Page [167.5-167.6]** (What does that mean...life only in your dreaming attention.")

SEE ALSO: *ATTENTION-DREAMING, WOMAN-CHURCH-(TOP)*

*ATTENTION-FIRST-[THE FIRST ATTENTION]: *(Warriors know that the first attention is the utilization of emphasized emanations from the narrow band where man's awareness is normally located; the glow of awareness fixed on the surface of man's luminous cocoon; the right side; normal*

awareness; the tonal; this world of solid objects; the known; animal awareness; reality; the description of the world; everything we are as average men; everything we think about; the attention of the tonal.)

SELECTED REFERENCES: The Eagle's Gift - Page [18.4-18.5] (In order to explain these concepts...the awareness of the physical body.) The Eagle's Gift - Page [20.4-21.8] (I could not, for instance, recall...They won't let you live in peace.") The Eagle's Gift - Page [141.5] ("This is the way I understand it...body has stored enough of it.") The Fire From Within - Page [65.5-65.7] (He explained that the first attention...it is even our only asset.) The Fire From Within - Page [66.2] ("In terms of what seers see...a glow that covers the known.) The Fire From Within - Page [76.1-76.2] ("I was explaining about the first...doesn't exist for the first attention.") The Fire From Within - Page [79.2] ("When the new seers arranged the...iota of energy is left free.") The Fire From Within - Page [109.5-109.8] (Don Juan explained that in order...calls it reality, rationality, common sense.) The Art of Dreaming - Page [16.8-17.1] (He pointed out that sorcerers really...an enormous number of new positions.)

SEE ALSO: AWARENESS-RIGHT, TONAL, KNOWN, REALITY-INTERPRETATION, ATTENTION-TONAL, AWARENESS-NORMAL-(ALL), ATTENTION-FIRST-(ALL)

ATTENTION-FIRST-BODY-PHYSICAL-[THE FIRST ATTENTION BELONGS TO THE PHYSICAL BODY]: (Warriors know that the first attention belongs to the physical body in the same way the second attention belongs to the luminous body.)

SELECTED REFERENCES: The Eagle's Gift - Page [252.8] (Zuleica must have seen what I...attention belongs to the physical body.)
SEE ALSO: ATTENTION-FIRST, BODY-PHYSICAL

ATTENTION-FIRST-COMPLACENCY-[THE COMPLACENCY OF THE FIRST ATTENTION]: SEE: COMPLACENCY-FIRST-ATTENTION-[THE COMPLACENCY OF THE FIRST ATTENTION]

ATTENTION-FIRST-ENTANGLEMENT-OBSESSIVE-[THE OBSESSIVE ENTANGLEMENT OF THE FIRST ATTENTION IN REASON OR SELF-ABSORPTION]: SEE: ATTENTION-FIRST-REASON-SELF-ABSORPTION-[THE OBSESSIVE ENTANGLEMENT OF THE FIRST ATTENTION IN REASON OR SELF-ABSORPTION]

ATTENTION-FIRST-FIXATION-[THE FIXATION OF THE FIRST ATTENTION]: (Warriors know that the fixation of the average man's first attention cannot be shut off while he is awake, and that that fixation acts as an interference to dreaming; warriors do what they can to minimize this interference and to overcome the fixation of their own first attention.)

SELECTED REFERENCES: The Eagle's Gift - Page [138.5-138.9] (Another topic of great significance was the...of those around us is dormant.)
SEE ALSO: INTERNAL-DIALOGUE-STOPPING, STOPPING-WORLD, DREAMING-TIME, BLACK-MAGICIANS

ATTENTION-FIRST-FOCUS-[THE FOCUS OF THE FIRST ATTENTION]: (Warriors know that the first attention is trained to focus doggedly, for that is how we maintain the world; the focus of the first attention can be on something in the world of solid objects or on simply an abstract proposition of reasonableness; the first attention has been taught to focus with great force on the items of the world in order to turn the chaotic realm of perception into the orderly world of awareness.)

SELECTED REFERENCES: The Eagle's Gift - Page [35.8-35.9] ("Our attention is trained to focus...instance, but rather propositions of reasonableness.) The Eagle's Gift - Page [139.1-139.2] (He explained, furthermore, that in dreaming...into the orderly world of awareness.)

SEE ALSO: *ATTENTION-FIRST, TONAL, DESCRIPTION-WORLD, ORDER-CHAOS, REASON*

ATTENTION-FIRST-GLOW-[THE GLOW OF THE FIRST ATTENTION]:
(Warriors know that the first attention is the glow of awareness developed to an ultra shine; it is a glow fixed on the surface of the luminous cocoon; the glow of the first attention covers the known.)
SELECTED REFERENCES: The Fire From Within - Page [66.2-66.3] ("In terms of what seers *see*...glow that covers the known.)
SEE ALSO: *ATTENTION-FIRST, AWARENESS-GLOW, ATTENTION-SECOND-GLOW, ATTENTION-THIRD-GLOW*

ATTENTION-FIRST-INTENT-ABANDON-[ABANDONING THE INTENT OF THE FIRST ATTENTION]: (Warriors know that in order to enter fully into the other self they must abandon the intent of the first attention at the moment of crossing.)
SELECTED REFERENCES: The Eagle's Gift - Page [301.7-301.8] (My mind was in a state...the *intent* of their first attention.)
SEE ALSO: *ATTENTION-FIRST, OTHER-SELF-ABANDON, WARRIOR-CROSSING-FREEDOM, ABANDON*

ATTENTION-FIRST-KNOWN-[THE FIRST ATTENTION WORKS ONLY WITH THE KNOWN]: (Warriors know that the first attention limits itself to working with only the known; it does everything possible to block and deny the existence of the unknown or the nagual.)
SELECTED REFERENCES: The Fire From Within - Page [76.1-76.3] ("I was explaining about the first attention...into existence in the first place.)
SEE ALSO: *ATTENTION-FIRST, KNOWN, UNKNOWN, INVENTORY, ATTENTION-TONAL*

ATTENTION-FIRST-ORDER-[THE ORDER OF THE FIRST ATTENTION]:
(Warriors know that the order of their perception belongs exclusively to the realm of the first attention, or to the realm of the tonal; warriors understand that stalkers represent the order of the tonal, the order of the first attention; they are peaceful and wise.)
SELECTED REFERENCES: Tales of Power - Page [173.7-174.1] ("Another thing one should do when facing...safeguard the order of the *tonal*.) Tales of Power - Page [196.2-196.3] ("An immortal being has all...a little time on this earth.") Tales of Power - Page [283.9-284.1] ("I must also add that few...is a most unappealing affair.) The Second Ring of Power - Page [1.7-1.9] (In my jump my perception went through...I had visions of order.) The Eagle's Gift - Page [15.4-15.7] ("The Atlanteans are the nagual; they...the opposite of the front row.")
SEE ALSO: *ATTENTION-FIRST, ORDER-CHAOS, ORDER-UNIVERSE, WARRIOR-ORDER, STALKING-ART, TONAL, ATLANTEANS*

ATTENTION-FIRST-REASON-SELF-ABSORPTION-[THE OBSESSIVE ENTANGLEMENT OF THE FIRST ATTENTION IN REASON OR SELF-ABSORPTION]: (Warriors know that the obsessive entanglement of the first attention in reason or self-absorption is a powerfully binding force; warriors must distract the first attention from its obsession with its inventory in order to free the assemblage point so it can move.)
SELECTED REFERENCES: The Fire From Within - Page [119.6-120.1] ("The new seers realize the true...the assemblage point loses its rigidity.)
SEE ALSO: *ATTENTION-FIRST, REASON, SELF-ABSORPTION, INVENTORY, OBSESSION, KNOWN-OBSESSIVE-MANIPULATION*

ATTENTION-FOCUSING-WOMB-[LEARNING TO FOCUS ATTENTION ON THE WOMB]: SEE: WOMB-[WOMB]

ATTENTION-HEIGHTENED-TEMPORARY-[TEMPORARY HEIGHTENED AWARENESS]: (Warriors know that the glow of awareness created by the luminous dent should rightfully be called temporary heightened attention because it emphasizes emanations that are so proximal to the habitual ones that the change is minimal; this shift of the assemblage point is significant enough, however, to produce in the warrior a greater capacity to understand and concentrate and above all, a greater capacity to forget.)

SELECTED REFERENCES: **The Fire From Within - Page [112.8-113.3]** (He said that the glow of awareness...which the experiences are immediately forgotten.)

SEE ALSO: *ATTENTION, AWARENESS-HEIGHTENED, LUMINOUS-DENT, FORGET-COMMAND, ASSEMBLAGE-POINT-SHIFT-LATERAL*

ATTENTION-IMMOBILIZING-[IMMOBILIZING ATTENTION]: SEE: ATTENTION-DREAMING-[THE DREAMING ATTENTION]

ATTENTION-NAGUAL-[THE ATTENTION OF THE NAGUAL]: (Warriors know that the attention of the nagual is the second attention; the second ring of power; the warriors' capacity to place awareness on the non-ordinary world; the attention under the table.)

SELECTED REFERENCES: **The Second Ring of Power - Page [275.2-275.5]** (The second domain was the "attention...or the "attention of the nagual.") **The Second Ring of Power - Page [277.8-279.1]** (Don Juan said that our "first ring...make it into an encumbering production.) **The Second Ring of Power - Page [282.3-282.5]** ("What's dona Soledad going to do...attention faster than any of us.) **The Second Ring of Power - Page [291.1-291.3]** (The Nagual said that death pushes...for that center to push out.") **The Second Ring of Power - Page [293.2-293.5]** (Since it was unthinkable to tackle the immensity...only after the warriors had swept the top of their tables clean.) **The Second Ring of Power - Page [293.8-293.9]** ("The attention under the table is...you were taught about power plants.)

SEE ALSO: *ATTENTION-SECOND, POWER-RING-SECOND, ATTENTION-NAGUAL, AWARENESS-LEFT, NAGUAL*

ATTENTION-PREREQUISITE-[THE PREREQUISITE TO ENTER ANY OF THE THREE STAGES OF ATTENTION]: (Warriors know that the possession of the life force is the prerequisite to entering any of the three stages of attention; without it, warriors have no direction or purpose.)

SELECTED REFERENCES: **The Eagle's Gift - Page [247.7-247.9]** (He told me that I had...just before the Eagle devours it.)

SEE ALSO: *ATTENTION-FIRST, ATTENTION-SECOND, ATTENTION-THIRD, LIFE-FORCE*

*ATTENTION-SECOND-[THE SECOND ATTENTION]: (Warriors know that the second attention is the utilization of normally unused emanations inside man's luminous cocoon; a more specialized state of the glow of awareness resulting from the utilization of unused emanations inside man's luminous cocoon; left side awareness; the nagual; the other world; the unknown; the attention of the nagual; the battlefield of the warrior; the training ground for the third attention.)

SELECTED REFERENCES: **The Second Ring of Power - Page [326.7-327.3]** ("Yes we will go as we...focus indefinitely on anything we wanted.) **The Eagle's Gift - Page [13.5-13.9]** ("He said that she no longer...there is nothing more horrendous.") **The Eagle's Gift - Page [18.5-18.7]** (Another larger portion he called the...the awareness of the physical and luminous bodies.) **The Eagle's Gift - Page [27.1-27.4]** (I said that the custodian who...the Atlanteans would walk at night.) **The Eagle's Gift - Page [135.7-135.8]** (The residue of consciousness, which don Juan...harnessed through exercises of *not-doing*.) **The Eagle's Gift - Page [138.9-139.3]** (This lead to his description of the...possibility of getting the desired result.) **The Eagle's Gift - Page [140.9-143.4]** ("I think the Nagual must have told...command it, to make it do things.) **The Fire From Within - Page [66.3-66.9]** ("The second attention, on the other...and its lure nearly irresistible.") **The Fire From Within - Page [109.9-110.1]** (The disregarded emanations within man's band...world, the unknown, the second attention.) **The Power of Silence - Page [101.3-101.4]** (I remembered at that moment scores...the counterpart of my normal attentiveness.) **The Art of Dreaming - Page [vii.9-viii.1]** (Don Juan was indeed an intermediary...the supernatural but the second attention.) **The Art of Dreaming - Page [15.9-16.1]** (This was the first time, in my...state he called the second attention.) **The Art of Dreaming - Page [28.8-29.1]** ("What's the difference between the dreaming...aware of the items of our dreams.") **The Art of Dreaming - Page [37.8-37.9]** (One, we would free our energy...the actual grandeur of the universe.) **The Art of Dreaming - Page [51.7-51.9]** (In this fashion, he divided me...surround and insulate the second attention.)

SEE ALSO: *AWARENESS-LEFT, NAGUAL, UNKNOWN, ATTENTION-NAGUAL, WARRIOR-BATTLEFIELD, AWARENESS-HEIGHTENED, ATTENTION-SECOND-(ALL)*

ATTENTION-SECOND-ANTITHETICAL-[THINGS THAT ARE ANTITHETICAL TO THE SECOND ATTENTION]: *(Warriors know not to practice dreaming in flat areas or by rivers, lakes or the sea, because water and flat areas are antithetical to dreaming.)*

SELECTED REFERENCES: **The Eagle's Gift - Page [249.7-249.9]** (Zuleica told me that if dreaming...were antithetical to the second attention.)

SEE ALSO: *DREAMING-ART, DREAMING-TECHNIQUES, ATTENTION-SECOND-(ALL), ATTENTION-DREAMING*

ATTENTION-SECOND-ASSEMBLING-[ASSEMBLING THE SECOND ATTENTION]: *(Warriors know that assembling the second attention is a process connected to the secret of the formless Toltec dreamers; the movement of the opening of the crack between the world acts to assemble the second attention.)*

SELECTED REFERENCES: **The Second Ring of Power - Page [298.7-298.9]** ("Did he disappear like that...Toltec dreamers once they are formless.")

SEE ALSO: *TOLTEC-SECRET-DREAMERS-FORMLESS, ATTENTION-SECOND, CRACK-WORLDS, DOOR-ONLY*

ATTENTION-SECOND-BALANCING-[BALANCING THE SECOND ATTENTION]: *(Warriors know that if they have used power plants to gather their second attention, they must eventually balance the second attention in order to survive; power plants gather the first face of the second attention, the menacing side; dreaming is the only way to gather the second attention without injuring it.)*

SELECTED REFERENCES: **The Second Ring of Power - Page [284.9-287.2]** ("And this brings me to the next...them you'd be a great warrior.")

SEE ALSO: *ATTENTION-SECOND-TRAPPING, POWER-PLANTS, GAZING, DREAMING-ART*

ATTENTION-SECOND-BECKONER-[THE SECOND ATTENTION IS THE BECKONER OF CHANCES]: *(Warriors know that the second attention serves the function of beckoner, the caller of chances; the more the second attention is exercised, the greater the possibility of getting the desired result.)*

ATTENTION-SECOND-BECOMING-ALL-[BECOMING ALL SECOND ATTENTION]: *(Warriors know that when the physical body, or the first attention becomes the second attention, it simply goes into the other world; warriors becomes all second attention when they leave the world as they are, with their bodies and the totality of their being.)*

SELECTED REFERENCES: **The Second Ring of Power - Page [326.5-327.3]** ("The Nagual told us that our...focus indefinitely on anything we wanted.)

SEE ALSO: *ATTENTION-SECOND, ATTENTION-FIRST, BODY-PHYSICAL, EAGLE-GIFT, TOTALITY, FREEDOM-TOTAL*

SELECTED REFERENCES: The Eagle's Gift - Page [139.2-139.4] (Don Juan also told us that...attention having beckoned the event.)
SEE ALSO: *ATTENTION-SECOND, ATTENTION-BECKONING-POWER*

ATTENTION-SECOND-CENTER-STROKING-[STROKING THE CENTER OF ASSEMBLAGE FOR THE SECOND ATTENTION-(TOP)

ATTENTION-SECOND-COLLAPSING-BOUNDARY-[COLLAPSING THE BOUNDARY OF THE SECOND ATTENTION]: (Warriors know that as they continue on the path of knowledge and begin to more fully exercise their sorcerers' recollections, the boundary of the second attention begins to collapse and cause them a great deal of first attention confusion and distress.)

SELECTED REFERENCES: The Art of Dreaming - Page [183.7-184.5] (At home, I soon realized that...of mind can awareness be enhanced.")
SEE ALSO: *ATTENTION-SECOND, RECOLLECTION-SORCERER*

ATTENTION-SECOND-DENT-[THE DENT OF THE SECOND ATTENTION]-(TOP): SEE: DENT-LUMINOUS-[THE LUMINOUS DENT]-(TOP)

ATTENTION-SECOND-DOOR-[THE DOOR TO THE SECOND ATTENTION]: SEE: ATTENTION-DREAMING [THE DREAMING ATTENTION]

ATTENTION-SECOND-FACES-TWO-[THE TWO FACES OF THE SECOND ATTENTION]: (Warriors know there are two "faces" of the second attention; the first and easiest face is the aberrant face, the face resulting from the focus of dreaming on items of the world; the second is the more difficult face resulting from the focus of dreaming on items neither in nor from this world.)

SELECTED REFERENCES: The Second Ring of Power - Page [284.9-285.9] ("And this brings me to the next thing...sing to it to calm it down.) The Second Ring of Power - Page [314.4-314.6] (That was the alternative of power...The second face was the second attention.) The Eagle's Gift - Page [19.9-20.2] ("The Nagual said that the fixation of the second...impeccability in order to reach this face.") The Eagle's Gift - Page [20.3-21.8] (I could not, for instance, recall...won't let you live in peace.") The Eagle's Gift - Page [22.7-22.9] ("It is easy for me to...he was protecting my *dreaming body*.")
SEE ALSO: *ABERRATION-MORBIDITY, POWER-OBJECTS, OBSESSION, ATTENTION-SECOND-FIXATION*

**ATTENTION-SECOND-FIXATION-[THE FIXATION OF THE SECOND ATTENTION]:* (Warriors know that the fixation of the second attention is the uncontrolled focus of the second attention.)

SELECTED REFERENCES: The Eagle's Gift - Page [17.6-17.8] ("Then another kind of warrior must have...they did, it was too late.") The Eagle's Gift - Page [19.9-20.4] ("The Nagual said that the fixation...the fixation of attention in general.) The Eagle's Gift - Page [21.6-21.8] ("When you worry about what to...won't let you live in peace.") The Eagle's Gift - Page [26.4-27.4] (I then told them that I had...the Atlanteans would walk at night.) The Eagle's Gift - Page [141.8-142.4] (Next he recommended that I should...focuses on anything, one loses control.)
SEE ALSO: *ATTENTION-SECOND, ABERRATION-MORBIDITY, OBSESSION, ATLANTEANS, ATTENTION-SECOND-FACES-TWO*

ATTENTION-SECOND-FORERUNNER-[THE FORERUNNER OF THE SECOND ATTENTION]: SEE: DREAMING-SETTING-UP [SETTING UP DREAMING]

ATTENTION-SECOND-GATHERING-[GATHERING THE SECOND

ATTENTION]: SEE: ATTENTION-SECOND-TRAPPING-[TRAPPING THE SECOND ATTENTION]

ATTENTION-SECOND-GLOW-[THE GLOW OF THE SECOND ATTENTION]: (Warriors know that the second attention is a more specialized state of the glow of awareness; it is a glow that has to do with the unknown, with the unused emanations inside man's cocoon.)
SELECTED REFERENCES: **The Fire From Within - Page [66.3-66.5]** ("The second attention, on the other...that require supreme discipline and concentration.")
SEE ALSO: *ATTENTION-SECOND, AWARENESS-GLOW, ATTENTION-FIRST-GLOW, ATTENTION-THIRD-GLOW*

ATTENTION-SECOND-HANDLING-WITHOUT-PREPARATION-[HANDLING THE SECOND ATTENTION WITHOUT PREPARATION]-(TOP)

ATTENTION-SECOND-INTENDING-[INTENDING IN THE SECOND ATTENTION]: (Warriors know the secret of the twin positions; when dreamers fall asleep in a first dream and then dream again, the second dream is intending in the second attention; the only way to cross the fourth gate of dreaming; intending in the second attention allows the dreamer to transcend time and move forward or backward on the universe's luminous filaments of energy.)
SELECTED REFERENCES: **The Art of Dreaming - Page [248.8-249.3]** (Carol paused and asked me whether...cross the fourth gate of dreaming.") **The Art of Dreaming - Page [253.3-253.5]** ("Your energy body is moving forward...In a time yet to come.") **The Art of Dreaming - Page [254.1-254.4]** (Carol laughed, undisturbed by my accusation...but then the vortex swallowed me.) **The Art of Dreaming - Page [258.1-258.9]** (What he was saying had no meaning...of that maneuver and much more.")
SEE ALSO: *POSITIONS-TWIN, DREAMING-GATE-FOURTH, INTENT-FLYING-WINGS, INTENT-PROJECTION, TIME*

ATTENTION-SECOND-INTRICACIES-[THE INTRICACIES OF THE SECOND ATTENTION]: SEE: UNKNOWN-INTRICACIES-[THE INTRICACIES OF THE UNKNOWN]

ATTENTION-SECOND-JOLT-[THE JOLT OF THE SECOND ATTENTION]: (Warriors know it is not unusual for them to lose control of their motor and speech control as a result of contact with the second attention.)
SELECTED REFERENCES: **The Art of Dreaming - Page [244.3-244.4]** ("When did I lose my motor control...your speech or of your limbs.")
SEE ALSO: *ATTENTION-SECOND, SORCERER-MUTENESS, WARRIOR-MOTOR-CONTROL-LOSS-OF*

ATTENTION-SECOND-LUMINOUS-BODY-[THE SECOND ATTENTION BELONGS TO THE LUMINOUS BODY]: (Warriors know that the second attention belongs to the luminous body in the same way the first attention belongs to the physical body.)
SELECTED REFERENCES: **The Eagle's Gift - Page [252.8]** (Zuleica must have seen what I...attention belongs to the physical body.)
SEE ALSO: *ATTENTION-SECOND, LUMINOUS-BODY-FEATURES, ENERGY-BODY, DREAMING-BODY*

ATTENTION-SECOND-LURE-[THE LURE OF THE SECOND ATTENTION]: (Warriors know that the lure of the second attention is nearly irresistible, it requires all of the warriors' sobriety and discipline to overcome it's powerful pull.)

SELECTED REFERENCES: **The Fire From Within - Page [48.7]** (Female warriors in particular fall prey...too soon for their own good. **The Fire From Within - Page [66.7-67.2]** (He said that the second attention...the quagmire of the second attention.)

SEE ALSO: *ATTENTION-SECOND, INORGANIC-BEINGS-TRICKERY, INORGANIC-BEINGS REFUSING*

ATTENTION-SECOND-MANAGING-[MANAGING THE SECOND ATTENTION]: SEE: ATTENTION-SECOND-MASTERY [THE MASTERY OF THE SECOND ATTENTION]

ATTENTION-SECOND-MASTERY-[THE MASTERY OF THE SECOND ATTENTION]: (Warriors know they must gain mastery over the second attention or they are merely witnessing acts of power; without mastery of the second attention, warriors cannot claim knowledge as power, they cannot perform with it.)

SELECTED REFERENCES: **The Second Ring of Power - Page [286.7-287.2]** ("Sure. By the time Eligio had to...them you'd be a great warrior.") **The Second Ring of Power - Page [289.4-289.6]** ("How can I do that...the two, as you are now.) **The Second Ring of Power - Page [322.9-323.4]** ("It's very hard to get into...we have absolute control over it.")

SEE ALSO: *ATTENTION-SECOND-BALANCING, ATTENTION-SECOND, POWER-ACTS, KNOWLEDGE-CLAIMING-POWER*

ATTENTION-SECOND-ORDER-[THE ORDER OF THE SECOND ATTENTION]: (Warriors know that the second attention is the portentous ability all human beings have, but only sorcerers use, to impart order to the nonordinary world; warriors know that dreamers represent the order of the nagual, the order of the second attention brought forward; they are fearsome and mysterious; they are creatures of war but not of destruction.)

SELECTED REFERENCES: **The Second Ring of Power - Page [275.2-275.4]** (The second domain was the...impart order to the nonordinary world.) **The Eagle's Gift - Page [15.5-15.7]** ("The Atlanteans are the nagual; they...the opposite of the front row.")

SEE ALSO: *ATTENTION-SECOND, ATTENTION-FIRST-ORDER, POWER-RING-SECOND, DREAMING-ART, NAGUAL, ATLANTEANS*

ATTENTION-SECOND-PERCEPTUAL-BIAS-[THE PERCEPTUAL BIAS OF THE SECOND ATTENTION]: (Warriors know that through their dreaming they learn the perceptual bias of the second attention; learning about this perceptual bias is a step toward the control of the second attention.)

SELECTED REFERENCES: **The Eagle's Gift - Page [265.4-265.7]** (Don Juan said that my journeys...me that his reluctance was functional.)

SEE ALSO: *ATTENTION-SECOND, DREAMING-ART, DREAMER-GLANCE*

ATTENTION-SECOND-PROGRESSION-[THE SECOND ATTENTION AS A PROGRESSION]: (Warriors know that the second attention evolves as a specific progression; it begins as an idea, a curiosity, then it turns into a sensation that can only be felt; finally, it becomes a state of being, a realm of practicalities, a preeminent force that opens the world beyond the warriors' wildest fantasies.)

SELECTED REFERENCES: **The Art of Dreaming - Page [20.7-20.8]** (As a preamble to his first...us worlds beyond our wildest fantasies.) **The Art of Dreaming - Page [21.1-21.3]** (Don Juan told me that what...awareness of the assemblage point's displacement.)

SEE ALSO: *UNKNOWN-JOURNEY, DREAMING-ART*

ATTENTION-SECOND-QUAGMIRE-[THE QUAGMIRE OF THE SECOND ATTENTION]: (*Warriors know that the second attention is a field so vast that it seems limitless; it is a quagmire so complex that sober seers only enter it under the strictest of circumstances; warriors also know that the lure of the left-side awareness is nearly irresistible and that without exercising the ultimate sobriety it is easy to become lost in the quagmire of the second attention.*)

SELECTED REFERENCES: **The Fire From Within - Page [66.7-67.2]** (He said that the second attention...the quagmire of the second attention.) **The Fire From Within - Page [83.9-84.1]** (They considered flames and fluidity to...a quagmire with no way out.) **The Fire From Within - Page [132.9-133.2]** ("But would it be possible to encourage...being caught in the clutches of rationality.") **The Fire From Within - Page [167.5-167.9]** (As we walked, don Juan told...scorn and reject their own tradition.)

SEE ALSO: *ATTENTION-SECOND-INTRICACIES, WARRIOR-SOBRIETY, INORGANIC-BEINGS-TRICKERY, UNKNOWN-INTRICACIES*

ATTENTION-SECOND-ROUNDING-UP-[ROUNDING UP THE SECOND ATTENTION]: SEE: ATTENTION-SECOND-TRAPPING-[TRAPPING THE SECOND ATTENTION]

ATTENTION-SECOND-SPINNING-[SPINNING WITH THE SECOND ATTENTION]: (*Warriors know that spinning with the second attention is another term for the activation of the second attention.*)

SELECTED REFERENCES: **The Second Ring of Power - Page [285.2]** (He said that that's what happens...that comes out of their heads.) **The Second Ring of Power - Page [289.4-289.9]** ("How can I do that...is hidden, waiting for that day.)

SEE ALSO: *ALLIES-SPINNING, ATTENTION-SECOND*

ATTENTION-SECOND-TAKING-CONTROLS-[EXPERIENCING THE SECOND ATTENTION TAKING OVER THE CONTROLS]-(TOP)

ATTENTION-SECOND-TRAPS-[THE TRAPS OF THE SECOND ATTENTION]: SEE: PYRAMIDS-[PYRAMIDS AND TOLTEC RUINS]

ATTENTION-SECOND-TRAPPING-[TRAPPING THE SECOND ATTENTION]: (*Warriors know that trapping the second attention is a process necessary to the art of dreaming; a process accomplished through a variety of activities or influences including power plants, not-doing, dreaming or gazing; liquor or madness can also act to gather or trap the second attention.*)

SELECTED REFERENCES: **Tales of Power - Page [160.1-160.5]** (I told him that my reaction...This is a terrible way of being.") **Tales of Power - Page [239.3-239.4]** ("A teacher must not leave anything...trap it as the case required.") **The Second Ring of Power - Page [289.2-289.6]** (That's perfect. That will give us...the two, as you are now.) **The Second Ring of Power - Page [293.8-294.2]** ("The attention under the table is...before they can trap their second attention.) **The Second Ring of Power - Page [295.5]** ("Everything the Toltecs do is very simple...the world by gazing at dry leaves.) **The Second Ring of Power - Page [301.6-301.7]** ("First of all, before I say...for the little sisters and me.") **The Second Ring of Power - Page [302.3]** (She hoped that by gazing at it...to round up my second attention.) **The Second Ring of Power - Page [304.7-304.8]** (She said that the Nagual used to make...of the jolt the body suffered.) **The Second Ring of Power - Page [322.9-323.4]** ("It's very hard to get into...we have absolute control over it.") **The Second Ring of Power - Page [323.5-324.7]** ("The Nagual told me," la Gorda...he had an awesome, fearsome side.") **The Second Ring of Power - Page [325.8-325.9]** (So, when it was time for...and focused it on that world.) **The Second Ring of Power - Page [326.6-326.9]** ("Do you mean, Gorda, that we...vision, perhaps for a whole eternity.")

SEE ALSO: *ATTENTION-SECOND-FIXATION, GAZING, DREAMING-ART, ATTENTION-TRAPPING*

ATTENTION-SECOND-WEAKENING-[THE WEAKENING OF THE SECOND ATTENTION]: (*Warriors know that in the hands of the sorcerers of antiquity, the handling of the second attention became debased and vitiated; aberration and morbidity weakened the second attention instead of strengthening it; without controls and without restraint, the second attention became weaker by virtue of its increased intricacy.*)

SELECTED REFERENCES: **The Eagle's Gift** - Page [187.1-187.6] (The second topic was the cultural context...under the harshest conditions of suppression.)

SEE ALSO: *ATTENTION-SECOND-FACES-TWO, ABERRATION-MORBIDITY, OBSESSION, SORCERER-ANTIQUITY, WARRIOR-SELF-RESTRAINT, WARRIOR-CONTROL, WARRIOR-SOBRIETY*

ATTENTION-TABLE-OVER-[THE ATTENTION OVER THE TABLE]: SEE: ATTENTION-TONAL-[THE ATTENTION OF THE TONAL], TABLE-WILDERNESS-[THE TABLE IN THE WILDERNESS]

ATTENTION-TABLE-UNDER-[THE ATTENTION UNDER THE TABLE]: SEE: ATTENTION-NAGUAL-[THE ATTENTION OF THE NAGUAL], TABLE-WILDERNESS-[THE TABLE IN THE WILDERNESS]

*ATTENTION-THIRD-[THE THIRD ATTENTION]: (*Warriors know that the third attention is the largest portion of attention; an immeasurable consciousness which engages undefinable aspects of awareness; to extend the glow of awareness beyond the bounds of the luminous cocoon in one single stroke; the somersault of thought into the inconceivable; total awareness; the unknowable; the totality of the self; total freedom; the Eagle's gift; an alternate way of dying; to burn with the fire from within.*)

SELECTED REFERENCES: **The Eagle's Gift** - Page [17.7-17.8] ("The Nagual believed that the new...the fixation of the second attention.) **The Eagle's Gift** - Page [18.6-18.9] (He called the last portion, which...at, but very fruitful once attained.) **The Eagle's Gift** - Page [178.8-179.5] (Don Juan explained that the rule was...the reality of the third attention.) **The Eagle's Gift** - Page [210.4-210.7] (Don Juan explained to me at...to enter into the third attention.) **The Eagle's Gift** - Page [219.6] (Don Juan said that his benefactor...group, however, but one by one.) **The Eagle's Gift** - Page [247.6-247.9] (He told me that I had...just before the Eagle devours it.) **The Eagle's Gift** - Page [273.9-274.2] (The Next time don Juan took...I saw the wall of fog.) **The Eagle's Gift** - Page [301.8-301.9] (Once they were in the awareness of...apprentices were in their normal awareness.) **The Fire From Within** - Page [66.9-67.9] (He said that the old seers...to the Eagle's beak to be devoured.") **The Fire From Within** - Page [113.9-114.1] (Yet it is nothing in comparison...emanations extend themselves beyond anything imaginable.) **The Fire From Within** - Page [123.3] ("The grand test that the new...is called regaining the totality of oneself.") **The Fire From Within** - Page [127.8] (Don Juan had defined the scope...when they attain total awareness.) **The Fire From Within** - Page [183.9-184.1] ("At any rate, the job of realigning...we will all be gone in an instant.") **The Power of Silence** - Page [112.6-112.8] ("Sorcerers defeat death and death acknowledges...somersault into the inconceivable," he said.)

SEE ALSO: *THOUGHT-SOMERSAULT, FREEDOM-TOTAL, AWARENESS-TOTAL, FIRE-WITHIN, EAGLE-GIFT, UNKNOWABLE, ATTENTION-THIRD-GLOW, WARRIOR-THIRD-ATTENTION*

ATTENTION-THIRD-GLOW-[THE GLOW OF THE THIRD ATTENTION]: (*Warriors know that the third attention is attained when the glow of awareness becomes the fire from within; this glow kindles not just one band at a time but all the emanations inside man's cocoon in a single stroke.*)

SELECTED REFERENCES: **The Fire From Within** - Page [67.4] (The third attention is attained when...the Eagle's emanations inside man's cocoon.")

SEE ALSO: *ATTENTION-THIRD, AWARENESS-GLOW, FIRE-WITHIN, ATTENTION-FIRST-GLOW, ATTENTION-SECOND-GLOW*

ATTENTION-TONAL-[THE ATTENTION OF THE TONAL]: *(Warriors know that the attention of the tonal is the first attention; the first ring of power; the capacity of the average man to place his awareness on the ordinary world of common sense and solid objects; the attention over the table.)*

SELECTED REFERENCES: The Second Ring of Power - Page [274.9-275.2] (The first one was the "attention...our perception of our daily world.) **The Second Ring of Power - Page [275.8-276.1]** (What don Juan had struggled to...maintain those images, the world collapses.) **The Second Ring of Power - Page [277.8]** (Don Juan had said that our...is all there is to us.) **The Second Ring of Power - Page [292.8]** (He pointed out to them that...or their attention attention over the table.)

SEE ALSO: *ATTENTION-FIRST, POWER-RING-FIRST, AWARENESS-RIGHT, KNOWN, WORLD-SOLID-OBJECTS*

ATTENTION-TONAL-DISENGAGING-[DISENGAGING THE ATTENTION OF THE TONAL]: *(Warriors must learn to disengage the attention of the tonal; in other words they must learn to stop the internal dialogue.)*

SELECTED REFERENCES: The Second Ring of Power - Page [306.6-306.7] (Don Juan had asserted time and...disengaging the attention of the tonal.)

SEE ALSO: *INTERNAL-DIALOG-STOPPING, ATTENTION-TONAL, STOPPING-WORLD*

ATTENTION-TRAPPING-[TRAPPING ATTENTION]: *(Warriors know that sometimes they must employ devices to trap their attention and maintain it in focus; these devices are not themselves responsible for any sorcery effects, they merely act to trap attention to allow for the appropriate not-doing to occur; sometimes warriors' attention also becomes trapped inadvertently by things around them.)*

SELECTED REFERENCES: The Power of Silence - Page [3.8-4.2] (I should have been chilled to the bone...attention and maintain it in focus.) **The Power of Silence - Page [71.6-71.8]** ("Don't waste energy," don Juan commanded..."Don't look at that man.") **The Power of Silence - Page [158.7-159.1]** ("The only concrete help you get from me...increased energy and not on instruction.")

SEE ALSO: *ATTENTION, SORCERY, NOT-DOING, ATTENTION-SECOND-TRAPPING*

ATTENTION-VANQUISHING-[VANQUISHING ATTENTION]: *SEE: REASON-VANQUISHING-[VANQUISHING REASON]*

ATTENTIONS-UNIFYING-TWO-[UNIFYING THE TWO ATTENTIONS]: *(Warriors know that eventually they must unify the attention of the tonal with the attention of the nagual and fuse them into a single unit [the totality of themselves].)*

SELECTED REFERENCES: Tales of Power - Page [245.3-245.4] ("I gave you enough of the... ordinary man or to a sorcerer.) **The Second Ring of Power - Page [291.1-291.6]** (He explained to me that the...tonal and the nagual until then.") **The Second Ring of Power - Page [293.5-293.8]** (He said that reaching the second...requirement for unifying the two attentions.) **The Eagle's Gift - Page [166.3-166.4]** (The task of remembering, then, was...rearranging *intensity* into a linear sequence.) **The Eagle's Gift - Page [299.5-299.7]** (Don Juan tried to the very...the event in more encompassing terms.) **The Eagle's Gift - Page [300.7-300.9]** (As la Gorda spoke I felt...and I fell to the floor.) **The Art of Dreaming - Page [124.9-125.2]** (Don Juan added that, unless I...second attention I was a lunatic.)

SEE ALSO: *WARRIOR-TOTALITY, TOTALITY-REGAINING, PERCEPTION-WINGS, DREAMING-ATTENTION-UNIFYING, WARRIOR-CONTRADICTION-KNOWLEDGE*

ATTENTION-VANQUISHING-[VANQUISHING ATTENTION]: *SEE: REASON-VANQUISHING-[VANQUISHING REASON]*

ATTRIBUTES-WARRIOR-[THE WARRIORS' ATTRIBUTES]: SEE:
WARRIOR-ATTRIBUTES-[THE WARRIORS' ATTRIBUTES]

AUDACITY-ULTIMATE-[THE ULTIMATE AUDACITY]: (*Warriors know*
that to dart past the Eagle and be free is the ultimate audacity.)
   SELECTED REFERENCES: The Eagle's Gift - Page [296.4] It's wrong to say that...be
free is the ultimate audacity.)
   SEE ALSO: *EAGLE-GIFT, FREEDOM-TOTAL, ATTENTION-THIRD, WARRIOR-*
TOTAL-FREEDOM

AUDITORY-VIGIL-WARRIOR-[THE WARRIORS' AUDITORY VIGIL]:
(*Warriors know that the auditory vigil is a "not doing" exercise which helps*
separate the sense of hearing from the sense of sight.)
   SELECTED REFERENCES: The Eagle's Gift - Page [235.5-235.7] (The second not-
doing consisted of...the entire night in auditory vigil.)
   SEE ALSO: *NOT-DOING, EARS-RELIEVE-BURDEN-EYES*

AURA-MAN-[MAN'S AURA]: SEE : MAN-AURA-[MAN'S AURA]

AVAILABILITY-WARRIOR-[THE WARRIORS' AVAILABILITY]: SEE:
WARRIOR-AVAILABILITY-[THE WARRIORS' AVAILABILITY]

AWARENESS-[AWARENESS]: (*Warriors know that awareness is a glow in*
the cocoon of a living being which is more intense than the rest of its
luminous structure; the portion of the Eagle's emanations inside man's
cocoon that is there only for awareness; awareness is matching that portion
of emanations with the same portion of the emanations at large.)
   SELECTED REFERENCES: Tales of Power - Page [93.7-93.8] ("That night that you
met the...of luminous fibers that have awareness.) The Second Ring of Power - Page [274.8-
275.2] (Don Juan said that the core...our perception of our daily world.) The Fire From Within -
Page [ix.5-ix.8] (The organization for don Juan's instruction...and teachings for the left side.) The
Fire From Within - Page [2.7-3.1] ("We are going to be talking...freedom, but to their doom.")
The Fire From Within - Page [9.5-9.7] (He explained. One of the simplest...Real learning takes
place there.) The Fire From Within - Page [37.7-37.9] ("I've used the term 'the world'...and yet
unchanged, eternal.") The Fire From Within - Page [38.8] (They *saw* that it is the...it at the
moment of death.) The Fire From Within - Page [49.5-49.6] ("No. I mean that a
nagual...benefactor said, but in a different way.") The Fire From Within - Page [50.6-51.1] ("I've
mentioned to you that the...the cocoon inward across its width.) The Fire From Within - Page
[56.5-57.5] (Don Juan said that the pressure...the emanations at large carry it.") The Fire From
Within - Page [64.2-64.4] ("How do seers know that man's...attention the end product of
maturation.) The Fire From Within - Page [72.5-72.8] (In the meantime, lets go back ..."What
stops death is awareness.") The Fire From Within - Page [79.1-79.6] ("Things that are still
difficult if...it or even to remember it.") The Fire From Within - Page [102.5] ("You'd be
surprised what men are...routine for them to encounter allies.) The Fire From Within - Page
[128.5-128.6] ("What are we truly doing...are nothing do they become everything.") The Fire
From Within - Page [206.5-206.9] ("The unknown is not really inside...same portion of
emanations at large.) The Power of Silence - Page [xv.6-xviii.1] (Don Juan's instructions on the
art...issue by not thinking about it.)
   SEE ALSO: *ALIGNMENT, PERCEPTION, HAUNTED-HOUSE-ANALOGY,*
AWARENESS-(ALL)

AWARENESS-ALIGNMENT-[AWARENESS AND ALIGNMENT]:
(*Warriors know through their "seeing" that awareness takes place when the*
emanations inside man's luminous cocoon align themselves with the same
emanations outside the cocoon; warriors also know that alignment alone
does not fully explain the process that lights up the emanations within
man's cocoon; emanations do not need to be aligned to be lit up; the force
that energizes them is an independent force; it is not awareness per se,

because awareness is the glow of the emanations being lit up; the warrior calls this independent force will, or intent.)
    SELECTED REFERENCES: **The Power of Silence** - Page [102.2-103.2] (On another occasion don Juan had...has with everything in the universe.)
    SEE ALSO: *AWARENESS, ALIGNMENT, WILL, INTENT*

AWARENESS-VS-ATTENTION-[AWARENESS VS ATTENTION]:
(Warriors know that the consciousness of adult human beings matured by the process of growth, can no longer be called awareness; as the individual matures, awareness is modified into something more intense and complex, which seers call attention; awareness is the raw material and attention is the end product of maturation.)
    SELECTED REFERENCES: **The Fire From Within** - Page [63.9-64.7] (Suddenly, don Juan began his explanation...the whole scope of man's possibilities.)
    SEE ALSO: *AWARENESS, ATTENTION*

AWARENESS-BASTION-ULTIMATE-[THE ULTIMATE BASTION OF AWARENESS]: SEE: AWARENESS-PRESERVATION-[THE PRESERVATION OF AWARENESS]

AWARENESS-BESTOWAL-[THE BESTOWAL OF AWARENESS]:
(Warriors know that the Eagle's command decrees that sex is for the bestowal of the glow of awareness; during intercourse, the emanations inside the cocoons of both partners undergo a profound agitation which culminates in a fusing of two pieces of the glow of awareness, one from each partner, that have separated from their cocoons.)
    SELECTED REFERENCES: **The Fire From Within** - Page [58.5-59.3] (He told them that they could...partner, that separate from their cocoons.)
    SEE ALSO: *SEX, AWARENESS-GLOW, AWARENESS-BESTOWAL-CONSOLIDATION*

AWARENESS-BESTOWAL-CONSOLIDATION-[THE CONSOLIDATION OF THE BESTOWAL OF AWARENESS]: *(Warriors know that through sexual intercourse the Eagle bestows awareness and that consequently, sex is a bestowal of awareness whether or not that bestowal is consolidated; the Eagle's emanations don't know about sex for fun.)*
    SELECTED REFERENCES: **The Fire From Within** - Page [58.9-59.4] (We're talking about the Eagle's command...don't know of intercourse for fun.")
    SEE ALSO: *SEX, AWARENESS, EAGLE, AWARENESS-BESTOWAL, SEX-LUMINOUS REALITY*

AWARENESS-BUBBLE-[BUBBLES OF AWARENESS]: *(Warriors know that organic beings are bubbles that grow around a group of the Eagle's emanations.)*
    SELECTED REFERENCES: **The Fire From Within** - Page [158.3-159.3] (Organic beings are bubbles that grow...are the organic bubbles of awareness.)
    SEE ALSO: *AWARENESS, LUMINOUS-COCOON, PERCEPTION-BUBBLE*

*AWARENESS-BUNDLING-[BUNDLING AWARENESS]: SEE: DREAMING-DESCRIPTION-[A DESCRIPTION OF DREAMING]

AWARENESS-COLOR-[THE COLOR OF AWARENESS]: *(Warriors know that there are giant bundles of the Eagle's emanations that run through the eight great bands and make seers "feel" a hue.)*
    SELECTED REFERENCES: **The Second Ring of Power** - Page [240.1-240.3] ("A human being, or any other...else. All of us are amber.) **The Fire From Within** - Page [159.7-161.9] (He said that the way the Eagle...pink or peach or amber emanations.

SEE ALSO: *AWARENESS-GLOW, EAGLE-EMANATIONS, AWARENESS, EAGLE EMANATIONS-BUNDLES*

AWARENESS-COMPELLED-INTERPRET-EAGLE-[AWARENESS IS COMPELLED TO INTERPRET WHAT OUR BODY WITNESSES ABOUT THE EAGLE]: *(Warriors know that it is possible for the body to witness the energetic essence of the universe; the problem with being able to grasp that perception is that awareness is compelled to interpret that perception into something manageable for the senses; in reality, what is out there is beyond anything living creatures can grasp.)*

SELECTED REFERENCES: **The Fire From Within - Page [41.1-41.5]** ("It goes without saying that the...that no living creature can grasp.")

SEE ALSO: *EAGLE, EAGLE-EMANATIONS, SEEING, UNKNOWABLE, AWARENESS*

AWARENESS-CONCEALED-WARRIOR-[THE WARRIORS' CONCEALED AWARENESS]: SEE: WARRIOR-AWARENESS-CONCEALED-[THE WARRIORS' CONCEALED AWARENESS]

AWARENESS-CONCEPTION-[AWARENESS AND CONCEPTION]: *(Warriors know that seers have determined that awareness begins at the moment of conception, when the awareness of the two sexual partners is consolidated.)*

SELECTED REFERENCES: **The Fire From Within - Page [57.5-57.7]** (After a long interruption, don Juan...from the moment of conception," he replied.)

SEE ALSO: *AWARENESS, SEX-LUMINOUS-REALITY, AWARENESS-BESTOWAL-CONSOLIDATION*

AWARENESS-DEATH-FORESTALLS-[AWARENESS FORESTALLS DEATH]: *(Warriors know that the emanations within the luminous cocoon are fighting to break free, fighting to die; all living beings are struggling to die and what stops death is awareness itself; one of the most profound contradictions of the warriors' world is that awareness forestalls death while at the same time inducing it by being "food" for the Eagle.)*

SELECTED REFERENCES: **The Fire From Within - Page [72.5-72.9]** (He reiterated that awareness begins with...knowledge is composed of contradictory propositions.)

SEE ALSO: *AWARENESS, DEATH, WARRIOR-CONTRADICTION-KNOWLEDGE, AWARENESS-DEATH-STOPS*

AWARENESS-DEATH-STOPS-[AWARENESS STOPS DEATH]: *(Warriors know that all living beings are struggling to die and that the only thing that stops death is awareness; inside us there are only emanations struggling to break the cocoon and that aberrates us whether we're average men or warriors.)*

SELECTED REFERENCES: **The Fire From Within - Page [72.6-72.7]** (This pressure produces the first act...What stops death is awareness.") **The Fire From Within - Page [125.1-125.2]** ("The mystery is outside us...the new seers get around this.)

SEE ALSO: *DEATH, AWARENESS, ABERRATION-MORBIDITY, EAGLE-EMANATIONS, AWARENESS-DEATH-FORESTALLS*

AWARENESS-DEGREE-[THE DEGREE OF AWARENESS]: *(Warriors know that every sentient beings' degree of awareness depends on the degree to which it is capable of letting the pressure of the emanations at large carry it.)*

SELECTED REFERENCES: **The Fire From Within - Page [57.4]** ("The degree of awareness of every...the emanations at large carry it.")

SEE ALSO: EAGLE-EMANATIONS, EAGLE-EMANATIONS-PRESSURE, AWARENESS, AWARENESS-FIXATION

AWARENESS-DETACHES-SELF-REFLECTION-[AWARENESS DETACHES ITSELF FROM SELF-REFLECTION]: (Warriors know that conserving energy through the eradication of unnecessary habits detaches the glow of awareness from self-reflection and allows it the freedom to focus on the unknown which is always present.)
SELECTED REFERENCES: The Fire From Within - Page [79.1-79.6] ("Things that are still difficult if not...enough free energy to grasp it.)
SEE ALSO: AWARENESS, HABITS-UNNECESSARY, ENERGY, SELF-REELECTION, UNKNOWN, SELF-IMPORTANCE-LOSING

AWARENESS-DREAMING-[DREAMING AWARENESS]: SEE: DREAMING-AWARENESS-[DREAMING AWARENESS]

AWARENESS-ENERGETIC-ELEMENT-[AWARENESS AS AN ENERGETIC ELEMENT]: (Warriors know that awareness is an energetic element of the universe; awareness is a glow, a mode of transportation, through which warriors can transport themselves to the ends of the universe; warriors can hitch their energy body to the glow of awareness and go with it; sorcerers perceive the energetic elements of the universe because they are taught to do so; the average man does not perceive them because he has been taught only to perceive the physical elements of the universe; the use of awareness as an energetic element is the essence of sorcery; the use of awareness as an energetic element bypasses the influence of the inorganic beings, but still uses their energy.)
SELECTED REFERENCES: The Art of Dreaming - Page [184.9-186.8] ("I'm going to propose a line...it still uses their energy.") The Art of Dreaming - Page [197.7-198.3] ("There is a question that's burning...two were already in another world.")
SEE ALSO: AWARENESS, AWARENESS-GLOW, ENERGY-BODY, PERCEPTION, DESCRIPTION-WORLD, AWARENESS-MASTERY, STALKING-ULTIMATE, SORCERY

AWARENESS-ENHANCING-[ENHANCING AWARENESS]: (Warriors know that awareness is enhanced and enriched by the process of being alive; at a given time in the growth of human beings, man's band of emanations begins to glow as the individual accumulates experience; this enhancement of awareness is so dramatic that man's band of emanations eventually fuses with the emanations outside the cocoon, transforming awareness into something that seers call attention; awareness is an endless area of exploration for warriors; in order to enhance their awareness there is no risk warriors should not run, no means they should refuse, [bearing in mind of course that only in soundness of mind can awareness be enhanced].)
SELECTED REFERENCES: The Fire From Within - Page [57.5-57.6] (After a long interruption, don Juan...different ways, but with equal consistency.) The Fire From Within - Page [63.9-64.5] (Suddenly, don Juan began his explanation...process of being alive," he replied.) The Art of Dreaming - Page [184.3-184.4] ("Every sorcerer goes through the same...of mind can awareness be enhanced.")
SEE ALSO: ATTENTION, AWARENESS-CONCEPTION, AWARENESS, EXISTENCE-REASON, SANITY, WARRIOR-SOBRIETY

AWARENESS-EXPLANATION-[THE EXPLANATION OF AWARENESS]: (Warriors know that the explanation of awareness is in fact the explanation of the mastery of awareness; the truths about awareness.)
SELECTED REFERENCES: The Fire From Within - Page [32.8-33.1] ("He said that there were a...the total sequence of such truths.) The Fire From Within - Page [108.2-108.6] (He

then began his explanation. He...point is located on our cocoon.") **The Fire From Within - Page [141.1-141.2]** ("I've explained to you that man...different from the world we know.") **The Fire From Within - Page [256.3-256.9]** (Right after lunch, don Juan and...align another great band of emanations.) **The Power of Silence - Page [xv.6-xvi.8]** (Don Juan's instruction on the art...implies an alternative way of dying.)

SEE ALSO: *AWARENESS-TRUTHS, AWARENESS-MASTERY, AWARENESS, AWARENESS-TRUTH-(ALL)*

AWARENESS-FIXATION-[THE FIXATION OF AWARENESS]: (Warriors know that the fixation of awareness is the property of the Eagle's emanations outside the luminous cocoon to attract and fixate the matching emanations inside the cocoon; the pressure which the emanations at large exert on those inside man's luminous cocoon, a pressure which produces the first act of consciousness and stops the motion of the trapped emanations; the fixation or the movement of the assemblage point is all there is to us and the world we witness; the average man is taught to dull himself in order to keep the assemblage point fixed in one spot.)

SELECTED REFERENCES: **Journey to Ixtlan - Page [viii.9-ix.3]** (He pointed out that everyone who...conforming to that description, validate it.) **The Eagle's Gift - Page [20.3-21.5]** (I could not, for instance, recall...knew, but the principle was sound.) **The Fire From Within - Page [49.5-49.7]** ("What do the new seers say...look like bubbles of whitish light.") **The Fire From Within - Page [50.1-50.3]** (When seers *see* perception, they witness...the awareness of every specific being.) **The Fire From Within - Page [56.5-57.2]** (Don Juan said that the pressure...are - fluid, forever in motion, eternal.) **The Fire From Within - Page [72.5-72.7]** ("In the meantime, let's go back...break the cocoon, fighting to die.") **The Fire From Within - Page [73.8-73.9]** ("What is an inventory, don Juan...first attention begins to watch itself.) **The Fire From Within - Page [118.3]** (He affirmed that one of the...on that specific spot by habit.) **The Fire From Within - Page [119.1-119.2]** ("The assemblage point of man appears...point is fixated at that spot.") **The Fire From Within - Page [123.4-123.6]** (He went on to say that... point shift is a genuine triumph.) **The Fire From Within - Page [132.2-133.4]** (We were silent for a few...our command, our gift of magic.") **The Fire From Within - Page [135.3-135.5]** (Don Juan restated, as if on...the assemblage point is free to move.) **The Fire From Within - Page [148.7-148.9]** ("In order to be unbiased witnesses...assemblage point fixes on one spot.") **The Art of Dreaming - Page [64.9-65.3]** ("Why do some of us hear...the fixation of our assemblage points.")

SEE ALSO: *AWARENESS-TRUTH-FOURTH, ASSEMBLAGE-POINT-FIXATION, AWARENESS, DULL-OURSELVES, WARRIOR-WITNESS-UNBIASED*

AWARENESS-FREEING-[FREEING AWARENESS]: SEE: MAN-EVOLUTION-[MAN IS CAPABLE OF EVOLVING]

**AWARENESS-GLOW-[THE GLOW OF AWARENESS]:* (Warriors know that the glow of awareness is the glow in the luminous cocoon of living beings; the glow of awareness is also sometimes used as another term for the assemblage point; the assemblage point and its surrounding glow are the marks of life and consciousness.)

SELECTED REFERENCES: **The Fire From Within - Page [50.7-51.1]** ("I've said to you that they unraveled...the cocoon inward across its width.) **The Fire From Within - Page [51.2-51.4]** ("Genaro doesn't give a fig about...want with the glow of awareness.") **The Fire From Within - Page [66.2-67.4]** ("In terms of what seers *see*...Eagle's emanations inside man's cocoon.") **The Fire From Within - Page [111.8-114.3]** (Don Juan further said that the dent...at large, and glide into eternity.") **The Fire From Within - Page [160.6]** ("I've told you that the glow...are not colors but casts of amber.") **The Fire From Within - Page [170.5-170.6]** (They began by *seeing* how the...to handle that alignment of emanations.) **The Art of Dreaming - Page [6.7-7.1]** (Next, they *saw* that a spherical...and perceiving in an unfamiliar manner.) **The Art of Dreaming - Page [7.9-8.3]** (Don Juan stated that, *seeing* that...and the glow that surrounds it.) **The Art of Dreaming - Page [8.7-8.9]** (The effect of the assemblage point's...is, perception is automatically assembled there.) **The Art of Dreaming - Page [45.8-45.9]** ("For sorcerers, having life means having...as the precondition of being alive.")

SEE ALSO: *AWARENESS-MYSTERY, LUMINOUS-BEINGS-MYSTERY, ASSEMBLAGE-POINT, AWARENESS, ATTENTION-FIRST-GLOW, ATTENTION-SECOND-GLOW, ATTENTION-THIRD-GLOW*

AWARENESS-GLOW-CONSUMED-FIRST-ATTENTION-*[THE FIRST ATTENTION CONSUMES THE GLOW OF AWARENESS]:* (*Warriors know that the first attention consumes all of the glow of awareness so that not one iota of energy is left free for warriors to use in pursuit of the quest for freedom.*)

SELECTED REFERENCES: The Fire From Within - Page [79.1-79.3] ("Things that are still difficult if not...seers say, from eradicating unnecessary habits.")
SEE ALSO: *AWARENESS-GLOW, ATTENTION-FIRST, ENERGY, WARRIOR-IMPECCABLE, INVENTORY, AWARENESS, ATTENTION-FIRST-GLOW*

AWARENESS-GLOW-EXTENDING-*[EXTENDING THE GLOW OF AWARENESS]:* (*Warriors know that one of the critical errors of the old seers was the method they used to extend the glow of their awareness; the old seers succeeded in extending awareness by lighting up the emanations inside their cocoons one band at a time; rather than leading them to freedom, their success with this task only became instrumental in imprisoning the old seers in the quagmire of the second attention; the new seers corrected that error by allowing the mastery of awareness to develop to its natural end; this means that the new seers extend the glow of awareness beyond the bounds of the luminous cocoon in one single stroke; extending the glow of awareness is really another term for moving the assemblage point.*)

SELECTED REFERENCES: The Fire From Within - Page [66.9-67.3] (He said that the old seers...luminous cocoon in one single stroke.)
SEE ALSO: *AWARENESS-GLOW, AWARENESS-MASTERY, FIRE-WITHIN, ATTENTION-SECOND-QUAGMIRE, ATTENTION-THIRD, ASSEMBLAGE-POINT-MOVING, AWARENESS*

AWARENESS-GLOW-SHIFT-SUDDEN-*[A SUDDEN SHIFT IN THE GLOW OF AWARENESS]:* (*Warriors know that a sudden shift in the glow of awareness can have a weakening effect.*)

SELECTED REFERENCES: The Fire From Within - Page [70.9-71.2] (Don Juan patted my back gently...had succeeded by making me rage.)
SEE ALSO: *AWARENESS-GLOW, ASSEMBLAGE-POINT-MOVEMENT, AWARENESS*

AWARENESS-GLOW-WORKING-*[WORKING THE GLOW OF AWARENESS]-(TOP)*

AWARENESS-GROWTH-*[AWARENESS IS INTRINSICALLY COMPELLED TO GROW]:* (*Warriors know that consciousness is intrinsically compelled to grow, and that the only way it can grow is through strife, through life-or-death confrontations.*)

SELECTED REFERENCES: The Art of Dreaming - Page [101.3-101.4] (Don Juan explained that in the...through life-or-death confrontations.)
SEE ALSO: *AWARENESS, WARRIOR-PAPER, WARRIOR-DURESS-EXTREME-BENEFITS*

AWARENESS-HANDLING-VS-UNDERSTANDING-*[HANDLING AWARENESS VS UNDERSTANDING]:* (*Warriors know that there are only eight points that a man is capable of handling; they also understand that handling those points does not imply the understanding of them all.*)

SELECTED REFERENCES: A Separate Reality - Page [258.7-258.9] ("As far as I know there are...Your stumbling block is intact.) **The Fire From Within - Page [50.6-50.8]** ("I've mentioned to you that the old...called it the glow of awareness.") **The Fire From Within - Page [101.9-102.6]** (He assured me that experienced seers...old seers never made that realization.")
SEE ALSO: *AWARENESS, UNDERSTANDING, TOLTEC-LEVELS*

AWARENESS-HARNESSING-ATTENTION-[ATTENTION IS THE HARNESSING AND ENHANCEMENT OF AWARENESS]: SEE: ATTENTION-AWARENESS-ENHANCEMENT-[ATTENTION IS THE ENHANCEMENT OF AWARENESS]

**AWARENESS-HEIGHTENED-[HEIGHTENED AWARENESS]:* (Warriors know that heightened awareness is a lateral shift of the assemblage point characterized by a unique perceptual clarity; the emphasized emanations of heightened awareness are extremely close to the habitual ones, yet the shift produces a much greater capacity to understand and concentrate, as well as an overpowering tendency to forget; the portal of intent; the point of assemblage where real learning takes place; the only position of the assemblage point which warriors allow themselves to make a permanent shift to; heightened awareness is like a springboard, because from that position one can jump into infinity; warriors know there is no survival value in heightened awareness, otherwise the whole human race would be there; heightened awareness is a very difficult state to achieve, and there is only the remotest possibility that an average man would enter into such a state; heightened awareness eventually brings with it feelings of aloofness and detachment; events which occur in heightened awareness are outside the realm of everyday judgment.)

SELECTED REFERENCES: The Eagle's Gift - Page [165.3-165.5] (Another feature of those states of...an inherent need for economy and speed.) **The Eagle's Gift - Page [166.6-167.4]** (The pragmatic step that don Juan took...which had been veiled by *intensity*.) **The Eagle's Gift - Page [204.7-204.9]** (Due to something inexplicable in his...into that other world of awareness.) **The Eagle's Gift - Page [246.1-246.2]** (The left side instruction had been...the other half with don Juan.) **The Fire From Within - Page [xi.7-xi.8]** (In order for don Juan to...his hand on my upper back.) **The Fire From Within - Page [xii.5-xiii.4]** (Every time I entered into heightened...details of the action at hand.) **The Fire From Within - Page [9.7]** ("The old seers figured out," he...Real learning takes place there.") **The Fire From Within - Page [10.1-10.7]** (He said that the clarity and...new seers meant them to have.) **The Fire From Within - Page [52.2-52.7]** (The sensation I experienced then, once...if your life depends on it.) **The Fire From Within - Page [112.8-112.9]** (He said that the glow of...all, a greater capacity to forget.) **The Fire From Within - Page [122.2-122.4]** ("The assemblage point of man is located...on the surface of the cocoon.") **The Fire From Within - Page [277.7-277.9]** (Don Juan talked to me very...to let my assemblage point move.) **The Fire From Within - Page [298.9-299.2]** (One of the most fortunate decisions that...to choose total consciousness, total freedom.) **The Fire From Within - Page [300.2-300.3]** (We know now that we were...the greater our doubts, the greater our turmoil.) **The Power of Silence - Page [xii.8-xiii.5]** (Sorcery at this level could be...standards of awareness of everyday life.) **The Power of Silence - Page [xvii.8-xvii.9]** (It took me years to be able...of heightened awareness and direct knowledge.) **The Power of Silence - Page [14.1-14.2]** (He responded cuttingly that I was...edifice of sorcery knowledge was completed.) **The Power of Silence - Page [27.1]** ("I took you to that cave on purpose...the apprentice deep into heightened awareness.) **The Power of Silence - Page [29.3-29.5]** (Sometimes don Juan exasperated me so...the immensity that surrounds us reasonable.") **The Power of Silence - Page [68.1-68.2]** ("Of course," he replied with a grin...but are very difficult to arrange.") **The Power of Silence - Page [72.3-72.7]** (He said that heightened awareness was...I have lent you my energy.") **The Power of Silence - Page [83.4-84.3]** (Don Juan continued talking, but I was...it as such. Think about it.") **The Power of Silence - Page [113.7-113.9]** (In the early evening, don Juan...of my shift to heightened awareness.) **The Power of Silence - Page [119.8-120.3]** (I told him that his assertions...spirit move my assemblage point.) **The Power of Silence - Page [121.9-122.1]** (When she cut the body open...outside the realm of everyday judgment.) **The Art of Dreaming - Page [15.8-16.1]** ("How can I do that?

Borrow...state he called the second attention.) **The Art of Dreaming - Page [17.1-17.4]** (Don Juan helped me to experience...that normal awareness paled by comparison.)

SEE ALSO: *AWARENESS-LEFT, INTENT-PORTAL, LEARNING, WARRIOR-ALOOFNESS, WARRIOR-DETACHMENT, AWARENESS*

AWARENESS-IMMEASURABLE-AREA-[THE IMMEASURABLE AREA OF AWARENESS]: (Warriors know that the immeasurable area of awareness is the unused area of the Eagle's emanations outside of man's band; an area of emanations that can only be perceived in really indescribable ways; the unknown where human traits don't figure at all; the non-human unknown.)

SELECTED REFERENCES: **The Fire From Within - Page [66.7-66.9]** (He said that the second attention...and its lure nearly irresistible.") **The Fire From Within - Page [124.8-124.9]** ("How about the emanations that are inside...would be hard put to describe it.") **The Fire From Within - Page [260.2-260.4]** (He also said that there was...another by gripping feelings of defeat.)

SEE ALSO: *UNKNOWN, EAGLE-EMANATIONS, UNKNOWN-NON-HUMAN, UNKNOWN-INTRICACIES, ATTENTION-SECOND*

AWARENESS-LEFT-[THE LEFT SIDE AWARENESS]: (Warriors know that the left side awareness is the mysterious side of man; the state of awareness needed to function as a sorcerer and seer; the nagual; the other world; the unknown; the second attention.)

SELECTED REFERENCES: **The Eagle's Gift - Page [83.3]** (Eligio wants us to remember our...remember weird things now and then.") **The Eagle's Gift - Page [185.1-185.2]** (He warned me about a common error...all, a general ability to forget.) **The Eagle's Gift - Page [299.7-299.9]** (He warned me repeatedly that to...to handle themselves in that state..) **The Eagle's Gift - Page [311.5]** (Don Juan had told me that...the very depths of the universe.) **The Fire From Within - Pages [ix.5-ix.7]** (The organization of don Juan's instruction...to function as sorcerer and seer.) **The Fire From Within - Pages [xi.2-xii.1]** (In his teachings for the left...through a staggering effort of recovery.) **The Fire From Within - Pages [66.7-66.9]** (He said that the second attention...easy and its lure nearly irresistible.") **The Fire From Within - Page [109.8-110.1]** (The emphasized emanations compose a large...world, the unknown, the second attention.) **The Power of Silence - Page [xiv.8-xiv.9]** (In his teaching scheme, which was...practiced solely in states of heightened awareness.) **The Power of Silence - Page [xvii.4-xvii.8]** (In compliance with his tradition, it was...once I returned to my normal consciousness.)

SEE ALSO: *NAGUAL, ATTENTION-SECOND, UNKNOWN, ATTENTION-NAGUAL, POWER-RING-SECOND, NAGUAL, AWARENESS*

AWARENESS-LEFT-ADVANTAGES-DRAWBACKS-[THE ADVANTAGES AND DRAWBACKS OF THE LEFT SIDE AWARENESS]: (Warriors know that there are certain advantages and drawbacks to the left side awareness; it is an advantage only insofar as the warriors' grasp of things is accelerated; it is a disadvantage because it allows warriors to focus with inconceivable lucidity on one thing at a time, which renders them dependent and vulnerable; unless warriors have gained the totality of themselves, it is dangerous for them to be left in that state.)

SELECTED REFERENCES: **The Eagle's Gift - Page [299.7-299.9]** (He warned me repeatedly that to...to handle themselves in that state.)

SEE ALSO: *AWARENESS-LEFT, AWARENESS-HEIGHTENED, AWARENESS*

AWARENESS-LEFT-LEFT-[THE LEFT LEFT SIDE AWARENESS]:
(Warriors know that the left left side awareness is a special state of awareness, the site of the keenest form of attention; one of the primary features of the left left side is the wall of fog.)

SELECTED REFERENCES: **The Eagle's Gift - Page [154.6-154.9]** (On that occasion, at the request...don Juan called the "wall of fog.")

SEE ALSO: *FOG-WALL, AWARENESS-LEFT*

AWARENESS-LEFT-LURE-FEMALE-WARRIOR-[THE LURE OF THE LEFT-SIDE AWARENESS]: (*Warriors know that female warriors are particularly susceptible to the lure of the left-side awareness; women are so nimble that they can move in and out of it with no effort, often too soon for their own good.*)

SELECTED REFERENCES: The Fire From Within - Page [48.7] (Female warriors in particular fall prey...too soon for their own good.)

SEE ALSO: *AWARENESS-LEFT, WARRIOR-FEMALE, MENSTRUAL-PERIOD, CRACK-WORLDS*

AWARENESS-LEFT-TRANSITION-[THE TRANSITION TO THE LEFT SIDE AWARENESS]: (*Warriors know that there is an intermediate stage, before they enter fully into the left-side awareness; at this stage, warriors are capable of tremendous concentration but they are also subject to every conceivable influence, both good and bad; the deepest learning takes place during this transition period and it is during this time that warriors require accurate explanations so that they can evaluate them properly; if these explanations are not forth coming before warriors enter into the left-side awareness, they will be great sorcerers but poor seers, much like the ancient Toltecs.*)

SELECTED REFERENCES: The Fire From Within - Page [48.2-48.6] (Don Juan was reading me like...seers, as the ancient Toltecs were.)

SEE ALSO: *AWARENESS-LEFT, AWARENESS-RIGHT, AWARENESS-LEFT-RIGHT, AWARENESS-HEIGHTENED, TOLTECS, SEER-OLD, EXPLANATION, LEARNING, AWARENESS*

AWARENESS-MANIPULATION-[THE MANIPULATION OF AWARENESS]: (*Warriors know that awareness itself can be manipulated; the differences in the ways that awareness is manipulated are the differences between sorcery and warriorship; psychic healers are individuals capable of moving the assemblage points of the exact number of people in their audience.*)

SELECTED REFERENCES: The Fire From Within - Page [2.3-2.4] ("I have to emphasize an important...is that awareness can be manipulated.") The Fire From Within - [297.9-298.4] ("The old seers used to say that...*dreaming position* called total freedom.) The Power of Silence - Page [121.3-121.8] (Don Juan immediately pointed out that...and force them into heightened awareness.) The Power of Silence - Page [161.1-161.2] ("The nagual's presence is enough to...the apprentice who is being manipulated.") The Art of Dreaming - Page [15.8-16.1] ("How can I do that? Borrow...state he called the second attention.) The Art of Dreaming - Page [73.6-74.1] ("We are back again, harping on...manipulate the assemblage point for gain.)

SEE ALSO: *ASSEMBLAGE-POINT-MOVING, NAGUAL-BLOW, SORCERER-CURSE, WARRIORSHIP-VS-SORCERY, AWARENESS, SHADOWS-CIRCLE-(TOP)*

AWARENESS-MANIPULATION-SEER-NEW-[THE NEW SEERS' MANIPULATION OF AWARENESS]: (*Warriors know that the new seers manipulate awareness and the position of the assemblage point without any focus on the personal self; instead, they accomplish the detached manipulation of intent through sober commands; for the new seers this means darting past the Eagle to a dreaming position known as total freedom; the new seers discovered the futility of the old seers self-centered manipulation of awareness; instead of simply choosing an alternate world in which to die, the new seers choose total consciousness, total freedom.*)

SELECTED REFERENCES: The Fire From Within - [297.9-299.6] ("The old seers used to say that...that total freedom means total awareness.")

SEE ALSO: *SEER-NEW, FREEDOM-TOTAL, AWARENESS-TOTAL, FIRE-WITHIN, EAGLE-GIFT, AWARENESS-MANIPULATION, WARRIOR-DEATH-COMMAND, AWARENESS*

AWARENESS-MANIPULATION-SEER-OLD-[THE OLD SEERS' MANIPULATION OF AWARENESS]: *(Warriors know that the old seers' manipulation of awareness was directed towards the enhancement of their own self-reflection; the old seers moved their assemblage points to inconceivable dreaming positions but in the end they only succeeded in changing the locales of their deaths; the old seers tremendous feats of daring in this area lacked any sobriety and eventually sealed their doom because they could never retract the movement of their assemblage points, perhaps because they never wanted to.)*

SELECTED REFERENCES: **The Fire From Within** - [297.9-298.9] ("The old seers used to say that...all, the futility of self-importance.) **The Art of Dreaming - Page** [15.8-16.1] ("How can I do that? Borrow...state he called the second attention.) **The Art of Dreaming - Page** [73.6-74.1] ("We are back again, harping on...manipulate the assemblage point for gain.)

SEE ALSO: *SORCERY-WARRIORSHIP, SELF-REFLECTION, SEER-OLD, DEATH-DEFIERS, TOLTEC-DOOM, WARRIOR-SOBRIETY, AWARENESS, AWARENESS-MANIPULATION-SEER-NEW*

AWARENESS-MAP-[A MAP TO AWARENESS]: SEE: AWARENESS-TRUTHS-[THE TRUTHS ABOUT AWARENESS]

AWARENESS-MASTERY-[THE MASTERY OF AWARENESS]: *(The warriors' understanding and internalization of the sequence of truths about awareness; the riddle of the mind.)*

SELECTED REFERENCES: **The Fire From Within** - Page [xii.8-xiii.5] (The organization of his teachings for...tradition of the ancient Toltec seers.) **The Fire From Within - Page** [9.5-10.7] (He explained. One of the simplest...the new seers meant them to have.) **The Fire From Within - Page** [11.4-30.5] (Don Juan did not discuss the...of the petty tyrants for life.") **The Fire From Within - Page** [32.9-33.2] (He explained that the mastery of...a universe of the Eagle's emanations.) **The Fire From Within - Page** [50.8-51.1] (He explained that the old seers...the cocoon inward across its width.) **The Fire From Within** - [Page 67.3] ("The new seers corrected that error...luminous cocoon in one single stroke. **The Fire From Within - Page** [115.6-115.7] ("Genaro has something to tell you...its position by the nagual's blow.") **The Fire From Within** - [Page 168.3-168.8] (He explained that what the new...a long series of explanations.) **The Fire From Within** - [Page 258.6-258.7] ("You're in a position now to...point fixed at a certain position.) **The Fire From Within - Page** [259.6-259.7] (There was a long pause before...of recovery. Remember what you've done!") **The Power of Silence** - [Page xv.2] (The mastery of awareness is the...and scope of awareness and perception.) **The Power of Silence - Page** [xvi.9-xvii.2] (A level of practical knowledge was...*stalking*, the control of behavior.)

SEE ALSO: *AWARENESS-EXPLANATION, AWARENESS-TRUTHS , AWARENESS, LUMINOUS-COCOON-MAN-MANIPULATION*

AWARENESS-MASTERY-TEACHING-[TEACHING THE MASTERY OF AWARENESS]: *(Warriors know that they are taught the mastery of awareness in two ways; the teachings for the right side loosen the assemblage point from its original position and teach warriors the warriors' way; the teachings for the left side force the assemblage point to shift to as many new positions as possible and provide warriors with a long series of explanations.)*

SELECTED REFERENCES: **The Fire From Within** - Page [168.5-168.8] (He told me that he had...me a long series of explanations.)

SEE ALSO: *AWARENESS-MASTERY, TEACHERS-TEACHING, AWARENESS-RIGHT-SIDE, AWARENESS-LEFT-SIDE, AWARENESS*

AWARENESS-MERGING-RIGHT-LEFT-[MERGING THE RIGHT AND LEFT SIDE AWARENESS]: SEE: AWARENESS-PREDOMINANCE-SWITCHING-[SWITCHING THE ORDER OF THE PREDOMINANCE OF AWARENESS], DREAMING-DESCRIPTION-[A DESCRIPTION OF DREAMING]

AWARENESS-MYSTERY-[THE MYSTERY OF AWARENESS]: (Warriors know that awareness is a glow in the luminous cocoon of living beings.)
SELECTED REFERENCES: **The Fire From Within** - [Page 10.4-10.5] ("The best effort of the new...the apprentices are in heightened awareness.") **The Fire From Within** - [Page 50.6-50.8] ("I've mentioned to you that the...called it the glow of awareness.") **The Fire From Within** - Page [72.3-72.5] ("Oh, there is the mystery...mystery of awareness I'm referring to.) **The Fire From Within** Page [185.2-185.3] ("This indeed is the mystery of...apologize for either; both are needed.)
SEE ALSO: *LUMINOUS-BEINGS-MYSTERY, AWARENESS-GLOW, AWARENESS*

AWARENESS-NORMAL-[NORMAL AWARENESS]: (Warriors know that man's normal state of awareness is the world of solid objects; the known; the first attention; the attention of the tonal; normal reality.)
SELECTED REFERENCES: **The Eagle's Gift** - Page [301.8-301.9] (Once they were in the awareness of...apprentices were in their normal awareness.) **The Fire From Within** - Page [79.5-79.6] ("The unknown is forever present...enough free energy to grasp it.) **The Art of Dreaming** - Page [17.1-17.4] (Don Juan helped me to experience...that normal awareness paled by comparison.) **The Art of Dreaming** - Page [75.8-76.6] (Don Juan changed the subject and...are fixed on the same spot.)
SEE ALSO: *AWARENESS-RIGHT, ATTENTION-FIRST, TONAL, REALITY-INTERPRETATION, KNOWN, WORLD-SOLID OBJECTS, ATTENTION-TONAL, AWARENESS*

AWARENESS-NORMAL-LIMITATIONS-[THE LIMITATIONS OF NORMAL AWARENESS]: (Warriors know that existence is incomprehensibly complex and that our normal awareness maligns it with its limitations.)
SELECTED REFERENCES: **The Fire From Within** - Page [53.6-53.7] ("I don't blame you," he said...awareness maligns it with its limitations.")
SEE ALSO: *AWARENESS-RIGHT, BOUNDARIES, ETERNITY, AWARENESS*

AWARENESS-ORDERLY-WORLD-VS-PERCEPTION-CHAOTIC-REALM-[THE ORDERLY WORLD OF AWARENESS VS THE CHAOTIC REALM OF PERCEPTION: SEE: ATTENTION-FIRST-FOCUS-[THE FOCUS OF THE FIRST ATTENTION]

AWARENESS-OTHER-[THE OTHER AWARENESS]: (Warriors know that the other awareness is a term for the third attention.)
SELECTED REFERENCES: **The Eagle's Gift** - Page [298.8-299.1] (It was only by a strange...to each of them individually.)
SEE ALSO: *ATTENTION-THIRD, AWARENESS*

AWARENESS-PERCEPTION-GIVES-RISE-[AWARENESS GIVES RISE TO PERCEPTION]: (Warriors know that awareness gives rise to perception when the emanations inside man's cocoon align themselves with the corresponding emanations at large.)
SELECTED REFERENCES: **The Fire From Within** - Page [108.4-108.5] (That awareness gives rise to perception...with the corresponding emanations at large.)
SEE ALSO: *AWARENESS, PERCEPTION, ALIGNMENT, ASSEMBLAGE-POINT*

AWARENESS-PERCEPTION-UNIT-[AWARENESS AND PERCEPTION AS A SINGLE UNIT]: (Warriors know that awareness and perception are a single, functional, inextricable unit; this unit has two domains, the attention of the tonal and the attention of the nagual, or the first and second rings of power; awareness and perception go together and are tied to the assemblage point and the glow that surrounds it.)
    SELECTED REFERENCES: **The Second Ring of Power - Page [274.8-275.4]** (Don Juan said that the core...impart order to the nonordinary world.) **The Art of Dreaming - Page [8.2-8.3]** (The inescapable conclusion of the sorcerers...and the glow that surrounds it.)
    SEE ALSO: *BEING-CORE, BEING-MAGIC-OF-OUR, PERCEPTION, AWARENESS, ATTENTION-TONAL, ATTENTION-NAGUAL, POWER-RING-FIRST, POWER-RING-SECOND, ASSEMBLAGE-POINT, AWARENESS-GLOW*

AWARENESS-PERSISTENCE-[THE PERSISTENCE OF AWARENESS]: SEE: AWARENESS-PRESERVATION-[THE PRESERVATION OF AWARENESS]

AWARENESS-PLAYING-WITH-[PLAYING WITH AWARENESS]-(TOP)

AWARENESS-POLARITY-APPLYING-[APPLYING THE POLARITY OF AWARENESS]: (Warriors know that the polarity created between the states of right and left side awareness can be used in two ways; the old seers used it to force their sorcery apprentices to achieve the concentration necessary to learn sorcery techniques; the new seers use it to lead their apprentices to the conviction that there are unrealized possibilities in man.)
    SELECTED REFERENCES: **The Fire From Within - Page [9.5-10.3]** (He explained. One of the simplest...there are unrealized possibilities in man.)
    SEE ALSO: *AWARENESS-LEFT, AWARENESS-RIGHT, AWARENESS-RIGHT-LEFT, AWARENESS-HEIGHTENED, HUMAN-ALTERNATIVES-POTENTIAL-POSSIBILITIES, AWARENESS, POWER-HIDDEN, EQUILIBRIUM*

AWARENESS-PREDOMINANCE-SWITCHING-[SWITCHING THE ORDER OF THE PREDOMINANCE OF AWARENESS]: (Warriors know that in order to do dreaming they must merge the right and left side awareness so that the normal order of predominance can be switched, giving the left supremacy; when dreamers revert back to their normal awareness, the process reverses and the right side awareness is once again left holding the reins.)
    SELECTED REFERENCES: **The Eagle's Gift - Page [259.7-259.8]** (Zuleica also said that the feeling...with the right holding the reins.)
    SEE ALSO: *DREAMING-DESCRIPTION, AWARENESS-LEFT, AWARENESS-RIGHT, LUMINOUS-DENT, DREAMING-ART, ATTENTION-DREAMING, AWARENESS*

AWARENESS-PRESERVATION-[THE PRESERVATION OF AWARENESS]: (Warriors know that it is possible to preserve awareness beyond death; the old and new seers each had techniques to accomplish this; the old seers used the tumbler's boost, the new seers use the boost from the earth; the new seers make the world of everyday awareness vanish, they burn with the fire from within but somewhat retain the sense of being themselves; sorcerers, by manipulating their assemblage points in specific ways to certain locations within their total energy fields have been able to allow their awareness and life force to persist.)
    SELECTED REFERENCES: **The Fire From Within - Page [248.8-249.6]** (Very early the next morning, at...and usually meant a struggle for supremacy.) **The Fire From Within - Page [290.1]** ("Los Angeles will vanish like a puff..."But you will remain.) **The Fire From Within**

- Page [295.6-295.7] (What you are going to do is...retain the sense of being themselves.") **The Power of Silence - Page [58.1-58.2]** (For all the sorcerers of don Juan's...awareness and life force to persist.)

SEE ALSO: *EAGLE-GIFT, INTENDING-DEATH-AWAY, TUMBLER-BOOST, EARTH-BOOST, FIRE-WITHIN, WARRIOR-DEATH-COMMAND, AWARENESS*

AWARENESS-RELINQUISHING-[RELINQUISHING AWARENESS]: (Warriors know that they must die and relinquish their awareness; but they also know it is possible to change just a tinge of that, a change that enables warriors to experience great mysteries.)

SELECTED REFERENCES: **The Fire From Within - Page [287.1-287.2]** ("Who cares about sadness, he said...mysteries await us! What mysteries!")

SEE ALSO: *DEATH, AWARENESS-SURROGATE, RECAPITULATION, EAGLE-GIFT, WARRIOR-DEATH-COMMAND, AWARENESS-PRESERVATION, AWARENESS*

AWARENESS-RETAINING-[RETAINING AWARENESS]: SEE: AWARENESS-PRESERVING-[THE PRESERVATION OF AWARENESS]

AWARENESS-RIGHT-[THE RIGHT SIDE AWARENESS]: (Warriors know that the right side awareness is the state of normal awareness necessary for everyday life; normal awareness; the attention of the tonal; this world; the known; the first attention; reality; rationality; common sense.)

SELECTED REFERENCES: **The Eagle's Gift - Page [183.8-184.1]** (His benefactor put him under the direct...rational ballast to hold them back.) **The Fire From Within - Page [ix.5-ix.6]** (The organization of don Juan's instruction...normal awareness necessary for everyday life.) **The Fire From Within [Page 10.1]** (He said that the clarity and...of his normal state of awareness.) **The Fire From Within - Page [109.7-109.8]** (The new seers call the emphasized...calls it reality, rationality, common sense.) **The Power of Silence - Page [xiv.8-xiv.9]** (In his teaching scheme, which was...practiced solely in states of heightened awareness.) **The Art of Dreaming - Page [75.8-76.6]** (Don Juan changed the subject and...are fixed on the same spot.)

SEE ALSO: *TONAL, ATTENTION-FIRST, ATTENTION-TONAL, KNOWN, REALITY-INTERPRETATION, AWARENESS*

**AWARENESS-RIGHT-LEFT-[THE RIGHT AND THE LEFT SIDE AWARENESS]:* (Warriors know that as part of their training they must move between the right and the left side awareness; the first effect of sorcery is the shift between normal and heightened awareness.)

SELECTED REFERENCES: **The Fire From Within - Page [9.2-10.3]** ("The ancient seers were very fortunate...there are unrealized possibilities in man.) **The Fire From Within - Page [47.4-48.3]** (Don Juan, don Genaro, and I...I was being influenced by suspicion,) **The Fire From Within - Page [51.9-52.6]** (Don Juan had come into the kitchen...even if my life depended on it.) **The Power of Silence - Page [53.3-53.4]** ("The story says that the spirit...needed to strengthen his connecting link.") **The Power of Silence - Page [105.3-105.6]** (I understood don Juan's explanation with...him that I resented my fate.) **The Power of Silence - Page [107.9-108.2]** (I begged don Juan not to...than I was at that moment.) **The Power of Silence - Page [113.3-113.4]** (I said as much to don Juan...I was neither fish nor fowl.) **The Power of Silence - Page [118.6]** ("The first principle should not be...shift between normal and heightened awareness.")

SEE ALSO: *AWARENESS-RIGHT, AWARENESS-LEFT, AWARENESS-HEIGHTENED, AWARENESS, AWARENESS-POLARITY-APPLYING, EQUILIBRIUM*

AWARENESS-SUBLIMINAL-[THE SUBLIMINAL AWARENESS OF OUR POSSIBILITIES]: (Warriors know that man is subliminally aware of his potential.)

SELECTED REFERENCES: **The Fire From Within - Page [216.6-216.7]** (Genaro walked ahead of us and...are subliminally aware of our possibilities.)

SEE ALSO: *AWARENESS, HUMAN-ALTERNATIVES-POSSIBILITIES-POTENTIAL, MAN-MALADY, CYNICISM, EQUILIBRIUM, MAN-MALADY*

AWARENESS-SURROGATE-WARRIOR-[THE WARRIORS' SURROGATE AWARENESS]: (Warriors know that they can create a replica of awareness through a perfect recapitulation; the Eagle will accept this replicated awareness as a surrogate of the warriors' consciousness; the sorcerers of antiquity based their rationale for the recapitulation on the concept of offering a surrogate awareness to the Eagle as a facsimile of their life experience; the warriors of the new cycle use their surrogate awareness to dart past the Eagle to freedom.)

SELECTED REFERENCES: The Eagle's Gift - Page [178.8-179.1] (Don Juan explained that the rule...of the totality of the body.) **The Eagle's Gift** - Page **[287.7-287.8]** (The reason why stalkers must recapitulate...perfect recapitulation in place of consciousness.) **The Eagle's Gift** - Page **[292.1-292.3]** (Florinda said that Soledad had been...because I had no more energy.) **The Power of Silence** - Page **[192.4-192.6]** ("I died in that field," he said...to go back and try again.) **The Art of Dreaming** - Page **[149.7-149.9]** (Don Juan stated that the old...the confines of time and space.)

SEE ALSO: *AWARENESS, RECAPITULATION, EAGLE-GIFT*

AWARENESS-SURVIVAL-FIRE-WITHIN-[THE SURVIVAL OF AWARENESS AFTER BURNING WITH THE FIRE FROM WITHIN]-(TOP)

AWARENESS-TOTAL-[TOTAL AWARENESS]: (Warriors know that total awareness is the culmination of the warriors' search for total freedom; the warriors' struggle to become fully aware; the ultimate bastion of awareness; the aim of warriors is to experience all the perceptual possibilities available to man, including an alternate way of dying.)

SELECTED REFERENCES: The Eagle's Gift - Page [178.8-179.3] (Don Juan explained that the rule...exists such an awareness at all.) **The Eagle's Gift** - Page **[265.7-265.9]** (Under Zuleica's guidance during her instruction...having my own tales of eternity.) **The Fire From Within** - Page **[67.2-67.3]** ("The new seers corrected that error...luminous cocoon in one single stroke.) **The Fire From Within** - Page **[113.8-114.3]** (He went on to explain that a...at large, and glide into eternity.) **The Fire From Within** - Page **[127.7-127.8]** (Don Juan had defined the scope...comes when they attain total awareness.) **The Fire From Within** - Page **[128.5-128.6]** ("What are we really doing, don...are nothing do they become everything." **The Fire From Within** - Page **[295.6]** ("What you are going to do...retain the sense of being themselves.") **The Fire From Within** - Page **[299.5-299.6]** ("The new seers burn with the...that total freedom means total awareness.") **The Power of Silence** - Page **[xvi.8]** (The aim of sorcerers is to...implies an alternative way of dying.)

SEE ALSO: *FREEDOM-TOTAL, FIRE-WITHIN, ATTENTION-THIRD, EAGLE-GIFT, HUMAN-ALTERNATIVES-POSSIBILITIES-POTENTIAL, AWARENESS-TRUTH-NINTH, WARRIOR-DEVELOPMENT-STAGES-THREE, AWARENESS*

AWARENESS-TRANSFERRING-[TRANSFERRING AWARENESS]: (Warriors know that transferring awareness is merely a matter of intending the total transfer of our normal awareness to our energy body; this transfer is accomplished by warriors voicing their intent and having sufficient energy to facilitate the transfer.)

SELECTED REFERENCES: The Art of Dreaming - Page [189.4-189.8] (Don Juan pulled us to...the trick. It'll tip the scales.") **The Art of Dreaming** - Page **[196.2-196.7]** (He confirmed our conjectures..."You bet your life," he replied.)

SEE ALSO: *AWARENESS, INTENT-VOICING, SCALES-TIP, INORGANIC-BEINGS-REALM-TRANSPORTED, AWARENESS-PREDOMINANCE-SWITCHING*

AWARENESS-TRICK-[THE TRICK OF AWARENESS]: (Warriors know that since the emanations at large are made to fixate what is inside man's cocoon, the trick of awareness is to let the fixating emanations merge with what is inside us; when that happens, warriors know that they become what they really are, fluid, forever in motion and eternal.)

SELECTED REFERENCES: **The Fire From Within - Page [56.9-57.2]** (He said that seers maintain, naturally...are - fluid, forever in motion, eternal.)

SEE ALSO: *AWARENESS, ASSEMBLAGE-POINT-MOVING, ATTENTION-THIRD*

AWARENESS-TRUTH-EIGHTH-[THE EIGHTH TRUTH ABOUT AWARENESS]: (Warriors know that the eighth truth about awareness is that intent is the pervasive force that causes us to perceive; we do not become aware because we perceive; rather, we perceive as a result of the pressure and intrusion of intent.)

SELECTED REFERENCES: **The Eagle's Gift - Page [148.3-148.7]** ("The Nagual said that *intent* is...had been waiting around for us.") **The Fire From Within - Page [258.4-258.5]** (I had always wondered, however, how...what makes the assemblage point move.) **The Power of Silence - Page [xvi.7]** (*Intent* is the pervasive force that...of the pressure and intrusion of intent.) **The Power of Silence - Page [31.2]** ("Meanwhile, let's continue with the element...nor any warriors in search of knowledge.") **The Power of Silence - Page [99.7-99.8]** (Don Juan repeated that his benefactor...was intent, the force that permeates everything.) **The Power of Silence - Page [103.7-103.9]** (In a calm voice don Juan...he said, is the essence of sorcery.)

SEE ALSO: *INTENT-INTERVENTION, PERCEPTION, ALIGNMENT, AWARENESS, AWARENESS-TRUTHS, AWARENESS-TRUTH-(ALL)*

AWARENESS-TRUTH-FIFTH-[THE FIFTH TRUTH ABOUT AWARENESS]: (Warriors know that the fifth truth about awareness is that perception occurs when the energy fields in the small group immediately surrounding the point of brilliance extend their light to illuminate identical energy fields outside the ball.)

SELECTED REFERENCES: **The Fire From Within - Page [46.1]** ("To perceive is to match the emanations inside our cocoon with those that are outside.") **The Fire From Within - Page [49.6-49.7]** ("They say that perception is a...to be cultivated by every living creature.") **The Fire From Within - Page [56.7-57.2]** ("Now," he went on, "when seers...are - fluid, forever in motion, eternal.) **The Fire From Within - Page [108.3]** (That awareness is achieved by the...exert on those inside our cocoons.) **The Fire From Within - Page [214.5-214.6]** ("We living beings are perceivers...the earth's boost is the key.) **The Fire From Within - Page [238.7-283.9]** (Don Juan stated that a displacement...world is just the force of alignment.) **The Power of Silence - Page [xvi.2]** (Perception occurs when the energy fields...identical energy fields outside the ball.) **The Power of Silence - Page [101.9-102.1]** (He had explained that normal perception...filaments extending into infinity outside our cocoon.)

SEE ALSO: *PERCEPTION, ALIGNMENT, ALIGNMENT-MYSTERY, AWARENESS, AWARENESS-TRUTHS, AWARENESS-TRUTH-(ALL)*

AWARENESS-TRUTH-FIRST-[THE FIRST TRUTH ABOUT AWARENESS]: (Warriors know that the first truth about awareness is that the universe is an infinite agglomeration of energy fields, resembling threads of light; the world out there is not what the average man thinks it is, because he thinks it is a world of objects and it is not; in fact there is no world of objects but a universe of the Eagle's emanations.)

SELECTED REFERENCES: **The Fire From Within - Page [33.1-33.2]** (The first truth, he said, was...a universe of the Eagle's emanations.) **The Fire From Within - Page [36.5-36.6]** ("The first truth about awareness, as...world of objects and it's not.") **The Fire From Within - Page [37.2-37.9]** ("The first truth is that the...in motion, and yet unchanged, eternal.") **The Fire From Within - Page [46.2-46.4]** ("No. Not at all. That would be...each of them is an eternity unto itself.") **The Fire From Within - Page [221.3-221.5]** (I followed his command...myriads of fibers came out of them.) **The Power of Silence - Page [xv.7]** ("The universe is an infinite agglomeration of energy fields resembling threads of light."] **The Power of Silence - Page [98.5-98.8]** (As I stared at the wondrous sight...all of them were inextricably bundled together.) **The Power of Silence - Page [101.7-101.8]** (Don Juan had explained that the universe...they were made out of light that was alive.) **The Art of Dreaming - Page [3.7]** ("Everything is energy. The whole universe...that energy is all there is.) **The Art of Dreaming - Page [4.9-5.4]** ("To perceive the essence of everything...for the human mind to comprehend.)

SEE ALSO: *EAGLE-EMANATIONS, LINES-WORLD, AWARENESS, AWARENESS-TRUTHS, WORLD-SOLID-OBJECTS, REALITY-INTERPRETATION, AWARENESS-TRUTHS, AWARENESS-TRUTH-(ALL), ENERGY*

AWARENESS-TRUTH-FOURTH-[THE FOURTH TRUTH ABOUT AWARENESS]: *(Warriors know that the fourth truth about awareness is that only a very small group of the energy fields inside the luminous ball are lit up by a point of intense brilliance located on the ball's surface.)*

SELECTED REFERENCES: **The Fire From Within - Page [43.5-43.7]** (He went on to say that the new seers...pressure organisms construct their perceivable world.) **The Fire From Within - Page [50.1-50.6]** ("When seers *see* perception, they witness...web and thereby directs the pressure.") **The Fire From Within - Page [72.5-72.7]** (He reiterated that awareness begins...breaking the cocoon, fighting to die.) **The Fire From Within - Page [108.3-108.4]** (That awareness is achieved by the constant pressure...exert on those inside our cocoons.) **The Fire From Within - Page [283.9]** (Certain emanations are routinely aligned...all there is to our world.) **The Power of Silence - Page [xvi.1]** (Only a very small group of the...brilliance located on the ball's surface.)

SEE ALSO: *AWARENESS-FIXATION, AWARENESS, EAGLE-EMANATIONS, AWARENESS-TRUTHS, AWARENESS-TRUTH-(ALL)*

AWARENESS-TRUTH-NINTH-[THE NINTH TRUTH ABOUT AWARENESS]: *(Warriors know that the ninth truth about awareness is that the aim of warrior-sorcerers is to reach a state of total awareness in order to experience all the possibilities of perception available to man; this state of awareness even implies an alternate way of dying.)*

SELECTED REFERENCES: **The Fire From Within - Page [67.2-67.3]** ("The new seers corrected that error...the luminous cocoon in one single stroke.") **The Fire From Within - Page [127.8-127.9]** (Don Juan had defined the scope...the only release that her spirit had.) **The Fire From Within - Page [128.5-128.6]** ("What are we really doing don Juan...are nothing do they become everything.") **The Fire From Within - Page [295.6-295.7]** ("What you are going to do...somewhat retain the sense of being themselves.") **The Power of Silence - Page [xvi.8]** (The aim of sorcerers is to reach...an alternative way of dying.)

SEE ALSO: *WORLDS-OTHER-ASSEMBLE-TOTAL, FREEDOM-TOTAL, AWARENESS, WARRIOR-DEATH-COMMAND, AWARENESS-TRUTHS, AWARENESS-TRUTH-(ALL)*

AWARENESS-TRUTH-SECOND-[THE SECOND TRUTH ABOUT AWARENESS]: *(Warriors know that the second truth about awareness is that the energy fields called the Eagle's emanations radiate from a source of inconceivable proportions metaphorically called the Eagle.)*

SELECTED REFERENCES: **The Fire From Within - Page [33.1-33.2]** (The first truth he said, was that...but a universe of the Eagle's emanations.) **The Fire From Within - Page [37.2-37.4]** ("The first truth is that the world...the same kind, because we learn what to perceive.") **The Fire From Within - Page [43.8-43.9]** ("In our case as human beings...isn't possible for us to disregard our perceptions.") **The Fire From Within - Page [45.7]** (The new seers on the other hand...utilize them to construct their perceivable world.) **The Fire From Within - Page [48.8-48.9]** (After a long silence, Genaro fell...truths have been verified by *seeing*.) **The Fire From Within - Page [50.5]** ("The Eagle's emanations are more...Each of them is a source of boundless energy.") **The Fire From Within - Page [108.3]** (That human beings are made of the...that encloses a small portion of these emanations.) **The Power of Silence - Page [xv.7-xv.8]** (These energy fields, called the Eagle's emanations...inconceivable proportions metaphorically called the Eagle.)

SEE ALSO: *EAGLE, EAGLE-EMANATIONS, AWARENESS, AWARENESS-TRUTHS, AWARENESS-TRUTH-(ALL)*

AWARENESS-TRUTH-SEVENTH-[THE SEVENTH TRUTH ABOUT AWARENESS]: *(Warriors know that the seventh truth about awareness is that the assemblage point can be moved from its usual position on the surface of the luminous ball to another position on the surface, or into the interior; since the brilliance of the assemblage point can light up whatever*

energy fields it comes in contact with, when it moves to a new position it immediately brightens up new energy fields, making them perceivable; this perception is known as "seeing"; when the assemblage point shifts, it makes possible the perception of an entirely different world, as objective and factual as the one we normally perceive; sorcerers go into that other world to get energy, power, solutions to general and particular problems, or to face the unimaginable.)

SELECTED REFERENCES: **The Fire From Within** - Page [125.3-125.5] ("I've mentioned to you that the...human senses perceive in inconceivable ways.") **The Fire From Within** - Page [141.1-141.3] ("I've explained to you that man...different from the world we know.") **The Fire From Within** - Page [144.7-144.8] ("But today, we are going to examine...after it moves from its original position.) **The Fire From Within** - Page [163.8-163.9] ("There are other complete worlds that...the other five are something else.") **The Fire From Within** - Page [164.5-164.8] (He said that a true change...and consequently we perceive other worlds.") **The Fire From Within** - Page [213.2-213.3] ("I mean that when man's assemblage...aided by the boost from the earth.") **The Fire From Within** - Page [283.5-284.2] (He said that now I needed...of a mirage as the old fixation.") **The Power of Silence** - Page [xvi.3-xvi.8] (The assemblage point can be moved...particular problems, or to face the unimaginable.) **The Power of Silence** - Page [56.9-57.1] (Don Juan said that perception is...perception of the world changes accordingly.) **The Art of Dreaming** - Page [6.8-7.1] (Finally, they *saw* two things...are perceiving in an unfamiliar manner.)

SEE ALSO: *ASSEMBLAGE-POINT-MOVING, AWARENESS, AWARENESS-TRUTHS, AWARENESS-TRUTH-(ALL)*

AWARENESS-TRUTH-SIXTH-[THE SIXTH TRUTH ABOUT AWARENESS]: (Warriors know that the sixth truth about awareness is that since the only energy fields perceivable are those lit by the point of brilliance, that point is named "the point where perception is assembled" or simply "the assemblage point.")

SELECTED REFERENCES: **The Fire From Within** - Page [108.5-108.6] ("The next truth is that perception...assemblage point is located on our cocoon.") **The Fire From Within** - Page [110.9] (He also said that the old seers...luminous shell, in the cocoon itself.) **The Fire From Within** - Page [118.2] ("Every living being has an assemblage point...points have selected are the same.") **The Fire From Within** - Page [119.1-119.2] ("The assemblage point of man appears...that point is fixated at that spot.") **The Fire From Within** - Page [123.6-124.1] (Don Juan said that the assemblage...as bundles, with the emanations at large.) **The Fire From Within** - Page [148.8] ("In order to be unbiased witnesses...witness, whatever that world might be.") **The Fire From Within** - Page [216.3] (Just before we came into the square...leave room for anything except realness.) **The Power of Silence** - Page [xvi.2] (Since the only energy fields perceivable...or simply "the assemblage point.") **The Art of Dreaming** - Page [6.8-7.1] (Finally, they *saw* two things...are perceiving in an unfamiliar manner.)

SEE ALSO: *ASSEMBLAGE-POINT, PERCEPTION, ALIGNMENT, AWARENESS, AWARENESS-TRUTHS, AWARENESS-TRUTH-(ALL)*

AWARENESS-TRUTH-THIRD-[THE THIRD TRUTH ABOUT AWARENESS]: (Warriors know that the third truth about awareness is that human beings are also composed of an incalculable number of the same threadlike energy fields; these Eagle's emanations form an encased agglomeration that manifests itself as a ball of light the size of a person's body with the arms extended laterally, like a giant luminous egg.)

SELECTED REFERENCES: **A Separate Reality** - Page [23.2-23.5] ("Men look different when you "see"...changed in that luminous egg? What?") **A Separate Reality** - Page [106.1-106.2] (He said that he had already told...utmost importance in the life of a man.) **The Eagle's Gift** - Page [17.9-18.1] (Don Juan said that our total being...the appearance of giant luminous eggs.) **The Fire From Within** - Page [45.8-46.1] ("It's so simple it sounds idiotic...encased, is what makes us men.") **The Fire From Within** - Page [49.8-50.1] ("The emanations inside and the emanations...to have inside their luminous cocoons.) **The Fire From Within** - Page [50.8-50.9] (He explained that the old seers...the cocoon, running along its entire length.) **The Fire From Within - Page [108.3]** (That human beings are made of the...that encloses a small portion of these emanations.) **The Power of Silence - Page [xv.8-xv.9]** (Human beings are also composed of an...extended laterally, like a giant luminous egg.)

SEE ALSO: *LUMINOUS BEINGS, LUMINOUS-COCOON, AWARENESS, AWARENESS-TRUTHS, AWARENESS-TRUTH-(ALL), LUMINOUS-EGG*

AWARENESS-TRUTHS-[THE TRUTHS ABOUT AWARENESS]: (Warriors know that the truths about awareness are certain conclusions reached through "seeing" about the nature of man and the world; the explanation of awareness.)

SELECTED REFERENCES: **The Fire From Within - [Page 32.9-33.1]** (He said that there were a...the total sequence of such truths) **The Fire From Within - Page [33.3]** (Most of the truths about awareness...order those truths were nearly incomprehensible.) **The Fire From Within - [Page 35.6-35.7]** (Don Juan said that *seeing* was...awareness he was explaining to me.) **The Fire From Within - Page [108.2-108.6]** (He then began his explanation...point is located on our cocoon.) **The Fire From Within - Page [109.3]** (He said that the new seers...order for the truths about awareness.) **The Fire From Within - Page [118.4-118.7]** ("The nagual's blow is of great...simply don't know about their possibilities.") **The Fire From Within - Page [141.1-141.2]** ("I've explained to you that man...different from the world we know.") **The Power of Silence - Page [xv.7-xvi.9]** (1. The universe is an infinite field...implies an alternative way of dying.) **The Art of Dreaming - Page [4.9-5.2]** ("To perceive the essence of everything...and *see* the essence of everything.)

SEE ALSO: *AWARENESS-EXPLANATION, AWARENESS-TRUTH-(ALL)*

AWARENESS-ULTIMATE-BASTION-[THE ULTIMATE BASTION OF AWARENESS]: (Warriors know that to make this world vanish while still remaining somewhat themselves is the ultimate bastion of awareness; to burn with consciousness while still retaining the sense of being oneself.)

SELECTED REFERENCES: **The Fire From Within - Page [295.5-295.7]** ("What you are going to do is...retain the sense of being themselves.")

SEE ALSO: *FIRE-WITHIN, AWARENESS-TOTAL*

AWARENESS-WE-ARE-[WE ARE AN AWARENESS]: (Warriors know that they are an awareness, a perceiver; warriors know they are boundless and not solid objects; warriors knows they have no solidity.)

SELECTED REFERENCES: **Tales of Power - Page [97.7-97.8]** (We are perceivers. We are an...we rarely emerge in a lifetime.)

SEE ALSO: *PERCEIVERS-WE-ARE, AWARENESS, WORLD-SOLID-OBJECTS*

AWARENESS-WRAPPED-[WRAPPED IN AWARENESS]: SEE: WARRIOR-IMPECCABILITY-TICKET-WRAPPED-AWARENESS-[THE WARRIORS' TICKET TO IMPECCABILITY MUST BE WRAPPED IN AWARENESS]

AWARENESS-WRAPPING-[WRAPPING AWARENESS]: SEE: DREAMING-DESCRIPTION-[A DESCRIPTION OF DREAMING]

B

BACKBONE-WARRIOR-[THE BACKBONE OF THE WARRIOR]: SEE: WARRIOR-BACKBONE-[THE BACKBONE OF THE WARRIOR]

BAD-LUCK-[BAD LUCK]: SEE: LUCK-BAD-[BAD LUCK]

BAFFLEMENT-WARRIOR-[THE BAFFLEMENT OF THE WARRIOR]: SEE: WARRIOR-BAFFLEMENT-[THE BAFFLEMENT OF THE WARRIOR]

BALANCE-[BALANCE]: (*Warriors know that they begin life with their spirits somewhat off balance and that they must spend a lifetime doing their ultimate best to regain that balance; the balance and harmony of the warriors' way; the harmony between actions and thought; the harmony between the tonal and the nagual; the luminous equilibrium of the world and the universe; women have an inherent balance which men do not; with regard to the movement of the assemblage point, warriors know that human beings are experts at compensating for these movements and that we all re-balance ourselves constantly so that we can go on as if nothing has happened to us; eventually, warriors must have the assuredness to balance the tenuousness of their new continuity.*)

SELECTED REFERENCES: **A Separate Reality - Page [23.4-23.6]** ("Is that the way everyone looks...changed in that luminous egg? What?) **A Separate Reality - Page [99.4]** ("Talking is not Genaro's predilection," he...you about the equilibrium of things.") **A Separate Reality - Page [219.3]** (Don Juan laughed and said that...done harmoniously and with great patience.) **Journey to Ixtlan - Page [53.7-54.1]** ("To be a hunter means that...your family all ate the game.") **Journey to Ixtlan - Page [267.6]** ("Only as a warrior can one...the wonder of being a man.") **Tales of Power - Page [26.8-27.1]** (As you already know, your spirit...ultimate best to gain this balance.) **Tales of Power - Page [91.6]** ("Good, good," don Juan said, patting...is to balance terror and wonder.") **Tales of Power - Page [142.7]** ("What is a *proper tonal* ?" I asked...is just right, balanced and harmonious.) **Tales of Power - Page [155.9]** (Now there is no longer a war...the harmony between *tonal* and *nagual.*) **Tales of Power - Page [160.9]** (Because of its inherent weakness the...order to prop up the *tonal.*) **The Second Ring of Power - Page [136.9-137.2]** (Once a sorcerer regains his completeness...had three sons and one daughter.) **The Second Ring of Power - Page [152.7]** (The Nagual taught me to be...and not to seek anything eagerly.) **The Eagle's Gift - Page [222.7-222.8]** (Don Juan told us that the reason...to which she happens to belong.) **The Fire From Within - Page [266.7-266.9]** (Soon he became aware that since...if nothing has happened to us.) **The Power of Silence - Page [35.8-35.9]** (Well, your assemblage point moves almost...sexual energy is not in balance.")

SEE ALSO: *HARMONY, ACT-LEARNING, TONAL-NAGUAL-DICHOTOMY, WARRIOR-EQUILIBRIUM, WARRIOR-ASSUREDNESS, SPIRIT-BALANCE, BALANCE-(ALL), CONTINUITY, EQUILIBRIUM, WARRIOR-COMPLETENESS*

BALANCE-SOBRIETY-ABANDON-WARRIOR-[WARRIORS BALANCE SOBRIETY AND ABANDON]: SEE: WARRIOR-BALANCE-SOBRIETY-ABANDON-[WARRIORS BALANCE SOBRIETY AND ABANDON]

BALANCE-WARRIOR-[THE WARRIORS' BALANCE]: SEE: WARRIOR-BALANCE-[THE WARRIORS' BALANCE]

BARKING-DOG-SADNESS-[THE NOCTURNAL VOICE OF MAN]-(TOP)

BASES-FOUR-[THE FOUR BASES]: (*Warriors know that the four bases is another term for the four moods of stalking; in order to protect themselves, warriors cultivate the perfect blend of ruthlessness, cunning, patience, and*

sweetness; the four bases are inextricably bound together and warriors cultivate them by intending them.)
    SELECTED REFERENCES: **The Power of Silence - Page [244.2-244.6]** ("In order to protect themselves from...points to move to specific positions.")
    SEE ALSO: *STALKING-MOODS-FOUR, RUTHLESSNESS, CUNNING, PATIENCE, SWEETNESS*

BATTLE-LAST-WARRIOR-[THE WARRIORS' LAST BATTLE]: SEE: WARRIOR-LAST STAND-[THE WARRIORS' LAST STAND]

BATTLE-POWER-[THE BATTLE OF POWER]: SEE: WARRIOR-BATTLE-[THE WARRIORS' BATTLE OF POWER]

BATTLE-SOUL-[THE BATTLE FOR THE SOUL]: (TOP) SEE: SOUL-BATTLE-[THE BATTLE FOR THE SOUL]-(TOP)

BATTLEFIELD-WARRIOR-[THE WARRIORS' BATTLEFIELD]: SEE: WARRIOR-BATTLEFIELD-[THE WARRIORS' BATTLEFIELD]

BEAUTY-[BEAUTY]: *(Warriors know that they must develop a peculiar appreciation for beauty; they lavish beauty on those around them, retaining for themselves only their longing; this shock of beauty is called stalking; the warriors' sense of beauty is part of their sobriety, it distinguishes warriors from those who have been aberrated by their contact with power.)*
    SELECTED REFERENCES: **The Second Ring of Power - Page [285.5-285.7]** ("How do I balance my second attention...you decided to go with us.") **The Second Ring of Power - Page [326.1]** (The Nagual and Genaro liked beauty. They went there for there sheer enjoyment.") **The Power of Silence - Page [82.3-82.6]** ("The real challenge for those sorcerers...that, they need morality and beauty.") **The Power of Silence - Page [109.7-109.8]** ("You must agree, don Juan, not...no order, no sobriety, no beauty.) **The Power of Silence - Page [111.6-111.8]** ("As I hear the words," don...this shock of beauty, is stalking. ")
    SEE ALSO: *WARRIOR-SOBRIETY, POETRY, STALKING-JOLT, MORALITY*

BEAUTY-DEMON-[THE DEMON OF PERSONAL BEAUTY]: *(Warriors know that personal beauty is a demon that proliferates and breeds when admired; it is by far one of the hardest demons to overcome; those who are beautiful are often wretched because of their struggle with their own demon beauty.)*
    SELECTED REFERENCES: **The Eagle's Gift - Page [271.6-272.3]** (She said that she had been born...Everybody said so, especially men.") **The Eagle's Gift - Page [286.1-286.2]** (Even though her benefactor made her...that she was impervious to change.)
    SEE ALSO: *BEAUTY, SELF-IMPORTANCE*

BED-STRINGS-[THE BED OF STRINGS]-(TOP)

BEETLE-DEATH-WARRIOR-[THE BEETLE AND THE WARRIOR'S DEATH]-(TOP)

BEGINNING-[THE BEGINNING OF THINGS]: *(Warriors know there is no beginning; the beginning of things exists only in man's thoughts.)*
    SELECTED REFERENCES: **A Separate Reality - Page [177.7]** ("You always insist on knowing things...beginning is only in your thought.")
    SEE ALSO: *TIME, KNOWLEDGE-VS-LANGUAGE*

BEHAVIOR-UNUSUAL-[UNUSUAL BEHAVIOR]: SEE: ROUTINES-DISRUPTING-[DISRUPTING ROUTINES]

BEHAVIOR-WARRIOR-[THE WARRIORS' BEHAVIOR]: SEE: WARRIOR-BEHAVIOR-[THE WARRIORS' BEHAVIOR]

BEING-CORE-[THE CORE OF OUR BEING]: (Warriors know that perception is the core of man's being.)
> SELECTED REFERENCES: **The Second Ring of Power** - Page **[274.8-274.9]** (Don Juan said that the core...being was the act of awareness.)
> SEE ALSO: *PERCEPTION, AWARENESS-PERCEPTION-UNIT*

BEING-DIE-[THE BEING THAT IS GOING TO DIE]: (Warriors know that the being which is going to die is another term for the energy body.)
> SELECTED REFERENCES: **Journey to Ixtlan** - Page **[200.4-200.5]** ("It may hook you to another...the *not-doing* of the self.") **Journey to Ixtlan** - Page **[247.3-247.4]** (We are both beings who are...taught you and *stop the world*.")
> SEE ALSO: *ENERGY-BODY*

BEING-MAGIC-OF-OUR-[THE MAGIC OF OUR BEING]: (Warriors know that the act of awareness is the magic of our being.)
> SELECTED REFERENCES: **The Second Ring of Power** - Page **[274.9]** (Don Juan said that the core...being was the act of awareness.)
> SEE ALSO: *AWARENESS, AWARENESS-PERCEPTION-UNIT, MAGIC*

BEING-THEMSELVES-WARRIOR-[THE WARRIORS' CHALLENGE TO BE THEMSELVES WITHOUT BEING THEMSELVES]: SEE: WARRIOR-BEING-THEMSELVES-[THE WARRIORS' CHALLENGE TO BE THEMSELVES WITHOUT BEING THEMSELVES]

BEING-TOTAL-[THE WARRIORS' TOTAL BEING]: SEE: TOTAL-BEING-[THE WARRIORS' TOTAL BEING]

BEINGS-AWARENESS-MOVING-VS-STATIONARY-[THE AWARENESS OF MOVING BEINGS VS STATIONARY BEINGS]: (Warriors know that the awareness of moving beings is filled with strife, but there is no sense of strife in the awareness of a tree.)
> SELECTED REFERENCES: **The Eagle's Gift** - Page **[236.5-236.6]** (Silvio Manuel told us that the...filled to the brim with it.)
> SEE ALSO: *TREES, AWARENESS, STRIFE*

BEINGS-DOUBLE-[DOUBLE BEINGS]: SEE: DOUBLE-BEINGS-[DOUBLE BEINGS]

BEINGS-INORGANIC-[INORGANIC BEINGS]: SEE: INORGANIC-BEINGS-[THE INORGANIC BEINGS]

BEINGS-LUMINOUS-[LUMINOUS BEINGS]: SEE: LUMINOUS-BEINGS-[LUMINOUS BEINGS]

BEINGS-MAGICAL-[MAGICAL BEINGS]: SEE: MAGICAL-BEINGS-[MAGICAL BEINGS]

BEINGS-ORGANIC-[ORGANIC BEINGS]: SEE: ORGANIC-LIFE-[ORGANIC LIFE]

*BELIEVE-HAVING-TO-[HAVING TO BELIEVE]: (Warriors know they must evolve a specific perspective on believing; they do this as a choice, as an expression of their innermost predilection; the warriors' secret of believing is that they believe without believing.)
> SELECTED REFERENCES: **Tales of Power** - Page **[52.3-52.5]** (A warrior acts as if nothing had...in such a manner dissipates obsession.") **Tales of Power** - Page **[107.7-107.9]** (I was told that the only...believe, a warrior *has* to believe.") **Tales of Power** - Page **[114.5-114.7]** ("What an exquisite omen this is...is the predilection of my spirit.") **Tales of Power** - Page **[115.9]** (Don Juan was right. Having to...predilection. Without it he had nothing.)

SEE ALSO: *WARRIOR-PREDILECTION, WARRIOR-CONTRADICTION-KNOWLEDGE*

BELLY-BUTTON-BRACE-[BELLY BUTTON BRACE]: (Warriors know that in dreaming they pay attention with their belly button; by bracing the belly button and having something pressing on it, warriors can better hold the images of their dreams.)
SELECTED REFERENCES: The Second Ring of Power - Page [163.4-163.7] ("The Nagual told me to find...to hold images in my dreams.)
SEE ALSO: *BELLY-PUSHING-DOWN*

BELLY-PUSHING-DOWN-[PUSHING THE BELLY DOWN]: (Warriors know that pushing down with the belly is a breathing technique used in moments of danger, fear or stress.)
SELECTED REFERENCES: Tales of Power - Page [166.3-166.7] (I felt don Juan's head next...accelerated fashion, depending on one's preference.) Tales of Power - Page [189.5] (I began the breathing exercises and held...I was not listening to him.)
SEE ALSO: *BREATH*

BENCH-WARRIOR-[THE BENCH OF A WARRIOR]-(TOP)

BENEFACTOR-[THE WARRIORS' BENEFACTOR]: (Warriors know that the benefactor is one of two mentors that every sorcery apprentice has; the benefactor is the teacher who shows the apprentice the nagual; the apprentice is the benefactor's "protegido", his "protected one".)
SELECTED REFERENCES: The Teachings of Don Juan - Page [14.8-14.9] (I had known don Juan for...the training was long and arduous.) Journey to Ixtlan - Page [90.1-90.2] (We then had a long conversation...to become a "man of knowledge.") Journey to Ixtlan - Page [216.1-216.3] ("If we wouldn't be tricked, we...lot more in order to survive.") Tales of Power - Page [175.1-175.6] ("Can you tell me, don Juan...been to work with your tonal.") Tales of Power - Page [176.3-176.4] ("When an ordinary man is ready,...benefactor, and he becomes a sorcerer.") Tales of Power - Page [187.2] ("Genaro is very warm," don Juan...that you found a gentle benefactor.") Tales of Power - Page [187.9-188.9] (The main topic was don Genaro...not more so than the teacher.) Tales of Power - Page [230.7-230.9] ("I've already told you that I am...show how to get to it.") Tales of Power - Page [243.3-243.5] ("What would have happened if I...the necessary avenues. That is the rule.") Tales of Power - Page [246.8-247.4] (Don Juan was talking about a time... fear and yet drooling at her.) Tales of Power - Page [270.7-271.2] (He began to talk about Pablito and...kind teacher and a stern benefactor.) The Power of Silence - Page [10.6-10.7] ("Why are the naguals called 'benefactors'...guides them through unimaginable areas.")
SEE ALSO: *TEACHERS-TEACHING, NAGUAL, PROTEGIDO, BENEFACTOR-DELIVER-WARD-POWER*

BENEFACTOR-DELIVER-WARD-POWER-[THE BENEFACTOR DELIVERS HIS WARD TO POWER]: (Warriors know that a benefactor is responsible for delivering his ward to power; in doing so, the benefactor imparts his personal touch to the neophyte, as much, if not more so than the teacher.)
SELECTED REFERENCES: Tales of Power - Page [188.8-188.9] (Don Juan said that it was...not more so than the teacher.)
SEE ALSO: *BENEFACTOR, TEACHERS-TEACHING, POWER*

BENEFACTOR-OMEN-[THE OMEN OF THE BENEFACTOR]-(TOP): SEE: OMEN-BENEFACTOR-[THE OMEN OF THE BENEFACTOR]-(TOP)

BENEFICIAL-SPOT-[THE WARRIORS' BENEFICIAL SPOT]: SEE: POWER-SPOT-[THE WARRIORS' POWER SPOT]

BENIGNO-EYES-PRESSES-[BENIGNO PRESSES WITH HIS EYES]-(TOP)

BENIGNO-VOICE-BOOMING-[BENIGNO'S FAVORITE VOICE]-(TOP)

BEST-WARRIOR-[WARRIORS AT THEIR BEST]: SEE: WARRIOR-BEST-[WARRIORS AT THEIR BEST]

BEWITCHING-[BEWITCHING]: (Warriors know that bewitching is the activity of an aberrant sorcerer; bewitching is for rendering people harmless or sick or dumb; warriors have no interest in directing their power towards others in such a way.)
SELECTED REFERENCES: **A Separate Reality - Page [76.6-76.8]** ("Can you bewitch him, don Juan...you have a man of courage!")
SEE ALSO: *DIABLERO, WITCHES, WARRIOR-DESIRE*

BID-POWER-WARRIOR-[THE WARRIORS' BID FOR POWER]: SEE: WARRIOR-POWER-BID-[THE WARRIORS' BID FOR POWER]

BIGOT-WAY-[THE BIGOT'S WAY]: (Warriors know that the bigot's way is one of the three bad habits which are used over and over by the average man when he is confronted by unusual life situations; the bigot's way is to disregard what's happening and feel as if it never occurred; warriors strive to live their lives the warriors' way.)
SELECTED REFERENCES: **Tales of Power - Page [52.1-52.2]** ("There are three kinds of bad...That one is the bigot's way.)
SEE ALSO: *HABITS-BAD-THREE, WARRIOR-WAY*

BIRD-FREEDOM-[THE BIRD OF FREEDOM]: Warriors speak of the path of knowledge as a magical, mysterious bird which pauses in its flight for a moment in order to give man hope and purpose; warriors live under the wing of that bird, which is called the bird of freedom; warriors nourish that bird with their dedication and impeccability; the bird of freedom always flies in a straight line, it can never circle back; the bird of freedom can do only two things, take warriors along or leave them behind.)
SELECTED REFERENCES: **The Power of Silence - Page [22.8-23.2]** (The woman did not respond. And...sorcerers along, or leave them behind.) **The Power of Silence - Page [23.7-24.2]** (Don Juan commented that that was not surprising...it flew away, it never returned.)
SEE ALSO: *FREEDOM, KNOWLEDGE-PATH, WARRIOR-WAY, WARRIOR-IMPECCABILITY, WARRIOR-CHANCE-MINIMAL, WARRIOR-DECISIONS, WARRIOR-CHOICE, WARRIOR-PURPOSE, WARRIOR-FREEDOM*

BLACK-DOG-[THE IRIDESCENT BLACK DOG]-(TOP): SEE: OMEN-ESCOGIDO-[THE OMEN OF THE ESCOGIDO]-(TOP)

BLACK-LAKE-[THE BLACK LAKE]-(TOP)

BLACK-MAGICIANS-[THE BLACK MAGICIANS]: (Warriors know that the black magicians are our fellow men; those who would keep warriors tied down with their thoughts and first attention agendas.)
SELECTED REFERENCES: **Journey to Ixtlan - Page [12.8-12.9]** ("Don't you see?" he asked dramatically...pins you down with their thoughts.") **Journey to Ixtlan - Page [15.8-15.9]** ("What's wrong is that once they...way people know you, for instance.") **Tales of Power - Page [20.8-21.3]** ("You're again confusing issues. Solace, haven...time and your power fearing me.")
SEE ALSO: *FREEDOM, SLAVERY*

BLACK-SHADOW-DEATH-[THE BLACK SHADOW OF DEATH]: SEE: SHADOW-BLACK-DEATH-[THE BLACK SHADOW OF DEATH]

BLACK-WORLD [THE BLACK WORLD]: SEE: WORLD-BLACK-[THE BLACK WORLD]

BLACK-WORLD-TALES-[TALES OF THE BLACK WORLD]-(TOP): SEE: WORLD-BLACK-TALES-[TALES OF THE BLACK WORLD]-(TOP)

BLACKNESS-HEIGHTS-ASCENDING-[ASCENDING THE HEIGHTS OF BLACKNESS]-(TOP)

BLACKNESS-MOMENT-[THE MOMENT OF BLACKNESS]: (Warriors know that the moment of blackness is a moment of supreme silence that gives rise to intent; a moment more silent than the moment of shutting off the internal dialogue.)
SELECTED REFERENCES: The Eagle's Gift - Page [143.2-143.4] ("Have you ever felt that moment...it, to make it do things.)
SEE ALSO: *INNER SILENCE, INTERNAL-DIALOGUE-STOPPING*

BLEEDING-TOGETHER-[WE ARE BLEEDING TOGETHER]: SEE: DAGGER-METAPHORICAL-[THE METAPHORICAL DAGGER]

BLOW-DEATH-[THE BLOW OF DEATH]: SEE: NAGUAL-BLOW-DEATH-[THE NAGUAL'S BLOW OF FREEDOM CAN BE THE BLOW OF DEATH]

BLOW-FREEDOM-[THE BLOW OF FREEDOM]: SEE: NAGUAL-BLOW-DEATH-[THE NAGUAL'S BLOW OF FREEDOM CAN BE THE BLOW OF DEATH]

BLOW-NAGUAL-[THE NAGUAL'S BLOW]: SEE: NAGUAL-BLOW-[THE NAGUAL'S BLOW]

BLUE-ENERGY-[BLUE ENERGY]: (Warriors know that blue energy doesn't exist in a natural state in our world; blue energy is like ours, it wavers, but it is blue instead of white.)
SELECTED REFERENCES: The Art of Dreaming - Page [179.2-179.3] ("Where does the blue scout stand...a natural state in our world.)
SEE ALSO: *ENERGY, SCOUT-BLUE-(TOP)*

BLUE-SCOUT-[THE BLUE SCOUT]-(TOP): SEE: SCOUT-BLUE-[THE BLUE SCOUT]-(TOP)

BLUEPRINT-EVENTS-[THE BLUEPRINTS OF EVENTS]: (Warriors know that the abstract cores of the sorcery stories are blueprints for complete chains of events.)
SELECTED REFERENCES: The Power of Silence - Page [6.4-6.5] (Don Juan explained that sorcerers...blueprints of complete chains of events.)
SEE ALSO: *ABSTRACT-CORES, SORCERY-STORIES*

BODY-ENERGY-[THE ENERGY BODY]: SEE: ENERGY-BODY-[THE ENERGY BODY]

BODY-PHYSICAL-[THE PHYSICAL BODY]: (Warriors know that the awareness of the physical body is one of two perceivable segments of the warriors' total being; without the energy body, one is merely a lump of organic matter that can easily be manipulated by awareness; the physical body of the average man is somehow dormant and unaware of a great many things.)
SELECTED REFERENCES: Journey to Ixtlan - Page [19.5-19.7] (He seemed to have read my thoughts...not really stupid but somehow dormant.) Journey to Ixtlan - Page [160.2-160.4] (I told him that I was simply...rather in what you don't do.") Journey to Ixtlan - Page [180.1-180.4] (The reason you keep on coming...me because I am its friend.") Journey to Ixtlan - Page [181.5] (He explained the event, saying that...soaked for hours in "not-doing.") Journey to

Ixtlan - Page [194.5-194.6] ("When one does something with people...cares whether or not you understand?") **Tales of Power** - Page [77.6-77.7] ("So, as you may very well...I deviated some of your crap.") **Tales of Power** - Page [82.3-82.4] ("Watch those muscles," he said. "They...before the *will* is a functioning unit.") **Tales of Power** - Page [93.6-93.8] ("That night that you met the...of luminous fibers that have awareness.) **Tales of Power** - Page [94.3-94.4] ("Everything that you've witnessed so far...together in a most praiseworthy manner.) **Tales of Power** - **Page [95.6-95.8]** (I remarked that the diagram was...the fibers of a luminous being.) **Tales of Power** - **Page [136.4]** ("There is no need to treat...I have called that indulging.) **Tales of Power** - **Page [157.5-157.6]** ("No. I wasn't. But it 's useless...with the body, not the reason.") **Tales of Power** - **Page [195.6-195.7]** ("The reason why you're afraid of...run away every time Genaro is around.") **Tales of Power** - **Page [217.9-218.2]** (Genaro says that the reason why...the same choice, it doesn't work.") **Tales of Power** - **Page [245.5]** ("Here is where I varied from...above all, without injuring one's body.) **The Second Ring of Power** - **Page [326.6]** ("Yes, we will go as we...simply goes into the other world.) **The Eagle's Gift** - **Page [17.9-18.1]** (Don Juan had said that our...the appearance of giant luminous eggs.) **The Eagle's Gift** - **Page [18.4]** (In order to explain these concepts...passes the awareness of the physical body.) **The Eagle's Gift** - **Page [163.6]** (Don Juan had also told us that...are in the human body itself.) **The Fire From Within** - **Page [64.8-65.2]** (Don Juan replied that human alternatives are...have, therefore, nearly an inexhaustible scope.) **The Fire From Within** - **Page [123.6-123.7]** (Don Juan said that the assemblage...human body as we perceive it.) **The Art of Dreaming** - **Page [11.4-11.5]** (In his teachings he put a...egg, which is our energy self.) **The Art of Dreaming** - **Page [132.5]** (Don Juan added that without the...can be easily manipulated by awareness.)
      SEE ALSO: *ATTENTION-FIRST, TONAL, ATTENTION-TONAL, ATTENTION-FIRST-BODY-PHYSICAL, BODY-PHYSICAL-(ALL)*

BODY-PHYSICAL-CENTERS-[THE CENTERS OF THE PHYSICAL BODY]: (Warriors know that the centers for the physical body are located in the midsection and in the calves, especially the right calf.)

      SELECTED REFERENCES: **The Eagle's Gift** - **Page [155.7-155.9]** (Moved by the boundless fear I was feeling...at the midpoint of my body.) **The Eagle's Gift** - **Page [238.7-238.8]** (In my case, on one occasion...on the midpoint of my body.) **The Eagle's Gift** - **Page [257.7-258.2]** (One day, for no reason I...my body in my sitting position.)The **Eagle's Gift** - **Page [259.1-259.2]** (Second, in order to dislodge the...possible until they seem to join.)
      SEE ALSO: *BODY-PHYSICAL-MIDPOINT, DREAMER-PONCHO*

BODY-PHYSICAL-IMAGES-[THE PHYSICAL BODY HOLDS THE IMAGES OF THE EVERYDAY WORLD]: (Warriors know that our bodies hold the images of our daily world, even though we have no idea how they do it.)

      SELECTED REFERENCES: **The Second Ring of Power** - **Page [163.1-163.4]** ("The next thing the Nagual wanted me...to glance and yet hold the image.)
      SEE ALSO: *BODY-PHYSICAL, ATTENTION-FIRST*

BODY-PHYSICAL-KNOWING-[KNOWING WITH THE PHYSICAL BODY]: SEE: BODY-PHYSICAL-WITNESSING-[WITNESSING AND KNOWING WITH THE PHYSICAL BODY]:

BODY-PHYSICAL-MIDPOINT-[THE MIDPOINT OF THE PHYSICAL BODY]: (Warriors know that the midpoint of the body is the center for the will.)

      SELECTED REFERENCES: **The Eagle's Gift** - **Page [155.7-155.9]** (Moved by the boundless fear I was feeling...at the midpoint of my body.) **The Eagle's Gift** - **Page [238.7-238.8]** (In my case, on one occasion...on the midpoint of my body.) **The Eagle's Gift** - **Page [259.1-259.2]** (Second, in order to dislodge the...possible until they seem to join.) **The Eagle's Gift** - **Page [257.4-258.2]** (Zuleica started then on another facet...my body in my sitting position.) **The Eagle's Gift** - **Page [260.3-260.4]** (She ordered me to stand up by...to lift up my whole body.) **The Fire From Within** - **Page [107.4-107.6]** (Don Juan came to my side...the man let go of me.)
      SEE ALSO: *WILL, BODY-PHYSICAL-CENTERS, BODY-PHYSICAL*

BODY-PHYSICAL-NEEDS-LEARN-[WHAT THE PHYSICAL BODY NEEDS TO LEARN]: (Warriors are aware that the body needs to learn things that are independent of the understanding of reason.)

SELECTED REFERENCES: **Journey to Ixtlan - Page [180.1-180.4]** (The reason you keep on coming...me because I am its friend.")
SEE ALSO: *BODY-PHYSICAL, REASON, REASON-VS-BODY, LEARNING*

BODY-PHYSICAL-POINTS-SORCERER-DIAGRAM-[THE CORRESPONDING LOCATIONS ON THE PHYSICAL BODY FOR THE EIGHT POINTS OF THE SORCERERS' DIAGRAM]: SEE: SORCERER-DIAGRAM-BODY-[THE CORRESPONDING LOCATIONS ON THE PHYSICAL BODY FOR THE EIGHT POINTS OF THE SORCERERS' DIAGRAM]

BODY-PHYSICAL-PROTECTING-[PROTECTING THE PHYSICAL BODY]: (Warriors know it is unnecessary to treat the physical body so badly; warriors know that human beings have learned to perfection how to make their tonals weak through self-indulging; warriors protect their physical bodies by avoiding their tendencies to indulge themselves.)
SELECTED REFERENCES: **Tales of Power - Page [136.4-136.5]** ("There is no need to treat the body...I have called that indulging.")
SEE ALSO: *BODY-PHYSICAL, TONAL, SELF-INDULGING, WARRIOR-IMPECCABILITY*

BODY-PHYSICAL-REMEMBERING-[REMEMBERING WITH THE PHYSICAL BODY]: SEE: REMEMBER-BODY-[REMEMBERING WITH THE BODY]

BODY-PHYSICAL-REMOVING-[REMOVING THE PHYSICAL BODY]: SEE: BODY-PHYSICAL-TAKING-AWAY-[TAKING THE PHYSICAL BODY AWAY]

BODY-PHYSICAL-SEEING-[SEEING WITH THE BODY]: (Warriors know that seeing with the physical body is another way to describe "seeing"; a way of perceiving things through a bodily sense.)
SELECTED REFERENCES: **The Power of Silence - Page [99.3-99.4]** (Yet in spite of the total blackness...I was, rather, a bodily sense.)
SEE ALSO: *SEEING, BODY-PHYSICAL-WITNESSING, BODY-PHYSICAL*

BODY-PHYSICAL-STRONG-SECRET-[THE SECRET OF A STRONG BODY]: (Warriors know that the secret of a strong body is not in what one does but rather in what one "does not do.")
SELECTED REFERENCES: **Journey to Ixtlan - Page [180.5-181.5]** ("I've told you that the secret...been soaked for hours in "not-doing.")
SEE ALSO: *NOT-DOING*

BODY-PHYSICAL-TAKING-AWAY-[TAKING THE PHYSICAL BODY AWAY]: (Warriors know that taking the physical body away is another term for moving the assemblage point to the position of the dreaming body.)
SELECTED REFERENCES: **The Teachings of Don Juan - Page [139.8-140.8]** (The smoke, on the other hand, is...anything because of the little smoke.) **The Teachings of Don Juan - Page [164.1-164.4]** (Don Juan did not talk about my...to the ground, wherever you fall.") **The Teachings of Don Juan - Page [176.2]** ("Perhaps by now you know it...fear to understand what I mean.") **A Separate Reality - Page [6.9-7.2]** (In order to become a man of...as the "ally removing one's body.") **A Separate Reality - Page [9.3-9.6]** (Don Juan used this condition of inapplicability...remove the body of the practitioner.") **A Separate Reality - Page [124.4-124.7]** ("I know now that it was...cannot be stopped or locked in.")
SEE ALSO: *DREAMING-BODY, ASSEMBLAGE-POINT-MOVING, LITTLE-SMOKE*

BODY-PHYSICAL-TUNING-[TUNING THE PHYSICAL BODY]: SEE: WARRIOR-SUSPENDING-[SUSPENDING THE WARRIOR]

BODY-PHYSICAL-WILL-UNIT-[THE BODY AND THE WILL AS A FUNCTIONING UNIT]: (Warriors know that the body must be perfection before the will is a functioning unit.)
 SELECTED REFERENCES: **Tales of Power - Page [82.3-82.4]** ("Watch those muscles," he said...the will is a functioning unit.")
 SEE ALSO: *BODY-PHYSICAL, WILL*

BODY-PHYSICAL-WITNESSING-[WITNESSING AND KNOWING WITH THE PHYSICAL BODY]: Warriors experience first-hand the physical body's ability to do and know things that reason cannot comprehend; the body's ability to store experiences and memories; the body's ability to witness the nagual; the bodily knowledge known as "seeing".)
 SELECTED REFERENCES: **Journey to Ixtlan - Page [194.5-194.6]** ("When one does something with people...cares whether or not you understand?") **Journey to Ixtlan - Page [213.7]** ("Very drastic things have to happen...all you have learned," he said.) **Journey to Ixtlan - Page [246.3-247.2]** (The next day as soon as I...let your body decide what's what.") **Journey to Ixtlan - Page [252.8-253.9]** (I stayed on the hilltop in...it because the world had collapsed.") **Journey to Ixtlan - Page [255.8-255.9]** ("But how did he force me to...and allow your body to *see*.") **Journey to Ixtlan - Page [256.2-256.5]** ("Power plants are only an aid...is the way of the sorcerer.") **Tales of Power - Page [64.5-64.7]** ("But how did you know that you...it, shines it, and keeps it running.") **Tales of Power - Page [84.1-84.3]** ("It isn't, but we made...the ally that night, right here.") **Tales of Power - Page [132.2-132.3]** (The idea is that at the...without the binding force of life.") **Tales of Power - Page [157.5-157.6]** (Whatever I say doesn't make sense...with the body, not the reason.") **Tales of Power - Page [195.6]** ("The reason why you're afraid of...away every time Genaro is around.") **The Second Ring of Power - Page [63.4-63.5]** (But you fooled my floor by liking it...Your body knew what to do.) **The Second Ring of Power - Page [179.3-179.9]** (He remained quiet, while I frantically...minute I walked through that door.") **The Second Ring of Power - Page [233.1-233.9]** (Her statements put me in a very...knew beyond the shadow of a doubt.) **The Eagle's Gift - Page [37.2-37.5]** (La Gorda was right. I...recall perceiving two separate scenes simultaneously.) **The Eagle's Gift - Page [85.8-85.9]** (The force behind my explosion...the house that had intrigued me.) **The Eagle's Gift - Page [113.7-113.9]** (I speculated with la Gorda that the...the intellect played a minimal part.) **The Eagle's Gift - Page [178.8-179.1]** (Don Juan explained that the rule was...of the totality of the body.) **The Fire From Within - Page [41.1-41.3]** ("It goes without saying that the...only revert back to his components.) **The Art of Dreaming - Page [26.4-26.5]** ("No it isn't. Intending is much...all the cells of your body.")
 SEE ALSO: *SEEING, ENERGY-BODY, INFORMATION-EXPERIENCE-STORAGE, RECOLLECTION-SORCERER, PERCEIVING-BODY-ENTIRE*

BODY-REMEMBERING-[REMEMBERING WITH THE PHYSICAL BODY]: SEE: REMEMBERING BODY-[REMEMBERING WITH THE BODY]

BODY-TOTAL-[THE TOTAL BODY]: (Warriors know that the total body is the physical body and its luminous periphery; some of the points on the luminous periphery are as much as three feet away from the physical body; the total being of the warrior; the physical body and the energy body together.)
 SELECTED REFERENCES: **The Eagle's Gift - Page [163.4-163.5]** (Don Juan had told us that...body, thus its resistance to conceptualization.) **The Eagle's Gift - Page [178.8-179.1]** (Don Juan explained that the rule was...of the totality of the body.) **The Eagle's Gift - Page [196.1-196.4]** (This pattern coincides with hundreds of...Juan Tuma, I forgot my anger.)
 SEE ALSO: *TOTAL-BEING, BODY-PHYSICAL, ENERGY-BODY*

BONES-WARRIOR-[THE WARRIORS' BONES]: SEE: WARRIOR-BONES-[THE WARRIORS' BONES]

BOOST-EARTH-[THE BOOST FROM THE EARTH]: SEE: EARTH-BOOST-[THE BOOST FROM THE EARTH]

BOOZE-[BOOZE]: (Warriors know that alcohol is what makes people crazy, it blurs their images of our world; alcohol acts to trap the second attention.)
    SELECTED REFERENCES: **A Separate Reality** - Page [66.1-66.2] ("It does make sense," don Juan...so very well. So very well!") **The Second Ring of Power** - Page [324.1-324.2] ("There are no hallucinations," la Gorda...maybe it's the Nagual's smoking mixture.)
    SEE ALSO: *MESCALITO, ATTENTION-SECOND-TRAPPING*

BOREDOM-[BOREDOM]: (Warriors know that they must turn their backs on boredom, the boredom of the first attention's limited description of the world.)
    SELECTED REFERENCES: **Journey to Ixtlan** - Page [17.2-17.3] ("You see," he went 0n...will pop out, not even ourselves.") **Journey to Ixtlan** - Page [69.6-69.9] ("The art of the hunter is to...became tired and bored with people.) **Journey to Ixtlan** - Page [81.3] (I insisted that to be bored...you are as good as dead.") **Tales of Power** - Page [156.1-156.3] ("In the beginning, one has to...which only plunge it into boredom.) **Tales of Power** - Page [173.2-173.5] (Your obsession, or better yet, everyone's...or to peek into that infinity.") **Tales of Power** - Page [174.7] ("In your case, for instance, you...to have everything under its control.) **Tales of Power** - Page [248.3-249.1] (My happy mood did not last...and drove back to his house.) **The Fire From Within** - Page [148.1-148.3] (He explained that what makes the...has welcomed the world of boredom.)
    SEE ALSO: *DESCRIPTION-WORLD, LIMITS, BOUNDARIES*

BOTTLED-UP-[THE FEELING OF BEING BOTTLED UP]: (Warriors know that the sensation of feeling bottled up is experienced by every human being and is a reminder of our existing connection with intent.)
    SELECTED REFERENCES: **The Power of Silence** - Page [108.9-109.1] ("That sensation of being bottled up...sorcerers relieve it by *stalking* themselves.")
    SEE ALSO: *WARRIOR-INTENT-LINK*

BOUNDARIES-AFFECTION-[THE BOUNDARIES OF AFFECTION]: (Warriors know that their feelings make boundaries around everything; these are the boundaries of affection; the stronger the feeling, the stronger the boundary.)
    SELECTED REFERENCES: **The Eagle's Gift** - Page [80.6-80.9] (The questions that I wanted to...But I could not concentrate.) **The Eagle's Gift** - Page [84.8-85.3] ("Never again will you get us...the way we did," Nestor replied.) **The Eagle's Gift** - Page [106.1-106.3] (Nestor made a gesture of solidarity...be pleasant but deadly for them.)
    SEE ALSO: *FEELINGS, WARRIOR-LOVE, BOUNDARIES*

BOUNDARIES-AFFECTION-CROSSING-[CROSSING THE BOUNDARIES OF AFFECTION]-(TOP)

BOUNDARIES-ATTENTION-FIRST-[THE BOUNDARIES OF THE FIRST ATTENTION]: (Warriors know that the boundaries of the first attention are the physical limits of the first attention; the boundaries of the physical body; the boundaries of the known or the tonal.)
    SELECTED REFERENCES: **The Teachings of Don Juan** - Page [53.2-53.3] ("An ally is a power capable...reveal matters no human being could.") **Tales of Power** - Page [8.9-9.3] ("You didn't have this knowledge before...a feeling, an awareness encased here.") **Tales of Power** - Page [94.5-94.8] ("When we arrived at the rock...into the world of your reason.) **Tales of Power** - Page [97.6-97.8] ("Today I have to pound the nail...we rarely emerge in our lifetime.) **Tales of Power** - Page [191.4-191.5] (You want to explain the *nagual*...are not applicable to the *nagual*. ") **The Eagle's Gift** - Page [84.8-85.3] ("Never again will you get us...never be back, we broke it.") **The Eagle's Gift** - Page [106.7-106.8] ("The course of a warrior's destiny is...destiny the breadth

of one hair.") **The Fire From Within - Page [96.9-97.3]** (Never in my life had I...that it can bring about death.)

SEE ALSO: *BODY-PHYSICAL, WARRIOR-LIMITS, BOUNDARIES-SELF, KNOWN*

BOUNDARIES-SELF-[THE BOUNDARIES OF THE INDIVIDUAL SELF]:
Warriors use the recapitulation to transcend the narrow boundaries of their person; when the recapitulation is complete, warriors no longer abide by the limitations of the personal self.)

SELECTED REFERENCES:: **The Eagle's Gift - Page [287.3-287.6]** (She explained that a recapitulation is...by the limitations of her person.)

SEE ALSO: *TONAL, WARRIOR-LIMITS, BOUNDARIES, RECAPITULATION*

BOY-BUTTON-NOSED-PROMISE-[THE PROMISE TO THE BUTTON NOSED BOY]-(TOP)

BREATH-[BREATH]: (Warriors know that breath is a magical life-giving function with a cleansing capacity; breath is the key element in the warriors' recapitulation; breathing is a magical life-giving act, a vehicle for the warriors' energy when used in conjunction with the warriors' recapitulation; the exhalation of a breath ejects foreign energy from the body while the inhalation pulls back energy that has been left behind.)

SELECTED REFERENCES: **Tales of Power - Page [166.3-166.7]** (I felt don Juan's head next...accelerated fashion, depending on one's preference.) **The Eagle's Gift - Page [164.5-165.3]** (He never pushed or massaged me...as I filled up my lungs.) **The Eagle's Gift - Page [288.4]** (Florinda explained that the key element...because it was a life-giving function.) **The Eagle's Gift - Page [288.7-289.4]** (Florinda said that her benefactor directed...involved in the event being recollected.) **The Eagle's Gift - Page [289.8]** (Florinda emphasized that the rule defined...a recapitulation into a practical matter.) **The Art of Dreaming - Page [148.9-149.4]** (Don Juan taught me that the...themselves left behind during the interaction.)

SEE ALSO: *RECAPITULATION, STALKER-BREATH, LUMINOUS-FILAMENTS*

BREATH-STALKER-[THE STALKERS' BREATH]: SEE: STALKER-BREATH-[THE STALKERS' BREATH]

BREATHING-DREAMING-[LEARNING TO BREATHE IN DREAMING]-(TOP): SEE: DREAMING-BREATHING-[LEARNING TO BREATHE IN DREAMING]-(TOP)

BRIDGE-DREAMING-[THE BRIDGE FOR SURFACING FROM DREAMING]: (Warriors know that dreamers should wear a gold ring, preferably a bit tight-fitting; this ring serves as a bridge for surfacing from dreaming or for sinking from daily awareness into the realm of the inorganic beings; the ring attracts and releases energy that aids in the transport of dreamers; it also helps insure their return to this world by giving them a constant familiar sense on their fingers.)

SELECTED REFERENCES: **The Art of Dreaming - Page [94.2-94.6]** ("Dreamers should wear a gold ring...constant, familiar sense on his fingers.)

SEE ALSO: *DREAMING-ART, DREAMING-TECHNIQUES*

BRIDGE-FOG-[THE FOG BRIDGE]-(TOP)

BRIDGE-SORCERER-[THE SORCERERS' BRIDGE]: (Warriors know that warrior-sorcerers can never make a bridge to join the people of the world; but if people desire to do so, the people of the world can make a bridge to join the warrior-sorcerers.)

SELECTED REFERENCES: **The Power of Silence - Page [192.9-193.1]** (He wanted to explain that his...to make abridge to join sorcerers.)

SEE ALSO: *WARRIOR-CONTRADICTION-KNOWLEDGE, BLACK-MAGICIANS, WARRIOR-DETACHMENT*

BRIDGE-TWO-ONE-WAY-[THE TWO ONE WAY BRIDGES]: *(Warriors know there are two one-way bridges; one extends from silent knowledge to reason, and is known as "concern"; the other is a one way bridge from reason to silent knowledge, and is known as "pure understanding".)*
SELECTED REFERENCES: **The Power of Silence - Page [240.5-240.9]** (The nagual Elias assured don Juan...force that made both positions possible.)
SEE ALSO: *CONCERN, UNDERSTANDING-PURE, REASON, KNOWLEDGE-SILENT*

BRIDGE-UNKNOWN-[THE BRIDGE TO THE UNKNOWN]-(TOP)

BRIDGE-WARRIOR-[THE WARRIORS' BRIDGE]: SEE: WARRIOR-BRIDGE [THE WARRIORS' BRIDGE]

BRIDGE-WORLD-[THE BRIDGE BETWEEN THE WORLDS]: *(Warriors know that the dreaming emissary, because it is a voice, is the perfect bridge between the world of inorganic beings and the world of men.)*
SELECTED REFERENCES: **The Art of Dreaming - Page [93.3-93.6]** (Don Juan had said that inorganic...old sorcerers' preference for concrete practices.)
SEE ALSO: *DREAMING-EMISSARY, INORGANIC-BEINGS-REALM*

BRINK-INFINITY-[ON THE BRINK OF INFINITY]: *(Warriors know that heightened awareness places them on the brink of infinity, from there they can push the assemblage point beyond the threshold of no return.)*
SELECTED REFERENCES: **The Power of Silence - Page [72.3-72.6]** (He said that heightened awareness was...forward I would fall into it.)
SEE ALSO: *AWARENESS-HEIGHTENED, ASSEMBLAGE-POINT-THRESHOLD, ASSEMBLAGE-POINT-PUSHING*

BRUJO-[BRUJO]: *(Warriors know that brujo is a Spanish word for sorcerer, medicine man or curer.)*
SELECTED REFERENCES: **The Teachings of Don Juan - Page [105.1]** ("No, that is not true...but anyone can partake of Mescalito.") **The Teachings of Don Juan - Page [129.8-129.9]** ("The trouble with you is that...does he or doesn't he fly?") **The Teachings of Don Juan - Page [186.5]** (Most of the time, though, one...who have very little to teach.) **A Separate Reality - Page [5.5-5.6]** (In 1961, a year after our...teach me the mysteries of sorcery.) **A Separate Reality - Page [69.8-70.4]** ("My grandfather is too old...tired of his evil sorcery and killed him.")
SEE ALSO: *SORCERY, DIABLERO-DIABLERA, SORCERER*

BRUJO-SURVIVES-WARRIOR-[THE BRUJO SURVIVES ONLY AS A WARRIOR]: *(Warriors know that brujos can only survive if they live like warriors.)*
SELECTED REFERENCES: **A Separate Reality - Page [180.4-180.6]** ("You abandoned yourself. You willed to...aware of what he is doing.")
SEE ALSO: *BRUJO, WARRIOR, WARRIORSHIP-VS-SORCERY*

BUMPKIN-OUTSMART-EVERYONE-[THE BUMPKIN WHO OUTSMARTED EVERYONE]-(TOP)

BURY-EARTH-HEALING-[THE HEALING PROPERTIES OF BEING BURIED IN THE EARTH]: SEE: EARTH-[THE EARTH]

BUSH-SPIRIT-[THE BUSH TOUCHED BY THE SPIRIT]-(TOP)

BUSINESS-DOWN-TO-[GETTING DOWN TO BUSINESS]: *(Warriors know there is only one way to learn, and that is to get down to business; to talk about power is useless, warriors must tackle everything themselves.)*

SELECTED REFERENCES: Journey to Ixtlan - Page [177.2-177.3] ("There is only one way to learn...it you must tackle everything yourself.")
SEE ALSO: *ACTING-VS-TALKING, KNOWLEDGE-VS-LANGUAGE*

C

CALCULATING-*[CALCULATING]:* *(Warriors know that calculating is another term for explaining.)*
    SELECTED REFERENCES: Tales of Power - Page [174.6-174.8] ("In your case, for instance, you...we can do to change that condition.")
    SEE ALSO: *EXPLANATION, REASON, UNDERSTANDING, WARRIOR-BAFFLEMENT, TALKING*

CALIXTO-MUNI-*[CALIXTO MUNI]*-*(TOP)*

CALMNESS-ATTENTION-SECOND-*[CALMNESS AND THE SECOND ATTENTION]:* *(Warriors know that the second attention is calmness itself; fretting is proper only to the first attention.)*
    SELECTED REFERENCES: The Eagle's Gift - Page [260.5-260.6] (Zuleica finally spoke to me...attention: the second attention was calmness itself.)
    SEE ALSO: *FRETTING, WARRIOR-CALMNESS, ATTENTION-FIRST, ATTENTION-SECOND*

CALMNESS-WARRIOR-*[THE WARRIORS' CALMNESS]: SEE: WARRIOR-CALMNESS*-*[THE WARRIORS' CALMNESS]*

CAR-DISAPPEARING-*[THE DISAPPEARING CAR]*-*(TOP)*

CAR-WON'T-START-WILL-*[WILL AND THE CAR THAT WON'T START]*-*(TOP)*

CARING-FOR-ANOTHER-WARRIOR-*[CARING FOR ANOTHER WARRIOR]: SEE: WARRIOR-CARING-FOR-ANOTHER*-*[CARING FOR ANOTHER WARRIOR]*

CARING-NOT-CARING-*[CARING AND NOT CARING]: SEE: PEOPLE-GROUPS*-*[THE STALKERS' TWO MAIN GROUPS OF HUMAN BEINGS]*

CARING-THOSE-WHO-*[THOSE WHO CARE ABOUT THEIR FELLOW MEN]: SEE: PEOPLE-GROUPS*-*[THE STALKERS' TWO MAIN GROUPS OF HUMAN BEINGS]*

CARING-THOSE-WHO-DON'T-*[THOSE WHO DON'T CARE ABOUT THEIR FELLOW MEN]: SEE: PEOPLE-GROUPS*-*[THE STALKERS' TWO MAIN GROUPS OF HUMAN BEINGS]*

CARLOS-BLOND-FRIEND-*[CARLOS' BLOND GIRL FRIEND]*-*(TOP)*

CARLOS-BOY-*[THE LITTLE BOY IN CARLOS' LIFE]*-*(TOP)*

CARLOS-CHANCES-FOUR-*[CARLOS' FOUR CHANCES]*-*(TOP)*

CARLOS-CROW-TRANSFORMATION-*[CARLOS' TRANSFORMATION INTO A CROW]*-*(TOP): SEE: CROW-TRANSFORMATION-CARLOS*-*[CARLOS' TRANSFORMATION INTO A CROW]*-*(TOP)*

CARLOS-DEATH-*[CARLOS' DEATH]: SEE: DEATH-CARLOS*-*[CARLOS' DEATH]*-*(TOP)*

CARLOS-DOUBLE-*[CARLOS'-DOUBLE]: SEE: DOUBLE-CARLOS*-*[THE EMERGENCE OF CARLOS' DOUBLE]*-*(TOP)*

CARLOS-ENERGY-BLOWING-BODY-[BLOWING ENERGY INTO CARLOS' BODY]-(TOP): SEE: ENERGY-BLOWING-INTO-CARLOS-[BLOWING ENERGY INTO CARLOS' BODY]-(TOP)

CARLOS-FINDING-[HOW POWER FOUND CARLOS]-(TOP): SEE: FINDING-CARLOS-[HOW POWER FOUND CARLOS]-(TOP)

CARLOS-FLYING-[CARLOS' FLYING]-(TOP)

CARLOS-INFANT-MEMORIES-[CARLOS' MEMORIES AS AN INFANT]-(TOP)

CARLOS-POLICEMAN-[CARLOS AND THE FLEET-FOOTED POLICEMAN]-(TOP)

CARLOS-STRANGULATION-[CARLOS' STRANGULATION]-(TOP)

CARLOS-SWIMMING-FATHER-[CARLOS' SWIMMING STORY WITH HIS FATHER]-(TOP)

CARLOS-VISION-MOTHER-[CARLOS' VISION OF HIS MOTHER]-(TOP)

CARPENTER-METAPHOR-[THE MASTER CARPENTER METAPHOR]-(TOP)

CARRY-HANDS-[CARRYING THINGS WITH THE HANDS]: (Warriors know that carrying things in the hands while walking has a deleterious effect on the body; whenever possible, warriors carry things on their backs or over their shoulders in order to avoid holding them in the hands.)
    SELECTED REFERENCES: Journey to Ixtlan - Page [89.5-89.8] (He asked if I usually carried...your body carrying all this around.)
    SEE ALSO: *BODY-PHYSICAL*

CATALINA-PIERCING-[PIERCING LA CATALINA]-(TOP)

CATALINA-TALES-[TALES OF LA CATALINA]-(TOP)

CATCHERS-INTENT-[THE CATCHERS OF INTENT]: SEE: EYES-FUNCTION-[THE TRUE FUNCTION OF THE EYES]

CATS-STORY-[THE STORY OF THE TWO CATS]-(TOP)

CAVE-[CAVES]: (Warriors know that the earth is a sentient being and that its awareness can effect the awareness of human beings; the sorcerers of antiquity discovered that the most effective way to utilize that influence was through certain caves.)
    SELECTED REFERENCES: The Power of Silence - Page [100.6-101.1] (Don Juan asked me to pay close...until it reached a lull of perception.)
    SEE ALSO: *EARTH, PERCEPTION-LULL, CAVE-SORCERER-(TOP)*

CAVE-SORCERER-[THE SORCERERS' CAVE OF UNDERSTANDING]-(TOP)

CEMETERY-[CEMETERY]: (Warriors know not to be concerned with cemeteries because there is no power in them.)
    SELECTED REFERENCES: Journey to Ixtlan - Page [106.9] (I did not mean dead people's...There is no power in them.)
    SEE ALSO: *EARTH, WARRIOR-BONES*

CHAINS-SELF-REFLECTION-[THE CHAINS OF OUR SELF-REFLECTION]: *(Warriors know that every man is held by the chains of his self-reflection; warriors struggle to cut those chains and then deal with the consequences; the fourth abstract core is the spirit cutting the chains of self-reflection; cutting those chains is marvelous but also very undesirable because nobody wants to be free; once those chains are cut we are no longer bound by the concerns of the daily world; warriors then find themselves in this world but not of it because in order to belong they must share the concerns of people and without their chains, they simply can't.)*
    SELECTED REFERENCES: The Power of Silence - Page [89.8-90.6] (Sorcerers say that the fourth abstract...and without chains we can't.")
    SEE ALSO: *SELF-REFLECTION, ABSTRACT-CORE-FOURTH, SPIRIT-DESCENT, WORLD-IN-NOT-OF, BLACK-MAGICIANS*

CHAIR-PABLITO-[PABLITO'S CHAIR]-(TOP)

CHALLENGE-WARRIOR [THE WARRIORS' CHALLENGE]: SEE: WARRIOR-CHALLENGE-[THE WARRIORS' CHALLENGE]

CHANCE-[CHANCE OR LUCK]: SEE: WARRIOR-CHANCE-MINIMAL-[THE WARRIORS" MINIMAL CHANCE]

CHANCE-HAVE-[A CHANCE TO HAVE A CHANCE]: *(Warriors know that the Eagle's gift it is not a bestowal but a chance to have a chance for freedom.)*
    SELECTED REFERENCES: The Eagle's Gift - Page [181.1-5-181.6] (Don Juan said that his benefactor's...a chance to have a chance.)
    SEE ALSO: *EAGLE-GIFT, POWER-PROMISE, FREEDOM, WARRIOR-CHANCE, WARRIOR-CHANCE-MINIMAL*

CHANCE-MINIMAL-WARRIOR-[THE WARRIORS' MINIMAL CHANCE]: SEE: WARRIOR-CHANCE-MINIMAL-[THE WARRIORS' MINIMAL CHANCE]

CHANCE-WARRIOR-[THE WARRIORS' CHANCE]: SEE: WARRIOR-CHANCE-[THE WARRIORS' CHANCE]

CHANCES-CALLER-OF-[THE CALLER OF CHANCES]: SEE: ATTENTION-SECOND-BECKONER-[THE SECOND ATTENTION IS THE BECKONER OF CHANCES]

CHANGE-[CHANGE]: *(Warriors know they must struggle to change themselves, to transform the island of the tonal by altering rather than obliterating the use of its assigned elements; warriors change their idea of the world; the contradiction of change is that no matter how warriors struggle to change themselves, they are still no more than luminous beings and there is nothing to change in a luminous egg.)*
    SELECTED REFERENCES: The Teaching of Don Juan - Page [50.8-50.9] ("Seek and see the marvels all...will come to you of itself.") A Separate Reality - Page [23.4-23.5] ("Is that the way everyone...changed in that luminous egg? What?") A Separate Reality - Page [63.6-63.9] ("In what way would peyote change...leading is no life at all.) A Separate Reality - Page [219.4] ("A warrior is aware that the...be prepared for that monumental jolt.") A Separate Reality - Page [263.3.263.7] (Don Juan slowly walked around me...really changed in you," he said.) Journey to Ixtlan - Page [55.3-55.8] (I protested that I did not...didn't figure it out for myself.") Journey to Ixtlan - Page [56.8-57.1] (One day I found out that if...should I have to change it?") Journey to Ixtlan - Page [78.8-79.2] (Around mid-afternoon, after we had...was to really want to change.") Journey to Ixtlan - Page [80.2-80.3] ("You won't be able to stop...you

finally succeed in changing yourself.") **Journey to Ixtlan - Page [82.7-83.1]** ("Don't just agree with me," he...of my interest in convincing you.") **Journey to Ixtlan - Page [266.4]** ("Spinning with your ally will change...that changes, the world itself changes.") **Tales of Power - Page [7.5-7.7]** ("There are lots of things that...and routines stand in your way.") **Tales of Power - Page [8.2]** ("Everything we do, everything we are...change the course of our lives.) **Tales of Power - Page [13.8]** ("To change our idea of the...the only way to accomplish it.) **Tales of Power - Page [23.7]** ("Knowledge and power. Men of knowledge...at a given moment everything changed.") **Tales of Power - Page [54.6-54.8]** ("Genaro is a man," don Juan..."Of course, you yourself are changing.") **Tales of Power - Page [64.6]** ("You yourself know that something in...shines it, and keeps it running.") **Tales of Power - Page [231.1-231.2]** ("I mean the total change which...You have accomplished that task.") **Tales of Power - Page [241.4-241.6]** (Don Juan pointed out then that...the use assigned to those elements.) **Tales of Power - Page [246.9-247.1]** (But she's a great warrior and...acts sent you into another realm.) **The Second Ring of Power - Page [159.1-159.5]** ("What is the point of losing your...Once it leaves, you are nothing.) **The Second Ring of Power - Page [174.5-174.8]** ("No. Unfortunately, understanding is not their...but an impeccable warrior survives, always.") **The Second Ring of Power - Page [203.8-204.1]** ("Is he really shy," I asked...ourselves and not worry about anything.) **The Fire From Within - Page [114.8]** ("I've explained to you that the...that warriors must purposely seek change.) **The Fire From Within - Page [118.7-118.9]** ("How can one accomplish that change...as a consequence of new habits.") **The Fire From Within - Page [218.8-219.1]** (He remarked that one of the most...And none of us wants to be.") **The Power of Silence - Page [251.2-251.5]** (I interrupted him to ask whether...supreme accomplishment of magic, of *intending*.)
SEE ALSO: *TONAL-ISLAND, HUMAN-FORM-LOSING, FREEDOM, FACADE-TRANSFORMING, WARRIOR-TRANSFORMATION, WARRIOR-CHANGE-MUST, WARRIOR-CONTRADICTION-KNOWLEDGE, CHANGE-(ALL), CHANGING-(ALL)*

CHANGE-DEATH-SYMBOLIC-[CHANGE AND THE WARRIORS' SYMBOLIC DEATH]: *(Warriors know that some teachers believe that the apprentice to nagualism can only really change if he dies a symbolic death.)*
SELECTED REFERENCES: **The Power of Silence - Page [251.5-251.6]** ("I was the same. For a...only really change if we die.")
SEE ALSO: *WARRIOR-IMPECCABILITY-TICKET, SELF-IMPORTANCE-MONSTER-THREE-THOUSAND-HEADS, WARRIOR-DEATH-SYMBOLIC*

CHANGE-DIE-[CHANGE OR DIE]: *(Warriors know that they have no choice but to change or die.)*
SELECTED REFERENCES: **The Second Ring of Power - Page [52.4-52.5]** (In the case of my girls...Gorda changed more than anyone else.)
SEE ALSO: *CHANGE, DEATH*

CHANGE-DIRECTION-WARRIOR-[WARRIORS CHANGE DIRECTION]: SEE: WARRIOR-CHANGE-DIRECTION-[WARRIORS CHANGE DIRECTION]

CHANGE-LIGHT-ASSEMBLAGE-POINT-[THE LIGHT SHIFT WHICH MARKS THE MOVEMENT OF THE ASSEMBLAGE POINT]: SEE: ASSEMBLAGE-POINT-LIGHT-[THE LIGHT SHIFT WHICH MARKS THE MOVEMENT OF THE ASSEMBLAGE POINT]

CHANGE-MUST-WARRIOR-[WARRIORS MUST CHANGE]: SEE: WARRIOR-CHANGE-MUST-[WARRIORS MUST CHANGE]

CHANGE-WITHIN-[THE CHANGE FROM WITHIN]: *(Warriors know that they must use the technique of realization in order to accomplish the change from within.)*
SELECTED REFERENCES: **The Fire From Within - Page [118.4-118.9]** ("The nagual's blow is of great...as a consequence of new habits.")
SEE ALSO: *REALIZATION-TECHNIQUE, HABITS, CHANGE, FACADE-TRANSFORMATION*

CHANGING-DIRECTION-WARRIOR-[CHANGING THE WARRIORS'
DIRECTION]-(TOP) SEE: WARRIOR-DIRECTION-CHANGING-
[CHANGING THE WARRIORS' DIRECTION]-(TOP)

CHANGING-SPEED-[SPEEDING OR CHANGING SPEED]: SEE: SPEED-
[SPEEDING OR CHANGING SPEED]

CHEESE-ANALOGY-[THE JACK CHEESE ANALOGY]: (Warriors know
that the jack cheese analogy is a descriptive analogy of man's band of
emanations and how it relates to the overall structure of man's luminous
cocoon.)
    SELECTED REFERENCES: The Fire From Within - Page [121.4-122.4] (I told him
that I couldn't understand...on the surface of the cocoon.")
    SEE ALSO: *EAGLE-EMANATIONS-MAN-BAND, LUMINOUS-COCOON*

CHEESE-CARLOS-LOVE-OF-[CARLOS' LOVE OF CHEESE]-(TOP)

CHICKEN-LIDIA-BLOUSE-[THE CHICKEN IN LIDIA'S BLOUSE]-(TOP)

CHILDHOOD-PAIN-ESCAPING-[ESCAPING THE PAIN OF
CHILDHOOD]-(TOP)

CHILDREN-SEE-[CHILDREN WHO SEE]: SEE: SEE-CHILDREN-
[CHILDREN WHO SEE]

CHILDREN-SUN-[CHILDREN OF THE SUN]: SEE: SUN-PIECES-[PIECES
OF THE SUN]

CHOICE-SECOND-WARRIOR-[THE WARRIORS' SECOND CHOICE]:
SEE: WARRIOR-CHOICE-SECOND-[THE WARRIORS' SECOND
CHOICE]

CHOICE-SORCERER-[THE SORCERERS' CHOICE]: SEE: INORGANIC-
BEINGS-REFUSING-[REFUSING THE INORGANIC BEINGS]

CHOICE-WARRIOR-[THE WARRIORS' CHOICE]: SEE: WARRIOR-
CHOICE-[THE WARRIORS' CHOICE]

CHOICES-MATCHING-REASON-[MATCHING THE CHOICES OF
REASON]: (Warriors know that reason makes us choose what seems sound
to the mind, even though these choices have nothing to do with the warriors'
connection to the spirit; warriors must learn to match their rational choices
with choices dictated by silent knowledge.)
    SELECTED REFERENCES: The Power of Silence - Page [201.3-202.1] ("Reason
makes us choose what seems...of how unreasonable it may seem.")
    SEE ALSO: *REASON, WARRIOR-DECISIONS, WARRIOR-CHOICES, WARRIOR-*
CHOOSES-WELL

CHOOSES-WELL-WARRIOR-[THE WARRIOR CHOOSES WELL]: SEE:
WARRIOR-CHOOSES-WELL-[THE WARRIOR CHOOSES WELL]

CHURCH-VISION-[A VISION OF THE CHURCH]-(TOP)

CHURCH-WOMAN-[THE WOMAN IN THE CHURCH]-(TOP): SEE:
WOMAN-CHURCH-[THE WOMAN IN THE CHURCH]-(TOP)

CIRCULAR-FORCE-[THE CIRCULAR FORCE]: SEE: FORCE-CIRCULAR-
[THE CIRCULAR FORCE]

CITY-UNKNOWN-DREAM-[CARLOS' DREAM OF THE UNKNOWN CITY]-(TOP): SEE: DREAM-CITY-UNKNOWN-[CARLOS' DREAM OF THE UNKNOWN CITY]-(TOP)

CLARIFICATION-WARRIOR-[THE WARRIORS' CLARIFICATION]: SEE: WARRIOR-CLARIFICATION-[THE WARRIORS' CLARIFICATION]

CLARITY-[CLARITY]: (Warriors know that clarity is the property of mind that erases fear; this make-believe power of the warrior must be defied and used only to "see"; a point before the warriors' eyes and nothing more; the second natural enemy of the warrior.)
     SELECTED REFERENCES: The Teachings of Don Juan - Page [84.9-85.9] ("No. Once a man has vanquished...eyes. It will be true power.) The Teachings of Don Juan - Page [106.8-107.1] (Therefore you must always keep in mind...your heart tells you to do.) A Separate Reality - Page [115.3-115.5] ("You don't want to lose your...you call that fear." He chuckled.) A Separate Reality - Page [260.7-260.8] (He explained that the leaf had fallen...affair, so very small," he said.)
     SEE ALSO: WARRIOR-ASSUREDNESS, WARRIOR-ENEMIES-FOUR-NATURAL, SEEING

CLOUD-GAZING-[CLOUD GAZING]: SEE: GAZING-[GAZING]

CLUSTER-WORLDS-[THE CLUSTER OF CONSECUTIVE WORLDS]: SEE: WORLD-OTHER-[OTHER WORLDS]

COCOON-LUMINOUS-[THE LUMINOUS COCOON]: SEE: LUMINOUS-COCOON-[THE LUMINOUS COCOON]

COFFEE-SHOP-DREAMING-JOURNEY-[CARLOS' DREAMING JOURNEY TO THE COFFEE SHOP]-(TOP): SEE: DREAMING-JOURNEY-COFFEE-SHOP-[CARLOS' DREAMING JOURNEY TO THE COFFEE SHOP]-(TOP)

COHESION-[ENERGETIC UNIFORMITY AND COHESION]: SEE: ENERGETIC-UNIFORMITY-COHESION-[ENERGETIC UNIFORMITY AND COHESION]

COINCIDENCE-[COINCIDENCE]: SEE: ATTENTION-BECKONING-POWER-[THE BECKONING POWER OF ATTENTION]

COLLAPSES-REASSEMBLES-WORLD-[THE WARRIOR COLLAPSES AND REASSEMBLES THE WORLD]: SEE: WARRIOR-WORLD-COLLAPSES-[THE WARRIOR COLLAPSES AND REASSEMBLES THE WORLD]

COLOR-AWARENESS-[THE COLORS OF AWARENESS]: SEE: AWARENESS-COLOR-[THE COLOR OF AWARENESS]

COLORS-WARRIOR-[THE WARRIORS' COLORS]: SEE: WARRIOR-COLORS-[THE WARRIORS' COLORS]

COMMAND-EAGLE-[THE EAGLE'S COMMAND]: SEE: EAGLE-COMMAND-[THE EAGLE'S COMMAND]

COMMAND-FORGET-[THE COMMAND TO FORGET]: SEE: FORGET-COMMAND-[THE COMMAND TO FORGET]

COMMAND-WARRIOR-[THE WARRIORS' COMMAND]: SEE:
WARRIOR-COMMAND-[THE WARRIORS' COMMAND]

COMPANIONS-WARRIOR-UNKNOWN-[THE WARRIORS'
COMPANIONS IN THE IMMENSITY OF THE UNKNOWN]: SEE:
WARRIOR-COMPANIONS-UNKNOWN-[THE WARRIORS'
COMPANIONS IN THE IMMENSITY OF THE UNKNOWN]

COMPASSION-WARRIOR-[THE WARRIORS' COMPASSION]: SEE:
WARRIOR-COMPASSION-[THE WARRIORS' COMPASSION]

COMPLACENCY-FIRST-ATTENTION-[THE COMPLACENCY OF THE
FIRST ATTENTION]: (Warriors know they must battle against the natural
complacency of the first attention.)
     SELECTED REFERENCES: The Power of Silence - Page [48.7] (Now the question is,
how are...fit into your scheme of complacency?")
     SEE ALSO: *ATTENTION-FIRST, SELF-COMPASSION, SELF-CONGRATULATING*

COMPLAINTS-WARRIOR-[THE WARRIORS' COMPLAINTS]: SEE:
WARRIOR-COMPLAINTS-[THE WARRIORS' COMPLAINTS]

COMPLETENESS-WARRIOR-[THE WARRIORS' COMPLETENESS]: SEE:
WARRIOR-COMPLETENESS-[THE WARRIORS' COMPLETENESS]

CONCEIT-WARRIOR-[THE WARRIORS' CONCEIT]: SEE: WARRIOR-
CONCEIT-[THE WARRIORS' CONCEIT]

CONCERN-[CONCERN]: (Warriors know that the one-way bridge
extending from silent knowledge to reason is called concern.)
     SELECTED REFERENCES: The Power of Silence - Page [240.5-240.9] (The nagual
Elias assured don Juan...force that made both positions possible.)
     SEE ALSO: *BRIDGES-TWO-ONE-WAY, UNDERSTANDING-PURE, REASON,*
KNOWLEDGE-SILENT, ASSEMBLAGE-POINT-POSITION

CONCERN-FIRST-WARRIOR-[THE WARRIORS' FIRST CONCERN]: SEE:
WARRIOR-CONCERN-[THE WARRIORS' FIRST CONCERN]

CONCERN-PLACE-[THE PLACE OF CONCERN]: (Warriors know that the
place of concern is the counterpoint to "the place of no pity"; a position of
the assemblage point which is the forerunner of reason.)
     SELECTED REFERENCES: The Power of Silence - Page [199.2] (He also said that
"the place...concern," was the forerunner of reason.)
     SEE ALSO: *REASON, PITY-PLACE-NO, ASSEMBLAGE-POINT-POSITION*

CONCEPTION-[CONCEPTION]: SEE: AWARENESS-CONCEPTION-
[AWARENESS AND CONCEPTION]

CONCRETENESS-[CONCRETENESS]: (Warriors know that concreteness is
the practical art of sorcery; the obsessive fixation of the mind on practices
and techniques; the obsessive manipulation of the known; the unwarranted
influence over people; concreteness belongs to the realm of the sorcerers of
antiquity.)
     SELECTED REFERENCES: The Power of Silence - Page [187.8-188.1] (But the most
draining pain...opposite of his own concrete needs.) The Art of Dreaming - Page [2.3-2.6]
(During one of our conversations, don...have no interest in concrete gains.) The Art of
Dreaming - Page [93.3-93.6] (Don Juan had said that inorganic...old sorcerers' preference for

concrete practices.) **The Art of Dreaming - Page [124.6-124.9]** ("I am very pleased, but very...to concreteness, a most undesirable state.")
SEE ALSO: *KNOWN-OBSESSIVE-MANIPULATION, ABERRATION-MORBIDITY, SORCERER-ANTIQUITY, OBSESSION, GAZING*

CONDITION-WARRIOR-[THE WARRIORS' CONDITION]: SEE: WARRIOR-CONDITION-[THE WARRIORS' CONDITION]

CONDITIONING-ENERGETIC-[ENERGETIC CONDITIONING]: SEE: ENERGETIC-CONDITIONING-[ENERGETIC CONDITIONING]

CONFIDENCE-WARRIOR-[THE WARRIORS' CONFIDENCE]: SEE: WARRIOR-SELF-CONFIDENCE-[THE WARRIORS' SELF-CONFIDENCE], WARRIOR-ASSUREDNESS [THE WARRIORS' ASSUREDNESS]

CONFUSION-WARRIOR-[THE WARRIORS' CONFUSION]: SEE: WARRIOR-CONFUSION-[THE WARRIORS' CONFUSION]

CONJECTURE-MASTERS-[THE MASTERS OF CONJECTURE]: (Warriors know that the old seers were the masters of conjecture; they made a series of terrible assumptions about their invulnerability which eventually lead to their downfall.)
SELECTED REFERENCES: **The Fire From Within - Page [34.3-34.7]** (Don Juan explained that the new...total certainty that they were invulnerable.)
SEE ALSO: *SEER-OLD, TOLTECS, TOLTECS-DOOM*

CONSCIOUSNESS-ALIEN-[ALIEN ENERGY THAT HAS CONSCIOUSNESS]: SEE: DREAMING-EMISSARY-[THE DREAMING EMISSARY]

CONSCIOUSNESS-HAVING-[THE PROPERTY OF HAVING CONSCIOUSNESS]: SEE: LIFE-HAVING-[HAVING LIFE]

CONSCIOUSNESS-MARK-[THE MARK OF CONSCIOUSNESS]: SEE: AWARENESS-GLOW-[THE GLOW OF AWARENESS]

CONSISTENCY-WARRIOR-[THE WARRIORS' CONSISTENCY]: SEE: WARRIOR-CONSISTENCY-[THE WARRIORS' CONSISTENCY]

CONTINUITY-[CONTINUITY]: (Warriors know that continuity is the idea that we are a solid block; continuity is the underlying order of our self-reflection that sustains our world; the certainty that we are unchangeable; continuity is so important in the life of the average man that if it breaks, it's always repaired; once the warriors' assemblage point reaches the place of no pity, though, continuity is never the same again; warriors must eventually create a new sense of continuity for themselves; they must become capable of intelligently utilizing their new continuity while invalidating the continuity of their old lives; the process of invalidating their old continuity is called the ticket to impeccability or the sorcerers' symbolic but final death.)
SELECTED REFERENCES: **A Separate Reality - Page [7.3-7.5]** (Don Juan's method of teaching required...something we can take for granted.) **A Separate Reality - Page [262.3-262.9]** (Before I left I sat down...indulge too much," he said softly.) **Journey to Ixtlan - Page [83.9-84.5]** (I disagreed with him. Happiness for...not make you happy or powerful.") **The Eagle's Gift - Page [37.7-37.8]** (That was the only time I really...caressing the backs of my hands.) **The Eagle's Gift - Page [83.3-83.5]** (Her conclusions were logical given the...lives where we could fit them.) **The Eagle's Gift - Page [119.4-119.7]** (Up to that night, I could...that moment, I

had never met.) **The Eagle's Gift - Page [312.9-313.4]** (Don Juan said then that...in the continuum of my time.) **The Fire From Within - Page [171.1-171.3]** (Don Juan said that the new...rerouted to reinforce some choice alignments.) **The Power of Silence - Page [13.8-14.1]** (I argued that very few of my....present was that of knowing him.) **The Power of Silence - Page [70.5-70.6]** (I repeated the same things I...the movement of the assemblage point.) **The Power of Silence - Page [163.9-165.4]** ("What happened to you that day...points were ready to be moved.) **The Power of Silence - Page [165.9-166.3]** ("Sorcerers know that when an average...they knew him as an old man.) **The Power of Silence - Page [168.2-168.5]** (He remarked that that day in...break every vestige of my continuity.) **The Power of Silence - Page [169.1-169.6]** (He pointed out that my assemblage...struggle of your reason, of course.") **The Power of Silence - Page [171.2-171.5]** ("Your uncertainty is to be expected...victims go after a ferocious struggle.") **The Power of Silence - Page [191.9-192.3]** (He explained that in order for...new continuity cost me my life.") **The Power of Silence - Page [210.4-210.7]** (He said that possibly every human being...the prescribed position of normal living.) **The Power of Silence - Page [227.3-227.8]** (He said my disadvantage in the...the solution. Why? No one knows.") **The Power of Silence - Page [228.6-228.8]** ("When a movement of the assemblage...things are there for the asking.") **The Power of Silence - Page [251.5-251.8]** ("Consider what happens to you," he...shattering blow to his psychological continuity.) **The Art of Dreaming - Page [xi.2-xi.6]** (During the fulfillment of my dreaming...is a result of that rearrangement.)
    SEE ALSO: *DESCRIPTION-WORLD, WARRIOR-IMPECCABILITY-TICKET, WARRIOR-DEATH-SYMBOLIC*

CONTRADICTION-KNOWLEDGE-WARRIOR-*[THE CONTRADICTIONS OF THE WARRIORS' QUEST FOR KNOWLEDGE]: SEE: WARRIOR-CONTRADICTION-KNOWLEDGE-[THE CONTRADICTIONS OF THE WARRIORS' QUEST FOR KNOWLEDGE]*

CONTROL-*[CONTROL]:* (Warriors know that control is one of the four attributes of warriorship.)
    SELECTED REFERENCES: **The Fire From Within - Page [23.5]** ("My benefactor developed a strategy using...warriorship: control, discipline, forbearance, and timing.")
    SEE ALSO: *WARRIOR-CONTROL, WARRIOR-ATTRIBUTES, DISCIPLINE, FORBEARANCE, TIMING, WILL*

CONTROL-WARRIOR-*[THE WARRIORS' CONTROL]: SEE: WARRIOR-CONTROL-[THE WARRIORS' CONTROL]*

CONTROL-WITHOUT-CONTROL-*[CONTROL WITHOUT CONTROL]:* (Warriors know they must develop a way of being in control without controlling anything; the warriors' way of calculating their actions and then letting go once those calculations are over; the warriors' exercise of controlled abandon; the warriors' decisiveness and humility in the face of power.)
    SELECTED REFERENCES: **A Separate Reality - Page [181.4-181.7]** ("It seems to me it is...would be battling to the end.") **Journey to Ixtlan - Page [120.2-120.3]** ("A warrior, on the other hand...the best of all possible fashions.") **Tales of Power - Page [52.5]** (He acts as if he is...in such a manner dissipates obsession.") **Tales of Power - Page [58.5]** (So, you see, a man of...is in control without controlling anything.")
    SEE ALSO: *WARRIOR-CONTROL, ACT-LEARNING LETTING GO, WARRIOR-DECISIONS, WARRIOR-ABANDON-CONTROLLED, WARRIOR-HUMILITY, CALCULATING, WARRIOR-CONTROLLED-FOLLY*

CONTROLLED-ABANDON-*[THE WARRIORS' CONTROLLED ABANDON]: SEE: WARRIOR-ABANDON-[THE WARRIORS' CONTROLLED ABANDON]*

CONTROLLED-FOLLY-*[THE WARRIORS' CONTROLLED FOLLY]: SEE: WARRIOR-CONTROLLED-FOLLY-[THE WARRIORS' CONTROLLED FOLLY], WARRIOR-FOLLY-[THE WARRIORS' FOLLY]*

CONTROLLED-FOLLY-ART-[THE ART OF CONTROLLED FOLLY]:
(Warriors know that the art of controlled folly is another term for the art of stalking.)
> SELECTED REFERENCES: The Power of Silence - Page [82.7-82.9] ("Some sorcerers object to the term...awkward to say *controlled folly maker*.")
> SEE ALSO: STALKING-ART

CONTROLLED-FOLLY-MAKER-[THE CONTROLLED FOLLY MAKER]:
(Warriors know that controlled folly maker is another term for stalker.)
> SELECTED REFERENCES: The Power of Silence - Page [82.8-82.9] ("It's also called the art of stealth...awkward to say *controlled folly maker*.")
> SEE ALSO: STALKING-ART, WARRIOR-CONTROLLED-FOLLY

CONVENTIONS-BREAKING-[BREAKING AWAY FROM CONVENTIONS]: *(Warriors know that breaking away from conventions means breaking away from the conventions which bind our perception; a euphemism for shifting the assemblage point.)*
> SELECTED REFERENCES: The Power of Silence - Page [210.5-211.5] (He said that possibly every human...no devil. There is only perception.")
> SEE ALSO: FACADE-TRANSFORMING, ASSEMBLAGE-POINT-MOVING, WARRIOR-TRANSFORMATION

CONVICTION-NEW-SEER-[THE CONVICTION OF THE NEW SEERS]: SEE: IMPECCABILITY-SOBRIETY-ASSEMBLAGE-POINT-MOVE-[IMPECCABILITY, SOBRIETY AND THE MOVEMENT OF THE ASSEMBLAGE POINT]

CONVINCING-WARRIOR-[CONVINCING THE WARRIOR]: SEE: WARRIOR-CONVINCING-[CONVINCING THE WARRIOR]

CORE-GOOD-ROTTEN-[THE CORE OF EVERYTHING GOOD AND THE CORE OF EVERYTHING ROTTEN]: *(Warriors know that addressing the dilemma of everything good and rotten within themselves means addressing the dilemma of eliminating their own self-importance; self-importance is at the core of everything good and at the core of everything rotten in men; to eliminate the self-importance that is rotten while maintaining the good requires a masterpiece of strategy.)*
> SELECTED REFERENCES: The Fire From Within - Page [14.7-14.8] ("Self-importance is not something simple...to those who have accomplished it.")
> SEE ALSO: SELF-IMPORTANCE, STALKING-ONESELF, SELF-IMPORTANCE-LOSING

CORN-MAN-PLANTS-[THE MAN WHO PLANTS CORN]-(TOP)

CORN-SORCERY-[CORN SORCERY)-(TOP)

COUNTERPOINT-WARRIOR-[THE WARRIORS' COUNTERPOINT]: SEE: WARRIOR-COUNTERPOINT-[THE WARRIORS' COUNTERPOINT]

COURAGE-WARRIOR-[THE WARRIORS' COURAGE]: SEE: WARRIOR-COURAGE-[THE WARRIORS' COURAGE]

COURIER-WARRIOR-[THE WARRIOR COURIER]: SEE: WARRIOR-COURIER-[THE WARRIOR COURIER]

COYOTE-[COYOTES]: *(Warriors know that a coyote knows much more about the world than the average man; a coyote is capable of "seeing" another coyote's death.)*
    SELECTED REFERENCES: A Separate Reality - Page [41.2-41.7] ("Very simple," he said, "We men...crow it looks like a pointed hat.)
    SEE ALSO: *DEATH LINGERS, CROW-SEEING-(TOP)*

COYOTE-MAGICAL-[THE MAGICAL COYOTE]-(TOP): SEE: MAGICAL-COYOTE-[THE MAGICAL COYOTE]-(TOP)

COYOTE-SORCERER-[A COYOTE SORCERER]: SEE: SORCERER-COYOTE-[A COYOTE SORCERER]

CRACK-WORLDS-[THE CRACK BETWEEN THE WORLDS]: *(Warriors know that there is a crack between the world of sorcerers and the world of average men; a place where the two worlds overlap; the gateway to the second attention; the twilight, or the door to the unknown; the crack between the worlds is more than a metaphor, it represents the capacity to change levels of attention, and to travel between its two domains.)*
    SELECTED REFERENCE : The Teachings of Don Juan - Page [94.8] ("The twilight is the crack between the worlds," he said softly, without turning to me.) The Teachings of Don Juan - Page [115.5] (I thought of don Juan's words...there's the crack between the worlds!") The Teachings of Don Juan - Page [185.4-185.9] ("The particular thing to learn is...weak man journeys long and precariously.) Tales of Power - Page [294.5-294.6] ("The twilight is the crack between...beyond that abyss is the unknown.") The Second Ring of Power - Page [47.3-47.7] (Women have their own ways...it, but it took them years.") The Second Ring of Power - Page [164.3-164.5] (And like the Nagual showed us...a man has to make it.) The Second Ring of Power - Page [172.2-172.3] ("She laughed. Her laughter was not...is none in front of yours.") The Second Ring of Power - Page [247.2-247.9] ("I've told you already what the...days until the crack would open.") The Second Ring of Power - Page [279.3-279.7] (Genaro could go in and out...and Genaro went through that crack.") The Second Ring of Power - Page [298.5-299.1] ("I know about it," she said...of her hand on my mouth.) The Second Ring of Power - Page [325.8-326.1] (So, when it was time for him...went there for their sheer enjoyment.") The Eagle's Gift - Page [40.7] (The last hour of the afternoon...have to be at that time.) The Eagle's Gift - Page [241.7-243.8] (Silvio Manuel had conceived the idea...of awareness you ever had.") The Fire From Within - Page [58.6-58.9] ("One day, without any warning at all...it is a curtain," don Juan replied.)
    SEE ALSO: *PARALLEL-LINES, VAGINA-COSMIC, DOOR-OTHER, ATTENTION-DOMAINS-TWO, WARRIOR-DEVELOPMENT-STAGES-THREE*

CRACKING-SOUND-NECK-[THE CRACKING SOUND AT THE BASE OF THE NECK]-(TOP): SEE: DOUBLE-SOUND-[THE SOUND OF THE DOUBLE]-(TOP)

CRATE-[THE CRATE]: *(Warriors know that the crate is one of the key elements of the stalkers' recapitulation; a wooden crate large enough to accommodate the warrior; the crate reduces the area of stimulation around the body.)*
    SELECTED REFERENCES: The Eagle's Gift - Page [234.8-235.4] (For our first not-doing, Silvio...of sitting with our knees up.) The Eagle's Gift - Page [284.7-285.8] (Her two servants left the next...task he had called the "recapitulation.") The Eagle's Gift - Page [287.4-287.7] (She explained that a recapitulation is...recollecting, every moment of their lives.) The Eagle's Gift - Page [288.4-288.5] (Florinda explained that the key element...would foster deeper and deeper memories.)
    SEE ALSO: *RECAPITULATION, STALKING-ART, CRIB-DREAMER*

CREATIVITY-[A DEMONSTRATION OF CREATIVITY AND THE NAGUAL]-(TOP) SEE: NAGUAL-DEMONSTRATION-[A

DEMONSTRATION OF CREATIVITY AND THE NAGUAL]-(TOP)

CREATIVITY-MOLDING-[MOLDING AND CREATIVITY]: *(Warriors know the difference between the pure creativity of the nagual and the superb molding abilities of the tonal; the nagual is the only part of the warrior that can create; the tonal cannot create anything, it can only witness and assess and mold things, personally or in conjunction with other tonals.)*
SELECTED REFERENCES: **Tales of Power** - Page [123.8-124.2] ("The *tonal* is what makes the...of speaking, it creates the world.") **Tales of Power** - Page [137.1-137.3] (I did not remember all the...that was accountable for creativity.) **Tales of Power** - Page [140.6-141.8] ("One can say that the nagual...did not remember having stood up.)
SEE ALSO: *TONAL, NAGUAL*

CREATURES-OBSESSED-MOVEMENT-[THE CREATURES OBSESSED WITH MOVEMENT]-(TOP)

CRIB-DREAMER-[THE DREAMERS' CRIB]: *(Warriors know that if dreaming is going to be done indoors it is best to do it sitting inside a coffin like crib.)*
SELECTED REFERENCES: **The Eagle's Gift** - Page [249.7-249.8] (Zuleica told me that if *dreaming*...while sitting inside a coffin like crib.) **The Eagle's Gift** - Page [251.1-251.2] (She led me to an alcove...I thought was a hard cushion.)
SEE ALSO: *DREAMING-ART, DREAMING-TECHNIQUES, DREAMER-PONCHO, CRATE*

*CROSSING-EYES-[CROSSING THE EYES]: SEE: PERCEPTION-DOUBLE-[DOUBLE PERCEPTION OF THE WORLD]

CROSSING-FREEDOM-WARRIOR-[THE WARRIOR CROSSES OVER TO FREEDOM]: SEE: WARRIOR-CROSSING-FREEDOM-[THE WARRIOR CROSSES OVER TO FREEDOM]

CROW-EMISSARY-WARRIOR-[THE EMISSARY CROWS OF ONE WARRIOR'S FATE]-(TOP)

CROW-SEEING-AS-[SEEING AS A CROW SEES]-(TOP)

CROW-TRANSFORMATION-CARLOS-[CARLOS' TRANSFORMATION INTO A CROW]-(TOP)

CRUELTY-[CRUELTY]: *(Warriors know that the position of self-reflection forces the assemblage point to assemble a world of sham compassion but very real cruelty and self-centeredness.)*
SELECTED REFERENCES: **The Power of Silence** - Page [154.4-154.5] ("The position of self-reflection." don Juan...or self-importance. Ruthlessness is sobriety.")
SEE ALSO: *VIOLENCE, SELF-REFLECTION, SELF-IMAGE, SELF-COMPASSION, CYNICISM, CUNNING*

CRYSTALS-FOG-[THE FOG OF CRYSTALS]: SEE: FOG-CRYSTALS-[THE FOG OF CRYSTALS]

CRYSTALS-POWER-[POWER CRYSTALS]-(TOP)

CUBIC-CENTIMETER-CHANCE-[THE WARRIORS' CUBIC CENTIMETER OF CHANCE]: SEE: WARRIOR-CHANCE-MINIMAL-[THE WARRIORS' MINIMAL CHANCE]

CUNNING-[CUNNING]: *(Warriors know that cunning is one of the four moods of stalking; the warriors' ability to be skillful, clever and ingenious*

without being cruel; the courage of warriors empowers them to be cunning without being conceited.)
    SELECTED REFERENCES: **The Power of Silence - Page [68.2-68.6]** (Don Juan said that his benefactor...acts this way he's being prissy.'") **The Power of Silence - Page [69.3-69.4]** ("In the past few days, I...what I taught you about them.) **The Power of Silence - Page [78.5-78.8]** ("You're neither ruthless nor cunning...be taught in careful, meticulous steps.) **The Power of Silence - Page [81.8]** ("The very first principle of stalking...himself ruthlessly, cunningly, patiently, and sweetly.") **The Power of Silence - Page [109.2-109.3]** ("I'll try to help you clarify...behavior in a ruthless, cunning way.") **The Power of Silence - Page [110.2-110.3]** ("Yes," he went on. "The idea...be ruthless without being self-important.") **The Art of Dreaming - Page [51.6-51.8]** (The cunningness of sorcerers, cultivated through...it all made sense to me.)
    SEE ALSO: *STALKING-MOODS-FOUR, CRUELTY, RUTHLESSNESS*

CURIOSITY-WARRIOR-[THE WARRIORS' CURIOSITY]: SEE: WARRIOR-CURIOSITY-[THE WARRIORS' CURIOSITY]

CYCLE-DREAMING-[THE CYCLE OF DREAMING]: SEE: WARRIOR-CYCLE -THE WARRIORS' CYCLE]

CYCLE-NEW-[THE NEW CYCLE]: (Warriors know that the new cycle is the cycle of the new seers; the cycle that began after the distinction between the unknown and the unknowable was realized.)
    SELECTED REFERENCES: **The Eagle's Gift - Page [187.1-187.6]** (The second topic was the cultural...under the harshest conditions of suppression.) **The Fire From Within - Page [xiii.5-xiii.7]** (Although he felt that he was...as if they had never existed.) **The Fire From Within - Page [2.7-3.5]** ("We are going to be talking...like entering a dead-end street.) **The Fire From Within - Page [5.7-6.2]** ("Who were those conquerors, don Juan...practitioners of the art of stalking.") **The Fire From Within - Page [35.5]** ("What happened after the distinction between...done stems from understanding that distinction.") **The Fire From Within - Page [61.2-61.4]** (I asked him if there was....to come, must come of itself.") **The Fire From Within - Page [90.7-90.8]** ("I am a seer of the new cycle...I'm telling you what they believed.") **The Fire From Within - Page [170.1-171.4]** ("*Stalking* belongs exclusively to the new...of *will*, the energy of alignment.)
    SEE ALSO: *SEER-NEW, UNKNOWN-VS-UNKNOWABLE, UNKNOWN, UNKNOWABLE*

CYCLE-SORCERER-[THE SORCERERS' CYCLE]: SEE: SORCERER-CYCLE-FIRST [THE FIRST SORCERERS' CYCLE] , SORCERER-CYCLE-SECOND [THE SECOND SORCERERS' CYCLE]

CYCLE-WARRIOR-[THE WARRIORS' CYCLE]: SEE: WARRIOR-CYCLE-[THE WARRIORS' CYCLE]

CYCLES-WARRIOR-[THE WARRIORS' CYCLES]: SEE: WARRIOR-CYCLES-[THE WARRIORS' CYCLES]

CYNICISM-[CYNICISM]: (Warriors know the reason for man's cynicism and despair is the bit of silent knowledge left in him; this knowledge does two things; first, it gives man an inkling of his connection with intent and second, it makes man feel that without this connection he has no hope for peace, satisfaction or attainment in his life.)
    SELECTED REFERENCES: **The Power of Silence - Page [149.7-150.1]** (As the feeling of the individual self...of peace, of satisfaction, of attainment.) **The Art of Dreaming - Page [171.9-172.4]** ("Your problem is your cynicism...this in a bona fide manner.)
    SEE ALSO: *WARRIOR-ATTAINMENT, PEACE, KNOWLEDGE-SILENT, CRUELTY, SELF-IMAGE, AWARENESS-SUBLIMINAL*

D

DAGGER-METAPHORICAL-[THE METAPHORICAL DAGGER]:
(Warriors know that average men share a metaphorical dagger, the concerns of their self-reflection; with this dagger they cut themselves and bleed, and it is the job of their self-reflection to make them feel as if they are bleeding together, sharing some sort of wonderful act of humanity; in reality though, they are not sharing anything, they are bleeding alone; when man cuts himself with his metaphorical dagger, he is only toying with his manageable but unreal, man-made reflection.)
　　SELECTED REFERENCES: The Power of Silence - Page [90.7-90.9] (Don Juan said that the nagual...our manageable, unreal, man-made reflection.)
　　SEE ALSO: *SELF-REFLECTION, BLACK-MAGICIANS, SELF-IMAGE, ENERGY, ENERGY-DRAINAGE*

DAMNATION-SORCERER-[THE SORCERERS' DAMNATION]: SEE: SORCERER-DAMNATION [THE SORCERERS' DAMNATION]

DANCE-LAST-POWER-WARRIOR-[THE WARRIORS' LAST DANCE OF POWER]: SEE: WARRIOR-DANCE-LAST-POWER-[THE WARRIORS' LAST DANCE OF POWER]

DARING-WARRIOR-[THE WARRIOR MUST BE DARING]: SEE: WARRIOR-ABANDON-[THE WARRIORS' CONTROLLED ABANDON]

DARK-ENERGY-[DARK ENERGY]: SEE: ENERGY-DARK-[DARK ENERGY]

DARK-REGIONS-[THE DARK REGIONS]: (Warriors know that the dark regions is another term for the realm of the inorganic beings.)
　　SELECTED REFERENCES: The Fire From Within - Page [81.4-81.5] ("The counterpart of the earth was...it together with all organic beings.)
　　SEE ALSO: *INORGANIC-BEINGS-REALM*

DARK-SIDE-MAN-[THE DARK SIDE OF MAN]: SEE: MAN-DARK-SIDE-[THE DARK SIDE OF MAN]

DARKNESS-DAY-[THE DARKNESS OF THE DAY]: (Warriors know that the darkness of the day is another term for the night.)
　　SELECTED REFERENCES: A Separate Reality - Page [24.8-25.3] (I told don Juan how much...late to go into it then.) Journey to Ixtlan - Page [165.3-165.4] ("Today you are going to hunt...the darkness they are not hills.")
　　SEE ALSO: *SEEING-DARKNESS-DAY*

DARKNESS-WARRIOR-[THE WARRIOR OF THE DARKNESS]-(TOP)

DATURA-[DATURA]: SEE: DEVIL'S-WEED-[DEVIL'S WEED]

DAUGHTERS-SONS-[DAUGHTERS AND SONS]: SEE: MEN-[MEN], WOMEN-[WOMEN]

DAY-EDGE-[THE EDGE OF THE DAY]: (Warriors know that the edge of the day is another term for twilight; when warriors find themselves at the edge of the day it means that the hour of the nagual is approaching, the edge of the day is the warriors' hour of power.)

SELECTED REFERENCES: Tales of Power - Page [144.4-144.6] (I wanted to question him further...edge of the day is an omen.) Tales of Power - Page [145.1-145.6] ("For a *proper tonal* everything on the...I wouldn't have it any other way.")
SEE ALSO: TWILIGHT, WARRIOR-HOUR-POWER

DEAD-COMPANY-WARRIOR-[THE WARRIOR AND THE COMPANY OF THE DEAD]: SEE: WARRIOR-COMPANY-DEAD-[THE WARRIOR AND THE COMPANY OF THE DEAD]

*DEATH-[DEATH]: (Warriors know that the moment of dying is when all of their being disintegrates under the attraction of the immense force of the Eagle; death is the only worthy opponent that warriors have; an active force in the life of warriors; the force which challenges warriors; the force that sets the pace for the warriors' actions; the force which pushes warriors relentlessly until it breaks them or until they manage to rise above all possibilities by countermanding it.)

SELECTED REFERENCES: The Teachings of Don Juan - Page [161.4] (It does not take much to...seek death is to seek nothing.") A Separate Reality - Page [195.6-195.8] (I admitted that I was too...it is, made his life expand.") A Separate Reality - Page [196.1-196.4] ("Death has two stages. The first...it dissolves our lives into nothing.") A Separate Reality - Page [197.1-197.8] ("The second stage of your death...of tiny crystals moving, moving away.") Journey to Ixtlan - Page [40.1-40.3] ("Look at me ," he said...There is only time for decisions.") Journey to Ixtlan - Page [43.6-43.7] ("It doesn't matter what the decision...the face of our inevitable death.") Journey to Ixtlan - Page [153.6-155.5] ("What do you mean by my...to the south. To the vastness.") Journey to Ixtlan - Page [155.8-157.4] ("Is death a personage, don Juan...he lives and how he dies.") Journey to Ixtlan - Page [249.7-249.9] (The beetle emerged from a deep...Our death made us equal.) Tales of Power - Page [75.2-75.4] ("Write, write. Or you'll die...does not give himself to it.") Tales of Power - Page [84.6-84.7] ("Why is the ally waiting for...point what is meant by that.) Tales of Power - Page [112.5-112.6] ("I would rather be with you...death is going to find him.) Tales of Power - Page [113.7-113.9] ("The world upheld by *will* makes...tautness and vanishing one by one.) Tales of Power - Page [114.5-114.7] (It is only because death is...that is the predilection of my spirit.") Tales of Power - Page [132.4-132.5] ("The totality of ourselves is a very...not, then, live with that totality?") Tales of Power - Page [272.6-273.2] (This is the sorcerers' explanation...they had never been a unit.) The Second Ring of Power - Page [234.4-234.9] (I had an attack of profound...behind the best of my feelings.) The Eagle's Gift - Page [243.6-243.7] ("There is nothing gorgeous or peaceful...flicker of awareness you have ever had.") The Fire From Within - Page [42.2-42.4] ("Look at what some seers have...the attraction of that immense force.) The Fire From Within - Page [72.5-72.9] (He reiterated that awareness begins...knowledge is composed of contradictory propositions.) The Fire From Within - Page [226.7-226.9] (Don Juan said that in cases...it open and makes it collapse.") The Fire From Within - Page [254.5-254.7] ("What happens at the moment of...except to escape through the gap.") The Power of Silence - Page [17.4-17.5] (Don Juan explained again something...the person to whom it belonged.) The Power of Silence - Page [46.6-46.7] (What he was saying was that...making the assemblage point change positions.) The Power of Silence - Page [109.5-110.3] ("The idea of death therefore is of...be ruthless without being self-important.) The Power of Silence - Page [111.9-112.5] ("Would you say, don Juan, that...above all possibilities and defeat death.) The Power of Silence - Page [206.8-207.5] ("Don't worry," he said...had been made, they stood forever.)
SEE ALSO: WORTHY-OPPONENT, DEATH-ADVISER, DEATH-(ALL)

DEATH-ACTIVE-FORCE-[DEATH IS THE ACTIVE FORCE]: (Warriors know that death is not an enemy; death is our only worthy opponent, our only real challenger; death is the active force while life is the arena.)

SELECTED REFERENCES: The Power of Silence - Page [111.9-112.3] ("Would you say, don Juan, that...at any time: oneself and death.")
SEE ALSO: DEATH, DEATH-WORTHY-OPPONENT, DEATH-ADVISER, KNOWLEDGE-POWER-DEATH, MAN-PASSIVE, LIFE ARENA

*DEATH-ADVISER-[DEATH AS AN ADVISER]: (Warriors know that it is the idea of death that tempers their spirit; death is the central force behind

every bit of knowledge that becomes power; warriors consider themselves already dead, so they are clear and calm and without anything to lose; warriors have an awareness of the presence of death because without it there is no power, no mystery; the knowledge of death from which warriors draw the courage to face anything.)

SELECTED REFERENCES: **A Separate Reality** - Page [47.8-47.9] ("A warrior thinks of his death...only thing that tempers our spirit.") **A Separate Reality** - Page [96.5] (The two of them had another...his death?"" he said to me.) **A Separate Reality** - Page [150.2-150.6] ("By the time knowledge becomes a...becoming an obsession, becomes an indifference.") **A Separate Reality** - Page [151.1-151.6] ("Only the idea of death makes...with gusto and lusty efficiency.) **Journey to Ixtlan** - Page [34.1-36.2] ("You're the boy who stalked...you feel its presence around you.") **Journey to Ixtlan** - Page [37.3-37.5] ("Is it possible to see our...is sitting with me right here.") **Journey to Ixtlan** - Page [39.1-39.2] ("Think of your death now," don...of us have time for that.) **Journey to Ixtlan** - Page [80.6-81.2] ("You always feel compelled to explain...witnessing all the marvels of it.") **Journey to Ixtlan** - Page [84.8-85.1] ("Use it. Focus your attention on...the acts of a timid man.") **Tales of Power** - Page [27.7-27.8] ("There is nothing in this world...suspect that he has witnessed everything.") **Tales of Power** - Page [114.5-114.6] (Power is showing you that death...the world is an unfathomable mystery.) **Tales of Power** - Page [115.8] ("So you see, without an awareness...there is no power, no mystery.") **Tales of Power** - Page [196.7-196.8] ("It's not as complicated as you...are no survivors on this earth!") **Tales of Power** - Page [240.7-240.8] (He explained that in order to...dubious about himself and his actions.) **Tales of Power** - Page [241.3-241.4] (Obviously, after an untold struggle you...is nothing in comparison to death.") **Tales of Power** - Page [241.8-242.1] ("Take self-pity again...witness your acts and advise you.) **The Second Ring of Power** - Page [234.4-234.5] (Don Juan had always maintained that...and our fears of the unknown.) **The Fire From Within** - Page [241.7-241.9] (Don Juan had drilled into me...no longer have anything to fear.) **The Power of Silence** - Page [109.4-110.3] (He explained that when a sorcerer's...be ruthless without being self-important.") **The Power of Silence** - Page [111.8-112.2] (I was very moved. Don Juan's...about it; average men do not.")

SEE ALSO: *DEATH, DEATH-WORTHY-OPPONENT, WARRIOR-SPIRIT, WARRIOR-DEATH-SYMBOLIC, DEATH-ACTIVE-FORCE*

DEATH-ALAMEDA-PARK-[DEATH FINDS A MAN IN ALAMEDA PARK]-(TOP)

DEATH-ALLIES-MERGE-[THE ALLIES TRY TO MERGE WITH THE WARRIORS' DEATH]-(TOP): SEE: ALLIES-DEATH-MERGE-[THE ALLIES TRY TO MERGE WITH THE WARRIORS' DEATH]-(TOP)

DEATH-ATTENTION-THIRD-[DEATH AND THE THIRD ATTENTION]:

(Warriors know that at the moment of dying, awareness enters into the third attention as a purging action before that awareness is reclaimed by the Eagle.)

SELECTED REFERENCES: **The Eagle's Gift** - Page [247.7-247.9] (He told me that I had...just before the Eagle devours it.)

SEE ALSO: *DEATH, ATTENTION-THIRD, EAGLE*

DEATH-AVOIDING-[AVOIDING DEATH]: *(Warriors know that through the art of dreaming, sorcerers tighten their luminous layers and unify their two attentions; by doing so sorcerers act to avoid their own deaths.)*

SELECTED REFERENCES: **The Second Ring of Power** - Page [291.1-291.5] (He explained to me that the center...together that perhaps they'll never die.") **The Power of Silence** - Page [213.5-213.7] (I asked don Juan to explain...fluctuate between reason and silent knowledge.)

SEE ALSO: *DEATH, DREAMING-ART, LUMINOUS-LAYERS, ATTENTIONS-UNIFYING-TWO, WARRIOR-DEATH-COMMAND*

DEATH-AWARENESS-[THE AWARENESS OF DEATH]: SEE: DESPAIR-DETERRENT-[THE ONLY DETERRENT TO DESPAIR]

DEATH-AWARENESS-STOPS-[AWARENESS STOPS DEATH]: SEE: *AWARENESS-DEATH-STOPS-[AWARENESS STOPS DEATH]*

DEATH-BLACK-SHADOW-[THE BLACK SHADOW OF DEATH]: SEE: *SHADOW-BLACK-DEATH-[THE BLACK SHADOW OF DEATH]*

DEATH-CARLOS-[CARLOS' DEATH]-(TOP)

DEATH-CHOOSE-NOT-WARRIOR-[THE WARRIOR DOES NOT CHOOSE DEATH]: SEE: *WARRIOR-DEATH-CHOOSE-NOT-[THE WARRIOR DOES NOT CHOOSE DEATH]*

DEATH-COMMAND-WARRIOR-[WARRIORS COMMAND THEIR DEATH]: SEE: *WARRIOR-DEATH-COMMAND-[WARRIORS COMMAND THEIR DEATH]*

DEATH-VS-DECISIONS-WARRIOR-[THE WARRIORS' DEATH VS THE WARRIORS' DECISIONS]: SEE: *WARRIOR-DEATH-VS-DECISIONS-[THE WARRIORS' DEATH VS THE WARRIORS' DECISIONS]*

*DEATH-DEFIERS-[THE DEATH DEFIERS]: (*Warriors know that the death defiers are certain old seers, who through their aberrant practices, learned to intend death away; seers who found a way to utilize the rolling force, and instead of succumbing to the onslaughts of the tumbler, let the boost of the tumbler move their assemblage points to the extremes of human possibilities.*)
      SELECTED REFERENCES: **The Fire From Within** - Page **[230.5-230.6]** ("They chose to live," he repeated...beak of the Eagle to be devoured.") **The Fire From Within** - Page **[232.7-233.7]** ("As Genaro told you, the old...the seers who practiced them are.") **The Fire From Within** - Page **[237.6-237.9]** (Don Juan remarked how easy it...elongate those periods to cover millennia.) **The Fire From Within** - Page **[247.8-250.5]** ("You claim that they are alive...about your being revolted. It's embarrassing!") **The Fire From Within** - Page **[289.6-289.8]** ("Where will I be don Juan...you won't be in this world.") **The Fire From Within** - Page **[298.5-299.3]** (He explained that the old seers...the quintessence of the death defiers.) **The Art of Dreaming** - Page **[12.4-13.9]** (Don Juan went on to explain...potentials are nothing to sneeze at.")
      SEE ALSO: *TENANT, TUMBLER, FORCE-ROLLING, TOLTEC-GHOULS, SEER-OLD, TOLTECS, WARRIOR-DEATH-DEFIER-QUINTESSENCE, INTENDING-DEATH-AWAY*

DEATH-DEFIERS-COURT-[THE DEATH DEFIERS AND THEIR COURT]-(TOP): SEE: *TOLTEC-GHOULS-[THE TOLTEC GHOULS]-(TOP)*

DEATH-DEFIERS-QUINTESSENCE-WARRIOR-[THE WARRIOR BECOMES THE QUINTESSENCE OF THE DEATH DEFIERS]: SEE: *WARRIOR-DEATH-DEFIERS-QUINTESSENCE-[THE WARRIOR BECOMES THE QUINTESSENCE OF THE DEATH DEFIERS]*

DEATH-ENEMY-NOT-[DEATH IS NOT AN ENEMY]: (*Warriors know that death is not an enemy, even though it appears to be so; death is the active force and life is the arena.*)
      SELECTED REFERENCES: **The Power of Silence** - Page **[111.9-112.3]** ("Would you say, don Juan, that...at any time: oneself and death.")
      SEE ALSO: *DEATH, DEATH-ACTIVE-FORCE*

DEATH-EXPERIENCE-[EXPERIENCING A TRUE SENSE OF DEATH]-(TOP)

DEATH-GESTURE-WARRIOR-[THE GESTURE WHICH DEATH MAKES TO THE IMPECCABLE WARRIOR]: (Warriors know they are only human and cannot change the designs of their death; but impeccable warriors who have stored power over a lifetime are capable of holding back death for a moment, long enough to rejoice in recalling their power; death will sit and watch warriors as they do their last dance of power.)
> SELECTED REFERENCES: **Journey to Ixtlan - Page [154.1-154.7]** ("If a dying warrior has limited...those who have an impeccable spirit.")
> SEE ALSO: *WARRIOR-DANCE-LAST-POWER, WARRIOR-PREDILECTION-PLACE*

DEATH-GIFT-[THE GIFT OF DEATH]: (Warriors know that the powers that guide men's lives lead all living creatures to their deaths; the death of any given being has the capacity to be a gift for something or someone else.)
> SELECTED REFERENCES: **Journey to Ixtlan - Page [88.1-88.6]** (I felt nauseated. He very patiently...to roam in this marvelous desert.")
> SEE ALSO: *DEATH, POWERS-GUIDE-MEN*

DEATH-HUNTER-[DEATH IS THE HUNTER]: (Warriors know that the world of the warrior is a world in which death is the hunter, a world in which there is no time for regrets or doubts; warriors know that they are not immortal, they only have time for decisions.)
> SELECTED REFERENCES: **Journey to Ixtlan - Page [40.3-40.4]** ("You, on the other hand, feel...There is only time for decisions.") **Journey to Ixtlan - Page [43.6-43.7]** ("It doesn't matter what the decision...the face of our inevitable death.")
> SEE ALSO: *DEATH, WARRIOR-REGRETS, IMMORTALITY, WARRIOR-DECISIONS*

DEATH-INDIFFERENCE-[DEATH AS AN INDIFFERENCE]: (Warriors know they must be keenly aware of death because death is the central force behind every bit of knowledge that becomes power in their lives; but warriors must also maintain a sense of detachment about death so that they won't become debilitated by a preoccupation with death; warriors develop a detachment which turns the idea of imminent death from an obsession into an indifference.)
> SELECTED REFERENCES: **A Separate Reality - Page [150.3-150.6]** ("A man who follows the paths of...becoming an obsession, becomes an indifference.")
> SEE ALSO: *DEATH, WARRIOR-DETACHMENT, OBSESSION*

DEATH-INTENDING-AWAY-[INTENDING DEATH AWAY]: SEE: INTENDING-DEATH-AWAY-[INTENDING DEATH AWAY]

DEATH-INTENT-SUSPENDING-[SUSPENDING THE INTENT OF DEATH]: (Warriors know that death exists only because we have intended it since the moment of birth; warriors also knows that the intent of death can be suspended by making the assemblage point move.)
> SELECTED REFERENCES: **The Power of Silence - Page [46.6-46.7]** (With his last bit of consciousness...making the assemblage point change positions.)
> SEE ALSO: *DEATH, INTENDING-DEATH-AWAY, INTENT*

DEATH-JUAN-[DON JUAN'S DEATH]-(TOP): SEE: JUAN-DEATH-[THE STORY OF DON JUAN'S DEATH]-(TOP)

DEATH-JUAN-PARENTS-[THE DEATH OF DON JUAN'S PARENTS]-(TOP): SEE: JUAN-PARENTS-DEATH-[THE DEATH OF DON JUAN'S PARENTS]-(TOP)

DEATH-KNOWLEDGE-[THE KNOWLEDGE OF DEATH]: *(Warriors know that the knowledge of their unavoidable death is what gives them their sobriety.)*
      SELECTED REFERENCES: **The Power of Silence - Page [109.5-109.7]** ("The idea of death therefore is...we can protect ourselves from it.")
      SEE ALSO: *DESPAIR-DETERRENT, DEATH, DEATH-ADVISER, WARRIOR-SOBRIETY, IMMORTALITY*

DEATH-LEFT-[DEATH IS TO THE WARRIORS' LEFT]: *(Warriors know that death hovers to their left, over their left shoulder.)*
      SELECTED REFERENCES: **Journey to Ixtlan - Page [153.8-153.9]** ("And finally, one day when his...there the warrior dances to his death.) **Journey to Ixtlan - Page [225.5]** ("You should have known that it...You shouldn't have run either.") **Journey to Ixtlan - Page [226.6-226.7]** ("Of course , you know that from...moment when you are unaware and weak.") **Tales of Power - Page [170.8-171.5]** (I began to breath frantically...risks more dangerous than they already were.) **Tales of Power - Page [195.7-195.9]** (I mentioned that I was curious to...deliberately taking as a suicidal plunge.)
      SEE ALSO: *DEATH, DEATH-TAP, NAGUAL-FACING*

DEATH-LIGHTS-HEAD-[THE LIGHTS ON THE HEAD OF DEATH]-(TOP)

DEATH-LINGERS-[DEATH LINGERS]: *(Warriors know that death lingers on the spot where it occurs, even though the average man cannot "see" it.)*
      SELECTED REFERENCES: **A Separate Reality - Page [41.5-41.6]** (A good hunter knows that and...but we never *see* it.")
      SEE ALSO: *DEATH, SEEING*

DEATH-PACE-[DEATH SETS THE PACE]: *(Warriors know the true nature of life and death; death is the active force, while life is the arena where only two contenders struggle, the warrior and death; death sets the pace for warriors' actions and pushes relentlessly until it either breaks them or until they rise above all possibilities and defeat death.)*
      SELECTED REFERENCES: **The Power of Silence - Page [112.3-112.6]** ("Life is the process by means...above all possibilities and defeat death.)
      SEE ALSO: *DEATH, LIFE, WARRIOR-DEATH-COMMAND, FIRE-WITHIN, HUMAN-ALTERNATIVES-POSSIBILITIES-POTENTIAL, DEATH-ACTIVE-FORCE*

DEATH-PAIN-[THE PAIN OF DEATH]: *(Warriors know that death is painful only when it happens in one's bed, in sickness; in a fight for their lives, warriors feel no pain; if they feel anything, it's exaltation.)*
      SELECTED REFERENCES: **The Power of Silence - Page [206.8-206.9]** ("Don't worry," he said. "Death is...If you feel anything, it's exaltation.)
      SEE ALSO: *DEATH, WARRIOR-PAIN*

DEATH-PARALLEL-LINES-LAND-[DEATH IN THE LAND BETWEEN THE PARALLEL LINES]-(TOP)

DEATH-REVELATION-[THE REVELATION OF DEATH]-(TOP)

DEATH-SEEING-[SEEING DEATH]: SEE: SEEING-DEATH-[SEEING DEATH]

DEATH-SEEKING-NOT-WARRIOR-[THE WARRIOR DOES NOT SEEK DEATH]: SEE: WARRIOR-DEATH-SEEKING-NOT-[THE WARRIOR DOES NOT SEEK DEATH]

DEATH-SHADOW-[THE SHADOW OF DEATH]-(TOP): SEE: SHADOW-DEATH-[THE SHADOW OF DEATH]-(TOP)

DEATH-SIGN-[THE SIGN THAT HERALDS THE WARRIORS' DEATH]:
(Warriors know that they will have a sign when it is time for them to go; it
does not have to be something great, anything the warrior likes will do.)
　　　SELECTED REFERENCES: **The Eagle's Gift - Page [74.1-74.8]** ("The Nagual Juan
Matus said that...idiotic tune, the same peerless trumpeter.)
　　　SEE ALSO: *DEATH, TRUMPETER-PEERLESS-(TOP)*

DEATH-SIGNIFICANCE-[THE SIGNIFICANCE OF DEATH]: (Warriors
know they are lost unless they understand the true significance of death.)
　　　SELECTED REFERENCES: **The Second Ring of Power - Page [189.6-190.1]** (Pablito's
statements made me remember something...is stupidly the same to him.")
　　　SEE ALSO: *DEATH-ADVISER, DEATH*

DEATH-STOP-WARRIOR-[THE WARRIOR STOPS DEATH]-(TOP): SEE:
WARRIOR-DEATH-STOP-[THE WARRIOR STOPS DEATH]-(TOP)

DEATH-SULFUR-DUNES-[DEATH IN THE LAND OF THE SULFUR
DUNES]-(TOP): SEE: DEATH-PARALLEL-LINES-LAND-[DEATH IN THE
LAND BETWEEN THE PARALLEL LINES]-(TOP)

DEATH-SYMBOLIC-WARRIOR-[THE WARRIORS' SYMBOLIC DEATH]:
SEE: WARRIOR-DEATH-SYMBOLIC-[THE WARRIORS' SYMBOLIC
DEATH]

DEATH-TAP-[THE TAP OF DEATH]: (Warriors know that when death
comes it will tap them on the left shoulder.)
　　　SELECTED REFERENCES: **Journey to Ixtlan - Page [153.8-153.9]** ("And finally, one
day when his...there the warrior dances to his death.) **Journey to Ixtlan - Page [225.5]** ("You
should have known that it...You shouldn't have run either.") **Journey to Ixtlan - Page [226.6-
226.7]** ("Of course , you know that from...moment when you are unaware and weak.") **Tales of
Power - Page [170.8-171.5]** (I began to breath frantically...risks more dangerous than they already
were.) **Tales of Power - Page [195.7-195.9]** (I mentioned that I was curious to...deliberately
taking as a suicidal plunge.)
　　　SEE ALSO: *DEATH, WARRIOR-DANCE-LAST-POWER, DEATH-LEFT*

DEATH-WAITING-FOR-[WAITING FOR DEATH]-(TOP)

DEATH-WAITS-[DEATH IS WAITING]: (Warriors know that death is
always waiting for them when they journey into the unknown; to venture
into the unknown without any power is stupid because warriors knows they
will only find death.)
　　　SELECTED REFERENCES: **Journey to Ixtlan - Page [135.6-135.7]** ("Death is always
waiting, and when...One will only find death.")
　　　SEE ALSO: *DEATH, UNKNOWN*

DEATH-WARRIOR-[THE WARRIORS' DEATH]: SEE: WARRIOR-
DEATH-[THE WARRIORS' DEATH]

DEATH-WORTHY-OPPONENT-[DEATH IS THE ONLY WORTHY
OPPONENT]: (Warriors know that death is the challenger, the only worthy
opponent that they have.)
　　　SELECTED REFERENCES: **The Power of Silence - Page [112.1-112.2]** (Death is not
our destroyer...about it; average men do not.")
　　　SEE ALSO: *DEATH, WORTHY-OPPONENT*

DECISIONS-EMPOWERING-[EMPOWERING DECISIONS]: SEE:
WARRIOR-DECISIONS-EMPOWERING-[WARRIORS EMPOWER THEIR
DECISIONS]

DECISIONS-FINAL-WARRIOR-[THE FINALITY OF THE WARRIORS' DECISIONS]: SEE: WARRIOR-DECISIONS-FINAL-[THE FINALITY OF THE WARRIORS' DECISIONS]

DECISIONS-WARRIOR-[THE WARRIORS' DECISIONS]: SEE: WARRIOR-DECISIONS-[THE WARRIORS' DECISIONS]

DEDICATION-WARRIOR-[THE WARRIORS' DEDICATION AND SINGLE-MINDEDNESS]: SEE: WARRIOR-DEDICATION-[THE WARRIORS' DEDICATION AND SINGLE-MINDEDNESS]

DEFEAT-[DEFEAT]: (Warriors know there are various ways they can be defeated by their four natural enemies or by other forces in the warriors' world of power.)
SELECTED REFERENCES: The Teachings of Don Juan - Page [51.3-51.5] ("A man goes to knowledge as he...be no pitiful regrets over that.) The Teachings of Don Juan - Page [84.1-87.8] ("He slowly begins to learn - bit...clarity, power and knowledge is enough.") A Separate Reality - Page [27.3-27.5] ("Why do you have to push...it perhaps even harder than you.") A Separate Reality - Page [88.7-88.8] ("Everything is filled to the brim," he...my struggle was worth my while.) A Separate Reality - Page [138.3-138.6] ("You haven't been defeated yet...for reasons other than defeat itself.) A Separate Reality - Page [147.4-147.6] ("Is the will an object...to the moon, if he wants.") Journey to Ixtlan - Page [227.5-227.6] ("What a terrible way of putting it...that *doing* there are only actions.") Tales of Power - Page [284.2-284.3] ("If you choose not to return...the command over the totality of yourselves.") The Second Ring of Power - Page [84.3-84.8] (There was no doubt left in my...human nature, he was probably right.) The Fire From Within - Page [30.1-30.5] (I explained to don Juan that...of the petty tyrants for life.") The Fire From Within - Page [260.2-260.3] (He also said that there was…another by gripping feelings of defeat.)
SEE ALSO: *FAILURE, WARRIOR-ENEMIES-FOUR-NATURAL, LEARNING-HARDSHIPS, VICTORY-(ALL), WARRIOR-DEFEAT-FEELING-COMBATING, WARRIOR-REGRETS*

DEFEAT-FEELING-COMBATING-WARRIOR-[HOW WARRIORS CAN COMBAT THEIR FEELINGS OF DEFEAT]: SEE: WARRIOR-DEFEAT-FEELING-COMBATING-[HOW WARRIORS CAN COMBAT THEIR FEELINGS OF DEFEAT]

DEFEND-NOTHING-WARRIOR-[WARRIORS HAVE NO POINTS TO DEFEND]: SEE: WARRIOR-DEFEND-NOTHING-[WARRIORS HAVE NO POINTS TO DEFEND]

DEFINITIVE-JOURNEY-[THE WARRIORS' DEFINITIVE JOURNEY]: SEE: WARRIOR-DEFINITIVE-JOURNEY-[THE WARRIORS' DEFINITIVE JOURNEY]

DELICACY-WARRIOR-[THE WARRIORS' DELICACY]: SEE: WARRIOR-DELICACY-[THE WARRIORS' DELICACY]

DENIAL-[DENIAL]: (Warriors know that denial is one of the worst forms of self-indulgence; the indulgence of denying forces warriors to believe they are doing great things, when in fact, they are only fixed within themselves.)
SELECTED REFERENCES: A Separate Reality - Page [146.7-146.9] ("No," he said. "Denying yourself is...we are only fixed within ourselves.) A Separate Reality - Page [151.1-151.2] ("Only the idea of death makes...and for all things of life.)
SEE ALSO: *SELF-INDULGENCE*

DENT-LUMINOUS-[THE LUMINOUS DENT]: SEE: LUMINOUS-DENT-[THE LUMINOUS DENT]

DENT-LUMINOUS-FEELING-[FEELING THE LUMINOUS DENT]-(TOP):
SEE: ATTENTION-SECOND-CONTROLS-[EXPERIENCING THE
SECOND ATTENTION TAKING OVER THE CONTROLS]-(TOP)

DEPRESSION-MELANCHOLY-[DEPRESSION AND MELANCHOLY]:
(Warriors experience first-hand an overwhelming feeling of sadness when their luminous being senses its final destination as the boundaries of the known are broken; the warriors' melancholy is brought on by bouts of self-importance; the sign that warriors have received their "eviction notice" from the unknown; warriors know that experiencing melancholy and depression is a sign that they are beginning to learn.)

SELECTED REFERENCES: **The Teachings of Don Juan** - Page **[48.2-48.5]** (I told don Juan how I felt..."You are beginning to learn.") **Journey to Ixtlan** - Page **[89.4]** (The post effects of that experience...of exceptionally vivid dreams and nightmares.) **Journey to Ixtlan** - Page **[89.9]** (I complained again about the feeling...and said, "You're beginning to learn.") **The Fire From Within** - Page **[96.9-97.7]** (Never in my life had I...be ready for the definitive journey.") **The Fire From Within** - Page **[129.2-129.3]** (When they had calmed down, don...there only to make them laugh.) **The Fire From Within** - Page **[152.6-153.6]** (My experience with la Catalina delayed...get another pad," don Juan replied.) **The Power of Silence** - Page **[110.3-110.5]** (He smiled again and nudged me...you read me to *stalk* yourself.")

SEE ALSO: *SADNESS, SELF-IMPORTANCE, OBSESSION, WARRIOR-EVICTION NOTICE, WARRIOR-HUMOR*

DEPTH-ACTION-[THE DEPTH OF THE WARRIORS' ACTIONS]:
(Warriors know that they must cultivate a tri-dimensionality to their actions; the depth of the third point of reference; the warriors' ability to perceive two places at once.)

SELECTED REFERENCES: **The Power of Silence** - Page **[221.1-221.8]** (I urged him to try to...must perceive two places at once.")

SEE ALSO: *POINT-THIRD, HERE-HERE*

DEPTH-VIEW-[A VIEW OF THE DEPTHS]: *(When warriors face the nagual, they experience first-hand the depths of the unknown; those depths give warriors a glimpse of their final destination whenever the boundaries of the known are broken; on such occasions, warriors get a glimpse of eternity and its absolute loneliness.)*

SELECTED REFERENCES: **The Fire From Within** - Page **[96.9-97.3]** (Never in my life had I...that it can bring about death.) **The Fire From Within** - Page **[97.6-98.1]** ("Something is finally getting through to you...could actually face the loneliness of eternity.")

SEE ALSO: *NAGUAL-FACING, UNKNOWABLE, DEPRESSION-MELANCHOLY, WARRIOR-EVICTION-NOTICE, WARRIOR-LONELINESS, UNKNOWN*

DESCRIPTION-WORLD-[THE DESCRIPTION OF THE WORLD]:
(Warriors know that the description of the world is the "common sense" view of the world; a description, an interpretation of the world that our human senses make; the first attention's view of reality; the description of reason; the limited view of eternity which traps the totality of human beings in a vicious circle.)

SELECTED REFERENCES: **A Separate Reality** - Page **[10.5-10.6]** (Don Juan's task ,as a practitioner...because it is only an interpretation.) **Journey to Ixtlan** - Page **[viii.7-viii.8]** (For the purpose of presenting my...all know, is only a description.) **Journey to Ixtlan** - Page **[xiii.5-xiii.8]** (In summing up I can say...other words, I had gained *membership.*) **Tales of Power** - Page **Tales of Power** - Page **[23.1-23.3]** (The world, according to don Juan...is referred to, or is intended.) **Tales of Power** - Page **[24.3-24.5]** ("That's the flaw with words," he...where new acts have new reflections.") **Tales of Power** - Page **[47.4-47.5]** ("Think of this," he went on...just passed. We recollect, recollect, recollect.") **Tales of Power** - Page **[97.6-97.8]** ("Today I have to pound the nail...we rarely emerge in our lifetime.) **Tales of Power** - Page **[98.2-98.9]** ("We are perceivers," he proceeded...to get to the totality of yourself.) **Tales of Power - Page [244.5-245.4]** ("That's a difficult point to explain...ordinary man or to a sorcerer.) **Tales of Power - Page [252.4-253.2]** ("The sorcerers' explanation, of course," he...opens the bubble from the outside.") **The Fire From Within - Page [41.1-41.5]** ("There is nothing visual about the....that no living creature can grasp.")

  SEE ALSO: *ATTENTION-FIRST, REASON, REALITY-INTERPRETATION, POWER-RING-FIRST, ATTENTION-TONAL, SORCERER-DESCRIPTION-WORLD, DESCRIPTION-WORLD-(ALL)*

DESCRIPTION-WORLD-MEMORIES-[MEMORIES OF THE DESCRIPTION OF THE WORLD]: *(Warriors know that their memories of the world include everything they feel about the world; the memories warriors accumulate concerning the description of the world; the warriors' solidity.)*

  SELECTED REFERENCES: **Tales of Power - Page [48.7-48.9]** ("Certainly," don Juan said. "Solidity, corporealness...you feel me as being solid.")

  SEE ALSO: *DESCRIPTION-WORLD, WARRIOR-SOLIDITY*

DESCRIPTION-WORLD-SORCERER-[THE SORCERERS' DESCRIPTION OF THE WORLD]: *(Warriors know that sorcerers describe the world in entirely new and sophisticated terms; sorcerers "see" energy directly, they "see" the energetic essence of everything, they "see" the Eagle's emanations.)*

  SELECTED REFERENCES: **The Art of Dreaming - Page [4.8-5.3]** (But this is not the only...see the essence of the universe.)

  SEE ALSO: *SEEING, ENERGETIC-ESSENCE, SORCERY-PREMISE-BASIC*

DESCRIPTION-WORLD-TWO-[THE TWO DESCRIPTIONS OF THE WORLD]: *(Warriors know that there are two descriptions of the world; the most fundamental is that first this is a world of energy, and then secondly, it's a world of solid objects; warriors learn to pit these two descriptions one against the other.)*

  SELECTED REFERENCES: **Journey to Ixtlan - Page [xiii.8-xiv.2]** (Don Juan stated that in order...world, is not to be questioned.) **Tales of Power - Page [98.2-98.8]** ("We are perceivers," he proceeded...to get to the totality of yourself.) **Tales of Power - Page [244.5-244.9]** ("That's a difficult point to explain...in enlarging their views of the world.) **The Art of Dreaming - Page [4.3-4.6]** ("I can't conceive the world in...pointed out: the hardness of objects.")

  SEE ALSO: *DESCRIPTION-WORLD; DESCRIPTION-WORLD-SORCERER, WARRIOR-CONTRADICTION-KNOWLEDGE, WARRIOR-EQUILIBRIUM, REALITY, EQUILIBRIUM*

DESIRE-INTERVENTION-POWER-[POWER MOVES INDEPENDENT OF THE INTERVENTION OF DESIRE]: *(Warriors know that the intervention of desire has no effect on the designs of power; the body rallies its knowledge without the intervention of desire through a process independent of the warriors' volition.)*

  SELECTED REFERENCES: **The Eagle's Gift - Page [273.5-273.6]** (She said that there is no...knowledge without the intervention of desire.)

  SEE ALSO: *POWER-DESIGNS, KNOWLEDGE-RALLYING, WARRIOR-VOLITION, BODY-PHYSICAL-NEEDS-LEARN*

DESIRE-WARRIOR-[THE WARRIORS' DESIRE]: SEE: WARRIOR-DESIRE-[THE WARRIORS' DESIRE]

DESPAIR-DETERRENT-WARRIOR-[THE ONLY DETERRENT TO THE WARRIORS' DESPAIR]: SEE: WARRIOR-DESPAIR-DETERRENT-[THE ONLY DETERRENT TO THE WARRIORS' DESPAIR]

DESPAIR-MAN-[MAN'S DESPAIR]: SEE: MAN-DESPAIR-[MAN'S DESPAIR]

DESPAIR-WARRIOR-[THE WARRIORS' DESPAIR]: SEE: WARRIOR-DESPAIR-DETERRENT-[THE ONLY DETERRENT TO THE WARRIORS' DESPAIR]

DESPERATE-ONES-[THE DESPERATE ONES]: (Warriors know that some people come to warriorship from a position of desperation; those warriors are already almost dead and may even have tried to commit suicide; they are the desperate ones; there are other warriors who do not come from such desperate life experience.)
    SELECTED REFERENCES: The Second Ring of Power - Page [189.1-189.6] ("Those women hate me because they've...body and freedom to my spirit.)
    SEE ALSO: *WARRIORSHIP, WARRIOR-DESPAIR-DETERRENT, WARRIOR-DESPERATE-NEVER*

DESPERATE-WARRIOR-NEVER-[WARRIORS ARE NEVER DESPERATE]: SEE: WARRIOR-DESPERATE-NEVER-[WARRIORS ARE NEVER DESPERATE]

DESTINY-WARRIOR-[THE WARRIORS' DESTINY]: SEE: WARRIOR-DESTINY-[THE WARRIORS' DESTINY]

DESTROY-VS-BUILD-MAINTAIN-[DESTROYING SOMETHING VS BUILDING AND MAINTAINING IT]: (Warriors know it is infinitely easier to destroy something than it is to build and maintain it.)
    SELECTED REFERENCES: The Fire From Within - Page [227.9] ("They realized that it is infinitely...to giving it and nourishing it.)
    SEE ALSO: *ROLLING-FORCE, FORCE-CIRCULAR, TUMBLER*

DETACHMENT-MOMENT-[THE MOMENT OF DETACHMENT]: (Warriors know that the moment of detachment is the moment's pause which arises from the warriors' sense of detachment; a moment which allows warriors to reassess situations; a moment which warriors struggle a lifetime to utilize correctly.)
    SELECTED REFERENCES: The Eagle's Gift - Page [113.3-113.5] (He had said that detachment did...to struggle unyieldingly for a lifetime.) The Eagle's Gift - Page [124.9-125.1] (Having a sense of detachment, as don...strive to use that pause correctly.)
    SEE ALSO: *WARRIOR-DETACHMENT, WARRIOR-PAUSE-ATTENTION*

DETACHMENT-WARRIOR-[THE WARRIORS' DETACHMENT]: SEE: WARRIOR-DETACHMENT-[THE WARRIORS' DETACHMENT]

DETAIL-TRAP-[THE TRAP OF DETAIL]: SEE: ENERGY-BODY-PERFECTING-[PERFECTING THE ENERGY BODY]

DETERMINATION-WARRIOR-[THE WARRIORS' DETERMINATION]: SEE: WARRIOR-DETERMINATION-[THE WARRIORS' DETERMINATION]

DETHRONE-TONAL-GENTLE-[GENTLY DETHRONING THE TONAL]: SEE: TONAL-OVERSEER-PROTECTED-[THE TONAL AS A PROTECTED OVERSEER]

DEVELOPMENT-THREE-STAGES-WARRIOR-[THE THREE STAGES OF THE WARRIORS' DEVELOPMENT]: SEE: WARRIOR-DEVELOPMENT-THREE-STAGES-[THE THREE STAGES OF THE WARRIORS' DEVELOPMENT]

DEVIL-[DEVIL]: SEE: EVIL-[EVIL]

DEVIL-SELLING-SOUL-[SELLING ONE'S SOUL TO THE DEVIL]:

(Warriors know that the idea of selling one's soul to the devil is a carryover of the transcendental observations of the sorcerers of antiquity; an observation based on the relationship between those ancient sorcerers and the inorganic beings who offer to maintain an individual's self-awareness for nearly an eternity in exchange for imprisoning the individual in their realm.)

SELECTED REFERENCES: **The Art of Dreaming** - Page [173.4-173.6] (He remarked that of all the...self-awareness for nearly an eternity.)

SEE ALSO: *INORGANIC-BEINGS-TRICKERY, INORGANIC-BEINGS-REALM*

DEVIL'S-WEED-[THE DEVIL'S WEED]: *(Warriors know that the devil's weed is a psychotropic plant also called Datura or Jimson weed; a power plant capable of moving the warriors' assemblage point; the devil's weed flatters men and blinds them with ambition; the devil's weed entices men and gives them a sense of power, making them believe they can do things that no ordinary man can.)*

SELECTED REFERENCES: **The Teachings of Don Juan** - Page [52.7-52.9] (On the other hand, the acquiring...benefactor had taught him its secrets.) **The Teachings of Don Juan - Page [54.8-56.6]** ("The devil's weed [Jimson weed] was...learning to tame an ally power.) **The Teachings of Don Juan - Page [65.9-66.9]** (Perhaps the devil's weed would be...For what? to frighten the Indians?) **The Teachings of Don Juan - Page [69.2]** ("The devil's weed is for those who bid for power.) **The Teachings of Don Juan - Page [72.8-79.7]** (The specific time to replant the..."No, I will do that for you.") **The Teachings of Don Juan - Page [109.7-121.3]** (We returned to his room where...on, then you must simply stop.") **The Teachings of Don Juan - Page [153.5-161.4]** (Don Juan seemed to want me...seek death is to seek nothing.") **Tales of Power - Page [243.7-243.9]** ("Did the power plants help me...especially with the devil's weed.")

SEE ALSO: *POWER-PLANTS*

DEVIL'S-WEED-TALES-[TALES OF THE DEVIL'S WEED]-(TOP)

DIABLERO-DIABLERA-[THE DIABLERO AND THE DIABLERA]:

(Warriors know that diablero is a term used to describe an evil person who practices black sorcery and is capable of transforming into an animal.)

SELECTED REFERENCES: **The Teachings of Don Juan** - Page [14.9-15.5] (In describing his teacher, don Juan...that follow indicate what they felt.) **The Teachings of Don Juan - Page [184.2-185.2]** ("Very simple. She is a *diablera* and...the paths of life is everything.) **The Teachings of Don Juan - Page [186.3-187.6]** (Once on the other side,...recognize it. But I could not.)

SEE ALSO : *BRUJO, SORCERER, DIABLERO-VS-WARRIOR, DIABLERO-WORLD*

DIABLEROS-TALES-[TALES OF THE DIABLEROS]-(TOP)

DIABLERO-VS-WARRIOR-[THE DIABLERO VS THE WARRIOR]:

(Warriors know the differences between a diablero and a warrior; the diablero seeks power and the warrior seeks to "see"; the diablero is inclined towards the force and violence of the world while warriors seek to abstract themselves through the actions of an impeccable life.)

SELECTED REFERENCES: **The Teachings of Don Juan - Page [184.6-185.2]** ("To know that, you have to...the paths of life is everything.)

SEE ALSO: *POWER-PURSUIT, SEEING-VS-PURSUIT-POWER, SEEING, WARRIORSHIP-VS-SORCERY, ABSTRACT-RETURN, WARRIOR-IMPECCABILITY, DIABLERO-DIABLERA, WARRIOR*

DIABLERO-WORLD-[THE WORLD OF THE DIABLERO]: (Warriors know that the world beyond the parallel lines is the world of the diablero; the other side.)
SELECTED REFERENCES: The Teachings of Don Juan - Page [184.7] (That other side is the world of the diableros.) The Teachings of Don Juan - Page [185.4-185.5] ("The particular thing to learn is...and the world of living men.)
SEE ALSO: WORLD-OTHER, PARALLEL-LINES,-LAND, SORCERER, OTHER-SIDE, DIABLERO-DIABLERA

DIALOGUE-SEER-NEW-WARRIOR-[THE WARRIORS' DIALOGUE OF THE NEW SEERS]: SEE: WARRIOR-DIALOGUE-[THE WARRIORS' DIALOGUE OF THE NEW SEERS]

DIALOGUE-SEER-OLD-WARRIOR-[THE WARRIORS' DIALOGUE OF THE OLD SEERS]: SEE: WARRIOR-DIALOGUE-SEER-OLD-[THE WARRIORS' DIALOGUE OF THE OLD SEERS]

DIALOGUE-WARRIOR-[THE WARRIORS' DIALOGUE]: SEE: WARRIOR-DIALOGUE-[THE WARRIORS' DIALOGUE OF THE NEW SEERS]

DIAPHRAGM-SPASMS-[THE SPASMS OF THE DIAPHRAGM]-(TOP): SEE: ATTENTION-SECOND-CONTROLS-[EXPERIENCING THE SECOND ATTENTION TAKING OVER THE CONTROLS]-(TOP)

DIE-STRUGGLING-TO-[WE ARE ALL STRUGGLING TO DIE]: SEE: AWARENESS-DEATH-STOPS [AWARENESS STOPS DEATH]

DIMPLE-LUMINOUS-[THE LUMINOUS DIMPLE]: SEE: LUMINOUS-DENT-TYPE-[THE TYPES OF LUMINOUS DENTS]

DIRECTION-WARRIOR-[THE WARRIORS' DIRECTION]: SEE: WARRIOR-DIRECTION-[THE WARRIORS' DIRECTION]

DISAPPEARANCE-WARRIOR-[THE WARRIORS' DISAPPEARANCE]: SEE: WARRIOR-DISAPPEARANCE-[THE WARRIORS' DISAPPEARANCE]

DISAPPOINTMENT-WARRIOR-[THE WARRIORS' DISAPPOINTMENT]: SEE: WARRIOR-DISAPPOINTMENT-[THE WARRIORS' DISAPPOINTMENT]

DISASSOCIATION-WARRIOR-[THE WARRIORS' DISASSOCIATION]: SEE: WARRIOR-DISASSOCIATION-[THE WARRIORS' DISASSOCIATION]

DISCIPLINE-[DISCIPLINE]: (Warriors know that discipline is one of the four attributes of warriorship.)
SELECTED REFERENCES: The Fire From Within - Page [23.5] ("My benefactor developed a strategy using...warriorship: control, discipline, forbearance, and timing.")
SEE ALSO: WARRIOR-DISCIPLINE, WARRIOR-ATTRIBUTES, CONTROL, FORBEARANCE, TIMING, WILL

DISCIPLINE-WARRIOR-[THE WARRIORS' DISCIPLINE]: SEE WARRIOR-DISCIPLINE-[THE WARRIORS' DISCIPLINE]

DISCONNECTING-RECONNECTING-WORLD-[DISCONNECTING AND RECONNECTING THE WORLD]: SEE: WARRIOR-WORLD-COLLAPSES-[WARRIORS COLLAPSE AND REASSEMBLE THE WORLD]

DISEASE-[DISEASE]: (*Warriors know there are no diseases, there is only indulging.*)
SELECTED REFERENCES: Journey to Ixtlan - Page [246.7] ("It's like a disease," I said..."There is only indulging.)
SEE ALSO: *SELF-INDULGING, WARRIOR-WELL-BEING, ILL-BEING*

DISGUISE-WARRIOR-[THE WARRIORS' DISGUISE]: SEE: WARRIOR-DISGUISE-[THE WARRIORS' DISGUISE]

DISPASSIONATE-WARRIOR-[THE DISPASSIONATE WARRIOR]: SEE: WARRIOR-DISPASSIONATE-[THE DISPASSIONATE WARRIOR]

DISPOSITION-WARRIOR-THE WARRIORS' DISPOSITION]: SEE: WARRIOR-DISPOSITION-[THE WARRIORS' DISPOSITION]

DISSOLVING-FORCE-[THE DISSOLVING FORCE]: SEE: EAGLE-[EAGLE]

DIVINATION-[DIVINATION]: (*Warriors know that sorcerers have the ability to divine information about matters of their concern.*)
SELECTED REFERENCES: The Teachings of Don Juan - Page [111.1-111.2] (He told me again to ask...that I was losing my breath.) The Teachings of Don Juan - Page [121.4-121.5] (I brought up the subject of...portion is used for other purposes.) The Teachings of Don Juan - Page 153.5-153.7] (Don Juan seemed to want me...to divine about some stolen objects
SEE ALSO: *SORCERY, LIZARD-SORCERY-(TOP)*

DIVINING-LIBRARY-THIEF-[DIVINING THE LIBRARY THIEF]-(TOP)

DIZZY-APPEARING-[APPEARING TO BE DIZZY]: SEE: DRUNK-APPEARING-[APPEARING TO BE DRUNK OR DIZZY]

DO-NOTHING-WARRIOR-[WARRIORS DO NOTHING]: SEE: WARRIOR-DO-NOTHING-[WARRIORS DO NOTHING]

DOER-VS-EXPLAINER-[DOER VS EXPLAINER]: (*Warriors know that doers and explainers are manifestations of the two variations of the fundamental teaching method of the new seers; one involves the extremes of talking while the other involves the extremes of stalking.*)
SELECTED REFERENCES: The Fire From Within - Page [51.2-51.4] ("Genaro doesn't give a fig about...want with the glow of awareness.") The Fire From Within - Page [52.8-53.1] ("The explanation is coming," he said...all action and no real knowledge.") The Fire From Within - Page [109.2-109.5] (He said that the new seers looked...understand and to corroborate those truths.) The Fire From Within - Page [145.5-145.6] (Genaro turned to me and assured me...and let them fend for themselves.) The Fire From Within - Page [193.1-194.3] ("I really don't understand, don Juan...yanks the point from its location.)
SEE ALSO: *TEACHERS-TEACHING, TALKING, STALKING-ART, EXPLANATION, KNOWLEDGE-VS-LANGUAGE, TEACHING-VARIATIONS-TWO*

DOG-BLACK-[THE IRIDESCENT BLACK DOG]-(TOP): SEE: OMEN-ESCOGIDO-[THE OMEN OF THE ESCOGIDO]-(TOP)

DOG-STOLE-CHEESE-[THE DOG WHO STOLE CHEESE]-(TOP): SEE DIABLERO-TALES-[TALES OF THE DIABLEROS]-(TOP)

DOING-[DOING]: (Warriors know that a doing is something which contributes to making the world of solid objects; warriors know that an object is an object because we know how to "do" to it; this process is called " doing"; if warriors don't want a rock to be a rock, all they have to do is "not-doing".)
SELECTED REFERENCES: **Journey to Ixtlan - Page [188.4-189.8]** (Don Juan looked around and then...*stop the world* you must *stop* doing.") **Journey to Ixtlan - Page [190.6-191.3]** ("*Doing* makes you separate the pebble...it is merely a small rock.) **Journey to Ixtlan - Page [227.3-227.7]** ("You are in a terrible bind...the mercy of people," he replied.) **The Second Ring of Power - Page [228.2-228.4]** (Don Juan had taught me the...order to be a live activity.) **The Power of Silence - Page [165.5-165.7]** (He reminded me that he had...not belong in that charted whole.)
SEE ALSO: *NOT-DOING, DOING-VS-NOT-DOING*

DOING-DISASSEMBLING-[DISASSEMBLING A DOING]: (Warriors know that a doing has many parts, all of which are necessary for that doing to function; if any of those parts are missing, the doing is disassembled and cannot continue as a live activity.)
SELECTED REFERENCES: **The Second Ring of Power - Page [228.1-228.4]** (Don Juan had taught me the same...order to be alive activity.)
SEE ALSO: *ROUTINES-DISRUPTING, HABITS, DOING*

DOING-VS-NOT-DOING-[DOING VS NOT-DOING]: (Warriors know the difference between doing and not-doing , just as they know the difference between looking and "seeing" and the difference between knowledge and language; doing is the activation of the first attention while not-doing is the activation of the second attention.)
SELECTED REFERENCES: **Journey to Ixtlan - Page [188.1-191.9]** ("I don't know what you're talking...*not-doing.* See what I mean?") **Journey to Ixtlan - Page [191.2-191.9]** ("You've been watching it for a...*not-doing.* See what I mean?") **Journey to Ixtlan - Page [197.7-197.9]** (I described the unusual sensation I..."doing" was a manner of succumbing.) **Journey to Ixtlan - Page [211.2-212.9]** (Don Juan seemed relaxed; his eyes...*not-doing* is equally miraculous, and powerful.")
SEE ALSO: *LOOKING-VS-SEEING, ACTING-VS-TALKING, ATTENTION-FIRST, ATTENTION-SECOND, KNOWLEDGE-VS-LANGUAGE, WARRIOR-DOING-NOT-DOING*

DOING-NOT-DOING-WARRIOR-[THE DOING AND THE NOT-DOING OF WARRIORS]: SEE: WARRIOR-DOING-NOT-DOING-[THE DOING AND THE NOT-DOING OF WARRIORS]

DOING-NOTHING-WARRIOR-[WARRIORS DO NOTHING]: SEE: WARRIOR-DOING-NOTHING-[THE WARRIORS DO NOTHING]

DOING-RING-[THE RING OF DOING]: (Warriors know that the ring of doing is another term for the first ring of power.)
SELECTED REFERENCES: **Journey to Ixtlan - Page [211.6-211.8]** ("Let's say that when every one...into being at this very moment.")
SEE ALSO: *POWER-RING-FIRST, ATTENTION-FIRST, ATTENTION-TONAL*

DOING-WORLD-ESCAPING-[ESCAPING THE DOING OF THE WORLD]: (Warriors know that there is no way to escape the doing of the world, so they turn their world into a hunting ground instead.)
SELECTED REFERENCES: **Journey to Ixtlan - Page [214.1-214.2]** (And out there, in that world...he is used and taken himself.")
SEE ALSO: *DOING*

DOMED-WORLD-[THE DOMED WORLD]-(TOP)

DON-GENARO-[DON GENARO]-(TOP) SEE: GENARO-[DON GENARO]-(TOP)

*DON-JUAN-[DON JUAN]: SEE: JUAN-DON-[DON JUAN]

DOOR-ONLY-[THE ONLY DOOR THERE IS]: (Warriors know that the movement of the assemblage point beyond a certain limit results in the assemblage of other total worlds; the threshold of this critical movement is known as the only door there is.)
SELECTED REFERENCES: Tales of Power - Page [231.9-232.2] (It is early afternoon, the day...no way to close it again.") The Fire From Within - Page [213.2-213.3] ("What do you mean, don Juan...by the boost from the earth.")
SEE ALSO: CRACK-WORLDS, ASSEMBLAGE-POINT-MOVING, WORLD-OTHER, AWARENESS-TRUTH-SEVENTH, ASSEMBLAGE-POINT-THRESHOLD, WORLDS-OTHER-ASSEMBLE-TOTAL

DOOR-PARALLEL-LINES-[THE DOOR ACROSS THE PARALLEL LINES]: SEE: PARALLEL-LINES-DOOR-[THE DOOR ACROSS THE PARALLEL LINES]

DOORWAY-OTHER-[THE DOOR TO THE OTHER WORLD]: (Warriors know that certain power spots can act as bridges to cross from one parallel line to the other.)
SELECTED REFERENCES: The Eagle's Gift - Page [97.4-97.5] ("It's simplicity itself," la Gorda...world, a door to the other.) The Eagle's Gift - Page [100.2-100.4] (La Gorda speculated that the airline...the line I came from, this world.)
SEE ALSO: POWER-SPOT, HOLE-WORLD, PARALLEL-LINES, CRACK-WORLD

DOUBLE-[THE DOUBLE]: (Warriors know that the double is another term for the energy body, the dreaming body, or the other.)
SELECTED REFERENCES: Tales of Power - Page [40.5-48.9] (The moth had not been don Genaro...you feel me as being solid.") Tales of Power - Page [54.6-57.8] ("Genaro is a man," don Juan said...to be unobtrusive and gentle.) Tales of Power - Page [60.8-65.5] (Don Genaro was leaning against the...another chance I should be prepared.) Tales of Power - Page [76.5-78.3] ("Why not, don Juan?'...think he understands," don Genaro said.) Tales of Power - Page [274.9] (You saw everything. Genaro and I...all about the double, the other.") The Second Ring of Power - Page [82.8-83.5] (I heard again, as I had heard...peal of a large cracked bell.) The Second Ring of Power - Page [163.7-163.9] ("Then the Nagual gave me the task...I felt cheated. Now I don't care.) The Second Ring of Power - Page [168.8-169.3] (With my flying I was supposed...he had run out of time.") The Second Ring of Power - Page [224.2-225.3] ("What art is that. Gorda...sisters tried to take your luminosity.") The Second Ring of Power - Page [226.9-227.3] (She then reiterated the reason,...and that makes you the Nagual. That's all.) The Second Ring of Power - Page [284.9-285.9] ("And this brings me to the next...to it to calm it down.) The Eagle's Gift - Page [23.3-23.9] (Don Juan had explained to me...man's dreaming body is more possessive.")
SEE ALSO: DREAMING-BODY, DREAMING-ART, ENERGY-BODY, OTHER-SELF, DOUBLE-POWER-PLANTS, DOUBLE-(ALL)

DOUBLE-ATTENTION-[THE ATTENTION OF THE DOUBLE]: (Warriors know that the double requires a tremendous amount of attention; the sounds and sights of the double can be missed if one does not have the attention for them.)
SELECTED REFERENCES: The Second Ring of Power - Page [168.9-169.4] (I saw your whole maneuver from...time to put my notes away.)
SEE ALSO: DOUBLE, DREAMING-ATTENTION

DOUBLE-BEING-ACT-[THE ACT OF BEING DOUBLE]: (Warriors know that the act of being double allows the warrior to be in both the place of *reason and the place of silent knowledge, either separately or at the same time.)*

SELECTED REFERENCES: **The Power of Silence - Page [238.6-238.8]** (The old nagual explained that the...alternately or at the same time.)

SEE ALSO: *POINT-THIRD, KNOWLEDGE-SILENT, REASON, PERCEPTION-SPLIT, POINT-SECOND, HERE-HERE, PERCEPTUAL-DUALISM*

DOUBLE-BEINGS-[DOUBLE BEINGS]: *(Warriors know that a double being is man or woman who possesses a characteristic double luminosity; unlike the average man or woman who has two luminous segments to their cocoon, the double man has four (or sometimes three) compartments instead.)*

SELECTED REFERENCES: **The Eagle's Gift - Page [215.6-215.7]** (Don Juan said that double beings...Her own reactions scared her.) **The Eagle's Gift - Page [220.9-221.3]** (Don Juan and his warriors did arrive...thought they had already found it.) **The Eagle's Gift - Page [222.9-223.3]** (After don Juan and his party of warriors...to find one who is available.) **The Eagle's Gift - Page [228.3-228.9]** (A double being has a great advantage...to be lived with the spirit.) **The Fire From Within - Page [x.9-xi.2]** (He had also explained that seers...become naguals after learning to *see*.) **The Power of Silence - Page [13.4-13.5]** (The nagual Julian immediately evaluated the...candidate to be his apprentice nagual.)

SEE ALSO: *NAGUAL-MAN-WOMAN, NAGUAL-THREE-PRONGED-(TOP),*

DOUBLE-CARLOS-[THE EMERGENCE OF CARLOS' DOUBLE]-(TOP)

DOUBLE-DREAMING-[DREAMING THE DOUBLE]-(TOP): SEE: DREAMING-DOUBLE-[DREAMING THE DOUBLE]-(TOP)

DOUBLE-EYES-[THE EYES OF THE DOUBLE]-(TOP): SEE: EYES-DOUBLE-[THE EYES OF THE DOUBLE]-(TOP)

*DOUBLE-FACING-[FACING THE DOUBLE]: *(Warriors know that they cannot face the double and survive; warriors who finds themselves face to face with the double are dead warriors.)*

SELECTED REFERENCES: **Tales of Power - Page [46.2-46.6]** ("Well, a sorcerer can double up...things up. No one knows why.") **Tales of Power - Page [55.2-55.3]** ("Why am I so afraid of...be faced in any other way.") **Tales of Power - Page [67.7-67.9]** ("Then I heard the sound of people approaching...deadly for me to awaken myself.)

SEE ALSO: *DREAMING-BODY, DOUBLE*

DOUBLE-MAN-WOMAN-[THE DOUBLE MAN AND DOUBLE WOMAN]: SEE: DOUBLE-BEING-[DOUBLE BEINGS]

DOUBLE-MORTAL-COMBAT-[THE MORTAL COMBAT OF THE DOUBLE]-(TOP)

DOUBLE-VS-NAGUAL-[THE DOUBLE VS THE NAGUAL]-(TOP)

DOUBLE-POWER-PLANTS-[THE DOUBLE AND POWER PLANTS]: *(Warriors know that if they use power plants to gather the second attention, the menacing side of that attention will be brought together in one clump; that clump of attention is the double that comes out of the top of the warriors' head.)*

SELECTED REFERENCES: **The Second Ring of Power - Page [284.9-285.9]** ("And this brings me to the next thing...sing to it to calm it down.)

SEE ALSO: *DOUBLE, POWER-PLANTS, ATTENTION-SECOND-TRAPPING, DREAMING-BODY, NAGUAL*

DOUBLE-SECRET-[THE SECRET OF THE DOUBLE]: SEE: RIDDLE-

DREAMER-DREAMED-[THE RIDDLE OF THE DREAMER AND THE DREAMED]

DOUBLE-SOUND-[THE SOUND OF THE DOUBLE]-(TOP)

DOUBLE-STEPS-TO-[THE STEPS TO THE DOUBLE]: (Warriors know there are no steps to get to the double; in the act of engaging the attention of the nagual, the dreamer finds the steps.)
SELECTED REFERENCES: **The Second Ring of Power** - Page [278.8-279.1] (Don Juan had told me that...make it into an encumbering production.)
SEE ALSO: *DOUBLE, DREAMING-BODY, ATTENTION-NAGUAL*

DOUBLE-TRAVELS-[THE TRAVELS OF THE DOUBLE]-(TOP)

DOUBT-POINT-NO-[THE POINT OF NO DOUBT]: (Warriors know that the point of no doubt is a position of the assemblage point characterized by a peculiar feeling of having no doubts about things; a position of the assemblage point deeper into the left from the position of normal awareness where the only thing one can "see" is blobs of energy; there are actually two points of no doubt for warriors; one is where they have no doubts because they know everything silently; the other is normal awareness where they have no doubts because they don't know anything.)
SELECTED REFERENCES: **The Fire From Within** - Page [179.3-179.5] (I asked him how he was...to the point of no doubt.") **The Fire From Within** - Page [260.2-260.4] (He also said that there was an immeasurable...another by gripping feelings of defeat.) **The Fire From Within** - Page [281.5-281.6] ("That day you accomplished a marvelous...doubts because you don't know anything.) **The Fire From Within** - Page [282.4-282.6] (He explained that I had to...as long as the emotion lasts.) **The Power of Silence** - Page [122.3-122.4] ("I explained to you then, although...the realm where miracles are commonplace.")
SEE ALSO: *ASSEMBLAGE-POINT-MOVING, AWARENESS-LEFT, SEEING, ASSEMBLAGE-POINT-POSITION*

DOUBT-POINT-PERCEPTION-BARRIER-[THE POINT OF NO DOUBT AND THE BARRIER OF PERCEPTION]: (Warriors know that there is an immeasurable area between the customary position of the assemblage point and the point of no doubt; the point of no doubt is almost the place where the barrier of perception appears.)
SELECTED REFERENCES: **The Fire From Within** - Page [260.2-260.4] (He also said that there was an immeasurable...another by gripping feelings of defeat.)
SEE ALSO: *DOUBT-POINT-NO, PERCEPTION-BARRIER*

DOUBT-REMOVING-[REMOVING ALL DOUBT]: SEE: MAGIC-[MAGIC]

DOUBTS-REMORSE-WARRIOR-[THE WARRIORS' DOUBTS AND REMORSE]: SEE: WARRIOR-DOUBTS-REMORSE-[THE WARRIORS' DOUBTS AND REMORSE]

DRAINAGE-ENERGY-[PLUGGING POINTS OF ENERGY DRAINAGE]: SEE: ENERGY-DRAINAGE-[PLUGGING POINTS OF ENERGY DRAINAGE]

DREAD-SHEER-[SHEER DREAD]: (Warriors know that the most dangerous facet of the sorcerers' knowledge is contact with the inorganic beings.)
SELECTED REFERENCES: **The Art of Dreaming** - Page [44.9-45.2] ("You have entered now into the...you're going off the deep end.")
SEE ALSO: *INORGANIC-BEINGS, KNOWLEDGE-INTRICACIES*

DREAM-CITY-UNKNOWN-[CARLOS' DREAM OF THE UNKNOWN CITY]-(TOP)

DREAM-FARM-MOUNTAINS-[CARLOS' DREAM OF THE FARM AND THE MOUNTAINS]-(TOP)

DREAM-HAND-[THE DREAM HAND]-(TOP)

DREAM-IRIDIUM-WALKING-STICK-[CARLOS' DREAM OF THE IRIDIUM WALKING STICK]-(TOP)

DREAM-JOURNAL-CARLOS-[CARLOS' DREAM JOURNAL]: (Carlos was teased by don Juan for keeping a meticulous dream diary called "My Dreams" during the time Carlos was supposedly struggling to battle self-importance.)
SELECTED REFERENCES: The Art of Dreaming - Page [36.9-37.2] (As I gained proficiency in setting up...superpersonal diary called "My Dreams.")
SEE ALSO: WRITING-SORCERY

DREAM-ORDINARY-[ORDINARY DREAMS]: SEE: DREAMING-DREAMS-[DREAMING VS ORDINARY DREAMS]

DREAM-PULLED-[BEING PULLED INTO A DREAM]: (When sorcerers are capable of projecting their intent, they can easily pull anyone into their intent or into their dream; when someone is pulled into a dream they are pulled into a total realm that the dreamer alone has visualized .)
SELECTED REFERENCES: The Art of Dreaming - Page [232.2-232.7] (From a simple object, those sorcerers...to be an ultimately personal item.)
SEE ALSO: DREAMING-GATE-FOURTH, INTENT-PROJECTING

DREAM-SABRE-TOOTHED-TIGER-[THE DREAM OF THE SABRE-TOOTHED TIGER]-(TOP)

DREAM-TOPAZ-[CARLOS' DREAM OF THE GLOWING TOPAZ]-(TOP)

DREAMER-ALERTNESS-[THE ALERTNESS OF THE DREAMER]: (Warriors know that dreamers touch and enter real worlds with all-inclusive effects; any deviation from total alertness imperils the dreamer in dreadful ways.)
SELECTED REFERENCES: The Art of Dreaming - Page [174.7-175.3] (He warned me, that since dreamers...a fraction of an inch leeway.")
SEE ALSO: DREAMING-REALITY, WARRIOR-ALERTNESS, DREAMING-ART

*DREAMER-ART-[THE ART OF THE DREAMER]: (Warriors know that the art of dreamers is to be able to hold the image of their dreams; warriors accomplish this by merely glancing yet somehow holding the image of their dreams; the art of the dreamer is the art of attention.)
SELECTED REFERENCES: The Second Ring of Power - Page [163.1-163.4] ("The next thing the Nagual wanted...to glance and yet hold the image.) The Second Ring of Power - Page [274.3-274.4] ("The Nagual told us to show...dreamer is the art of attention.")
SEE ALSO: DREAMING-ART, STALKING-ART, DREAMER-GLANCE

DREAMER-CRIB-[THE DREAMERS' CRIB]: SEE: CRIB-DREAMER-[THE DREAMERS' CRIB]

DREAMER-DECISION-[THE DREAMERS' DECISION]: (Warriors know it is the dreamers' responsibility to continue dreaming until they have entered *the universe behind the second gate of dreaming; once accomplished, it is up to dreamers to either accept or reject the lure of the inorganic beings; the dreamers' decision is an ultra personal one and depends solely on the strengths and weaknesses of the individual.)*

SELECTED REFERENCES: **The Art of Dreaming - Page [109.3-109.6]** ("You have to continue your dreaming...that it is a final affair.")

SEE ALSO: *DREAMING-ART, INORGANIC-BEINGS-REFUSING, WARRIOR-DECISIONS-FINALITY, WARRIORSHIP-VS-SORCERY*

DREAMER-DEVELOPMENT-[THE DEVELOPMENT OF DREAMERS]: SEE: DREAMING-CONTROL [THE CONTROL OF DREAMING]

DREAMER-DREAMED-[THE DREAMER AND THE DREAMED]-(TOP)

DREAMER-DREAMED-RIDDLE-[THE RIDDLE OF THE DREAMER AND THE DREAMED]: SEE: RIDDLE-DREAMER-DREAMED-[THE RIDDLE OF THE DREAMER AND THE DREAMED]

DREAMER-DUAL-STAND-[THE DUAL STAND OF THE DREAMER]: SEE: DREAMING-REALITY-METAMORPHOSIS-[DREAMING AND THE METAMORPHOSIS OF REALITY]

DREAMER-FORTIFYING-[FORTIFYING THE DREAMER]: *(Warriors know that the warriors' way is designed to help fortify dreamers and give them the inner strength they need to handle dreaming without becoming weak, compulsive and capricious; the warriors' way gives dreamers their sobriety.)*

SELECTED REFERENCES: **The Fire From Within - Page [175.7-176.2]** (He said that at first the...all these traits of character sobriety.)

SEE ALSO: *WARRIOR-WAY, WARRIOR-SOBRIETY, DREAMING-PITFALL, WARRIORSHIP-VS-SORCERY, DREAMING-LEARN*

DREAMER-GAZE-[THE DREAMERS' GAZE]: SEE: DREAMER-GLANCE-[THE DREAMERS' GLANCE]

DREAMER-GLANCE-[THE DREAMERS' GLANCE]: *(Warriors know that dreamers must take quick, deliberate glances at everything present in their dreams; if they focus on something specific, it is only as a point of departure.)*

SELECTED REFERENCES: **The Second Ring of Power - Page [163.1-163.4]** ("The next thing the Nagual wanted...to glance and yet hold the image.) **The Eagle's Gift - Page [50.4-53.1]** (I *dreamed* once that I woke up...a chance to talk to him.) **The Eagle's Gift - Page [141.8-142.4]** (Next he recommended that I should...focuses on anything, one loses control.) **The Fire From Within - Page [88.2-88.6]** (He commanded me to empty myself...repeatedly ordered me in a forceful whisper.) **The Fire From Within - Page [94.3-95.1]** ("What do we do now...on the other end of the mirror.) **The Art of Dreaming - Page [27.4-27.6]** (He told me that dreamers take...departure as many times as possible.) **The Art of Dreaming - Page [30.4-31.1]** (During another discussion at a different...item and start all over again.") **The Art of Dreaming - Page [36.4-36.6]** (I told him that in practice..."It's the first gate of dreaming.) **The Art of Dreaming - Page [38.1-38.3]** (It occurred to me that the...at the elements of my dreams.)

SEE ALSO: *DREAMING-ART, DREAMING-STARTING-ITEM*

DREAMER-GUIDE-THEMSELVES-[DREAMERS CAN GUIDE THEMSELVES]: SEE: DREAMING-LEARN-[LEARNING DREAMING]

DREAMER-HAVEN-[THE DREAMERS' HAVEN]: *(Warriors know that the diabolical part of the inorganic beings realm is that it might well be the only haven and sanctuary for dreamers in a hostile universe; nevertheless,*

warriors must remain warriors and not succumb to self-indulgence; they must stand without props or railings and clearly know exactly what they are.)
    SELECTED REFERENCES: The Art of Dreaming - Page [96.5-96.8] ("This is rally diabolical, don Juan...learned to say, So be it!")
    SEE ALSO: *INORGANIC-BEINGS-REALM, INORGANIC-BEINGS-REFUSING*

DREAMER-HEADBAND-[THE DREAMERS' HEADBAND]: (Warriors know that dreamers must wear a headband to sleep which they must make from scratch based on a vision they have had of that headband in dreaming; just wearing an ordinary hat or head cover to sleep will not serve the same function as the dreamers' headband; those objects will only cause intense dreams, not dreaming.)
    SELECTED REFERENCES: Journey to Ixtlan - Page [131.7-132.4] (I explained to him how difficult...water, the clouds, and so on.)
    SEE ALSO: *DREAMING-ART, DREAMING-TECHNIQUES, DREAMING-VS-DREAMS*

DREAMER-INVOCATION-[THE DREAMERS' INVOCATION]: (Warriors know the formula or invocation of dreamers; that invocation is, "The hinge of sorcery is the mystery of the assemblage point."; dreamers who repeat this invocation incessantly to themselves will allow unseen forces to make appropriate changes within them with regard to the movement of the assemblage point.)
    SELECTED REFERENCES: The Art of Dreaming - Page [172.1-172.5] ("I propose that you do one...but you have to repeat it.") The Art of Dreaming - Page [175.4-175.7] (This was the end of our...out loud my intent to *see*.)
    SEE ALSO: *DREAMING-ART, SORCERY-HINGE, DREAMING-TECHNIQUES*

DREAMER-OPTIONS-[THE DREAMERS OPTIONS]: (Warriors know that dreamers face two options as their reality begins to undergo the metamorphosis resulting from their dreaming practices; they can either carefully revamp their system of sensory input interpretation or they can completely discard it; to revamp their interpretation system means that dreamers deliberately attempt to enlarge its capabilities, their reality becomes fluid and its scope becomes enhanced without threatening the integrity of the system; if dreamers chooses to discard their system, the scope of what they can perceive expands inordinately and to such gigantic degrees that they are left with a sense of infinite unrealness that could be real but is not.)
    SELECTED REFERENCES: The Art of Dreaming - Page [97.2-97.8] (Dreaming of that world, I became...well be real but is not.)
    SEE ALSO: *REALITY-INTERPRETATION, WARRIORSHIP-VS-SORCERY*

DREAMER-PONCHO-[THE DREAMERS' PONCHO]: (Warriors know the dreamers' poncho is a poncho-like garment which aids dreamers in focusing their dreaming attention.)
    SELECTED REFERENCES: The Eagle's Gift - Page [255.3-256.4] (Zuleica was very demanding from the...fond of it. Neither was I.)
    SEE ALSO: *DREAMING-ART, BODY-PHYSICAL-CENTERS, DREAMING-TECHNIQUE*

DREAMER-SAFETY-VALVE-[THE DREAMERS' SAFETY VALVE]:
(Warriors know that as they cross the second gate of dreaming, dreamers must intend a greater and more sober control over their dreams; this is the

only safety valve that dreamers have to prevent them from becoming lost in the mortal depths of dreaming.)

SELECTED REFERENCES: **The Art of Dreaming - Page [42.1-42.4]** ("What's the implication of all this...dreaming attention must make them surface.")

SEE ALSO: *WARRIOR-SOBRIETY, WARRIORSHIP-VS-SORCERY, UNKNOWN-INTRICACIES*

DREAMER-VIGILANCE-[THE DREAMERS' VIGILANCE]: *(Warriors know that dreamers must always be on guard against the trickery of the inorganic beings; dreamers must handle everything related to dreaming with kid gloves and above all they must be vigilant because they can never foretell where the inorganic beings' attack will come from.)*

SELECTED REFERENCES: **The Art of Dreaming - Page [110.1-110.4]** ("If you fall, you pay the...where the attack will come from.")

SEE ALSO: *DREAMING-ART, INORGANIC-BEINGS-TRICKERY*

*DREAMING-ART-[THE ART OF DREAMING]: *(Warriors know that the art of dreaming is the control of the natural shift that the assemblage point undergoes in sleep; the art of handling the dreaming body; the ultimate use of the nagual; the art of training the tonal to let go for a moment and then grab again; the art of dreaming is concerned with the movement or displacement of the assemblage point; one of the warriors' avenues to power; the art of transforming ordinary dreams into controlled awareness by virtue of the second attention; dreaming is the exercise of the second attention; the not-doing of sleep; a unique state of awareness arrived at by focusing the second attention on the elements or features of one's dreams; the most important of the sorcery arts; dreaming is a process of awakening, a process of gaining control; dreaming is sustaining the position where the assemblage point has shifted in dreams; dreaming is perceiving more than we believe it is possible to perceive; dreaming is a journey of unthinkable dimensions, a journey that after making us perceive everything we can humanly perceive, makes the assemblage point jump outside the human domain and perceive the inconceivable; dreaming is tainted with the mood of the sorcerers of antiquity; warriors must learn dreaming because that is the pattern set out by the old sorcerers; dreaming is the old sorcerers' invention and has to be played by their rules; intending is the secret to dreaming; dreaming can also be defined as the process by which dreamers intend to find adequate positions of the assemblage point, positions which permit them to perceive energy-generating items in dreamlike states; dreaming is real, it is an energy-generating condition; by inducing a systematic displacement of the assemblage point, dreaming liberates perception, enlarging the scope of what can be perceived; dreaming opens the doors to other perceivable worlds and prepares the dreamer to enter those worlds in full awareness; dreaming is the gateway to the light and darkness of the universe; dreaming is one of the eight points on the sorcerers' diagram; warriors must practice dreaming without allowing their fear to make it into an encumbering production; dreaming is the only way to trap the second attention without injuring it.)*

SELECTED REFERENCES: **Journey to Ixtlan - Page [90.9-93.1]** ("Nothing. Let them pass," he said...."And so does hunting, walking, laughing.") **Journey to Ixtlan - Page [98.5-99.2]** (Don't think it's a joke...Do you see what I mean?") **Tales of Power - Page [9.8-10.1]** ("And now,

suppose you tell me...a dream from reality became inoperative.) **Tales of Power - Page [11.8-11.9]** ("Each warrior has his own way....of all the barriers and disappointments.") **Tales of Power - Page [96.2-96.9]** ("We may say that every one..."dreaming" were on the right side.) **Tales of Power - Page [250.5-250.8]** (He explained that disrupting routines, the...the ultimate use of the *nagual."*) **The Second Ring of Power - Page [2.6-2.7]** (In those few days they revealed...the core of the present work.) **The Second Ring of Power - Page [224.1-224.3]** (That was why I interfered with...are dreamers. Your double is *dreaming.*") **The Second Ring of Power - Page [276.3-276.4]** ("Can all of you go into...None of us has that much power.) **The Second Ring of Power - Page [277.8-279.1]** (Don Juan said that our "first...make it into an encumbering production.) **The Second Ring of Power - Page [291.2-291.3]** (Sorcerers have to do their best...for that center to push out.") **The Eagle's Gift - Page [4.5-4.6]** (La Gorda and the three little sisters...Genaro called the *second attention.)* **The Eagle's Gift - Page [17.5-17.6]** (They were not lodgings but places...*dreaming* and exercise their second attention.) **The Eagle's Gift - Page [22.7-23.3]** ("It is easy for me to understand...alleged extra body, the *dreaming body.)* **The Eagle's Gift - Page [135.6-135.8]** (One night we sat down and,... "*not doing* of talking to oneself.") **The Eagle's Gift - Page [138.9-139.1]** (Don Juan explained to us...turn an ordinary dream into *dreaming.)* **The Eagle's Gift - Page [141.5-142.6]** (This is the way I understand it...into my world of everyday life.) **The Fire From Within - Page [66.5-66.6]** (He said that he had told...to deal with the daily world.) **The Fire From Within - Page [172.6-172.7]** (That was the time when they...way to move the assemblage point.) **The Fire From Within - Page [172.8-173.4]** ("Why do the new seers command...art of handling the *dreaming body.)* **The Fire From Within - Page [173.6-173.8]** (He said that seers, old and...enormous effort and concentration to accomplish.) **The Fire From Within - Page [174.1-175.9]** (After observing *dreamers* while they slept...warriors' way, or the warriors' path.) **The Fire From Within - Page [180.8-181.1]** ("The development of *dreamers* is indirect,"...as our ordinary dreams are chaotic.) **The Power of Silence - Page [xvii.1]** (The two great systems devised by...and *stalking,* the control of behavior.) **The Power of Silence - Page [36.1]** ("Our sexual energy is what governs...it. There is no other way.) **The Power of Silence - Page [101.3-101.6]** (I remembered at that moment scores...therefore I had to be *dreaming.)* **The Art of Dreaming - Page [viii.1-viii.2]** (His role as a teacher was to...is called the art of dreaming **The Art of Dreaming - Page [viii.6-ix.5]** (Believing that our energetic conditioning is...seek an outlet in its practices.) **The Art of Dreaming - Page [18.7-19.3]** (Another monumental breakthrough that the old...scope of what can be perceived.") **The Art of Dreaming - Page [28.7-28.8]** ("You certainly can reach the same...the door to the second attention.") **The Art of Dreaming - Page [46.9-47.1]** ("Dreaming is sustaining the position where...assemblage point has shifted in dreams.) **The Art of Dreaming - Page [49.4-49.5]** ("You are a religious man to...believe it is possible to perceive.") **The Art of Dreaming - Page [49.7-49.8]** (It seemed at that time that...in my dreams was no exception.) **The Art of Dreaming - Page [69.4-69.6]** (Don Juan expressed his bewilderment...location to which it is displaced.) **The Art of Dreaming - Page [73.5-73.6]** (He added that what dreaming does...human domain and perceive the inconceivable.) **The Art of Dreaming - Page [79.9-81.7]** ("I haven't gotten to that yet...what it is: a mere candle.") **The Art of Dreaming - Page [108.5]** (He reiterated that dreaming, being the...to be played by their rules.) **The Art of Dreaming - Page [109.4-109.6]** (I confessed to him that I...that it is a final affair.") **The Art of Dreaming - Page [161.3-161.4]** (He explained that since everything related...from which it can finally emerge.) **The Art of Dreaming - Page [164.4-164.6]** (Don Juan then gave me another...energy-generating items in dreamlike states.) **The Art of Dreaming - Page [173.6-175.1]** ("As you know, succumbing to the...start any of your weird maneuvers.") **The Art of Dreaming - Page [221.1-221.3]** (Don Juan was right in saying that...to the darkness of the universe.) **The Art of Dreaming - Page [260.3-260.4]** (I must have had an expression of...are final. Carol Tiggs is gone.")
SEE ALSO: *DREAMING-BODY, SLEEP, NAGUAL, ATTENTION-SECOND , NOT-DOING, ROUTINES-DISRUPTING, GAIT-POWER, ENERGY-BODY-CONDENSING, DREAMING-VS-STALKING, ASSEMBLAGE-POINT-MOVING, PERCEPTION, SORCERER-DIAGRAM, DREAMER-(ALL), DREAMING-(ALL)*

DREAMING-ATTENTION-[THE DREAMING ATTENTION]: SEE: ATTENTION-DREAMING-[THE DREAMING ATTENTION]

DREAMING-ATTENTION-SECOND-[DREAMING AND THE SECOND ATTENTION]: (The second attention is available to everyone, but willfully holding on to reason and the first attention keeps the second attention at arm's length; warriors understand that dreaming brings down the barriers that surround and insulate the second attention.)

SELECTED REFERENCES: The Art of Dreaming - Page [51.8-51.9] (His contention was that the second...surround and insulate the second attention.)

SEE ALSO: *PERCEPTION-BARRIER-BREAKING, ATTENTION-SECOND, DREAMING-ART, REASON-CLINGING, ATTENTION-DREAMING*

DREAMING-ATTENTION-UNIFYING-[DREAMING AND UNIFYING THE TWO ATTENTIONS]: (*Warriors know the practice of dreaming tightens the warriors' luminous layers and ties together the two attentions; this means that the attention of the nagual which is at the center of our luminosity, ceases pushing out and loosening the layers of luminosity.*)

SELECTED REFERENCES: The Second Ring of Power - Page [291.1-291.3] (He explained to me that the...for that center to push out.")

SEE ALSO: *ATTENTIONS-UNIFYING-TWO, DREAMING-ART, ATTENTION-NAGUAL, LUMINOUS-LAYERS*

DREAMING-AWARENESS-[DREAMING AWARENESS]: (*Warriors know dreaming as a sensation that allows them to perceive other worlds; they can't describe what makes them perceive in this way, it is a process in their bodies, an awareness in their minds; warriors understand that dreams are a realm of real events.*)

SELECTED REFERENCES: The Art of Dreaming - Page [ix.1-ix.3] (On another occasion don Juan said...bodies, an awareness in our minds.") The Art of Dreaming - Page [69.1-69.3] (On one of my visits to him...as a realm of real events.)

SEE ALSO: *DREAMING-ART*

DREAMING-AWARENESS-NORMAL-[DREAMING AND NORMAL AWARENESS]: (*Warriors know that it is absolutely essential that they learn dreaming while in a state of normal awareness; in this way the shields and defenses of the first attention act to safeguard the dreamer from the force of the unused emanations that suddenly become aligned in dreaming.*)

SELECTED REFERENCES: The Fire From Within - Page [172.7-173.1] ("One of the strictest commands of...that suddenly become aligned in *dreaming* .")

SEE ALSO: *DREAMING-ART, AWARENESS-NORMAL*

**DREAMING-BODY-[THE DREAMING BODY]:* (*Warriors know that the dreaming body is the double or the other; the energy body; the other self; the not-doing of the self; the awareness of our state as luminous beings; a position of the assemblage point; the energy of a luminous being, projected by the fixation of the second attention into a variety of forms including a three-dimensional image of the physical body, a whitish, phantom-like emanation; dreamers find in the dreaming body an endless source of youth and energy.*)

SELECTED REFERENCES: The Teachings of Don Juan - Page [129.8-129.9] ("The trouble with you is that...does he or doesn't he fly?") Tales of Power - Page [44.3-44.7] ("Tell me more about the double...time you've been with his double.") Tales of Power - Page [48.6-48.8] ("Is the double solid? I asked...you feel me as being solid.") Tales of Power - Page [54.8-55.3] ("Do you mean that I will...be faced in any other way.") Tales of Power - Page [56.5-56.8] ("The double is one of those...."It is the self, damn it!") Tales of Power - Page [57.6-57.8] ("Genaro is a man of knowledge...to be unobtrusive and gentle.) Tales of Power - Page [61.3-61.9] ("Well, if you're going to tell me...he is a dream," he retorted.) The Second Ring of Power - Page [278.2-279.3] (Don Juan said that there are no...go in and out a door.") The Eagle's Gift - Page [22.7-23.6] ("It is easy for me to...the use of our first attention.) The Eagle's Gift - Page [143.7-143.8] (*Will* is very quiet, unnoticeable...but we are not complete yet.") The Eagle's Gift - Page [145.1-145.8] ("Holy Jesus! We are remembering the...of eating, or drinking," she replied.) The Eagle's Gift - Page [151.9] (The realization struck me then that...spontaneously entered into our *dreaming bodies*.) The Eagle's Gift - Page [294.9-295.4] (Dona Soledad had not only made...endless source of youth and energy.) The Fire From Within - Page [173.2-173.4] (Don Juan explained that *dreaming*...art of handling the *dreaming body*.) **The Fire From Within - Page [177.3-178.1]** ("Let's talk now about the *dreaming body*...what the *dreaming body* really is.) **The Fire From Within - Page [179.2]** (Don Juan remarked that my animal...really is, a blob of light.) **The Fire From Within - Page [180.3-180.8]** (Don Juan then outlined the procedure...more and more manageable, even orderly.) **The Fire From Within - Page [251.2-251.7]** ("Right at this juncture is where...that were equally personal, humanized.) **The Fire From Within - Page [271.9-273.6]** (He repeated over and over that...the ground ready to zoom away.) **The Power of Silence - Page [33.5-33.7]** (Don Juan laughed, and since he...his natural self be a recluse.")

SEE ALSO: *DREAMING-ART, DREAMING-TRAVELING, LUMINOUS-BEINGS-MYSTERY, POINT-THIRD, DOUBLE, OTHER-SELF, PARALLEL-BEING*

DREAMING-BODY-DEMONSTRATIONS-PURPOSE-[THE PURPOSE OF THE DEMONSTRATIONS OF THE DREAMING BODY]: (*Warriors know that the purpose of their being shown another warriors' dreaming body is to make the assemblage point move, not from a position of heightened awareness, but from its normal position.*)

SELECTED REFERENCES: **The Fire From Within - Page [177.7-177.9]** (Don Juan stated that Genaro, being...awareness, but from its normal setting.)

SEE ALSO: *DREAMING-BODY, AWARENESS-HEIGHTENED, AWARENESS-NORMAL, ASSEMBLAGE-POINT-MOVING*

DREAMING-BODY-EYES-[THE EYES OF THE DREAMING BODY]-(TOP): SEE: EYES-DREAMING BODY-[THE EYES OF THE DREAMING BODY]-(TOP)

DREAMING-BODY-JOURNEY-[THE JOURNEY OF THE DREAMING BODY-(TOP)

DREAMING-BODY-OBSERVING-[OBSERVING THE DREAMING BODY]-(TOP)

DREAMING-BODY-PROCEDURE-GETTING-TO-[THE PROCEDURE FOR GETTING TO THE DREAMING BODY]: (*Warriors know that the procedure for getting to the dreaming body begins with an initial act, which by the fact of being sustained breeds unbending intent; unbending intent then leads to internal silence; internal silence leads to the internal strength needed to make the assemblage point shift to suitable positions in dreams; all in all, warriors know the only procedure necessary to get to the dreaming body is impeccability throughout the course of daily life.*)

SELECTED REFERENCES: **The Fire From Within - Page [180.3-181.1]** (Don Juan then outlined the procedure...is impeccability in our daily life.")

SEE ALSO: *DREAMING-BODY, INTENT-UNBENDING, INNER-SILENCE, WARRIOR-STRENGTH, ASSEMBLAGE-POINT-MOVING, WARRIOR-IMPECCABILITY*

DREAMING-BODY-PROTECTING-[PROTECTING THE DREAMING BODY]: (*Warriors know that eliminating one's material possessions is a way of protecting the dreaming body; it is not good for the dreaming body to focus on the weak face of the second attention.*)

SELECTED REFERENCES: **The Eagle's Gift - Page [22.2-22.9]** ("Your compulsion to possess and hold...he was protecting my *dreaming body*.")

SEE ALSO: *WARRIOR-FOCUS-MATERIAL-ABERRANT, DREAMING-BODY, ATTENTION-SECOND-FACES-TWO, WARRIOR-RECOMMENDATION*

DREAMING-BODY-SEER-NEW-[THE NEW SEERS' DREAMING BODY]: (*Warriors know that the new seers have no interest in replicating the physical body with the dreaming body; for the new seers, the dreaming body is simply a feeling, a surge of energy that is transported by the movement of the assemblage point to any place in the seven worlds available to man; the dreaming body of the new seers is a result of a shift of the assemblage point along the midsection of man's band of emanations, which at a certain depth, becomes a blob of light; a blob of light is the dreaming body of the new seers; this impersonal dreaming body is conducive to understanding and examination, which is the basis of everything the new seers do.)*

SELECTED REFERENCES: The Fire From Within - Page [179.6-180.3] (When we were back in Silvio Manuel's...the seven worlds available to man.") The Fire From Within - Page [250.9-251.7] (He explained that during normal sleep...answers that were equally personal, humanized.)

SEE ALSO: *DREAMING-BODY, SEER-NEW, EAGLE-EMANATIONS-MAN-BAND-MIDSECTION, DREAMING-BODY-TOLTEC, POWER-BID-SEPARATE*

DREAMING-BODY-SEER-OLD-[THE OLD-SEERS' DREAMING BODY]: SEE: DREAMING-BODY-TOLTECS-[THE TOLTECS' DREAMING BODY]

DREAMING-BODY-SHOOTING-OFF-[SHOOTING OFF THE DREAMING BODY]-(TOP)

DREAMING-BODY-STRENGTH-[THE STRENGTH OF THE DREAMING BODY]: (Warriors know that the inherent strength of the dreaming body represents a formidable potential pitfall to the dreamer; it is very easy for the dreaming body to gaze uninterruptedly at the Eagle's emanations, but it is also very easy for the dreaming body to be consumed by them.)

SELECTED REFERENCES: The Fire From Within - Page [181.5-181.7] (Don Juan said that there is...stood by ready to end their *seeing*.)

SEE ALSO: *DREAMING-BODY, EAGLE-EMANATIONS, DREAMING-PITFALLS*

DREAMING-BODY-TOLTECS-[THE TOLTECS' DREAMING BODY]: (Warriors know that the ancient Toltecs concentrated all their efforts on exploiting the dreaming body and using it as a more practical body; in other words, they succeeded in recreating themselves in increasingly weird ways; the old seers wanted a replica of the body but with more physical strength, so they made their assemblage points shift along the right edge of man's band of emanations; the deeper they moved along the right edge, the more bizarre their dreaming bodies became.)

SELECTED REFERENCES: The Fire From Within - Page [177.3-177.7] ("Lets talk now about the *dreaming body*...his chin to ask the question.) The Fire From Within - Page [179.6-180.3] (When we were back in Silvio Manuel's...the seven worlds available to man.") The Fire From Within - Page [250.9-251.7] (He explained that during normal sleep...answers that were equally personal, humanized.)

SE ALSO: *DREAMING-BODY, TOLTECS, DREAMING-BODY-SEER-NEW, EAGLE-EMANATIONS-MAN-BAND-RIGHT-EDGE, POWER-BID-SEPARATE*

DREAMING-BODY-TRAVELS-NAGUAL-WOMAN-[CARLOS' DREAMING BODY TRAVELS TO THE HOME OF THE NAGUAL WOMAN]-(TOP): SEE: DREAMING-BODY-JOURNEY-[THE JOURNEY OF THE DREAMING BODY]-(TOP)

DREAMING-BRANDS-[THE OLD AND NEW SORCERERS' BRANDS OF DREAMING]: (Warriors know that the sorcerers of antiquity invented dreaming and concentrated their dreaming activities on the human unknown; the use of dreaming techniques in the everyday world was one of the old sorcerers' most effective devices; the new sorcerers must begin with the old sorcerers' brand of dreaming as an exercise, but at a given moment they deviate onto new ground and re-concentrate themselves on the non-human unknown; the new sorcerers are the warriors for total freedom.)

SELECTED REFERENCES: The Art of Dreaming - Page [79.2-79.4] (He asserted that to use dreaming...thing that had happened to me.) The Art of Dreaming - Page [79.6-81.7] ("Do you mean, don Juan, that...what it is: a mere candle.")
SEE ALSO: *UNKNOWN-HUMAN-VS-NON-HUMAN, DREAMING-ART, WARRIORSHIP-VS-SORCERY, ASSEMBLAGE-POINT-SHIFT-VS-MOVEMENT*

DREAMING-BREATHING-[LEARNING TO BREATHE IN DREAMING]-(TOP)

DREAMING-CELESTIAL-[CELESTIAL DREAMING]-(TOP): SEE: ZULEICA-CELESTIAL-DREAMING-[ZULEICA'S CELESTIAL DREAMING]-(TOP)

DREAMING-COLORS-[COLORS TO INITIATE DREAMING-(TOP)

DREAMING-COMMAND-[COMMANDING DREAMING]: *(Warriors know they cannot command their dreams; to consciously or semi-consciously manipulate one's dreams unavoidably interferes with the natural shift of the assemblage point; warriors know they cannot command their dreams per se, all they can do is direct the fixation of the assemblage point; dreamers are like fishermen equipped with a line that casts itself wherever it may; the only thing they can do is keep the line anchored at the place where it sinks.)*

SELECTED REFERENCES: The Fire From Within - Page [173.2-175.1] (Don Juan explained that *dreaming*, like...at the place where it sinks.)
SEE ALSO: *DREAMING-ART, ASSEMBLAGE-POINT-FIXATION-DREAMER-DIRECTS, DREAMING-CONTROL*

DREAMING-CONCENTRATION-[THE CONCENTRATION NECESSARY TO DO DREAMING]: *(Warriors know that supreme discipline and concentration are necessary in order to do dreaming; the concentration needed to be aware that one is having a dream is the forerunner of the second attention, a form of consciousness in a different category from the consciousness used to deal with the daily world.)*

SELECTED REFERENCES: The Fire From Within - Page [66.4-66.6] ("The reason I called the second attention...to deal with the daily world.)
SEE ALSO: *DREAMING-ART, ATTENTION-SECOND, ATTENTION-DREAMING, WARRIOR-DISCIPLINE*

DREAMING-CONDITIONS-FIVE-[THE FIVE CONDITIONS OF DREAMING]: *(Warriors know that the art of dreaming is anchored on five conditions that seers observe in the energy flow of human beings as it regards the displacement of the assemblage point.)*

SELECTED REFERENCES: The Art of Dreaming - Page [19.4-19.8] (He said that the old sorcerers...systematic displacement of the assemblage point.)
SEE ALSO: *DREAMING-ART, ASSEMBLAGE-POINT-MOVING, EAGLE-EMANATIONS, PERCEPTION*

DREAMING-CONTROL-[THE CONTROL OF DREAMING]: *(Warriors know that they cannot consciously or sub-consciously control their dreams without interfering with the movement of the assemblage point; the development of control in dreaming comes after the groundwork for dreaming has been laid; warriors must develop the necessary inner strength through impeccability in their daily lives; the development of dreamers is*

indirect, and the control necessary to do dreaming develops indirectly as well.)

SELECTED REFERENCES: **The Fire From Within - Page [173.2-175.1]** (Don Juan explained that *dreaming*, like...at the place where it sinks.) **The Fire From Within - Page [180.3-181.1]** (Don Juan then outlined the procedure...is impeccability in our daily life.")

SEE ALSO: *DREAMING-BODY-PROCEDURE-GETTING-TO, DREAMING-COMMAND, WARRIOR-STRENGTH, WARRIOR-SOBRIETY, WARRIOR-IMPECCABILITY, DREAMING-GATES, DREAMING-SETTING-UP*

DREAMING-DESCRIPTION-[A DESCRIPTION OF DREAMING]:

(Warriors know that in order to do dreaming, dreamers must "bundle" or wrap together their right and left side awareness and allow them to come to rest in a single bundle inside the dent in the luminous shell; this means that dreamers are able to manipulate both their luminous and physical bodies; first dreamers must make the center for assembling their second attention accessible by having it pushed in from the outside by someone else or sucking it in from within on their own; then they must dislodge the first attention by placing the centers of the physical body as close together as possible until they seem to join; then the sensation of being bundled takes place and the second attention automatically takes over.)

SELECTED REFERENCES: **The Eagle's Gift - Page [258.8-259.8]** (I understood then the impossibility of...with the right holding the reins.)

SEE ALSO: *LUMINOUS-DENT, ATTENTION-SECOND, ATTENTION-FIRST, ASSEMBLAGE-CENTERS, DREAMING-ART, AWARENESS-BUNDLING-(TOP)*

DREAMING-DISUSE-WHY-[WHY DREAMING FELL INTO DISUSE]:

(Warriors theorize that dreaming fell into disuse because it upsets the precarious mental balance of susceptible people.)

SELECTED REFERENCES: **The Power of Silence - Page [35.3-35.4]** ("The nagual Elias had great respect...precarious mental balance of susceptible people.)

SEE ALSO: *SANITY, INSANITY, DREAMING-ART*

DREAMING-DOOR-[THE DOOR OF DREAMING]: *(Warriors know that dreaming is the door between the realm of the inorganic beings and the world of men; dreaming is the vehicle that brings men to that world; everything sorcerers know about dreaming was taught to them by the inorganic beings; inorganic beings know how to pass through the door of dreaming, but men don't; men have to learn how to pass through that doorway.)*

SELECTED REFERENCES: **The Art of Dreaming - Page [117.4-117.5]** ("Dreaming is the vehicle that brings...men don't. they have to learn it.")

SEE ALSO: *DREAMING-ART, INORGANIC-BEINGS-REALM, PARALLEL-LINES*

DREAMING-DOUBLE-[DREAMING THE DOUBLE]-(TOP)

DREAMING-VS-DREAMS-[DREAMING VS ORDINARY DREAMS]:

(Warriors know that dreaming and normal dreams are very different affairs; in fact, dreaming is the warriors' practical way of putting ordinary dreams to use; dreams are the basis of dreaming just as controlled folly is the basis of stalking; dreams become dreaming only after warriors have learned to engage their dreaming attention; scouts are numerous in dreams only when they are normal dreams; the dreams of dreamers are strangely free from scouts; dreamers can determine if worlds they are perceiving are real worlds or phantom worlds; if the dreamers' energy body is complete, they will "see"

energy every time they gaze at an item in the daily world; in dreams, if they "see" the energy of an item they know they are dealing with a real world, no matter how distorted that world may appear to their dreaming attention; if they can't "see" the energy of an item, dreamers know they are not in a real world.)

    SELECTED REFERENCES: Journey to Ixtlan - Page [90.8-91.4] ("Don't concern yourself. They are only...nothing or very little about it.) **Journey to Ixtlan - Page [198.8-198.9]** ("When you first started dreaming you...you will also progress in *dreaming*.) **Tales of Power - Page [9.8-10.1]** (His sudden shift caught me...a dream from reality became inoperative.) **The Second Ring of Power - Page [277.8-278.2]** (Don Juan said that our first ring...dreams, change those dreams into "dreaming.") **The Eagle's Gift - Page [138.9-139.1]** (Don Juan explained to us...turn an ordinary dream into *dreaming*.) **The Eagle's Gift - Page [209.8-209.9]** (The *stalkers* are the practitioners of...as dreams are the basis for *dreaming*.) **The Art of Dreaming - Page [viii.8]** ("Let's then do away with metaphors...of putting ordinary dreams to use.") **The Art of Dreaming - Page [ix.1-ix.2]** (On another occasion don Juan said...it daydreaming or wishing or imagining.) **The Art of Dreaming - Page [21.3-22.2]** ("I am going to teach you...dreams actually be turned into dreaming.") **The Art of Dreaming - Page [25.4-25.5]** ("Where were we don Juan...your reason but your energy body.) **The Art of Dreaming - Page [69.1-69.4]** (On one of my visits to him...thousands of positions it can adopt.") **The Art of Dreaming - Page [84.9-85.5]** (When I told don Juan about...dreamers catch the presence of scouts.") **The Art of Dreaming - Page [164.1-165.2]** ("Dreamers have a rule of thumb...the simplicity and directness of sorcery.) **The Art of Dreaming - Page [166.8-167.6]** (The first time I put into...life only in your dreaming attention.) **The Art of Dreaming - Page [174.6-174.7]** ("I am saying all this because you...energy-generating condition we call dreaming.")

    SEE ALSO: *DREAMING-ART, ATTENTION-DREAMING, SLEEP, DREAMS-ORDINARY-(ALL)*

DREAMING-EMISSARY-[THE DREAMING EMISSARY]: *(An energetic entity; an impersonal and constant force that comes to dreamers from the realm of the inorganic beings; upon crossing the first or second gate of dreaming, dreamers reach a threshold and begin to "see" things or hear a voice, that voice is the dreaming emissary; an alien energy that has consciousness; an impersonal force that we turn into something personal because it has a voice; an alien energy that purports to aid dreamers by telling them things, even though it can only tell dreamers things that they already know or should know; warriors who choose to take its words as advice are incurable fools; warriors are aware that they experience the emissary because they are successfully able to fix the assemblage point on a specific new position; the more intense that fixation, the more intense the experience of the emissary; the dreaming emissary does not really advise sorcerers, it can only tell them what's what; all dreamers hear the dreaming emissary, but very few "see" it or feel it; sometimes the dreamer finds it necessary to control the interference of the emissary by threatening to get rid of it forever; the emissary will sometimes propose an alternate solution which is more convenient for the warrior-dreamer.)*

    SELECTED REFERENCES: The Art of Dreaming - Page [38.3-39.2] (This new capacity of looking in..."Some do," he answered uninterestedly.) **The Art of Dreaming - Page [64.4-67.9]** (He was not impressed in the...bent is to teach, to guide.") **The Art of Dreaming - Page [68.2-68.4]** ("Do I gather, don Juan, that...disagreed with him about the emissary.) **The Art of Dreaming - Page [74.7-75.4]** (The return to my dreaming practices...I had been interested in them.) **The Art of Dreaming - Page [93.3-93.6]** (Don Juan had said that inorganic...old sorcerers' preference for concrete practices.) **The Art of Dreaming - Page [95.3-95.9]** (I received a profusion of instructions...refuse to listen to my accounts.) **The Art of Dreaming - Page [119.7-119.9]** (I heard the emissary's voice. It...fact, no one wants to leave.") **The Art of Dreaming - Page [146.6-146.9]** (Secretly, I felt somehow exonerated from...to do to liberate the blue scout.) **The Art of Dreaming - Page [158.1-159.7]** (The voice of the dreaming emissary...without any

meddling from the emissary.) **The Art of Dreaming - Page [173.4-173.6]** (He remarked that of all the...self-awareness for nearly an eternity.) **The Art of Dreaming - Page [180.5-180.6]** ("Why did they believe that...our awareness for nearly an eternity.")
    SEE ALSO: *INORGANIC-BEINGS, ALLIES, SEEING-VOICE*

DREAMING-EMISSARY-VOICE-[THE VOICE OF THE DREAMING EMISSARY]: SEE: DREAMING-EMISSARY [THE DREAMING EMISSARY], INORGANIC-BEINGS-VOICE-[THE VOICE OF THE INORGANIC BEINGS], SEEING-VOICE-[THE VOICE OF SEEING]

DREAMING-EXPLANATION-[AN EXPLANATION OF THE PRACTICE OF DREAMING]: *(Warriors know that the practice of dreaming can only be accomplished if it is faced as a task which is entertaining instead of solemn and morbid; dreaming has to be performed with integrity and seriousness but also with laughter as well; warriors must be light as a feather to dream well, they must have the confidence of someone who doesn't have a care in the world.)*
    SELECTED REFERENCES: **The Art of Dreaming - Page [21.8-22.2]** (For instance, I expressed my feelings...dreams actually be turned into dreaming.")
    SEE ALSO: *DREAMING-ART, ABERRATION-MORBIDITY, WARRIOR-LIGHTNESS, DREAMING-FEAR, EXPLANATION*

DREAMING-FEAR-[THE FEAR OF DREAMING]: *(Warriors know they must learn to practice dreaming without letting fear turn it into an encumbering production.)*
    SELECTED REFERENCES: **The Second Ring of Power - Page [278.9-279.1]** (He urged me to practice...make it into an encumbering production.)
    SEE ALSO: *DREAMING-ART, FEAR, DREAMING-EXPLANATION*

DREAMING-GATE-FIRST-[THE FIRST GATE OF DREAMING]:
(Warriors know that the first gate of dreaming is a threshold warriors must cross; one reaches the first gate by becoming aware that one is falling asleep or by having a gigantically "real" dream; the barrier of the first gate of dreaming is more than a psychological obstacle created by our socialization; the first gate of dreaming has to do with the flow of energy in the universe, and as such it is a natural obstacle.)
    SELECTED REFERENCES: **The Second Ring of Power - Page [278.2-278.8]** (Don Juan said that there are no...as oneself, but made in "dreaming.") **The Art of Dreaming - Page [23.1-23.9]** ("The first gate is a threshold...it to know what I mean.") **The Art of Dreaming - Page [25.8-26.1]** ("In this particular instance, since we're...aware that you are falling asleep.") **The Art of Dreaming - Page [26.6-27.7]** (He assured me that intending the...anything I focused my attention on.) **The Art of Dreaming - Page [30.4-31.3]** (During another discussion, at a different...they also reach the energy body.") **The Art of Dreaming - Page [32.7]** (He reiterated that reaching, with deliberate...gain is predicated on energy alone.) **The Art of Dreaming - Page [36.4-36.7]** (I commented that the difficult part...the universe. It's a natural obstacle.") **The Art of Dreaming - Page [41.9]** (A dreamer on crossing the first gate has already reached the energy body.)
    SEE ALSO: *DREAMING-SETTING-UP, DREAMING-PRAXIS, SLEEP, DREAMING-GATES-SEVEN*

DREAMING-GATE-FOURTH-[THE FOURTH GATE OF DREAMING]: *(Warriors know that at the fourth gate of dreaming the energy body travels to specific, concrete places; there are three ways of using the fourth gate; 1) to travel to concrete places in this world; 2) to travel to concrete places out of this world, and; 3) to travel to places that exist only in the intent of others; to cross the fourth gate and travel to places that exist only in someone else's intent is very dangerous because every item in such a dream is an ultimately personal item.)*

SELECTED REFERENCES: **The Second Ring of Power - Page [278.2-278.8]** (Don Juan said that there are no...as oneself, but made in "dreaming.") **The Art of Dreaming - Page [200.4-200.8]** (Don Juan explained that, at the...cross the fourth gate by myself.) **The Art of Dreaming - Page [205.5-205.6]** ("And what's the lesson in dreaming...those naguals' personal bents of character.") **The Art of Dreaming - Page [231.3-231.4]** (She explained that as long as...gate of dreaming, dreaming my dream.") **The Art of Dreaming - Page [232.6-232.7]** (She warned me, then, that to...to be an ultimately personal item.) **The Art of Dreaming - Page [248.4-248.7]** ("So what do you think happened...exists today, only in her intent.")

SEE ALSO: *AWARENESS-TRANSFERRING, DREAMING-TRAVELING, INTENT-PROJECTING, POSITIONS-TWIN, PERCEPTION-TOTAL, DREAM-PULLED, DREAMING-GATES-SEVEN*

DREAMING-GATE-SECOND-[THE SECOND GATE OF DREAMING]:

(Warriors know that they have reached the second gate of dreaming when they are able to wake up from one dream to another; they can have as many dreams as they are capable of; the second gate of dreaming presents the problem of indulging to warriors; if they are unable to exercise their sobriety they will sink to mortal depths in their dreaming and never again wake up in this world; the second gate is reached and crossed only when dreamers learn to isolate and follow a foreign energy scout; the rule of the second gate is a series of three steps; 1) through practicing the drill of changing dreams, dreamers learn about the scouts; 2) by following the scouts, dreamers enter into another veritable universe; 3) in that universe, by means of their actions, dreamers learn the governing laws of the universe; the universe behind the second gate of dreaming is closest to our own, it is crafty and heartless; the universe behind the second gate is so powerful and aggressive that it serves as a natural screen where dreamers are probed for their weaknesses; if dreamers survive the test of the universe behind the second gate, they can proceed to the next gate, if not, they remain forever trapped in that universe; the real dreaming task of the second gate is to be transported by a scout.)

SELECTED REFERENCES: **The Second Ring of Power - Page [278.2-278.8]** (Don Juan said that there are no...as oneself, but made in "dreaming.") **The Art of Dreaming - Page [40.8-42.4]** ("Let's get on with our business...dreaming attention must make them surface.") **The Art of Dreaming - Page [43.8-44.7]** ("You have reached the second gate...My falling into dark, deep slumber.) **The Art of Dreaming - Page [46.9-47.2]** ("Dreaming is sustaining the position where...wait for a sign from them.") **The Art of Dreaming - Page [107.6-108.1]** ("I mean that it's not true...the key that opens that door.) **The Art of Dreaming - Page [108.5-108.7]** (He described the rule of the second...laws and regulations of that universe.) **The Art of Dreaming - Page [109.3-109.4]** ("You have to continue your dreaming...ever comment on your dreaming practices.") **The Art of Dreaming - Page [110.6-111.3]** (I only know that the universe behind...remain forever trapped in that universe.) **The Art of Dreaming - Page [156.8-156.9]** ("As you know, to be transported...hinges on really seeing yourself asleep.")

SEE ALSO: *DREAMING-ART, SCOUTS-ISOLATING-FOLLOWING, DREAMING-GATES-SEVEN*

DREAMING-GATE-THIRD-[THE THIRD GATE OF DREAMING]:

(Warriors know that the third gate of dreaming is reached when dreamers finds themselves in a dream staring at someone else who is asleep and that someone turns out to be themselves; at the third gate of dreaming, dreamers begin to deliberately merge their dreaming reality with the reality of their daily world; this merging of realities is called completing the energy body; as warriors consolidate their energy bodies, they must avoid the

overwhelming temptation to plunge into detail; warriors must also devise a valid guide to determine if they are actually "seeing" their bodies asleep in their beds; this is the only way they can tell if they are really dreaming and not just having an ordinary dream; the drill of the third gate of dreaming is moving the energy body by itself; the real task of the third gate of dreaming is "seeing" energy with the energy body.)

SELECTED REFERENCES: The Second Ring of Power - Page [278.2-278.8] (Don Juan said that there are no...as oneself, but made in "dreaming.") The Art of Dreaming - Page [141.7] (The third gate of dreaming is...to be you," don Juan said.) The Art of Dreaming - Page [142.3-143.7] ("At the third gate of dreaming...irrational abandon to counteract that insistence.") The Art of Dreaming - Page [147.4-147.6] (I hurried to change the subject..."You must recapitulate your life further.") The Art of Dreaming - Page [151.3-154.5] (The result of my second recapitulation...moves in the inorganic beings' world.) The Art of Dreaming - Page [155.7-157.9] (At the first opportunity I had...floating, going from to item to item.) The Art of Dreaming - Page [162.6-165.2] (He asked me then to tell...the simplicity and directness of sorcery.) The Art of Dreaming - Page [184.9-185.4] ("I'm going to propose a line...to the ends of the universe.") The Art of Dreaming - Page [186.5-186.6] ("By yourself, you don't have enough...do what I have in mind.")

SEE ALSO: *DREAMING-ART, ENERGY-BODY-COMPLETING, ENERGY-BODY-MOVING, DREAMING-GATES-SEVEN*

DREAMING-GATES-SEVEN-[THE SEVEN GATES OF DREAMING]:

(Warriors know there are seven gates of dreaming which dreamers must open one at a time if they are to dream; these seven gates are entrances to the energy flow of the universe and are experienced by dreamers as obstacles which must be overcome; there are two phases to each gate of dreaming; the first is to reach the gate and the second is to cross it.)

SELECTED REFERENCES: The Second Ring of Power - Page [278.2-278.8] (Don Juan said that there are no...as oneself, but made in "dreaming.") The Art of Dreaming - Page [22.6-22.9] ("There are seven gates," he said...sorcerers call the seven gates of dreaming.) The Art of Dreaming - Page [107.4-107.5] ("You already understand that the gates...what that gate is all about.") The Art of Dreaming - Page [108.4-108.5] (Don Juan admitted that I was...to be played by their rules.) The Art of Dreaming - Page [142.1-142.2] ("There are two phases to each...the second is to cross it.)

SEE ALSO: *DREAMING-ART, DREAMING-GATE-FIRST, DREAMING-GATE-SECOND, DREAMING-GATE-THIRD, DREAMING-GATE-FOURTH*

DREAMING-GHOST-[GHOST DREAMING]: *(Warriors know ghost dreaming is a type of dreaming peculiar to individuals with violent or destructive tendencies; a ghost dreamer is marked by fate to have ghost helpers and allies.)*

SELECTED REFERENCES: The Eagle's Gift - Page [54.4-54.8] ("It seems to me that the Nagual...to have ghost helpers and allies.")

SEE ALSO: *DREAMING-ART, SPIRIT-HELPERS, ALLIES, INORGANIC-BEINGS*

DREAMING-GOAL-[THE GOAL OF DREAMING]: *(Warriors know that the goal of dreaming is to intend and perfect the energy body.)*

SELECTED REFERENCES: The Art of Dreaming - Page [25.7-26.1] ("Is the goal of dreaming to intend...and that you are a dreamer.) The Art of Dreaming - Page [42.2-.42.3] ("You will find out for yourself...is to perfect the energy body.)

SEE ALSO: *DREAMING-ART, ENERGY-BODY, INTENDING*

DREAMING-GORDA-[LA GORDA'S DREAMING]-(TOP)

DREAMING-GROUNDWORK-[THE GROUNDWORK OF DREAMING]: SEE: DREAMING-BODY-PROCEDURE-GETTING-TO-[THE PROCEDURE FOR GETTING TO THE DREAMING BODY]

DREAMING-GUIDE-*[A VALID GUIDE FOR DREAMING]*: *(Warriors know that dreamers must devise a valid guide to determine whether they are actually dreaming or not; the warriors' extraordinary exploration of perception hinges on whether or not warriors really "see" themselves asleep; "seeing" energy with the energy body is the most accurate gauge for determining whether or not the dreamer is really dreaming or not.)*
    SELECTED REFERENCES: The Art of Dreaming - Page [151.6-151.9] ("You have to establish some valid...be on your own very soon.") The Art of Dreaming - Page [155.7-157.9] (At the first opportunity I had...floating, going from to item to item.) The Art of Dreaming - Page [164.1-165.2] ("Dreamers have a rule of thumb...the simplicity and directness of sorcery.)
    SEE ALSO: *DREAMING-ART, DREAMING-VS-DREAMS, ENERGY-BODY-PERCEPTION, DREAMING-GATE-THIRD*

DREAMING-IMAGES-HOLDING-*[HOLDING THE IMAGES OF A DREAM AS WE HOLD THE IMAGES OF THE WORLD]*: SEE: IMAGES-HOLDING-DREAM-WORLD-*[HOLDING THE IMAGES OF A DREAM AS WE HOLD THE IMAGES OF THE WORLD]*

DREAMING-IMAGINATION-*[DREAMING AND IMAGINATION]*: *(Warriors know that dreamers have to be imaginative and avoid being stuck at the level of interpretation when faced with a riddle.)*
    SELECTED REFERENCES: The Art of Dreaming - Page [153.7-154.3] ("Dreamers have to be imaginative," he said...again at the level of interpretation.)
    SEE ALSO: *DREAMING-ART, WARRIOR-IMAGINATION, RIDDLE-DREAMER-DREAMED, RIDDLE-HEART, RIDDLE-MIND, RIDDLE-SPIRIT*

DREAMING-INDULGING-*[INDULGING IN DREAMING]*: *(Warriors know that if dreaming is overemphasized, it becomes what it was for the sorcerers of antiquity, a source of inexhaustible indulging.)*
    SELECTED REFERENCES: The Art of Dreaming - Page [122.2-122.3] (He remarked that if dreaming is...sorcerers: a source of inexhaustible indulging.)
    SEE ALSO: *DREAMING-ART, SELF-INDULGENCE, WARRIOR-SOBRIETY*

DREAMING-INSTRUCTION-[THE WARRIORS' INSTRUCTION IN DREAMING]*: *(Warriors know that instruction in dreaming should be conducted without interference and with only the occasional pointer.)*
    SELECTED REFERENCES: The Eagle's Gift - Page [137.4] ("From then on he never put...instruction in *dreaming* should be conducted.")
    SEE ALSO: *DREAMING-ART, DREAMING-LEARN*

DREAMING-INTRICACIES-*[THE INTRICACIES OF DREAMING]-(TOP)*

DREAMING-JOURNEY-COFFEE-SHOP-*[CARLOS' DREAMING JOURNEY TO THE COFFEE SHOP]-(TOP)*

DREAMING-LEARN-[LEARNING TO DO DREAMING]*: *(Warriors know that since dreaming uses a natural built-in shift of the assemblage point, warriors should be able to learn dreaming by themselves alone; the development of dreamers is indirect; what dreamers need more than anything else is sobriety, and no one can give that to them, they must create it for themselves.)*
    SELECTED REFERENCES: The Fire From Within - Page [180.8-181.1] ("The development of *dreamers* is indirect...is impeccability in our daily life.")
    SEE ALSO: *DREAMING-ART, WARRIOR-SOBRIETY, WARRIOR-STRENGTH, IMPECCABLE-MAN-NO-GUIDE, DREAMING-INSTRUCTION, DREAMING-FORTIFYING*

DREAMING-LEARN-PURPOSE-NEW-SEER-[THE PURPOSE OF THE NEW SEERS IN LEARNING DREAMING]: (*Warriors know that the new seers overrode their hesitancy to explore dreaming for two reasons; 1) they realized that it was imperative for them to be able to "see" the Eagle's emanations and; 2) they wanted to move their assemblage points.*)
　　　SELECTED REFERENCES: The Fire From Within - Page [172.4-173.6] (The new seers deemed it imperative...help them move their assemblage points.)
　　　SEE ALSO: *DREAMING-ART, SEER-NEW, EAGLE-EMANATIONS-SEEING*

DREAMING-LESSON-[A DREAMING LESSON]-(TOP)

DREAMING-METAPHORS-[METAPHORS FOR DREAMING]: (*Warriors know that dreaming can be described as the "gateway to infinity" or the "sorcerers' way of saying good-night to the world"; less poetically, it can be described as the practical way of putting normal dreams to use.*)
　　　SELECTED REFERENCES: The Art of Dreaming - Page [viii.7-ix.1] (With the perspective time gives, I...I'm doing the same with you.")
　　　SEE ALSO: *DREAMING-ART*

DREAMING-MOOD-NEFARIOUS-[THE NEFARIOUS MOOD OF DREAMING]: (*Warriors know that dreaming is tainted with the mood of the sorcerers of antiquity; the new seers realize that dreaming has the capacity to make the dreamer weak, compulsive, and capricious, since the old seers were like that; in order to offset the nefarious effect of dreaming, the new seers developed the warriors' way as a method of fortifying the dreamer and enhancing his sobriety.*)
　　　SELECTED REFERENCES: The Fire From Within - Page [175.4-175.9] ("I have to make it clear to...warrior's way, or the warrior's path.)
　　　SEE ALSO: *TOLTECS, SEER-OLD, SORCERER-ANTIQUITY, WARRIOR-WAY, WARRIOR-SOBRIETY, SEER-OLD-MOOD, SORCERER-ANTIQUITY-MOOD*

DREAMING-MUSCULAR-[BECOMING MORE MUSCULAR THROUGH DREAMING]-(TOP)

DREAMING-NORMAL-AWARENESS-[DREAMING AND NORMAL AWARENESS]: (*Warriors know that one of the strictest commands of the new seers is that dreaming must be learned in a state of normal awareness.*)
　　　SELECTED REFERENCES: The Fire From Within - Page [172.7-173.1] ("One of the strictest commands of the new...that suddenly become aligned in dreaming.)
　　　SEE ALSO: *DREAMING-ART, AWARENESS-NORMAL*

DREAMING-NOT-DOING-[THE NOT-DOING OF DREAMING]: (*Warriors know that dreaming is the not-doing of ordinary dreams.*)
　　　SELECTED REFERENCES: Journey to Ixtlan - Page [198.8-198.9] ("When you first started dreaming you...you will also progress in *dreaming*.)
　　　SEE ALSO: *DREAMING-VS-DREAMS, DOING-VS-NOT-DOING, NOT-DOING, DREAMING-ART*

DREAMING-ORDINARY-[ORDINARY DREAMS]: SEE: DREAMING-DREAMS-[DREAMING VS ORDINARY DREAMS]

DREAMING-PARADOX-[THE PARADOX OF DREAMING]: (*Warriors know that they must resolve a fundamental paradox of dreaming by striking a very subtle balance; dreams cannot be interfered with, nor can they be commanded by the conscious effort of the dreamer, and yet the shift of the assemblage point must obey the dreamer's command.*)

SELECTED REFERENCES: **The Fire From Within - Page [173.8-173.9]** (Don Juan explained that dreamers have...but must be resolved in practice.)
SEE ALSO: *DREAMING-ART, WARRIOR-CONTRADICTION-KNOWLEDGE, DREAMING-CONTROL, DREAMING-COMMAND, BALANCE, WARRIOR-EQUILIBRIUM, EQUILIBRIUM*

DREAMING-PITFALLS-[THE PITFALLS OF DREAMING]: (Warriors know that the path of dreaming is filled with pitfalls because dreaming was invented by the sorcerers of antiquity and is tainted with their mood; to avoid those pitfalls or fall into them is a personal and final affair of each dreamer; there is really no way to direct the movement of the assemblage point in dreaming; the only thing that directs that shift is the inner strength or weakness of the dreamer.)
SELECTED REFERENCES: **The Fire From Within - Page [175.4-175.9]** ("I have to make it clear to...warrior's way, or the warrior's path.) **The Fire From Within - Page [181.5-181.7]** (Don Juan said that there is...stood by ready to end their *seeing*.) **The Art of Dreaming - Page [109.4-109.9]** (I confessed to him that I...way of plummeting into a pitfall.")
SEE ALSO: *DREAMING-ART, WARRIOR-WAY, SEER-OLD-MOOD, WARRIORSHIP-VS-SORCERY, DREAMING-CONTROL, DREAMING-COMMAND*

DREAMING-POSITION-[THE DREAMING POSITION]: (Warriors know that the dreaming position is the spot to where the assemblage point moves in dreams; a position of the assemblage point beyond the known; the position of a dream; a position of the assemblage point characterized by a shift or movement deeper into the left side awareness; warriors are able to fixate the assemblage point on a dreaming position by sustaining the view of any item in their dreams or by changing dreams at will.)
SELECTED REFERENCES: **The Fire From Within - Page [175.2-175.4]** ("Wherever the assemblage point moves in dreams...up at a new *dreaming position*.) **The Fire From Within - Page [177.4-177.6]** (Don Juan maintained that it is...kind of contorted shape or manner.) **The Fire From Within - Page [179.3-179.5]** (I asked him how he was…to the point of no doubt.") **The Fire From Within - Page [180.3-180.7]** (Don Juan then outlined the procedure…more and more manageable, even orderly.) **The Fire From Within - Page [219.1-219.4]** (He told me then that I was…as if nothing is happening to them.) **The Fire From Within - Page [230.5-230.6]** ("They chose to live," he repeated...of the Eagle to be devoured.") **The Fire From Within - Page [275.7-275.8]** ("I want you to realign the proper...in a *dreaming position*," he said.) **The Fire From Within - Page [281.7-281.8]** ("It was too soon then for...traveled an enormous distance that day.") **The Fire From Within - Page [282.7-283.3]** ("You traveled because you woke up…emanations that are inside the cocoon.") **The Fire From Within - Page [285.8-285.9]** (I told don Juan that since both…took off into the unknown in packs.) **The Fire From Within - Page [298.3-298.5]** (The fact that such a maneuver…*dreaming position* called total freedom.) **The Art of Dreaming - Page [69.2-70.3]** ("Dreams are analyzed for their meaning...any particular dream you are having.") **The Art of Dreaming - Page [70.8]** ("Remember that, in your dreams, once...dreaming position of your assemblage point.) **The Art of Dreaming - Page [170.1-170.3]** (Don Juan said that in special dreams...that it resembles an ordinary dream.)
SEE ALSO: *DREAMING-BODY, DREAMING-TRAVELING, ASSEMBLAGE-POINT-FIXATION, DREAMING-GATE-SECOND, DREAMER-GLANCE, DREAMING-ART, ASSEMBLAGE-POINT-POSITION*

DREAMING-POSITION-FIXATION-[THE FIXATION OF THE DREAMING POSITION]: SEE: ASSEMBLAGE-POINT-FIXATION-DREAMER-DIRECTS-[THE DREAMER DIRECTS THE FIXATION OF HIS ASSEMBLAGE POINT]

DREAMING-POSITION-INTENT-[INTENT AND THE DREAMING POSITION]: (Warriors know that intent, through the dreamers' sobriety, maintains the alignment of whatever emanations are lit up by the movement of the dreamer's assemblage point.)

SELECTED REFERENCES: **The Fire From Within - Page [180.3-181.5]** (Don Juan then outlined the procedure...the movement of the assemblage point.)
SEE ALSO: *DREAMING-SOBRIETY, INTENT, DREAMING-POSITION, ASSEMBLAGE-POINT-MOVING, DREAMING-ART*

DREAMING-POSITION-PHYSICAL-[THE PHYSICAL POSITION ONE ASSUMES TO DO DREAMING]: (Warriors know they can maximize the effectiveness of their dreaming by adopting specific physical positions; for a woman, it is to sit with the legs crossed and let the body fall; for a man it is to sit up on a soft thin mat with the soles of the feet together and the thighs as close to the mat as possible.)
SELECTED REFERENCES: **The Eagle's Gift - Page [137.9-138.4]** (The position one assumes to do *dreaming*...my forehead would rest on my feet.) **The Eagle's Gift - Page [153.1]** (Both of us were so exhausted...quite spontaneously adopted the *dreaming* position.)
SEE ALSO: *DREAMING-ART, DREAMING-TECHNIQUES*

DREAMING-POSITION-UNIMAGINABLE-[UNIMAGINABLE DREAMING POSITIONS]: SEE: DREAMING POSITION-[THE DREAMING-POSITION]

DREAMING-PRACTICES-COHESION-[DREAMING PRACTICES AND COHESION]: (Warriors know that through their dreaming practices, they are really exercising their ability to be cohesive; the dreamers' capacity to hold a new energy shape by holding the assemblage point fixed on a particular new dreaming position.)
SELECTED REFERENCES: **The Art of Dreaming - Page [70.1-70.3]** ("How do we fixate the assemblage...any particular dream you are having.")
SEE ALSO: *ENERGETIC-UNIFORMITY-COHESION, ENERGY-SHAPE, ASSEMBLAGE POINT-FIXATION, DREAMING-POSITION, STALKING-ART, DREAMING-ART*

DREAMING-PRAXIS-[THE PRAXIS OF DREAMING]: (Warriors know that the praxis of dreaming consists of the exercise of finding one's hands [or some other body part] in a dream; an exercise in which one deliberately looks for and finds oneself in a dream by simply intending to do so.)
SELECTED REFERENCES: **Journey to Ixtlan - Page [98.1-98.5]** ("You must start by doing something...thing in this awesome, mysterious world.") **Tales of Power - Page [10.2]** (Don Juan's praxis of "dreaming" was...to the level of the eyes.) **The Art of Dreaming - Page [21.3-22.3]** ("I am going to teach you...thing but engaging my dreaming attention.) **The Art of Dreaming - Page [26.6-27.7]** (He assured me that intending the...anything I focused my attention on.)
SEE ALSO: *DREAMING-SETTING-UP, DREAMING-STAGES-FOUR*

DREAMING-PROJECTION-[PROJECTING ONESELF IN DREAMING]: (Warriors know that their ability to project themselves in dreaming depends on their level of impeccability; the stronger and more impeccable dreamers are, the farther they can project the second attention and the longer those projections will last.)
SELECTED REFERENCES: **The Eagle's Gift - Page [265.3-265.4]** (The only thing Zuleica told me...longer their *dreaming* projection would last.)
SEE ALSO: *DREAMING-POSITION, DREAMING-ART*

DREAMING-PURPOSE-[THE PURPOSE OF DREAMING]: (The warrior knows that the purpose of dreaming is control and power.)
SELECTED REFERENCES: **Journey to Ixtlan - Page [112.5]** ("Drop it!" he said imperatively...*dreaming*, which is control and power.")
SEE ALSO: *WARRIOR-CONTROL, POWER, DREAMING-ART*

DREAMING-RATIONAL-STATE-[DREAMING IS A RATIONAL STATE]:
(Warriors know that dreaming is in fact a rational undertaking because the right side or rational awareness of the dreamer is bundled together with the left side awareness during dreaming; dreamers' rational awareness gives them a sense of sobriety and rationality but that rationality has to be minimized and used only as an inhibiting mechanism to protect dreamers from their own aberrations.)
    The Eagle's Gift - Page [261.1-261.3] (The more I practiced, the clearer...*dreamer* from excess and bizarre undertakings.)
    SEE ALSO: *DREAMING-ART, REASON, DREAMING-DESCRIPTION, WARRIOR-SOBRIETY, ABERRATION-MORBIDITY, STALKING-STALKERS*

DREAMING-REALITY-[THE REALITY OF DREAMING]: *(Warriors know that dreaming is not just an idea; dreaming is real; dreaming is an energy generating condition.)*
    SELECTED REFERENCES: **The Eagle's Gift - Page [265.4-265.9]** (Don Juan said that my journeys...having my own tales of eternity.) **The Art of Dreaming - Page [173.6-174.5]** ("As you know, succumbing to the...believe in the reality of dreaming.")
    SEE ALSO: *DREAMING-ART, REALITY-NON-ORDINARY, DREAMING-REALITY-(ALL)*

DREAMING-REALITY-INCLUSIVE-[DREAMING AS AN ALL-INCLUSIVE REALITY]: *(The art of the old sorcerers; the most frightening thing there is is that dreams can be spun which constitute all-inclusive realities.)*
    SELECTED REFERENCES: **The Art of Dreaming - Page [259.5-259.9]** (Before we arrived at the house...crowning lesson in dreaming, didn't I?")
    SEE ALSO: *DREAMING-ART, DREAMING-REALITY*

DREAMING-REALITY-METAMORPHOSIS-[DREAMING AND THE METAMORPHOSIS OF REALITY]: *(Warriors know that under the influence of the practice of dreaming, the dreamers' reality suffers a metamorphosis; dreaming truly opens the door for dreamers into other aspects of what is real.)*
    SELECTED REFERENCES: **The Art of Dreaming - Page [97.2-98.7]** (Dreaming of that world, I became...foremost assailant of our rationality.)
    SEE ALSO: *DREAMERS-OPTIONS-TWO, DREAMING-DOOR, DREAMING-REALITY*

DREAMING-VS-RECAPITULATION-[DREAMING VS THE RECAPITULATION]: SEE: WARRIOR-PREOCCUPATION-[THE WARRIORS' PREOCCUPATION]

DREAMING-REQUISITES-[THE REQUISITES FOR DREAMING]:
(Warriors know that a redeployment of energy is necessary to begin dreaming; warriors accomplish this redeployment of energy by redefining their personal premises and conserving their personal power; this redeployment of energy is also known as "setting up dreaming".)
    SELECTED REFERENCES: **The Art of Dreaming - Page [181.6-181.9]** ("Can you explain to me, don Juan...need loads of dark, alien energy.")
    SEE ALSO: *DREAMING-SETTING-UP, WARRIOR-IMPECCABILITY, POWER-PERSONAL, FACADE-TRANSFORMING, WARRIOR-EMPHASIS*

*DREAMING-SEEING-[SEEING IN DREAMING]: SEE: SEEING-DREAMING-[SEEING IN DREAMING]

DREAMING-SELECTING-TOPIC-[SELECTING A TOPIC FOR DREAMING]: *(Warriors know dreamers can select a topic for dreaming by deliberately holding a topic in their minds after shutting off the internal dialogue.)*

SELECTED REFERENCES: Tales of Power - Page [11.9-12.2] (The sorcerers explanation of how to...you were not aware of it.")
SEE ALSO: *DREAMING-ART, DREAMING-SETTING-UP, DREAMING-TECHNIQUES*

DREAMING-SETTING-UP-[SETTING UP DREAMING]: *(Warriors know they must develop a concise, pragmatic control over the general situation of a dream, comparable to the control one has while awake; the warriors' first step to power.)*

SELECTED REFERENCES: Journey to Ixtlan - Page [97.8-100.3] ("I am going to teach you... long time to perfect this technique.") Journey to Ixtlan - Page [111.6-113.4] (I gave him a detailed report...the exact time of your traveling.") Journey to Ixtlan - Page [131.7-132.2] (After a moment's pause he casually...only cause intense dreams, not *dreaming.*") Journey to Ixtlan - Page [152.4-153.3] (I tried to insist, but he...most important place in your life".) Journey to Ixtlan -Page [198.8-199..1] ("When you first started dreaming you...without believing he is *not-doing.*") Tales of Power - Page [10.4-10.5] (Don Juan wanted to know the...prevent the fulfillment of my task.) Tales of Power - Page [10.9-11.3] (One night, quite unexpectedly, I found...street in some unknown foreign city.) The Second Ring of Power - Page [162.2-162.9] ("I learned that in *dreaming*...was the beginning. The rest was easy.") The Second Ring of Power - Page [278.2-278.8] (Don Juan said that there are no...as oneself, but made in "dreaming.") The Second Ring of Power - Page [295.3-295.4] ("He combined gazing at dry leaves...that's all there is to gazing.") The Eagle's Gift - Page [141.8] (I told la Gorda that in my case...to find my hands in *dreaming.*) The Fire From Within - Page [66.4-66.6] ("The reason I called the second attention...to deal with the daily world.) The Art of Dreaming - Page [21.3-22.3] ("I am going to teach you...thing but engaging my dreaming attention.)
SEE ALSO: *DREAMING, DREAMING-PRAXIS, DREAMING-STAGES-FOUR, DREAMING-ART, DREAMING-CONTROL, DREAMING-COMMAND, DREAMING-REQUISITES*

DREAMING-SNATCHING-ANOTHER-DREAMER-[SNATCHING ANOTHER DREAMER IN DREAMING]-(TOP)

DREAMING-SOBRIETY-[DREAMING AND SOBRIETY]: *(Warriors know that their sobriety is all they have to offset the nefarious effects of dreaming; warriors know that a life of impeccability by itself leads unavoidably to a sense of sobriety, and sobriety in turn leads to the movement of the assemblage point; it is the dreamers' sobriety which enables intent to maintain the alignment of whatever emanations have been lit up by the movement of the dreamers' assemblage point.)*

SELECTED REFERENCES: The Fire From Within - Page [175.7-176.3] (He said that at first the...the movement of the assemblage point.) The Fire From Within - Page [180.3-181.5] (Don Juan then outlined the procedure...the movement of the assemblage point.)
SEE ALSO: *WARRIOR-WAY, WARRIOR-SOBRIETY, DREAMING-MOOD-NEFARIOUS, DREAMING-PITFALL, DREAMING-ART, WARRIOR-SOBRIETY, WARRIOR-IMPECCABLE, ASSEMBLAGE-POINT-MOVING, INTENT, ALIGNMENT*

DREAMING-STAGES-FOUR-[THE FOUR STAGES OF DREAMING]: *(Carlos Castaneda's outline for the four stages of dreaming; restful vigil, dynamic vigil, passive witnessing, and dynamic initiative.)*

SELECTED REFERENCES: The Eagle's Gift - Page [128.9-129.6] (Years before, when I had acquired a...I called this state *dynamic initiative.*) The Eagle's Gift - Page [150.7-151.1] (In unison, we arrived then at the...I could switch on and off.) The Eagle's Gift - Page [251.3-263.3] (Speaking from behind me , she ordered...of the state of *restful vigil,*.)

SEE ALSO: *DREAMING-ART, DREAMING-PRAXIS, DREAMING-TOGETHER, DREAMING-TRAVELING*

DREAMING-VS-STALKING-[DREAMING VS STALKING]: *(Warriors know that there is a key distinction between the arts of dreaming and stalking; dreaming is concerned with the displacement of the assemblage point while stalking is concerned with the fixation of the assemblage point on any location to which it is displaced; one art cannot exist without the other; intending is the secret to both dreaming and stalking; warriors displace their assemblage points through intending and fixate them equally through intending; there is no technique for intending, warriors intend through usage; the intensive practice of stalking tends to create in the warrior a feeling of lightheartedness and joviality while the practice of dreaming tends to make the dreamer more somber and morose; the conservation of sexual energy is vital for dreamers but not so critical for stalkers.)*

SELECTED REFERENCES: **The Eagle's Gift - Page** [248.4-248.6] (Moreover, la Gorda deduced on her...became progressively more somber and morose.) **The Power of Silence - Page** [36.2-36.3] ("The same thing happened to me...average man and as a nagual.") **The Art of Dreaming - Page** [69.4-69.6] (Don Juan expressed his bewilderment...location to which it is displaced.) **The Art of Dreaming - Page** [77.5-77.9] ("The art of stalking," he continued...which the old sorcerers were involved.) **The Art of Dreaming - Page** [161.3-161.9] (He explained that since everything related...for intending. One intends through usage.")

SEE ALSO: *DREAMING-ART, STALKING-ART, DREAMING-PRACTICES-COHESION, ASSEMBLAGE-POINT-FIXATION, ASSEMBLAGE-POINT-MOVING, INTENDING, ASSEMBLAGE POINT-POSITION-OPTIMUM, SEX-ENERGY-CONSERVING*

DREAMING-STALKING-END-SAME-[DREAMING AND STALKING LEAD TO THE SAME END]: *(Warriors know that a perfect recapitulation can change a warrior as much if not more than the total control of the dreaming body; both arts lead warriors to the third attention and it is important for warriors to know and practice both.)*

SELECTED REFERENCES: **The Eagle's Gift - Page** [288.1-288.2] (She assured me that a perfect...however, to know and practice both.)

SEE ALSO: *DREAMING-ART, STALKING-ART, ATTENTION-THIRD, RECAPITULATION, DREAMING-BODY*

DREAMING-STALKING-PRACTICE-[THE PRACTICE OF DREAMING AND STALKING BY MEN AND WOMEN]: *(Warriors know that it takes different configurations in the luminous body of a woman to master either dreaming or stalking; men can practice both with a degree of ease but they can never attain the level of proficiency that women can attain in either art.)*

SELECTED REFERENCES: **The Eagle's Gift - Page** [288.2-288.3] (In this respect, *dreaming* and *stalking*...the women attained in each art.)

SEE ALSO: *DREAMING-ART, STALKING-ART, MEN, WOMEN*

DREAMING-STARTING-ITEM-[THE STARTING POINT ITEM FOR DREAMING]: *(In order to offset the evanescent quality of dreams, sorcerers have devised the use of the starting point item because dreamers get a surge of energy every time they isolate that particular item in their dream; when dreamers begin to feel they are losing control of their dream, they can return to their starting point item and begin again.)*

SELECTED REFERENCES: **The Art of Dreaming - Page** [30.8-31.1] ("This is precisely what I am...item and start all over again.")

SEE ALSO: *DREAMER-GLANCE, DREAMING-TECHNIQUES*

DREAMING-TALKING-IN-[TALKING IN DREAMING]-(TOP)

DREAMING-TASK-[THE WARRIORS' TASK TO FULFILL IN DREAMING]: *(Warriors know they will be given a specific dreaming task to fulfill.)*
SELECTED REFERENCES: The Eagle's Gift - Page [54.1-54.3] (They had particular *dreaming* tasks...had nothing of substance to report.) The Eagle's Gift - Page [139.5-140.6] (Our discussion of the second attention...didn't know what was going on.") The Eagle's Gift - Page [141.8-142.6] (I told la Gorda that in my...into my world of everyday life.)
SEE ALSO: *DREAMING-ART, WRITING-SORCERY-EXERCISE*

DREAMING-TECHNIQUES-[TECHNIQUES FOR PERFECT DREAMING]: *(Warriors know there are a series of mechanical techniques which optimize the entrance into dreaming and the control of the dreaming attention.)*
SELECTED REFERENCES: The Eagle's Gift - Page [249.7-250.1] (Zuleica told me that if dreaming...monotonous chanting, intricate repetitious movements.) The Art of Dreaming - Page [93.6-95.2] ("For perfect dreaming, the first thing...terms of controlling the dreaming attention.)
SEE ALSO: *DREAMING-ART, DREAMER-HEADBAND, RITUAL, BRIDGE-DREAMING, DREAMING-ATTENTION, DREAMING-TIME, DREAMING-STARTING-ITEM, DREAMING-SETTING-UP, DREAMING-PRAXIS, DREAMING-POSITION-PHYSICAL*

DREAMING-TIME-[THE TIME TO DO DREAMING]: *(Warriors know that late night or early morning hours are the best time to do dreaming; these times provide the best conditions of solitude and a minimum of first attention interference.)*
SELECTED REFERENCES: The Eagle's Gift - Page [138.5-138.9] (Another topic of great significance was the...of those around us is dormant.)
SEE ALSO: *DREAMING-TECHNIQUES , DREAMING-POSITION*

*DREAMING-TOGETHER-[DREAMING TOGETHER]: *(Warriors know that dreaming together is the process whereby two or more individual dreamers can dream together; a phenomenon based on the mysterious tendency of one dreaming body to follow another in dreaming.)*
SELECTED REFERENCES: The Eagle's Gift - Page [127.7-128.6] ("What kind of dreaming do you...more difficult it seems to be.") The Eagle's Gift - Page [132.7-133.3] (I had suddenly realized that la...were younger and I was fat.") The Fire From Within - Page [181.5-182.2] (Don Juan said that there is...the left side, while *dreaming together*.) The Fire From Within - Page [285.8-286.2] (I told don Juan that since...because I wanted to be with you.") The Fire From Within - Page [294.8-295.1] (The inquisitive, rational part of me...been there alone with the allies.") The Power of Silence - Page [96.2-96.9] (The young actor, hearing his own...was quite out of the ordinary.)
SEE ALSO: *DREAMING-ART, DREAMING-TRAVELING*

DREAMING-TRAVEL-GUIDES-[THE GUIDES OF THE DREAMING TRAVELER]: *(Warriors know that strong emotion, unbending intent or great interest and need serve as guides to the dreaming traveler.)*
SELECTED REFERENCES: The Fire From Within - Page [283.2-283.3] ("How does a journey like that...emanations that are inside the cocoon.") The Fire From Within - Page [290.2-290.3] (He said that I could not as...to serve me as a launcher.)
SEE ALSO: *EMOTION, WARRIOR-INTENT-UNBENDING, DREAMING-TRAVELING, DREAMING-POSITION*

DREAMING-TRAVELING-[TRAVELING IN DREAMING]: *(Warriors know that traveling in dreaming is a phenomenon based on the ability of the dreaming body to transport itself over great distances; the ability of dreamers to fly over incredible distances to points within this world or*

beyond it; the ability of dreamers to allow themselves to be pulled to a new dreaming position; dreaming is the sorcerer's jet plane.)
SELECTED REFERENCES: **Journey to Ixtlan - Page [152.5-153.3]** (I had begun to dream about...most important place in your life.") **Tales of Power - Page [41.5-41.7]** ("Genaro is a man of knowledge,"...Genaro but his double," he said.) **Tales of Power - Page [158.3-158.4]** (I could not answer any of...my material corporeality inside the market.) **The Eagle's Gift - Page [141.9-142.1]** (Next he recommended that I should...second attention would zero in on.) **The Fire From Within - Page [280.6-281.8]** (Don Juan had caught up with...traveled an enormous distance that day.") **The Fire From Within - Page [282.8-283.3]** ("You traveled because you woke up...emanations that are inside the cocoon.") **The Power of Silence - Page [33.6-33.7]** ("*Dreaming* is a sorcerer's jet plane...his natural self be a recluse.")
SEE ALSO: *DREAMING-ART, DREAMING-POSITION, DREAMING-BODY-JOURNEY-(TOP)*

DREAMING-TREE-[THE DREAMING TREE]-(TOP)

DREAMING-TRIALS-[THE TRIALS OF DREAMING]: *(Warriors know that there is no point in emphasizing the trials of dreaming; if they have the same vision three times, they should then pay attention to it; otherwise a neophyte's attempts are merely stepping stones to building the second attention.)*
SELECTED REFERENCES: **The Eagle's Gift - Page [50.2-50.3]** (I related to them the events...stone to building the second attention.)
SEE ALSO: *DREAMING-ART, ATTENTION-SECOND, DREAMING-VS-DREAMS*

*DREAMING-VOICE-[A VOICE FROM DREAMING]: *(Warriors know that the voice of their dreaming instructor is sometimes heard by the dreamer as a disembodied voice, similar to the voice of "seeing".)*
SELECTED REFERENCES: **The Eagle's Gift - Page [249.5-249.7]** (Zuleica was very effective as my...thought she had heard in *dreaming*.)
SEE ALSO: *DREAMING-ART, SEEING-VOICE*

DREAMING-WAR-ZONE-[THE WAR ZONE OF DREAMING]: *(Warriors know that the realm of the inorganic beings is always ready to strike; that realm must be entered into as if it were a war zone.)*
SELECTED REFERENCES: **The Art of Dreaming - Page [110.8-110.9]** ("The universe of the inorganic beings...were venturing into a war zone.")
SEE ALSO: *INORGANIC-BEINGS-TRICKERY, DREAMING-GATE-SECOND*

DREAMING-WOMAN-[A WOMAN'S DREAMING]: *(A woman's dreaming has to come from her womb because that is her center; she learns to feel the inside of it; the hardest part for her is to learn to begin; she stops her internal dialogue by concentrating her attention on her womb.)*
SELECTED REFERENCES: **The Eagle's Gift - Page [136.4-137.3]** (In a woman both the attention...He said it had been *dreaming*.)
SEE ALSO: *DREAMING-ART, WOMB*

DREAMS-ORDINARY-[ORDINARY DREAMS]: SEE: DREAMING-VS-DREAMS-[DREAMING VS ORDINARY DREAMS]

DREAMS-ORDINARY-VS-DREAMING-[ORDINARY DREAMS VS DREAMING]: SEE: DREAMING-VS-DREAMS [DREAMING VS ORDINARY DREAMS]

DREAMS-ORDINARY-NO-POWER-[ORDINARY DREAMS HAVE NO POWER]: *(Warriors know that ordinary dreams have no power; ordinary dreams may be weird, poignant or frightening but they are not "dreaming.")*

SELECTED REFERENCES: Journey to Ixtlan - Page [90.8-91.2] ("Don't concern yourself. They are only...poignant but they are not *dreaming*.) Journey to Ixtlan - Page [112.1-112.5] (I told him that I had been...*dreaming*, which is control and power.")
SEE ALSO: *DREAMING-VS-DREAMS*

DREAMS-ORDINARY-SIGNIFICANCE-[THE SIGNIFICANCE OF ORDINARY DREAMS]: *(Warriors know that the details of dreams must be sorted out by the dreamer before interpretations are made from them; some items are of key importance because they are associated with the spirit, while others are entirely unimportant because they are associated with indulging personalities.)*

SELECTED REFERENCES: The Art of Dreaming - Page [85.5-85.8] (Don Juan advised me to pay...being associated with our indulging personality.)
SEE ALSO: *DREAMING-VS-DREAMS, DREAMING-TRIALS*

DREAMS-STREET-TWO-WAY-[DREAMS ARE A TWO-WAY STREET]: SEE: DREAMING DREAMS-[DREAMING VS DREAMS]

DREAMS-WARRIOR-[THE WARRIORS DREAMS]: SEE: WARRIOR-DREAMS-[THE WARRIORS' DREAMS]

DRINKING-LUCIO-[DRINKING WITH LUCIO]-(TOP)

DROPPING-THINGS-LIVES-[DROPPING THINGS FROM OUR LIVES]: *(Warriors know that at any given moment they can drop anything from their lives that they choose; they can simply let things go; it is important for warriors to reduce to a minimum all things that are unnecessary in their lives in order to withstand the impact of their encounter with the nagual.)*

SELECTED REFERENCES: A Separate Reality - Page [43.7-43.8] (Then he explained that the allies...bringing out the worst in a person.) Journey to Ixtlan - Page [8.1-8.2] ("People hardly ever realize that we...all if we want to drop them.")
SEE ALSO: *LETTING-GO, PETTINESS-DROPPING*

DRUNK-APPEARING-[APPEARING TO BE DRUNK OR DIZZY]: *(Warriors know that technically, when the assemblage point moves, the individual is then asleep; to people in a state of normal awareness, warriors in such a condition appear to be a bit drunk or dizzy.)*

SELECTED REFERENCES: The Fire From Within - Page [250.5-251.1] (Don Juan left me alone in the...slumber, yet a *dreamer* is asleep.)
SEE ALSO: *ASSEMBLAGE-POINT-MOVE, SLEEP-AWAKE, SLEEP, SEEING-DRUNKARD-LOOK*

DRUNKARDS-[THE DRUNKARDS]-(TOP)

DUALISM-PERCEPTUAL-[PERCEPTUAL DUALISM]: SEE: PERCEPTUAL-DUALISM-[PERCEPTUAL DUALISM]

DUALISM-WARRIOR-[THE WARRIORS' DUALISM]: SEE: WARRIOR-DUALISM-[THE WARRIORS' DUALISM]

DUALITY-RECOLLECTION-WARRIOR-[THE RECOLLECTION OF THE WARRIORS' DUALITY]: SEE: WARRIOR-DUALITY-RECOLLECTION-[THE RECOLLECTION OF THE WARRIORS' DUALITY]

DULLING-OURSELVES-[DULLING OURSELVES]: *(Warriors know that the average man is taught to talk to himself; this internal dialogue is the*

means by which he dulls himself and keeps his assemblage point fixed in its habitual position.)

SELECTED REFERENCES: The Fire From Within - Page [148.9] ("The new seers say that when...assemblage point fixed on one spot.")

SEE ALSO: *INTERNAL-DIALOGUE, TALKING, ASSEMBLAGE-POINT-FIXATION*

DURESS-EXTREME-BENEFITS-WARRIOR-[THE BENEFITS OF EXTREME DURESS FOR WARRIORS]: SEE: WARRIOR-DURESS-EXTREME-BENEFITS-[THE BENEFITS OF EXTREME DURESS FOR WARRIORS]

DUTY-WARRIOR-[THE WARRIORS' DUTY]: SEE: WARRIOR-DUTY-[THE WARRIORS' DUTY]

DYNAMIC-INITIATIVE-[DYNAMIC INITIATIVE]: SEE: DREAMING-STAGES-[THE FOUR STAGES OF DREAMING]

DYNAMIC-VIGIL-[DYNAMIC VIGIL]: SEE: DREAMING-STAGES-[THE FOUR STAGES OF DREAMING]

DYNAMISM-WARRIOR-[THE WARRIORS' DYNAMISM]: SEE: WARRIOR-DYNAMISM-[THE WARRIORS' DYNAMISM]

E

EAGLE-[THE EAGLE]: *(Warriors know that the Eagle is the metaphorical name for the indescribable force which is the source of all sentient beings; the Eagle is the unknowable, a force which no human being can grasp; the power that governs the destiny of all living beings; the Eagle is not a literal "eagle", nor does it have anything to do with a literal eagle; the Eagle only manifests itself to seers as something which resembles an eagle of infinite proportions; the Eagle bestows awareness on all living creatures and re-absorbs that same enriched awareness after making sentient beings relinquish it at the moment of death; the Eagle is not God, but it is a power that reflects equally and at once on all living things; there is no way for man to pray to the Eagle, to ask favors or to hope for grace from the Eagle because the human part of the Eagle is to insignificant to move the whole; the inconceivable dissolving force in the universe which makes organisms live by lending them awareness and also makes them die by extracting their awareness; this force is seeking our life experience and when the warrior provides that force with a facsimile of his life experience through recapitulation, then the dissolving force lets the warrior go free to expand his capacity to perceive in the fullest sense possible.)*
SELECTED REFERENCES: **The Eagle's Gift - Page [172.8-173.6]** (The power that governs the destiny...too insignificant to move the whole.) **The Eagle's Gift - Page [243.6-243.7]** ("There is nothing gorgeous or peaceful...of awareness you ever had.") **The Fire From Within - Page [38.6-39.2]** (He said that the old seers,...awareness that is the Eagle's food.") **The Fire From Within - Page [40.2-42.8]** (I told him that I was...or it, a more accurate one.") **The Fire From Within - Page [44.4-44.7]** ("Genaro is the one who should...have been made half in fun.) **The Fire From Within - Page [45.1-45.4]** ("How did the old seers come...as there is of the Eagle.") **The Art of Dreaming - Page [149.6-149.9]** (Don Juan stated that the old...the confines of time and space.)
SEE ALSO: *UNKNOWABLE, GOD, INTENT, RECAPITULATION, WARRIOR-FREEDOM-TOTAL, EAGLE-(ALL)*

EAGLE-AWARENESS-BESTOWS-[THE EAGLE BESTOWS AWARENESS]: *(Warriors know that the Eagle bestows awareness by means of three giant bundles of emanations that run through the eight great bands.)*
SELECTED REFERENCES: **The Fire From Within - Page [159.3-160.1]** ("What makes those eight bands produce...it is either pink, peach, or amber.)
SEE ALSO: *EAGLE-EMANATIONS-BUNDLES, SEX-LUMINOUS-REALITY, EAGLE*

EAGLE-COMMANDS-[THE EAGLE'S COMMANDS]: *(The Eagle's emanations; the concept that the warriors' command can be heard and obeyed as if it were the Eagle's command; the essence of the mastery of intent; the detached manipulation of intent through sober commands, a manipulation that begins with a command given to oneself and ends when the command is repeated until it mysteriously becomes the Eagle's command.)*
SELECTED REFERENCES: **The Fire From Within - Page [42.9-43.1]** ("Seers who *see* the Eagle's...what they really are, commands.") **The Fire From Within - Page [74.1-74.4]** ("I don't mean to say that human...commands us to take it, that's all.") **The Fire From Within - Page [119.1-119.4]** ("The assemblage point of man appears...assemblage points and make them move.) **The Fire From Within - Page [123.4-123.6]** (He went on to say that...point shift is a genuine

triumph.) **The Fire From Within - Page [131.7]** ("The explanation is simplicity itself,"...became the Eagle's command.) **The Fire From Within - Page [133.2-133.5]** (Don Juan went on to express...command, our gift of magic.") **The Fire From Within - Page [259.9-260.1]** ("It will be a long time before...if it were the Eagle's command.") **The Fire From Within - Page [297.8-298.2]** ("In a moment, you're going to...the moment warriors reach inner silence.)
SEE ALSO: *EAGLE-EMANATIONS, INTENT-MASTERY, EAGLE, POWER-COMMANDS*

EAGLE-DESCRIPTION-HOW-WHY-[HOW AND WHY THE OLD SEERS CAME TO DESCRIBE THE EAGLE AND WHY THERE IS NO PAT VERSION OF THE EAGLE'S EMANATIONS]: (Warriors know that the old seers needed a minimal set of guidelines about the unknown for the purposes of instruction; they resolved that need with a sketchy description of the Eagle itself but not of its emanations; the emanations cannot be rendered in a language of comparisons; there is no pat version of the emanations as there is of the Eagle.)
SELECTED REFERENCES: **The Fire From Within - Page [45.1-45.4]** ("How did the old seers come...as there is of the Eagle.")
SEE ALSO: *EAGLE-EMANATIONS, UNKNOWABLE, SEER-OLD, EAGLE*

EAGLE-DICTUMS-FINALITY-[THE FINALITY OF THE EAGLE'S DICTUMS]: (Warriors know that the Eagle is real and final, and the force of the warriors' actions originates from this knowledge.)
SELECTED REFERENCES: **The Eagle's Gift - Page [211.4-211.5]** (Don Juan said that the force...the finality of the Eagle's dictums.)
SEE ALSO: *EAGLE*

*EAGLE-EMANATIONS-[THE EAGLE'S EMANATIONS]: (Warriors know that the Eagle's emanations are an immutable thing which engulfs everything that exists, both knowable and unknowable; a presence, a mass of sorts, a pressure that creates a dazzling sensation; an indescribable presence that must be witnessed because there is no way to describe what it is; a brilliant array of live compelling fibers, each of which is an infinity unto itself; the fabric of the luminous universe; the energetic essence of everything; the essence of the universe; incandescent threads that are conscious of themselves in a way impossible for the human mind to comprehend; energy fields which defy description; they resemble threads of light that exude awareness, they seem to be made out of light that is alive.)
SELECTED REFERENCES: **A Separate Reality - Page [23.2-23.6]** ("What's this other mode of seeing...changed in that luminous egg? What?") **A Separate Reality - Page [106.1-106.4]** (Don Juan then explained don Genaro's...to talk about something thoroughly unrelated.) **Tales of Power - Page [172.9-173.5]** ("When one is dealing with the nagual...or to peak into that infinity.") **Tales of Power - Page [222.8-223.1]** (Then my left eye image of don Juan...had a light of their own.) **The Fire From Within - Page [32.9-33.2]** (He explained that the mastery of...a universe of the Eagle's emanations.) **The Fire From Within - Page [40.3-41.5]** ("But what kind of a force...that no living creature can grasp.") **The Fire From Within - Page [43.2-43.9]** (Don Juan said that to see...after courting tremendous dangers.) **The Fire From Within - Page [45.2-46.4]** ("They needed a minimal set of...them is an eternity in itself.") **The Fire From Within - Page [49.8-50.6]** (The emanations inside and the emanations...web and thereby directs the pressure.) **The Fire From Within - Page [80.7-80.9]** ("What is that mysterious force...*will* of the Eagle's emanations, or *intent*.") **The Fire From Within - Page [105.1-105.2]** (They were given to me for...that immensity that is the Eagle's emanations.") **The Fire From Within - Page [108.2-108.5]** (He then began his explanation...with the corresponding emanations at large.) **The Fire From Within - Page [221.2-221.5]** (I would have gone on *seeing*...not interfere with my ordinary view.) **The Power of Silence - Page [xv.6-xv.9]** (Don Juan's instruction on the art...like a giant luminous egg.) **The Power of Silence - Page [101.6-101.8]** (Don Juan had explained that the...withstand the impact of that sight.) **The Art of Dreaming - Page [5.2-5.4]** (For such sorcerers, the most

significant act...for the human mind to comprehend.) **The Art of Dreaming - Page [16.2-16.5]** (Suddenly, I was looking or I...dreaming the filaments of the universe.)
    SEE ALSO: *EAGLE-COMMANDS, EAGLE, LINES-WORLD, EAGLE-EMANATIONS-(ALL)*

EAGLE-EMANATIONS-ALIGNING-ALL-[ALIGNING ALL THE EAGLE'S EMANATIONS INSIDE MAN'S COCOON AT ONCE]: SEE: EAGLE-EMANATIONS-LIGHTING-ALL-[LIGHTING UP ALL THE EAGLE'S EMANATIONS IN MAN'S COCOON AT ONCE], FIRE-WITHIN-[THE FIRE FROM WITHIN]

EAGLE-EMANATIONS-AWARENESS-[THE EAGLE'S EMANATIONS AND AWARENESS]: (Warriors know that the portion of emanations inside man's cocoon is there only for awareness; awareness is matching that portion of emanations with the same portion of emanations at large.)
    SELECTED REFERENCES: **The Fire From Within - Page [206.5-206.9]]** ("The unknown is not really inside...same portion of emanations at large.)
    SEE ALSO: *EAGLE-EMANATIONS, AWARENESS, ALIGNMENT, LUMINOUS-COCOON, EAGLE*

EAGLE-EMANATIONS-BANDS-AWARENESS-EIGHT-[THE EIGHT BANDS OF EMANATIONS THAT PRODUCE AWARENESS]: (Warriors know that there are eight bands of emanations which produce awareness; one of them produces all organic life and the other seven produce inorganic life.)
    SELECTED REFERENCES: **The Fire From Within - Page [158.6-159.9]** ("As you can understand, organic beings...of being amber, like clear honey.)
    SEE ALSO: *EAGLE-EMANATIONS, ORGANIC-LIFE, INORGANIC-LIFE, EAGLE, EAGLE-EMANATIONS-BANDS-GREAT*

EAGLE-EMANATIONS-BANDS-EARTH-FORTY-EIGHT-[THE FORTY-EIGHT BANDS OF EMANATIONS IN THE EARTH]: (Warriors know that there are forth-eight bands of emanations in the earth; eight of those bands produce awareness, both organic and inorganic; the other forty bands produce configurations of inanimate energy.)
    SELECTED REFERENCES: **The Fire From Within - Page [158.7-159.1]** ("Are there many of these great...are bands that generate only organization.) **The Fire From Within - Page [163.5]** ("The total world is made of the forty-eight bands," he said.)
    SEE ALSO: *FORTY-EIGHT, EAGLE-EMANATIONS, EAGLE, EAGLE-EMANATIONS-BANDS-GREAT*

*EAGLE-EMANATIONS-BANDS-GREAT-[THE GREAT BANDS OF THE EAGLE'S EMANATIONS]: (Warriors know that the great bands of the Eagle's emanations are the "clustered" structure of the Eagle's emanations; the forty-eight types of clusters or structures on the earth, eight of which produce awareness and forty of which generate only organization; bubbles or containers filled with emanations are formed on eight of these bands, one of which produces organic life and seven of which produce inorganic life.)
    SELECTED REFERENCES: **The Fire From Within - Page [157.6-161.9]** (He then told me that we were going...pink or peach or amber emanations.) **The Fire From Within - Page [164.5-164.8]** (He said that a true change...and consequently we perceive other worlds.")
    SEE ALSO: *EAGLE-EMANATIONS-MAN-BAND, PERCEPTION-BUBBLE EARTH, EAGLE-EMANATIONS-CLUSTERING, EAGLE*

EAGLE-EMANATIONS-BAND-MAN-[MAN'S BAND OF EMANATIONS]:

SEE: EAGLE-EMANATIONS-MAN-BAND-[MAN'S BAND OF EMANATIONS]

EAGLE-EMANATIONS-BANDS-ORGANIZATION-FORTY-[THE FORTY BANDS OF EMANATIONS THAT GENERATE ONLY ORGANIZATION]: (*Warriors know that there are forty bands of the Eagle's emanations that generate only organization; the product of those forty great bands is not awareness at all but a configuration of inanimate energy.*)
    SELECTED REFERENCES: **The Fire From Within - Page [158.9-159.1]** ("No, not at all. The old...are bands that generate only organization.) **The Fire From Within - Page [163.1-163.3]** (He explained next that the product...from the energy of the encased emanations.)
    SEE ALSO: *EAGLE-EMANATIONS, EAGLE, EAGLE-EMANATIONS-BANDS-GREAT*

EAGLE-EMANATIONS-BANDS-NORMAL-PERCEPTION-TWO-[THE TWO BANDS OF EMANATIONS THAT MAKE UP THE WORLD OF NORMAL PERCEPTION]: (*Warriors know that the world the assemblage point assembles for normal perception is made up of two bands; one is the organic band and the other is a band of only structure.*)
    SELECTED REFERENCES: **The Fire From Within - Page [163.5-163.6]** ("The total world is made of...of the world we normally perceive.")
    SEE ALSO: *PERCEPTION-NORMAL-SYSTEM, EAGLE, EAGLE-EMANATIONS-BANDS-GREAT*

EAGLE-EMANATIONS-BUNDLES-[THE BUNDLES OF THE EAGLE'S EMANATIONS]: (*Warriors know that the Eagle bestows awareness by means of three giant bundles of emanations which run through the eight great bands; these bundles are quite peculiar, because they make seers feel a hue; one bundle gives a feeling of beige-pink, one peach and one clear amber; the three bundles crisscross the eight bands; in the organic band, the pink bundle belongs mainly to plants, the peach bundle mostly to insects, and the amber band to man and other animals.*)
    SELECTED REFERENCES: **The Fire From Within - Page [159.3-161.2]** ("What makes those eight bands produce...each of the seven great bands.")
    SEE ALSO: *EAGLE-EMANATIONS, EAGLE, EAGLE-EMANATIONS-BANDS-GREAT, AWARENESS-COLOR*

EAGLE-EMANATIONS-CLUSTERING-[THE CLUSTERING OF THE EAGLE'S EMANATIONS]: (*Warriors know that a clustering characteristic of the assemblage point is responsible for the fact that human beings perceive the emanations dealt with by the first attention in terms of groups or clusters; the assemblage point radiates a glow that groups together bundles of encased emanations and aligns them as bundles with the emanations at large; the assemblage point is like a luminous magnet that picks emanations and groups them together for perception as it moves within the bounds of man's band of emanations; clustering is limited to the huge portion of emanations characterized by seers as the "known" and the "unknown"; the "unknowable", on the other hand, is an eternity where our assemblage point has no way of clustering anything.*)
    SELECTED REFERENCES: **Tales of Power - Page [93.7-93.8]** ("That night that you met the...of luminous fibers that have awareness.) **Tales of Power - Page [272.5]** (The second time you experienced...You are a cluster.) **Tales of Power - Page [273.3-273.7]** ("There is no way to refer to...cluster the bubble of perception.) **Tales of Power - Page [276.2]** ("Those leaps were only the beginning...are a nameless cluster of feelings.) **Tales of Power - Page [278.4]** ("Now you should sit on Genaro's...that binds that cluster of feelings.) **The Fire From Within - Page**

[123.6-124.5] (Don Juan said that the assemblage...unknown in a new light.) **The Fire From Within - Page [133.4-133.5]** ("The force of the emanations at large...is our command, our gift of magic.") **The Fire From Within - Page [157.8]** ("The Eagle's emanations are always...really bands, but the name stuck.) **The Fire From Within - Page [259.4-259.5]** ("The mold of man is a...only inside the cocoon of man.) **The Power of Silence - Page [102.1]** (Extraordinary perception, *seeing*, occurs when by...*see* the energy fields themselves.)
SEE ALSO: *SKIMMINGS, EAGLE*

EAGLE-EMANATIONS-DESCRIPTION-NO-PAT-[WHY THERE IS NO PAT VERSION OF THE EAGLE'S EMANATIONS]: SEE: EAGLE-DESCRIPTION-HOW-WHY [HOW AND WHY THE OLD SEERS CAME TO DESCRIBE THE EAGLE AND WHY THERE IS NO PAT VERSION OF THE EAGLE'S EMANATIONS]

EAGLE-EMANATIONS-DORMANT-[THE DORMANT PORTION OF THE EAGLE'S EMANATIONS]: (Warriors know that there is a large portion of the Eagle's emanations trapped inside man's cocoon that is not utilized as part of the average man's normal perception; normally these emanations lie dormant for a lifetime; at the moment of death all these emanations suddenly become aligned, producing an inconceivable force that floods the warriors' being; these disregarded emanations are known as the left side awareness, the nagual, the other world, the unknown, the second attention.)
SELECTED REFERENCES: **The Fire From Within - Page [109.8-110.1]** (The emphasized emanations compose a large...world, the unknown, the second attention.) **The Fire From Within - Page [122.2-122.4]** ("The assemblage point of man is located...on the surface of the cocoon.") **The Fire From Within - Page [254.4-254.7]** (He said that the energy locked...except to escape through the gap.)
SEE ALSO: *EAGLE-EMANATIONS, EAGLE-EMANATIONS-EMPHASIZED, EAGLE-EMANATIONS-MAN-BAND, AWARENESS-LEFT, NAGUAL, UNKNOWN, ATTENTION-SECOND, EAGLE, FORCE-EAGLE-EMANATIONS-DORMANT*

EAGLE-EMANATIONS-EARTH-[THE EMANATIONS OF THE EARTH]: (Warriors know that the first attention is hooked to the emanations of the earth in contrast to the second attention which is hooked to the emanations of the universe.)
SELECTED REFERENCES: **The Eagle's Gift - Page [262.6-262.7]** (During one of the dreaming sessions...to the emanations of the universe.)
SEE ALSO: *EAGLE-EMANATIONS, ATTENTION-FIRST, EARTH, EAGLE*

EAGLE-EMANATIONS-EMPHASIZED-[THE EMPHASIZED EMANATIONS]: (Warriors know that in order for the first attention to bring into focus the world we perceive, it has to emphasize certain emanations from man's band of emanations; these emphasized emanations are the tonal and represent barely on tenth of the emanations encased inside man's cocoon; the emphasized emanations are the first attention, the known, the right-side awareness, the daily world, and compose a large portion of man's band of awareness [but a small portion of the total spectrum of emanations present inside man's cocoon]; the disregarded emanations represent man's left-side awareness, the unknown, the nagual, the other world, the second attention; the process of emphasizing certain emanations was discovered and practiced by the old seers through a technique known as the nagual's blow; this technique involves "pushing" the emphasis of the emanations away from the usual ones and making it shift to the neighboring dormant emanations.)

SELECTED REFERENCES: The Fire From Within - Page [109.6-110.2] (Don Juan explained that in order...and practiced by the old seers.) **The Fire From Within - Page [254.4-254.5]** (He said that the energy locked within...the emanations encased in man's cocoon.)
SEE ALSO: *EAGLE-EMANATIONS, EAGLE-EMANATIONS-MAN-BAND, TONAL, ATTENTION-FIRST, REALITY-INTERPRETATION, REASON, AWARENESS-RIGHT, KNOWN, UNKNOWN, NAGUAL, ATTENTION-SECOND, AWARENESS-LEFT, NAGUAL-BLOW, EAGLE, WARRIOR-EMPHASIS*

EAGLE-EMANATIONS-EMPLOYING-[EMPLOYING AND INTERPRETING THE EAGLE'S EMANATIONS]: *(Warriors know that the Eagle's emanations have a compelling power and all living beings are forced to employ them without ever knowing what they are; human beings employ the emanations and interpret them as reality.)*

SELECTED REFERENCES: The Fire From Within - Page [43.5-43.9] (He went on to say that...hard way - after courting tremendous dangers.")
SEE ALSO: *EAGLE-EMANATIONS, REALITY-INTERPRETATION, PERCEPTION, EAGLE*

EAGLE-EMANATIONS-ENCOUNTER-[AN ENCOUNTER WITH THE EAGLE'S EMANATIONS]-(TOP)

EAGLE-EMANATIONS-INORGANIC-LIFE-[THE IMMEASURABLE CLUSTERS OF EMANATIONS THAT PRODUCE INORGANIC LIFE]: *(Warriors know that there are seven bands of the Eagle's emanations that produce inorganic awareness.)*

SELECTED REFERENCES: The Fire From Within - Page [158.9-159.2] ("Does that mean that there are...most juicy, luscious fruit there is.")
SEE ALSO: *EAGLE-EMANATIONS, INORGANIC-BEINGS, INORGANIC-LIFE, EAGLE-EMANATIONS-BANDS-GREAT*

EAGLE-EMANATIONS-LARGE-AT-[THE EMANATIONS AT LARGE]: *(Warriors know that the emanations at large are the portion of the Eagle's emanations outside man's cocoon; these emanations are immense and are known as the unknowable.)*

SELECTED REFERENCES: The Fire From Within - Page [50.1-50.2] (When seers *see* perception, they witness...the awareness of every specific being.) **The Fire From Within - Page [57.4]** ("The degree of awareness of every...the emanations at large carry it.") **The Fire From Within - Page [108.2-108.5]** (He then began his explanation...with the corresponding emanations at large.) **The Fire From Within - Page [133.4-133.5]** ("The force of the emanations at large...is our command, our gift of magic.") **The Fire From Within - Page [206.8-207.3]** (Don Juan restated over and over...is perceived and becomes the known.)
SEE ALSO: *UNKNOWABLE, EAGLE-EMANATIONS, EAGLE*

EAGLE-EMANATIONS-LARGE-FORCE-[THE FORCE OF THE EMANATIONS AT LARGE]: *(Warriors know that the force of the emanations at large is the rolling force, the life-giver and enhancer of awareness.)*

SELECTED REFERENCES: The Fire From Within - Page [227.6-227.8] (I asked him a lot of...of life-giver and enhancer of awareness.)
SEE ALSO: *ROLLING-FORCE, FORCE-CIRCULAR, EAGLE-EMANATIONS-LARGE-AT, EAGLE*

EAGLE-EMANATIONS-LIGHTING-ALL-[LIGHTING UP ALL THE EAGLE'S EMANATIONS IN MAN'S COCOON AT ONCE]: *(Warriors know that when they burn with the force of alignment, with the fire from within, they light up all the emanations inside the luminous cocoon at once.)*

SELECTED REFERENCES: **The Fire From Within - Page [183.9-184.1]** ("At any rate, the job of...all be gone in an instant.") **The Fire From Within - Page [299.3-299.5]** (He explained that the new seers...all the emanations inside the cocoon at once.)
SEE ALSO: *FIRE-WITHIN, EAGLE-EMANATIONS, EAGLE-GIFT*

EAGLE-EMANATIONS-MAN-BAND-[MAN'S BAND OF EMANATIONS]:
(Warriors know that man's band of emanations is a vertical "band" of the Eagle's emanations located on the extreme right hand side of man's luminous cocoon; a thin bundle of luminous filaments inside the luminous egg; a bundle called the band of man or the purely human aspect of the universe's energy.)

SELECTED REFERENCES: **The Fire From Within - Page [50.8-51.1]** (He explained that the old seers...of the cocoon inward across its width.) **The Fire From Within - Page [109.6-110.1]** (Don Juan explained that in order...the unknown, the second attention.) **The Fire From Within - Page [121.3-123.2]** (He remarked that my flaw was my emotional...wherever it ends up is always virgin ground.) **The Fire From Within - Page [134.4-135.2]** (He stopped talking and looked at me....complete view of that human junk pile.") **The Fire From Within - Page [206.8-207.3]** (Don Juan restated over and over...unknown is perceived and becomes the known.) **The Fire From Within - Page [220.6-220.9]** (That afternoon, I *saw* ten luminous beings...that it was the assemblage point.) **The Fire From Within - Page [251.2-251.6]** ("Right at this juncture is where the new...is the *dreaming body of* the new seers.) **The Fire From Within - Page [293.2-293.3]** ("It's the easiest world to assemble,"...make as they approach a crucial position.") **The Art of Dreaming - Page [217.4-217.5]** (Don Juan further explained that most...purely human aspect of the universe's energy.)
SEE ALSO: *LUMINOUS-COCOON, EAGLE-EMANATIONS, ASSEMBLAGE-POINT, EAGLE, CHEESES-ANALOGY, EAGLE-EMANATIONS-MAN-BAND-(ALL)*

EAGLE-EMANATIONS-MAN-BAND-EDGES-[THE EDGES OF MAN'S BAND OF EMANATIONS]: *(Warriors know that the edges of man's band of emanations are sometimes called the human julkpile; the right edge has endless visions of physical activity, violence, killing and sensuality; the left edge has visions of spirituality, religion and God; this area of man's band of emanations is also sometimes known as the preamble to the unknown .)*

SELECTED REFERENCES: **The Fire From Within - Page [134.5-135.2]** ("That's exactly what I meant,"...complete view of that human junkpile.") **The Fire From Within - Page [251.2-251.6]** ("Right at this juncture is where...*dreaming body* of the new seers.)
SEE ALSO: *HUMAN-JUNKPILE, EAGLE-EMANATIONS-MAN-BAND, PREAMBLE-UNKNOWN, EAGLE*

EAGLE-EMANATIONS-MAN-BAND-LEFT-EDGE-[THE LEFT EDGE OF MAN'S BAND OF EMANATIONS]: *(Warriors know that on the left edge of man's band of emanations they will find visions of spirituality, religion and God.)*

SELECTED REFERENCES: **The Fire From Within - Page [134.5-135.2]** ("That's exactly what I meant,"...complete view of that human junkpile.") **The Fire From Within - Page [251.2-251.6]** ("Right at this juncture is where...*dreaming body* of the new seers.)
SEE ALSO: *HUMAN-JUNKPILE, DREAMING-BODY, EAGLE, GOD*

EAGLE-EMANATIONS-MAN-BAND-MIDSECTION-[THE MIDSECTION OF MAN'S BAND OF EMANATIONS]: *(Warriors know that when the assemblage point moves into the midsection of man's band of emanations, those moves are not coupled with slumber, yet the dreamer is asleep; warriors also know that the new seers focus the movement of their assemblage points along this midsection in order to create their impersonal dreaming bodies; this type of shift is characterized by a slight vulnerability to emotions such as fear and doubt, and at a certain depth, the dreamer who is shifting along the midsection becomes a blob of light.)*

SELECTED REFERENCES: The Fire From Within - Page [251.2-251.6] ("Right at this juncture is where...*dreaming body* of the new seers.)
SEE ALSO: *HUMAN-JUNKPILE, DREAMING-BODY-NEW-SEER, SLEEP, EAGLE*

EAGLE-EMANATIONS-MAN-BAND-OUTSIDE-[THE EMANATIONS OUTSIDE MAN'S BAND]: SEE: UNKNOWN-IMMEASURABLE-[THE IMMEASURABLE UNKNOWN

EAGLE-EMANATIONS-MAN-BAND-RIGHT-EDGE-[THE RIGHT EDGE OF MAN'S BAND OF EMANATIONS]: (Warriors know that the right edge of man's band of emanations is characterized by an emphasis on the physical side of life; it is on this edge that the old seers focused their assemblage points in order to create their bizarre dreaming bodies; on the right edge are endless visions of physical activity, violence, killing, and sensuality.)

SELECTED REFERENCES: The Fire From Within - Page [134.5-135.2] ("That's exactly what I meant,"...complete view of that human junkpile.") **The Fire From Within - Page [251.2-251.6]** ("Right at this juncture is where...*dreaming body* of the new seers.)
SEE ALSO: *HUMAN-JUNKPILE, DREAMING-BODY, DREAMING-BODY-TOLTECS, EAGLE*

EAGLE-EMANATIONS-MAN-SEEING-[SEEING MAN'S BAND OF EMANATIONS]-(TOP)

EAGLE-EMANATIONS-MERGING-[THE MERGING OF THE EAGLE'S EMANATIONS]: (Warriors know that the emanations at large are made to fixate and merge with the emanations inside us; the trick of awareness is to allow the merging of this awareness to the greatest degree possible.)

SELECTED REFERENCES: The Fire From Within - Page [56.9-57.2] (He said that seers maintain, naturally...are - fluid, forever in motion, eternal.) **The Fire From Within - Page [74.5-74.7]** ("The emanations inside the cocoon of...scarabs' emanations expanding to great size.)
SEE ALSO: *EAGLE-EMANATIONS, EAGLE-EMANATIONS-LARGE-AT, AWARENESS-TRICK, EAGLE*

EAGLE-EMANATIONS-NOT-WORLD-FORTY-SIX-[THE FORTY-SIX BANDS OF THE EAGLE'S EMANATIONS THAT ARE NOT PART OF THE WORLD WE NORMALLY PERCEIVE]: (Warriors know that there are forty six bands of the Eagle's emanations that are not part of the world which we normally perceive.)

SELECTED REFERENCES: The Fire From Within - Page [163.5-163.6] ("The total world is made of...of the world we normally perceive.")
SEE ALSO: *EAGLE-EMANATIONS-BANDS-NORMAL-PERCEPTION-TWO, EAGLE*

EAGLE-EMANATIONS-ONE-TENTH-[THE GROUP OF EMANATIONS USED FOR NORMAL PERCEPTION IS ONE TENTH OF THE TOTAL EMANATIONS ENCASED WITH IN THE COCOON OF MAN: SEE: EAGLE-EMANATIONS-EMPHASIZED-[THE EMPHASIZED EMANATIONS]

EAGLE-EMANATIONS-ORGANIC-LIFE-[THE IMMEASURABLE CLUSTER OF EMANATIONS THAT PRODUCES ORGANIC LIFE]: (Warriors know that the emanations of the organic band are "fluffy" and have a unique transparency and light of their own.)

SELECTED REFERENCES: The Fire From Within - Page [157.8-158.8] ("For instance, there is an immeasurable...Organic life is one of them.")

SEE ALSO: EAGLE-EMANATIONS-GREAT-BANDS, EAGLE

EAGLE-EMANATIONS-ORGANISM-RANGE-[THE RANGE OF EMANATIONS WHICH EACH ORGANISM CAN GRASP]: *(Warriors know that every individual species of organism has a definite range of the Eagle's emanations which it has been designed to grasp; these specific emanations exert great pressure on the organisms, and through that pressure the organisms construct their perceivable world.)*

SELECTED REFERENCES: **The Fire From Within** - Page **[43.5-43.7]** (He went on to say that...hard way - pressure organisms construct their perceivable world.)

SEE ALSO: *ORGANIC-LIFE, INORGANIC-LIFE, EAGLE-EMANATIONS, EAGLE*

EAGLE-EMANATIONS-PERCEPTION-NORMAL-[THE EMANATIONS USED FOR NORMAL PERCEPTION]: SEE: EAGLE-EMANATIONS-EMPHASIZED-[THE EMPHASIZED EMANATIONS]

EAGLE-EMANATIONS-POWER-COMPELLING-[THE COMPELLING POWER OF THE EAGLE'S EMANATIONS]: SEE: EAGLE-EMANATIONS-EMPLOYING-[EMPLOYING AND INTERPRETING THE EAGLE'S EMANATIONS]

EAGLE-EMANATIONS-PRESSURE-[THE PRESSURE OF THE EAGLE'S EMANATIONS]: *(Warriors know that the pressure of the Eagle's emanations is responsible for awareness; awareness is the result of the intrusion of intent.)*

SELECTED REFERENCES: **The Fire From Within** - Page **[50.3-50.6]** (Seers can also see how the emanations...web and thereby directs the pressure.) **The Fire From Within** - Page **[56.4-57.4]** (After dinner don Juan went on...the emanations at large carry it.") **The Fire From Within** - Page **[72.6-72.7]** (He reiterated that awareness begins with..."what stops death is awareness.") **The Fire From Within** - Page **[108.2-108.5]** (He then began his explanation...with the corresponding emanations at large.) **The Fire From Within** - Page **[133.4-133.5]** ("The force of the emanations at large...is our command, our gift of magic.") **The Fire From Within** - Page **[145.8-145.9]** ("Without enough energy, the force of...never take place under ordinary circumstances.")

SEE ALSO: *AWARENESS-TRUTH-EIGHTH, INTENT, EAGLE-EMANATIONS, EAGLE*

EAGLE-EMANATIONS-QUIETING-[THE QUIETING OF THE EAGLES EMANATIONS]: *(Warriors know that all organic beings except man quiet down their trapped emanations so that they can align themselves with the matching emanations outside the luminous cocoon; human beings do not do this because the first attention intervenes and takes an inventory of the emanations inside the cocoon; human beings actually quiet down their emanations but not for the purpose of matching them with the emanations outside; human beings quiet their emanations and reflect on them.)*

SELECTED REFERENCES: **The Fire From Within** - Page **[73.6-74.7]** (Don Juan continued his explanation and...them. The emanations focus on themselves.")

SEE ALSO: *INVENTORY, ATTENTION-FIRST, ALIGNMENT, EAGLE, SELF-REFLECTION*

EAGLE-EMANATIONS-RECALL-CONCENTRATION-TOTAL-[THE EMANATIONS OF TOTAL RECALL AND CONCENTRATION: *(Warriors know that when they align certain emanations they can concentrate and recall things with their totality.)*

SELECTED REFERENCES: **The Fire From Within** - Page **[157.4-157.6]** (Days later, in his house in...of total concentration and total recall.)

SEE ALSO: RECOLLECTION-SORCERER, EAGLE-EMANATIONS

EAGLE-EMANATIONS-RECALL-TOTAL-[THE TOTAL RECALL OF THE EAGLE'S EMANATIONS]: SEE: FIRE-WITHIN-[THE FIRE FROM WITHIN]

EAGLE-EMANATIONS-SAME-SELECT-REASONS-[THE REASONS WHY HUMAN BEINGS REPEATEDLY SELECT THE SAME EMANATIONS FOR PERCEIVING]: (*Warriors know that there are two reasons why human beings repeatedly select the same emanations for perceiving; the first and most important reason is that those emanations are perceivable and the second is that our assemblage points select and prepare those emanations for being used.*)
SELECTED REFERENCES: The Fire From Within - Page [117.9-118.1] (He explained that human beings repeatedly...prepare those emanations for being used.)
SEE ALSO: EAGLE-EMANATIONS, ASSEMBLAGE-POINT, PERCEPTION, AWARENESS-RIGHT, ATTENTION-TONAL, ATTENTION-FIRST, ASSEMBLAGE-POINT-POSITION-NORMAL, EAGLE

*EAGLE-EMANATIONS-SEEING-[SEEING THE EAGLE'S EMANATIONS]: (*Warriors know that it is very dangerous to "see" the Eagle's emanations; gazing at those emanations is something that warriors must do under the protection of dreaming; the mold of man is the only portion of the Eagle's emanations that seers can "see" without any danger to themselves; when a crucial number of emanations are lit up as part of the warriors' extraordinary perception, they are able to "see" the emanations themselves.*)
SELECTED REFERENCES: A Separate Reality - Page [106.1-106.4] (Don Juan then explained don Genaro's...to talk about something thoroughly unrelated.) The Fire From Within - Page [43.2-43.9] (Don Juan said that to see...after courting tremendous dangers.") The Fire From Within - Page [172.4-172.6] (The new seers deemed it imperative...way to move the assemblage point.) The Fire From Within - Page [173.4-173.5] (He remarked that there is hardly...help them move their assemblage points.) The Fire From Within - Page [181.5-181.7] (Don Juan said that there is...stood by ready to end their *seeing*.) The Fire From Within - Page [218.5] ("I want you to try *seeing*...you *see* the cocoon of man.") The Fire From Within - Page [222.2-222.4] ("Were those fibers I *saw* the...longer it would have blasted you.") The Fire From Within - Page [258.8-259.5] (Don Juan reminded me that he...directly without any danger to themselves.") The Power of Silence - Page [97.5-98.9] (By the time it became completely dark...vision and plunged me into darkness.) The Power of Silence - Page [101.5-101.6] (I had just *seen* the Eagle's...therefore I had to be *dreaming*.) The Power of Silence - Page [102.1-102.2] (Extraordinary perception, *seeing*, occurs when...to *see* the energy fields themselves.)
SEE ALSO: DREAMING-ART, SEEING, EAGLE-EMANATIONS, FLOW-OF-THINGS-SEEING, PERCEPTION-EXTRAORDINARY, EAGLE

EAGLE-EMANATIONS-STRUGGLE-DIE-[THE EMANATIONS INSIDE THE LUMINOUS COCOON ARE STRUGGLING TO DIE]: SEE: AWARENESS-DEATH-STOPS [AWARENESS STOPS DEATH]

EAGLE-EMANATIONS-UNIVERSE-[THE EMANATIONS OF THE UNIVERSE]: (*Warriors know that the second attention is hooked to the emanations of the universe in contrast to the first attention which is hooked to the emanations of the earth.*)
SELECTED REFERENCES: The Eagle's Gift - Page [262.6-262.7] (During one of the dreaming sessions...to the emanations of the universe.)
SEE ALSO: EAGLE-EMANATIONS, ATTENTION-SECOND, EAGLE, ATTENTION-FIRST, EARTH

EAGLE-GIFT-[THE EAGLE'S GIFT]: (Warriors know that the Eagle's gift is an opportunity provided by the Eagle to all living beings, an opportunity to keep the flame of awareness; every living being has been granted the power, if it so desires, to disobey the summons to die and be consumed; every living being has been granted the power to seek an opening to freedom and go through it; the opportunity warriors have to enter into the third attention while retaining the life-force as a reward for their attainment; the Eagle's gift to man is contingent on the creation of a surrogate awareness which the Eagle will accept in lieu of the warriors' own awareness; total freedom, total awareness is the Eagle's gift to man.)

SELECTED REFERENCES: The Eagle's Gift - Page [173.6-173.8] (The Eagle, although it is not moved...in order to perpetuate awareness.) The Eagle's Gift - Page [178.8-179.3] (Don Juan explained that the rule...exists such an awareness at all.) The Eagle's Gift - Page [181.4-181.6] (According to don Juan, he and...a chance to have a chance.) The Eagle's Gift - Page [292.1-292.3] (Florinda said that Soledad had been...because I had no more energy.) The Eagle's Gift - Page [303.7-303.8] (The next thing I knew...Eagle would let us go through.) The Eagle's Gift - Page [307.5-307.6] (*I am already given to the...past the Eagle to be free.*) The Fire From Within - Page [67.5-67.7] (Don Juan expressed his awe for the...like a reward for an attainment.) The Fire From Within - Page [227.4-227.6] (He said that the same force can...is their total and instantaneous disintegration.) The Fire From Within - Page [299.5-299.7] ("The new seers burn with the force...gift, is to have sufficient energy.") The Fire From Within - Page [300.4] (So far, it is as if...to accept the Eagle's gift ourselves.) The Power of Silence - Page [192.4-192.6] ("I died in that field," he said...to go back and try again.)

SEE ALSO: FREEDOM-TOTAL, AWARENESS-TOTAL, ATTENTION-THIRD, FIRE-WITHIN, EAGLE, POWER-PROMISE, AWARENESS-SURROGATE

EAGLE-GLIMPSING-[GLIMPSING THE EAGLE]-(TOP)

EAGLE-MAN-[THE EAGLE AND THE FAINT REFLECTION OF MAN]:
(Warriors know that it is possible to find in the Eagle the faint reflection of man; the human part of the Eagle is too insignificant to move the whole; the Eagle does not care about man's actions and yet it provides him with a passageway to freedom; because of the Eagle's lack of concern for the individual warrior, warriors have to make sure that their chances for freedom are enhanced, perhaps by their own dedication and impeccability.)

SELECTED REFERENCES: The Eagle's Gift - Page [173.4-173.5] (The Eagle, that power that governs...too insignificant to move the whole.) The Eagle's Gift - Page [178.5-178.8] (I had confronted don Juan with the...the form of a governing body.) The Eagle's Gift - Page [181.1-181.4] (He said that there are two types...enhanced, perhaps by my own dedication.)

SEE ALSO: EAGLE, WARRIOR-PRAYER, WARRIOR-IMPECCABILITY, GOD

EAGLE-METAPHOR-LAXNESS-[THE LAXNESS OF THE METAPHOR OF THE EAGLE]: *(Warriors know that there is a definite laxness in the description of the Eagle as something which devours all living beings at the moment of death; a more abstract description would be much more appropriate for such an incomprehensible force.)*

SELECTED REFERENCES: The Fire From Within - Page [42.2-42.8] ("Look at what some seers have done...for it, a more accurate one.") The Fire From Within - Page [44.4-44.7] ("Genaro is the one who should...it literally, and that terrified me.)

SEE ALSO: EAGLE, SEER-MISERABLE, HUMAN-CONDITION

EAGLE-MIRRORING-[MIRRORING THE EAGLE]: *(Warriors know that their apparent control is only an illusion created by the Eagle; the actions of impeccable warriors are merely their humble attempts to mirror the Eagle.)*

SELECTED REFERENCES: The Eagle's Gift - Page [211.2-211.3] (Don Juan told us that at...humble attempt to mirror the Eagle.)

SEE ALSO: *WARRIOR-CONTROL, WARRIOR-IMPECCABILITY, EAGLE, RULE, WARRIOR-HUMBLENESS*

EAGLE-WITHSTANDING-[WITHSTANDING THE EAGLE'S PRESENCE]: (*Warriors know that the key to withstanding the presence of the Eagle is the potency of their intent; without intent, warriors have nothing.*)

SELECTED REFERENCES: **The Eagle's Gift** - Page [243.6-244.2] ("There is nothing gorgeous or peaceful...but that he was not around.)

SEE ALSO: *INTENT, EAGLE, EAGLE-GLIMPSING-(TOP)*

EARS-RELIEVE-BURDEN-EYES-[THE EARS RELIEVE THE BURDEN ON THE EYES]: (*Warriors know that the ears can relieve some of the burden from the eyes; in certain situations of darkness and quietude the eyes become subsidiary to the ears.*)

SELECTED REFERENCES: **A Separate Reality** - Page [219.1-219.2] ("First of all you must use...the sounds of the world.") **The Eagle's Gift** - Page [236.6-236.8] (His contention was that perception suffers...eyes become subsidiary to the ears.)

SEE ALSO: *EYES, PERCEPTION-QUIETUDE-DARKNESS, WARRIOR-HEARING, WORLD-SOUNDS-OF*

EARTH-[EARTH]: (*Warriors know the earth is an enormous sentient being; a lovely, nurturing being, alive to its last recesses; the earth understands, soothes and cures the warrior; the earth is a magnificent being that teaches warriors freedom and liberates their spirit; warriors know that they can bury themselves in the earth to gain enlightenment and power; warriors consider the earth to be the ultimate source of everything we are.*)

SELECTED REFERENCES: **Journey to Ixtlan** - Page [106.1-108.4] (I examined the rock and was wondering..."For enlightenment and for power.") **Journey to Ixtlan** - Page [110.8-110.9] (He sat cross-legged and told me...weep with self-pity," he said.) **Journey to Ixtlan** - Page [191.4-191.5] ("Can I do that now...let the earth absorb its heaviness.") **Tales of Power** - Page [270.3-270.5] (Don Juan walked me slowly, pushing down...earth had again consolidated my form.) **Tales of Power** - Page [291.3-291.5] ("It's almost time for us to...I will show you now.") **Tales of Power** - Page [292.4-293.1] ("Genaro's love is the world," he...for it, it taught me freedom.") **Tales of Power** - Page [293.9-294.3] ("The antidote that kills that poison...only then does it make sense.) **The Second Ring of Power** - Page [211.5-211.6] (In order to calm myself down...the warmth and protection of the earth.) **The Eagle's Gift** - Page [11.8-12.3] ("What happened to you, Gorda, after...she could only get better. Which she did.") **The Eagle's Gift** - Page [26.1-26.2] (He *saw* the phantoms and pulled the...squatted around waiting for their chance.) **The Fire From Within** - Page [158.7-159.4] ("Are there many of these great bands?"...through its emanations," he replied.) **The Fire From Within** - Page [163.4] ("You must bear in mind that everything...containers of inorganic beings at all.") **The Fire From Within** - Page [203.5-204.2] ("I've been telling you all along...earth is indeed our ultimate source.) **The Fire From Within** - Page [205.8-206.3] (He explained that what he called...allows them to enter unimaginable worlds.) **The Fire From Within** - Page [236.3-237.1] (Don Juan said that those seers...in the spirit of defying it.") **The Fire From Within** - Page [237.5-237.9] (Don Juan remarked how easy it...elongate those periods to cover millennia.) **The Fire From Within** - Page [289.6-289.8] ("Where will I be don Juan...you won't be in this world.") **The Power of Silence** - Page [100.6-101.1] (Don Juan asked me to pay...until it reached a lull of perception.)

SEE ALSO: *EARTH-BOOST, CAVES, EARTH-(ALL)*

EARTH-AWARENESS-SUPREME-[THE SUPREME AWARENESS OF THE EARTH]: (*Warriors know that it is the supreme awareness of the earth that makes it possible for human beings to access other great bands of awareness.*)

SELECTED REFERENCES: **The Fire From Within** - Page [213.9-214.6] ("There's one thing you haven't understood...the earth's boost is the key.)

SEE ALSO: *EARTH, EARTH-BOOST, EAGLE-EMANATIONS-BANDS-GREAT*

*EARTH-BOOST-[THE EARTH'S BOOST]: (Warriors know that the earth's boost is a force which warriors can obtain from the earth itself; the force of alignment of only the amber emanations; a boost which heightens awareness to unthinkable degrees; a blast of unlimited consciousness; total freedom; the earth's boost is an impulse that comes from the awareness of the earth itself at the instant in which the emanations inside the warriors' cocoon are aligned with the appropriate emanations inside the earth's cocoon; the main thing warriors learn through the earth's boost is a lesson about alignment; only when a state of total silence is attained can warriors use the boost from the earth; in order to withstand the impact of the earth's boost, warriors must be impeccable.)

SELECTED REFERENCES: The Second Ring of Power - Page [276.4-277.2] ("No," la Gorda replied. "Dreaming takes too...fingers clawed in an upright position.) The Fire From Within - Page [205.8-205.9] (He explained that what he called...appropriate emanations inside the earth's cocoon.) The Fire From Within - Page [212.2-212.3] ("And what do you think was...the same time I said it to myself.) The Fire From Within - Page [213.2-213.7] ("I mean that when man's assemblage...of individual existence don't go together.) The Fire From Within - Page [214.3-214.5] (When they had quieted down...the earth's boost is the key.) The Fire From Within - Page [216.8-216.9] ("When the assemblage point assembles a...new alignment makes the world vanish.) The Fire From Within - Page [237.6-237.8] (Don Juan remarked how easy it...ceaseless strikes of the rolling force.) The Fire From Within - Page [249.3-249.4] (I asked him about the difference...which they call total freedom.) The Fire From Within - Page [290.2-290.3] (He said that I could not as...to serve me as a launcher.) The Art of Dreaming - Page [32.2-32.3] ("What about the other way you...and off it goes with them.")

SEE ALSO: EARTH, TUMBLER-BOOST

EARTH-BOOST-LOOKING-SEEING-[THE THREE WAYS THE ENERGY BODY DEALS WITH ENERGY IN DREAMING]: SEE: ENERGY-BODY-DREAMING-[THE THREE WAYS THE ENERGY BODY DEALS WITH ENERGY IN DREAMING]

*EARTH-DOORS-MAGIC-KEY-[THE MAGIC KEY TO THE EARTH'S DOORS]: (Warriors know that the magic key that opens the earth's doors is made of internal silence and anything that shines.")

SELECTED REFERENCES: The Fire From Within - Page [204.8-205.9] (He pointed to the mountain range...appropriate emanations inside the earth's cocoon.)

SEE ALSO: EARTH, INNER-SILENCE, EARTH-BOOST

EARTH-EMBRACE-[THE EMBRACE OF THE EARTH]-(TOP): SEE: GENARO-EARTH-EMBRACES [DON GENARO EMBRACES THE EARTH]-(TOP)

EARTH-ENERGY-CRISSCROSS-[ENERGY THAT CRISSCROSSES THE EARTH]: (TOP): SEE: ENERGY-CRISSCROSS-EARTH-[ENERGY THAT CRISSCROSSES THE EARTH]-(TOP)

EARTH-ENERGY-FIELD-[THE EARTH'S ENERGY FIELD]: (Warriors know that the earth has its own gigantic luminous energy field.)

SELECTED REFERENCES: The Second Ring of Power - Page [276.4-276.5] ("No," la Gorda replied. "Dreaming takes too...from the light of the earth.) The Fire From Within - Page [205.8-205.9] (He explained that what he called...appropriate emanations inside the earth's cocoon.) The Fire From Within - Page [249.3-249.4] (I asked him about the difference...which they call total freedom.) The Art of Dreaming - Page [5.6]("When sorcerers see a human being...had a taproot that was dragging.)

SEE ALSO: EARTH

EARTH-ENERGY-FROM-[ENERGY FROM THE EARTH]: SEE: EARTH-BOOST-[THE EARTH'S BOOST]

EARTH-HEALING-[THE HEALING PROPERTIES OF THE EARTH]: SEE: EARTH -[THE EARTH]

EARTH-MAN-CONNECTION-[MAN'S CONNECTION TO THE EARTH]: (Warriors know that human beings are like trees, we are somehow rooted to the ground; even though our roots are transportable that does not free us from the ground.)
    SELECTED REFERENCES: The Eagle's Gift - Page [235.7-235.8] (Silvio Manuel was then ready to...not free us from the ground.)
    SEE ALSO: WARRIOR-SUSPENDING , EARTH, LUMINOUS-TAPROOT

EARTH-POWER-LINE-[A NATURAL POWER LINE ON THE EARTH]: (Warriors know that there are some natural power lines on the earth which can give warriors strength and knowledge if they can become one with them; some animal trails naturally follow these power lines.)
    SELECTED REFERENCES: The Eagle's Gift - Page [67.7-67.9] (She said that the Nagual Juan...it and become one with it.)
    SEE ALSO: POWER-SPOT

EARTH-PULL-[THE PULL OF THE EARTH]-(TOP)

EARTH-ROLLING-FORCE-[THE EARTH AND THE ROLLING FORCE]: SEE: FORCE-ROLLING-EARTH [THE EARTH AND THE ROLLING FORCE]

EARTH-SIGN-[THE SIGN THE EARTH MAKES WHEN WARRIORS JUMP INTO THE ABYSS]-(TOP)

*EAST-[EASTERLY WOMEN]: (Warriors know that the easterly woman is the first of a nagual's party of female warriors; she is called order; she is optimistic, light-hearted, smooth, persistent like a steady breeze; easterly women are fresh and funny, a true delight to the eyes and ears.)
    SELECTED REFERENCES: The Eagle's Gift - Page [174.5-174.8] (The female warriors are called the...shy, warm, like a hot wind.) The Eagle's Gift - Page [185.6-186.2] (A group composed of two sets of...lose their composure and be raving mad.) The Eagle's Gift - Page [192.7] (Don Juan said that the east...women the next day at midmorning.)
    SEE ALSO: WARRIORS-FEMALE

EAT-WARRIOR-[HOW WARRIORS EAT]: SEE: WARRIOR-EAT-[HOW WARRIORS EAT]

EDGE-DAY-[THE EDGE OF THE DAY]: SEE: DAY-EDGE-[THE EDGE OF THE DAY]

EDGE-REVERTS-[THE EDGE OF A PERSON WHO DIES REVERTS BACK TO THE GIVER OF THAT EDGE]: SEE: WARRIOR-EDGE-[THE EDGE OF THE WARRIOR]

EDGE-WARRIOR-[THE WARRIORS' EDGE]: SEE: WARRIOR-EDGE-[THE WARRIORS' EDGE]

EFFECTIVENESS-WARRIOR-[THE WARRIORS' EFFECTIVENESS]: SEE: WARRIOR-EFFECTIVENESS-[THE WARRIORS' EFFECTIVENESS]

EFFICIENCY-WARRIOR-[THE WARRIORS' EFFICIENCY]: SEE:
WARRIOR-EFFICIENCY-[THE WARRIORS' EFFICIENCY]

EFFORT-SUSTAINED-[SUSTAINED EFFORT]: SEE: WARRIOR-
QUALITIES-TWO-BASIC [THE TWO BASIC QUALITIES OF WARRIORS]

EGO-IMPERICAL-[THE IMPERICAL EGO]: (Warriors know that there is
no imperical ego, there is only the tonal.)
    SELECTED REFERENCES: Tales of Power - Page [139.6-140.4] (I felt compelled at
that point...my nagual was acting upon you.")
    SEE ALSO: TONAL, NAGUAL

EGO-TRANSCENDENTAL-[THE TRANSCENDENTAL EGO]: (Warriors
know there is no transcendental ego, there is only the tonal.)
    SELECTED REFERENCES: Tales of Power - Page [139.6-140.4] (I felt compelled at
that point...my nagual was acting upon you.")
    SEE ALSO: TONAL, NAGUAL

EGOMANIA-[EGOMANIA]: (Warriors know that egomania is an
expression of the first attention's sense of self and that as warriors they
must work ceaselessly to dethrone it.)
    SELECTED REFERENCES: The Power of Silence - Page [73.1-73.5] (He told me to
drive across the...must work ceaselessly to dethrone it.")
    SEE ALSO: ATTENTION-FIRST, SELF, SELF-IMAGE

EGOTIST-HOMICIDAL-[MAN IS A HOMICIDAL EGOTIST]: SEE: SELF-
IMAGE-[THE SELF-IMAGE]

EIGHT-POINTS-LUMINOUS-BEING-SORCERER-DIAGRAM-[THE
EIGHT POINTS ON THE FIBERS OF A LUMINOUS BEING]: SEE:
SORCERER-DIAGRAM-BODY-[THE CORRESPONDING LOCATIONS
ON THE PHYSICAL BODY FOR THE EIGHT POINTS OF THE
SORCERERS' DIAGRAM]

ELIAS-AMALIA-INORGANIC BEINGS-[THE INORGANIC BEINGS' TRAP
FOR ELIAS AND AMALIA]-(TOP): SEE: INORGANIC-BEINGS-TRAP
[THE TRAP OF THE INORGANIC BEINGS]-(TOP)

ELIAS-NAGUAL-DUAL-LIFE-[THE DUAL LIFE OF THE NAGUAL ELIAS]-
(TOP)

ELIAS-NAGUAL-ETERNITY-OBJECTS-[THE ETERNITY OBJECTS OF THE
NAGUAL ELIAS]-(TOP)

ELIAS-NAGUAL-IMPECCABILITY-[THE IMPECCABILITY OF THE
NAGUAL ELIAS]-(TOP)

ELIAS-NAGUAL-TALES-[TALES OF THE NAGUAL ELIAS]-(TOP)

ELIGIO-DREAMING-AVAILABILITY-[ELIGIO'S AVAILABILITY IN
DREAMING]-(TOP)

ELIGIO-MESSAGE-[ELIGIO'S MESSAGE]-(TOP)

ELIGIO-POWER-AWAY-[POWER TAKES ELIGIO AWAY]-(TOP)

ELIGIO-TALES-[TALES OF ELIGIO]-(TOP)

EMILITO-TALES-[TALES OF EMILITO]-(TOP)

EMOTIONS-[EMOTIONS]: SEE: FEELINGS-[FEELINGS]

EMPHASIS-WARRIOR-[THE WARRIORS' EMPHASIS]: SEE: WARRIOR-EMPHASIS-[THE WARRIORS' EMPHASIS]

EMPTINESS-WARRIOR-[THE WARRIORS' EMPTINESS]: SEE: WARRIOR-EMPTINESS-[THE WARRIORS' EMPTINESS]

ENCASED-EVERYTHING-EARTH-[EVERYTHING ON THE EARTH IS ENCASED]: (Warriors know that everything on the earth is encased; whatever we perceive is made up of cocoons or vessels with emanations; even the earth itself is enclosed in a gigantic ball which encases the Eagle's emanations.)
    SELECTED REFERENCES: The Fire From Within - Page [163.1-163.4] (He explained next that the product...containers of inorganic beings at all.") The Fire From Within - Page [203.8-203.9] ("The old seers saw that the...to the same forces we are.")
    SEE ALSO: LUMINOUS-COCOON-RECEPTACLE, EARTH

ENEMY-COLOR-WARRIOR-[THE WARRIORS' ENEMY COLOR]: SEE: WARRIOR-ENEMY-COLOR-[THE WARRIORS' ENEMY COLOR]

ENEMY-FIRST-[THE FIRST ENEMY OF THE WARRIOR]: SEE: FEAR, WARRIOR-ENEMIES-FOUR-NATURAL-[THE FOUR NATURAL ENEMIES OF THE WARRIOR]

ENEMY-FOURTH-[THE FOURTH ENEMY OF THE WARRIOR]: SEE: OLD-AGE [OLD AGE], WARRIOR-ENEMIES-FOUR-NATURAL-[THE FOUR NATURAL ENEMIES OF THE WARRIOR]

ENEMY-GREAT-WARRIOR-[THE GREAT ENEMY OF THE WARRIOR]: SEE: WARRIOR-ENEMY-GREAT-[THE GREAT ENEMY OF THE WARRIOR]

ENEMY-RELENTLESS-WOMEN-[WOMEN ARE RELENTLESS ENEMIES]: (Warriors know that women make the most relentless enemies because they never forget; men are usually too busy to be relentless enemies; our fellow men are our most worthy opponents; other entities have no volition of their own and the warrior must take the initiative to meet them and lure them out; our fellow men, on the other hand are relentless.)
    SELECTED REFERENCES: A Separate Reality - Page [211.5-211.6] ("What happened back there?" I finally...and she was a relentless enemy.) A Separate Reality - Page [212.2] ("You could never touch her...too busy to be relentless enemies.") Journey to Ixtlan - Page [179.8-179.9] ("Unfortunately only our fellow men are...men, on the contrary, are relentless.)
    SEE ALSO: WOMEN

ENEMY-SORCERER-SUPREME-[THE SORCERERS' SUPREME ENEMY]: SEE: MAN-NEMESIS-[THE NEMESIS OF MAN]

ENEMY-SECOND-[THE SECOND ENEMY OF THE WARRIOR]: SEE: CLARITY-[CLARITY], WARRIOR-ENEMIES-FOUR-NATURAL-[THE FOUR NATURAL ENEMIES OF THE WARRIOR]

ENEMY-SPOT-[THE WARRIORS' ENEMY SPOT]: (Warriors know that an enemy spot is the opposite of a warriors' power spot; a place that drains the warriors' energy.)

SELECTED REFERENCES: The Teachings of Don Juan - Page [34.2-34.9] ("You have found the spot...was by detecting their respective colors.) **Journey to Ixtlan** - Page [48.3-52.5] (In the early evening, however, he...You must learn that yourself.")
SEE ALSO: *POWER-SPOT*

ENEMY-THIRD-[THE THIRD ENEMY OF THE WARRIOR]: SEE: POWER [POWER], WARRIOR-ENEMIES-FOUR-NATURAL-[THE FOUR NATURAL ENEMIES OF THE WARRIOR]

ENEMIES-FOUR-NATURAL-WARRIOR-[THE FOUR NATURAL ENEMIES OF THE WARRIOR]: SEE: WARRIOR-ENEMIES-FOUR-NATURAL-[THE FOUR NATURAL ENEMIES OF THE WARRIOR]

ENERGETIC-AVAILABILITY-[ENERGETIC AVAILABILITY]: (Warriors know they must live impeccable lives and conserve their precious energy so that the barrier of the second attention will not make experiences in dreaming energetically unavailable to them; when warriors have stored enough energy, they are capable of returning their assemblage points to the precise spot necessary to fully recollect their experiences in heightened awareness.)
SELECTED REFERENCES: The Art of Dreaming - Page [xi.2-xi.6] (During the fulfillment of my dreaming...is a result of that rearrangement.)
SEE ALSO: *RECOLLECTION-SORCERER, ASSEMBLAGE-POINT-MOVING, WARRIOR-IMPECCABILITY, ENERGETIC-CONDITIONING*

ENERGETIC-CONDITIONING-[ENERGETIC CONDITIONING]: (Warriors know that their energetic conditioning is responsible for the relative inaccessibility of the worlds of the second attention; because of that conditioning, the average man is compelled to assume that the world of daily life is the only possible world; warriors strive to recondition their energetic capabilities to perceive, so that they can change their perception at its social base.)
SELECTED REFERENCES: The Art of Dreaming - Page [viii.4-viii.7] (Don Juan explained to me that...of practices the art of dreaming.)
SEE ALSO: *WORLDS-OTHER, PERCEPTION-CHANGING-SOCIAL-BASE*

ENERGETIC-COHESION-[ENERGETIC UNIFORMITY AND COHESION]: SEE: ENERGETIC-UNIFORMITY-COHESION-[ENERGETIC UNIFORMITY AND COHESION]

ENERGETIC-ESSENCE-[THE ENERGETIC ESSENCE OF THINGS]: (Warriors know that energy is all there is, energy is the essence of everything; the whole universe is energy; everything is energy.)
SELECTED REFERENCES: The Art of Dreaming - Page [2.9-3.8] (Don Juan explained that their most...have both alternatives at our fingertips.")
SEE ALSO: *ENERGY, AWARENESS-TRUTH-FIRST, EAGLE-EMANATIONS*

ENERGETIC-ESSENCE-PERCEIVING-[PERCEIVING THE ENERGETIC ESSENCE OF THINGS]: (Warriors know that the warriors' way is specifically designed to teach a new way of perceiving; first by making it clear that normal perception is processed to fit a mold and second by fiercely guiding the apprentice to perceive energy directly; the process of perceiving energy directly is known as "seeing".)
SELECTED REFERENCES: The Art of Dreaming - Page [2.9-3.2] (Don Juan explained that their most...things, a capacity they call *seeing*.) The Art of Dreaming - Page [3.7-3.9] ("How then should we perceive the...guiding us to perceive energy directly.)

SEE ALSO: *SEEING*

ENERGETIC-INTERFERENCES-*[ENERGETIC INTERFERENCES]:*
(Warriors know that among the multitude of items in our dreams, there exist real energetic interferences, things that have been put in our dreams extraneously by an alien force; to be able to find them and follow them is sorcery.)
    SELECTED REFERENCES: The Art of Dreaming - Page [29.1-30.2] (He said that among the multitude...collapses, leaving only the foreign energy.) The Art of Dreaming - Page [84.1-84.2] (From time to time, however, as...about shopping in a department store.)
    SEE ALSO: *INORGANIC-BEINGS, SCOUTS, SCOUTS-ISOLATING-FOLLOWING*

ENERGETIC-UNIFORMITY-COHESION-*[ENERGETIC UNIFORMITY AND COHESION]:* *(Warriors know that man's energy shape has uniformity because every human being on earth has the form of either a luminous ball or egg; the energy body has cohesion because it is able to hold itself together in whatever shape it takes; average men share an energetic uniformity and cohesion which is attained automatically in the course of their rearing; sorcerers strive to attain a new energetic uniformity and cohesion in order to perceive coherently and totally; the key to the acquisition of either form of uniformity and cohesion is the fixation of the assemblage point; the dreaming attention, the energy body, the second attention, the relationship with the inorganic beings, and the dreaming emissary are all by-products of acquiring cohesion [or by-products of fixating the assemblage point on a number of dreaming positions]; the clarity of the dreamers' perception is the gauge by which they measure their cohesion, the clearer the view of their dreams, the greater their cohesion; the act of acquiring uniformity and cohesion outside the normal worlds is called stalking perception.)*
    SELECTED REFERENCES: The Art of Dreaming - Page [13.9-15.7] (Another topic of don Juan's explanations...individuals, alone, surrounded by the boundless.) The Art of Dreaming - Page [40.5-40.7] ("My confusion comes when you...attributes are the key to perceiving.") The Art of Dreaming - Page [69.6-69.9] ("To fixate the assemblage point on...on a number of dreaming positions.") The Art of Dreaming - Page [70.1-70.6] ("How do we fixate the assemblage...our dreams, the greater our cohesion.) The Art of Dreaming - Page [77.2-77.5] ("We are again, don Juan, at...the normal world stalking perception.) The Art of Dreaming - Page [78.1-78.7] (Don Juan said that those activities...another person, a bird, or anything.) The Art of Dreaming - Page [216.7-218.1] ("They are called gifts of power...specific knowledge required to do this.") The Art of Dreaming - Page [230.2-230.5] ("What does that do?" I asked...what total perception means," I lied.)
    SEE ALSO: *PERCEPTION, ENERGY-BODY, LUMINOUS-LINE,* LUMINOUS-BALL, ENERGETIC-UNIFORMITY-COHESION-REARRANGING, ASSEMBLAGE-POINT-FIXATION, ATTENTION-DREAMING, INORGANIC-BEINGS, DREAMING EMISSARY, PERCEPTION-*STALKING*

ENERGETIC-UNIFORMITY-COHESION-REARRANGING-
[REARRANGING ENERGETIC UNIFORMITY AND COHESION]:
(Warriors know they must learn to rearrange the uniformity and cohesion of their perception by maintaining the position of the assemblage point on a spot which allows them to enter the second attention; warriors accomplish this by fixing the new position of the assemblage point and not letting it slide back into its original spot; this rearranging is known as "seeing".)
    SELECTED REFERENCES: The Art of Dreaming - Page [16.4-16.7] (He remarked that I was not ready...sliding back to its original spot.") The Art of Dreaming - Page [18.3-18.4] (Judging from where I stand today...me to rearrange my uniformity and cohesion.)

ENERGY-[ENERGY]: *(Warriors know that energy is the luminous essence of man; personal power; one of the primary focuses of warriors is energy and the ability to save and rechannel it; the goal of impeccability; the commodity which governs the warriors' ability to move the assemblage point and command the spirit; warriors must learn to re deploy their energy in a more intelligent manner; there is no more energy for warriors anywhere so they are forced to conserve the energetic resources which they already have.)*

SELECTED REFERENCES: The Eagle's Gift - Page [165.4-165.5] (Another feature of those states of...inherent need for economy and speed.) The Fire From Within - Page [15.5-15.8] (Don Juan choked with laughter,...in terms of expanding their energy.") The Fire From Within - Page [16.2-16.4] (Don Juan said then that in...action of rechanneling that energy is impeccability.") The Fire From Within - Page [57.7-57.9] ("Awareness develops from the moment of...saving and rechanneling energy.") The Fire From Within - Page [79.1-79.3] ("Things that are still difficult...from eradicating unnecessary habits.") The Fire From Within - Page [112.6-112.7] ("Your flaw is to remain glued...in another bubble of energy.") The Fire From Within - Page [120.7-120.8] ("Energy! Impeccability! Impeccable warriors...friends or with strangers.") The Fire From Within - Page [145.7-145.9] ("I once told you that the nagual...take place under ordinary circumstances.") The Fire From Within - Page [153.1-153.8] ("I'll tell you what the nagual...will solidify that new position.") The Power of Silence - Page [x.2-xi.2] (He stopped for a moment...the ordinary world we know.) The Power of Silence - Page [53.3-53.4] ("The story says that the spirit...needed to strengthen his connecting link.") The Power of Silence - Page [144.6-144.7] (He then said something which I already...energy sorcerers had at their command.) The Power of Silence - Page [158.7-159.1] ("The only concrete help you get from me...increased energy and not on instruction.") The Power of Silence - Page [228.2] ("Sorcerers say that in order to...for us is our impeccability.") The Power of Silence - Page [228.7-228.8] ("How do you maximize that movement?"...things are there for the asking.") The Power of Silence - Page [265.6-265.7] (Moving the assemblage point is everything...the place of silent knowledge.") The Art of Dreaming - Page [3.7] ("Everything is energy. The whole universe is energy.) The Art of Dreaming - Page [9.7-9.9] ("There is only one thing for...yourself that it can be done.) The Art of Dreaming - Page [32.7-33.2] (But to maintain that gain is...we can find it, he replied.) The Art of Dreaming - Page [37.2-37.4] (Every time he had an opportunity...existing energy, by any means available.)
SEE ALSO: *POWER-PERSONAL, WARRIOR-IMPECCABILITY, WARRIOR-ENERGY, ENERGY-(ALL), AWARENESS-TRUTH-FIRST, EAGLE-EMANATIONS*

ENERGY-AMPLIFICATION-[THE AMPLIFICATION OF ENERGY]:
(Warriors know that the movement of the assemblage point involves an amplification of energy which is felt as a killing anxiety.)

SELECTED REFERENCES: The Power of Silence - Page [148.9-149.3] (Don Juan then started a most...felt as a killing anxiety.)
SEE ALSO: *ENERGY, ASSEMBLAGE-POINT-MOVE, WARRIOR-ANXIETY*

ENERGY-ASSEMBLAGE-POINT-MOVE-[THE ENERGY NECESSARY TO MOVE THE ASSEMBLAGE POINT]: *(Warriors know that the energy necessary to move the assemblage point comes from the realm of the inorganic beings; there is no other viable energy for sorcerers; in order to "see" energy directly, to forge the energy body, and to fly into other realms, sorcerers need loads of dark, alien energy, the only source of which is the realm of the inorganic beings.)*

SELECTED REFERENCES: The Art of Dreaming - Page [180.8-182.3] ("You are ready then for one final...he waved good-bye to me.) The Art of Dreaming - Page [198.1-198.2] (He explained to us again, as if...medium of awareness into another world.)
SEE ALSO: *WARRIORSHIP-VS-SORCERY, INORGANIC-BEINGS-REALM, ENERGY-DARK, ASSEMBLAGE-POINT-MOVING*

ENERGY-BLOWING-INTO-CARLOS-[BLOWING ENERGY INTO CARLOS' BODY]-(TOP)

ENERGY-BLUE-[BLUE ENERGY]: SEE: BLUE-ENERGY-[BLUE ENERGY]

ENERGY-BODY-[THE ENERGY BODY]: *(Warriors know that the energy body is the energetic essence of man; man's luminous body; the energy body is the counterpart of the physical body, a ghostlike configuration made up of pure energy; the energy body has appearance but no mass and is capable of feats beyond the possibilities of the physical body; the dreaming body; dreamers begin forging the energy body by fulfilling the drills of the first and second gates of dreaming; when they reach the third gate, the energy body is ready to act; the energy body knows immensities.)*

SELECTED REFERENCES: The Eagle's Gift - Page [196.1-196.4] (This pattern coincides with hundreds of...Juan Tuma, I forgot my anger.) The Art of Dreaming - Page [5.4-5.8] (From *seeing* the essence of the universe...akin to people of ancient times.) The Art of Dreaming - Page [11.4-11.5] (In his teachings he put a...egg, which is our energy self.) The Art of Dreaming - Page [23.6-23.8] ("For sorcerers, because the statement I...body. For that you need energy.") The Art of Dreaming - Page [25.2-26.1] ("I lent you my energy, and...and that you are a dreamer.") The Art of Dreaming - Page [31.4-31.9] ("What exactly is the energy body...as we ordinarily perceive the world.") The Art of Dreaming - Page [41.9] (A dreamer on crossing the first gate has already reached the energy body.) The Art of Dreaming - Page [142.6-143.7] ("The given drill, at the third...irrational abandon to counteract that insistence.") The Art of Dreaming - Page [144.5-144.6] ("I was tickled pink when your...show you how much it knows.") The Art of Dreaming - Page [186.8-186.9] (He did not want to give...capable of taking care of itself.)

SEE ALSO: *LUMINOUS-BEINGS, DREAMING-BODY, DOUBLE, OTHER*

ENERGY-BODY-ARRIVING-SUSTAINING-[ARRIVING AT AND SUSTAINING THE ENERGY BODY]: *(Warriors know that reaching the first gate of dreaming is a way of arriving at the energy body; warriors mold their life situations by conserving enough energy to reach and sustain the energy body.)*

SELECTED REFERENCES: The Art of Dreaming - Page [32.7] (He reiterated that reaching, with deliberate...of arriving at the energy body.) The Art of Dreaming - Page [33.8-33.9] ("When sorcerers talk about molding one's...direction and consequences of our lives.")

SEE ALSO: *DREAMING-GATE-FIRST, ENERGY-BODY, WARRIOR-IMPECCABILITY*

ENERGY-BODY-COMPLETING-[COMPLETING THE ENERGY BODY]: *(Warriors know that at the third gate of dreaming, dreamers begin to merge dreaming reality with the reality of the daily world; this merging of realities is called completing the energy body; the completion of the energy body is accomplished the moment the energy body moves all by itself.)*

SELECTED REFERENCES: The Art of Dreaming - Page [142.3-142.4] ("At the third gate of dreaming...gate with great care and curiosity.") The Art of Dreaming - Page [163.2-163.7] (Don Juan smiled and said...body curtailed its obsession with detail.") The Art of Dreaming - Page [164.1-164.3] ("Dreamers have a rule of thumb...and not in a real world.") The Art of Dreaming - Page [170.6-170.8] (I remarked that I had *seen*...items that nearly ended your life.)

SEE ALSO: *DREAMING-GATE-THIRD*

ENERGY-BODY-CONDENSING-[CONDENSING THE ENERGY BODY]: *(Warriors know that through dreaming, they condense the energy body into a unit capable of its own unique perception.)*

SELECTED REFERENCES: The Eagle's Gift - Page [253.3-254.5] (Zuleica warned me that if I did...time fully awake, aware of everything.) The Art of Dreaming - Page [31.7] ("Through dreaming we condense the energy...it's a unit capable of perceiving.)

SEE ALSO: *ENERGY-BODY, DREAMING-ART*

ENERGY-BODY-DISCIPLINE-[DISCIPLINING THE ENERGY BODY]:
(Warriors know that they must maintain discipline over the energy body in order to perform the sorcerers' maneuver of entering another total world with their entire being.)
SELECTED REFERENCES: **The Art of Dreaming** - Page [190.2-190.4] ("What exactly do we have to...explained away as insanity or hallucination.")
SEE ALSO: *ENERGY-BODY, WORLDS-OTHER-ASSEMBLE-TOTAL, STALKING-ULTIMATE, WARRIOR-DISCIPLINE*

ENERGY-BODY-DREAMING-DEALS-THREE-[THE THREE WAYS THE
ENERGY BODY DEALS WITH ENERGY IN DREAMING]: *(Warriors know*
there are three ways which the energy body deals with energy in dreaming; 1) one is to perceive energy as it flows ["seeing"]; 2) another is to use energy from the earth to boost itself into unexpected realms [the earth's boost]; 3) the third is to perceive as we normally perceive the world.)
SELECTED REFERENCES: **The Art of Dreaming** - Page [31.8-31.9] (The energy body deals with energy...as we ordinarily perceive the world.")
SEE ALSO: *ENERGY-BODY, LOOKING-VS-SEEING, EARTH-BOOST*

ENERGY-BODY-JOURNEY-[THE JOURNEY OF THE ENERGY BODY]:
(Warriors know that journeys of the energy body occur when the assemblage point moves to the proper dreaming position; the energy body can travel in a split second over incredible distances.)
SELECTED REFERENCES: **The Art of Dreaming** - Page [170.1-171.9] (Don Juan said that in special dreams...feel that we are always right.")
SEE ALSO: *ENERGY-BODY, DREAMING-TRAVELING*

*ENERGY-BODY-MOVING-[MOVING THE ENERGY BODY]: *(Warriors*
know that the energy body does not move as if it were in the daily world; the energy body can move like energy moves, fast and directly; the energy body itself knows exactly how to move; the warriors' ability to move the energy body represents the optimum position of the assemblage point.)
SELECTED REFERENCES: **The Art of Dreaming** - Page [153.9-154.5] (Since I was not going to...moves in the inorganic beings' world.) **The Art of Dreaming** - Page [160.3-161.8] (At the first free moment I...position and you will be stalking.")
SEE ALSO: *ENERGY-BODY, ASSEMBLAGE-POINT-POSITION-OPTIMUM, WILL-MOVING-BY-(TOP)*

ENERGY-BODY-PERCEPTION-[THE PERCEPTION OF THE ENERGY
BODY]: *(Warriors know that the perception of the energy body, although*
affected by normal perception, is in reality its own independent perception; it has its own sphere of perception, the sphere of energy; there are three ways the energy body deals with the perception of energy in dreaming; 1) one is to perceive energy as it flows; 2) another is to use energy to boost to unexpected realms; 3) yet another is to perceive as we normally perceive the world; the energy body is capable of perceiving energy that is quite different from the energy of the ordinary world; it is also capable of determining whether or not the items perceived during dreaming belong to a real world or not.)
SELECTED REFERENCES: **The Art of Dreaming** - Page [31.7-31.9] ("Through dreaming we condense the energy...as we ordinarily perceive the world.") **The Art of Dreaming** - Page [164.1-165.2] ("Dreamers have a rule of thumb...the simplicity and directness of sorcery.)
SEE ALSO: *ENERGY-BODY, PERCEPTION,*

ENERGY-BODY-PERFECTING-[PERFECTING THE ENERGY BODY]:
(Warriors know that dreamers take a long time to perfect their energy bodies; the energy body must mature through its own "dreaming experience" until it is complete; until that time, the energy body is self-absorbed and cannot get free from the compulsion to be absorbed by everything; this compulsion of the dreaming body is called the trap of detail.)
        SELECTED REFERENCES: The Art of Dreaming - Page [42.2-42.4] ("You will find out for yourself...dreaming attention must make them surface.") The Art of Dreaming - Page [159.7-161.3] (He was right. I continued my...is to say, by stalking it.") The Art of Dreaming - Page [162.6-163.7] (He asked me then to tell...body curtailed its obsession with detail.") The Art of Dreaming - Page [177.6-177.8] (He was right again. Without much...if they were filled with pressurized gas.)
        SEE ALSO: *ENERGY-BODY, ENERGY-BODY-COMPLETING*

ENERGY-BODY-SEEING-[SEEING THE ENERGY BODY]: (Warriors know that "seeing" the energy body refers to the indescribable way in which the energy body is perceived by seers.)
        SELECTED REFERENCES: The Art of Dreaming - Page [15.4-15.7] ("To understand all this certainly isn't..."You must see that for yourself!")
        SEE ALSO: *SEEING, ENERGY-BODY*

ENERGY-BODY-SELF-ABSORPTION-[THE SELF-ABSORPTION OF THE ENERGY BODY]: SEE: ENERGY-BODY-PERFECTING-[PERFECTING THE ENERGY BODY]

ENERGY-BODY-STALKING-[STALKING THE ENERGY BODY]: (Warriors know that they must perfect the energy body and overcome the trap of detail by learning to stalk the energy body; instead of resisting the energy body's compulsion with detail before it matures, warriors lend it a hand by directing the energy body's behavior through stalking; warriors stalk the energy body through their intent; they let the energy body intend to reach the optimum dreaming position and then let the energy body intend to stay in that position.)
        SELECTED REFERENCES: The Art of Dreaming - Page [161.1-161.8] ("Until the energy body is complete and...position and you will be stalking.")
        SEE ALSO: *ENERGY-BODY, STALKING-ART, INTENDING*

ENERGY-BODY-UNDERSTANDING-[THE UNDERSTANDING OF THE ENERGY BODY]: (Warriors know that understanding extends beyond the realm of reason to include the realm of energy; the energy body is capable of "understanding" things in terms entirely different from those of the mind; this type of understanding is experienced as a bodily feeling.)
        SELECTED REFERENCES: The Art of Dreaming - Page [23.3-23.9] ("Intent or intending is something very...it to know what I mean.")
        SEE ALSO: *UNDERSTANDING, KNOWLEDGE-VS-LANGUAGE, BODY-PHYSICAL-WITNESSING, KNOWLEDGE-SILENT, ENERGY BODY*

ENERGY-CHARACTERISTICS-[THE CHARACTERISTICS OF DIFFERENT ENERGIES IN THE UNIVERSE]: (Warriors know that they must learn to recognize the characteristic properties of the various energies in the universe; the energy of the daily world wavers and scintillates; the energy of the realm of the inorganic beings sizzles.)
        SELECTED REFERENCES: The Art of Dreaming - Page [164.1-165.2] ("Dreamers have a rule of thumb...the simplicity and directness of sorcery.) The Art of Dreaming - Page [175.9-177.8] (I discovered that the energy of...they were filled with pressurized gas.)

SEE ALSO: *ENERGY-BODY-PERCEPTION, ENERGY BODY*

ENERGY-CENTER-[THE ENERGY CENTER OF THE BODY]: SEE: BODY-MIDPOINT [THE MIDPOINT OF THE BODY]

ENERGY-CONSERVING-[CONSERVING ENERGY]: SEE: ENERGY-[ENERGY], ENERGY-DRAINAGE-[PLUGGING POINTS OF ENERGY DRAINAGE], WARRIOR-IMPECCABILITY-[THE WARRIORS' IMPECCABILITY]

ENERGY-CRISSCROSS-EARTH-[ENERGY THAT CRISSCROSSES THE EARTH]-(TOP)

ENERGY-CUMULATIVE-[ENERGY IS CUMULATIVE]: (Warriors know that the acquisition of energy tends to be cumulative; if warriors follow an impeccable path, their energy will accumulate and one day their world will be transformed as their memories open up.)

SELECTED REFERENCES: The Art of Dreaming - Page [138.9-139.1] ("Energy tends to be cumulative; if you...come when your memory opens up.")
SEE ALSO: *ENERGY, RECOLLECTION-SORCERER, WARRIOR-IMPECCABILITY*

ENERGY-CURRENTS-UNKNOWN-[ENERGY CURRENTS FROM THE UNKNOWN]: (Warriors know that jolts of energy may originate either outside or inside the energy body; the average man pays no attention to them but they are felt as a vague sensation of sadness followed by an immediate sense of euphoria; these jolts are energy jolts sent by the inorganic beings.)

SELECTED REFERENCES: The Art of Dreaming - Page [11.6-11.9] ("How is it displaced?" I asked...but as unexplainable, ill-founded moodiness.") The Art of Dreaming - Page [47.3-47.4] ("What would the sign be, don...to you by the inorganic beings.") The Art of Dreaming - Page [47.9-48.2] ("I'm not clear, don Juan, about...themselves right in front of us.)
SEE ALSO: *ASSEMBLAGE-POINT-MOVING, ENERGY-BODY, INORGANIC-BEINGS*

ENERGY-DARK-[DARK ENERGY]: (Warriors know that dark energy is energy from the realm of the inorganic beings; this dark energy is tainted with the mood of the sorcerers of antiquity but is necessary to the warrior on his path to freedom; warriors must eventually access this dark energy to complete their definitive journey, but in the process warriors must manage to avoid the influence of the inorganic beings and their realm.)

SELECTED REFERENCES: The Art of Dreaming - Page [180.8-182.3] ("You are ready then for one final...he waved good-bye to me.) The Art of Dreaming - Page [198.1-198.2] (He explained to us again, as if...medium of awareness into another world.)
SEE ALSO: *ENERGY, ASSEMBLAGE-POINT-MOVEMENT-ENERGY, INORGANIC-BEINGS-REALM, WARRIORSHIP-VS-SORCERY, INORGANIC-BEINGS-REFUSING, WARRIOR-JOURNEY-DEFINITIVE*

ENERGY-DRAINAGE-[PLUGGING POINTS OF ENERGY DRAINAGE]: (Warriors know they must learn to store personal power by plugging up all their points of energy drainage; they don't have to be deliberate about it because power finds a way to accomplish this process; warriors assist the process by living the most impeccable life they possibly can even though power is unnoticeable to them as it is being stored.)

SELECTED REFERENCES: Journey to Ixtlan - Page [177.8-178.1]. ("But how can I store personal power...unnoticeable when it is being stored.") The Eagle's Gift - Page [303.8-304.2] (As we walked back to his house...not a matter of my volition.)

SEE ALSO: *WARRIOR-IMPECCABILITY, ENERGY, POWER-PERSONAL, WARRIOR-WAY*

ENERGY-DREAMING-[ENERGY FOR DREAMING]: (Warriors know that for a man, the energy needed in order to move and seek in dreaming comes from the area below the navel; in women, this energy originates from the womb.)
SELECTED REFERENCES: **The Eagle's Gift - Page [136.2-136.4]** (Later on, when I had succeeded...for dreaming originate from the womb.)
SEE ALSO: *ENERGY, DREAMING-ART*

ENERGY-FIELDS-INACCESSIBLE-AVAILABLE-[ENERGY FIELDS THAT ARE AVAILABLE BUT INACCESSIBLE]: (Warriors know that one of the keys to sorcery is that the warrior begins to make use of energy fields which are available but inaccessible to the average man.)
SELECTED REFERENCES: **The Power of Silence - Page [xi.7-xi.9]** ("Once we have reached it, it....silent knowledge, depends on our own temperament.")
SEE ALSO: *ENERGY, WARRIOR-IMPECCABILITY, SORCERY*

ENERGY-GENERATING-CONDITION-[ENERGY GENERATING CONDITION]: SEE: DREAMING -ART-[THE ART OF DREAMING]

ENERGY-INCREASED-WARRIOR-[THE WARRIORS' INCREASED ENERGY]: SEE: WARRIOR-ENERGY-INCREASED-[THE WARRIORS' INCREASED ENERGY]

ENERGY-INORGANIC-BEINGS-VS-ORGANIC-BEINGS-[THE ENERGY OF INORGANIC BEINGS VS ORGANIC BEINGS]: (Warriors know that the energy of inorganic beings is more like an electric current while the energy of organic beings is like heat waves.)
SELECTED REFERENCES: **The Fire From Within - Page [102.7-102.8]** (I told don Juan that from...beings are more like heat waves.")
SEE ALSO: *ENERGY, INORGANIC-BEINGS, ORGANIC-BEINGS*

ENERGY-INSTRUCTION-ASSEMBLAGE-POINT-MOVE-[ENERGY, INSTRUCTION AND THE MOVEMENT OF THE ASSEMBLAGE POINT]: (Warriors know that the movement of the assemblage point depends on the warriors' increased energy and not on instruction.)
SELECTED REFERENCES: **The Power of Silence - Page [158.7-159.1]** ("The only concrete help you get from me...increased energy and not on instruction.")
SEE ALSO: *ENERGY, INSTRUCTION-WARRIOR, ASSEMBLAGE-POINT-MOVING*

ENERGY-INTENT-LINK-[ENERGY AND THE CONNECTING LINK WITH INTENT]: (Warriors know that once the energy that is ordinarily used to maintain the fixed position of the assemblage point becomes liberated, it automatically focuses on the connecting link with intent; this is an instantaneous shift of energy that takes place once a certain level of proficiency has been attained; this level of proficiency is known as pure understanding.)
SELECTED REFERENCES: **The Power of Silence - Page [114.1-114.5]** (He said that as the energy...to *intend* it through pure understanding.) **The Power of Silence - Page [144.6-144.7]** (He then said something which I already...energy sorcerers had at their command.)
SEE ALSO: *ENERGY, WARRIOR-IMPECCABILITY, WARRIOR-LINK-INTENT, UNDERSTANDING-PURE*

ENERGY-JOURNEYS-TWO-[THE TWO KINDS OF ENERGY JOURNEYS INTO OTHER WORLDS]: (*Warriors know there are two kinds of energy journeys into other worlds; one is when awareness picks up the energy body and takes it wherever it may; the other is when the warrior makes a conscious decision to use the avenue of awareness to make a journey.*)
    SELECTED REFERENCES: The Art of Dreaming - Page [186.2-186.9] ("There are two kinds of energy...capable of taking care of itself.)
    SEE ALSO: *WORLDS-OTHER-ASSEMBLE-TOTAL, AWARENESS, DREAMING-ART, AWARENESS-ENERGETIC-ELEMENT*

ENERGY-MASS-[THE ENERGY MASS]: (*Warriors know that the energy mass is another term for the energy body.*)
    SELECTED REFERENCES: The Art of Dreaming - Page [78.1-78.2] (Don Juan said that those activities...and thus retain their cohesiveness, indefinitely.)
    SEE ALSO: *ENERGY-BODY*

ENERGY-MAXIMUM-WARRIOR-[THE WARRIORS' MAXIMUM ENERGY LEVEL]: SEE: WARRIOR-ENERGY-MAXIMUM-[THE WARRIORS' MAXIMUM ENERGY LEVEL]

ENERGY-MISER-WARRIOR-[WARRIORS MUST BECOME MISERS WITH THEIR ENERGY]: SEE: WARRIOR-ENERGY-MISER-[WARRIORS MUST BECOME MISERS WITH THEIR ENERGY]

ENERGY-SEEING-DREAMING-[SEEING ENERGY IN DREAMING]: (*Warriors know that "seeing" energy with the energy body is the real task of the third gate of dreaming.*)
    SELECTED REFERENCES: The Art of Dreaming - Page [163.8-164.8] ("What comes next for you is...world nothing sizzles; everything here wavers.)
    SEE ALSO: *SEEING, DREAMING-GATE-THIRD*

ENERGY-SELF-[THE ENERGY SELF]: SEE: ENERGY-BODY-[THE ENERGY BODY]

ENERGY-SHAPE-[THE ENERGY SHAPE]: (*Warriors know that the energy shape is another term for the energy body.*)
    SELECTED REFERENCES: Tales of Power - Page [32.5-32.7] (He said that the mushroomlike formation...in this specific type of *seeing*.") Tales of Power - Page [35.5-35.6] ("Why are those people shaped differently...and not pegged down to the ground.") The Art of Dreaming - Page [12.1-12.4] ("What happens when the assemblage point...becomes a thin line of energy.) The Art of Dreaming - Page [70.1-70.5] ("How do we fixate the assemblage...all of them is a triumph.") The Art of Dreaming - Page [103.9-104.1] ("We are energy that is kept...of that energy will change accordingly.)
    SEE ALSO: *ENERGY-BODY*

ENERGY-SHAPE-TRANSFORMATION-[THE TRANSFORMATION OF THE ENERGY SHAPE]: (*Warriors know that the energy shape of sorcerers changes as they learn to move the assemblage point; the energy shape transforms itself from a ball to a shape resembling a smoking pipe, and in the most extreme cases, to a thin luminous line; the energy shape can also be contorted to transform the dreamers sexual orientation.*)
    SELECTED REFERENCES: The Art of Dreaming - Page [5.7] (Don Juan had the impression that...shape keeps on changing through time.) The Art of Dreaming - Page [12.1-12.8] ("What happens when the assemblage point...like a dog chasing its tail.") The Art of Dreaming - Page [234.7-234.8] (She was thoroughly right. That was...a cleavage that ran its length.)

SEE ALSO: *ENERGY-BODY, SORCERER-LUMINOSITY-CHANGE, MALENESS-VS-FEMALENESS*

ENERGY-SHIFT-INSTANTANEOUS-[THE INSTANTANEOUS SHIFT OF ENERGY]: (Warriors know that the energy ordinarily used to maintain the fixed position of the assemblage point, eventually becomes liberated through the warriors' unrelenting efforts; once that energy is free, it automatically focuses itself on the warriors' connecting link with intent; there are no techniques to be learned to accomplish this shift of energy; it is rather a matter of an instantaneous shift taking place once a certain level of proficiency has been attained; that level of proficiency is known as pure understanding.)

SELECTED REFERENCES: **The Power of Silence - Page [113.9-114.4]** (We left the house and strolled around...*intend* it through pure understanding.)

SEE ALSO: *WARRIOR-ATTAINMENT, ENERGY, UNDERSTANDING-PURE*

ENERGY-SLIPS-SECOND-ATTENTION-DAILY-WORLD-[ENERGY SLIPPING BETWEEN THE SECOND ATTENTION AND THE DAILY WORLD]: (Warriors know that energy occasionally slips between the wall which separates the realm of the second attention and the everyday world of men.)

SELECTED REFERENCES: **The Art of Dreaming - Page [136.2-136.7]** (A serious query, which don Juan's...in such an overt, volitional way.")

SEE ALSO: *SCOUT-BLUE-(TOP), CRACK-WORLDS*

ENERGY-SORCERY-[ENERGY AND SORCERY]: (Warriors know that sorcery is beyond the reach of the average man because the average man lacks the energetic resources to deal with it.)

SELECTED REFERENCES: **The Power of Silence - Page [ix.9-xi.2]** ("From where the average man stands...perceive something which ordinary perception cannot.) **The Power of Silence - Page [144.6-144.7]** (He then said something which I already...energy sorcerers had at their command.) **The Power of Silence - Page [158.7-159.1]** ("The only concrete help you get from me...increased energy and not on instruction.")

SEE ALSO: *ENERGY, SORCERY, PERCEPTION-SORCERER*

ENERGY-SURPLUS-WARRIOR-[THE WARRIORS' SURPLUS ENERGY]: (Warriors know that they cannot begin to move the assemblage point away from its customary position until they have accumulated some surplus energy through the actions of an impeccable life.)

SELECTED REFERENCES: **The Fire From Within - Page [108.8-108.9]** (He said that for me to have...because I had enough surplus energy.) **The Power of Silence - Page [144.6-144.7]** (He then said something which I already...energy sorcerers had at their command.)

SEE ALSO: *ENERGY, WARRIOR-IMPECCABLE, ASSEMBLAGE-POINT-MOVING*

ENERGY-WORLD-DAILY-ARRANGEMENT-COLORS-[THE ARRANGEMENT OF COLORS IN THE ENERGY OF THE DAILY WORLD]: (Warriors know that the energy of the daily world consists of layers of shimmering hues; the top layer is white, another adjacent layer is chartreuse, and another, more distant layer is amber; the whitish layer is the hue of the present position of mankind's assemblage point; the chartreuse layer is the hue of the position of mankind's assemblage point at another time; the amber layer is characteristic of the ruling energy of a position of the assemblage point from an extremely ancient time in man's past; the color of sorcerers is amber, which means they are energetically associated with the men who existed in the ancient past.)

SELECTED REFERENCES: **The Art of Dreaming - Page [175.9-176.6]** (I discovered that the energy of...who existed in a distant past.")
SEE ALSO: *AWARENESS-COLOR, FOG-GREEN*

ENLIGHTENMENT-[ENLIGHTENMENT]: *(Warriors know that enlightenment is the result of the true acquisition of knowledge, a process which occurs independent of language; the flaw with words is that they force us to feel enlightened, even though we are not.)*

SELECTED REFERENCES: **Tales of Power - Page [24.4-24.6]** ("That's the flaw with words," he...where new acts have new reflections.")
SEE ALSO: *TALKING, KNOWLEDGE-VS-LANGUAGE, KNOWLEDGE, WORDS-FLAW*

ENTERPRISE-WARRIOR-[THE WARRIORS' ENTERPRISE]: SEE: WARRIOR-ENTERPRISE-[THE WARRIORS' ENTERPRISE]

ENTITIES-NIGHT-[THE ENTITIES OF THE NIGHT]: *(Warriors know that the entities of the night are the allies, the inorganic beings, spirits; these entities may be more properly called entities of the mountains because they really don't belong to the night; they are called entities of the night because they can be perceived more easily in the dark, but they are around us all the time; these entities are real and ordinarily kill someone who stumbles upon them without any personal power; the cry of an owl brings out the entities of the night; they are not naturally malevolent and are dangerous only to someone who is not impeccable.)*

SELECTED REFERENCES: **Journey to Ixtlan - Page [172.1-172.8]** (I felt relieved and asked him...that sent chills through my body.) **Journey to Ixtlan - Page [176.6-177.8]** ("It doesn't look too good...you have stored enough personal power.") **Journey to Ixtlan - Page [177.4-177.8]** ("The road to knowledge and power...you have stored enough personal power.") **Journey to Ixtlan - Page [178.2-179.1]** ("The entities of the night moved along...of an owl brings them out.) **Journey to Ixtlan - Page [179.8-179.9]** ("Unfortunately only our fellow men are...men, on the contrary, are relentless.) **Journey to Ixtlan - Page [181.9-182.2]** (After a day's rest he announced...to be cleansed and restored.) **The Eagle's Gift - Page [68.8-69.2]** ("We are doomed," she said to...entities at large in the world.) **The Eagle's Gift - Page [157.9-158.1]** (Silvio Manuel thought you needed to...And other things even more fierce.")
SEE ALSO: *ALLIES, INORGANIC BEINGS, SPIRITS*

EQUAL-UNIMPORTANT-[EQUAL AND UNIMPORTANT]: *(Warriors who have learned to "see", realize that everything is equal and unimportant.)*

SELECTED REFERENCES: **A Separate Reality - Page [82.8-82.9]** (For example, don Juan, do you...by being equal they are unimportant.") **A Separate Reality - Page [88.6-88.9]** (Don Juan stood up and extended...realize then that nothing matters.") **A Separate Reality - Page [168.1-168.3]** ("I've told you already," he said..."The unimportance of everything.") **Journey to Ixtlan - Page [121.2-121.3]** ("I know, I know," don Juan...It takes power to do that.") **Journey to Ixtlan - Page [249.7-250.1]** (The beetle emerged from a deep...no more important than a beetle.) **The Second Ring of Power - Page [235.2-235.6]** (I told her that my sadness in leaving...of us had accepted our fate.) **The Eagle's Gift - Page [279.2-279.7]** ("Warriors don't have the world to cushion...One is equal to everything.)
SEE ALSO: *SEEING*

EQUALITY-AMONG-WARRIORS-[EQUALITY AMONG WARRIORS]: SEE: WARRIOR-EQUALITY-AMONG-[EQUALITY AMONG WARRIORS]

EQUILIBRIUM-[EQUILIBRIUM]: *(Warriors begin with the certainty that their luminous energy is off balance; by living in full control and awareness, warriors then do their ultimate best to regain their balance or their equilibrium; every human being's imbalance is a result of the sum total of*

their actions; all human beings sense from the moment of birth that there are two parts to our being, we silently know of the existence of the true pair; once individuals have become all tonal, they begins making pairs because they sense their two sides; the problem is that we represent the true pair with items from the tonal alone and believe in our madness that we are making perfect sense; warriors counteract their imbalance and regain their equilibrium not by making pairs on the island, but by living impeccably through the warriors' way in order that one day they might sneak off that island and face the nagual; warriors have personally experienced the unfathomable balance of things, the imperatives or "commands" of the equilibrium of the universe, the harmony and mystery of the Eagle's emanations, the totality of the knowable and the unknowable; the totality of ourselves is something the tonal cannot obliterate all together; there are moments in the lives of warriors when this totality becomes apparent; these are the moments of the warriors' equilibrium, moments when we can surmise and assess what we really are; the key to the warriors' equilibrium is the bridge between contradictions, that which allows warriors to pit two opposing views of the world against each other and somehow slip in between them to find themselves; equilibrium is a mirror of the state of the warriors' totality, an impossible state of awareness that reflects the true balance of the energetic universe; at a given moment there is no longer a war within the warrior, because the warriors' way is harmony, first the harmony between actions and decisions and then the harmony between the tonal and the nagual.)

SELECTED REFERENCES: **Tales of Power - Page [26.8-27.2]** ("We've never talked about moths...proper light to talk about moths.") **Tales of Power - Page [33.2-33.3]** ("Don't waste your power on trifles...nonsense is petty and downright disastrous.") **Tales of Power - Page [126.7-127.4]** ("The *nagual* is there," he said...believe ourselves to be making perfect sense.") **Tales of Power - Page [131.8-132.1]** ("On certain occasions, however, or under...and assess what we really are.) **Tales of Power - Page [155.9]** (Now there is no longer a war...then the harmony between *tonal* and *nagual*.) **The Fire From Within - Page [42.6-43.2]** ("The real impact can't be measured...that's what they really are, commands.") **The Fire From Within - Page [72.8-73.5]** (Don Juan said that the new seers...sobriety, love, or even kindness.")

SEE ALSO: *WARRIOR-EQUILIBRIUM, WARRIOR-BRIDGE, BALANCE, KNOWABLE, UNKNOWABLE, EAGLE, EAGLE-EMANATIONS, EAGLE-COMMANDS, TONAL-ISLAND, WARRIOR-CONTRADICTION-KNOWLEDGE, TONAL-NAGUAL-DICHOTOMY, WARRIOR-DUALISM, AWARENESS-SUBLIMINAL, FORCE-POSITIVE-NEGATIVE, SOBRIETY-DREAMING, SNEAKING-WORLD-MEN-WORLD-SORCERER, WARRIOR-COUNTERPOINT, WARRIOR-JOURNEY-DEFINITIVE, AWARENESS-POLARITY-APPLYING, SNEAKING-WORLD-MEN-WORLD-SORCERER, WARRIOR-BALANCE-SOBRIETY-ABANDON, SORCERER-EXPLANATION, WARRIOR-WAR-VS-PEACE, WARRIOR-FLUIDITY*

EQUILIBRIUM-WARRIOR-[THE WARRIORS' LUMINOUS EQUILIBRIUM]: SEE: WARRIOR-EQUILIBRIUM-[THE WARRIORS' LUMINOUS EQUILIBRIUM]

ERASING-WARRIOR-[WARRIORS ERASE THEMSELVES]: SEE: PERSONAL-HISTORY-ERASING-[ERASING PERSONAL HISTORY]

ESCOGIDO-[ESCOGIDO]: *(The warrior knows that the escogido is a teacher's "chosen one", the apprentice to whom he shows the tonal.)*

SELECTED REFERENCES: **The Teachings of Don Juan - Page [49.1-49.5]** ("What kind of an indication...lot of a man of knowledge.") **Tales of Power - Page [199.2-199.4]** (He quickly changed the subject..."protegido" meant the protected one.)

SEE ALSO: *PROTEGIDO*

ETERNITY-[ETERNITY]: (*Warriors define eternity as the immeasurable immensity which surrounds us; the third attention.*)
SELECTED REFERENCES: **Tales of Power - Page [8.6-8.9]** ("There! Eternity is there!"...yourself forever in any direction.") **Tales of Power - Page [33.2-33.4]** ("Don't waste your power on...is petty and outright disastrous.") **The Fire From Within - Page [97.1-97.7]** (Don Juan remarked that in the life...you'll be ready for the definitive journey.") **The Power of Silence - Page [29.5-29.6]** ("At this stage you enter into heightened...immensity that surrounds us reasonable.")
SEE ALSO: *ATTENTION-THIRD*

ETERNITY-GLIMPSING-[GLIMPSING ETERNITY]: SEE: DEPTH-VIEW-[A VIEW OF THE DEPTHS]

ETERNITY-GUARDIAN-[THE GUARDIAN OF ETERNITY]: (*Warriors know that the guardian of eternity can be many things, from a moth to a gnat; the herald of eternity; the depository of the gold dust of eternity.*)
SELECTED REFERENCES: **Tales of Power - Page [28.4]**("The moths are the heralds or...of the gold dust of eternity.")
SEE ALSO: *ETERNITY, KNOWLEDGE, KNOWLEDGE-DUST, ALLIES*

ETERNITY-VS-HUMANNESS-[ETERNITY VS HUMANNESS]: (*Warriors know that there is nothing more lonely than eternity and nothing more cozy than to be a human being; warriors must somehow overcome this contradiction and keep the bonds of their humanness while purposefully adventuring into the absolute loneliness of eternity.*)
SELECTED REFERENCES: **The Fire From Within - Page [97.6-98.1]** ("Something is finally getting through to you...could actually face the loneliness of eternity.")
SEE ALSO: *WARRIOR-CONTRADICTION-KNOWLEDGE, ETERNITY, INVENTORY, HUMAN-CONDITION, WARRIOR-LONELINESS, WARRIOR-SOLITUDE*

ETERNITY-ROAD-[THE ROAD TO ETERNITY]: (*Warriors know that all roads lead to eternity, all warriors have to do is follow any one of them in total silence.*)
SELECTED REFERENCES: **The Fire From Within - Page [295.7-295.8]** (He smiled and pointed to a street...It's time. Go now! Go!")
SEE ALSO: *INNER-SILENCE*

*ETERNITY-TALES-[TALES OF ETERNITY]: (*The warriors' tales of the unknown.*)
SELECTED REFERENCES: **The Eagle's Gift - Page [191.5-191.192.1]** (Nonetheless, she was definitely on the ...he passed on to the others.).
SEE ALSO: *ETERNITY, UNKNOWN*

ETHOS-WARRIOR-[THE ETHOS OF WARRIORS]: SEE: WARRIOR-ETHOS-[THE ETHOS OF WARRIORS]

EVERYTHING-FILLED-BRIM-[EVERYTHING IS FILLED TO THE BRIM]: (*Warriors know that everything in their lives is equal and filled to the brim; there is no defeat or victory or emptiness, there is only the sense that everything is filled to the brim and that the warriors' struggle is worth while.*)
SELECTED REFERENCES: **A Separate Reality - Page [88.7-88.8]** ("Everything is filled to the brim...my struggle was worth my while.)
SEE ALSO: *EQUAL-UNIMPORTANT, VICTORY-DEFEAT-EQUAL*

EVERYTHING-LOST-THOSE-[THOSE WHO HAVE LOST EVERYTHING]: **(Warriors know that they are already dead and they draw courage from this realization; the worst thing that can happen to them is that they will die, and since they consider that they have already lost everything in that sense, warriors are free and have nothing to fear.)**
SELECTED REFERENCES: The Fire From Within - Page [241.8-241.9] (Don Juan had drilled into me...no longer have anything to fear.)
SEE ALSO: *DEATH, DEATH-ADVISER, WARRIOR-IMPECCABILITY-TICKET*

EVERYTHING-NOTHING-[EVERYTHING AND NOTHING]: NOTHING-EVERYTHING-[NOTHING AND EVERYTHING]

EVICTION-NOTICE-WARRIOR-[THE WARRIORS' EVICTION NOTICE]: SEE: WARRIOR-EVICTION-NOTICE-[THE WARRIORS' EVICTION NOTICE]

EVIL-[EVIL]: **(Warriors know that there is no evil, there is only perception; warriors know without a shadow of a doubt that only energy exists in the universe; evil is merely a concatenation of the human mind, overwhelmed by the fixation of the assemblage point on its habitual position; the realm of extraordinary perception; that which the average man does not have energy to perceive; the human interpretation of the aberration of power; warriors know that there is no evil, no devil, no witch craft because they have turned everything into what it really is: the abstract, the spirit, the nagual.)**
SELECTED REFERENCES: **Journey to Ixtlan** - Page [182.9-183.3] (The soothing feeling of peace and plenitude...an unwarranted importance on the self.) **Tales of Power** - Page [54.9-55.2] ("No one develops a double...that awareness such a unique challenge.") **The Fire From Within** - Page [15.1-15.3] (My discomfort made me argue that...my impeccability, that's all," he said.) **The Power of Silence** - Page [211.2-211.5] (Don Juan pushed his argument further...There is only perception.") **The Power of Silence** - Page [263.4-263.6] ("Of course, there is a dark side...yes, and it's called stupidity.") **The Art of Dreaming** - Page [49.4-49.5] ("You are a religious man to...we believe it is possible to perceive.") **The Art of Dreaming** - Page [238.8-239.3] (I was again more than terrified...not be able to wake up.)
SEE ALSO: *ABERRATION-MORBIDITY, ATTENTION-SECOND, ASSEMBLAGE-POINT-FIXATION, WITCHCRAFT, EVIL-ATTENTION-SECOND, EVIL, STUPIDITY-IGNORANCE*

EVIL-SECOND-ATTENTION-[THE EVILNESS OF THE SECOND ATTENTION]: **(Warriors know that the evilness of the second attention is another term for the aberration of the second attention; the second attention in itself is not evil, but the misguided fixation of the second attention can be.)**
SELECTED REFERENCES: The Eagle's Gift - Page [17.4-17.8] ("The Nagual said that it was...they did, it was too late.") The Eagle's Gift - Page [20.2-20.4] (I said to them that I...the fixation of attention in general.)
SEE ALSO: *EVIL, ATTENTION-SECOND*

EVOLUTION-MAN-[MAN IS CAPABLE OF EVOLVING]: SEE: MAN-EVOLUTION-[MAN IS CAPABLE OF EVOLVING]

EXAGGERATION-WARRIOR-[THE WARRIORS' EXAGGERATION]: SEE: WARRIOR-EXAGGERATION-[THE WARRIORS' EXAGGERATION]

EXCITATION-WARRIOR-[THE WARRIORS' EXCITATION]: SEE: WARRIOR-EXCITATION-[THE WARRIORS' EXCITATION]

EXHAUSTION-[EXHAUSTION]: (Warriors know that being unavailable means to avoid exhausting themselves and others; warriors are not desperate or clinging.)
SELECTED REFERENCES: **Journey to Ixtlan - Page [69.9-70.3]** ("To be unavailable means that you...or whatever you are clinging to.") **The Fire From Within - Page [26.1-26.4]** ("The foreman at the house followed...trampling on you is called control.)
SEE ALSO: *DESPERATION, WARRIOR-UNAVAILABILITY*

EXISTENCE-REASON-[THE REASON FOR EXISTENCE]: (Warriors know that the reason for the existence of all sentient beings is to enhance awareness; the Eagle creates sentient beings so that they will live and enrich the awareness it gives them with life.)
SELECTED REFERENCES: **A Separate Reality - Page [181.5-181.7]** ("Life for a warrior is an...he would be battling to the end.") **A Separate Reality - Page [194.5]** ("True. It's not the same...not a single thing is the same.") **The Fire From Within - Page [37.9-38.1]** (He stopped me with a gesture...Don Juan called it a colossal discovery.) **The Fire From Within - Page [38.7-39.2]** (They *saw* that it is the Eagle...the awareness that is the Eagle's food.") **The Art of Dreaming - Page [45.8-45.9]** ("For sorcerers, having life means having...as the precondition of being alive.")
SEE ALSO: *AWARENESS, EAGLE*

EXPECTATION-[EXPECTATION]: (Warriors know it is stupidity that forces man to discard everything that does not conform to his self-reflective expectations.)
SELECTED REFERENCES: **The Power of Silence - Page [219.2-219.4]** (He said that one of the...the fact that it could move.)
SEE ALSO: *STUPIDITY-IGNORANCE, SELF-REFLECTION*

EXPECTATION-GAUGING-[GAUGING ONE'S EXPECTATIONS]: (Warriors know that when dealing with the inorganic beings, they must gauge their expectations to allow for the vast barrier between the world of men and the world of the inorganic beings.)
SELECTED REFERENCES: **The Art of Dreaming - Page [47.4-47.6]** ("What should I do...as it takes to be acknowledged.)
SEE ALSO: *INORGANIC-BEINGS-ENTICING-DREAMING, EXPECTATION*

EXPECTATION-WARRIOR-[THE WARRIORS' EXPECTATION]: SEE: WARRIOR-EXPECTATION-[THE WARRIORS' EXPECTATION]

EXPECTED-UNEXPECTED-[THE EXPECTED AND THE UNEXPECTED]: (Warriors know they must learn to balance themselves and control things in their lives without controlling anything; warriors strive to meet any conceivable situation, either expected or unexpected, with equal efficiency.)
SELECTED REFERENCES: **The Eagle's Gift - Page [306.9-307.2]** (Vicente came to my side next...and the unexpected with equal efficiency.)
SEE ALSO: *WARRIOR-BALANCE, WARRIOR-CONTROL, WARRIOR-EFFICIENCY, WARRIOR-PREPAREDNESS, EXPECTATION, EQUILIBRIUM, WARRIOR-CONTROLLED-FOLLY, CONTROL-WITHOUT-CONTROL*

EXPERIENCE-EXPERIENCES-[THE EXPERIENCE OF EXPERIENCES]: SEE: WARRIOR-EXPERIENCE-[THE EXPERIENCE OF EXPERIENCES IS BEING A WARRIOR]

EXPLANATION-[EXPLANATION]: (Warriors know that explanations stem from the tonal's sterile and boring insistence on having everything under its control; warriors learn to do without explanations because the road to power is filled with things that are beyond words, things that can only be experienced or utilized; warriors know that explanations are never wasted because they are imprinted in us for immediate or later use or to help prepare the way to reach silent knowledge.)

SELECTED REFERENCES: **A Separate Reality - Page [126.7-127.5]** ("You really know how to talk...not sure of your explanations either.") **A Separate Reality - Page [257.5-257.8]** ("I think I understand what don...one side of this," he said.) **A Separate Reality - Page [262.3-262.9]** (Before I left I sat down...indulge too much," he said softly.) **Journey to Ixtlan - Page [39.3-39.4]** (I told him that his explanation...really wanted to learn about plants.) **Journey to Ixtlan - Page [246.5-247.2]** (I told don Juan that my insistence...so let your body decide what's what.") **Tales of Power - Page [5.9-6.1]** ("I was under the impression that...he's not as stiff as you.") **Tales of Power - Page [174.6-175.7]** ("In your case, for instance, you have...to have everything under its control.) **Tales of Power - Page [191.2-191.5]** ("I've never put a ban on talking,"...are not applicable to the *nagual.")* **Tales of Power - Page [195.1-195.3]** ("That's a meaningless statement,"...if your life would be different.) **Tales of Power - Page [246.1-246.2]** ("I don't want to emphasize those events...this time a much larger view.") **Tales of Power - Page [276.8-277.6]** ("To make *reason* feel safe...it is that we are witnessing.") **The Fire From Within - Page [49.3-49.5]** (I asked him why he had...said, but in a different way.") **The Power of Silence - Page [49.5]** ("I like poems for many reasons,"...what can hardly be explained.") **The Power of Silence - Page [81.5-81.6]** ("Sorcerers have a rule of thumb...tongue-tied, confused, and evasive.") **The Power of Silence - Page [85.5-85.8]** (But before I could savor...could only make use of it.) **The Power of Silence - Page [132.9-133.1]** ("What about all the explanations...are the result of my ruthlessness.") **The Power of Silence - Page [198.5-198.7]** (Don Juan, displaying great patience, discussed...our way to reaching silent knowledge.) **The Art of Dreaming - Page [8.4-8.6]** ("I can't explain to you why...is far too great to resist.)
SEE ALSO: *REASON, TALKING, KNOWLEDGE-SILENT*

EXPLANATION-ABSTRACT-[ABSTRACT EXPLANATIONS]: (Warriors know that abstract explanation is another term for the teachings for the left side; the apprentice receives abstract explanations from the nagual while in states of heightened awareness.)

SELECTED REFERENCES: **The Art of Dreaming - Page [17.4-17.5]** (Don Juan justified the indispensability of...gives them abstract and detailed explanations.) **The Art of Dreaming - Page [18.1-18.3]** (In the second attention, don Juan...something we've learned very early in life.")
SEE ALSO: *TEACHERS-TEACHING, AWARENESS-LEFT*

EXPLANATION-LEFT-SIDE-[THE IMPORTANCE OF EXPLANATIONS BEFORE THE WARRIOR ENTERS THE LEFT-SIDE AWARENESS]: SEE: AWARENESS-LEFT-TRANSITION [THE TRANSITION TO THE LEFT SIDE AWARENESS]

EXPLORATION-NEW-AREA-WARRIOR-[THE NEW AREA OF EXPLORATION FOR THE WARRIOR]-(TOP)

EYE-DOOR-OPENING-[OPENING THE EYE-DOOR]-(TOP)

EYE-DREAMING-[THE EYE OF DREAMING]-(TOP)

EYES-[EYES]: (Warriors experience first-hand the magical properties of the eyes; the eyes are linked with intent; the freedom of the warriors' eyes; intent is experienced with the eyes, not the reason.)

SELECTED REFERENCES: **A Separate Reality - Page [219.1-219.2]** ("First of all you must use your ears...listens to the sounds of the world.") **A Separate Reality - Page [252.7-252.8]** (I told him that it had...and shook his head in disbelief.) **Tales of Power - Page [173.1-173.5]** (Our eyes are the eyes of the *tonal*...to peek into that infinity.) **Tales of Power - Page [192.2-192.6]** (Anyone who sees can witness that...apprehend and the *tonal* cannot explain.") **The Second Ring of Power - Page [159.5-160.8]** ("The Nagual told me that a warrior...I'm like you, a bit stubborn and lazy.") **The Eagle's Gift - Page [308.1-309.1]** (Silvio Manuel smiled, cognizant of my problem....physical bodies when I closed my eyes.) **The Eagle's Gift - Page [310.5]** (The setting for the poem was...to be focused in their eyes.) **The Fire From Within - Page [178.4-**

178.5] (I gently shook Genaro. He slowly...my back and restored my equilibrium.) **The Fire From Within - Page [273.6-273.7]** (Another thing I had done that...merely odd, unknown, strange.) **The Power of Silence - Page [125.4-125.5]** (Our assemblage points are constantly...let their eyes beckon it.") **The Power of Silence - Page [126.1-126.9]** Ruthlessness makes sorcerer's eyes shine,...to move their assemblage points.") **The Power of Silence - Page [166.9-167.6]** (He said that as soon as he had *intended*...with the eyes, not with the reason.") **The Power of Silence - Page [243.3-243.5]** ("Intensity, being an aspect of *intent*...But I have already explained that.")
SEE ALSO: *INTENT, EYES-(ALL), WARRIOR-INTENT-BECKONS-EYES*

EYES-CONNECTION-TRUE-[THE TRUE CONNECTION OF THE EYES]:
(Warriors know that the eyes are only superficially connected to the world of everyday life; their deeper connection is to the abstract; the eyes are directly connected with intent; the warriors' eyes are focused on intent while still being on the world, looking for food.)
SELECTED REFERENCES: **The Power of Silence - Page [126.3-126.9]** (He explained that the reason sorcerers...eyes to move their assemblage points.") **The Power of Silence - Page [130.4-131.4]** (Don Juan began to explain what...is especially true for the naguals.")
SEE ALSO: *EYES, INTENT, ABSTRACT, LOOKING-SEEING, SEEING*

*EYES-CROSSING-[CROSSING THE EYES]: SEE: PERCEPTION-DOUBLE-[DOUBLE PERCEPTION OF THE WORLD]

EYES-DREAMING BODY-[THE EYES OF THE DREAMING BODY]-(TOP)

EYES-ENERGY-GAINING-[GAINING ENERGY THROUGH THE EYES]:
(Warriors know that they can boost their energy by allowing the light of the sun [or any other light for that matter] into their eyes.)
SELECTED REFERENCES: **The Second Ring of Power - Page [276.5-276.7]** (The Nagual said that the best...light that could shine on the eyes.) **The Second Ring of Power - Page [287.2-287.9]** (I wanted to tell her more on the...casually pushed my pad out of reach.)
SEE ALSO: *ENERGY, SUN-ENERGY*

EYES-FOCUS-INTENT-[THE EYES FOCUS ON INTENT]: SEE: EYES-CONNECTION-TRUE-[THE TRUE CONNECTION OF THE EYES]

EYES-FOCUS-WORLD-[THE EYES FOCUS ON THE EVERYDAY WORLD]:
(Warriors know that under normal conditions, people's eyes are focused on the world, looking for food, looking for shelter, looking for love; the focus of the warriors' eyes is on intent, and yet their eyes remain focused on the world as well, looking for food.)
SELECTED REFERENCES: **The Power of Silence - Page [130.5-130.9]** (Under normal conditions, however, people's eyes...on the world, looking for food.")
SEE ALSO: *WORLD-IN-NOT-OF, LOOKING-SEEING, SEEING, EYES-CONNECTION-TRUE, ATTENTION-FIRST, DESCRIPTION-WORLD*

EYES-FUNCTION-TRUE-[THE TRUE FUNCTION OF THE EYES]: *(The warrior knows that the true function of the eyes is to serve as the catchers of intent; the warrior beckons intent with his eyes and also uses them to beckon another aspect of intent called "seeing".)*
SELECTED REFERENCES: **The Eagle's Gift - Page [308.3-308.6]** (He turned one more time into a...the eyes, the catchers of intent.)
SEE ALSO: *INTENT, WARRIOR-INTENT-BECKON-EYES, SEEING, EYES*

EYES-INTENT-BECKON-[THE EYES BECKON INTENT]: SEE: WARRIOR-INTENT-BECKON-EYES-[THE WARRIOR BECKONS INTENT

EYES-INTENT-CONNECTION-[THE EYES CONNECTION WITH INTENT]: SEE: EYES-CONNECTION-TRUE-[THE TRUE CONNECTION OF THE EYES]

WITH HIS EYES]

EYES-MANIPULATING-[MANIPULATING THE EYES]: SEE: STALKER-EYES-MANIPULATE-[STALKERS MANIPULATE THE EYES]

EYES-MEMORY-[THE EYES' MEMORY]: SEE: EYES-SHINE-INTENT-BECKON-[THE SHINE OF THE WARRIORS' EYES BECKONS INTENT]

EYES-ROLLING-[ROLLING THE EYES]: (Warriors know they can roll their eyes as a simple procedure to help relieve feelings of impatience, anger, sadness or despair; a movement of the eyes which causes the assemblage point to move momentarily in lieu of the true mastery of intent.)
    SELECTED REFERENCES: **The Fire From Within** - Page [260.4-260.6] ("The new seers recommend a very simple...in lieu of true mastery of *intent.*") **The Fire From Within** - Page [261.1-261.3] (He urged me to relax and move...had *seen* the mold of man.) **The Power of Silence** - Page [71.6-71.8] ("Don't waste energy," don Juan commanded..."Don't look at that man.")
    SEE ALSO: *INTENT-MASTERY, ASSEMBLAGE-POINT-MOVING, EYES*

EYES-SHIFTING-[SHIFTING THE EYES]: (Warriors know that shifting the eyes is a facet of the warriors' controlled folly; when warriors wish, they can shift their eyes and choose to "see" rather than look upon a scene.)
    SELECTED REFERENCES: **A Separate Reality** - Page [83.4-83.6] ("Would a man of knowledge cry...funny I look and I laugh.") **A Separate Reality** - Page [90.4-91.4] ("How does a man of knowledge exercise...he said. "It's hard work.") **Tales of Power** - Page [173.8-174.1] ("Another thing one should do when facing...safeguard the order of the *tonal.*)
    SEE ALSO: *LOOKING-VS-SEEING, SEEING, WARRIOR-CONTROLLED-FOLLY*

EYES-SHINE-[THE VARIOUS TYPES OF SHINE IN THE WARRIORS' EYES]: SEE: EYES-SHINE-INTENT-BECKON-[THE SHINE OF THE WARRIORS' EYES BECKONS INTENT]

EYES-SHINE-INTENT-BECKON-[THE SHINE OF THE WARRIORS' EYES BECKONS INTENT]: (Warriors know that the shine of their eyes beckons intent; each spot to which the warriors' assemblage point moves is indicated by its own distinctive shine; since the eyes have a memory of their own, they can recall any spot by recollecting the specific shine associated with that position of the assemblage point.)
    SELECTED REFERENCES: **The Power of Silence** - Page [126.1-126.3] (Ruthlessness makes sorcerers' eyes shine...specific shine associated with that spot.") **The Power of Silence** - Page [167.3-167.6] ("The only way of talking about...the eyes, not with the reason.") **The Power of Silence** - Page [243.3-243.5] ("Intensity, being an aspect of *intent*...But I have already explained that.")
    SEE ALSO: *WARRIOR-INTENT-BECKON-EYES, INTENT, RUTHLESSNESS-SHINE, ASSEMBLAGE-POINT-MOVING-EYES-SHINE*

EYES-SOOTHING-[SOOTHING WITH THE EYES]: (Warriors know they can soothe themselves or others with their eyes.)
    SELECTED REFERENCES: **Tales of Power** - Page [17.9-18.7] (He gave me furtive glances from....He rubbed his umbilical region.)
    SEE ALSO: *EYES*

EYES-UNKNOWN-KEY-[THE EYES ARE THE KEY TO ENTERING THE UNKNOWN]: (Warriors know that the eyes are the key to entering the unknown; it is the eyes that open the way.)
    SELECTED REFERENCES: **The Fire From Within** - Page [90.4] (They believed that our eyes are...the eyes to open the way.")
    SEE ALSO: *EYES, UNKNOWN*

EYES-WALKED-ON-["MY EYES WALKED ON"]: (Warriors know that the expression "my eyes walked on", is an expression used by the tenant to describe his "seeing".)

SELECTED REFERENCES: The Art of Dreaming - Page [215.8-215.9] (Don Juan reminded me of time...the helmets of the Spanish conquerors.")

SEE ALSO: *SEEING, TENANT*

EYES-WINDOW-[THE EYES AS WINDOWS]: (Warriors know that the eyes are the windows of the tonal; the warriors' task is to convince the tonal that the nagual can pass in front of those same windows; warriors can set their eyes free, they can let them be windows to peer into boredom or to peer into infinity.)

SELECTED REFERENCES: Tales of Power - Page [173.4-173.5] (The point is to convince the...or to peek into that infinity.")

SEE ALSO: *EYES, PERCEPTION, TONAL, NAGUAL*

EYES-WITNESSED-ALL-[EYES THAT HAVE WITNESSED ALL THERE IS TO SEE]-(TOP)

F

FACADE-TRANSFORMING-[TRANSFORMING THE FACADE]: (Warriors know that transforming the facade refers to the sustained act of shifting the place of prominence of specific elements on the island of the tonal; warriors learn to emphasize the things that are truly important, like impeccability, and to de-emphasize those things that drain their power, like self-importance.)
> SELECTED REFERENCES: **A Separate Reality - Page [156.2-156.3]** ("Your life is getting complicated...stay here quietly and rearrange yourself.") **Tales of Power - Page [241.4-242.5]** (Don Juan pointed out then that...were there, without ever being used.")
> SEE ALSO: *WARRIOR-EMPHASIS, TONAL-ISLAND, SELF-IMPORTANCE, WARRIOR-IMPECCABILITY, WARRIOR-TRANSFORMATION, CHANGE*

FACE-FIRST-[THE FIRST FACE OF THE SECOND ATTENTION]: SEE: ATTENTION-SECOND-FACES-TWO-[THE TWO FACES OF THE SECOND ATTENTION]

FACES-SECOND-ATTENTION-TWO-[THE SECOND FACE OF THE SECOND ATTENTION]: SEE: ATTENTION-SECOND-FACES-TWO-[THE TWO FACES OF THE SECOND ATTENTION]

FAILURE-[FAILURE]: (Warriors know specific ways in which to measure failure or defeat; the warriors' struggle is to keep from abandoning the quest for knowledge.)
> SELECTED REFERENCES: **The Teachings of Don Juan - Page [86.5-87.1]** ("A man who is defeated by power...never have really abandoned himself to it.") **Tales of Power - Page [55.8-56.2]** ("But you yourself told me,...will not let you go either way.") **The Second Ring of Power - Page [174.5-174.8]** ("No. Unfortunately, understanding is not their...but an impeccable warrior survives, always.") **The Fire From Within - Page [30.1-30.5]** (I explained to don Juan that...ranks of the petty tyrants for life.") **The Fire From Within - Page [260.2-260.4]** (He also said that there was...by gripping feelings of defeat.) **The Power of Silence - Page [48.9-49.5]** (He said that we, as average...simple anger at having missed out.)
> SEE ALSO: *VICTORY-(ALL), DEFEAT-(ALL), DEPRESSION-MELANCHOLY, ABANDON, WARRIOR-STRUGGLE*

FAITH-RELIGIOUS-[RELIGIOUS FAITH]: (Warriors know that "seeing", the pragmatic basis for nagualism, is not a matter of faith, it is a matter of experience; seers do not have faith in the principles of their teachings, they have verified them with their own "seeing" experience.)
> SELECTED REFERENCES: **The Fire From Within - Page [38.2-38.9]** (In a half-serious tone he asked...faith or deduction. They *saw* it.) **The Fire From Within - Page [261.3-261.4]** (I moved my eyes as he suggested...sacrilegious statements I had ever heard.) **The Fire From Within - Page [262.8-263.5]** (As I heard don Juan's explanation...man as often as they please.) **The Power of Silence - Page [121.1-121.3]** (I had narrated all of this...an atmosphere of almost religious faith.)
> SEE ALSO: *SEEING-(ALL), GOD, EAGLE, EXISTENCE-REASON, MOLD-MAN*

FALCON-WHITE-[THE WHITE FALCON]-(TOP)

FANNING-EVENT-[FANNING THE EVENT]: (Warriors know that fanning the event is part of the recapitulation; a breathing procedure which involves the movement of the head coupled with rhythmical natural breathing; long exhalations are performed as the head moves slowly from right to left; long inhalations are taken as the head moves from slowly from left to right.)

SELECTED REFERENCES: **The Art of Dreaming - Page [148.9-149.4]** (Don Juan taught me that the...themselves left behind during the interaction.)
SEE ALSO: *RECAPITULATION, BREATHING*

FAREWELL-WARRIOR-[THE WARRIORS' FAREWELL]: SEE: WARRIOR-FAREWELL-[THE WARRIORS' FAREWELL]

FART-[FART]: (Warriors know that a fart is another term for the stalkers' second classification of personality types, the self-centered personality.)
SELECTED REFERENCES: **The Power of Silence - Page [247.7-248.3]** ("Don't give me that combination nonsense...himself seriously, while you still do.")
SEE ALSO: *PEOPLE-TYPES*

FATE-PREOCCUPATION-HEREDITARY-[THE HEREDITARY PREOCCUPATION WITH FATE]: (Warriors know it is man's connecting link with intent which is responsible for his hereditary preoccupation with fate.)
SELECTED REFERENCES: **The Power of Silence - Page [48.9-49.1]** (He said that we, as average...us our hereditary preoccupation with fate.)
SEE ALSO: *WARRIOR-FATE, WARRIOR-INTENT-LINK, AWARENESS-SUBLIMINAL*

FATE-WARRIOR-[THE WARRIORS' FATE]: SEE: WARRIOR-FATE-[THE WARRIORS' FATE]

FATIGUE-[FATIGUE]: SEE: TIREDNESS-[TIREDNESS]

FAVORS-POWER-[THE FAVORS OF POWER]: SEE: WARRIOR-POWER-FAVOR-[WARRIORS AND THE FAVORS OF POWER]

FEAR-[FEAR]: (Warriors know that fear is one of the greatest forces in life, a force that makes us perceive things in a different way; fright never injures anyone; what injures the spirit is having someone always on your back beating you; fear is the first enemy of warriors; warriors must defy their fear and take the next step in learning in spite of the things they fear; warriors learn to vanquish fear through the power of their decisions; when the moment of truth comes, fear is the only worthwhile condition of the warrior.)
SELECTED REFERENCES: **The Teachings of Don Juan - Page [48.6-48.7]** (All I know is that it makes...you see things in a different way.") **The Teachings of Don Juan - Page [49.7-50.5]** (I asked him again what this new...that instead of on your fear?") **The Teachings of Don Juan - Page [54.2-54.3]** (He said that fears are natural;...without an ally, or without knowledge.) **The Teachings of Don Juan - Page [84.1-85.3]** ("He slowly begins to learn...dispels fear, but also blinds.) **The Teachings of Don Juan - Page [107.1]** (But your decision to keep on...be free of fear or ambition) **The Teachings of Don Juan - Page [160.9]** ("I have told you that to choose...blinds you with ambition") **The Teachings of Don Juan - Page [176.2-176.3]** ("Perhaps by now you know it...fear to understand what I mean.") **The Teachings of Don Juan - Page [188.5]** (And, although don Juan has not...enemy of a man of knowledge.) **A Separate Reality - Page [27.7-29.5]** ("You ought to let the smoke guide...to be around here for that.") **A Separate Reality - Page [47.6]** ("Once you decided to come to...to come should have vanquished them.) **A Separate Reality - Page [190.1-190.2]** (He laughed at me, saying that...before you shit in your pants.") **A Separate Reality - Page [251.7-251.9]** ("Fright is something one can never...is the master at all times.") **Journey to Ixtlan - Page [xii.3]** (Fright never injures anyone. what injures...do and what not to do.) **Tales of Power - Page [20.6-21.3]** (His expression was deliberately comical...time and your power fearing me.") **Tales of Power - Page [27.8-28.1]** (Don Juan's words, and above all...knowledge he cancels out its awesomeness.") **The Fire From Within - Page [44.7-44.8]** ("One of the greatest forces..."It spurs them to learn.") **The Fire From Within - Page [49.3-49.5]** (I asked him why he had...said, but in a different way.") **The Fire From**

Within - Page [92.4-92.8] (My fear was so terrifying that...constructs they controlled their fear instead.) **The Fire From Within - Page [107.9-108.1]** (I commented on my abrupt change...certain threshold inside man's cocoon.) **The Fire From Within - Page [194.3-194.7]** (Don Juan said that when the...as if don Juan were alone.) **The Fire From Within - Page [246.2-246.3]** (He added that I had performed two...that warriors have nothing to fear.) **The Fire From Within - Page [260.9-261.1]** (He winked at me and said...me remember *seeing* the mold of man.) **The Fire From Within - Page [271.8-271.9]** ("Freedom is like a contagious disease,"...for this moment. And so will you.") **The Art of Dreaming - Page [47.7-47.9]** ("Yes, but for a perfect result...is unnecessary, to say the least.") **The Art of Dreaming - Page [48.4]** ("Fear can settle down in our...be mavericks to deal with it.) **The Art of Dreaming - Page [250.8-251.6]** (I stretched my legs and put...Are sorcerers people in love now?")
    SEE ALSO: *WARRIOR-ENEMIES-FOUR-NATURAL, WARRIOR-DECISIONS, WARRIOR-CONDITION, LEARNING-HARDSHIPS*

FEAR-CARRY-NEW-ALIGNMENT-[CARRYING FEAR TO A NEW POSITION OF ALIGNMENT]: (Warriors know that fear is only prevalent among the emanations of daily life and that to carry those feeling from the usual state of awareness into new positions of the assemblage point is indeed a travesty.)

    SELECTED REFERENCES: **The Fire From Within - Page [244.5-245.1]** ("Don't pay any more attention to those...such a preposterous thing as that.)
    SEE ALSO: *FEAR, ASSEMBLAGE-POINT-MOVING, ALIGNMENT*

FEAR-CHANNEL-[THE CHANNEL OF FEAR]: (Warriors know an emotional connection exists between the daily world of men and the world of the second attention; fear can act as a conduit or channel through which beings from the other world can follow dreamers back into the world of men.)

    SELECTED REFERENCES: **The Art of Dreaming - Page [48.2-48.3]** (Since at the beginning of dreaming...world, with disastrous results for us.")
    SEE ALSO: *FEAR, WORLD-OTHER, FRIGHT-AVENUE*

FEAR-JOLTS-[JOLTS OF PHYSICAL FEAR]: SEE: WARRIOR-SHIVER-[THE SHIVER OF THE WARRIOR]

FEAR-NAGUAL-LOSING-[THE FEAR OF LOSING THE NAGUAL]: (Warriors know there are times when the only thing that keeps them on the warriors' path is the fear of losing the nagual.)

    SELECTED REFERENCES: **The Art of Dreaming - Page [250.8-251.4]** (I stretched my legs and put my...is the fear of losing the nagual.")
    SEE ALSO: *FEAR, NAGUAL*

FEAR-NOTHING-WARRIOR-[WARRIORS HAVE NOTHING TO FEAR]: SEE: WARRIOR-FEAR-NOTHING-[THE WARRIORS HAVE NOTHING TO FEAR]

FEAR-PARCELING-OUT-[PARCELING OUT ONE'S FEAR]: (Warriors know that it is possible for sorcerers to control their allies by parceling out fear and other emotions to them.)

    SELECTED REFERENCES: **The Fire From Within - Page [102.9-103.6]** ("But why did they chase you...actually held the allies in bondage.) **The Fire From Within - Page [191.6-192.2]** (Don Juan said that when he...made a deal with the creature.")
    SEE ALSO: *FEAR, ALLIES, ALLIES-EMOTIONS, TOLTECS, SORCERER-ANTIQUITY, TOLTEC-GHOULS, ALLIES-FEAR-FEED*

FEAR-RATIONAL-[RATIONAL FEARS]: SEE: IMPECCABILITY-STATE-OF-BEING-[AN IMPECCABLE STATE OF BEING]

FEAR-THRESHOLD-[THE THRESHOLD OF FEAR]: *(Warriors know that fear does not exist as soon as the assemblage point moves beyond a certain threshold inside man's cocoon.)*

SELECTED REFERENCES: **The Fire From Within - Page [107.9-108.1]** (I was terribly disturbed by the...a certain threshold inside man's cocoon.) **The Fire From Within - Page [108.8-108.9]** (He said that for me to have...because I had enough surplus energy.)
SEE ALSO: *FEAR, ASSEMBLAGE-POINT-THRESHOLD*

FEATHER-[FEATHERS]-(TOP)

FEELING-[FEELING]: SEE: WEST-[WESTERLY WOMEN]

FEELING-RIGHT-ALWAYS-[FEELING THAT WE ARE ALWAYS RIGHT]: *(Warriors know that the cynicism of the average man does not allow him to reorder his understanding of the world; it forces him to feel that he is always right.)*

SELECTED REFERENCES: **The Art of Dreaming - Page [171.9]** ("Your problem is your cynicism...feel that we are always right.")
SEE ALSO: *CYNICISM, FACADE-TRANSFORMING*

FEELING-WORLD-[FEELING THE WORLD]: SEE: KNOWLEDGE-DIRECT-[DIRECT KNOWLEDGE]

FEELINGS-[FEELINGS]: *(Warriors know that feelings or emotions create cobweb-like filaments which are projected out of the luminous body; these filaments are potentially draining to the luminous body and are of great concern to the warrior; warriors know they are no more than a "feeling" and that what we call our body is a cluster of luminous filaments that have awareness; feeling is one of the eight points on the sorcerers' diagram.)*

SELECTED REFERENCES: **Journey to Ixtlan - Page [196.1-196.3]** ("You may say that there is...them shadows is merely our *doing* .") **Tales of Power - Page [9.3]** ("These are the boundaries I'm talking about...a feeling, an awareness encased here.") **Tales of Power - Page [93.8]** (Genaro demonstrated for you with tremendous...luminous fibers that have awareness.) **Tales of Power - Page [96.2-96.9]** ("We may say that every one..."dreaming" were on the right side.) **Tales of Power - Page [276.3]** (Your *reason* cannot fight the physical...you are a nameless cluster of feelings.) **The Second Ring of Power - Page [235.2-235.6]** (I told her that my sadness in leaving...of us had accepted our fate.) **The Eagle's Gift - Page [85.1-85.3]** ("Our feelings make boundaries around anything,"...we'll never be back, we broke it.") **The Eagle's Gift - Page [174.5-174.8]** (The female warriors are called the...like a cold gust of wind.) **The Eagle's Gift - Page [289.1-289.2]** (Florinda claimed that the luminous body...potentially draining to the luminous body.) **The Fire From Within - Page [121.3-121.4]** (He remarked that my flaw was...moved into man's band of emanations.) **The Fire From Within - Page [283.2-283.3]** ("How does a journey like that...emanations that are inside the cocoon.") **The Art of Dreaming - Page [147.9-148.2]** ("The recapitulation of our lives never...them that is not quite clear.")
SEE ALSO: *RECAPITULATION, REMEMBERING, BREATHING, ENERGY, SORCERER-DIAGRAM, LUMINOUS-FILAMENTS, WARRIOR-FEELINGS, BOUNDARIES-AFFECTION, FEELINGS-(ALL)*

FEELINGS-HUMAN-[HUMAN FEELINGS]: SEE HUMAN-FORM-[THE HUMAN FORM]

FEELINGS-INTENDING-BACK-[INTENDING FEELINGS BACK]: SEE: INFORMATION-EXPERIENCE-STORAGE-[THE STORAGE OF INFORMATION AND EXPERIENCE IN THE POSITION OF THE ASSEMBLAGE POINT]

FEELINGS-INTERVENTION-[THE INTERVENTION OF FEELINGS]:
(Warriors know that they are capable of intuiting things directly and unerringly; mistakes occur only when warriors' feelings intervene and cloud their link with intent.)
SELECTED REFERENCES: The Power of Silence - Page [14.5-14.7] (He said that the feeling everyone...knowledge is totally accurate and functional.)
SEE ALSO: *WARRIOR-INTUITION, WARRIOR-LINK-INTENT, FEELINGS, OMENS*

FEELINGS-NAMELESS-CLUSTER-[A NAMELESS CLUSTER OF
FEELINGS]: (Warriors know that they are no more than a nameless cluster of feelings.)
SELECTED REFERENCES: Tales of Power - Page [276.2-276.4] ("Those leaps were only the beginning...although one can never explain it.) Tales of Power - Page [278.4-278.5] ("Now you should sit on Genaro's place...life that binds that cluster of feelings.")
SEE ALSO: *EAGLE-EMANATIONS, EAGLE-EMANATIONS-CLUSTERING, FEELINGS*

FEELINGS-WARRIOR-[WARRIORS PIN THEMSELVES DOWN WITH THEIR FEELINGS]: SEE: WARRIOR-FEELINGS-[WARRIORS PIN THEMSELVES DOWN WITH THEIR FEELINGS]

FEMALE-[FEMALE]: SEE: WOMEN-[WOMEN]

FEMALE-MALE-[FEMALENESS VS MALENESS]: SEE: MALE-FEMALE-[MALENESS VS FEMALENESS]

FEMALE-PERSONALITY-[FEMALE PERSONALITIES]: SEE: WARRIOR-FEMALE-[FEMALE WARRIORS]

FEMALE-UNIVERSE-[THE FEMALE UNIVERSE]: (Warriors know that the universe is markedly female, and that maleness, being an offshoot of femaleness, is almost scarce and thus coveted; consequently, the inorganic beings, as a rule, are not the slightest bit interested in women; women also have much more of a natural facility with the nagual; the inorganic beings believe that the female principle has such pliability and so vast a scope that its members are impervious to their traps and set ups.)
SELECTED REFERENCES: The Eagle's Gift - Page [157.8-158.2] ("Why did the Nagual woman go...protection," she said. "I'm a woman.) The Art of Dreaming - Page [103.3-103.4] (He stated that the nagual Rosendo...femaleness, is almost scarce, thus, coveted.) The Art of Dreaming - Page [188.1-188.8] ("Women in general have a natural bent...even if I stood on my head.) The Art of Dreaming - Page [246.1-246.3] (The death defier was unavoidably caught...out of the inorganic beings' realm.)
SEE ALSO: *INORGANIC-BEINGS, WARRIOR-FEMALE*

FEMALE-WARRIOR-[FEMALE WARRIORS]: SEE: WARRIOR-FEMALE-[FEMALE WARRIORS]

FEROCITY-WOMEN-[WOMEN'S FEROCITY]: SEE: WOMEN-TALENT-[WOMEN'S TALENT], ENEMY-RELENTLESS-WOMEN-[WOMEN ARE RELENTLESS ENEMIES]

FIGHTING-FORM-WARRIOR-[THE WARRIORS' FIGHTING FORM]:
SEE: WARRIOR-FIGHTING-FORM [THE WARRIORS' FIGHTING FORM]

FIGHTING-POSTURE-WARRIOR-[THE WARRIORS' FIGHTING POSTURE]: SEE: VIGIL-POSITION [THE POSITION OF SITTING "IN

VIGIL"], WARRIOR-FIGHTING-FORM-[THE WARRIORS' FIGHTING FORM]

FINDING-CARLOS-[HOW POWER FOUND CARLOS]-(TOP)

FINDING-CAROL-[HOW POWER FOUND CAROL THE NAGUAL WOMAN]-(TOP): SEE: FINDING-NAGUAL-WOMAN-[HOW POWER FOUND CAROL THE NAGUAL WOMAN AND OLINDA THE NAGUAL WOMAN]-(TOP)

FINDING-ELIGIO-[HOW POWER FOUND ELIGIO]-(TOP)

FINDING-GORDA-[HOW POWER FOUND GORDA]-(TOP)

FINDING-JOSEPHINA-[HOW POWER FOUND JOSEPHINA]-(TOP)

FINDING-LIDIA-[HOW POWER FOUND LIDIA]-(TOP)

FINDING-NAGUAL-WOMAN-[HOW POWER FOUND CAROL THE NAGUAL WOMAN AND OLINDA THE NAGUAL WOMAN]-(TOP)

FINDING-OLINDA-[HOW POWER FOUND OLINDA THE NAGUAL WOMAN]-(TOP): SEE: FINDING-NAGUAL-WOMAN-[FINDING CAROL THE NAGUAL WOMAN AND OLINDA THE NAGUAL WOMAN]-(TOP)

FINDING-PABLITO-[HOW POWER FOUND PABLITO]-(TOP)

FINDING-ROSA-[HOW POWER FOUND ROSA]-(TOP)

FINESSE-WARRIOR-[THE WARRIORS' FINESSE]: SEE: WARRIOR-FINESSE-[THE WARRIORS' FINESSE]

FIRE-GAZING-[FIRE GAZING]: SEE: GAZING-[GAZING]

FIRE-TRANSPORTED-[TRANSPORTED ON THE POWER OF FLAME]-(TOP): SEE: FLAME-TRANSPORTED [TRANSPORTED ON THE POWER OF FLAME]-(TOP)

*FIRE-WITHIN-[THE FIRE FROM WITHIN]: (Warriors know that the fire from within is the force of the Eagle's emanations which enables warriors to burn with complete consciousness; the movement of the warriors' assemblage point across the entire field of luminous energy; a single stroke which creates a force so intense that it consumes the warriors' entire luminous mass; the natural end of the mastery of awareness; the extension of the glow of awareness beyond the bounds of the luminous cocoon in one single stroke; an expansion of the glow of awareness that kindles not just one band at a time, but all the Eagle's emanations inside the warriors' cocoon; a burst of incandescence inside the luminous cocoon, an explosion of light of such magnitude that the boundaries of the luminous cocoon are diffused and the emanations inside extend themselves beyond anything imaginable; the way in which warriors fuse themselves with the emanations at large and glide into eternity in a state of full awareness; the physical result of burning with the fire from within is the warriors' total and instantaneous disintegration; the new seers discovered that if the assemblage point is made to move constantly to the confines of the unknown and made to return to the limit of the known, then when it is finally released

it moves like lightening across the entire cocoon and aligns all the emanations inside the cocoon at once.)

SELECTED REFERENCES: The Second Ring of Power - Page [300.6-300.7] (The last series was fire,...and have color and movement in them.) The Eagle's Gift - Page [219.7-219.8] (As the two of them dissolved into...had witnessed of their benefactor's world.) The Fire From Within - Page [xiii.5-xiii.7] (Although he felt that he was inextricably...free, as if they had never existed.) The Fire From Within - Page [57.2-57.3] (There was a long pause...It passed and he went on talking.) The Fire From Within - Page [67.4-67.5] ("The third attention is attained...Eagle's emanations inside man's cocoon.") The Fire From Within - Page [113.8-114.3] (Yet it is nothing in comparison...emanations at large, and glide into eternity.") The Fire From Within - Page [181.6-181.7] (Seers who gazed at the Eagle's...burned with the fire from within.) The Fire From Within - Page [227.4-227.6] (He said that the same force can produce...their total and instantaneous disintegration.) The Fire From Within - Page [295.6-295.7] ("What you are going to do...retain the sense of being themselves.") The Fire From Within - Page [299.3-299.6] (He explained that the new seers...that total freedom means total awareness.") The Power of Silence - Page [104.8] (So in the end sorcerers concerned themselves...free to light the fire from within.) The Power of Silence - Page [207.9-208.3] (Or they could move their assemblage...lacked the speed to pull me out.) The Art of Dreaming - Page [220.8-221.1] (I took a moment to reconsider what...unknown, and they had made it.)

SEE ALSO: ATTENTION-THIRD, AWARENESS-TOTAL, FREEDOM-TOTAL, EAGLE-GIFT, ALIGNMENT-FORCE, EAGLE-EMANATIONS-LIGHTING-ALL

FIRE-WITHIN-PREPARATION-ASSEMBLAGE-POINT-[PREPARING THE ASSEMBLAGE POINT TO BURN WITH THE FIRE FROM WITHIN]:

(Warriors know that if the assemblage point is made to shift constantly to the confines of the unknown but is made to return to a position at the limit of the known, then when it is finally released it moves like lightening across the entire cocoon of man aligning all the emanations inside the cocoon at once.)

SELECTED REFERENCES: The Fire From Within - Page [299.3-299.4] (He explained that the new seers...all the emanations inside the cocoon at once.)

SEE ALSO: FIRE-WITHIN, ASSEMBLAGE-POINT-MOVING, AWARENESS-TOTAL, FREEDOM-TOTAL, ASSEMBLAGE-POINT-THRESHOLD

FIRING-SQUAD-[THE WARRIOR'S FIRING SQUAD]-(TOP) SEE: WARRIOR-WALK-TREES [THE WARRIOR'S WALK TO THE EDGE OF THE TREES]-(TOP)

FIRST-ATTENTION-[THE FIRST ATTENTION]: SEE: ATTENTION-FIRST-[THE FIRST ATTENTION]

FIRST-ENEMY-[THE WARRIORS' FIRST ENEMY]: SEE: FEAR [FEAR]

FIRST-EVENT-[THE FIRST EVENT OF A SERIES]: *(Warriors know that the first event of any series is a blueprint or map of what will develop subsequently; the first event of such a series is an omen proper.)*

SELECTED REFERENCES: The Second Ring of Power - Page [216.7-216.8] (He explained that my first vision...what was going to develop subsequently.)

SEE ALSO: OMENS

FIRST-FACE-[THE FIRST FACE OF THE SECOND ATTENTION]: SEE: ATTENTION-SECOND-FACES-TWO-[THE TWO FACES OF THE SECOND ATTENTION]

FIRST-POINT-[THE FIRST POINT]: SEE: REASON-RATIONALITY-[REASON AND RATIONALITY]

FISH-FACED-MAN-[THE FISH FACED MAN]-(TOP)

FISHERMAN-LINE-CAST-ITSELF-*[THE FISHERMAN WITH A LINE THAT CASTS ITSELF]*: *SEE: ASSEMBLAGE-POINT-FIXATION-DREAMER-DIRECTS-[THE DREAMER DIRECTS THE FIXATION OF HIS ASSEMBLAGE POINT]*

FLAME-TRANSPORTED-*[TRANSPORTED ON THE POWER OF FLAME]*-*(TOP)*

FLAT-AREAS-*[FLAT GEOGRAPHICAL AREAS]*: *SEE: ATTENTION-SECOND-ANTITHETICAL-[THINGS THAT ARE ANTITHETICAL TO THE SECOND ATTENTION]*

FLIGHT-UNKNOWN-INTO-*[THE WARRIORS' FLIGHT INTO THE UNKNOWN]*: *(Warriors know that the flight into the unknown is another term for the warriors' definitive journey.)*
SELECTED REFERENCES: The Eagle's Gift - Page [21.6-21.8] ("When you worry about what to...won't let you live in peace.")
SEE ALSO: *WARRIOR-JOURNEY-DEFINITIVE, WARRIOR-JOURNEY-UNKNOWN, FIRE-WITHIN, UNKNOWN*

FLOOR-SOLEDAD-MAGICAL-*[DONA SOLEDAD'S MAGICAL FLOOR]*-*(TOP) SEE: SOLEDAD-FLOOR-MAGICAL-[DONA SOLEDAD'S MAGICAL FLOOR]-(TOP)*

FLORINDA-*[FLORINDA]*-*(TOP)*

FLORINDA-LEG-*[HEALING FLORINDA'S LEG]*-*(TOP)*

FLOW-THINGS-SEEING-*[SEEING THE FLOW OF THINGS]*: *(Warriors know that the flow of things is another term for "seeing" the Eagle's emanations, the lines of the world; "seeing" the spirit or "seeing" intent.)*
SELECTED REFERENCES: The Power of Silence - Page [99.6-99.9] (He coughed a couple of times...but not the way he meant it.)
SEE ALSO: *SEEING, INTENT, SPIRIT, EAGLE-EMANATIONS-SEEING, LINES-WORLD*

FLUIDITY-ASSEMBLAGE-POINT-*[THE ASSEMBLAGE POINT'S MARGIN OF FLUIDITY]*: *SEE: ASSEMBLAGE POINT-FLUIDITY-[THE ASSEMBLAGE POINT'S MARGIN OF FLUIDITY]*

FLUIDITY-WARRIOR-*[THE WARRIORS' FLUIDITY]*: *SEE: WARRIOR-FLUIDITY-[THE WARRIORS' FLUIDITY]*

FLYING-CARLOS-*[CARLOS' FLYING]*-*(TOP)*

FLYING-DEVIL'S-WEED-*[FLYING WITH THE DEVIL'S WEED]*-*(TOP)*

FLYING-DREAMING-*[FLYING IN DREAMING]*-*(TOP)*

FLYING-GENARO-CARLOS-*[DON GENARO'S FLIGHT WITH CARLOS] WITH CARLOS]*-*(TOP)*

FLYING-GORDA-*[LA GORDA'S FLYING]*-*(TOP)*

FLYING-INTENT-*[THE INTENT OF FLYING]*-*(TOP): SEE: INTENT-FLYING-[THE INTENT OF FLYING]-(TOP)*

FLYING-JUAN-*[DON JUAN'S FLYING]*-*(TOP)*

FOCUS-MATERIAL-ABERRANT-WARRIOR-[THE WARRIORS'
ABERRANT MATERIAL FOCUS]: SEE: WARRIOR-FOCUS-MATERIAL-
ABERRANT-[THE WARRIORS' ABERRANT MATERIAL FOCUS]

FOCUS-SPIRIT-WARRIOR-[THE WARRIORS' FOCUS ON THE SPIRIT]:
SEE: WARRIOR-FOCUS-SPIRIT-[THE WARRIORS' FOCUS ON THE
SPIRIT]

FOCUS-WARRIOR-[THE WARRIORS' FOCUS]: SEE: WARRIOR-
FOCUS-[THE WARRIORS' FOCUS]

FOG-[FOG]: (Warriors know that fog has strange properties and must be
treated with the utmost respect; the fog is akin to smoke for the warrior.)
SELECTED REFERENCES: **Journey to Ixtlan** - **Page [125.4-129.8]** (I followed his
instructions and wrote...And then I fell asleep.) **Journey to Ixtlan** - **Page [133.4-133.5]** ("What
happened to you last night...because it had not been real.) **Journey to Ixtlan** - **Page [134.1-134.7]**
(Two things could have happened to you...time my hate nearly destroyed me.) **Journey to
Ixtlan** - **Page [137.3-139.4]** ("It is early," he said...shoved me gently down the slope.) **Journey to
Ixtlan** - **Page [178.6-178.8]** ("Don't tax yourself with explanations...when you have enough
personal power.")
SEE ALSO: *SMOKE, LIGHTNING*

FOG-BRIDGE-[THE FOG BRIDGE]-(TOP): SEE: BRIDGE-FOG-[THE FOG
BRIDGE]-(TOP)

FOG-CREATE-WARRIOR-[WARRIORS CREATE A FOG AROUND
THEMSELVES]: SEE: WARRIOR-FOG-CREATE-[WARRIORS CREATE A
FOG AROUND THEMSELVES]

FOG-CRYSTALS-[THE FOG OF CRYSTALS]-(TOP)

FOG-GREEN-[THE GREEN FOG]: (Warriors know that like the guardian,
the green fog is something which is unavoidably there for them; there is no
great accomplishment in "seeing" it, but warriors must be extremely careful
not to be trapped by its clutches.)
SELECTED REFERENCES: **A Separate Reality** - **Page [168.5-169.2]** (I realized then
that I had forgotten...trying to find out something else.") **A Separate Reality** - **Page [169.7-169.8]**
("Nothing. For you, the green fog is...temperament to deal with the guardian.") **A Separate
Reality** - **Page [171.4-171.7]** (Don Juan made me smoke twice...fog and listen to my voice.") **A
Separate Reality** - **Page [180.1-180.6]** ("When did I indulge...aware of what he is doing.")
SEE ALSO: *FOG*

*FOG-WALL-[THE WALL OF FOG]: (Warriors know that the wall of fog is
one of several "perceived" manifestations of the barrier of perception; a
lateral shift of the assemblage point; the wall of fog is not another total
world.)
SELECTED REFERENCES: **The Eagle's Gift** - **Page [58.2-58.4]** ("I close my eyes and I
see this...that wall. We've done that twice.") **The Eagle's Gift** - **Page [88.9-89.2]** ("I know what's
missing," she shouted...thought that wall was after me.") **The Eagle's Gift** - **Page [104.2-105.4]**
(What they were saying was nothing...because then it does not move.) **The Eagle's Gift** - **Page
[154.6-157.8]** (On that occasion, at the request...who journey into the unknown.") **The Eagle's
Gift** - **Page [227.6-228.7]** (When she regained consciousness, she was...like Silvio Manuel, she
never returned.) **The Eagle's Gift** - **Page [236.9-237.6]** (He then told la Gorda and me...is part of
our total being.) **The Eagle's Gift** - **Page [292.5-293.1]** (I had already learned with la Gorda...a
mountainous area, rugged and inhospitable.) **The Fire From Within** - **Page [257.1-257.8]** (He
explained that when the assemblage...I *saw* the wall of fog.) **The Fire From Within** - **Page [292.9-
293.3]** (I refused to think about don...as they approach a crucial position.")
SEE ALSO: *PERCEPTION-BARRIER-BREAKING, FOG-WALL-PIERCING*

FOG-WALL-PIERCING -*[PIERCING THE WALL OF FOG]*: *(Warriors know it is a great accomplishment to be able to divide the world in two with the wall of fog; it is an even greater accomplishment to be able to stop the rotation of that wall and go through it; warriors know it is easier to pierce the wall of fog in dreaming because then it does not move.)*
 SELECTED REFERENCES: **The Eagle's Gift - Page [104.9-105.4]** (There was still one more facet...because then it does not move.) **The Eagle's Gift - Page [236.9-237.2]** (He then told la Gorda and me...the world between the parallel lines.) **The Eagle's Gift - Page [238.7-239.1]** (In my case, on one occasion...into the fog and beyond it.) **The Eagle's Gift - Page [292.4-293.2]** (Dona Soledad and I met several...woman who laughed uproariously at me.)
 SEE ALSO: *FOG-WALL, PERCEPTION-BARRIER-BREAKING*

FOG-WALL-SNATCHED-BEHIND-[BEING SNATCHED BEHIND THE WALL OF FOG]-(TOP)

FOG-WARRIOR-CREATE-[WARRIORS CREATE A FOG AROUND THEMSELVES]: SEE: WARRIOR-FOG-CREATE-[WARRIORS CREATE A FOG AROUND THEMSELVES]

FOLLY-WARRIOR-[THE WARRIORS' FOLLY]: SEE: WARRIOR-FOLLY [THE WARRIORS' FOLLY], WARRIOR-CONTROLLED-FOLLY [THE WARRIORS' CONTROLLED]

FOOL-WAY-[THE FOOL'S WAY]: *(Warriors know that the fool's way is one of the three bad habits of life which warriors struggle to avoid; the fool's way is to become obsessed with an event because it cannot be disregarded or accepted wholeheartedly; warriors strive to live the warriors' way.)*
 SELECTED REFERENCES: **The Teachings of Don Juan - Page [51.4-51.5]** (I asked him why was it...be no pitiful regrets over that.) **Tales of Power - Page [52.1-52.3]** ("There are three kinds of bad habits...we cannot accept it wholeheartedly. That the fool's way.)
 SEE ALSO: *WARRIOR-WAY, HABITS-BAD-THREE*

FORBEARANCE-[FORBEARANCE]: *(Warriors know that forbearance is the ability to hold back with the spirit something which we know is rightfully due; forbearance does not involve plotting mischief or settling past scores; forbearance works in conjunction with control, discipline and timing to assure giving whatever is due to whoever deserves it.)*
 SELECTED REFERENCES: **Tales of Power - Page [287.6-287.7]** ("You have learned that the backbone...you'll need you ultimate forbearance.") **The Eagle's Gift - Page [177.5-177.8]** (The Nagual and his warriors were...seek and face their definitive journey.) **The Fire From Within - Page [23.5-23.6]** ("My benefactor developed a strategy using...warriorship: control, discipline, forbearance, and timing.") **The Fire From Within - Page [29.4-29.6]** ("My benefactor explained something very interesting...due to whoever deserves it.") **The Fire From Within - Page [30.5]** ("Anyone who joins the petty tyrant...no forbearance, is to be defeated.")
 SEE ALSO: *WARRIOR-ATTRIBUTES, WARRIOR-FORBEARANCE, WARRIOR-CONTROL, WARRIOR-DISCIPLINE, CONTROL, TIMING, WILL*

FORCE-CIRCULAR-[THE CIRCULAR FORCE]: *(Warriors know that the circular force is the life-giving aspect of the rolling force; the force that maintains life and awareness, fulfillment and purpose; a force that strikes all living beings ceaselessly in order to give them strength, direction, awareness and life; a circular force, that when dreamed, gives the feeling of rings; an indivisible force that fits all living beings, organic and inorganic; the force of the emanations at large that acts as life-giver and as the enhancer of awareness.)*

SELECTED REFERENCES: The Fire From Within - Page [227.6-227.8] (I asked him a lot of...life-giver and enhancer of awareness.) The Fire From Within - Page [228.4-228.5] ("Those first new seers served everybody...seers who were filled with morbidity.") The Fire From Within - Page [228.6-229.6] (Don Juan said that these new...all living beings, organic and inorganic.")
SEE ALSO: FORCE-ROLLING, TUMBLER

FORCE-DISSOLVING-[THE INCONCEIVABLE DISSOLVING FORCE IN THE UNIVERSE]: SEE: EAGLE-[THE EAGLE]

FORCE-EAGLE-EMANATIONS-DORMANT-[THE FORCE OF THE DORMANT EMANATIONS]: (Warriors know that the force of the dormant emanations within the luminous cocoon is inconceivable in scope; this force can vaguely be assessed by realizing that the energy required for normal perception and activity in the daily world is the product of the alignment of barely one-tenth of the emanations encased inside man's cocoon; it is the force of these emanations being activated all at once that lies at the basis of normal death, the burning with the fire from within, and the process which the tenant uses to prolong his ally-like existence.)
SELECTED REFERENCES: The Fire From Within - Page [254.2-254.8] (Don Juan also said that his benefactor...taps a limited but gigantic jolt.)
SEE ALSO: EAGLE-EMANATIONS-DORMANT, EARTH-BOOST, FIRE-WITHIN, EAGLE-EMANATIONS-LIGHTING-ALL, TENANT

FORCE-LIFE-[THE LIFE FORCE]: SEE: LIFE-FORCE-[THE LIFE FORCE]

FORCE-MYSTERIOUS-[THE MYSTERIOUS FORCE]: (Warriors know that the mysterious force is another term for will or intent; the "mysterious force" of the ancient Toltecs.)
SELECTED REFERENCES: The Fire From Within - Page [80.5-80.8]("They are very obscure formulas, incantations...of the Eagle's emanations, or intent.")
SEE ALSO: WILL, INTENT

FORCE-POSITIVE-NEGATIVE-[THE WARRIORS' POSITIVE AND NEGATIVE FORCES]: (Warriors know they must learn to arrive at a subtle balance of positive and negative forces; warriors strive to be prepared to meet any conceivable situation.)
SELECTED REFERENCES: The Eagle's Gift - Page [306.9-307.2] (Vicente came to my side next...and the unexpected with equal efficiency.)
SEE ALSO: WARRIOR-BALANCE, WARRIOR-PREPAREDNESS, EXPECTED-UNEXPECTED, BALANCE, EQUILIBRIUM

FORCE-PREVAILING-[THE PREVAILING FORCE IN THE UNIVERSE]: (Warriors know that intent is the prevailing force in the universe.)
SELECTED REFERENCES: The Power of Silence - Page [10.8-10.9] ("For you, teaching is talking about patterns...or keeps them as they are.)
SEE ALSO: INTENT

*FORCE-ROLLING-[THE ROLLING FORCE]: (Warriors know that the rolling force is a ceaseless force from the Eagle's emanations that strikes us every instant of our lives; the rolling force is the means through which the Eagle distributes life and awareness for safekeeping and also the means through which it figuratively "collects the rent"; an eternal line of iridescent rings or balls of fire that roll onto living beings ceaselessly; there are two aspects to the rolling force, the tumbling aspect and the circular aspect; death is the tumbling aspect of the rolling force, when it finds a weakness in the gap of a luminous being it automatically cracks it open and makes it collapse; the circular aspect is the circular force, the life-giving part of the rolling force that distributes strength, direction and awareness to luminous beings; if at any time an individual feels the tumbling force strikes harder than the circular one, it means that the balance between the two aspects is upset; the tumbling force strikes harder and harder from then on, until it cracks the living being's gap and makes it die; the rolling force never enters the cocoon, it only makes it collapse.)

SELECTED REFERENCES: The Fire From Within - Page [219.4-219.6] (After a moment's pause he added...that stems from the emanations themselves.) The Fire From Within - Page [221.3-222.8] (I followed his command. Almost instantaneously...known as losing the human form.) The Fire From Within - Page [223.4-230.6] (He asked me then to describe...of the Eagle to be devoured.") The Fire From Within - Page [233.3-233.5] (The old seers realized, don Juan...offer no ideal configuration to it.) The Fire From Within - Page [237.5-237.9] (Don Juan remarked how easy it...elongate those periods to cover millennia.) The Fire From Within - Page [248.9-249.2] (He immediately started his explanation. He...the boost that the tumbler gives.) The Fire From Within - Page [254.5-254.6] ("What happens at the moment of...cocoon; it only makes it collapse.) The Power of Silence - Page [19.7-19.9] (Don Juan made a digression at...them with a dagger-like thrust.)

SEE ALSO: TUMBLER, FORCE-CIRCULAR , AWARENESS, GAP, DEATH, LUMINOUS-COCOON, LUMINOUS-BEINGS, FORCE-ROLLING-(ALL)

FORCE-ROLLING-BALANCE-[THE BALANCE OF THE TWO ASPECTS OF THE ROLLING FORCE]:

(Warriors know that the two aspects of the rolling force must remain in balance; if at any time warriors feel that the tumbling force is striking harder than the circular force, then it means that the balance between the two is upset; from then on the tumbling force strikes harder and harder until it cracks the individual's gap and causes death.)

SELECTED REFERENCES: The Fire From Within - Page [228.6-229.4] (Don Juan said that these new seers...being's gap and makes it die.")

SEE ALSO: FORCE-TUMBLING, FORCE-CIRCULAR, FORCE-ROLLING, BALANCE

FORCE-ROLLING-EARTH-[THE EARTH AND THE ROLLING FORCE]:

(Warriors know that the earth has an inexplicable capacity to deflect the ceaseless strikes of the rolling force.)

SELECTED REFERENCES: The Fire From Within - Page [237.6-237.9] (Not only did they discover and...elongate those periods to cover millennia.)

SEE ALSO: FORCE-ROLLING, EARTH, DEATH-DEFIER, TOLTEC-GHOULS

FORCE-ROLLING-HANDLING-[HANDLING THE ROLLING FORCE]:

(Warriors know that a shift of the assemblage point is all that is needed to open oneself to the rolling force; the old seers opened themselves to the rolling force and handled it for purposes guided mostly by self-importance and obsession; the new seers also endeavor to open themselves to the rolling force, but they become familiar with it by handling it without any self-importance; the results of these efforts are the staggering consequences of burning with the fire from within; the old seers were imprisoned by the rolling force while the new seers are rewarded for their toils with the gift of freedom; at a given moment the rolling force floods the warriors' cocoon instead of curling it up on itself and the result is the warriors' total and instantaneous disintegration.)

SELECTED REFERENCES: The Fire From Within - Page [225.6-227.5] ("You're such an exaggerated fellow," he said...is their total and instantaneous disintegration.) The Fire From

Within - Page [252.8-253.1] ("We're deviating from our subject...he uses exclusively to close his gap.")
SEE ALSO: *ROLLING-FORCE, SELF-IMPORTANCE, OBSESSION, FIRE-WITHIN, EAGLE-GIFT, TENANT, GAP*

FORCE-ROLLING-IMPRISON-REWARD-[THE ROLLING FORCE CAN EITHER ACT TO IMPRISON OR REWARD THE WARRIOR]: SEE: ROLLING-FORCE-HANDLING-[HANDLING THE ROLLING FORCE]

FORCE-ROLLING-OPENING-[OPENING ONESELF TO THE ROLLING FORCE]: SEE: ROLLING-FORCE-HANDLING-[HANDLING THE ROLLING FORCE]

FORCE-ROLLING-SEEING-[SEEING THE ROLLING FORCE]-(TOP)

FORCE-RULES-LIVES-[THE FORCE THAT RULES OUR LIVES]:
(Warriors know that power is the force that moves the luminous universe; a force outside ourselves that has nothing to do with our acts or volition; a force which dictates our acts whether we realize it or not; warriors address this force by living life as a series of impeccable acts.)
SELECTED REFERENCES: **Journey to Ixtlan - Page [91.4-91.5]** ("The decision as to who can be...realm of the powers that guide men.") **The Second Ring of Power - Page [283.4-284.1]** (I narrated to her the way don Juan...in my tying my shoelaces impeccably.) **The Fire From Within - Page [45.2-45.4]** ("They needed a minimal set of guidelines...as there is of the Eagle.") **The Power of Silence - Page [50.9-51.2]** (I think the poet senses...that is determining our fate.")
SEE ALSO : *POWER, NAGUAL, WARRIOR-IMPECCABILITY, WARRIOR-FATE, WARRIOR-DESTINY, SPIRITS*

FORCE-TUMBLING-[THE TUMBLING FORCE]: (Warriors know that the rolling force is actually two forces which are so close together that they seem the same; the tumbling force is the force which relates exclusively to destruction and death, the force that acts to break open the luminous cocoon and cause it to collapse; any time the tumbling force begins to strike an individual harder than the circular force, the balance between the two forces is upset and the being is in danger of dying.)
SELECTED REFERENCES: **The Fire From Within - Page [227.6-229.9]** (I asked him a lot of...they were neither invulnerable or immortal.)
SEE ALSO: *TUMBLER, FORCE-ROLLING, FORCE-CIRCULAR*

FORCE-WORLD-[THE FORCE OF THE WORLD]: (Warriors know that everything in the world is a force, a pull or a push.)
SELECTED REFERENCES: **The Second Ring of Power - Page [156.9-157.1]** ("The Nagual said that everything...and never acts upon us.)
SEE ALSO: *FORCE-(ALL)*

FORCES-FOUR-[THE FOUR FORCES]-(TOP)

FORCES-GUIDE-LIVES-[THE FORCES THAT GUIDE MEN'S LIVES]: SEE: SPIRITS-[SPIRITS], FORCE-RULES-LIVES

FORCES-INEXPLICABLE-[THE INEXPLICABLE FORCES OF THE UNIVERSE]: (The inexplicable forces with which warriors are always battling; the mysterious forces of the universe which are beyond the warriors' reason.)
SELECTED REFERENCES: **A Separate Reality - Page [213.8-213.9]** ("You forget too easily," he said...inexplicable forces will come to you.)
SEE ALSO: *MYSTERY, INTENT, FORCE-RULES-LIVES, FORCE-MYSTERIOUS*

FORCES-SPIRITS-[SPIRITS AND FORCES]: SEE: SPIRITS [SPIRITS]

FOREST-MAGICAL-TRAIL-[THE TRAIL IN THE MAGICAL FOREST-(TOP): SEE: MAGICAL-FOREST-TRAIL-[THE TRAIL IN THE MAGICAL FOREST]-(TOP)

FORGET-COMMAND-TO-[THE COMMAND TO FORGET]: (Warriors know that the Eagle commands all warriors to forget that which they have learned about the left side; the warriors' task then becomes to remember themselves and to remember the Eagle.)
SELECTED REFERENCES: **The Eagle's Gift - Page [177.5-177.8]** (The Nagual and his warriors were...seek and face their definitive journey.) **The Eagle's Gift - Page [185.1-185.2]** (He warned me about a common error...all, a general ability to forget.) **The Eagle's Gift - Page [219.8-220.2]** (As the two of them dissolved into...only helping us to help ourselves.) **The Fire From Within - Page [10.4-10.7]** (He said that the value of the...new seers meant them to have.) **The Fire From Within - Page [112.8-113.5]** (He said that the glow of awareness...used during states of heightened awareness.) **The Fire From Within - Page [183.7-183.8]** ("It is an internal knowledge," he said...every nagual is left to do.)
SEE ALSO: *REMEMBERING-TASK, WARRIOR-TASK, AWARENESS-HEIGHTENED*

FORM-WARRIOR-[THE WARRIORS' FORM]: SEE: WARRIOR-FORM-[THE WARRIORS' FORM]

FORMLESS-WARRIOR-[FORMLESS WARRIORS]: SEE: WARRIOR-FORMLESS-[FORMLESS WARRIORS]

FORMALITY-RIGIDITY-[FORMALITY AND RIGIDITY]: SEE: RECAPITULATION-[RECAPITULATION]

FORMAT-LIFE-WARRIOR-[THE FORMAT OF THE WARRIORS' LIFE]: SEE: WARRIOR-FORMAT-LIFE-[THE FORMAT OF THE WARRIORS' LIFE]

FORMAT-WARRIOR-[THE FORMAT OF THE WARRIORS' LIFE]: SEE: WARRIOR-FORMAT-[THE FORMAT OF THE WARRIORS' LIFE]

FORMULA-WARRIOR-[THE WARRIORS' FORMULA]: SEE: WARRIOR-FORMULA-[THE WARRIORS' FORMULA]

FORTUNE-GREAT-WARRIOR-[THE WARRIORS' GREAT FORTUNE]: SEE: WARRIOR-FORTUNE-GREAT-[THE WARRIORS' GREAT FORTUNE]

FORTY-EIGHT-[FORTY-EIGHT IS THE WARRIORS' NUMBER]: (Forty-eight is the warriors' number.)
SELECTED REFERENCES: **Tales of Power - Page [35.7-36.1]** (You've called forty-seven people...waste your power in idiotic questions.") **The Fire From Within - Page [158.6-159.1]** ("Are there many of these great...are bands that generate only organization.)
SEE ALSO: *EAGLE-EMANATIONS-BANDS-EARTH-FORTY-EIGHT, CORN-SORCERY-(TOP),*

FOUR-[FOUR IS A POWER NUMBER]: (Four is a power number for sorcerers.)
SELECTED REFERENCES: **The Second Ring of Power - Page [40.4-40.5]** ("How many kinds of winds are...Four is a power number for them.) **The Eagle's Gift - Page [178.3-178.5]** (While in the world, the...be added in multiples of four.)
SEE ALSO: *SORCERY*

FOUR-ENEMIES-NATURAL-WARRIOR-[THE FOUR NATURAL ENEMIES OF THE WARRIOR]: SEE: WARRIOR-ENEMIES-FOUR-NATURAL-[THE FOUR NATURAL ENEMIES OF THE WARRIOR]

FOUR-STAGES-WARRIOR-[THE FOUR STAGES OF THE WARRIOR]: SEE: WARRIOR-STAGES-FOUR-[THE FOUR STAGES OF THE WARRIOR]

FOUR-TULIOS-[THE FOUR TULIOS]-(TOP): SEE: TULIOS-FOUR-[THE FOUR TULIOS]-(TOP)

FOURTH-ENEMY-[THE WARRIORS' FOURTH ENEMY]: SEE: OLD-AGE-[OLD AGE]

FREEDOM-BIRD-[THE BIRD OF FREEDOM]: SEE: BIRD-FREEDOM-[THE BIRD OF FREEDOM]

FREEDOM-COMMITMENT-SEEK-[THE COMMITMENT TO SEEK FREEDOM]: (Warriors know that they must sustain their commitment to seek freedom above all else.)
    SELECTED REFERENCES: The Eagle's Gift - Page [213.3-213.4] (Although don Juan regretted immensely the...their commitment to seek their freedom.)
    SEE ALSO: *FREEDOM-TOTAL, WARRIOR-TOTAL-FREEDOM*

FREEDOM-DISEASE-CONTAGIOUS-[FREEDOM IS A CONTAGIOUS DISEASE]: (Warriors know that freedom is a contagious disease; it is transmitted and its carrier is an impeccable nagual.)
    SELECTED REFERENCES: The Fire From Within - Page [271.6-271.9] (During our long walk into the city...this moment. And so will you.")
    SEE ALSO: *FREEDOM-TOTAL, NAGUAL-MAN-WOMAN*

FREEDOM-FIGHT-WARRIOR-[THE WARRIORS' FIGHT FOR FREEDOM]: SEE: WARRIOR-FREEDOM-FIGHT-[THE WARRIORS' FIGHT FOR FREEDOM]

FREEDOM-FRIGHTENING-[FREEDOM IS FRIGHTENING]: SEE: FREEDOM-TOTAL-VIGOR-[THE VIGOR OF TOTAL FREEDOM]

FREEDOM-IMPLICATIONS-[THE IMPLICATIONS OF FREEDOM]: (Warriors know that freedom has devastating implications, among which is that warriors must purposely seek change; cutting the chains of self-reflection makes freedom possible and it is a marvelous thing; but warriors also know that it is undesirable at the same time because nobody wants to be free.)
    SELECTED REFERENCES: The Fire From Within - Page [114.8-115.1] ("I've explained to you that the...the other side of the coin.") The Fire From Within - Page [271.6-271.9] (During our long walk into the city...this moment. And so will you.") The Power of Silence - Page [89.8-89.9] ("Sorcerers say that the fourth abstract...for nobody wants to be free.)
    SEE ALSO: *CHANGE, WARRIOR-SEEKS-OTHER-SIDE-COIN, WARRIOR-FREEDOM, ETERNITY-HUMANNESS, WARRIOR-LONELINESS, FEAR, WARRIOR-EVICTION-NOTICE, WARRIOR-CONTRADICTION-KNOWLEDGE*

FREEDOM-INORGANIC-BEINGS-[FREEDOM AND THE INORGANIC BEINGS]: (Warriors know that the quest for freedom and the inorganic beings are antithetical; the inorganic beings love slavery and warriors love freedom; the inorganic beings love to buy but warriors are not selling;

warriors are aware of the terrible price they must pay for the knowledge of the inorganic beings; they must pay with their energy and their freedom.)
SELECTED REFERENCES: **The Art of Dreaming - Page [58.6-58.7]** ("Do you fear them now, don...to buy, and I don't sell.") **The Art of Dreaming - Page [67.5-67.7]** ("Do these relationships with inorganic beings...such a sustained journey is staggering.") **The Art of Dreaming - Page [68.2-68.3]** ("Do I gather, don Juan, that...will agree with me. you'll see.")
SEE ALSO: *FREEDOM, INORGANIC-BEINGS-TRICKERY, INORGANIC-BEINGS-REFUSING, , SORCERY-PRICE, WARRIORSHIP-VS-SORCERY,*

FREEDOM-LOSING-HUMAN-FORM-[FREEDOM AND LOSING THE HUMAN FORM]: *(Warriors know that losing the human form brings freedom to the warrior, the freedom of remembering the self.)*
SELECTED REFERENCES: **The Eagle's Gift - Page [60.5-60.9]** ("The Nagual told me that losing...go and talk to the Genaros?")
SEE ALSO: *FREEDOM, HUMAN-FORM-LOSING, SELF-REMEMBERING*

FREEDOM-QUEST-WARRIOR-[THE WARRIORS' QUEST FOR FREEDOM]: SEE: WARRIOR-QUEST-FREEDOM-[THE WARRIORS' QUEST FOR FREEDOM]

FREEDOM-TOTAL-[TOTAL FREEDOM]: *(Warriors know that their ultimate challenge is to dart past the Eagle and be free; the freedom of total awareness; a blast of unlimited consciousness; the Eagle's gift to man; the third attention; for warriors, dreaming is the freedom to perceive worlds beyond imagination; freedom is an adventure with no end; freedom is the driving force of the warrior; the freedom to fly off into infinity, the freedom to dissolve, to lift off; freedom is like the flame of a candle, which, in spite of being lit up against the light of a billion stars, remains intact, because it never pretended to be more than what it is, a mere candle; there is no risk too great for warriors in search of total freedom, even though no warrior knows exactly what total freedom is; total freedom is a dreaming position of the assemblage point; total freedom means total awareness.)*
SELECTED REFERENCES: **Tales of Power - Page [21.2-21.3]** (That is slavery....your time and your power fearing me.") **Tales of Power - Page [294.2-294.3]** ("Only the love for this splendorous...That is the last lesson.") **The Second Ring of Power - Page [189.5-189.6]** (His words plunged me into body and freedom to my spirit.) **The Eagle's Gift - Page [178.8-179.1]** (Don Juan explained that the rule was...of the totality of the body.) **The Eagle's Gift - Page [218.9-219.6]** (His benefactor explained to don Juan...group, however, but one by one.) **The Eagle's Gift - Page [296.4-296.5]** ("It's wrong to say that,"...and be free is the ultimate audacity.") **The Fire From Within - Page [127.7-127.8]** (Don Juan had defined the scope...they attain total awareness.) **The Fire From Within - Page [249.3-249.4]** (He explained that the earth's boost...which they call total freedom.) **The Fire From Within - Page [271.7-271.9]** (There was something festive about...for this moment. And so will you.") **The Fire From Within - Page [298.1-298.5]** (He said over and over again...*dreaming position* called total freedom.) **The Fire From Within - Page [298.9-299.2]** (One of the most fortunate decisions...choose total consciousness, total freedom.) **The Fire From Within - Page [299.5-299.7]** ("The new seers burn with the force...is to have sufficient energy.) **The Power of Silence - Page [ix.5-ix.7]** (At various times don Juan attempted...admitted it was not really accurate.) **The Power of Silence - Page [22.8-23.2]** (And the nagual Elias was obliged...sorcerers along, or leave them behind.) **The Power of Silence - Page [264.3-264.5]** (Sorcerers, however, were capable of finding...awareness needed to reach freedom.) **The Power of Silence - Page [264.7-264.9]** ("What was the nagual Elias's reason...their freedom from perceptual convention.) **The Art of Dreaming - Page [81.2-81.7]** ("For the sorcerers who practice dreaming...what it is: a mere candle.") **The Art of Dreaming - Page [181.5-181.6]** ("We can't have dealings with them...sorcerer knows what freedom really is.") **The Art of Dreaming - Page [204.5-204.6]** (He did not answer me...or indolence, but out of conviction.")

SEE ALSO: *AWARENESS-TOTAL, ATTENTION-THIRD, EAGLE-GIFT, FIRE-WITHIN, EARTH-BOOST, WARRIOR-CHALLENGE, WARRIOR-FREEDOM-TOTAL, SLAVERY, AWARENESS-MANIPULATION-SEER-NEW*

FREEDOM-TOTAL-VIGOR-[THE VIGOR OF TOTAL FREEDOM]:
(Warriors know that despite its implications, freedom has an unrestrainable vigor of its own; freedom is frightening, but only because people don't want to be free.)
SELECTED REFERENCES: The Fire From Within - Page [271.7-271.9] (During our long walk into the city...this moment. And so will you.")
SEE ALSO: *FREEDOM-TOTAL, FEAR, FREEDOM-IMPLICATIONS, WARRIOR-VIGOR*

FREEDOM-WARRIOR-[THE WARRIORS' FREEDOM]: SEE: WARRIOR-FREEDOM-[THE WARRIORS' FREEDOM]

FRETTING-[FRETTING]: (Warriors know that fretting is proper only to the first attention; warriors also know that it is wasteful to fret and get agitated when trying to deal with the second attention; the second attention is calmness itself.)
SELECTED REFERENCES: The Eagle's Gift - Page [260.5-260.6] (Zuleica finally spoke to me...attention: the second attention was calmness itself.) The Eagle's Gift - Page [291.6-291.6-291.7] ("Applying these principles brings about three...have an endless capacity to improvise.") The Power of Silence - Page [233.5-233.7] (The current dragged him a long distance...the river was follow its flow.)
SEE ALSO: *WARRIOR-CALMNESS, WORRY, STALKING-RESULTS-THREE, WARRIOR-WORRY-NOT*

FRIGHT-AVENUE-[THE AVENUE OF FRIGHT]: (Warriors know that fright has the power to shrink the tonal.)
SELECTED REFERENCES: Tales of Power - Page [195.6-195.7] ("The reason why you're afraid of Genaro...away every time Genaro is around.")
SEE ALSO: *TONAL-SHRINKING, FEAR, FEAR-CHANNEL*

FRONT-PLATE-[THE FRONT PLATE]: (Warriors know that the front plate is a lid-like protective shield on the front face of the luminous cocoon; it protects human beings throughout their lives from the force of the tumbler.)
SELECTED REFERENCES: The Fire From Within - Page [219.4-219.6] (After a moment's pause he added...that stems from the emanations themselves.) The Fire From Within - Page [220.9-221.2] (When I *saw* each luminous creature...the thickness of the total cocoon.)
SEE ALSO: *LUMINOUS-COCOON, TUMBLER, FORCE-TUMBLING*

FULFILLMENT-WARRIOR-[THE WARRIORS' FULFILLMENT]: SEE: WARRIOR-FULFILLMENT-[THE WARRIORS' FULFILLMENT]

FUTILITY-OF-IT-ALL-[THE FUTILITY OF IT ALL]: (Warriors know the futility of it all; the futility of struggling to control their fellow man; the futility of assembling other worlds; and above all, the futility of self-importance; warriors resolve the dilemma of futility by choosing total awareness, total freedom.)
SELECTED REFERENCES: The Fire From Within - Page [298.7-299.2] (Don Juan said that adventurous men,...to choose total consciousness, total freedom.)
SEE ALSO: *SORCERY-FUTILITY-PITFALLS, SORCERY-FUTILITY-RESOLUTION, SELF-IMPORTANCE, AWARENESS-TOTAL, FREEDOM-TOTAL, WORLDS-OTHER-ASSEMBLE-TOTAL*

FUTILITY-PITFALLS-SORCERY-[THE FUTILITY AND PITFALLS OF SORCERY]: SEE: SORCERY-FUTILITY-PITFALLS-[THE FUTILITY AND PITFALLS OF SORCERY]

G

GAIT-POWER-[THE GAIT OF POWER]: (*Warriors know that the gait of power is a high stepping gait used to "walk the assemblage point"; the rhythm of the muffled steps catches the alignment force of the emanations inside the cocoon which has been disconnected by inner silence; one of three techniques used by warriors for learning new ways of perceiving the world; one of three techniques which lead warriors to the knowledge of a separate and pragmatic world of dreaming.*)

SELECTED REFERENCES: **Journey to Ixtlan - Page [169.2-171.4]** (He then proceeded to demonstrate a...as I could in the daytime.) **Journey to Ixtlan - Page [180.7]** (He said that running in the darkness...that knew how "to not do.") **Journey to Ixtlan -Page [199.6-199.7]** ("During the day shadows are the...taught you the gait of power.") **Journey to Ixtlan - Page [210.4-210.6]** (My stomach felt a force coming...Then he came to a halt.) **Tales of Power - Page [250.5-250.6]** (He explained that disrupting routines,...the use of those three techniques.) **Tales of Power - Page [261.6-261.7]** (Before we reached the place, don...to wash away my tiredness.) **The Second Ring of Power - Page [147.3-147.4]** (Don Juan had called that particular action...that and pointed in front of us.) **The Fire From Within - Page [129.3-129.8]** ("Genaro has something to show you...I felt extraordinarily aggressive, muscular, daring.) **The Fire From Within - Page [131.3-131.5]** (While we were having lunch the...point fixed to its original position.) **The Fire From Within - Page [133.5-133.8]** (He said that in the light of what...of emanations, thus new perceptions.) **The Fire From Within - Page [134.8-135.1]** (I asked him to explain the...of the band," he went on.) **The Fire From Within - Page [207.4-207.6]** (Genaro stood up and started doing...his chest every time he stepped.) **The Fire From Within - Page [253.5-253.7]** ("Did anybody ever get hurt in...look young or old at will.")

SEE ALSO: *ROUTINES-DISRUPTING, NOT-DOING, ASSEMBLAGE-POINT-MOVING, ASSEMBLAGE-POINT-WALKING, GAIT-POWER-VISION-(TOP)*

GAIT-POWER-VISION-[A VISION OF THE GAIT OF POWER]-(TOP)

GAP-[THE GAP]: (*Warriors know that there is a gap in the luminous cocoon of men; like the soft spot on the top of a child's head, this gap opens as warriors develop their will; the most sensitive and important part of man; a natural bowl-like flaw or "dent" in the otherwise smooth cocoon of man; the spot where the tumbler strikes us ceaselessly and where the cocoon eventually cracks; if the gap develops a crack of large enough proportions, the cocoon collapses and curls in on itself, resulting in the death of the individual; death enters the luminous cocoon right through the gap of the will.*)

SELECTED REFERENCES: **A Separate Reality - Page [147.1-147.4]** (Our will operates in spite of...to shoot out, like an arrow.") **A Separate Reality - Page [197.9-198.1]** ("Death enters through the belly,"...most important and sensitive part of man.) **A Separate Reality - Page [216.8-217.9]** (Whenever a sorcerer has an encounter...close your gap and make you solid.") **A Separate Reality - Page [247.6-247.7]** (I asked him the meaning of my experience...you're healed and your gap is closed.") **Tales of Power - Page [81.2-81.3]** ("Will" was another concept which don Juan...opening he had called the "gap".) **The Eagle's Gift - Page [63.6-63.8]** ("The Nagual Juan Matus left us...she's merely riding on your back.") **The Fire From Within - Page [221.9]** (Don Juan said that I had...had dangerously opened up my gap.) **The Fire From Within - Page [226.1-227.3]** ("When the assemblage point shifts...are infinitely more durable than we are.) **The Fire From Within - Page [229.3-229.4]** ("What the new seers discovered is...being's gap and makes it die.") **The Fire From Within - Page [233.2-233.7]** ("How did they *intend* death away?"...more durable that a bowl-like one.") **The Fire From Within - Page [251.8-251.9]** ("There is another death defier,"...and close his gap whenever he wants.") **The Fire From Within - Page [254.5-255.1]** ("What happens at the moment of death...he takes it into his own gap.") **The Power of Silence - Page [19.6-19.8]** (The nagual was laughing and

pondering...them with a dagger-like thrust.) **The Power of Silence - Page [147.2-147.5]** ("Silent knowledge is something that all...the more ephemeral *intent* becomes.")
    SEE ALSO: *LUMINOUS-COCOON, TUMBLER, FORCE-ROLLING , DEATH, DEATH-DEFIERS, LUMINOUS-COCOON-INORGANIC-BEINGS, GAP-INORGANIC-BEINGS, LUMINOUS-DENT*

GAP-INORGANIC-BEINGS-*[THE INORGANIC BEINGS' GAP]: (Warriors know that the inorganic beings are practically immortal because they have only a line for a gap; this luminous configuration presents only a very small surface to the rolling force and is by far more durable than the bowl-like dent of man; the old seers intended death away by mimicking this luminous configuration which they saw in their allies.)*
    SELECTED REFERENCES: **The Fire From Within - Page [233.2-233.6]** ("How did they *intend* death away?"...more durable that a bowl-like one.")
    SEE ALSO: *GAP, INORGANIC-BEINGS, LUMINOUS-COCOON, INTENDING-DEATH-AWAY, LUMINOUS-COCOON-INORGANIC-BEINGS*

GARDEN-EDEN-*[THE GARDEN OF EDEN]: (Warriors know that the story of the Garden of Eden is an allegory for man's loss of silent knowledge, his knowledge of intent; at one time ancient man was close to the abstract, but then something happened that pulled man away from it and now he can't get back to it; the warriors' path represents a going back to the beginning, a return to paradise, a return to silent knowledge, a return to the abstract.)*
    SELECTED REFERENCES: **The Power of Silence - Page [37.1-37.3]** ("The nagual Elias used to tell me...can exist independent of each other.") **The Power of Silence - Page [103.3-103.4]** (Don Juan had stated his belief...the beginning, a return to paradise.) **The Power of Silence - Page [147.1-147.5]** ("Silent knowledge is something that...more ephemeral intent becomes.") **The Power of Silence - Page [149.5-150.1]** (Then he talked about ancient man...peace, of satisfaction, of attainment.)
    SEE ALSO: *KNOWLEDGE-SILENT, MAN-ANCIENT, ABSTRACT-RETURN, REASON-VS-INTENT, KNOWLEDGE-VS-LANGUAGE, WARRIOR-JOURNEY-RETURN*

GATE-DREAMING-*[THE GATES OF DREAMING]: SEE: DREAMING-GATES-[THE SEVEN GATES OF DREAMING]*

*GATE-DREAMING-FIRST-[THE FIRST GATE OF DREAMING]: SEE: DREAMING-GATE-FIRST-[THE FIRST GATE OF DREAMING]

GATE-DREAMING-FOURTH-*[THE FOURTH GATE OF DREAMING]: SEE: DREAMING-GATE-FOURTH-[THE FOURTH GATE OF DREAMING]*

*GATE-DREAMING-SECOND-[THE SECOND GATE OF DREAMING]: SEE: DREAMING-GATE-SECOND-[THE SECOND GATE OF DREAMING]

*GATE-DREAMING-THIRD-[THE THIRD GATE OF DREAMING]: SEE: DREAMING-GATE-THIRD-[THE THIRD GATE OF DREAMING]

GATE-INTENT-TONAL-NAGUAL-*[INTENT AS A GATE BETWEEN THE TONAL AND THE NAGUAL]: INTENT-GATE-TONAL-NAGUAL-[INTENT AS A GATE BETWEEN THE TONAL AND THE NAGUAL]*

GATE-WARRIOR-*[THE WARRIORS' GATE]: WARRIOR-GATE-[THE WARRIORS' GATE]*

GATEWAY-LIGHT-DARKNESS-*[GATEWAY TO THE LIGHT AND TO THE DARKNESS OF THE UNIVERSE]: SEE: DREAMING-ART-[THE ART OF DREAMING]*

GAZE-DREAMER-[THE DREAMERS' GAZE]: SEE: DREAMER-GLANCE-[THE DREAMERS' GLANCE]

GAZE-WARRIOR-[THE DREAMERS' GAZE]: SEE: WARRIOR-GAZE-[THE DREAMERS' GAZE]

GAZING-[GAZING]: (*Warriors know that gazing is a method used to trap the second attention and aid in dreaming; the not-doing of looking; when warriors have learned to stop the world they have become "gazers"; gazing was the old sorcerers' technique, they were able to get to their energy bodies in the blink of an eye simply by gazing at objects of their predilection; this impressive technique is useless to warriors because it does nothing to increase their sobriety or capacity to seek freedom; gazing only pins warriors down in the state of concreteness.*)
    SELECTED REFERENCES: The Second Ring of Power - Page [152.7-152.8] (Tonight, for instance, I knew which...They are a pain in the neck.") The Second Ring of Power - Page [202.7-202.8] ("To say they're bad is only...eyes for hours, sometimes for days.") The Second Ring of Power - Page [247.5-247.9] ("How is that done, Gorda...days until the crack would open.") The Second Ring of Power - Page [284.4-284.8] (She did not answer. She took...tie ourselves to them," she replied.) The Second Ring of Power - Page [288.5-288.8] (She said that she had not seen...and gave me a gentle shove.) The Second Ring of Power - Page [293.9-301.5] (I don't know what they did...there is to gazing," she said.) The Second Ring of Power - Page [306.1-306.5] (From la Gorda's statements about gazing...gaze as la Gorda had prescribed.) The Fire From Within - Page [90.2-90.4] ("What really took place out there...the eyes to open the way.") The Fire From Within - Page [101.9-102.2] (He assured me that experienced seers...I had *seen* in the mirror.) The Fire From Within - Page [127.3-127.6] (It was a clear sunny day...at these shadows in the afternoons.") The Art of Dreaming - Page [70.6-70.9] (He said then that it was...the awareness of our daily world.") The Art of Dreaming - Page [124.4-124.9] (While I remained with don Juan...to concreteness, a most undesirable state.")
    SEE   ALSO: STOPPING-WORLD, NOT-DOING, DREAMING-ART, CONCRETENESS, GAZING-(ALL)

GAZING-ACTIONS-FOUR-[THE FOUR ACTIONS OF GAZING]:
(*Warriors are familiar with the four separate actions of gazing.*)
    SELECTED REFERENCES: The Second Ring of Power - Page [302.4-302.7] (She sat down very close to...of light fibers on my eyelashes.)
    SEE ALSO: *GAZING*

GAZING-CLOTH-[THE GAZING CLOTH]: (*Warriors are familiar with the gazing cloth, a small piece of fabric used to aid individuals in gazing at geological formations.*)
    SELECTED REFERENCES: The Second Ring of Power - Page [303.4-303.9] (I struggled for a moment to keep...the mechanics of my phantom perception.)
    SEE ALSO: *GAZING*

GAZING-PEOPLE-BEHIND-[GAZING AT PEOPLE FROM BEHIND]:
(*Warriors know that in order to "see" human beings as luminous entities they must gaze at them from behind, as they walk away; it is the luminous cocoon's front plate that makes it useless to gaze at people face to face.*)
    SELECTED REFERENCES: The Fire From Within - Page [219.4-219.6] (After a moment's pause he added that...that stems from the emanations themselves.)
    SEE ALSO: *GAZING, FRONT-PLATE, SEEING*

GAZING-ROPE-[THE OLD SEERS' GAZING ROPE]: (*Warriors know the ancient seers had a very elaborate tool which they used to descend to what they believed to be the other levels; it was a rope of special twine which the*

old seers tied around themselves and which was held by the their assistants
as the seers became lost in their dreaming.)
 SELECTED REFERENCES: The Fire From Within - Page [102.2-102.4] ("The old
seers had a very elaborate...what we did with the mirror.")
 SEE ALSO: *TOLTEC-LEVELS, GAZING*

GAZING-VS-WALKING-RIGHT-WAY-*[GAZING VS THE RIGHT WAY OF*
WALKING]: (Warriors know that gazing and the right way of walking
represent opposite paths to the same end, stopping the internal dialogue.)
 SELECTED REFERENCES: The Second Ring of Power - Page [306.1-306.5] (From la
Gorda's statements...as la Gorda had prescribed.)
 SEE ALSO: *INTERNAL DIALOGUE-STOPPING, WALKING-RIGHT-WAY,*
GAZING

GENARO-ALLY-MEET-*[DON GENARO MEETS HIS ALLY]-(TOP)*

GENARO-BENCH-*[DON GENARO GETS UP OFF A BENCH WITHOUT*
GETTING UP]-(TOP)

GENARO-BOULDER-*[DON GENARO'S DREAM BOULDER]-(TOP)*

GENARO-CALLING-*[THE CALLING OF DON GENARO]-(TOP)*

GENARO-CARLOS-MEET-*[DON GENARO MEETS CARLOS]-(TOP)*

GENARO-DREAMING-BODY-ANTICS-*[THE ANTICS OF DON*
GENARO'S DREAMING BODY]-(TOP)

GENARO-DREAMING-BODY-EXPERIENCE-*[DON GENARO'S FIRST*
FOUR EXPERIENCES WITH HIS DREAMING BODY]-(TOP)

GENARO-EARTH-EMBRACES-*[DON GENARO EMBRACES THE*
EARTH]-(TOP)

GENARO-FLYING-CARLOS-*[DON GENARO'S FLIGHT WITH CARLOS]-*
(TOP): SEE: FLYING-GENARO-CARLOS-[DON GENARO'S FLIGHT
WITH CARLOS]-(TOP)

GENARO-FURRY-CROCODILE-*[THE FLIGHT OF DON GENARO'S*
BROWN FURRY CROCODILE-(TOP)

GENARO-GREEN-STUFF-*[DON GENARO'S GREEN STUFF]-(TOP)*

GENARO-HIDING-*[DON GENARO'S TECHNIQUE FOR HIDING]-(TOP)*

GENARO-LEAP-*[DON GERNARO'S PRODIGIOUS LEAP]-(TOP)*

GENARO-MOUNTAINS-TREMBLE-*[DON GENARO MAKES THE*
MOUNTAINS TREMBLE]-(TOP)

GENARO-RIDDLE-*[THE RIDDLE OF DON GENARO]-(TOP)*

GENARO-SEEING-MOUNTAINS-MILES-AWAY-*[SEEING DON GENARO*
IN THE MOUNTAINS TEN MILES AWAY]-(TOP)

GENARO-TOUCH-CRUSHING-*[DON GENARO'S CRUSHING TOUCH]-*
(TOP)

GENARO-VANISHES-*[DON GENARO VANISHES LIKE A PUFF OF AIR]-*
(TOP)

GENARO-WALK-EUCALYPTUS-TREES-[DON GENARO WALKS IN THE EUCALYPTUS TREES]-(TOP)

GENARO-WATERFALL-[DON GENARO SCALES THE WATERFALL]-(TOP)

GENAROS-[THE GENAROS]-(TOP)

GESTURE-SPIRIT-FOR-[A GESTURE FOR THE SPIRIT]: SEE: SPIRIT-GESTURE-[A GESTURE FOR THE SPIRIT]

GESTURE-SPIRIT-OF-[A GESTURE OF THE SPIRIT]: SEE: OMEN-[OMENS]

GETTING-DOWN-TO-BUSINESS-[GETTING DOWN TO BUSINESS]: SEE: BUSINESS-GETTING-DOWN-[GETTING DOWN TO BUSINESS]

GETTING-INTO-THINGS-[GETTING INTO THINGS]: (Warriors know that getting into things means that they can shift the assemblage point to the position of the dreaming body and are therefore capable of getting into and through physical objects and structures because the dreaming body knows the intent of performing such feats.)
    SELECTED REFERENCES: The Teachings of Don Juan - Page [139.3-139.4] ("No, not with the smoke. Later on...went *into* and *through* that wall.")
    SEE ALSO: *DREAMING-BODY, ASSEMBLAGE-POINT-MOVING,*

GIANT-TEN-FOOT-FEELING-[FEELING LIKE A TEN FOOT GIANT]-(TOP)

GIVERS-LIFE-[THE GIVERS OF LIFE]: (Warriors know that the givers of life are a thick bundle of luminous filaments that resemble a lion's tail and grow inward in women from the place of the genitalia; the embryo attaches itself to those nurturing roots and thoroughly consumes them through the course of its development in the womb; the consumption of this luminous structure leaves a hole in both the mother's and father's luminosity.)
    SELECTED REFERENCES: The Eagle's Gift - Page [45.8-46.] (Our visions differed in that she...the luminous mass of their bodies.)
    SEE ALSO: *WOMB, FORCE-CIRCULAR, EAGLE-EMANATIONS-LARGE-FORCE*

GLORY-TALES-[TALES OF GLORY]-(TOP)

GOALS-WARRIOR-[THE WARRIORS' GOALS]: SEE: WARRIOR-GOAL [THE WARRIORS' GOALS]

GOD-[GOD]: (Warriors know that God is an item of the warriors' personal tonal and of the tonal of the times; God is not the nagual; what man calls God is the mold of man; the mold is our God because we are what it stamps us with and not because it has created us from nothing in its own likeness and image; the mold of man is a static prototype of humanness without any power, a mold of our human pattern that groups together a bunch of luminous elements which we call man; the mold of man cannot under any circumstances help us by intervening in our behalf, or punish us for our wrongdoings, or reward us in any way; we are simply the product of its stamp, we are its impression; seers know that the belief in the existence of God is based on hearsay and not on actual "seeing".)

SELECTED REFERENCES: The Teachings of Don Juan - Page [89.7-90.2] ("All I want to know is if...He is not the same for everybody.) A Separate Reality -Page [64.1-64.3] (You don't have a protector!"...force you to listen," don Juan said.) Tales of Power - Page [125.9-126.5] ("Is the *nagual* the Supreme Being...but it cannot be talked about.") The Second Ring of Power - Page [157.4-157.9] (Did you ever see the mold,...The mold is God. What do you think?") The Fire From Within - Page [100.4-100.5] ("And what happened to your promise...way to make promises to them.) The Fire From Within - Page [130.6-131.3] (I was left facing the side of...we walked lazily around the patio.) The Fire From Within - Page [159.4-160.1] (His answer made me argue with...it is either pink, peach, or amber.) The Fire From Within - Page [258.8-259.7] (Don Juan reminded me that he had...Remember what you've done!") The Fire From Within - Page [261.3-265.9] (I moved my eyes as he suggested..."God is a male. What a relief!") The Fire From Within - Page [267.5-267.8] (I remembered then that I had...order to examine what they *saw*.) The Fire From Within - Page [290.6-291.2] (I recalled then that don Juan...gleaming with a blinding white light.) The Power of Silence - Page [86.1-86.2] (For a moment I believed that *intent*...not be described, much less represented.) The Power of Silence - Page [263.4-263.6] ("Of course, there is a dark side...yes, and it's called stupidity.")

SEE ALSO: *MOLD-MAN, FAITH-RELIGIOUS, EAGLE, NAGUAL, EVIL, STUPIDITY-IGNORANCE, GOD-(ALL)*

GOD-VS-EAGLE-EMANATIONS-[GOD VS THE EAGLE'S EMANATIONS]: (Warriors know that there is no God to hear our prayers or promises, there are only the Eagle's emanations.)

SELECTED REFERENCES: The Fire From Within - Page [100.5-100.6] ("And what happened to your promise to...way to make promises to them.")

SEE ALSO: *GOD, EAGLE, EAGLE-EMANATIONS, WARRIOR-PRAYER, MOLD-MAN*

GOD-INVENTORY-[GOD AND THE HUMAN INVENTORY]: (Warriors know that man's idea of God is one of the most sturdy aspects of the human inventory which binds the assemblage point to its original position.)

SELECTED REFERENCES: The Fire From Within - Page [258.8-258.9] (Don Juan reminded me that he...assemblage point to its original position.)

SEE ALSO: *GOD, INVENTORY, ASSEMBLAGE-POINT-FIXATION*

GOOD-BYE-WARRIOR-[THE WARRIORS' GOOD-BYE]: SEE: WARRIOR-FAREWELL-[THE WARRIORS' FAREWELL]

GORDA-[LA GORDA]-(TOP)

GORDA-CARING-[CARING FOR LA GORDA]-(TOP)

GORDA-COMPLETENESS-[LA GORDA REGAINS HER COMPLETENESS]-(TOP)

GORDA-DREAMING-[LA GORDA'S DREAMING]-(TOP): SEE: DREAMING-GORDA-[LA GORDA'S DREAMING]-(TOP)

GORDA-FLYING-[LA GORDA'S FLYING]-(TOP): SEE: FLYING-GORDA [LA GORDA'S FLYING]-(TOP)

GORDA-PETTY-TYRANT-[LA GORDA AS A PETTY TYRANT]-(TOP)

GORDA-POWER-ROCK-[LA GORDA AND THE POWER ROCK FROM MONTE ALBAN]-(TOP)

GORDA-PURPOSE-[LA GORDA'S PURPOSE]-(TOP)

GORDA-SEARCH-CARLOS-CITY-[LA GORDA SEARCHES IN THE CITY FOR CARLOS]-(TOP)

GORDA-SPARKS-[LA GORDA'S SPARKS]-(TOP)

GORDA-STORY-[LA GORDA'S STORY]-(TOP)

GORDA-WEAKNESS-DISASSEMBLE-[LA GORDA DISASSEMBLES HER WEAKNESS]-(TOP)

GOURD-FOOD-YOUNG-MAN-[THE GOURDS OF FOOD AND THE YOUNG MAN]-(TOP)

GOURD-SORCERER-[THE SORCERERS' GOURD]: (*Warriors know that the sorcerers' gourd is a magical focus of the second attention; a link which sorcerers have with intent; this focus can be "seen" as something resembling a gourd or a rag or a button-like object hanging from the sorcerers' belt; a sorcerers' "guaje"; sorcerers carry their allies in their gourd.*)
  SELECTED REFERENCES: Tales of Power - Page [263.6-263.9] (Don Juan spoke first;...not judging anything in a rational manner.) **The Second Ring of Power - Page [37.4-38.5]** (In desperation, I suppose, he introduced...In both cases his gourd helped him.) **The Second Ring of Power - Page [52.1-52.3]** ("How did the girls manage to stop...two allies and makes them help him.) **The Second Ring of Power - Page [145.5-145.7]** (She whispered that the cave was...don Juan's and don Genaro's belts.) **The Second Ring of Power - Page [151.3-152.1]** ("What do you know about the allies...allies become an aid to the sorcerer.) **The Second Ring of Power - Page [152.6-152.8]** ("I don't bother with them one...They are a pain in the neck.") **The Second Ring of Power - Page [154.7-154.8]** (But the others are easy prey...come all the time looking for you.)
  SEE ALSO: *ALLIES, MESCALITO, WARRIOR-GOURD-(TOP)*

GOURD-WARRIOR-[THE WARRIORS' GOURD]: SEE: WARRIOR-GOURD-[THE WARRIORS' GOURD]: (TOP)

GRATITUDE-WARRIOR-[THE WARRIORS' GRATITUDE]: SEE: WARRIOR-GRATITUDE-[THE WARRIORS' GRATITUDE]

GREED-[GREED]: (*Warriors know that greed works only in the world of ordinary affairs, a world which warriors strive to detach themselves from; the actions of the warrior are not motivated by greed.*)
  SELECTED REFERENCES: The Fire From Within - Page [250.1-250.4] (I say that they were afraid...your being revolted. It's embarrassing!")
  SEE ALSO: *SEER-OLD, TOLTECS, LOVE*

GREEN-FOG-[THE GREEN FOG]: SEE: FOG-GREEN-[THE GREEN FOG]

GROWTH-[GROWTH]: SEE: SOUTH-[SOUTHERLY WOMEN]

GUAJE-[GUAJE]: SEE: WARRIOR-GOURD-[THE WARRIORS' GOURD]

GUARDIAN-[THE GUARDIAN]-(TOP)

GUAYMAS-STROKE-[A STROKE IN GUAYMAS]-(TOP): SEE: JUAN-STROKE-GUAYMAS-[DON JUAN'S STROKE IN GUAYMAS]-(TOP)

H

HABITS-BAD-THREE-[THE THREE BAD HABITS OF LIFE]: (Warriors know the three bad habits of life are the bigot's way, the pious man's way, and the fool's way.)
SELECTED REFERENCES: Tales of Power - Page [52.1-52.3] ("There are three kinds of bad...the correct one, the warrior's way.)
SEE ALSO: *BIGOT-WAY, PIOUS-MAN-WAY, FOOL-WAY, WARRIOR-WAY*

HABITS-UNNECESSARY-[UNNECESSARY HABITS]: (Warriors know they must maintain an objective perspective on their own habits and behavior as they relate to the quest for impeccability; warriors struggle to eliminate the habit of having the world conform to their thoughts; the warriors' understanding that the eradication of unnecessary habits detaches the glow of awareness from self-refection and allows it the freedom to focus on other things of greater importance to the warrior; the warriors' realization that the world we perceive is the result of the specific location of the assemblage point, and that the assemblage point can move almost at will as a consequence of new habits; the warriors' realization that his command can become the Eagle's command.)
SELECTED REFERENCES: Tales of Power - Page [7.5-7.6] ("There are lots of things that you...habits and routines stand in your way.") Tales of Power - Page [22.2-23.2] ("Your knowledge of the world...in terms he called "habits".) The Second Ring of Power - Page [159.2] ("A warrior must drop the human form...that one can change one's habits.) The Second Ring of Power - Page [228.1-228.4] (Don Juan had taught me the same...order to be alive activity.) The Fire From Within - Page [79.2-79.5] (When the new seers arranged the...to focus on something else.) The Fire From Within - Page [118.3-118.4] (He affirmed that one of the...arrive at new usages, new habits.) The Fire From Within - Page [118.7-119.3] ("The new seers say that realization...We'll come back to that later on.")
SEE ALSO: *WARRIOR-IMPECCABILITY, SELF-REFLECTION, AWARENESS-GLOW, ROUTINES-DISRUPTING, STALKING-ART, EAGLE-COMMANDS, ROUTINES-DISRUPTING, ASSEMBLAGE-POINT-MOVING, WILL-VS-INTENT*

HABITUATION-[HABITUATION]: (Warriors know that the normal or habitual position of the assemblage point is not innate but is brought about by a process of habituation; human beings are drafted into a system of perceiving and strive to adjust their perception from the moment of birth to conform to the demands of that system; normally, this system rules us for life; countermanding that system and perceiving energy directly is what transforms an average man into a sorcerer.)
SELECTED REFERENCES: The Fire From Within - Page [118.3-118.4] (He affirmed that one of the most...arrive at new usages, new habits.) The Art of Dreaming - Page [75.8-76.6] (Don Juan changed the subject and...are fixed on the same spot.)
SEE ALSO: *ASSEMBLAGE-POINT-FIXATION, ASSEMBLAGE-POINT-POSITION-NORMAL, SORCERER, SEEING*

HALLUCINATIONS-[HALLUCINATIONS]: (Warriors know that there are no hallucinations, there are only shifts of the assemblage point; if an individual "sees" something different that was not there before it is because he has trapped the second attention and focused it on something.)
SELECTED REFERENCES: The Second Ring of Power - Page [324.1-324.2] ("There are no hallucinations," la Gorda...maybe it's the Nagual's smoking mixture.)
SEE ALSO: *ATTENTION-SECOND-TRAPPING, ATTENTION-SECOND, ASSEMBLAGE-POINT-SHIFT-LATERAL*

HAND-CARRY-[CARRYING THINGS WITH THE HANDS]: SEE: CARRY -HANDS-[CARRYING THINGS WITH THE HANDS]

HAND-DREAM-[THE DREAM HAND]-(TOP): SEE: DREAM-HAND-[THE DREAM HAND]-(TOP)

HAND-JOINING-DREAMING-[JOINING HANDS IN DREAMING]-(TOP)

HAND-JOINING-PLANETS-[THE WARRIORS OF THE INDIVIDUAL PLANETS JOIN HANDS]: (Warriors know that the four members of the right or left planets should only join hands under special circumstances because their collective touch fuses them into a single being; this joining of hands should only be used in cases of dire need or at the moment of leaving the world.)
> SELECTED REFERENCES: **The Eagle's Gift - Page [176.8-177.1]** (The only time when the four dreamers...the moment of leaving this world.)
> SEE ALSO: *PLANETS-WARRIORS, WARRIOR-FEMALE*

HAPPINESS-WARRIOR-[THE WARRIORS' HAPPINESS]: SEE: WARRIOR-HAPPINESS-[THE WARRIORS' HAPPINESS]

HARMONY-[HARMONY]: (Warriors know that harmony is the balance of the warrior; the natural harmony of intent; at a given moment there is no longer a war within the warrior, because the warriors" way is harmony, first the harmony between actions and decisions and then the harmony between the tonal and the nagual.)
> SELECTED REFERENCES: **A Separate Reality - Page [219.3]** (I put my notes away. Don...done harmoniously and with great patience.) **Tales of Power - Page [107.5-107.7]** ("You'll get used to it...is neither one nor the other.) **Tales of Power - Page [155.9]** (Now there is no longer a war...then the harmony between *tonal* and *nagual*.) **The Power of Silence - Page [xiii.7]** (Because of their extraordinary energy, naguals...and transmit them to their companions.)
> SEE ALSO: *WARRIOR-BALANCE, WARRIOR-EQUILIBRIUM, BALANCE, EQUILIBRIUM, WARRIOR-WAR-VS-PEACE*

HAT-WARRIOR-[THE WARRIORS' HAT]: SEE: WARRIOR-HAT-[THE WARRIORS' HAT]

HAUNTED-HOUSE-ANALOGY-[THE HAUNTED HOUSE ANALOGY]: (Warriors know that human awareness can be described as an immense haunted house; normal awareness is like being sealed in one room of that house for life; we enter that room through one magical opening, birth; we exit that room from another magical opening, death; warrior-sorcerers are capable of finding still another opening to that single room and can leave it while still alive; when they escape the sealed room they choose freedom; they choose to leave that immense haunted house instead of getting lost in other parts of it.)
> SELECTED REFERENCES: **The Power of Silence - Page [264.2-264.5]** (Don Juan said that human awareness...lost in other parts of it.)
> SEE ALSO: *AWARENESS, DEATH, WARRIORSHIP-VS-SORCERY, FREEDOM*

HEARING-SPECIAL-WARRIOR-[THE WARRIORS' SPECIAL SENSE OF HEARING]: SEE: WARRIOR-HEARING-SPECIAL-[THE WARRIORS' SPECIAL SENSE OF HEARING]

HEART-MUST-KNOW-WARRIOR-[THE WARRIOR MUST KNOW HIS HEART]: SEE: WARRIOR-HEART-MUST-KNOW-[THE WARRIOR MUST

KNOW HIS HEART]

HEART-PATH-WITH-[THE PATH WITH HEART]: SEE: PATH-HEART-WITH-[THE PATH WITH HEART]

HEART-PATH-WITHOUT-[THE PATH WITHOUT A HEART]: SEE: PATH-HEART-WITHOUT-[THE PATH WITHOUT A HEART]

HEART-STRENGTH-[THE STRENGTH OF THE HEART]: SEE: LITTLE-SMOKE-VS-DEVIL'S-WEED-[THE LITTLE SMOKE VS THE DEVIL'S WEED]

HEAVEN-[HEAVEN]: SEE: WORLD-APPARITIONS-[THE WORLD OF APPARITIONS]

HEAVEN-VISIONS-[VISIONS OF HEAVEN]-(TOP): SEE: WORLD-APPARITIONS-[THE WORLD OF APPARITIONS]-(TOP)

HELL-[HELL]: (Warriors know that hell is an element of the tonal; a lateral shift of the assemblage point within man's band of emanations which manifests itself as a desolate landscape of sulfur dunes; the land of the sulfur dunes is not another total world.)
> SELECTED REFERENCES: The Fire From Within - Page [290.5-290.9] (The moment I recollected that,...They had seen hell in the sulfur dunes.) The Power of Silence - Page [159.9-160.1] ("As I have already said to you,"...Understanding is one of our trophies.")
> SEE ALSO: *PARALLEL-LINES-LAND, WORLD-APPARITIONS, INORGANIC-BEINGS-REALM*

HELL-VISIONS-[VISIONS OF HELL]-(TOP)

HELP-NEED-NO-WARRIOR-[WARRIORS NEED NO HELP]: SEE: WARRIOR-HELP-NEED-NO-[WARRIORS NEED NO HELP]

HELP-OTHERS-[HELPING OTHERS]: SEE: WARRIOR-INTERVENTION-[THE WARRIORS' INTERVENTION], WARRIOR-COMPASSION-[THE WARRIORS' COMPASSION]

HERE-HERE-[THE HERE AND HERE]: (Warriors know that the term "here and here" is a description of the peculiar perception attained in the place of silent knowledge; the perception of being two places at the same instant; the overriding of the normal axis of perception, instead of perceiving "here and there", warriors are able to perceive "here and here" as a result of the movement of the assemblage point to the place of silent knowledge.)
> SELECTED REFERENCES: The Power of Silence - Page [216.6-216.8] (I was very curious to hear...I had perceived "here and here.") The Power of Silence - Page [222.2-222.6] (Thinking about my recollection,...perception of "there" was gained.)
> SEE ALSO: *PERCEPTION-SPLIT, PERCEPTION-WINGS, POINT-THIRD*

HERE-THERE-[THE HERE AND THERE]: SEE: HERE-HERE-[THE HERE AND HERE]

HERMANITAS-[LAS HERMANITAS]: (Warriors know that las hermanitas is another term for the four little sisters, Lidia, Rosa, Josephina and la Gorda.)
> SELECTED REFERENCES: The Second Ring of Power - Page [70.1-70.7] (Don Juan used to call them...I was almost afraid of them.)
> SEE ALSO: *WARRIOR-FEMALE, LIDIA-(TOP), ROSA-(TOP), JOSEPHINA-(TOP), GORDA-(TOP)*

HERMANITAS-BID-POWER-[LAS HERMANITAS' BID FOR POWER]-(TOP)

HERMANITAS-BOUT-[A BOUT WITH LAS HERMANITAS]-(TOP)

HERMIT-[HERMIT]: (Warriors know that by detaching themselves, they do not seek to become hermits; to be a hermit is an indulgence all its own; a hermit is not detached because he willfully abandons himself to being a hermit.)
> SELECTED REFERENCES: A Separate Reality - Page [150.8-151.1] ("Now you must detach yourself," he...abandons himself to being a hermit.)
> SEE ALSO: *WARRIOR-DETACHMENT, SELF-INDULGENCE*

HIDING-SHOWING-[HIDING AND SHOWING ONESELF]: SEE: WARRIOR-FOG [WARRIORS CREATE A FOG AROUND THEMSELVES], WARRIOR-UNAVAILABILITY [THE WARRIORS' UNAVAILABILITY]

HINGE-PERCEPTION-[PERCEPTION IS THE HINGE OF EVERYTHING]: SEE: PERCEPTION-HINGE-EVERYTHING-[PERCEPTION IS THE HINGE FOR EVERYTHING]

HINGE-SORCERY-[THE HINGE OF SORCERY]: SEE: SORCERY-HINGE-[THE HINGE OF SORCERY]

HOLDINGS-GIVING-UP-WARRIOR-[GIVING UP THE WARRIORS' HOLDINGS]: SEE: WARRIOR-HOLDINGS-GIVING-UP-[GIVING UP THE WARRIORS' HOLDINGS]

HOLE-SOUND-[THE HOLES IN THE SOUNDS]-(TOP)

HOLE-WORLD-[A HOLE IN THE WORLD]: (Warriors know that a hole in the world is a power spot; a crack in the world; a door to the other; a point to cross the parallel lines; a hole in the unknown.)
> SELECTED REFERENCES: A Separate Reality - Page [221.6-226.5] (When I had finished smoking he said...the worms give him truthful messages.) Journey to Ixtlan - Page [201.9-202.6] (Don Juan said in a very soft...it also became windy and cold.) The Second Ring of Power - Page [303.1-305.5] (La Gorda told me then to...gazing had been thoroughly dissipated.) The Eagle's Gift - Page [82.8-82.9] ("Where's that spot?" "Somewhere in the...in are on two parallel lines.) The Eagle's Gift - Page [97.4-97.5] ("It's simplicity itself," la Gorda said...this world, a door to the other.)
> SEE ALSO: *HOLE-WORLD, CRACK-WORLDS, POWER-SPOT, PARALLEL-LINES, DOOR-OTHER*

HOLE-UNKNOWN-[A HOLE IN THE UNKNOWN]: SEE: HOLE-WORLD-[HOLE IN THE WORLD]

HOMICIDAL-EGOTIST-[MAN IS A HOMICIDAL EGOTIST]: SEE: SELF-IMAGE-[THE SELF-IMAGE]

HONGUITOS-[LOS HONGUITOS]: (Warriors know that los honguitos is a term for the little mushrooms needed to prepare the smoking mixture used to reach the little smoke.)
> SELECTED REFERENCES: The Teachings of Don Juan - Page [71.5-71.6] ("What kind of mixture is it...year, and only in certain places.")
> SEE ALSO: *LITTLE-SMOKE*

HOUR-POWER-[THE WARRIORS' HOUR OF POWER]: SEE: WARRIOR-HOUR-POWER-[THE WARRIORS' HOUR OF POWER]

HOUSE-LEFT-SIDE-[THE HOUSE ON THE LEFT SIDE]-(TOP)

HOUSE-SHADOWS-[THE HOUSE OF SHADOWS]-(TOP)

HUMAN-ALTERNATIVES-POSSIBILITIES-POTENTIAL-[HUMAN ALTERNATIVES, POSSIBILITIES AND POTENTIAL]: (Warriors know they must cultivate a comprehensive perspective on the limited "alternatives" presented to them by the first attention and the unlimited and incredible "possibilities" and "potential" of the second and third attentions; warriors struggle to extend themselves beyond the bounds of their first attention "alternatives" by discovering the unimaginable nature of their true potential; warriors know that all the possibilities of sorcery from the simplest to the most astounding are in the human body itself; warriors struggle to rise above all their possibilities and defeat death.)

SELECTED REFERENCES: **A Separate Reality** - Page **[91.7]** ("You're thinking again," he said...he cannot encounter that possibility.) **A Separate Reality** - Page **[153.6-153.8]** ("The sole idea of being detached...the most frightening waste there is.) **Tales of Power** - Page **[92.6-92.7]** ("As you know," he said,...you could stop talking to yourself.) **Tales of Power** - Page **[177.6-177.8]** ("As a rule the *tonal* must defend...the *tonal* from shrinking out of the picture.") **Tales of Power** - Page **[250.5]** (He explained that disrupting routines,...inkling of incredible possibilities of action.) **The Eagle's Gift** - Page **[163.6]** (Don Juan had also told us that...are in the human body itself.) **The Eagle's Gift** - Page **[180.5]** (The impact of knowing them and...the magnitude of our unknown possibilities.) **The Fire From Within** - Page **[10.1-10.3]** (He said that the clarity and freedom...are unrealized possibilities in man.) **The Fire From Within** - Page **[118.5-118.7]** ("The nagual's blow is of great...They simply don't know about their possibilities.") **The Fire From Within** - Page **[176.4-176.9]** ("I've said that the new seers...the warrior realizes his full potential.) **The Power of Silence** - Page **[xvi.8]** (9. The aim of sorcerers is to reach...implies an alternative way of dying.) **The Power of Silence** - Page **[112.4-112.5]** ("I would think, don Juan, that...above all possibilities and defeat death.) **The Power of Silence** - Page **[126.4-126.5]** (Don Juan's reply was that man's...no hope of ever understanding them.) **The Power of Silence** - Page **[145.2]** (He emphasized over and over that...the position of the assemblage point.) **The Power of Silence** - Page **[219.6-219.8]** (He added that for the rational...And freedom is at his fingertips.) **The Power of Silence** - Page **[244.1-244.2]** (Their trump card as *stalkers*, though,...outlandish possibilities of human awareness.) **The Art of Dreaming** - Page **[2.5-2.6]** ("And what do you call the abstract...without obsessions, all that's humanly possible.) **The Art of Dreaming** - Page **[3.7-3.8]** ("How then should we perceive the...have both alternatives at our fingertips.") **The Art of Dreaming** - Page **[79.5-79.6]** ("I've been saying this to you...become real. But new worlds exist!)

SEE ALSO: *ATTENTION-FIRST, ATTENTION-SECOND, ATTENTION-THIRD, POWER-HIDDEN*

HUMAN-BEINGS-ACCOMPLISHMENT-[THE SUPREME ACCOMPLISHMENT OF HUMAN BEINGS]: SEE: WARRIOR-ATTAINMENT-[THE WARRIORS' ATTAINMENT]

HUMAN-BEINGS-DIVIDED-[HUMAN BEINGS ARE DIVIDED IN TWO]: (Warriors know that all human beings are divided in two; the right side is the tonal and the left side is the nagual; warriors know it takes great discipline and determination to break the seal and go from one side to the other.)

SELECTED REFERENCES: **The Eagle's Gift** - Page **[163.4-163.5]** (Don Juan told us that human...body, thus its resistance to conceptualization.) **The Eagle's Gift** - Page **[228.2-228.3]** (He explained to her that the...from one side to the other.) **The Eagle's Gift** - Page **[230.6-230.8]** (There was another striking anomaly that...they staggered around without muscular coordination.)

SEE ALSO: *TONAL-NAGUAL-DICHOTOMY, TONAL*

HUMAN-CONDITION-[THE HUMAN CONDITION]: (Warriors know that once they understand the nature of awareness, they cease to be persons and the human condition is no longer part of their view; seers must be paragons in order to override the nearly invincible laxness of the human condition; the human condition forces the glow of awareness to focus on the same emanations that others are using in both the right and left side awareness; for sorcerers, the abstract is something with no parallel in the human condition.)

SELECTED REFERENCES: **Journey to Ixtlan - Page [81.3]** (I insisted that to be bored...you are as good as dead.") **The Eagle's Gift - Page [306.5-306.9]** (Don Juan called everyone to come...understood and had accepted my fate.) **The Fire From Within - Page [41.9-42.1]** ("The characteristic of miserable seers is...invincible laxness of our human condition.) **The Fire From Within - Page [181.9-182.2]** (He added that in *dreaming together,* something...the left side, while *dreaming together.*) **The Power of Silence - Page [xv.5]** (The mastery of *intent* is the riddle...projected beyond our human condition.) **The Power of Silence - Page [38.4]** ("Whereas for a sorcerer an abstract...in the human condition," he said.)

SEE ALSO: *AWARENESS-TOTAL, SEER, WARRIOR-SOBRIETY, AWARENESS-GLOW, AWARENESS-RIGHT, AWARENESS-LEFT, HUMAN-(ALL), INDOLENCE, MANKIND-CONDITION, EAGLE-METAPHOR-LAXNESS*

HUMAN-FEELING-[HUMAN FEELING]: SEE: HUMAN-FORM-[THE HUMAN FORM]

*HUMAN-FORM-[THE HUMAN FORM]: (Warriors know that the human form is a force without form that makes human beings what they are; a force that possesses people all during their lives and normally doesn't leave them until the moment of death; normal human experience is all sifted through the human form; we act as humans because we cling to the human form; the compelling force of alignment of the emanations lit by the glow of awareness on the precise spot where man's assemblage point is normally fixed; the force that makes us into persons; the compelling force of alignment of the emanations lit by the glow of awareness on the precise spot on which man's assemblage point is normally fixated; to be a person is to be affiliated with that force of alignment and consequently with the precise spot where it originates.)

SELECTED REFERENCES: **Tales of Power - Page [273.5]** (The human form or human feeling...forms which the cluster may adopt.) **The Second Ring of Power - Page [154.8-155.4]** ("The Nagual told me that as long as..."And the human mold is...well...a mold.) **The Second Ring of Power - Page [158.4-158.5]** ("But if the human mold is what...I have felt it in my body.") **The Second Ring of Power - Page [160.5-160.7]** (The Nagual said that everything...I'm like you, a bit stubborn and lazy.) **The Second Ring of Power - Page [172.6-172.7]** ("Everything we say," she went on,...when they fight to kill one another.") **The Second Ring of Power - Page [283.1-283.3]** ("Maybe we don't have to do anything...only way to scare away the human form.) **The Fire From Within - Page [123.6-123.7]** (Don Juan said that the assemblage...is the human body as we perceive it.) **The Fire From Within - Page [222.8-223.2]** (I asked him to explain to me once...precise spot where it originates.)

SEE ALSO: *ATTENTION-FIRST, BODY-PHYSICAL, ALIGNMENT-HUMAN-FORM*

HUMAN-FORM-CLINGING-[CLINGING TO THE HUMAN FORM]: (Warriors know that clinging to the human form is responsible for the self-centered actions and thoughts of mankind.)

SELECTED REFERENCES: **The Second Ring of Power - Page [172.6-172.7]** ("Everything we say," she went on...they fight to kill one another.") **The Second Ring of Power - Page [237.1-239.8]** (She doesn't do those things out of...if she were delighted at my sadness.) **The Eagle's Gift - Page [73.6-73.9]** ("We are coming to the end...go as we should. We cling.")

SEE ALSO: *HUMAN-FORM, REASON-CLINGING, CYNICISM, SELF-IMAGE*

HUMAN-FORM-IMPECCABILITY-[THE HUMAN FORM AND IMPECCABILITY]: SEE: IMPECCABILITY-HUMAN-FORM-

[IMPECCABILITY AND THE HUMAN FORM]

*HUMAN-FORM-LOSING-[LOSING THE HUMAN FORM]: *(Warriors know they must struggle to become formless through the actions of an impeccable life; something warriors must accomplish in order to really change or transform themselves; an essential requirement for unifying the two attentions; losing the human form is the only way to effectively break the shell of luminosity and release the luminous core.)*
    SELECTED REFERENCES: The Second Ring of Power - Page [52.4-52.5] (And la Gorda changed more than...like her. I'm afraid of her.) The Second Ring of Power - [153.8-154.5] ("That's no mystery," she said...dreadful creatures of the night.) The Second Ring of Power - Page [159.1-159.8] ("What is the point of losing...form begins to see an eye.) The Second Ring of Power - Page [167.6-167.7] (Her knees were up and I...possibly think of her as a woman.) The Second Ring of Power - Page [174.5-174.8] ("No. Unfortunately, understanding is not their...an impeccable warrior survives, always.") The Second Ring of Power - Page [203.8-204.1] ("Is he really shy," I asked...ourselves and not worry about anything.) The Second Ring of Power - Page [235.2-235.6] ("We are human creatures," she said....that neither of us had accepted our fate.) The Second Ring of Power - Page [237.1-237.2] (She doesn't do those things out of...get angry. They can't help themselves.") The Second Ring of Power - Page [293.5-293.8] (La Gorda said that his demonstration...for unifying the two attentions.) The Eagle's Gift - Page [29.4-29.8] (For several weeks after my return...of your human form step by step.") The Eagle's Gift - Page [35.3-36.2] (If you would only rally your...concept too vague for immediate consideration.) The Eagle's Gift - Page [60.3-60.9] ("Maybe we should go back...human form unless you remember first.) The Eagle's Gift - Page [112.7-113.8] (La Gorda, upon hearing my report...case, the intellect played a minimal part.) The Eagle's Gift - Page [124.7-125.9] (For the first time in the memory...self-discipline and courage to utilize it.) The Eagle's Gift - Page [220.8-220.9] (Don Juan told us that losing...arriving at the totality of oneself.) The Fire From Within - Page [222.8-223.4] (I asked him to explain to me,...force that makes us persons.)
    SEE ALSO: *HUMAN-FORM, WARRIOR-TRANSFORMATION, ATTENTIONS-UNIFYING-TWO, HUMAN-FORM-CLINGING, LUMINOUS-SHELL, LUMINOUS-CORE*

HUMAN-INTERACTION-CORE-[THE CORE OF HUMAN INTERACTION]: *(Warriors know that coming face to face with the boring repetition of one's self-esteem is the core of all human interaction.)*
    SELECTED REFERENCES: The Eagle's Gift - Page [289.6-289.7] (Florinda said that one of the...the core of all human interaction.)
    SEE ALSO: *SELF-REFLECTION, SELF-ESTEEM*

HUMAN-JUNKPILE-[THE HUMAN JUNKPILE]: *(Warriors know that the human junkpile is a strange storehouse of the refuse of man's luminous being; an incalculable pile of human junk; a morbid, sinister storehouse on both edges of man's band of emanations; on the right edge are endless visions of physical activity, violence, killing, sensuality; on the left edge are visions of spirituality, religion and God; a lateral shift of the assemblage point; this area of man's band of emanations is also sometimes known as the prelude to the unknown.)*
    SELECTED REFERENCES: The Fire From Within - Page [134.5-135.3] ("That's exactly what I meant,"...complete view of that human junkpile.")
    SEE ALSO: *ASSEMBLAGE-POINT-LATERAL-SHIFT, DREAMING-ART, UNKNOWN-PRELUDE, EAGLE-EMANATIONS-MAN-BAND*

HUMBLENESS-WARRIOR-[THE WARRIORS' HUMBLENESS]: SEE: WARRIOR-HUMBLENESS-[THE WARRIORS' HUMBLENESS]

HUMILIATION-[HUMILIATION]: SEE: MEANNESS-HUMILIATION-[MEANNESS AND HUMILIATION]

HUMILITY-WARRIOR-[THE WARRIORS' HUMILITY]: SEE: WARRIOR-HUMBLENESS-[THE WARRIORS' HUMBLENESS]

HUMITO-[HUMITO]: SEE: LITTLE-SMOKE-[THE LITTLE SMOKE]

HUMOR-WARRIOR-[THE WARRIORS' HUMOR]: SEE: WARRIOR-HUMOR-[THE WARRIORS' HUMOR]

HUNTER-[THE HUNTER]: (Warriors know that to be a hunter means that one can see the world in different ways; the hunter knows a great deal and is in perfect balance with everything else.)
    SELECTED REFERENCES: **Journey to Ixtlan - Page [53.4-53.9]** ("Your hunter's spirit has returned to...One of them fed us today.") **Journey to Ixtlan - Page [54.5-56.9]** ("I really think that you have...worth living...so I changed it.") **Journey to Ixtlan - Page [85.4-85.6]** ("Our death is waiting and this...It dulls the edge of his fright.")
    SEE ALSO: *HUNTER-POWER-BECOMING, HUNTER-VS-WARRIOR, WARRIOR, HUNTER-(ALL), BALANCE*

HUNTER-ART-[THE ART OF THE HUNTER]: (Warriors know that the art of the hunter is to become inaccessible; to interact with the world in the most sparing way possible; the hunter taps the world lightly, stays as long as he needs to, and then moves swiftly away leaving hardly a mark.)
    SELECTED REFERENCES: **Journey to Ixtlan - Page [69.6-70.8]** ("The art of a hunter is...moves away leaving hardly a mark.")
    SEE ALSO: *WARRIOR-INACCESSIBILITY, WARRIOR-FOG-CREATE, WARRIOR-FINESSE, WARRIOR-DELICACY*

HUNTER-BALANCE-[THE BALANCE OF THE HUNTER]: SEE: BALANCE-[BALANCE]

HUNTER-BECOMING-[BECOMING A HUNTER]-(TOP)

HUNTER-POWER-BECOMING-[BECOMING A HUNTER OF POWER]: (Warriors know they cannot escape the "doing" of the world, so they transform the world into their hunting ground and use every bit of it; warriors are hunters, they calculate everything and when their calculations are over they let go with impeccable abandon; warriors are tuned to survive and they survive in the best of all possible fashions.)
    SELECTED REFERENCES: **Journey to Ixtlan - Page [81.5]** ("You have never taken the responsibility...perhaps you'll never be a hunter,") **Journey to Ixtlan - Page [91.1-92.1]** ("I've never told you about *dreaming*...taking something for being something else.) **Journey to Ixtlan - Page [98.5]** (Imagine all the inconceivable things you...almost no limits in his *dreaming.* ") **Journey to Ixtlan - Page [99.8-99.9]** ("I am not trying to make you...the strong clean life of a hunter.) **Journey to Ixtlan - Page [104.8-104.9]** (I whispered in his ear, "What...know it was made to collapse.) **Journey to Ixtlan - Page [107.1-107.2]** ("Who is a man of knowledge, don...can be a man of knowledge.") **Journey to Ixtlan - Page [113.6]** ("You've been asking me the same...it and I'm just guiding you.") **Journey to Ixtlan - Page [120.2-120.4]** ("A warrior, on the other hand,...best of all possible fashions.") **Journey to Ixtlan - Page [121.9-122.2]** ("What are we going to do...certain times and at certain places.) **Journey to Ixtlan - Page [122.5-122.6]** ("A hunter of power entraps it...he becomes a man of knowledge.") **Journey to Ixtlan - Page [132.4-132.6]** ("A hunter of power watches everything...power one must live with power.") **Journey to Ixtlan - Page [139.8-155.5]** ("We're going to go on a little...to the south. To the vastness.") **Journey to Ixtlan - Page [157.3-157.6]** ("It doesn't matter how one was...you haven't been convinced so far.") **Journey to Ixtlan - Page [158.6]** ("Hunting power is a peculiar event...and then, bingo! It happens.") **Journey to Ixtlan - Page [159.4-159.5]** ("Hunting power is a very strange...act in the most appropriate fashion.") **Journey to Ixtlan - Page [164.8-164.9]** ("Everything a man does hinges on...you have very little personal power.") **Journey to Ixtlan - Page [165.3]** ("Today you are going to hunt power...he said and sat down.) **Journey to Ixtlan - Page [177.3-177.4]** ("There is only one way to...it you must tackle everything yourself.") **Journey to Ixtlan - Page [214.3-**

214.2] (And out there, in that world,...he is used and taken himself.") **Journey to Ixtlan - Page** [216.1-216.3] ("If we wouldn't be tricked, we...a lot more in order to survive.")

    SEE ALSO: *ABANDON, LETTING-GO, WARRIOR-CONTROL, WARRIOR-ACCESSIBILITY, WARRIOR-BALANCE-SOBRIETY, ABANDON, WARRIOR-ABANDON-CONTROLLED, WARRIOR-SURVIVE*

HUNTER-SECRET-[THE SECRET OF THE HUNTER]: *(The warrior knows that to learn to be available and unavailable at the precise turn of the road is the secret of great hunters.)*

    SELECTED REFERENCES: **Journey to Ixtlan - Page [66.3]** ("Therein lies the secret of great...the precise turn of the road.")

    SEE ALSO: *WARRIOR-ACCESSIBILITY, WARRIOR-FOG-CREATE, WARRIOR-AVAILABILITY, HUNTER, HUNTER-ART*

HUNTER-VS-WARRIOR-[THE HUNTER VS THE WARRIOR]: *(Warriors know that a hunter is not concerned with the manipulation of power; a warrior is on his way to power, while a hunter knows nothing or very little about it.)*

    SELECTED REFERENCES: **Journey to Ixtlan - Page [91.1-91.9]** ("I've never told you about *dreaming*...or to make a wrong move.) **Journey to Ixtlan - Page [99.7-99.9]** ("I am not trying to make you...the impeccable life of a warrior.)

    SEE ALSO: *WARRIOR, HUNTER-POWER-BECOMING, HUNTER*

HUNTER-WARRIOR-VS-AVERAGE-MAN-[THE WARRIOR-HUNTER VS THE AVERAGE MAN]: SEE: WARRIOR-HUNTER-VS-AVERAGE-MAN-[THE WARRIOR-HUNTER VS THE AVERAGE MAN]

HUNTER-WATCHES-EVERYTHING-[THE HUNTER WATCHES EVERYTHING]: *(Warrior-hunters watch everything and everything tells them some secret.)*

    SELECTED REFERENCES: **Journey to Ixtlan - Page [132.4-132.6]** ("A hunter of power watches everything...power one must live with power.")

    SEE ALSO: *HUNTER-POWER-BECOMING*

HUNTING-GROUND-WARRIOR-[THE WARRIORS' HUNTING GROUND]: SEE: WARRIOR-HUNTING-GROUND-[THE WARRIORS' HUNTING GROUND]

HUNTING-LION-[LION HUNTING]-(TOP): SEE: LION-HUNTING-[LION HUNTING]-(TOP)

HUNTING-RATTLESNAKE-[HUNTING A RATTLESNAKE]-(TOP): SEE: RATTLESNAKE-HUNTING-[HUNTING A RATTLESNAKE]-(TOP)

I

I-WISH ["I WISH"]: *(Warriors know they cannot possibly wish they were somewhere else or that their circumstances were different; warriors have no interest in the sentiment "I wish", because they live by challenge and never know where their deaths will find them.)*
> SELECTED REFERENCES: **Tales of Power - Page [58.9-59.2]** (Don Juan gave me a long...ourselves into one or the other.) **Tales of Power - Page [112.3-112.6]** (Don Juan sighed. "What a magnificent...his death is going to find him.)
> SEE ALSO: *WARRIOR-CHALLENGE, DEATH-HUNTER*

IDEA-WORLD-[THE IDEA OF THE WORLD]: SEE: CONTINUITY-[CONTINUITY]

IDEALITIES-KNOWLEDGE-[IDEALITIES VS FIRSTHAND KNOWLEDGE]: SEE: KNOWLEDGE-IDEALITIES-[IDEALITIES VS FIRSTHAND KNOWLEDGE]

IDIOCY-[IDIOCY]: (Warriors know that many of the feelings of the average man are idiocy, and it takes all of the warriors' energy to conquer that idiocy within themselves.)
> SELECTED REFERENCES: **Tales of Power - Page [196.7-196.9]** ("But don Juan, my point is...are no survivors on this earth!") **The Second Ring of Power - Page [243.6-243.8]** ("If your grandfather and father would...proper for you to choose wisely.")
> SEE ALSO: *STUPIDITY-IGNORANCE*

IGNORANCE-[IGNORANCE]: SEE: STUPIDITY-IGNORANCE-[STUPIDITY AND IGNORANCE]

ILL-BEING-[THE STATE OF ILL-BEING]: (Warriors know that it requires just as much intense work to achieve a state of ill-being as it does to achieve a state of well-being; the trick in distinguishing between the two is in what warriors emphasize; warriors either makes themselves miserable or they make themselves strong.)
> SELECTED REFERENCES: **Journey to Ixtlan - Page [183.8-184.1]** ("You don't know what well-being...the amount of work is the same.")
> SEE ALSO: *WARRIOR-WELL-BEING, WARRIOR EMPHASIS, WARRIOR-CHOICE, WARRIOR-IMPECCABILITY*

ILLUSION-[ILLUSION]: (Warriors know that the new worlds which they assemble are not illusions, they are real, but only in the sense that are the products of the fixation of the assemblage point; the world of solid objects seems real because it is created by a description that was told to us since the moment we were born.)
> SELECTED REFERENCES: **Tales of Power - Page [98.2-98.3]** ("We are perceivers," he proceeded...since the moment we were born.) **The Fire From Within - Page [283.9-284.4]** ("The soundness of the world is not...particular spot where you are now.")
> SEE ALSO: *MIRAGE, DESCRIPTION-WORLD, REALITY-INTERPRETATION, WORLDS-OTHER-ASSEMBLE-TOTAL*

IMAGES-HOLDING-DREAM-WORLD-[HOLDING THE IMAGES OF A DREAM AS WE HOLD THE IMAGES OF THE WORLD]: (Warriors know that with their attention they can hold the images of their dreams as well as they hold the images of the world.)

SELECTED REFERENCES: **(The Second Ring of Power - Page [274.3-274.4]** ("The Nagual told us to show...dreamer is the art of attention.") **The Second Ring of Power - Page [275.8-276.2]** (What don Juan struggled to vanquish...hold the images of any dream.") **The Second Ring of Power - Page [277.3-277.6]** (La Gorda said that holding the images...of attention had the same value.) **The Eagle's Gift - Page [138.9-139.1]** (Don Juan explained to us...turn an ordinary dream into *dreaming*.)

SEE ALSO: *ATTENTION, STALKING-ART, DREAMING-ART*

IMAGINATION-WARRIOR-[THE WARRIORS' IMAGINATION]: SEE: WARRIOR-IMAGINATION-[THE WARRIORS' IMAGINATION]

IMMENSITY-ROAMING-[ROAMING THE INCOMPREHENSIBLE IMMENSITY]: *(Warriors know that the boost from the earth can be purposely used to propel an individual into the immensity of the unknown.)*

SELECTED REFERENCES: **The Fire From Within - Page [213.6-213.8]** ("The speed of that boost will dissolve...still roaming is some incomprehensible immensity.")

SEE ALSO: *UNKNOWN-IMMEASURABLE, WARRIOR-COMPANION-UNKNOWN, EARTH-BOOST*

IMMORTALITY-[IMMORTALITY]: *(Warriors know that they must reject the notion of immortality because they cannot cling to the misconception that they have all the time in the world for doubts, bewilderment and fears; warriors cannot indulge in feelings of immortality because they know the totality of themselves has but a little time on this earth; warriors realize the idiocy of feeling that they have all the time in the world because they know there are no survivors on this earth; warriors can actually circumvent the issue of immortality through the attainment of the third attention, not because they achieve immortality but because they take a somersault into the inconceivable where death no longer challenges them at all; warriors have no sense of immortality, they struggle to realize on the deepest possible level that there is no assurance whatsoever that life will continue beyond the moment.)*

SELECTED REFERENCES: **Journey to Ixtlan - Page [35.2-35.3]** ("Yes" he said softly after a...if death will never tap them.") **Journey to Ixtlan - Page [40.1-40.3]** ("Look at me," he said...There is only time for decisions.") **Journey to Ixtlan - Page [81.6-81.8]** ("You're wrong again. You can do...why the hesitation to change?") **Journey to Ixtlan - Page [84.8-85.3]** ("Use it. focus your attention on...and exploiting our lot as men.") **Tales of Power - Page [196.1-196.9]** (I made an involuntary gesture...There are no survivors on this earth!") **Tales of Power - Page [242.2-242.3]** ("Erasing personal history and its three...to feel sorry for yourself.) **The Fire From Within - Page [229.7-230.6]** ("Why did the old seers focus...beak of the Eagle to be devoured.") **The Power of Silence - Page [109.6-109.7]** (Our most costly mistake as average...we can protect ourselves from it.") **The Power of Silence - Page [112.6-112.8]** ("Sorcerers defeat death and death acknowledges...somersault into the inconceivable," he said.) **The Art of Dreaming - Page [173.4-173.6]** (He remarked that of all the...self-awareness for nearly an eternity.)

SEE ALSO: *SELF-INDULGENCE, ATTENTION-THIRD, THOUGHT-SOMERSAULT, WARRIOR-DEATH-COMMAND, LIFE-ETERNAL*

IMPATIENCE-WARRIOR-[THE WARRIORS' IMPATIENCE]: SEE: WARRIOR-IMPATIENCE-[THE WARRIORS' IMPATIENCE]

IMPECCABILITY-FIGHT-WARRIOR-[THE WARRIORS' FIGHT FOR IMPECCABILITY]: SEE: WARRIOR-IMPECCABILITY-FIGHT-[THE WARRIORS' FIGHT FOR IMPECCABILITY]

IMPECCABILITY-HUMAN-FORM-[IMPECCABILITY AND THE HUMAN FORM]: *(Warriors know that impeccability is the only way to scare away the human form.)*

SELECTED REFERENCES: **The Second Ring of Power - Page [283.3]** (She told me how the Nagual...to scare away the human form.)
SEE ALSO: *WARRIOR-IMPECCABILITY, HUMAN-FORM, HUMAN-FORM-LOSING*

IMPECCABILITY-NAGUAL-ELIAS-[THE IMPECCABILITY OF THE NAGUAL ELIAS]-(TOP): SEE: NAGUAL-ELIAS-IMPECCABILITY-[THE IMPECCABILITY OF THE NAGUAL ELIAS]-(TOP)

IMPECCABILITY-RESOLUTION-WARRIOR-[IMPECCABILITY AND THE WARRIORS' RESOLUTION]: SEE: WARRIOR-RESOLUTION-[THE WARRIORS' RESOLUTION]

IMPECCABILITY-SOBRIETY-ASSEMBLAGE-POINT-MOVE-[IMPECCABILITY, SOBRIETY AND THE MOVEMENT OF THE ASSEMBLAGE POINT]: (Warriors know that an impeccable life by itself leads to an unavoidable sense of sobriety, which in turn leads to the movement of the assemblage point.)
SELECTED REFERENCES: **The Fire From Within - Page [176.3-176.5]** ("The conviction that the new seers have...the possibilities that seers have unraveled.")
SEE ALSO: *WARRIOR-IMPECCABILITY, WARRIOR-SOBRIETY, ASSEMBLAGE-POINT-MOVING*

IMPECCABILITY-STATE-OF-BEING-[AN IMPECCABLE STATE OF BEING]: (Warriors know that seers who travel into the unknown to "see" the unknowable must be in an impeccable state of being; to be in an impeccable state of being is to be free from rational assumptions and rational fears.)
SELECTED REFERENCES: **The Fire From Within - Page [260.8-261.1]** (He went back then to discussing the...remember *seeing* the mold of man.) **The Fire From Within - Page [282.2-282.3]** ("When we first sat down here...of awareness you are in now.)
SEE ALSO: *WARRIOR-IMPECCABILITY, REASON, FEAR*

*IMPECCABILITY-TICKET-WARRIOR-[THE WARRIORS' TICKET TO IMPECCABILITY]: SEE: *WARRIOR-IMPECCABILITY-TICKET-[THE WARRIORS' TICKET TO IMPECCABILITY]

IMPECCABILITY-TICKET-WRAPPED-AWARENESS-WARRIOR-[THE WARRIORS' TICKET TO IMPECCABILITY MUST BE WRAPPED IN AWARENESS]: SEE: WARRIOR-IMPECCABILITY-TICKET-WRAPPED-AWARENESS-[THE WARRIORS' TICKET TO IMPECCABILITY MUST BE WRAPPED IN AWARENESS]

IMPECCABILITY-WARRIOR-[THE WARRIORS' IMPECCABILITY]: SEE: WARRIOR-IMPECCABILITY-[THE WARRIORS' IMPECCABILITY]

IMPECCABLE-MAN-NO-GUIDE-[AN IMPECCABLE MAN NEEDS NO ONE TO GUIDE HIM]: (Warriors know that impeccable human beings need no one to guide them; by saving energy on their own, they are capable of doing everything that seers do; all they need is a minimal chance to be cognizant of the possibilities that seers have unraveled; warriors know that any human being who follows a specific and simple sequence of actions can learn to move the assemblage point; the difficulty with this simple progression is that most of us are so unwilling to accept that we need so little to get on with the most important work of our lives.)

SELECTED REFERENCES: The Fire From Within - Page [176.3-176.5] ("The conviction that the new seers have...the possibilities that seers have unraveled.") **The Power of Silence - Page [159.1-160.5]** (He then made an incongruous statement...do it ourselves? Big question, eh?")

SEE ALSO: *WARRIOR-IMPECCABILITY, WARRIOR-SOBRIETY, ASSEMBLAGE-POINT-MOVING, WARRIOR-CHANCE-MINIMAL, HUMAN-ALTERNATIVES-POSSIBILITIES-POTENTIAL, ASSEMBLAGE-POINT-SHIFT-NEED-IMPERATIVE, WARRIOR-HELP-NEED-NO, LIFE-SUFFICIENT, MAN-DEPENDENT*

IMPOSSIBLE-BECOMES-POSSIBLE-[THE IMPOSSIBLE BECOMES POSSIBLE]: SEE: SORCERY-PRACTICAL-SIDE-[THE PRACTICAL SIDE OF SORCERY]

IMPOSSIBILITY-TASK-WARRIOR-[THE IMPOSSIBILITY OF THE WARRIORS' TASK]: SEE: WARRIOR-SURRENDER-IMPECCABILITY-[WARRIORS SURRENDER TO THEIR IMPECCABILITY]

IMPROVISATION-WARRIOR-[THE WARRIORS' IMPROVISATION]: SEE: WARRIOR-IMPROVISATION-[THE WARRIORS' IMPROVISATION]

*INACCESSIBILITY-WARRIOR-[THE WARRIORS' INACCESSIBILITY]: SEE: WARRIOR-FOG-CREATE-[WARRIORS CREATE A FOG AROUND THEMSELVES]

INACCESSIBLE-BEING-[BEING INACCESSIBLE]: (TOP)

INCANTATION-[INCANTATION]: SEE: RITUAL-[RITUAL], WARRIOR-FORMULA-[THE WARRIORS' FORMULA]

INCOMPLETENESS-WARRIOR-[THE WARRIORS' INCOMPLETENESS]: SEE: WARRIOR-COMPLETENESS-[THE WARRIORS' COMPLETENESS]

INCOMPREHENSIBLE-RENDERING-COMPREHENSIBLE-DESIRE-[THE DESIRE TO RENDER THE INCOMPREHENSIBLE IN COMPREHENSIBLE TERMS]: SEE: ASSEMBLAGE-POINT-SHIFT-LATERAL-[LATERAL SHIFTS OF THE ASSEMBLAGE POINT]

INDEPENDENCE-BARRIER-[THE BARRIER OF INDEPENDENCE]: (Warriors know that feelings of independence are just a disguise for complacency; one of many barriers which bar warriors from silent knowledge.)

SELECTED REFERENCES: **The Power of Silence - Page [47.9-48.1]** (He remarked that each of us was...to disguise my complacency as independence.)

SEE ALSO: *COMPLACENCY, PERCEPTION-BARRIER-BREAKING*

INDICATIONS-SPIRIT-[INDICATIONS OF THE SPIRIT]: (Warriors know that the indications of the spirit is another term for omens.)

SELECTED REFERENCES: **The Power of Silence - Page [12.4-12.5]** (Don Juan explained that every act...or, more simply, indications or omens.) **The Power of Silence - Page [13.1-13.4]** (The indications the spirit gave the...less a nagual, should ever make.)

SEE ALSO: *OMENS*

INDIFFERENCE-WARRIOR-[THE WARRIORS' INDIFFERENCE]: SEE: WARRIOR-INDIFFERENCE-[THE WARRIORS' INDIFFERENCE]

INDIFFERENT-STALKER-CLASSIFICATIONS-THREE-[THE INDIFFERENT CLASSIFICATION OF PERSONALITY]: SEE: PEOPLE-TYPES-[THE STALKERS' CLASSIFICATIONS OF PERSONALITY TYPES

INDIVIDUAL-SELF-[THE INDIVIDUAL SELF]: SEE: WARRIOR-SELF-
INDIVIDUAL-[THE WARRIORS' INDIVIDUAL SELF]

INDIVIDUALITY-RELINQUISHING-[RELINQUISHING
INDIVIDUALITY]: **(Warriors know that as part of the process of going to**
knowledge, they must eventually relinquish their individuality.)
    SELECTED REFERENCES: The Power of Silence - Page [48.6-48.7] ("An apprentice
is someone who is...his individuality. That is the hard part.")
    SEE ALSO: *WARRIOR-INTENT-LINK, VOLUNTEERS, WARRIOR-INDIVIDUAL-*
SELF

INDOLENCE-[INDOLENCE, LAZINESS AND SELF-IMPORTANCE]:
(Warriors know that indolence, laziness and self-importance are all parts of
the daily world; warriors struggle to overcome these enemies that tend to
muddle their aims, destroy their purpose and make them weak.)
    SELECTED REFERENCES: The Fire From Within - Page [167.5-167.9] (As we
walked, don Juan told...scorn and reject their own tradition.)
    SEE ALSO: *SELF-IMPORTANCE, WARRIOR-ENEMIES-FOUR-NATURAL,*
HUMAN-CONDITION

INERTIA-[INERTIA]: SEE : WARRIOR-INERTIA-[THE WARRIORS'
INERTIA]

INFANT-INTERNAL-DIALOGUE-[THE INTERNALIZATION OF THE
INTERNAL DIALOGUE BY INFANTS AND CHILDREN]: **(Warriors know**
infants and children are taught by everyone around them to repeat an
endless dialogue to themselves; infants and children have hundreds of
teachers who teach them exactly where to place their assemblage points; the
way that older humans condition young children by forcing their assemblage
points to become more and more steady through an increasingly complex
internal dialogue.)
    SELECTED REFERENCES: Journey to Ixtlan - Page [viii.8-ix.3] (For the sake of
validating this premise...conforming to that description, validate it.) The Fire From Within -
Page [131.8-132.9] ("This is one of the most extraordinary...the position of their assemblage
points.") The Fire From Within - Page [137.9-138.3] ("Is the assemblage point of other
organisms...same happens to every other organism.)
    SEE ALSO: *INTERNAL-DIALOGUE, ASSEMBLAGE-POINT-FIXATION,*
ASSEMBLAGE-POINT-POSITION-TRAINED-ALL-CREATURES

INFANT-MEMORIES-CARLOS-[CARLOS' MEMORIES AS AN INFANT]-
(TOP): SEE: CARLOS-INFANT-MEMORIES-[CARLOS' MEMORIES AS
AN INFANT]-(TOP)

INFINITY-GATEWAY-[THE GATEWAY TO INFINITY]: SEE: DREAMING-
METAPHORS-[METAPHORS FOR DREAMING]

INFINITY-JUNKYARD-[THE JUNKYARD OF INFINITY]-(TOP): SEE:
NAGUAL-ELIAS-ETERNITY-OBJECTS-[THE ETERNITY OBJECTS OF THE
NAGUAL ELIAS]-(TOP)

INFORMATION-EXPERIENCE-STORAGE-[THE STORAGE OF
INFORMATION AND EXPERIENCE IN THE POSITION OF THE
ASSEMBLAGE POINT]: **(Warriors know that dialogue and experience can**
be stored in unused emanations, and then recalled by reemphasizing those
same emanations that were used for the storage of that information; the
warriors' ability [by moving the assemblage point] to store information in

totally isolated islands of perception, and then to completely relive that information by moving the assemblage point back to the precise spot where the information is stored.)
    SELECTED REFERENCES: The Eagle's Gift - Page [20.4-21.5] (I told them then what don Juan...but the principle was sound.) The Fire From Within - Page [113.5-113.7] (He reminded me that Genaro was always...reemphasizing the emanations that were used.) The Power of Silence - Page [70.4-70.7] (My recollection was so phenomenal...the movement of the assemblage point.") The Power of Silence - Page [85.1-85.2] ("You're going the wrong way,"...recall them by *intending* them back.") The Power of Silence - Page [108.6-108.9] (He assured me that he had...can make it function at will.) The Power of Silence - Page [242.1-243.2] (He told me that sorcerers counted...the way sorcerers store information.") The Art of Dreaming - Page [17.7-17.9] (Sorcerers explain this seeming peculiarity of...lifetime to fulfilling this task of remembering.) The Art of Dreaming - Page [144.4-146.2] ("My intention was to explain to you...an accomplishment of the highest magnitude.)
    SEE ALSO: RECOLLECTION-SORCERER, INTENSITY, REMEMBERING, RECAPITULATION, AWARENESS-MASTERY, BODY-PHYSICAL-WITNESSING

INFORMATION-SCATTERED-WARRIOR-[INFORMATION IS SCATTERED AMONG WARRIORS]: SEE: WARRIOR-INFORMATION-SCATTERED-[INFORMATION IS SCATTERED AMONG WARRIORS]

INITIATIVE-DYNAMIC-[DYNAMIC INITIATIVE]: SEE: DREAMING-STAGES-[THE FOUR STAGES OF DREAMING]

INNER-SILENCE-[INNER SILENCE]: *(Warriors know it is possible to reach a state of complete inner silence; a moment of blackness still more silent than the moment of shutting off the internal dialogue; this silence gives rise to the intent to direct the second attention; once silence is attained, everything is possible because silence breaks the bonds that tie the assemblage point to a particular spot and give it freedom to move; internal silence gives rise to the inner strength needed to make the assemblage point shift to suitable dreaming positions.)*
    SELECTED REFERENCES: Tales of Power - Page [30.5-30.6] (After struggling for a few minutes...I was thoroughly silent.) The Eagle's Gift - Page [46.3-46.5] (After la Gorda and I had sat...remain passive, thoughtless, and without desires.) The Eagle's Gift - Page [143.1-143.4] (Both can bring the moment of silence...to make it do things.) The Fire From Within - Page [131.3-131.5] (While we were having lunch...everything is possible," he said.) The Fire From Within - Page [135.3-135.4] (Don Juan restated, as if on second thought,...the assemblage point is free to move.) The Fire From Within - Page [180.3-180.4] (He said that it starts with...in dreams to suitable positions.) The Fire From Within - Page [204.9-205.1] ("There is enough glitter in those mountains...silence plus anything that shines.") The Fire From Within - Page [213.4-213.5] ("Of course. This difficulty for the average...to use that boost by yourself.") The Fire From Within - Page [219.6-219.8] (He also told me not to...between my hipbone and my ribcage.) The Fire From Within - Page [290.3-290.6] (Don Juan looked up at the sky...of what seemed to be sulfur.) The Fire From Within - Page [295.8] ("That street, like any other,...It's time. Go now! Go!") The Fire From Within - Page [296.1-296.3] (I started to follow them, but...windlike force blew the world away.) The Fire From Within - Page [298.2] (He said over and over again...the moment warriors reach inner silence.) The Art of Dreaming - Page [187.3-187.4] ("You haven't told me yet...go to the realm of the inorganic beings.)
    SEE ALSO: STOPPING-WORLD, INTERNAL-DIALOGUE-STOPPING, ASSEMBLAGE-POINT-FIXATION, DREAMING-POSITION, BLACKNESS-MOMENT

INNER-STATE-WARRIOR-[THE WARRIORS' INNER STATE]: SEE: WARRIOR-INNER-STATE-[THE WARRIORS' INNER STATE]

*INORGANIC-BEINGS-[THE INORGANIC BEINGS]: *(Warriors know that the inorganic beings are entities without organic life as we know it; formless energy fields; living creatures that are present on the earth and*

populate it together with organic beings; creatures characterized by a particular kind of emotional dependency, sadness, joy, wrath and a kind of love that man can't even conceive of; entities with awareness but no life as we understand it; the allies; spirits; forces; winds; airs; the consciousness of inorganic beings is incomprehensible to us because is it infinitely slower than ours; inorganic beings last longer than we do, they are immobile, they make everything move around them; what dreamers perceive in dreaming as bright or dark sticks, or the voice of the dreaming emissary, or scouts, are in fact only the projections of the inorganic beings; the inorganic beings create phantom projections to please dreamers or frighten them; in our world, the inorganic beings are like moving pictures of rarefied energy projected through the boundaries of two worlds; but in their own realm, the inorganic beings are as real as anything in our own world; the inorganic beings are female and only go after males, they don't pursue females.)

    SELECTED REFERENCES: **A Separate Reality - Page [232.3-233.6]** (Don Juan was sitting outside,...which were almost inaccessible.) **Tales of Power - Page [25.3-25.4]** (Humans have a brightness peculiar only...apart from other luminous living beings.) **The Fire From Within - Page [79.7-79.9** (He explained that at the site...by a legion of strange things.) **The Fire From Within - Page [81.4-81.5]** ("The counterpart of the earth was...form of life present on this earth.") **The Fire From Within - Page [82.1-82.6]** ("Organic living beings have a cocoon...there is no possible interaction.") **The Fire From Within - Page [91.2-91.9]** ("What they pursued with the technique...of the creature at the window.") **The Fire From Within - Page [92.9-93.8]** ("What else are we going to...weird ways to go beyond it.") **The Fire From Within - Page [102.6-102.9]** (I told don Juan that from...beings are more like heat waves.") **The Fire From Within - Page [158.8-159.2]** ("Does that mean that there are...most juicy, luscious fruit there is.") **The Fire From Within - Page [160.1-160.3]** ("Man, for example, is attached...the most exciting things you'll ever do.") **The Fire From Within - Page [161.2-161.4]** ("The same situation is prevalent...but not to human *seeing.*") **The Fire From Within - Page [161.7-163.1]** (Continuing, he explained that inorganic beings...produced as many organism as possible.) **The Fire From Within - Page [165.6-165.7]** ("What about the inorganic beings?"...to man and other organic creatures.") **The Fire From Within - Page [191.6-192.2]** (Don Juan said that when he...made a deal with the creature.") **The Fire From Within - Page [200.4-200.5]** (Don Juan said that the nagual Julian...could adopt a grotesque human form.) **The Power of Silence - Page [55.3-55.7]** (When he had recovered enough and...inorganic being, a formless energy field.") **The Power of Silence - Page [104.3-104.5]** (So in a judicious mood, sorcerers decided...failed to bring them wisdom.) **The Art of Dreaming - Page [44.7-49.7]** (Everything went smoothly in my practices...I had no fear at all.) **The Art of Dreaming - Page [58.3-58.9]** ("A most trying subject," he said...This way you don't commit yourself.) **The Art of Dreaming - Page [67.4-67.9]** ("The problem with the old sorcerers...bent is to teach, to guide.") **The Art of Dreaming - Page [83.7]** (Don Juan believed that the existence...a foremost assailant of our rationality.) **The Art of Dreaming - Page [86.6-87.1]** ("They come in search of potential...And so are their scouts.") **The Art of Dreaming - Page [98.6-98.7]** (This bona fide split was a...the foremost assailant of our rationality.) **The Art of Dreaming - Page [99.1-100.5]** (When my objective inquiry into the...Through the boundaries of two worlds.") **The Art of Dreaming - Page [106.7-107.3]** (You must be extremely careful, for...in control of my dreaming practices.) **The Art of Dreaming - Page [111.5-118.3]** (On one occasion, a scout guided...was fully awake, in my bed.) **The Art of Dreaming - Page [132.6]** ("The inorganic beings are glued together...their awareness together, they are unbeatable.) **The Art of Dreaming - Page [146.9-147.3]** ("The regularity of your dreams is...don Juan said in a serious tone.) **The Art of Dreaming - Page [154.5-155.5]** ("And this brings us to the...are still bidding for your awareness.") **The Art of Dreaming - Page [179.7-179.9]** (During our next discussion of dreaming...journey by himself to their realm." **The Art of Dreaming - Page [188.2-188.5]** (I thought I had caught don Juan...their enhanced awareness and their femaleness.)

    SEE ALSO: *ALLIES, SPIRITS, GHOSTS, ENTITIES-NIGHT, INORGANIC-BEINGS-(ALL), FEMALE-UNIVERSE*

INORGANIC-BEINGS-ALLIES-[INORGANIC BEINGS VS THE ALLIES]:
(Warriors know that once the barrier of communication is broken between
the inorganic beings and man, the inorganic beings change and become what
seers call allies.)
    SELECTED REFERENCES: The Fire From Within - Page [162.1-162.3] ("Those
emanations, under certain circumstances," he...subtle thoughts or moods or fears.)
    SEE ALSO: INORGANIC-BEINGS, ALLIES

INORGANIC-BEINGS-AVAILABILITY-[THE AVAILABILITY OF THE
INORGANIC BEINGS]: (Warriors know that the inorganic beings make
themselves known to both warriors and to average men all the time; but it
is only warriors who have conserved enough energy to be aware of their
presence.)
    SELECTED REFERENCES: The Fire From Within - Page [82.5-82.6] ("If those beings
are alive...circumstances there is no possible interaction.")
    SEE ALSO: INORGANIC-BEINGS, INVENTORY, ENERGY

INORGANIC-BEINGS-BARRIER-TO-[THE BARRIER TO THE
INORGANIC BEINGS]: SEE: INORGANIC-BEINGS-AVAILABILITY-[THE
AVAILABILITY OF THE INORGANIC BEINGS]

INORGANIC-BEINGS-COMBAT-[COMBAT WITH THE INORGANIC
BEINGS]: (Warriors know that if personal circumstance leads them to a
situation in which the inorganic beings target them as an attractive addition
to their realm, sooner or later those warriors will have to engage in mortal
combat with the inorganic beings in a fight for their being and the chance for
freedom.)
    SELECTED REFERENCES: The Art of Dreaming - Page [131.4-131.7] ("You are not
sick with an...you have survived their death blow.")
    SEE ALSO: INORGANIC-BEINGS-REFUSING, INORGANIC-BEINGS-ENTICING-
DREAMING

INORGANIC-BEINGS-DREAM-[INORGANIC BEINGS AND DREAMS]:
SEE: SCOUTS-DREAMS-[THE PRESENCE OF SCOUTS IN VARIOUS
TYPES OF DREAMS]

INORGANIC-BEINGS-ENTICING-DREAMING-[ENTICING THE
INORGANIC BEINGS IN DREAMING]: (Warriors know that the inorganic
beings are compelled to interact with dreamers through their dreaming
activities; the shift of the assemblage point accomplished in dreaming
creates a distinctive energy charge which attracts the inorganic beings'
attention; by crossing the first two gates of dreaming, warriors make their
bidding known to them; dreamers mingle with the inorganic beings and turn
them into allies; they form extraordinary associations with them.)
    SELECTED REFERENCES: The Art of Dreaming - Page [46.4-47.2] ("I warned you
that the subject...wait for a sign from them.") The Art of Dreaming - Page [47.7-47.9] ("Do you
mean, don Juan, that...is unnecessary, to say the least.") The Art of Dreaming - Page [48.4-48.6]
("What do sorcerers do with inorganic...unavoidably seek the company of consciousness.) The
Art of Dreaming - Page [83.4-83.5] (It took but a few sessions...was simply following his sorcery
training.)
    SEE ALSO: DREAMING-ART, DREAMING-GATE-FIRST, DREAMING-GATE-
SECOND, INORGANIC-BEINGS, WARRIOR-POWER-BID, SOCIAL-BEINGS-DREAMERS

INORGANIC BEINGS-FREEDOM-[INORGANIC BEINGS AND
FREEDOM]: SEE: FREEDOM-INORGANIC-BEINGS-[FREEDOM AND
THE INORGANIC BEINGS]

INORGANIC-BEINGS-IMMOBILITY-[THE IMMOBILITY OF THE INORGANIC BEINGS]: SEE: INORGANIC-BEINGS-[INORGANIC BEINGS]

INORGANIC-BEINGS-INSIDE-[INSIDE THE INORGANIC BEINGS]-(TOP)

INORGANIC-BEINGS-JOLTS-[JOLTS FROM THE INORGANIC BEINGS]: SEE: ENERGY-CURRENT-UNKNOWN-[ENERGY CURRENTS FROM THE UNKNOWN]

INORGANIC-BEINGS-VS-ORGANIC-BEINGS-[INORGANIC BEINGS VS ORGANIC BEINGS]: (Warriors know that life and consciousness are a matter of energy and as such belong to both organic and inorganic beings; energetically speaking, inorganic beings are long, candle-like and opaque while organic beings are round, and much brighter; organic beings are short-lived because they are made to hurry, while inorganic beings live infinitely longer with a consciousness that is much calmer and deeper; the old seers believed that plants have the most intense communication with the inorganic beings and used the awareness of plants to assemble the worlds of inorganic life.)

SELECTED REFERENCES: **The Fire From Within - Page [161.9-163.1]** (Don Juan said that the only similarity...produced as many organisms as possible.) **The Fire From Within - Page [164.9-166.4]** ("This may seem like an oddity...to become trees to do that.") **The Art of Dreaming - Page [45.2-45.5]** (Don Juan very solemnly explained that...consciousness infinitely more calm and deeper.)

SEE ALSO: *INORGANIC-BEINGS, ORGANIC-LIFE*

INORGANIC-BEINGS-PRICE-[THE PRICE EXTRACTED BY THE INORGANIC BEINGS: SEE: INORGANIC BEINGS-TEACHINGS-[THE TEACHINGS OF THE INORGANIC BEINGS]

INORGANIC-BEINGS-PROJECTION-[THE PROJECTIONS OF THE INORGANIC BEINGS]: SEE: INORGANIC-BEINGS-[INORGANIC BEINGS]

INORGANIC-BEINGS-REALM-[THE REALM OF THE INORGANIC BEINGS]: (Warriors know that in terms of the physicality of the universe, the realm of the inorganic beings exists in a particular position of the assemblage point, just as the world of men exists in the habitual position of the assemblage point; the realm of the inorganic beings is the old sorcerers' field; in their own realm, the inorganic beings are as real as they can be, but in our world they are like moving pictures of rarefied energy projected through the boundaries of two worlds; the realm of the inorganic beings is sometimes referred to as the netherworld; in the realm of the inorganic beings, anyone who has life force can give it to another by blowing on them; allies roam the deserted plain between the parallel lines; the realm of the inorganic beings is sealed, no one can enter or leave without the inorganic beings consent.)

SELECTED REFERENCES: **The Eagle's Gift - Page [157.8-158.3]** ("Why did the Nagual woman go...That was what Silvio Manuel said.) **The Eagle's Gift - Page [244.6-244.8]** (La Gorda added that they did...of the Nagual Juan Matus' party.) **The Fire From Within - Page [81.4-81.5]** ("The counterpart of the earth was...it together with all organic beings.) **The Power of Silence - Page [xvi.5-xvi.6]** (7. When the assemblage point shifts...problems, or to face the

unimaginable.) **The Art of Dreaming - Page [63.8-64.1]** (I wished to give don Juan...habitual position of the assemblage point.") **The Art of Dreaming - Page [67.8-68.2]** ("Do you mean, don Juan...We'll talk about that realm someday.") **The Art of Dreaming - Page [87.8]** ("Remember, the realm of the inorganic beings as the old sorcerers' field.) **The Art of Dreaming - Page [88.1-92.3]** (At home, I tired of searching...it replied. "Energy is like blood.") **The Art of Dreaming - Page 100.3-100.8]** ("you are contradicting yourself, don Juan...Do you think you are unique?") **The Art of Dreaming - Page [122.6-122.7]** ("Why do you say that I am...like fish take to the water.) **The Art of Dreaming -Page [139.3]** (You certainly know more than any...the exclusive concern of the old sorcerers.) **The Art of Dreaming - Page [179.7-181.3]** (During our next discussion of dreaming...to that world, like a magnet.") **The Art of Dreaming - Page [180.8-181.1]** ("You are ready then for one final...hurrying to get it over with.) **The Art of Dreaming - Page [187.3-187.4]** ("You haven't told me yet...go to the realm of the inorganic beings.) **The Art of Dreaming - Page [245.8-245.9]** (Carol related then a most intriguing story...which people called the netherworld.)
    SEE ALSO: WORLDS-OTHER-ASSEMBLE-TOTAL, INORGANIC-BEINGS, ATTENTION-SECOND, LABYRINTH-PENUMBRA, DREAMING-GATE-SECOND, HELL, PARALLEL-LINES-LAND, ALLIES

INORGANIC-BEINGS-REALM-RESCUE-[THE RESCUE FROM THE REALM OF THE INORGANIC BEINGS]-(TOP)

INORGANIC-BEINGS-REALM-TRANSPORTED-[BODILY TRANSPORTATION TO THE REALM OF THE INORGANIC BEINGS]: (Warriors know it is possible for a dreamer to be transported bodily to the realm of the inorganic beings; if the position of the assemblage point changes appropriately, the dreamer is off like a bullet, shoes, hat and all.)
    SELECTED REFERENCES: The Art of Dreaming - Page [102.8-104.1] ("Well, the nagual Elias and the love...a bullet, shoes, hat, and all.") The Art of Dreaming - Page [132.1-132.7] ("The inorganic beings snatched you, body...conspicuous and available, like he did.") The Art of Dreaming - Page [179.7-180.2] (During our next discussion of dreaming...realm, they haven't lost their power.")
    SEE ALSO: INORGANIC-BEINGS-REALM, WARRIOR-TOTALITY-COMMAND

INORGANIC-BEINGS-REFUSING-[REFUSING THE INORGANIC BEINGS]: (Warriors know that at a given point on the path of knowledge they must make a choice; warriors must choose either to concentrate on the inorganic beings or choose to refuse it all; this is the choice between self-indulgence and sobriety; this is the choice between sorcery and warriorship; warriors will always choose sobriety and warriorship because to refuse the inorganic beings is to choose freedom.)
    SELECTED REFERENCES: The Art of Dreaming - Page [66.5-67.3] ("No. Besides, I really don't care...well the reasons for his rejection.) The Art of Dreaming - Page [68.2-68.3] ("Do I gather, don Juan, that...will agree with me. You'll see.") The Art of Dreaming - Page [69.2-69.4] ("Dreams are analyzed for their meaning...thousands of positions it can adopt.") The Art of Dreaming - Page [95.7-96.8] (It did not take much for me...learned to say, So be it!") The Art of Dreaming - Page [109.3-109.9] ("You have to continue your dreaming until...way of plummeting into a pitfall.") The Art of Dreaming - Page [173.6-173.8] ("As you know, succumbing to the...the total implication of it yet.")
    SEE ALSO: INORGANIC-BEINGS, SORCERY-FUTILITY-PITFALLS, SORCERY-PRICE, WARRIORSHIP-VS-SORCERY, FREEDOM-INORGANIC-BEINGS, ALLIES-ANTITHETICAL

INORGANIC-BEINGS-SECRETIVENESS-[THE SECRETIVENESS OF THE INORGANIC BEINGS]: (Warriors know that the nature of the realm of inorganic beings is to foster secretiveness; inorganic beings veil themselves in mystery and darkness.)
    SELECTED REFERENCES: The Art of Dreaming - Page [99.1-99.4] (When my objective inquiry into the...to a light or a fire.)

SEE ALSO: INORGANIC-BEINGS-REFUSING, INORGANIC-BEINGS-TEACHINGS

INORGANIC-BEINGS-SEEING-NOT-[NOT BEING ABLE TO SEE THE INORGANIC BEINGS]-(TOP)

INORGANIC-BEINGS-TEACHINGS-[THE TEACHINGS OF THE INORGANIC BEINGS]: (Warriors know that the entire realm of the inorganic beings is poised to teach; perhaps because they have a deeper consciousness than man's, the inorganic beings feel compelled to take us under their wings; warriors are aware, however, of the terrible price which the inorganic beings exact for their teachings; warriors must pay for their knowledge with their energy, their devotion, their total being and ultimately their freedom; warriors also realize that the teaching method of the inorganic beings is based on their evaluation of our basic first attention self as a gauge of what we need; this teaching method focuses on the fearful, envious, greedy self and teaches what is necessary to fulfill that horrible state of being; this is obviously a dreadful dead-end procedure.)

SELECTED REFERENCES: The Art of Dreaming - Page [66.7-67.3] (He did not answer me...well the reasons for his rejection.) The Art of Dreaming - Page [68.2-68.3] ("Do I gather, don Juan, that...will agree with me. You'll see.") The Art of Dreaming - Page [90.1-91.1] (The emissary modulated its voice and...voice your intent, loud and clear.") The Art of Dreaming - Page [93.3-93.6] (Don Juan had said that inorganic...old sorcerers' preference for concrete practices.) The Art of Dreaming - Page [99.1-99.9] (When my objective inquiry into the...creating projections, phantasmagorical projections at times.") The Art of Dreaming - Page [109.6-109.9] ("Are those pitfalls the result of...way of plummeting into a pitfall.") The Art of Dreaming - Page [119.7-119.9] (I heard the emissary's voice...fact, no one wants to leave.") The Art of Dreaming - Page [124.6-125.2] ("I am very pleased, but very...second attention I was a lunatic.)

SEE ALSO: INORGANIC-BEINGS, INORGANIC-BEINGS-REFUSING, SORCERY-FUTILITY-PITFALLS, FREEDOM-INORGANIC-BEINGS, SORCERY-PRICE

*INORGANIC-BEINGS-TRAP-[THE TRAP OF THE INORGANIC BEINGS]: SEE: INORGANIC-BEINGS-TEACHINGS-[THE TEACHINGS OF THE INORGANIC BEINGS], INORGANIC-BEINGS-TRICKERY-[THE TRICKERY OF THE INORGANIC BEINGS]

INORGANIC-BEINGS-TRICKERY-[THE TRICKERY OF THE INORGANIC BEINGS]: (Warriors know they must never underestimate the trickery of the inorganic beings; it is absurd to trust the inorganic beings, they have their own rhythm and it isn't human.)

SELECTED REFERENCES: The Art of Dreaming - Page [103.7-104.3] (What the nagual Rosendo did not...own rhythm, and it isn't human.") The Art of Dreaming - Page [106.7-107.3] (You must be extremely careful, for...in control of my dreaming practices.) The Art of Dreaming - Page [108.7-109.9] (Don Juan said that my dealings...way of plummeting into a pitfall.") The Art of Dreaming - Page [119.7-119.9] (I heard the emissary's voice. It...fact, no one wants to leave.") The Art of Dreaming - Page [122.1-124.1] (He asked me to describe my...fishermen; they attract and catch awareness.") The Art of Dreaming - Page [154.5-155.4] ("And this brings us to the...are still bidding for your awareness.") The Art of Dreaming - Page [173.4-173.6] (He remarked that of all the...self-awareness for nearly an eternity.) The Art of Dreaming - Page [196.2-196.9] (He confirmed our conjectures...the same trap for you two.") The Art of Dreaming - Page [217.6-217.9] ("The inorganic beings tricked you and...like those most knowledgeable old sorcerers.) The Art of Dreaming - Page [245.7-246.5] ("She took me into another facet...think it's possible to fear anything.")

SEE ALSO: INORGANIC BEINGS

INORGANIC-BEINGS-TYPES-[THE TYPES OF INORGANIC BEINGS]:
(Warriors know that there are different types of inorganic beings with different individual characteristics; watery inorganic beings are more given to excesses, yet they are more loving, more capable of imitating or even having feelings and they are dependent, possessive and relentless; the fiery inorganic beings, on the other hand, are more serious, more contained and more pompous than the others.)
SELECTED REFERENCES: The Art of Dreaming - Page [54.9-55.5] (It took me more than twenty-four...the others, but also more pompous.") The Art of Dreaming - Page [111.5-112.5] (On one occasion, a scout guided...and scouts are like candle flames.") The Art of Dreaming - Page [114.1-114.5] ("This is the shadows' world," the...would have to provide that energy.") The Art of Dreaming - Page [117.6-117.7] ("The protuberances on the tunnels' walls...the tunnels, which is our energy.") The Art of Dreaming - Page [123.1-123.4] ("I assure you, don Juan, that...with you. It knows you intimately.")
SEE ALSO: *SPIRITS, ALLIES*

INORGANIC-BEINGS-VOICE-[THE VOICE OF THE INORGANIC BEINGS]: (Warriors know that the voice of the inorganic beings is the voice of "seeing"; the voice of an inorganic being in dreaming; the voice of the dreaming emissary.)
SELECTED REFERENCES: The Art of Dreaming - Page [59.2] ("I didn't want to discuss this...the voice of an inorganic being.") The Art of Dreaming - Page [63.5-66.6] (A few months later, my dreaming...I've never regretted that decision.")
SEE ALSO: *SEEING-VOICE, DREAMING-EMISSARY-VOICE, DREAMING-VOICE*

INORGANIC-BEINGS-WORLD-[THE WORLD OF THE INORGANIC BEINGS]-(TOP)

INORGANIC-BEINGS-WORLD-LOST-[LOST IN THE WORLD OF THE INORGANIC BEINGS]-(TOP)

INORGANIC-LIFE-[INORGANIC LIFE]: (Warriors know that there are seven great bands of the Eagle's emanations that produce inorganic bubbles of awareness.)
SELECTED REFERENCES: The Fire From Within - Page [158.8-159.3] ("Does that mean that there are...the organic bubbles of awareness.)
SEE ALSO: *ORGANIC-LIFE, INORGANIC-BEINGS, EAGLE-EMANATIONS*

INSANE-RELATIVE-[THE INSANE RELATIVE]: (Warriors know that the insane relative is a metaphor for the nagual, the second attention; the nagual is like an insane relative kept under lock and key in the dungeon of our being; this wild part of our nature, this "insane relative" tends to burst in on us unless we shield ourselves with our endless internal dialogue; warriors strive to recognize and work with the wild, untrained second attention, rather than struggling to keep it stifled throughout their lives.)
SELECTED REFERENCES: The Second Ring of Power - Page [306.7-307.2] (Don Juan had also said that once we stop...with our endless internal dialogue.) The Power of Silence - Page [37.8-37.9] (I kept quiet. And he continued...then that the spirit manifested itself.)
SEE ALSO: *NAGUAL, ATTENTION-SECOND, SHIELDS, INTERNAL-DIALOGUE, SPIRIT-ANIMAL-WILD*

INSANITY-[INSANITY]: (Warriors know that they must learn to redefine the term "insanity"; warriors make a deliberate effort to detach themselves in some respects from the things which define "sanity" to the average man; warriors create a new perspective for themselves that incorporates many elements that might be called "insane" by someone without enough personal power to recognize their true character; the warriors' delicate state of mental balance; warriors are no longer "sane" but they are not crazy either; the insane bring chaos into chaos, they have no preconceived purpose to the reality they perceive; warriors know that to be "healthy and sane" in the terms of the average man means that the assemblage point is immovable; when the assemblage point shifts, it literally means that the warrior is "deranged" to some degree.)

SELECTED REFERENCES: The Teachings of Don Juan - Page [110.7-110.8] (I explained to him that what...he was capable of controlling them.) The Teachings of Don Juan - Page [139.5] ("I think I really went out of my mind." "No you didn't.") The Teachings of Don Juan - Page [141.7-141.8] ("Your ally is very frightening, don...I felt was its unimaginable power.) The Teachings of Don Juan - Page [176.2-176.3] ("Perhaps by now you know it...fear to understand what I mean.") A Separate Reality - Page [65.8-68.1] ("But if it doesn't taste good...broke out laughing, including don Juan.) Journey to Ixtlan - Page [99.3-99.9] (I confessed that although I understood...the impeccable life of a warrior.) Tales of Power - Page [7.5-7.7] ("There are lots of things that you do...routines stand in your way.") Tales of Power - Page [63.5-63.8] ("You see," don Juan said...I was very much like you.) Tales of Power - Page [84.3] (You were not mad, neither were...the ally that night, right here.") Tales of Power - Page [155.7-155.9] ("This is your world. You can't...the harmony between *tonal* and *nagual.*) The Second Ring of Power - Page [324.1-324.2] ("There are no hallucinations," la Gorda...maybe it's the Nagual's smoking mixture.) The Eagle's Gift - Page [183.8-184.1] (His benefactor put him under the direct...rational ballast to hold them back.) The Eagle's Gift - Page [204.3-204.5] (Don Juan advised me that I should...a performance staged by someone else.) The Eagle's Gift - Page [213.8-213.9] (Don Juan could not figure out...loses his mind under any circumstances.) The Eagle's Gift - Page [265.1-265.3] (Zuleica took us systematically on voyages...rational causes or reasons for anything.) The Fire From Within - Page [32.6-32.7] ("I had always been oppressed, so...thought I had lost my mind.") The Fire From Within - Page [120.5-121.3] ("What if the assemblage point doesn't…than if you had kept it.") The Fire From Within - Page [154.5-154.9] ("The position of the assemblage point...lose anything, they lose their dimple.") The Power of Silence - Page [21.8-22.3] (The first thing the nagual Elias did...the man from losing his life.) The Power of Silence - Page [165.9-166.2] ("Sorcerers know that when an average...break the mirror of self-reflection.") The Art of Dreaming - Page [48.4] ("Fear can settle down in our...can easily drive us raving mad.") The Art of Dreaming - Page [78.8-79.1] ("But isn't that what mentally ill...anything we know to be real.")

SEE ALSO: *SANITY, REASON, ASSEMBLAGE-POINT-MOVING, DREAMING-DISUSE-WHY*

INSECT-GAZING-[INSECT GAZING]: SEE: GAZING-[GAZING]

INSTRUCTION-VALUE-[THE VALUE OF INSTRUCTION]: *(Warriors know that there is very little value in instruction; the movement of the assemblage point is all that matters, and that movement depends on personal power and not on instruction; if warriors can benefit from anything, it is not from methods but from emphasis; if we become aware of the need to curtail our self-importance, then that help is real.)*

SELECTED REFERENCES: The Power of Silence - Page [158.8-159.1] ("You've taught me, don Juan, more...increased energy and not on instruction.") The Power of Silence - Page [160.1-160.5] (I told him that his sequence...do it ourselves? Big question, eh?")

SEE ALSO: *ASSEMBLAGE-POINT-MOVING, KNOWLEDGE-VS-LANGUAGE, WARRIOR-EMPHASIS*

INSTRUCTION-WARRIOR-[THE WARRIORS' INSTRUCTION]: SEE: WARRIOR-INSTRUCTION-[THE WARRIORS' INSTRUCTION]

INSTRUMENTS-[INSTRUMENTS]: SEE: SENSES-CAPABLE-EVERYTHING [OUR SENSES ARE CAPABLE OF EVERYTHING]

INTEGRATION-MEMORIES-WARRIOR-[THE INTEGRATION OF THE WARRIORS' MEMORIES]: SEE: WARRIOR-INTEGRATION-

MEMORIES-[THE INTEGRATION OF THE WARRIORS' MEMORIES]

INTELLECT-DALLIANCE-[THE DALLIANCE OF THE INTELLECT]:
(Warriors know that it is always the intellect that fools warriors; instead
of acting on things immediately, it always dallies with them instead.)
　　　　SELECTED REFERENCES: The Second Ring of Power - Page [57.9-58.4] (Don Juan
had always said to me...immediately, it dallies with it instead.)
　　　　SEE ALSO: REASON, WORDS-FLAW, TALKING, REASON-DILEMMA

INTELLECT-SHIELD-[THE SHIELD OF INTELLECT]: (Warriors know that
the intellect is merely a part of the shields of the first attention; the shield of
the intellect is not sufficient to withstand the impact of the nagual, the
impact of silent knowing and remembering with the body.)
　　　　SELECTED REFERENCES: The Eagle's Gift - Page [124.4-124.5] (I wanted to start a
debate...than even the fear of dying.)
　　　　SEE ALSO: REASON, WORDS-FLAW, WARRIOR-SHIELDS, KNOWLEDGE-VS-
LANGUAGE, NAGUAL, KNOWLEDGE-SILENT, RECOLLECTION-SORCERER

INTELLECTUAL-EXERCISE-[THE WARRIORS' INTELLECTUAL
EXERCISE]: SEE: WARRIOR-INTELLECTUAL-EXERCISE-[THE
WARRIORS' INTELLECTUAL EXERCISE]

INTENDING-[INTENDING]: (Warriors know that to intend is to wish
without wishing, to do without doing; there is no technique for intending;
warriors intend through usage; intending is the secret to both dreaming and
stalking; only when warriors learn to intend can they move the assemblage
point at will; the way in which human beings maintain their continuity,
their description of the world, is a supreme accomplishment of magic, of
intending.)
　　　　SELECTED REFERENCES: The Fire From Within - Page [289.2-289.5] ("The only
force that can temporarily cancel...in any of the seven worlds.") The Power of Silence - Page
[80.5-80.7] (In a very low voice don Juan...could they move their assemblage point at will.) The
Power of Silence - Page [251.4-251.5] ("Consider what happens to you," he...supreme
accomplishment of magic, of intending.) The Art of Dreaming - Page [25.5-25.9] ("At this point,
you can't yet...without wishing, to do without doing.) The Art of Dreaming - Page [26.4-26.5]
("No it isn't. Intending is much...all the cells of your body.") The Art of Dreaming - Page [161.5-
161.9] (Don Juan said that the moment...for intending. One intends through usage.") The Art of
Dreaming - Page [189.8-189.9] (Don Juan explained that to tip...of intending and having enough
energy.) The Art of Dreaming - Page [193.9-194.2] (She reminded me that don
Juan...assemblage point by intending its displacement.)
　　　　SEE ALSO: INTENT, NOT-DOING, DREAMING-ART, STALKING-ART,
INTENDING-(ALL)

*INTENDING-APPEARANCES-[INTENDING APPEARANCES]: SEE:
APPEARANCES-INTENDING-[INTENDING APPEARANCES]

INTENDING-CHALLENGE-[THE CHALLENGE OF INTENDING]:
(Warriors know that they must learn to accept the challenge of intending;
warriors place their silent determination without a single thought on a
specific task or goal.)
　　　　SELECTED REFERENCES: The Art of Dreaming - Page [25.5-25.9] ("At this point,
you can't yet...without wishing, to do without doing.)
　　　　SEE ALSO: INTENT, INTENDING

INTENDING-DEATH-AWAY-[INTENDING DEATH AWAY]: (Warriors
know that it is possible to intend death away; the old seers succeeded in
intending death away by patterning themselves after their allies but they
still had to die; the old seers developed bizarre techniques to alter their

luminous configurations to more closely resemble those of the inorganic beings.)
SELECTED REFERENCES: **The Fire From Within - Page [232.6-233.7]** ("As Genaro told you, the old...the seers who practiced them are.") **The Power of Silence - Page [46.6-46.7]** (With his last bit of consciousness...making the assemblage point change positions.)
SEE ALSO: *DEATH-DEFIER, INTENDING, INTENDING-CHALLENGE, WARRIOR-DEATH-COMMAND, WARRIOR-DEATH-DEFIER-QUINTESSENCE, DEATH-INTENT-SUSPENDING*

INTENDING-MEMORIES-BACK-[INTENDING MEMORIES BACK]:
(Warriors know that intending back memories is a another term for remembering with the body.)
SELECTED REFERENCES: **The Power of Silence - Page [84.3-85.2]** (I was staring at each of them...recall them by *intending* them back.")
SEE ALSO: *REMEMBERING-BODY, INTENDING, RECOLLECTION-SORCERER*

INTENDING-MYSTERY-[THE MYSTERY OF INTENDING IN THE SECOND ATTENTION]: *(Warriors know that two dreamers can work together to project their intent in the second attention; this is the mystery of intending in the second attention and is the most real dreaming of all.)*
SELECTED REFERENCES: **The Art of Dreaming - Page [237.3-237.7]** (She ended her talk with a most...of intending in the second attention.) **The Art of Dreaming - Page [239.6-240.1]** (To fend off my worries, I...real that they even have thoughts.")
SEE ALSO: *INTENDING, DREAMING-GATE-FOURTH, INTENT-PROJECTING*

INTENDING-OBJECTS-[INTENDING OBJECTS]: *(Warriors know sorcerers can intend objects for which they know the complete intent.)*
SELECTED REFERENCES: **Tales of Power - Page [45.2-45.5]** (In the style of stage magic...off with the tail of his shirt.) **The Eagle's Gift - Page [148.9-149.5]** ("The Nagual showed all of us...the *intent* of hundreds of things.)
SEE ALSO: *INTENDING, INTENT-CALLING*

INTENSITY-[INTENSITY]: *(Warriors know it is possible to compress and decompress time; intensity is an automatic result of the movement of the assemblage point; warriors can store "intensity", they can store information in an experience itself; sorcerers count their lives in terms of hours and know that in one hour it is possible to live the equivalent in intensity of a normal life; this intensity is an advantage when it comes to storing information in the movement of the assemblage point.)*
SELECTED REFERENCES: **The Eagle's Gift - Page [165.7-166.6]** (La Gorda and I discerned at one moment...we had lived a thousand years.) **The Eagle's Gift - Page [167.1-167.3]** (At last la Gorda and I...which had been veiled by *intensity*.) **The Eagle's Gift - Page [281.3-281.4]** ("You've done just that....Warriors don't waste an instant.") **The Power of Silence - Page [242.5-243.2]** ("The assemblage point, with even the most...That is the way sorcerers store information.")
SEE ALSO: *INFORMATION-EXPERIENCE-STORAGE, TIME, INTENSITY-(ALL), STALKING-MOODS*

INTENSITY-BRANDS-[THE FOUR BRANDS OF INTENSITY]: SEE: STALKING-MOODS-[THE FOUR MOODS OF STALKING]

INTENSITY-EYES-[INTENSITY AND THE EYES]: *(Warriors know that intensity is an aspect of intent, and as such it is connected naturally to the shine in the warriors' eyes.)*
SELECTED REFERENCES: **The Power of Silence - Page [243.3-243.5]** ("Intensity, being an aspect of *intent*...But I have already explained that.")
SEE ALSO: *INTENSITY, INTENT, EYES-SHINE-INTENT-BECKON*

INTENSITY-WOMEN-[WOMEN'S INTENSITY]: SEE: WOMEN-TALENT-
[WOMEN'S TALENT], ENEMY-RELENTLESS-WOMEN-[WOMEN ARE
RELENTLESS ENEMIES]

INTENT-[INTENT]: (Warriors know that intent is the abstract, the element
that propels the warrior; intent is the flow of things, intent is the pervasive
force that causes us to perceive; the force that permeates everything; intent
is what makes the world, it is everywhere; all living creatures are the slaves
of intent, but for warriors, intent becomes their friend; intent is what makes
the assemblage point move; intent is not something one might use or
command or move in any way, nevertheless, warriors use it, command it or
move it as they desire; this contradiction is the essence of sorcery and
warriorship; intent is the prevailing force in the universe, the force that
changes things or keeps them as they are; intent is the personalized force of
alignment that makes the assemblage point shift; warriors know that intent
begins with a command.)

SELECTED REFERENCES: **The Eagle's Gift - Page [143.2-143.5]** ("Have you ever felt
that moment...flying produces the effect of flying.") **The Eagle's Gift - Page [148.3-148.6]** ("The
Nagual said that *intent* is...had been waiting around for us.) **The Fire From Within - Page [5.8-
5.9]** ("After the world of the first...happened to them with power plants.) **The Fire From Within
- Page [80.7-80.8]** ("What is that mysterious force...of the Eagle's emanations or *intent*.") **The Fire
From Within - Page [171.1-171.4]** (Don Juan said that the new...of *will*, the energy of alignment.)
The Fire From Within - Page [181.3-181.5] (I asked him how *intent* helps...the movement of the
assemblage point.) **The Fire From Within - Page [218.7-218.9]** (He repeated, as if he were...at the
service of each individual.) **The Fire From Within - Page [258.4-258.5]** (I had always wondered,
however, how...is what makes the assemblage point move.) **The Fire From Within - Page
[294.4-294.8]** ("To assemble other worlds is not...of getting stranded in inconceivable aloneness.)
The Fire From Within - Page [297.8] ("In a moment you're going to...that *intent* begins with a
command.) **The Fire From Within - Page [299.5-299.6]** ("The new seers burn with the
force...total freedom means total awareness.") **The Power of Silence - Page [xii.5-xiii.8]** (I had
entered into a wondrous...of one's connection with *intent*.) **The Power of Silence - Page [xvi.7]**
(*Intent* is the pervasive force that causes...the pressure and intrusion of *intent*.) **The Power of
Silence - Page [10.8-11.5]** ("For you, teaching is talking about patterns...the spirit, *intent*, the
abstract.") **The Power of Silence - Page [31.2]** ("Meanwhile, let's continue with the element...any
warriors in search of knowledge.") **The Power of Silence - Page [80.5-80.7]** (In a very low voice
don Juan...could they move their assemblage point at will.) **The Power of Silence - Page [99.7-
99.8]** (Don Juan repeated that his benefactor...*intent*, the force that permeates everything.) **The
Power of Silence - Page [101.8-102.2]** (He had explained that normal perception...to *see* the
energy fields themselves.) **The Power of Silence - Page [103.7-103.9]** (In a calm voice don
Juan...said, is the essence of sorcery.) **The Power of Silence - Page [147.5]** ("It means that normal
perception...the more ephemeral *intent* becomes.") **The Power of Silence - Page [167.2-167.4]** (I
asked him to clarify the idea...and mysterious than our wildest fantasies.") **The Power of
Silence - Page [210.2-210.3]** (He said that men of antiquity...in that fashion were called *intent*.)
The Power of Silence - Page [223.5-223.9] (I voiced the first question that came...feature shared
by everything there is.")
SEE ALSO: *ABSTRACT, ALIGNMENT-FORCE, WARRIOR-INTENT-LINK,
ASSEMBLAGE-POINT-MOVING, WILL-VS-INTENT, INTENT-(ALL), WARRIOR-
CONTRADICTION-KNOWLEDGE*

INTENT-AREAS-FOCUS-FOUR-[THE FOUR AREAS OF FOCUS FOR
INTENT]: SEE: SORCERY-REDUCTIONS-[THE FOUR REDUCTIONS OF
SORCERY]

INTENT-AVAILABILITY-[THE AVAILABILITY OF INTENT]: (Warriors
know that the natural knowledge of intent is available to everyone, but the
command of that knowledge belongs only to those who probe it.)

SELECTED REFERENCES: **The Power of Silence - Page [85.8-85.9]** (There was still
another piece of knowledge...belonged to those who probed it.)

SEE ALSO: *INTENT, KNOWLEDGE-CLAIMING-POWER, KNOWLEDGE-SILENT*

INTENT-AWARENESS-[THE AWARENESS OF INTENT]: (Warriors know that the awareness of intent is the warriors' minimal chance.)
SELECTED REFERENCES: **The Power of Silence - Page [158.6-158.7]** ("But there are examples of people...shatter people's mirrors of self-reflection.)
SEE ALSO: *WARRIOR-CHANCE-MINIMAL, WARRIOR-INTENT-LINK, INTENT, AWARENESS*

INTENT-BECKONS-EYES-[BECKONING INTENT WITH THE EYES]: SEE: WARRIOR-INTENT-BECKONS-EYES-[WARRIORS BECKON INTENT WITH THEIR EYES]

INTENT-BODY-PHYSICAL-[THE INTENT OF THE PHYSICAL BODY]: (Warriors know that it is possible to learn the intent of the physical body with the dreaming body; there are certain things the dreaming body cannot do because it cannot handle the intent of those things; the dreaming body cannot handle the intent of eating, drinking or defecating.)
SELECTED REFERENCES: **The Eagle's Gift - Page [145.6-146.2]** ("I never knew he was in...for his *dreaming body* to eat.")
SEE ALSO: *INTENT, DREAMING-BODY, INTENT-DREAMING-BODY, BODY-PHYSICAL*

INTENT-CALLING-[CALLING INTENT]: (Warriors know it is possible to make things appear by "calling intent"; warriors can "intend" something when they know the intent of that thing; a total concentration on that which is intended.)
SELECTED REFERENCES: **The Eagle's Gift - Page [148.6-149.7]** ("He said that when we become warriors,...the time they didn't do anything.") **The Power of Silence - Page [231.3-231.4]** ("The nagual Julian insisted that the...beckon something that does not exist.) **The Power of Silence - Page [262.3-262.8]** (Don Juan asked Tuliuno how they...dark closets, and black tables.)
SEE ALSO: *INTENT, WARRIOR-INTENT-UNBENDING, INTENDING-OBJECTS*

INTENT-CATCHER-[THE CATCHERS OF INTENT]: SEE: EYES-FUNCTION-[THE TRUE FUNCTION OF THE EYES]

INTENT-COMMAND-BEGINS-[INTENT BEGINS WITH A COMMAND]: (Warriors know that intent begins with a command; a nagual, by the force of his position, is obliged to command his knowledge of intent to echo the designs of the spirit; the natural knowledge of intent is available to everyone, but the command of intent belongs only to those who probe it.)
SELECTED REFERENCES: **The Fire From Within - Page [297.8]** ("In a moment, you're going to...that *intent* begins with a command.) **The Power of Silence - Page [70.7-70.8]** (He affirmed that although I possessed...command his knowledge in this manner.) **The Power of Silence - Page [85.8-85.9]** (There was still another piece of knowledge...belonged to those who probed it.) **The Power of Silence - Page [101.8]** (Don Juan had maintained in the past...withstand the impact of that sight.) **The Power of Silence - Page [103.7-103.9]** (In a calm voice don Juan told...of sorcerers unimaginable pain and sorrow.)
SEE ALSO: *EAGLE-COMMAND, INTENT, SPIRIT-DESIGNS, KNOWLEDGE-COMMAND*

INTENT-CONNECTION-EVERYTHING-[INTENT'S CONNECTION WITH EVERYTHING]: SEE: INTENT-LINK-EVERYTHING-[INTENT'S LINK WITH EVERYTHING]

INTENT-CONTACT-DIRECT-[DIRECT CONTACT WITH INTENT]: (Warriors know that direct contact with intent is another term for silent knowledge.)

SELECTED REFERENCES: The Power of Silence - Page [104.9-105.1] (A nagual has to struggle especially...nothing but direct contact with intent.)
SEE ALSO: *KNOWLEDGE-SILENT, INTENT*

INTENT-CONTRADICTION-[THE CONTRADICTION OF INTENT]:
(Warriors know that the contradiction of intent is the essence of sorcery; intent is not something that one might move or command in any way, and yet one can use it, command it, or move it as one desires.)
SELECTED REFERENCES: The Power of Silence - Page [103.7-103.9] (In a calm voice don Juan...said, is the essence of sorcery.)
SEE ALSO: *INTENT, WARRIOR-CONTRADICTION-KNOWLEDGE, WILL-VS-INTENT, SORCERY-ESSENCE*

INTENT-DESIRE-[THE DESIRE OF INTENT]: *(Warriors know that intent has no desire of its own.)*
SELECTED REFERENCES: The Eagle's Gift - Page [149.5-149.6] (The problem was that he had no...rely on the Nagual for volition.)
SEE ALSO: *INTENT*

INTENT-DREAMING-BODY-[THE INTENT OF THE DREAMING BODY]:
(Warriors know that the dreaming body has its own intent, different from the physical body; for instance, the dreaming body knows the intent of disappearing into thin air.)
SELECTED REFERENCES: The Eagle's Gift - Page [145.6-146.2] ("I never knew he was in...for his *dreaming body* to eat.")
SEE ALSO: *INTENT-BODY-PHYSICAL, INTENT, DREAMING-BODY, BODY-PHYSICAL*

INTENT-EAGLE-EMANATIONS-AMBER-[INTENT AND THE AMBER EMANATIONS]: *(Warriors know that intent is the alignment of all the amber emanations of awareness, so it is correct to say that total freedom means total awareness.)*
SELECTED REFERENCES: The Fire From Within - Page [299.5-299.6] ("The new seers burn with the...that total freedom means total awareness.")
SEE ALSO: *INTENT, EAGLE-EMANATIONS-COLOR, AWARENESS-COLOR, AWARENESS-TOTAL, FREEDOM-TOTAL*

INTENT-EDIFICE-[THE EDIFICE OF INTENT]: *(Warriors recognize the way intent causes things to happen around them; intent creates edifices and invites warriors to enter them; the underlying and abstract order of knowledge; the edifice which intent creates and the signs it gives warriors so they won't get lost once they are inside; the customs house within which warriors find the silent knowledge that allows for the clearing of their connecting link with intent; another term for the abstract cores; the first abstract core, the manifestations of the spirit is the edifice that intent builds and places before sorcerers as an invitation, or the edifice of intent "seen" by sorcerers; the knock of the spirit is the same edifice "seen" by the beginner who is forced rather than invited to enter.)*
SELECTED REFERENCES: The Power of Silence - Page [2.1-12.5] (Don Juan explained that every act...more simply, indications or omens.) The Power of Silence - Page [27.8-27.9] ("The nagual Elias's story is another matter...what is happening around them.") The Power of Silence - Page [28.2-28.5] ("You really don't think too well...actions to the edifices of *intent*.") The Power of Silence - Page [29.9-30.1] (Obviously, what sorcerers recognize as an...the ulterior arrangement of the abstract.") The Power of Silence - Page [40.7-40.8] ("The second abstract core of the...invited - or rather forced - to enter.) The Power of Silence - Page [42.2-42.3] ("After a lifetime of practice,"...the spirit has in store for them.") The Power Silence - Page [47.1-47.4] (Don Juan then said that he had...an indefinite sense of needing something.)

SEE ALSO: *WARRIOR-INTENT-LINK, KNOWLEDGE-SILENT, KNOWLEDGE-ABSTRACT-ORDER, ABSTRACT-CORES, ABSTRACT-CORE-FIRST, ABSTRACT-CORE-SECOND, SPIRIT-MANIFESTATIONS, SPIRIT-KNOCK, INTENT*

INTENT-ELONGATING-[ELONGATING INTENT]: (Warriors know they can increase the potency of their intent by elongating it in an indescribable way; warriors must change their intent to elongate it and this must be done through forced practice.)
SELECTED REFERENCES: **The Eagle's Gift - Page [243.7-244.2]** (Silvio Manuel prepared la Gorda and...but that he was not around.)
SEE ALSO: *INTENT, EAGLE-GLIMPSING-(TOP)*

INTENT-ENGAGING-[ENGAGING INTENT] (Warriors know that in order to make the assemblage point shift to precise spots, they must engage intent.)
SELECTED REFERENCES: **The Power of Silence - Page [125.4-125.5]** ("Our assemblage points are constantly shifting...sorcerers let their eyes beckon it.")
SEE ALSO: *WARRIOR-INTENT-BECKON-EYES, ASSEMBLAGE-POINT-MOVING, INTENT*

INTENT-ENTRANCE-[THE ENTRANCE OF INTENT]: SEE: INTENT-PORTAL-[THE PORTAL OF INTENT]

INTENT-EPHEMERAL-[INTENT IS EPHEMERAL]: (Warriors know that intent is ephemeral with respect to reason; the more man clings to the world of reason, the more ephemeral intent becomes.)
SELECTED REFERENCES: **The Power of Silence - Page [147.2-147.5]** ("Sorcerers believe that when man became...the more ephemeral *intent* becomes.")
SEE ALSO: *INTENT, REASON, REASON-CLINGING*

INTENT-EXAMINE-[EXAMINING INTENT]: (Warriors know that establishing a point of reference by examining the past means getting a chance to examine intent.)
SELECTED REFERENCES: **The Power of Silence - Page [2.2-2.9]** ("Sorcerers are vitally concerned with their past...basic abstract order of their knowledge.)
SEE ALSO: *ABSTRACT-CORES, SORCERY-STORIES, WARRIOR-PAST*

INTENT-EXPRESSING-[EXPRESSING INTENT]: SEE: INTENT-HANDLING [HANDLING INTENT]

INTENT-FAMILIAR-WARRIOR-[THE WARRIORS' FAMILIARITY WITH INTENT]: SEE: WARRIOR-INTENT-FAMILIAR-[THE WARRIORS' FAMILIARITY WITH INTENT]

INTENT-FEELINGS-[INTENT AND FEELINGS]: (Warriors know that the sorcerers of antiquity knew through silent knowledge of the power to be obtained through the movement of the assemblage point; on a reduced scale, warriors of today recapture that old power; with a movement of their assemblage points they can manipulate their feelings and change things; feelings processed in that fashion are called intent.)
SELECTED REFERENCES: **The Power of Silence - Page [210.1-210.3]** (He said that men of antiquity became...in that fashion were called *intent*.) **The Power of Silence - Page [216.4-216.5]** (He explained that that afternoon...reached the position of silent knowledge.) **The Power of Silence - Page [223.5-223.9]** (I voiced the first question that came...feature shared by everything there is.")
SEE ALSO: *INTENT, FEELINGS, KNOWLEDGE-SILENT, ASSEMBLAGE-POINT-MOVING*

INTENT-FIRE-WITHIN-[INTENT AND THE FIRE FROM WITHIN]:
(Warriors know that the four reductions of sorcery are equally corrupting and that they must instead focus themselves exclusively on the capacity which the connecting link with intent has to set them free to light the fire from within.)
      SELECTED REFERENCES: The Power of Silence - Page [104.7-104.8] (Don Juan said that although there...to light the fire from within.)
      SEE ALSO: _SORCERY-REDUCTIONS, INTENT, FIRE-WITHIN_

INTENT-FLYING-[THE INTENT OF FLYING]-(TOP)

*INTENT-FLYING-WINGS-[FLYING ON THE WINGS OF INTENT]:
(Warriors know that dreamers are capable of flying on the wings of intent; they can dream themselves in another place and time.)
      SELECTED REFERENCES: The Art of Dreaming - Page [253.4-253.6] ("Your energy body is moving forward...In a time yet to come.") **The Art of Dreaming - Page [254.1-254.4]** (Carol laughed, undisturbed by my accusation...but then the vortex swallowed me.) **The Art of Dreaming - Page [258.1-258.9]** (What he was saying had no meaning...of that maneuver and much more.") **The Art of Dreaming - Page [260.4-260.5]** ("But where do you think she...flying on the wings of intent.")
      SEE ALSO: _DREAMING-GATE-FOURTH, INTENT-PROJECTING, ATTENTION-SECOND-INTENDING, INTENT_

INTENT-GATE-TONAL-NAGUAL-[INTENT AS A GATE BETWEEN THE WORLDS OF THE TONAL AND THE NAGUAL]: *(Warriors know that intent serves as a sort of customs house for warriors; whenever the are in the world of the tonal, they have no time for irrational crap; whenever they are in the world of the nagual, they have no time for rational crap; intent is the gate between the worlds of the tonal and the nagual; it closes completely behind warriors when they go either way and they must learn to be equally impeccable standing on either side.)*
      SELECTED REFERENCES: Tales of Power - Page [173.6-173.7] ("I say that it is a very...him when he goes either way.)
      SEE ALSO: _INTENT, ATTENTION-TONAL, ATTENTION-NAGUAL_

INTENT-GIFT-[THE GIFT OF INTENT]-(TOP): SEE: TENANT-GIFT [THE TENANT'S GIFT]-(TOP)

INTENT-GOD-NOT-[INTENT IS NOT GOD]: *(Warriors know that intent is not God, because intent is a force that cannot be described, much less represented.)*
      SELECTED REFERENCES: The Power of Silence - Page [85.9-86.2] (I was terribly tired by this...not be described, much less represented.)
      SEE ALSO: _GOD, INTENT, NAGUAL_

*INTENT-HANDLING-[HANDLING INTENT]: *(Warriors know that intent is an abstract which can't even be conceived of; yet without the slightest chance or desire to understand it, warriors beckon it, become familiar with it and expresses it with their acts.)*
      SELECTED REFERENCES: The Power of Silence - Page [38.5-38.7] ("We are not," he insisted...and expresses it with his acts.)
      SEE ALSO: _INTENT, SPIRIT_

INTENT-INDICATIONS-[THE INDICATIONS OF INTENT]: *(Warriors know that the indications of intent is another term for omens or gestures of the spirit.)*
      SELECTED REFERENCES: The Power of Silence - Page [6.4-6.5] (Don Juan explained that sorcerers...blueprints of complete chains of events.)

SEE ALSO: *OMENS, SPIRIT-GESTURE-OF, INTENT-EDIFICE, INTENT*

INTENT-INTERVENTION-[THE INTERVENTION OF INTENT]: *(Warriors know they must not worry about procedures because they know that the real direction of their lives is dictated by the intervention of intent.)*

SELECTED REFERENCES: **The Fire From Within - Page [238.6-238.7]** (After a moment's thought he whispered...with only the intervention of *intent*.)

SEE ALSO: *INTENT, AWARENESS-TRUTH-EIGHTH, SPIRIT-INTERVENTION, WARRIOR-INERTIA*

INTENT-INTRUSION-[THE INTRUSION OF INTENT]: SEE: AWARENESS-TRUTH-EIGHTH-[THE EIGHTH TRUTH ABOUT AWARENESS]

INTENT-KNOWING-[KNOWING WHAT INTENT IS]: *(For warriors, knowing what intent is means that one can, at any time, explain that knowledge or use it; the natural knowledge of intent is available to everyone but the command of intent belongs only to those who probe it; warriors know that silent knowledge is the knowledge of intent; warriors know that since there is no rational way of "knowing" intent, the eyes must be allowed to beckon it.)*

SELECTED REFERENCES: **The Power of Silence - Page [70.7-70.8]** (He affirmed that although I possessed...command his knowledge in this manner.) **The Power of Silence - Page [85.8-85.9]** (There was still another piece of knowledge...belonged to those who probed it.) **The Power of Silence - Page [103.3-103.5]** (Don Juan had stated his belief...the beginning, a return to paradise.) **The Power of Silence - Page [125.4-125.5]** ("Our assemblage points are constantly shifting...sorcerers let their eyes beckon it.")

SEE ALSO: *INTENT, KNOWLEDGE, KNOWLEDGE-SILENT, INTENT-COMMAND, GARDEN-EDEN, WARRIOR-INTENT-BECKON-EYES*

INTENT-KNOWLEDGE-[THE KNOWLEDGE OF INTENT]: SEE: INTENT-KNOWING-[KNOWING WHAT INTENT IS]

INTENT-LETTING-GO-[LETTING GO OF INTENT]: *(Warriors know that they must learn how to let go of the intent of everyday life; to accomplish this they evoke intent with their eyes.)*

SELECTED REFERENCES: **The Eagle's Gift - Page [307.9-308.3]** (He told me that he was going...one's attention on the luminous shell.)

SEE ALSO: *WARRIOR-BECKONS-INTENT-EYES, LETTING-GO, INTENT*

INTENT-LEVELS-[THE LEVELS OF INTENT]: *(Warriors know that intent is comprised of many levels, which the warrior may or may not attain in a lifetime.)*

SELECTED REFERENCES: **The Power of Silence - Page [166.6]** ("The nagual's ruthlessness has many aspects...of *intent* that the nagual attains.)

SEE ALSO: *WARRIOR-ATTAINMENT, INTENT*

INTENT-LINK-CLEANING-[CLEANING THE LINK WITH INTENT]: *(Warriors know that the average man's link with intent has been numbed by the ordinary concerns of daily life; warriors strive to clean that link with intent by discussing, understanding and employing it; the connecting link of the average man is practically dead because it does not respond voluntarily; the warriors' path is a drastic process, the purpose of which is to bring the connecting link with intent to order; in order to revive the link with intent, warriors need a fierce purpose called unbending intent; the warriors' goal is to sensitize the connecting link with intent until it functions at will.)*

SELECTED REFERENCES: The Power of Silence - Page [xii.7-xiii.2] (Sorcerers, or warriors, as he called...the distracting intervention of spoken language.) **The Power of Silence - Page [54.4-54.5]** ("I've already told you the story...he taught me to *stalk* myself.) **The Power of Silence - Page [108.6-108.9]** (He assured me that he had...can make it function at will.) **The Power of Silence - Page [159.7-159.9]** (Once the assemblage point has moved...from the spirit in the first place.)
SEE ALSO: *INTENT, WARRIOR-INTENT-LINK, WARRIOR-INTENT-UNBENDING, WILL-INTENT, INTENT-COMMANDING, WARRIOR-PATH, WARRIOR-PURPOSE, WARRIOR-DIALOGUE*

INTENT-LINK-DUSTING-[DUSTING THE LINK WITH INTENT]: SEE: INTENT-LINK-CLEANING-[CLEANING THE LINK WITH INTENT]

INTENT-LINK-EVERYTHING-[INTENT'S LINK WITH EVERYTHING]: (Warriors know that intent is linked with everything in the universe; warriors focus their second attention on that link.)

SELECTED REFERENCES: The Power of Silence - Page [102.9-103.2] (They decided then that *intent* was...has with everything in the universe.) **The Power of Silence - Page [104.2-104.3]** (Don Juan explained that at one...needed to manage all that power.)
SEE ALSO: *WARRIOR-INTENT-LINK, INTENT, ATTENTION-SECOND*

INTENT-LINK-JOLT-[JOLTING THE LINK WITH INTENT]: SEE: NAGUAL-TRICKERY-APPRENTICE-[THE NAGUAL TRICKS HIS APPRENTICE], STALKING-JOLT-[THE JOLT OF STALKING]

INTENT-LINK-POETS-[THE POET'S LINK WITH INTENT]: (Warriors know that poets have no firsthand knowledge of the spirit; they are aware of it intuitively, however, but not in the pragmatic way that sorcerers are.)

SELECTED REFERENCES: The Power of Silence - Page [49.6-49.7] ("I like poems for many reasons...They hit pretty close to it though.")
SEE ALSO: *POETS, WARRIOR-INTENT-LINK, INTENT*

INTENT-LINK-SELF-REFLECTION-[SELF-REFLECTION AND THE LINK TO INTENT]: (Warriors know that once the assemblage point has moved, that movement, in and of itself, entails moving away from self-reflection; this in turn, assures a clear connecting link to the spirit.)

SELECTED REFERENCES: The Power of Silence - Page [159.7-159.9] (Once the assemblage point has moved...from the spirit in the first place.)
SEE ALSO: *INTENT-LINK, SELF-REFLECTION, ASSEMBLAGE-POINT-MOVING, INTENT*

INTENT-LINK-WARRIOR-[THE WARRIORS' LINK WITH INTENT]: SEE: WARRIOR-INTENT-LINK-[THE WARRIORS' LINK WITH INTENT]

INTENT-MANIPULATION-DETACHED-[THE DETACHED MANIPULATION OF INTENT]: SEE: WARRIOR-COMMAND-[THE WARRIORS' COMMAND]

INTENT-MASTERY-[THE MASTERY OF INTENT]: (Warriors know that the mastery of intent is the riddle of the spirit; the paradox of the abstract; the warrior-sorcerers' thoughts and actions projected beyond the human condition; one of the warriors' three masteries; the warriors' ability to make their command the Eagle's command; the manipulation of intent that begins with a command given to oneself, a command that is repeated until it becomes the Eagle's command.)

SELECTED REFERENCES: The Fire From Within - Page [144.6] ("What la Catalina does,"...*stalking*, and the mastery of *intent*.) **The Fire From Within - Page [227.3-227.5]** ("There is something hauntingly appealing about...result in their total and instantaneous disintegration.) **The Fire From Within - Page [259.9-260.2]** ("It will be a long time before...as if it were the

Eagle's command.") **The Fire From Within** - Page **[298.2-298.5]** (He said over and over again...*dreaming position* called total freedom.) **The Fire From Within** - Page **[299.3-299.6]** (He explained that the new seers...freedom means total awareness.") **The Power of Silence** - Page **[ix.5-ix.7]** (At various times don Juan attempted...admitted it was not really accurate.) **The Power of Silence** - Page **[xv.5]** (The mastery of *intent* is the riddle...projected beyond our human condition.) **The Power of Silence** - Page **[85.8-85.9]** (There was still another piece...to those who probed it.) **The Art of Dreaming** - Page **[21.1-21.3]** (Don Juan told me that what...awareness of the assemblage point's displacement.)
    SEE ALSO: *RIDDLE-SPIRIT, WARRIOR-MASTERIES-THREE, EAGLE-COMMANDS, HUMAN-CONDITION, WILL-VS-INTENT*

INTENT-MASTERY-IN-LIEU-[IN LIEU OF THE MASTERY OF INTENT]: *(Warriors know that rolling the eyes will make the assemblage point shift momentarily in lieu of the mastery of intent.)*
    SELECTED REFERENCES: **The Fire From Within** - Page **[260.4-260.6]** ("The new seers recommend a very simple...in lieu of true mastery of *intent*.)
    SEE ALSO: *INTENT-MASTERY, INTENT, ASSEMBLAGE-POINT-MOVING, EYES-ROLLING*

INTENT-MOLDING-[MOLDING INTENT]: *(Warriors know that without the nagual's molding intent, there would be no awe or wonder for the warrior; the molding of intent is responsible for the warriors' magical journey of rediscovery.)*
    SELECTED REFERENCES: **The Power of Silence** - Page **[11.1-11.2]** (Without the nagual's molding of *intent*...healer, sorcerer, diviner, charlatan, or whatever.")
    SEE ALSO: *INTENT, NAGUAL-MAN-WOMAN, WARRIOR-JOURNEY-RETURN*

INTENT-MOVED-BY-[BEING MOVED BY INTENT]: SEE: SPIRIT-DESCENT-[THE DESCENT OF THE SPIRIT], ABSTRACT-CORE-FOURTH-[THE FOURTH ABSTRACT CORE]

INTENT-PORTAL-[THE PORTAL OF INTENT]: *(Warriors know that the portal of intent is another term for heightened awareness.)*
    SELECTED REFERENCES: **The Power of Silence** - Page **[84.2-84.3]** ("Sorcerers say that heightened awareness is the...it as such. Think about it.") **The Power of Silence** - Page **[85.5-85.6]** (My mind, however, instead of focusing...I also understood what *intent* was.)
    SEE ALSO: *AWARENESS-HEIGHTENED, INTENT*

INTENT-PROJECTION-[PROJECTING INTENT]: *(Warriors know that it is possible, although thoroughly incomprehensible, to project one's intent at the fourth gate of dreaming and create a total "real" world that is solely the result of the dreamer's intent; projecting intent is the art of projecting the dreamer's thoughts in order to accomplish the truthful reproduction of any object or structure of the dreamer's choice.)*
    SELECTED REFERENCES: **The Art of Dreaming** - Page **[231.3-232.7]** ("Why is that?" I asked daringly...to be an ultimately personal item.) **The Art of Dreaming** - Page **[248.4-248.7]** ("So what do you think happened...exists today, only in her intent.") **The Art of Dreaming** - Page **[253.3-253.5]** ("Your energy body is moving forward...In a time yet to come.") **The Art of Dreaming** - Page **[254.1-254.4]** (Carol laughed, undisturbed by my accusation...but then the vortex swallowed me.) **The Art of Dreaming** - Page **[258.1-258.9]** (What he was saying had no meaning...of that maneuver and much more.")
    SEE ALSO: *INTENT, DREAMING-GATE-FOURTH*

INTENT-PULLED-[BEING PULLED INTO SOMEONE'S INTENT]: SEE: DREAM-PULLED-[BEING PULLED INTO A DREAM]

INTENT-REASON-[INTENT AND REASON]: *(Warriors know that reason exists independent of intent; the more man clings to the world of reason, the more ephemeral intent becomes.)*

SELECTED REFERENCES: **The Power of Silence - Page [147.2-147.5]** ("Sorcerers believe that when man became...the more ephemeral *intent* becomes.")
SEE ALSO: *KNOWLEDGE-VS-LANGUAGE, INTENT, REASON, REASON-CLINGING*

INTENT-REQUIREMENTS-[THE REQUIREMENTS OF INTENT]-(TOP)

INTENT-SETTING-[SETTING A NEW INTENT]: SEE: WILL-INTENT-SETTING-[WILL AND SETTING A NEW INTENT]

INTENT-SLAVES-[THE SLAVES OF INTENT]: (Warriors know that all living creatures are in the clutches of intent; intent makes us act in the world and do whatever it wants, it even makes us die.)

SELECTED REFERENCES: **The Eagle's Gift - Page [148.5-148.6]** ("I can't remember when," she said...world. It even makes us die.)
SEE ALSO: *INTENT, POWER-PRISONER*

INTENT-SORCERER-DOMAIN-EXCLUSIVE-[INTENT IS THE EXCLUSIVE DOMAIN OF SORCERERS]: (Warriors know that in one sense, intent is the exclusive domain of sorcerers even though this is not a true statement at all; it is just the actual situation in the realm of practicality; the real condition is that sorcerers are simply more aware of their connection to intent and strive to manipulate it.)

SELECTED REFERENCES: **The Power of Silence - Page [223.6-223.9]** ("Only sorcerers can turn their feelings into...feature shared by everything there is.")
SEE ALSO: *INTENT-SORCERER, INTENT, SORCERY, AWARENESS*

INTENT-TRIANGLE-[THE TRIANGLE OF INTENT]-(TOP)

INTENT-UNBENDING-WARRIOR-[THE WARRIORS' UNBENDING INTENT]: SEE: WARRIOR-INTENT-UNBENDING-[THE WARRIORS' UNBENDING INTENT]

INTENT-UNIVERSAL-[THE UNIVERSAL LINK WITH INTENT]: (Warriors know that the connecting link with intent is the universal feature shared by everything there is.)

SELECTED REFERENCES: **The Power of Silence - Page [223.7-223.9]** ("The misleading part of all this...feature sheared by everything there is.")
SEE ALSO: *INTENT-LINK-EVERYTHING], INTENT*

INTENT-VAGUE-[VAGUE INTENT]: (Warriors know that when apprentices begin on the path of knowledge their intent is vague and their purpose is faulty; they are unclear about their objectives and hopes for rewards that will never materialize because they know nothing of the hardships of learning.)

SELECTED REFERENCES: **The Teachings of Don Juan - Page [83.9-84.7]** ("When a man starts to learn...is no longer a terrifying task.) **The Power of Silence - Page [42.3-42.5]** (Don Juan said that progress along...because it does not respond voluntarily.)
SEE ALSO: *INTENT, LEARNING-HARDSHIPS, WARRIOR-PURPOSE, INTENT-LINK-CLEARING, APPRENTICESHIP-NAGUALISM*

INTENT-VIEW-[A VIEW OF INTENT]: (Warriors know that nothing gives us a better view of intent than examining stories of other sorcerers battling to understand the same force of intent.)

SELECTED REFERENCES: **The Power of Silence - Page [2.7-2.8]** ("For sorcerers, establishing a point of...battling to understand the same force.")
SEE ALSO: *INTENT, SORCERY-STORIES, ABSTRACT-CORES*

INTENT-VOICING-[VOICING INTENT]: (Warriors know they must exercise their irreversible intent by voicing it in dreaming; this includes the intent to follow the scouts in dreaming as well as the intent to remain in the realm of the inorganic beings.)
SELECTED REFERENCES: The Art of Dreaming - Page [87.8-88.4] ("Remember, the realm of inorganic beings...off I went into another world.) The Art of Dreaming - Page [90.6-91.1] (The voice of the emissary sounded...voice your intent, loud and clear.") The Art of Dreaming - Page [92.9-93.3] (From that day on, in spite...beyond what I can normally imagine.) The Art of Dreaming - Page [94.8-94.9] (The emissary explained that the skin...our intent out loud, in dreaming.) The Art of Dreaming - Page [96.4-96.5] ("I went through the same turmoil...cater to your most secret wishes.") The Art of Dreaming - Page [114.6-114.8] (I knew that the emissary was...in this world is for keeps.") The Art of Dreaming - Page [158.9-159.7] ("How can I stop it...sure the emissary won't interfere anymore.") The Art of Dreaming - Page [166.7-167.9] (Don Juan told me that in...later, you'll hit the right note.") The Art of Dreaming - Page [175.4-175.8] (This was the end of our...every time I deemed it necessary.) The Art of Dreaming - Page [179.7-180.2] (During our next discussion of dreaming...realm, they haven't lost their power.") The Art of Dreaming - Page [187.3-187.5] ("You haven't told me yet what...go to the inorganic beings' world.) The Art of Dreaming - Page [233.8-234.3] (Still feeling absurdly bashful, I automatically...yell like an asshole works too.")
SEE ALSO: *WARRIOR-DEATH-VS-DECISIONS, INTENT, WORDS*

INTENT-WAKING-UP-[WAKING UP INTENT]: (Warriors know that waking up intent is their way of making a gesture for the spirit, or announcing their intentions to the spirit; words are of supreme importance to stalkers and they must state their aims before attempting to achieve them; they cannot reveal their true aim at the outset, however, and must word things carefully to conceal their main thrust.)
SELECTED REFERENCES: The Power of Silence - Page [238.1-238.2] (The nagual Elias called this act...spirit was and how to define it.)
SEE ALSO: *INTENT, WORDS, INTENT-VOICING, STALKING-ART*

INTERMEDIARY-[INTERMEDIARY]: (Warriors know that the nagual acts as an intermediary for his apprentices between the realms of the first and second attentions; some people need no intermediaries; the intermediary provides a minimal chance [the awareness of intent] as well as assistance in shattering the apprentice's mirror of self-reflection.)
SELECTED REFERENCES: The Power of Silence - Page [158.5-158.7] ("But there are examples of people...shatter people's mirrors of self-reflection.) The Art of Dreaming - Page [vii.7-viii.2] (In anthropological works, shamanism is described...is called the art of dreaming.)
SEE ALSO: *WARRIOR-CHANCE-MINIMAL, SELF-REFLECTION, ATTENTION-FIRST, ATTENTION-SECOND, NAGUAL-MAN-WOMAN*

INTERNAL-DIALOGUE-INTERNALIZING-[INTERNALIZING THE INTERNAL DIALOGUE]: SEE: INFANTS-INTERNAL-DIALOGUE-[THE INTERNALIZATION OF THE INTERNAL DIALOGUE BY INFANTS AND CHILDREN]

INTERNAL-DIALOGUE-STOPPING-[STOPPING THE INTERNAL DIALOGUE]: (Warriors know that the internal dialogue is man's internal conversation, the conversation we carry on with ourselves about the world; most people maintain their world with their internal dialogue, they renew and uphold the world with their internal talking; the world is as it is because we tell ourselves that it is so; warriors understand that if they are to have an internal dialogue it should at least be a proper one; the proper internal dialogue of a warrior should focus on the detached manipulation of intent through sober commands; warriors strive to stop the internal dialogue because they know that once they stop talking to themselves, everything becomes attainable and all things are possible; the two major techniques which warriors use to accelerate the effects of stopping the internal dialogue are erasing personal history and dreaming; stopping the internal dialogue is an operational way of describing the act of disengaging the attention of the tonal.)

SELECTED REFERENCES: **A Separate Reality - Page [218.5-219.1]** ("You think and talk to much...you want to live like a warrior.") **A Separate Reality - Page [219.4-219.6]** ("The world is such-and-such...you must start slowly to undo the world.") **Tales of Power - Page [13.5-13.8]** (I mentioned to don Juan that...dialogue is the only way to accomplish it.) **Tales of Power - Page [30.3-30.5]** ("The problem for tonight is *seeing*...*see* the person you've selected.") **Tales of Power - Page [33.7-33.8]** ("I don't see why you make...tell yourself that you are that way.") **Tales of Power - Page [92.6-92.7]** ("As you know," he said,...you could stop talking to yourself.) **Tales of Power - Page [182.4]** (Don Juan spoke to me...and should stop my internal dialogue.) **Tales of Power - Page [236.2-236.6]** ("The first act of a teacher...to stop your internal dialogue.") **Tales of Power - Page [238.2-238.3]** ("Stopping the internal dialogue is,...erasing personal history and "dreaming.") **Tales of Power - Page [243.8-243.9]** ("Did the power plants help me?"...especially with the devil's weed.) **The Second Ring of Power - Page [306.6-306.7]** (Don Juan had asserted time and...disengaging the attention of the tonal.) **The Eagle's Gift - Page [46.4-46.5]** (But I also had to consider...passive, thoughtless, and without desires.) **The Eagle's Gift - Page [143.2-143.4]** ("Have you ever felt that moment...shutting off the internal dialogue.") **The Fire From Within - Page [131.8-133.2]** ("This is one of the most extraordinary...caught in the clutches of rationality.") **The Fire From Within - Page [134.8-134.9]** (I asked him to explain the act...what traps their assemblage points.) **The Fire From Within - Page [148.9]** ("The new seers say that when...assemblage point fixed on one spot.") **The Fire From Within - Page [154.5-154.9]** ("The position of the assemblage point...lose anything, they lose their dimple.") **The Fire From Within - Page [258.6-258.8]** (After all, there is really very little...the assemblage point becomes free.") **The Fire From Within - Page [290.3-290.6]** (Don Juan looked up at the sky...of what seemed to be sulfur.) **The Fire From Within - Page [297.9-298.1]** ("The old seers used to say that if...of *intent* through sober commands.") **The Art of Dreaming - Page [93.6-94.1]** ("For perfect dreaming, the first thing...the enhancing of one's dreaming attention.")

SEE ALSO: *INVENTORY, INTENT-MASTERY, INNER-SILENCE, STOPPING-WORLD, PERSONAL-HISTORY-ERASING, DREAMING-ART, WARRIOR-DIALOGUE*

INTERNAL-DIALOGUE-WILL-[WILL AND THE INTERNAL DIALOGUE]:
(Warriors know that the internal dialogue stops in the same way it begins, with an act of will.)

SELECTED REFERENCES: **The Fire From Within - Page [131.3-132.2]** (While we were having lunch the...*will* it, we must *intend* it.")

SEE ALSO: *WILL, INTERNAL-DIALOGUE-STOPPING*

INTERVENTION-WARRIOR-[THE WARRIORS' INTERVENTION]: SEE: WARRIOR-INTERVENTION [THE WARRIORS' INTERVENTION]

INTRICACIES-KNOWLEDGE-[THE INTRICACIES OF KNOWLEDGE]: SEE: KNOWLEDGE-INTRICACIES-[THE INTRICACIES OF KNOWLEDGE]

INTUITION-WARRIOR-[THE WARRIORS' INTUITION]: SEE: WARRIOR-INTUITION-[THE WARRIORS' INTUITION]

INVENTORY-[MAN'S INVENTORY]: *(Warriors know that the inventory is the mind of man; the inventory is the result of the way the first attention watches itself and takes notes about itself in whatever aberrant ways it can; the inventory is the mind; the way a human being's emanations focus on themselves; once one becomes deeply involved with the inventory, two states of mind may result, one is a unique state known as reason and the other is called self-absorption; the Eagle commands that man take his*

inventory; it is the warriors' choice, however, as to the disposition of the inventory once it has been taken; warriors can either worship the inventory or cast it aside; an inventory is also all the details of perception involved in becoming any particular animal or person or anything.)

SELECTED REFERENCES: The Fire From Within - Page [73.6-75.1] (Don Juan continued his explanation...a specialized way is known as self-absorption.) The Fire From Within - Page [76.2-76.3] ("That is not quite right,"...into existence in the first place.") The Fire From Within - Page [114.8-115.1] ("I've explained to you that the new seers...the other side of the coin.") The Fire From Within - Page [121.1-121.3] ("By all ordinary measures, you were indeed...stronger life that if you had kept it.") The Fire From Within - Page [134.3] ("Those visions are the product of...lateral shift of the assemblage point.") The Fire From Within - Page [185.7-185.8] ("The purpose of *stalking* is twofold:...that may be offensive to reason.") The Fire From Within - Page [258.6-258.9] (After all, there is really very...the assemblage point becomes free.") The Power of Silence - Page [165.8-166.2] ("Sorcerers, because they are *stalkers*,...to break the mirror of self-reflection.") The Art of Dreaming - Page [78.3-78.5] (He explained that the cohesiveness...insect, et cetera, et cetera.)

SEE ALSO: MIND, SANITY, INTERNAL-DIALOGUE, REASON, SELF-ABSORPTION, WARRIOR-CHOICE, INVENTORY-(ALL)

INVENTORY-COZINESS-DISRUPT-[DISRUPTING THE COZINESS OF THE INVENTORY]: SEE: DEPTHS-VIEW-[A VIEW OF THE DEPTHS], DEPRESSION-MELANCHOLY-[DEPRESSION-MELANCHOLY], WARRIOR-EVICTION-NOTICE-[THE WARRIORS' EVICTION NOTICE], ETERNITY-VS-HUMANNESS-[ETERNITY VS HUMANNESS]

INVENTORY-EXTREMES-TWO-[THE TWO EXTREMES OF TAKING THE INVENTORY]: SEE: REASON-VS-SELF-ABSORPTION-[REASON VS SELF-ABSORPTION]

INVENTORY-FAILURE-[THE FAILURE OF THE INVENTORY]: (Warriors know that when the inventory fails, an individual either enlarges his inventory or the world of his self-reflection collapses; the average person is willing to incorporate new items into the inventory as long as they don't contradict his continuity; if the underlying order of the inventory is contradicted, a person's mind collapses; sorcerers count on this when they attempt to shatter the mirror of self-reflection.)

SELECTED REFERENCES: The Power of Silence - Page [165.8-166.2] ("Sorcerers, because they are *stalkers*,...to break the mirror of self-reflection.")

SEE ALSO: INVENTORY, CONTINUITY, MIND, SELF-REFLECTION-MIRROR-SHATTERING

INVENTORY-INVULNERABILITY-[THE INVENTORY AND THE INVULNERABILITY OF THE AVERAGE MAN]: (Warriors know that the inventory makes the average man invulnerable; that is why the inventory came into existence in the first place; the inventory of the first attention blocks and denies the unknown so fiercely that the nagual simply doesn't exist for the tonal.)

SELECTED REFERENCES: The Fire From Within - Page [76.1-76.3] ("I was explaining about the first attention...into existence in the first place.)

SEE ALSO: INVENTORY, ATTENTION-FIRST, KNOWN, UNKNOWN, TONAL, NAGUAL

INVENTORY-REASON-EXISTENCE-[THE REASON FOR THE INVENTORY'S EXISTENCE]: (Warriors know that the inventory came into existence to keep man's awareness separated from the unknown.)

SELECTED REFERENCES: The Fire From Within - Page [76.1-76.3] ("I was explaining about the first attention...into existence in the first place.)

SEE ALSO: *INVENTORY, ATTENTION-FIRST, UNKNOWN*

INVENTORY-STRATEGIC-WARRIOR-[THE WARRIORS' STRATEGIC INVENTORY]: SEE: WARRIOR-INVENTORY-STRATEGIC-[THE WARRIORS' STRATEGIC INVENTORY]

INVENTORY-VISIONS-[THE VISIONS OF MAN'S INVENTORY]: SEE: VISIONS-MAN [MAN'S VISIONS]

INVENTORY-WORSHIP-THROW-AWAY-[THE WARRIOR CAN WORSHIP HIS INVENTORY OR THROW IT AWAY]: (Warriors know they cannot disobey the Eagle's command to take an inventory, but they do have control over the disposition of that inventory once it has been taken; warriors know they can either worship their inventory or throw it away; the new seers make accurate inventories and then laugh at them because they know that without the inventory the assemblage point becomes free.)

SELECTED REFERENCES: **The Fire From Within** - Page [74.1-74.4] ("I don't mean to say that human...commands us to take it, that's all.") **The Fire From Within** - Page [257.9-258.8] (Don Juan had commented that that...inventory the assemblage point becomes free.")

SEE ALSO: *INVENTORY, EAGLE-COMMANDS*

INVULNERABILITY-WARRIOR-[THE WARRIORS' INVULNERABILITY]: SEE: WARRIOR-INVULNERABILITY-[THE WARRIORS' INVULNERABILITY]

IRIDIUM-WALKING-STICK-[CARLOS' DREAM OF THE IRIDIUM WALKING STICK]-(TOP): SEE: DREAM-IRIDIUM-WALKING-STICK-[CARLOS' DREAM OF THE IRIDIUM WALKING STICK]-(TOP)

IRREVERENCE-WARRIOR-[THE WARRIORS' IRREVERENCE]: SEE: WARRIOR-HUMOR-[THE WARRIORS' HUMOR], WARRIOR-LIGHTNESS-[THE WARRIORS' LIGHTNESS]

ITCH-OUTSIDE-BODY-[THE ITCH OUTSIDE OF THE BODY]-(TOP): SEE: ATTENTION-SECOND-CONTROLS-[EXPERIENCING THE SECOND ATTENTION TAKING OVER THE CONTROLS]-(TOP)

J

JACK-CHEESE-ANALOGY-[THE JACK CHEESE ANALOGY]: SEE: CHEESE-ANALOGY-[THE JACK CHEESE ANALOGY]

JAGUAR-CHASE-NOT-DOING-[THE NOT-DOING OF BEING CHASED BY A JAGUAR]-(TOP)

JAGUAR-CHOICES-MATCHING-[MATCHING THE JAGUAR'S CHOICES]-(TOP)

JAGUAR-MAGICAL-[THE MAGICAL JAGUAR]-(TOP): SEE: POINT-THIRD [THE THIRD POINT]-(TOP)

JAPANESE-SQUIRREL-[THE JAPANESE SQUIRREL]-(TOP): SEE: NAGUAL-CREATIVITY-[THE NAGUAL AND A DEMONSTRATION OF CREATIVITY)-(TOP)

JILTED-BRIDE-PIGLET-[THE JILTED BRIDE AND HER PIGLET]-(TOP)

JIMSON-WEED-[JIMSON WEED]: SEE: DEVIL'S-WEED-[DEVIL'S WEED]

JOINING-HANDS-[JOINING HANDS]: SEE: HANDS-JOINING-PLANETS-[THE WARRIORS OF THE INDIVIDUAL PLANETS JOIN HANDS]

JOINING-HANDS-DREAMING-[JOINING HANDS IN DREAMING]-(TOP): SEE: HANDS-JOINING-DREAMING-[JOINING HANDS IN DREAMING]-(TOP)

JOINING-LEFT-RIGHT-AWARENESS-[JOINING THE LEFT AND RIGHT SIDES OF AWARENESS]: SEE: REMEMBERING-TASK-[THE TASK OF \ REMEMBERING], ATTENTION-UNIFYING-[UNIFYING THE TWO ATTENTIONS]

JOSEPHINA-DREAMING-[JOSEPHINA'S DREAMING]-(TOP)

JOSEPHINA-PRANKS-[JOSEPHINA'S PRANKS]-(TOP)

JOSEPHINA-STALKING-[JOSEPHINA'S STALKING MANEUVERS]-(TOP)

JOURNEY-DEFINITIVE-WARRIOR-[THE WARRIORS' DEFINITIVE JOURNEY]: SEE: WARRIOR-JOURNEY-DEFINITIVE-[THE WARRIORS' DEFINITIVE JOURNEY]

JOURNEY-EXTRAVAGANT-WARRIOR-[THE WARRIORS' EXTRAVAGANT JOURNEY]: SEE: WARRIOR-JOURNEY-EXTRAVAGANT-[THE WARRIORS' EXTRAVAGANT JOURNEY]

JOURNEY-IXTLAN-[JOURNEY TO IXTLAN]-(TOP)

JOURNEY-JOYFUL-WARRIOR-[THE WARRIORS' JOYFUL JOURNEY]: SEE: WARRIOR-JOURNEY-JOYFUL-[THE WARRIORS' JOYFUL JOURNEY]

JOURNEY-POWER-PATH-HEART-WARRIOR-[THE WARRIORS'
JOURNEY WITH POWER AND HIS PATH WITH HEART]: SEE:
WARRIOR-JOURNEY-POWER-PATH-HEART-[THE WARRIORS'
JOURNEY WITH POWER AND HIS PATH WITH HEART]

JOURNEY-RECOVERY-WARRIOR-[THE WARRIORS' JOURNEY OF
RECOVERY]: SEE: WARRIOR-JOURNEY-RECOVERY-[THE WARRIORS'
JOURNEY OF RECOVERY]

JOURNEY-RETURN-WARRIOR-[THE WARRIORS' JOURNEY OF
RETURN]: SEE: WARRIOR-JOURNEY-RETURN-[THE WARRIORS'
JOURNEY OF RETURN]

JOURNEY-UNKNOWN-WARRIOR-[THE WARRIORS' JOURNEY INTO
THE UNKNOWN]: SEE: WARRIOR-JOURNEY-UNKNOWN-[THE
WARRIORS' JOURNEY INTO THE UNKNOWN], UNKNOWN-JOURNEY-
[JOURNEY INTO THE UNKNOWN]

JOY-WARRIOR-[THE WARRIORS' JOY]: SEE: WARRIOR-JOY-[THE
WARRIORS' JOY]

JUAN-CARLOS-MEET-[HOW CARLOS MET DON JUAN]-(TOP)

JUAN-DEATH-[THE STORY OF DON JUAN'S DEATH]-(TOP)

JUAN-DESTINY-[DON JUAN'S DESTINY]-(TOP)

JUAN-DON-[DON JUAN MATUS]: (The nagual Juan Matus; a Yaqui Indian
sorcerer and warrior; the teacher of Carlos Castaneda.)
    SELECTED REFERENCES: The Teachings of Don Juan - Page [18.2-18.5] (Although
don Juan categorized his benefactor...to determine his precise cultural milieu.) The Teachings
of Don Juan - Page [18.9] (I carried out the apprenticeship first...during the course of my
training.) The Art of Dreaming - Page [vii.3-vii.5] (Over the past twenty years, I...spells, or
rituals to produce supernatural effects.)
    SEE ALSO: NAGUAL-MAN-WOMAN, TEACHERS-TEACHING

JUAN-DOUBLE-BEING-[DON JUAN EXPERIENCES BEING DOUBLE]-
(TOP)

JUAN-GENARO-STALKING-TEAM-[THE STALKING TEAM OF DON
JUAN AND DON GENARO]-(TOP)

JUAN-HUSBAND-FATHER-[DON JUAN AS HUSBAND AND FATHER]-
(TOP)

JUAN-INTUITION-[DON JUAN'S INTUITION]-(TOP)

JUAN-JULIAN-FINDING-[HOW THE NAGUAL JULIAN FOUND DON
JUAN]-(TOP)

JUAN-JULIAN-HOUSE-[DON JUAN'S STAY AT THE NAGUAL JULIAN'S
HOUSE]-(TOP)

JUAN-JULIAN-PARTY-MEET-[HOW DON JUAN MET THE NAGUAL
JULIAN'S PARTY]-(TOP)

JUAN-LEGS-LOSE-[IF DON JUAN LOST HIS LEGS]-(TOP)

JUAN-PARALYSIS-[DON JUAN'S PARALYSIS]-(TOP)

JUAN-PARENTS-[DON JUAN'S PARENTS]-(TOP)

JUAN-PARENTS-DEATH-*[THE DEATH OF DON JUAN'S PARENTS]*-*(TOP)*

JUAN-PIRATE-DISGUISE-*[DON JUAN'S PIRATE DISGUISE]: SEE: SHADOWS-CIRCLE-[A CIRCLE OF SHADOWS]-TOP*

JUAN-RAGE-*[DON JUAN'S RAGE]-(TOP)*

JUAN-RECAPITULATION-*[DON JUAN'S RECAPITULATION]-(TOP)*

JUAN-RIVER-BOUT-*[DON JUAN'S BOUT WITH THE RAGING RIVER]-(TOP)*

JUAN-RUTHLESSNESS-MASK-*[DON JUAN'S MASK OF RUTHLESSNESS]-(TOP)*

JUAN-STROKE-GUAYMAS-*[DON JUAN'S STROKE IN GUAYMAS]-(TOP)*

JUAN-TRANSFORMATION-*[DON JUAN'S TRANSFORMATION]-(TOP)*

JUAN-WOMAN-DISGUISE-*[DON JUAN'S WOMAN DISGUISE]-(TOP)*

JUDGMENT-WARRIOR-*[WARRIORS DO NOT PASS JUDGMENT]: SEE: WARRIOR-JUDGMENT-[WARRIORS DO NOT PASS JUDGMENT]*

JULIAN-NAGUAL-*[THE NAGUAL JULIAN]-(TOP)*

JULIAN-NAGUAL-AGE-*[THE ABILITY OF THE NAGUAL JULIAN TO APPEAR YOUNG OR OLD AT WILL]-(TOP)*

JULIAN-NAGUAL-IMPECCABILITY-*[THE IMPECCABILITY OF THE NAGUAL JULIAN]-(TOP)*

JULIAN-NAGUAL-INTENT-WAKES-UP-*[THE NAGUAL JULIAN WAKES UP INTENT]-(TOP)*

JULIAN-NAGUAL-JOKES-*[THE JOKES OF THE NAGUAL JULIAN]-(TOP)*

JULIAN-NAGUAL-JOY-*[THE JOY OF THE NAGUAL JULIAN]-(TOP)*

JULIAN-NAGUAL-LAST-SEDUCTION-*[THE LAST SEDUCTION OF THE NAGUAL JULIAN]-(TOP)*

JULIAN-NAGUAL-MAGIC-*[THE MAGIC OF THE NAGUAL JULIAN]-(TOP)*

JULIAN-NAGUAL-SEX-CHANGE-*[THE NAGUAL JULIAN'S SEX CHANGE]-(TOP)*

JULIAN-NAGUAL-SPIRIT-DESCENT-*[THE DESCENT OF THE SPIRIT ON THE NAGUAL JULIAN]-(TOP)*

JULIAN-NAGUAL-STALKING-*[THE STALKING OF THE NAGUAL JULIAN]-(TOP)*

JULIAN-NAGUAL-TALES-*[TALES OF THE NAGUAL JULIAN]-(TOP)*

JULIAN-NAGUAL-TEARS-*[THE TEARS OF THE NAGUAL JULIAN]-(TOP)*

JULIAN-NAGUAL-TRANSFORMATION-*[THE TRANSFORMATION OF THE NAGUAL JULIAN]-(TOP)*

JUMP-RAVINE-CARLOS-IN-OUT-*[CARLOS JUMPS IN AND OUT OF THE RAVINE-(TOP)*

JUMP-WARRIOR-[THE WARRIORS' JUMP INTO THE ABYSS]: SEE: WARRIOR-JUMP-[THE WARRIORS' JUMP INTO THE ABYSS]

K

KEY-EVERYTHING-[THE KEY TO EVERYTHING]: SEE: EARTH-BOOST-[THE EARTH'S BOOST]

KINDNESS-[KINDNESS]: (Warriors know that kindness is one name for the bridge between contradictions; the counterpoint to wisdom; that which makes wisdom useful and meaningful.)
SELECTED REFERENCES: **The Fire From Within - Page [xii.7-xii.8]** (Don Juan had told me that there...and knowledge without sobriety are useless.) **The Fire From Within - Page [73.5-73.6]** ("Only a feeling of supreme sobriety...art, affection, sobriety, love or even kindness.") **The Fire From Within - Page [228.4-228.5]** ("Those first new seers served everybody...seers who were filled with morbidity.") **The Power of Silence - Page [106.8-107.1]** (I answered it was very kind of him...be able to suspect his ruthlessness.) **The Power of Silence - Page [127.6-127.9]** (Years before, I had been both..."Nothing you would understand," he replied.)
SEE ALSO: *INTERVENTION, WARRIOR-SOBRIETY, WARRIOR-LOVE, WARRIOR-BRIDGE, WARRIOR-CONTRADICTION-KNOWLEDGE*

KING-PRONUNCIATION-[THE KING OF PRONUNCIATION]-(TOP)

KNOW-WORLD-[KNOWING THE WORLD]: SEE: WORLD-PREDICTABILITY-[THE PREDICTABILITY OF THE WORLD]

KNOWLEDGE-[KNOWLEDGE]: (Warriors think of knowledge as the knowledge of nagualism; also referred to as the mastery of intent, the search for total freedom, or sorcery.)
SELECTED REFERENCES: **The Teachings of Don Juan - Page [53.5-54.1]** (He looked at me for a long time...would only bring harm to me.) **A Separate Reality - Page [5.7-5.9]** (Our conversations were conducted in Spanish,...who "knows" to categorize a sorcerer.) **A Separate Reality - Page [10.8-11.7]** (Don Juan had once told me...impossible to talk about dancing or *seeing*.) **Tales of Power - Page [8.2-8.3]** ("It doesn't matter what one reveals...won't make a damn bit of difference.) **Tales of Power - Page [27.9]** ("Out there, there is only knowledge," he said in a factual tone.) **The Fire From Within - Page [72.8-72.9]** (Don Juan said that the new seers...is composed of contradictory propositions.) **The Fire From Within - Page [80.3-81.1]** ("The new seers were simply terrified...and more intricate as time passed.) **The Power of Silence - Page [ix.5-ix.7]** (At various times don Juan attempted...admitted it was not really accurate.) **The Power of Silence - Page [x.1-xi.2]** (He stopped for a moment before...in perceiving the ordinary world we know.)
SEE ALSO: *INTENT-MASTERY, FREEDOM-TOTAL, SORCERY, MAN-KNOWLEDGE, KNOWLEDGE-PATH, KNOWLEDGE-(ALL), ENLIGHTENMENT, SORCERER-KNOWLEDGE-MOST-SOPHISTICATED*

KNOWLEDGE-ABSTRACT-[THE ABSTRACT ORDER OF KNOWLEDGE]: (Warriors know that the abstract order of knowledge is the underlying order of nagualism, the edifice that intent places in front of warriors and the signs that it gives them so they won't get lost once they are inside; the ulterior arrangement of the abstract; silent knowledge; knowledge independent of language; the direct knowledge of the abstract.)
SELECTED REFERENCES: **The Teachings of Don Juan - Page [19.9-20.1]** (It had been evident to me...a most difficult task for me.) **The Power of Silence - Page [2.9-3.2]** (He explained that as they examined...abstract cores and the sorcery stories.") **The Power of Silence - Page [27.9-28.4]** (Don Juan reminded me that I had...won't get lost once we are inside.) **The Power of Silence - Page [30.4-30.7]** ("The rule says that the abstract cores...abstract directly, without the intervention of language.")
SEE ALSO: *ABSTRACT-CORES, KNOWLEDGE-SILENT, INTENT-EDIFICE, KNOWLEDGE, KNOWLEDGE-DIRECT*

KNOWLEDGE-ACCEPTING-PROPOSITIONS-*[ACCEPTING THE PROPOSITIONS OF KNOWLEDGE]:* (*Warriors know that actually accepting the propositions of knowledge is not as easy as saying one accepts them; the crux of man's difficulty in returning to the abstract is his refusal to accept that knowledge can exist independent of language or thoughts.*)
SELECTED REFERENCES: The Power of Silence - Page [36.8-37.4] (He said that the nagual Elias...without words or even without thoughts.)
SEE ALSO: *KNOWLEDGE-VS-LANGUAGE, ABSTRACT-RETURNING*

KNOWLEDGE-ACCURACY-*[THE ACCURACY OF KNOWLEDGE]:* (*Warriors know that barring the intervention of their personal feelings, direct knowledge, or silent knowledge is completely accurate and functional.*)
SELECTED REFERENCES: The Power of Silence - Page [14.6-14.7] (Reading omens is commonplace for sorcerers...knowledge is totally accurate and functional.)
SEE ALSO: *KNOWLEDGE, KNOWLEDGE-SILENT, FEELINGS-INTERVENTION, KNOWLEDGE-DIRECT*

KNOWLEDGE-APPOINTMENT-*[AN APPOINTMENT WITH KNOWLEDGE]-(TOP)*

KNOWLEDGE-AVAILABILITY-*[THE AVAILABILITY OF KNOWLEDGE]:* (*Warriors know that knowledge remains unavailable to them until their energy level comes on par with the importance of what they know; energy tends to be cumulative, and if warriors follow an impeccable path, a moment will come one day when their memories will open up.*)
SELECTED REFERENCES: The Art of Dreaming - Page [138.8-139.3] ("Do you mean that I can...what makes you hide your knowledge.)
SEE ALSO: *RECOLLECTION-SORCERER*

KNOWLEDGE-BEATING-ONESELF-*[BEATING KNOWLEDGE OUT OF ONESELF]:* (*Warriors know they must struggle to find knowledge; it can never be just given to them, they must beat it out of themselves.*)
SELECTED REFERENCES: A Separate Reality - Page [263.3.263.7] (Don Juan slowly walked around me...really changed in you," he said.)
SEE ALSO: *KNOWLEDGE, LEARNING-HARDSHIPS, KNOWLEDGE-CLAIMING-POWER*

KNOWLEDGE-CLAIMING-POWER-*[CLAIMING KNOWLEDGE AS POWER]:* (*Warriors know that they must claim knowledge as part of a personal internalization process; warriors know that they must accumulate personal power in order to claim their knowledge; this process applies to both the tonal and the nagual; warriors must claim "informational" knowledge through reason and claim the knowledge of "mysteries" by doing that which they have been shown.*)
SELECTED REFERENCES: The Teachings of Don Juan - Page [21.4-21.7] (He related the use of *Lophophora williamsii*...and the only means of acquiring power.) The Teaching of Don Juan - Page [24.6-24.7] ("Don't get me wrong, don Juan,"...of knowing things that are useless?") The Teachings of Don Juan - Page [53.7-53.8] (He said that while I remained...Thus, knowledge was indeed power.) Tales of Power - Page [6.1-6.7] ("How can I arrive at the sorcerers' explanation...personal power to tip the scales.") Tales of Power - Page [23.7] ("What is the rest, don Juan?"...at a given moment everything changed.) Tales of Power - Page [81.5-81.7] ("Can't don Genaro, being a sorcerer...position to claim knowledge as power.) The Second Ring of Power - Page [126.1-126.3] ("Why is the Nagual trying to...the little sisters to stalk you.) The Second Ring of Power - Page [269.5-269.8] (There was an abyss between our understanding...by doing what he has been shown.) The Second Ring of Power - Page [289.4-289.6] (I don't know. You are very...the two, as you are now.) The Eagle's Gift - Page [268.7-

268.9] (I asked her if she minded...woman can liberate you from that.) **The Power of Silence - Page [216.1-216.3]** (I told him everything made sense...to the place of silent knowledge.)
SEE ALSO: *LEARNING, KNOWLEDGE-INSINUATING, KNOWLEDGE-VS-POWER, REASON, DOER-VS-EXPLAINER, KNOWLEDGE-BEATING-ONESELF, TONAL, NAGUAL*

KNOWLEDGE-COMMAND-[COMMANDING KNOWLEDGE]: *(Warriors know they must learn to command their knowledge before they can really evaluate what's what.)*

SELECTED REFERENCES: **The Power of Silence - Page [86.2-86.3]** ("Don't be presumptuous," don Juan said...knowledge, then decide what is what.")
SEE ALSO: *INTENT-COMMAND, KNOWLEDGE-CLAIMING-POWER*

KNOWLEDGE-CONTRADICTION-[THE CONTRADICTIONS OF THE WARRIORS' QUEST FOR KNOWLEDGE]: SEE: WARRIOR-CONTRADICTION-KNOWLEDGE-[THE CONTRADICTIONS OF THE WARRIORS' QUEST FOR KNOWLEDGE]

KNOWLEDGE-COST-[THE COST OF KNOWLEDGE]: *(Warriors know that the old seers were forced to pay a tremendous price for their knowledge; that knowledge forced them to believe that their choices were infallible, and as a result they chose to live at any cost.)*

SELECTED REFERENCES: **The Fire From Within - Page [230.2-230.4]** (In spite of all the knowledge that...chose to live at any cost.")
SEE ALSO: *SEER-OLD, KNOWLEDGE, DEATH-DEFIERS*

KNOWLEDGE-CRUCIAL-[THE CRUCIAL PIECE OF KNOWLEDGE]: *(Warriors know the fact that the assemblage point exists and that it is capable of moving is the most crucial piece of knowledge available to any human being.)*

SELECTED REFERENCES: **The Power of Silence - Page [219.3-219.6]** (It was stupidity that forced us...entertaining the thought of its existence.")
SEE ALSO: *KNOWLEDGE, ASSEMBLAGE-POINT, ASSEMBLAGE-POINT-MOVING*

KNOWLEDGE-DEFINITION-CHANGING-[THE CHANGING DEFINITION OF KNOWLEDGE]: *(Warriors know that the definition of knowledge changes as they progress on the path of knowledge and their energetic capabilities increase.)*

SELECTED REFERENCES: **The Power of Silence - Page [ix.5-x.1]** (At various times don Juan attempted...the energy to deal with sorcery.")
SEE ALSO: *KNOWLEDGE, KNOWLEDGE-PATH, ENERGY, WARRIOR-IMPECCABILITY*

KNOWLEDGE-DIRECT-[DIRECT KNOWLEDGE]: *(Warriors know that direct knowledge is obtained directly from intent; direct knowledge is silent knowledge; warriors know how to feel the world and experience it directly, this is the basis for silent knowing; warriors know the spirit as an abstract simply because they know it without words or even thoughts.)*

SELECTED REFERENCES: **A Separate Reality - Page [4.5-46]** ("Do you know anything about the world...otherwise the world loses its sense.") **The Power of Silence - Page [xii.9-xiii.3]** (Sorcerers, therefore, divided their instruction into...generation to generation to the present.) **The Power of Silence - Page [xvii.8-xvii.9]** (It took me years to be able...of heightened awareness and direct knowledge.) **The Power of Silence - Page [14.5-14.7]** (He said that the feeling that...direct knowledge is totally accurate and functional.) **The Power of Silence - Page [30.1-30.7]** (I said I understood ulterior to mean...directly, without the intervention of language.) **The Power of Silence - Page [38.5-38.7]** ("We are not," he insisted...and expresses it with his acts.")

SEE ALSO: *KNOWLEDGE-SILENT, INTENT, KNOWLEDGE-VS-LANGUAGE, KNOWLEDGE, INTENT*

KNOWLEDGE-DUST-[THE DUST OF KNOWLEDGE]: *(Warriors know that knowledge comes floating like specks of dust carried on the wings of an ally moth, it rains over the warrior like a shower of gold dust.)*
SELECTED REFERENCES: Tales of Power - Page [28.5-29.1] ("The moths carry a dust on their wings,"...on their wings be knowledge?" "You'll see.")
SEE ALSO: *ALLIES, KNOWLEDGE, MOTH-(TOP)*

KNOWLEDGE-FRIGHTENING-[KNOWLEDGE IS FRIGHTENING]: *(Warriors know that knowledge itself is a frightening affair.)*
SELECTED REFERENCES: The Teachings of Don Juan - Page [54.2-54.3] (He said that fears are natural...without an ally, or without knowledge.) The Teachings of Don Juan - Page [83.9-84.8] ("When a man starts to learn...has defeated his first natural enemy.") The Art of Dreaming - Page [68.4-68.5] ("You like me because you find...and beliefs of your daily world.")
SEE ALSO: *FEAR, KNOWLEDGE, WARRIOR-ENEMIES-FOUR-NATURAL, ETERNITY-VS-HUMANNESS*

KNOWLEDGE-GOING-TO-REQUISITES-[THE FOUR REQUISITES OF GOING TO KNOWLEDGE]: *(Warriors know they must go to knowledge with four requisites in mind, or they will surely live to regret their steps; warriors go to knowledge as they go to war, wide-awake, with fear, with respect, and with absolute assurance.)*
SELECTED REFERENCES: The Teachings of Don Juan - Page [51.1-51.5] (Last night don Juan proceeded to...be no pitiful regrets over that.) A Separate Reality - Page [88.4-88.5] "So now you're afraid of me...trust in yourself, not in me.)
SEE ALSO: *WAR-WARRIOR, KNOWLEDGE, WARRIOR-ALERTNESS, FEAR, WARRIOR-RESPECT, WARRIOR-ASSURANCE*

KNOWLEDGE-HANDING-DOWN-[HANDING DOWN KNOWLEDGE]: *(Warriors know that knowledge which is simply handed down is never there when warriors need it; knowledge must be claimed through struggle by warriors if they are to have it at their command.)*
SELECTED REFERENCES: The Power of Silence - Page [250.6-250.7] ("My benefactor didn't believe in handing down...devise ways to claim that knowledge.")
SEE ALSO: *KNOWLEDGE-CLAIMING-POWER, KNOWLEDGE-INSINUATING, LEARNING-HARDSHIPS, KNOWLEDGE-BEATING-ONESELF*

KNOWLEDGE-VS-IDEALITIES-FIRST-HAND-KNOWLEDGE-[IDEALITIES VS FIRST-HAND KNOWLEDGE]: *(Warriors talk and think a great deal about the strange accomplishments of the sorcerers of antiquity; it is next to impossible for warriors to understand or believe these accomplishments until they have carried them beyond the realm of idealities into the realm of firsthand knowledge.)*
SELECTED REFERENCES: The Art of Dreaming - Page [208.2-208.4] ("We have been discussing the strange...have any practical knowledge of it.")
SEE ALSO: *KNOWLEDGE, SORCERER-ANTIQUITY, TOLTECS,-SEER-OLD, NAGUAL-FACING, WARRIOR-DIALOGUE*

KNOWLEDGE-INSINUATING-[INSINUATING KNOWLEDGE]: *(Warriors know that insinuating knowledge is a technique employed by a teacher or benefactor to spur students to learn; if knowledge is only insinuated, students will often devise ways of claiming that knowledge for themselves.)*
SELECTED REFERENCES: The Power of Silence - Page [250.6-250.7] ("My benefactor didn't believe in handing...to claim that knowledge.")
SEE ALSO: *KNOWLEDGE-CLAIMING-POWER, LEARNING, KNOWLEDGE*

KNOWLEDGE-INTERNAL-[INTERNAL KNOWLEDGE]: (Warriors know
that internal knowledge is another term for silent knowledge or direct
knowledge; knowledge without language.)
SELECTED REFERENCES: The Fire From Within - Page [183.7] ("How do you know
that you...is an internal knowledge," he said.)
SEE ALSO: KNOWLEDGE-SILENT, KNOWLEDGE-DIRECT

KNOWLEDGE-INTRICACIES-[THE INTRICACIES OF KNOWLEDGE]:
(Warriors know that it is very easy to become lost in intricacies and
morbidity on the path of knowledge; these intricacies can muddle warriors'
aims, destroy their purpose and make them weak.)
SELECTED REFERENCES: The Fire From Within - Page [167.5-167.9] (As we
walked, don Juan told...scorn and reject their own tradition.)
SEE ALSO: KNOWLEDGE, ABERRATION-MORBIDITY, WARRIOR-ENEMIES-
FOUR-NATURAL, UNKNOWN-INTRICACIES, OBSESSION

KNOWLEDGE-VS-LANGUAGE-[KNOWLEDGE VS LANGUAGE]:
(Warriors know that knowledge exists independent of language or
information; there is no way to talk about the abstract, the abstract can
only be experienced; the deeper the assemblage point moves, the greater the
feeling that warriors have knowledge and no words to explain it; sometimes
the assemblage points of average people move without a known cause and
without the individual's knowing it; this causes the person to become
tongue-tied for no apparent reason.)
SELECTED REFERENCES: Tales of Power - Page [191.2-191.5] ("I've never put a ban
on talking...are not applicable to the nagual.") The Eagle's Gift - Page [92.9-93.2] ("What are the
conclusions you reached...talk, we know," la Gorda said.) The Eagle's Gift - Page [124.4-124.5] (I
wanted to start a debate...than even the fear of dying.) The Eagle's Gift - Page [144.3-144.8] (We
sustained the feeling of community...or how to organize my knowledge.) The Eagle's Gift -
Page [273.5-273.6] (She said that there is no...knowledge without the intervention of desire.) The
Power of Silence - Page [37.2-37.8] (He used you to say that...Most of the time it seems
indifferent.") The Power of Silence - Page [38.9-39.1] (I was furious with don Juan...perhaps I
could see the light.) The Power of Silence - Page [80.7-81.7] (I knew exactly what he was
talking...become tongue-tied, confused and evasive.") The Power of Silence - Page [84.3-84.9] (I
was staring at each of them...had flooded me just moments ago.) The Power of Silence - Page
[85.5-85.8] (And then I understood not only...One could only make use of it.)
SEE ALSO: KNOWLEDGE-SILENT, TALKING, REASON, TONGUE-TIED,
SORCERER-MUTENESS, KNOWLEDGE-VS-WORDS, WORDS-FLAW

KNOWLEDGE-MAN-[MAN'S KNOWLEDGE]: (Warriors know that when
man became aware of his silent knowledge and wanted to be conscious of
what he knew, he lost sight of what he knew; man's error was to want to
know silent knowledge directly, the way he knows everyday life; the more
man tried to know silent knowledge, the more ephemeral it became; in the
end man gave up silent knowledge for the world of reason.)
SELECTED REFERENCES: The Power of Silence - Page [147.2-147.5] ("Sorcerers
believe that when man became...the more ephemeral intent becomes.")
SEE ALSO: KNOWLEDGE-SILENT, REASON, INTENT, GARDEN-EDEN, POINT-
THIRD-INVERSION, INTENT-EPHEMERAL, MAN-ANCIENT

KNOWLEDGE-MAN-OF-[MAN OF KNOWLEDGE]: SEE: MAN-
KNOWLEDGE-[MAN OF KNOWLEDGE]

KNOWLEDGE-MAN-ORIGINAL-[THE ORIGINAL MEN OF
KNOWLEDGE]: (Warriors know that the original men of knowledge were
the original Toltecs; these individuals lived in a vast geographical area

north and south of the valley of Mexico; they also were employed in specific lines of work including, curing, bewitching, storytelling, dancing, preparing food and being an oracle; some of these individuals eventually learned to "see" and then to teach others how to "see".)

SELECTED REFERENCES: The Fire From Within - Page [4.2-4.8] (Don Juan explained then that his...men of knowledge how to *see.*)

SEE ALSO: MAN-KNOWLEDGE, TOLTECS, TOLTEC-KNOWLEDGE-ORIGIN

KNOWLEDGE-PATH-[THE PATH OF KNOWLEDGE]: (Warriors know that the path to knowledge is the road to total awareness; a forced path, a path on which warriors are always fighting something, avoiding something or preparing for something that is inexplicable and greater than themselves; the warriors' journey with power, a path on which only impeccability matters; a path that leads warriors to their own hidden power.)

SELECTED REFERENCES: A Separate Reality - Page [152.1-152.3] (I would say that the warrior...progresses on the path of knowledge.) A Separate Reality - Page [213.8-214.7] ("You forget too easily," he said...the strength of being a warrior.) Journey to Ixtlan - Page [157.9-158.3] ("It's funny the way you sometimes...even become a man of knowledge.) Journey to Ixtlan - Page [267.6] ("Only as a warrior can one...the wonder of being a man.") Tales of Power - Page [105.5] ("Only as a warrior can one...or bad. Challenges are simply challenges.") Tales of Power - Page [249.4-249.5] ("In the life of a warrior...true measure of a warrior's spirit.") The Fire From Within - Page [18.3-18.4] (I would certainly say that the...counts in the path of knowledge.") The Fire From Within - Page [23.6-23.9] (Don Juan said that his benefactor...fourth step and have become seers.) The Fire From Within - Page [54.2-54.3] ("There are untold dangers in the...*seeing,* but not with your eyes.") The Fire From Within - Page [152.8-153.1] (Don Juan and Genaro laughed until...advance in the path of knowledge.) The Fire From Within - Page [167.6-167.9] (As we walked, don Juan told...scorn and reject their own tradition.) The Power of Silence - Page [xi.4-xi.5] (What a strange paradox! Every warrior...and that he can reach it.")

SEE ALSO: WARRIOR-PATH, WARRIOR-JOURNEY-POWER-PATH-HEART, APPRENTICESHIP-NAGUALISM, WARRIOR, KNOWLEDGE, MAN-KNOWLEDGE, SEER, KNOWLEDGE-PATH-STEPS-FOUR, POWER-HIDDEN, WARRIOR-JOURNEY-RETURN, AWARENESS-TOTAL, KNOWLEDGE-PATH-(ALL)

KNOWLEDGE-PATH-DANGER-[DANGERS ON THE PATH OF KNOWLEDGE]: (Warriors know that there are untold dangers on the path of knowledge for those without sober understanding.)

SELECTED REFERENCES: The Fire From Within - Page [54.2-54.3] ("There are untold dangers in the...*seeing,* but not with your eyes.")

SEE ALSO: KNOWLEDGE-PATH, WARRIOR-SOBRIETY, UNDERSTANDING

KNOWLEDGE-PATH-DIFFICULTY-REAL-[THE REAL DIFFICULTY ON THE PATH OF KNOWLEDGE]: (Warriors know that moving the assemblage point or breaking one's continuity is not the real difficulty on the path of knowledge; the real difficulty is having energy; if the warriors' assemblage point moves, inconceivable things are there for the asking if warriors have the energy to actualize them.)

SELECTED REFERENCES: The Power of Silence - Page [228.7-228.8] ("How do you maximize that movement...things are there for the asking.")

SEE ALSO: KNOWLEDGE-PATH, ENERGY, WARRIOR-IMPECCABILITY

KNOWLEDGE-PATH-STEPS-FOUR-[THE FOUR STEPS ON THE PATH OF KNOWLEDGE]: (Warriors know that the first step on the path of knowledge is the decision to become an apprentice; the second step is to become a warrior; the third step is to become a man of knowledge [a sorcerer]; the fourth step is to become a seer.)

SELECTED REFERENCES: A Separate Reality - Page [152.4-152.6] ("When the convulsions cease the warrior...and that he has acquired will.") A Separate Reality - Page

[153.3-153.6] ("My benefactor was a sorcerer of...from absolutely everything he knew before.") **The Fire From Within - Page** [23.6-23.9] (Don Juan said that his benefactor...fourth step and have become seers.)
      SEE ALSO: *APPRENTICESHIP-NAGUALISM, WARRIOR, MAN-KNOWLEDGE, SEER*

KNOWLEDGE-PITFALLS-*[THE PITFALLS OF KNOWLEDGE]: SEE: SORCERY-FUTILITY-PITFALL-[THE FUTILITY AND PITFALLS OF SORCERY]*

KNOWLEDGE-VS-POWER-*[KNOWLEDGE VS POWER]: (Warriors know that knowledge and power are not directly proportional; men of great power are not necessarily men of knowledge and by the same token, the power that a man of knowledge possesses rests on the kind of knowledge which that individual holds.)*
      SELECTED REFERENCES: **The Teachings of Don Juan - Page** [24.6-24.7] ("Don't get me wrong, don Juan...of knowing things that are useless?") **Tales of Power - Page** [244.8-245.2] (I would say that sorcerers, by using...to that evasive totality of oneself.) **The Art of Dreaming - Page** [68.4-68.5] ("You like me because you find...and beliefs of your daily world.")
      SEE ALSO: *KNOWLEDGE, POWER, KNOWLEDGE-POWER-(ALL)*

KNOWLEDGE-POWER-DEATH-*[KNOWLEDGE, POWER AND DEATH]: (Warriors know that every bit of knowledge that becomes power has death as its central force; whatever is touched by death indeed becomes power; death lends the necessary potency to the warriors' acts; death gives warriors the concentration necessary to transform ordinary time on earth into magical power.)*
      SELECTED REFERENCES: **A Separate Reality - Page** [150.2-150.4] ("By the time knowledge becomes a...time on earth into magical power.)
      SEE ALSO: *KNOWLEDGE, POWER, DEATH, MAGIC, DEATH-ACTIVE-FORCE*

KNOWLEDGE-POWER-PROTECTING-*[PROTECTING ONESELF FROM KNOWLEDGE AND POWER]: (Warriors know that once they embark on the path of knowledge they open themselves to powers which can easily overwhelm them if they do not know what they are doing; warriors learn to access knowledge and power only when they have adequately prepared themselves to deal with these acquisitions and their consequences.)*
      SELECTED REFERENCES: **A Separate Reality - Page** [34.3-34.8] (Don Juan shook his head from...you chucked it. What a pity!")
      SEE ALSO: *KNOWLEDGE, POWER, KNOWLEDGE-PATH, WARRIOR-AVAILABILITY, WARRIOR-PREPAREDNESS*

KNOWLEDGE-POWER-SECRETS-COME-THEMSELVES-*[THE SECRETS OF KNOWLEDGE AND POWER COME BY THEMSELVES]: (Warriors know that knowledge and power come of themselves; warriors cannot say how they have acquired knowledge and power except to say that they kept on acting like warriors and one day everything changed.)*
      SELECTED REFERENCES: **The Teachings of Don Juan - Page** [82.4-82.5] ("A man of knowledge is one who...the secrets of power and knowledge.") **Journey to Ixtlan - Page** [90.2-90.4] (I sensed that something dreadful was...will come to you of itself.") **Journey to Ixtlan - Page** [152.4] ("This is not the time to talk...power to even talk about it.") **Tales of Power - Page** [23.6-23.7] ("All of us go through the same...at a given moment everything changed.")
      SEE ALSO: *KNOWLEDGE, POWER, KNOWLEDGE-VS-LANGUAGE, POWER-DESIGNS, WARRIOR-WAITS, CHANGE, WARRIOR-TRANSFORMATION*

KNOWLEDGE-QUEST-*[THE WARRIORS' QUEST FOR KNOWLEDGE]: SEE: WARRIOR-CONTRADICTION-[THE CONTRADICTIONS OF THE*

WARRIORS' QUEST FOR KNOWLEDGE]

KNOWLEDGE-RALLYING-[RALLYING KNOWLEDGE]: *(Warriors know they are capable of rallying their knowledge to perform complex maneuvers which require "seeing"; warriors are not always consciously aware of what they do when they rally their knowledge in this way; there is no way warriors can order anyone including themselves to rally knowledge; rallying knowledge is a slow affair; the body rallies its knowledge at the right time and under the proper circumstances of impeccability and without the intervention of desire.)*
    SELECTED REFERENCES: The Eagle's Gift - Page [35.3-36.4] ("If you would only rally your...performed complex maneuvers which required *seeing*.) The Eagle's Gift - Page [37.2-37.6] (La Gorda was right. I...recall perceiving two separate scenes simultaneously.) The Eagle's Gift - Page [273.6-273.7] (She said that there is no...knowledge without the intervention of desire.)
    SEE ALSO: KNOWLEDGE, KNOWLEDGE-SILENT, ATTENTION-SECOND-TRAPPING, BODY-PHYSICAL, WARRIOR-IMPECCABILITY

KNOWLEDGE-ROAD-WARRIOR-[THE WARRIORS' ROAD TO KNOWLEDGE]: SEE: WARRIOR-KNOWLEDGE-ROAD-[THE WARRIORS' ROAD TO KNOWLEDGE]

KNOWLEDGE-ROMANCE-[THE WARRIORS' ROMANCE WITH KNOWLEDGE]: SEE: UNDERSTANDING-SHEER-[SHEER UNDERSTANDING]

*KNOWLEDGE-SILENT-[SILENT KNOWLEDGE]: *(Warriors know that silent knowledge is a position of the assemblage point; the warriors' direct knowledge; the knowledge of the body; "seeing"; internal knowledge; knowing something without a shadow of a doubt; one of the bewildering effects of the connecting link with intent, a sense of knowing things directly; the knowledge that exists independent of language; the third point; direct contact with intent; what the older side of man knows; it takes an inordinate amount of energy to voice one's silent knowledge; silent knowledge is something all of us have; silent knowledge has complete mastery, but it cannot think, therefore it cannot speak of what it knows; silent knowledge is intent, the spirit, the abstract; silent knowledge was the normal position of man's assemblage point long ago, and for some indeterminable reason, the assemblage point has now moved away from that position to the position of reason.)*
    SELECTED REFERENCES: A Separate Reality - Page [56.5-56.6] (I was absorbed in a series...of my relationship with my mother.) Tales of Power - Page [123.4-123.5] (He lifted his ayes and asked...my thoughts had been crystal clear.) Tales of Power - Page [153.6-153.9] ("Do you think that my visions...of knowledge the deeper it sank.) The Second Ring of Power - Page [168.1-168.2] ("How did you do it, Gorda...how I did it, I can't.) The Fire From Within - Page [3.8-4.2] (Isn't all this a conjecture on...we are so closely bound together.) The Power of Silence - Page [xi.6-xi.9] ("Exactly. I'm trying to convince you...knowledge, depends on our own temperament.") The Power of Silence - Page [xii.9-xiii.9] (Don Juan stressed that this cleaning procedure...process of understanding as very difficult.) The Power of Silence - Page [xiv.1-xiv.2] ("You will need a lifetime to remember...of the unfathomable mysteries of awareness.") The Power of Silence - Page [14.3-14.7] (Then he answered my question about...knowledge is totally accurate and functional.) The Power of Silence - Page [30.1-30.7] (I said I understood ulterior to mean...directly, without the intervention of language.) The Power of Silence - Page [36.6-36.9] ("The nagual Elias explained that my...exist without words to explain it.) The Power of Silence - Page [38.5-38.7] ("For a sorcerer, the spirit is...and expresses it with his acts.") The

Power of Silence - Page [38.9-39.1] (I was furious with don Juan...perhaps I could see the light.) The Power of Silence - Page [41.4-41.5] ("I can say that this is...you and make you feel secure.") The Power of Silence - Page [47.1-48.1] (Don Juan then said that he...to disguise my complacency as independence.) The Power of Silence - Page [80.7-81.7] (I knew exactly what he was talking...become tongue-tied, confused and evasive.") The Power of Silence - Page [84.3-84.9] (I was staring at each of them...had flooded me just moments ago.) The Power of Silence - Page [103.3-103.5] (Don Juan had stated his belief...the beginning, a return to paradise.) The Power of Silence - Page [104.1-104.3] (Don Juan explained that at one...needed to manage all that power.) The Power of Silence - Page [104.9-105.2] (He asserted that all modern-day...of our being aware of *intent.*) The Power of Silence - Page [126.6-126.7] ("Of course!" he exclaimed. You know...to explain it, even to yourself.) The Power of Silence - Page [144.6-145.1] (He then said something which I...to make the assemblage point move.) The Power of Silence - Page [146.2] (The old, dark, heavy part of...to stop fretting, and to enjoy.) The Power of Silence - Page [146.5-147.5] (He said that when the assemblage...the more ephemeral *intent* becomes.") The Power of Silence - Page [148.8-148.9] (When I had calmed down, I...to articulate what I myself knew.) The Power of Silence - Page [149.5-150.1] (Then he talked about ancient man...of peace, of satisfaction, of attainment.) The Power of Silence - Page [198.5-199.5] (Don Juan, displaying great patience, discussed...not question my capacity to understand.) The Power of Silence - Page [201.5-201.9] ("A better but less rational choice...choices are dictated by silent knowledge.) The Power of Silence - Page [213.5-213.7] (I asked don Juan to explain...fluctuate between reason and silent knowledge.) The Power of Silence - Page [237.5-237.6] (The nagual Elias maintained that while...to enter directly into silent knowledge.) The Power of Silence - Page [244.7-248.1] ("I am just considering how our...therefore the possibility of buttressing themselves.) The Power of Silence - Page [265.6-265.7] (Moving the assemblage point is everything...reach the place of silent knowledge.") The Art of Dreaming - Page [74.6-74.7] (I was too numb to follow...finding its way back to me.)

SEE ALSO: *SEEING, POINT-THIRD, WARRIOR-INTENT-LINK, KNOWLEDGE-VS-LANGUAGE, BODY-PHYSICAL, KNOWLEDGE-DIRECT, KNOWLEDGE-INTERNAL, POINT-THIRD-INVERSION, INTENT-KNOWING, KNOWLEDGE-SILENT-(ALL)*

KNOWLEDGE-SILENT-AGE-[THE AGE OF SILENT KNOWLEDGE]:
(Warriors know that man has spent the greater part of his complete history in the position of silent knowledge, hence, his greater longing for it; the age of man before the inversion of the third point.)

SELECTED REFERENCES: The Power of Silence - Page [239.6-240.6] (The nagual said there had been...from the position of silent knowledge.)

SEE ALSO: *REASON, POINT-FIRST, POINT-THIRD, POINT-THIRD-INVERSION, KNOWLEDGE-SILENT-AGE*

KNOWLEDGE-SILENT-BARRIERS-[THE PERSONAL BARRIERS TO SILENT KNOWLEDGE]: (Warriors know that all human beings are barred from silent knowledge by natural barriers specific to each of us as individuals.)

SELECTED REFERENCES: The Power of Silence - Page [47.9-48.1] (He remarked that each of us was...to disguise my complacency as independence.)

SEE ALSO: *KNOWLEDGE-SILENT*

KNOWLEDGE-SILENT-LOSS-[THE LOSS OF SILENT KNOWLEDGE]: SEE: GARDEN-EDEN-[THE GARDEN OF EDEN]

KNOWLEDGE-SILENT-MASTERY-COMPLETE-[THE COMPLETE MASTERY OF SILENT KNOWLEDGE]: (Warriors know that silent knowledge has complete mastery, complete knowledge of everything; but silent knowledge cannot think, and therefore it cannot speak of what it knows.)

SELECTED REFERENCES: The Power of Silence - Page [147.1-147.2] ("Silent knowledge is something that all of...cannot speak of what it knows.)

SEE ALSO: *KNOWLEDGE-SILENT*

KNOWLEDGE-SILENT-LAKE-*[THE LAKE OF SILENT KNOWLEDGE]:*
(Warriors know that every human being carries a gigantic dark lake of silent knowledge, a lake which is accessible to the individual under the appropriate conditions.)
SELECTED REFERENCES: The Power of Silence - Page [144.8-145.1] (I mentioned to don Juan that I...to make that assemblage point move.)
SEE ALSO: *KNOWLEDGE-SILENT, WARRIOR-INTUITION, POWER-HIDDEN*

KNOWLEDGE-SILENT-REASON-*[REASON VS SILENT KNOWLEDGE]:*
SEE: CHOICES-MATCHING-REASON-[MATCHING THE CHOICES OF REASON]

KNOWLEDGE-SILENT-REASON-FLUCTUATING-*[FLUCTUATING BETWEEN REASON AND SILENT KNOWLEDGE]:* *(Warriors know that when they can manipulate the assemblage point at will, they can fluctuate between reason and silent knowledge at will as well.)*
SELECTED REFERENCES: The Power of Silence - Page [213.5-213.7] (I asked don Juan to explain the...fluctuate between reason and silent knowledge.) The Power of Silence - Page [216.1-216.3] (I told him everything made sense...to the place of silent knowledge.)
SEE ALSO: *WARRIOR-DEATH-COMMAND, KNOWLEDGE-SILENT, REASON*

KNOWLEDGE-SILENT-THINKING-*[THINKING AND SILENT KNOWLEDGE]:* *(Warriors know that silent knowledge has complete mastery, complete knowledge of everything; but silent knowledge cannot think, and therefore it cannot speak of what it knows.)*
SELECTED REFERENCES: The Power of Silence - Page [147.1-147.2] ("Silent knowledge is something that all of...cannot speak of what it knows.)
SEE ALSO: *KNOWLEDGE-SILENT, REASON, THINKING-(ALL)*

KNOWLEDGE-STEPS-*[THE FOUR STEPS TO KNOWLEDGE]: SEE: KNOWLEDGE-PATH-[THE FOUR STEPS ON THE PATH OF KNOWLEDGE]*

KNOWLEDGE-TALKING-*[TALKING ABOUT KNOWLEDGE]: (Warriors know that there is no point in trying to talk about knowledge because true knowledge, silent knowledge, is independent of language and the faculties of reason.)*
SELECTED REFERENCES: The Teaching of Don Juan - Page [53.8-54.1] (Don Juan said then that every...would only bring harm to me.)
SEE ALSO: *TALKING, KNOWLEDGE-VS-LANGUAGE, KNOWLEDGE-SILENT*

KNOWLEDGE-USELESS-*[USELESS KNOWLEDGE]: (Warriors know that certain kinds of knowledge are useless in the quest for total freedom; warriors' power rests on the kind of knowledge they hold and the level of impeccability they are able to maintain in the application of that knowledge.)*
SELECTED REFERENCES: The Teachings of Don Juan - Page [24.6-24.7] ("Don't get me wrong, don Juan...of knowing things that are useless?") The Art of Dreaming - Page [139.5-139.7] ("I am not flattering or humoring...I shudder at the mere thought.")
SEE ALSO: *KNOWLEDGE, POWER, WARRIOR-IMPECCABILITY, FREEDOM-TOTAL, KNOWLEDGE-CLAIMING-POWER*

KNOWLEDGE-VS-WORDS-*[KNOWLEDGE VS WORDS]: (Warriors know that knowledge cannot be turned into words; knowledge exists for everyone, to be felt, to be used but not to be explained.)*

SELECTED REFERENCES: **The Power of Silence - Page [85.6-85.8]** (And, above all, I understood that...One could only make use of it.)
SEE ALSO: *KNOWLEDGE-SILENT, KNOWLEDGE-VS-LANGUAGE, EXPLANATION, WORDS-FLAW, TALKING*

KNOWLEDGE-WORLD-[THE WORLD OF KNOWLEDGE]: (Warriors know that the knowledge of the world is our description of the world; our habit of having the world conform to our thoughts.)

SELECTED REFERENCES: **Tales of Power - Page [22.1-22.8]** ("How was I operating my knowledge...forced to understand it as talking.")
SEE ALSO: *DESCRIPTION-WORLD, REALITY-INTERPRETATION, ATTENTION-FIRST, ATTENTION-SECOND*

KNOWLEDGE-WORLD-OPERATING-[THE OPERATING KNOWLEDGE OF THE WORLD]: (The warriors' knowledge of the world is the first attention description of the world, the world of reason and solid objects.)

SELECTED REFERENCES: **Tales of Power - Page [21.8-22.5]** ("I should say that tonight, when...really took place at those times.")
SEE ALSO: *KNOWLEDGE, ATTENTION-FIRST, DESCRIPTION-WORLD, REALITY-INTERPRETATION, WORLD-SOLID-OBJECTS, KNOWLEDGE-WORLD*

KNOWN-[KNOWN]: (Warriors know that the known is the minute fraction of the Eagle's emanations within the reach of normal human awareness; the first attention; right side awareness; the attention of the tonal.)

SELECTED REFERENCES: **The Fire From Within - Page [33.5-33.6]** (They set up boundaries and defined...becomes the known at a given time.) **The Fire From Within - Page [34.9-35.1]** (By steadily practicing *seeing,* the new seers...given moment and enter into the unknown.) **The Fire From Within - Page [43.3-43.5]** (Only a small portion of those...incalculable rest is the unknowable.) **The Fire From Within - Page [76.1-76.3]** ("I was explaining about the first attention,'...doesn't exist for the first attention.) **The Fire From Within - Page [109.5-109.9]** (Don Juan explained that in order...present inside the cocoon of man.) **The Fire From Within - Page [206.8 207.3]** (Don Juan restated over and over...is perceived and becomes the known.) **The Fire From Within - Page [299.3-299.5]** (He explained that the new seers discovered...aligning all the emanations inside the cocoon at once.)
SEE ALSO: *ATTENTION-FIRST, AWARENESS-RIGHT, TONAL, ATTENTION-TONAL, AWARENESS-NORMAL*

KNOWN-LIMIT-[THE LIMIT OF THE KNOWN]: SEE: ASSEMBLAGE-POINT-THRESHOLD-[THE THRESHOLD OF THE ASSEMBLAGE POINT]

KNOWN-OBSESSIVE-MANIPULATION-[THE OBSESSIVE MANIPULATION OF THE KNOWN]: (Warriors know that it is the obsessive manipulation of the known which is responsible for turning men and women into petty tyrants.)

SELECTED REFERENCES: **The Fire From Within - Page [18.7-18.8]** ("Because *will* belongs to another sphere,...obsessive manipulation of the known")
SEE ALSO: *PETTY-TYRANT, OBSESSION, ABERRATION-MORBIDITY*

KNOWN-UNKNOWN-BODY-LUMINOUS-EGG-[THE BODY AND THE KNOWN, THE LUMINOUS EGG AND THE UNKNOWN]: (Warriors know that they tackle the known with the body as an object and that they tackle the unknown with the body as a luminous egg.)

SELECTED REFERENCES: **The Fire From Within - Page [64.8-65.2]** (Don Juan replied that human alternatives are...have, therefore, nearly an inexhaustible scope.)
SEE ALSO: *HUMAN-ALTERNATIVES-POSSIBILITIES-POTENTIAL, KNOWN, BODY-PHYSICAL, UNKNOWN, LUMINOUS-BODY, ENERGY-BODY, LUMINOUS-EGG*

L

LA-CATALINA-[LA CATALINA]-(TOP): SEE: CATALINA-[LA CATALINA]-(TOP)

LA-GORDA-[LA GORDA]-(TOP): SEE: GORDA-[LA GORDA]-(TOP)

LABYRINTH-PENUMBRA-[THE LABYRINTH OF PENUMBRA]:
(Warriors know that the labyrinth of penumbra is the sorcerers' term for the realm of the inorganic beings; a blob of cavernous pores floating in some dark space; the inorganic beings are portrayed by sorcerers as hollow canes bound together like the cells of our bodies; this immense bundle is called the labyrinth of penumbra.)
    SELECTED REFERENCES: The Art of Dreaming - Page [100.5-100.8] ("But what about inorganic beings in...Do you think you are unique?")
    SEE ALSO: INORGANIC-BEINGS, INORGANIC-BEINGS-REALM

LAND-PARALLEL-LINES-[THE LAND BETWEEN THE PARALLEL LINES]: SEE: PARALLEL-LINES-LAND-[THE LAND BETWEEN THE PARALLEL LINES]

LAND-SULFUR-DUNES-[THE LAND OF THE SULFUR DUNES]: SEE: PARALLEL-LINES-LAND-[THE LAND BETWEEN THE PARALLEL LINES]

LANGUAGE-VS-KNOWLEDGE-[LANGUAGE VS KNOWLEDGE]: SEE: KNOWLEDGE-LANGUAGE-[KNOWLEDGE VS LANGUAGE]

*LAST-BATTLE-EARTH-WARRIOR-[THE WARRIORS' LAST BATTLE ON EARTH]: SEE: WARRIOR-LAST-STAND-[THE WARRIORS' LAST STAND]

LAST-SEDUCTION-NAGUAL-JULIAN-[THE LAST SEDUCTION OF THE NAGUAL JULIAN]-(TOP): SEE: JULIAN-NAGUAL-LAST-SEDUCTION-[THE LAST SEDUCTION OF THE NAGUAL JULIAN]-(TOP)

LAST-STAND-WARRIOR-[THE WARRIORS' LAST STAND]: SEE: WARRIOR-LAST-STAND-[THE WARRIORS' LAST STAND]

LAUGHING-AT-ONESELF-[LAUGHING AT ONESELF]: SEE: WARRIOR-HUMOR-[THE WARRIORS' HUMOR], STALKING-RESULTS-THREE-[THE THREE RESULTS OF STALKING], WARRIOR-LIGHTNESS-[THE WARRIORS' LIGHTNESS]

LAUGHTER-[LAUGHTER]: (Warriors know that the funny edge of the world is part of the realm of the tonal; warriors must look with their eyes in order to laugh, because when they "see" everything is equal and nothing is funny.)
    SELECTED REFERENCES: A Separate Reality - Page [83.2-84.4] ("For instance, we need to look...the former was indeed more important.) A Separate Reality - Page [85.4] (A man of knowledge chooses...and then he sees and knows.) A Separate Reality - Page [89.7-89.8] ("There is one more thing...Their laughter is not roaring.") The Fire From Within - Page [120.6-120.8] ("What determines whether it is one...with their friends or with strangers.") The Art of Dreaming - Page [21.8-22.2] (For instance, I expressed my feelings...dreams actually be turned into dreaming.")

SEE ALSO: *WARRIOR-HUMOR, WARRIOR-JOY, WARRIOR-LIGHTNESS, STALKING-RESULTS-THREE*

LAWYER-BITTER-[A BITTER LAWYER]-(TOP)

LAXNESS-HUMAN-CONDITION-[THE LAXNESS OF THE HUMAN CONDITION]: SEE: HUMAN-CONDITION-[THE HUMAN CONDITION], EAGLE-METAPHOR-LAXNESS-[THE LAXNESS OF THE METAPHOR OF THE EAGLE]

LAZINESS-[LAZINESS]: SEE: INDOLENCE-[INDOLENCE, LAZINESS AND SELF-IMPORTANCE]

LEAF-FELL-THREE-TIMES-[THE LEAF THAT FELL THREE TIMES FROM THE SAME TREE]-(TOP)

LEAF-GAZING-[LEAF GAZING]: SEE: GAZING-[GAZING]

LEAF-RAZOR-[THE LEAF THAT CUT LIKE A RAZOR]-(TOP)

LEARN-ONE-WAY-[THERE IS ONLY ONE WAY TO LEARN]: SEE: BUSINESS-DOWN-TO-[GETTING DOWN TO BUSINESS]

LEARNING-[LEARNING]: (Warriors know that learning is their lot in life, to learn and to be hurled into inconceivable new worlds; the warriors' sincere desire to learn.)
 SELECTED REFERENCES: **The Teachings of Don Juan** - Page [28.1-28.7] ("Would you teach me about peyote...few Indians have such a desire.") **The Teachings of Don Juan** - Page [48.2-49.8] (I told don Juan how I felt...in the two sessions with him.) **The Teachings of Don Juan** - Page [50.3-50.5] ("All this is very easy to understand...there was nothing else I could do but learn.) **The Teachings of Don Juan** - Page [53.8-53.9] (Don Juan said then that every time...his learning are determined by his own nature.) **The Teachings of Don Juan** - Page [69.8] (And the man attempting to learn...by leading a hard, quiet life.) **The Teachings of Don Juan** - Page [83.9-84.7] ("When a man starts to learn...Learning is no longer a terrifying task.) **The Teachings of Don Juan** - Page [86.9-87.1] ("No, that is not true...have really abandoned himself to it.") **The Teachings of Don Juan** - Page [110.7-110.8] (I explained to him that what...he was capable of controlling them.) **The Teachings of Don Juan** - Page [161.1-161.2] (I argued that one needs ambition...ambition, because you are not bidding to know.) **A Separate Reality** - Page [85.2] ("I told you once that our lot...for good or bad," he said.) **A Separate Reality** - Page [153.9] ("We are men and our lot...into inconceivable new worlds.") **A Separate Reality** - Page [213.8] ("You forget too easily," he said...to learn we must be spurred.) **Journey to Ixtlan** - Page [55.6-55.6] ("Let's put it this way...that anyone can tell you. True?") **Journey to Ixtlan** - Page [180.1-180.2] (The reason you keep on coming...come back to me to learn more.) **Journey to Ixtlan** - Page [213.6-213.7] ("Very drastic things have to happen...all you have learned," he said.) **The Fire From Within** - Page [138.8-139.2] ("The skimmings of men," don Juan...the old seers paid for theirs.") **The Power of Silence** - Page [x.9-xi.2] ("Think of it this way," he...perceive something which ordinary perception cannot.) **The Power of Silence** - Page [xii.9-xiii.9] (Don Juan stressed that this cleaning procedure...process of understanding as very difficult.)
 SEE ALSO: *KNOWLEDGE, LEARNING-HARDSHIPS, BODY-PHYSICAL-NEEDS-LEARN, LEARNING-(ALL)*

LEARNING-ASSEMBLING-WARRIOR-[WARRIORS ASSEMBLE WHAT THEY'VE LEARNED]: SEE: WARRIOR-LEARNING-ASSEMBLING-[WARRIORS ASSEMBLE WHAT THEY'VE LEARNED]

LEARNING-FRIGHTENING-[LEARNING IS FRIGHTENING]: SEE: KNOWLEDGE-FRIGHTENING-[KNOWLEDGE IS FRIGHTENING]

LEARNING-HARDSHIPS-[THE HARDSHIPS OF LEARNING]: (Warriors know that learning is the most difficult task a person can undertake;

warriors must undergo a process through which they no longer perceive learning as a terrifying task.)

SELECTED REFERENCES: **The Teachings of Don Juan - Page [53.5]** (He looked at me for a long time...difficult task a man could undertake.) **The Teachings of Don Juan - Page [83.9-84.7]** ("When a man starts to learn...Learning is no longer a terrifying task.) **A Separate Reality - Page [27.4-27.5]** ("I feel that I'm betraying you...it perhaps even harder than you.") **A Separate Reality - Page [28.2-29.5]** (Don Juan patted me gently on...have to be around here for that.") **Journey to Ixtlan - Page [177.3-177.4]** ("There is only one way to learn...is very difficult and very long.) **Journey to Ixtlan - Page [213.7]** ("Very drastic things have to happen...all you have learned," he said.) **Tales of Power - Page [144.9]** ("What's going to happen to me,...You are now at the edge of the day.")

SEE ALSO: *LEARNING, KNOWLEDGE-PATH, KNOWLEDGE-FRIGHTENING, LEARNING-LIMITS*

<u>LEARNING-LIMITS</u>-*[THE LIMITS OF LEARNING]: (Warriors know that the limits of our ability to learn are determined by our own nature; warriors must claim knowledge for themselves, based on their own impeccability.)*

SELECTED REFERENCES: **The Teachings of Don Juan - Page [53.8-53.9]** (Don Juan said then that every...are determined by his own nature.)

SEE ALSO: *LEARNING, WARRIOR-LIMITS, KNOWLEDGE-PATH, WARRIOR-IMPECCABILITY, KNOWLEDGE-CLAIMING-POWER*

<u>LEARNING-PRAGMATIC</u>-*[PRAGMATIC LEARNING]: (The warriors' form of pragmatic learning; a type of learning that takes place independent of language or reason; the acquisition of silent knowledge.)*

SELECTED REFERENCES: **The Teachings of Don Juan - Page [21.6-21.8]** (Don Juan believed that states of...with the states of nonordinary reality.)

SEE ALSO: *KNOWLEDGE-SILENT, LEARNING, KNOWLEDGE, KNOWLEDGE-VS-LANGUAGE*

<u>LEARNING-SPITE-WARRIOR</u>-*[WARRIORS LEARN IN SPITE OF THEMSELVES]: SEE: WARRIOR-LEARN-IN-SPITE-[WARRIORS LEARN IN SPITE OF THEMSELVES]*

<u>LEARNING-TASK-WARRIOR</u>-*[THE WARRIORS' TASK OF LEARNING]: SEE: WARRIOR-LEARNING-TASK-[THE WARRIORS' TASK OF LEARNING]*

<u>LEDGE-WARRIOR</u>-*[THE WARRIORS' LEDGE]: SEE: WARRIOR-LEDGE-[THE WARRIORS' LEDGE]*

<u>LEFT-AWARENESS</u>-*[LEFT SIDE AWARENESS]: SEE: AWARENESS-LEFT-[LEFT SIDE AWARENESS]*

<u>LEFT-LEFT-AWARENESS</u>-*[THE LEFT LEFT SIDE AWARENESS]: SEE: AWARENESS-LEFT-LEFT-[THE LEFT LEFT SIDE AWARENESS]*

<u>LEFT-SIDE-REMEMBERING</u>-*[REMEMBERING THE LEFT SIDE]-(TOP): SEE: REMEMBERING-LEFT-SIDE [REMEMBERING THE LEFT SIDE]-(TOP)*

<u>LENIENCY-WARRIOR</u>-*[LENIENCY IS NOT PERMISSIBLE FOR WARRIORS]: SEE: WARRIOR-LENIENCY-[LENIENCY IS NOT PERMISSIBLE FOR WARRIORS]*

LESSON-WORLDS-TWO-[THE LESSON OF THE TWO WORLDS]:
(Warriors know that there is only one world for them, and that is the world of men; warriors find their way through the world of men by following one path, the warriors' path with heart.)
    SELECTED REFERENCES: The Teachings of Don Juan - Page [152.7-153.3] (Don Juan listened to my explanations..."I believe that was the lesson.")
    SEE ALSO: *PATH-HEART, WARRIOR-PATH, ,WORLD-MEN*

LETTING-GO-[LETTING GO]: (Warriors know they must learn to act with abandon, to let go of their first attention agendas and inventory; the warriors' ability to let go of the desire to cling to things, people, self-reflection and other specifics of the world of solid objects.)
    SELECTED REFERENCES: A Separate Reality - Page [156.4-157.1] (My first impulse was to fret again,..."Good, good work," he said reassuringly.) Journey to Ixtlan - Page [120.2-120.3] ("A warrior, on the other hand,...in the best of all possible fashions.") Tales of Power - Page [42.4-42.5] ("Let go!" he commanded me dryly...Genaro, is one of those deeds.") Tales of Power - Page [156.3-156.4] (The whole trouble is that the...easier it is to shrink it.) Tales of Power - Page [250.7-250.8] (*"Dreaming* is a practical aid devised...to let go without losing your marbles.) The Second Ring of Power - Page [123.7-123.8] (All I felt was a sense of loss...you must forget him," he said.) The Eagle's Gift - Page [14.1] (The Nagual said that if the man...have been any fear in him.") The Eagle's Gift - Page [35.6-36.1] ("What do you think I should...so hard that you paralyze yourself.") The Eagle's Gift - Page [59.7-59.9] (Don Juan used to stress the need...everything we knew. She was inflexible.) The Eagle's Gift - Page [60.5-60.9] ("The Nagual told me that losing...go and talk to the Genaros?") The Power of Silence - Page [167.8-168.2] (I've told you over and over...to my experiences in is world.) The Power of Silence - Page [226.8-227.1] ("I understand exactly what you are...structures. Don't you do the same.")
    SEE ALSO: *ABANDON, WARRIOR-DECISIONS, ACT-LEARNING, DROPPING-THINGS-LIVES, ATTENTION-FIRST, INVENTORY, SELF-REFLECTION, WORLD-SOLID-OBJECTS, INTENT, APPRENTICE-INDIVIDUALITY-RELINQUISH*

LIDIA-EYES-CURE-[CURING LIDIA'S EYES]-(TOP)

LIDIA-RAPE-[THE ATTEMPTED RAPE OF LIDIA]-(TOP)

LIENS-MORTGAGES-[LIENS AND MORTGAGES]: (Warriors know that their liens and mortgages are the edifices of morbidity, obsession and self-importance; the things which weigh heavily on warriors and impede their progress on the path of knowledge.)
    SELECTED REFERENCES: The Power of Silence - Page [263.7-264.2] (After a moment's pause, don Juan...liens and mortgages on our awareness.")
    SEE ALSO: *ABERRATION-MORBIDITY, OBSESSION, SELF-IMPORTANCE, KNOWLEDGE-PATH, LETTING-GO, DROPPING-THINGS-LIVES*

LIES-[LIES]: (Warriors know there is no need for a true warrior to lie; lies are only for those who have never witnessed the utterly impersonal unknown that's waiting for them; in the world of the inorganic beings, lies do not exist; there, only intent exists and a lie has no intent behind it.)
    SELECTED REFERENCES: The Art of Dreaming - Page [63.2-63.3] ("How do you know he was telling...what's out there waiting for them.") The Art of Dreaming - Page [114.8-115.2] (I could not help thinking that...but that intention is not intent.)
    SEE ALSO: *TRUTH, ETERNITY, UNKNOWABLE, INORGANIC-BEINGS-REALM*

LIFE-[LIFE]: (Warriors know that life is the arena; death challenges the warrior through the process of life.)
    SELECTED REFERENCES: The Power of Silence - Page [122.2-112.3] ("I personally would say, don Juan,...at any time: oneself and death.")
    SEE ALSO: *DEATH*

LIFE-ARENA-[LIFE IS THE ARENA]: (Warriors know that death is the active force and life is the arena; life is the means by which death challenges

us; in that arena there are only two contenders at any given time: oneself and death.)
    SELECTED REFERENCES: **The Power of Silence - Page [111.9-112.3]** ("Would you say, don Juan, that...at any time: oneself and death.")
    SEE ALSO: *LIFE*

LIFE-BAD-HABITS-*[THE THREE BAD HABITS OF LIFE]: SEE: HABITS-BAD-THREE-[THE THREE BAD HABITS OF LIFE]*

LIFE-VS-BEING-ALIVE-*[LIFE VS BEING ALIVE]: (Warriors are thoroughly involved with the themes of life and being alive; this makes warriors acutely aware of the difference between life as a consequence of biological forces and the act of being alive as a matter of cognition.)*
    SELECTED REFERENCES: **The Art of Dreaming - Page [33.7-33.8]** (He said that his interest, as...alive, as a matter of cognition.)
    SEE ALSO: *PROACTIVITY, LIFE*

LIFE-CHOOSING-*[CHOOSING LIFE]: (Warriors know they must choose life, not because it matters, but because to live is the bent of their nature; it is the warriors' will that makes them go on living in spite of the things they may "see".)*
    SELECTED REFERENCES: **A Separate Reality - Page [84.5-84.8]** (He stubbornly maintained that his preference...living in spite of anything I may *see.)*
    SEE ALSO: *WARRIOR-PREDILECTION, EXISTENCE-REASON, WARRIOR-CHOICE, WARRIOR-WILL , DEATH-CHOOSING, WARRIOR-DEATH-SEEK-NOT*

LIFE-DEATH-*[LIFE AND DEATH]: SEE: STAKES-ULTIMATE-[STAKES BEYOND LIFE AND DEATH]*

LIFE-DEATH-VISION-*[LIFE AND DEATH ARE ONE LONG VISION]: (Warriors know the true character of reality and understand that life and death on this earth are nothing more than a kind of long vision, a vision no different than the experiences one has in the second attention.)*
    SELECTED REFERENCES: **The Second Ring of Power - Page [220.1-221.4]** ("You have already died," Nestor said...my earth. It's my indulging perhaps.")
    SEE ALSO: *LIFE, DEATH, DREAMING-ART, VISIONS-MAN*

LIFE-ETERNAL-*[ETERNAL LIFE]: (The rule states that warriors may keep the awareness which is normally relinquished at the moment of dying; but preserving this awareness does not constitute eternal life as this concept is commonly understood; warriors cannot explain or even conceive of what is meant by being able to keep that awareness.)*
    SELECTED REFERENCES: **The Eagle's Gift - Page [178.8-178.9]** (Don Juan explained that the rule...could not even conceive of it.)
    SEE ALSO: *IMMORTALITY, EAGLE-GIFT, ATTENTION-THIRD, FIRE-WITHIN, WARRIOR-DEATH-COMMAND*

LIFE-FORCE-*[THE LIFE FORCE]: (The life force is the force which binds the warriors' cluster of feelings together and prevents them from disintegrating back to the nagual from which they came; the force which pops a luminous being into the tonal; a force which is intimately related to the circular force of the tumbler; the life-giving force of creation.)*
    SELECTED REFERENCES: **Tales of Power - Page [97.5-97.6]** ("Learning the warrior's way...force of your life will take you.") **Tales of Power - Page [132.1-132.4]** ("I was concerned with those jolts...without the binding force of life.") **Tales of Power - Page [268.8-269.4]** (I again had the sensation of being...one another was my life force.) **Tales of Power - Page [272.6-273.2]** (This is the sorcerers' explanation. The...as if they had never been a unit.") **Tales of Power -**

Page [278.4-278.5] ("Now you should sit on Genaro's...that binds that cluster of feelings.") **The Second Ring of Power** - Page [154.8-154.9] ("The Nagual told me that as long as one...we see them as heavy, ugly creatures.") **The Second Ring of Power** - Page [156.1-156.2] (He described the mold as being...itself into the shape of man.) **The Eagle's Gift** - Page [189.5-189.6] (I had to begin by approaching...leaves us flowing toward the north.) **The Eagle's Gift** - Page [244.6-244.8] (La Gorda added that they did...of the Nagual Juan Matus' party.) **The Fire From Within** - Page [67.7-67.9] (He added that at the moment...Eagle's beak to be devoured.") **The Power of Silence** - Page [58.1-58.2] (For all the sorcerers of don Juan's...awareness and life force to persist.) **The Power of Silence** - Page [92.9-93.1] ("When I struck your back...removing the plug with another blow.)

SEE ALSO: *FORCE-CIRCULAR, FEELINGS, LIFE, NAGUAL, TONAL*

LIFE-GIVER-[THE GIVERS OF LIFE]: SEE: GIVER-LIFE-[THE GIVERS OF LIFE]

LIFE-HABITS-BAD-[THE THREE BAD HABITS OF LIFE]: SEE: HABITS-BAD-THREE-[THE THREE BAD HABITS OF LIFE]

LIFE-HAVING-[HAVING LIFE]: (Warriors know that having life means having consciousness.)

SELECTED REFERENCES: **The Art of Dreaming** - Page [45.8-45.9] ("For sorcerers, having life means having...as the precondition of being alive.")

SEE ALSO: *EXISTENCE-REASON, AWARENESS*

LIFE-INTERACTIONS-DAILY-[THE INTERACTIONS OF DAILY LIFE]: (Warriors know about the overwhelming amount of energy normally consumed by the actions and interactions of daily life; it becomes the warriors' unbending intent to conserve that precious energy through an impeccable way of being.)

SELECTED REFERENCES: **The Eagle's Gift** - Page [165.4-165.5] (Another feature of those states...inherent need for economy and speed.) **The Power of Silence** - Page [103.2-103.3] (Don Juan had asserted that our great...of being linked to everything else.)

SEE ALSO: *WARRIOR-IMPECCABILITY, LIFE-MODERN, LIFE-TURNING-AWAY, LULL-DAILY-AFFAIRS*

LIFE-LUST-WARRIOR-[THE WARRIORS' LUST FOR LIFE]: SEE: WARRIOR-LIFE-LUST-[THE WARRIORS' LUST FOR LIFE]

LIFE-MARK-[THE MARK OF LIFE]: SEE: AWARENESS-GLOW-[THE GLOW OF AWARENESS]

LIFE-MEANING-[THE MEANING OF LIFE]: SEE: EXISTENCE-REASON-[THE REASON FOR EXISTENCE]

LIFE-MODERN-TURNING-AWAY-[TURNING AWAY FROM MODERN LIFE]: (Warriors know that modern man has exchanged the realm of the mysterious for the realm of the functional; warriors live in the midst of the modern world but turn their backs on the focus of the modern man; warriors embrace the world of the foreboding and the exulting in favor of the world of boredom.)

SELECTED REFERENCES: **The Fire From Within** - Page [148.1-148.3] (He explained that what makes the warrior's...has welcomed the world of boredom.)

SEE ALSO: *WARRIOR-PATH, BOREDOM, WORLD-IN-NOT-OF, WORLD-MYSTERIOUS, BLACK-MAGICIANS, WARRIOR-WAY*

LIFE-REGURGITATING-[REGURGITATING OUR LIVES]: SEE: RECAPITULATION-[RECAPITULATION]

LIFE-STRONG-[A STRONG LIFE]: *(Warriors know that in order to withstand their encounters with power they must live strong lives; without the strength and sobriety fostered by the warriors' way, warriors' lives would be smashed to bits.)*
    SELECTED REFERENCES: The Teachings of Don Juan - Page [141.8-142.1] (And to handle that power, he...life would be shattered to bits.) The Teachings of Don Juan - Page [173.6-173.7] (He reminded me again that in order...to lead a strong, quiet life.)
    SEE ALSO: WARRIOR-WAY, WARRIOR-LIFE-(ALL)

LIFE-SUFFICIENT-[LIFE IS SUFFICIENT]: *(Warriors know that life in and of itself is sufficient for their extravagant journey.)*
    SELECTED REFERENCES: The Teachings of Don Juan - Page [185.1-185.2] (A diablero is a diablero, and...the paths of life is everything.) Tales of Power - Page [52.8-52.9] ("I never thought that you needed...is sufficient, self-explanatory and complete.)
    SEE ALSO: LIFE, WARRIOR-JOURNEY-EXTRAVAGANT, IMPECCABLE-MAN-NO-GUIDE

LIFE-TIGHT-WARRIOR-[THE WARRIORS' TIGHT LIFE]: SEE: WARRIOR-LIFE-TIGHT-[THE WARRIORS' TIGHT LIFE]

LIFE-TRUTHFUL-[A TRUTHFUL LIFE]: *(Warriors know that in order to be strong, they must live truthful lives; a life lived with deliberateness, a good strong life.)*
    SELECTED REFERENCES: The Teachings of Don Juan - Page [105.5] ("You have to be a strong man...with deliberateness, a good, strong life.")
    SEE ALSO: WARRIOR-WAY, LIFE-STRONG, TRUTH, WARRIOR-LIFE-TIGHT

LIFE-WARRIOR-[THE WARRIORS' LIFE]: SEE: WARRIOR-LIFE-[THE WARRIORS' LIFE]

LIFE-WAYS-FACING-TWO-[THE TWO WAYS OF FACING LIFE]: *(Warriors know they have two ways of facing being alive; one is to surrender to it by acquiescing or fighting life's demands; the other is to mold our individual life situation to fit its own configurations.)*
    SELECTED REFERENCES: The Art of Dreaming - Page [33.4-33.5] ("There are two ways of facing...situation to fit our own configurations.")
    SEE ALSO: PROACTIVITY, VICTIM, WARRIOR-CHOICE, WARRIOR-DECISIONS, WARRIOR-IMPECCABILITY

LIGHTNESS-WARRIOR-[THE WARRIORS' LIGHTNESS]: SEE: WARRIOR-LIGHTNESS-[THE WARRIORS' LIGHTNESS]

LIGHTNING-[LIGHTNING]: *(Warriors know that fog and lightning are often in cahoots with each other.)*
    SELECTED REFERENCES: Journey to Ixtlan - Page [127.7-129.8] (There was a sudden flash of lightning...And then I fell asleep.) Journey to Ixtlan - Page [133.4-133.5] ("What happened to you last night...because it had not been real.) Journey to Ixtlan - Page [178.6-178.8] ("Don't tax yourself with explanations...when you have enough personal power.")
    SEE ALSO: FOG

LIGHTS-DANCING-EYES-[LIGHTS DANCING BEFORE THE EYES]: SEE: SPIRIT-SEEING-PRELUDE-[PRELUDE TO SEEING THE SPIRIT]

LIKES-WARRIOR-[THE WARRIORS' LIKES]: SEE: WARRIOR-LIKES-[THE WARRIORS' LIKES]

LIMBO-[LIMBO]: *(Warriors know that limbo is another term for the land between the parallel lines.)*

SELECTED REFERENCES: **The Eagle's Gift - Page [154.5-154.6]** (La Gorda was right, we had...we had not been in *dreaming.*)
SEE ALSO: *PARALLEL-LINES-LAND, WARRIOR-LIMBO*

LIMBO-WARRIOR-[THE WARRIORS' LIMBO]: SEE: WARRIOR-LIMBO-[THE WARRIORS' LIMBO]

LIMITS-WARRIOR-[THE WARRIORS' LIMITS]: SEE: WARRIOR-LIMITS-[THE WARRIORS' LIMITS]

LINE-MAKING-[MAKING A LINE]-(TOP)

*LINES-WORLD-[THE LINES OF THE WORLD]: (Warriors know that the lines of the world are a visual manifestation of the Eagle's emanations which warriors can "hook" themselves on to and use to move their bodies.)

SELECTED REFERENCES: **A Separate Reality - Page [23.2-23.6]** ("What's this other mode of seeing...changed in that luminous egg? What?") **A Separate Reality - Page [106.1-106.4]** (Don Juan then explained don Genaro's...to talk about something thoroughly unrelated.) **Journey to Ixtlan - Page [193.4-193.9]** (Whenever your hand remains warm...one feels the world through its lines.") **Journey to Ixtlan - Page [194.2]** (I mentioned that I felt nauseated...of the world with his eyes.) **Journey to Ixtlan - Page [196.1]** ("You may say that there is...say that feelings come from them.") **Journey to Ixtlan - Page [198.2-198.3]** (I had to confess I was...as a door into "not-doing.") **Journey to Ixtlan - Page [201.6-202.4]** (I was tired. I wanted to...saw the web of light fibers.) **Journey to Ixtlan - Page [252.4-252.8]** (Suddenly I felt that my body...I looked away from the sun.) **Journey to Ixtlan - Page [253.9]** ("The world was like it is today...cannot *see* the lines of the world.) **Journey to Ixtlan - Page [255.2]** (I wanted to keep on asking..."You have seen a luminous being.) **Tales of Power - Page [180.1-180.3]** (That was true *seeing* on your...on the spot he focused on.) **Tales of Power - Page [182.5-182.7]** (I saw him leap to a low...had sipped him through its lines.) **Tales of Power - Page [223.2-223.3]** (The two luminous beings shivered...my eyes and with my body.) **Tales of Power - Page [224.6-225.3]** (I had the clear perception that he had...the lines bent outward and down.) **Tales of Power - Page [258.6-258.8]** (They said that I should not be...up from the ravine to the rock.) **The Second Ring of Power - Page [160.8-162.4]** ("The Nagual taught me how to use my body...Everything for a woman warrior starts in *dreaming.)* **The Second Ring of Power - Page [164.6-164.7]** ("Well, it was during my periods...have learned in *dreaming* so far.") **The Second Ring of Power - Page [272.4-273.3]** (And then I suddenly recalled something...recollection to the other in my mind.) **The Second Ring of Power - Page [277.7-277.8]** ("You know that as well as...do what you *saw* us doing.") **The Power of Silence - Page [97.5-98.9]** (By the time it became completely dark...vision and plunged me into darkness.)
SEE ALSO: *EAGLE-EMANATIONS, FLYING-(TOP), LINES-WORLD-(ALL)*

LINES-WORLD-DURABLE-[THE DURABLE LINES OF THE WORLD]: (Warriors know that there are an infinite number of lines that join us to things; the man of knowledge uses the middle of the body and the eyes to produce the most durable lines for practical purposes; the lines cast from other parts of the body such as the hand are not as durable.)

SELECTED REFERENCES: **The Second Ring of Power - Page [193.2-193.9]** ("Did I do something wrong...feels the world through its lines.")
SEE ALSO: *EAGLE-EMANATIONS, LINES-WORLD, DREAM-HAND*

LINES-WORLD-FEELING-[FEELING THE LINES OF THE WORLD]-(TOP): SEE: NOT-DOING-EXERCISE-[THE EXERCISE OF NOT-DOING]-(TOP)

LION-HUNTING-[HUNTING LIONS]-(TOP)

LISTENING-[LISTENING]: (Warriors know that unless they are vigilant and pay strict attention to the things that are said to them, they will have the tendency to listen to things in their own way and hear only what they want to hear.)

SELECTED REFERENCES: **The Eagle's Gift** - Page [19.7-19.9] ("The Nagual never explained this to me...heard what he wanted to hear.)
SEE ALSO: *WARRIOR-ALERTNESS*

LITTLE-SISTERS-[THE LITTLE SISTERS]-(TOP)

LITTLE-SMOKE-[THE LITTLE SMOKE]: (Warriors know that the little smoke is a psychotropic smoking mixture made from certain mushrooms and other plants; the little smoke, when prepared and ingested properly, can lead the warrior to an ally.)

SELECTED REFERENCES: **The Teachings of Don Juan** - Page [53.1] (His own ally was in the...on the nature of the smoke.) **The Teachings of Don Juan** - Page [68.5-72.5] ("Can your ally protect you from...house to put his pipe away.) **The Teachings of Don Juan** - Page [79.8-82.3] (As soon as I got to his...piece of fog in his mind.") **The Teachings of Don Juan** - Page [130.8-143.6] (Collecting the ingredients and preparing them...the subject were of no importance.) **The Teachings of Don Juan** - Page [161.6-176.3] (In the month of December, 1964...fear to understand what I mean.") **A Separate Reality** - Page [6.6-7.3] (Don Juan considered the Jimson weed...as the "ally removing one's body.") **A Separate Reality** - Page [8.9-9.3] (During the second cycle of apprenticeship...the cessation of the pertinence of my world view.) **A Separate Reality** - Page [23.2] ("What's this other mode of seeing men,...you to *see men* as fibers of light.") **A Separate Reality** - Page [39.1-39.3] (I reminded him that he had at first...little smoke for reasons of my own.") **A Separate Reality** - Page [40.1] ("The ally is not in the smoke,"...you don't ever have to smoke again.) **A Separate Reality** - Page [132.5-133.1] ("Is smoking the only way to...something you can fool around with.") **The Second Ring of Power** - Page [324.1-324.2] ("There are no hallucinations," la Gorda...maybe it's the Nagual's smoking mixture.)
SEE ALSO: *POWER-PLANTS, LITTLE-SMOKE-VS-DEVIL'S WEED*

LITTLE-SMOKE-VS-DEVIL'S-WEED-[THE LITTLE SMOKE VS THE DEVIL'S WEED]: (Warriors know the essential differences between the devil's weed and the little smoke; warriors understand that these differences parallel the differences between sorcery and warriorship; the devil's weed represents a path with out a heart; it flatters warriors and makes them feel good even though it is full of passions, jealousy and violence; the little smoke, on the other hand, reinforces the heart, by requiring only that warriors have strength of the heart; the little smoke is constant and never takes a human being prisoner.)

SELECTED REFERENCES: **The Teachings of Don Juan** - Page [161.8-162.4] ("Now that you know a bit...about forgetting something along the line.")
SEE ALSO: *PATH-HEART-WITH, PATH-HEART-WITHOUT, WARRIORSHIP-VS-SORCERY, LITTLE-SMOKE, DEVIL'S WEED*

LITTLE-SMOKE-TALES-[TALES OF THE LITTLE SMOKE]-(TOP)

LIVE-RIGHT-[THE RIGHT WAY TO LIVE]: (Warriors know that Mescalito teaches the right way to live; the warriors' way; the way of the impeccable action.)

SELECTED REFERENCES: **The Teachings of Don Juan** - Page [21.3-21.4] (He related the use of *Lophophora williamsii*...knowledge of the right way to live.) **The Teachings of Don Juan** - Page [88.9] ("What does he teach?" "He teaches you to live properly.") **The Teachings of Don Juan** - Page [139.8] (Mescalito is a protector because he...him because he is outside you.) **A Separate Reality** - Page [6.5-6.6] (He called peyote "Mescalito"...lesson on the right way to live.) **A Separate Reality** - Page [25.5-25.7] (I said that I believed a...of Mescalito and his specific lesson.) **A Separate Reality** - Page [63.9] ("Peyote drives you out of your mind,"...fellows are leading is no life at all.) **A Separate Reality** - Page [63.8-64.1] ("How can it change us?" Eligio insisted...You don't have a protector!") **A Separate Reality** - Page [65.5-66.7] ("If Lucio would seek the protector...how to live a better life.") **A Separate Reality** - Page [125.4-125.7] ("You'll be in one piece again...there is no other way to live.") **Journey to Ixtlan** - Page [55.2-55.3] ("Hunters must be exceptionally tight individuals...perhaps through it you will change.")

SEE ALSO: *MESCALITO, WARRIOR-WAY, WARRIOR-IMPECCABILITY, ACT-LEARNING*

LIVE-WARRIOR-[LIVE LIKE A WARRIOR]: SEE: WARRIOR-LIVE-[LIVE LIKE A WARRIOR]

LIVE-WAY-NO-OTHER-[NO OTHER WAY TO LIVE]: SEE: LIVE-RIGHT-[THE RIGHT WAY TO LIVE]

LIVING-ALLIES-REALM-[LIVING IN THE ALLIES' REALM]: (Warriors know that the sorcerers of antiquity, in order to follow their allies' example, had to spend their lives in the realm of the inorganic beings; this type of involvement curtailed their quest for freedom by consuming all their available energy; the ancient sorcerers "lived" in the realm of the inorganic beings in the sense that they retained their awareness, their individuality.)

SELECTED REFERENCES: The Art of Dreaming - Page [67.4-67.9] ("The problem with the old sorcerers...bent is to teach, to guide.")
SEE ALSO: *ALLIES, INORGANIC-BEINGS, INORGANIC-BEINGS-REALM*

LIVING-WITH-DEATH-[WARRIORS LIVE WITH DEATH]: SEE: WARRIOR-LIVES-WITH-DEATH-[WARRIORS LIVE WITH DEATH]

LIZARD-SORCERY-[THE SORCERY OF THE LIZARDS]-(TOP)

LONELINESS-WARRIOR-[THE WARRIORS' LONELINESS]: SEE: WARRIOR-LONELINESS-[THE WARRIORS' LONELINESS]

LONGING-WARRIOR-[THE WARRIORS' LONGING]: SEE: WARRIOR-LONGING-[THE WARRIORS' LONGING]

LOOKING-VS-SEEING-[LOOKING VS SEEING]: (Warriors know about the distinctions between the two separate manners of perceiving; "looking" refers to the way we normally perceive the world of solid objects through the eyes of the first attention; "seeing" refers to the way warriors perceive the world with their entire body and are able to view the luminous essence of the world instead; "looking" involves viewing the tonal which is in everything; "seeing" involves viewing the nagual which is in everything; when an average person observes the world he "looks"; when a sorcerer observes the world he "sees"; shifting the eyes from "looking" to "seeing" is a technique of the warriors' controlled folly.)

SELECTED REFERENCES: A Separate Reality - Page [8.1-8.3] (Apparently in his system of knowledge...of the things of the world.) A Separate Reality - Page [10.8-11.3] (Don Juan had once told me that...to know; others do other things.") A Separate Reality - Page [36.8-38.1] ("What's it like to *see*, don Juan...spot that they were not people.") A Separate Reality - Page [39.5-39.6] (We involved ourselves in a long discussion...stemmed from my insistence on talking.) A Separate Reality - Page [40.7-40.8] ("I think we are all clowns...eyes only to look at things.") A Separate Reality - Page [81.4-81.5] ("We learn to think about everything...what he looks at everything becomes unimportant.") A Separate Reality - Page [82.9-83.6] (I asked him if his statements were...something funny I look and I laugh.") A Separate Reality - Page [90.6-91.4] ("Take my son Eulalio, that's a better example..."Lucky, bull!" he said. "It's hard work.") A Separate Reality - Page [252.3-252.8] ("Genaro is determined to help you...and shook his head in disbelief.) Journey to Ixtlan - Page [ix.8-ix.9] (His contention was that he was...was the first step to "seeing".) Journey to Ixtlan - Page [188.9] ("Take that rock for instance...to *see* it is *not-doing*.") The Second Ring of Power - Page [226.5-226.9] (She said that the tonal...had to be properly called the nagual.) The Second Ring of Power - Page [273.3-273.4] (When I told them about my...with what I had looked at.) The Fire From Within - Page [54.5-54.8] ("What is *seeing*, then?"

I asked...way *seeing* is labeled and described.) **The Fire From Within - Page [273.6-273.8]** (Another thing I had done that night...as merely odd, unknown, strange.)

    SEE ALSO: *SEEING, WARRIOR-CONTROLLED-FOLLY, EYES-SHIFTING, LOOKING-SEEING-SIMULTANEOUSLY, LOOKING-(ALL)*

LOOKING-SEEING-EARTH-[LOOKING AND SEEING AND THE BOOST FROM THE EARTH]: SEE: ENERGY-BODY-DREAMING [THE THREE WAYS THE ENERGY BODY DEALS WITH ENERGY IN DREAMING]

LOOKING-SEEING-SIMULTANEOUSLY-[LOOKING AND SEEING AT THE SAME TIME]: (Warriors know it is possible for them to "look" and "see" at the same time; in that state warriors are not fully their usual selves, but at the same time they are still capable of operating their normal knowledge of the world.)

    SELECTED REFERENCES: **Tales of Power - Page [21.8-21.9]** ("I should say that tonight, when...operate your knowledge of the world.") **The Eagle's Gift - Page [63.6-63.7]** ("The Nagual Juan Matus left us...she's merely riding on your back.") **The Fire From Within - Page [224.7-225.1]** (As don Juan spoke to me...were bright and bursting with energy.) **The Power of Silence - Page [155.8-156.9]** (Around noon, we continued on up...perceive is simply average sensory perception.")

    SEE ALSO: *LOOKING-VS-SEEING, SEEING*

*LOSING-HUMAN-FORM-[LOSING THE HUMAN FORM]: SEE: HUMAN-FORM-LOSING-[LOSING THE HUMAN FORM]

LOS-QUE-NO-SON-GENTE-["LOS QUE NO SON GENTE"]: (Warriors know that "those who are not men" is another term for the allies.)

    SELECTED REFERENCES: **A Separate Reality - Page [39.4]** (Don Juan said that the three...were in reality don Vicente's allies.) **Journey to Ixtlan - Page [260.3-264.3]** ("Then I looked around to find out...We were quiet for a long time.")

    SEE ALSO: *ALLIES, INORGANIC-BEINGS*

LOT-WARRIOR-[THE WARRIORS' LOT]: SEE: WARRIOR-LOT-[THE WARRIORS' LOT]

LOVE-ALLIES -[THE LOVE OF THE ALLIES]: SEE: ALLIES-LOVE-[THE LOVE OF THE ALLIES]

LOVE-LOOKING-FOR-[LOOKING FOR LOVE]-(TOP)

LOVE-UNCONDITIONAL-[UNCONDITIONAL LOVE]: SEE: AFFECTION-REAL-[REAL AFFECTION]

LOVE-WARRIOR-[THE WARRIORS' LOVE]: SEE: WARRIOR-LOVE [THE WARRIORS' LOVE]

LOVE-WARRIOR-POWER-[THE WARRIORS' POWER TO LOVE]: SEE: WARRIOR-LOVE-POWER-[THE WARRIORS' POWER TO LOVE]

LUCK-[LUCK]: SEE: WARRIOR-CHANCE-MINIMAL-[THE WARRIORS' MINIMAL CHANCE]

*LUCK-BAD-[BAD LUCK]: (Warriors know that bad luck is a reflection of a loss of personal power; warriors feel that they are jinxed when this occurs.)

    SELECTED REFERENCES: **The Eagle's Gift - Page [19.3-19.7]** ("What exactly did he say would...rotten twice and fall on us?")

    SEE ALSO: *PYRAMIDS, POWER-PERSONAL*

LULL-DAILY-AFFAIRS-[THE LULL OF DAILY AFFAIRS]: (Warriors know that the average man has a preoccupation with the lull of daily affairs; a preoccupation that leads to tiredness and boredom.)

SELECTED REFERENCES: The Power of Silence - Page [48.9-49.3] (He said that we, as average men...begins to take on a different character.) The Power of Silence - Page [103.2-103.3] (Don Juan had asserted that our...being linked to everything else.)

SEE ALSO: TIREDNESS, BOREDOM, LIFE-INTERACTIONS-DAILY

LUMINOUS-BALL-[THE LUMINOUS BALL]: (Warriors know that the luminous ball is one of the shapes which the energetic essence of man adopts.)

SELECTED REFERENCES: The Fire From Within - Page [291.3-291.4] (I saw don Juan walking by...me and I saw inside it.) The Fire From Within - Page [294.8-294.9] (The inquisitive, rational part of me...be in that world with people.) The Art of Dreaming - Page [5.7-5.8] (Don Juan had the impression that...akin to people of ancient times.) The Art of Dreaming - Page [12.2-12.4] (Don Juan explained that the end...ball becomes a thin line of energy.) The Art of Dreaming - Page [13.3-13.5] ("Do you mean monstrous...circles, which they couldn't quite make.) The Art of Dreaming - Page [14.3-14.4] (I asked him what uniformity and...an egg proves it has cohesion.) The Art of Dreaming - Page [15.2-15.7] (On his insistence, I made giant...individuals, alone, surrounded by the boundless.)

SEE ALSO: ENERGY-BODY, ENERGY-SHAPE

LUMINOUS-BEINGS-[LUMINOUS BEINGS]: (Warriors know that all organic and inorganic life forms are luminous beings.)

SELECTED REFERENCES: Journey to Ixtlan - Page [255.2] (I wanted to keep on asking..."You have seen a luminous being.) Tales of Power - Page [25.3-25.4] (Humans have a brightness peculiar only...apart from other luminous living beings.) Tales of Power - Page [32.5-32.7] (He said that the mushroomlike formation...in this specific type of seeing.") Tales of Power - Page [46.8-46.9] ("A fluid warrior can no longer...luminous being existing in a luminous world.) Tales of Power - Page [93.7-93.8] ("That night that you met the...of luminous fibers that have awareness.) Tales of Power - Page [158.8-158.9] ("But did they see me disappear...are only extraordinary for the tonal.) Tales of Power - Page [222.8-223.3] (Then my left eye image of don Juan...my eyes and with my body.) The Eagle's Gift - Page [220.3-220.9] (To this effect, he trained la Gorda...arriving at the totality of oneself.) The Fire From Within - Page [45.8-46.4] ("How are those emanations utilized by...them is an eternity in itself.") The Fire From Within - Page [220.1-221.3] (Don Juan said that a man was going to walk...the barrier and I was seeing the emanations.) The Power of Silence - Page [207.7-207.8] (He said that for a seer...any place in their luminous mass.) The Art of Dreaming - Page [5.5-5.8] (From seeing the essence of the universe...akin to people of ancient times.)

SEE ALSO: LUMINOUS-COCOON, EAGLE-EMANATIONS, AWARENESS-TRUTH-THIRD, ENERGY-BODY, INORGANIC-BEINGS, ORGANIC-LIFE

LUMINOUS-BEINGS-LUMINOUS-WORLD-[WE ARE LUMINOUS BEINGS IN A LUMINOUS WORLD]: (Warriors know that every human being is a luminous being in a luminous world.)

SELECTED REFERENCES: Tales of Power - Page [46.8-46.9] ("A fluid warrior can no longer make...luminous being existing in a luminous world.)

SEE ALSO: LUMINOUS-BEINGS, EAGLE-EMANATIONS, WORLD-MYSTERIOUS

LUMINOUS-BEINGS-MYSTERY-[THE MYSTERY OF THE LUMINOUS BEINGS]: (Warriors know that the luminous beings are very mysterious; the mysteries of the luminous beings include the mystery of awareness, the mystery of the dreamer and the dreamed, the mystery of human beings as perceivers, the mystery of alignment, and the mystery of how will becomes intent.)

SELECTED REFERENCES: Journey to Ixtlan - Page [25.3] ("The world around us is a mystery,"...are no better than anything else.) Journey to Ixtlan - Page [135.8-136.1] ("Don't tax yourself trying to figure it out,"...make it into a familiar scene.") Tales of Power - Page [76.9-77.1] ("I told you that Genaro came to show...is the double who dreams the self.") Tales of Power - Page [78.1] ("But how can that be possible,...mystery of us as luminous beings.) Tales of Power - Page **[97.4]** ("I'm saying that we all are unfathomable...by a purpose that is not our decision.") **Tales of Power - Page [255.1-255.3]** (We have one single issue left,"...is what goes through our *reason.)* **The Fire From Within - Page [125.1-125.3]** (I insisted once more that it seemed...but what makes us perceive.) **The Fire From Within - Page [218.8-219.1]** (He remarked that one of the most...And none of us wants to be.") **The Power of Silence - Page [29.5-29.6]** ("At this stage you enter into heightened...the immensity that surrounds us reasonable.") **The Power of Silence - Page [167.8-167.9]** ("I've told you over and over...we find a sorcerer underneath.)

SEE ALSO: *MYSTERY, RIDDLE-MIND, RIDDLE-HEART, RIDDLE-SPIRIT, RIDDLE-DREAMER-DREAMED, MYSTERY-AWARENESS, ALIGNMENT-MYSTERY*

**LUMINOUS-BEINGS-PARADOX-*[THE PARADOX OF THE LUMINOUS BEINGS]: (Warriors confront the paradox of the tonal and the nagual; the tonal is a reflection of the indescribable unknown filled with order; the nagual is a reflection of that indescribable void that contains everything.)*
SELECTED REFERENCES: **Tales of Power - Page [278.1-278.3]** ("We have arrived at the last part...indescribable void that contains everything.)
SEE ALSO: *TONAL-NAGUAL-DICHOTOMY, PAIR-TRUE, TONAL, NAGUAL*

**LUMINOUS-BEINGS-POINTS-*[THE EIGHT POINTS ON THE FIBERS OF A LUMINOUS BEING]: SEE: SORCERER-DIAGRAM [THE SORCERERS' DIAGRAM]*

**LUMINOUS-BEINGS-POSSIBILITIES-TWO-*[THE TWO POSSIBILITIES OPEN TO LUMINOUS BEINGS]: (Warriors know that there are two possibilities open to us as luminous beings; one is the world of reason and the other is the world of will.)*
SELECTED REFERENCES: **Tales of Power - Page [113.7-114.3]** ("The world upheld by *reason* makes...with your *reason*, I with my *will.*)
SEE ALSO: *REASON-WORLD, WILL-WORLD-UPHELD, REASON, WILL*

***LUMINOUS-BEINGS-SECRET-*[THE SECRET OF THE LUMINOUS BEINGS]: (Warriors know that the secret of the luminous beings is that we are perceivers.)*
SELECTED REFERENCES: **Tales of Power - Page [255.1-255.4]** ("We have one single issue left...you will know the two remaining points.")
SEE ALSO: *PERCEIVERS-WE-ARE, POWER-RING-SECOND*

**LUMINOUS-BEINGS-SEEING-*[SEEING THE LUMINOUS BEINGS]-(TOP)*

**LUMINOUS-BODY-*[THE LUMINOUS BODY]: SEE: ENERGY-BODY-[THE ENERGY BODY]*

**LUMINOUS-BODY-FEATURES-*[THE FEATURES OF THE LUMINOUS BODY]: (Warriors know that the Eagle showed the original nagual man and woman the specific features in the luminous bodies of the four types of men and the four types of women; the nagual man and nagual woman also have their own specific luminous features as do dreamers and stalkers.)*
SELECTED REFERENCES: **The Eagle's Gift - Page [175.3-176.6]** (In order to make things easier...consists of countless small, round protuberances.)
SEE ALSO: *WARRIOR-FEMALE, WARRIOR-MALE, ENERGY-BODY, LUMINOUS-COCOON*

**LUMINOUS-BUBBLE-*[THE LUMINOUS BUBBLE]: (Warriors know that human beings are made of the Eagle's emanations and are, in essence, bubbles of luminescent energy, wrapped in a cocoon that encloses a small portion of those emanations.)*
SELECTED REFERENCES: **The Fire From Within - Page [108.2-108.3]** (He then began his explanation...a small portion of these emanations.)

SEE ALSO: *AWARENESS-TRUTH-THIRD, EAGLE-EMANATIONS, LUMINOUS-COCOON, PERCEPTION-BUBBLE, AWARENESS-BUBBLE*

LUMINOUS-CHANGE-SORCERER-[THE CHANGE IN THE SORCERERS' LUMINOSITY]: SEE: SORCERER-LUMINOSITY-CHANGE-[THE CHANGE IN THE SORCERERS' LUMINOSITY]

LUMINOUS-CHARACTERISTICS-REASON-SELF-ABSORPTION-[THE LUMINOUS CHARACTERISTICS OF REASON AND SELF-ABSORPTION]: SEE: REASON-SELF-ABSORPTION-[REASON VS SELF-ABSORPTION]

LUMINOUS-COCOON-[THE LUMINOUS COCOON]: (Warriors know that the luminous cocoon is a transparent structure shared by human beings and all sentient beings; the configurations of these cocoons vary, but all sentient beings are alike insofar as their emanations are encased inside some kind of luminous cocoon; the luminous shell.)

SELECTED REFERENCES: **A Separate Reality - Page [23.2-23.5]** ("What's this other mode of seeing...changed in that luminous egg? What?") **The Eagle's Gift - Page [17.9-18.3]** (Don Juan had said that our total being...systematic exertion he called *not-doing*.) **The Eagle's Gift - Page [41.1-41.6]** (Then all at once the people...have thought that we were drunk.) **The Eagle's Gift - Page [220.3-220.9]** (To this effect, he trained la Gorda...arriving at the totality of oneself.) **The Fire From Within - Page [45.8-46.1]** ("How are the emanations utilized...cocoon with those that are outside.) **The Fire From Within - Page [82.1-82.7]** ("Organic beings have a cocoon...circumstances there is no possible interaction.") **The Fire From Within - Page [108.2-108.3]** (He then began his explanation...a small portion of these emanations.) **The Fire From Within - Page [110.8-112.4]** (He also said that the old...to spread to the neighboring ones.") **The Fire From Within - Page [122.4-122.5]** (He repeated his analogy three or four...along the thickness of man's band.) **The Fire From Within - Page [163.1-163.4]** (He explained next that the product...perceive the containers of inorganic beings at all.") **The Fire From Within - Page [165.5-165.7]** ("But the real difference between plants...to man and other organic creatures.") **The Fire From Within - Page [203.8-203.9]** ("The old seers *saw* that the...to the same forces we are.") **The Fire From Within - Page [259.5]** ("The mold of man is the portion...without any danger to themselves.") **The Power of Silence - Page [xv.8-xv.9]** (3. Human beings are also composed of...like a giant luminous egg.) **The Power of Silence - Page [207.7-207.8]** (He said that for a seer...any place in their luminous mass.)

SEE ALSO: *ENERGY-BODY, LUMINOUS-BEINGS, EAGLE-EMANATIONS, ENERGY-BODY, ENCASED-EVERYTHING-EARTH, LUMINOUS-BUBBLE, LUMINOUS-COCOON-(ALL)*

LUMINOUS-COCOON-INORGANIC-BEINGS-[THE LUMINOUS COCOON OF THE INORGANIC BEINGS]: (Warriors know about the peculiarities of the luminous structure of the inorganic beings; the inorganic beings have only a hairline gap and no inner glow or mobility to their luminosity.)

SELECTED REFERENCES: **The Fire From Within - Page [163.3-163.4]** ("You must bear in mind that...the containers of inorganic beings at all.") **The Fire From Within - Page [291.7-292.2]** (They crowded me. I became annoyed...the allies, it was quite brilliant.) **The Fire From Within - Page [296.1-296.3]** (I started to follow them, but...windlike force blew the world away.)

SEE ALSO: *INORGANIC-BEINGS, ALLIES, ENCASED-EVERYTHING-EARTH, GAP, LUMINOUS-COCOON*

LUMINOUS-COCOON-INVENTORY-TOUGHENING-[THE TOUGHENING OF THE LUMINOUS COCOON]: (Warriors know that the inventory not only consumes all of the average person's energy but it also toughens the luminous cocoon to the point where it becomes inflexible;

under these circumstances there is no possibility of interaction between man and the inorganic beings.)

    SELECTED REFERENCES: **The Fire From Within - Page [82.5-82.7]** ("If those beings are alive...circumstances there is no possible interaction.")

    SEE ALSO: *INVENTORY, INORGANIC-BEINGS, LUMINOUS-COCOON*

LUMINOUS-COCOON-MAN-LUMINOUS-COCOON-EARTH-[THE LUMINOUS COCOONS OF MAN AND THE EARTH]: (Warriors know that the earth's boost is an impulse that comes from the awareness of the earth itself at the instant that the emanations inside the warriors' cocoon become aligned with the emanations inside the earth's cocoon.)

    SELECTED REFERENCES: **The Fire From Within - Page [205.8-207.3]** (He explained that what he called...is perceived and becomes the known.)

    SEE ALSO: *LUMINOUS-COCOON, EARTH, EARTH-BOOST*

LUMINOUS-COCOON-MAN-MANIPULATION-[THE STRUCTURE OF MAN'S LUMINOUS COCOON]: (Warriors know that the mastery of awareness is essentially the manipulation of the structure of man's luminous cocoon.)

    SELECTED REFERENCES: **The Fire From Within - Page [50.6-50.8]** ("I've mentioned to you that the old...called it the glow of awareness.")

    SEE ALSO: *LUMINOUS-COCOON, AWARENESS-MASTERY*

LUMINOUS-COCOON-MIDLINE-[THE MIDLINE OF THE LUMINOUS COCOON]: SEE: ASSEMBLAGE-POINT-THRESHOLD-[THE THRESHOLD OF THE ASSEMBLAGE POINT]

LUMINOUS-COCOON-RECEPTACLE-[THE LUMINOUS COCOON AS A RECEPTACLE]: (Warriors know that the luminous cocoon is a receptacle incapable of withstanding the onslaughts of the tumbler indefinitely.)

    SELECTED REFERENCES: **The Fire From Within - Page [82.1-82.2]** ("Organic living beings have a cocoon...life other than reproduction and metabolism.") **The Fire From Within - Page [108.2-108.3]** (He then began his explanation...a small portion of these emanations.) **The Fire From Within - Page [161.7-161.8]** (Continuing, he explained that inorganic beings...like luminous balls bursting with energy.) **The Fire From Within - Page [163.1-163.4]** (He explained next that the product...containers of inorganic beings at all.") **The Fire From Within - Page [230.1-230.2]** (Don Juan explained that the old...onslaught of the rolling force forever.)

    SEE ALSO: *LUMINOUS-COCOON, TUMBLER, LUMINOUS-SHELL, FORCE-TUMBLING*

LUMINOUS-CORE-[THE LUMINOUS CORE]: (Warriors know that although human beings appear to seers as luminous eggs, the egg-like shape is actually an external shell of luminosity which houses a most intriguing and mesmeric core of luminosity; this core appears to be like a series of concentric circles of yellowish luminosity, the color of a candle's flame; the only means of liberating this luminous core is by breaking the luminous shell in the right way through the loss of the human form; the liberation of the luminous core is the act of regaining the totality of oneself.)

    SELECTED REFERENCES: **The Eagle's Gift - Page [220.3-220.9]** (To this effect, he trained la Gorda...arriving at the totality of oneself.)

    SEE ALSO: *LUMINOUS SHELL, LUMINOUS-COCOON, LUMINOUS-EGG, HUMAN-FORM-LOSING, TOTALITY-REGAINING, AWARENESS-COLOR*

LUMINOUS-CREVICE-[THE LUMINOUS CREVICE]: SEE: LUMINOUS-DENT-DREAMING-[THE LUMINOUS DENT NECESSARY FOR DREAMING]

LUMINOUS-DENT-[THE LUMINOUS DENT]-(TOP)

LUMINOUS-DENT-ATTENTION-FIRST-[THE LUMINOUS DENT AND THE FIRST ATTENTION]: (Warriors know that the luminous dent acts on the first attention by displacing the glow of awareness; the dent presses on the emanations inside the luminous shell and shifts the emphasis of the assemblage point under the force of that pressure; the luminous dent, through this displacement, makes the assemblage point fall on emanations which are ordinarily inaccessible to the first attention.)

SELECTED REFERENCES: The Fire From Within - Page [111.7-112.4] (Don Juan further said that the...to spread to other neighboring ones.")
SEE ALSO: *LUMINOUS-DENT-TYPES, ATTENTION-FIRST, ASSEMBLAGE-POINT, NAGUAL-BLOW*

LUMINOUS-DENT-DREAMING-[THE LUMINOUS DENT NECESSARY FOR DREAMING]: (Warriors know that the luminous dent is the dent of the second attention; in order to do dreaming, the right and left side must be wrapped up together and come to rest in one single bundle in this luminous dent.)

SELECTED REFERENCES: The Eagle's Gift - Page [253.3-259.9] (Zuleica warned me that if I...I had other things to do.)
SEE ALSO: *LUMINOUS-BODY-FEATURES, ENERGY-BODY, LUMINOUS-DIMPLE*

LUMINOUS-DENT-FEELING-[FEELING THE LUMINOUS DENT]-(TOP): SEE: ATTENTION-SECOND-CONTROLS [EXPERIENCING THE SECOND ATTENTION TAKING OVER THE CONTROLS]-(TOP)

LUMINOUS-DENT-TYPES-[THE TYPES OF LUMINOUS DENTS]: (Warriors know that the position of the assemblage point is infinitely stronger once it begins to move in the luminous cocoon because it creates a dimple in its luminosity; this dimple houses the assemblage point from then on; the nagual's blow can also create a type of luminous dent or dimple in the luminous cocoon that is felt like a blow to the right shoulder blade; these dents can either be bowl-like depressions or crevices which run the width or length of the luminous cocoon; these crevices make the luminous shell look like it has curled up on itself; the luminous dent is an inexplicable affair, a matter of a glow creating a dent in another glow.)

SELECTED REFERENCES: The Eagle's Gift - Page [253.3-259.9] (Zuleica warned me that if I...I had other things to do.) The Fire From Within - Page [110.8-112.9] (He also said that the old...all, a greater capacity to forget.) The Fire From Within - Page [118.4-118.7] ("The nagual's blow is of great...simply don't know about their possibilities.") The Fire From Within - Page [154.8-154.9] (He said that the position of...lose anything, they lose their dimple.")
SEE ALSO: *LUMINOUS-COCOON, ASSEMBLAGE-POINT, LUMINOUS-DENT-(ALL), AWARENESS-GLOW*

LUMINOUS-EGG-[THE LUMINOUS EGG]: (Warriors know that the luminous egg is one of the shapes which the energetic essence of man adopts; the shape of an average human being is like that of a transparent luminous egg; sorcerers are more like tombstones, round at both ends; more often than not, the luminous shape of human beings resembles a ball or a tombstone; individuals with an egg-like luminous shape are more akin to the sorcerers of antiquity.)

SELECTED REFERENCES: Tales of Power - Page [32.5-32.6] (He said that the mushroomlike formation...egglike cluster of luminous fibers.) The Second Ring of Power -

Page [240.2-240.4] ("What color are you Gorda...we are round at both ends.") **The Fire From Within - Page [xi.1-xi.2]** (He had also explained that seers...become naguals after learning to *see*.) **The Fire From Within - Page [64.8-65.2]** (Don Juan replied that human alternatives are...have, therefore, nearly an inexhaustible scope.) **The Fire From Within - Page [122.4-122.6]** (He repeated his analogy three or four...along the thickness of man's band.) **The Power of Silence - Page [xv.6-xv.9]** (Don Juan's instruction on the art...like a giant luminous egg.) **The Art of Dreaming - Page [5.4-5.8]** (From *seeing* the essence of the universe...akin to people of ancient times.) **The Art of Dreaming - Page [11.4-11.6]** (In his teachings he put a...egg, which is our energy self.) **The Art of Dreaming - Page [14.3-14.4]** (I asked him what uniformity and...an egg proves it has cohesion.)
      SEE ALSO: *ENERGY-BODY, LUMINOUS-TOMBSTONE, LUMINOUS-BALL, SORCERER-ANTIQUITY, LUMINOUS-COCOON, AWARENESS-TRUTH-THIRD*

LUMINOUS-EQUILIBRIUM-WARRIOR-[THE WARRIORS' LUMINOUS EQUILIBRIUM]: SEE: WARRIOR-EQUILIBRIUM-[THE WARRIORS' LUMINOUS EQUILIBRIUM]

LUMINOUS-FIBERS-JOIN-MAN-SURROUNDINGS-[THE LUMINOUS FIBERS THAT JOIN MAN TO HIS SURROUNDINGS]: (Warriors know that we are connected to everything around us through a bunch of long fibers that shoot out from the center of the abdomen; these fibers join us to our surroundings and give us balance and stability.)
      SELECTED REFERENCES: **A Separate Reality - Page [23.4-23.6]** ("Is that the way everyone looks...changed in that luminous egg? What?")
      SEE ALSO: *WILL-GRABBING, EAGLE-EMANATIONS, LINES-WORLD-DURABLE, WARRIOR-EQUILIBRIUM, LUMINOUS-TENTACLE*

LUMINOUS-FILAMENTS-[THE LUMINOUS FILAMENTS]: (Warriors know that the luminous body is constantly creating cobweb-like filaments which are projected out of the luminous mass by emotions of any sort; the stalkers' breath enables warriors to retrieve lost filaments as well as to expel filaments left in us by other luminous bodies with which we have interacted; through the recapitulation, we must reject the luminous filaments left in us by others because those filaments are the basis for our limitless capacity for self-importance.)
      SELECTED REFERENCES: **The Eagle's Gift - Page [288.8-289.6]** (The *stalker* then takes the event...one's limitless capacity for self-importance.).)
      SEE ALSO: *STALKER-BREATH, RECAPITULATION, SELF-IMPORTANCE, BREATH, FEELINGS*

LUMINOUS-LAYERS-[THE LUMINOUS LAYERS]: (Warriors know that human beings are creatures composed of many layers of luminosity, not unlike an onion; various kinds of jolts are always acting to separate those layers, but they normally get back together again; if the jolt is too great, however, the layers separate for good and the individual dies.)
      SELECTED REFERENCES: **The Second Ring of Power - Page [290.2-291.4]** (The Nagual told me that human...for that center to push out.") **The Art of Dreaming - Page [171.2-171.6]** (Don Juan insisted on talking about...in another skin of the onion.")
      SEE ALSO: *LUMINOUS-COCOON, ENERGY-BODY*

LUMINOUS-LIGHTNESS-[LUMINOUS LIGHTNESS]: (Warriors know that human beings are born with a lightness to their luminosity, but as they grow they become earthbound and fixed; as warriors accumulate more personal power, their luminosity becomes less connected to the ground.)
      SELECTED REFERENCES: **Tales of Power - Page [35.5-35.7]** ("Why are those people shaped differently...differently because they live like warriors.)
      SEE ALSO: *WARRIOR-LIGHTNESS, LUMINOUS-COCOON, POWER-PERSONAL*

LUMINOUS-LINE-[THE LUMINOUS LINE]: (Warriors know that the luminous line is the extreme limit of the sorcerers' energy shape transformation; a transformation of this type was only accomplished by the sorcerers of antiquity in their efforts to achieve an ally-like existence and defy death; these sorcerers succeeded in changing the configuration of their gaps to more closely mirror the gaps of the allies; by stretching their energetic shapes they also succeeded in stretching the duration of their consciousness; the goal of these sorcerers was to bend their lines of energy into circles, but they were never quite able to accomplish this.)

SELECTED REFERENCES: The Art of Dreaming - Page [12.2-12.8] (Don Juan explained that the end...like a dog chasing its tail.") The Art of Dreaming - Page [13.2-13.5] ("Were all those sorcerers like the...circles, which they couldn't quite make.) The Art of Dreaming - Page [14.3-15.2] (I asked him what uniformity and...filaments that passed through that line.)

SEE ALSO: ENERGY-SHAPE-TRANSFORMATION, SORCERER-LUMINOSITY-CHANGE, GAP, INORGANIC-BEINGS, DEATH-DEFIERS, ENERGY-BODY, ENERGY-SHAPE

LUMINOUS-MAGNET-[THE LUMINOUS MAGNET]: (Warriors know that the assemblage point is like a luminous magnet that selects emanations and groups them together for perception.)

SELECTED REFERENCES: The Fire from Within - Page [124.4-124.5] (He explained that the assemblage point...the unknown in a new light.)

SEE ALSO: ASSEMBLAGE-POINT, EAGLE-EMANATIONS, PERCEPTION

LUMINOUS-SHELL-[THE LUMINOUS SHELL]: (Warriors know that the luminous core is contained within a luminous shell; this shell of luminosity is itself dull, and in fact dulls the radiance of the luminous core; the luminous shell must be broken in order to liberate the warriors' total being; the shell must be broken at just the right time, however, just as with creatures that hatch out of shells; if warriors fail to break out of their shells at the appropriate time, they die; losing the human form is the only means of liberating the warriors' luminous core; to break the luminous shell means to remember the other self or to arrive at the totality of oneself.)

SELECTED REFERENCES: The Eagle's Gift - Page [220.3-220.9] (To this effect, he trained la Gorda...arriving at the totality of oneself.)

SEE ALSO: LUMINOUS-COCOON, LUMINOUS-BEINGS, TOTAL-BEING, HUMAN-FORM-LOSING, SELF-OTHER, TOTALITY-REGAINING, LUMINOUS-CORE, LUMINOUS-SHELL-DIFFUSION

LUMINOUS-SHELL-DIFFUSION-[THE DIFFUSION OF THE LUMINOUS SHELL]: (Warriors know that when they burn with the fire from within the boundaries of the luminous cocoon are diffused and the inside emanations extend themselves beyond anything imaginable.)

SELECTED REFERENCES: The Fire From Within - Page [113.8-114.3] (He went on to explain that a...at large, and glide into eternity.")

SEE ALSO: LUMINOUS-SHELL, LUMINOUS-COCOON, FIRE-WITHIN, AWARENESS-TOTAL

LUMINOUS-SMOKING-PIPE-[THE LUMINOUS SMOKING PIPE]: (Warriors know that the movement of the assemblage point results in a total change in the shape of the energy body; the energy body transforms from a ball into a shape resembling a smoking pipe.)

SELECTED REFERENCES: The Art of Dreaming - Page [12.2-12.4] (Don Juan explained that the end...ball becomes a thin line of energy.)

SEE ALSO: ENERGY-BODY, SORCERER-LUMINOSITY-CHANGE, ENERGY-SHAPE, LUMINOUS-BALL

LUMINOUS-TAPROOT-[THE LUMINOUS TAPROOT]: (Warriors know that the energy bodies of men make a deep furrow in the energy of the earth when they move, as if they had a taproot that was dragging.)
SELECTED REFERENCES: The Art of Dreaming - Page [5.6-5.7]("When sorcerers see a human being...had a taproot that was dragging.)
SEE ALSO: ENERGY-BODY

LUMINOUS-TENTACLE-[THE LUMINOUS TENTACLE]: (Warriors know that every human being has a set of long, tentacle-like fibers, that protrude out from the area around the navel; these fibers tell a lot about individuals, whether they are sick or healthy, whether they are kind or treacherous, whether they can "see" or not; these tentacle-like fibers are of the utmost importance in the life of any human being.)
SELECTED REFERENCES: A Separate Reality - Page [23.4-23.5] ("Is that the way everyone...changed in that luminous egg? What?") A Separate Reality - Page [106.1-108.6] (Don Juan then explained don Genaro's...knew that you had not seen.") The Eagle's Gift - Page [155.7-155.9] (Moved by the boundless fear I was feeling...at the midpoint of my body.) The Eagle's Gift - Page [257.4-258.2] (Zuleica started then on another facet...my body in my sitting position.) The Eagle's Gift - Page [260.3-260.4] (She ordered me to stand up by...to lift up my whole body.)
SEE ALSO: EAGLE-EMANATIONS, LUMINOUS-COCOON, WILL, SEEING, LUMINOUS-FIBERS-JOIN-MAN-SURROUNDINGS

LUMINOUS-TOMBSTONE-[THE LUMINOUS TOMBSTONE]: (Warriors know that the luminous tombstone is one of the shapes which the energetic essence of man adopts; the characteristic luminous configuration of sorcerers; sorcerers are shaped more like luminous tombstones than like luminous balls.)
SELECTED REFERENCES: The Second Ring of Power - Page [240.2-240.4] ("What color are you, Gorda...we are round at both ends.")
SEE ALSO: LUMINOUS-COCOON, ENERGY-BODY, LUMINOUS-EGG, ENERGY-SHAPE, SORCERER-LUMINOSITY-CHANGE

LUMINOUS-WORLD-[THE LUMINOUS WORLD]: (Warriors know that they are not objects in a world of objects; warriors know they are luminous beings in a luminous world.)
SELECTED REFERENCES: Tales of Power - Page [46.8-46.9] ("A fluid warrior can no longer...luminous being existing in a luminous world.)
SEE ALSO: EAGLE-EMANATIONS

LUST-WARRIOR-LIFE-[THE WARRIORS' LUST FOR LIFE]: SEE: WARRIOR-LIFE-LUST-[THE WARRIORS' LUST FOR LIFE]

M

MAESTRO-[MAESTRO]: (Warriors know that "maestro" is a term of respect between warriors.)
SELECTED REFERENCES: The Second Ring of Power - Page [177.6-177.8] ("You look very fine yourself, Maestro...be glad to see you again.)
SEE ALSO: WARRIOR

MAGIC-[MAGIC]: (Warriors know that magic is the true heritage of man; magic can be described as the simple act of awareness, the ability of human beings to keep the assemblage point fixed; the ability of human beings to impart order to that which they perceive; the force that fills warriors and banishes doubt from their minds; the indescribable abstract essence of the world; warriors know that they must allow magic to get hold of them and banish doubt from their minds; once our doubts have been banished, anything is possible; without magic there can be no elation, no lesson, no realization; the way in which human beings keep their continuity in tact is a supreme accomplishment of magic, of intending.)
SELECTED REFERENCES: Tales of Power - Page [254.7] (That is the order that should prevail;...magical heritage and reduces us to nothing.") The Second Ring of Power - Page [274.8-274.9] (Don Juan said that the core...was the act of awareness.) The Fire From Within - Page [83.9-84.1] (They considered flames and fluidity to...transportation to the realm of non organic life.) The Fire From Within - Page [133.2-133.5] (Don Juan went on to express...is our command, our gift of magic.") The Power of Silence - Page [106.9-107.1] (A warrior was magical and ruthless,...be able to suspect his ruthlessness.) The Power of Silence - Page [120.4] ("What we need to do to allow...doubts are banished, anything is possible.") The Power of Silence - Page [121.6-122.5] (Her dramatic trance and the accompanying...the realm where miracles are commonplace.") The Power of Silence - Page [167.8] ("I've told you over and over...have a very deep sense of magic.) The Power of Silence - Page [222.8-222.9] ("That big cat came unnoticed out of nowhere...had no elation, no lesson, no realizations.") The Power of Silence - Page [251.5] ("Consider what happens to you,"...supreme accomplishment of magic, of intending.)
SEE ALSO: ABSTRACT, BEING-MAGIC-OF-OUR, WARRIOR-MAGIC, WARRIOR-JOY, INTENDING

MAGIC-WARRIOR-[THE MAGIC OF THE WARRIOR]: SEE: WARRIOR-MAGIC-[THE MAGIC OF THE WARRIOR]

*MAGICAL-BEINGS-[MAGICAL BEINGS]: (Warriors know that certain animals are impossible to track because they have no routines; sometimes a hunter is fortunate enough to come across a magical being once in a lifetime.)
SELECTED REFERENCES: Journey to Ixtlan - Page [76.1-76.7] ("There are certain animals, however, that...enough to cross paths with one.)
SEE ALSO: ROUTINES-HUNTER

MAGICAL-COYOTE-[THE MAGICAL COYOTE]-(TOP)

MAGICAL-DEER-[THE MAGICAL DEER]-(TOP)

MAGICAL-FOREST-TRAIL-[THE TRAIL IN THE MAGICAL FOREST]-(TOP)

MAIZ-PINTO-[MAIZ PINTO]-(TOP): SEE: CORN-SORCERY-[CORN SORCERY]-(TOP)

MALE-[MALE]: SEE: MEN-[MEN]

MALE-MALENESS-[MALENESS]: (Don Juan's theory that perhaps the relative scarcity of maleness in the universe is the reason for the male gender's unwarranted dominion on our planet.)
SELECTED REFERENCES: The Art of Dreaming - Page [103.3-103.5] (He stated that the nagual Rosendo's...men's unwarranted dominion on our planet.)
SEE ALSO: FEMALE-UNIVERSE, MALENESS-FEMALENESS, WARRIOR-MALE

MALE-PERSONALITY-[MALE PERSONALITIES]: SEE: WARRIOR-MALE-[MALE WARRIORS]

MALE-RATIONALES-WARRIOR-[THE RATIONALES OF THE MALE WARRIOR]: SEE: WARRIOR-MALE-RATIONALES-[THE RATIONALES OF THE MALE WARRIOR]

MALE-STRENGTH-[THE INHERENT STRENGTH OF MALE WARRIORS]: SEE: MEN-[MEN]

MALE-WARRIORS-[MALE WARRIORS]: SEE: WARRIOR-MALE-[MALE WARRIORS]

MALENESS-VS-FEMALENESS-[MALENESS VS FEMALENESS]: (Warriors know that maleness and femaleness are not final states, but are instead, the result of a specific act of positioning the assemblage point; this positioning is actually a matter of volition and training; the positioning of the assemblage point is what determines maleness or femaleness; the shiniest part of the assemblage point faces outward in females and inward in males; sexual orientation can be totally changed if sorcerers can change the position of their assemblage point; this is accomplished by twisting the energy shape to look like a shell that has curled up on itself.)
SELECTED REFERENCES: The Art of Dreaming - Page [210.6-212.3] ("The first part of the dreaming lesson...has been tailored just for you.") The Art of Dreaming - Page [219.6-219.8] ("I have already said to you...that has curled up on itself.")
SEE ALSO: MALENESS, ASSEMBLAGE-POINT-POSITION

MAN-ACCOUNTABLE-SOCIETY-[MEN ARE ACCOUNTABLE TO SOCIETY]: SEE: MEN-ACCOUNTABLE-[MEN ARE HELD ACCOUNTABLE]

*MAN-ACTION-[THE MAN OF ACTION]: (Warriors know that the man of action is the second male personality; a highly volatile man; a great humorous fickle companion,)
SELECTED REFERENCES: The Eagle's Gift - Page [174.9-175.3] (The three male warriors and the...who cannot stand on his own.)
SEE ALSO: WARRIOR-MALE

MAN-ALTERNATIVES-POSSIBILITIES-POTENTIAL-[MAN'S ALTERNATIVES, POSSIBILITIES AND POTENTIAL]: SEE: HUMAN-ALTERNATIVES-POSSIBILITIES-POTENTIAL-[HUMAN ALTERNATIVES, POSSIBILITIES, AND POTENTIAL]

MAN-ANCIENT-[ANCIENT MAN]: (Warriors know that man's ancient ancestors chose the arbitrary position of modern man's assemblage point; those individuals who unwittingly began the development of the sense of "self", a development which as it progressed eventually severed man's natural connection with silent knowledge.)

SELECTED REFERENCES: **A Separate Reality - Page [40.8-41.2]** ("This is like asking me what we men..."We men know very little about the world.) **The Fire From Within - Page [133.6-133.8]** (The explanations behind all these complex...alignments of emanations, thus new perceptions.) **The Power of Silence - Page [37.1-37.2]** ("The nagual Elias used to tell me...Now we can't get back to it.) **The Power of Silence - Page [47.4-47.6]** (He explained that the events...knock of the spirit were examples.) **The Power of Silence - Page [147.3-147.5]** ("Sorcerers believe that when man became aware...the more ephemeral *intent* becomes.") **The Power of Silence - Page [149.5-150.1]** (Then he talked about ancient man....of peace, of satisfaction, of attainment.) **The Power of Silence - Page [159.8-159.9]** (Once the assemblage point has moved,...to the spirit, having descended into hell.) **The Power of Silence - Page [198.7-199.1]** (When I asked him to talk about...had been squarely on that location either.)
SEE ALSO: *GARDEN-EDEN, KNOWLEDGE-SILENT-AGE, SELF, KNOWLEDGE-MAN, KNOWLEDGE-SILENT*

MAN-AURA-[MAN'S AURA]: (*Warriors know that man is not the unknowable, that his luminosity can be "seen" almost as if one were using the eyes alone.*)
SELECTED REFERENCES: **The Fire From Within - Page [122.7]** ("Man is not the unknowable,"...if one were using the eyes alone.")
SEE ALSO: *LUMINOUS-BEINGS-, AWARENESS-COLOR*

MAN-AWAKENING-[THE AWAKENING OF THE AVERAGE MAN]: (*Warriors know that the awakening of the average man occurs only when he begins to lose energy because of aging; when the awakening occurs this late in life the individual usually doesn't have enough energy left to turn this realization into a pragmatic discovery.*)
SELECTED REFERENCES: **The Power of Silence - Page [48.9-49.5]** (He said that we, as average...simple anger at having missed out.)
SEE ALSO: *AGE-OLD, WARRIOR-ENEMIES-FOUR-NATURAL*

MAN-BAND-[MAN'S BAND OF EMANATIONS]: SEE: EAGLE-EMANATIONS-MAN-BAND-[MAN'S BAND OF EMANATIONS]

MAN-BEHIND-SCENES-[THE MAN BEHIND THE SCENES]-(TOP)

MAN-BEST-[MAN AT HIS BEST]: (*Warriors know that human beings are at their best in the face of the unknown; the unknown invigorates us and draws the best from us; warriors thrive in a mysterious state in which they cannot predict the outcome of their actions.*)
SELECTED REFERENCES: **The Fire From Within - Page [33.8-33.9]** ("There is a simple rule of thumb...in the face of the unknown.")
SEE ALSO: *UNKNOWN, WARRIOR-FOG-CREATE*

MAN-COMMAND-VS-EAGLE-COMMAND-[MAN'S COMMAND VS THE EAGLE'S COMMAND] : (*Warriors know that the Eagle's commands do not have to box warriors in, we can disobey them by obeying them; human beings also have to learn to protect themselves from their own commands.*)
SELECTED REFERENCES: **The Fire From Within - Page [133.4-133.5]** ("The force of the emanations at large...our command, our gift of magic.") **The Fire From Within - Page [138.4-139.2]** ("When we, as serious adult human...the old seers paid for theirs.")
SEE ALSO: *MAGIC, INVENTORY-WORSHIP-THROW-AWAY; EAGLE-COMMAND*

MAN-CORE-[THE CORE OF MAN'S BEING]: SEE: BEING-CORE-[THE CORE OF OUR BEING]

MAN-CORN-PLANTS-[THE MAN WHO PLANTS CORN]-(TOP): SEE: CORN-MAN-PLANTS-[THE MAN WHO PLANTS CORN]-(TOP)

MAN-DARK-SIDE-[THE DARK SIDE OF MAN]: (*Warriors know that the dark side of man is the somber and foreboding portion of the unknown which is not only the unknown but the "who-cares-to-know-it"; the first face of the second attention; the silent side of man; the area of the unknown that breeds aberration and morbidity; that portion of the unknown that is steeped with the obsessive mood of the ancient Toltecs; the dark and heavy character of the older side of man, or the second point*)

SELECTED REFERENCES: **The Fire From Within** - Page [124.6-124.7] ("Those were visions of the dark side...but the who-cares-to-know-it.") **The Power of Silence** - Page [145.6-146.9] (I abruptly pulled over to the...knowledge that you cannot yet voice.") **The Power of Silence** - Page [262.9-263.6] (He said he had *seen* that my body,...yes, and it's called stupidity.")

SEE ALSO: *ATTENTION-SECOND-FACES-TWO, UNKNOWN-HUMAN-VS-NON-HUMAN, ABERRATION-MORBIDITY*

MAN-DEPENDENT-[MAN IS DEPENDENT]: (*Warriors know that human beings are dependent; we crave someone to guide us when we can accomplish everything by ourselves; we are unwilling to accept that we need so little to get on with the most essential work of our lives.*)

SELECTED REFERENCES: **The Power of Silence** - Page [160.2-160.5] ("Our difficulty with this simple progression...do it ourselves? Big question, eh?")

SEE ALSO: *MAN-ERROR, IMPECCABLE-MAN-NO-GUIDE*

MAN-DESPAIR-[MAN'S DESPAIR]: (*Warriors know that man's despair springs from the bit of silent knowledge left in us which does two things; first that knowledge gives us an inkling of our ancient connection with intent; second, it makes us feel that without that connection we will find no peace, no satisfaction, no attainment.*)

SELECTED REFERENCES: **The Power of Silence** - Page [149.7-150.1] (As the feeling of the individual self...peace, of satisfaction, of attainment.)

SEE ALSO: *MAN-ERROR, SELF-ORIGIN, KNOWLEDGE-SILENT, SELF-IMAGE, CYNICISM, CRUELTY*

MAN-ERROR-[MAN'S ERROR]: (*Warriors know the error of ancient man was his desire to know intent directly, the way he knew everyday life; when man became aware of what he knew and then wanted to become "conscious" of what he knew, he immediately began to lose sight of what he knew [as a result of wanting to try to understand it directly]; man's error is to fail to realize that the more he clings to reason, the more ephemeral intent becomes; in the end man gave up silent knowledge for the world of reason.*)

SELECTED REFERENCES: **The Power of Silence** - Page [147.2-147.5] ("Sorcerers believe that when man...the more ephemeral *intent* becomes.") **The Power of Silence** - Page [149.5-150.1] (Then he talked about ancient man...peace, of satisfaction, of attainment.)

SEE ALSO: *GARDEN-EDEN, MAN-ANCIENT, KNOWLEDGE-SILENT, REASON, POINT-THIRD-INVERSION*

MAN-EVOLUTION-[MAN IS CAPABLE OF EVOLVING]: (*Warriors know that man is capable of evolving; in order to do so, we must free our awareness from the bindings of the social order; once our awareness is free, intent will redirect it onto a new evolutionary path; sorcerers are the proof that this evolution is possible.*)

SELECTED REFERENCES **A Separate Reality** - Page [219.4-220.4] ("A warrior is aware that the world...people do as an endless folly.") **The Power of Silence** - Page [210.4-210.7] (He said that possibly every human...the prescribed position of normal living.) **The Art of Dreaming** - Page [176.6-176.8] ("Do you think, don Juan, that...import of evolving is another matter.")

SEE ALSO: *SORCERY-TASK-GRAND, AWARENESS, INTENT, WARRIOR-FREEDOM-TOTAL, PERCEPTION-SOCIAL-BASE, PERCEPTION-CHANGING-SOCIAL-BASE, ENERGY, ASSEMBLAGE-POINT-MOVING-STRESS*

MAN-EXPERIENCE-[THE EXPERIENCE OF BEING A MAN]: (*Warriors know that the experience of being a human being is simply the extravagant journey of life; the warriors' understanding of the sufficiency of life and awareness.*)
SELECTED REFERENCES: Tales of Power - Page [52.7-52.9] (I never thought that you needed...is sufficient, self-explanatory and complete.)
SEE ALSO: *EXISTENCE-REASON*

MAN-FALLACY-[THE FALLACY OF MAN]: (*Warriors know that the average man is inclined to totally disregard his link with intent and the magic of existence; the average man believes in his madness that he is all tonal, and totally disregards the nagual.*)
SELECTED REFERENCES: Tales of Power - Page [127.2-127.4] ("From the moment we become all...ourselves to be making perfect sense.") The Fire From Within - Page [59.6-59.7] (Don Juan fought not to laugh...drive that one can twist at will.)
SEE ALSO: *WARRIOR-INTENT-LINK, LUMINOUS-BEINGS-MYSTERY, WORLD-MYSTERIOUS, AWARENESS-MYSTERY, INTENT, MAGIC*

MAN-FLAW-[THE FLAWS OF THE AVERAGE MAN]: (*Warriors know that man's great collective flaw is to completely disregard his connection with intent; the fatal flaw of the average man is to take himself too seriously; the flaw of the average man is that he remains glued to the inventory of his reason, he doesn't deal with himself as energy; the flaw of the average man is to think that the shift of the assemblage point is purely mental instead of being an actual realignment of his fundamental energetic being.*)
SELECTED REFERENCE: The Fire From Within - Page [24.6-24.9] (Don Juan explained that the mistake...had over the simple-minded Spaniards.) The Fire From Within - Page [112.5-112.7] ("In some inexplicable way, it is...dent in another bubble of energy.) The Fire From Within - Page [121.3-121.4] (He remarked that my flaw was...moved into man's band of emanations.) The Fire From Within - Page [133.8-134.1] ("I used to give you power...It isn't, as you yourself can attest.") The Fire From Within - Page [138.8-139.2] ("The skimmings of men," don Juan...the old seers paid for theirs.") The Power of Silence - Page [103.2-103.3] (Don Juan had asserted that our great...of being linked to everything else.)
SEE ALSO: *MAN-FALLACY, SELF-SERIOUSNESS, INVENTORY, REASON, ASSEMBLAGE-POINT-MOVING, ENERGY*

MAN-FRIENDS-NO-[MAN HAS NO FRIENDS ON THIS EARTH]: (*Warriors know why man has no friends on the earth; man is destructive, he has antagonized every living being on this earth; that is why he has no friends.*)
SELECTED REFERENCES: The Art of Dreaming - Page [87.3-87.4] (We have no friends on this...that's why we have no friends.")
SEE ALSO: *MAN-MALADY*

MAN-HELL-PRIVATE-[MAN'S PRIVATE HELL]: (*Warriors know that when men create their own private hells, they are born out of their own stupidity.*)
SELECTED REFERENCES: The Power of Silence - Page [191.2-191.3] (The spirit could not possibly have cared...for the spirit to pay attention.)
SEE ALSO: *STUPIDITY, HELL*

MAN-INTENT-DISCONNECTED-[MAN IS DISCONNECTED FROM INTENT]: (*Warriors know that as man's sense of self developed he lost his natural connection to intent; modern man, being heir to that development, therefore finds himself so hopelessly removed from the source of everything that all he can do is express his despair in violent and cynical acts of self-destruction.*)

SELECTED REFERENCES: **The Power of Silence** - Page [149.5-150.1] (Then he talked about ancient man...peace, of satisfaction, of attainment.)

SEE ALSO: *INTENT, GARDEN-EDEN, MAN-ERROR, CYNICISM*

MAN-KNOWLEDGE-[MAN OF KNOWLEDGE]: (*Warriors know that a man of knowledge is a warrior who follows truthfully the hardships of learning; a human being who has, without rushing or faltering, gone as far as one can go in unraveling the secrets of power and knowledge; a warrior who has defeated the four natural enemies of the warrior; a warrior who "knows"; a warrior who succeeds in hunting power; a warrior who possesses both knowledge and power; a warrior who is in control without controlling anything.*)

SELECTED REFERENCES: **The Teachings of Don Juan** - Page [51.3-51.5] ("A man goes to knowledge as he goes...there will be no pitiful regrets over that.) **The Teachings of Don Juan** - Page [82.4-83.1] (In our conversations, don Juan consistently...formidable; most men succumb to them.") **The Teachings of Don Juan** - Page [87.7-87.8] ("But if the man sloughs off his tiredness,...clarity, power, and knowledge is enough.") **A Separate Reality** - Page [5.8-5.9] (In the context of more serious..."one who knows" to categorize a sorcerer.) **A Separate Reality** - Page [6.9-7.1] (I order to become a man of knowledge...one had to become familiar with it.) **A Separate Reality** - Page [10.8-11.8] (Don Juan had once told me that a man...to *see* that it is his peculiar way of knowing.") **A Separate Reality** - Page [22.2-23.2] ("Do you think that your very rich world...to change anything about them.") **A Separate Reality** - Page [28.6-28.9] (I've told you already, only a crackpot...Perhaps it's time to trick you again.") **A Separate Reality** - Page [65.2] ("Sacateca is a man of knowledge,..."He dances because that's the bent of his nature.) **A Separate Reality** - Page [85.3-85.9] (You should know by now that a man...that would also be his controlled folly.") **A Separate Reality** - Page [88.8-88.9] ("In order to become a man of...to realize then that nothing matters.") **A Separate Reality** - Page [126.7-126.8] ("You really know how to talk...to confuse yourself with riddles.) **A Separate Reality** - Page [148.8-148.9] ("Is will the same as *seeing*...will and also with his *seeing*. ") **Journey to Ixtlan** - Page [106.9-107.2] (And there is even more power...can be a man of knowledge.") **Journey to Ixtlan** - Page [158.3-158.4] (I asked him to explain what...unraveling the secrets of personal power.) **Journey to Ixtlan** - Page [194.3-194.4] (*"Not-doing* is very simple...though the technique of *not-doing."*) **Tales of Power** - Page [23.6-23.7] ("All of us go through the same shenanigans,"...at a given moment everything changed.") **Tales of Power** - Page [41.4-41.5] ("Genaro is a man of knowledge,"...transporting himself over great distances.") **Tales of Power** - Page [58.1-58.5] ("There is no hypothetical sense when...is in control without controlling anything.") **Tales of Power** - Page [84.1-84.2] ("Our reason is petty and it is...now that your reason cannot comprehend.) **Tales of Power** - Page [139.5-139.6] (The men of knowledge of today...he doesn't even have the idea it exists.") **The Fire From Within** - Page [4.7-5.3] (Don Juan said that after some of these...into other worlds and never came back.) **The Fire From Within** - Page [23.6-23.9] (Don Juan said that his benefactor...fourth step and have become seers.)

SEE ALSO: *KNOWLEDGE, POWER, LEARNING-HARDSHIPS, WARRIOR-ENEMIES-FOUR-NATURAL, HUNTER-POWER-BECOMING, MAN-KNOWLEDGE-SECRETS, MAN-KNOWLEDGE-(ALL)*

MAN-KNOWLEDGE-ACCOMPLISHMENT-[THE FINAL ACCOMPLISHMENT OF A MAN OF KNOWLEDGE]: (*Warriors know that "seeing" is the final accomplishment of a man of knowledge and that "seeing" is attained after the individual first learns to stop the world through the technique of not-doing.*)

SELECTED REFERENCES: **Journey to Ixtlan** - Page [194.4-194.5] ("*Not-doing* is very simple but...through the technique of *not-doing*.")

SEE ALSO: NOT-DOING, SEEING, STOPPING-WORLD

MAN-KNOWLEDGE-INDIFFERENT-WARRIOR-[THE MAN OF KNOWLEDGE IS THE INDIFFERENT WARRIOR]: SEE: MAN-KNOWLEDGE-SORCERY-[THE MAN OF KNOWLEDGE IS BEYOND SORCERY]

MAN-KNOWLEDGE-LYRIC-[LYRIC MAN OF KNOWLEDGE]: (Warriors know that a lyric man of knowledge is another term for sorcerer; a person with a knowledge of nagualism; a man of knowledge.)
SELECTED REFERENCES; A Separate Reality - Page [33.4-34.1] (Don Vicente had only words of praise...Why did you go see him?")
SEE ALSO: MAN-KNOWLEDGE

MAN-KNOWLEDGE-PERCEPTION-[THE THREE FOLD PERCEPTION OF A MAN OF KNOWLEDGE]: (The warrior-sorcerer-seers perceive the world in three ways, with their senses, with their will and with their "seeing".)
SELECTED REFERENCES: A Separate Reality - Page [148.8-148.9] ("No. Will is a force, a power...will and also with his *seeing*.")
SEE ALSO: MAN-KNOWLEDGE, WILL, LOOKING-VS-SEEING

MAN-KNOWLEDGE-SECRETS-[THE SECRETS OF A MAN OF KNOWLEDGE]: (Warriors know that "tengo secretos" are the secrets which a man of knowledge learns in conjunction with his encounters with power.)
SELECTED REFERENCES: The Teachings of Don Juan - Page [159.9-160.1] (Don't take her with passion...There are other paths.) The Teachings of Don Juan - Page [176.1-176.3] ("It takes a very long time...fear to understand what I mean.") Journey to Ixtlan - Page [13.5-13.9] (His tone was firm. I felt...thighs and laughed with great delight.) Journey to Ixtlan - Page [155.2-155.4] ("And thus you will dance to your...will sit here and watch you.)
SEE ALSO: MAN-KNOWLEDGE

MAN-KNOWLEDGE-SEER-[BECOMING A SEER AND CEASING TO BE A MAN OF KNOWLEDGE]: (Warriors know it is possible for a man of knowledge to become a seer and then cease to be a man of knowledge; if seers' obsessions with what they "see" become too intense, then they cease to be men of knowledge and get lost in the intricacies of the unknown; "seeing" can actually undermine the strength of a man of knowledge and force him to become obsessed with what he "sees".)
SELECTED REFERENCES: The Fire From Within - Page [4.7-5.4] (Don Juan said that after some...were as defenseless as everyone else.)
SEE ALSO: MAN-KNOWLEDGE, SEER, OBSESSION, UNKNOWN-INTRICACIES, WARRIORSHIP-VS-SORCERY

MAN-KNOWLEDGE-SENSES-[THE SENSES OF A MAN OF KNOWLEDGE]: (Warriors know that only men of knowledge perceive the world in three different ways, with their first attention senses, with their will and with their "seeing".)
SELECTED REFERENCES: A Separate Reality - Page [148.8-148.9] ("Is will the same as seeing...will and also with his seeing.")
SEE ALSO: WILL, SEEING, SENSES-(ALL)

MAN-KNOWLEDGE-SORCERY-[THE MAN OF KNOWLEDGE IS BEYOND SORCERY]: (Warriors know that a man of knowledge is impeccable in his actions and would never use his power to create or resolve ordinary situations; the man of knowledge is the indifferent warrior.)

SELECTED REFERENCES: **Tales of Power** - Page [57.6-57.9] ("Genaro is a man of knowledge...for you, only tales of power.")

SEE ALSO: *WARRIOR-INDIFFERENCE, MAN-KNOWLEDGE, WARRIORSHIP-VS-SORCERY*

MAN-KNOWLEDGE-TEMPORARY-[BECOMING A MAN OF KNOWLEDGE IS A TEMPORARY THING]: *(Warriors know that being a man of knowledge is not a permanent condition; rather, warriors become men of knowledge for a brief instant after defeating their four natural enemies.)*

SELECTED REFERENCES: **The Teachings of Don Juan** - Page [83.6-83.7] ("To be a man of knowledge has...after defeating the four natural enemies.")

SEE ALSO: *WARRIOR-ENEMIES-FOUR-NATURAL*

MAN-LOT-[MAN'S LOT IN LIFE]: *(Warriors know that man's lot in life is to learn and to be hurled into inconceivable new worlds; our lot as human beings is to want to know, for good or bad.)*

SELECTED REFERENCES: **The Teachings of Don Juan** - Page [161.2] ("The desire to learn is not ambition...because you are not bidding to know.) **A Separate Reality** - Page [85.2] ("I told you once that our lots...for good or bad," he said.) **A Separate Reality** - Page [153.9] ("We are men and our lot...be hurled into inconceivable new worlds.") **A Separate Reality** - Page [258.8-258.9] ("Your problem is that you want...Your stumbling block is intact.) **Journey to Ixtlan** - Page [84.8-85.3] ("Use it. focus your attention on...and exploiting our lot as men.") **Journey to Ixtlan** - Page [108.6-108.7] (He laughed and threatened to cover...as one acted as a warrior.)

SEE ALSO: *LEARNING-(ALL), WARRIOR-LOT*

MAN-MAGIC-GIFT-[MAN'S GIFT OF MAGIC]: *(Warriors know that man's gift of magic is two-fold; first, we have the ability to keep the assemblage point unwaveringly fixed in its normal position and second we have the power to assign the meaning we give to all that we perceive.)*

SELECTED REFERENCES: **The Fire From Within** - Page [133.4-133.5] ("The force of the emanations at large...our command, our gift of magic.") **The Fire From Within** - Page [138.4-139.2] ("When we, as serious adult human...the old seers paid for theirs.")

SEE ALSO: *MAGIC, ASSEMBLAGE-POINT-FIXATION, INVENTORY-WORSHIP-THROW-AWAY, BEING-MAGIC-OF-OUR*

MAN-MALADY-[THE MALADY OF MAN]: *(Warriors know that man's malady is that he knows infinitely more about the mystery of the universe than he rationally suspects.)*

SELECTED REFERENCES: **The Art of Dreaming** - Page [65.6-65.7] ("I'm afraid I can't claim that...of the universe than we suspect.")

SEE ALSO: *MYSTERY, DREAMING-EMISSARY, AWARENESS-SUBLIMINAL, CYNICISM, MAN-PREDICAMENT*

MAN-MARK-[THE MARK OF MODERN MAN]: *(Warriors know that excessive concern with the individual self is the mark of modern man; it is this total involvement with the self-image that accounts for man's tendency to be a homicidal egotist.)*

SELECTED REFERENCES: **The Power of Silence** - Page [150.4-150.7] (He explained that sorcerers had discovered...self-reflection and its concomitant: self-importance.)

SEE ALSO: *SELF, SELF-IMAGE, WARRIOR-MARK*

MAN-MISERY-[THE SOURCE OF MAN'S MISERY]: *(Warriors know that self-pity is their true enemy and the source of man's misery; self-pity leads to self-importance which in turn develops its own momentum and gives rise to man's fake sense of worth.)*

SELECTED REFERENCES: The Power of Silence - Page [151.1-151.3] ("It doesn't sound possible, but that...gives it its fake sense of worth.)
SEE ALSO: *SELF-PITY, SELF-IMPORTANCE*

MAN-MODERN-VS-ANTIQUITY-[MODERN MAN VS THE MEN OF 'ANTIQUITY]: *(Warriors know that the sorcerers of antiquity had a very realistic view of perception based on what they "saw" of the universe around them; modern man, on the other hand, has an absurd and unrealistic view of perception based on his observations of the social order and his dealings with it.)*

SELECTED REFERENCES: The Art of Dreaming - Page [172.9-173.6] (He pointed out, first, that there...self-awareness for nearly an eternity.)
SEE ALSO: *SORCERER-ANTIQUITY, PERCEPTION, SEEING, REALITY-INTERPRETATION*

MAN-MOLD-[THE MOLD OF MAN]: SEE: MOLD-MAN-[THE MOLD OF MAN]

MAN-NEEDS-[WHAT MAN NEEDS NOW]: *(Warriors know that what man needs now is be taught ideas pertaining to facing the unknown; human beings need to be taught ideas that will pull them away from the outer world and reconnect them with the inner world of the abstract; human beings need to be taught the secrets of the assemblage point; human beings need to be taught how to abstract themselves; what we needs is to allow magic to get hold of us and banish all doubt from our minds; once those doubts have been erased, anything is possible; human beings need help in reconnecting with the abstract, not through methods, but through emphasis; if someone makes a human being aware of the need to curtail self-importance, then that help is real.)*

SELECTED REFERENCES: The Power of Silence - Page [120.4] ("What we need to do to allow...doubts are banished, anything is possible.") The Power of Silence - Page [160.1-160.4] (I told him that his sequence...self-importance, that help is real.) The Power of Silence - Page [228.8-229.2] (Don Juan explained that man's predicament...the secrets of the assemblage point.) The Art of Dreaming - Page [3.3-3.5] (Whatever we are perceiving is energy...must change at its social base.") The Art of Dreaming - Page [xi.9] (The definitive reason for this work...and our commitment to his quest.)
SEE ALSO: *AWARENESS-TRUTHS, UNKNOWN, ASSEMBLAGE-POINT-SECRETS*

MAN-NEMESIS-[THE NEMESIS OF MAN]: *(Warriors know that self-importance is the nemesis of mankind and the sorcerers' supreme enemy.)*

SELECTED REFERENCES: The Art of Dreaming - Page [37.6] (He was of the opinion that...enemy but the nemesis of mankind.)
SEE ALSO: *SELF-IMPORTANCE, SELF-IMPORTANCE-LOSING, WARRIOR-WAR*

MAN-PASSIVE-[MAN IS INHERENTLY PASSIVE]: *(Warriors know that man is inherently passive; if he moves, its only when he feels the pressure of his death; death sets the pace for man's actions and pushes him relentlessly until it breaks him; warriors struggle to rise above all their possibilities and defeat death.)*

SELECTED REFERENCES: The Power of Silence - Page [112.4-112.5] ("I would think, don Juan, that...above all possibilities and defeat death.)
SEE ALSO: *DEATH-ACTIVE-FORCE, LIFE-ARENA, WARRIOR-DEATH-COMMAND*

MAN-PITFALL-[MAN'S PITFALL]: *(Warriors know that the skimmings of the first attention are the average man's pitfall; they are so real to him that*

he forgets that he has constructed them by commanding his assemblage point to appear where it does; the average man does not have the power to protect himself from his own commands.)
SELECTED REFERENCES: The Fire From Within - Page [138.8-139.2] ("The skimmings of men," don Juan...the old seers paid for theirs.")
SEE ALSO: *MAN-FLAW, SKIMMINGS, ATTENTION-FIRST*

MAN-PLANTS-CORN-[THE MAN WHO PLANTS CORN]-(TOP): SEE: CORN-MAN-PLANTS-[THE MAN WHO PLANTS CORN]-(TOP)

MAN-PLIGHT-[MAN'S PLIGHT]: *(Warriors know that man's plight is the counterpoint between his stupidity and his ignorance.)*
SELECTED REFERENCES: The Power of Silence - Page [228.8-229.2] (Don Juan explained that man's predicament...the secrets of the assemblage point.)
SEE ALSO: *STUPIDITY-IGNORANCE*

MAN-POSSIBILITIES-EXPLORING-UNDERSTANDING-[EXPLORING MAN'S POSSIBILITIES WITHOUT TRYING TO UNDERSTAND THEM]: *(Warriors know that man's possibilities are so vast and mysterious that rather than thinking about them, the warrior chooses to explore them with no hope of ever understanding them.)*
SELECTED REFERENCES: The Power of Silence - Page [126.4-126.5] (Don Juan's reply was that man's...no hope of ever understanding them.)
SEE ALSO: *HUMAN-ALTERNATIVES-POSSIBILITIES-POTENTIAL, THINKING-ACTING*

MAN-PREDICAMENT-[THE ESSENCE OF MAN'S PREDICAMENT]: *(Warriors know that man's predicament is that he intuits his hidden resources but is afraid to use them; the position of man's assemblage point is so overwhelming that it creates a fog which obliterates the memory of the world which we came from and what our purpose was for coming here; the immobility of man's assemblage point prevents it from returning to its original habitual position.)*
SELECTED REFERENCES: The Power of Silence - Page [228.8-229.2] (Don Juan explained that man's predicament...the secrets of the assemblage point.) The Art of Dreaming - Page [197.1-197.4] (He explained that since we entered...our purpose was in coming here.")
SEE ALSO: *MAN-PREDICAMENT, POINT-THIRD-INVERSION, POWER-HIDDEN, FEAR, MAN-ANCIENT, MAN-MALADY, AWARENESS-SUBLIMINAL, CYNICISM*

MAN-PURPOSE-[THE PURPOSE OF THE AVERAGE MAN]: SEE: PURPOSE-MAN-[THE PURPOSE OF THE AVERAGE MAN]

MAN-SEEING-[SEEING A MAN[: SEE: SEEING-MAN-[SEEING A MAN]

MAN-SILENT-SIDE-[THE SILENT SIDE OF MAN]: *(Warriors know that the silent side of man is the unknown aspect of man's great band of emanations; the side of man whose intricacies can trap him in his own aberration and morbidity.)*
SELECTED REFERENCES: The Fire From Within - Page [132.9-133.2] ("But would it be possible to encourage...being caught in the clutches of rationality.")
SEE ALSO: *MAN-DARK-SIDE, REASON-ANTECEDENTS, ATTENTION-SECOND-QUAGMIRE, UNKNOWN-IMMEASURABLE, UNKNOWN-INTRICACIES*

MAN-SPIRIT-ACCOUNT-[PAYING BACK TO THE ACCOUNT OF THE SPIRIT OF MAN]: *(Warriors make deposits to the account of the spirit of man as their way of repaying the kindness and generosity of others they*

*have encountered on their path; the account of the spirit of man is very
small, but whatever one puts in is always more than enough.)*
    SELECTED REFERENCES: **Tales of Power - Page** [138.4-138.6] ("Where are they
from, don Juan...personally was moved by those three.) **The Second Ring of Power - Page**
[124.5-124.8] (I wanted to believe that I...in it is more than enough.")
    SEE ALSO: *SPIRIT*

*MAN-SPIRIT-DISCONNECT-[WHAT DISCONNECTED MAN FROM THE
SPIRIT]: (Warriors know it was self-reflection that disconnected man from
the spirit in the first place.)*
    SELECTED REFERENCES: **The Power of Silence - Page** [159.7-159.9] (Once the
assemblage point has moved...from the spirit in the first place.)
    SEE ALSO: *SELF-REFLECTION, POINT-THIRD-INVERSION*

*MAN-SURVIVAL-[MAN'S SURVIVAL]: (Warriors know that the survival
of man depends on our ability to change our perception at its social base.)*
    SELECTED REFERENCES: **The Art of Dreaming - Page** [3.3-3.5] (Whatever we are
perceiving is energy...must change at its social base.")
    SEE ALSO: *PERCEPTION-CHANGING-SOCIAL-BASE, WARRIOR-SURVIVE*

*MAN-THORN-SIDE-[THE THORN IN MAN'S SIDE]: (Warriors know that
the thorn in man's side is that he does not know that the assemblage point
exists and is therefore obliged to take the by-product of its habitual position
as something final and indisputable; this misconception is the thorn in
man's side.)*
    SELECTED REFERENCES: **The Art of Dreaming -Page -** [73.6-74.1] ("We are back
again, harping on...manipulate the assemblage point for gain.)
    SEE ALSO: *ASSEMBLAGE-POINT, ATTENTION-FIRST, DESCRIPTION-WORLD*

*MAN-UNKNOWABLE-NOT-[MAN IS NOT THE UNKNOWABLE]:
(Warriors know that man is not the unknowable; man's luminosity can be
"seen" almost as if one were using the eyes alone.)*
    SELECTED REFERENCES: **The Fire From Within - Page** [122.7] ("Man is not the
unknowable...one were using the eyes alone.")
    SEE ALSO: *UNKNOWABLE, SEEING*

*MAN-VISUAL-[MAN IS A VISUAL CREATURE]: SEE: PERCEPTION-
PREDATOR-[A PREDATOR'S WAY OF PERCEIVING]*

**MANIFESTATIONS-SPIRIT-[THE MANIFESTATIONS OF THE SPIRIT]:
SEE: SPIRIT-MANIFESTATION [THE MANIFESTATIONS OF THE
SPIRIT], ABSTRACT-CORE-FIRST [THE FIRST ABSTRACT CORE]*

*MANKIND-AUDIENCE-[THE AUDIENCE OF MANKIND]: (Warriors
know that the audience of mankind is the great majority of people whose
assemblage points are not precisely on the points of reason or silent
knowledge; in our day, they are the lovers of reason, in the past they were
the lovers of silent knowledge; these are the people who have admired and
sung odes to the heroes of either position.)*
    SELECTED REFERENCES: **The Power of Silence - Page** [239.4-239.9] (The old
nagual went on to explain...to the heroes of either position.)
    SEE ALSO: *MANKIND-LEADERS, REASON, KNOWLEDGE-SILENT, POINT-
FIRST, POINT-THIRD*

*MANKIND-CONDITIONS-[THE CONDITIONS OF MANKIND]: (Warriors
know it is useless to single out the wretched conditions of a group of people
or individuals because the life conditions of man in general are so*

horrendous; *warriors do not feel sorry for themselves or for other oppressed people; instead they feel a detached compassion for all of mankind.*)
SELECTED REFERENCES: **The Fire From Within** - Page [31.6-32.2] (I told him that it had...don't have a chance in hell.")
SEE ALSO: *OPPRESSED-ADVANTAGES, SELF-PITY, SELF-COMPASSION, HUMAN-CONDITION, WARRIOR-COMPASSION*

MANKIND-LEADERS-[THE TRUE LEADERS OF MANKIND]: *(Warriors know that humanity is now on the first point, but not every human being is squarely on the position of reason; those who are on the spot itself are the true leaders of mankind; most of these people are unknown individuals whose genius is the exercising of their reason; when silent knowledge was the first point, the same condition prevailed; this means that through the ages, the true leaders of mankind have always been the few human beings whose assemblage points happened to be exactly on the point of reason or of silent knowledge; the rest of humanity is merely an audience.*)
SELECTED REFERENCES: **The Power of Silence** - Page [239.4-239.9] (The old nagual went on to explain...to the heroes of either position.)
SEE ALSO: *MANKIND-AUDIENCE, REASON, KNOWLEDGE-SILENT, POINT-FIRST, POINT-THIRD*

MARK-LIFE-[THE MARK OF LIFE AND CONSCIOUSNESS]: SEE: AWARENESS-GLOW-[THE GLOW OF AWARENESS]

MARK-WARRIOR-[THE WARRIORS' MARK]: SEE: WARRIOR-MARK-[THE WARRIORS' MARK]

MASTERIES-THREE-WARRIOR-[THE THREE MASTERIES OF THE WARRIOR: SEE: WARRIOR-MASTERIES-THREE-[THE THREE MASTERIES OF THE WARRIOR]

MASTERY-WARRIOR-[THE WARRIORS' MASTERY]: SEE: WARRIOR-MASTERY-[THE WARRIORS' MASTERY]

MATTERS-NOTHING-WARRIOR-[NOTHING MATTERS TO THE WARRIOR]: SEE: WARRIOR-NOTHING-MATTERS-[NOTHING MATTERS TO THE WARRIOR]

MATTERS-WHAT-WARRIOR-[WHAT MATTERS TO THE WARRIOR]: SEE: WARRIOR-MATTERS-WHAT-[WHAT MATTERS TO THE WARRIOR]

MATURATION-END-PRODUCT-[THE END PRODUCT OF MATURATION]: SEE: AWARENESS-ATTENTION-[AWARENESS VS ATTENTION]

MAX-CAT-[MAX THE CAT]-(TOP): SEE: CATS-STORY-[THE STORY OF THE TWO CATS]-(TOP)

MEANING-LIFE-[THE MEANING OF LIFE]: SEE: EXISTENCE-REASON-[THE REASON FOR EXISTENCE]

MEANNESS-HUMILIATION-[MEANNESS AND HUMILIATION]:
(*Warriors know that the person who has never been truly humiliated is the person who is likely not to be really mean.*)

SELECTED REFERENCES: A Separate Reality - Page [138.1-138.2] (I talked for a long time...reason I was not really mean.)
SEE ALSO: *DEFEAT*

MELANCHOLY-[MELANCHOLY]: SEE: DEPRESSION-MELANCHOLY-[DEPRESSION AND MELANCHOLY]

MEMBERSHIP-[MEMBERSHIP]: (Warriors know that membership is a term which denotes that an individual has conformed to a particular description of the world, or that he has "gained membership"; when a child knows the description of the world of solid objects and is capable of making all the perceptual interpretations necessary to validate that description, then he is a full-fledged "member" of the first attention world; when warriors have learned a new description of the world in a convincing and authentic manner and have become capable of eliciting a new perception of the world that matches that description, then they become "members" in the world of the man of knowledge.)
SELECTED REFERENCES: Journey to Ixtlan - Page [viii.6-viii.7] (In the case of my work with...acquiring *membership* in his knowledge.) Journey to Ixtlan - Page [ix.2-ix.4] (From that moment on, however,...have learned to make in common.) Journey to Ixtlan - Page [xiii.7-xiii.8] (The termination of the apprenticeship meant...I had gained *membership*.)
SEE ALSO: *DESCRIPTION-WORLD*

MEMORABLE DATES-[THE MEMORABLE DATES]: (Warriors know that Yaqui Indians have a collection of historical events which they call the memorable dates; the memorable dates are a series of oral accounts of the history of the Yaqui nation during the time they waged a war for their homeland against the Spanish and Mexican invaders.)
SELECTED REFERENCES: The Power of Silence - Page [114.6-114.9] (He said that some sorcerers were...accounts of their defeats and disintegration.)
SEE ALSO: *SORCERER-STORYTELLERS*

MEMORY-DESCRIPTION-[MEMORIES OF THE DESCRIPTION OF THE WORLD]: (Warriors know that each of the things we feel about the world is really only a memory of the description of the world which we have come to accept as reality.)
SELECTED REFERENCES: Tales of Power - Page [48.7-47.8] ("Does the double have corporealness?"...you feel me as being solid.")
SEE ALSO: *DESCRIPTION-WORLD, REALITY-INTERPRETATION*

MEMORY-TYPES-[THE TWO TYPES OF MEMORIES]: SEE: REMEMBERING-BODY-VS-REMEMBERING-NORMAL-[REMEMBERING WITH THE BODY VS NORMAL REMEMBERING]

MEN-[MEN]: (Warriors know the strengths and weaknesses of men as a gender.)
SELECTED REFERENCES: Tales of Power - Page [144.2-144.4] (His statements aroused my curiosity...The rest is the same.") The Second Ring of Power - Page [42.1-42.4] ("A woman, of course, is much more supple...an empty woman. He must be right.) The Second Ring of Power - Page [95.6-95.8] ("There is a hole there on the right side,"...they know for a fact who emptied them.") The Second Ring of Power - Page [171.5-172.3] ("The men will give you very little...there is none in front of yours.") The Second Ring of Power - Page [247.3-247.4] ("We hold the images of the world...Especially during her menstrual period.) The Second Ring of Power - Page [277.1-277.2] (In order for a man to be energized...the fingers clawed in an upright position.) The Second Ring of Power - Page [300.4-300.6] ("By the time Benigno and Nestor were cured,...for I needed to be contained.) The Eagle's Gift - Page [23.8-23.9] ("The Nagual said that the *dreaming body...dreaming body* is more possessive.") The Eagle's Gift - Page [174.8-175.3] (The three male warriors and the courier...but who cannot stand on his own.) The

Eagle's Gift - Page [222.3-223.1] (Don Juan marveled that this realization...a double man he could approach.) **The Eagle's Gift - Page [269.5-270.5]** ("That applies only to men," she said...you go around giving lectures.") **The Eagle's Gift - Page [271.1-271.2]** ("Oh, it's perfectly understandable," she went on....makes things even more difficult.")
SEE ALSO: *WOMEN-(ALL), MEN-(ALL)*

MEN-ACCOUNTABLE-SOCIETY-[MEN ARE HELD ACCOUNTABLE BY SOCIETY]: *(Warriors know that men are characterized by having a solid history; a man's history pins him down with the thoughts and feelings of all his family and friends; he is held accountable and cannot erase himself without a lot of work; men must resort to becoming protective, secretive and forever on guard against themselves; secrecy is the price the male warrior pays for being important to society; men resent having to erase themselves and will find strange ways of popping up in spite of it all.)*
SELECTED REFERENCES: **The Eagle's Gift - Page [269.3-270.5]** ("I beg your pardon," I said...you go around giving lectures.)
SEE ALSO: *WOMEN, MEN, PERSONAL-HISTORY-ERASING, WOMEN-ACCOUNTABLE-SOCIETY, WARRIOR-SECRETS, WARRIOR-UNAVAILABILITY*

MEN-TALENT-[MEN'S TALENT]: SEE: WOMEN-TALENT-[WOMEN'S TALENT]

MENSTRUAL-PERIOD-[A WOMAN'S MENSTRUAL PERIOD]: *(Warriors know that menstruation is a door for women; during that time they become something else; during that time they can "see" the crack between the worlds; during their periods the disguise of women falls away and they are bare; two days before her period a woman can open the crack between the worlds and step through it; when a woman menstruates she cannot focus her attention.)*
SELECTED REFERENCES: **The Second Ring of Power - Page [47.1-47.7]** ("You caught a glimpse of the other...do it, but it took them years.") **The Second Ring of Power - Page [164.1-164.5]** (I close my eyes and fall asleep...a man has to make it.) **The Second Ring of Power - Page [247.1-247.7]** (Her laughter was clear and contagious...or by gazing at the clouds.)
SEE ALSO: *WOMEN, CRACK-WORLDS, WOMB*

MENTAL-BALANCE-[MENTAL BALANCE]: SEE: SANITY-[SANITY], MIND-[THE MIND]

MERCHANTS-THREE-ASPIRING-[THE THREE ASPIRING MERCHANTS]-(TOP)

MERGING-[MERGING]: *(Warriors know that merging is another term for "seeing"; a process that consists of a true silence from within followed by an outward elongation of something from within which meets and merges with anything within one's field of awareness.)*
SELECTED REFERENCES: **Tales of Power - Page [136.5-136.8]** (He put his hand on my...anything within one's field of awareness.) **The Eagle's Gift - Page [152.1-152.2]** (Because I had some experience moving...merged until something broke our hold.) **The Art of Dreaming - Page [258.1-258.6]** (What he was saying had no...wings of intent, I believe forward.)
SEE ALSO: *SEEING*

MERGING-LUMINOSITY-[MERGING LUMINOSITY]-(TOP)

MERGING-REALITIES-[MERGING REALITIES]: SEE: DREAMING-GATE-THIRD-[THE THIRD GATE OF DREAMING]

MESCALITO-[MESCALITO]: (*Warriors know that Mescalito is a unique power; a protector and a teacher for certain warriors; a power connected with the ingestion of peyote.*)

SELECTED REFERENCES: The Teaching of Don Juan - Page [28.1-28.7] ("Would you teach me about peyote,...Very few Indians have such a desire.") The Teachings of Don Juan - Page [35.4-35.7] ("You asked me to teach you...Mescalito requires a very serious intent.") The Teachings of Don Juan - Page [36.7-37.3] (Don Juan whispered that we were...one can do," don Juan said.) The Teachings of Don Juan - Page [43.5-48.1] (After we had finished eating and were resting..."Goddammit! It was not a dog!") The Teachings of Don Juan - Page [52.1-53.4] ("Is Mescalito your ally?"...An ally takes you out to give you power.") The Teachings of Don Juan - Page [68.6-68.7] ("How about Mescalito? Can he protect...to be used for personal reasons.") The Teachings of Don Juan - Page [88.2-105.5] (Don Juan seldom spoke openly about...with deliberateness ,a good strong life.") The Teachings of Don Juan - Page [139.8] (Mescalito is a protector because he...him because he is outside you.) A Separate Reality - Page [6.5-6.6] (He called peyote "Mescalito" and he...on the right way to live.) A Separate Reality - Page [60.3-69.8] ("Carlos is learning about Mescalito,..."Yeah, he's too old," Benigno echoed.) A Separate Reality - Page [77.9-78.4] (I began by asking him: Did I...are you turning your back on Mescalito?") A Separate Reality - Page [91.4-92.1] ("If I have understood you correctly...his reasons are incomprehensible to me.") Journey to Ixtlan - Page [89.1-89.4] (Two weeks before, on August 4th...of exceptionally vivid dreams and nightmares.) Journey to Ixtlan - Page [90.1-90.4] (We then had a long conversation...will come to you of itself.") The Second Ring of Power - Page [37.6-38.6] ("Mescalito is the Nagual's guaje,"...Mescalito told him never to bring me around.)

SEE ALSO: POWER PLANTS

MESCALITO-ELIGIO-[ELIGIO MEETS MESCALITO]-(TOP)

MESCALITO-ENCOUNTER-FIRST-[THE FIRST ENCOUNTER WITH MESCALITO]-(TOP)

MESCALITO-ENCOUNTER-SECOND-[THE SECOND ENCOUNTER WITH MESCALITO]-(TOP)

MESCALITO-LIGHT-[MESCALITO'S LIGHT]-(TOP)

MESCALITO-SPIRIT-[THE SPIRIT OF MESCALITO]: (*Warriors know that Mescalito is like a spirit, although whatever he is does not become truly clear until the warrior has experienced Mescalito for himself.*)

SELECTED REFERENCES: A Separate Reality - Page [62.9-63.3] ("Don Juan says there is a spirit...animal-like is to get drunk.")
SEE ALSO: MESCALITO

MESSAGE-DREAMER-ALLIES-[THE DREAMER'S MESSAGE FOR THE ALLIES]-(TOP): SEE: ALLIES-MESSAGE-DREAMER-[THE DREAMER'S MESSAGE FOR THE ALLIES]-(TOP)

METAPHORICAL-DAGGER-[THE METAPHORICAL DAGGER]: SEE: DAGGER-METAPHORICAL-[THE METAPHORICAL DAGGER]

MIDPOINT-BODY-PHYSICAL-[THE MIDPOINT OF THE PHYSICAL BODY]: SEE: BODY-PHYSICAL-MIDPOINT-[THE MIDPOINT OF THE PHYSICAL BODY]

MIND-[THE MIND]: (*Warriors know that the mind is nothing more than the self-reflection of the inventory of man; the mind is our rationality, and our rationality is our self-reflection; warriors actually set out to lose the self-reflective aspect of themselves without losing their underpinnings; in this way they are actually able to "lose their minds" without anyone knowing it, and in the process, live an infinitely stronger life than if they had kept their minds intact; mental balance is nothing more than the fixing of*) *the assemblage point on one spot we're accustomed to; warriors understand the flimsiness of the mind's underlying order or continuity; the mind is tremendously vague and yet we trust it simply because we are familiar with it.)*

SELECTED REFERENCES: Tales of Power - Page [125.3-125.4] ("Would you say that the *nagual*...the mind is the chili sauce,") The Fire From Within - Page [121.1-121.3] ("By all ordinary measures, you were...infinitely stronger life than if you had kept it.") The Fire From Within - Page [154.5-154.9] ("The position of the assemblage point...lose anything, they lose their dimple.") The Power of Silence - Page [35.4-35.6] ("I've taught you *dreaming* the same...point erratically and lose their minds.") The Power of Silence - Page [164.3-164.7] ("Finally, when it became impossible to...was the key idea," he replied.) The Power of Silence - Page [166.2] (The inventory is the mind...to break the mirror of self-reflection.") The Power of Silence - Page [225.4-225.5] ("To discover the possibility of being...what kind of persons we are.") The Power of Silence - Page [242.6] ("But how can information be stored...are familiar with it," he retorted.) The Art of Dreaming - Page [2.8] (I personally detest the darkness and morbidity...I like the immensity of thought.) The Art of Dreaming - Page [72.9-73.4] (Upon awakening I gave don Juan...world, of being able to predict.)
SEE ALSO: *INVENTORY, SELF-REFLECTION*

MIND-BODY-[MIND AND BODY]: *(Warriors know that the actions of seers are more complex than dividing man into mind and body; the memories of the left side are not trapped in our minds, they are locked away in other areas of our total being, areas that are used for "seeing", or more specifically, in positions of the assemblage point.)*

SELECTED REFERENCES: The Fire From Within - Page [53.1-53.5] ("Are those memories trapped in my...those other areas is to *see*.")
SEE ALSO: *MIND, BODY-PHYSICAL, REMEMBERING-BODY, INFORMATION-EXPERIENCE-STORAGE*

MIND-CULTIVATING-[CULTIVATING THE MIND]: *(Warriors know the importance of cultivating the mind in whatever form they can so that they might overcome their inherent naiveté.)*

SELECTED REFERENCES: The Art of Dreaming - Page [8.4-8.6] ("I can't explain to you why...is far too great to resist.)
SEE ALSO: *MIND*

MIND-FRAMES-FOUR-[THE FOUR FRAMES OF MIND]: *(Warriors know that the four frames of mind is another term for the four moods of stalking.)*

SELECTED REFERENCES: The Power of Silence - Page [244.5-244.6] ("Sorcerers use the four moods of...points to move to specific positions.")
SEE ALSO: *STALKING-MOODS-FOUR*

MIND-SEEKS-ONE-SIDE-ONLY-[THE MIND SEEKS ONLY ONE SIDE OF THINGS]: *(Warriors know that the mind has limits to its capacity to understand and make things comprehensible; it seeks only the first attention side of things.)*

SELECTED REFERENCES: A Separate Reality - Page [257.5-257.8] ("I think I understand what don...one side of this," he said.)
SEE ALSO: *UNDERSTANDING, EXPLANATION, INVENTORY, ATTENTION-FIRST, TONAL*

MIND-SOUNDNESS-[SOUNDNESS OF MIND]: SEE WARRIOR-SOBRIETY-[THE SOBRIETY OF THE WARRIOR], SANITY-[SANITY]

MINIMAL-CHANCE-WARRIOR-[THE WARRIORS' MINIMAL CHANCE]: SEE: WARRIOR-MINIMAL-CHANCE-[THE WARRIORS' MINIMAL CHANCE]

MIRACLE-[MIRACLE]: (Warriors know that a miracle is a manifestation of the nagual; a manifestation of the spirit perceived in conjunction with a movement of the assemblage point; when the tonal shrinks, extraordinary things are possible, but these miracles are only extraordinary for the tonal.)
SELECTED REFERENCES: The Power of Silence - Page [122.3-122.5] ("I explained to you then,...where miracles are commonplace.) Tales of Power - Page [158.8-158.9] ("But did they see me disappear...are only extraordinary for the tonal.)
SEE ALSO: NAGUAL, MAGIC, ABSTRACT, TONAL, TONAL-SHRINKING

MIRAGE-[MIRAGE]: (Warriors know that a mirage infiltrates our perspective as human beings; the soundness of the world is not the mirage; the mirage is the fixation of the assemblage point in any one spot; any new world which warriors may assemble is just as much a mirage as the world of our old fixation.)
SELECTED REFERENCES: Tales of Power - Page [98.2-98.7] ("We are perceivers," he proceeded...by your reason or by your will.) Tales of Power - Page [232.1-232.3] (But before we venture beyond this point...no way to close it again.") Tales of Power - Page [276.8-277.2] (Genaro and I have labored to give...nagual but also the indescribable tonal.) Tales of Power - Page [288.1-288.2] (Don Juan's voice brought forth another...blow that no one can parry.) The Fire From Within - Page [36.5] ("The first truth about awareness,...world of objects and it's not.) The Fire From Within - Page [37.2-37.9] ("The first truth is that the world...and yet unchanged, eternal.") The Fire From Within - Page [283.5-284.2] (He said that now I needed to have...a mirage as the old fixation.)
SEE ALSO: ASSEMBLAGE-POINT-FIXATION

MIRROR-NOT-REFLECT-IMAGE-[THE MIRROR THAT DOES NOT REFLECT OUR IMAGE]: (To the warrior apprentice, a man of knowledge appears to be a creature totally unlike the other human beings of the world in both demeanor and abilities; the man of knowledge appears to be a mirror, a mirror that does not reflect its own image.)
SELECTED REFERENCES: The Power of Silence - Page [181.1-181.3] (Everything had occurred so smoothly that...mirrors that did not yield reflection.) The Power of Silence - Page [226.3-226.8] ("You are not like any one...that he was just like us.)
SEE ALSO: MAN-KNOWLEDGE

MIRROR-SELF-REFLECTION-[THE MIRROR OF SELF-REFLECTION]: SEE: SELF-REFLECTION-MIRROR-[THE MIRROR OF SELF-REFLECTION]

MIRROR-STREAM-[THE MIRROR AND THE STREAM]-(TOP)

MITOTE-[MITOTE]: (Warriors know that a mitote is a ceremonial gathering for the purpose of encountering Mescalito.)
SELECTED REFERENCES: The Teachings of Don Juan - Page [143.8-144.1] (My last encounter with Mescalito was...ritual food was consumed each day.) A Separate Reality - Page [6.5-6.6] (He called peyote "Mescalito" and he...on the right way to live.) A Separate Reality - Page [25.4-26.7] (As soon as I woke up in the...another mitote and see for yourself?") A Separate Reality - Page [44.3-44.8] (On June 10, 1968, I started on...did not conform to his system.) A Separate Reality - Page [49.4-57.6] (We arrived in northeastern Mexico...on my part than being around.)
SEE ALSO: MESCALITO

MODERATION-WARRIOR-[THE WARRIORS' MODERATION]: SEE: WARRIOR-MODERATION-[THE WARRIORS' MODERATION]

MODERN-LIFE-[TURNING AWAY FROM MODERN LIFE]: SEE: LIFE-TURNING-AWAY-[TURNING AWAY FROM MODERN LIFE]

MOLD-ANIMALS-[THE MOLD OF THE ANIMALS]-(TOP)

MOLD-MAN-[THE MOLD OF MAN]: (Warriors know that the mold of man is that portion of the Eagle's emanations which seers can "see" directly without any danger to themselves; a pattern of energy that serves to stamp the qualities of humanness on an otherwise amorphous blob of biological matter; that which we call God; a static prototype of humanness without any power; a cast which groups together a bunch of fiber-like elements which we call man; the mold of man is always found in water holes and gullies because without water there is no mold; the mold of man feeds on water; the mold of man is the origin of man, the source of man; without the mold of man and the force of life there is no way for that force to assemble itself into the shape of man; the mold of man is a huge cluster of emanations in the great band of organic life; it is called the mold of man because it only appears inside the cocoon of man; the mold is not an omniscient creator, but the pattern of every human attribute conceivable; the mold stamps us with what we are but does not create us from nothing and make us in its image and likeness.)

SELECTED REFERENCES: The Second Ring of Power - Page [155.3-156.7] ("You don't know about the human mold...But your emptiness prevented you from seeing anything.) The Second Ring of Power - Page [157.4-158.4] ("Did you ever see the mold, Gorda?...what is the human form?") The Fire From Within - Page [258.8-259.5] (Don Juan reminded me that he...directly without any danger to themselves.") The Fire From Within - Page [261.8-263.7] (He gave me a detailed explanation of what...fiber-like elements, which we call man.) The Fire From Within - Page [265.1-265.3] (It was at that point that I realized...divinity that was in front of me.) The Fire From Within - Page [267.5-268.2] (I remembered then that I had...see the mold as a woman.) The Fire From Within - Page [269.3-270.2] ("There are two ways of seeing...me that my promise was worthless.) The Fire From Within - Page [290.8-291.1] (As that sacred light bathed me...the glory of heaven in the diaphanous light.)
SEE ALSO: GOD

*MOLD-MAN-SEEING-MALE-FEMALE-LIGHT-[SEEING THE MOLD OF MAN AS A MALE OR FEMALE OR SEEING IT AS A LIGHT]: (Warriors know that if they "see" the mold of man as a male or female figure instead of as an abstract entity, it is because their assemblage point does not have the stability to maintain its position and shifts laterally within man's band; if the assemblage point shifts into the midsection of man's band, the mold is seen as a light.)

SELECTED REFERENCES: The Fire From Within - Page [267.8-268.2] (I asked him why it was...see the mold as a woman.) The Fire From Within - Page [269.3-269.6] ("There are two ways of seeing....of man be seen and understood.)
SEE ALSO: ASSEMBLAGE-POINT-SHIFT-LATERAL, MOLD-MAN, GOD, EAGLE-EMANATIONS-MAN-BAND-MIDSECTION, MOLD-MAN-SEEING-WHY

MOLD-MAN-SEEING-WHY-[WHY SEERS RECOMMEND SEEING THE MOLD OF MAN]: SEE: ASSEMBLAGE-POINT-POSITION-MOLD-MAN-[THE POSITION OF THE ASSEMBLAGE-POINT WHERE THE MOLD OF MAN APPEARS]

MOLD-ORGANIC-SPECIES-[EVERY ORGANIC SPECIES HAS ITS OWN MOLD]: (Warriors know that every species has its own mold, and that every individual molded by this process shows characteristics particular to its own kind.)

SELECTED REFERENCES: The Fire From Within - Page [262.2] (He also said that every species has...characteristics particular to its own kind.)
SEE ALSO: MOLD-MAN, MOLD-ANIMALS-(TOP), MOLD-PLANTS-(TOP)

MOLD-PLANTS-[THE MOLD OF PLANTS]-(TOP)

MOMENT-SILENCE-[THE MOMENT OF SILENCE]: SEE: INNER-SILENCE-[INNER SILENCE]

MOMENTUM-WORLD-[THE MOMENTUM OF THE DAILY WORLD]: (*Warriors know that the momentum of the everyday world tends to carry us through our lives; warriors must make a sustained effort to break that momentum by no longer clinging to the world of reason.*)
      SELECTED REFERENCES: The Power of Silence - Page [226.8-227.1] ("I understand exactly what you are...structures. Don't you do the same.")
      SEE ALSO: *REASON-CLINGING, WORLD-EVERYDAY*

MONSTROUS-MAN-[THE MONSTROUS MAN]-(TOP): SEE: FISH-FACED-MAN-[THE FISH FACED MAN]-(TOP)

MOOD-FORMLESS-[MOOD SWINGS AND FORMLESSNESS]: SEE: SOBRIETY-FORMLESSNESS-[SOBRIETY AND FORMLESSNESS]

MOOD-FOUR-[THE FOUR MOODS]: SEE: WARRIOR-FEMALE-[FEMALE WARRIORS]

MOOD-SORCERER-ANCIENT-[THE MOOD OF THE ANCIENT SORCERERS]: SEE: SORCERER-ANTIQUITY-MOOD-[THE MOOD OF THE SORCERERS OF ANTIQUITY

MOOD-WARRIOR-[THE WARRIORS' MOOD]: SEE: WARRIOR-MOOD-[THE WARRIORS' MOOD]

MORALITY-[MORALITY]: (*Warriors know they must cultivate a sense of detachment from the concept of morality, a concept which they replace with the concept of impeccability; warriors are not concerned with morality, instead, they are concerned with frugality, thoughtfulness, simplicity, innocence and a lack of self-reflection as these attributes apply to an impeccable life; these qualities resemble morality but they are not; they simply represent the best use of the warriors' energy.*)
      SELECTED REFERENCES: Tales of Power - Page [135.1-135.2] ("What does it entail to see...that he is hopeless or helpless.) Tales of Power - Page [227.8-228.2] (Don Juan remained quiet for a moment...like a manual for monastic life, but it isn't.) The Fire From Within - Page [15.2-15.6] ("Warriors fight self-importance as a matter...you have to save enough energy yourself.") The Fire From Within - Page [57.7-57.9] ("Awareness develops from the moment of...terms of saving and rechanneling energy.") The Fire From Within - Page [198.9-199.2] ("He seems like a very selfish person...I envied him in that order.) The Power of Silence - Page [82.3-82.6] ("The real challenge for those sorcerers...that, they need morality and beauty.")
      SEE ALSO: *WARRIOR-IMPECCABILITY, BEAUTY*

MORTALITY-RATE-WARRIOR-[THE MORTALITY RATE OF WARRIORS]: SEE: WARRIOR-MORTALITY-RATE-[THE MORTALITY RATE OF WARRIORS]

MORTGAGES-[MORTGAGES]: SEE: LIENS-MORTGAGES-[LIENS AND MORTGAGES]

MOTH-[MOTH]: (*Warriors know that moths are friends and helpers to sorcerers.*)
      SELECTED REFERENCES: The Power of Silence - Page [92.9-93.6] (It started the last time you were...such a great emphasis on you.)
      SEE ALSO: *MOTH-(ALL)*

MOTH-CALL-[THE MOTH'S CALL]-(TOP): SEE: MOTH-SONG-[THE SONG OF THE MOTH]-(TOP)

MOTH-NIGHT-[THE NIGHT OF THE MOTH]-(TOP): SEE: KNOWLEDGE-APPOINTMENT-[AN APPOINTMENT WITH KNOWLEDGE]-(TOP)

MOTH-SONG-[THE SONG OF THE MOTH]-(TOP)

MOTH-STEP-CARLOS-NECK-[THE MOTH STEPS ON CARLOS' NECK]-(TOP)

MOTH-TALES-[TALES OF THE MOTH]-(TOP)

MOTOR-CONTROL-LOSS-OF-WARRIOR-[WARRIORS LOSE THEIR MOTOR CONTROL]: SEE: WARRIOR-MOTOR-CONTROL-LOSS-OF-[WARRIORS LOSE THEIR MOTOR CONTROL]

MOUNTAIN-GAZING-[MOUNTAIN GAZING]: SEE: GAZING-[GAZING]

MOUTH-ROOF-[THE AREA BEHIND THE ROOF OF THE MOUTH]: SEE: ATTENTION-DREAMING-[THE DREAMING ATTENTION]

MOVING-DREAMING-[MOVING IN DREAMING]-(TOP): SEE: WILL-MOVING -[MOVING BY THE WILL]-(TOP

MOVING-WILL-[MOVING BY THE WILL]-(TOP): SEE: WILL-MOVING-[MOVING BY THE WILL]-(TOP)

MUNI-CALIXTO-[CALIXTO MUNI]-(TOP): SEE: CALIXTO-MUNI-[CALIXTO MUNI]-(TOP)

MUSCULAR-DREAMING-[BECOMING MORE MUSCULAR THROUGH DREAMING]-(TOP): SEE: DREAMING-MUSCULAR-[BECOMING MORE MUSCULAR THROUGH DREAMING]-(TOP)

MUSEUM-OBJECTS-GAZING-[GAZING AT OBJECTS IN THE MUSEUM OF ANTHROPOLOGY AND HISTORY]-(TOP)

MUSHROOMS-[MUSHROOMS]: SEE: LITTLE-SMOKE-[LITTLE SMOKE]

MUTENESS-SORCERER-[THE SORCERERS' MUTENESS]: SEE: SORCERER-MUTENESS-[THE SORCERERS' MUTENESS]

MYSTERIES-RECEIVE-WARRIOR-[WARRIORS RECEIVE MYSTERIES]: SEE: WARRIOR-MYSTERIES-RECEIVES-[WARRIORS RECEIVE MYSTERIES]

MYSTERIOUS-FORCE-[THE MYSTERIOUS FORCE]: SEE: FORCE-MYSTERIOUS-[THE MYSTERIOUS FORCE]

MYSTERY-[MYSTERY]: SEE : WORLD-MYSTERIOUS-[THE MYSTERIOUS WORLD], MYSTERY-ULTIMATE-[THE ULTIMATE MYSTERY]

MYSTERY-ACCEPT-WARRIOR-[WARRIORS ACCEPT THE MYSTERY OF THEMSELVES]: SEE: WARRIOR-MYSTERY-ACCEPTS-[WARRIORS ACCEPT THE MYSTERY OF THEMSELVES]

MYSTERY-IS-PERCEIVING-[THE MYSTERY IS PERCEIVING]: *(Warriors know that the mystery is perceiving itself; not so much what we perceive, but what makes us perceive in the first place.)*

SELECTED REFERENCES: The Fire From Within - Page [125.1-125.5] ("The mystery is outside us...human senses perceive in inconceivable ways.")

SEE ALSO: *WORLD-MYSTERIOUS, PERCEPTION*

MYSTERY-ULTIMATE-[THE ULTIMATE MYSTERY]: *(Warriors know that the ultimate mystery is the mystery of the third attention.)*

SELECTED REFERENCES: The Eagle's Gift - Page [310.5-310.6] (The courier Juan Tuma said very...usher me into the ultimate mystery.)

SEE ALSO: *MYSTERY, WARRIOR-JOURNEY-DEFINITIVE, ATTENTION-THIRD*

N

NAGUAL-[THE NAGUAL]: (Warriors know that the nagual, pronounced (nah-wa'hl), is the abstract, intent, the indescribable, the second attention, the spirit; the nagual is one of the eight points on the sorcerers' diagram; the nagual is the left side, a realm of indescribable features, a realm impossible to contain in words.)

SELECTED REFERENCES: Tales of Power - Page [124.9-126.7] ("If the *tonal* is everything we know...The *nagual* is there, where power hovers.) Tales of Power - Page [127.8-128.6] ("I'm afraid I haven't asked the right...of the true pair, the *nagual*.") Tales of Power - Page [130.2-130.4] ("Does the *nagual* have consciousness?...but to simply recount its effects.") Tales of Power - Page [132.2-13.4] (The idea is that at the...without the binding force of life.") Tales of Power - Page [139.3-141.8] ("Let's say that they turned over...although I did not remember having stood up.) Tales of Power - Page [145.2-145.3] (But power comes from the nagual...the warrior's hour of power.") Tales of Power - Page [156.7-157.2] ("Once the man has been shoved...That was the time to watch.) Tales of Power - Page [158.8-159.1] ("But did they see me disappear...Can you feel what it is?") Tales of Power - Page [159.9-161.4] ("The *nagual*, once it learns to...Genaro may show you the *nagual*.") Tales of Power - Page [172.7-175.6] ("No. There's no explanation...been to work with your *tonal*.") Tales of Power - Page [177.9-180.6] ("The nagual can perform extraordinary things...will keep everything suspended," he said.) Tales of Power - Page [190.2-191.5] ("The *nagual* is gone," don Juan said...are not applicable to the *nagual*.") Tales of Power - Page [194.1-194.3] ("Through the air?...The two things don't jibe.") Tales of Power - Page [244.5-245.7] ("If they are used only to...excursions into the *nagual*, the unknown.") Tales of Power - Page [249.1-249.3] ("What would have happened if I...in the realm of the *nagual*.) Tales of Power - Page [250.7-250.8] ("*Dreaming* is a practical aid devised...the ultimate use of the *nagual*.") Tales of Power - Page [271.6-273.9] ("What Genaro wanted to show you...followed to arrive at that point.) Tales of Power - Page [276.2-278.3] ("Those leaps were only the beginning...indescribable void that contains everything.) Tales of Power - Page [283.9-284.1] ("I must also add that few...is a most appealing affair.) The Eagle's Gift - Page [15.5-15.7] ("The Atlanteans are the nagual; they...the opposite of the front row.") The Eagle's Gift - Page [163.4-163.5] (Don Juan had told us that...body, thus its resistance to conceptualization.) The Power of Silence - Page [11.2-11.5] ("Can you explain *intent* to me...the spirit, *intent*, the abstract.")

SEE ALSO: ABSTRACT, ATTENTION-SECOND, INTENT, SORCERER-DIAGRAM, EAGLE-EMANATIONS-DORMANT, NAGUAL-(ALL)

NAGUAL-APPRENTICE-COMPLIANCE-[THE COMPLIANCE OF THE APPRENTICE NAGUAL]-(TOP)

NAGUAL-ASSAULT-[THE ASSAULT OF THE NAGUAL]: (Warriors know that the actions of the nagual are deadly; if the nagual takes them by surprise and if they do not have enough energy to parry the nagual's assault, warriors know they will die; it is the warriors' tonal that protects warriors from the assaults of the nagual.)

SELECTED REFERENCES: A Separate Reality - Page [261.5-261.8] (The bafflement I experienced was as...in his effort to help me.) Tales of Power - Page [190.4-190.7] ("Tonight the nagual tried to make you...of my help or Genaro's concern.") The Power of Silence - Page [90.3-90.4] ("I know that at this moment your...from the onslaughts of the unknown.")

SEE ALSO: NAGUAL, TONAL-OVERSEER-PROTECTED

*NAGUAL-BLOW-[THE NAGUAL'S BLOW]: (Warriors know that the nagual's blow is a way in which the spirit touches the apprentice through the conduit of the nagual man or nagual woman; a "sorcerer's maneuver"; the apprentices' assemblage point is moved into a state of heightened awareness as a result of the nagual's blow; the physical blow delivered by the nagual is only a pacifier, a way of removing the apprentices' doubts and *jolting their bodies to give them confidence as they are being manipulated; the nagual's blow is a technique whereby a nagual man or nagual woman, by virtue of their extra strength, push the emphasis of the assemblage point away from the usual emanations of the first attention and make it shift to the neighboring dormant emanations; the new seers use this technique to guide their apprentices to learn about man's possibilities.)*

SELECTED REFERENCES: **The Eagle's Gift - Page [164.1-165.3]** (She said that sometimes he would even give...clear as I filled up my lungs.) **The Eagle's Gift - Page [245.6-245.8]** (Afterward I did not see don Juan...of my association with don Juan.) **The Eagle's Gift - Page [312.3-312.5]** (Don Juan pressed my back and relieved...but a movement of those emanations.) **The Fire From Within - Page [xi.7-xi.8]** (In order for don Juan to impart...palm of his hand on my upper back.) **The Fire From Within - Page [110.1-110.5]** ("This process of emphasizing certain...apprentices to learn about man's possibilities.) **The Fire From Within - Page [118.4-118.7]** ("The nagual's blow is of great...simply don't know about their possibilities.") **The Fire From Within - Page [122.2-123.2]** ("The assemblage point of man is located...ends up is always virgin ground.) **The Fire From Within - Page [145.5-145.9]** (Genaro turned to me and assured me...which never take place under ordinary circumstances.") **The Fire From Within - Page [178.4-178.6]** (I gently shook Genaro. He slowly...my back and restored my equilibrium.) **The Fire From Within - Page [224.7-224.8]** (As don Juan spoke to me...of awareness. And then I saw.) **The Fire From Within - Page [247.3-247.6]** ("It's time for you to shift that...and suddenly began to move again.) **The Fire From Within - Page [263.9-264.2]** (The more he talked, the greater...the most peaceful and exquisite beatitude.) **The Fire From Within - Page [265.5-265.6]** (The fervor I felt on *seeing*...and I lost sight of God.) **The Power of Silence - Page [xii.1-xii.5]** (On another occasion, he gave me...been hard as well as unexpected.) **The Power of Silence - Page [xvii.2-xvii.4]** (Moving one's assemblage point was...in a state of heightened awareness.) **The Power of Silence - Page [21.1-21.3]** (The nagual Elias, having made his decision,...and there he stopped dying.) **The Power of Silence - Page [21.8-22.2]** (The first thing the nagual Elias did...shift erratically once it was loose.) **The Power of Silence - Page [58.6-58.8]** (Don Juan used to repeat every chance he could...with the moving of the assemblage point.) **The Power of Silence - Page [66.3]** (So Belisario bid him good-bye...back repeatedly and with considerable force.) **The Power of Silence - Page [68.6-68.8]** (And as if to make sure...was being manipulated into heightened awareness.) **The Power of Silence - Page [71.4-71.5]** (By the time I realized it was a crude...found myself in a state of heightened awareness.) **The Power of Silence - Page [91.9-93.3]** (Again I interrupted don Juan...his fear, and he passed out.) **The Power of Silence - Page [119.4-120.4]** ("I've told you the nagual is...doubts are banished, anything is possible.") **The Power of Silence - Page [160.9-161.3]** ("You are forgetting something essential,"...tone of someone about to lose his patience.) **The Power of Silence - Page [161.9-162.9]** ("Let us see how you figure...mere presence of an impeccable nagual.") **The Power of Silence - Page [218.3-218.5]** (I asked him if he wanted to hear...a blow between my shoulder blades.) **The Art of Dreaming - Page [16.1-16.4]** (So, to make my assemblage point shift...see stars," he doubled up laughing.) **The Art of Dreaming - Page [17.1-17.5]** (Don Juan helped me to experience...he gives them abstract and detailed explanations.) **The Art of Dreaming - Page [23.9-24.1]** (I wanted a more precise explanation...sworn that his touch hypnotized me.)

SEE ALSO: *ASSEMBLAGE-POINT-MOVING, AWARENESS-HEIGHTENED, AWARENESS-MANIPULATION, RECOLLECTION-SORCERER, EAGLE-EMANATIONS-EMPHASIZED, NAGUAL, NAGUAL-BLOW-(ALL)*

NAGUAL-BLOW-ABERRANT-[THE ABERRANT USE OF THE NAGUAL'S BLOW BY THE OLD SEERS]: (Warriors know that the old seers used the nagual's blow in a practical way to keep their apprentices in bondage; they made them shift into heightened awareness, and while in that highly impressionable state, taught them aberrant techniques which made them into sinister men.)

SELECTED REFERENCES: **The Fire From Within - Page [110.1-110.5]** ("This process of emphasizing certain emanations...sinister men, just like their teachers.)

SEE ALSO: *NAGUAL-BLOW, SEER-OLD, ABERRATION-MORBIDITY, AWARENESS-HEIGHTENED, TOLTEC-GHOULS*

NAGUAL-BLOW-DEATH-*[THE NAGUAL'S BLOW OF FREEDOM CAN BE THE BLOW OF DEATH]:* (*Warriors know that if the recipient of the nagual's blow does not have sufficient energy to allow for the shift of the assemblage point, the nagual's blow is not the blow of freedom but the blow of death instead; the recipient of the nagual's blow must have energy to sustain the pressure of alignments which never take place under normal circumstances.*")
    SELECTED REFERENCES: The Fire From Within - Page [145.6-145.9] ("I once told you that the...never take place under ordinary circumstances.")
    SEE ALSO: NAGUAL-BLOW, ALIGNMENT-FORCE, NAGUAL

NAGUAL-BLOW-POSITIVE-*[THE POSITIVE USE OF THE NAGUAL'S BLOW BY THE NEW SEERS]: SEE: NAGUAL-BLOW-[THE NAGUAL'S BLOW]*

NAGUAL-BLOW-REQUISITES-*[THE REQUISITES OF THE NAGUAL'S BLOW]:* (*Warriors know that the nagual's blow must be delivered by a person with the strength of a nagual and with the ability to "see" the precise spot where the assemblage point is located on any given individual; it is equally useless to have the strength of a nagual and not "see" as it is to "see" and not have the strength of a nagual; without both requisites the results are just blows.*)
    SELECTED REFERENCES: The Fire From Within - Page [110.5-110.8] (Don Juan explained that the nagual's...able to strike the precise spot.)
    SEE ALSO: NAGUAL-BLOW, SEEING, NAGUAL-MAN-WOMAN, NAGUAL

NAGUAL-CREATIVITY-*[THE NAGUAL AND A DEMONSTRATION OF CREATIVITY]-(TOP)*

NAGUAL-ELIAS-*[THE NAGUAL ELIAS]-(TOP): SEE: ELIAS-NAGUAL-[THE NAGUAL ELIAS]-(TOP)*

NAGUAL-ENCOUNTERING-*[ENCOUNTERING THE NAGUAL]: SEE NAGUAL-FACING-[FACING THE NAGUAL]*

NAGUAL-ENERGY-LOAN-*[THE NAGUAL LOANS HIS ENERGY]-(TOP)*

NAGUAL-EXPRESSION-*[THE EXPRESSION OF THE NAGUAL]:* (*Warriors know that the expression of the nagual is a personal matter; it is up to individual warriors to arrange and rearrange their cluster of emanations, or the bubble of their perception.*)
    SELECTED REFERENCES: Tales of Power - Page [273.4-273.7] (I've said to you that the...is no way to reassemble that cluster.)
    SEE ALSO: NAGUAL, ANIMAL-FORMS-ADOPTING, PERCEPTION-BUBBLE

NAGUAL-EYES-[THE NAGUAL'S EYES]: SEE: NAGUAL-MAN-WOMAN-[THE NAGUAL MAN AND THE NAGUAL WOMAN]*

NAGUAL-FACING-[FACING THE NAGUAL]:* (*Warriors know that facing the nagual is a potentially deadly proposition; warriors know that one should never turn to one's left when facing the nagual because death is always to the warriors' left.*)
    SELECTED REFERENCES: Tales of Power - Page [171.4-171.5] (Don Juan extended his hand and...more dangerous than they already were.) Tales of Power - Page [172.8-172.9] "When one is dealing with the...in order to break the fixation.") Tales of Power - Page [173.7-174.6] ("Another thing one should do when facing...could even conceive witnessing the *nagual*.) Tales of Power - Page [179.3-179.8] (Genaro always cracks me up because...could admit

everything without admitting anything.) **Tales of Power - Page [186.6-186.7]** ("I must warn you," don Juan...direct physical contact with the *nagual*.") **Tales of Power - Page [188.5-188.7]** (He reminded me that once, years...of us in a different guise.) **Tales of Power - Page [190.2-190.7]** ("The nagual is gone," he said...of my help or Genaro's concern.") **Tales of Power - Page [229.6-229.7]** (Yesterday you let the wings of your...the last issue, the sorcerers' explanation.) **The Fire From Within - Page [72.3-72.4]** ("Oh, there is the mystery," he...The mystery can only be witnessed.") **The Fire From Within - Page [97.3-97.5]** (He said that the best way to...focusing all its power on sadness.)

SEE ALSO: *DEATH-TAP, DEPTH-VIEW, DEATH-LEFT, NAGUAL, POWER-ENCOUNTER*

NAGUAL-FEAR-[THE FEAR OF LOSING THE NAGUAL]: SEE: FEAR-NAGUAL-[THE FEAR OF LOSING THE NAGUAL]

NAGUAL-HEALING-[THE HEALING POWER OF THE NAGUAL]-(TOP)

NAGUAL-HOUR-[THE HOUR OF THE NAGUAL]: SEE: WARRIOR-HOUR-POWER-[THE WARRIORS' HOUR OF POWER]

NAGUAL-HYPNOTIC-SPELL-[THE HYPNOTIC SPELL OF THE NAGUAL]: (Warriors know that the spell of the nagual is more of a problem for men than it is for women; women deal with the second attention in a much more natural and intuitive way than men.)

SELECTED REFERENCES: **The Eagle's Gift - Page [268.7-268.9]** (I asked her if she minded...woman can liberate you from that.)

SEE ALSO: *WOMEN, NAGUAL, FEMALE-UNIVERSE*

NAGUAL-INDESCRIBABLE-[THE INDESCRIBABLE NAGUAL]: SEE: TONAL-INDESCRIBABLE-[THE INDESCRIBABLE TONAL], SORCERER-EXPLANATION-[THE SORCERERS' EXPLANATION]

NAGUAL-JULIAN-[THE NAGUAL JULIAN]-(TOP): SEE: JULIAN-NAGUAL-[THE NAGUAL JULIAN]-(TOP)

NAGUAL-KNOWLEDGE-DIFFICULT-[THE MOST DIFFICULT ASPECT OF THE NAGUAL'S KNOWLEDGE]: (Warriors know that the most difficult part of the nagual's knowledge is reaching out for the third point; the nagual intends the free movement of the assemblage point and the spirit channels to the nagual the means to accomplish it; as difficult as it is for the nagual to intend that free movement, it is nothing compared to the difficulty his disciples have in understanding what he is doing.)

SELECTED REFERENCES: **The Power of Silence - Page [224.3-224.5]** ("The most difficult aspect of the...effort to intend it for me.)

SEE ALSO: *NAGUAL-MAN-WOMAN, POINT-THIRD, ASSEMBLAGE-POINT-FREE-MOVEMENT, NAGUAL*

NAGUAL-LUMINOUS-[THE LUMINOUS ESSENCE OF THE NAGUAL]: (Warriors know that the luminous essence of the nagual is in everything and that a nagual man or woman can actually deposit some of that luminosity onto another person.)

SELECTED REFERENCES: **The Second Ring of Power - Page [33.1-33.3]** ("His touch changed people," she said...the Nagual more than death itself.) **The Second Ring of Power - Page [66.5-66.7]** ("The Nagual said that if I failed...more. You are the Nagual himself.") **The Second Ring of Power - Page [86.1-87.2]** (I automatically took her hand again...and made me jog on the spot.) **The Second Ring of Power - Page [89.1-89.3]** (I sat for a long while...in Rosa's hand with my blows.) **The Second Ring of Power - Page [119.8-120.8]** ("You said that I had a hole...and that we both were empty.") **The Second Ring of Power - Page [135.3-135.7]** ("Soledad has to take her edge...would then have come after us.) **The Second Ring of Power - Page [136.7-137.8]** ("Were they supposed to kill me too...you were about to annihilate them.") **The Second**

Ring of Power - Page [152.5] ("You're not a complete sorcerer yet...of place. They are no joke.") The Second Ring of Power - Page [164.9-165.1] ("The allies must come to you...even gave you his own call.") The Second Ring of Power - Page [224.6-226.9] (La Gorda said that I had more...to be properly called the nagual.)
  SEE ALSO: NAGUAL

NAGUAL-MAN-WOMAN-[THE NAGUAL MAN AND THE NAGUAL WOMAN]: (Warriors know that a nagual man or woman is a double being to whom the rule has been revealed; the nagual comes in male and female pairs; the pair becomes the nagual only after the rule has been told to each of them and each has understood it fully; to be a nagual entails being a leader, a teacher and a guide; a nagual has extraordinary energy, sobriety, endurance and stability; a nagual acts as an intermediary, channeling peace, harmony, laughter and knowledge directly from intent to their companions; a nagual is a conduit of the spirit; without the nagual's intervention, there can be no freedom; the nagual uses many types of maneuvers to act as a conduit for the spirit, many of which involve the use of a masterful sense of artifice and subterfuge; naguals cannot plan their course of action rationally, they must allow the spirit to decide their course; naguals can move their own assemblage point or the assemblage point of others with the shine of their eyes; in order to accomplish this movement naguals must be ruthless and thoroughly familiar with the place of no pity; underneath their mask of ruthlessness naguals are as cold as ice because that's what ruthlessness is, a total lack of pity.)

SELECTED REFERENCES: The Second Ring of Power - Page [93.4-93.9] ("Do you envy la Gorda for...the Nagual was a new life.) The Eagle's Gift - Page [117.2-124.9] (La Gorda and I went through a...We must snap out of it.") The Eagle's Gift - Page [173.8-174.5] (For the purpose of guiding living...nourish, enhance, and lead to freedom.) The Eagle's Gift - Page [218.5-218.6] (The Nagual woman and don Juan...were one and the same being.) The Eagle's Gift - Page [223.7-223.9] (Almost immediately after finding me...as partners in an inconceivable enterprise.) The Eagle's Gift - Page [228.7-228.9] (When Don Juan put the Nagual woman...to be lived with the spirit.) The Eagle's Gift - Page [312.3-312.5] (Don Juan pressed my back and relieved...but a movement of those emanations.) The Fire From Within - Page [x.9-xi.2] (He had also explained that seers...being a leader, being a teacher and a guide.) The Fire From Within - Page [112.8-113.2] (He said that the glow of awareness...after which the experiences are immediately forgotten.) The Fire From Within - Page [264.9-265.1] ("You can't tell the nagual off,"...The nagual is the guide.") The Power of Silence - Page [xiii.5-xiii.8] (Then he explained the role of the...the awareness of one's connection with intent.) The Power of Silence - Page [10.6-10.7] ("Why are the naguals called 'benefactors'...guides them through unimaginable areas.") The Power of Silence - Page [20.2-20.4] (And then the nagual saw that in relaxing...not been for the black shadow of death.) The Power of Silence - Page [42.5-43.2] (He stressed that in order to...simple or the most complex labyrinths.") The Power of Silence - Page [119.5-119.6] ("I've told you the nagual is the conduit...spirit express itself through him.) The Power of Silence - Page [130.4-131.4] (Don Juan began to explain what...is especially true for the naguals.") The Power of Silence - Page [133.3-133.9] ("I'm not a rational man," he continued...gives you the impression of warmth.) The Power of Silence - Page [151.8-152.1] (He then took my experience of...tell him what I could remember.) The Power of Silence - Page [161.9-162.9] ("Let us see how you figure...mere presence of an impeccable nagual.") The Power of Silence - Page [176.2] ("I am the nagual Julian...there is no way to freedom.") The Power of Silence - Page [188.4-188.7] (For the first time since he had...his chance to be with them.) The Art of Dreaming - Page [10.2-10.6] (Don Juan was certainly right about...leader of a party of sorcerers.) The Art of Dreaming - Page [143.9-144.3] (Yet all this wealth of experience...of the assemblage point ." he said.) The Art of Dreaming - Page [188.1-188.2] ("Women in general have a natural bent...the nagual woman, has superb energy.") The Art of Dreaming - Page [202.4-202.7] (He seemed to making a serious effort...nagual Julian to compare you with.") The Art of Dreaming - Page [205.1-205.2] ("Judging by the way you're talking...I am merely its agent.") The Art of Dreaming - Page [210.3-210.4] ("I can't tell you what to do...it or to ask without asking.")

SEE ALSO: *RULE, NAGUAL, SPIRIT-CONDUIT, ARTIFICE-SUBTERFUGE, RUTHLESSNESS-MASK*

NAGUAL-MAN-WOMAN-DUTY-[THE DUTIES OF A NAGUAL MAN OR A NAGUAL WOMAN]: (The duties of the nagual man and the nagual woman.)
SELECTED REFERENCES: **The Fire From Within** - Page [49.3-49.5] (I asked him why he had changed...said, but in a different way.")
SEE ALSO: *EXPLANATION, WARRIOR-TERMS, NAGUAL-MAN-WOMAN*

NAGUAL-MAN-WOMAN-FREEDOM-[THE FREEDOM THAT MAKES A NAGUAL]: (Warriors know that a nagual comes and goes without leaving a trace; it is that freedom that makes a nagual.)
SELECTED REFERENCES: **The Fire From Within** - Page [210.4-210.5] ("A nagual never lets anyone know...is what makes him a nagual.")
SEE ALSO: *NAGUAL-MAN-WOMAN, WARRIOR-FREEDOM, WARRIOR-FINESSE, WARRIOR-LIGHTNESS, WARRIOR-INACCESSIBILITY, WARRIOR-DELICACY*

NAGUAL-MANEUVER-[THE NAGUAL'S MANEUVERS]: SEE: *NAGUAL-MAN-WOMAN*-[THE NAGUAL MAN AND THE NAGUAL WOMAN]

NAGUAL-MASQUERADE-[THE NAGUAL'S MASQUERADE]: (Warriors know that naguals always give the impression of being something they are not; and they do it so completely that everyone believes their masquerade.)
SELECTED REFERENCES: **The Power of Silence** - Page [131.4-131.7] (He said that each nagual developed...know them best, believe their masquerade.")
SEE ALSO: *NAGUAL, RUTHLESSNESS-MASK*

**NAGUAL-PARTY-WARRIORS*-[THE NAGUAL'S PARTY OF WARRIORS]: (Warriors know that the nagual is a leader of a group of seers known as the nagual's party; that party of seers is composed of a nagual man and woman, a group of female warriors, a group of male warriors and at least one courier.)
SELECTED REFERENCES: **The Eagle's Gift** - Page [173.8-178.5] (For the purpose of guiding living...must be added in multiples of four.) **The Eagle's Gift** - Page [188.4-229.2] (When don Juan judged that the time...members of don Juan's own party.) **The Fire From Within** - Page [xi.2-xi.7] (In his teachings for the left side...together with the nagual woman Carol.) **The Fire From Within** - Page [171.4-171.5] ("Silvio Manuel, Genaro, and Vicente were...is why Genaro is helping you.") **The Power of Silence** - Page [74.4-75.7] (Two men, perhaps in their mid-fifties...other two, yet seemed infinitely stronger.) **The Art of Dreaming** - Page [ix.5-ix.8] (I have already described all this...I was supposed to lead them.)
SEE ALSO: *RULE, NAGUAL-MAN-WOMAN, WARRIOR-FEMALE, WARRIOR-MALE*

NAGUAL-PERCEPTION-[THE NAGUAL'S PERCEPTION]: (Warriors know that the lines of the world guide the nagual's perception in the same way as the eyes guide the tonal's perception.)
SELECTED REFERENCES: **Tales of Power** - Page [258.6-258.8] (They said that I should not be...up from the ravine to the rock.)
SEE ALSO: *LINES-WORLD, TONAL-PERCEPTION, SEEING, NAGUAL*

NAGUAL-PLUNGING-[PLUNGING INTO THE NAGUAL]: (Warriors know that plunging into the nagual is another term for being hurled into the unknown.)
SELECTED REFERENCES: **Tales of Power** - Page [245.4-245.7] ("Here is where I varied from the...true excursions into the *nagual*, the unknown.") **Tales of Power** - Page [273.7-273.9] ("I have called that cluster the...followed to arrive at that point.")
SEE ALSO: *NAGUAL, UNKNOWN-JOURNEY, UNKNOWN*

NAGUAL-PRESENCE-[THE PRESENCE OF THE NAGUAL]: (Warriors know that an apprentice can experience a shift in the position of the assemblage point simply as a result of the presence of the nagual.)
SELECTED REFERENCES: The Power of Silence - Page [119.3-119.7] (I remarked that his statements that...It is as simple as that.")
SEE ALSO: SPIRIT-CONTACT, NAGUAL, SPIRIT, INTENT, NAGUAL-BLOW, NAGUAL-MAN-WOMAN

NAGUAL-PROPS-TONAL-[THE NAGUAL PROPS UP THE TONAL]: (Warriors know they must learn to balance talking with action so that the tonal and nagual come to balance each other; the tonal has to be convinced with reasons while the nagual must be convinced with actions until one props up the other.)
SELECTED REFERENCES: Tales of Power - Page [160.8-161.1] ("Any threat to the tonal always...That boosting is called personal power.")
SEE ALSO: NAGUAL, TONAL, TALKING, WARRIOR-ACTING, BALANCE

NAGUAL-ROSENDO-[THE NAGUAL ROSENDO]-(TOP): SEE: ROSENDO-NAGUAL-[THE NAGUAL ROSENDO]-(TOP)

NAGUAL-RULE-[THE RULE OF THE NAGUAL]-(TOP): SEE: RULE-NAGUAL [THE RULE OF THE NAGUAL]-(TOP)

NAGUAL-RUMBLE-[THE RUMBLE OF THE NAGUAL]-(TOP)

NAGUAL-SURFACES-[THE NAGUAL SURFACES]: (Warriors know that the moment when the nagual surfaces is the moment when it becomes fully operative and the tonal becomes aware of the totality of the self.)
SELECTED REFERENCES: Tales of Power - Page [132.1-132.2] ("I was concerned with those jolts...aware of the totality of oneself.) Tales of Power - Page [158.7-160.6] ("What did the people in the...it does, it terrifies the tonal.)
SEE ALSO: NAGUAL, INSANE-RELATIVE, PAIR-TRUE, TONAL

NAGUAL-SUSPENDS-EVERYTHING-[THE NAGUAL SUSPENDS EVERYTHING]: (An inexplicable effect of the nagual; the nagual can keep the normal time of the tonal suspended during its "time", the time of the nagual.)
SELECTED REFERENCES: Tales of Power - Page [180.5-180.6] ("We are going back to the...will keep everything suspended," he said.)
SEE ALSO: NAGUAL, NAGUAL-TIME

NAGUAL-TASK-[THE NAGUAL'S TASK]: (Warriors know that every nagual must face the task of being left behind to reorganize everything that has been done to him by his teacher and his benefactor; the most crucial part of the nagual's task is reaching out for the third point; the nagual intends the free movement of the assemblage point and the spirit channels to the nagual the means to accomplish it.)
SELECTED REFERENCES: The Fire From Within - Page [212.7-212.8] ("That's precisely the point," don Juan...task every nagual has to face.) The Power of Silence - Page [224.3-224.5] ("The most difficult aspect of the...effort to intend it for me.)
SEE ALSO: NAGUAL, BENEFACTOR, TEACHERS-TEACHING

*NAGUAL-THREE-PRONGED-[THE THREE-PRONGED NAGUAL]: (Warriors know that instead of having four compartments of energy, the three-pronged nagual has only three; such an unstable natural configuration makes the three-pronged nagual more akin to the sorcerers of antiquity.)
SELECTED REFERENCES: The Eagle's Gift - Page [230.4-232.4] (Don Juan and his warriors sat...of what to do about it.) The Fire From Within - Page [x.9-xi.2] (He had also

explained that seers...become naguals after learning to *see*.) **The Power of Silence - Page [131.4-131.6]** (He said that each nagual developed...behind a mask of indulgence and laxness.) **The Art of Dreaming - Page [ix.8-x.1]** (However, working with me he realized...more akin to my energetic structure.)
    SEE ALSO: *NAGUAL-MAN-WOMAN, DOUBLE-BEINGS*

NAGUAL-TIME-[IN NAGUAL'S TIME]: (*Warriors know that nagual's time is the specialized time frame of the nagual; a time frame independent of reason and the parameters of the tonal; the recipient of the nagual's energy is no longer in his own time, he is in the time of the nagual.*)
    SELECTED REFERENCES: **Tales of Power - Page [157.5-157.6]** ("But you were next to me...with the body, not the reason.") **Tales of Power - Page [194.1-194.3]** ("No. For the *nagual* there is no...The two things don't jibe.") **The Eagle's Gift - Page [243.4-243.5]** (I assume that the whole event...on our way to Mexico City.) **The Power of Silence - Page [72.7-72.8]** ("Your assemblage point moved to heightened...are in mine. I drink water.")
    SEE ALSO: *TIME, NAGUAL, NAGUAL-SUSPENDS-EVERYTHING*

NAGUAL-TONNAGE-[THE NAGUAL TONNAGE]-(TOP)

NAGUAL-TRACE-LEAVES-NO-[THE NAGUAL LEAVES NO TRACE]: SEE: *NAGUAL-MAN-WOMAN-FREEDOM-[THE FREEDOM THAT MAKES A NAGUAL], WARRIOR-DELICACY-[THE WARRIORS' DELICACY]*

NAGUAL-TRICKS-APPRENTICE-[THE NAGUAL TRICKS HIS APPRENTICE]: (*Warriors know the first thing the nagual does with his prospective apprentice is to trick him; in other words, he gives him a jolt on his connecting link to the spirit; the nagual can do this in two ways, one through semi-normal channels and the other through outright sorcery.*)
    SELECTED REFERENCES: **The Power of Silence - Page [54.5-54.6]** (The first thing a nagual does...which my benefactor used on me.) **The Power of Silence - Page [55.3-55.7]** (When he had recovered enough and...inorganic being, a formless energy field.")
    SEE ALSO: *SPIRIT-TRICKERY, NAGUAL-MAN-WOMAN, ARTIFICE-SUBTERFUGE*

NAGUAL-TRUSTING-[TRUSTING THE NAGUAL]: (*Warriors know that the apprentice must learn to trust the nagual implicitly and accept him without bias as the nagual; trusting the nagual is absolutely necessary if the warrior is to have any possibility of clearing the debris from his life in order to find freedom.*)
    SELECTED REFERENCES: **The Art of Dreaming - Page [10.2-11.4]** (Don Juan was certainly right about...he was striving to teach me.)
    SEE ALSO: *NAGUAL-MAN-WOMAN*

NAGUAL-UNCONTESTED-AWARENESS-[THE NAGUAL IS THE LAST UNCONTESTED AREA OF AWARENESS]: (*Warriors know that the nagual is the last uncontested area of awareness; for warriors with the proper spirit, the tyranny of the first attention can drive them mercilessly to discover this final refuge of the tonal.*)
    SELECTED REFERENCES: **Tales of Power - Page [138.6-139.6]** ("Indians are the losers of our time...even have the idea that it exists.")
    SEE ALSO: *TONAL-REFUGE-NAGUAL, TYRANNY-HELL-BLISS, ATTENTION-FIRST*

*NAGUAL-WHISPERING-[THE WHISPERING OF THE NAGUAL]:
(Warriors know that listening for the nagual involves a particular range of auditory perception around one ear which allows warriors to hear everything with incredible fidelity.)
SELECTED REFERENCES: Tales of Power - Page [194.3-194.8] (As don Juan spoke I felt...sensations. I know you will succeed.)
SEE ALSO: NAGUAL

NAGUAL-WIND-[THE NAGUAL WIND]: (Warriors know that the nagual wind is a real wind which is capable of blowing one's life away; it is a wind that blows everything on earth; the wind that heralds the arrival of the dreaming body; the wind that spins the warrior with the ally; the wind that blows through the crack in the world.)
SELECTED REFERENCES: The Teachings of Don Juan - Page [185.7-186.3] (When the convulsions do not stop...blown to the ends of the other world.) Tales of Power - Page [177.3-177.5] (But when his *tonal* shrinks,...You took it as a joke, though.") The Second Ring of Power - Page [166.5-166.7] (I had the clear impression...through the door she had opened.) The Second Ring of Power - Page [168.4-168.5] (Once the door was opened...instead of blowing me away.) The Second Ring of Power - Page [213.8-213.9] ("What did Soledad say Eligio did?"...any of them, so they let him go.) The Second Ring of Power - Page [257.8-257.9] (I also knew that la Gorda...like a giant, weightless leaf.) The Eagle's Gift - Page [223.7-223.9] (Almost immediately after finding me...as partners in an inconceivable enterprise.) The Eagle's Gift - Page [228.7-228.9] (When Don Juan put the Nagual woman...to be lived with the spirit.) The Eagle's Gift - Page [295.8-295.9] (The result of our last meeting was even...something that held no meaning for me.) The Eagle's Gift - Page [314.2] (And then there was only...And then the lights were gone.) The Fire From Within - Page [76.8-76.9] ("Do you notice anything in the room...was nothing to notice in there.) The Fire From Within - Page [117.3-117.4] (But just before it hit me...wind carried with me tremendous speed.) The Fire From Within - Page [131.2] (I was only a few feet...people when something swished me away.) The Fire From Within - Page [211.8-211.9] (The next thing I knew, I...I was with don Juan and don Genaro.) The Fire From Within - Page [245.8] (I felt extraordinarily sad for those...sort of wind scooped them away.) The Fire From Within - Page [272.5-273.1] ("The *dreaming body* is known by...and nearly scared me to death.) The Fire From Within - Page [274.4-274.6] (I watched in fascination and realized that...as if trying to blow him away.) The Fire From Within - Page [296.2-296.3] (My assemblage point was moving...windlike force blew the world away.) The Art of Dreaming - Page [24.9-25.1] (I was about to realize what was...I wanted to tell don Juan.) The Art of Dreaming - Page [42.7-42.8] (As I was watching a window...through the window to the outside.) The Art of Dreaming - Page [155.9] (Then something like a wind came...disarranged everything, and erased my view.) The Art of Dreaming - Page [157.6-157.7] (A notable feature of these dreams...hover over it, like a hummingbird.)
SEE ALSO: DREAMING-BODY, CRACK-WORLDS, ALLIES-SPINNING, NAGUAL

NAGUAL-WITNESSES-FOUR-[THE FOUR WITNESSES TO THE NAGUAL]-(TOP)

NAGUAL-WITNESSES-THREE-[THREE WITNESSES TO THE NAGUAL]-(TOP)

NAGUAL-WITNESSING-[WITNESSING THE NAGUAL]: SEE: NAGUAL-FACING-[FACING THE NAGUAL]

NAGUAL-WOMAN-[THE NAGUAL WOMAN]-(TOP)

NAGUAL-WOMAN-FINDING-[FINDING CAROL THE NAGUAL WOMAN AND OLINDA THE NAGUAL WOMAN]-(TOP): SEE: FINDING-NAGUAL-WOMAN-[HOW POWER FOUND CAROL THE NAGUAL WOMAN AND OLINDA THE NAGUAL WOMAN]-(TOP)

NAGUAL-WOMAN-LEAVING-[LEAVING THE NAGUAL WOMAN]-(TOP)

NAGUAL-WOMAN-REMEMBERING-[REMEMBERING THE NAGUAL WOMAN]-(TOP)

NAGUALISM-[NAGUALISM]: (Warriors know that nagualism is the most appropriate name for the warrior-sorcerer's knowledge.)
SELECTED REFERENCES: The Power of Silence - Page [ix.5-ix.7] (At various times don Juan attempted...although he admitted it was not really accurate.)
SEE ALSO: *KNOWLEDGE, INTENT-MASTERY, TOTAL-FREEDOM, SORCERY*

NAGUALS-TWO-[THE TWO NAGUALS]-(TOP)

NAMES-CALLING-[THE CALLING OF NAMES]: (Warriors know that the calling of names is a serious matter, reserved for times of great stress or need.)
SELECTED REFERENCES: The Teachings of Don Juan - Page [56.5-56.6] (He also said there were other...the life of whoever seeks knowledge.)
SEE ALSO: *TALKING*

NATURAL-REALM-[THE NATURAL REALM]: (Warriors know that the natural realm is another term for the first attention.)
SELECTED REFERENCES: The Art of Dreaming - Page [vii.7-vii.9] (In anthropological works, shamanism is described...between the natural and supernatural realms.)
SEE ALSO: *ATTENTION-FIRST, SUPERNATURAL-REALM*

NEEDS-[NEEDS]: (Warriors know that any individual's attachment to self-reflection is felt as need; there are some people who need no one, they get peace, harmony, laughter and knowledge directly from the spirit, they need no intermediaries, whereas those who are needy do need an intermediary to provide a minimal chance to help shatter the mirror of their self-reflection.)
SELECTED REFERENCES: The Power of Silence - Page [158.4-158.8] ("Each of us has a different degree...real help you've gotten from me.")
SEE ALSO: *INTERMEDIARY, SELF-REFLECTION, WORLD-EVERYDAY*

NEEDS-CONCRETE-[CONCRETE NEEDS]: (Warriors know they must learn to trade their concrete needs for the warriors' abstract purpose, the pursuit of freedom.)
SELECTED REFERENCES: The Power of Silence - Page [187.9-188.4] (As he lay helpless in bed...when his concrete needs overpowered him.)
SEE ALSO: *WARRIOR-ABSTRACT-PURPOSE, FREEDOM*

NELIDA-[NELIDA]-(TOP): SEE: NORTH-[NORTHERLY WOMEN]-(TOP)

NESTOR-TEETH-[NESTOR'S TEETH]-(TOP)

NETHERWORLD-[NETHERWORLD]: SEE: INORGANIC BEINGS-REALM-[THE REALM OF THE INORGANIC BEINGS]

NIGHT-EDGE-[THE EDGE OF THE NIGHT]: (Warriors know that the edge of the night is another term for the edge of the unknown.)
SELECTED REFERENCES: Journey to Ixtlan - Page [166.9-167.2] (Then don Juan came very close..."The night is out there.")
SEE ALSO: *DARKNESS-DAY*

NINCOMPOOP-DIE-FRIGHT-[A NINCOMPOOP WHO COULD DIE OF FRIGHT]-(TOP)

NON-ORDINARY-REALITY-[NON-ORDINARY REALITY]: SEE: REALITY-NON-ORDINARY-[NON-ORDINARY REALITY]

NORMALCY-RETURN-[THE RETURN TO NORMALCY]: *(Warriors know that the average man craves a return to normalcy after experiencing a dramatic movement of his assemblage point; the warriors' need to close the gap after coming into dramatic contact with the unknown.)*
SELECTED REFERENCES: The Power of Silence - Page [228.3-228.5] (Don Juan remarked that we do not...craving the return to normalcy.)
SEE ALSO: *GAP, WARRIOR-SHIELDS, WARRIOR-PATH, NAGUAL-FACING*

*NORTH-[NORTHERLY WOMEN]: *(Warriors know that the northerly woman is the second of a nagual's party of female warriors; she is called strength; she is resourceful, blunt, direct, tenacious, like a hard wind; northerly women are utterly womanly, vain, coquettish, concerned with their aging, and terribly direct and impatient.)*
SELECTED REFERENCES: The Eagle's Gift - Page [174.5-174.8] (The female warriors are called the...shy, warm, like hot wind.) The Eagle's Gift - Page [185.6-186.2] (A group composed of two sets of...lose their composure and be raving mad.)
SEE ALSO: *WARRIOR-FEMALE*

*NOT-DOING-[NOT-DOING]: *(Warriors know that not-doing is any unfamiliar act which engages our total being by forcing it to become conscious of its luminous segment; the opposite of doing; doing is anything that is part of a whole for which we have a cognitive account, while not-doing is an element that does not belong to the charted whole; one of three techniques warriors use to stop the world; any activity designed to engage the second attention.)*
SELECTED REFERENCES: Journey to Ixtlan - Page [160.2-160.4] (I told him that I was simply...rather in what you don't do.") Journey to Ixtlan - Page [180.5-181.5] ("I've told you that the secret...been soaked for hours in "not-doing.") Journey to Ixtlan - Page [194.4-194.5] (*"Not-doing* is very simple...through the technique of *not-doing."*) Journey to Ixtlan - Page [195.8-195.9] ("Look at the shadow of that boulder,"...like doors, the doors of *not-doing.*) Journey to Ixtlan - Page [212.1-212.2] ("You see," he continued, "every one of us...he can spin another world.") Journey to Ixtlan - Page [212.8-212.9] ("We all have been taught to agree...is equally miraculous, and powerful.") Journey to Ixtlan - Page [213.2-213.4] (I changed the subject and asked...It would have only injured you.") Journey to Ixtlan - Page [247.3-247.4] (We are both beings who are...taught you and *stop the world.*") Tales of Power - Page [105.8-105.9] ("It depends on your personal power,"...I should say that you're doing fine.") Tales of Power - Page [250.2-250.9] (Don Juan then gave me a step-by-step...forced me to engage in the gait of power.) The Eagle's Gift - Page [17.5-17.6] ("The Nagual said that it was...figures that were put on the walls.) The Eagle's Gift - Page [18.2-18.3] (He had also said that one...conscious of its luminous segment.) The Eagle's Gift - Page [20.7-21.5] (We had discussed this in detail...but the principle was sound.) The Eagle's Gift - Page [22.9-23.2] (Don Juan had described *dreaming* to me...portion of their lives spent in slumber.) The Eagle's Gift - Page [135.7-135.9] (The residue of consciousness, which don Juan... "*not doing* of talking to oneself.") The Power of Silence - Page [165.4-165.7] (He reminded me that he had described...did not belong in that charted whole.) The Art of Dreaming - Page [25.9] (To intend is to wish without wishing, to do without doing.)
SEE ALSO: *DOING, STOPPING-WORLD, NOT-DOING-(ALL), DOING*

NOT-DOING-BODY-[THE BODY DOES NOT-DOING]: *(Warriors know that it is the body that does not-doing; there is no way for warriors to really talk about not doing because not-doing implies the disconnection from all logical and rational processes of "doing".)*
SELECTED REFERENCES: Journey to Ixtlan - Page [188.1-188.2] ("I don't know what you're talking about...is the body that does it.") Journey to Ixtlan - Page [212.5] ("Your difficulty is that you haven't...doesn't know *not-doing*," he said.)
SEE ALSO: *KNOWLEDGE-VS-LANGUAGE, DOING-VS-NOT-DOING, BODY-PHYSICAL*

NOT-DOING-DEVICE-[THE NOT-DOING DEVICE]-(TOP)

NOT-DOING-DOORS-[THE DOORS OF NOT-DOING]: (Warriors know that shadows are like the doors of not-doing; warriors can tell a man's innermost feelings by watching his shadow.)
SELECTED REFERENCES: Journey to Ixtlan - Page [195.8-195.9] ("Look at the shadow of that boulder,"...feelings of men by watching their shadows.") Journey to Ixtlan - Page [199.5-199.6] ("During the day shadows are the...taught you the gait of power.")
SEE ALSO: NOT-DOING, SHADOWS

NOT-DOING-EXERCISE-[THE EXERCISE OF NOT-DOING]-(TOP)

NOT-DOING-EXERCISE-PHYSICAL-[THE NOT-DOING OF PHYSICAL EXERCISE]: (Warriors know that once they have reached a certain level of personal power, physical exercise becomes unnecessary; at that point, warriors need only engage themselves in not-doing to remain in impeccable form.)
SELECTED REFERENCES: Journey to Ixtlan - Page [194.9-195.1] (I felt terribly embarrassed that don Juan...to engage oneself in "not-doing.")
SEE ALSO: NOT-DOING

NOT-DOING-FEELING-[FEELING THE LINES OF THE WORLD]-(TOP): SEE: NOT-DOING-EXERCISE [THE EXERCISE OF NOT-DOING-(TOP)

NOT-DOING-NOTES-[THE NOT-DOING OF TAKING NOTES]: (The process of taking notes by writing with the tip of the finger; rather than focusing the first attention on the process of remembering, this procedure focuses the second attention on the task of remembering instead.)
SELECTED REFERENCES: The Eagle's Gift - Page [20.6-21.5] (We had discussed this in detail...but the principle was sound.) The Fire From Within - Page [113.5-113.7] (He reminded me that Genaro was always...reemphasizing the emanations that were used.)
SEE ALSO: NOT-DOING, WRITING-SORCERY-EXERCISE

NOT-DOING-PERSONAL-LIFE-[THE NOT-DOING OF A MALE WARRIORS' PERSONAL LIFE]: (Warriors know that the not-doing of their personal lives consists of telling endless stories, but not a single one about their real self.)
SELECTED REFERENCES: The Eagle's Gift - Page [269.3-269.6] ("I beg your pardon," I said...you needed a lot of work.)
SEE ALSO: NOT-DOING, PERSONAL-HISTORY-ERASING, WARRIOR-FOG-CREATE

NOT-DOING-PLACES-[PLACES OF NOT-DOING]: (Warriors know there are places of not-doing, places like the pyramids where warriors can do their dreaming and exercise their second attention; these places are traps of the second attention.)
SELECTED REFERENCES: The Eagle's Gift - Page [17.4-17.6] ("The Nagual said that it was a guide...that were put on the walls.)
SEE ALSO: PYRAMIDS, NOT-DOING, SECOND-ATTENTION-TRAPPING

NOT-DOING-RING-[THE RING OF NOT-DOING]: (Warriors know that the ring of not-doing is the second ring of power; the warriors' ring of power.)
SELECTED REFERENCES: Journey to Ixtlan - Page [212.1-212.2] ("You see," he continued, "every one...he can spin another world.")
SEE ALSO: POWER-RING-SECOND, NOT-DOING, ATTENTION-SECOND

<u>NOT-DOING-SEEING</u>-[NOT-DOING, STOPPING THE WORLD AND SEEING]: *(Warriors know that "seeing" is the final accomplishment of a man of knowledge and that "seeing" is attained only after one has stopped the world through the technique of not-doing.)*
    SELECTED REFERENCES: **Journey to Ixtlan - Page [194.4-194.5]** ("*Not-doing* is very simple but...through the technique of *not-doing*.") **Journey to Ixtlan - Page [247.3-247.4]** (We are both beings who are...taught you and *stop the world*.")
    SEE ALSO: NOT-DOING, SEEING, STOPPING-WORLD

<u>NOT-DOING-SELF</u>-[THE NOT-DOINGS OF THE SELF]: *(Warriors know that the not-doings of the self are various techniques which are used to develop the second attention; these techniques include such things as erasing personal history, losing self importance, and disrupting routines.)*
    SELECTED REFERENCES: **The Eagle's Gift - Page [290.4-290.5]** (Her benefactor thought that a profound...losing self-importance, breaking routines and so forth.)
    SEE ALSO: ATTENTION-SECOND, PERSONAL-HISTORY-ERASING, SELF-IMPORTANCE-LOSING, ROUTINES-DISRUPTING, RECAPITULATION, BEING-DIE

<u>NOT-DOING-SILVIO-MANUEL</u>-[THE NOT-DOINGS OF SILVIO MANUEL]-(TOP)

<u>NOT-DOING-SLEEP</u>-[THE NOT-DOING OF SLEEP]: *(Warriors know that dreaming is intrinsically the not-doing of sleep.)*
    SELECTED REFERENCES: **The Eagle's Gift - Page [22.9-23.3]** (Don Juan had described *dreaming*... alleged extra body, the *dreaming body*.)
    SEE ALSO: NOT-DOING, DREAMING-ART, SLEEP

<u>NOT-DOING-SOAKING-BODY</u>-[SOAKING THE BODY IN NOT-DOING]-(TOP)

<u>NOT-DOING-TALKING</u>-[THE NOT-DOING OF TALKING TO ONESELF]: *(Warriors know that stopping the internal dialogue is the not-doing of talking to oneself.)*
    SELECTED REFERENCES: **The Eagle's Gift - Page [135.7-135.9]** (The residue of consciousness, which don Juan... "*not doing* of talking to oneself.")
    SEE ALSO: NOT-DOING, INTERNAL-DIALOGUE

<u>NOT-DOING-WALKING-BACKWARDS</u>-[THE NOT-DOING OF WALKING BACKWARD]-(TOP): SEE: NOT-DOING-DEVICE-[THE NOT-DOING DEVICE]-(TOP)

<u>NOTES-BUNDLES-WALKING</u>-[BUNDLES OF WALKING NOTES]-(TOP)

<u>NOTHING-BECOME-WARRIOR</u>-[WARRIORS BECOME NOTHING]: SEE: WARRIOR-NOTHING-BECOME-[WARRIORS BECOME NOTHING]

<u>NOTHING-EVERYTHING</u>-[NOTHING AND EVERYTHING]: *(Warriors know that when they experience "seeing", everything becomes nothing; everything is here and yet it isn't here at all; warriors prepare themselves to be aware, and full awareness comes only when there is no more self-importance left in them; only when warriors are nothing can they hope to become everything.)*
    SELECTED REFERENCES: **A Separate Reality - Page [153.3-153.6]** ("My benefactor was a sorcerer...from absolutely everything he knew before.") **A Separate Reality - Page [159.6-159.9]** ("Let's say that *seeing* is somewhat...I didn't become nothing in front of you.) **A Separate Reality - Page [170.1-170.6]** (If you have no feeling toward it,...as I said before, is learned by *seeing*.) **A Separate Reality - Page [194.4-195.2]** ("Hardly. When a man learns to *see*,...yet it isn't here at all.") **Tales of Power - Page [268.8-269.7]** (I again had the sensation of being...disintegrate

and be nothing once more.) **Eagle's Gift - Page [279.3-279.4]** ("Celestino's arrogance was his undoing and...to what we really are - nothing.) **The Fire From Within - Page [128.5-128.6]** ("What are we really doing, don Juan?"...are nothing do they become everything.") **The Fire From Within - Page [213.6-213.8]** ("The speed of that boost will dissolve...still roaming is some incomprehensible immensity.")

    SEE ALSO: *SEEING, SELF-IMPORTANCE, WARRIOR-EMPTINESS, SELF-IMPORTANCE-LOSING*

NOTHING-EVERYTHING-EXPERIENCING-[EXPERIENCING NOTHING AND EVERYTHING]-(TOP)

NOTHING-LOSE-THOSE-[THOSE WITH NOTHING TO LOSE]: *(Warriors know they can become courageous only after they have realized they have nothing to lose; the average man remains timid only because he has something to cling to.)*

    SELECTED REFERENCES: **The Second Ring of Power - Page [106.7-106.8]** ("It's a very simple procedure...something we can still cling to.")

    SEE ALSO: *REASON-CLINGING, WARRIOR-COURAGE, TIMIDITY*

NOTHING-MATTERS-WARRIOR-[NOTHING MATTERS TO WARRIORS]: SEE: WARRIOR-NOTHING-MATTERS-[NOTHING MATTERS TO WARRIORS]

NOTHING-PENDING-LIFE-WARRIOR-[NOTHING IS PENDING IN THE LIVES OF WARRIORS]: SEE: WARRIOR-LIFE-NOTHING-PENDING-[NOTHING IS PENDING IN THE LIVES OF WARRIORS]

NOTHING-SURE-[NOTHING IS FOR SURE]: SEE: WARRIOR-FOG-CREATE-[WARRIORS CREATE A FOG AROUND THEMSELVES]

NOTICES-EVERYTHING-WARRIOR-[WARRIORS NOTICE EVERYTHING]: SEE: WARRIOR-NOTICES-EVERYTHING-[WARRIORS NOTICE EVERYTHING]

NUNS-PRIESTS-[NUNS AND PRIESTS]: *(Warriors know there is little inherent difference between the lifestyle of the warrior and the lifestyle of a true nun or priest; true nuns and priests are usually complete and do not weaken themselves with sexual acts.)*

    SELECTED REFERENCES: **The Second Ring of Power - Page [242.4-242.8]** (I objected to her religious connotation...them that they can do it.")

    SEE ALSO: *WARRIOR-WAY, WARRIOR-COMPLETENESS, WARRIOR-IMPECCABILITY*

O

OBJECT-NO-LONGER-WARRIOR-[WARRIORS ARE NO LONGER OBJECTS]: SEE: WARRIOR-OBJECT-NO-LONGER-[WARRIORS ARE NO LONGER OBJECTS]

OBJECTIVITY-WARRIOR-[THE OBJECTIVITY OF THE WARRIOR]: SEE: WARRIOR-OBJECTIVITY-[THE OBJECTIVITY OF THE WARRIOR]

OBJECTS-INTENDING-[INTENDING OBJECTS]: SEE: INTENDING-OBJECTS-[INTENDING OBJECTS]

OBLIVION-[OBLIVION]: (Warriors know that the only thing that soothes those who journey into the unknown is the oblivion of normal awareness.)
SELECTED REFERENCES: The Fire From Within - Page [281.4-281.5] (As I was telling don Juan...to be in the ordinary world!)
SEE ALSO: WARRIOR-SHIELDS

OBSESSION-[OBSESSION]: (Warriors know that obsession is the obsessive manipulation of the known; the inability to let go; the first face of the second attention; the aberrant and morbid focus of attention on any particular thing; the obsessive entanglement of attention in self-absorption or reason; warriors stalk themselves to break the power of their obsessions.)
SELECTED REFERENCES: Tales of Power - Page [13.8-14.1] ("To change our idea of the world...would only breed obsession and morbidity.") Tales of Power - Page [51.5-52.5] ("I've got to talk about this,"...in such a manner dissipates obsession.") Tales of Power - Page [173.1-173.3] (One of the sources of your bafflement...make our eyes stiff and intransigent.) Tales of Power - Page [244.7-245.7] (Sorcerers, however, can learn to perceive...excursions into the nagual, the unknown.") The Eagle's Gift - Page [20.4-21.8] (He stressed to me that all archaeological...They won't let you live in peace.") The Eagle's Gift - Page [22.2-22.6] ("Your compulsion to possess and hold...found your bundles walking around.") The Fire From Within - Page [4.7-5.1] (Don Juan said that after some...to be obsessed with what they saw.) The Fire From Within - Page [40.1] (When I told you that a nagual...that a nagual has no obsessions.") The Fire From Within - Page [119.9-120.1] (He added that the obsessive entanglement...assemblage point loses its rigidity.) The Fire From Within - Page [124.5-124.6] (The new seers noticed that some...dark side of man," he asserted.) The Power of Silence - Page [10.4-10.5] ("The fact is that you're still...them you don't become morbidly obsessed.") The Power of Silence - Page [110.4-110.5] ("Your problem is very simple,"...poems you read me to stalk yourself.") The Power of Silence - Page [263.7-263.9] (After a moment's pause, don Juan explained...free of liens and mortgages.) The Art of Dreaming - Page [2.4-2.5] ("What do you call concreteness, don...of the sorcerers of the past.") The Art of Dreaming - Page [13.1-13.8] ("In what way was it unusual...pinned down by their own machinations.)
SEE ALSO: ABERRATION-MORBIDITY, SELF-ABSORPTION, KNOWN-OBSESSIVE-MANIPULATION, LETTING-GO, LIENS-MORTGAGES

OCEANS-[OCEANS, RIVERS AND LAKES]: SEE: ATTENTION-SECOND-ANTITHETICAL-[THINGS THAT ARE ANTITHETICAL TO THE SECOND ATTENTION]

OFFENDED-NOT-WARRIOR-[WARRIORS ARE NOT OFFENDED]: SEE: WARRIOR-OFFENDED-NOT-[WARRIORS ARE NOT OFFENDED]

OLD-AGE-[OLD AGE]: (Warriors know that old-age is their fourth enemy; it is the cruelest enemy of all because warriors can never defeat it completely, they can only fight it away.)
SELECTED REFERENCES: The Teachings of Don Juan - Page [87.4-87.7] ("The man will be, by then,...overrule all his clarity, his power, and his knowledge.) A Separate Reality -

Page [198.5-198.6] ("It is his will which assembles...expanding fog moving beyond its limits.")
The Power of Silence - Page [49.1-49.5] (He asserted that during our active lives...and simple anger at having missed out.) **The Power of Silence - Page [50.8-51.2]** (I reread the poem to myself...that is determining our fate.")
    SEE ALSO: *WARRIOR-ENEMIES-FOUR-NATURAL*

OLINDA-[OLINDA]-(TOP): SEE NAGUAL-WOMAN-FINDING-[HOW POWER FOUND CAROL THE NAGUAL WOMAN AND OLINDA THE NAGUAL WOMAN]-(TOP)

*OMEN-[OMENS]: (Warriors know that omens are acts of power, indications of the spirit; the cubic centimeter of chance; manifestations of the spirit; gestures of the spirit; the edifice of intent.)
    SELECTED REFERENCES: The Teachings of Don Juan - Page [50.6-50.7] ("Was it so unusual?"...And that produces a terrible fatigue.") **Tales of Power - Page [106.7-106.8]** ("You are going to sit here...itself up and give an indication.") **Tales of Power - Page [113.6-113.7]** (I really felt that the whole thing...is an omen, an act of power.) **Tales of Power - Page [114.1-114.7]** (We came to this park, after you had...that is the predilection of my spirit.") **The Second Ring of Power - Page [216.7-216.8]** (He explained that my first vision...what was going to develop subsequently.) **The Eagle's Gift - Page [139.3-139.4]** (Don Juan also told us that...our attention having beckoned the event.) **The Power of Silence - Page [6.1-6.2]** ("The spirit, in order to shake...to anything but his self-concern.") **The Power of Silence - Page [12.4-12.5]** (Don Juan explained that every act performed...more simply, indications of omens.) **The Power of Silence - Page [13.5-13.8]** (This brought up a nagging rational concern...my experiences in the sorcerers' world.) **The Power of Silence - Page [14.3-14.7]** (Then he answered my question...direct knowledge is totally accurate and functional.) **The Power of Silence - Page [42.1-42.3]** (But once the willingness of the spirit...the spirit has in store for them.")
    SEE ALSO: *SPIRIT-GESTURES, WARRIOR-CHANCE-MINIMAL, INTENT-EDIFICE, INTENT-INDICATIONS, OMEN-(ALL), OMENS-(ALL)*

OMEN-ACCEPTANCE-SECOND-[THE SECOND OMEN OF ACCEPTANCE]-(TOP): SEE: CARLOS-VISION-MOTHER [CARLOS' VISION OF HIS MOTHER]-(TOP)

OMEN-VS-AGREEMENT-[OMENS VS AGREEMENTS]: (Warriors know the difference between an omen and an agreement from one's surroundings.)
    SELECTED REFERENCES: Journey to Ixtlan - Page [19.7-20.6] (At that moment an enormous crow...and broke into a belly laugh.) **Journey to Ixtlan - Page [22.5-22.6]** ("This is very weird," I said...that was an agreement," he said.)
    SEE ALSO: *OMENS, SPIRIT-GESTURE-OF*

OMEN-ALLIES-[OMENS AND ALLIES]: SEE: ALLIES-OMEN [THE ALLIES AS OMENS]

OMEN-APPRENTICE-NAGUAL-JUAN-[THE OMENS OF THE APPRENTICE NAGUAL JUAN MATUS]-(TOP)

OMEN-APPRENTICE-NAGUAL-JULIAN-[THE OMENS OF THE APPRENTICE NAGUAL JULIAN]-(TOP)

OMEN-BENEFACTOR-[OMEN OF THE BENEFACTOR]-(TOP)

OMEN-CHOLLA-[OMEN OF THE CHOLLA]-(TOP): SEE: FINDING-ELIGIO-[HOW POWER FOUND ELIGIO]-(TOP)

OMEN-CROW-[OMEN OF THE CROW]-(TOP)

OMEN-ESCOGIDO-[THE OMEN OF THE ESCOGIDO]-(TOP)

OMEN-HARDNESS-TRANSFORMATION-[THE OMEN OF HARDNESS AND TRANSFORMATION]-(TOP): SEE: OMEN-WAITRESS-[THE OMEN OF THE WAITRESS]-(TOP)

OMEN-HUNT-POWER-*[THE OMEN TO HUNT FOR POWER]-(TOP)*

OMEN-INTERPRETING-*[INTERPRETING OMENS]: (Warriors know that reading omens is commonplace for sorcerers; their direct knowledge is totally accurate and functional unless their personal feelings cloud their connecting link with intent; everything that happens to warriors can be interpreted as an omen.)*

SELECTED REFERENCES: **Journey to Ixtlan - Page [132.4-132.6]** ("A hunter of power watches everything...power one must live with power.") **The Second Ring of Power - Page [171.4-171.7]** (She smiled coyly and said that...always a couple of days behind.") **The Power of Silence - Page [13.5-13.8]** (This brought up a nagging rational...my experiences in the sorcerers' world.) **The Power of Silence - Page [14.3-14.7]** (Then he answered my question about...knowledge is totally accurate and functional.)
SEE ALSO: *OMENS, KNOWLEDGE-DIRECT, KNOWLEDGE-SILENT, FEELINGS, SEEING-UNMISTAKABILITY*

OMEN-LIDIA-*[LIDIA'S OMEN]-(TOP)*

OMEN-MOTH-*[THE OMEN OF THE MOTH]-(TOP)*

OMEN-MOTHS-CIRCLE-*[THE OMEN OF LA GORDA'S CIRCLE OF MOTHS]-(TOP): SEE: FINDING-GORDA-[HOW POWER FOUND LA GORDA]-(TOP)*

OMEN-POWER-ROUNDS-UP-*[POWER ROUNDS UP AN OMEN]: (Warriors know that power is capable of gathering itself in order to give warriors an indication of its designs.)*

SELECTED REFERENCES: **Tales of Power - Page [106.7-106.8]** ("You are going to sit here...round itself up and give an indication.") **Tales of Power - Page [114.1-114.4]** (And yet, how can you discard...have plucked it, but have you?")
SEE ALSO: *OMENS, POWER-DESIGNS*

OMEN-POWER-SPOT-*[THE OMEN OF THE POWER SPOT]-(TOP)*

OMEN-RETURN-*[THE OMEN OF RETURN]-(TOP)*

OMEN-SOLEDAD-*[DONA SOLEDAD'S OMENS]-(TOP)*

OMEN-SUN-*[THE OMEN OF THE SUN]-(TOP)*

OMEN-WAITRESS-*[THE OMEN OF THE WAITRESS]-(TOP)*

OMEN-WARRIOR-RITUAL-*[THE OMEN OF THE WARRIORS' RITUAL]-(TOP)*

ON-GUARD-*[BEING ON GUARD]: SEE: WARRIOR-PREPAREDNESS-[THE WARRIORS' PREPAREDNESS]*

ONLY-DOOR-*[THE ONLY DOOR THERE IS]: SEE: DOOR-ONLY-[THE ONLY DOOR THERE IS]*

OPENINGS-AWARENESS-MAGICAL-TWO-*[THE TWO MAGICAL OPENINGS TO AWARENESS]: (Warriors know that human awareness can be described as an immense haunted house; normal awareness is like being sealed in one room of that house for life; we enter that room through one magical opening, birth; we exit that room from another magical opening, death.)*

SELECTED REFERENCES: **The Power of Silence - Page [264.2-264.3]** (Don Juan said that human awareness...through another such magical opening: death.)
SEE ALSO: *AWARENESS, DEATH, HAUNTED-HOUSE-ANALOGY*

OPENNESS-WARRIOR-[THE WARRIORS' OPENNESS]: SEE:
WARRIOR-OPENNESS-[THE WARRIORS' OPENNESS]

OPPRESSED-ADVANTAGES-[THE ADVANTAGES IN BEING
OPPRESSED]: (Warriors know that there are specific advantages to being
oppressed; when a man is oppressed he may, because of that oppression,
come out triumphant in the end; but the petty tyrant that treads on him
doesn't have a chance in hell.)
    SELECTED REFERENCES: The Fire From Within - Page **[31.6-32.2]** (I told him that
it had...don't have a chance in hell.")
    SEE ALSO: *WARRIOR-DURESS-EXTREME-BENEFITS, PETTY-TYRANT,*
OPPRESSED-OPPRESSORS-OPPORTUNITIES

OPPONENT-WORTHY-[WORTHY OPPONENT]: SEE: WORTHY-
OPPONENT-[WORTHY OPPONENT]

OPPRESSED-OPPRESSORS-OPPORTUNITIES-[THE OPPRESSED AND
THEIR OPPRESSORS]: (Warriors know that the oppressed have special
opportunities that come with their oppression should they choose to exercise
them; the oppressed at least have a chance for freedom while the oppressors
don't have a chance in hell.)
    SELECTED REFERENCES: The Fire From Within - Page **[32.1-32.2]** ("Don't just feel
sorry for the poor...don't have a chance in hell.") **The Fire From Within** - Page **[170.2-170.5]**
(Don Juan said next that the...energy of alignment is that force.)
    SEE ALSO: *PETTY-TYRANT, OPPRESSED-ADVANTAGES*

OPTIMISM-WARRIOR-[THE WARRIORS' OPTIMISM]: SEE:
WARRIOR-OPTIMISM-[THE WARRIORS' OPTIMISM]

OPTIONS-WARRIOR-ASSEMBLAGE-POINT-MOVE-[THE TWO
OPTIONS OPEN TO THE WARRIOR WHOSE ASSEMBLAGE POINT HAS
MOVED]: SEE: WARRIOR-OPTIONS-ASSEMBLAGE-POINT-MOVE-
[THE TWO OPTIONS OPEN TO THE WARRIOR WHOSE ASSEMBLAGE
POINT HAS MOVED]

ORDER-[ORDER]: SEE: EAST-[EASTERLY WOMEN]

ORDER-ATTENTION-FIRST-[THE ORDER OF THE FIRST ATTENTION]:
SEE: ATTENTION-FIRST-ORDER-[THE ORDER OF THE FIRST
ATTENTION]

ORDER-ATTENTION-SECOND-[THE ORDER OF THE SECOND
ATTENTION]: SEE: ATTENTION-SECOND-ORDER-[THE ORDER OF
THE SECOND ATTENTION]

ORDER-CHAOS-[ORDER OUT OF CHAOS]: (Warriors know that the
average man has a magical capacity to impart order to the chaos of the
Eagle's emanations and to keep his assemblage point fixed.)
    SELECTED REFERENCES: The Fire From Within - Page **[133.2-133.3]** (Don Juan
went on to express...keep our assemblage point unwaveringly fixed.) **The Art of Dreaming** -
Page **[78.9-79.1]** (Sorcerers, on the contrary, bring order...anything we know to be real.")
    SEE ALSO: *ATTENTION-FIRST-ORDER*

ORDER-UNIVERSE-[THE ORDER OF THE UNIVERSE] (Warriors know
that they must learn to bring order to the chaos of the universe; warrior-
sorcerers have a transcendental purpose, to free their perception; sorcerers
don't make up the world they are perceiving, they perceive energy directly; it

is insane people that bring only chaos to chaos because they have no preconceived purpose.)

SELECTED REFERENCES: **Tales of Power** - Page [27.3-27.4] ("I caught a glimpse of the moth...figure reflecting your lack of order.") **Tales of Power** - Page [272.1-272.3] ("One thing has nothing to...but the only one we've got.) **Tales of Power** - Page [276.8-278.3] ("To make *reason* feel safe is...of that indescribable void that contains everything.) **Tales of Power** - Page [291.1-291.2] ("We have enjoyed ourselves and laughed...it should always come to an end.") **The Second Ring of Power** - Page [1.7-2.2] (In my jump my perception went...say anything to clarify their nature.) **The Second Ring of Power** - Page [274.8-275.2] (Don Juan said that the core...our perception of our daily world.) **The Fire From Within** - Page [33.3-33.5] (He told me then that before...the unknowable are the same thing.) **The Power of Silence** - Page [109.7-109.8] ("You must agree, don Juan, not...no order, no sobriety, no beauty.) **The Art of Dreaming** - Page [78.8-79.1] ("But isn't that what mentally ill...anything we know to be real.")

SEE ALSO: *ORDER, PERCEPTION, FREEDOM, INSANITY, SEEING, ATTENTION-FIRST-ORDER*

ORDER-WARRIOR-[THE WARRIORS' ORDER]: SEE: WARRIOR-ORDER-[THE WARRIORS' ORDER]

ORDINARY-NO-LONGER-WARRIOR-[WARRIORS ARE NO LONGER ORDINARY]: SEE: WARRIOR-ORDINARY-NO-LONGER-[WARRIORS ARE NO LONGER ORDINARY]

ORGANIC-BEINGS-INORGANIC-BEINGS-[ORGANIC BEINGS VS INORGANIC BEINGS]: SEE: INORGANIC-BEINGS-ORGANIC-BEINGS-[INORGANIC BEINGS VS ORGANIC BEINGS]

ORGANIC-BEINGS-[ORGANIC BEINGS]: SEE: ORGANIC-LIFE-[ORGANIC LIFE]

ORGANIC-LIFE-[ORGANIC LIFE]: *(Warriors know that organic life is only one of the forty-eight types of luminous organizations or structures on the earth; organic life as we know it.)*

SELECTED REFERENCES: **The Fire From Within** - Page [157.8-159.3] ("For instance, there is an immeasurable...the organic bubbles of awareness.) **The Fire From Within** - Page [162.9-163.1] (He said that the old seers also...produced as many organisms as possible.) **The Fire From Within** - Page [258.8-259.5] (Don Juan reminded me that he...directly without any danger to themselves.")

SEE ALSO: *INORGANIC-BEINGS, EAGLE-EMANATIONS*

ORGANIZATION-TONAL-[THE ORGANIZATION OF THE TONAL]: *(Warriors know that the organization of the tonal is the order and organization of perception.)*

SELECTED REFERENCES: **Tales of Power** - Page [272.8] (The *tonal* is where all the unified organization exists.)

SEE ALSO: *ORDER, TONAL*

ORGANIZER-[THE ORGANIZER]: *(Warriors know that the organizer is the third male personality; the organizer behind the scenes; a mysterious unknowable man.)*

SELECTED REFERENCES: **The Eagle's Gift** - Page [174.8-175.3] (The three male warriors and the...who cannot stand on his own.)

SEE ALSO: *WARRIOR-MALE*

OTHER-[THE OTHER SELF]: SEE: OTHER-SELF-[THE OTHER SELF]

*OTHER-SELF-[THE OTHER SELF]: *(Warriors know that the other self is the dreaming body; the double; an identical being as oneself, but made in dreaming.)*

SELECTED REFERENCES: Tales of Power - Page [42.4-43.5] ("Let go!" he commanded me dryly...a sorcerer who *sees*, the double is brighter.") Tales of Power - Page [60.8-61.2] (Don Genaro was leaning against the...about the other," don Juan said.) Tales of Power - Page [274.9] (You *saw* everything. Genaro and I...all about the double, the other.") The Second Ring of Power - Page [278.7-278.8] (The result of engaging the "attention...as oneself, but made in "dreaming.") The Eagle's Gift - Page [143.6-145.7] (*Will* is very quiet, unnoticeable...going to shit and make the mountains tremble.") The Eagle's Gift - Page [274.6-274.9] (She told me then that to...immeasurable vastness of the other self.) The Eagle's Gift - Page [301.8-301.9] (Once they were in the awareness of...apprentices were in their normal awareness.) The Eagle's Gift - Page [312.7-313.9] (The systematic interaction that warriors go through...I had entered into the other self.) The Fire From Within - Page [272.6] (The old seers said that the other always comes shrouded in wind.")
SEE ALSO: *DREAMING-BODY*

OTHER-SELF-REMEMBERING-[REMEMBERING THE OTHER SELF]:
(Warriors know that remembering the other self is another term for regaining the totality of oneself.)
SELECTED REFERENCES: The Eagle's Gift - Page [220.8-220.9] (Don Juan told us that losing the...arriving at the totality of oneself.)
SEE ALSO: *TOTALITY-REGAINING, TOTAL-BEING*

OTHER-SIDE-[THE OTHER SIDE]: *(Warriors know that the other side is another term for the second attention.)*
SELECTED REFERENCES: The Teachings of Don Juan - Page [184.7] (The other side is the world of the diableros.) The Teachings of Don Juan - Page [185.4-185,5] ("The particular thing to learn is...and the world of living men.) The Teachings of Don Juan - Page [186.3] (All he needs is a gentle shove...the ends of the other world.) The Art of Dreaming - Page [74.1-74.5] ("I still don't understand. What is...driven by expectations of power and gain.)
SEE ALSO: *WORLD-OTHER, ATTENTION-SECOND, DIABLERO-WORLD*

OTHER-WORLD-[THE OTHER WORLD]: SEE: WORLD-OTHER-[THE OTHER WORLD], OTHER-SIDE-[THE OTHER SIDE]

OTHER-WORLD-ARRANGEMENT-[THE ARRANGEMENT OF THE OTHER WORLD]: SEE: WORLD-OTHER-LAYERS-[THE TEN LAYERS OF THE OTHER WORLD]

OTHER-WORLD-CURTAIN-[THE CURTAIN OF THE OTHER WORLD: SEE: WORLD-OTHER-CURTAIN-[THE CURTAIN OF THE OTHER WORLD]

OVER-ANALYSIS-[OVER-ANALYSIS]: *(Warriors know the importance of remaining quiet and not over-analyzing their energetic gains and the acts of power which herald them; this kind of over-analysis only leads to the wasting of the warriors' power and the reversal of their gains.)*
SELECTED REFERENCES: The Eagle's Gift - Page [47.9-48.4] (I drove all night. I wanted...must allow ourselves time to heal.") The Eagle's Gift - Page [59.6-60.3] (True to her practice of waiting before...we can't talk about something else.") The Eagle's Gift - Page [62.6-62.8] (I asked them if they also...Pablito said. "You're the Nagual!")
SEE ALSO: *POWER-ACTS, WARRIOR-IMPECCABILITY, ENERGY, WARRIOR-SILENCE*

OVERCONFIDENCE-WARRIOR-[THE WARRIORS' OVERCONFIDENCE]: SEE: WARRIOR-OVERCONFIDENCE-[THE WARRIORS' OVERCONFIDENCE]

P

PABLITO-ATTEMPTED-ESCAPE-[PABLITO'S ATTEMPTED ESCAPE]-(TOP)

PABLITO-BASKET-[PABLITO'S BASKET AND HIS ENCOUNTER WITH THE NAGUAL]-(TOP)

PABLITO-BID-NAGUAL-[PABLITO'S BID TO BE THE NAGUAL]-(TOP)

PABLITO-TUG-OF-WAR-GAME-[PABLITO'S TUG OF WAR GAME]-(TOP)

PABLITO-MANUELITA-[PABLITO'S SWEET MANUELITA]-(TOP)

PABLITO-VANISHES-[PABLITO VANISHES INTO THIN AIR]-(TOP)

PAIN-AVOIDING-[AVOIDING PAIN]: (Warriors know they can learn to avoid pain by utilizing a special way of "grabbing on to things"; warriors avoid needless pain by selecting a path with heart and remaining on it; warriors have vanquished their problems; it is not an issue that warriors do not have time to grab onto all the things they would like, it is only a pity.)
SELECTED REFERENCES: The Teachings of Don Juan - Page [106.6-107.5] (And yet, I could have avoided...you strong; the other weakens you.") A Separate Reality - Page [5.2-5.4] ("You think about yourself too much...no despair or self-pity in it.)
SEE ALSO: *PATH-HEART-WITH, PATHS-MILLION*

PAIN-WARRIOR-[THE WARRIORS' PAIN]: SEE: WARRIOR-PAIN-[THE WARRIORS' PAIN]

PAIR-TRUE-[THE TRUE PAIR]: (Warriors know that the tonal and the nagual are the members of true pair; the two components of the warriors' totality.)
SELECTED REFERENCES: Tales of Power - Page [127.8-127.9] ("I'm afraid I haven't asked the...the island, one finds the *nagual*.) Tales of Power - Page - [128.1-128.6] ("But, when you call it the...of the true pair, the *nagual*.) Tales of Power - Page [132.1-132.4] ("I was concerned with those jolts...without the binding force of life.") Tales of Power - Page [160.5-160.6] ("What can I do...it does, it terrifies the *tonal*.) The Second Ring of Power - Page [1.6-1.7] (Prior to that jump don Juan...the tonal and the nagual.)
SEE ALSO: *TONAL, NAGUAL, TOTALITY*

PAPER-WARRIOR-[THE PAPER WARRIOR]: SEE: WARRIOR-PAPER-[THE PAPER WARRIOR]

*PARALLEL-BEING-[THE PARALLEL BEING]: (Warriors know that the parallel being is another term for the dreaming body, the double, the other, the other self; another person of the same sex inextricably joined to the first one; a person and their parallel being coexist in the world at the same time and are like two ends of the same pole; warriors find in their parallel being an endless source of youth and energy.)
SELECTED REFERENCES: The Eagle's Gift - Page [294.6-294.8] (Florinda told me, in the spirit...techniques, had found her parallel being.) The Eagle's Gift - Page [294.9-295.4] (Dona Soledad had not only made...endless source of youth and energy.)
SEE ALSO: *DREAMING-BODY, OTHER*

PARALLEL-LINES-[THE PARALLEL LINES]: (Warriors know that the world of the tonal and the world of the nagual are on two parallel lines; warriors understand that it is possible to cross those lines in a state of full awareness, to burn with the fire from within.)
  SELECTED REFERENCES: The Eagle's Gift - Page [75.9-76.9] (She broke her silence and spoke...not breathe and everything went black.) The Eagle's Gift - Page [78.3-78.4] (I told them then about my...it was the same for them.) The Eagle's Gift - Page [82.8-83.5] ("Where's that spot?" Somewhere in the...lives where we could fit them.) The Eagle's Gift - Page [84.1-84.2] (Dona Soledad had used an appropriate...on two different lines of thought.) The Eagle's Gift - Page [94.8-94.9] ("I've told you already that I...from that time, from that world.") The Eagle's Gift - Page [97.4-97.6] ("It's simplicity itself," la Gorda said...We could see only his eyes.") The Eagle's Gift - Page [100.2-104.2] (La Gorda speculated that the airline...to do was to talk about him.) The Eagle's Gift - Page [152.2-153.7] (I felt a command to examine...that area with our whole bodies.") The Eagle's Gift - Page [292.4-293.2] (Dona Soledad and I met several...woman who laughed uproariously at me.) The Eagle's Gift - Page [299.1-299.2] (He had helped everyone impeccably... the parallel lines in one's totality.) The Eagle's Gift - Page [301.1-301.2] (She had just remembered that we...once more to cross the bridge.)
  SEE ALSO: PARALLEL LINES-(ALL), TONAL, NAGUAL

PARALLEL-LINES-DOOR-[THE DOOR ACROSS THE PARALLEL LINES]: (Warriors know that certain power spots are doorways across the parallel lines, doorways to the other world.)
  SELECTED REFERENCES: The Eagle's Gift - Page [97.4-97.5] ("It's simplicity itself," la Gorda said...world, a door to the other.) The Eagle's Gift - Page [100.2-100.4] (La Gorda speculated that the airline...line I came from, this world.)
  SEE ALSO: PARALLEL-LINES, DOOR-ONLY, CRACK-WORLDS

PARALLEL-LINES-JOURNEY-[JOURNEY TO THE LAND BETWEEN THE PARALLEL LINES]-(TOP)

PARALLEL-LINES-LAND-[THE LAND BETWEEN THE PARALLEL LINES]: (Warriors know that the land between the parallel lines is a lateral alignment of the assemblage point which helps define the barrier of perception; a land of pale yellow sandstone or rough granules of sulfur with a yellow oppressive sky and banks of yellow vapor; the land between the parallel lines is real because it is part of the total world, as the luminous body is part of the warriors' total being; the land of the sulfur dunes is not another total world.)
  SELECTED REFERENCES: A Separate Reality - Page [130.6-130.9] (I was confronted with a very...plateau filled with vapors of sulfur.) The Eagle's Gift - Page [152.2-153.7] (We stayed merged until something broke...the area with our whole bodies.") The Eagle's Gift - Page [157.7-158.1] ("The nagual woman was special...And other things even more fierce.") The Eagle's Gift - Page [236.9-237.5] (He then told la Gorda and me...is part of our total being.) The Eagle's Gift - Page [237.8-241.7] (Silvio Manuel had la Gorda and...world entails engaging our total being.) The Eagle's Gift - Page [293.2-293.6] (My incapacity to remember what we...but I could not pinpoint them.) The Fire From Within - Page [290.3-290.6] (Don Juan looked up at the sky...of what seemed to be sulfur.) The Fire From Within - Page [293.1-293.3] ("It's the easiest world to assemble...as they approach a crucial position.")
  SEE ALSO: PERCEPTION-BREAKING-BARRIER, PARALLEL-LINES, ASSEMBLAGE-POINT-SHIFT-LATERAL, INORGANIC-BEINGS-REALM

PARALLEL-LINES-LAND-ENTERING-[ENTERING THE LAND BETWEEN THE PARALLEL LINES]: (The warrior knows that to enter the land between the parallel lines without awareness only brings death, because without consciousness, the physical pressure of that world exhausts the life force.)
  SELECTED REFERENCES: The Eagle's Gift - Page [244.4-244.6] (His plan was to take me...the physical pressure of that world.)
  SEE ALSO: LIFE-FORCE. PARALLEL-LINES-LAND, INORGANIC-BEINGS-REALM, PARALLEL-LINES

PARTY-HUNTERS-[A PARTY OF HUNTERS]-(TOP)

PASSIONATE-WARRIOR-[THE PASSIONATE WARRIOR]: SEE: WARRIOR-PASSIONATE-[THE PASSIONATE WARRIOR]

PASSIVE-WITNESSING-[PASSIVE WITNESSING]: SEE: DREAMING-STAGES-[THE FOUR STAGES OF DREAMING]

PAST-WARRIOR-[THE WARRIORS' PAST]: SEE: WARRIOR-PAST-[THE WARRIORS' PAST]

PATH-HEART-WITH-[THE PATH WITH HEART]: (For warriors there is only traveling on paths with heart; the path with heart makes for a joyful journey; as long as warriors follow their path with heart, they are one with it; the path with heart makes the warrior strong; warriors choose a path with heart to remain at their best; warriors choose a path with heart and follow it; and then they look and rejoice and laugh and then they "see" and know; the things warriors select to make their shields are the items of their path with heart.)

SELECTED REFERENCES: **The Teachings of Don Juan - Page [11.3-11.4]** (*[For me there is only the...there I travel looking, looking, breathlessly.]*) **The Teachings of Don Juan - Page [28.1-28.7]** ("Would you teach me about peyote...few Indians have such a desire.") **The Teachings of Don Juan - Page [106.8-107.5]** (Therefore you must always keep in...you strong; the other weakens you.") **The Teachings of Don Juan - Page [160.2-161.4]** ("But how do you know when...seek death is to seek nothing.") **The Teachings of Don Juan - Page [184.7-185.3]** (I think it would be best...there I travel - looking, looking, breathlessly.") **A Separate Reality - Page [84.2-84.3]** (I have said this to you...perhaps so one can always laugh.") **A Separate Reality - Page [85.3-85.4]** (You should know by now that...and then he *sees* and knows.) **A Separate Reality - Page [217.9-218.3]** ("Years ago I told you that...will perish in the next encounter.") **A Separate Reality - Page [225.3-225.5]** (At that crucial instant a thought...I could see his entire face.) **Journey to Ixtlan - Page [266.9]** ("That is the feeling Genaro is...just the path where he walks.)

SEE ALSO: *WARRIOR-PATH, WARRIOR-JOY, WARRIOR-SHIELDS, WARRIOR-JOURNEY-POWER-PATH-HEART*

PATH-HEART-WITHOUT-[THE PATH WITHOUT A HEART]: (Warriors know that the path without a heart will make them curse their lives and weaken them as long as they remain on it; warriors must exchange such a path for a path with heart.)

SELECTED REFERENCES: **The Teachings of Don Juan - Page [107.4-107.5]** (My benefactor's question has meaning now...you strong; the other weakens you.") **The Teachings of Don Juan - Page [161.2-161.4]** (Don't let the devil's weed blind...seek death is to seek nothing.")

SEE ALSO: *PATH-HEART-WITH*

PATH-KNOWLEDGE-[THE PATH OF KNOWLEDGE]: SEE: KNOWLEDGE-PATH-[THE PATH OF KNOWLEDGE]

PATH-KNOWLEDGE-FOUR-STEPS-[THE FOUR STEPS ON THE PATH OF KNOWLEDGE]: SEE: KNOWLEDGE-PATH-STEPS-[THE FOUR STEPS ON THE PATH OD KNOWLEDGE]

PATH-MOST-DIFFICULT-THING-WARRIOR-[THE MOST DIFFICULT THING ON THE WARRIORS' PATH]: SEE: WARRIOR-PATH-MOST-DIFFICULT-THING-[THE MOST DIFFICULT THING ON THE WARRIORS' PATH]

PATH-WARRIOR-[THE WARRIORS' PATH]: SEE: WARRIOR-PATH-[THE WARRIORS' PATH

PATHS-MILLION-[THE MILLION PATHS]: *(Warriors know there are millions of options open to every man; warriors evaluate the million paths and select from them the path with heart.)*
    SELECTED REFERENCES: The Teachings of Don Juan - Page [106.8-106.9] (The devil's weed is only one...stay with it under any conditions.)
    SEE ALSO: *PATH-HEART-WITH, PATH-HEART-WITHOUT*

PATIENCE-[PATIENCE]: *(Warriors know that patience is one of the four moods of stalking; one of the three results of stalking.)*
    SELECTED REFERENCES: A Separate Reality - Page [219.3] (I put my notes away. Don...done harmoniously and with great patience.) The Eagle's Gift - Page [291.6-291.7] ("Applying these principles brings about three...have an endless capacity to improvise.") The Power of Silence - Page [68.2-68.6] (Don Juan said that his benefactor...acts this way he's being prissy.'") The Power of Silence - Page [69.3-69.4] ("In the past few days...bring you into a total recollection.") The Power of Silence - "Page [78.5-78.8] (You're not patient either. If you...be taught in careful, meticulous steps.) The Power of Silence - Page [81.8] ("The very first principle of *stalking*...himself ruthlessly, cunningly, patiently, and sweetly.")
    SEE ALSO: *STALKING-MOODS-FOUR, STALKING-RESULTS-THREE, WARRIOR-PATIENCE*

PATIENCE-WARRIOR-[THE WARRIORS' PATIENCE]: SEE: WARRIOR-PATIENCE-[THE WARRIORS' PATIENCE]

PAUSE-WARRIOR-ATTENTION-[THE PAUSE IN THE WARRIORS' ATTENTION]: SEE: WARRIOR-PAUSE-ATTENTION-[THE PAUSE IN THE WARRIORS' ATTENTION]

PAUSE-WARRIOR-DETACHMENT-[THE PAUSE OF THE WARRIORS' DETACHMENT]: SEE: WARRIOR-PAUSE-DETACHMENT-[THE PAUSE OF THE WARRIORS' DETACHMENT]

PEACE-WARRIOR-[PEACE FOR WARRIORS]: SEE: WARRIOR-PEACE-[PEACE FOR WARRIORS]

PEACE-WARRIOR-WAR-[PEACE VS WAR FOR WARRIORS]: SEE: WARRIOR-WAR-PEACE-[WAR VS PEACE FOR WARRIORS]

PENDING-NOTHING-WARRIOR-[NOTHING IS PENDING IN THE LIVES OF WARRIORS]: SEE: WARRIOR-NOTHING-PENDING-[NOTHING IS PENDING IN THE LIVES OF WARRIORS]

PEOPLE-GROUPS-[THE STALKERS' TWO MAIN GROUPS OF HUMAN BEINGS]: *(Warriors know that there are only two main groups of people, those who care about their fellow men and those who don't; the people who care about their fellow men don't feel comfortable with generosity and don't like to think they are imposing their will on them in any way; those who don't care about people are more comfortable helping people in a covert way; people who help their fellow men overtly don't really care about them at all.)*
    SELECTED REFERENCES: The Fire From Within - Page [186.8-188.4] (Don Juan explained that the new seers...But that's not the same.")
    SEE ALSO: *PEOPLE-TYPES, WARRIOR-INTERVENTION*

PEOPLE-TYPES-[THE STALKERS' CLASSIFICATIONS OF PERSONALITY TYPES]: *(Warriors know that the entire human race falls into three categories of personality; the first classification includes the nicest people one could hope to find, but they have one huge flaw, they can't function* alone; the second classification includes people who are insecure and never pleased, the more insecure they become the nastier they are and their fatal flaw is that they would kill to be leaders; the third category includes people who are indifferent, those who serve no one and impose themselves on no one; those who always promise to deliver but who never do because they simply do not have the resources; the avenue of redemption that remains open for all three personality types is that it is only our personal self-reflection that falls into these categories; when the warriors' self-importance is destroyed, it doesn't matter which category of personality they fall into because they no longer take themselves seriously.)

SELECTED REFERENCES: The Power of Silence - Page [246.2-248.4] ("*Stalkers* who practice controlled folly believe...himself seriously, while you still do.")

SEE ALSO: *SELF-REFLECTION*

PERCEIVE-ENERGY-[PERCEIVING THE ENERGETIC ESSENCE OF THINGS]: SEE: ENERGETIC-ESSENCE-PERCEIVING-[PERCEIVING THE ENERGETIC ESSENCE OF THINGS], SEEING-[SEEING]

PERCEIVE-KEY-[THE KEY TO PERCEIVING]: SEE: ENERGETIC-UNIFORMITY-[ENERGETIC UNIFORMITY AND COHESION]

PERCEIVE-LEARN-WHAT-TO-[WARRIORS LEARN WHAT TO PERCEIVE]: SEE: PERCEIVE-WE-[WE PERCEIVE]

PERCEIVERS-WE-ARE-[WE ARE PERCEIVERS]: (Warriors know they are perceivers, that they an awareness; human beings have no solidity, we are boundless; the fact that we perceive is a hard fact, but what we perceive is not a fact of the same kind; warriors learn what to perceive.)

SELECTED REFERENCES: Tales of Power - Page [97.7-97.8] (We are perceivers. We are an...we rarely emerge in a lifetime.) Tales of Power - Page [98.2] ("We are perceivers," he proceeded...since the moment we were born.) The Fire From Within - Page [37.3-37.4] (Pay close attention to this, for...because we learn what to perceive.) The Fire From Within - Page [214.5-214.6] ("We living beings are perceivers," he said...the earth's boost is the key.) The Power of Silence - Page [243.8-244.2] (Don Juan fixed me with his stare...possibilities than the mind can conceive.")

SEE ALSO: *AWARENESS-WE-ARE, PERCEPTION, LUMINOUS-BEINGS-SECRET, REALITY-INTERPRETATION*

PERCEIVING-ALL-INCLUSIVE-[PERCEIVING IS AN ALL-INCLUSIVE AFFAIR]: (Warriors know that perceiving is an all-inclusive act when the assemblage point has been immobilized on one position; this immobility is what makes our perception of the world so inclusive and overpowering that it cannot be normally escaped; if warriors are to break this totally inclusive force, they must do it by intending the displacement of the assemblage point.)

SELECTED REFERENCES: The Art of Dreaming - Page [193.7-194. ("Why am I so frightened?" she asked...assemblage point by intending its displacement.)

SEE ALSO: *PERCEPTION, DESCRIPTION-WORLD, ASSEMBLAGE-POINT-MOVING*

PERCEIVING-BODY-ENTIRE-[PERCEIVING WITH THE ENTIRE BODY]: (Warriors know that "seeing" with the entire body is another term for "seeing".)

SELECTED REFERENCES: The Power of Silence - Page [157.9-158.1] (He said that sorcerers are capable of...senses a greater range of perception.)

SEE ALSO: *SEEING, LOOKING-SEEING-SIMULTANEOUSLY, BODY-PHYSICAL-WITNESSING*

PERCEIVING-VEHICLE-*[THE VEHICLE TO PERCEIVING]:* *(Warriors know how to recognize expressions of magic for what they really are; such occurrences are seen, not as oddities, but as vehicles to perceiving, as sources of awe.)*

SELECTED REFERENCES: The Power of Silence - Page [223.1-223.3] (Don Juan observed that for an...on oddity, but a source of awe.)
SEE ALSO: *PERCEPTION, SPIRIT, SPIRIT-MANIFESTATIONS, MAGIC, OMENS, SPIRIT-GESTURES-OF*

PERCEPTION-*[PERCEPTION]:* *(Warriors know that perception takes place when the Eagle's emanations inside the luminous cocoon align themselves with the corresponding emanations at large; perception takes place because the assemblage point selects internal and external emanations for alignment; perception is the precondition of being alive.)*

SELECTED REFERENCES: Tales of Power - Page [97.6-98.2] ("What is Genaro doing in this...since the moment we were born.) **Tales of Power** - Page [252.4-252.5] ("What do you mean...round walls is our own reflection.") **Tales of Power** - Page [255.1-255.4] ("We have one single issue left...you will know the two remaining points.") **Tales of Power** - Page [272.1-172.2] ("One thing has nothing to do...but the only one we've got.) **The Second Ring of Power** - Page [274.8-275.4] (Don Juan said that the core...to impart order to the nonordinary world.) **The Fire From Within** - Page [37.2-37.5] ("The first truth is that the...awareness forces them to do so.") **The Fire From Within** - Page [43.5-43.9] (He went on to say that...after courting tremendous dangers.") **The Fire From Within** - Page [45.8-46.2] ("How are those emanations utilized...the outside emanations would match them.") **The Fire From Within** - Page [49.4-49.7] ("Do you mean that a nagual...look like bubbles of whitish light.") **The Fire From Within** - Page [108.3-108.5] (That awareness gives rise to perception...internal and external emanations for alignment.) **The Fire From Within** - Page [125.1-125.4] ("The mystery is outside us...senses perceive in inconceivable ways.") **The Fire From Within** - Page [133.2-133.5] (Don Juan went on to express...our command, our gift of magic.") **The Power of Silence** - Page [xvi.1-xvi.3] (5. Perception occurs when the energy...or simply "the assemblage point.") **The Power of Silence** - Page [56.9-57.2] (Don Juan said that perception is...could become anything he wanted.) **The Power of Silence** - Page [58.4-58.5] (Don Juan had explained that sorcerers...classic example of an aberration.) **The Art of Dreaming** - Page [6.3-7.2] ("What does the assemblage point do...evidently, the consequent awareness and perception.) **The Art of Dreaming** - Page [45.8-45.9] ("For sorcerers, having life means having...as the precondition of being alive.")
SEE ALSO: *AWARENESS, ALIGNMENT, EAGLE-EMANATIONS, AWARENESS-TRUTH-FIFTH, PERCEPTION-(ALL)*

PERCEPTION-ALIGNMENT-*[PERCEPTION IS ALIGNMENT]:* *(Warriors know that perception is alignment.)*

SELECTED REFERENCES: The Fire From Within - Page [204.7-204.8] (He didn't answer me. He kept...from knowing what they had accomplished.)
SEE ALSO: *PERCEPTION, ALIGNMENT*

PERCEPTION-AWARENESS-UNIT-*[AWARENESS AND PERCEPTION AS A SINGLE UNIT]: SEE: AWARENESS-PERCEPTION-UNIT-[AWARENESS AND PERCEPTION AS A SINGLE UNIT]*

PERCEPTION-BARRIER-BREAKING-[BREAKING THE BARRIER OF PERCEPTION]:* *(Warriors know that when the assemblage point moves away from its customary position to a certain degree, it breaks a barrier that momentarily disrupts its capacity to align emanations; this threshold is experienced as a moment of perceptual blankness; the old seers referred to that moment as the wall of fog because a bank of fog appears whenever the alignment of emanations falters; actually there are three ways for warriors to deal with this threshold of assembly; the first is to take it abstractly as a*

barrier of perception; the second is to feel it as the act of piercing a tight paper screen with the entire body; the third is to "see" it as a wall of fog; breaking the barrier of perception is the culmination of everything that warriors do, and it confirms their ability to move the assemblage point to the degree necessary to actually assemble other worlds; for the warriors of don Juan's lineage, breaking the barrier of perception was used as a final test, a test which consisted of the warrior jumping from a mountaintop into an abyss while in a state of normal awareness; if warriors are not capable of erasing the daily world and assembling another one before they reach the bottom, they die; breaking the barrier of perception is the descent of the spirit; the act of executing a somersault of thought into the inconceivable; the moment in which man's perception reaches its outer limits; once the barrier of perception is broken, fate takes on a new meaning for warriors.)

SELECTED REFERENCES: The Teachings of Don Juan - Page [186.1-186.4] (On top of that plateau is...man will have to wander around.) Tales of Power - Page [55.1-55.2] (All of us luminous beings have...that awareness such a unique challenge.") Tales of Power - Page [89.6-89.8] (The next thing I knew don Juan...audible and their meaning crystal clear.) Tales of Power - Page [141.2-141.3] (It took me an incredibly long...place my sight on his hand.) Tales of Power - Page [177.2-177.5] ("No. After the *tonal* shrinks, the...took it as a joke, though.") Tales of Power - Page [188.9-189.3] (During a short pause in our talk...for a chance to break through.) The Second Ring of Power - Page [90.1-90.4] (The ticklishness was like a shield...means to that suspension of judgment.) The Second Ring of Power - Page [272.1-272.4] (It was at that instant that...memory had taken possession of me.) The Eagle's Gift - Page [230.6-230.8] (There was another striking anomaly that...they staggered around without muscular coordination.) The Fire From Within - Page [166.2s-166.4] ("They taxed their awareness to the...to become trees to do that.") The Fire From Within - Page [215.5-215.6] (I felt a great pressure all over...found myself facing a luminescent world.) The Fire From Within - Page [216.1-216.2] (He said that the sobriety needed...the barrier of perception with impunity.) The Fire From Within - Page [248.2] (The seers felt that they were relatively...perception set by the assemblage point.) The Fire From Within - Page [256.8-257.4] ("Now, the only thing left for...seen as a wall of fog.) The Fire From Within - Page [259.6-259.7] ("To break the barrier of perception is...of recovery. Remember what you've done!") The Fire From Within - Page [260.2-260.4] (He also said that there was...by gripping feelings of defeat.) The Fire From Within - Page [272.3-272.4] (Then he smiled and remarked that...in order to assemble another world.) The Fire From Within - Page [289.6-289.6] ("What about the people around me...you won't be in this world.") The Fire From Within - Page [294.4-294.5] ("To assemble other worlds is not...the world. See what I mean?") The Fire From Within - Page [295.3-295.5] (He said that breaking the barrier...before he reaches bottom, he dies.) The Power of Silence - Page [113.5] ("A somersault of thought into the...which man's perception reaches its limits.) The Art of Dreaming - Page [51.8-51.9] (His contention was that the second...surround and insulate the second attention.)

SEE ALSO: *FOG-WALL, PERCEPTION, ALIGNMENT, ASSEMBLAGE-POINT-SHIFT-LATERAL, OTHER-WORLDS-ASSEMBLE-TOTAL, WARRIOR-JUMP, SPIRIT-DESCENT, WARRIOR-FATE, PERCEPTION-BARRIER-SEEING-FOG-WALL*

PERCEPTION-BARRIER-SEEING-FOG-WALL-[SEEING THE BARRIER OF PERCEPTION AS A WALL OF FOG]: (Warriors know that if they "see" the barrier of perception as a wall of fog instead of as an abstract entity, it means that the assemblage point does not have the stability to maintain its position and it shifts laterally within man's band.)

SELECTED REFERENCES: The Fire From Within - Page [267.8-268.2] (I asked him why it was...see the mold as a woman.)

SEE ALSO: *PERCEPTION-BARRIER, FOG-WALL, ASSEMBLAGE-POINT-SHIFT-LATERAL*

PERCEPTION-BARRIER-WARRIOR-PERCEPTION-[THE WARRIORS' PERCEPTION OF THE BARRIER OF PERCEPTION]: (Warriors know that the perception of the barrier of perception is variable; it can be seen as a

wall of fog, it can be felt as the act of piercing a tight paper screen or it can be taken abstractly as a barrier of perception.)

SELECTED REFERENCES: **The Fire From Within** - **Page [257.1-257.9]** (He explained that when the assemblage...something else, I couldn't change it.)

SEE ALSO: *PERCEPTION-BARRIER, PERCEPTION-BARRIER-SEEING-FOG-WALL, ASSEMBLAGE-POINT-MOVING, FOG-WALL*

PERCEPTION-BUBBLE-[THE BUBBLE OF PERCEPTION]: *(Warriors know that the bubble of perception is a part of the sorcerers' explanation; all men are placed inside a bubble of perception at the moment of birth, a bubble which is open at first, but which soon closes up and seals us in; we live inside that bubble all our lives and what we witness on its round walls is our own reflection; that view is first a description, which is given to us from the moment of birth until all of our attention is caught by it and the description becomes a view; the task of warriors is to somehow rearrange that view by expanding their perception beyond that bubble; the bubble must be opened in order to give warriors a view of their totality; the only problem with the bubble of perception is that as men we are perceivers, and our mistake is to believe that the only perception worthy of acknowledgment is what goes through our reason; warriors understand that there is much more to their total being than reason, and so they struggle to expand their awareness to include all perceptual possibilities; the cluster of emanations which warriors can arrange and rearrange)*

SELECTED REFERENCES: **Tales of Power** - **Page [252.5-255.3]** (Sorcerers say that we are inside...shouldn't take so much for granted.) **Tales of Power** - **Page [272.3-272.5]** "Last night your bubble of perception...true nature. You are a cluster.) **Tales of Power** -**Page [273.7-273.9]** ("I have called that cluster the...followed to arrive at that point.") **Tales of Power** - **Page [275.2-275.3]** ("The secret of the double is...*here* and the *there* at once.")

SEE ALSO: *SORCERER-EXPLANATION, TONAL, NAGUAL, DESCRIPTION-WORLD, PERCEPTION-BARRIER-BREAKING, AWARENESS-TOTAL, AWARENESS-BUBBLE*

PERCEPTION-BUBBLE-OPENING-[THE SECRET OF OPENING THE BUBBLE OF PERCEPTION]: *(Warriors know that the bubble of perception opens only when one plunges into the nagual.)*

SELECTED REFERENCES: **Tales of Power** - **Page [272.3-272.5]** "Last night your bubble of perception...true nature. You are a cluster.) **Tales of Power** - **Page [273.7-273.9]** ("I have called that cluster the bubble...have followed to arrive at that point.")

SEE ALSO: *PERCEPTION-BUBBLE, NAGUAL*

PERCEPTION-CHANGING-SOCIAL-BASE-[CHANGING THE SOCIAL BASE OF PERCEPTION]: *(Warriors know it is necessary for man to learn to separate the social part of his perception; he must learn to modify the foundation of his perception from a base of concreteness to a basis predicated on the abstract; everything is energy, the whole universe is energy; the social base of our perception should be the physical certainty that energy is all there is.)*

SELECTED REFERENCES: **The Power of Silence** - **Page [264.3-264.9]** (Sorcerers, however, were capable of finding...their freedom from perceptual convention.) **The Art of Dreaming** - **Page [3.2-3.7]** ("What would it mean to me...certainty that energy is all there is.)

SEE ALSO: *DESCRIPTION-WORLD, WORLD-SOLID-OBJECTS, AWARENESS-TRUTH-FIRST, ENERGETIC-CONDITIONING, CONCRETENESS, PERCEPTION-SOCIAL-BASE, SORCERY-TASK-GRAND, WARRIOR-FREEDOM-TOTAL, MAN-EVOLUTION, ENERGY*

PERCEPTION-CONTENT-[THE CONTENT OF PERCEPTION]: (Warriors know that the content of perception depends on the position of the assemblage point.)
SELECTED REFERENCES: The Power of Silence - Page [145.2-145.3] (He emphasized over and over that...the position of the assemblage point.)
SEE ALSO: PERCEPTION. ASSEMBLAGE-POINT-MOVING, ASSEMBLAGE-POINT-POSITION

PERCEPTION-DOUBLE-OF-[THE PERCEPTION OF THE DOUBLE]-(TOP)

PERCEPTION-DOUBLE-WORLD-[DOUBLE PERCEPTION OF THE WORLD]: (Warriors know they can use the technique of crossing the eyes and squinting to create a double perception of the world; this double perception allows warriors the opportunity to judge changes in their surroundings that they would be normally incapable of perceiving; warriors learn to separate the double images and focus their attention on the area between them, which they then evaluate with their feelings to determine the correct place to rest.)
SELECTED REFERENCES: Journey to Ixtlan - Page [49.5-49.9] (After a long pause don Juan...eyes were ordinarily capable of perceiving.) Journey to Ixtlan - Page [160.7-160.9] (I put away my writing pad and...a couple of steps behind me.) Journey to Ixtlan - Page [196.5-197.7] (He marked a spot for me to...blocked the sunlight with his body.) Tales of Power - Page [222.6-223.1] (Don Genaro signaled Pablito and Nestor...had a light of their own.)
SEE ALSO: PERCEPTION, DOING-VS-NOT-DOING, EQUILIBRIUM, EYES-CONNECTION-TRUE

*PERCEPTION-DUAL-[DUAL PERCEPTION]: SEE: PERCEPTUAL-DUALISM-[PERCEPTUAL DUALISM]

PERCEPTION-ENERGY-INCREASED-[PERCEPTION AND THE WARRIORS' INCREASED ENERGY]: (Warriors know that their increased energy level, derived from the curtailment of self-reflection, allows the senses a greater range of perception.)
SELECTED REFERENCES: The Power of Silence - Page [157.9-158.1] (He said that sorcerers are capable of...senses a greater ranger of perception.)
SEE ALSO: PERCEPTION, ENERGY, SELF-REFLECTION, WARRIOR-IMPECCABILITY

PERCEPTION-EXTRAORDINARY-[EXTRAORDINARY PERCEPTION]: (Warriors know that extraordinary perception, or "seeing", occurs when by the force of intent, a different cluster of emanations from the ordinary is energized and lit up; when a critical number of those emanations are lit up, sorcerers are able to "see" the emanations themselves.)
SELECTED REFERENCES: The Power of Silence - Page [102.1-102.2] (Extraordinary perception, seeing, occurs when...to see the energy fields themselves.)
SEE ALSO: SEEING, PERCEPTION, PERCEPTION-NORMAL, EAGLE-EMANATIONS

PERCEPTION-FINAL-NEVER-[THE PERCEPTION OF THE WORLD IS NEVER FINAL]: (Warriors know that their perception of the world is never final; warriors understand the true concept of reality and perception and do not attach undue importance to their perceptions of the world.)
SELECTED REFERENCES: The Fire From Within - Page [267.2-267.4] (Don Juan said then that he...of the world is never final.)
SEE ALSO: PERCEPTION, REALITY-INTERPRETATION

PERCEPTION-FORCE-[THE FORCE OF PERCEPTION]: (Warriors know that the force of perception is the force capable of separating warriors from the world as we know it; the force of perception allows warriors to assemble other worlds, and as they perceive them, the force of their perception leaves room for nothing else; when the assemblage point assembles a world, that world is total; the world disappears like a puff of air when a new total alignment makes them perceive another total world.)
SELECTED REFERENCES: **The Fire From Within - Page [216.4-216.8]** ("Genaro will let his assemblage point...of perception," don Juan said quietly.)
SEE ALSO: *PERCEPTION, WORLDS-OTHER-ASSEMBLE-TOTAL, ASSEMBLAGE-POINT-MOVING*

PERCEPTION-FREEING-[FREEING PERCEPTION]: (Warriors know that their preconceived transcendental purpose is to free perception by changing it at its social base.)
SELECTED REFERENCES: **The Art of Dreaming - Page [78.9-79.1]** (Sorcerers, on the contrary, bring order...anything we know to be real.")
SEE ALSO: *WARRIOR-PURPOSE, PERCEPTION-CHANGING-SOCIAL BASE*

PERCEPTION-HINGE-EVERYTHING-[PERCEPTION IS THE HINGE FOR EVERYTHING]: (Warriors know that perception is the hinge for everything man is or does.)
SELECTED REFERENCES: **The Power of Silence - Page [56.9-57.2]** ("I don't quite understand what you're...point could become anything he wanted.)
SEE ALSO: *PERCEPTION, SORCERY-HINGE*

PERCEPTION-INCONCEIVABLE-[WARRIORS ARE CAPABLE OF INCONCEIVABLE PERCEPTION]: (Warriors know that when the assemblage point moves and aligns emanations different from the normal ones, their senses perceive the world in inconceivable ways.)
SELECTED REFERENCES: **The Fire From Within - Page [125.3-125.5]** ("I've mentioned to you that the...human senses perceive in inconceivable ways.")
SEE ALSO: *PERCEPTION, ASSEMBLAGE-POINT-MOVING, SEEING, WORLD-OTHER*

PERCEPTION-LULL-[THE LULL OF PERCEPTION]: (Warriors know that there is a lull of perception between normal and heightened awareness; a blackness of non-perception between two perceptual possibilities.)
SELECTED REFERENCES: **Tales of Power - Page [132.1-132.2]** ("I was concerned with those jolts...being that is going to die.) **The Power of Silence - Page [100.4-100.6]** (He said that at that very...of the sorcerers who carved it.)
SEE ALSO: *PERCEPTION-BARRIER-BREAKING, ASSEMBLAGE-POINT-SHIFT-LATERAL, AWARENESS-HEIGHTENED*

PERCEPTION-MOLD-[THE MOLD OF PERCEPTION]: (Warriors know that since the average man cannot perceive energy directly, he processes his perception to fit a mold; the description of the world.)
SELECTED REFERENCES: **The Art of Dreaming - Page [3.2-3.5]** ("What would it mean to me...our perception is all that exists.) **The Art of Dreaming - Page - [4.1-4.9]** (Don Juan's conception was that our...essence of everything, energy itself, directly.)
SEE ALSO: *DESCRIPTION-WORLD, PERCEPTION-SOCIAL-BASE, PERCEPTION*

PERCEPTION-NORMAL-[NORMAL PERCEPTION]: (Warriors know that normal perception occurs when intent lights up a portion of the emanations inside man's luminous cocoon while at the same time brightening a long extension of those same emanations extending into infinity outside the cocoon; human beings are drafted into a system of perception from the moment of birth; the assemblage point's normal position is not innate, but rather is brought about by a process of habituation; most people spend their lives striving to adjust their perception to conform to the demands of that system, a system which normally rules them for life; the act of countermanding that system and perceiving energy directly is what transforms an average person into a sorcerer.)

SELECTED REFERENCES: The Power of Silence - Page [101.8-102.1] (He had explained that normal perception...extending into infinity outside our cocoon.) The Art of Dreaming - Page [75.8-76.6] (Don Juan changed the subject and...are fixed on the same spot.)

SEE ALSO: ASSEMBLAGE-POINT, INTERNAL-DIALOGUE, ATTENTION-FIRST, PERCEPTION, SORCERY, HABITUATION, DESCRIPTION-WORLD, SORCERY, AWARENESS-NORMAL

PERCEPTION-POSSIBILITIES-[THE POSSIBILITIES OF PERCEPTION]: (Warriors know that perception has more possibilities than the mind can conceive.)

SELECTED REFERENCES: The Power of Silence - Page [243.8-244.2] (Don Juan fixed me with his stare...possibilities than the mind can conceive.")

SEE ALSO: PERCEPTION, HUMAN-ALTERNATIVES-POSSIBILITIES-POTENTIAL

PERCEPTION-PREDATOR-[A PREDATOR'S WAY OF PERCEIVING]: (Warriors know that normal perception is a predator's way of perceiving; a very efficient manner of appraising and classifying food and danger.)

SELECTED REFERENCES: The Art of Dreaming - Page [4.8] ("Our way of perceiving is a...appraising and classifying food and danger.) The Art of Dreaming - Page [7.5] (Don Juan pointed out that we...what the predator's eye normally sees.)

SEE ALSO: PERCEPTION, AWARENESS-NORMAL

PERCEPTION-PURE-[PURE PERCEPTION]: (Warriors know that pure perception is the awareness of warriors as they fly on the wings of perception and experience the scope of the true pair.)

SELECTED REFERENCES: The Second Ring of Power - Page [1.6-1.7] (Prior to that jump don Juan...creation, the tonal and the nagual.)

SEE ALSO: PERCEPTION-WINGS, UNKNOWN-JOURNEY, TONAL-NAGUAL-DICHOTOMY

PERCEPTION-QUIETUDE-DARKNESS-[PERCEPTION IN STATES OF QUIETUDE AND DARKNESS]: (Warriors know that perception suffers a profound jolt when placed into a context of quietude and darkness; hearing takes the lead then and signals from the living entities around us can be detected with a combination of our auditory and visual senses; in darkness, especially while suspended, the eyes become subsidiary to the ears.)

SELECTED REFERENCES: The Eagle's Gift - Page [236.6-236.8] (His contention was that perception suffers...eyes become subsidiary to the ears.)

SEE ALSO: WARRIOR-SUSPENDING, EARS, WARRIOR-HEARING

PERCEPTION-REALITY-[THE REALITY OF PERCEPTION]: (Warriors know they cannot believe in the final reality of their perception; warriors become aware that perception is merely a product of the position of the assemblage point.)

SELECTED REFERENCES: A Separate Reality - Page [189.7-189.8] (This was the first time I...of my head with his knuckles.)

SEE ALSO: REALITY-INTERPRETATION, PERCEPTION, ASSEMBLAGE-POINT, ASSEMBLAGE POINT-MOVING, ASSEMBLAGE-POINT-POSITION

PERCEPTION-REALM-CHAOTIC-VS-AWARENESS-WORLD-ORDERLY-
[THE CHAOTIC REALM OF PERCEPTION VS THE ORDERLY WORLD
OF AWARENESS]: SEE: ATTENTION-FIRST-FOCUS-[THE FOCUS OF
THE FIRST ATTENTION]

PERCEPTION-RECONCILING-[RECONCILING PERCEPTION]:
(Warriors know that they must reconcile the two distinct forms of
perception into a unified whole; this is the task of consolidating the totality
of oneself.)
    SELECTED REFERENCES: The Eagle's Gift - Page [166.3-166.4] (The task of
remembering, then, was...rearranging *intensity* into a linear sequence.)
    SEE ALSO: *PERCEPTION, REMEMBERING-TASK*

PERCEPTION-REGARDING-DISREGARDING-[THE REGARDING AND
DISREGARDING OF NORMAL PERCEPTION]: (Warriors know that
employing the Eagle's emanations and interpreting them as reality is a
tricky affair because what man senses is such a small portion of the total
scope of those emanations; for that reason, warriors know it is ridiculous to
put much stock in those perceptions, and yet it isn't possible to disregard
those perceptions either; warriors must wriggle their way in between these
contradictory truths as they learn the mastery of awareness.)
    SELECTED REFERENCES: The Fire From Within - Page [43.5-43.9] (He went on to
say that...hard way - after courting tremendous dangers.")
    SEE ALSO: *PERCEPTION, INVENTORY, EAGLE-COMMAND, AWARENESS-*
MASTERY, WARRIOR-CONTRADICTION-KNOWLEDGE, EQUILIBRIUM

PERCEPTION-SOCIAL-BASE-[THE SOCIAL BASIS OF PERCEPTION]:
(Warriors know that the social base of perception is the physical certainty
that the world is made of concrete objects; a fierce effort is put forth by all
the black magicians to guide the warrior in perceiving the world this way;
warriors struggle to expand their perception beyond its social base.)
    SELECTED REFERENCES: The Power of Silence - Page [264.3-264.9] (Sorcerers,
however, were capable of finding...their freedom from perceptual convention.) The Art of
Dreaming - Page [3.2-3.6] ("What would it mean to me...the world the way we do.")
    SEE ALSO: *PERCEPTION, DESCRIPTION-WORLD, WORLD-SOLID-OBJECTS,*
CONCRETENESS, ATTENTION-TONAL, PERCEPTION-CHANGING-SOCIAL-BASE,
SORCERY-TASK-GRAND, ENERGY

PERCEPTION-SOCIAL-BASE-CHANGING-[CHANGING PERCEPTION
AT ITS SOCIAL BASE]: SEE: PERCEPTION-CHANGING-SOCIAL BASE-
[CHANGING PERCEPTION AT ITS SOCIAL BASE]

PERCEPTION-SORCERER-[THE SORCERERS' PERCEPTION]: (Warriors
know that the sorcerers' perception is the physical certainty that energy is
all there is; warriors struggle to learn to perceive energy directly, to learn to
"see".)
    SELECTED REFERENCES: The Art of Dreaming - Page [3.7-3.9] ("How then should
we perceive the...guiding us to perceive energy directly.)
    SEE ALSO: *SEEING, ENERGETIC-ESSENCE-PERCEIVING*

PERCEPTION-SORCERY-[PERCEPTION AND SORCERY]: (Warriors
know that the average man lacks the energy necessary to deal with sorcery;
perceiving the worlds that sorcerers perceive requires employing a cluster of
energy fields not normally used; the average man is not capable of using

that cluster of energy fields because he does not have enough energy to do so.)

SELECTED REFERENCES: The Power of Silence - Page [x.6-xi.2] ("This is what I mean when I say...perceive something which ordinary perception cannot.)
SEE ALSO: *PERCEPTION, ENERGY, SORCERY*

PERCEPTION-SPLIT-[*SPLIT PERCEPTION*]: *(Warriors know that split perception is the simultaneous awareness of both reason and silent knowledge; split perception, when accomplished by the warriors' own means, is called the free movement of the assemblage point; the all-out effort to encourage this free movement is called "reaching out for the third point.")*

SELECTED REFERENCES: Tales of Power - Page [47.1-47.9] ("Can an outsider, looking at a...time is no longer binding him.") The Power of Silence - Page [145.6-147.2] (I abruptly pulled over to the...cannot speak of what it knows.) The Power of Silence - Page [224.1-224.3] (Split perception, if accomplished by one's...reaching out for the third point.") The Power of Silence - Page [238.6-238.8] The old nagual explained that the...alternately or at the same time.)
SEE ALSO: *ASSEMBLAGE-POINT-MOVEMENT-FREE, POINT-THIRD, KNOWLEDGE-SILENT, REASON*

PERCEPTION-STALKING-[*STALKING PERCEPTION*]: *(Warriors know that the act of acquiring energetic uniformity and cohesion outside the normal world is called stalking perception.)*

SELECTED REFERENCES: The Art of Dreaming - Page [77.5] (The old sorcerers called the entire...outside the normal world stalking perception.) The Art of Dreaming - Page [78.6-78.7] (He said that the old sorcerers...another person, a bird, or anything
SEE ALSO: *ENERGETIC-UNIFORMITY-COHESION, PERCEPTION, STALKING-ART, POWER-GIFTS*

PERCEPTION-STEADY-WORLD-[*THE STEADY PERCEPTION OF THE WORLD*]: *(Warriors know that the mystery of alignment accounts inexplicably for the ability of the assemblage point and its glow of awareness to assemble a select cluster of the Eagle's emanations into a steady perception of the world.)*

SELECTED REFERENCES: The Art of Dreaming - Page [7.5-7.8] (After *seeing* what the assemblage point...them how or why energy moves.)
SEE ALSO: *PERCEPTION, ALIGNMENT-MYSTERY, ASSEMBLAGE-POINT, EAGLE-EMANATIONS-CLUSTERING*

PERCEPTION-SYSTEM-NORMAL-[*THE SYSTEM OF NORMAL PERCEPTION*]: SEE: PERCEPTION-NORMAL-[NORMAL PERCEPTION]

PERCEPTION-SYSTEMS-OLD-NEW-[*THE OLD AND NEW SYSTEMS OF PERCEPTION*]: *(Warriors know that at the moment when the assemblage point is displaced beyond a certain threshold, there is no longer any sense to what is perceived because our normal system of perception becomes inoperative; but then, the old system rallies and helps transform our incomprehensible new perceptions into a thoroughly comprehensible world; in other words, we create a new system of perception.)*

SELECTED REFERENCES: The Art of Dreaming - Page [76.6-77.2] (He went on to say that...in front of a new world.")
SEE ALSO: *PERCEPTION, ATTENTION-FIRST, ATTENTION-SECOND*

PERCEPTION-TOTAL-[TOTAL PERCEPTION]: (*Warriors know that total perception is a matter of complete energetic uniformity and cohesion; total perception is the successful stalking of perception.*)
SELECTED REFERENCES: **The Art of Dreaming** - Page [230.1-230.4] ("Start your dreaming by lying on...what total perception means," I lied.) **The Art of Dreaming** - Page [231.7-232.7] (She told me then that she...to be an ultimately personal item.)
SEE ALSO: PERCEPTION, ENERGETIC-UNIFORMITY-COHESION, PERCEPTION-STALKING, INTENT-PROJECTING

PERCEPTION-TOTAL-STEP-FIRST-[THE FIRST STEP TO TOTAL PERCEPTION]: (*Warriors know that the first step to total perception is the act of dreaming and creating an object in a dream, from the point of view of a total materialization of the object from the dreamer's own perception.*)
SELECTED REFERENCES: **The Art of Dreaming** - Page [231.9-232.1] (The next thing in their developing...the first step to total perception.)
SEE ALSO: PERCEPTION-TOTAL, PERCEPTION-STALKING, DREAMING-ART

PERCEPTION-TRI-DIMENSIONAL-[TRI-DIMENSIONAL-PERCEPTION]: (*Warriors know that sorcerers perceive their actions with depth; those actions are tri-dimensional because they have a third point of reference; in order to achieve the third point of reference, warriors must perceive two places at once.*)
SELECTED REFERENCES: **The Power of Silence** - Page [221.6-221.9] ("A sorcerer perceives his actions with...must perceive two places at once.")
SEE ALSO: DEPTH, PERCEPTION, PERCEPTION-TWO-DIMENSIONAL, POINT-THIRD, HERE-HERE

PERCEPTION-TWO-DIMENSIONAL-[TWO-DIMENSIONAL PERCEPTION]: (*Warriors know that the world of daily life consists of two points of reference; for example, here and there, in and out, up and down, good and evil; properly speaking, our daily lives are two-dimensional; none of what the average man perceives has any "depth", in the way sorcerers describe the term.*)
SELECTED REFERENCES: **The Power of Silence** - Page [221.2-221.3] ("The world of daily life consists...we perceive ourselves doing has depth.")
SEE ALSO: DEPTH, PERCEPTION

PERCEPTION-UNIVERSAL-[THE UNIVERSAL HOMOGENEITY OF PERCEPTION]: (*Warriors know that human perception is universally homogenous because the assemblage points of the entire human race are fixed on the same spot.*)
SELECTED REFERENCES: **The Art of Dreaming** - Page [76.5-76.6] (He assured me that human perception...are fixed on the same spot.)
SEE ALSO: PERCEPTION, POINT-FIRST, ASSEMBLAGE-POINT-FIXATION

*PERCEPTION-WINGS-[THE WINGS OF PERCEPTION]: (*Warriors know they have wings with which they can touch their totality; the wings of perception carry warriors as they explore the perceptual possibilities within and beyond man's band of emanations; the wings of perception can transport warriors either to the most recondite confines of the nagual or to the most inconceivable worlds of the tonal; it is the wings of perception that warriors use to journey into the unknown.*)
SELECTED REFERENCES: **Tales of Power** - Page [156.5-159.7] ("The *tonal* shrinks at given times...moment before a cab came along.) **Tales of Power** - Page [272.3-272.5] "Last night your bubble of perception...true nature. You are a cluster.) **Tales of Power** - Page [277.7-277.9] ("Last night was the first time...back a bag of rocks, though.") **Tales of Power** - Page [278.5-

278.6] ("Tomorrow's task is to plunge into...perception and fly into that infinitude.") **The Second Ring of Power - Page [1.5-2.2]** (Toward the end we all said...say anything to clarify their nature.) **The Second Ring of Power - Page [326.7-327.4]** (But Eligio was stronger and his...the experience of my own journey.)
SEE ALSO: *UNKNOWN-JOURNEY, PERCEPTION-BARRIER-BREAKING, PERCEPTION-BUBBLE, HERE-HERE*

PERCEPTUAL-BLANKNESS-MOMENT-*[THE MOMENT OF PERCEPTUAL BLANKNESS]: SEE: PERCEPTION-BARRIER-BREAKING-[BREAKING THE BARRIER OF PERCEPTION]*

PERCEPTUAL-DUALISM-*[PERCEPTUAL DUALISM]: (Warriors know that perceptual dualism is an awareness of the true duality of our luminous being; a split perception; a simultaneous perception of both the first and second points; a simultaneous awareness of both reason and the antecedents of reason; a simultaneous awareness of each member of the true pair.)*
SELECTED REFERENCES: **The Second Ring of Power - Page [275.6-275.8]** (Perhaps all of us are continually perceiving...two distinct memories of one event.) **The Eagle's Gift - Page [238.7-239.1]** (In my case, on one occasion...into the fog and beyond it.) **The Eagle's Gift - Page [308.6-309.1]** (I then used my eyes deliberately...bodies when I closed my eyes.) **The Fire From Within - Page [272.7-279.6]** (Over the years don Juan and...really was, where I really belonged.) **The Power of Silence - Page [145.6-147.2]** (I abruptly pulled over to the side...therefore, it cannot speak of what it knows.)
SEE ALSO: *WARRIOR-DUALISM, PERCEPTION-SPLIT, POINT-THIRD, PAIR-TRUE, PERCEPTION-WINGS, REASON, KNOWLEDGE-SILENT*

PERCEPTUAL-INPUT-WEIGHT-*[THE WEIGHT OF THE WARRIORS' PERCEPTUAL INPUT]: (Warriors know that when their awareness becomes bogged down with the weight of their perceptual input, the best remedy is to deliver themselves a stalking jolt with the idea of their own death.)*
SELECTED REFERENCES: **The Power of Silence - Page [109.4-109.5]** (He explained that when a sorcerer's...death to deliver that *stalking* jolt.)
SEE ALSO: *STALKING-ONESELF, STALKING-JOLT, DEATH-ADVISER*

PERSECUTOR-VICTIM-*[PERSECUTORS VS VICTIMS]: SEE: VICTORY-DEFEAT-[VICTORY VS DEFEAT]*

PERSISTENCE-WARRIOR-*[THE WARRIORS' PERSISTENCE]: SEE: WARRIOR-PERSISTENCE-[THE WARRIORS' PERSISTENCE]*

PERSONAL-HISTORY-ERASING-[ERASING PERSONAL HISTORY]: (Warriors know the freedom which comes with the loss of personal history; as they lose their personal history, warriors free themselves from the encumbering thoughts of other people and create a fog around themselves; warriors must erase themselves until nothing in their world is any longer for sure or real, including themselves; warrior don't take things for granted, they erase themselves instead.)*
SELECTED REFERENCES: **Journey to Ixtlan - Page [9.9-17.5]** (I asked him if I was interfering...drive him to the nearby town.) **Journey to Ixtlan - Page [37.4-37.5]** ("I'm an old man; with age...is sitting with me right here.") **Journey to Ixtlan - Page [80.6-81.2]** ("You always feel compelled to explain...witnessing all the marvels of it.") **Tales of Power - Page [242.1-242.3]** ("Erasing personal history and its three...you to feel sorry for yourself.)
SEE ALSO: *, LETTING-GO, WARRIOR-FOG-CREATE, WARRIOR-SECRETS, PERSONAL-HISTORY-ERASING-TECHNIQUES-THREE, WARRIOR-FREEDOM*

PERSONAL-HISTORY-ERASING-TECHNIQUES-THREE-[THE THREE TECHNIQUES FOR ERASING PERSONAL HISTORY]: (Warriors know there are three techniques which will help erase personal history without making warriors become shifty, evasive and unnecessarily dubious about themselves and their actions; the first is losing self-importance; the second is assuming responsibility; the third is using death as an adviser.)

SELECTED REFERENCES: **Tales of Power** - Page [240.7-240.8] (He explained that in order to help...dubious about himself and his actions.)

SEE ALSO: *SELF-IMPORTANCE-LOSING, RESPONSIBILITY-ASSUMING, DEATH-ADVISER*

PERSONAL-POWER-[PERSONAL POWER]: SEE: POWER-PERSONAL-[PERSONAL POWER]

PERSONALITIES-WARRIOR-[THE PERSONALITIES OF WARRIORS]: SEE: WARRIOR-PERSONALITIES-[THE PERSONALITIES OF WARRIORS]

PERSONALITY-FEMALE-[THE FOUR FEMALE PERSONALITIES]: SEE: WARRIOR-FEMALE-[FEMALE WARRIORS]

PERSONALITY-MALE-[THE FOUR MALE PERSONALITIES]: SEE: WARRIOR-MALE-[MALE WARRIORS]

PERSONALITY-TYPES-[THE STALKERS' CLASSIFICATIONS OF PERSONALITY TYPES]: SEE: PEOPLE-TYPES-[THE STALKERS' CLASSIFICATIONS OF PERSONALITY TYPES]

PETTINESS-DROPPING-[DROPPING ONE'S PETTINESS]: (Warriors know that using death as an adviser helps him drop his pettiness.)

SELECTED REFERENCES: **Journey to Ixtlan** - Page [34.4-35.1] ("The thing to do when you're...in the light of my death.)

SEE ALSO: *DEATH-ADVISER, SELF-IMPORTANCE-LOSING, DROPPING-THINGS-LIVES, LETTING-GO*

*PETTY-TYRANT-[THE PETTY TYRANT]: (Warriors know the petty tyrant is a critical ingredient of the new seer's strategy for ridding warriors of self-importance and helping them realize that impeccability is the only thing that matters on the path of knowledge; the petty tyrant is a tormentor, someone who either holds the power of life and death over warriors or simply annoys them to distraction; the petty tyrant is utilized in conjunction with the attributes of the warrior to temper the spirit of the warrior; nothing prepares warriors to face the presence of the unknowable as much as the challenge of dealing with impossible people in positions of power; warriors know that it is the obsessive manipulation of the known that turns people into petty tyrants.)

SELECTED REFERENCES: **The Eagle's Gift Page** - Page [130.1-130.5] (Don Juan went on explaining...fulfillment of my true task.) **The Eagle's Gift Page** - Page [134.6-134.8] (As far as the *dreaming* scene...don Juan's orders to the letter.) **The Fire From Within** - Page [16.4-30.6] (He said that the most effective strategy...of the petty tyrants for life.") **The Fire From Within** - Page [32.6-32.7] ("I had always been oppressed...thought I had lost my mind.") **The Fire From Within** - Page [108.7-108.8] ("I've mentioned to you...is to move their assemblage points.")

SEE ALSO: *WARRIOR-ATTRIBUTES, PROGRESSION-THREE-PHASE, WARRIOR-SPIRIT, KNOWN-OBSESSIVE-MANIPULATION, PETTY-TYRANT-(ALL)*

PETTY-TYRANT-ASSEMBLAGE-POINT-MOVING-[THE PETTY TYRANT AS A METHOD OF MOVING THE ASSEMBLAGE POINT]: *(Warriors know that the reason the new seers placed such a high value on the interaction with petty tyrants was because the petty tyrant forces warriors to use the principles of stalking and in so doing move the assemblage point.)*
    SELECTED REFERENCES: The Fire From Within - Page [108.7-108.8] ("I've mentioned to you," he continued...is to move their assemblage points.") The Fire From Within - Page [169.8-169.9] (He said that I could now understand...seers to move their assemblage points.)
    SEE ALSO: PETTY-TYRANT, ASSEMBLAGE-POINT-MOVING, STALKING-ART

PETTY-TYRANT-AWARENESS-[PETTY TYRANTS AND AWARENESS]: *(Warriors know that their knowledge of the true function of petty tyrants is merely an introduction to the larger topic of awareness.)*
    SELECTED REFERENCES: The Fire From Within - Page [31.5-32.7] (As we strolled leisurely, don Juan...thought I had lost my mind.")
    SEE ALSO: PETTY-TYRANT, AWARENESS

PETTY-TYRANT-KING-SIZE-[DON JUAN'S KING-SIZE PETTY TYRANT]- (TOP)

PHYSICAL-BODY-[THE PHYSICAL BODY]: SEE: BODY-PHYSICAL-[THE PHYSICAL BODY]

PIECES-SUN-[PIECES OF THE SUN]: SEE: SUN-PIECES-[PIECES OF THE SUN]

PIOUS-MAN-WAY-[THE PIOUS MAN'S WAY]: *(Warriors know that the pious man's way is the second of the three bad habits of life; the pious man's way is to accept everything at face value and feel as if we know what's going on.)*
    SELECTED REFERENCES : Tales of Power - Page [52.1-52.2] ("There are three kinds of bad...on. That's the pious man's way.) Tales of Power - Page [75.5-75.8] ("What Genaro showed you yesterday is...one can find flaws in it.") The Fire From Within - Page [265.6-265.7] (I was left with a tantalizing feeling...what I had *seen* to everyone.)
    SEE ALSO : HABITS-BAD-THREE, BIGOT-WAY, FOOL-WAY, WARRIOR-WAY

*PITY-PLACE-NO-[THE PLACE OF NO PITY]: *(Warriors know that the place of no pity is a specific position of the assemblage point that shines in the eyes of sorcerers; the site of ruthlessness; the forerunner of silent knowledge; the second point; the point warriors must pass in order to reach the third point; when the spirit descends on a human being it allows its presence to move the individual's assemblage point to the place of no pity; when the assemblage point reaches the place of no pity it is forced to abandon its customary place of self-reflection.)*
    SELECTED REFERENCES: The Power of Silence - Page [118.3-118.5] ("As I have already told you...way, the first principle of sorcery.) The Power of Silence - Page [124.4-124.8] ("What new position is that, don...position, the more the eyes shone.) The Power of Silence - Page [125.9-126.1] ("You must recollect the first time...you then. Ruthlessness possessed you then.) The Power of Silence - Page [131.3-131.4] ("But for sorcerers to use the shine...is especially true for the naguals.") The Power of Silence - Page [238.6-238.7] (The old nagual explained that the...point, the place of no pity.) The Power of Silence - Page [143.8-144.1] ("I never just make conversation," he...who makes his assemblage point move.) The Power of Silence - Page [154.3-154.4] (He said that from the moment...its customary place of self-reflection.) The Power of Silence - Page [164.3-164.4] ("Finally, when it became impossible to...reach the place of no pity.") The Power of Silence - Page [168.4-168.7] ("But puncturing your rationality was not...had forgotten about your violent outbursts.") The Power of Silence - Page [169.4-169.5] ("Continuity is so important in our...pity, continuity is never the same.) The Power

of Silence - Page [199.2-199.3] (He also said that "The place...concern," was the forerunner of reason.) **The Power of Silence - Page [213.5]** (I asked don Juan to explain...the energy to manipulate it myself.) **The Power of Silence - Page [249.6-250.2]** (Don Juan said that in the...he had not responded at all.) **The Power of Silence - Page [259.3-259.5]** (Don Juan understood with perfect clarity...would return to its point of departure.)
SEE ALSO: *RUTHLESSNESS, POINT-SECOND, CONCERN-PLACE, RUTHLESSNESS-SHINE, SPIRIT-DESCENT*

PLACE-CONCERN-[THE PLACE OF CONCERN]: SEE: CONCERN-PLACE-[THE PLACE OF CONCERN]

PLACE-PITY-[THE PLACE OF NO PITY]: SEE: PITY-PLACE-NO-[THE PLACE OF NO PITY]

PLAN-WARRIOR-[THE WARRIORS' PLAN]: SEE: WARRIOR-PLAN-[THE WARRIORS']

PLANET-LEFT-[THE LEFT PLANET]: SEE: PLANETS-WARRIORS-[THE PLANETS OF WARRIORS]

PLANET-RIGHT-[THE RIGHT PLANET]: SEE: PLANETS-WARRIOR-[THE PLANETS OF WARRIORS]

PLANETS-WARRIORS-[THE PLANETS OF WARRIORS]: (Warriors know that the eight female warriors of the nagual's party are divided into two bands called the right and left planets; the right planet is made up of four stalkers, the left planet of four dreamers.)
SELECTED REFERENCES: **The Eagle's Gift - Page [176.6-176.7]** (The eight female warriors are divided...stalking; the dreamers were taught dreaming.) **The Eagle's Gift - Page [209.6-209.7]** (He said that all the members of his...foremost authorities on their respective activities.)
SEE ALSO: *STALKING-ART, DREAMING-ART, WARRIOR-FEMALE*

PLANS-OF-ACTION-[PLANS OF ACTION]: (Warriors know that plans of action are appropriate only if one is dealing with average human beings; in the face of the unknown, however, the only hope for survival is to acquiesce and understand.)
SELECTED REFERENCES: **The Power of Silence - Page [60.1-60.3]** (Don Juan asked Belisario to recommend...survival was to acquiesce and understand.)
SEE ALSO: *WARRIOR-ACQUIESCENCE, UNDERSTANDING, WARRIOR-PLAN*

PLANT-[PLANTS]: (Warriors know the true nature of plants; plants [especially trees] are much closer to man than many animals; trees and men can develop a great relationship because they share emanations; plants have the most intense communication with inorganic beings.)
SELECTED REFERENCES: **Journey to Ixtlan - Page [5.9-6.2]** (We hiked in the surrounding desert...the wind are agreeing with me.") **Journey to Ixtlan - Page [23.3-25.4]** ("I am going to talk to my..."Thank you," in a loud voice.) **The Fire From Within - Page [164.8-166.4]** (Don Juan abruptly changed the subject...to become trees to do that.") **The Power of Silence - Page [39.7-40.6]** It was as cool and quiet...as we discuss my definitive journey.")
SEE ALSO: *PLANT-(ALL), POWER-PLANTS, GAZING, WARRIOR-TREES, TOLTECS-DESCENT-DEPTHS, TREES*

PLANT-GAZING-[PLANT GAZING]: SEE: GAZING-[GAZING]

PLANT-POWER-[POWER PLANTS]: SEE: POWER-PLANTS-[POWER PLANTS]

PLANT-TALKING-[TALKING TO PLANTS]: (Warriors know they can use the act of talking to plants as an exercise in losing self-importance and appreciating the mystery of the world.)
SELECTED REFERENCES: Journey to Ixtlan - Page [23.3-23.8] ("I am going to talk to...do it in front of others.) Journey to Ixtlan - Page [25.3-25.4] ("The world around us is a mystery..."Thank you," in a loud voice.) Journey to Ixtlan - Page [26.8-27.2] (After a long hike we came to a..."What are you trying to do?") Journey to Ixtlan - Page [36.1-36.2] (Be still. There is no need...that you feel its presence around you.")
SEE ALSO: PLANT, SELF-IMPORTANCE-LOSING, WORLD-MYSTERIOUS

PLATE-FRONT-[THE FRONT PLATE]: SEE: FRONT PLATE-[THE FRONT PLATE]

PLAYER-REAL-[THE REAL PLAYER]: (Warriors know that the spirit is the only real player in our lives; we are not really players.)
SELECTED REFERENCES: The Art of Dreaming - Page [200.2] ("I don't know that, and neither...are mere pawns in its hands.)
SEE ALSO: SPIRIT, POWER-PRISONER, SPIRIT-COMMANDS, SPRIT-DESIGNS

*PLUMED-SERPENT-[THE PLUMED SERPENT]: (Warriors know that the plumed serpent is another term for the luminous configuration of the nagual's party as they leave the world and burn with the fire from within.)
SELECTED REFERENCES: The Eagle's Gift - Page [311.8-312.3] (Don Juan and don Genaro very swiftly...slit that had appeared in the room.) The Eagle's Gift - Page [313.7-314.3] (Don Juan made me jump at...And then the lights were gone.)
SEE ALSO: NAGUAL-PARTY-WARRIORS, FIRE-WITHIN

POETRY-[POETRY]: (Warriors know that the power of poetry is to provide a release for the warriors' spirit; a tool which warriors use to stalk themselves; warriors can jolt themselves with the shock of beauty which an appropriate poem can provide; warriors can borrow from a poet's longing.)
SELECTED REFERENCES: The Teachings of Don Juan - Page [11.2-11.4] (Para mi solo recorrerlos caminos que...there I travel looking, looking, breathlessly.) The Teachings of Don Juan - Page [137.7-137.9] (He came even closer and started...recall the forgotten memories of childhood.) Journey to Ixtlan - Page [109.5-109.7] (That was exactly the way I...quisiera llorar, quisiera rier de sentimiento.) Journey to Ixtlan - [266.5-266.8] (He reminded me that I had...recondite corner of my flowery garden.) Tales of Power - Page [0.3-0.5] (The conditions of a solitary bird...fifth, that it sings very softly.) Tales of Power - [114.8-115.3] ("I remember a poem that you...up an indescribable melancholy for me.) The Eagle's Gift - Page [39.5-40.6] (I recounted for her the great...they were not soothing at all.) The Eagle's Gift - Page [118.9-119.2] (I am already given to the power...past the Eagle to be free.) The Eagle's Gift - Page [123.4-123.7] (I had remembered that don Juan...I read poems to don Juan.) The Eagle's Gift - Page [307.4-307.8] (Silvio Manuel came to my side...el aguila pasar a la libertad.) The Eagle's Gift - Page [309.8-310.4] (Don Genaro, who had always made jokes...was overpowering. I felt a shiver.) The Fire From Within - Page [43.9-44.2] (Don Juan was sitting where he...from the works of Spanish-speaking poets.) The Fire From Within - Page [127.7-128.4] (Don Juan had defined the scope...breaks loose and flows into infinity.) The Fire From Within - Page [241.2-241.9] ("Let's sing again," he added. "Let's...no longer have anything to fear.) The Power of Silence - Page [49.5-51.2] ("I like poems for many reasons...simplicity, that is determining our fate.") The Power of Silence - Page [110.4-111.8] ("Your problem is very simple," he...this shock of beauty, is stalking. The Art of Dreaming - Page [201.3-201.6] (Don Juan asked me to read...the air, leave me half-blind.)
SEE ALSO: STALKING-JOLT, WARRIOR-SPIRIT, STALKING-ART

POETS-[POETS]: (Warriors know that some poets have an intuitive grasp of the nature of the universe; many poets are keenly aware of the connecting link with the spirit, but they are aware of it intuitively, not in the deliberate, pragmatic way of warrior-sorcerers; poets catch the mood of warriors and explain what can hardly be explained, even though they don't have firsthand

knowledge of the spirit; poets intuit with great certainty, that there is some unnamed factor determining our fate.)
> SELECTED REFERENCES: The Power of Silence - Page [49.5-49.7] ("I like poems for many reasons...They hit pretty close to it though.") The Power of Silence - Page [111.6-111.8] ("As I hear the words," don Juan...this shock of beauty is *stalking*.")
> SEE ALSO: *POETRY, WARRIOR-MOOD , WARRIOR-PASSIONATE, BEAUTY*

POINT-DOUBT-[THE POINT OF NO DOUBT]: SEE: DOUBT-POINT-[THE POINT OF NO DOUBT][

POINT-FIRST-[THE FIRST POINT]: *(Warriors know that the first point is another term for reason; not every human being is squarely on the position of reason; those who are on the spot itself are the true leaders of mankind.)*
> SELECTED REFERENCES: The Power of Silence - Page [145.6-146.9] (I abruptly pulled over to the...knowledge that you cannot yet voice.") The Power of Silence - Page [239.4-239.5] (The old nagual went on to...was the exercising of their reason.)
> SEE ALSO: *REASON, POINT-SECOND, POINT-THIRD, POINT-THIRD-INVERSION*

POINT-SECOND-[THE SECOND POINT]: *(Warriors know that the second point is another term for the position of the assemblage point known as the place of no pity or ruthlessness)*
> SELECTED REFERENCES: The Power of Silence - Page [145.6-146.9] (I abruptly pulled over to the...knowledge that you cannot yet voice.") The Power of Silence - Page [238.6-238.7] (The old nagual explained that the...point, the place of no pity.)
> SEE ALSO: *PITY-PLACE-NO, RUTHLESSNESS, POINT-FIRST, POINT-THIRD*

*POINT-THIRD-[THE THIRD POINT, THE THIRD POINT OF REFERENCE]: *(Warriors know that the third point is another term for silent knowledge; the third point of reference is intent; it is the spirit; it is the somersault of thought into the inconceivable; it is the act of reaching beyond our boundaries and touching the inconceivable.)*
> SELECTED REFERENCES: Tales of Power - Page [46.2-47.3] ("Well, a sorcerer can double up...has no notion of his duality.") The Power of Silence - Page [198.7-199.1] (When I asked him to talk about...been squarely on that location either.") The Power of Silence - Page [213.5-213.7] (I asked don Juan to explain...fluctuate between reason and silent knowledge.) The Power of Silence - Page [216.2-216.9] (He insisted that for a movement...I had perceived "here and here.") The Power of Silence - Page [219.6-219.9] (He added that for the rational...point can be made to move.") The Power of Silence - Page [221.1-221.9]) (I urged him to try to...must perceive two places at once.") The Power of Silence - Page [224.2-224.9] (He assured me that every nagual...our boundaries and touching the inconceivable.") The Power of Silence - Page [238.6-241.1] (The old nagual explained that the...especially the power he was addressing.)
> SEE ALSO: *KNOWLEDGE-SILENT, POINT-FIRST, POINT-SECOND, ASSEMBLAGE-POINT-MOVEMENT-FREE*

POINT-THIRD-INVERSION-[THE INVERSION OF THE THIRD POINT]: *(Warriors know that the third point became inverted at some point in man's ancient past; reason, which is now the first point, used to be the third point and silent knowledge, which used to be the first point, is now the third point; the age of reason came into being because the position of reason can be clearly "seen" from the position of silent knowledge and vice versa.)*
> SELECTED REFERENCES: The Power of Silence - Page [198.7-199.3] (When I asked him to talk...concern," was the forerunner of reason.) The Power of Silence - Page [239.6-240.8] (The nagual said there had been...in an endless sea of islands.)
> SEE ALSO: *POINT-FIRST, POINT-THIRD, BRIDGES-TWO-ONE-WAY, GARDEN-EDEN, ABSTRACT-RETURN, REASON-AGE*

POINT-THIRD-REACHING-[REACHING OUT FOR THE THIRD POINT]: SEE: ASSEMBLAGE-POINT-MOVEMENT-FREE-[THE FREE MOVEMENT

OF THE ASSEMBLAGE POINT]

POLICEMAN-FLEET-FOOTED-[THE FLEET-FOOTED POLICEMAN]:
SEE: CARLOS-POLICEMAN-[CARLOS AND THE FLEET-FOOTED
POLICEMAN]-(TOP)

*POPULATIONS-LEAVE-WORLD-[POPULATIONS LEAVE THE
WORLD]: (Warriors know that at one time in the history of the ancient
Toltecs, entire populations left the world under the auspices of the
movement of the assemblage point.)
    SELECTED REFERENCES: The Fire From Within - Page [5.1-5.3] ("There were seers,
however, who escaped...other worlds and never came back.) The Fire From Within - Page
[177.4-177.6] (Don Juan maintained that it is...kind of contorted shape or manner.) The Fire
From Within - Page [285.8-286.2] (I told don Juan that since...because I wanted to be with you.")
    SEE ALSO: ASSEMBLAGE-POINT-MOVING, MAN-KNOWLEDGE

PORFIRIO-[PORFIRIO]-(TOP)

PORTAL-INTENT-[THE PORTAL OF INTENT]: SEE: AWARENESS-
HEIGHTENED-[HEIGHTENED AWARENESS]

POSITIONS-TWIN-[THE TWIN POSITIONS]: (Warriors know that
together, the twin positions are the initial position in which dreamers hold
their physical bodies to begin dreaming and the position in which they hold
their energy bodies to fixate the assemblage point on the dreaming position
of their choosing; the two positions make a unit and a perfect relationship
exists between any two positions; the only way to have absolute control of
dreams is to use the technique of the twin positions.)
    SELECTED REFERENCES: The Art of Dreaming - Page [228.8-230.6] (She urged me
to sit down...said were not possible to foretell.) The Art of Dreaming - Page [231.5-231.6] (She
told me that her art...but it cannot be explained or comprehended.) The Art of Dreaming - Page
[232.7-233.2] ("Do you still want to go..."It just happens. Like everything else.")
    SEE ALSO: DREAMING-ART, ENERGY-BODY, ASSEMBLAGE-POINT-FIXATION

POSSESSIVENESS-[POSSESSIVENESS]: (Warriors know they must rid
themselves of the fixation to possess things; warriors protect their dreaming
bodies by eliminating material possessions from their lives.)
    SELECTED REFERENCES: The Eagle's Gift - Page [22.2-22.9] ("Your compulsion to
possess and hold...he was protecting my dreaming body.")
    SEE ALSO: ATTENTION-SECOND-FACES-TWO, OBSESSION, DREAMING-
BODY

POSSIBILITIES-HUMAN-[HUMAN ALTERNATIVES, POSSIBILITIES
AND POTENTIAL]: SEE: HUMAN-ALTERNATIVES-POSSIBILITIES-
POTENTIAL-[HUMAN ALTERNATIVES, POSSIBILITIES AND
POTENTIAL]

POSTURE-WARRIOR-[THE WARRIORS' POSTURE]: SEE: WARRIOR-
FORM [THE WARRIORS' FORM], WARRIOR-PROTECT-POSITION-
[THE WARRIORS' PROTECTIVE POSITION], WARRIOR-FIGHTING-
FORM-[THE WARRIORS' FIGHTING FORM], WARRIOR-VIGIL-
POSITION-[THE WARRIORS' POSITION OF SITTING "IN VIGIL"]

POTENTIAL-HUMAN-[HUMAN ALTERNATIVES, POSSIBILITIES AND
POTENTIAL]: SEE: HUMAN-ALTERNATIVES-POSSIBILITIES-
POTENTIAL-[HUMAN ALTERNATIVES, POSSIBILITIES AND
POTENTIAL]

POWER-[POWER]: (*Warriors know power is something they simply deal with; an incredible far-fetched affair; at first warriors may not have it or even fully realize that it exists, yet still they know that something is there, something that was not noticeable before; next power manifests itself to warriors as something uncontrollable that comes to them; it is nothing and yet it makes marvels appear before their eyes; and finally power is something inside warriors, something that controls their acts and at the same time obeys their commands; power is what warriors seek, but at the same time power is also the warriors' great enemy because the easiest thing to do is to give in to power and not handle it with ultimate sobriety and humbleness; power is a feeling one has about certain things; power commands warriors and yet it obeys them.*)
SELECTED REFERENCES: **The Teachings of Don Juan - Page [24.6-24.7]** ("Don't get me wrong don Juan...of knowing things that are useless?") **The Teachings of Don Juan - Page [53.2-53.8]** ("What kind of a power is...thus, knowledge was indeed power.) **The Teachings of Don Juan - Page [86.1-86.5]** ("He will know at this point...or how to use his power.") **A Separate Reality - Page [95.1]** ("You fail to understand that a...*see*, he attempts to gain power.") **Journey to Ixtlan - Page [97.3-97.7]** ("There are certain things we will...acts and yet obeys one's command.") **Journey to Ixtlan - Page [104.3-104.5]** (He said that the spirit...but always with great caution.) **Journey to Ixtlan - Page [122.3-122.5]** ("Power is a very peculiar affair...you and yet it obeys you.) **Tales of Power - Page [23.7]** ("Knowledge and power. Men of knowledge...at a given moment everything changed.") **Tales of Power - Page [92.1-92.2]** ("Genaro's power was like a tide...was testing you and you failed.") **The Fire From Within - Page [170.2-170.5]** (Don Juan said next that the...energy of alignment is that force.) **The Power of Silence - Page [xi.3-xi.5]** ("Everything I've put you through," don...and that he can reach it.")
SEE ALSO: *ENEMY-THIRD, WARRIORSHIP-VS-SORCERY, POWER-(ALL)*

**POWER-ACCESSIBLE-[BECOMING ACCESSIBLE TO POWER]: SEE: WARRIOR-ACCESSIBILITY-[THE ACCESSIBILITY OF THE WARRIOR]*

POWER-ACQUIRING-[ACQUIRING POWER]: (*Warriors know that acquiring power is a reflection of one's relationship with the abstract; as warriors clear their link with intent, they appear to acquire power.*)
SELECTED REFERENCES: **The Teachings of Don Juan - Page [21.6-21.7]** (Don Juan believed that states of...incidental to the acquisition of power.)
SEE ALSO: *POWER, WARRIOR-INTENT-LINK*

POWER-ACTS-[ACTS OF POWER]: (*Warriors know that acts of power are expressions of the nagual; expressions of the warriors' intent.*)
SELECTED REFERENCES: **Tales of Power - Page [44.5-44.6]** ("A double is the sorcerer himself...only a tale of power to you.) **Tales of Power - Page [113.6-113.7]** ("The world adjusts itself to itself...an omen, an act of power.)
SEE ALSO: *POWER-TALES*

POWER-ACTS-WITNESS-[A WITNESS TO ACTS OF POWER]-(TOP)

POWER-AFFAIR-[AN AFFAIR OF POWER]: (*Warriors know that an affair of power is another term for an act of power.*)
SELECTED REFERENCES: **Tales of Power - Page [73.6-73.9]** (There don Genaro demonstrated his great...my tension whenever I needed to.)
SEE ALSO: *POWER, POWER-ACTS*

POWER-AIDS-WARRIOR-[POWER AIDS THE WARRIOR]: (*Warriors know they must learn to relax and abandon themselves, because only if they fear nothing will power open the road and aid them.*)
SELECTED REFERENCES: **The Eagle's Gift - Page [280.7-280.8]** ("Good," Florinda said. "I see that...road and aid us. Only then.)

SEE ALSO: *POWER, POWER-FLOW, POWER-DESIGNS, ABANDON, WARRIOR-ABANDON-CONTROLLED*

POWER-APPOINTMENT-*[AN APPOINTMENT WITH POWER]-(TOP):* SEE: *DREAMER-ART-[THE ART OF THE DREAMER]-(TOP)*

POWER-AVENUES-*[THE AVENUES TO POWER]:* (*Warriors know that power provides avenues to us in accordance with our impeccability.*)
SELECTED REFERENCES: **Journey to Ixtlan** - Page [91.1-91.4] ("I've never told you about *dreaming*...nothing or very little about it.) **Tales of Power** - Page [243.4-243.5] ("Power provides according to your impeccability...the necessary avenues. That is the rule.")
SEE ALSO: *POWER, WARRIOR-IMPECCABILITY, DREAMING-ART*

POWER-BATTLE-*[A BATTLE OF POWER]-(TOP)*

POWER-BATTLE-WARRIOR-*[THE WARRIORS' BATTLE OF POWER]:* SEE: *WARRIOR-POWER-BATTLE-[THE WARRIORS' BATTLE OF POWER]*

POWER-BIDS-SEPARATE-*[THE SEPARATE BIDS FOR POWER]:* (*Warriors know the old and new seers made separate bids for power with regard to the development of their dreaming bodies; the old seers sought a replica of the body with more physical strength while the new seers seek a dreaming body which is merely a blob of light; the dreaming body of the old seers was personal and intensely humanized while the dreaming body of the new seers is impersonal and more conducive to understanding and examination.*)
SELECTED REFERENCES: **The Fire From Within** - Page [251.2-251.7] ("Right at this juncture is where...answers that were equally personal, humanized.)
SEE ALSO: *DREAMING-BODY, DREAMING-BODY-SEER-NEW, DREAMING-BODY-TOLTECS, SEER-OLD, SEER-NEW, POWER*

POWER-BID-WARRIOR-*[THE WARRIORS' BID FOR POWER]:* SEE: *WARRIOR-POWER-BID-[THE WARRIORS' BID FOR POWER]*

POWER-BREATHES-LIFE-TWIG-*[POWER BREATHES LIFE INTO A TWIG]-(TOP)*

POWER-CENTER-*[THE CENTER OF POWER]:* (*Warriors know that a power center is another term for a power spot or a place where power objects may be found.*)
SELECTED REFERENCES: **Journey to Ixtlan** - Page [202.9-203.1] (He pointed to one of the...where power objects might be found.)
SEE ALSO: *POWER SPOT, POWER-OBJECTS*

POWER-CHECK-KEEPING-*[KEEPING POWER IN CHECK]:* (*Warriors know that they must maintain an appropriate control over the power that they accesses on the path of knowledge; warriors must keep their power in check.*)
SELECTED REFERENCES: **The Teachings of Don Juan** - Page [87.5-87.8] ("This is the time when a man...clarity, power, and knowledge is enough.")
SEE ALSO: *POWER, POWER-MANAGING*

POWER-CLAIMING-*[CLAIMING POWER]:* SEE: *KNOWLEDGE-CLAIMING-POWER-[CLAIMING KNOWLEDGE AS POWER*

POWER-COMMANDS-*[THE COMMANDS OF POWER]:* (*Warriors know that they must obey the commands of power.*)

SELECTED REFERENCES: **The Second Ring of Power** -Page [54.6] ("He bothered with you," she went...told him to do with you.")
SEE ALSO: *POWER, POWER-DESIGNS, SPIRIT-DESIGNS, EAGLE-COMMANDS*

POWER-CRYSTAL-QUARTZ-[POWER QUARTZ CRYSTALS]: (Warriors know that power quartz crystals are power objects used for sorcery purposes; quartz crystals that have been touched by a spirit giver of power or ally; these power objects are usually used to kill, but can also be used to aid the dreamer with his dreaming.)
SELECTED REFERENCES: **Journey to Ixtlan** - Page [204.1-206.7] (Once I engaged them in...if you can't find anything else.")
SEE ALSO: *POWER-OBJECTS, ALLIES*

POWER-DANCING-[POWER DANCING]-(TOP): SEE: JUAN-FLYING- [DON JUAN'S FLYING]-(TOP)

POWER-DESIGNS-[THE DESIGNS OF POWER]: (Warriors know that they must humbly accept the nature and designs of power; warriors understand that no one can discern the designs of power, because the spirit always decides its own course; power is and power moves, these are the only things that warriors know for sure.)
SELECTED REFERENCES: **Journey to Ixtlan** - Page [164.1-164.2] ("You found the right place...without any plan on your part.") **Tales of Power** - Page [55.4-55.7] (Have you ever asked yourself, why...stop the fulfillment of that design.") **Tales of Power** - Page [97.4-97.6] ("I'm saying that we all are...of your life will take you.") **Tales of Power** - Page [176.4-176.6] ("What makes a man ready, so...has a benefactor. Power decides that.") **Tales of Power** - Page [187.2] ("Genaro is very warm,": don Juan...that you found a gentle benefactor.") **Tales of Power** - Page [188.3-188.5] ("If you're dumb enough not to...of predicting the quirks of power.") **The Second Ring of Power** - Page [54.6] ("He bothered with Juan," she went...told him to do with you.") **The Eagle's Gift** - Page [206.9-207.1] (I asked don Juan why there...is impossible to know its designs.) **The Power of Silence** - Page [151.8-151.9] (He then took my experience of...lets the spirit decide his course.) **The Power of Silence** - Page [158.3] (He added that each apprentice was...the spirit decide about the particulars.) **The Power of Silence** - Page [226.3-226.7] ("You are not like any one...accept the designs of the abstract.")
SEE ALSO: *POWER, WARRIOR-INTENT-LINK, SPIRIT-DESIGNS, POWER-FLOW*

POWER-DICTUMS-[THE DICTUMS OF POWER]: SEE: POWER-DESIGNS-[THE DESIGNS OF POWER]

POWER-DIRECTION-[THE DIRECTION OF POWER]: (Warriors know that power flows from the south towards the north.)
SELECTED REFERENCES: **Journey to Ixtlan** - Page [155.4-155.5] ("The dying sun will glow on...to the south. To the vastness.")
SEE ALSO: *POWER, SOUTH-DIRECTION*

POWER-DISPLAY-[THE DISPLAY OF POWER]: (Warriors know that a display of power is another term for the movements which a sorcerer performs in order to demonstrate his connection with the flow of power.)
SELECTED REFERENCES: **A Separate Reality** - Page [203.2-203.4] (There was a fairly steady wind...not mind spending the night there.) **A Separate Reality** - Page [211.9-212.1] (He commended my resolution and called it...show off in front of her.)
SEE ALSO: *POWER*

POWER-ENCOUNTER-[AN ENCOUNTER WITH POWER]: (Warriors know it is their great fortune to have an encounter with power; but if warriors do not have sufficient personal power to meet power, they are surely lost.)

SELECTED REFERENCES: **Journey to Ixtlan - Page [133.4-134.4]** ("What happened to you last night...power the bridge would have collapsed.") **Journey to Ixtlan - Page [155.2-155.4]** ("And thus you will dance to your...will sit here and watch you.)
SEE ALSO: *WARRIOR-BATTLE-POWER, POWER, NAGUAL-FACING*

POWER-EXTRA-RING-[THE EXTRA RING OF POWER]: SEE: POWER-RING-EXTRA-[THE EXTRA RING OF POWER]

POWER-FAVORS-WARRIOR-[WARRIORS AND THE FAVORS OF POWER]: SEE: WARRIOR-POWER-FAVORS-[WARRIORS AND THE FAVORS OF POWER]

POWER-FEELING-[POWER IS STORED AS A FEELING]: SEE: POWER-PERSONAL-[PERSONAL POWER]

POWER-FIRST-RING-[THE FIRST RING OF POWER]: SEE: POWER-RING-FIRST-[THE FIRST RING OF POWER]

POWER-FLOW-[THE FLOW OF POWER]: (Warriors know they can never guess or determine how power will flow to them; no man can say that power would flow to him if his life would be different.)
SELECTED REFERENCES: **Tales of Power - Page [195.1-195.3]** ("You once told me that if...if your life would be different.) **The Power of Silence - Page [233.5-23.7]** (The current dragged him a long distance...the river was follow its flow.)
SEE ALSO: *POWER, POWER-DESIGNS*

POWER-FOOD-[POWER FOOD]: (Warriors define power food as the meat of an animal that had power.)
SELECTED REFERENCES: **Journey to Ixtlan - Page [122.8-123.2]** (He picked up the gourds with...power sink slowly into your body.") **Journey to Ixtlan - Page [132.7-133.4]** ("Eat your power food," he urged...it, because of your own stupidity.) **Journey to Ixtlan - Page [214.6-214.7]** (Don Juan had told me, as we...I could dry for "power food.")
SEE ALSO: *POWER*

POWER-FULFILLING-BID-[FULFILLING THE WARRIORS' BID FOR POWER]: (Warriors remain detached from thoughts regarding the fulfillment of their bid for power; warriors understand that they will not fulfill their destiny because there is no destiny; all they can hope for instead is that someday they may fulfill their power in a way that is completely beyond reason or comprehension.)
SELECTED REFERENCES: **Tales of Power - Page [10.5-10.6]** (He had warned me that the...melancholy, or even a suicidal depression.) **Tales of Power - Page [145.3-145.5]** ("I still don't understand the meaning...you're about to fulfill your power.) **The Eagle's Gift - Page [306.9-307.3]** (Vicente came to my side next...the fulfilling of a sacred trust.)
SEE ALSO: *POWER, WARRIOR-POWER-BID, POWER-PROMISE*

POWER-GIFTS-[THE GIFTS OF POWER]: (Warriors know that the gifts of power are the challenges that power gives to the warrior; the opportunities that power gives warriors to learn and progress on the path of knowledge; when gifts of power are given by another sorcerer who preselects the nature of the gift, the warrior is bound to that sorcerer and the negative results of his gift; once such a gift is accepted, the warrior becomes an indulging and dependent sorcerer; these preselected gifts of power have to do with the procedures necessary to manipulate the energy body in such a way as to allow for complete perception and cohesion in a given position of the assemblage point.)
SELECTED REFERENCES: **A Separate Reality - Page [30.4-36.5]** (I told don Juan that once...can do to salvage your gift.") **Tales of Power - Page [229.7-229.8]** ("Pablito and you

will go into...accompanied by such a fine warrior.") **The Second Ring of Power - Page [282.2-282.3]** (The Nagual said that if you...those bouts were gifts of power.") **The Power of Silence - Page [122.1-122.2]** (I had asked don Juan how the...which had moved those assemblage points.) **The Art of Dreaming - Page [62.6-62.7]** (Don Juan said that what transpired...gladly and proudly accepting their gifts.) **The Art of Dreaming - Page [204.8-205.1]** ("I think I can understand detachment...to put aside such a gift.") **The Art of Dreaming - Page [213.6-213.8]** ("You have to understand that only you...either, the gifts or the price.) **The Art of Dreaming - Page [214.7-215.5]** (He said that the tenant was...line of very indulging, dependent sorcerers.") **The Art of Dreaming - Page [216.6-217.4]** ("Why do you call the death defier's...to work a very complex machine.) **The Art of Dreaming - Page [217.9-218.6]** ("Every grand shift has different inner...that finished off the old sorcerers.") **The Art of Dreaming - Page [224.1-224.5]** (Gathering all the energy I could...me a thing of similar value.) **The Art of Dreaming - Page [229.2-229.6]** (She began then to whisper in my...had a most remarkable crystalline sound.) **The Art of Dreaming - Page [230.7-231.2]** (She abruptly changed the subject and asked...taking you deeper into my dream.")
    SEE ALSO: *WARRIOR-CHALLENGE, LEARNING-HARDSHIPS, WARRIORSHIP-VS-SORCERY, POWER*

POWER-HIDDEN-[MAN'S HIDDEN POWER]: (Warriors know that power is accessible to every human being at all times; the warriors' path of knowledge really involves nothing more than allowing ourselves to be convinced that power is hidden in our being and that it is possible for us to access it.)

    SELECTED REFERENCES: **The Second Ring of Power - Page [84.3-84.8]** (There was no doubt left in my...human nature, he was probably right.) **The Second Ring of Power - Page [234.9-235.2]** (I was almost embarrassed to tell...kind of power we may have?") **The Power of Silence - Page [xi.3-xi.9]** ("Everything I've put you through...silent knowledge, depends on your own temperament.") **The Power of Silence - Page [46.6-46.7]** (What he was saying was that...making the assemblage point change positions.) **The Power of Silence - Page [72.3-72.5]** (He said that heightened awareness was...from which there is no return.) **The Power of Silence - Page [228.8-228.9]** (Don Juan explained that man's...between his stupidity and his ignorance.)
    SEE ALSO: *HUMAN-ALTERNATIVES-POSSIBILITIES-POTENTIAL, POWER-REACHING, WARRIOR-AWARENESS-CONCEALED, AWARENESS-POLARITY-APPLYING*

POWER-HINGE-[EVERYTHING WARRIORS DO HINGES ON PERSONAL POWER]: (Warriors know that everything they do hinges on their personal power.)

    SELECTED REFERENCES: **Journey to Ixtlan - Page [164.8-164.9]** ("Everything a man does hinges on...you have very little personal power.")
    SEE ALSO: *POWER-PERSONAL, POWER, SORCERY-HINGE*

POWER-HOUR-WARRIOR-[THE WARRIORS' HOUR OF POWER]: SEE: WARRIOR-HOUR-POWER-[THE WARRIORS' HOUR OF POWER]

POWER-HUNTER-[BECOMING A HUNTER OF POWER]: SEE: HUNTER-POWER-[BECOMING A HUNTER OF POWER]

POWER-INDICATIONS-[THE INDICATIONS OF POWER]: (Warriors know that an indication of power is another term for an omen.)

    SELECTED REFERENCES: **Tales of Power - Page [106.7-106.9]** ("You are going to sit here...round itself up and give an indication.")
    SEE ALSO: *OMENS*

POWER-IS-POWER-MOVES-[POWER IS AND POWER MOVES]: (Warriors know that there is no explanation for the fact that power exists and that it moves inexplicably and of its own accord.)

    SELECTED REFERENCES: **The Art of Dreaming - Page [7.7-7.8]** ("How are those filaments you talk...them how or why energy moves.")
    SEE ALSO: *POWER, POWER-DESIGNS*

POWER-KNOWLEDGE-[POWER AND KNOWLEDGE]: (*Warriors know that knowledge is not power; power rests on the kind of knowledge one holds and the manner in which one applies it.*)
  SELECTED REFERENCES: **The Teachings of Don Juan - Page [24.6-24.7]** ("Don't get me wrong, don Juan...of knowing things that are useless?")
  SEE ALSO: *KNOWLEDGE, POWER, KNOWLEDGE-VS-POWER*

POWER-VS-KNOWLEDGE-[POWER VS KNOWLEDGE]: SEE: KNOWLEDGE-VS-POWER-[KNOWLEDGE VS POWER]

POWER-LITTLE-RING-[THE LITTLE RING OF POWER]: SEE: POWER-RING-FIRST-[THE FIRST RING OF POWER]

POWER-MANAGING-[MANAGING POWER]: (*Warriors know that it takes ultimate sobriety to manage the power that flows through their renewed link with intent.*)
  SELECTED REFERENCES: **The Power of Silence - Page [104.1-104.3]** (Don Juan explained that at one...needed to manage all that power.)
  SEE ALSO: *WARRIOR-SOBRIETY, WARRIOR-INTENT-LINK, WARRIORSHIP-VS-SORCERY, POWER-CHECK-KEEPING*

POWER-MOVEMENTS-[THE MOVEMENTS OF POWER]: (*Warriors define the movements of power as the individual movements that make up the warriors' last dance of power; each of these movements is obtained through a struggle with power, so that the warriors' last dance becomes a story which grows as that individual grows in personal power.*)
  SELECTED REFERENCES: **Journey to Ixtlan - Page [154.4-154.6]** ("Can you teach me that dance...as he grows in personal power.")
  SEE ALSO: *WARRIOR-DANCE-LAST-POWER, POWER-PERSONAL*

POWER-MOVES-[POWER IS AND POWER MOVES]: SEE: POWER-IS-POWER-MOVES-[POWER IS AND POWER MOVES]

POWER-MOVES-DESIRE-[POWER MOVES INDEPENDENT OF THE INTERVENTION OF DESIRE]: SEE: DESIRE-INTERVENTION-POWER-[POWER MOVES INDEPENDENT OF THE INTERVENTION OF DESIRE]

POWER-NUMBERS-[POWER NUMBERS]: SEE FOUR-[FOUR IS A POWER NUMBER], FORTY-EIGHT-[FORTY-EIGHT IS THE WARRIORS' NUMBER]

*POWER-OBJECT-[POWER OBJECTS]: (*Warriors know that certain objects are permeated with power; these power objects are in the realm of war objects designed for strife; power objects are fostered by powerful men with the aid of friendly spirits; anything can become a power object, and the power that it has depends on its owner's power; the nature of these objects is to be at war, because the part of our attention which focuses on them to give them power is a very dangerous and belligerent part of ourselves; the fixation of the second attention is poured into power objects to make them what they are.*)
  SELECTED REFERENCES: **The Teachings of Don Juan - Page [21.8-24.7]** (Throughout my field notes there are...are like a game for children.") **The Teachings of Don Juan - Page [26.4-27.5]** (I then told them that I...the Atlanteans would walk at night.) **A Separate Reality - Page [233.2-233.4]** (I asked him how people enticed...produce the auditory illusion of noise.) **Journey to Ixtlan - Page [191.2-191.4]** ("You've been watching it for a ...that pebble into a power object.") **Journey to Ixtlan - Page [202.9-203.5]** (He pointed to one of the...should polish

and care for it.) **Journey to Ixtlan - Page [204.1-206.7]** (Once I engaged them in...if you can't find anything else.") **The Second Ring of Power - Page [313.6-313.9]** (She explained that the particular formation...the east, in his right hand.) **The Eagle's Gift - Page [10.6-14.1]** ("Something happened to me in the...have been any fear in him.") **The Eagle's Gift - Page [22.2-22.7]** ("Your compulsion to possess and hold...weak face of the second attention.)

SEE ALSO: *OBSESSION, ATTENTION-SECOND-FIXATION, ATTENTION-SECOND-FACES-TWO, ALLIES, POWER-OBJECT-HURLING*

POWER-OBJECT-HURLING-[HURLING A POWER OBJECT]: (Warriors know that hurling a power object at an enemy is a last means of defense when one's life is threatened.)

SELECTED REFERENCES: **The Teachings of Don Juan - Page [178.4-178.8]** (He warned me that the form had to...only under "severe conditions of seriousness.")

SEE ALSO: *POWER-OBJECT*

POWER-PERMANENT-[PERMANENT POWER]: SEE: POWER-SEAT-[THE SEAT OF POWER]

POWER-PERSONAL-[PERSONAL POWER]: (Warriors know that personal power is like a mood or a feeling, something like being lucky; personal power is something that every human being acquires regardless of their origin; warriors hunt for power and they learn to store it and use it in the best way possible; warriors store personal power by living and acting impeccably; they plug up all the points of drainage through which their power would otherwise escape; personal power has the peculiarity that it is unnoticeable when it is being stored; warriors understand that they are only the sum of their personal power; that sum determines how they live and how they die; warriors store power but clearly understand that power does not belong to anyone; warriors learn to trust their personal power because it is all they have in this mysterious world; warriors are impeccable when they trust their personal power whether it is small or enormous; the boosting of the tonal so the nagual can emerge is called personal power; power is personal, it belongs to oneself alone; warriors store power away as a personal finding; power is stored through a feeling; in order to have power one must live with power.)

SELECTED REFERENCES: **Journey to Ixtlan - Page [122.3-122.8]** ("Power is a very peculiar affair..."You have to do it yourself.") **Journey to Ixtlan - Page [132.4-132.6]** ("A hunter of power watches everything...power one must live with power.") **Journey to Ixtlan - Page [153.6-154.7]** ("This is the site of your...those who have an impeccable spirit.") **Journey to Ixtlan - Page [155.3-155.4]** ("And thus you will dance to your...will sit here and watch you.) **Journey to Ixtlan - Page [157.3-157.6]** ("It doesn't matter how one was...you haven't been convinced so far.") **Journey to Ixtlan - Page [158.3-158.5]** (I asked him to explain what...the idea of storing personal power.") **Journey to Ixtlan - Page [159.3-159.7]** ("What are we going to do...don't need to have a plan.") **Journey to Ixtlan - Page [164.2-165.1]** "What kind of leaves did you...Power will find a way.") **Journey to Ixtlan - Page [167.5]** ("Trust your personal power," he said...has in this whole mysterious world.") **Journey to Ixtlan - Page [168.3-168.5]** (Don Juan put his hand over...whether it is small or enormous.") **Journey to Ixtlan - Page [170.3-170.8]** (Don Juan came back and jogged...brought back my feelings of insecurity.) **Journey to Ixtlan - Page [177.7-178.1]** (Since the natural abodes of the...unnoticeable when it is being stored.") **Journey to Ixtlan - Page [178.7]** ("Don't tax yourself with explanations," he...have begun to happen to you.) **Tales of Power - Page [6.1-6.7]** ("How can I arrive at the...personal power to tip the scales.") **Tales of Power - Page [8.9-9.5]** ("You didn't have this knowledge before...my explanation will not explain it.") **Tales of Power - Page [23.6-23.7]** ("All of us go through the...at a given moment everything changed.") **Tales of Power - Page [85.5-85.6]** ("There's no need to be confused...it's up to your personal power.") **Tales of Power - Page [105.6-105.9]** ("Now that you are here, what...should say that you're doing fine.") **Tales of Power - Page [115.3-115.4]** (Don Juan whispered that he *had*...as the place of his death.) **Tales of Power - Page [160.8-161.1]** ("Any threat to the *tonal* always...That boosting is called personal power.") **Tales of Power - Page [231.5-231.7]** (Personal power decides who can...personal power to profit by their acts.) **Tales of Power - Page [287.1-287.5]** (Your only chance is your impeccability...will be for either of you.") **The Second Ring of Power - Page [230.3-230.5]** ("Everybody has enough personal power for...when he thought I was indulging.) **The Second Ring of Power - Page [232.4-234.3]** ("Where are you going to go...Do you see what I mean?") **The Eagle's Gift - Page [30.3-30.6]** (The pressure in my life also...life was coming to an end.)

SEE ALSO: *POWER, WARRIOR-IMPECCABILITY*

POWER-PERSONAL-STORING-[STORING PERSONAL POWER]: SEE: ENERGY-DRAINAGE-[PLUGGING POINTS OF ENERGY DRAINAGE], POWER-PERSONAL

POWER-PLANTS-[POWER PLANTS]: (Warriors know that there are three power plants used by the nagual to move the apprentice's assemblage point, Mescalito, the devil's weed and the little smoke; power plants are only an aid, they cause untold damage to the body and their use must be indicated by power itself; power plants are used by warriors to get a final and total boost of such unimaginable magnitude that it is impossible to understand; the use of power plants has been de-emphasized by the seers of the new cycle; power plants function as they do in part because of their particular luminous structures; power plants share the largest amount of emanations with man, not the emanations of awareness, but other emanations in general.)

SELECTED REFERENCES: **The Teachings of Don Juan - Page [20.9-21.7]** (Don Juan used, separately and on...reality was differentiated from ordinary reality.) **A Separate Reality - Page [5.5-7.3]** (In 1961, a year after our...as the "ally removing one's body.") **Journey to Ixtlan - Page [vii.5-vii.9]** (I have already presented the case...don Juan was attempting to teach me.) **Journey to Ixtlan - Page [xii.9-xiii.2]** (That monumental event in my life...sensitivity which had fostered their use.) **Journey to Ixtlan - Page [256.1-256.3]** (I told him that the events...has been to show you that.) **Tales of Power - Page [3.5-3.9]** (Finally I managed to steer the...do not seem to need them.") **Tales of Power - Page [242.8-243.1]** ("That was your mistake," he said...us; we needed those power plants.") **Tales of Power - Page [243.7-245.7]** ("Did the power plants help me...excursions into the *nagual*, the unknown.") **Tales of Power - Page [246.2-246.5]** (Don Juan said that after the...get out of the whole mess.) **The Second Ring of Power - Page [264.6-265.8]** ("That must be the woman who...would be staggering to the mind.) **The Second Ring of Power - Page [286.7-287.2]** ("Sure. By the time Eligio had to...them you'd be a great warrior.") **The Second Ring of Power - Page [289.4-289.9]** ("How can I do that...is hidden, waiting for that day.") **The Second Ring of Power - Page [293.8-294.1].** ("The attention under the table is...*dreaming*, the Nagual taught us gazing.) **The Second Ring of Power - Page [322.9-323.4]** ("It's very hard to get into...we have absolute control over it.") **The Second Ring of Power - Page [323.5-324.7]** ("The Nagual told me," a Gorda...he had an awesome, fearsome side.") **The Fire From Within - Page [3.6-3.8]** (I asked him then about the...were very daring, but very mistaken.") **The Fire From Within - Page [4.7-5.9]** (Don Juan said that after some...happened to them with power plants.) **The Fire From Within - Page [133.8-133.9]** ("I used to give you power plants...that can have a similar effect.) **The Fire From Within - Page [165.1-165.3]** ("How big are their cocoons?" I...awareness, but other emanations in general.) **The Fire From Within - Page [267.2-267.4]** (Don Juan said then that he had...of the world is never final.) **The Art of Dreaming - Page [18.9-19.1]** (Don Juan said that this observation...even knowing it, they created dreaming.)

SEE ALSO: *MESCALITO, DEVIL'S-WEED, LITTLE SMOKE*

POWER-PLANTS-BOOST-[THE BOOST OF POWER PLANTS]: (Warriors know that when they are complete, they are given a final boost with power plants.)

SELECTED REFERENCES: **The Second Ring of Power - Page [286.5-286.9]** ("Eligio also went on a different...plants to Eligio until the very last.") **The Second Ring of Power - Page [289.7-289.9]** (Since you took another path, you...is hidden, waiting for that day.)

SEE ALSO: *POWER-PLANTS, EARTH-BOOST*

POWER-PRISONER-[THE PRISONER OF POWER]: *(Warriors know that power sets up the limits within which warriors must operate; in this sense, every warrior is a prisoner of power, a prisoner who has one free choice, the choice to act either like an impeccable warrior or to act like a nincompoop; in the final analysis, warriors progress even beyond that choice, and in another sense become slaves of power because even that choice is no longer a choice for them; eventually warriors cannot act in any way but impeccably; to act in any other way would drain their power and cause their demise.)*

SELECTED REFERENCES: **Tales of Power - Page [55.4-56.2]** (Have you ever asked yourself, why...not let you go either way.") **Tales of Power - Page [195.4-195.6]** ("Genaro and I have to act...drain him and cause his demise.) **Tales of Power - Page [287.7-287.8]** ("A warrior must be always ready...particular, but what a great fortune!") **The Art of Dreaming - Page [200.1-200.2]** ("Will she continue my dreaming practices...are mere pawns in its hands.)

SEE ALSO: *POWER, WARRIOR-CHOICE, INTENT-SLAVES*

POWER-PROMISE-[THE PROMISE OF POWER]: *(Warriors know that the promise of power is the fulfillment of the designs of power for the warrior; the promise of power is a promise that power makes to all men and women as luminous beings; every warrior has a different fate and there is no way of telling what the promise of power will be for any given individual.)*

SELECTED REFERENCES: **Tales of Power - Page [55.6-55.7s]** ("To make it into an ordinary...stop the fulfillment of that design.") **Tales of Power - Page [287.2-287.5]** (You must wait without looking back...will be for either of you.") **The Power of Silence - Page [227.6-227.8]** ("None of us resolves anything," he...the solution. Why? No one knows.")

SEE ALSO: *POWER, POWER-FULFILLING-BID, POWER-PROMISE-FALSE, WARRIOR-DESTINY, WARRIOR-FATE, REDEMPTION-AVENUE*

POWER-PROMISES-FALSE-[THE FALSE PROMISES OF POWER]: *(Warriors know that the inorganic beings try and lure dreamers to remain in their world with false promises of power, promises which appeal to the dreamers' sense of self-indulgence.)*

SELECTED REFERENCES: **The Art of Dreaming - Page [109.6-109.9]** ("Are those pitfalls the result of...way of plummeting into a pitfall.") **The Art of Dreaming - Page [123.1]** ("I assure you, don Juan, that...interested in either, and that's that.")

SEE ALSO: *INORGANIC-BEINGS-TRICKERY, POWER-PROMISE*

POWER-PROTECTION-[THE PROTECTION OF POWER]-(TOP)

POWER-PURSUIT-[THE PURSUIT OF POWER]: *(Warriors know that the sorcerers of antiquity were given to the pursuit of power; their selfish pursuit of power was their downfall however, because it kept them from the attainment of total freedom.)*

SELECTED REFERENCES: **The Teachings of Don Juan - Page [65.6-65.7]** (My benefactor used to say that...was good reason to be powerful.") **The Teachings of Don Juan - Page [66.1-66.4]** ("I don't like its power...root goes deeper into the ground.) **The Teachings of Don Juan - Page [66.5-66.7s]** (I myself do not seek it...moving at the top of the trees.) **The Teachings of Don Juan - Page [106.3-106.4]** ("Can a man actually fly through...you that. Every man is different.") **The Teachings of Don Juan - Page [175.5]** (As I have already told you...not for those who seek power.)

SEE ALSO: *POWER, SORCERY-FUTILITY-PITFALLS, LITTLE-SMOKE, SORCERER-ANTIQUITY*

POWER-REACHING-[REACHING POWER]: *(Warriors know that they must learn that they are capable of reaching power.)*

SELECTED REFERENCES: **The Power of Silence - Page [xi.3-xi.9]** ("Everything I've put you through...silent knowledge, depends on your own temperament.")

SEE ALSO: *POWER, POWER-HIDDEN*

POWER-REASON-[THE REASON TO WANT POWER]: *(Warriors know that before they succeed in accessing power, they may not have a reason to want power; however, if they store enough power, power itself will supply them with a good reason.)*
    SELECTED REFERENCES: **Journey to Ixtlan - Page [136.3-136.4]** ("But why should I want power...good reason. Sounds crazy, doesn't it?")
    SEE ALSO: *POWER*

POWER-RING-[THE RING OF POWER]-(TOP)

POWER-RING-EXTRA-[THE EXTRA RING OF POWER]: *(Warriors know that the extra ring of power is another term for the second ring of power.)*
    SELECTED REFERENCES: **Journey to Ixtlan - Page [212.5]** ("Your difficulty is that you haven't...doesn't know *not-doing*," he said.) **Journey to Ixtlan - Page [255.8-255.9]** ("But how did he force me to...and allow your body to *see*.")
    SEE ALSO: *POWER-RING-SECOND*

POWER-RING-FIRST-[THE FIRST RING OF POWER]: *(Warriors know that the first ring of power is the ring of power that they consciously bring into the world very soon after they are born; the little ring of power; the ring of power that is hooked to the "doing" of the world; the ring of power with which we create the world of solid objects and circumstance; reason is the first ring of power and its companion is talking; the attention of the tonal; the ring of doing; our awesome but taken-for-granted ability to impart order to the perception of the daily world.)*
    SELECTED REFERENCES: **Journey to Ixtlan - Page [211.6-211.8]** ("Let's say that when every one...into being at this very moment.") **Tales of Power - Page [98.3-98.5]** ("We, the luminous beings, are born...reason learns to accept and defend.) **The Second Ring of Power - Page [274.8-275.2]** (Don Juan said that the core...our perception of the daily world.) **The Second Ring of Power - Page [277.8]** (Don Juan said that our "first...is all there is to us.)
    SEE ALSO: *REASON, TALKING, ATTENTION-TONAL, DOING, POWER, DOING-RING*

*POWER-RING-SECOND-[THE SECOND RING OF POWER]: *(Warriors know that the second ring of power is the ring of power developed by a man of knowledge; the ring of "not-doing"; the will; with the second ring of power a warrior can spin another world; the second ring of power is the secret of the luminous beings; the attention of the nagual.)*
    SELECTED REFERENCES: **Journey to Ixtlan - Page [212.1-212.5]** ("You see", he continued, "every one...doesn't know *not-doing*," he said.) **Tales of Power - Page [98.3-98.7]** ("We, the luminous beings, are born...*will* is more engulfing than *reason*.) **The Second Ring of Power - Page [275.3-275.6]** (The second domain was the "attention...or the "attention of the nagual.") **The Second Ring of Power - Page [277.8-277.9]** (Don Juan had said that our...death is it revealed to us.)
    SEE ALSO: *POWER, POWER-RING-FIRST, NOT-DOING, MAN-KNOWLEDGE, NAGUAL, ALLIES-SPINNING, ATTENTION-NAGUAL, LUMINOUS-BEINGS-SECRET*

POWER-RING-SORCERER-[THE SORCERERS' RING OF POWER]-(TOP)

POWER-RING-WARRIOR-[THE WARRIORS' RING OF POWER]: SEE: POWER-RING-SECOND-[THE SECOND RING OF POWER]

POWER-SEAT-[THE SEAT OF]: *(Warriors know that the seat of power is power without end; the seat of a warriors' personal battle with power; the scenes that will characterize the warriors' individual battle with power.)*

SELECTED REFERENCES: **The Teachings of Don Juan - Page [66.4]** (When one arrives to a depth of...of permanent power, power without end.) **Journey to Ixtlan - Page [135.2-135.3]** ("What happened to you last night...you; those scenes are most meaningful.")
SEE ALSO: *WARRIOR-BATTLE-POWER*

POWER-SECRETS-[THE SECRETS OF POWER]: (The secrets of a man of knowledge; a brujo's secrets.)
SELECTED REFERENCES: **A Separate Reality - Page [36.1]** ("What do I seem to know...power, of course; a brujo's knowledge.")
SEE ALSO: *MAN-KNOWLEDGE-SECRETS, POWER, BRUJO, WARRIOR-SECRETS*

POWER-SEEK-WARRIOR-[WARRIORS SEEK POWER]: SEE: WARRIOR-POWER-SEEK-[WARRIORS SEEK POWER]

POWER-SLAVE-[THE SLAVE OF POWER]: SEE: POWER-PRISONER-[THE PRISONER OF POWER]

POWER-SPOT-[THE WARRIORS' POWER SPOT]: (Warriors know that a power spot, or "sitio", is a hole in a sort of canopy that prevents the world from losing its shape; a power spot can be utilized as long as warriors have gathered enough second attention strength; a spot where warriors can feel naturally happy and strong; a spot where warriors can be at their very best; animals can detect areas with special levels of energy in their surroundings; most of them avoid those places with the exception of coyotes and mountain lions which lay and even sleep on such spots when they happen upon them; sorcerers are the only ones who deliberately seek out those spots for their effects; power spots give out imperceptible jolts of invigorating energy; sorcerers are capable of finding these spots by perceiving with their entire bodies.)
SELECTED REFERENCES: **The Teachings of Don Juan - Page [28.9-29.9]** (I asked him if there was...it from all the other places.) **The Teachings of Don Juan - Page [53.7-53.8]** (He said that while I remained...that might be harmful to me.) **Journey to Ixtlan - Page [48.3-52.5]** (In the early evening, however, he...You must learn that yourself.") **Journey to Ixtlan - Page [54.6-54.7]** (He reminded me that I had found...their spots at the same time.") **Tales of Power - Page [283.4-283.5]** ("Don't apologize," don Juan said to me...Be as fine as they were.") **The Eagle's Gift - Page [82.6-82.9]** ("I am not yet ready for...in are on two parallel lines.) **The Eagle's Gift - Page [83.5-83.6]** (La Gorda reclined on the bed...is no possible journey for us.") **The Eagle's Gift - Page [97.4-97.5]** ("It's simplicity itself," la Gorda said...world, a door to the other.) **The Eagle's Gift - Page [100.2]** (La Gorda speculated that the airline...one parallel line to the other.) **The Eagle's Gift - Page [241.7-241.8]** (Silvio Manuel had conceived the idea...to withstand a glimpse of the Eagle.) **The Eagle's Gift - Page - [243.8-243.9]** (He explained that power spots were...enough strength in the second attention.) **The Power of Silence - Page [156.1-158.1]** ("Tell me, which spot on the...senses a greater range of perception.)
SEE ALSO: *POWER, ATTENTION-SECOND-TRAPPING*

POWER-SPOT-TALES-LOCATING-[TALES OF LOCATING POWER SPOTS]-(TOP)

POWER-STEP-FIRST-[THE FIRST STEP TO POWER]: SEE: DREAMING-SETTING-UP-[SETTING UP DREAMING]

POWER-STRUGGLE-WARRIOR-[THE WARRIORS' STRUGGLE FOR POWER]: SEE WARRIOR-STRUGGLE [THE WARRIORS' STRUGGLE]

*POWER-TALES-[TALES OF POWER]: (For the warrior apprentice there is only witnessing acts of power and listening to tales of power; tales of power are the sorcery stories.)

SELECTED REFERENCES: **The Teachings of Don Juan** - Page **[66.1-66.7]** (In other times, like those my...moving at the top of the trees.") **Tales of Power** - Page **[44.5-44.6]** ("A double is the sorcerer himself...only a tale of power to you.) **Tales of Power** - Page **[56.2-56.5]** ("Why do you laugh," I asked...listening to tales, tales of power.) **Tales of Power** - Page **[57.6-57.9]** ("Genaro is a man of knowledge...for you, only tales of power.")
SEE ALSO: *POWER, POWER-ACTS, ABSTRACT-CORES, SORCERY-STORIES*

POWER-TRAPPING-*[TRAPPING AND STORING POWER]: SEE: POWER-PERSONAL-[PERSONAL POWER], HUNTER-POWER-[BECOMING A HUNTER OF POWER], ENERGY-DRAINAGE-[PLUGGING POINTS OF ENERGY DRAINAGE]*

POWER-UNIQUENESS-*[POWER AND UNIQUENESS]: (Warriors know that power and uniqueness are unbeatably corrupting forces; the inorganic beings use these forces against warriors to try and engage their sense of self and divert them away from their quest for freedom.)*

SELECTED REFERENCES: **The Art of Dreaming** - Page **[100.7-101.2]** ("Then every dreamer sees that world...and then I never went back.")
SEE ALSO: *POWER, INORGANIC-BEINGS-REFUSING, INORGANIC-BEINGS-TEACHINGS , FREEDOM-TOTAL*

POWER-UNNOTICEABILITY-*[THE UNNOTICEABILITY OF POWER]: SEE: ENERGY-DRAINAGE-[PLUGGING POINTS OF ENERGY DRAINAGE]*

POWER-WALK-FOR-*[THE WALK FOR POWER]-(TOP)*

POWER-WASTING-*[WASTING POWER]: (Warriors know they must make it a habit to never waste their power, to never waste their gains.)*

SELECTED REFERENCES: **The Eagle's Gift** - Page **[48.1-484]** (As she got out of the car...must allow ourselves time to heal.")
SEE ALSO: *POWER, ENERGY-CONSERVING, WARRIOR-IMPECCABILITY*

POWER-WEIRD-*[POWER IS A WEIRD AFFAIR]: (Warriors know that power and its acquisition is a very weird affair; in order to have power and command it, one must have power to begin with; in order to acquire power the warrior must store it little by little through an impeccable way of being.)*

SELECTED REFERENCES: **Journey To Ixtlan** - Page **[135.1-135.2]** ("Power is a very weird affair...oneself in a battle of power.")
SEE ALSO: *POWER, WARRIOR-IMPECCABILITY*

POWER-WORLD-*[THE WORLD OF POWER]: (Warriors know the world of power and make it into a familiar scene; the world of power is the warriors' world and is a world that admits very few mistakes.)*

SELECTED REFERENCES: **Journey to Ixtlan** - Page **[135.9-136.1]** (You and I are right here...make it into a familiar scene.") **The Power of Silence** - Page **[23.7-23.9]** (Don Juan commented that that was...world that admitted very few mistakes.)
SEE ALSO: *POWER*

POWER-WORLD-WARRIOR-*[WARRIORS IN THE WORLD OF POWER]: (Warriors know that it takes a lifelong struggle to function by ourselves in the world of power.)*

SELECTED REFERENCES: **Journey to Ixtlan** - Page **[136.9-137.1]** ("I have taught you nearly everything...oneself in the world of power.")
SEE ALSO: *WARRIOR-STRUGGLE, POWER*

POWERS-GUIDE-MEN-*[THE POWERS THAT GUIDE MEN'S LIVES]:*
(Warriors know that there are powers on this earth that guide men and animals and everything that is living; these are the powers that guide the

lives and deaths of men; forces, allies, spirits, airs, winds, shadows, entities of the night, or inorganic beings.)

SELECTED REFERENCES: Journey to Ixtlan - Page [79.8-79.9] ("A hunter must not only know...guide our lives and our deaths.") Journey to Ixtlan - Page [85.8-86.1] ("I've told you, this is a weird...airs, winds, or anything like that.") Journey to Ixtlan - Page [88.1-88.2] (I felt nauseated. He very patiently...gift for something or someone else.) Journey to Ixtlan - Page [91.4-91.7] ("The decision as to who can...even in my wildest fantasies.) Journey to Ixtlan - Page [99.8-99.9] ("I am not trying to make...the impeccable life of a warrior.) Journey to Ixtlan - Page [164.1-164.2] ("You found the right place...without any plan on your part.") Journey to Ixtlan - Page [172.1] (I felt relieved and asked him...he said in a whisper.) Journey to Ixtlan - Page [177.7] (Since the natural abodes of the...you have stored enough personal power.") The Eagle's Gift - Page [118.9] (*I am already given to the power...I will have nothing to defend.*)

SEE ALSO: *ALLIES, INORGANIC-BEINGS, SPIRITS*

PRACTICALITIES-QUEST-[THE QUEST FOR PRACTICALITIES]: SEE: STALKER-QUEST-PRACTICALITIES-[THE STALKERS' QUEST FOR PRACTICALITIES]

PRANKS-VS-MAGICAL-DRAMAS-[PRANKS VS MAGICAL DRAMAS]: *(Warriors know that a true stalker is not a prankster; the true stalker plays magical dramas that require a movement of the assemblage point.)*

SELECTED REFERENCES: The Fire From Within - Page [198.8-198.9] ("I can't shake off the feeling...a movement of the assemblage point.")

SEE ALSO: *STALKING-ART, ASSEMBLAGE-POINT-MOVING, MAGIC*

PRAYER-[PRAYER]: *(Warriors know that neither the mold of man nor the spirit itself will, under any circumstances, help us by intervening in our behalf; these incomprehensible forces cannot punish or reward us in any way, because they act in accordance with their own design.)*

SELECTED REFERENCES: The Fire From Within - Page [263.6-263.7] (They have seen, therefore, that what...or reward us in any way.) The Power of Silence - Page [191.2-191.3] (The spirit could not possibly have cared...for the spirit to pay attention.)

SEE ALSO: *GOD, MOLD-MAN, FAITH-RELIGIOUS, SPIRIT-DESIGN*

PRAYER-WARRIOR-[THE WARRIORS' PRAYER]: SEE: WARRIOR-PRAYER-[THE WARRIORS' PRAYER]

PREAMBLE-UNKNOWN-[THE PREAMBLE OF THE UNKNOWN]: SEE: AWARENESS-HEIGHTENED-[HEIGHTENED AWARENESS]

PREDATOR-PREY-[PREDATORS AND PREY]: SEE: UNIVERSE-PREDATORIAL-[THE PREDATORIAL UNIVERSE]

PREDICTABILITY-WORLD-[THE PREDICTABILITY OF THE WORLD]: SEE: WORLD-PREDICTABILITY-[THE PREDICTABILITY OF THE WORLD]

PREDILECTION-PLACE-WARRIOR-[THE WARRIORS' PLACE OF PREDILECTION]: SEE: WARRIOR-PREDILECTION-PLACE-[THE WARRIORS' PLACE OF PREDILECTION]

PREDILECTION-WARRIOR-[THE WARRIORS' PREDILECTION]: SEE: WARRIOR-PREDILECTION-[THE WARRIORS' PREDILECTION]

PREOCCUPATION-WARRIOR-[THE WARRIORS' PREOCCUPATION]: SEE: WARRIOR-PREOCCUPATION-[THE WARRIORS' PREOCCUPATION]

PREPARATION-WARRIOR-[THE WARRIORS' PREPARATION]: SEE: WARRIOR-PREPARATION-[THE WARRIORS' PREPARATION]

PREPAREDNESS-WARRIOR-[THE WARRIORS' PREPAREDNESS]: SEE: WARRIOR-PREPAREDNESS-[THE WARRIORS' PREPAREDNESS]

PRESSURE-RELIEVES-WARRIOR-[WARRIORS RELIEVE THEIR PRESSURE]: SEE: WARRIOR-PRESSURE-RELIEVES-[WARRIORS RELIEVE THEIR PRESSURE]

PRICE-SORCERY-[THE PRICE OF SORCERY]: SEE: SORCERY-PRICE-[THE PRICE OF SORCERY]

PRIDE-FALSE-[FALSE PRIDE]: (Warriors know that they must avoid being ripped apart by the activation of their false pride and the feelings of worthlessness that it brings.)
SELECTED REFERENCES: The Fire From Within - Page [26.1-26.4] ("The foreman at the house followed...trampling on you is called control.)
SEE ALSO: *SELF-IMPORTANCE-WEAR-TEAR, SELF-IMPORTANCE-LOSING*

PRIESTS-[PRIESTS]: SEE: NUNS-PRIESTS-[NUNS AND PRIESTS]

PROACTIVE-STANCE-[THE PROACTIVE STANCE]: SEE: WARRIOR-PROACTIVITY-[THE WARRIORS' PROACTIVITY]

PROACTIVITY-WARRIOR-[THE WARRIORS' PROACTIVITY]: SEE: WARRIOR-PROACTIVITY-[THE WARRIORS' PROACTIVITY]

PROGRESSION-THREE-PHASE-[THE THREE-PHASE PROGRESSION]: (Warriors know that nothing can temper their spirit as much as the challenge of dealing with impossible people in positions of power; this truth leads warriors to an incontestable three-phase conclusion; if warrior-seers can hold their own in the face of their petty tyrants then they can certainly face the unknown with impunity and if they can face the unknown with impunity then they can even stand the presence of the unknowable.)
SELECTED REFERENCES: The Fire From Within - Page [19.3-19.7] (He explained that one of the...stand the pressure of the unknowable.")
SEE ALSO: *PETTY-TYRANT, UNKNOWN, UNKNOWABLE*

PROFICIENCY-WARRIOR-[THE WARRIORS' PROFICIENCY]: SEE: WARRIOR-PROFICIENCY-[THE WARRIORS' PROFICIENCY]

PROMISE-BUTTON-NOSED-BOY-[THE PROMISE TO THE BUTTON-NOSED BOY]-(TOP): SEE: BOY-BUTTON-NOSED-PROMISE-[THE PROMISE TO THE BUTTON NOSED BOY]-(TOP)

PROMISE-CHILDHOOD-[THE PROMISE OF CHILDHOOD]-(TOP)

PROMISE-POWER-[THE PROMISE OF POWER]: SEE: POWER-PROMISE-[THE PROMISE OF POWER]

PROMISE-WORTHLESS-SERVANT-WORTHLESS-MASTER-[THE PROMISE OF A WORTHLESS SERVANT TO A WORTHLESS MASTER]-(TOP)

PROPS-WARRIOR-[THE WARRIORS' PROPS]: SEE: WARRIOR-PROPS-[THE WARRIORS' PROPS]

PROTECT-PERSON-WARRIOR-[WARRIORS PROTECT THEIR PERSON]: SEE: WARRIOR-PROTECT-PERSON-[WARRIORS PROTECT THEIR PERSON]

PROTECT-THEMSELVES-COMMANDS-WARRIOR-[WARRIORS MUST LEARN TO PROTECT THEMSELVES FROM THEIR OWN COMMANDS]: SEE: WARRIOR-PROTECT-THEMSELVES-COMMANDS-[WARRIORS MUST LEARN TO PROTECT THEMSELVES FROM THEIR OWN COMMANDS]

PROTECTIVE-POSITION-WARRIOR-[THE WARRIORS' PROTECTIVE POSITION]: SEE: WARRIOR-PROTECTIVE-POSITION-[THE WARRIORS' PROTECTIVE POSITION]

PROTECTOR-[THE PROTECTOR]: SEE: MESCALITO-[MESCALITO]

PROTEGIDO-[PROTEGIDO]: (Warriors know that the protegido is a benefactor's "protected one", the apprentice to whom he shows the nagual.)
SELECTED REFERENCES : **Tales of Power** - Page **[199.2-199.4]** (He quickly changed the subject and began...The word "protegido" meant the protected one.)
SEE ALSO : *ESCOGIDO*

PSYCHIC-SURGERY-[PSYCHIC SURGERY]-(TOP)

PULL-PUSH-[PULL AND PUSH]: (Warriors know that everything in the world is a force, a pull or a push; in order to be pushed or pulled, warriors must be complete, their luminous "sails" must be complete; if they have a hole in the middle of their luminosity, the forces of the world go through it and never act upon them.)
SELECTED REFERENCES: **The Second Ring of Power** - Page **[156.9-157.1]** ("The Nagual said that everything in...it and never acts upon us.)
SEE ALSO: *WARRIOR-COMPLETENESS, FORCE-MYSTERIOUS*

PURE-UNDERSTANDING-[PURE UNDERSTANDING]: SEE: UNDERSTANDING-PURE-[PURE UNDERSTANDING]

PURPOSE-MAN-[THE PURPOSE OF THE AVERAGE MAN]: (Warriors know it is useless to approach the average man with the challenge of warriorship; they feel no need to find a purpose in life because they believe they have already found it.)
SELECTED REFERENCES: **The Eagle's Gift** - Page **[221.2-221.3]** (Their quest for a new pair of...thought they had already found it.)
SEE ALSO: *WARRIOR-PURPOSE*

PURPOSE-WARRIOR-[THE WARRIORS' PURPOSE]: SEE: WARRIOR-PURPOSE-[THE WARRIORS' PURPOSE]

PUSHING-ARM-EXERCISE-[THE EXERCISE OF PUSHING WITH THE ARM]-(TOP): SEE: NOT-DOING-EXERCISE-[THE EXERCISE OF NOT-DOING]-(TOP)

*PYRAMIDS-[PYRAMIDS AND TOLTEC RUINS]: (Warriors know that the pyramids are ancient structures built as traps of the second attention; these structures are foreign expressions of thought and action and are harmful to modern men in general and formless warriors in particular.)
SELECTED REFERENCES: **The Eagle's Gift** - Page **[14.2-15.7]** ("Pablito and I have been in...the opposite of the front row.") **The Eagle's Gift** - Page **[16.7-17.8]** ("I really don't know

what it...they did, it was too late.") **The Eagle's Gift - Page [18.9-19.5]** ("The pyramids are harmful," Pablito went...visiting those ruins against his recommendations.) **The Eagle's Gift - Page [20.4-20.6]** (He stressed to me that all...obsessive concern had a harmful potential.)

SEE ALSO: *ATLANTEANS, ATTENTION-SECOND-FACES-TWO, OBSESSION, TOLTECS*

Q

QUAIL-FIVE-[THE STORY OF THE FIVE QUAIL]-(TOP)

QUALITIES-TWO-BASIC-WARRIOR-[THE TWO BASIC QUALITIES OF WARRIORS]: SEE: WARRIOR-QUALITIES-TWO-BASIC-[THE TWO BASIC QUALITIES OF WARRIORS]

QUARTZ-POWER-CRYSTALS-[POWER QUARTZ CRYSTALS]: SEE: POWER-CRYSTAL-[POWER QUARTZ CRYSTALS]

QUEST-COMPLETION-WARRIOR-[THE COMPLETION OF THE WARRIORS' QUEST]: SEE: WARRIOR-QUEST-COMPLETION-[THE COMPLETION OF THE WARRIORS' QUEST]

QUEST-FREEDOM-WARRIOR-[THE WARRIORS' QUEST FOR FREEDOM]: SEE: WARRIOR-QUEST-FREEDOM-[THE WARRIORS' QUEST FOR FREEDOM]

QUEST-FREEDOM-VS-ADVENTURE-UNKNOWN-WARRIOR-[THE WARRIORS' QUEST FOR FREEDOM VS THE HIGH ADVENTURE OF THE UNKNOWN]: SEE: WARRIOR-QUEST-FREEDOM-VS-ADVENTURE-UNKNOWN-[THE WARRIORS' QUEST FOR FREEDOM VS THE HIGH ADVENTURE OF THE UNKNOWN]

QUEST-KNOWLEDGE-[THE CONTRADICTIONS OF THE WARRIORS' QUEST FOR KNOWLEDGE]: SEE: WARRIOR-CONTRADICTION-KNOWLEDGE-[THE CONTRADICTIONS OF THE WARRIORS' QUEST FOR KNOWLEDGE]

QUEST-WARRIOR-[THE WARRIORS' QUEST]: SEE: WARRIOR-QUEST-[THE WARRIORS' QUEST]

QUESTION-ONLY-MEANINGFUL-[THE ONLY MEANINGFUL QUESTION]: (Warriors know that the only meaningful question they can ask is "where is the unknown?")
    SELECTED REFERENCES: The Fire From Within - Page [206.3-207.3] ("I've been waiting for you to...is perceived and becomes the known.)
    SEE ALSO: UNKNOWN-WHERE, KNOWN, AWARENESS, LUMINOUS-COCOON

QUESTIONS-WARRIOR-[THE WARRIORS' QUESTION]: SEE: WARRIOR-QUESTIONS-[THE WARRIORS' QUESTION]

QUIETNESS-CONTROLLED-WARRIOR-[THE WARRIORS' CONTROLLED QUIETNESS]: SEE: WARRIOR-QUIETNESS-CONTROLLED-[THE WARRIORS' CONTROLLED QUIETNESS]

QUIETNESS-TOTAL-[TOTAL QUIETNESS]: SEE: INNER-SILENCE-[INNER SILENCE]

R

RABBIT-LAST-BATTLE-[A RABBIT'S LAST BATTLE ON EARTH]-(TOP)

RAGE-WARRIOR-[THE WARRIORS' RAGE]: SEE: WARRIOR-RAGE-[THE WARRIORS' RAGE]

RAIN-GAZING-[RAIN GAZING]: SEE: GAZING

RATIONALES-WARRIOR-[THE WARRIORS' RATIONALES]: SEE: WARRIOR-RATIONALES-[THE WARRIORS' RATIONALES]

RATIONALITY-[RATIONALITY]: SEE: REASON-[REASON AND RATIONALITY]

RATIONALITY-ASSAILANT-[THE FOREMOST ASSAILANT OF RATIONALITY]: (Warriors know that the existence of the inorganic beings is the foremost assailant of our rationality.)
    SELECTED REFERENCES: The Art of Dreaming - Page [98.6-98.7] (This bona fide split was a...the foremost assailant of our rationality.)
    SEE ALSO: *INORGANIC-BEINGS, REASON*

RATIONALITY-DISPENSING-WITH-[DISPENSING WITH RATIONALITY]: SEE: IMPECCABILITY-STATE-OF-BEING-[AN IMPECCABLE STATE OF BEING]

RATIONALITY-EXTREMES-[THE EXTREMES OF RATIONALITY]: (Warriors know that the contradictory propositions of knowledge demand that they fluctuate between the extremes of rationality; warriors must be methodical, rational, beings and at the same time shy away from all those qualities to be free and open to the mysteries of the universe.)
    SELECTED REFERENCES: The Fire From Within - Page [73.2-73.4] ("For example, seers have to be...him how I understood his point.)
    SEE ALSO: *REASON, WARRIOR-SOBRIETY, WARRIOR-CONTRADICTION-KNOWLEDGE, WARRIOR-ABANDON-CONTROLLED*

RATIONALITY-HOLDING-BACK-[HOLDING BACK RATIONALITY]: (Warriors know that when they reach the third gate of dreaming they must actively engage in holding back their rationality; they must do so because rationality is responsible for the energy body's obsession with superfluous detail; therefore, warriors hold back their rationality to make things easier for the energy body.)
    SELECTED REFERENCES: The Art of Dreaming - Page [143.3-143.7.] (Don Juan added that his recommendations...irrational abandon to counteract that insistence.")
    SEE ALSO: *ABANDON, REASON, DREAMING-GATE-THIRD, WARRIOR-ABANDON-CONTROLLED*

RATIONALITY-VENEER-[THE VENEER OF RATIONALITY]: (Warriors know that they are part of the mysterious; rationality is only a veneer with human beings.)
    SELECTED REFERENCES: The Power of Silence - Page [167.8-167.9] ("I've told you over and over...others do it with total ease.)
    SEE ALSO: *REASON, WORLD-MYSTERIOUS*

RATTLESNAKE-HUNTING-[HUNTING A RATTLESNAKE]-(TOP)

RATTLESNAKE-PARTY-ARRANGEMENT-[THE ARRANGEMENT OF THE NAGUAL'S PARTY LIKE A RATTLESNAKE]-(TOP)

REACTIVE-STANCE-[THE REACTIVE STANCE]: (*Warriors know that the stance of the average man is a reactive stance; it is the stance of the victim; warriors deliberately avoid a reactive stance in life and work to establish a proactive position with regard to the world around them; warriors control their lives by not controlling anything; in transforming their facade, warriors change their position in life from reactive to proactive; warriors are not victims, they are not at the mercy of the wind.*)
    SELECTED REFERENCES: **Tales of Power - Page [154.1-154.3]** (We laughed at the image...You're not living like a warrior.")
    SEE ALSO: *WARRIOR-PROACTIVITY, CONTROL-WITHOUT-CONTROL, VICTIM, FACADE-TRANSFORMING*

REAFFIRMATIONS-WORLD-[REAFFIRMATIONS FROM THE WORLD AROUND US]-(TOP)

REAL-UNREAL-PERCEPTION-[THE REAL AND THE UNREAL PART OF NORMAL HUMAN PERCEPTION]: (*Warriors know that the real part of perception is that something out there is affecting our senses; the unreal part of our perception is what our senses tell us is there.*)
    SELECTED REFERENCES: **The Fire From Within - Page [37.2-37.6]** ("The first truth is that the...awareness forces them to do so.")
    SEE ALSO: *PERCEPTION, REALITY-INTERPRETATION, AWARENESS-TRUTH-FIRST*

REALITY-ALTERING-[ALTERING REALITY]: SEE: WORLD-STOPPING-[STOPPING THE WORLD]

REALITY-ASSEMBLAGE-POINT-[REALITY AND THE ASSEMBLAGE POINT]: SEE: REALITY-INTERPRETATION-[REALITY IS AN INTERPRETATION WE MAKE]

REALITY-DREAMER-[REVAMPING THE DREAMERS' REALITY]: SEE: DREAMER-OPTIONS-[THE DREAMERS' OPTIONS]

REALITY-INTERPRETATION-[REALITY IS AN INTERPRETATION WE MAKE]: (*Warriors know that reality is an interpretation we make based on the position of the assemblage point; in order to perceive "reality", people need cohesion to maintain the fixation of the assemblage point on a particular position; the position of the assemblage point is everything and the world it makes us perceive is so real that it does not leave room for anything except its realness.*)
    SELECTED REFERENCES: **A Separate Reality - Page [6.1-6.3]** (Through the separate ingestion of each...they were real but "as" real.) **A Separate Reality - Page [10.5-10.6]** (Don Juan's task, as a practitioner...because it is only an interpretation.) **Journey to Ixtlan - Page [viii.7-viii.8]** (For the purpose of presenting my argument...all know, is only a description.) **Journey to Ixtlan - Page [xiii.8-xiv.3]** (Don Juan stated that in order...we have learned to call reality.") **Journey to Ixtlan - Page [17.2-17.3]** ("You see," he went on...rabbit will pop out, not even ourselves.") **Journey to Ixtlan - Page [133.6-134.1]** ("And what is real?" don Juan...was the real thing last night.) **Tales of Power - Page [20.2-20.4]** ("Yes. There is something in myself...could agree with you about it.") **Tales of Power - Page [22.1-22.8]** ("How was I operating my knowledge...forced to understand it as talking.") **The Fire From Within - Page [24.8-24.9]** (Warriors, on the other hand, not...reality is an interpretation we make.) **The Fire From Within - Page [216.2-216.4]** (We were coming closer to the main...leave room for anything except

realness.) **The Power of Silence - Page [xv.3-xv.5]** (The art of *stalking* is the riddle...so unalterably objective and factual change.) **The Art of Dreaming - Page [40.5-40.7]** ("My confusion comes when you...attributes are the key to perceiving.") **The Art of Dreaming - Page [77.2-77.5]** ("We are again, don Juan, at...outside the normal world stalking perception.")

SEE ALSO: *REALITY-(ALL), ASSEMBLAGE-POINT, ENERGETIC-UNIFORMITY-COHESION, PERCEIVERS-WE-ARE, ASSEMBLAGE-POINT-POSITION-EVERYTHING, DESCRIPTION-WORLD-TWO, REALIZATION-TECHNIQUE, SORCERY-PREMISE-BASIC*

REALITY-MERGING-[MERGING REALITY]: SEE: DREAMING-GATE-THIRD-[THE THIRD GATE OF DREAMING]

REALITY-METAMORPHOSIS-DREAMING-[DREAMING AND THE METAMORPHOSIS OF REALITY]: SEE: DREAMING-REALITY-METAMORPHOSIS-[DREAMING AND THE METAMORPHOSIS OF REALITY]

REALITY-NON-ORDINARY-[NON-ORDINARY REALITY]: (Warriors know that states of non-ordinary reality are their only method of pragmatic learning and the only means through which they can acquire power; non-ordinary reality represents the separate reality of the warrior, the reality of the second and third attentions.)

SELECTED REFERENCES: **The Teachings of Don Juan - Page [21.4-21.8]** (The importance of the plants was...with the states of nonordinary reality.) **A Separate Reality - Page [6.1-6.3]** (Through the separate ingestion of each...they were real but "as" real.) **The Eagle's Gift - Page [101.8-101.9]** (Pablito made an attempt to talk...were no other people on the bridge.)

SEE ALSO: *REALITY-ORDINARY, REALITY-INTERPRETATION, ASSEMBLAGE POINT-MOVING, REALITY-SEPARATE-(TOP)*

REALITY-ORDINARY-[ORDINARY REALITY]: (Warriors know that things are real only after we have learned to agree on their "realness"; the reality of the average man revolves around his habit of making the world conform to his thoughts; reality is an interpretation that people make; reality for the average man is the reality of the first attention, the reality of the tonal; the world appears to be real to the average man; it appears to be unalterable and factual because of certain peculiarities of our awareness and perception, but if different peculiarities of perception come into play, the very things about the world that seem so real, change in the blink of an eye.)

SELECTED REFERENCES: **A Separate Reality - Page [6.1-6.3]** (Through the separate ingestion of each...they were real but "as" real.) **Tales of Power - Page [20.2-20.4]** ("Yes. There is something in myself...could agree with you about it.") **Tales of Power - Page [22.1-22.8]** ("How was I operating my knowledge...forced to understand it as talking.") **The Fire From Within - Page [24.7-24.9]** Don Juan explained that the mistake...had over the simple-minded Spaniards.) **The Power of Silence - Page [xv.3-xv.5]** (The art of *stalking* is the riddle...so unalterably objective and factual change.)

SEE ALSO: *REALITY-NON-ORDINARY, DESCRIPTION-WORLD-, RIDDLE-HEART, AWARENESS, PERCEPTION, REALITY-(ALL)*

REALITY-SEPARATE-[A SEPARATE REALITY]-(TOP)

REALITY-SEPARATE-WARRIOR-[THE SEPARATE REALITY OF THE WARRIOR]: SEE: REALITY-NON-ORDINARY-[NON-ORDINARY REALITY]

REALIZATION-[REALIZATION]: (Warriors know there are two kinds of realizations; one is just a pep talk, a great outburst of emotion and nothing more; the other is a product of a shift of the assemblage point; it is not coupled with an emotional outburst but with action; warriors place the highest value on deep, unemotional realizations; warriors know that emotional realizations mean nothing because to understand, one needs sobriety, not emotionality; warriors know that those who weep with realization have realized nothing; warriors know that realizations from the point of no doubts are commonplace and useless; it is equally useless to have a realization from the point of normal awareness because those realizations are just emotional outbursts and are valid only as long as the emotion lasts; without magic there can be no realizations; personal power determines when an individual can profit from a revelation and experience an emotionless realization.)

SELECTED REFERENCES: **Tales of Power - Page [75.4-75.6]** ("What Genaro showed you yesterday is...questions, today you are all acceptance.") **Tales of Power - Page [231.5-231.7]** (Personal power decides who can...personal power to profit by their acts.) **Tales of Power - Page [243.1-243.3]** (It had indeed taken me years...always done in states of sober consciousness.) **The Fire From Within - Page [13.8-13.9]** (I ran after him then, elated...he replied. "Realizations are always personal.") **The Fire From Within - Page [53.7-54.2]** (He reiterated that my concentration had...realization, for they have realized nothing.) **The Fire From Within - Page [118.7-118.9]** ("How can one accomplish that change...as a consequence of new habits.") **The Fire From Within - Page [121.3-121.4]** (He remarked that my flaw was...moved into man's band of emanations.) **The Fire From Within - Page [184.1-184.4]** (I felt I should be sad...then years later have the realization.") **The Fire From Within - Page [193.8]** ("That's the *stalkers'* method," don Juan...fosters not understanding but total realization.) **The Fire From Within - Page [199.9-200.1]** (He said that realizations are of...new position of their assemblage points.) **The Fire From Within - Page [212.3-212.5]** (I turned around in a reflex action...much later, after years of struggle.) **The Fire From Within - Page [246.5-246.6]** (I told him how sorry I was...out as the assemblage point shifts.) **The Fire From Within - Page [282.3-282.6]** (He explained that I had to...as long as the emotion lasts.) **The Fire From Within - Page [283.5-282.7]** (He said that now I needed...to be what it is to us.) **The Power of Silence - Page [222.8-222.9]** ("That big cat came out of nowhere...elation, no lesson, no realizations.")

SEE ALSO: *UNDERSTANDING, WARRIOR-SOBRIETY, KNOWLEDGE, ASSEMBLAGE-POINT-SHIFT, ACT-LEARNING, MAGIC, WARRIOR-ALONE*

REALIZATION-CANCELED-ASSEMBLAGE-POINT-MOVE- [REALIZATIONS ARE CANCELED BY THE MOVEMENT OF THE ASSEMBLAGE POINT]: *(Warriors know that certain kinds of realizations are canceled out by the movement of the assemblage point; such realizations are a dime a dozen for warriors.)*

SELECTED REFERENCES: **The Fire From Within - Page [246.5-246.6]** (I told him how sorry I...out as the assemblage point shifts.)
SEE ALSO: *REALIZATION, ASSEMBLAGE-POINT-MOVE*

REALIZATION-FINAL-WARRIOR-[THE FINAL REALIZATION]: SEE: WARRIOR-REALIZATION-FINAL-[THE WARRIORS' FINAL REALIZATION]

REALIZATION-SHADES-[SHADES OF REALIZATION]: *(Warriors know that the abstract cores of the sorcery stories are shades of realization, degrees of the warriors' awareness of intent.)*

SELECTED REFERENCES: **The Power of Silence - Page [105.1-105.2]** (Examined in this way, sorcery becomes...of our being aware of *intent.*)
SEE ALSO: *ABSTRACT-CORES, SORCERY-STORIES, KNOWLEDGE-VS-LANGUAGE, WARRIOR-INTENT-LINK*

REALIZATION-TECHNIQUE-[THE TECHNIQUE OF REALIZATION]: *(Warriors know that the technique of realization is the way that warriors accomplish the change from within; first warriors must be aware that the world they perceive is the result of the assemblage point's location on its*

habitual spot on the luminous cocoon; once that is understood, the assemblage point can move at will as a consequence of new habits.)
SELECTED REFERENCES: The Fire From Within - Page [118.7-118.9] ("How can one accomplish that change...as a consequence of new habits.")
SEE ALSO: *REALIZATION, CHANGE, FACADE-TRANSFORMING, ASSEMBLAGE-POINT-POSITION, REALITY-INTERPRETATION, ASSEMBLAGE-POINT-MOVING, HABITS-UNNECESSARY*

REASON-[REASON AND RATIONALITY]: *(Warriors know that reason or rationality is a condition of alignment, merely a by-product of the habitual position of the assemblage point; the first ring of power, the companion to talking; the first point; reason is merely reflecting an outside order, it cannot explain it; reason can only witness the effects of the tonal, it can never understand or unravel them; conclusions arrived at through reason have very little to do with altering the course of the life of warriors; the average man stimulates his reason by running through his inventory and pitting it against his friends' inventories; the more a man clings to reason, the more ephemeral intent becomes; to be too rational is a handicap because reason is just a veneer with men, scratch the surface and you find a sorcerer underneath; rationality puts warriors between a rock and a hard place because the tendency of reason is to ponder and question and find things out; there is simply no way to do this from within the discipline of the warriors' way because the goal of warriorship is to reach silent knowledge and silent knowledge can never be reasoned out; reason is one of the eight points on the sorcerers' diagram.)*
SELECTED REFERENCES: Journey to Ixtlan - Page [216.3-216.6] ("This is all crazy," I said...nothing about this mysterious unknown world.") Tales of Power - Page [5.9-6.1] ("I was under the impression that...he's not as stiff as you.") Tales of Power - Page [24.1-24.3] ("I'm really scared," I said...the evidence clung steadfast to "reason.") Tales of Power - Page [33.3-33.4] ("To turn that magnificence out there...nonsense is petty and outright disastrous.") Tales of Power - Page [45.8-45.9] ("I've told you time and time...that should be more than enough.") Tales of Power - Page [51.5-51.7] ("I've got to talk about this...think that now is the moment.") Tales of Power - Page [56.5-56.6] ("The double is one of those...as real as it can be.") Tales of Power - Page [83.7-84.3] ("I have no idea that I'm...the ally that night, right here.") Tales of Power - Page [96.2-96.9] ("We may say that every one..."dreaming" were on the right side.) Tales of Power - Page [98.3-98.7] ("We, the luminous beings, are born...your *reason* or by your *will.*) Tales of Power - Page [151.5-151.6] (He criticized, without getting angry, my...about it I was dissipating it.) Tales of Power - Page [157.5-157.6] ("But you were next to me...with the body, not the reason.") Tales of Power - Page [173.7-174.2] ("Another thing one should do when...That fear is ill founded.) Tales of Power - Page [195.2-195.3] (But to be a sorcerer...explanations which stand in your way.) Tales of Power - Page [244.6-244.7] (We function at the center of...therefore it is properly the *nagual*.) Tales of Power - Page [253.7-254.7] (By now you must have realized...magical heritage and reduces us to nothing.") Tales of Power - Page [276.3-277.4] (Your *reason* cannot fight the physical....that, or what the order is.") The Eagle's Gift - Page [113.7-113.8] (I speculated with la Gorda that the...the intellect played a minimal part.) The Eagle's Gift - Page [183.8-184.1] (His benefactor put him under the direct...rational ballast to hold them back.) The Eagle's Gift - Page [261.2-261.34] (The more I practiced, the clearer...*dreamer* from excess and bizarre undertakings.) The Eagle's Gift - Page [265.1-265.3] (Zuleica took us systematically on voyages...rational causes or reasons for anything.) The Eagle's Gift - Page [296.3-296.4] (It was then that I turned...the meagerness of my rationality.) The Fire From Within - Page [36.9-37.1] (He went on to say that...idea that to err is human.) The Fire From Within - Page [38.4-38.5] (What I was trying to point...turns into a matter of beliefs.) The Fire From Within - Page [73.2-73.4] ("For example, seers have to be...him how I understood his point.) The Fire From Within - Page [114.9-115.1] (You stimulate your reason by running...to examine yourself and your fate.) The Fire From Within - Page [282.4-282.5] (He explained that I had to...the position of the assemblage point.) The Power of Silence - Page [29.6] (As with everything else, we complicate...the immensity that surrounds us reasonable.") The Power of Silence - Page [115.8] ("Your argument is glib and convincing...see the flaw in your argument.")

The Power of Silence - Page [147.2-147.5] ("Sorcerers believe that when man became...the more ephemeral *intent* becomes.") The Power of Silence - Page [167.8-167.9] ("I've told you over and over...surface, we find a sorcerer underneath.) The Power of Silence - Page [198.7-198.9] (When I asked him to talk...adopted a new one called "reason.") The Power of Silence - Page [201.2-201.9] ("What can we do then...would need a gun to hold it.) The Power of Silence - Page [239.4-240.8] (The old nagual went on to...in an endless sea of islands.) The Power of Silence - Page [244.7-244.9] ("I am just considering how our...It can only be experienced.) The Art of Dreaming - Page [72.9-73.4] (Upon awakening I gave don Juan...world, of being able to predict.) The Art of Dreaming - Page [83.5-83.7] (He had remarked time and time...a foremost assailant of our rationality.) The Art of Dreaming - Page [143.6-143.7] ("Don't say anything. At the third...irrational abandon to counteract that insistence.") The Art of Dreaming - Page [173.8-173.9] (Don Juan said that my rationality...itself by suspending my dreaming practices.)

    SEE ALSO: *POINT-FIRST, ATTENTION-FIRST, ALIGNMENT, POWER-RING-FIRST, THINKING-TALKING-ENERGY, INVENTORY, REASON-VS-INTENT, KNOWLEDGE-SILENT, SORCERER-DIAGRAM, INTELLECT-(ALL), AWARENESS-RIGHT*

REASON-ABANDONING-[ABANDONING REASON]-(TOP)

REASON-ABERRATION-[THE ABERRATION OF REASON]: *(Warriors know that the aberration of reason is simply the overemphasis of reason; the distortions and limited perspective of reason.)*

    SELECTED REFERENCES: The Power of Silence - Page [27.2-27.4] ("You always say that your benefactor...heavily toward the aberrations of reason.")
    SEE ALSO: *REASON, ABERRATION-MORBIDITY*

REASON-AGE-[THE AGE OF REASON]: *(Warriors know that the age of reason is the current age of man; the age of reason was preceded by the age of silent knowledge, an age of longer duration which existed before the inversion of the third point.)*

    SELECTED REFERENCES: The Power of Silence - Page [239.6-240.6] (The nagual said there had been...from the position of silent knowledge.)
    SEE ALSO: *REASON, POINT-FIRST, POINT-THIRD, POINT-THIRD-INVERSION, KNOWLEDGE-SILENT-AGE*

REASON-ANTECEDENTS-[THE ANTECEDENTS OF REASON]: *(Warriors know that the antecedents of reason are the older, darker, silent side of man; the place of silent knowledge.)*

    SELECTED REFERENCES: The Power of Silence - Page [146.6-146.7] (He said that when the assemblage...view of the antecedents of reason.)
    SEE ALSO: *MAN-SILENT-SIDE, KNOWLEDGE-SILENT*

REASON-VS-BODY-[REASON VS THE BODY]: *(Warriors know that reason is petty and places itself at odds with the other parts of the warrior that are capable of perceiving things about the world; the body is capable of doing things which reason simply does not comprehend.)*

    SELECTED REFERENCES: Journey to Ixtlan - Page [180.1-180.4] (The reason you keep on coming...me because I am its friend.") Tales of Power - Page [83.8-84.2] ("Your reason is not aware of...now that your reason cannot comprehend.)
    SEE ALSO: *REASON, BODY-PHYSICAL*

REASON-CHAINS-[CHAINED TO REASON]: *(Warriors know they must struggle to break the chains which shackle them to their reason because they know that understanding is only a very small affair.)*

    SELECTED REFERENCES: A Separate Reality - Page [260.6-260.8] ("You're chained!" don Juan exclaimed...affair, so very small," he said.) A Separate Reality - Page [261.8-261.9] ("You are going to change directions...the centers of radiation in his diagram.)
    SEE ALSO: *UNDERSTANDING, EXPLANATION, REASON-CLINGING*

REASON-CHOICE-[REASON'S CHOICES]: SEE: CHOICES-MATCHING-REASON-[MATCHING THE CHOICES OF REASON]

REASON-CLINGING-[CLINGING TO REASON]: (Warriors know they must struggle to convince their reason, their tonal, to become free and fluid; the less reason clings to its doings, the easier it is for warriors to shrink the tonal; warriors know that the more they cling to the world of reason, the more ephemeral intent becomes.)
> SELECTED REFERENCES: Tales of Power - Page [24.1-24.3] ("I'm really scared," I said...the evidence clung steadfast to "reason.") Tales of Power - Page [156.3-156.4] (The whole trouble is that the...easier it is to shrink it.) The Power of Silence - Page [147.2-147.5] ("Sorcerers believe that when man became...the more ephemeral *intent* becomes.") The Power of Silence - Page [167.8-168.2] (I've told you over and over...to my experiences in his world.) The Power of Silence - Page [226.8-227.1] ("I understand exactly what you are...structures. Don't you do the same.")
> SEE ALSO: *TONAL-SHRINKING, REASON, WARRIOR-FLUIDITY, REASON-FLAW*

REASON-DILEMMAS-[THE DILEMMAS OF REASON]: (Warriors know they cannot afford to indulge in the dilemmas of reason.)
> SELECTED REFERENCES: Tales of Power - Page [105.2-105.3] ("For one thing," he said...cannot possibly afford to do that.")
> SEE ALSO: *REASON, SELF-INDULGENCE, INTELLECT-DALLIANCE*

REASON-FLAW-[THE FLAW' OF REASON]: (Warriors know that a person's argument can be glib and convincing and reasonable, but if the spirit of its proponent is dead, that individual will never be able to see the flaw in their argument; the flaw of reason is that reason remains glued to its inventory.)
> SELECTED REFERENCES: A Separate Reality - Page [4.7-5.4] ("You make it sound stupid," he...despair or self-pity in it.) Tales of Power - Page [191.7-191.8] ("You know damn well that you're...use it to win an argument.") The Fire From Within - Page [112.5-112.7] ("In some inexplicable way, it is...dent in another bubble of energy.) The Power of Silence - Page [13.7-13.8] (He pointed out that the flaw...my experiences in the sorcerers' world.) The Power of Silence - Page [115.8] ("Your argument is glib and convincing...see the flaw in your argument.")
> SEE ALSO: *REASON, UNDERSTANDING, KNOWLEDGE, INVENTORY, MAN-FLAW*

REASON-VS-INTENT-[REASON VS. INTENT]: (Warriors know they must come to understand the relationship between the first and third points; the more man clings to the world of reason, the more ephemeral intent becomes.)
> SELECTED REFERENCES: The Power of Silence - Page [xvii.8-xviii.1] (It took me years to be...issue by not thinking about it.) The Power of Silence - Page [147.1-147.5] ("Silent knowledge is something that all...the more ephemeral *intent* becomes.") The Power of Silence - Page [198.7-199.3] (When I asked him to talk...concern," was the forerunner of reason.) The Power of Silence - Page [200.9-202.1] ("It's not so easy," he said...of how unreasonable it may seem.") The Power of Silence - Page [239.4-240.8] (The old nagual went on to...in an endless sea of islands.) The Art of Dreaming - Page [60.6-60.9] (I told don Juan that I...remains purely a matter of energy.")
> SEE ALSO: *REASON, INTENT, POINT-FIRST, POINT-THIRD, POINT-THIRD-INVERSION, MAN-ERROR, LETTING-GO, REASON-VS-WILL*

REASON-VS-KNOWING-BODY-[REASON VS KNOWING WITH THE BODY]: (Warriors know that reason and the knowledge of the body are two different things; warriors know that direct knowledge is completely independent of language.)
> SELECTED REFERENCES: The Second Ring of Power -Page [179.3-179.9] (He remained quiet, while I frantically...minute I walked through that door.")
> SEE ALSO: *KNOWLEDGE-VS-LANGUAGE, BODY-PHYSICAL, BODY-PHYSICAL-WITNESSING, PERCEIVING-BODY-ENTIRE, RECOLLECTION-SORCERER, SEEING*

REASON-LADDER-[THE ENDLESS LADDER OF REASON]: (*Warriors know that the dilemmas of reason are only steps in an endless ladder which they cannot afford to emphasize on the road to knowledge.*)

SELECTED REFERENCES: Tales of Power - Page [105.2-105.3] ("For one thing," he said...cannot possibly afford to do that.")

SEE ALSO: *REASON, SELF-INDULGENCE, WARRIOR-EMPHASIS, REASON-DILEMMAS*

REASON-LIFE-COURSE-[REASON HAS LITTLE TO DO WITH ALTERING THE COURSE OF OUR LIVES]: (*Warriors know that reason has little to do with altering the course of our lives; this is why it is easy for the average man to have extremely clear convictions and yet act diametrically against them time after time.*)

SELECTED REFERENCES: The Fire From Within - Page [36.9-37.1] (He went on to say that...idea that to err is human.)

SEE ALSO: *SCHOLAR-ARRANGEMENT, REASON*

REASON-PARADOX-[THE PARADOX OF REASON]: (*Warriors know that the sorcerers' explanation forces them to face a great paradox of reason; warriors must not hurry or panic as they prepare themselves for the worst; they must realize that they don't have any time even though they're surrounded by eternity.*)

SELECTED REFERENCES: Tales of Power - Page [232.6-232.8] (I asked him to explain his...What a paradox for your *reason*.) The Power of Silence - Page [244.7-244.9] ("I am just considering how our...out. It can only be experienced.")

SEE ALSO: *SORCERER-EXPLANATION, REASON, DESCRIPTION-WORLD*

REASON-RUBRIC-[THE RUBRIC OF REASON]: (*Warriors know that the rubric of reason is the first attention description of the world; the world of reason.*)

SELECTED REFERENCES: Tales of Power - Page [113.9-114.1] ("Those are the two possibilities opened...everything under the rubric of *reason*.)

SEE ALSO: *REASON*

REASON-VS-SELF-ABSORPTION-[REASON VS SELF-ABSORPTION]: (*Warriors know that human beings carry the command of taking an inventory to its logical extreme and disregard everything else; once they are deeply involved with the inventory they do one of two things, they either ignore the impulses of the emanations at large or they use them in a very specialized way; ignoring the emanations results in a unique state known as reason; using the emanations in a specialized way is known as self-absorption; the obsessive entanglement of the first attention in reason and self-absorption is a powerfully binding force which tends to keep the assemblage point fixed on its habitual position.*)

SELECTED REFERENCES: The Fire From Within - Page [74.8-75.8] (He said that human beings carry...long pauses of dullness," he said.) The Fire From Within - Page [119.6-120.1] ("The new seers realized the true...the assemblage point loses its rigidity.) The Fire From Within - Page [132.9-133.2] ("But would it be possible to encourage...being caught in the clutches of rationality.")

SEE ALSO: *REASON, SELF-ABSORPTION, INVENTORY, EAGLE-EMANATIONS-QUIETING*

REASON-SNARLS-[THE SNARLS OF REASON]: SEE: REASON-DILEMMA-[THE DILEMMAS OF REASON]

REASON-TALKING-[REASON AND TALKING]: (*Warriors know that reason and talking are the companions of the first ring of power; between the two they concoct and maintain the world.*)
SELECTED REFERENCES: Tales of Power - Page [98.3-98.4] ("We, the luminous beings, are born...they concoct and maintain the world.)
SEE ALSO: *REASON, TALKING, POWER-RING-FIRST*

REASON-TRICKING-[TRICKING REASON]: (*Warriors know that the reason of the average man is tricked into believing that the tonal is accountable and predictable; in reality, that is a mirage because reason, like the will, is only a center of assemblage; reason is merely reflecting an outside order and is as unfathomable and unexplainable as the nagual; reason can only witness the effects of the tonal in the same way the will witnesses the effects of the nagual.*)
SELECTED REFERENCES: Tales of Power - Page [276.8-277.6] ("To make *reason* feel safe is...it is that we are witnessing.)
SEE ALSO: *REASON, TONAL, TONAL-INDESCRIBABLE, MIRAGE, WILL*

REASON-VANQUISHING-[VANQUISHING REASON]: (*Warriors know they must struggle to suppress or "vanquish" the attention of the tonal, not reason or the capacity for rational thought per se; the warriors' motive for doing so is based upon the understanding that once the attention of the tonal is dropped, the world as we know it collapses.*)
SELECTED REFERENCES: A Separate Reality - Page [5.3-5.4] ("I've vanquished my problems. Too bad...no despair or self-pity in it.) The Second Ring of Power - Page [274.4-274.8] (Thoughts came down on me like...that to him reason meant attention.) The Second Ring of Power - Page [275.8-276.1] (What don Juan had struggled to...maintain those images, the world collapses.) The Fire From Within - Page [73.3-73.4] (His example left me baffled...him how I understood his point.)
SEE ALSO: *ATTENTION-TONAL, REASON, ATTENTION, WARRIOR-WORLD-COLLAPSE-REASSEMBLE*

REASON-WARRIOR-[THE WARRIORS' REASONS]: SEE: WARRIOR-REASONS-[THE WARRIORS' REASONS]

REASON-WEIGHT-[THE WEIGHT OF REASON]: (*Warriors know the weight of reason and struggle to lighten their load by accepting the fact that reality extends far beyond the limits of rationality.*)
SELECTED REFERENCES: A Separate Reality - Page [262.3-262.9] (Before I left I sat down...indulge too much," he said softly.)
SEE ALSO: *REASON, LETTING-GO*

REASON-VS-WILL-[REASON VS WILL]: (*Warriors know that the relationship between reason and the will is the relationship between the two rings of power, the two descriptions of the world.*)
SELECTED REFERENCES: Tales of Power - Page [98.3-98.8] ("We, the luminous beings, are born...get to the totality of yourself.) Tales of Power - Page [244.5-244.9] ("That's a difficult point to explain...enlarging their views of the world.) The Art of Dreaming - Page [72.9-73.4] (Upon awakening I gave don Juan...world, of being able to predict.)
SEE ALSO: *REASON-VS-INTENT, REASON, WILL, POWER-RING-FIRST, POWER-RING-SECOND, DESCRIPTION-WORLD-TWO, LUMINOUS-BEINGS-SECRET, REASON-TRICKING*

REASON-WORLD-[THE WORLD OF REASON]: (*Warriors know that the world which reason wants to sustain is the world created by a description and its dogmatic and inviolable rules, rules which reason learns to accept and defend.*)

SELECTED REFERENCES: Tales of Power - Page [98.4-98.5] ("So, in essence, the world that...reason learns to accept and defend.) **The Art of Dreaming** - Page [4.1-4.9] (Don Juan's conception was that our...essence of everything, energy itself, directly.)
SEE ALSO: *REASON, DESCRIPTION-WORLD*

REASONABLENESS-PROPOSITIONS-[THE PROPOSITIONS OF REASONABLENESS]: SEE: ATTENTION-FIRST-FOCUS-[THE FOCUS OF THE FIRST ATTENTION], REASON-RATIONALITY-[REASON AND RATIONALITY]

REASONS-WARRIOR-[THE WARRIORS' REASONS]: SEE: WARRIOR-REASONS-[THE WARRIORS' REASONS]

RECAPITULATION-[RECAPITULATION]: **(Warriors know that the recapitulation is the forte of stalkers as the dreaming body is the forte of dreamers; the task of recapitulation consists of recollecting one's own life down to the most insignificant detail; the task of recapitulation is important to stalkers because the surrogate awareness of a perfect recapitulation can satisfy the Eagle in place of consciousness; there are three stalking techniques necessary for recapitulation, the crate, the list of events to be recapitulated and the stalker's breath; a profound recapitulation is the most expedient means to lose the human form; the recapitulation process never ends, no matter how well the warrior has accomplished it; through the recapitulation, warriors free themselves of heavily loaded emotions; recapitulation and dreaming go hand in hand; the recapitulation sets free energy which is necessary for dreaming; the recapitulation is actually the sorcerers' ploy to induce the steady but minute displacement of the assemblage point; there are two basic rounds to the recapitulation; the first is called formality and rigidity and the second is called fluidity.)**
SELECTED REFERENCES: **The Eagle's Gift** - Page [285.7-285.8] (Florinda laughed, describing her shock...task he called the "recapitulation.") **The Eagle's Gift** - Page [287.2-289.8] (Because of this her benefactor had...a recapitulation into a practical matter.) **The Eagle's Gift** - Page [290.3-290.5] (Florinda said that her benefactor considered...self-importance, breaking routines and so forth.) **The Art of Dreaming** - Page [147.6-151.3] ("You are not yet ready for...was a new, more relaxed attitude.)
SEE ALSO: *STALKING-ART, RECOLLECTION, BREATH, CRATE, AWARENESS-SURROGATE, STALKER-BREATH*

RECAPITULATION-DREAMING-BODY-[RECAPITULATION AND THE DREAMING BODY]: **(Warriors know that the recapitulation is the forte of stalkers in the same way that the dreaming body is the forte of dreamers.)**
SELECTED REFERENCES: **The Eagle's Gift** - Page [287.3-287.4] (She explained that a recapitulation is...*dreaming body* is the forte of dreamers.)
SEE ALSO: *RECAPITULATION, DREAMING-BODY, STALKING-ART, DREAMING-ART*

RECAPITULATION-STAGES-[THE FUNDAMENTAL STAGES OF THE RECAPITULATION]: **(Warriors know that there are two fundamental stages to the recapitulation; the first is a brief recounting of all the incidents in the warriors' life that stand out in an obvious manner for examination; the second stage is a more detailed recollection of every moment of the warriors' life from the moment of birth.)**
SELECTED REFERENCES: **The Eagle's Gift** - Page [287.8-288.1] (Florinda gave me then the fundamentals...extend to the moment of birth.)
SEE ALSO: *RECAPITULATION*

RECAPITULATION-TECHNIQUES-[THE THREE TECHNIQUES OF THE RECAPITULATION]: SEE: RECAPITULATION-[RECAPITULATION]

RECOLLECTION-[RECOLLECTION]: (Warriors know that the world does not yield itself directly to us, the description of the world stands in between; this means that warriors are always one step removed and their experience of the world is actually a recollection of that experience; this also means that we are perennially recollecting the instant that has just happened, just passed.)

SELECTED REFERENCES: **Tales of Power - Page [47.4-47.5]** ("Think of this," he went on...We recollect, recollect, recollect.") **The Power of Silence - Page [69.3-69.4]** ("In the past few days ,I...bring you into a total recollection.") **The Power of Silence - Page [124.8-125.3]** ("Try to recall what you already...point is known as the sorcerers' recollection.")

SEE ALSO: *DESCRIPTION-WORLD, INFORMATION-EXPERIENCE-STORAGE, INTENSITY*

RECOLLECTION-SORCERER-[THE SORCERERS' RECOLLECTION]: (Warriors know that the sorcerers' recollection is a way of bringing back a total event by means of shifting the assemblage point to the precise spot where it was located when the event took place; the way warriors store and retrieve information; sorcerer-dreamers understand this kind of recollection as an energetic configuration of awareness; one of the most complex and difficult of the traditional tasks of sorcery.)

SELECTED REFERENCES: **The Second Ring of Power - Page [272.1-273.7]** (It was at that instant that...remember at all a while ago.") **The Power of Silence - Page [xiv.1-xiv.2]** ("You will need a lifetime to remember...of the unfathomable mysteries of awareness.") **The Power of Silence - Page [xvii.8-xviii.1]** (It took me years to be...issue by not thinking about it.) **The Power of Silence - Page [125.3]** (Bringing back the total event by...point is known as sorcerers' recollection.") **The Power of Silence - Page [242.9-243.5]** ("Intensity is an automatic result of...But I have already explained that.") **The Art of Dreaming - Page [x.3-xi.6]** (We interacted with one another solely...is a result of that rearrangement.) **The Art of Dreaming - Page [17.4-17.9]** (Don Juan justified the indispensability of...to fulfilling this task of remembering.) **The Art of Dreaming - Page [18.5-18.7]** (I succeeded countless times in perceiving...such a state existed at all.) **The Art of Dreaming - Page [138.6-139.1]** (I confided to him that I was...come when your memory opens up.") **The Art of Dreaming - Page [144.4-146.2]** ("My intention was to explain to you...an accomplishment of the highest magnitude.)

SEE ALSO: *REMEMBERING-VS-RECOLLECTION, ASSEMBLAGE-POINT-MOVING, INFORMATION-EXPERIENCE-STORAGE, INTENSITY, SORCERY-TASKS TRADITIONAL*

RECOLLECTION-WARRIOR-DUALITY-[THE RECOLLECTION OF THE WARRIORS' DUALITY]: SEE: WARRIOR-DUALITY-RECOLLECTION-[THE RECOLLECTION OF THE WARRIORS' DUALITY]

RECOMMENDATION-WARRIOR-[THE RECOMMENDATION FOR WARRIORS]: SEE: WARRIOR-RECOMMENDATION-[THE RECOMMENDATION FOR WARRIORS]

RED-INSECTS-WORLD-[THE WORLD OF THE RED INSECTS]: SEE: DOMED-WORLD-[THE DOMED WORLD]

REDEMPTION-AVENUE-[THE AVENUE OF REDEMPTION]: (Warriors know that there is an avenue of redemption open to all men; it doesn't matter which personality type one is because it is only personal self-reflection that falls into the stalker's classifications of personality; once warriors have banished self-importance, it doesn't matter which classification they belong to.)

SELECTED REFERENCES: The Power of Silence - Page [248.1-248.3] (He agreed that that was exactly...himself seriously, while you still do.")
SEE ALSO: *PEOPLE-TYPES, SELF-REELECTION, SELF-SERIOUSNESS, POWER-PROMISE*

REGRETS-WARRIOR-[THE WARRIORS' REGRETS]: SEE: WARRIOR-REGRETS-[THE WARRIORS' REGRETS]

REJOICE-VICTORIES-SPIRIT-WARRIOR-[WARRIORS REJOICES IN VICTORIES OF THE SPIRIT]: SEE: WARRIOR-REJOICE-VICTORIES-SPIRIT-[WARRIORS REJOICE IN VICTORIES OF THE SPIRIT]

RELENTLESS-ENEMY-WOMEN-[WOMEN ARE RELENTLESS ENEMIES]: SEE: ENEMY-RELENTLESS-WOMEN-[WOMEN ARE RELENTLESS ENEMIES]

RELIGIOUS-BELIEF-[RELIGIOUS BELIEFS]: *(Warriors know they must create a new context for their religious beliefs, a context that takes into account the existence of the mold of man.)*
SELECTED REFERENCES: The Fire From Within - Page [261.3-265.9] (I moved my eyes as he suggested...God is a male. What a relief!")
SEE ALSO: *MOLD-MAN, GOD, FAITH-RELIGIOUS*

RELIGIOUS-FAITH-[RELIGIOUS FAITH]: SEE: FAITH-RELIGIOUS-[RELIGIOUS FAITH]

*REMEMBERING-BODY-[REMEMBERING WITH THE BODY]: *(Warriors know they are capable of remembering or recollecting events that are stored in the movement of the assemblage point; the systematic interaction warriors go through to entice the other self to reveal itself through memories; this type of remembering has nothing to do with normal memory, it has to do with the movement of the assemblage point; this type of remembering [or recollecting] is something that is within the realm of every human being; every one of us can go directly to the memories of our luminosity with unfathomable results; the process by which warriors move the assemblage point back to a position in which they have stored the memory of an experience; warriors know that sometimes rolling the eyes can facilitate the movement of the assemblage point necessary to remember with the body.)*
SELECTED REFERENCES: The Second Ring of Power - Page [272.1-272.4] (A wave of profound affection...alien memory had taken possession of me.) The Eagle's Gift - Page [46.6-47.2] ("I don't agree with you," she...it, myself. I know that much.") The Eagle's Gift - Page [166.1-166.3] (Our incapacity to remember was in...blocked by a wall of *intensity.*) The Eagle's Gift - Page [166.7-167.4] (Upon completing our remembering, la Gorda...which had been veiled by *intensity.*) The Eagle's Gift - Page [307.5-307.6] (*I am already given to the...past the Eagle to be free.*) The Eagle's Gift - Page [312.5-312.9] (Don Juan told me then that...of our luminosity with unfathomable results.) The Fire From Within - Page [10.5-10.7] (He said that the value of the...new seers meant them to have.) The Fire From Within - Page [53.1-53.5] ("Are those memories trapped in my...those other areas is to *see.*) The Fire From Within - Page [72.3-72.5] ("Oh, there is the mystery." he...back to our explanation of awareness.") The Fire From Within - Page [112.8-113.5] (He said that the glow of awareness...used during states of heightened awareness.) The Fire From Within - Page [183.7-183.8] ("It is an internal knowledge," he said...every nagual is left to do.) The Fire From Within - Page [184.6-185.1] (Don Juan began his elucidation by...so commonplace, so taken for granted.) The Fire From Within - Page [259.6-259.7] ("To break the barrier of perception is...of recovery. Remember what you've done!") The Fire From Within - Page [260.7] ("It will all come back to...an overstuffed closet had given way.") The Fire From Within - Page [261.1-261.3] (He urged me to relax and move...had *seen* the mold of man.) The Fire From Within - Page [266.1-266.5] (After recounting to don Juan what...a true

misunderstanding on my part.") **The Fire From Within - Page [275.7-275.8]** ("I want you to realign the proper...in a *dreaming position*," he said.) **The Fire From Within - Page [284.3-284.7]** ("Take yourself, for example; you are...thing for you to integrate it.") **The Fire From Within - Page [300.2-300.3]** (We know now that we were...the greater our doubts, the greater our turmoil.) **The Power of Silence - Page [70.2-71.1]** (Suddenly I began to remember with shattering...that had happened many years before.) **The Power of Silence - Page [84.3-85.2]** (I was staring at each of them...recall them by *intending* them back.") **The Power of Silence - Page [108.6-108.9]** (He assured me that he had...can make it function at will.) **The Power of Silence - Page [118.8-119.4]** (Ruthlessness is the first principle of...do with moving the assemblage point.") **The Power of Silence - Page [123.8-123.9]** ("I want you to recall something...take over and make you recollect.") **The Power of Silence - Page [124.9-125.3]** ("Recollecting is not the same as remembering...point is a known as sorcerers' recollection.") **The Power of Silence - Page [134.7-134.8]** (Don Juan told me that there...mountains, until I had recollected everything.) **The Power of Silence - Page [242.3-243.2]** (I demanded that he explain this...That is the way sorcerers store information.")

SEE ALSO: *RECOLLECTION-SORCERER, INFORMATION-EXPERIENCE-STORAGE, EYES-ROLLING, REMEMBERING-BODY-(ALL)*

REMEMBERING-BODY-BEST-WAY-[THE BEST WAY TO ENSURE A COMPLETE RECOLLECTION OF A BODILY MEMORY STORED IN THE ASSEMBLAGE POINT]: (Warriors know that the best way to ensure the complete recollection of a bodily memory stored in a position of the assemblage point is to walk around.)

SELECTED REFERENCES: **The Power of Silence - Page [134.7-134.8]** (Don Juan told me that there...mountains, until I had recollected everything.)

SEE ALSO: *REMEMBERING-BODY, RECOLLECTION-SORCERER, INTENDING-MEMORIES-BACK*

REMEMBERING-BODY-VS-REMEMBERING-NORMAL-[REMEMBERING WITH THE BODY VS NORMAL REMEMBERING]: (Warriors know that normal remembering is a function of day-to day thinking and that the facility to remember those things has to do with the fixity of the assemblage point on its normal position; remembering with the body, on the other hand, has to do with moving the assemblage point back to the precise spot where the memory is stored; warriors know that they records events in their everyday memory as well as in their left side emanations, and that they are capable of accessing both kinds of memories, albeit through different kinds of "remembering" processes.)

SELECTED REFERENCES: **The Fire From Within - Page [184.6-184.8]** (Don Juan began his elucidation by...the spot where it normally sets.) **The Fire From Within - Page [224.5-224.6]** (His assertion was so farfetched that...as in my left-side emanations.) **The Power of Silence - Page [84.3-85.2]** (I was staring at each of them...recall them by *intending* them back.") **The Power of Silence - Page [124.9-125.3]** ("Recollecting is not the same as...point is known as the sorcerers' recollection.")

SEE ALSO: *THINKING-VS-ASSEMBLAGE-POINT-MOVEMENT, INTENSITY*

REMEMBERING-LEFT-SIDE-[REMEMBERING THE LEFT SIDE]-(TOP)

REMEMBERING-TASK-[THE TASK OF REMEMBERING]: (Warriors know that the task of remembering is properly the task of rejoining the left and right sides and consolidating the totality of themselves.)

SELECTED REFERENCES: **The Eagle's Gift - Page [166.3-166.4]** (The task of remembering, then, was...rearranging *intensity* into a linear sequence.) **The Eagle's Gift - Page [177.5-177.8]** (The Nagual and his warriors were...seek and face their definitive journey.) **The Eagle's Gift - Page [302.3-302.6]** (La Gorda remembered that to prepare...a device that helped them remember.)

SEE ALSO: *RECOLLECTION-SORCERER, AWARENESS-LEFT, AWARENESS-RIGHT, FORGET-COMMAND, TOTALITY*

REMEMBERING-TRACKING-HIDING-SKILLS-*[REMEMBERING THE WARRIORS' TRACKING AND HIDING SKILLS]-(TOP)*

REMORSE-WARRIOR-*[THE WARRIORS' DOUBTS AND REMORSE]: SEE: WARRIOR-DOUBTS-REMORSE-[THE WARRIORS' DOUBTS AND REMORSE]*

REPETITION-WARRIOR-*[REPETITION FOR THE WARRIOR]: SEE: WARRIOR-REPETITION-[REPETITION FOR THE WARRIOR]*

REPLACEMENT-REPAIR-*[REPLACEMENT NOT REPAIR]:* (Warriors know that in a natural state, replacement, not repair prevails.)
  SELECTED REFERENCES: **The Power of Silence - Page [17.6-17.8]** (As he recognized the imminent presence...a display of such obvious waste.)
  SEE ALSO: *DEATH*

REQUISITES-KNOWLEDGE-GOING-*[THE FOUR REQUISITES OF GOING TO KNOWLEDGE]: SEE: KNOWLEDGE-GOING-REQUISITES-[THE FOUR REQUISITES OF GOING TO KNOWLEDGE]*

RESERVOIR-SECRET-WARRIOR-*[THE WARRIORS' SECRET RESERVOIR]: SEE: WARRIOR-RESERVOIR-SECRET-[THE WARRIORS' SECRET RESERVOIR]*

RESOLUTION-WARRIOR-*[THE WARRIORS' RESOLUTION]: SEE: WARRIOR-RESOLUTION-[THE WARRIORS' RESOLUTION]*

RESOURCEFULNESS-WARRIOR-*[THE WARRIORS' RESOURCEFULNESS]: SEE: WARRIOR-RESOURCEFULNESS-[THE WARRIORS' RESOURCEFULNESS]*

RESPECT-WARRIOR-*[THE WARRIORS' RESPECT]: SEE: WARRIOR-RESPECT-AWE-LIFE-[THE WARRIORS' RESPECT AND AWE FOR LIFE]*

RESPONSIBILITY-ASSUMING-[ASSUMING RESPONSIBILITY]: (Warriors know they must take full responsibility for each and every one of their actions; no matter what they do, they must first know why they are acting, and then they must proceed with their actions without having doubts or remorse about them; the average man complains all his life because he does not assume responsibility for his decisions; to assume responsibility for one's decisions is to be ready to die for them; warriors know they must assume responsibility to gain enough personal power to tip the scales.)
  SELECTED REFERENCES: **A Separate Reality - Page [133.9]** ("Live like a warrior!...your thoughts and that's wrong.) **A Separate Reality - Page [151.3-151.4]** ("A detached man, who knows he...permit him time to cling to anything.) **Journey to Ixtlan - Page [39.5-39.8]** ("What was wrong with you when...having doubts or remorse about them.") **Journey to Ixtlan - Page [40.1-40.3]** ("Look at me," he said...There is only time for decisions.") **Journey to Ixtlan - Page [43.2-43.5]** ("You are complaining," he said softly...is ready to die for them.") **Journey to Ixtlan - Page [80.6-81.5]** ("You always feel compelled to explain...perhaps you'll never be a hunter.") **Journey to Ixtlan - Page [227.1-227.3]** ("No, I don't mean that. You...the acts that he deems necessary.") **Tales of Power - Page [6.1-6.7]** ("How can I arrive at the sorcerers' explanation...personal power to tip the scales.") **Tales of Power - Page [240.7-240.8]** (He explained that in order to...dubious about himself and his actions.) **Tales of Power - Page [241.8-242.5]** ("One changes the facade by altering the...were there, without ever being used.")
  SEE ALSO: *WARRIOR-DECISIONS, ACT-LEARNING, POWER-PERSONAL*

RESTFUL-VIGIL-*[RESTFUL VIGIL]: SEE: DREAMING-STAGES-[THE FOUR STAGES OF DREAMING]*

<u>*RETREAT-MEANINGLESSNESS-[THE MEANINGLESSNESS OF*</u>
RETREAT]: (*Warriors know it is meaningless to retreat from the world and hide, because even in isolated deserted places the interference of our fellow men is still prevalent because the fixation of their first attention cannot be shut off.*)

SELECTED REFERENCES: The Eagle's Gift - Page [138.5-138.8] (Another topic of great significance was the...of those around us is dormant.)

SEE ALSO: *ATTENTION-FIRST, WARRIOR-RETREAT*

<u>*RETREAT-WARRIOR-[THE WARRIORS' RETREAT]: SEE: WARRIOR-*</u>
RETREAT-[THE WARRIORS' RETREAT]

<u>*RETURN-WARRIOR-[WILL THE WARRIOR RETURN FROM THE*</u>
UNKNOWN?]: SEE: WARRIOR-RETURN-[WILL THE WARRIOR RETURN FROM THE UNKNOWN?]

<u>*REVELATION-[REVELATION]:*</u> (*Warriors know that the ability to profit from a revelation is dependent on personal power; knowledge cannot be claimed by warriors unless the have the personal power to do so; the most magnificent piece of knowledge can be revealed to anyone, but without enough personal power, that revelation won't make the slightest bit of difference.*)

SELECTED REFERENCES: Tales of Power - Page [8.1-8.3] ("But maybe I'm revealing things I...make a damn bit of difference.") Tales of Power - Page [8.9-9.2] ("You didn't have this knowledge before...boundaries in which it is contained.") Tales of Power - Page [160.3-160.5] (What attracted and trapped my attention...is a terrible way of being.") Tales of Power - Page [231.5-231.7] (Personal power decides who can or...as empty as any other routine.)

SEE ALSO: *POWER-PERSONAL, KNOWLEDGE-VS-POWER, KNOWLEDGE-CLAIMING-POWER*

<u>*REWARD-WARRIOR-[THE WARRIORS' REWARD]: SEE: WARRIOR-*</u>
REWARD-[THE WARRIORS' REWARD]

<u>*RIDDLE-DREAMER-DREAMED-[THE RIDDLE OF THE DREAMER AND*</u>
THE DREAMED]: (*Warriors know that the art of dreaming is the riddle of the dreamer and the dreamed; the double dreams the self and the self dreams the double; once the self learns to dream the double a moment comes when one realizes that it is the double that dreams the self; warriors know that they themselves are a dream; the secret of the double is in the bubble of perception, the capacity of luminous beings to perceive here and there at the same time.*)

SELECTED REFERENCES: Tales of Power - Page [46.2-47.9] ("Well, a sorcerer can double up...time is no longer binding him.") Tales of Power - Page [61.9] (Then after a moment's pause he...he is a dream," he retorted.) Tales of Power - Page [73.5] (Don Juan said that it was...of the dreamer and the dreamed.) Tales of Power - Page [76.8-77.2] ("I told you that Genaro came...the double who dreams the self.") Tales of Power - Page [77.8-78.2] ("Last night Genaro guided you through...enough power even to understand that.") Tales of Power - Page [93.9-94.1] ("Last night you were back again...your reason refuses to believe it.) Tales of Power - Page [275.2-275.3] ("The secret of the double is in...the *here* and the *there* at once.") The Eagle's Gift - Page [50.4-50.6] (I *dreamed* once that I woke up...without knowing how, outside my room.) The Power of Silence - Page [221.6-221.9] ("A sorcerer perceives his actions with...must perceive two places at once.") The Power of Silence - Page [224.9] ("The third point of reference is...our boundaries and touching the inconceivable.") The Power of Silence - Page [238.7-238.8] (He said that don Juan's assemblage...alternately or at the same time.)

SEE ALSO: *DREAMING-BODY, SELF, TONAL-NAGUAL-DICHOTOMY, POINT-THIRD, LUMINOUS-BEINGS-MYSTERY, DOUBLE-FACING, PERCEPTION-BUBBLE, HERE-HERE*

RIDDLE-ENERGY-BODY-[THE RIDDLE OF MOVING THE ENERGY
BODY]: SEE: ENERGY-BODY-MOVING-[MOVING THE ENERGY BODY]

RIDDLE-FACED-WITH-[FACED WITH A RIDDLE]: SEE: DREAMING-
IMAGINATION-[DREAMING AND IMAGINATION]

RIDDLE-HEART-[THE RIDDLE OF THE HEART]: (Warriors know that the
art of stalking is the riddle of the heart, the riddle of awareness and
perception; the world appears to be unalterably factual and objective due to
certain peculiarities of perception and awareness; but if different
peculiarities of perception and awareness come into play, the things about
the world that seem so unalterable and factual change in the blink of an eye.)
SELECTED REFERENCES: Tales of Power - Page [20.1-20.5] ("I always think that I'm
being...he was making fun of me.) Tales of Power - Page [24.6-24.8] (He sat down by me
and...that I had seen a man.) Tales of Power - Page [97.7-97.8] (We are an awareness; we
are...we rarely emerge in a lifetime.) The Fire From Within - Page [37.4-37.6] ("Something out
there is affecting our...awareness forces them to do so.") The Power of Silence - Page [xv.3-
xv.5] (The art of stalking is the riddle...seem so unalterably objective and factual change.)
SEE ALSO: STALKING-ART, PERCEPTION, MIRAGE, ALIGNMENT,
AWARENESS

RIDDLE-MIND-[THE RIDDLE OF THE MIND]: (Warriors know that the
mastery of awareness is the riddle of the mind; the mystery of the luminous
beings.)
SELECTED REFERENCES: Tales of Power - Page [98.2] ("We are perceivers," he
proceeded...since the moment we were born.) The Fire From Within - Page [72.3] ("Oh, there is
the mystery...The mystery can only be witnessed.") The Fire From Within - Page [133.7-133.8]
(The explanation behind all these complex...alignments of emanations, thus new perceptions.)
The Fire From Within - Page [258.6] ("The mastery of awareness is what...point fixed at a certain
position.) The Fire From Within - Page [283.5-283.7] (He said that now I needed...where the
assemblage point is located.) The Power of Silence - Page [xv.2-xv.3] (The mastery of
awareness is the riddle...mystery and scope of awareness and perception.)
SEE ALSO: AWARENESS-MASTERY, LUMINOUS-BEINGS-MYSTERY,
AWARENESS-EXPLANATION

RIDDLE-SPIRIT-[THE RIDDLE OF THE SPIRIT]: (Warriors know that the
mastery of intent is the riddle of the spirit; the paradox of the abstract; the
somersault of thought into the inconceivable.)
SELECTED REFERENCES: Tales of Power - Page [273.3-273.6] ("There is no way to
refer...no way to reassemble that cluster.) The Fire From Within - Page [259.9-260.2] ("It will be
a long time...if it were the Eagle's command.") The Power of Silence - Page [xv.5] (The mastery
of intent is the riddle...projected beyond our human condition.) The Power of Silence - Page
[xviii.1-xviii.9] (Whatever I written about my sorcery...that was essential to understanding
them.) The Power of Silence - Page [11.3-11.4] ("Can you explain intent to me?" I...the spirit, the
abstract, the nagual.)
SEE ALSO: INTENT-MASTERY, THOUGHT-SOMERSAULT

RIDDLES-SORCERY-[THE RIDDLES OF SORCERY]: SEE: RIDDLE-
MIND-[THE RIDDLE OF THE MIND], RIDDLE-HEART-[THE RIDDLE OF
THE HEART], RIDDLE-SPIRIT-[THE RIDDLE OF THE SPIRIT], RIDDLE-
DREAMER-DREAMED-[THE RIDDLE OF THE DREAMER AND THE
DREAMED]

RIGHT-WAY-LIVE-[THE RIGHT WAY TO LIVE]: SEE: LIVE-RIGHT-[THE
RIGHT WAY TO LIVE]

RIGHT-WAY-WALKING-[THE RIGHT WAY OF WALKING]: SEE:
WALKING-RIGHT-WAY-[THE RIGHT WAY OF WALKING]

RIGIDITY-FORMALITY-[RIGIDITY AND FORMALITY]: SEE: RECAPITULATION-[RECAPITULATION]

RINGS-POWER-[THE RINGS OF POWER]: SEE: POWER-RING-FIRST [THE FIRST RING OF POWER], POWER-RING-SECOND [THE SECOND RING OF POWER], DOING-RING [THE RING OF DOING], NOT-DOING-RING [THE RING OF NOT-DOING]

RISK-WARRIOR-[THE WARRIORS' RISK]: SEE: WARRIOR-RISK-[THE WARRIORS' RISK]

RITUAL-[RITUAL]: (*Warriors know that ritual behavior is powerful because it is repetitive and forces the first attention to free some of its energy from watching the inventory; ritual behavior is necessary at some point in every warriors' life as a means of luring the first attention away from the power of self-absorption, which in turn helps the assemblage point lose some of its rigidity; there is no better way to make a direct hit on the second attention than through ritual acts, monotonous chanting, and intricate repetitious movements; in addition to its positive effects, ritual can also become a trap, it can force warriors to construct edifices of morbidity and obsession.*)

SELECTED REFERENCES: **The Eagle's Gift - Page [188.7-189.5]** (Don Juan said that he had the...pomp were out of character for me.) **The Eagle's Gift - Page [249.7-250.1]** (Zuleica told me that if dreaming...monotonous chanting, intricate repetitious movements.) **The Fire From Within - Page [119.5-120.1]** ("I've mentioned to you that sorcery...the assemblage point loses its rigidity.) **The Power of Silence - Page [120.1-120.3]** (He replied that striking my back...the spirit move my assemblage point.) **The Power of Silence - Page [262.7-262.8]** (I asked don Juan what he...candles, dark closets, and black tables.) **The Power of Silence - Page [263.7-264.2]** (After a moment's pause, don Juan...liens and mortgages on our awareness.")

SEE ALSO: *INVENTORY, ASSEMBLAGE-POINT-MOVING, OBSESSION, ABERRATION-MORBIDITY, ASSEMBLAGE-POINT-RIGIDITY*

RIVER-JUAN-SPIRIT-[DON JUAN MEETS THE SPIRIT BY BEING THROWN INTO THE RIVER]-(TOP): SEE: JUAN-RIVER-BOUT-[DON JUAN'S BOUT WITH THE RAGING RIVER]-(TOP)

ROCK-GAZING-[ROCK GAZING]: SEE: GAZING-[GAZING]

ROCKS-SCENT-[THE SCENT OF ROCKS]-(TOP)

*ROLLING-FORCE-[THE ROLLING FORCE]: SEE: FORCE-ROLLING-[THE ROLLING FORCE]

ROLLING-FORCE-SEEING-[SEEING THE ROLLING FORCE]-(TOP): SEE: FORCE-ROLLING-SEEING-[SEEING THE ROLLING FORCE]-(TOP)

ROMANCE-KNOWLEDGE-[THE WARRIORS' ROMANCE WITH KNOWLEDGE]: SEE: UNDERSTANDING-SHEER-[SHEER UNDERSTANDING]

ROOTS-[ROOTS]: (*Warriors know that roots are special luminous filaments connected with human reproduction; these structures differentiate men from women; women have thick bundles of filaments resembling a lion's tail that grow inward from the place of the genitalia; men have short filaments that are alive and floating almost independently from the luminous mass of their bodies.*)

SELECTED REFERENCES: The Eagle's Gift - Page [45.8-46.1] (Our visions differed in that she...the luminous mass of their bodies.) **The Fire From Within - Page [60.8-61.1]** ("How do seers know that having...*seen* superimposed on the body itself.")
SEE ALSO: *GIVERS-LIFE, WOMB, WARRIOR-COMPLETENESS*

ROSENDO-NAGUAL-TALES-[TALES OF THE NAGUAL ROSENDO]-(TOP)

ROUTINES-ACCESSIBILITY-[ROUTINES AND ACCESSIBILITY]:
(Warriors know that routines are what make them accessible.)
SELECTED REFERENCES: Journey to Ixtlan - Page [69.3-69.4] ("What is the point of all...your life was a routine one.")
SEE ALSO: *WARRIOR-ACCESSIBILITY, ROUTINES-DISRUPTING*

*ROUTINES-DISRUPTING-[DISRUPTING ROUTINES]: *(Warriors know they must develop a stalking strategy of disrupting routines; normal human behavior is routine and any behavior that breaks from that routine causes an unusual effect on our total being; that effect is what warriors seek, because it is cumulative; if unusual behavior is practiced systematically and directed wisely, it eventually forces the assemblage point to move; disrupting routines is one of the fundamental principles of the art of stalking; one of three techniques used by warriors to make possible a pragmatic world of dreaming; a routine is a doing which needs all of its parts in order to function; if some parts are missing, the routine is disassembled.)*
SELECTED REFERENCES: Journey to Ixtlan - Page [69.4-69.5] ("You lost her because you were...but I assure you it is.") **Journey to Ixtlan - Page [73.5-77.1]** ("You think I'm crazy don't you...men and the routines of hunters.") **Tales of Power - Page [250.5-250.9]** (He explained that disrupting routines, the...engage in the gait of power.) **The Second Ring of Power - Page [227.7-228.4]** ("A hunter just hunts," she said...order to be a live activity.) **The Eagle's Gift - Page [106.1-106.3]** (Nestor made a gesture of solidarity with...be pleasant but deadly for them.) **The Fire From Within - Page [118.3-118.9]** (He affirmed that one of the...as a consequence of new habits.") **The Power of Silence - Page [81.8-82.4]** (I wanted to laugh, but he...differentiates sorcerer seers from just plain witches.")
SEE ALSO: *DREAMING-ART, STALKING-ART, NOT-DOING, PERSONAL HISTORY-ERASING, HABITS, DOING-DISASSEMBLING*

ROUTINES-HUNTER-[ROUTINES AND THE HUNTER]: *(The hunter knows one thing above all else, he knows the routines of his prey.)*
SELECTED REFERENCES: Journey to Ixtlan - Page [74.5-74.6] ("You know a great deal about...what makes him a good hunter.") **Journey to Ixtlan - Page [75.3-75.4]** ("I don't care how you feel...like your prey, easy to predict.")
SEE ALSO: *ROUTINES-DISRUPTING, HUNTER*

ROUTINES-STALKING-[STALKING ROUTINES]: SEE: ROUTINES-DISRUPTING-[DISRUPTING ROUTINES]

RULE-[THE RULE]: *(Warriors know that the rule is an absolute truth; an endless map to the universe which covers every aspect of the warriors' behavior; being involved with the rule may be described as living a myth; the warrior at first conceptualizes the rule as a myth and later comes to understand it and accept it as a map.)*
SELECTED REFERENCES: The Teachings of Don Juan - Page [50.3-50.4] ("All this is very easy to...spite of yourself; that's the rule.") **The Teachings of Don Juan - Page [120.4]** ("I think this is all I...have told you is the rule.) **The Teaching of Don Juan - Page [142.9-143.5]** ("You will have to wait, the same...the subject were of no importance.) **A Separate Reality - Page [134.4-134.5]** (The rule is right. The steps...which of course is right for you.") **A Separate Reality - Page [211.7-211.8]** ("Whatever I have done to you today...I have tricked you into

learning.") **A Separate Reality - Page [212.7-212.8]** (Don Juan reminded me of the...ordinary trick. It was the rule.") **Tales of Power - Page [46.5-46.6]** ("Genaro is right," don Juan said...things up. No one knows why.") **Tales of Power - Page [192.7-192.9]** ("That was the best part of...the most impeccable warrior there is.") **Tales of Power - Page [243.3-243.5]** ("What would have happened if I...necessary avenues. That is the rule.") **The Second Ring of Power - Page [242.1]** ("The Nagual didn't make the rule...out there, and not by a man.") **The Eagle's Gift - Page [158.3-158.5]** (We were supposed to walk for quite...by little. That is the rule.) **The Eagle's Gift - Page [172.1-172.3]** (His total preeminence rested on the...northern Mexico lived at that time.) **The Eagle's Gift - Page [172.7-180.3]** (Don Juan did exactly the same...which in essence was a map.) **The Eagle's Gift - Page [180.9-181.6]** (In trying to explain to me...a chance to have a chance.) **The Eagle's Gift - Page [210.7-211.5]** (Don Juan said that his benefactor...the finality of the Eagle's dictums.) **The Eagle's Gift - Page [218.3-219.8]** (Olinda hesitated. Don Juan's benefactor reminded...had witnessed of their benefactor's world.) **The Eagle's Gift - Page [228.1-228.2]** (He then revealed the rule to...to her appropriate and self-evident.) **The Eagle's Gift - Page [230.4-233.6]** (Don Juan and his warriors sat...the rule. She was a *stalker*.) **The Eagle's Gift - Page [244.5-244.6]** (His idea was sound in the...the physical pressure of that world.) **The Eagle's Gift - Page [289.7-289.8]** (Florinda emphasized that the rule defined...a recapitulation into a practical matter.) **The Eagle's Gift - Page [297.4-297.5]** (Having accomplished every one of the...for me, was to witness it.) **The Power of Silence - Page [30.4-30.5]** ("The rule says that the abstract...to you by the stories themselves.")
SEE ALSO: *NAGUAL, RULE-(ALL)*

RULE-CARRIER-[THE CARRIER OF THE RULE]: *(Warriors know that a carrier of the rule is a particular individual who carries the rule for another warrior.)*
SELECTED REFERENCES: **The Eagle's Gift - Page [245.5-245.6]** (He also told me not to...order to reveal my true task.)
SEE ALSO: *RULE*

RULE-GOVERNING-BODY-[THE RULE AS A GOVERNING BODY]: *(Warriors know that the Eagle's irrevocable dictums have been apprehended by seers and accumulated into a governing body called the rule.)*
SELECTED REFERENCES: **The Eagle's Gift - Page [178.5-178.7]** (I had confronted don Juan with the...the form of a governing body.)
SEE ALSO: *RULE, EAGLE, EAGLE-DICTUMS-FINALITY*

RULE-INTERPRETATIONS-UNIVERSAL-INDIVIDUAL-[THE UNIVERSAL AND INDIVIDUAL INTERPRETATIONS OF THE RULE]: *(Warriors know there are two types of interpretations of the rule; universal interpretations take the statements that make up the body of the rule at face value; individual interpretations are current conclusions arrived at by seers using universal interpretations as premises.)*
SELECTED REFERENCES: **The Eagle's Gift - Page [181.1-181.4]** (He said that there are two types...enhanced, perhaps by my own dedication.)
SEE ALSO: *RULE*

RULE-MAP-[ACCEPTING THE RULE AS A MAP]: *(Warriors know that accepting the rule as a map is the first stage of the warriors' development; warriors must learn to accept the rule as a map.)*
SELECTED REFERENCES: **The Eagle's Gift - Page [179.9-186.8]** (In order to lead us through the first...also forced a shattering self-examination.) **The Eagle's Gift - Page [204.7-204.9]** (Due to something inexplicable in his...into that other world of awareness.) **The Eagle's Gift - Page [266.4-266.5]** (La Gorda and I were in total agreement...had accomplished what the rule prescribed.) **The Eagle's Gift - Page [279.3-279.7]** ("Warriors don't have the world to cushion...One is equal to everything.) **The Eagle's Gift - Page [298.3-298.9]** (Don Juan pointed out that not...the passageway into the other awareness.)
SEE ALSO: *RULE, WARRIOR-DEVELOPMENT-STAGES-THREE*

RULE-NAGUAL-[THE RULE OF THE NAGUAL]-(TOP)

RULE-PRECEPTS-FIRST-THREE-*[THE FIRST THREE PRECEPTS OF THE RULE]: (Warriors know the first three precepts of the rule; 1) everything that surrounds us is an unfathomable mystery; 2) we must each try to unravel these mysteries without ever hoping to accomplish this; 3) warriors, aware of the unfathomable mystery that surrounds them and aware of their duty to try and unravel it, take their rightful place among mysteries and regard themselves as one.)*
    SELECTED REFERENCES: **The Eagle's Gift** - Page [279.5-279.7] ("The first precept of the rule...One is equal to everything.) **The Fire From Within** - Page [185.2-185.3] ("This indeed is the mystery of awareness...apologize for either; both are needed.)
    SEE ALSO: *RULE, EQUAL-UNIMPORTANT*

RULE-STALKER-*[THE RULE FOR STALKERS]: SEE: STALKER-RULE-[THE THREE PRECEPTS OF THE RULE FOR STALKERS]*

RUTHLESSNESS-*[RUTHLESSNESS]: (Warriors know that ruthlessness is the first principle of sorcery; one of the four moods of stalking; the place of no pity is the site of ruthlessness; ruthlessness is a specific position of the assemblage point that shines in the eyes of sorcerers; ruthlessness is sobriety, it should not be harshness; death gives warriors the courage to be ruthless without being self-important; ruthlessness is the opposite of self-pity or self-importance; ruthlessness is a state of being, a level of intent that a warrior attains; the worldly task of warriors is to sharpen, yet disguise, their cutting edges so that no one would suspect their ruthlessness; ruthlessness is not cruelty, ruthlessness is sobriety.)*
    SELECTED REFERENCES: **The Power of Silence** - Page [68.2-68.8] (Don Juan said that his benefactor...acts this way he's being prissy.") **The Power of Silence** - Page [78.4-78.8] ("You are neither ruthless nor cunning...be taught in careful, meticulous steps.) **The Power of Silence** - Page [81.8] ("The very first principle of *stalking*....himself ruthlessly, cunningly, patiently, and sweetly.") **The Power of Silence** - Page [106.9-107.1] (A warrior, he said, was on...be able to suspect his ruthlessness.) **The Power of Silence** - Page [109.2-109.3] ("I'll try to help you clarify...behavior in a ruthless, cunning way.") **The Power of Silence** - Page [110.2-110.3] ("Yes," he went on. "The idea...be ruthless without being self-important.") **The Power of Silence** - Page [117.7-117.8] ("Don't you remember my teaching you..."Ruthlessness, the opposite of self-pity?") **The Power of Silence** - Page [118.1-119.1] ("All sorcerers are ruthless," he said...do with moving the assemblage point.") **The Power of Silence** - Page [122.5-122.6] (He asserted emphatically that the healer...people around her, especially the patient.) **The Power of Silence** - Page [122.9] ("I prefer the word 'ruthlessness' to...proper setting for the spirit's intervention.") **The Power of Silence** - Page [124.5-124.6] ("The place of no pity is...this moment, your eyes are dull.") **The Power of Silence** - Page [125.9-126.1] ("You must recollect the first time...shine, and that shine beckons *intent*.) **The Power of Silence** - Page [131.3-131.4] ("But, for sorcerers to use the...is especially true for the naguals.") **The Power of Silence** - Page [132.7-133.1] ("We've discussed ruthlessness before. Recollect it...are the result of my ruthlessness.") **The Power of Silence** - Page [150.3-151.8] (Don Juan said then that it...is merely self-pity in disguise.) **The Power of Silence** - Page [154.4-154.6] ("The position of self-reflection," don...or self-importance. Ruthlessness is sobriety.") **The Power of Silence** - Page [164.9-165.2] (I wanted to ask him if...point move was the nagual's ruthlessness.) **The Power of Silence** - Page [166.6] ("The nagual's ruthlessness has many aspects...of *intent* that the nagual attains.)
    SEE ALSO: *SORCERY-PRINCIPLE-FIRST, STALKING-MOODS-FOUR, PITY-PLACE-NO, RUTHLESSNESS-(ALL), SOBRIETY, INTENT, SELF-IMPORTANCE, SELF-PITY, CUNNING*

RUTHLESSNESS-MASK-*[THE MASK OF RUTHLESSNESS]: (Warriors know that there are a variety of masks which mask ruthlessness; naguals mask their ruthlessness automatically, even against their will; whatever the mask, it is always ruthlessness that underlies the facade, whether it be*

reasonableness, generosity, easy-goingness, or thoroughness; any kind of mask for a nagual's ruthlessness will do except the mask of generosity)
    SELECTED REFERENCES: **Journey to Ixtlan - Page [216.3]** ("This is all crazy," I said..."You're rational," he retorted. "I am not.") **The Power of Silence - Page [163.3-134.1]** ("But, for sorcerers to use the...false impression of attention and thoroughness.) **The Power of Silence - Page [163.2-163.9]** (Don Juan noted that in this...into exerting themselves to any degree.) **The Power of Silence - Page [169.5-170.6]** ("Since you are naturally slow, you...began to laugh at my dismay.)
    SEE ALSO: *RUTHLESSNESS-NAGUAL, RUTHLESSNESS*

RUTHLESSNESS-NAGUAL-[THE NAGUAL'S RUTHLESSNESS]: (Warriors know that the nagual's ruthlessness has many aspects, it's like a tool that adapts itself to many uses; the nagual's ruthlessness is a state of being; a level of intent which the nagual attains.)
    SELECTED REFERENCES: **The Power of Silence - Page [166.6-166.8]** ("The nagual's ruthlessness has many aspects...made my own assemblage point move.) **The Power of Silence - Page [169.6-170.6]** ("It was also that day that...began to laugh at my dismay.)
    SEE ALSO: *RUTHLESSNESS, NAGUAL-MAN-WOMAN*

RUTHLESSNESS-SHINE-[THE SHINE OF RUTHLESSNESS]: (Warriors know that ruthlessness is a specific position of the assemblage point that shines in the eyes of sorcerers; it is like a shimmering film over the eyes, making them brilliant; ruthlessness makes sorcerers' eyes shine and that shine beckons intent; for sorcerers to use the shine of their eyes to move their own or anyone else's assemblage point they have to be ruthless, that is they have to be familiar with the specific position of the assemblage point called the place of no pity.)
    SELECTED REFERENCES: **A Separate Reality - Page [3.6]** (Bill went on talking but I...his eyes. They had actually shone.) **The Eagle's Gift - Page [310.4-310.5]** (The setting for the poem was...seemed to be focused in their eyes.) **The Power of Silence - Page [124.5-124.6]** ("The place of no pity is...At this moment, your eyes are dull.") **The Power of Silence - Page [125.9-126.1]** ("You must recollect the first time...shine, and that shine beckons *intent.*) **The Power of Silence - Page [131.3-131.4]** ("But, for sorcerers to use the...This is especially true for the naguals.")
    SEE ALSO: *EYES, RUTHLESSNESS, ASSEMBLAGE-POINT-MOVING, PITY-PLACE-NO*

S

SABRE-TOOTHED-TIGER-DREAM-[THE DREAM OF THE SABRE-TOOTHED TIGER]-(TOP): SEE: DREAM-SABRE-TOOTHED-TIGER-[THE DREAM OF THE SABRE-TOOTHED TIGER]-(TOP)

SACATECA-WILL-[THE WILL OF SACATECA]-(TOP)

SADNESS-LAUGHTER-[THE WARRIORS' SADNESS IS THERE ONLY TO MAKE HIM LAUGH]: SEE: WARRIOR-SADNESS-[THE WARRIORS' SADNESS]

SADNESS-WARRIOR-[THE WARRIORS' SADNESS]: SEE: WARRIOR-SADNESS-[THE WARRIORS' SADNESS]

SANITY-[SANITY]: (Warriors know that the mind is nothing but the self-reflection of the inventory of man; warriors actually strive to lose that self-reflection without losing their underpinnings; if they accomplish this, warriors actually live an infinitely stronger life than if they had kept their minds as they originally were; mental balance is nothing but the fixing of the assemblage point on one spot that we're accustomed to; once the assemblage point has been moved, the normal parameters of "sanity" as we know it no longer apply.)
 SELECTED REFERENCES: Tales of Power - Page [250.7-250.8] ("Dreaming is a practical aid devised...let go without losing your marbles.) The Fire From Within - Page 120.1-121.3] ("What happens to the person whose...than if you had kept it.") The Fire From Within - Page [154.5-154.9] ("The position of the assemblage point...lose anything, they lose their dimple.") The Power of Silence - Page [35.5-35.7] (Mental balance is nothing but the...point erratically and lose their minds.") The Power of Silence - Page [104.1-104.3] (Don Juan explained that at one time...needed to manage all that power.) The Art of Dreaming - Page [72.9-73.4] (Upon awakening I gave don Juan...world, of being able to predict.) The Art of Dreaming - Page [203.3-203.9] ("For years now, I have been...or like the new ones," he said.) The Art of Dreaming - Page [211.7-211.9] (I reminded him that he himself...was an abhorrent and untenable position.)
 SEE ALSO: SELF-REFLECTION, INVENTORY, WARRIOR-SOBRIETY

SATISFACTION-WARRIOR-[THE WARRIORS' SATISFACTION]: SEE: WARRIOR-SATISFACTION-[THE WARRIORS' SATISFACTION]

SCALES-TIP-[TIP THE SCALES]: (Warriors know the term "tip the scales" refers to a level of personal power which enables them to cross a threshold of awareness through the shift or movement of the assemblage point; to add one's total physical mass to the energy body is referred to as "tipping the scales"; this transfer of awareness is dependent simply on intending and having enough energy.)
 SELECTED REFERENCES: Tales of Power - Page [6.5-6.7] (Again, you don't have enough personal...personal power to tip the scales.") Tales of Power - Page [77.4-77.6] ("That would have been the feat...almost didn't have enough to survive.) Tales of Power - Page [106.5-106.7] ("The basic difference between an ordinary...scales in favor of the warrior's way.") The Power of Silence - Page [233.7-233.8] (Don Juan contended that that simple...free movement of his assemblage point.) The Art of Dreaming - Page [189.8-190.5] ("What does it mean to tip...explained away as insanity or hallucination.")
 SEE ALSO: POWER-PERSONAL, AWARENESS-TRANSFERRING, AWARENESS-ENERGETIC-ELEMENT, INORGANIC-BEINGS-REALM-TRANSPORTED

SCARABS-[SCARABS]: (Warriors know that scarabs have the ability to merge themselves with the emanations at large and move with them.)
SELECTED REFERENCES: The Fire From Within - Page [74.5-74.7] ("The emanations inside the cocoon of...scarabs' emanations expanding to great size.)
SEE ALSO: *EAGLE-EMANATIONS-MERGING*

*SCHOLAR-[THE SCHOLAR]: (Warriors know the scholar is the first male personality; a noble, dependable, serene man, completely dedicated to accomplishing his task, whatever it may be.)
SELECTED REFERENCES: The Eagle's Gift - Page [174.8-175.3] (The three male warriors and the...who cannot stand on his own.) The Power of Silence - Page [165.7-165.9] ("Sorcerers, because they are *stalkers,* understand...or an expert in his field.)
SEE ALSO: *WARRIORS-MALE*

SCHOLAR-WORLD-ARRANGEMENT-[THE SCHOLAR'S ARRANGEMENT OF THE WORLD]: (Warriors know that the scholar arranges the world in a beautiful and enlightened manner from 8:00 A.M. to 5:00 P.M. and then he goes home in order to forget about his beautiful arrangement; the scholar's arrangement of the world is inadequate because words themselves are inadequate; the warrior knows that true knowledge is independent of language altogether.)
SELECTED REFERENCES: The Second Ring of Power - Page [150.9-151.1] (All my efforts had been no...order to forget his beautiful arrangement.)
SEE ALSO: *WORDS-FLAW, KNOWLEDGE-VS-LANGUAGE, REASON-LIFE-COURSE-*

SCOUT-BLUE-[THE BLUE SCOUT]-(TOP)

SCOUT-ENGAGING-DREAMING-[ENGAGING A SCOUT IN DREAMING]-(TOP)

SCOUTS-[FOREIGN ENERGY SCOUTS]: (Warriors know there are scouts from the realm of the second attention which enter into our dreams; they are reconnoiterers from the inorganic realm; we interpret them as items familiar or unfamiliar to us; scouts are foreign energies which invade our dreams; they normally appear as incongruous objects or blobs of light in our dreams.)
SELECTED REFERENCES: The Fire From Within - Page [101.8-101.9] (He said that the matching emanations give...with it they can even materialize themselves.) **The Art of Dreaming** - Page [29.3-29.5] ("Dreams are, if not a door, a...items familiar or unfamiliar to us.) **The Art of Dreaming** - Page [84.1-84.2] (From time to time, however, as...about shopping in a department store.) **The Art of Dreaming** - Page [84.9-85.5] (When I told don Juan about...dreamers catch the presence of scouts.") **The Art of Dreaming** - Page [85.8-87.1] ("The first scout you isolate will...And so are their scouts.") **The Art of Dreaming** - Page [176.8-179.9] (The other kind of energy I...journey by himself to their realm.")
SEE ALSO: *ENERGETIC-INTERFERENCES, ATTENTION-SECOND, SCOUTS-(ALL)*

SCOUTS-COLOR-[THE COLOR OF SCOUTS]: SEE: SCOUT-TYPES-[THE THREE TYPES OF SCOUTS]

SCOUTS-DREAMS-[THE PRESENCE OF SCOUTS IN VARIOUS TYPES OF DREAMS]: (Warriors know that scouts are much more prevalent in the dreams of ordinary dreamers than they are in the dreams of real dreamers; this happens because average people are subject to a much greater barrage from the unknown; this assault from the unknown is provoked by the strength of the barriers of the average man, barriers such as worries about

the self; the stronger the barrier, the greater the attack; in contrast, dreamers have fewer barriers and fewer scouts in their dreams.)
SELECTED REFERENCES: **The Art of Dreaming - Page [84.9-85.5]** (When I told don Juan about...dreamers catch the presence of scouts.")
SEE ALSO: *SCOUTS, DREAMING-ART, DREAMING-VS-DREAMS*

SCOUTS-ISOLATING-FOLLOWING-*[ISOLATING AND FOLLOWING SCOUTS IN DREAMING]*: *(Warriors know that to cultivate the ability to find, isolate and follow scouts in one's dreams is sorcery; these scouts come from other realms and act to guide sorcerers into areas of overwhelming mystery; sorcerers recognize scouts with their energy bodies; it is undesirable for dreamers to indulge in searching for scouts because one can easily become swayed by that search; in order to follow the scouts, dreamers fix their dreaming attention on the items of their dreams, and when they have the scout in focus, they shout their intent to follow it and off they go, pulled by the foreign energy; warriors also have the power to stop the process and not be pulled by the scouts if they so intend.)*
SELECTED REFERENCES: **The Art of Dreaming - Page [29.1-30.2]** (He heavily stressed that the dreaming...collapses, leaving only the foreign energy.") **The Art of Dreaming - Page [32.4-32.6]** ("I've mentioned to you before that...can get swayed by that search.) **The Art of Dreaming - Page [84.9-85.5]** (When I told don Juan about...dreamers catch the presence of scouts.") **The Art of Dreaming - Page [87.5-88.4]** (I felt so ill at ease...off I went into another world.) **The Art of Dreaming - Page [92.9-93.3]** (From that day on, in spite...beyond what I can normally imagine.) **The Art of Dreaming - Page [101.6-102.2]** ("What do you suggest I do...dreaming would follow the opposite course.) **The Art of Dreaming - Page [107.7-108.4]** ("Because the second gate of dreaming is...knowing why but with irrefutable authority.))
SEE ALSO: *ENERGETIC-INTERFERENCES, ATTENTION-SECOND, INTENT-VOICING*

SCOUTS-TALES-*[TALES OF THE SCOUTS]-(TOP)*

SCOUTS-TYPES-THREE-*[THE THREE TYPES OF SCOUTS]*: *(Warriors know there are three types of scouts; the first type is from the realm of the inorganic beings; the second and third types are from realms even more distant than the inorganic beings realm; the third type of scout is by far the most dangerous to the dreamer; these dangerous scouts hide behind the images of parents and close friends in our dreams.)*
SELECTED REFERENCES: **The Art of Dreaming - Page [176.8-179.9]** (The other kind of energy I...journey by himself to their realm.")
SEE ALSO: *SCOUTS*

SECOND-FACE-*[THE SECOND FACE OF THE SECOND ATTENTION]*: *SEE: ATTENTION-SECOND-FACES-[THE TWO FACES OF THE SECOND ATTENTION]*

SECOND-ENEMY-*[THE SECOND ENEMY OF THE WARRIOR]*: *SEE: CLARITY-[CLARITY], WARRIOR-ENEMIES-FOUR-NATURAL-[THE FOUR NATURAL ENEMIES OF THE WARRIOR]*

SECOND-POINT-*[THE SECOND POINT]*: *SEE: PITY-PLACE-[THE PLACE OF NO PITY]*

SECRETS-MAN-KNOWLEDGE-*[THE SECRETS OF A MAN OF KNOWLEDGE]*: *SEE: MAN-KNOWLEDGE-SECRETS-[THE SECRETS OF A MAN OF KNOWLEDGE]*

SECRETS-WARRIOR-[THE WARRIORS' SECRETS] SEE: WARRIOR-
SECRETS-[THE WARRIORS' SECRETS]

*SEEING-[SEEING]: (Warriors know that "seeing" is another term for
moving the assemblage point; "seeing" is a way of witnessing the world
with one's entire body; "seeing" is to lay bare the core of everything, to
witness the unknown and to glimpse into the unknowable; "seeing" is the
capacity of human beings to enlarge their perceptual field until they are
capable of assessing the essence of everything; "seeing" is contrary to
sorcery; "seeing" makes warriors realize the unimportance of everything;
"seeing" is perceiving energy as it flows; "seeing" is perceiving energy
directly, or "seeing" energy with the energy body; once warriors learn to
"see", they no longer need to live like warriors or be sorcerers; upon learning
to "see ", warriors become everything by becoming nothing; warrior-seers
can then get anything they desire, but they desire nothing; instead of playing
with their fellow men as if they were toys, warriors meet them in the midst
of their folly; warriors who "see" control their folly and no longer have any
active interest in their fellow men, because "seeing" has detached them from
everything they knew before; "seeing" is one of the eight points on the
sorcerers' diagram; "seeing" is a bodily knowledge; "seeing" was the crucial
element in both the destruction of the ancient seers' world and the in the
reconstruction of the new view.)

SELECTED REFERENCES: The Teachings of Don Juan - Page [69.2-69.3] ('The
devil's weed is for those who...who want to watch and see.') The Teachings of Don Juan - Page
[106.2] ("The second portion of the devil's...on at any place he chooses.") A Separate Reality -
Page [10.8-11.3] ("My predilection is to see," he said...to know; others do other things.") A
Separate Reality - Page [36.8-38.1] ("What's it like to see, don Juan...spot that they were not
people.") A Separate Reality - Page [81.5] (But when a man learns to...what he looks at
everything becomes unimportant.") A Separate Reality - Page [84.6-84.7] (On the other hand, I
choose to...spite of anything I may see.) A Separate Reality - Page [95.1] ("You fail to understand
that a sorcerer...see, he attempts to gain power.") A Separate Reality - Page [111.3-112.3] (Don
Juan was not at his house...the body and its strength in tact.") A Separate Reality - Page [138.3-
138.5] (Men were either victorious or defeated...having the memory of being humiliated.) A
Separate Reality - Page [148.8-148.9] ("Is will the same as seeing...will and also with his seeing.")
A Separate Reality - Page [149.5-149.8] (After a long pause he continued...your entire life like a
warrior.) A Separate Reality - Page [153.3-153.6] (My benefactor was a sorcerer of great...from
absolutely everything he knew before.") A Separate Reality - Page [159.4-160.2] (The next day I
insisted again on...and yet they are still there.") A Separate Reality - Page [168.1-168.3] ("I've
told you already," he said..."The unimportance of everything.") A Separate Reality - Page
[194.3-194.8] ("Maybe that's the way they understand...wrote is not crap at all.") A Separate
Reality - Page [252.3-252.8[("Genaro is determined to help you...and shook his head in
disbelief.) Journey to Ixtlan - Page [194.4-194.5] ("Not-doing is very simple but...through the
technique of not-doing.") Tales of Power - Page [96.2-96.9] ("We may say that every
one..."dreaming" were on the right side.) Tales of Power - Page [136.7-136.8] (I asked him to
explain what...anything within one's field of awareness.) Tales of Power - Page [153.3-153.7]
(Don Juan's comment was that my...it should be, a direct knowing.") The Eagle's Gift - Page
[37.2-37.6] (La Gorda was right. I...recall perceiving two separate scenes simultaneously.) The
Eagle's Gift - Page [307.5-307.6] (I am already given to the power...past the Eagle to be free.) The Fire
From Within - Page [x.8-xi.3] (Don Juan had already explained to...being a teacher and a guide.)
The Fire From Within - Page [4.7-5.6] (Don Juan said that after some...talking about, because
they're not seers.") The Fire From Within - Page [35.6-35.8] (Don Juan said that seeing
was...about awareness he was explaining to me.) The Fire From Within - Page [53.4-53.7]
(Patiently, he explained that everything I...awareness malings it with its limitations.) The Fire
From Within - Page [125.1-125.4] ("The mystery is outside us...human senses perceive in
inconceivable ways.") The Fire From Within - Page [233.5-223.6] (He pointed out that seeing
is...interpret then as having remembered them.) The Power of Silence - Page [xi.6-xi.9]
("Exactly. I'm trying to convince you that...depends on our own temperament.") The Power of

Silence - Page [xvi.3-xvi.5] (6. The assemblage point can be moved...This perception is known as *seeing*.) **The Power of Silence - Page [101.8-102.2]** (He had explained that normal perception...able to see the energy fields themselves.) **The Art of Dreaming - Page [2.9-3.2]** (Don Juan explained that the their...things, a capacity they call *seeing*.) **The Art of Dreaming - Page [7.2-7.5]** ("Notice that when I talk about...what the predator's eye normally sees.) **The Art of Dreaming - Page [15.4-15.7]** ("To understand all this certainly isn't..."You must *see* that for yourself!") **The Art of Dreaming - Page [31.8-32.1]** (The energy body deals with energy...sensation that can even be pain.") **The Art of Dreaming - Page [37.8-37.9]** (One, we would free our energy...the actual grandeur of the universe.) **The Art of Dreaming - Page [50.2-50.4]** (I knew that it was a dream...the energy essences of something unbelievable.) **The Art of Dreaming - Page [163.8-164.1]** ("What comes next for you is...are going to do it deliberately.)
　　　　SEE ALSO: *KNOWLEDGE-SILENT, LOOKING-VS-SEEING, ASSEMBLAGE-POINT-MOVING, BODY-PHYSICAL, WARRIOR-CONTROLLED-FOLLY, EVERYTHING-NOTHING, WARRIOR-DETACHMENT, SORCERERS-DIAGRAM, BODY-PHYSICAL-WITNESSING, KNOWLEDGE-DIRECT, FLOW-OF-THINGS-SEEING, SEEING-(ALL)*

SEEING-ALIGNMENT-[SEEING IS ALIGNMENT]: *(Warriors know that "seeing" is alignment, the alignment of the normally dormant portions of the Eagle's emanations.)*
　　　　SELECTED REFERENCES: **The Fire From Within - Page [54.5-54.9]** ("What is *seeing*, then," I asked...seer is engaged in isn't *seeing*.")
　　　　SEE ALSO: *SEEING, ALIGNMENT, EAGLE-EMANATIONS-DORMANT*

SEEING-ALL-THROUGH-[SEEING ALL THE WAY THROUGH]: *(Warriors know that seeing all the way through is another term for "seeing".)*
　　　　SELECTED REFERENCES: **The Second Ring of Power - Page [270.9-271.8]** ("Tonight was a special night for you...at least be assured of that.)
　　　　SEE ALSO: *SEEING*

SEEING-CHILDREN-[CHILDREN WHO SEE]: *(Warriors know that the assemblage points of young children are not fixed, so they have a great natural capacity to focus on emanations that will later be completely disregarded; as a result many children "see", but most of them are considered oddballs and every effort is made by the people around them to solidify their assemblage points.)*
　　　　SELECTED REFERENCES: **The Fire From Within - Page [9.2-9.8]** ("The ancient seers were very fortunate...centuries of that kind of concentration.") **The Fire From Within - Page [132.5-132.9]** (He said that seers *see* that...the position of their assemblage points.") **The Fire From Within - Page [137.9-138.2]** ("Is the assemblage point of other organisms...same happens to every other organism.) **The Art of Dreaming - Page [75.8-76.6]** (Don Juan changed the subject and...are fixed on the same spot.)
　　　　SEE ALSO: *SEEING, INFANTS-CHILDREN-INTERNAL-DIALOGUE*

SEEING-CONTROLLED-USE-[THE CONTROLLED USE OF SEEING]: SEE: UNKNOWN-MAPPING [MAPPING THE UNKNOWN]

SEEING-CROW-AS-[SEEING AS A CROW SEES]-(TOP): SEE: CROW-SEEING-AS-[SEEING AS A CROW SEES]-(TOP)

SEEING-DARKNESS-DAY-[SEEING AND THE DARKNESS OF THE DAY]: *(Warriors know that the best time to "see" is under the cover of darkness; warriors learn to use the darkness because the collective activity of the first attention is lessened while the majority of people around the warrior are asleep.)*
　　　　SELECTED REFERENCES: **A Separate Reality - Page [24.8-25.4]** (I told don Juan how much I enjoyed...late to go into it then.)
　　　　SEE ALSO: *SEEING, DARKNESS-DAY*

SEEING-DARKNESS-IN-[SEEING IN THE DARKNESS]-(TOP)

SEEING-DEATH-[SEEING DEATH]: (Warriors know that it is possible to "see" death.)
> SELECTED REFERENCES: Tales of Power - Page [113.8-113.9] ("The world upheld by *will* makes it...tautness and vanishing one by one.)
> SEE ALSO: SEEING, DEATH

SEEING-DESTRUCTION-RECONSTRUCTION-[SEEING WAS THE CRUCIAL ELEMENT IN THE DESTRUCTION OF THE WORLD OF THE SORCERERS OF ANTIQUITY AS WELL AS IN THE RECONSTRUCTION OF THE NEW VIEW]: (Warriors know that "seeing" was the key element in both the downfall of the old cycle and the origin of the new cycle; the aberrant fixation on "seeing" led the sorcerers of antiquity to their doom; correcting those mistakes and applying their "seeing" to a true understanding of the world, led the new seers to the discovery of the truths about awareness, which in turn made the new cycle possible.)
> SELECTED REFERENCES: The Fire From Within - Page [35.6-35.8] (Don Juan said that *seeing* was...about awareness he was explaining to me.)
> SEE ALSO: SEEING

SEEING-DREAMING-[SEEING AND DREAMING]: (Warriors know they should never attempt "seeing" unless they are aided by dreaming.)
> SELECTED REFERENCES: The Fire From Within - Page [219.1-219.2] (He told me then that I was...unless they are aided by *dreaming*.)
> SEE ALSO: SEEING, DREAMING-ART

*SEEING-DREAMING-IN-[SEEING IN DREAMING]: (Warriors know that sorcerers perceive energy directly; they "see" energy with the energy body; for some reason pertinent to the mind, "seeing" energy in dreaming is one of the most upsetting things one can think of; by pointing at things in their dreams, dreamers can indicate their intent to "see" the energetic essence of the things around them and whether or not they are energy-generating)
> SELECTED REFERENCES: The Art of Dreaming - Page [163.8-167.9] ("What comes next for you is...later, you'll hit the right note.") The Art of Dreaming - Page [168.9-169.3] (These images were so vivid that...drill and crossed into another world.) The Art of Dreaming - Page [170.1-170.8] (Don Juan said that in special dreams...items that nearly ended your life.") The Art of Dreaming - Page [175.4-175.7] (This was the end of our...out loud my intent to *see*.) The Art of Dreaming - Page [198.6-198.9] (Don Juan brought my dreaming practices...inanimate matter or of living beings.) The Art of Dreaming - Page [233.6-234.9] (Contrary to what had happened to...to do is just watch everything.") The Art of Dreaming - Page [252.4-252.5] (I opened the curtains of the window...had been erased from my memory.) The Art of Dreaming - Page [255.6-255.7] (Don Juan asked me to tell them...in her dream, my intent to *see*.)
> SEE ALSO: SEEING, ENERGY-BODY-PERCEPTION, SEEING-DREAMING-IN, SEEING-AND-DREAMING

SEEING-DRUNKARD-LOOK-[SEEING AND THE LOOK OF A DRUNKARD]: (Warriors know that sorcerers in the act of "seeing" sometimes appear to be drunk or sleepy.)
> SELECTED REFERENCES: A Separate Reality - Page [13.1-13.3] (Sacateca was standing in front of me...alert and aware of my presence.)
> SEE ALSO: SEEING, DRUNK-APPEARING

SEEING-EAGLE-EMANATIONS-[SEEING THE EAGLE'S EMANATIONS]-(TOP)

SEEING-EMPTINESS-[SEEING AND EMPTINESS]: (Warriors know that emptiness can prevent them from "seeing"; the forces of the world are like a push or a pull; in order for warriors to be pushed or pulled by those forces

they must be intact like a sail; if they are incomplete and have a hole in their middle, the force goes through them and never acts upon them.)
SELECTED REFERENCES: **The Second Ring of Power - Page [156.9-157.1]** ("The Nagual said that everything in...it and never acts upon us.)
SEE ALSO: *SEEING, PULL-PUSH, WARRIOR-COMPLETENESS, WARRIOR-EMPTINESS*

SEEING-ENERGY-*[SEEING AND ENERGY]: (Warriors know that the only thing necessary to break the barrier of perception and "see", is to conserve enough energy to do so; the hardest part about this process is convincing ourselves that it can be accomplished at all.)*
SELECTED REFERENCES: **The Art of Dreaming - Page [9.7-9.9]** ("There is only one thing for...yourself that it can be done.)
SEE ALSO: *SEEING, ENERGY, WARRIOR-IMPECCABILITY, PERCEPTION-BARRIER-BREAKING*

SEEING-EVERYONE-*[EVERYONE CAN SEE]: (Warriors know that everyone can "see", and yet most people choose not to remember what they "see"; all of us can "see", some of us more than others.)*
SELECTED REFERENCES: **The Second Ring of Power - Page [273.4-273.8]** (Is it possible, I thought to...can *see*, some more than others.") **The Second Ring of Power - Page [275.6-275.8]** (Perhaps all of us are continually perceiving...two distinct memories of one event.)
SEE ALSO: *SEEING, RECOLLECTION-SORCERER*

SEEING-FEELING-*[THE FEELING OF SEEING]: (Warriors know that the feeling of "seeing" is another term for the feeling of stopping the world.)*
SELECTED REFERENCES: **The Second Ring of Power - Page [238.2-238.6]** ("How did you see all that...particular way was incomprehensible to them.)
SEE ALSO: *STOPPING-WORLD-FEELING, SEEING*

SEEING-FORCE-LIFE-*[SEEING THE FORCE OF LIFE]-(TOP)*

SEEING-IMPORTANT-*[MORE IMPORTANT THAN SEEING ITSELF IS WHAT SEERS DO WITH WHAT THEY SEE]: (Warriors know that it is much more important for them to focus on what they do with their "seeing" than it is to focus on their ability to "see".)*
SELECTED REFERENCES: **The Fire From Within - Page [41.6-42.8]** ("This is simply the case of something...for it, a more accurate one.")
SEE ALSO: *SEEING, WARRIOR-SOBRIETY*

SEEING-INCOMPREHENSIBILITY-*[THE INCOMPREHENSIBILITY OF SEEING]: (Warriors are always baffled by what they "see" because "seeing" is beyond their capacity to understand; the man of knowledge learns to have no thoughts so he will "see".)*
SELECTED REFERENCES: **A Separate Reality - Page [91.7-92.2]** ("You're thinking again," he said...his reasons are incomprehensible to me.")
SEE ALSO: *THINKING, SEEING, KNOWLEDGE-VS-LANGUAGE, KNOWLEDGE-SILENT, UNDERSTANDING*

SEEING-ISOLATING-THINGS-FOR-*[ISOLATING THINGS FOR SEEING]: (Warriors know that it is an error to isolate anything for "seeing".)*
SELECTED REFERENCES: **The Fire From Within - Page [228.1-228.3]** ("How were they wrong, don Juan...freedom of the seers of today.)
SEE ALSO: *SEEING, SEER-OLD*

SEEING-KNOWING-*[SEEING AND KNOWING]: (Warriors on the path of knowledge make use of previously inaccessible energy fields and eventually* *begin to "see", thereby perceiving things beyond the ordinary world of men; then warriors begin to know silently without the use of words.)*

SELECTED REFERENCES: **The Power of Silence - Page [xi.7-xi.9]** ("Once we have reached it, it...silent knowledge, depends on our own temperament.")
SEE ALSO: *SEEING, KNOWLEDGE-SILENT, ENERGY*

SEEING-LOOKING-[LOOKING VS SEEING]: SEE: LOOK-SEE-[LOOKING VS SEEING]

SEEING-LOOKING-EARTH-[SEEING AND LOOKING AND THE BOOST FROM THE EARTH: SEE: ENERGY-BODY-DREAMING-[THE THREE WAYS THE ENERGY BODY DEALS WITH ENERGY IN DREAMING]

SEEING-LOOKING-SIMULTANEOUSLY-[LOOKING AND SEEING AT THE SAME TIME]: SEE: LOOKING-SEEING-SIMULTANEOUSLY-[LOOKING AND SEEING AT THE SAME TIME]

SEEING-MAN-[SEEING A MAN]: *(Warriors know that is possible to "see" a man as a luminous being resembling a luminous ball or egg.)*

SELECTED REFERENCES: **A Separate Reality - Page [23.1-23.6]** (Someday perhaps you'll be able...changed in that luminous egg? What?") **A Separate Reality - Page [40.3-40.6]** (How does an ally look to you...is never fooled, neither is a crow.") **A Separate Reality - Page [106.1-106.4]** (Don Juan then explained don Genaro's...to talk about something thoroughly unrelated.) **Tales of Power - Page [32.5-32.6]** (He said that the mushroomlike formation...egglike cluster of luminous fibers.) **Tales of Power - Page [136.4-137.2]** ("There is no need to treat...he did not remember it either.) **The Eagle's Gift - Page [41.1-41.5]** (Then all at once the people...moved deliberately and sat up straight.) **The Fire From Within - Page [122.7]** ("Man is not the unknowable...as if one were using the eyes alone.")
SEE ALSO: *LUMINOUS-COCOON, LUMINOUS-TENTACLE-, FRONT-PLATE, MAN-UNKNOWABLE-NOT, LUMINOUS-BEINGS, SEEING*

SEEING-PAST-[SEEING THE PAST]: *(Warriors can literally "see" the past; they can experience it as a peculiar feeling of knowing without a shadow of a doubt)*

SELECTED REFERENCES: **The Fire From Within - Page [3.8-4.2]** ("Isn't all this a conjecture on...we are so closely bound together.")
SEE ALSO: *SEEING*

SEEING-PEOPLE-[SEEING PEOPLE]-(TOP)

SEEING-PRELIMINARIES-[THE PRELIMINARIES OF SEEING]-(TOP)

SEEING-VS-PURSUIT-POWER-[THE PURSUIT OF POWER VS THE PURSUIT OF SEEING]: *(Warriors know the distinction between the pursuit of power and the pursuit of "seeing".)*

SELECTED REFERENCES: **The Teachings of Don Juan - Page [175.5]** (As I have already told you...for those who crave to see.)
SEE ALSO: *SEEING-VS-SORCERY, POWER-PURSUIT, SEEING, POWER*

SEEING-VS-REASON-[SEEING VS REASON]: *(Warriors know that "seeing" is antithetical to reason; "seeing" represents a direct way of knowing which is beyond language or rational understanding; "seeing" can only be experienced to be understood.)*

SELECTED REFERENCES: **The Art of Dreaming - Page [15.4--15.7]** ("To understand all this certainly isn't..."You must *see* that for yourself!")
SEE ALSO: *SEEING, REASON, KNOWLEDGE-VS-LANGUAGE*

SEEING-ROLLING-FORCE-[SEEING THE ROLLING FORCE]-(TOP): SEE: SEEING-TUMBLER-[SEEING THE TUMBLER]-(TOP)

SEEING-SORCERER-ANTIQUITY-VS-MODERN-[THE SEEING OF THE SORCERERS OF ANTIQUITY VS THE SEEING OF THE MODERN DAY SORCERERS]: (Warriors know that modern day sorcerers perceive energy directly as a matter of personal attainment, they maneuver the assemblage point through self-discipline; for the sorcerers of antiquity, the displacement of the assemblage point was a result of their subjugation to others who were their teachers; those teachers accomplished these displacements through dark operations and gave them to their disciples as gifts of power.)
SELECTED REFERENCES: The Art of Dreaming - Page [205.8-205.9] ("As you already know, for modern...their disciples as gifts of power.)
SEE ALSO: SEEING, WARRIOR-WAY, WARRIORSHIP-VS-SORCERY, POWER-GIFTS

SEEING-VS-SORCERY-[SEEING VS SORCERY]: (Warriors know that "seeing" is a process independent of the techniques of sorcery; "seeing" is contrary to sorcery; "seeing" has nothing to do with the manipulatory techniques of sorcery; "seeing" has no effect on men.)
SELECTED REFERENCES: A Separate Reality - Page [167.4-168.3] (He spoke about "seeing" as a..."The unimportance of everything.") A Separate Reality - Page [199.1-199.3] ("To be a sorcerer is a terrible...is how to use his will.")
SEE ALSO: SEEING, SORCERY, KNOWLEDGE-PATH-STEPS-FOUR

SEEING-SPIRIT-[SEEING THE SPIRIT]-(TOP): SEE: SPIRIT-SEEING-[SEEING THE SPIRIT]-(TOP)

SEEING-STARS-[SEEING STARS]: (Warriors know that the phenomenon of seeing stars is a result of a very small crack in the luminous cocoon; these blotches of color and contorted shapes remain in the warriors' vision even when the eyes are closed.)
SELECTED REFERENCES: The Fire From Within - Page [226.3-226.4] (He went on to explain that if...even if the eyes are closed.)
SEE ALSO: GAP, ASSEMBLAGE-POINT-MOVEMENT-INVOLUNTARY, WARRIOR-SOLIDITY, SPIRIT-SEEING-PRELUDE

SEEING-STOPPING-WORLD-[SEEING VS STOPPING THE WORLD]: SEE: STOPPING-WORLD-[STOPPING THE WORLD]

SEEING-TALKING-[TALKING ABOUT SEEING]: (Warriors know that there is no adequate way to talk about "seeing" because the seer "sees" without the use of his eyes; everything about "seeing" is so unique that there is no basis for comparison with the world of sights which we know; warriors nevertheless, strive to talk about "seeing" in ever new ways.)
SELECTED REFERENCES: A Separate Reality - Page [105.2] ("Seeing is very difficult," he said...matter of talk," he said imperatively.) Tales of Power - Page [26.5-26.7] ("Today you stopped your talk at...little moth come to you again.") The Fire From Within - Page [49.3-49.5] (I asked him why he had changed...said, but in a different way.") The Art of Dreaming - Page [7.2-7.5] ("Notice that when I talk about...what the predator's eye normally sees.)
SEE ALSO: SEEING, TALKING, KNOWLEDGE-VS-LANGUAGE, SEEING-VS-THINKING, REASON, WARRIOR-DIALOGUE

SEEING-TASK-[THE TASK OF SEEING]-(TOP)

SEEING-TEAMS-[SEEING IN TEAMS]: (Warriors know that "seeing" in teams is a method developed by the new seers to overcome the problems associated with gazing directly at the Eagle's emanations; dreaming together.)

SELECTED REFERENCES: **The Fire From Within** - Page **[181.5-182.3]** (Don Juan said that there is...the left side, while *dreaming together.*)
SEE ALSO: *DREAMING-TOGETHER, SEEING, DREAMING-BODY, EAGLE-EMANATIONS, EAGLE-EMANATIONS-SEEING*

SEEING-VS-THINKING-[SEEING VS THINKING]: (Warriors know that "seeing" is not something that they can think about; "seeing" is something that can only be experienced; the process of "seeing" exists independent of the process of thinking, just as knowledge exists independent of language.)
SELECTED REFERENCES: **A Separate Reality** - Page **[86.1-86.4]** ("You think about your acts," he...it is something you cannot think about.")
SEE ALSO: *THINKING, SEEING, KNOWLEDGE-VS-LANGUAGE, SEEING-TALKING, REASON*

SEEING-TOGETHER-[SEEING TOGETHER]-(TOP)

SEEING-TUMBLER-[SEEING THE TUMBLER]-(TOP)

SEEING-UNDERSTANDING-[SEEING IS NOT UNDERSTANDING]:
(Warriors know that being able to "see" something does not guarantee that they will understand it; understanding is a very long process that must be carried out at a snail's pace; dislodging the assemblage point in and of itself is not enough to bring about understanding.)
SELECTED REFERENCES: **The Fire From Within** - Page **[166.1-267.2]** (After recounting to don Juan what...by little at a snail's pace.)
SEE ALSO: *SEEING, UNDERSTANDING*

SEEING-UNMISTAKABILITY-[THE UNMISTAKABILITY OF SEEING]:
(Warriors know that there is no way they can be mistaken about their "seeing"; they can arrive at false conclusions about it if they are naive and uncultivated; when it comes to simply describing what they have "seen", warriors cannot err, because "seeing" is direct knowledge; it is only when they take their "seeing" and try to explain it that they may make a mistake.)
SELECTED REFERENCES: **The Art of Dreaming** - Page **[8.3-8.7]** ("Is there a chance that those...is far too great to resist.)
SEE ALSO: *SEEING, OMENS-MISINTERPRETING, MIND-CULTIVATING*

SEEING-VOICE-[THE VOICE OF SEEING]: (Warriors know that the voice of "seeing" is the voice of the nagual; a mysterious and inexplicable thing; a voice that tells the seer in his ear what's what; the glow of awareness playing on the Eagle's emanations as a harpist plays on a harp; a gauge warriors use to determine whether or not they are really "seeing"; if the voice of "seeing" is not present, then the warrior is not truly "seeing"; the voice of an inorganic being; the voice of the dreaming emissary.)
SELECTED REFERENCES: **The Teachings of Don Juan** - Page **[155.2-155.7]** (A flood of thoughts rushed into...about my feeling of being doomed.) **The Teachings of Don Juan** - Page **[156.1-157.5]** (Then I heard a "voice" in...touch it, I could move around.) **Tales of Power** - Page **[64.7-64.9]** (He was right. I had to...I had woken up a second time.) **Tales of Power** - Page **[131.9]** ("On certain occasions, however, or under...the depths, the voice of the *nagual.*) **The Second Ring of Power** - Page **[39.3-40 3]** ("One day, while we were in the...I had learned to distinguish them.") **The Eagle's Gift** - Page **[140.3]** (Little by little I started to...felt it was a woman's voice.) **The Fire From Within** - Page **[54.8-55.5]** ("When seers see, something explains everything...everything would become clear to me.) **The Fire From Within** - Page **[56.8-56.9]** (It means that the voice of...some of those which are outside.") **The Fire From Within** - Page **[89.1-89.4]** (Slowly I got my fear under control...in my ear said in Spanish.) **The Fire From Within** - Page **[91.9-92.1]** ("But I heard a voice in my ear...of the time they are deadly.") **The Fire From Within** - Page **[209.8-209.9]** (It was then that I *saw*...always let Genaro be the heavy.) **The Fire From Within** - Page **[215.5]** (I felt a great pressure all over...together with don Juan and Genaro.) **The Fire From Within** - Page **[220.5-220.9]** (Don Juan whispered in my ear...that it was the

assemblage point.) **The Fire From Within - Page [264.6-265.2]** (Suddenly, I heard don Juan's voice...Also, the voice was right.) **The Fire From Within - Page [292.6]** (I heard then the voice of...bands of emanations: a black world.) **The Power of Silence - Page [5.8-5.9]** ("The spirit tried, uselessly, to reveal...his own thoughts he was thinking.) **The Art of Dreaming - Page [59.2]** ("I didn't want to discuss this...the voice of an inorganic being.")
    SEE ALSO: *SEEING, AWARENESS-GLOW, INORGANIC-BEINGS, DREAMING-EMISSARY, DREAMING-EMISSARY-VOICE-(TOP), DREAMING-VOICE-(TOP)*

SEEING-VS-WARRIORSHIP-[SEEING VS WARRIORSHIP]: *(Warriors know that human beings who "see" don't have to live like warriors, or like anything else for that matter; if someone "sees", they can perceive the world directly and direct their lives accordingly.)*
    SELECTED REFERENCES: **A Separate Reality - Page [149.6-149.8]** (I understand the world and live...your entire life like a warrior.)
    SEE ALSO: *SEEING, WARRIORSHIP, WARRIOR-SORCERER-SEER*

SEEING-VS-WRITING-[SEEING VS WRITING]: *(Warriors know the futility of writing or talking about "seeing"; "seeing" exists beyond the realm of reason.)*
    SELECTED REFERENCES: **A Separate Reality - Page [105.5-105.6]** (He said that don Genaro, being a...unnecessary as standing on one's head.)
    SEE ALSO: *SEEING, SEEING-TALKING, SEEING-VS-THINKING, REASON*

SEEKING-OTHER-SIDE-COIN-WARRIOR-[THE WARRIOR SEEKS THE OTHER SIDE OF THE COIN]: SEE: WARRIOR-SEEKS-OTHER-SIDE-COIN-[THE WARRIOR SEEKS THE OTHER SIDE OF THE COIN]

SEER-[SEER]: *(Warriors know that seers are those who "see"; there are two categories of seers, those who are willing to exercise self-restraint and channel their activities towards pragmatic goals and those who are unwilling to do so; seers come in all shapes and sizes; seers are human beings full of foibles [or rather human beings full of foibles are capable of becoming seers].)*
    SELECTED REFERENCES: **A Separate Reality - Page [194.3-194.8]** ("Maybe that's the way they understand...wrote is no crap at all.") **The Fire From Within - Page [x.6-x.8]** (It was in his teachings for...a seer, but also a nagual.) **The Fire From Within - Page [14.4-14.6]** (He said that seers, old and new...to resolve the problem of self-importance.) **The Fire From Within - Page [23.6-23.9]** (Don Juan said that his benefactor...fourth step and have become seers.) **The Fire From Within - Page [41.6-42.2]** ("This is simply the case of...at the moment of our death.") **The Fire From Within - Page [251.2-251.7]** ("Right at this juncture is where...answers that were equally personal, humanized.)
    SEE ALSO: *SEEING, SEER-(ALL)*

SEER-ACCOMPLISHMENT-SUPREME-[THE SEERS' SUPREME ACCOMPLISHMENT]: SEE: WARRIOR-ACCOMPLISHMENT-SUPREME-[THE WARRIORS' SUPREME ACCOMPLISHMENT]

SEER-CONQUEST-[THE SEERS OF THE SPANISH CONQUEST]:
(Warriors know that the seers of the conquest were the progenitors of the new seers, the seers of the new cycle; the seers of the conquest were the unquestionable masters of stalking and were tested to the limit by their merciless Spanish persecutors; the seers of the conquest developed the strategy of the petty tyrant and the attributes of warriorship.)
    SELECTED REFERENCES: **The Fire From Within - Page [16.4]** (He said that the most effective strategy...Conquest, the unquestionable masters of *stalking*.) **The Fire From Within - Page [19.3]** (He explained that one of the...he called the three-phase progression.) **The Fire From Within - Page [19.8-20.3]** ("The difference is in something you...a petty tyrant with unlimited prerogatives.)

SEE ALSO: *SEER-NEW, CYCLE-NEW, STALKING-ART, PETTY-TYRANT, WARRIOR-ATTRIBUTES, WARRIOR-DURESS-EXTREME-BENEFITS*

SEER-FEMALE-[FEMALE SEERS]: *(Warriors know that female seers have a greater facility for bouncing in and out of the position of the shift below.)*
SELECTED REFERENCES: The Fire From Within - Page [137.3-137.8] ("Female seers have downshifts more often...woman seer, run for the hills!")
SEE ALSO: *SHIFT-BELOW*

SEER-MISERABLE-[MISERABLE SEERS]: *(Warriors know that seers come in all shapes and sizes and that there are scores of imbeciles who learn to "see"; the characteristic of these miserable seers is that they forget the wonder of the world, and become obsessed with what they believe to be their own genius.)*
SELECTED REFERENCES: The Fire From Within - Page [41.5-42.8] (I asked him if the source...for it, a more accurate one.")
SEE ALSO: *SEER, WARRIOR-SOBRIETY, WARRIORSHIP-VS-SORCERY*

*SEER-NEW-[THE NEW SEERS]: *(Warriors know that the new seers are the seers of the new cycle; "los nuevos videntes"; modern day sorcerers; the new seers are terribly practical men, they aren't involved in concocting rational theories; the new seers have corrected the mistakes of the old seers by applying what they've learned through "seeing".)*
SELECTED REFERENCES: The Fire From Within - Page [xiii.5-xiii.7] (Although he felt that he was...as if they had never existed.) The Fire From Within - Page [3.1-3.3] ("Do you know those practices yourself...The old seers were the sorcerers.) The Fire From Within - Page [5.7-8.1] ("Other Indians," he said. "When the...from the six who preceded them.) The Fire From Within - Page [92-9.4] ("The ancient seers were very fortunate...do is lost in Toltec time.") The Fire From Within - Page [10.3-10.7] ("The best effort of the new seers...new seers meant them to have.) The Fire From Within - Page [14.4-14.6] (He said that seers, old and new...to resolve the problem of self-importance.) The Fire From Within - Page [34.3-35.8] (Don Juan explained that the new...awareness he was explaining to me.) The Fire From Within - Page [45.4-45.8] ("The new seers seem to have...them to construct their perceivable world.) The Fire From Within - Page [90.7-90.8] ("I am a seer of the new cycle...I'm telling you what they believed.") The Fire From Within - Page [168.8-169.5] (Don Juan stopped talking and stared...quite deep into the left side.) The Fire From Within - Page [228.1-228.6] ("How were they wrong, don Juan...moment in their lives, was intolerable.) The Fire From Within - Page [251.2-251.7] ("Right at this juncture is where...answers that were equally personal, humanized.) The Art of Dreaming - Page [79.5-81.7] ("I've been saying this to you...what it is: a mere candle.")
SEE ALSO: *SEER, SEER-OLD, TOLTEC-HISTORY, CYCLE-NEW, SORCERER-MODERN, WARRIORSHIP-VS-SORCERY*

SEER-NEW-ACCOMPLISHMENTS-TWO-[THE TWO GREATEST ACCOMPLISHMENTS OF THE NEW SEERS]: *(Warriors know that the two greatest accomplishments of the new seers are the art of stalking and the mastery of intent.)*
SELECTED REFERENCES: The Fire From Within - Page [169.4] ("Stalking is one of the two greatest accomplishments of the new seers," he said.) The Fire From Within - Page [170.2-170.3] (Don Juan said next that the...arrival of the modern-day seers.)
SEE ALSO: *STALKING-ART, DREAMING-ART, INTENT-MASTERY*

SEER-OLD-[THE OLD SEERS]: *(Warriors know that the old seers are the ancient seers of the old cycle, the sorcerers of antiquity; most of the fundamental knowledge of the new seers was figured out by the old seers; the knowledge of the old seers led them to total destruction, so the new seers had to reevaluate the procedures of their immense tradition and sort out the errors the old seers had made; the old seers were masters of conjecture, they made several critical assumptions which led them to a most precarious position with regard to the unknown and the unknowable; the old seers became aberrant and morbidly obsessed; their bid is to dominate, to master everybody and everything.)*

SELECTED REFERENCES: The Fire From Within - Page [2.7-3.3] ("We are going to be talking...The old seers were the sorcerers.) **The Fire From Within** - Page [4.2-5.7] (Don Juan explained then that his...secure their place in a new cycle.") **The Fire From Within** - Page [9.2-9.4] ("The ancient seers were very fortunate...do is lost in Toltec time.") **The Fire From Within** - Page [14.4-14.6] (He said that seers, old and new...to resolve the problem of self-importance.) **The Fire From Within** - Page [19.5-19.6] ("A seer who can hold his...that assumption. We know better now.) **The Fire From Within** - Page [34.3-35.6] (Don Juan explained that the new...done stems from understanding that distinction.") **The Fire From Within** - Page [80.3-80.6] ("The new seers were simply terrified...more horrifying than it really is.") **The Fire From Within** - Page [103.2-103.7] (He said that it was the...dominate, to master everybody and everything.") **The Fire From Within** - Page [248.9-251.4] (He immediately started his explanation...deep shift along the right edge.")

SEE ALSO: *TOLTECS, SORCERER-ANTIQUITY, SEER, SEER-NEW, TOLTEC-HISTORY, CYCLE-NEW, ABERRATION-MORBIDITY, OBSESSION*

SEER-OLD-INVULNERABILITY-[THE INVULNERABILITY AND IMMORTALITY OF THE OLD SEERS]: *(Warriors know that the old seers were terribly mistaken in allowing themselves to believe that they had become invulnerable and immortal.)*

SELECTED REFERENCES: The Fire From Within - Page [229.7-229.9] ("Why did the old seers focus...they were neither invulnerable nor immortal.)

SEE ALSO: *SEER-OLD, TOLTECS, DEATH-DEFIERS*

SEER-OLD-MASTERY-[THE MASTERY OF THE OLD SEERS]: *(Warriors know that the mastery of the old seers was the art of handling awareness; they learned to move the glow of awareness from its original setting to new positions inward across the width of the luminous cocoon.)*

SELECTED REFERENCES: The Fire From Within - Page [50.6-51.1] ("I've mentioned to you that the...the cocoon inward across its width.)

SEE ALSO: *SEER-OLD-(ALL), TOLTECS, AWARENESS-MASTERY, WARRIOR-MASTERIES-THREE*

SEER-OLD-MOOD-[THE MOOD OF THE OLD SEERS]: *(Warriors know that sorcery is tainted by the mysterious mood of the old seers, a mood of darkness and shadows.)*

SELECTED REFERENCES: The Fire From Within - Page [272.4-272.6] ("The *dreaming body* is known by...other always comes shrouded in wind.")

SEE ALSO: *SEER-OLD, TOLTECS, DREAMING-MOOD-NEFARIOUS*

SEER-QUEST-[THE SEERS' QUEST]: *(Warriors know that the quest of sorcerer-seers is to proceed further on the path of knowledge once they have learned to make the assemblage point move; anyone who succeeds in moving the assemblage point to a new position is a sorcerer; the quest of sorcerer-seers is to go beyond that stand and to do that they need morality and beauty.)*

SELECTED REFERENCES: The Fire From Within - Page [195.3-195.4] ("It goes without saying that the...it is the seers' quest proper.") **The Fire From Within** - Page [228.1-228.4] ("It's an error to isolate anything...freedom of the seers of today.) **The Power of Silence** - Page [82.5-82.6] ("Anyone who succeeds in moving his...that, they need morality and beauty.")

SEE ALSO: *WARRIOR-QUEST-COMPLETION, ASSEMBLAGE-POINT-MOVING, MORALITY, BEAUTY*

SEER-RESPONSIBILITY-MAN-[SEERS' RESPONSIBILITY TO THEIR FELLOW MEN]: *(Warrior-seers know that their aim is to be free and to be unbiased witnesses, incapable of passing judgment; this detachment*

prevents them from assuming responsibility for anyone but themselves; humble warriors would never superimpose their own first attention agendas onto the agenda of power itself; warriors know that if a more adjusted cycle is to come, they cannot assume responsibility for it; warriors know that such an adjusted cycle must come of itself.)

SELECTED REFERENCES: The Fire From Within - Page [61.2-61.4] (I asked him if there was anything...to come, must come of itself.")

SEE ALSO: WARRIOR-WITNESS-UNBIASED, WARRIOR-DETACHMENT, RESPONSIBILITY-ASSUMING, WARRIOR-HUMBLENESS, WARRIOR-INTERVENTION, POWER-PROMISE

SEER-TYPES-SELF-IMPORTANCE-[THE TWO TYPES OF SEERS BASED ON THE PROBLEMS OF SELF-IMPORTANCE]: (Warriors know that seers, both old and new are divided into two categories; the first is comprised of those seers who are willing to exercise self-restraint and channel their activities toward pragmatic goals; the other category consists of those who don't care about self-restraint or pragmatic goals; the first category of seers are those who have succeeded in resolving the problems of self-importance while the members of the second category are those who have failed to resolve those same self-importance issues.)

SELECTED REFERENCES: The Fire From Within - Page [14.4-14.8] (He said that seers, old and...to those who have accomplished it.")

SEE ALSO: SEER, SELF-IMPORTANCE, SELF-IMPORTANCE-NICETIES, SELF-IMPORTANCE-LOSING

SEER-VS-WARRIOR-[WARRIOR VS SEER]: SEE: WARRIOR-VS-SEER-[WARRIOR VS SEER]

SEER-WITNESS-UNBIASED-[SEERS AIM TO BE AN UNBIASED WITNESS]: (Warrior-seers aim to be unbiased witnesses, incapable of passing judgment.)

SELECTED REFERENCES: The Fire From Within - Page [61.2-61.4] (I asked him if there was anything...to come, must come of itself.")

SEE ALSO: WARRIOR-WITNESS-UNBIASED, SEER, WARRIOR-JUDGMENT

SEIZURE-WARRIOR-[THE WARRIORS' SEIZURE]: SEE: WARRIOR-SEIZURE-[THE WARRIORS' SEIZURE]

SELF-[THE SELF]: (Warriors know that ancient man knew, in the most direct fashion, what to do and how to do it; but because he performed so well, he began to develop a feeling of "selfness" which gave him the feeling that he could predict and plan the actions he was used to performing, and thus the idea of an individual self appeared; this individual sense of self began to dictate the nature and scope of man's actions; the warrior battles to detach himself from the individual self that has deprived him of his power; the self is the sense of individual existence; the idea of the personal self is of no value to the warrior whatsoever.)

SELECTED REFERENCES: Tales of Power - Page [268.8-269.7] (I again had the sensation of being...disintegrate and be nothing once more.) The Fire From Within - Page [213.7] ("The speed of that boost will...individual existence don't go together.) The Power of Silence - Page [149.5-149.8] (Then he talked about ancient man...and cynical acts of self-destruction.) The Power of Silence - Page [150.2-150.3] ("That's right," he admitted. "But war...that has deprived man of his power.") The Power of Silence - Page [218.9-219.2] ("That is not the residue I am...aware of the need to abstract.)

SEE ALSO: ABSTRACT-TO, POINT-THIRD-[INVERSION, SELF-REFLECTION

SELF-ABSORPTION-[*SELF-ABSORPTION*]: (*Warriors know that self absorption is the result of the way human beings use the impulses of the Eagle's emanations and turn them into a force to stir the trapped emanations inside their cocoons; seers "see" that self-absorbed individuals shorten their lives because of the internal agitation created by self-absorption itself.*)
SELECTED REFERENCES: The Fire From Within - Page [74.8-75.8] (He said that human beings carry...long pauses of dullness," he said.) The Fire From Within - Page [119.9-120.1] (He added that the obsessive entanglement...the assemblage point loses its rigidity.)
SEE ALSO: *REASON, AGITATION, EAGLE-EMANATIONS, SELF-REFLECTION*

SELF-BEGINS-ENDS-WARRIOR-[*FOR THE WARRIOR EVERYTHING BEGINS AND ENDS WITH THE SELF*]: SEE: *WARRIOR-SELF-BEGINS-ENDS-[FOR THE WARRIOR EVERYTHING BEGINS AND ENDS WITH THE SELF]*

SELF-CENTERED-STALKER-CLASSIFICATION-TWO-[*THE SELF-CENTERED CLASSIFICATION OF PERSONALITY*]: SEE: *PEOPLE-TYPES-[THE STALKERS' CLASSIFICATIONS OF PERSONALITY TYPES]*

SELF-CENTEREDNESS-[*SELF-CENTEREDNESS*]: SEE: *SELF-COMPASSION-[SELF-COMPASSION]*

SELF-COMBAT-[*MORTAL COMBAT WITH THE SELF*]: (*Warriors know that there are times on the path of knowledge when they enter into mortal combat with themselves; part of themselves wants to go with the will while another part wants to stay with the reason; the trick of warriors is to enter into this combat without dying from its consequences.*)
SELECTED REFERENCES: Tales of Power - Page [94.8-94.9] (Then, of course, you entered into...outcome was dubious for a moment.")
SEE ALSO: *SELF, WARRIOR-WAR*

SELF-COMPASSION-[*SELF-COMPASSION*]: (*Warriors know self-compassion is a by-product of self-importance; self-compassion is self-pity in disguise; the position of self-reflection forces the assemblage point to assemble a world of sham compassion, but very real cruelty and self-centeredness.*)
SELECTED REFERENCES: The Power of Silence - Page [31.7-31.9] ("I never saw the reason for...force of self-pity, compassion is meaningless.) The Power of Silence - Page [151.6-151.7] (Sorcerers knew, by means of their...and with it their self-importance.) The Power of Silence - Page [154.4-154.5] ("The position of self-reflection," don Juan...for the one who feels them.)
SEE ALSO: *SELF, SELFISHNESS, SELF-IMAGE, SELF-PITY, SELF-IMPORTANCE, SELF-CONGRATULATING, CRUELTY, CYNICISM*

SELF-CONCERN-[*SELF-CONCERN*]: (*Warriors know that self-concern is another term for self-importance.*)
SELECTED REFERENCES: The Power of Silence - Page [6.1-6.2] ("The spirit, in order to shake him...to anything but his self-concern.")
SEE ALSO: *SELF-IMPORTANCE*

SELF-CONFIDENCE-WARRIOR-[*THE WARRIORS' SELF-CONFIDENCE*]: SEE: *WARRIOR-SELF-CONFIDENCE-[THE WARRIORS' SELF-CONFIDENCE]*

SELF-CONFIDENCE-HUMILITY-[*SELF-CONFIDENCE VS HUMILITY*]: SEE: *WARRIOR-SELF-CONFIDENCE-[THE WARRIORS' SELF-CONFIDENCE], WARRIOR-HUMILITY-[THE WARRIORS' HUMILITY]*

SELF-CONGRATULATING-[CONGRATULATING OURSELVES]:
(Warriors know they must be spurred mercilessly on the path to knowledge; otherwise the natural human tendency is to stop and congratulate ourselves on having covered so much ground; human beings have an odious tendency to be too easy on themselves.)
 SELECTED REFERENCES: **The Power of Silence - Page [249.3-249.5]** ("I can't repeat often enough that...he was, had not spared him.)
 SEE ALSO: *TEACHERS-TEACHING, SELF-COMPASSION, SELF-IMPORTANCE*

SELF-DESTRUCTION-[SELF-DESTRUCTION]: *(Warriors know that modern man has become hopelessly removed from intent and all he can do is express his despair in violent and cynical acts of self-destruction.)*
 SELECTED REFERENCES: **The Power of Silence - Page [149.7-150.1]** (As the feeling of the individual self...peace, of satisfaction, of attainment.)
 SEE ALSO: *MAN-ERROR, SELF-ORIGIN, CYNICISM, SELF-IMAGE*

SELF-ESTEEM-[SELF-ESTEEM]: (Warriors know that self-esteem is at the core of all human interaction and when confronted, self-esteem is found to be boring and repetitive; warriors learn to laugh in the face of their own self-reflection and self-esteem.)
 SELECTED REFERENCES: **The Eagle's Gift - Page [289.6-289.7]** (Florinda said that one of the...the core of all human interaction.)
 SEE ALSO: *SELF-REFLECTION, RECAPITULATION, WARRIOR-HUMOR, SELF-IMAGE*

SELF-EXAMINATION-WARRIOR-[THE WARRIORS' SELF-EXAMINATION]: SEE: WARRIOR-SELF-EXAMINATION-[THE WARRIORS' SELF-EXAMINATION]

SELF-FORGET-FEAR-NOTHING-[FORGET THE SELF AND YOU WILL FEAR NOTHING]: (Warriors know that one way to cope with fear is by forgetting the individual self.)
 SELECTED REFERENCES: **The Art of Dreaming - Page [190.7]** (Don Juan's parting words to us were invitations to ponder the statement.)
 SEE ALSO: *SELF, FEAR, WARRIOR-FORMULA*

SELF-IMAGE-[THE SELF-IMAGE]: (Warriors know that the average man is totally involved with his self-image; the self-image of man cannot be sustained once the assemblage point moves past a particular threshold; it is the way we cling to our self-image that insures the continuation of our abysmal ignorance; being totally involved with the self-image is what makes man a homicidal egotist; having lost hope of returning to the abstract, man seeks solace in selfness, and in doing so, succeeds in fixing the assemblage point on the exact position which perpetuates the self image; the only worthwhile course of action for warriors or for average men is to restrict their involvement with the self-image as much as possible; the human being who holds fast to his self-image insures his abysmal ignorance by doing so.)
 SELECTED REFERENCES: **The Power of Silence - Page [150.3-151.7]** (Don Juan said then that it...self-reflection and its concomitant: self-importance.) **The Power of Silence - Page [219.6-219.7]** (He added that for the rational...everything else that was humanly possible.) **The Art of Dreaming - Page [37.7-37.9]** (Don Juan's argument was that most...the actual grandeur of the universe.)
 SEE ALSO: *SELF, SELF-REFLECTION, SELF-ABSORPTION, CYNICISM, AWARENESS-SUBLIMINAL, CRUELTY, KNOWLEDGE-SILENT, STUPIDITY-IGNORANCE, SELF-IMPORTANCE-LOSING, DAGGER-METAPHORICAL, SELF-IMAGE-IGNORANCE*

SELF-IMAGE-IGNORANCE-[THE SELF-IMAGE AND MAN'S IGNORANCE]: (Warriors know that holding steadfastly to the self-image inures abysmal ignorance.)
SELECTED REFERENCES: The Power of Silence - Page [219.6-219.7] (He added that for the rational...everything else that was humanly possible.)
SEE ALSO: STUPIDITY-IGNORANCE, SELF-IMAGE

SELF-IMPORTANCE-[SELF-IMPORTANCE]: (Warriors know that self-importance is the force generated by man's self-image; it is the force that keeps the assemblage point fixed at its habitual position; the thrust of the warriors' way is to dethrone self-importance; self-importance is really self-pity masquerading as something else; the luminous filaments left in human beings by others are the basis for our limitless capacity for self-importance.)
SELECTED REFERENCES: The Power of Silence - Page [150.8-151.1] (Don Juan described self-importance as...self-pity masquerading as something else.)
SEE ALSO: SELF-IMAGE, SELF, SELF-PITY, WARRIOR-WAY, CORE-GOOD-ROTTEN, LUMINOUS-FILAMENTS, ASSEMBLAGE-POINT-FIXATION, SELF-IMPORTANCE-(ALL)

SELF-IMPORTANCE-DETHRONING-[DETHRONING SELF-IMPORTANCE]: SEE: SELF-IMPORTANCE-[SELF-IMPORTANCE], TONAL-OVERSEER-PROTECTED-[THE TONAL AS A PROTECTED OVERSEER], TONAL-TYRANT-[THE TONAL AS A TYRANT]

SELF-IMPORTANCE-FUTILITY-[THE FUTILITY OF SELF-IMPORTANCE]: (As a result of their "seeing", warriors know the futility of self-importance.)
SELECTED REFERENCES: The Fire From Within - [298.7-298.9] (Don Juan said that adventurous men...the futility of self-importance.)
SEE ALSO: SELF-IMPORTANCE, SORCERY-WARRIORSHIP

*SELF-IMPORTANCE-LOSING-[LOSING SELF-IMPORTANCE]: (Warriors know that self-importance is the force which keeps the assemblage point fixed in its customary position; for this reason, the thrust of the warriors' way is to dethrone self-importance; warriors cannot believe that they are above anyone because they know that they are really nothing; warriors cannot travel into the non-human unknown until they have completely lost their self-importance; the warriors' courage empowers them to be ruthless without being self-important; warriors know that as soon as the assemblage point moves, self-importance crumbles; without the customary position of the assemblage point, the self-image cannot be sustained, and without the self-image, self-compassion, self-pity and self-importance are all lost; if warriors need help it is not with methods but with emphasis, and if someone makes them aware of the need to curtail self-importance, that help is real.)
SELECTED REFERENCES: The Teachings of Don Juan - Page [72.6-72.7] ("No! I'm never angry at anybody...don't feel that way any longer.") A Separate Reality - Page [7.9-8.1] ("The reason you got scared and quit...one needs to be light and fluid.") A Separate Reality - Page [81.2-81.5] ("Your acts, as well as the acts...he looks at everything becomes unimportant.") Journey to Ixtlan - Page [21.6-21.9] ("You take yourself too seriously...he said in a dramatic tone.) Journey to Ixtlan - Page [23.2-23.3] ("This is not the time to explain it...is yourself apart from everything else.") Journey to Ixtlan - Page [26.6-26.7] (We went into the desert chaparral importance and of my personal history.) Journey to Ixtlan - Page [37.4-37.5] ("I'm an old man; with age...is sitting with me right here.") Journey to Ixtlan - Page [68.1] ("Don't stall," don Juan said dryly...cut off your feelings of importance.) Journey to Ixtlan - Page [80.6-81.2] ("You

always feel compelled to explain...witnessing all the marvels of it.") **Journey to Ixtlan - Page [182.6-182.7]** ("I can't believe that this is...the world is unknown and marvelous.) **Journey to Ixtlan - Page [182.9-183.3]** (The soothing feeling of peace and plenitude...an unwarranted importance on the self.) **Tales of Power - Page [42.3]** (Don Juan said in a severe...was too heavy and self-important.) **Tales of Power - Page [156.1-156.3]** ("In the beginning one has to talk...which only plunge it into boredom.) **Tales of Power - Page [218.7-218.9]** (I had never seen Nestor so light..."That's why he's younger.") **Tales of Power - Page [240.7-240.8]** (He explained that in order to...dubious about himself and his actions.) **The Eagle's Gift - Page [207.4-207.5]** (I raged at him that most of...had to lean against a wall.) **The Eagle's Gift - Page [279.3-279.4]** ("Celestino's arrogance was his undoing and...to what we really are - nothing.) **The Fire From Within - Page [12.5-13.7]** (Half-complaining, I told him that...self-importance is a terrible encumbrance.) **The Fire From Within - Page [14.3-15.3]** ("Self-importance can't be fought with...I say in terms of morality.") **The Fire From Within - Page [16.4-16.5]** (He said that the most effective...is fighting to lose self-importance.) **The Fire From Within - Page [18.3-18.4]** ("You haven't yet put together...that counts in the path of knowledge.") **The Fire From Within - Page [24.8-24.9]** (Warriors, on the other hand...seers had over the simple-minded Spaniards.) **The Fire From Within - Page [29.8-29.9]** ("The new seers used petty tyrants...on discussing the mastery of awareness.") **The Fire From Within - Page [129.2-129.3]** (When they had calmed down...there only to make them laugh.) **The Fire From Within - Page [225.7-225.8]** ("The new seers, on the other...result is staggering in its consequences.") **The Fire From Within - [298.7-298.9]** (Don Juan said that adventurous men...the futility of self-importance.) **The Power of Silence - Page [110.2-110.3]** ("Yes," he went on. "The idea...be ruthless without being self-important.") **The Power of Silence - Page [150.8-151.8]** (Don Juan described self-importance as...is merely self-pity in disguise.) **The Power of Silence - Page [160.1-160.4]** (I told him that his sequence...self-importance, that help is real.) **The Art of Dreaming - Page [37.2-37.9]** (Every time he had an opportunity...the actual grandeur of the universe.) **The Art of Dreaming -Page [80.9-81.2]** ("Where are those worlds, don Juan...price they couldn't afford to pay.)
    SEE ALSO: *SELF-IMAGE, SELF, SELF-IMPORTANCE-LOSING, INDOLENCE, NOTHING-EVERYTHING, SELF, SELF-PITY, SELF-IMAGE, SELF-COMPASSION, CORE-GOOD-ROTTEN, WARRIOR-WAY, RUTHLESSNESS, WARRIOR-SELF-INDIVIDUAL*

SELF-IMPORTANCE-MELANCHOLY-[SELF-IMPORTANCE AND MELANCHOLY]: (Warriors know that self-importance is the motivating force behind every attack of melancholy.)
    SELECTED REFERENCES: **The Fire From Within - Page [129.2-129.3]** (When they had calmed down, don...there only to make them laugh.)
    SEE ALSO: *SELF-IMPORTANCE, DEPRESSION-MELANCHOLY*

SELF-IMPORTANCE-MONSTER-THREE-THOUSAND-HEADS-[THE MONSTER OF SELF-IMPORTANCE WITH THREE THOUSAND HEADS]: (Warriors know that self-importance can be described as a monster with three thousand heads; warriors can face and destroy this monster in one of three ways; 1) one is to sever each head, one at a time; 2) another is to reach the place of no pity which destroys the monster by slowly starving it; 3) the last is to pay for the instantaneous annihilation of the monster with one's symbolic death; it is the spirit that chooses which alternative warriors will select, and it the warriors' duty to follow the indications of intent.)
    SELECTED REFERENCES: **The Power of Silence - Page [249.5-250.2]** (Don Juan said that in the...he had not responded at all.)
    SEE ALSO: *PITY-PLACE-NO, WARRIOR-IMPECCABILITY-TICKET, SELF-IMPORTANCE-LOSING, WARRIOR-DEATH-SYMBOLIC*

SELF-IMPORTANCE-NICETIES-[SELF-IMPORTANCE CAN'T BE FOUGHT WITH NICETIES]: (Warriors know that self-importance can't be fought with niceties; warriors must go to war with the negative aspects of self-importance; to eliminate the negative aspects of self-importance while retaining its positive aspects requires a masterpiece of strategy.)
    SELECTED REFERENCES: **The Fire From Within - Page [14.3]** ("Self-importance can't be fought with...expressed my concern about la Gorda.)

SEE ALSO: *SELF-IMPORTANCE, SELF-COMBAT, CORE-GOOD-ROTTEN, WAR-WARRIOR*

SELF-IMPORTANCE-RESTRAINED-REALITY-INTERPRETATION-[SELF-IMPORTANCE IS RESTRAINED BY THE WARRIORS' KNOWLEDGE THAT REALITY IS AN INTERPRETATION THAT WE MAKE]: (*Warriors restrain self-importance with the knowledge that reality is an interpretation that we make; this knowledge is the definitive advantage that warriors have over petty tyrants.*)

SELECTED REFERENCES: The Fire From Within - Page [24.7-24.9] (Don Juan explained that the mistake...had over the simple-minded Spaniards.)

SEE ALSO: *REALITY-INTERPRETATION, SELF-IMPORTANCE-LOSING, WARRIOR-ADVANTAGE*

SELF-IMPORTANCE-SELF-PITY-[SELF-IMPORTANCE AND SELF-PITY]: (*Warriors know that self-importance is self-pity in disguise.*)

SELECTED REFERENCES: The Power of Silence - Page [150.9-151.8] (He explained that sorcerers had unmasked...is merely self-pity in disguise.)

SEE ALSO: *SELF-IMPORTANCE, SELF-PITY, SELF-COMPASSION, RUTHLESSNESS, SELF-IMAGE*

SELF-IMPORTANCE-WEAR-TEAR-[THE WEAR AND TEAR OF SELF-IMPORTANCE]: (*Warriors know that they must exercise control to prevent the wear and tear of their own self-importance; what exhausts the average man is this wear and tear and the feeling of being ripped apart by pride and a sense of worthlessness.*)

SELECTED REFERENCES: The Fire From Within - Page [26.1-26.4] ("The foreman at the house followed...trampling on you is called control.)

SEE ALSO: *SELF-IMPORTANCE-LOSING, WARRIOR-CONTROL, PRIDE-FALSE, EXHAUSTION*

SELF-INDIVIDUAL-[THE INDIVIDUAL SELF]: SEE: SELF-[THE INDIVIDUAL SELF]

SELF-INDIVIDUAL-WARRIOR-[THE WARRIORS' INDIVIDUAL SELF]: SEE: WARRIOR-SELF-INDIVIDUAL-[THE WARRIORS' INDIVIDUAL SELF]

SELF-INDULGENCE-[SELF-INDULGENCE]: (*Warriors know that indulging is another name for the way the average man weakens his tonal; warriors refuse to weaken themselves in this way, and instead accept in humbleness what they are; warriors avoid self-indulgence because it drains their personal power which is stupid, wasteful and injurious to their total being; taking the easy way out is the indulging way, not the warriors' way.*)

SELECTED REFERENCES: A Separate Reality - Page [150.8-151.1] ("Now you must detach yourself," he...abandons himself to being a hermit.) A Separate Reality - Page [180.1] ("The spirit is a force...you became green in the water.") A Separate Reality - Page [251.6-251.7] ("Fright is something one can never...thus he cannot die of fright.) Tales of Power - Page [54.1-54.3] ("What's wrong with me, don Juan...accepts in humbleness what he is.") Tales of Power - Page [74.5-74.9] (Don Juan said that the night...the little power you have left.") Tales of Power - Page [77.6-77.7] ("So, as you may very well...body is not an indestructible affair.) Tales of Power - Page [136.4-137.2] ("There is no need to treat...he did not remember it either.) Tales of Power - Page [154.2-154.3] ("That is the easy way out...You're not living like a warrior.") Tales of Power - Page [156.1-156.3] ("In the beginning, one has to...which only plunge it into boredom.) Tales of Power - Page [159.8-160.5] ("Things like that are known to happen...This is a terrible way of being.") Tales of Power - Page [193.6-193.8] ("You indulge like a son of...warrior for doing his impeccable best.") Tales of Power - Page [288.4-288.5] (Don Juan was right again when...but only the indulging in them.) The Second Ring of Power - Page [174.5-174.8] ("No. Unfortunately, understanding is not their...but an impeccable warrior survives, always.") The

Fire From Within - Page [79.7-79.8] (He explained that at the site...legion of strange things with me.) **The Power of Silence** - Page [78.1-78.2] ("We tied you down," don Juan...indulger, just as I had said.) **The Art of Dreaming** - Page [41.6-42.2] ("There's one problem with the second...the only safety valve for dreamers.") **The Art of Dreaming** - Page [95.7-95.9] (It did not take much for me...refuse to listen to my accounts.) **The Art of Dreaming** - Page [215.1-215.5] ("I mean the negative results of...line of very indulgent, dependent sorcerers.")
    SEE ALSO: *SELF, SELF-REFLECTION, SELF-IMPORTANCE, WARRIOR-WAY*

SELFISHNESS-[SELFISHNESS]: (Warriors know they must seek to harness the power of selfishness by turning it around and putting it to good use; the surest way of doing that is through the daily activity of life; if they can truly extend their selfish concern to include others, then warriors maximize their chances for finding the clues to the fulfillment of their true task.)
    SELECTED REFERENCES: **The Eagle's Gift** - Page [129.9-130.5] (Don Juan was telling me that...the fulfillment of my true task.)
    SEE ALSO: *WARRIOR-TASK, WARRIOR-CARING-FOR-ANOTHER*

SELFISHNESS-HARNESSING-[HARNESSING SELFISHNESS]: SEE: WARRIOR-CARING-FOR-ANOTHER-[CARING FOR ANOTHER WARRIOR]

SELF-ORIENTATION-WARRIOR-[THE WARRIORS' SELF-ORIENTATION]: SEE: WARRIOR-SELF-ORIENTATION-[THE WARRIORS' SELF-ORIENTATION]

SELF-ORIGIN-[THE ORIGIN OF THE INDIVIDUAL SELF]: (Warriors know that ancient man knew, in a direct way, what to do and how best to do it; but he performed so well that he began to develop a sense of selfness, and thus the idea of an individual self appeared; the individual self then began to dictate the nature and scope of man's actions; as the feeling of the individual self became stronger, man lost his connection to silent knowledge.)
    SELECTED REFERENCES: **The Power of Silence** - Page [149.5-150.1] (Then he talked about ancient man...peace, of satisfaction, of attainment.)
    SEE ALSO: *SELF, MAN-ERROR, SELF-IMAGE, KNOWLEDGE-SILENT, MAN-ANCIENT*

*SELF-OTHER-[THE OTHER SELF]: SEE: OTHER-SELF-[THE OTHER SELF]

SELF-PITY-[SELF-PITY]: (Warriors know that self-pity is the real enemy and the source of man's misery; self-importance springs from a degree of pity for oneself.)
    SELECTED REFERENCES: **Journey to Ixtlan** - Page [110.9-111.2] ("A warrior buries himself in order...time it calls for abandoning himself.) **Tales of Power** - Page [240.8-242.5] (Don Juan asked me to tell him...were there, without ever being used.") **The Second Ring of Power** - Page [105.3-105.4] ("She thinks she is the only woman...no longer feels sorry for herself.") **The Second Ring of Power** - Page [235.2-235.7] (I told her that my sadness in leaving...had to cook his own food.) **The Fire From Within** - Page [185.2-185.3] ("This indeed is the mystery of awareness...apologize for either; both are needed.) **The Power of Silence** - Page [31.9] (Without the driving force of self-pity, self-compassion is meaningless.") **The Power of Silence** - Page [124.2-124.5] (He tried to put me at ease...the site of ruthlessness," he said.) **The Power of Silence** - Page [150.9-151.3] (He explained that sorcerers had unmasked...it its fake sense of worth.")
    SEE ALSO: *SELF-IMPORTANCE, SELF, SELF-IMAGE*

SELF-QUASI-MEMORIES-OTHER-[QUASI MEMORIES OF THE OTHER SELF]-(TOP)

<u>SELF-REFLECTION</u>-[SELF-REFLECTION]: (Warriors know the position of self-reflection is the mind of man, the self-reflection of man's inventory; self-reflection is a position of the assemblage point; warriors struggle to maximize the movement of the assemblage point by curtailing self-reflection; once the assemblage point reaches the place of no pity, it is forced to abandon its customary place of self-reflection.)

SELECTED REFERENCES: The Teachings of Don Juan - Page [50.6-50.7] ("You are the only person I...And that produces a terrible fatigue.") A Separate Reality - Page [5.2-5.4] ("You think about yourself too much...despair or self-pity in it.) The Fire From Within - Page [79.4-79.5] (He stopped talking and solicited questions...freedom to focus on something else.) The Fire From Within - Page [121.2-121.3] (The mind, for a seer, is...than if you had kept it.") The Power of Silence - Page [28.8-28.9] (The mere mention of my discomfort...those who were reflections of ourselves.) The Power of Silence - Page [89.8-89.9] ("Sorcerers say that the fourth abstract...for nobody wants to be free.) The Power of Silence - Page [90.3-91.1] ("I know that at this moment...longer prey to their self-reflection.") The Power of Silence - Page [154.3-154.5] (He said that from the moment...or self-importance. Ruthlessness is sobriety.") The Power of Silence - Page [158.1-158.8] (The sorcerers' increased energy, derived from...real help you've gotten from me.") The Power of Silence - Page [165.2-165.9] (He then compared the acts he...his world of self-reflection collapses.) The Power of Silence - Page [228.1-288.2] (Impeccability is simply the best use...for monastic life, but it isn't.) The Power of Silence - Page [228.6-228.8] ("When a movement of the assemblage...things are there for the asking.") The Power of Silence - Page [265.5-265.7] ("Go home and think about the basic...reach the place of silent knowledge.")

SEE ALSO: MIND, SELF-IMAGE, INVENTORY, ASSEMBLAGE-POINT-MOVING, EAGLE-EMANATIONS-QUIETING, SELF-REFLECTION-(ALL)

<u>SELF-REFLECTION-BEYOND</u>-[ANYTHING BEYOND SELF REFLECTION]: (Warriors know that anything beyond self-reflection either appalls or attracts warriors, depending on the type of person they are; or warriors may be appalled and attracted in the same measure.)

SELECTED REFERENCES: The Power of Silence - Page [225.4-225.9] ("To discover the possibility of being..."You and I are very much alike.")

SEE ALSO: SELF-REFLECTION, PERCEPTION-SPLIT

<u>*SELF-REFLECTION-MIRROR-SHATTERING</u>-[SHATTERING THE MIRROR OF SELF-REFLECTION]: (Warriors know they must strive to shatter the mirror of self-reflection and restrict their involvement with their own self-image; the only worthwhile course of action for warriors or for average men is to restrict their involvement with the self-image as much as possible; the only concrete help the apprentice receives from his apprenticeship is the way it helps to shatter the mirror of the apprentice's self-reflection.)

SELECTED REFERENCES: The Power of Silence - Page [158.2-158.8] ("I've been trying to make clear...real help you've gotten from me.") The Power of Silence - Page [159.7-159.9] (Once the assemblage point has moved...the spirit in the first place.) The Power of Silence - Page [162.5] (He stated that what seemed a...destroy the mirror of self-reflection.) The Power of Silence - Page [163.2-163.4] (Don Juan noted that in this...the sorcerers' world without any preparation.) The Power of Silence - Page [166.1-166.2] (The inventory is the mind...break the mirror of self-reflection.") The Power of Silence - Page [171.2-171.5] ("Your uncertainty is to be expected...victims go after a ferocious struggle.")

SEE ALSO: SELF-REFLECTION, SELF-IMAGE

<u>SELF-REFLECTION-PRISON</u>-[THE PRISON OF SELF-REFLECTION]: (Warriors know that the chains of self-reflection imprison us; they keep us pinned down on the comfortable spot of self-reflection, and by so doing they also defend us from the onslaughts of the unknown.)

SELECTED REFERENCES: The Power of Silence - Page [90.3-90.4] ("I know that at this moment your...from the onslaughts of the unknown.")

SEE ALSO: *CHAINS-SELF-REFLECTION, NAGUAL-ASSAULT, WARRIOR-SHIELDS*

SELF-REMEMBERING-[REMEMBERING THE SELF]: (Warriors know that if they remain on the path of knowledge they will eventually remember themselves, or remember their left side; remembering the self is a recollection of the body, not the mind.)
SELECTED REFERENCES: **The Eagle's Gift - Page [59.9-60.7]** ("We have to wait," she said...in turn makes you even freer.")
SEE ALSO: *REMEMBERING-LEFT-SIDE-(TOP), REMEMBERING-BODY, RECOLLECTION-SORCERER*

SELF-RESTRAINT-WARRIOR-[THE WARRIORS' SELF-RESTRAINT]: SEE: WARRIOR-SELF-RESTRAINT-[THE WARRIORS' SELF-RESTRAINT]

SELF-RETAINING-SENSE-OF-[RETAINING THE SENSE OF ONESELF]: SEE: AWARENESS-PRESERVING-[PRESERVING AWARENESS]

SELF-SERIOUSNESS-[SELF-SERIOUSNESS]: (Warriors know that they must learn to lose self-seriousness; it is debilitating for warriors to take themselves to seriously; warriors learn to laugh at themselves.)
SELECTED REFERENCES: **Journey to Ixtlan - Page [20.3-21.7]** ("You're very violent," he commented casually...That's nonsense! you're weak and conceited!") **The Fire From Within - Page [24.7-25.1]** (Don Juan explained that the mistake...deadly seriousness while warriors do not.) **The Power of Silence - Page [248.1-248.3]** (He agreed that that was exactly...himself seriously, while you do.)
SEE ALSO: *WARRIOR-HUMOR, STALKING-RESULTS-THREE, LAUGHTER, SELF, SELF-IMAGE, SERIOUSNESS, WARRIOR-SERIOUSNESS*

SELF-STRONGHOLDS-GIVING-UP-[GIVING UP THE STRONGHOLDS OF THE SELF]: (Warriors know that it is very difficult to make the self give up its strongholds except through practice; one of the self's strongest defenses is reason and rationality.)
SELECTED REFERENCES: **The Art of Dreaming - Page [83.5-83.7]** (He had remarked time and time...a foremost assailant of our rationality.)
SEE ALSO: *REASON, SELF, SELF-IMAGE, LETTING-GO, DROPPING-THINGS-LIVES, REASON-VANQUISHING, WARRIOR-HOLDINGS-GIVING-UP*

SELF-TOTALITY-[THE TOTALITY OF THE SELF]: SEE: TOTALITY-REGAINING-[REGAINING THE TOTALITY OF ONESELF]

SELF-WAR-[WAR AGAINST THE INDIVIDUAL SELF]: SEE: WARRIOR-WAR-[WAR FOR THE WARRIOR]

SELF-WORTH-[SELF-WORTH]: (Warriors know that self-pity is the real source of man's self-importance; once the force of self-importance is engaged, it develops an independent momentum which gives the self a fake sense of worth.)
SELECTED REFERENCES: **The Power of Silence - Page [151.1-151.3]** ("Self-pity is the real enemy and...it its fake sense of worth.")
SEE ALSO: *SELF-PITY, SELF-IMPORTANCE, SELF, SELF-IMAGE*

SENSES-DETECT-ANYTHING-[THE SENSES ARE CAPABLE OF DETECTING ANYTHING]: (Warriors know that the human senses are capable of perceiving everything which surrounds us; it is the position of the assemblage point that dictates what our senses perceive; it is possible for a human being to perceive in inconceivable ways if the assemblage point aligns emanations inside the cocoon in a position different from its normal one; unfortunately the average man taps only a very small portion of this potential.)

SELECTED REFERENCES: The Fire From Within - Page [125.3-125.5] ("I've mentioned to you that the...human senses perceive in inconceivable ways.")

SEE ALSO: *ASSEMBLAGE-POINT, ALIGNMENT, PERCEPTION, SENSES, HUMAN-ALTERNATIVES-POSSIBILITIES-POTENTIAL, SENSES-SUPERFICIAL-ROLE-PERCEPTION*

SENSES-EXPANSION-[THE EXPANSION OF THE PHYSICAL SENSES]:
(Warriors know that the physical senses can operate in cooperation with an expanded awareness and the will.)

SELECTED REFERENCES: A Separate Reality - Page [148.4-148.8] ("Yesterday you said that one can...or 'as real' as we think.") The Power of Silence - Page [156.6-156.9] (I told him that on the...perceive is simply average sensory perception.")

SEE ALSO: *BODY-PHYSICAL, WILL, LOOKING-VS-SEEING, PERCEPTION, SENSES-(ALL)*

SENSES-SUPERFICIAL-ROLE-PERCEPTION-[THE SENSES PLAY ONLY A SUPERFICIAL ROLE WITH REGARD TO PERCEPTION]:
(Warriors know that the senses play only a superficial role with regard to perceiving the universe as it really is; the senses of the average man perceive the way they do because a specific feature of awareness forces him to do so.)

SELECTED REFERENCES: The Fire From Within - Page [37.2-37.6] ("The first truth is that the...awareness forces them to do so.")

SEE ALSO: *AWARENESS-TRUTH-FIRST, PERCEPTION, SENSES-DETECT-ANYTHING*

SENSITIVITY-[SENSITIVITY]:
(Warriors know that sensitivity is a natural condition of certain people; but warriors understand that in the final analysis sensitivity matters very little; what matters to warriors is being impeccable.)

SELECTED REFERENCES: Tales of Power - Page [4.2-4.3] ("To be sensitive is a natural...warrior be impeccable," he finally said.) Tales of Power - Page [54.1-54.2] ("You indulge," he snapped. "You feel...accepts in humbleness what he is.") The Second Ring of Power - Page [190.1-190.2] (My life before I met don Juan...to appear as a sensitive man.)

SEE ALSO: *WARRIOR-IMPECCABILITY*

SENSUALITY-[SENSUALITY]:
(Warriors know there is nothing wrong with man's sensuality, but warriors maintain a larger perspective on those feelings; warriors know the magical nature of sex and refuse to recklessly waste the life-bestowing force that is dissipated as a result of sexual activity.)

SELECTED REFERENCES: The Fire From Within - Page [60.6-60.8] ("What can be done with man's...one taxes the glow of awareness.")

SEE ALSO: *SEX-LUMINOUS-REALITY, SEXUAL-ENERGY-CONSERVING, EAGLE-EMANATIONS, DREAMING-ART*

SENTIMENTAL-WARRIOR-[THE WARRIOR IS NOT SENTIMENTAL]: SEE: WARRIOR-SENTIMENTAL-[THE WARRIOR IS NOT SENTIMENTAL]

SERENITY-WARRIOR-[THE WARRIORS' SERENITY]: SEE: WARRIOR-SERENITY-[THE WARRIORS' SERENITY]

SERIOUSNESS-[SERIOUSNESS]:
(Warriors do not take themselves too seriously because they are free from self-importance; warriors attach their seriousness to what goes on outside them, not to their own self-reflection.)

SELECTED REFERENCES: **The Teachings of Don Juan - Page [50.6-50.7]** (You are the only person I...And that produces a terrible fatigue.") **The Fire From Within - Page [24.7-25.1]** (Don Juan explained that the mistake...deadly seriousness while warriors do not.)
SEE ALSO: *SELF-IMPORTANCE, WARRIOR-HUMOR, SELF-SERIOUSNESS, WARRIOR-SERIOUSNESS*

SERIOUSNESS-WARRIOR-[THE WARRIORS' SERIOUSNESS]: SEE: WARRIOR-SERIOUSNESS-[THE WARRIORS' SERIOUSNESS]

SEX-BORED-[BORED SEX]: (Warriors know that certain individuals are the product of "cojida aburrida", or bored sex; bored sex means that a person's parents were too tired and bored at the moment their child was conceived.)
SELECTED REFERENCES: **The Fire From Within - Page [58.3-58.4]** (He told me that I didn't...store the little energy we have.)
SEE ALSO: *SEXUAL-ENERGY-CONSERVING*

SEX-EAGLE-COMMAND-[THE EAGLE'S COMMAND ABOUT SEX]: (Warriors know that the Eagle's command about sex is that sexual energy be used for creating life.)
SELECTED REFERENCES: **The Fire From Within - Page [58.9-59.1]** (We're talking about the Eagle's command...new sentient being they are creating.")
SEE ALSO: *SEX-LUMINOUS-REALITY*

SEX-FUN-[SEX FOR FUN]: SEE: SEXUAL-INTERCOURSE-FUN-[THE EAGLE'S EMANATIONS DON'T KNOW ABOUT INTERCOURSE FOR FUN]

SEX-LUMINOUS-REALITY-[THE LUMINOUS REALITY OF SEX]: (Warriors know about the life-giving luminous structures in both men and women and the luminous process undergone by the Eagle's emanations during sex; it is the Eagle's command that sexual energy be used for creating life; sexual intercourse is always a bestowal of awareness, even though the bestowal is not always consolidated; warriors respect the mystery of existence and understand that sex is a sublime act of bestowing life and not merely a physical drive that one can twist at will.)
SELECTED REFERENCES: **The Eagle's Gift - Page [45.2-46.1]** (Many of those luminous eggs had...the luminous mass of their bodies.) **The Fire From Within - Page [58.9-60.8]** (We're talking about the Eagle's command...one taxes the glow of awareness.")
SEE ALSO: *SEXUAL-ENERGY-CONSERVING, ROOTS*

SEX-WARRIOR-[SEX FOR THE WARRIOR]: SEE: WARRIOR-SEX-[SEX FOR THE WARRIOR]

SEX-WARRIOR-WEAKEST-MOMENT-[SEX IS THE WARRIORS' WEAKEST MOMENT]: SEE: WARRIOR-SEX-WEAKEST-MOMENT-[SEX IS THE WARRIORS' WEAKEST MOMENT]

SEXUAL-ENERGY-BALANCING-[BALANCING SEXUAL ENERGY]: SEE: SEX-ENERGY-CONSERVING-[CONSERVING SEXUAL ENERGY]

SEXUAL-ENERGY-CONSERVING-[CONSERVING SEXUAL ENERGY]: (Warriors know that sexual energy is what governs dreaming; dreamers either make love with their sexual energy or they dream with it; if warriors want to have enough energy to "see" they must become misers with their sexual energy; warriors are also aware that in addition to the energy

dissipated during sex, a parent's glow of awareness diminishes with every child he or she has; as the awareness of any child becomes enhanced, a large dark spot develops on the luminous cocoon of their parents on the very place from which the glow was taken away; if dreamers do not conserve their sexual energy, they might as well get used to erratic shifts of the assemblage point because their sexual energy will not remain in balance.)

SELECTED REFERENCES: The Second Ring of Power - Page [242.4-242.8] (I objected to her religious connotation...them that they can do it.") The Eagle's Gift - Page [37.9-38.2] (They are more fierce than I...to it regardless of my discomfort.) The Eagle's Gift - Page [113.9-116.2] (One night la Gorda and I were...allowing myself no room for revision.) The Fire From Within - Page [57.5-61.1] (After a long interruption, don Juan...*seen* superimposed on the body itself.") The Fire From Within - Page [145.7-145.8] ("I once told you that the...freedom, but the blow of death.") The Power of Silence - Page [35.3-36.4] ("The nagual Elias had great respect...average man and as a nagual.")

SEE ALSO: SEX-LUMINOUS-REALITY, AWARENESS-GLOW, WARRIOR-EMPTINESS

SEXUAL-INTERCOURSE-FUN-[THE EAGLE'S EMANATIONS DON'T KNOW ABOUT INTERCOURSE FOR FUN]: (Warriors know that the Eagle's command about sex is that sexual energy be used for creating life and bestowing awareness;   sexual intercourse is always a bestowal of awareness, even though it may not always be consolidated;   the Eagles emanations don't know of sexual intercourse for fun.)

SELECTED REFERENCES: The Fire From Within - Page [58.9-59.4] (We're talking about the Eagle's command...don't know of intercourse for fun.")

SEE ALSO: SEX-LUMINOUS-REALITY AWARENESS, EAGLE, EAGLE-EMANATIONS

SHADOW-[SHADOWS]: (Warriors know that shadows are the "doors of not doing"; the lines of the world are shown in shadows, there is movement in them and feelings come out of them; warriors can tell the innermost feelings of a man by observing his shadow; a shadow can also be a power, an entity, an inorganic being; these powers are called shadows because they have the same lines as the shadows of objects; at night, everything is a shadow including the allies.)

SELECTED REFERENCES: Journey to Ixtlan - Page [195.4-197.7] ("Shadows are peculiar affairs," he said...blocked the sunlight with his body.) Journey to Ixtlan - Page [199.6-199.7] ("During the day shadows are the...taught you the gait of power.") Tales of Power - Page [250.2-250.3] (Don Juan then gave me a...such as the shadows of things.) The Second Ring of Power - Page [307.5-308.1] ("I'm a distance and shadow gazer...it up to me to learn.")

SEE ALSO: LINES-WORLD, INORGANIC-BEINGS, ALLIES, NOT-DOING, SHADOW-(ALL), SHADOWS-(ALL)

SHADOW-CIRCLE-[A CIRCLE OF SHADOWS]-(TOP)

SHADOW-DEATH-[THE SHADOW OF DEATH]-(TOP)

SHADOW-DEATH-BLACK-[THE BLACK SHADOW OF DEATH]: (Death is a black spot directly behind the left shoulder, a sign of the imminent presence of death; warriors know that when a person is close to dying a dark moving shadow the exact size and shape of the person becomes evident to those who "see".)

SELECTED REFERENCES: Journey to Ixtlan - Page [38.5-38.6] (I reviewed for him the sequence...he had said was my death.) The Second Ring of Power - Page [129.6-129.7] (I was dumbfounded; I couldn't believe...seen my death circling around me.) The Power of Silence - Page [17.3-17.7] (The nagual had to admit that...the black shadow of his death.) The

Power of Silence - Page [20.2-20.4] (And then the nagual *saw* that...for the black shadow of death.)
SEE ALSO: *DEATH, SHADOWS*

SHADOW-FOLLOW-[THE SHADOW THAT FOLLOWS]-(TOP)

SHADOW-GAZING-[SHADOW GAZING]: SEE: GAZING-[GAZING]

SHADOW-MERGING-[MERGING SHADOWS]-(TOP)

SHADOW-OBSERVING-[OBSERVING OBJECTS AND THEIR SHADOWS]-(TOP)

SHADOW-WORLD-[THE SHADOW'S WORLD]-(TOP)

SHAMANISM-[SHAMANISM]: (Warriors know that shamanism is a belief system prevalent among some native North American Indian tribes; shamanism maintains that an unseen world of spiritual forces is pervasive around us and can be summoned or controlled through intermediaries between the natural and supernatural realms.)
SELECTED REFERENCES: The Art of Dreaming - Page [vii.5-vii.9] (Following don Juan's suggestion, I have...between the natural and supernatural realms.)
SEE ALSO: *SORCERY, WORLD-UNSEEN*

SHAME-NO-BEING-YOURSELF-[THERE IS NO SHAME IN BEING YOURSELF]: (Warriors know that if they are impeccable, there is no shame in being what they are; if power and intuition guide warriors in a certain direction, then they must go without remorse or regrets.)
SELECTED REFERENCES: The Art of Dreaming - Page [213.3-213.4] ("You are at the end of...There is no shame in that.")
SEE ALSO: *WARRIOR-IMPECCABILITY, WARRIOR-DECISIONS, POWER-DESIGNS, WARRIOR-INTUITION*

SHAPE-SHIFTING-ALLIES-[THE ALLIES' SHAPE-SHIFTING CAPABILITIES]: SEE: ALLIES-SHAPE-SHIFTING-[THE ALLIES' SHAPE-SHIFTING CAPABILITIES]

SHIELDS-DROPPING-WARRIOR-[DROPPING THE WARRIORS' SHIELDS]-(TOP): SEE: HUMAN-FORM-LOSING-[LOSING THE HUMAN FORM]-(TOP)

SHIELDS-WARRIOR-[THE WARRIORS' SHIELDS]: SEE: WARRIOR-SHIELDS-[THE WARRIORS' SHIELDS]

*SHIFT-BELOW-[THE SHIFT BELOW]: (Warriors know the shift below is the movement of the assemblage point to a position below where it is customarily located; a downward shift of the assemblage point to the "place of the beast"; the shift below entails a view, not of another world, but of our same world of everyday life seen from another perspective; the shift below is counter to the warriors' best interests and is the key procedure involved in adopting animal forms; whenever we think of something unnamable lurking in the darkness, we're thinking, without knowing it, about an aberrant woman seer holding a position in the immeasurable area below; the shift below diminishes a seer's power considerably, and the lapses it causes make seers extremely morose and narrow-minded, and in certain cases, extremely rational; when a sorcerer's assemblage point has shifted to a position below, his or her vision becomes limited because their

view of the world becomes narrow and detailed to the point that it seems to be an entirely different world; it is a mesmerizing view with tremendous appeal for those driven by a desire for quick gains; in those positions of the assemblage point, seers are plagued by violent and brutal deaths, which happen even more quickly than they do in the world of the normal position of man's assemblage point.)

SELECTED REFERENCES: **The Fire From Within** - Page [135.4-137.8] (He said that the movement is ordinarily...aberrant woman seer, run for the hills!") **The Fire From Within** - Page [141.3-141.5] (Still in a whisper, he said...her sorcery antics, jolted it loose.") **The Fire From Within** - Page [147.6-147.8] (I became so despondent I was...the assemblage point to shift below.) **The Fire From Within** - Page [149.4-149.5] ("Sorcerers have their own quirks...see you standing, they'll attack you.") **The Fire From Within** - Page [156.1-156.5] (He also said that La Catalina...great band of the Eagle's emanations.) **The Fire From Within** - Page [163.9-164.5] (When we sat down to talk...place for cavorting, but that's all.")

SEE ALSO: *ASSEMBLAGE-POINT-MOVING, ANIMAL-FORMS-ADOPTING, ABERRATION-MORBIDITY, REASON, SHIFT-BELOW-UNWITTING*

SHIFT-BELOW-UNWITTING-[UNWITTING SHIFTS BELOW]: *(Warriors know that unwitting downshifts occur periodically to every seer; these downshifts become less and less frequent as the warriors' assemblage point moves toward the left; warriors must maintain a near constant vigil to avoid these downshifts; disciplined warriors are less prone to that kind of downshift; female seers have downshifts more often than men and they are capable of bouncing out of that position with no effort at all; male seers have a tendency to linger dangerously in the position below.)*

SELECTED REFERENCES: **The Fire From Within** - Page [136.7-137.3] (He further said that an unwitting...while males linger dangerously in it.")

SEE ALSO: *SHIFT-BELOW*

SHIFT-LEFT-[THE SHIFT TO THE LEFT]: *(Warriors know that a movement of the assemblage point is always in depth, into the luminous interior of the cocoon along the thickness of man's band, but the transparency of the cocoon gives the impression of movement towards the left; the only exception to this rule is the "lateral shift" of the assemblage point which is characterized as a shift from one side to the other along the width of man's band of emanations instead of a shift in depth; the shift of the assemblage point into the left side is what produces dreams.)*

SELECTED REFERENCES: **The Fire From Within** - Page [122.2-122.9] ("The assemblage point of man is...it a shift to the left.) **The Fire From Within** - Page [134.4-134.5] (He stopped talking and looked at...exactly what I meant," he said.) **The Fire From Within** - Page [174.1-174.6] (After observing *dreamers* while they slept...natural shift of the assemblage point.) **The Fire From Within** - Page [223.2-223.4] (By reason of their activities, at...the force that makes us persons.) **The Fire From Within** - Page [275.2-275.7] ("That night, as he had done...in a *dreaming position*," he said.)

SEE ALSO: *ASSEMBLAGE-POINT-MOVING, ASSEMBLAGE-POINT-SHIFT-LATERAL, EAGLE-EMANATIONS-MAN-BAND, LUMINOUS-COCOON*

SHIVER-WARRIOR-[THE WARRIORS' SHIVER]: SEE: WARRIOR-SHIVER [THE WARRIORS' SHIVER]

SHOE-LACES-TIE-[A WARRIOR STOPS TO TIE THE LACES OF HIS SHOES]-(TOP)

SHORTCOMINGS-WARRIOR-[THE WARRIORS' SHORTCOMINGS]: SEE: WARRIOR-SHORTCOMINGS-[THE WARRIORS' SHORTCOMINGS]

SHOVE-WARRIOR-[THE WARRIORS' SHOVE]: SEE: WARRIOR-SHOVE-[THE WARRIORS' SHOVE]

SIEGE-WARRIOR-[THE WARRIOR UNDER SIEGE]: SEE: WARRIOR-SIEGE-[THE WARRIOR UNDER SIEGE]

SILENCE-INNER-[INNER SILENCE]: SEE: INNER-SILENCE-[INNER SILENCE]

SILENCE-MOMENT-[THE MOMENT OF SILENCE]: SEE: INNER-SILENCE-[INNER SILENCE]

SILENCE-POWER-[THE POWER OF SILENCE]-(TOP)

SILENCE-WARRIOR-[THE WARRIORS' SILENCE]: SEE: WARRIOR-SILENCE-[THE WARRIORS' SILENCE]

*SILENT-KNOWLEDGE-[SILENT KNOWLEDGE]: SEE: KNOWLEDGE-SILENT-[SILENT KNOWLEDGE

SILENT-KNOWLEDGE-AGE-[THE AGE OF SILENT KNOWLEDGE]: SEE: REASON-AGE-[THE AGE OF REASON]

SILENT-PROTECTOR-[THE SILENT PROTECTOR]: (Warriors know that a silent protector is one of the sorcerers' options; a surge of inexplicable energy that comes to warriors when nothing else works; positions of the assemblage point that help strengthen the warriors' new continuity.)
    SELECTED REFERENCES: The Power of Silence - Page [184.9-185.5] ("Although I was only twenty-three...were to be my silent protectors.)
    SEE ALSO: *SORCERER-OPTIONS, CONTINUITY, WARRIOR-STRENGTH*

SILENT-SIDE-MAN-THE SILENT SIDE OF MAN]: SEE: MAN-SILENT-SIDE-[THE SILENT SIDE OF MAN]

SILVIO-MANUEL-BREATH-[SILVIO MANUEL'S BREATH]-(TOP)

SILVIO-MANUEL-EYES-[SILVIO MANUEL'S EYE]-(TOP)

SILVIO-MANUEL-MASTER-INTENT-[SILVIO MANUEL THE MASTER OF INTENT]-(TOP)

SILVIO-MANUEL-NOT-DOING-[THE NOT-DOINGS OF SILVIO MANUEL]-(TOP): SEE: NOT-DOING-SILVIO-MANUEL-[THE NOT-DOINGS OF SILVIO MANUEL]-(TOP)

SILVIO-MANUEL-TALES-[TALES OF SILVIO MANUEL]-(TOP)

SIMPLICITY-WARRIOR-[THE WARRIORS' SIMPLICITY]: SEE: WARRIOR-SIMPLICITY-[THE WARRIORS' SIMPLICITY]

SINGLE-MINDEDNESS-WARRIOR-[THE WARRIORS' DEDICATION AND SINGLE-MINDEDNESS]: SEE: WARRIOR-DEDICATION-[THE WARRIORS' DEDICATION AND SINGLE-MINDEDNESS]

SITIO-[SITIO]: (Warriors know that sitio is another term for power spot or power place.)
    SELECTED REFERENCES: The Teachings of Don Juan - Page [29.2-29.3] (Finally he told me that there...where I could sit without fatigue.) The Teachings of Don Juan - Page [34.2-34.9] ("You have found the spot...was by detecting their respective colors.)
    SEE ALSO: *POWER SPOT, ENEMY-SPOT*

SKIMMINGS-*[SKIMMINGS]*: *(Warriors know that skimmings are a tricky refinement of perception; a human construct with no parallel; the skimmings of men represent the further clustering of the clusters of the Eagle's emanations; man's assemblage point takes some part of the emanations already selected for alignment and makes an even more palatable construct with them; the skimmings of men are more "real" than what other creatures perceive, and to give those skimmings a free hand as we do is an error in judgment for which we pay dearly; it is our pitfall to forget our skimmings are real only because it is our command to perceive them as real.)*

SELECTED REFERENCES: The Fire From Within - Page [138.4-139.2] ("When we, as serious adult human...the old seers paid for theirs.")
SEE ALSO: *EAGLE-EMANATIONS-CLUSTERING, REALITY-INTERPRETATION, PERCEPTION*

SKIN-*[SKIN]*: *(Warriors know that the skin is the perfect organ for transposing energy waves between the daily world and the realm of the inorganic beings; the skin automatically screens energy and what dreamers need to do to make the skin exchange that energy is to voice their intent out loud.)*

SELECTED REFERENCES: The Art of Dreaming - Page [94.6-94.9] (During another dreaming session, the...our intent out loud, in dreaming.)
SEE ALSO: *INTENT-VOICING, DREAMING-ART*

SLAVERY-*[SLAVERY]* *[THE SLAVERY OF THE AVERAGE MAN]*:
(Warriors know that the black magicians are the captors and masters of the average man, his thoughts and his actions are fixed forever in their terms.)

SELECTED REFERENCES: Tales of Power - Page [21.1-21.3] ("Our fellow men are the black...time and your power fearing me.")
SEE ALSO: *BLACK-MAGICIANS, FREEDOM, SLAVERY*

SLEEP-*[SLEEP]*: *(Warriors know that the assemblage point undergoes a natural shift during sleep; this natural movement is the basis for the art of dreaming; to move the assemblage point away from its natural setting and to keep it fixed at its new location is to be asleep; with practice, seers learn to be asleep and yet behave as if nothing is happening to them.)*

SELECTED REFERENCES: Journey to Ixtlan - Page [99.1-99.2] ("Every time you look at anything...Do you see what I mean?") The Eagle's Gift - Page [23.1-23.3] (He said that *dreaming* is intrinsically...alleged extra body, the *dreaming body*.) The Eagle's Gift - Page [135.6-135.7] (First was the act itself. It...or the features, of one's dreams.) The Fire From Within - Page [173.2-173.8] (Don Juan explained that *dreaming*...enormous effort and concentration to accomplish.) The Fire From Within - Page [219.1-219.4] (He told me then that I was...if nothing is happening to them.) The Fire From Within - Page [232.1-232.2] (I wanted to laugh out loud...were sleeping with his eyes open.) The Fire From Within - Page [233.8-233.9] ("They're still alive to this day...an apparent state of deep sleep.) The Fire From Within - Page [250.6-251.1] (Don Juan left me alone in the...with slumber, yet a *dreamer* is asleep.) The Fire From Within - Page [277.7-277.9] (Don Juan talked to me very...the heaviness of being deeply asleep.) The Power of Silence - Page [25.7-26.5] (I got up and went to look...Something else is bothering you.") The Power of Silence - Page [86.5-86.6] (Don Juan was very understanding...return me to a normal state of awareness.) The Power of Silence - Page [101.3-101.5] (I remembered at that moment scores of...don Juan made in the past.) The Art of Dreaming - Page [18.7-18.8] (Another monumental breakthrough that the old...becomes very easily displaced during sleep.) The Art of Dreaming - Page [69.9-70.1] ("What is a dreaming position, don...point has been displaced during sleep.")
SEE ALSO: *DREAMING-ART, ASSEMBLAGE-POINT-MOVING, SLEEP-AWAKE*

SLEEP-AWAKE-[BEING ASLEEP WHILE BEING AWAKE]: (Warriors know that whenever the assemblage point shifts, we are technically asleep; when those shifts run along either edge of man's band they are always coupled with slumber; when those shifts occur along the midsection of man's band they are not coupled with slumber but the dreamer is still asleep.)

SELECTED REFERENCES: **The Fire From Within - Page [250.6-251.1]** (Don Juan left me alone in the...slumber, yet a *dreamer* is asleep.)

SEE ALSO: *DRUNK-APPEARING, EAGLE-EMANATIONS-MAN-BAND, ASSEMBLAGE-POINT-SHIFT, SLEEP*

SMOKE-[SMOKE]: (Warriors know that smoke is like fog for the warrior, but easier to handle; smoke can be used by the warrior-sorcerer to "see" people and to cure them; smoke has a cleansing effect on the luminosity of men and makes the warrior clear and direct.)

SELECTED REFERENCES: **The Teachings of Don Juan - Page [28.4-28.5]** ("The only reason I have is...matter now. I know your intentions.") **The Second Ring of Power - Page [267.3-269.4]** (La Gorda said that the Nagual...to take me into fog banks.)

SEE ALSO: *FOG, SMOKE-DIVINERS, LITTLE-SMOKE*

SMOKE-DIVINERS-[THE SMOKE OF DIVINERS]: (Warriors know that the smoke of diviners is another term for the little smoke.)

SELECTED REFERENCES: **The Teachings of Don Juan - Page [68.9-69.1]** ("What kind of smoke is it, don Juan? The smoke of diviners!")

SEE ALSO: *LITTLE-SMOKE, SMOKE*

SMOKE-GAZING-[SMOKE GAZING]: SEE: GAZING-[GAZING]

SMOKE-LITTLE-[LITTLE SMOKE]: SEE: LITTLE-SMOKE-[LITTLE SMOKE]

SNAIL-SIDEWALK-[A SNAIL ON THE SIDEWALK]-(TOP)

SNEAKING-WORLD-MEN-WORLD-SORCERER-[SNEAKING BETWEEN THE WORLD OF MEN AND THE WORLD OF SORCERERS]: (Warriors know that "seeing" occurs when warriors are able to sneak between the world of ordinary men and the world of sorcerers; sneaking between the worlds this way is what characterizes the warrior as a warrior.)

SELECTED REFERENCES: **Journey to Ixtlan - Page [254.3-254.6]** ("Yesterday the world became as sorcerers...in the realm of ordinary men.") **Journey to Ixtlan - Page [255.5-255.7]** (Don Juan looked at me with...thought you had found your car.")

SEE ALSO: *SEEING, SORCERY-VS -WARRIORSHIP, WARRIOR-WAY, WARRIOR-CONTRADICTION-KNOWLEDGE, EQUILIBRIUM, WARRIOR-BALANCE-SOBRIETY-ABANDON*

SO-BE-IT-["SO BE IT"]: SEE: INORGANIC-BEINGS-REFUSING-[REFUSING THE INORGANIC BEINGS]

SOBRIETY-ABANDON-BALANCE-[WARRIORS BALANCE SOBRIETY AND ABANDON]: SEE: WARRIOR-BALANCE-SOBRIETY-ABANDON-[WARRIORS BALANCE SOBRIETY AND ABANDON]-

SOBRIETY-DREAMER-[THE DREAMERS' SOBRIETY]: (Warriors know that the dreamers' sobriety is acquired only after inconceivable battles with the self; it is the dreamers' sobriety that defines the balance between sorcery and warriorship for the dreamer.)

SELECTED REFERENCES: **The Power of Silence - Page [36.5]** (He said that the nagual Elias...task of answering don Juan's questions.)

SEE ALSO: *WARRIOR-SOBRIETY, DREAMING-ART. WARRIORSHIP-VS-SORCERY, EQUILIBRIUM*

SOBRIETY-VS-EMOTIONALITY-WARRIOR-[THE WARRIORS' SOBRIETY VS THE WARRIORS' EMOTIONALITY]: SEE: WARRIOR-SOBRIETY-VS-EMOTIONALITY-[THE WARRIORS' SOBRIETY VS THE WARRIORS' EMOTIONALITY]

SOBRIETY-FORMLESSNESS-[SOBRIETY AND FORMLESSNESS]:
(*Warriors know that if anything, formlessness is a detriment to the warriors' sobriety and levelheadedness; the detachment and capacity to immerse oneself in whatever one is doing extends to everything the warrior does, including being inconsistent and outright petty.*)
SELECTED REFERENCES: **The Eagle's Gift - Page [125.7-125.8]** (Having lost my human form, I was...including being inconsistent, and outright petty.)
SEE ALSO: *HUMAN-FORM-LOSING, WARRIOR-SOBRIETY, WARRIOR-DETACHMENT, WARRIOR-FORMLESS*

SOBRIETY-UNDERSTANDING-VS-CAPRICIOUSNESS-SELF-IMPORTANCE-[SOBRIETY AND UNDERSTANDING VS CAPRICIOUSNESS AND SELF-IMPORTANCE]: (*Warriors know that sobriety and internal strength help direct the assemblage point to a position which fosters understanding; without that sobriety it is likely that the warriors' capriciousness will move the assemblage point to a position that fosters self-importance.*)
SELECTED REFERENCES: **The Fire From Within - Page [175.7-177.3]** (He said that at first the new...been the case many times before.)
SEE ALSO: *WARRIORSHIP-VS-SORCERY, WARRIOR-SOBRIETY, WARRIOR-STRENGTH, UNDERSTANDING, SELF-IMPORTANCE, ASSEMBLAGE-POINT-MOVING*

SOBRIETY-WARRIOR-[THE WARRIORS' SOBRIETY]: SEE: WARRIOR-SOBRIETY-[THE WARRIORS' SOBRIETY]

SOCIAL-BASE-PERCEPTION-CHANGING-[CHANGING THE SOCIAL BASE OF PERCEPTION]: SEE: PERCEPTION-CHANGING-SOCIAL-BASE-[CHANGING THE SOCIAL BASE OF PERCEPTION]

SOCIAL-BEINGS-DREAMERS-[DREAMERS ARE SOCIAL BEINGS]:
(*Warriors know that dreamers are inherently social beings; they unavoidably seek the company of consciousness, even the consciousness of inorganic beings in dreaming.*)
SELECTED REFERENCES: **The Art of Dreaming - Page [48.4-48.9]** ("What do sorcerers do with inorganic...this case. Dreamers seek them avidly.")
SEE ALSO: *DREAMING-ART, INORGANIC-BEINGS*

SOCIAL-ORDER-[FREEING ONESELF FROM THE BINDINGS OF THE SOCIAL ORDER]: SEE: MAN-EVOLUTION [MAN IS CAPABLE OF EVOLVING]

SOLEDAD-BATTLE-DEATH-[A BATTLE TO THE DEATH WITH DONA SOLEDAD]-(TOP): SEE: DOUBLE-MORTAL-COMBAT-[THE MORTAL COMBAT OF THE DOUBLE]-(TOP)

SOLEDAD-BID-POWER-[DONA SOLEDAD'S BID FOR POWER]-(TOP)

SOLEDAD-FLOOR-MAGICAL-[THE MAGICAL FLOOR OF DONA SOLEDAD]-(TOP)

SOLEDAD-RECAPITULATION-[THE RECAPITULATION OF DONA SOLEDAD]-(TOP)

SOLEDAD-TRANSFORMATION-[THE TRANSFORMATION OF DONA SOLEDAD]-(TOP)

SOLIDITY-WARRIOR-[THE WARRIORS' SOLIDITY]: SEE: WARRIOR-SOLIDITY-[THE WARRIORS' SOLIDITY]

SOLITUDE-WARRIOR-[THE WARRIORS' SOLITUDE]: SEE: WARRIOR-SOLITUDE-[THE WARRIORS' SOLITUDE]

*SOMERSAULT-THOUGHT-[THE SOMERSAULT OF THOUGHT]: SEE: THOUGHT-SOMERSAULT-[THE SOMERSAULT OF THOUGHT]

SONORA-[THE SONORA DESERT]: (Warriors know that the Sonora desert is a geographical area which naturally tends to promote downward shifts of the assemblage point from the customary position to the position of the beast.)
> SELECTED REFERENCES: The Fire From Within - Page [141.3-141.4] (Still in a whisper, he said...to the place of the beast.) The Fire From Within - Page [147.6-147.8] (I became so despondent I was...the assemblage point to shift below.)
> SEE ALSO: SHIFT-BELOW, ANIMAL-FORMS-ADOPTING

SONS-DAUGHTERS-[SONS AND DAUGHTERS]: SEE: MEN-[MEN], WOMEN-[WOMEN]

SORCERER-[SORCERER]: (Warriors know that a sorcerer is a person who succeeds in moving the assemblage point to a new position; a sorcerer is someone who can command an ally and use it to his advantage.)
> SELECTED REFERENCES: A Separate Reality - Page [167.4-168.2] (He spoke about "seeing" as a process...realize the unimportance of it all.") The Power of Silence - Page [162.3-162.5] ("What are you then?" he asked...movement that makes one a sorcerer.")
> SEE ALSO: SORCERER-(ALL), SORCERY (ALL), ASSEMBLAGE-POINT-MOVING-(ALL), SORCERER-ASSEMBLAGE-POINT-MOVEMENT, WARRIOR-SORCERER

SORCERER-ABSTRACT-[THE TRUE ABSTRACT SORCERER]: (The warrior-sorcerer is defined as a true abstract sorcerer; instead of merely being part of a morbid and ignorant audience of lovers of the unknown, true warrior-sorcerers have abstracted themselves.)
> SELECTED REFERENCES: The Power of Silence - Page [240.3-240.4] (At the same time, the nagual...audience of lovers of the unknown.)
> SEE ALSO: ABSTRACT-TO, WARRIORSHIP-VS-SORCERY, WARRIOR-SORCERER

SORCERER-ACCOMPLISHMENT-[THE SORCERER'S' GREATEST ACCOMPLISHMENT]: SEE: SORCERER-VIRTUOSITY-[THE SORCERERS' VIRTUOSITY]

SORCERER-ACCOMPLISHMENT-TRANSCENDENTAL-[THE SORCERER'S TRANSCENDENTAL ACCOMPLISHMENTS]: (Warrior-sorcerers train themselves to do two transcendental things; first, to conceive the existence of the assemblage point, and second, to make that assemblage point move.)
> SELECTED REFERENCES: The Power of Silence - Page [144.8-145.1] (I mentioned to don Juan that I...to make that assemblage point move.)
> SEE ALSO: ASSEMBLAGE-POINT, ASSEMBLAGE-POINT-MOVING, SORCERER-VIRTUOSITY

SORCERER-ACTION-[THE SORCERERS' ACTIONS]: (Warrior-sorcerers know their actions must be deliberate in thought and realization and be a blend of the four moods of stalking, (ruthlessness, cunning, patience and sweetness); the actions of warrior-sorcerers are executed as a consequence of a movement of the assemblage point, and such movements are determined by the amount of energy that they have at their command.)

SELECTED REFERENCES: **The Power of Silence - Page [144.6-144.7]** (He then said something which I...energy sorcerers had at their command.) **The Power of Silence - Page [244.4-244.5]** (He went on to say that...of the four foundations of *stalking*.)

SEE ALSO: *STALKING-MOODS-FOUR, ACT-LEARNING*

SORCERER-AFFECTION-[THE SORCERERS' AFFECTION]: (Warrior-sorcerers know love in their lives; the affection and love of warrior-sorcerers is not an inconsistency, it is just not emphasized in the teachings of nagualism because love and sex are so overemphasized in the everyday world of men.)

SELECTED REFERENCES: **The Art of Dreaming - Page [102.5-102.8]** (I am going to tell you...wanted to give you a break.)

SEE ALSO: *SORCERER, WARRIOR-LOVE, WARRIOR-LOVE-POWER*

*SORCERER-ANTIQUITY-[THE SORCERERS OF ANTIQUITY]: (Warriors know that the sorcerers of antiquity is another term for the old seers; the ancient Toltecs.)

SELECTED REFERENCES: **The Fire From Within - Page [9.2-9.3]** ("The ancient seers were very fortunate...that we can't even imagine today.") **The Art of Dreaming - Page [1.7-3.1]** (Don Juan stressed, time and time...into the basic premise of sorcery.) **The Art of Dreaming - Page [12.4-13.9]** (Don Juan went on to explain...potentials are nothing to sneeze at.") **The Art of Dreaming - Page [39.6-39.8]** ("You have a proclivity for behaving...A most real but dangerous journey.") **The Art of Dreaming - Page [57.9-58.4]** (We were engaged in some unrelated...do you think about them now?") **The Art of Dreaming - Page [59.7-61.1]** (I had forgotten my question about...that the two of you meet someday.) **The Art of Dreaming - Page [67.4-67.9]** ("The problem with the old sorcerers...bent is to teach, to guide.") **The Art of Dreaming - Page [69.3-69.4]** ("To my knowledge, only the old...thousands of positions it can adopt.") **The Art of Dreaming - Page [77.9-79.9]** ("The old sorcerers called them the...We are after the nonhuman unknown.") **The Art of Dreaming - Page [95.7-95.9]** (It did not take much for me...refuse to listen to my accounts.) **The Art of Dreaming - Page [122.6-122.7]** ("Why do you say that I am...like fish take to the water.) **The Art of Dreaming - Page [203.3-203.9]** ("For years now, I have been...or like the new ones," he said.) **The Art of Dreaming - Page [205.8-206.2]** ("As you already know, for modern...passed on from teacher to disciple.")

SEE ALSO: *SEER-OLD, TOLTECS, SORCERER-ANTIQUITY-(ALL)*

SORCERER-ANTIQUITY-ACTION-[THE ACTIONS OF THE SORCERERS OF ANTIQUITY]: (Warriors know that the sorcerers of antiquity were not given to thought, they leaned toward action.)

SELECTED REFERENCES: **The Power of Silence - Page [27.1-27.4]** ("I took you to that cave...heavily toward the aberrations of reason.")

SEE ALSO: *ACTING-VS-THINKING*

SORCERER-ANTIQUITY-MOOD-[THE MOOD OF THE SORCERERS OF ANTIQUITY]: (Warriors know the dark mood of the sorcerers of antiquity; the mood of the ancient Toltecs.)

SELECTED REFERENCES: **The Art of Dreaming - Page [68.2-68.3]** ("Do I gather, don Juan, that...will agree with me. You'll see.")

SEE ALSO: *TOLTEC-TRADITION, SORCERER-ANTIQUITY, SEER-OLD-MOOD, WARRIOR-MOOD, DREAMING-MOOD-NEFARIOUS*

SORCERER-ANTIQUITY-PREDILECTION-[THE PREDILECTION OF THE SORCERERS OF ANTIQUITY]: (Warriors know that the predilection of the sorcerers of antiquity was to utilize the fourth gate of dreaming to travel to places that exist only in the intent of others.)
SELECTED REFERENCES: The Art of Dreaming - Page [200.4-200.6] (Don Juan explained that, at the...by far, the old sorcerers predilection.)
SEE ALSO: *DREAMING-GATE-FOURTH, SORCERER-ANTIQUITY, WARRIOR-PREDILECTION*

SORCERER-APPROACH-ANYONE-[SORCERERS NEVER APPROACH ANYONE]: SEE: SORCERER-LOOK-FOR-ANYONE-NEVER-[SORCERERS NEVER LOOK FOR ANYONE]

SORCERER-ART-[THE SORCERERS' ART]: (The art of warrior-sorcerers is to be outside everything and to be unnoticeable; more than anything else the art of warrior-sorcerers is to be impeccable, to never waste their power.)
SELECTED REFERENCES: The Second Ring of Power - Page [246.8-246.9] ("The art of sorcerers is to...idiocies, like what you're doing now.)
SEE ALSO: *WARRIOR-INACCESSIBILITY, WARRIOR-IMPECCABILITY, WARRIOR-ART, WARRIOR-DELICACY, WORLD-IN-NOT-OF*

SORCERER-ASSEMBLAGE-POINT-MOVEMENT-[THE MOVEMENT OF THE ASSEMBLAGE POINT MAKES ONE A SORCERER]: (Warriors know that it is the movement of the assemblage point that makes anyone a sorcerer; both the average man or the warrior apprentice become sorcerers when the movement of the assemblage point is maximized, because by maximizing that movement, continuity is shattered beyond repair.)
SELECTED REFERENCES: The Power of Silence - Page [162.3-162.5] ("What are you then?" he asked...movement that makes one a sorcerer.") The Power of Silence - Page [228.3-228.6] (Don Juan remarked that we do...movement, continuity is shattered beyond repair.")
SEE ALSO: *ASSEMBLAGE-POINT-MOVING, CONTINUITY, SORCERERY-ALL-THERE-IS, WARRIORSHIP-VS-SORCERY, SORCERER*

SORCERER-ASSUREDNESS-STRUGGLE-[THE SORCERERS' STRUGGLE FOR ASSUREDNESS]: (Warrior-sorcerers know that the struggle for assuredness is the most dramatic struggle there is; in order to have this assuredness, warriors must have command of their new continuity and must invalidate the continuity of their old lives.)
SELECTED REFERENCES: The Power of Silence - Page [191.8-192.2] ("The sorcerers' struggle for assuredness is...and instability of his new continuity.)
SEE ALSO: *CONTINUITY, WARRIOR-IMPECCABILITY-TICKET, WARRIOR-ASSUREDNESS, WARRIOR-SORCERER*

SORCERER-BECOMING-[BECOMING A SORCERER]: SEE: SORCERER-ASSEMBLAGE-POINT-MOVE-[THE MOVEMENT OF THE ASSEMBLAGE POINT MAKES ONE A SORCERER]

SORCERER-CALL-[THE SORCERERS' CALL]: (Warriors know that sorcerers have specific calls with which they summon up the nagual.)
SELECTED REFERENCES: The Second Ring of Power - Page [164.7-165.6] (I laughed and told her that I...lantern and gathered up my notes.)
SEE ALSO: *ALLIES-CALLING-(TOP), MOTH-CALL-(TOP), WARRIOR-CRY-ANIMAL-(TOP)*

SORCERER-CAVE-[THE SORCERERS' CAVE]-(TOP): SEE: CAVE-SORCERER-[THE SORCERERS' CAVE OF UNDERSTANDING]-(TOP)

SORCERER-CHOICE-[THE SORCERERS' CHOICE]: SEE: INORGANIC-BEINGS-REFUSING-[REFUSING THE INORGANIC BEINGS]

SORCERER-CONTRADICTION-TERMS-PRACTICE-[THE SORCERERS' CONTRADICTIONS IN TERMS AND PRACTICE]: (Warrior-sorcerers know that the sorcerers' world is filled with contradictions in terms, but in practice there are no contradictions at all.)
SELECTED REFERENCES: The Power of Silence - Page [159.2-159.5] (I pointed out that he was...being made aware of the spirit.")
SEE ALSO: WARRIOR-CONTRADICTION-KNOWLEDGE, WARRIOR-SORCERER, EQUILIBRIUM

SORCERER-COYOTE-[A COYOTE SORCERER]: (Warriors know that a coyote sorcerer is a brujo who draws a lot of things from his coyote brothers.)
SELECTED REFERENCES: Journey to Ixtlan - Page [254.9-255.2] ("If I were you," he added...of things from his coyote brothers.")
SEE ALSO: SORCERER-LYRIC

SORCERER-CURSE-[THE SORCERERS' CURSE]: (Warriors know that the ancient sorcerers' curse was that they fell for the facility of the assemblage point to be manipulated; by believing that they could manipulate the movement of the assemblage point for their own gain, they sealed their doom.)
SELECTED REFERENCES: The Art of Dreaming - Page [73.6-74.1] ("We are back again, harping on...manipulate the assemblage point for gain.)
SEE ALSO: ASSEMBLAGE-POINT, ASSEMBLAGE-POINT-MOVING, SORCERER-ANTIQUITY

SORCERER-CYCLE-FIRST-[THE FIRST SORCERERS' CYCLE] (Warriors know that the first cycle of warrior-sorcerers is when they are still human, when they still have their human form; warriors are taught during his first cycle.)
SELECTED REFERENCES: The Second Ring of Power - Page [244.5-244.8] ("You fought against what the Nagual...little, Nagual, you've lost the game.") The Second Ring of Power - Page [264.2-2644] ("What is a cycle, Gorda?" I asked...are the second cycle to them.)
SEE ALSO: HUMAN-FORM-CLINGING, WARRIOR-SORCERER

SORCERER-CYCLE-FIRST-GOAL-[THE GOAL OF THE FIRST SORCERERS' CYCLE]: (The goal of the warrior-sorcerers' first cycle is to lose the human form; the loss of the human form is what differentiates the sorcerers' first and second cycles.)
SELECTED REFERENCES: The Second Ring of Power - Page [264.2-264.4] ("What is a cycle, Gorda?" I asked...are the second cycle to them.)
SEE ALSO: HUMAN-FORM-CLINGING, HUMAN-FORM-LOSING, WARRIOR-SORCERER, SORCERER-CYCLE-TWO

SORCERER-CYCLE-SECOND-[THE SECOND SORCERERS' CYCLE]: (Warriors know that the second cycle of warrior-sorcerers is when they are no longer human, when they have lost their human form; warriors teach during the second cycle.)
SELECTED REFERENCES: The Second Ring of Power - Page [264.2-264.4] ("What is a cycle, Gorda?" I asked...are the second cycle to them.) The Eagle's Gift - Page [231.7] (Thanks to the Nagual woman and myself...their cycle and were almost free.)
SEE ALSO: HUMAN-FORM-LOSING, TEACHERS-TEACHING, WARRIOR-SORCERER, SORCERER-CYCLE-TWO

SORCERER-CYCLE-TWO-[THE TWO CYCLES OF THE SORCERER]:
(Warrior-sorcerers know that there are two cycles of a warriors' life; these cycles are delineated by the loss of the human form.)
SELECTED REFERENCES : The Second Ring of Power - Page [244.5-244.8] ("You fought against what the Nagual...little, Nagual, you've lost the game.") The Second Ring of Power - Page [264.2-264.4] ("What is a cycle, Gorda...We are the second cycle to them.)
SEE ALSO : *HUMAN-FORM-LOSING, SORCERER-CYCLE-FIRST, SORCERER-CYCLE-FIRST-GOAL, SORCERER-CYCLE-SECOND, WARRIOR-SORCERER, SORCERER-CYCLE-(ALL)*

SORCERER-DAMNATION-[THE SORCERERS' DAMNATION]: (Warriors know that the sorcerers' damnation is the way in which the old sorcerers were taken by the inorganic beings to worlds from which they could not return.)
SELECTED REFERENCES: The Art of Dreaming - Page [196.7-196.9] ("You bet your life," he replied...the same trap for you two.")
SEE ALSO: *INORGANIC-BEINGS-TRICKERY, INORGANIC-BEINGS-REALM*

SORCERER-DEATH-[THE SORCERERS' DEATH]: (Warrior-sorcerers define an alternate way of dying for themselves, they do not die in the traditional sense; the two attentions of the warrior are so closely tied together that there is no longer any need for the attention of the nagual to push out against the luminous layers of his being.)
SELECTED REFERENCES: The Second Ring of Power - Page [291.2-291.5] (Sorcerers have to do their best...together that perhaps they'll never die.")
SEE ALSO: *WARRIOR-DEATH-COMMAND, DEATH, LUMINOUS-LAYERS, ATTENTIONS-UNIFYING-TWO, ATTENTION-NAGUAL, SPEED, WARRIOR-SORCERER*

SORCERER-DESCRIPTION-METAPHOR-[THE SORCERERS' METAPHORICAL DESCRIPTIONS]: (Warriors know that trying to reason out the sorcerers' metaphorical descriptions is as useless as trying to reason out silent knowledge.)
SELECTED REFERENCES: The Power of Silence - Page [220.8-221.1] (I must have looked dumbfounded...only made them more confusing.)
SEE ALSO: *KNOWLEDGE-SILENT, REASON*

SORCERER-DESCRIPTION-WORLD-[THE SORCERER'S DESCRIPTION OF THE WORLD]: (Warrior-sorcerers know that the dreamers' description of the world is a "non-ordinary" description of the world which is learned through "seeing".)
SELECTED REFERENCES: Journey to Ixtlan - Page [xiii.5-xiii.8] (In summing up I can say that...other words, I had gained *membership*.)
SEE ALSO: *DESCRIPTION-WORLD, SEEING, REALITY-NON-ORDINARY, WARRIOR-SORCERER*

SORCERER-DIAGRAM-[THE SORCERERS' DIAGRAM]: (Warriors know that the sorcerers' diagram is an outline of the eight points every man is capable of handling; a diagram of eight points on the fibers of a luminous being; those points are reason, talking, feeling, dreaming, "seeing", will, the tonal and the nagual.)
SELECTED REFERENCES: A Separate Reality - Page [258.1-258.8] (He turned and looked at me...not understanding, did you get that?") A Separate Reality - Page [261.9] ("Genaro and I are acting from...centers of radiation in his diagram.) Tales of Power - Page [95.2-97.2] (He then spilled some ashes on...be on your own, by yourself.")
SEE ALSO: *REASON, TALKING, FEELING, DREAMING-ART, SEEING, WILL, TONAL, NAGUAL, SORCERER-DIAGRAM-BODY*

SORCERER-DIAGRAM-BODY-[THE CORRESPONDING LOCATIONS ON THE PHYSICAL BODY FOR THE EIGHT POINTS OF THE SORCERERS' DIAGRAM]: (*Warriors know that the eight points on the sorcerers' diagram correspond to specific anatomical locations on the physical body; reason and talking correspond to the head; feeling corresponds to the tip of the sternum; the area below the navel corresponds to the will; dreaming corresponds to the area on the right side of the ribcage; seeing corresponds to the left side of the ribcage; in some warriors, seeing and dreaming are both on the right side of the ribs.*)

SELECTED REFERENCES: Tales of Power - Page [96.7-97.2] (I asked him if the eight points...will be on your own, by yourself.") **The Fire From Within - Page [219.7-219.9]** (He told me then to relax my muscles...of everything that was taking place.) **The Fire From Within - Page [247.4-247.6]** ("It's time for you to shift that...and suddenly began to move again.) **The Fire From Within - Page [263.9-264.2]** (The more he talked, the greater...the most peaceful and exquisite beatitude.) **The Fire From Within - Page [265.5-265.6]** (The fervor I felt on *seeing*...and I lost sight of God.) **The Power of Silence - Page [91.9-93.3]** (Again I interrupted don Juan...his fear, and he passed out.)

SEE ALSO: *SORCERER-DIAGRAM, BODY-PHYSICAL, REASON, TALKING, FEELING, DREAMING-ART, SEEING, WILL, TONAL, NAGUAL*

SORCERER-DISCIPLES-GIFT-[THE SORCERERS OF ANTIQUITY MADE GIFTS OF THEIR DISCIPLES TO THE INORGANIC BEINGS]: (*Warriors know that the sorcerers of antiquity made a practice of offering their disciples to the inorganic beings as "gifts" of awareness.*)

SELECTED REFERENCES: The Art of Dreaming - Page [104.3-104.7] (I asked don Juan what exactly...inorganic beings were under his control.)

SEE ALSO: *SORCERER-ANTIQUITY, INORGANIC-BEINGS, TOLTECS*

SORCERER-ENEMY-[THE SORCERERS' SUPREME ENEMY]: (*Warrior-sorcerers know that self-importance is our supreme enemy.*)

SELECTED REFERENCES: The Art of Dreaming - Page [37.6] (He was of the opinion that...enemy but the nemesis of mankind.)

SEE ALSO: *SELF-IMPORTANCE-LOSING, MAN-NEMESIS, WARRIOR-SORCERER, SELF-IMPORTANCE, WARRIOR-ENEMIES-FOUR-NATURAL*

SORCERER-EVENTS-UNLEASHED-[EVENTS UNLEASHED BY SORCERERS]: (*Warrior-sorcerers know that the events unleashed by sorcerers as a result of silent knowledge are so simple and yet so abstract that they can only be spoken of in symbolic terms; the symbolic retelling of these events is the reason behind the existence of the sorcery stories.*)

SELECTED REFERENCES: The Power of Silence - Page [47.4-47.6] (He explained that the events unleashed...knock of the spirit were examples.)

SEE ALSO: *SORCERY-STORIES, ABSTRACT-CORES, WARRIOR-SORCERER*

SORCERER-EVIL-[EVIL SORCERERS]: (*Warriors know an evil sorcerer is a "telecote", an owl; an evil sorcerer is a child of the night whose most useful animals are wild cats and night birds, especially owls.*)

SELECTED REFERENCES: A Separate Reality - Page [98.6-98.9] (I don't remember what prompted don...he had been listening in silence.)

SEE ALSO: *SORCERY, EVIL, ABERRATION-MORBIDITY, OBSESSION, WARRIORSHIP-VS-SORCERY*

SORCERER-EXPERIENCE-[THE SORCERERS' EXPERIENCE]: (*Warrior-sorcerers know their experience is so outlandish that they use it as an intellectual exercise with which to stalk themselves.*)

SELECTED REFERENCES: **The Power of Silence - Page [243.8-244.2]** (Don Juan fixed me with his stare...possibilities than the mind can conceive.") **The Art of Dreaming - Page [10.1-10.2]** (The marvel of sorcery is that...hope that you will practice them.")
SEE ALSO: *STALKING-ONESELF, SORCERER-REASONINGS*

SORCERER-EXPLANATION-[THE SORCERERS' EXPLANATION]: (The sorcerers' explanation is a personal experience of the warrior; the act of flying on the wings of perception; the paradox of the luminous beings; the warriors' silent understanding of the true pair; the experiential understanding that the tonal is nothing but a reflection of the indescribable unknown filled with order and the nagual is nothing but the a reflection of the indescribable void that contains everything.)

SELECTED REFERENCES: **Tales of Power - Page [5.7-6.3]** ("You don't have enough personal power...after the reflection of your ideas.") **Tales of Power - Page [11.9-12.2]** (The sorcerers explanation of how to...you were not aware of it.") **Tales of Power - Page [22.6-22.9]** ("When the sorcerers' explanation became clear...not opposed to the sorcerers' explanation.") **Tales of Power - Page [78.9-79.4]** ("We won't discuss this matter...be worthy of knowledge and power.) **Tales of Power - Page [80.5-80.7]** ("Genaro doesn't want me to tell you...we must honor and respect them.") **Tales of Power - Page [119.3-128.6]** ("I have put on my suit...of the true pair, the *nagual*.") **Tales of Power - Page [229.5-229.7]** (Yesterday you let the wings of your...the last issue, the sorcerers' explanation.) **Tales of Power - Page [231.4-233.3]** ("At this precise point a teacher...wings of your perception," he said.) **Tales of Power - Page [241.4-241.5]** (Don Juan pointed out then that...the use assigned to those elements.) **Tales of Power - Page [252.3-252.6]** ("This is another of the sorcerers'...looked at me askance. He giggled.) **Tales of Power - Page [271.7-273.9]** ("What Genaro wanted to show you...followed to arrive at that point.") **Tales of Power - Page [276.8-277.4]** ("To make *reason* feel safe is...that, or what the order is.") **Tales of Power - Page [278.1-278.6]** ("We have arrived at the last...perception and fly to that infinitude.") **Tales of Power - Page [288.1-288.5]** (Don Juan's voice brought forth another...could not bear to leave alone.) **Tales of Power - Page [294.1-294.2]** ("The sorcerers' explanation cannot at all...gives you shelter, aloneness is loneliness.)
SEE ALSO: *PERCEPTION-WINGS, TONAL, NAGUAL, TONAL-INDESCRIBABLE, EQUILIBRIUM*

SORCERER-FACE-SEEING-[SEEING A SORCERER'S FACE]-(TOP)

SORCERER-FIELD-[THE SORCERERS' FIELD]: SEE: INORGANIC-BEINGS-REALM-[THE REALM OF THE INORGANIC BEINGS]

SORCERER-FLIGHT-[A SORCERER IN FLIGHT]-(TOP)

SORCERER-GOAL-[THE SORCERERS' GOAL]: (The goal of warrior-sorcerers is to last; they don't take unnecessary risks and spend a lifetime sweeping clean the island of the tonal so that one day they can actually "sneak off of it" in a manner of speaking.)

SELECTED REFERENCES: **Tales of Power - Page [193.2-193.4]** ("In order to be an average...the gate for such an escape.)
SEE ALSO: *WARRIOR-IMPECCABILITY, TONAL-ISLAND, WARRIOR-GOAL, SORCERY-GOAL, WARRIOR-SORCERER*

SORCERER-GREAT-SEER-POOR-[A GREAT SORCERER BUT A POOR SEER]: SEE: AWARENESS-LEFT-TRANSITION-[THE TRANSITION TO THE LEFT SIDE AWARENESS]

SORCERER-HORDE-ANGRY-[A HORDE OF ANGRY SORCERERS]-(TOP)

SORCERER-INCOMPLETE-[INCOMPLETE SORCERERS]: (Warriors know that there are plenty of incomplete sorcerers; warrior-sorcerers must be complete if they are ever to enter into the nagual with their total being.)

SELECTED REFERENCES: **The Second Ring of Power - Page [240.9]** ("Not everybody has to do that...complete is only for us Toltecs.)

SEE ALSO: WARRIOR-COMPLETENESS, WARRIOR-EMPTINESS, WARRIOR-SORCERER

SORCERER-KILLING-[KILLING ANOTHER SORCERER]: (Warriors know that there is nothing more difficult than for one sorcerer to kill another; it is much easier for an average man to kill a sorcerer or for a sorcerer to kill an average man.)
SELECTED REFERENCES: The Teachings of Don Juan - Page [17.6-18.2] ("It could have been a diablero...was a huge pool of grease.") The Second Ring of Power - Page [126.5-126.9] (He told her that nothing could....not overpower you even with that.") The Second Ring of Power - Page [135.3-135.7] ("Soledad has to take her edge...would then have come after us.)
SEE ALSO: SORCERY, WARRIOR-SORCERER

SORCERER-KNOWLEDGE-DANGEROUS-[THE MOST DANGEROUS FACET OF THE SORCERER'S KNOWLEDGE]: SEE: DREAD-SHEER [SHEER DREAD]

SORCERER-KNOWLEDGE-MOST-SOPHISTICATED-[THE SORCERERS' MOST SOPHISTICATED-KNOWLEDGE]: (Warriors know that the most sophisticated knowledge they possess is the knowledge of their potential as perceiving beings and the fact that the content of perception depends on the position of the assemblage point.)
SELECTED REFERENCES: The Power of Silence - Page [145.2-145.3] (He emphasized over and over that...the position of the assemblage point.)
SEE ALSO: PERCEPTION, ASSEMBLAGE-POINT-MOVING, KNOWLEDGE

SORCERER-LEGACY-[THE LEGACY OF THE OLD SORCERERS]: (Warriors know that the legacy of the old sorcerers is the working knowledge that the energy necessary for warriors to complete their definitive journey must come from the realm of the inorganic beings.)
SELECTED REFERENCES: The Art of Dreaming - Page [180.8-182.3] ("You are ready then for one final...he waved good-bye to me.)
SEE ALSO: ENERGY-ASSEMBLAGE-POINT-MOVE, SORCERER-ANTIQUITY, WARRIOR-JOURNEY-DEFINITIVE, WARRIORSHIP-VS-SORCERY, INORGANIC-BEINGS-REALM

SORCERER-LINEAGE-[THE ENERGY BALANCE OF THE MEMBERS OF A SORCERER'S LINEAGE]: (Warriors know that the energy balance of the members of a sorcery lineage is the cumulative balance of the energies and impeccability of the various naguals of that line; this balance is directly effected by the choices of each new nagual.)
SELECTED REFERENCES: The Fire From Within - Page [7.3-8.1] (He explained that all the lines...from the six who proceeded them.) The Art of Dreaming - Page [218.5-218.6] ("Now it's your turn to meet...that finished off the old sorcerers.")
SEE ALSO: WARRIOR-IMPECCABILITY, NAGUAL-PARTY-WARRIORS

SORCERER-LOOK-FOR-ANYONE-NEVER-[SORCERERS NEVER LOOK FOR ANYONE]: (Warriors know that sorcerers never look for or approach anyone.)
SELECTED REFERENCES: The Power of Silence - Page [194.7-194.8] ("Did you go and look for them...and that sorcerers never approach anyone.)
SEE ALSO: TEACHERS-TEACHING

SORCERER-LUMINOSITY-CHANGE-[THE CHANGE IN THE SORCERER'S LUMINOSITY]: (Warriors know that sorcerers change both the color and shape of their luminosity as they progress on the path of knowledge.)

SELECTED REFERENCES: Tales of Power - Page [34.9-35.6] (A new series of forms emerged...not pegged down to the ground.") **Tales of Power** - Page [222.8-223.1] (Then my left eye image of don Juan...had a light of their own.) **The Second Ring of Power** - Page [240.2-240.4] ("What color are you, Gorda...we are round at both ends.") **The Fire From Within** - Page [160.8-160.9] ("Seers say that the amount of...Silvio Manuel are examples of that.") **The Art of Dreaming** - Page [5.7-5.8] (Don Juan had the impression that...akin to people of ancient times.) **The Art of Dreaming** - Page [12.1-12.4] ("What happens when the assemblage point...becomes a thin line of energy.)
SEE ALSO: *LUMINOUS-COCOON, LUMINOUS-TOMBSTONES, AWARENESS-COLOR, KNOWLEDGE-PATH*

SORCERER-LYRIC-[THE LYRIC SORCERERS]: *(Warriors know that the lyric sorcerers are the dilettante sorcerers, the sorcerers who do not take sorcery or themselves too seriously; the lyric sorcerers prefer animals other than those of the evil sorcerers, such as crows for example.)*
SELECTED REFERENCES: **A Separate Reality** - Page [98.6-98.9] (I don't remember what prompted don...he had been listening in silence.)
SEE ALSO: *WARRIOR, WARRIOR-SORCERER, WARRIOR-TOTAL-FREEDOM, SORCERER-ABSTRACT, SORCERER-EVIL, CROW-TRANSFORMATION-CARLOS-(TOP)*

SORCERER-VS-MAN-[THE SORCERER VS THE AVERAGE MAN]:
(Warriors know the only difference between warrior-sorcerers and average men is that sorcerers are more aware of their connection with the spirit than the average man, and strive to manipulate that connection in addition to being aware of it.)
SELECTED REFERENCES: **The Power of Silence** - Page [223.6-223.9] ("Only sorcerers can turn their feelings into...feature shared by everything there is.")
SEE ALSO: *SORCERER-ASSEMBLAGE-POINT-MOVEMENT, WARRIOR-SORCERER, WARRIOR-INTENT-LINK*

SORCERER-MANEUVER-[THE SORCERERS' MANEUVER]: *(Warriors know that the warrior-sorcerers' maneuver is the act of transferring awareness and transporting themselves in their physical and energetic entirety into another total world.)*
SELECTED REFERENCES: **The Art of Dreaming** - Page [190.2-190.6] ("What exactly do we have to...anything I had done so far.)
SEE ALSO: *AWARENESS-TRANSFERRING, INORGANIC-BEINGS-REALM-TRANSPORTED, WARRIOR-SORCERER, WORLDS-OTHER-ASSEMBLE-TOTAL*

SORCERER-MASTER-[MASTER SORCERER]: *(Warriors know a master sorcerer is capable of transforming himself into an eagle and transporting his disciple through the ten layers of the other world; evil and dilettante sorcerers can at best go through only three layers.)*
SELECTED REFERENCES: **A Separate Reality** - Page [98.6-99.2] (I don't remember what prompted don...said, go through only three layers.)
SEE ALSO: *OTHER-SIDE, WORLD-OTHER*

SORCERER-MODERN-[MODERN SORCERERS]: *(Warriors know that the new seers are the modern sorcerers; the seers of the new cycle; warriors for total freedom.)*
SELECTED REFERENCES: **The Art of Dreaming** - Page [1.9-2.1] (Modern sorcerers, by contrast, don Juan...sorcery if they deemed it necessary.)
SEE ALSO: *SEER-NEW, WARRIOR-TOTAL-FREEDOM*

SORCERER-MUTENESS-[THE SORCERER'S MUTENESS]: *(Warriors know that man's speech faculty is extremely flimsy and attacks of muteness are extremely common among sorcerers who venture beyond the limits of normal perception.)*

SELECTED REFERENCES: **The Fire From Within - Page [226.5-226.6]** (If the shift is considerable...they have been frozen from the inside.) **The Art of Dreaming - Page [72.6-72.7]** (I instantly realized I had entered...beyond the limits of normal perception.)
SEE ALSO: *TALKING, WARRIOR-MOTOR-CONTROL-LOSS-OF, ATTENTION-SECOND-JOLT, KNOWLEDGE-VS-LANGUAGE, NAGUAL-FACING*

SORCERER-OLD-POSITION-[THE POSITION OF THE OLD SORCERERS]: (Warriors know that the position of the old sorcerers corresponds to the stage in dreaming where dreamers are trying to pass the tests which manifest themselves in the universe beyond the second gate of dreaming; dreamers must decide for themselves how they will respond to being in that position.)

SELECTED REFERENCES: **The Art of Dreaming - Page [122.4-123.3]** (When he finally spoke, he said...their hooks, they never give up.")
SEE ALSO: *DREAMING-GATE-SECOND*

SORCERER-OPTIONS-[THE SORCERERS' OPTIONS]: (Warriors know the sorcerers' options are positions of the assemblage point; an infinite number of positions which the assemblage point can reach; each of these positions can act to strengthen a warrior-sorcerers' new continuity; the effect of these shifts of the assemblage point is cumulative.)

SELECTED REFERENCES: **The Power of Silence - Page [185.1-185.8]** ("What did he mean, don Juan...sorcerers were and what they did.)
SEE ALSO: *ASSEMBLAGE-POINT-MOVING, CONTINUITY*

SORCERER-PASSAGEWAY-[THE PASSAGEWAY TO THE WORLD OF SORCERERS]: (Warriors know that the passageway to the world of sorcerers opens up after warriors have learned to stop their internal dialogue.)

SELECTED REFERENCES: **Tales of Power - Page [13.7-13.8]** (Don Juan explained that the passageway...the only way to accomplish it.)
SEE ALSO: *SORCERER-WORLD-KEY, INTERNAL-DIALOGUE-STOPPING*

SORCERER-PATH-[THE ESSENCE OF THE SORCERERS' PATH]: SEE: SPIRIT-TRICKERY [THE TRICKERY OF THE SPIRIT]

SORCERER-PIPE-[THE SORCERERS' PIPE]: (Warriors know that the sorcerers' pipe is given to the apprentice by his benefactor for the purpose of calling the little smoke.)

SELECTED REFERENCES: **The Teachings of Don Juan - Page [69.3-72.5]** (It takes years alone to become...house to put his pipe away.) **The Second Ring of Power - Page [289.7-289.9]** (Since you took another path, you...is hidden, waiting for that day.)
SEE ALSO: *LITTLE SMOKE, BENEFACTOR*

SORCERER-PROBLEM-[THE SORCERERS' PROBLEM]: (Warrior-sorcerers know they must learn to overcome a specific two-fold problem; first they must deal with the impossibility of restoring their shattered continuity and second they must deal with the impossibility of using the continuity dictated by the new position of the assemblage point; warriors do not consciously resolve this impossible problem; the spirit either resolves it or it doesn't.)

SELECTED REFERENCES: **The Power of Silence - Page [227.4-227.6]** (He described the specific problem of sorcerers...in the world of everyday life.)
SEE ALSO: *CONTINUITY, WARRIOR-RESOLUTION*

SORCERER-PURPOSE-TRANSCENDENTAL-*[THE SORCERERS'*
TRANSCENDENTAL PURPOSE]: (Warrior-sorcerers' transcendental
purpose is to free perception and learn to "see".)
SELECTED REFERENCES: The Art of Dreaming - Page [78.9-79.1] (Sorcerers, on the contrary, bring order...anything we know to be real.")
SEE ALSO: *SEEING, WARRIOR-PURPOSE, WARRIOR-SORCERER*

SORCERER-REASONINGS-*[THE SORCERERS' REASONINGS]:*
(Warriors know they must adopt the sorcerers' reasoning strategy after they
have experienced the premises of sorcery in normal awareness.)
SELECTED REFERENCES: The Power of Silence - Page [14.1-14.3] (He responded cuttingly that I was...edifice of sorcery knowledge was completed.)
SEE ALSO: *REASON, SORCERER-EXPERIENCE, AWARENESS-NORMAL*

SORCERER-RECOLLECTION-*[THE SORCERERS' RECOLLECTION]:*
SEE: *RECOLLECTION-SORCERER-[THE SORCERERS' RECOLLECTION]*

SORCERER-REFERENCE-POINT-*[THE SORCERERS' POINT OF*
REFERENCE]: (Warrior-sorcerers know that establishing a point of
reference means getting a chance to examine intent; sorcerers are vitally
concerned with their past but only as a point of reference.)
SELECTED REFERENCES: The Power of Silence - Page [2.2-2.8] ("Sorcerers are vitally concerned with their past...battling to understand the same force.")
SEE ALSO: *WARRIOR-PAST, WARRIOR-SORCERER, INTENT, SORCERY-STORIES*

SORCERER-RESIDUE-*[THE SORCERERS' RESIDUE]: (The residue of*
concern to the warrior-sorcerer is the idea of the abstract, the idea of the
spirit; the idea of the personal self has no value to the warrior-sorcerer
whatsoever.)
SELECTED REFERENCES: The Power of Silence - Page [218.5-219.2] ("*Intending* the movement of your assemblage point...the spirit by being aware of it.")
SEE ALSO: *WARRIOR-SORCERER, ABSTRACT, INTENT, SPIRIT, SELF,*
WARRIOR-WAR

SORCERER-RESOLUTION-*[THE SORCERERS' RESOLUTION]: (Warrior-*
sorcerers do not concentrate on resolving the fundamental problem of their
new emerging continuity; instead they rely on the spirit to either resolve it
or not.)
SELECTED REFERENCES: The Power of Silence - Page [227.6-227.8] ("How do sorcerers resolve this problem...the solution. Why? No one knows.")
SEE ALSO: *POWER-FLOW, CONTINUITY, WARRIOR-SORCERER, SORCERER-*
RESOLUTION, SPIRIT-DESIGNS

SORCERER-SAFETY-VALVE-*[THE SORCERERS' SAFETY VALVE]: (The*
safety valve of warrior-sorcerers' is that by the time they are truly focused
on intent, they no longer have any desire to utilize that capability for their
own purposes.)
SELECTED REFERENCES: The Power of Silence - Page [131.1-131.2] (He added, seriously, that the sorcerers'...no longer interested in mesmerizing anyone.)
SEE ALSO: *WARRIOR-DESIRE, WARRIOR*

SORCERER-SEER-WARRIOR-*[WARRIOR-SORCERER-SEERS]:*
(Warriors know that the warrior-sorcerer-seers are the new seers, warriors
who "see" and who struggle to differentiate themselves from aberrant seers;
the challenge of warrior-sorcerer-seers remains to define a system of
behavior that is neither petty or capricious and which is characterized by the

sense of beauty that differentiates warrior-sorcerer-seers from just plain witches.)
    SELECTED REFERENCES: The Power of Silence - Page [82.3-82.4] ("The real challenge for those sorcerer...differentiates sorcerer seers from just plain witches.")
    SEE ALSO: *SEER-NEW, WARRIOR-WAY*

SORCERER-SEND-OFF-[A SORCERER'S SEND-OFF]-(TOP)

SORCERER-SHAM-[SHAM SORCERERS]: *(Warriors know that the sham sorcerers are those sorcerers who have only copied the procedures of the Toltec seers without ever having acquired their inner knowledge.)*
    SELECTED REFERENCES: The Fire From Within - Page [5.4-5.6] ("Those conquerors," he went on, "took...talking about, because they're not seers.")
    SEE ALSO: *TOLTECS, SORCERERY*

SORCERER-SMOKING-FACE-[SMOKING A SORCERER'S FACE]-(TOP): SEE: SORCERER-FACE-SEEING-[SEEING A SORCERER'S FACE]-(TOP)

*SORCERER-SONGS-[THE SORCERERS' SONGS]: *(Warriors know that the sorcerers' songs are those he learns from Mescalito himself.)*
    SELECTED REFERENCES: The Teachings of Don Juan - Page [104.3-104.5] ("Can you teach me the words...songs that belong to another man.") The Teachings of Don Juan - Page [150.5-150.9] (I said, "Take the songs for instance...for other purposes, don Juan said.)
    SEE ALSO: *MESCALITO*

SORCERER-STORYTELLERS-[SORCERER STORYTELLERS]: *(Warriors know that some sorcerers are storytellers; storytelling is these warriors' path to the spirit, their path to perfection; sorcerer storytellers can manipulate the elusive link with intent and actually change things; under the auspices of the spirit they can let their thoughts somersault into the inconceivable, and know without a shadow of a doubt, that somewhere in that infinity the spirit has descended and changed things.)*
    SELECTED REFERENCES: The Power of Silence - Page [114.6-116.5] (He said that some sorcerers were...His goal has transcended his person.")
    SEE ALSO: *WARRIOR-INTENT-LINK, THOUGHT-SOMERSAULT, SPIRIT-DESCENT*

SORCERER-STRATEGY-[THE STRATEGY OF A SORCERER]-(TOP)

SORCERER-SYMBOLIC-DEATH-[THE SORCERERS' SYMBOLIC BUT FINAL DEATH]: SEE: WARRIOR-IMPECCABILITY-TICKET-[THE WARRIORS' TICKET TO IMPECCABILITY]

SORCERER-THUNDERBOLT-[A THUNDERBOLT SORCERER]-(TOP)

SORCERER-TOPIC-[THE MOST IMPORTANT SORCERERS' TOPIC]: *(Warriors know that the position of the assemblage point is the most important topic of the sorcerers' world; this topic was both the old sorcerers' curse and the current thorn in mankind's side; the ancient sorcerer and the average man both fall prey to the position of the assemblage point, albeit for different reasons; the sorcerers of antiquity knew all about the assemblage point but fell for its facility to be manipulated by believing they could manipulate it for personal gain; the average man doesn't even know that the assemblage point exists so he is obliged to take the first attention as something final and indisputable.)*
    SELECTED REFERENCES: The Art of Dreaming - Page [73.6-74.1] ("We are back again, harping on...manipulate the assemblage point for gain.)

SEE ALSO: *ASSEMBLAGE-POINT, ATTENTION-FIRST, WARRIOR-SORCERER, SORCERER-ANTIQUITY*

SORCERER-TRANSFORMATION-[THE SORCERERS' TRANSFORMATION]: *(Warriors know that sorcerers are capable of accomplishing actual physical transformations; they can adopt a wide variety of forms including those of animals and people; in fact, sorcerers who know exactly where to place their assemblage points can become anything they want.)*

SELECTED REFERENCES: **The Power of Silence - Page [56.9-57.9]** ("I don't quite understand what you're...said and looked at me questioningly.)

SEE ALSO: *ANIMAL-FORMS-ADOPTING, SHIFT-BELOW, ASSEMBLAGE-POINT-MOVING, CROW-TRANSFORMATION-CARLOS-(TOP), WORM-CAVORTING-WITH-(TOP)*

SORCERER-TRICK-[THE SORCERERS' TRICK]: *(Warrior-sorcerers do not think of explaining or changing the forces of the world; their trick is that they learn instead to use such forces by redirecting themselves and adapting to the direction of those forces; the sorcerers' grand trick is to be aware that they are dead; the ticket to impeccability must be wrapped in awareness.)*

SELECTED REFERENCES: **A Separate Reality - Page [214.2-214.4]** ("The world is indeed full of...to their direction. That's his trick.) **The Power of Silence - Page [195.3-195.5]** ("Am I dead too," don Juan...I've kept mine in mint condition.")

SEE ALSO: *WARRIOR-TRANSFORMATION, WARRIOR-SORCERER, SORCERER-TRICK, WARRIOR-DEATH-SYMBOLIC, WARRIOR-IMPECCABILITY-TICKET, POWER-FLOW*

SORCERER-UNDERNEATH-[THE SORCERER UNDERNEATH THE SURFACE]: *(Warriors know that human beings are all part of a most mysterious world, scratch the surface of the average man and you'll find a sorcerer underneath.)*

SELECTED REFERENCES: **The Power of Silence - Page [167.8-167.9]** ("I've told you over and over...others do it with total ease.)

SEE ALSO: *WORLD-MYSTERIOUS, SORCERY, RATIONALITY-VENEER*

SORCERER-VIEW-[THE SORCERERS' VIEW]: *(Warrior-sorcerers, by using their will, have succeeded in enlarging their view of the world; warriors understand that the bounds of those enormous views are powerful and they struggle to break them instead of being imprisoned by them; warriors understand that they must reach beyond the sorcerers' view if they are to reach the totality of themselves.)*

SELECTED REFERENCES: **Tales of Power - Page [244.5-245.4]** ("That's a difficult point to explain...ordinary man or to a sorcerer.)

SEE ALSO: *WARRIOR-TOTALITY, WARRIOR-SORCERER, KNOWLEDGE-VS-POWER, DESCRIPTION-WORLD*

SORCERER-VIRTUOSITY-[THE SORCERERS' VIRTUOSITY]: *(Warrior-sorcerers know that their virtuosity is to know precisely what is needed from the world of the inorganic beings; to take only what is needed from that realm is the warrior-sorcerers' greatest accomplishment.)*

SELECTED REFERENCES: **The Art of Dreaming - Page [109.3-109.9]** ("You have to continue your dreaming until...way of plummeting into a pitfall.")

SEE ALSO: *INORGANIC-BEINGS-REFUSING, WARRIOR-SORCERER, STALKING-STALKERS, WARRIORSHIP-VS-SORCERY, SORCERER-ACCOMPLISHMENT-TRANSCENDENTAL*

SORCERER-VITAL-ISSUES-DANGEROUS-[THE MOST DANGEROUS OF THE SORCERERS' VITAL ISSUES]: (Dealing with awareness as an energetic element open to the energy body is the most dangerous of the sorcerers' vital issues.)

SELECTED REFERENCES: The Art of Dreaming - Page [186.3-186.4] (After a long silence, don Juan...vital, and dangerous of those issues.)

SEE ALSO: *AWARENESS-ENERGETIC-ELEMENT, ENERGY-JOURNEYS-TWO, AWARENESS-MASTERY*

SORCERER-WARRIOR-[THE WARRIOR-SORCERER]: SEE: WARRIOR-SORCERER-[THE WARRIOR-SORCERER]

SORCERER-WARRIOR-FROM-[FROM WARRIOR TO SORCERER]: SEE: WARRIOR-SORCERER-FROM-[FROM WARRIOR TO SORCERER]

SORCERER-WARRIOR-SEER-[FROM WARRIOR TO SORCERER TO SEER]: SEE: WARRIOR-SORCERER-SEER-[FROM WARRIOR TO SORCERER TO SEER]

SORCERER-WAY-[THE SORCERERS' WAY]: SEE: WARRIOR-WAY-[THE WARRIORS' WAY]

SORCERER-WORLD-[THE SORCERERS' WORLD]: SEE: POWER-WORLD-[THE WORLD OF POWER]

SORCERER-WORLD-KEY-[THE KEY TO THE SORCERERS' WORLD]: (Warriors know that stopping the internal dialogue is the key to the sorcerers' world; the rest of the warriors' activities only act to accelerate the effect of stopping the internal dialogue.)

SELECTED REFERENCES: Tales of Power - Page [283.2-238.3] ("Stopping the internal dialogue is, however...effect of stopping the internal dialogue.")

SEE ALSO: *SORCERER-PASSAGEWAY, INTERNAL-DIALOGUE-STOPPING, STOPPING-WORLD*

SORCERER-WORLD-PASSAGEWAY-[THE PASSAGEWAY INTO THE WORLD OF SORCERERS]: SEE: SORCERER-PASSAGEWAY [THE PASSAGEWAY TO THE WORLD OF SORCERERS]

SORCERESS-CAPABILITY-[THE CAPABILITY OF A SORCERESS]: (Warriors know a true sorceress has capabilities far beyond those of any man when it comes to dreaming; a sorceress doesn't need any props.)

SELECTED REFERENCES: The Art of Dreaming - Page [187.6-188.2] (Don Juan chucked and said...the nagual woman has superb energy.")

SEE ALSO: *WOMEN, SORCERY, WARRIOR-FEMALE*

SORCERY-[SORCERY]: (Warriors know that sorcery is the application of knowledge and power by the individual; sorcery is a state of awareness; sorcery is the attempt to reestablish our knowledge of intent, the act of reaching the place of silent knowledge; sorcery can be a dead-end street or the key to a warriors' totality, depending on the warriors' temperament; the act of countermanding the normal system of perception and perceiving energy directly is what transforms a person into a sorcerer; anyone who succeeds in moving the assemblage point to a new position is a sorcerer, and from that position he can do all kinds of good and bad things to his fellow men; ideally, sorcery is a journey of return; we return victorious to the spirit, having descended into hell; the ability to find and follow the *energetic interferences in one's dreams is sorcery; sorcery is action; when the time comes, sorcerers will act their passion; sorcery is to apply one's will to a key joint; sorcerers don't have to "see" to be sorcerers, they simply have to know how to use their will; sorcery is not incantations and hocus-pocus; sorcery is the freedom to perceive the world in all the ways that are humanly possible.)*

SELECTED REFERENCES: **A Separate Reality** - Page **[10.2-10.7]** (By "practitioner" I mean a participant...of meaning with which it deals.) **A Separate Reality** - Page **[199.1-199.5]** ("To be a sorcerer is a...it and your car won't work.") **A Separate Reality** - Page **[214.2-214.7]** ("The world is indeed full of...the strength of being a warrior.) **Journey to Ixtlan** - Page **[viii.4-vii.6]** (I have maintained the practice of...to the points I want to raise.) **Tales of Power** - Page **[244.6-245.2]** (*Reason can* actually account in one...to that evasive totality of oneself.) **The Fire From Within** - Page **[x.6-x.8]** (It was in his teachings for...a seer, but also a nagual.) **The Fire From Within** - Page **[2.7-3.5]** ("We are going to be talking...like entering a dead-end street.") **The Fire From Within** - Page **[119.3-119.8]** (He stated once again that the...keeps your assemblage point rigidly fixed.") **The Fire From Within** - Page **[141.3-141.6]** (Still in a whisper, he said...her sorcery antics, jolted it loose.") **The Power of Silence** - Page **[ix.5-xi.9]** (At various times don Juan attempted...knowledge, depends on our own temperament.") **The Power of Silence** - Page **[xii.5-xii.9]** (Then don Juan began a most...cleaning one's connecting link to *intent*.) **The Power of Silence** - Page **[82.5-82.6]** ("Anyone who succeeds in moving his...that, they need morality and beauty.") **The Power of Silence** - Page **[103.4-103.5]** (Don Juan had stated his belief...the beginning, a return to paradise.) **The Power of Silence** - Page **[105.1-105.2]** (Examined in this way, sorcery becomes...of our being aware of *intent* .) **The Power of Silence** - Page **[159.9]** ("As I have already said to...spirit, having descended into hell.) **The Power of Silence** - Page **[219.6-219.7]** (He added that for the rational man...everything else that was humanly possible.) **The Power of Silence** - Page **[244.7-244.9]** ("I am just considering how our...out. It can only be experienced.") **The Art of Dreaming** - Page **[vii.3-vii.7]** (Over the past twenty years, I...he presented to me in his teachings.) **The Art of Dreaming** - Page **[29.1-29.2]** (He heavily stressed that the dreaming...them and follow them is sorcery.) **The Art of Dreaming** - Page **[76.3]** (Consequently, the old sorcerers were thoroughly...transforms a person into a sorcerer.) **The Art of Dreaming** - Page **[137.6]** ("Don't worry," he said laughing...the same way I act mine.) **The Art of Dreaming** - Page **[165.1-165.2]** (He said that I'd had, at...the simplicity and directness of sorcery.)

SEE ALSO: *SHAMANISM, KNOWLEDGE-PATH, ABSTRACT-RETURN, WARRIOR-INTENT-LINK, WARRIORSHIP-VS-SORCERY, WARRIOR-SORCERER, SORCERY-(ALL), SORCERER-(ALL)*

SORCERY-ACCOMPLISHMENT-MOST-DIFFICULT-[THE MOST DIFFICULT ACCOMPLISHMENT IN SORCERY]: *(Warriors know that the most difficult accomplishment in sorcery is moving the assemblage point beyond the sphere of the world we know in order to assemble another total world.)*

SELECTED REFERENCES: The Power of Silence - Page **[94.3-94.5]** (The nagual Elias then shifted his...sphere of the world we know.)
SEE ALSO: *SORCERY, WORLDS-OTHER-ASSEMBLING-TOTAL*

SORCERY-ALL-THERE-IS-[ALL THERE IS TO SORCERY]: *(Warriors know there are no procedures, methods or steps to sorcery; the only thing that matters is the movement of the assemblage point and no procedure can cause that; the movement of the assemblage point is something that happens all by itself.)*

SELECTED REFERENCES: **The Power of Silence** - Page **[161.7-161.8]** ("I have insisted to the point...effect that happens all by itself.")
SEE ALSO: *SORCERY, ASSEMBLAGE-POINT-MOVING, INTENT, WARRIOR-INSTRUCTION, WARRIOR-STEPS*

SORCERY-APPRENTICESHIP-[A SORCERY APPRENTICESHIP]:
(Warriors know that a sorcery apprenticeship is the way the spirit instructs man on the mysteries of sorcery; a route of artifice and subterfuge.)

SELECTED REFERENCES: **The Power of Silence - Page [52.9-53.3]** ("And again, as with the first...a route of artifice and subterfuge.)
SEE ALSO: *APPRENTICESHIP-NAGUALISM, SPIRIT-TRICKERY, ABSTRACT CORE-THIRD, SORCERY, ARTIFICE-SUBTERFUGE*

SORCERY-CHALLENGE-[SORCERY IS AN ENDLESS CHALLENGE]:
(Warriors know that they are faced with an ever-changing series of challenges with regard to their progress on the path of knowledge; if one thing does not work, another will, because in the end, it doesn't really matter.)
SELECTED REFERENCES: **The Art of Dreaming - Page [197.9]** ("You are going to postpone stalking...Sorcery is an endless challenge.)
SEE ALSO: *SORCERY, WARRIOR-CHALLENGE, KNOWLEDGE-PATH*

SORCERY-EFFECT-FIRST-[THE FIRST EFFECT OF SORCERY]: *(Warriors know that the first effect of the sorcery apprenticeship is the shift between normal and heightened awareness, which should not be confused with the first principle of sorcery, which is ruthlessness.)*
SELECTED REFERENCES: **The Power of Silence - Page [118.6-118.9]** ("The first principle should not be...only trying to help you remember.")
SEE ALSO: *SORCERY, ASSEMBLAGE-POINT-MOVING, AWARENESS-NORMAL, AWARENESS-HEIGHTENED, AWARENESS-RIGHT-LEFT, RUTHLESSNESS*

SORCERY-ESSENCE-[THE ESSENCE OF SORCERY]: *(Warriors know that the contradiction of intent is the essence of sorcery; intent is not something that one might move or command in any way, and yet one can use it, command it, or move it as one desires; the use of awareness as an energetic element is the essence of sorcery; the essential feature of sorcery is stopping the internal dialogue.)*
SELECTED REFERENCES: **The Second Ring of Power - Page [306.6-306.7]** (Don Juan had asserted time and...disengaging the attention of the tonal.) **The Power of Silence - Page [103.7-103.9]** (In a calm voice don Juan...said, is the essence of sorcery.) **The Art of Dreaming - Page [184.9-186.1]** ("I'm going to propose a line...all our physicality into other worlds.)
SEE ALSO: *INTERNAL-DIALOGUE-STOPPING, AWARENESS-ENERGETIC-ELEMENT, WARRIOR-CONTRADICTION-KNOWLEDGE, SORCERER-CONTRADICTIONS-TERMS-PRACTICE, INTENT-CONTRADICTION*

SORCERY-EXPERIENCE-[SORCERY CAN ONLY BE EXPERIENCED]:
(Warrior-sorcerers know that sorcery is the act of reaching the place of silent knowledge; this act cannot be reasoned out, it can only be experienced.)
SELECTED REFERENCES: **The Power of Silence - Page [244.7-244.9]** ("I am just considering how our...It can only be experienced.") **The Art of Dreaming - Page [10.1-10.2]** (The marvel of sorcery is that...hope that you will practice them.")
SEE ALSO: *SORCERY, KNOWLEDGE-SILENT, REASON, SORCERER-EXPERIENCE, WARRIOR-EXPERIENCE, WARRIOR-SORCERER*

SORCERY-EXPLANATIONS-TWO-[THE TWO EXPLANATIONS OF SORCERY]: *(Warriors can attempt to explain sorcery in two different ways; one is to speak of it in metaphorical terms as a world of magical dimensions; the other is to explain it in abstract terms proper to sorcery; neither of these explanations is adequate in truly explaining sorcery however; sorcery must be experienced to be understood because the sorcerers' realm is a realm of silent knowledge.)*
SELECTED REFERENCES: **The Art of Dreaming - Page [20.9-21.1]** (When explaining sorcery, sorcerers have two...rational mind of a western man.)
SEE ALSO: *SORCERY, KNOWLEDGE-SILENT, KNOWLEDGE-VS-LANGUAGE*

SORCERY-EXPLAINING-DESIRE-[THE DESIRE TO EXPLAIN SORCERY]: (*Warriors know that the desire to explain sorcery in cogent, well-reasoned terms is a typical affliction among sorcerers; the warrior must utilize this desire as an intellectual exercise to stalk themselves with, all the while remembering that perception has more possibilities than the mind can conceive.*)

SELECTED REFERENCES: The Power of Silence - Page [243.8-244.2] (Don Juan fixed me with his stare...possibilities than the mind can conceive.")
SEE ALSO: *EXPLANATIONS, SORCERY, KNOWLEDGE-VS-LANGUAGE, STALKING-ONESELF, WARRIOR-DIALOGUE, SORCERY-EXPLANATIONS-TWO*

SORCERY-FEAR-[THE FEAR OF SORCERY]: (*Warriors know that man's natural fear of sorcery is seated in his stupidity; man is afraid of sorcery because he is afraid of freedom, afraid of the freedom which is forever at his fingertips.*)

SELECTED REFERENCES: The Power of Silence - Page [219.7-219.9] ("Here is where the average man's...point can be made to move.")
SEE ALSO: *STUPIDITY-IGNORANCE, FEAR, FREEDOM, POWER-HIDDEN*

SORCERY-FUTILITY-PITFALLS-[THE FUTILITY AND PITFALLS OF SORCERY]: (*Warriors know that they do not need anyone to teach them sorcery, because there is really nothing to learn; warriors are also aware that sorcery practices have no intrinsic value, their worth is indirect since their real function is to make the assemblage point shift; sorcery removed from the context of sober and impeccable warriorship is a dead-end street; the manipulatory techniques of sorcery only serve to act upon our fellow men and the warrior has no interest in this kind of manipulation whatsoever; sorcery is an essentially futile endeavor with many pitfalls; sorcery does not help sorcerers live a better life but rather it hinders them and makes their lives more cumbersome and precarious; sorcery can distort us by giving us a taste of power without fortifying our hearts; this makes us domineering and weak in the face of the power we command; sorcery flatters sorcerers and caters only to their self-reflection; sorcery entices men and makes them prisoners; sorcery requires strength, but not the strength of the heart; sorcery is not constant, it is full of passions, jealousies and violence.*)

SELECTED REFERENCES: The Teachings of Don Juan - Page [24.4-24.7] ("Maizpinto, crystals and feathers...of knowing things that are useless?") The Teachings of Don Juan - Page [55.2] ("She distorts men. She gives them...the middle of their great power.") The Teachings of Don Juan - Page [66.1-67.2] ("I don't like its power...Perhaps he said quietly.) The Teachings of Don Juan - Page [186.7-186.9] (My benefactor was such a man...will not be able to return.) A Separate Reality - Page [167.6-167.7] (He felt there was no reason...hand, had no effect on men.) A Separate Reality - Page [199.1] ("To be a sorcerer is a terrible...the sorcerer is a sad fellow.") A Separate Reality - Page [214.4-214.5] ("A sorcerer is only slightly better...it makes his life cumbersome, precarious.") Tales of Power - Page [57.8-57.9] ("It was my error to mislead you...for you, only tales of power.") Tales of Power - Page [244.8-245.2] (I would say that sorcerers, by...to that evasive totality of oneself.) The Fire From Within - Page [119.5-119.8] ("I've mentioned to you that sorcery...keeps your assemblage point rigidly fixed.) The Fire From Within - Page [230.1-230.6] (Don Juan explained that the old seers...of the Eagle to be devoured.") The Fire From Within - [298.7-298.9] (Don Juan said that adventurous men...the futility of self-importance.) The Power of Silence - Page [xi.4-xi.5]] ("We don't need anyone to teach...and that he can reach it.") The Power of Silence - Page [104.1-105.2] (Don Juan explained that at one...of our being aware of *intent*.) The Art of Dreaming - Page [32.4-32.6] ("I've mentioned to you before that...can get swayed by that search.)

SEE ALSO: *SORCERY, POWER-PURSUIT, WARRIORSHIP-VS-SORCERY, SELF-REFLECTION, ASSEMBLAGE-POINT-MOVING, IMPECCABLE-MAN-NO-GUIDE, WARRIOR-SOBRIETY, WARRIOR-IMPECCABILITY, INORGANIC-BEINGS-TEACHINGS*

SORCERY-FUTILITY-RESOLUTION-[THE RESOLUTION OF THE FUTILITY OF SORCERY]: *(Warriors know that the new seers resolved the dilemmas of the futility of sorcery from a position of heightened awareness; the solution is not to simply choose an alternate world in which to die, but instead to choose total consciousness, total freedom.)*

SELECTED REFERENCES: **The Fire From Within - Page [298.9-299.2]** (One of the most fortunate decisions...but to choose total consciousness, total freedom.)

SEE ALSO: *WARRIORSHIP-VS-SORCERY, WARRIOR-DEATH-COMMAND*

SORCERY-GOAL-[THE GOAL OF SORCERY]: *(Warrior-sorcerers know that one of the most important goals of sorcery is to reach the luminous cocoon; this goal is fulfilled through the use of dreaming and a systematic exertion of "not-doing".)*

SELECTED REFERENCES: **The Eagle's Gift - Page [18.2-18.4]** (He had also said that one...become conscious of its luminous segment.)

SEE ALSO: *LUMINOUS-COCOON, DREAMING-ART, NOT-DOING*

SORCERY-HINGE-[THE HINGE OF SORCERY]: *(Warriors know that the hinge of sorcery is the mystery of the assemblage point.)*

SELECTED REFERENCES: **The Art of Dreaming - Page [172.1-172.5]** ("I propose that you do one...but you have to repeat it.")

SEE ALSO: *ASSEMBLAGE-POINT, LUMINOUS-BEINGS-MYSTERY, DREAMER-INVOCATION, POWER-HINGE*

SORCERY-LEARNING-[LEARNING SORCERY]: *(Warriors know that by learning sorcery, they are simply learning to save their energy; this energy, once they learn to conserve it, enables sorcerers to handle energy fields that were inaccessible to them before; that is sorcery, the ability to perceive emanations that are not employed in perceiving the ordinary world we know.)*

SELECTED REFERENCES: **The Power of Silence - Page [x.9-xi.2]** ("Think of it this way," he...perceive something which ordinary perception cannot.)

SEE ALSO: *SORCERY, PERCEPTION, ENERGY, WARRIOR-SORCERER, WARRIOR-IMPECCABILITY*

SORCERY-LEARNING-NOT-[THE APPRENTICE IS NOT LEARNING SORCERY]: *(Warriors know that they are not really learning sorcery, but how to master three aspects of the sorcerers' ancient knowledge, the mastery of awareness, the mastery of stalking, and the mastery of intent; true warriors are not just sorcerers, they are also seers.)*

SELECTED REFERENCES: **The Fire From Within - Page [x.6-x.8]** (It was in his teachings for...seer, but also a nagual.)

SEE ALSO: *WARRIORSHIP-VS-SORCERY, WARRIOR-MASTERIES-THREE*

SORCERY-LEGACY-[THE LEGACY OF SORCERY]: *(Warriors know that the legacy of sorcery is the sustained use of heightened awareness over thousands of years of painful struggle; sorcerers have gained specific insights into intent, and have passed this direct knowledge on from generation to generation.)*

SELECTED REFERENCES: **The Power of Silence - Page [xiii.3-xiii.4]** (Don Juan explained that by using...generation to generation to the present.)

SEE ALSO: *AWARENESS-HEIGHTENED, INTENT, KNOWLEDGE-SILENT, KNOWLEDGE-DIRECT, APPRENTICESHIP-NAGUALISM*

SORCERY-LINEAGE-CONCURRENT-[THE EXISTENCE OF CONCURRENT SORCERY LINEAGES]: (*Warriors know that members of concurrent sorcery lineages do not cross paths; each of the existing lineages was founded by a surviving Toltec and the number of lines are few; the members of those lineages now live like solitary birds because the seers who lived during the Spanish conquest set it up that way in order to avoid extermination at the hands of their Spanish oppressors.*)
SELECTED REFERENCES: The Fire From Within - Page [6.4-7.5] ("Were there a great many new...eleven, and some up to fifteen.)
SEE ALSO: *TOLTECS*

SORCERY-MARVEL-[THE MARVEL OF SORCERY]: (*Warriors know that the marvel of sorcery is that every sorcerer has to prove everything with personal experience.*)
SELECTED REFERENCES: The Art of Dreaming - Page [10.1-10.2] (The marvel of sorcery is that...hope that you will practice them.")
SEE ALSO: *SORCERY, WARRIOR-SORCERER, SORCERER-EXPERIENCE, WARRIOR-EXPERIENCE*

SORCERY-PARADOX-[THE PARADOX OF SORCERY]: (*Warriors know that the paradox of sorcery is that there is really nothing for warriors to learn about sorcery; warriors just go about the process of becoming convinced that they can reach the incalculable hidden power in their being; warriors don't need anyone to teach them sorcery.*)
SELECTED REFERENCES : The Power of Silence - Page [xi.3-xi.7] ("Everything I've put you through...hard to convince as you are.) The Power of Silence - Page [105.1-105.2] (Examined in this way, sorcery becomes...of our being aware of *intent*.)
SEE ALSO : *SORCERY, NAGUALISM, POWER-HIDDEN, WARRIOR-INSTRUCTION, WARRIOR-SORCERER, WARRIOR-CONVINCING, IMPECCABLE-MAN-NO-GUIDE, WARRIOR-CONTRADICTION-KNOWLEDGE*

SORCERY-PERCEPTION-[SORCERY AND PERCEPTION]: (*Warriors know that sorcery is the act of embodying some specialized premises about the nature and role of perception in molding the sorcerers' world; sorcerers learn to change perception at its social base.*)
SELECTED REFERENCES: The Art of Dreaming - Page [vii.5] (For don Juan, sorcery was the...in molding the universe around us.)
SEE ALSO: *SORCERY, PERCEPTION, PERCEPTION-CHANGING-SOCIAL-BASE*

SORCERY-PITFALL-[THE PITFALLS OF SORCERY]: SEE: SORCERY-FUTILITY-PITFALL-[THE FUTILITY AND PITFALLS OF SORCERY]

SORCERY-PRACTICAL-[THE PRACTICAL PART OF SORCERY]: (*Warriors know that the practical part of sorcery is another term for concreteness.*)
SELECTED REFERENCES: The Art of Dreaming - Page [2.4-2.5] ("What do you call concreteness, don...of the sorcerers of the past.")
SEE ALSO: *CONCRETENESS, WARRIOR-SORCERER*

SORCERY-PRACTICAL-SIDE-[THE PRACTICAL SIDE OF SORCERY]: (*Warriors know that sorcery is a practical art and that it exists as a practical reality; the principles of the normal world no longer function as soon as the position of the assemblage point is displaced beyond certain boundaries; this means that sorcerers are actually capable of accomplishing impossible acts because they are no longer bound by the forces which bind the average man.)*

SELECTED REFERENCES: **The Art of Dreaming - Page [211.2-211.9]** ("I understand all that," he said...was an abhorrent and untenable position.)

SEE ALSO: *SORCERY, ASSEMBLAGE-POINT-MOVING, ASSEMBLAGE POINT-POSITION, WARRIOR-SORCERER, SORCERY-PRAGMATIC-INTENT-LINK, SORCERY-TRAJECTORY, WARRIOR-DETERMINATION*

SORCERY-PRACTICE-[THE PRACTICE OF SORCERY]: *(Warriors know that the principles of sorcery are not meant to be memorized, they are meant to be practiced.)*

SELECTED REFERENCES: **The Art of Dreaming - Page [10.1-10.2]** (The marvel of sorcery is that...hope that you will practice them.")

SEE ALSO: *SORCERY, WARRIOR-ARTS, SORCERY-PRINCIPLES, WARRIOR-SORCERER*

SORCERY-PRACTICE-VALUE-TRUE-[THE TRUE VALUE OF SORCERY PRACTICE]: *(Warriors know that the true value of sorcery practices is to make the assemblage point shift by making the first attention release its control on that point.)*

SELECTED REFERENCES: **The Fire From Within - Page [119.5-119.8]** ("I've mentioned to you that sorcery...keeps your assemblage point rigidly fixed.")

SEE ALSO: *SORCERY-PRACTICE, ATTENTION-FIRST, WARRIOR-SORCERER*

SORCERY-PRAGMATIC-INTENT-LINK-[THE PRAGMATIC SIDE OF THE SORCERERS' LINK WITH INTENT]: *(Warriors know that sorcerers are keenly aware of their link with intent, not in an intuitive or theoretical way, but in the very pragmatic and deliberate way of sorcerers.)*

SELECTED REFERENCES: **The Power of Silence - Page [49.6]** (He conceded that poets ere keenly...the deliberate, pragmatic way of sorcerers.)

SEE ALSO: *SORCERY-PRACTICAL-SIDE, WARRIOR-SORCERER, WARRIOR-INTENT-LINK*

SORCERY-PREMISE-BASIC-[THE BASIC PREMISE OF SORCERY]: *(For warrior-sorcerers, the basic premise of sorcery is that the world is not real as we believe it is; reality for sorcerers is only a description; the capacity to perceive the energetic essence of things is the basic premise of sorcery; this capacity is known as "seeing".)*

SELECTED REFERENCES: **Journey to Ixtlan - Page [viii.7-ix.6]** (For the purpose of presenting my argument...be taken as a serious proposition.) **The Art of Dreaming - Page [2.9-3.2]** (Don Juan explained that the their...things, a capacity they call *seeing*.)

SEE ALSO: *SEEING, WARRIOR-SORCERER, REALITY-INTERPRETATION, ENERGETIC-ESSENCE, DESCRIPTION-WORLD-SORCERER, RULE-PRECEPTS*

SORCERY-PRICE-[THE PRICE OF SORCERY]: *(Warriors know the terrible price they must pay for the knowledge of the inorganic beings; they must pay with their energy, their lives, their devotion to the inorganic beings, and ultimately by forfeiting their chance for freedom.)*

SELECTED REFERENCES: **The Art of Dreaming - Page [66.8-66.9]** ("I didn't see any point in...In other words, our freedom.") **The Art of Dreaming - Page [68.2-68.3]** ("Do I gather, don Juan, that...will agree with me. You'll see.")

SEE ALSO: *FREEDOM-INORGANIC-BEINGS, INORGANIC-BEINGS-TEACHINGS, INORGANIC-BEINGS-TRICKERY*

SORCERY-PRINCIPLE-[SORCERY PRINCIPLES]: *(Warriors know that the sorcery principles are the practicing arts of the sorcerer.)*

SELECTED REFERENCES: **The Art of Dreaming - Page [10.1-10.2]** (The marvel of sorcery is that...hope that you will practice them.") **The Art of Dreaming - Page [210.9-211.1]** ("That being in the church is...embodied all the principles of sorcery.")
SEE ALSO: *SORCERY, WARRIOR-SORCERER, WARRIOR-ARTS*

SORCERY-PRINCIPLE-FIRST-[THE FIRST PRINCIPLE OF SORCERY]:
(Warriors know that ruthlessness is the first principle of sorcery.)
SELECTED REFERENCES : **The Power of Silence - Page [118.6-118.9]** ("The first principle should not be...only trying to help you remember.")
SEE ALSO : *RUTHLESSNESS*

SORCERY-PROCEDURES-[SORCERY PROCEDURES]: (Warriors know that there are no procedures in sorcery, no methods, no steps; there is only the movement of the assemblage point and no procedure can cause that; it is an effect that happens all by itself.)
SELECTED REFERENCES: **The Power of Silence - Page [161.7-161.8]** ("I have insisted to the point of...effect that happens all by itself.")
SEE ALSO: *ASSEMBLAGE-POINT-MOVING*

SORCERY-REDUCTIONS-[THE FOUR REDUCTIONS OF SORCERY]:
(Warriors know that the four reductions of sorcery are the various ways in which sorcerers have focused their connecting link with intent; although there are remarkable differences between these four areas of interest, they are all equally corrupting; in the end the warrior must instead focus his connecting link with intent on its capacity to set him free to light the fire from within.)
SELECTED REFERENCES: **The Power of Silence - Page [104.1-104.8]** (Don Juan explained that at one...to light the fire from within.)
SEE ALSO: *INTENT, FIRE-WITHIN, WARRIOR-SORCERER, WARRIOR-INTENT-LINK*

SORCERY-RIDDLES-[THE RIDDLES OF SORCERY]: SEE: RIDDLE-MIND-[THE RIDDLE OF THE MIND] , RIDDLE-HEART-[THE RIDDLE OF THE HEART], RIDDLE-SPIRIT-[THE RIDDLE OF THE SPIRIT], RIDDLE-DREAMER-DREAMED-[THE RIDDLE OF THE DREAMER AND THE DREAMED]

SORCERY-STORIES-[THE SORCERY STORIES]: (Warriors know that the sorcery stories are the best way for warriors to examine their past for a point of reference, a chance to examine intent; nothing gives warriors a better view of intent than examining stories of other warriors battling to understand the same force; the abstract cores of the sorcery stories are shades of realization, degrees of being aware of intent; the sorcery stories are essentially no more than pacifiers for those who are uncomfortable with the silence of the abstract.)
SELECTED REFERENCES: **The Power of Silence - Page [xviii.5-xix.1]** (I have not pursued the subjects directly...arranged in an increasing level of complexity.) **The Power of Silence - Page [1.5-3.4]** (Don Juan, whenever it was pertinent, used...relive them, so to speak.") **The Power of Silence - Page [6.9-7.6]** (He said, for example, that I...that caps and seals a pyramid.") **The Power of Silence - Page [41.5]** ("You like words," he said accusingly...you and make you feel secure.") **The Power of Silence - Page [105.1-105.2]** (Examined in this way, sorcery becomes...of our being aware of *intent*.) **The Power of Silence - Page [204.6]** ("Both the jaguar and I can read thoughts...get the maximum effect from them.") **The Art of Dreaming - Page [139.3-139.4]** (You certainly know more than...source of sorcerers' stories for us.")
SEE ALSO: *WARRIOR-PAST, ABSTRACT-CORES, WARRIOR-INTENT-LINK, ABSTRACT-SILENCE*

SORCERY-TASK-GRAND-[THE GRAND TASK OF SORCERY]: (Warriors know that the grand task of sorcerers is to bring forth the idea that, in order to evolve, man must first free his awareness from its bindings to the social order.)
SELECTED REFERENCES: **The Art of Dreaming - Page [176.6-176.8]** ("Do you think, don Juan, that...import of evolving is another matter.")
SEE ALSO: *WARRIOR-FREEDOM-TOTAL, MAN-EVOLUTION, PERCEPTION-CHANGING-SOCIAL-BASE, PERCEPTION-SOCIAL-BASE*

SORCERY-TASKS-TRADITIONAL-[THE TRADITIONAL TASKS OF SORCERY]: (Warrior-sorcerers know that remembering what has happened to them in the second attention is one of the most difficult and complex traditional tasks of sorcery and warriorship; from the spirit's point of view, this task consists of clearing the connecting link with intent.)
SELECTED REFERENCES: **The Power of Silence - Page [xiii.3-xiii.4]** (He said that the task of...the standards of awareness of everyday life.) **The Power of Silence - Page [47.1-47.4]** (Don Juan then said that he...an indefinite sense of needing something.) **The Art of Dreaming - Page [17.5-17.9]** (Ordinarily, apprentices do not remember these...lifetime to fulfilling this task of remembering.)
SEE ALSO: *RECOLLECTION-SORCERER, WARRIOR-SORCERER, WARRIOR-INTENT-LINK, REMEMBERING-BODY*

SORCERY-TECHNIQUES-[SORCERY TECHNIQUES]: (Warriors know that the sorcery techniques are the practices of the old seers; the legacy of the ancient Toltecs; obscure formulas, incantations and procedures that have to do with the handling of intent; the new seers realized that these practices are not only useless but injurious to the warriors' total being; when the new seers reevaluated the ancient Toltecs' knowledge, they shifted their emphasis away from those bizarre techniques.)
SELECTED REFERENCES: **The Fire From Within - Page [80.1-80.8]** ("In explaining awareness," he said...of the Eagle's emanations, or *intent.*) **The Fire From Within - Page [119.3-119.8]** (He stated once again that the...keeps your assemblage point rigidly fixed.") **The Fire From Within - Page [165.7-166.4]** (He added that the old seers...to become trees to do that.") **The Fire From Within - Page [234.7-235.9]** (Don Juan said that the new...both show you the same sample.") **The Art of Dreaming - Page [2.4-2.5]** (What do you call concreteness, don...of the sorcerers of the past.")
SEE ALSO: *SEER-OLD, TOLTECS, CYCLE-NEW, SORCERY-FUTILITY-PITFALLS, SORCERY-FUTILITY-RESOLUTION*

SORCERY-TRAJECTORY-[THE TRAJECTORY OF SORCERY]: (Warriors know that in practical terms, the trajectory of sorcery is threefold; 1) first, sorcery frees the existing energy in warriors through the impeccable following of the warriors' way; 2) second, sorcery enables warriors to use that energy to develop the energy body by means of dreaming; 3) third, sorcery enables warriors to use awareness as an element of the environment in order to travel with both their energy bodies and physical bodies into other total worlds.)
SELECTED REFERENCES: **The Art of Dreaming - Page [185.9-186.1]**(Don Juan explained that the use...all our physicality into other worlds.)
SEE ALSO: *WARRIOR-WAY, WARRIOR-IMPECCABILITY, DREAMING-SETTING-UP, DREAMING-ART, ENERGY-BODY, AWARENESS-ENERGETIC-ELEMENT, WORLD-OTHER, SORCERY-PRACTICAL-SIDE*

SORCERY-VS-WARRIORSHIP-[WARRIORSHIP VS SORCERY]: SEE: WARRIORSHIP-VS-SORCERY-[WARRIORSHIP VS SORCERY]

SORCERY-WILL-[SORCERY AND THE WILL]: (*Warriors know that sorcerers don't have to "see" to be sorcerers; all they have to know is how to use their will.*)
SELECTED REFERENCES: A Separate Reality - Page [19.2-19.3] ("Sorcery is to apply one's will...is how to use his will.")
SEE ALSO: SORCERY, SEEING, WILL

SOUL-BATTLE-[A BATTLE FOR THE SOUL]-(TOP)

SOUL-LOSS-[THE LOSS OF THE SOUL]-(TOP)

SOUNDNESS-MIND-[SOUNDNESS OF MIND]: SEE: SANITY-[SANITY]

*SOUTH-[SOUTHERLY WOMEN]: (*Warriors know that the southerly woman is the fourth of a nagual's party of female warriors; she is called growth; she is nurturing, loud, shy and warm, like a hot wind; southerly women are friendly and warm.*)
SELECTED REFERENCES: The Eagle's Gift - Page [174.5-174.8] (The female warriors are called the...shy, warm, like hot wind.) The Eagle's Gift - Page [185.6-186.2] (A group composed of two sets of...lose their composure and be raving mad.) The Eagle's Gift - Page [192.4-192.6] (The south was really the night...they did not light their lanterns.)
SEE ALSO: WARRIOR-FEMALE, POWER-DIRECTION

SOUTH-DIRECTION-[THE SOUTHERLY DIRECTION]: (*Warriors know that the southerly direction is important because power flows from south to north in its ceaseless flux; the warriors' life force flows from the south and leaves flowing towards the north; the opening to the nagual's world is from the south.*)
SELECTED REFERENCES: Journey to Ixtlan - Page [155.4-155.5] ("The dying sun will glow on...to the south. To the vastness.") The Eagle's Gift - Page [189.5-189.7] (He conceded, however, that a minimal...go through if they so decided.) The Eagle's Gift - Page [242.3-242.4] (My task was to take them...as a group into the unknown.) The Power of Silence - Page [191.3-191.5] ("I knelt and faced the southeast...was finally dead! I was finally free!")
SEE ALSO: POWER-FLOW, POWER-DIRECTION

SPARKS-GORDA-[LA GORDA'S SPARKS]-(TOP): SEE: GORDA-SPARKS-[LA GORDA'S SPARKS]-(TOP)

SPEED-[SPEEDING OR CHANGING SPEED]: (*Warriors define speed as the quickness necessary to grasp the fleeting world of the second attention; the characteristic "speeding" sensation of left side awareness; warriors have a sense of grasping things with precision and directness, of moving at breakneck speed; the warrior commands his death with his speed.*)
SELECTED REFERENCES: A Separate Reality - Page [112.1-112.3] ("What do you mean by a...the body and its strength intact.") A Separate Reality - Page [132.5-133.1] ("Is smoking the only way to...something you can fool around with.") A Separate Reality - Page [177.6] ("You moved very fast," he said...hard time keeping up with you.") A Separate Reality - Page [211.5-211.6] (He giggled like a child without answering...and she was a relentless enemy.) A Separate Reality - Page [226.2-226.3] ("Everything is meaningful for a sorcerer...can give us that grasping speed.) Journey to Ixtlan - Page [234.2-234.4] ("There is something you ought to...speed, the prowess to pick it up.) The Second Ring of Power - Page [83.3-83.4] (The peculiar sound at the base...having experienced it in his company.) The Second Ring of Power - Page [211.6-211.8] ("Hours must have passed. Suddenly I...to accomplish anything that one needed.) The Eagle's Gift - Page [58.7-58.8] (Josephina has just told you what...but my body cannot understand him.) The Eagle's Gift - Page [164.1-164.2] (She said that sometimes he would even...in the world had been changed.) The Eagle's Gift - Page [165.4-165.7] (Another feature of those states of...Gorda and I understood as speeding.) The Eagle's Gift - Page [292.9-293.1] (I would experience the...a mountainous area, rugged and inhospitable.) The Fire From Within - Page [208.1-208.3] ("Don't look at Genaro," a voice...moving around us, at great speed.) The Fire From Within - Page [213.7-213.8] ("The speed of that boost will dissolve...still roaming

is some incomprehensible immensity.") **The Fire From Within - Page [219.6-219.7]** (He also told me not to...extremely fast by my *seeing* window.) **The Fire From Within - Page [296.1-296.3]** (I started to follow them, but...windlike force blew the world away.) **The Power of Silence - Page [207.2-208.3]** ("The greatest difference between an average...the speed to pull me out.)
SEE ALSO: *SORCERER-DEATH, POINT-THIRD, FIRE-WITHIN, ATTENTION-SECOND, WARRIOR-DEATH-COMMAND*

SPINNING-ALLIES-[SPINNING WITH THE ALLY]: SEE: ALLIES-SPINNING-[SPINNING WITH THE ALLY]

SPIRIT-[SPIRIT]: *(Warriors know the spirit is the abstract, the spirit is intent; the spirit is something with no parallel in the human condition; warriors meet the spirit without thinking about it or seeing it or touching it or feeling its presence; the spirit is the force that sustains the universe; the spirit is nothing that can be seen or felt, but it is always looming over us; sometimes it comes to some of us, but most of the time it seems indifferent; the spirit is not an entity or a presence; it has no essence and yet it can be beckoned and enticed to come forward.)*

SELECTED REFERENCES: **A Separate Reality - Page [63.7-63.8]** ("Mescalito changes everything," don Juan said...sometime even against our will.") **Journey to Ixtlan - Page [9.2-9.4]** (I staged a weak final complaint...he said softly and waved good-bye.) **The Eagle' Gift - Page [21.6-21.8]** ("When you worry about what to...won't let you live in peace.") **The Power of Silence - Page [11.2-11.5]** ("Can you explain *intent* to me...it the spirit, *intent,* the abstract.") **The Power of Silence - Page [14.8-14.9]** (All of a sudden he said...particular, are tuned to such revelations.") **The Power of Silence - Page [36.6-39.3]** ("The nagual Elias explained that my...touching it or feeling its presence.") **The Power of Silence - Page [49.5-49.7]** ("I like poems for many reasons...hit pretty close to it, though.") **The Power of Silence - Page [103.7-103.9]** (In a calm voice don Juan...said, is the essence of sorcery.) **The Power of Silence - Page [115.8]** ("Your argument is glib and convincing...see the flaw in your argument.") **The Power of Silence - Page [119.1-119.7]** (He waited a moment to see...It is as simple as that.") **The Power of Silence - Page [122.1-122.2]** (I had asked don Juan how...which had moved those assemblage points.) **The Power of Silence - Page [160.9-161.3]** ("You are forgetting about something essential...one about to lose his patience.) **The Power of Silence - Page [162.5-162.9]** (He stated that what seemed a...mere presence of an impeccable nagual.") **The Power of Silence - Page [191.2-191.3]** (The spirit could not possibly have cared...for the spirit to pay attention.) **The Power of Silence - Page [223.5-223.9]** (I voiced the first question that...feature shared by everything there is.") **The Power of Silence - Page [227.6-227.8]** ("How do sorcerers resolve this problem...Why? No one knows.") **The Power of Silence - Page [231.1-231.4]** ("I thought he was talking nonsense...beckon something that does not exist.") **The Art of Dreaming - Page [200.1-200.2]** ("Will she continue my dreaming practices...are mere pawns in its hands.)
SEE ALSO: *INTENT, ABSTRACT-THE, POWER, FORCE-RULES-LIVES, SPIRIT-(ALL)*

SPIRIT-ANIMAL-WILD-[THE SPIRIT IS LIKE A WILD ANIMAL]: *(Warriors know that in many ways the spirit is like a wild animal; most of the time it keeps its distance until a moment when something entices it forward.)*

SELECTED REFERENCES: **The Power of Silence - Page [37.8-37.9]** (I kept quiet. And he continued...then that the spirit manifested itself.)
SEE ALSO: *SPIRIT, INSANE-RELATIVE*

SPIRIT-AWARENESS-[THE AWARENESS OF THE SPIRIT]: *(Warriors know that their minimal chance is not instruction, but rather the process of being made aware of the spirit.)*

SELECTED REFERENCES: **The Power of Silence - Page [159.3-159.5]** ("In the sorcerers' world there are only...being made aware of the spirit.")
SEE ALSO: *SPIRIT, WARRIOR-CHANCE-MINIMAL, WARRIOR-INSTRUCTION*

SPIRIT-AWARENESS-CAPACITY-ADJUST-[THE SPIRIT MAKES FINAL

ADJUSTMENTS IN THE WARRIORS' CAPACITY FOR AWARENESS]-
(TOP)

SPIRIT-BALANCE-[THE BALANCE OF THE SPIRIT]: (Warriors know they
must live in keeping with the warriors' way in order to balance the spirit.)
      SELECTED REFERENCES: Tales of Power - Page [26.8-27.2] ("We've never talked
about moths...proper light to talk about moths.")
      SEE ALSO: WARRIOR-SPIRIT, WARRIOR-WAY, WARRIOR-IMPECCABILITY,
WARRIOR-BALANCE, BALANCE

SPIRIT-CATCHER-[A SPIRIT CATCHER]: (Warriors know a spirit
catcher is a fiber with which warriors may call allies or spirits; spirit
catchers may be of many varied configurations but they are not made out of
anything per se; a spirit catcher is the thing itself.)
      SELECTED REFERENCES: A Separate Reality - Page [160.8-163.3] (He then took a
sort of whitish..."You will know that very soon.") A Separate Reality - Page [166.1-166.8] (He
took his string and tensed it...and came around to my side.) A Separate Reality - Page [221.8-
221.9] (He said that he was going to...me the message I was seeking.) A Separate Reality - Page
[223.8-223.9] (I heard again the piercing wail...a hole, a very large hole.) A Separate Reality -
Page [224.9-225.1] (I heard once more the eerie wail...as I had seen him before.) A Separate
Reality - Page [226.6-227.3] ("But all this is not important...will to hold them at bay.") A
Separate Reality - Page [227.8-228.4] ("Can I use water at another place...after you know him
very well.") Tales of Power - Page [88.2-88.4] (I believed that don Genaro had...between the
thumb and index finger.) Tales of Power - Page [219.1-219.7] (Pablito and Nestor nearly died
laughing...he did not have one himself.) Tales of Power - Page [289.9-290.3] ("Witness, please
squeeze your spirit catcher...helpful in the best way he could.) The Second Ring of Power -
Page [313.6-313.9] (She explained that the particular formation...the east, in his right hand.)
      SEE ALSO: ALLIES, SPIRITS

SPIRIT-CATCHER-SEARCH-[IN SEARCH OF A SPIRIT CATCHER]-(TOP)

SPIRIT-COMMANDS-[THE COMMANDS OF THE SPIRIT]: (Warriors
know that the manifestations of the spirit can either be almost indiscernible
or they can be like commands; with regard to apprentices to the nagual, the
more difficult the command of the spirit, the more difficult the disciple will
turn out to be.)
      SELECTED REFERENCES: The Power of Silence - Page [41.6-42.2] (Then he
reminded me that I...spared no effort to satisfy it.) The Power of Silence - Page [43.4-43.9] ("The
difference is discernible in the manifestations...door, it nearly banged it down.") The Art of
Dreaming - Page [200.1-200.2] ("Will she continue my dreaming practices...are mere pawns in its
hands.)
      SEE ALSO: SPIRIT, OMENS, SPIRIT-MANIFESTATIONS, SPIRIT-
COMMANDING

SPIRIT-COMMANDING-[COMMANDING THE SPIRIT]: (Warriors know
that commanding the spirit is another term for the handling of the spirit; the
spirit is an abstract which warriors know without words or thoughts, yet
without the slightest chance or desire to understand it, warriors recognize
and command the spirit; they beckon it, they entice it, they become familiar
with it, and they express it with their acts; when warriors command the
spirit, they in essence command the movement of the assemblage point; the
moment of blackness, the moment of silence gives rise to the intent to direct
the spirit, to command it and make it do things; this is why it's called will,
the intent and the effect are will, they are tied together; for instance the
intent of flying produces the effect of flying; commanding the spirit is
another term for commanding the assemblage point; in order to command

the spirit one needs energy and the only thing that stores energy for the warrior is impeccability.)

SELECTED REFERENCES: **The Eagle's Gift** - **Page [143.3-143.5]** (The Nagual said that it is a...flying produces the effect of flying.") **The Power of Silence** - **Page [38.5-38.7]** ("For a sorcerer, the spirit is...and expresses it with his acts.") **The Power of Silence** - **Page [103.7-103.8]** (In a calm voice don Juan...or move it as one desires.) **The Power of Silence** - **Page [228.2-228.3]** ("Sorcerers say that in order to...energy for us is our impeccability.")

SEE ALSO: *INTENT, INTENT-BECKONING, ASSEMBLAGE-POINT-MOVING INNER-SILENCE, STOPPING-WORLD, WILL, WARRIOR-IMPECCABILITY, ASSEMBLAGE-POINT-MOVING-INTENT, SPIRIT*

SPIRIT-CONDUIT-[THE CONDUIT OF THE SPIRIT]: *(Warriors know naguals are living conduits of the spirit; since they spend a lifetime impeccably redefining their connecting link with intent, and since they possess more energy than the average man, naguals can let the spirit express itself through them; naguals can be conduits only after the spirit has manifested its willingness to be used, either almost imperceptibly or through outright commands; once the willingness of the spirit has been revealed, naguals spare no effort to satisfy it.)*

SELECTED REFERENCES: **The Power of Silence** - **Page [5.6-5.8]** ("That first abstract core is a story...inclination really to examine the matter.) **The Power of Silence** - **Page [41.6-42.2]** (Then he reminded me that I...spared no effort to satisfy it.) **The Power of Silence** - **Page [53.4-53.5]** (Don Juan told me that if...and subterfuge in order to teach.) **The Power of Silence** - **Page [119.4-119.5]** ("I've told you the nagual is...the spirit expresses itself through him.) **The Power of Silence** - **Page [122.1-122.3]** (I had asked don Juan how the...which had moved the assemblage points.)

SEE ALSO: *SPIRIT, NAGUAL-MAN-WOMAN, WARRIOR-INTENT-LINK, SPIRIT-WILLINGNESS, OMENS, SPIRIT-COMMANDS*

SPIRIT-CONTACT-[CONTACT WITH THE SPIRIT]: *(Warriors know that mere contact with the spirit can bring about a movement of the assemblage point.)*

SELECTED REFERENCES: **The Power of Silence** - **Page [119.3-120.3]** (I remarked that his statements that...the spirit move my assemblage point.)

SEE ALSO: *SPIRIT, ASSEMBLAGE-POINT-MOVING, ASSEMBLAGE-POINT-MOVING-SPIRIT*

SPIRIT-DEER-[SPIRIT DEER]-(TOP): SEE: MAGICAL-DEER-[MAGICAL DEER]-(TOP)

*SPIRIT-DESCENT-[THE DESCENT OF THE SPIRIT]: *(Warriors know that the fourth abstract core is the descent of the spirit or the act of the spirit revealing itself to the warrior; sorcerers describe it as the spirit lying in ambush for us and then descending on us, its prey; the spirit's descent is always shrouded, it happens but it seems not to have happened at all; the somersault of thought is the descent of the spirit; the descent of the spirit is being moved by intent; the spirit chooses a moment when the man is unguarded and lets its presence by itself move the assemblage point to the place of no pity.)*

SELECTED REFERENCES: **The Power of Silence** - **Page [88.5-88.9]** ("Before we leave for the cave...seems not to have happened at all.") **The Power of Silence** - **Page [96.2-96.9]** (The young actor, hearing his own...was quite out of the ordinary.) **The Power of Silence** - **Page [118.3-118.6]** ("As I have already told you...way, the first principle of sorcery.)

SEE ALSO: *ABSTRACT-CORE-FOURTH, SPIRIT, THOUGHT-SOMERSAULT, PITY-PLACE-NO, RUTHLESSNESS*

SPIRIT-DECISIONS-[THE DECISIONS OF THE SPIRIT]: (*Warriors know that the decisions of the spirit is another abstract core; warriors do their utmost and then, without any remorse or regrets, let the spirit decide the outcome.*)

SELECTED REFERENCES: The Power of Silence - Page [194.1-194.4] (He reminded me that he had taught...get to discussing that basic core.)

SEE ALSO: *ABSTRACT-CORES, SPIRIT, SPIRIT-DESIGNS, WARRIOR-DECISIONS*

SPIRIT-DESIGNS-[THE DESIGNS OF THE SPIRIT]: (*Warriors know they must move through life watching for the designs of the spirit to reveal themselves; instead of allowing pettiness to choose all the things in their lives, they become silent and proceed as the spirit directs them to proceed.*)

SELECTED REFERENCES: The Power of Silence - Page [43.1-43.2] ("Reviving an apprentice's link is a nagual's...simple or the most complex labyrinths.") The Power of Silence - Page [189.6-189.7] (One day, however, don Juan thought...to work under the scorching sun.) The Power of Silence - Page [193.9-194.1] ("I did that with my feelings for...could decide the outcome of that affection.") The Art of Dreaming - Page [150.6-150.7] ("But it's going to be a mess...the event the spirit points out.") The Art of Dreaming - Page [200.1-200.2] ("Will she continue my dreaming practices...are mere pawns in its hands.)

SEE ALSO: *LETTING-GO, SPIRIT, SPIRIT-GESTURES-OF, POWER-DESIGNS, SPIRIT-DECISIONS*

SPIRIT-DUSTING-LINK-[DUSTING THE LINK WITH THE SPIRIT]-(TOP)

SPIRIT-GESTURE-FOR-[A GESTURE FOR THE SPIRIT]: (*Warriors know that a gesture for the spirit is a display warriors make for the spirit; the spirit only listens when the speaker speaks in gestures, gestures in the sense of acts of true abandon, acts of largesse and humor; through gestures for the spirit, the warrior brings out the best of himself and offers it to the spirit.*)

SELECTED REFERENCES: Journey to Ixtlan - Page [43.7-44.1] ("Why do you tell me all...properly have a gesture with you.") Journey to Ixtlan - Page [56.6-56.7] ("Why are you doing all this...say that it is my turn.) The Power of Silence - Page [49.6-49.7] (He conceded that poets were keenly...hit pretty close to it though.") The Power of Silence - Page [190.4-191.5] ("I sat there in view of all those...was finally dead! I was finally free!") The Power of Silence - Page [240.8-241.3] (The nagual added that a human...silently offer it to the abstract.)

SEE ALSO: *ABANDON, WARRIOR-HUMOR*

SPIRIT-GESTURE-OF-[A GESTURE OF THE SPIRIT]: (*Warriors know a gesture of the spirit is another term for an omen.*)

SELECTED REFERENCES: The Power of Silence - Page [12.4-12.5] (Don Juan explained that every act...or, more simply, indications or omens.)

SEE ALSO: *OMENS*

SPIRIT-GIVER-POWER-[THE SPIRIT GIVER OF POWER]: (*Warriors know that the spirit giver of power is another term for an ally who touches a power object and gives it power.*)

SELECTED REFERENCES: Journey to Ixtlan - Page [206.1-206.7] (Next he talked about the search...if you can't find anything else.")

SEE ALSO: *POWER-OBJECTS, ALLIES, INORGANIC-BEINGS*

SPIRIT-GO-AFTER-[TO GO AFTER THE SPIRIT]: (*Warriors know that to go after the spirit is another way of referring to commanding the spirit, or moving the assemblage point.*)

SELECTED REFERENCES: The Power of Silence - Page [228.2-228.3] ("Sorcerers say that in order...energy for us is our impeccability.) The Power of Silence - Page [230.9-231.1] (During one of those nighttime excursions...to me: go after the spirit.)

SEE ALSO: *SPIRIT-COMMANDING, ASSEMBLAGE-POINT-MOVING*

SPIRIT-HANDLING-[HANDLING THE SPIRIT]: SEE: SPIRIT-COMMANDING-[COMMANDING THE SPIRIT]

SPIRIT-HELPER-[SPIRIT HELPER]: *(Warriors know a spirit helper is a spirit that lives on the other side of the world and helps an aberrant sorcerer to cause sickness and pain and death.)*
SELECTED REFERENCES: The Teachings of Don Juan - Page [184.3-184.6] ("Is a helper on the other side...think I could get a helper?") The Teachings of Don Juan - Page [186.3-187.2] (Once on the other side, the man...it to her helper, for keeps.") A Separate Reality - Page [226.9-227.8] ("What is a spirit catcher...it, the spirit will take you.")
SEE ALSO: *DIABLERO, SORCERY-FUTILITY-PITFALLS, ABERRATION-MORBIDITY*

SPIRIT-HELPERS-ALLIES-[SPIRIT HELPER VS ALLY]: SEE: ALLIES-SPIRIT-HELPERS-[ALLY VS SPIRIT HELPERS]

SPIRIT-INJURING-[INJURING THE SPIRIT]: *(Warriors know that what injures the spirit is having someone always on our backs, beating us, telling us what to do and what not to do.)*
SELECTED REFERENCES: Journey to Ixtlan - Page [xii.3] (Fright never injures anyone. what injures...do and what not to do.)
SEE ALSO: *SPIRIT*

SPIRIT-INTERVENTION-[THE INTERVENTION OF THE SPIRIT]: *(Warriors know that the intervention of the spirit is another term for the manifestations and the knock of the spirit.)*
SELECTED REFERENCES: The Power of Silence - Page [41.6-42.2] (Then he reminded me that I...spared no effort to satisfy it.)
SEE ALSO: *ABSTRACT-CORE-FIRST, ABSTRACT-CORE-SECOND, SPIRIT-MANIFESTATIONS, SPIRIT-KNOCK, SPIRIT-CONDUIT, NAGUAL-MAN-WOMAN, OMENS, INTENT-INTERVENTION*

*SPIRIT-KNOCK-[THE KNOCK OF THE SPIRIT]: *(Warriors know that the knock of the spirit is the second abstract core of the sorcery stories; the knock of the spirit is the edifice of intent "seen" by the beginner who is forced, rather than invited to enter into it.)*
SELECTED REFERENCES: The Power of Silence - Page [40.7-40.8] ("The second abstract core of the...or rather forced-to enter.) The Power of Silence - Page [41.6-42.2] (Then he reminded me that I...spared no effort to satisfy it.) The Power of Silence - Page [52.9-53.3] ("And again as with the first...a route of artifice and subterfuge.)
SEE ALSO: *ABSTRACT-CORE-SECOND, INTENT-EDIFICE*

SPIRIT-LAST-ARTIFICE-[THE SPIRIT'S LAST ARTIFICE]: SEE: ARTIFICE-SPIRIT-LAST-[THE SPIRIT'S LAST ARTIFICE]

SPIRIT-LINK-JOLT-[JOLTING THE LINK WITH THE SPIRIT]: SEE: NAGUAL-TRICKS-APPRENTICE-[THE NAGUAL TRICKS HIS APPRENTICE], STALKING-JOLT-[THE JOLT OF STALKING]

SPIRIT-LIVING-WITH-[LIVING WITH THE SPIRIT]: *(Warriors know that any minute may be their last and so their lives must be lived with the spirit.)*
SELECTED REFERENCES: The Eagle's Gift - Page [228.8-228.9] (He told us that we had...to be lived with the spirit.)
SEE ALSO: *SPIRIT, DEATH-ADVISER*

SPIRIT-MAN-ACCOUNT-[THE ACCOUNT OF THE SPIRIT OF MAN]: SEE: MAN-SPIRIT-ACCOUNT-[PAYING BACK TO THE ACCOUNT OF THE SPIRIT OF MAN]

***SPIRIT-MANIFESTATIONS*-*[MANIFESTATIONS OF THE SPIRIT]*:**
(Warriors know that the manifestations of the spirit is another term for omens; the spirit tends to keep its distance until something entices it forward; it is then that the spirit manifests itself; the manifestations of the spirit is the edifice that intent builds and places before the sorcerer as an invitation; it is the edifice of intent "seen" by the sorcerer.)
SELECTED REFERENCES: **The Power of Silence - Page [12.4-12.5]** (Don Juan explained that every act...or, more simply, indications or omens.) **The Power of Silence - Page [14.7-14.9]** (All of a sudden he said...particular, are tuned to such revelations.") **The Power of Silence - Page [21.7-21.9]** (Don Juan admitted that he had...important part of the spirit's manifestation.) **The Power of Silence - Page [37.8-37.9]** (I kept quiet. And he continued...then that the spirit manifested itself.) **The Power of Silence - Page [40.7-40.8]** ("The second abstract core of the...or rather forced-to enter.) **The Power of Silence - Page [52.9-53.3]** ("And again as with the first...a route of artifice and subterfuge.) **The Power of Silence - Page [208.6]** (I told don Juan I was...a true manifestation of the spirit.)
SEE ALSO: *OMENS, INTENT-EDIFICE, ABSTRACT-CORE-FIRST*

***SPIRIT-NASTY-ENCOUNTER*-*[AN ENCOUNTER WITH A NASTY SPIRIT]*-(TOP)**

***SPIRIT-NOTHING-GIVE-ENCOUNTER*-*[AN ENCOUNTER WITH THE SPIRIT WITH NOTHING TO GIVE]*-(TOP)**

***SPIRIT-PERFECTING*-*[PERFECTING THE SPIRIT]*:** *(Warriors know they must sustain an impeccable effort to fix, purge and perfect the spirit; there is no more worthwhile task; to not act to perfect the spirit is to seek nothing, to seek death.)*
SELECTED REFERENCES: **Journey to Ixtlan - Page [108.8-108.9]** (Lowering his voice to almost a...to overtake us regardless of anything.) **The Second Ring of Power - Page [52.4-52.5]** (And la Gorda changed more than...like her. I'm afraid of her.)
SEE ALSO: *WARRIOR-INTENT-LINK, WARRIOR-SPIRIT*

***SPIRIT-SEEING*-*[SEEING THE SPIRIT]*-(TOP)**

***SPIRIT-SEEING-PRELUDE*-*[PRELUDE TO SEEING THE SPIRIT]*:**
(Warriors know that if they "see" lights dancing before their faces, it may be because they are about to enter a dreaming state and "see" the spirit all by themselves.)
SELECTED REFERENCES: **The Power of Silence - Page [170.3-170.5]** (Until that moment I had not...yourself, like Talia and my benefactor.")
SEE ALSO: *SPIRIT, INTENT, SEEING, DREAMING-ART, SEEING-STARS*

***SPIRIT-SHINING*-*[SHINING THE SPIRIT]*-(TOP)**

***SPIRIT-TALKING*-*[TALKING ABOUT THE SPIRIT]*:** *(Warriors know there is really no way to talk about the spirit because the spirit can only be experienced.)*
SELECTED REFERENCES: **The Power of Silence - Page [37.7-37.8]** ("I told you there is no way...of the time it seems indifferent.")
SEE ALSO: *SPIRIT, ACTING-TALKING, KNOWLEDGE-VS-LANGUAGE*

***SPIRIT-TOUCH*-*[THE TOUCH OF THE SPIRIT]*: SEE: SPIRIT-CONTACT-[CONTACT WITH THE SPIRIT]**

***SPIRIT-TRAP*-*[THE TRAP OF THE SPIRIT]*: SEE: SPIRIT-TRICKERY-[THE TRICKERY OF THE SPIRIT]**

***SPIRIT-TRICKERY*-*[THE TRICKERY OF THE SPIRIT]*:** *(Warriors know that the trickery of the spirit is the third abstract core.)*

SELECTED REFERENCES: The Teachings of Don Juan - Page [238.2-238.4] (Nearly six years after I had...that they were not an oddity.) **A Separate Reality - Page [28.2-29.5]** (Don Juan patted me gently on...have to be around here for that.") **A Separate Reality - Page [211.7-213.1]** ("Whatever I have done to you today...the pressure of my irrational fear.) **Journey to Ixtlan - Page [215.6-216.3]** (Over a month before, I had...lot more in order to survive.") **Tales of Power - Page [20.1]** ("I always think that I'm being tricked..."That cannot be your problem.) **Tales of Power - Page [233.8-233.9]** (He said at that point a teacher...he was doing make sense to me.) **Tales of Power - Page [238.5-240.4]** (He explained that the art of...trick! Uh?" he said and laughed.) **Tales of Power - Page [271.6]** ("Today I have to accomplish a most crucial...you must fall for my tricking.") **The Second Ring of Power -Page [84.3-84.8]** (There was no doubt left in my...human nature, he was probably right.) **The Second Ring of Power - Page [192.2-194.6]** ("Why did they go to all...be making his green stuff today.") **The Eagle's Gift - Page [283.9-284.1]** ("As you yourself know," Florinda went...Don't we all do that?") **The Power of Silence - Page [6.3-6.4]** ("I've just told you the first...But that is another story.") **The Power of Silence - Page [40.9-41.1]** ("This second abstract core could be...the spirit knocked on the door.) **The Power of Silence - Page [52.8-53.5]** ("We are going to talk now about...and subterfuge in order to teach.) **The Power of Silence - Page [54.5-54.6]** (The first thing a nagual does...which my benefactor used on me.) **The Power of Silence - Page [94.8-95.1]** (Then the nagual Elias had another...sorcery in order to help them.) **The Power of Silence - Page [224.5-224.7]** ("Difficult as it is for a nagual...the trickery of the nagual Julian.)
SEE ALSO: *ABSTRACT-CORE-THIRD, SPIRIT, ARTIFICE-SUBTERFUGE*

SPIRIT-UNDERSTANDING-[UNDERSTANDING THE SPIRIT]: (Warriors battle to understand the spirit in two ways; first they must understand indirectly what the spirit is; second, they must come to understand the spirit directly; the sorcery stories are tales of warriors battling to understand the spirit.)

SELECTED REFERENCES: The Power of Silence - Page [2.9-3.2] ("In sorcery there are twenty-one...abstract cores and the sorcery stories.") **The Power of Silence - Page [36.6-37.4]** ("The nagual Elias explained that my...know without words or even thoughts.)
SEE ALSO: *SORCERY-STORIES, SPIRIT, KNOWLEDGE-SILENT, KNOWLEDGE-DIRECT*

SPIRIT-VOICE-SILENT-[THE SILENT VOICE OF THE SPIRIT]: (The warrior knows that the silent voice of the spirit is another term for the abstract cores.)

SELECTED REFERENCES: The Power of Silence - Page [29.9-30.1] (Obviously, what sorcerers recognize as an...the ulterior arrangement of the abstract.")
SEE ALSO: *ABSTRACT-CORES*

SPIRIT-WARRIOR-[THE WARRIORS' SPIRIT]: SEE: WARRIOR-SPIRIT-MEASURE-[THE TRUE MEASURE OF THE WARRIORS' SPIRIT]

SPIRIT-WARRIOR-MEASURE--[THE TRUE MEASURE OF THE WARRIORS' SPIRIT]: SEE: WARRIOR-SPIRIT-MEASURE-[THE TRUE MEASURE OF THE WARRIORS' SPIRIT]

SPIRIT-WATER-HOLE-[THE SPIRIT OF THE WATER HOLE]-(TOP)

SPIRIT-WILLINGNESS-[THE WILLINGNESS OF THE SPIRIT]: (Warriors know that the nagual can only be a conduit for the spirit after the spirit has manifested its willingness to be used, either almost imperceptibly or through outright commands.)

SELECTED REFERENCES: The Power of Silence - Page [41.6-42.2.] (Then he reminded me that I...spared no effort to satisfy it.)
SEE ALSO: *SPIRIT, SPIRIT-CONDUIT, NAGUAL-MAN-WOMAN, OMENS, SPIRIT-COMMANDS*

SPIRITS-[SPIRITS]: (Warriors define spirits as inexplicable and unbending powers that guide the lives of warriors; allies; forces, airs, winds.)

SELECTED REFERENCES: A Separate Reality - Page [37.9-38.7] (If you were capable of seeing...allies of a man of knowledge.) A Separate Reality - Page [62.9-63.2] ("Don Juan says that there is a...clear until one knows about him.) A Separate Reality - Page [180.1] ("The spirit is a force...you became green in the water.") A Separate Reality - Page [217.5-217.6] ("A warrior encounters those inexplicable and unbending...will irresistibly escape through it.) Journey to Ixtlan - Page [60.9-64.5] ("There it is," he said, as...hard and constantly all the time. Journey to Ixtlan - Page [86.1] ("Certainly. There are powers that guide...airs, winds, or anything like that.") Journey to Ixtlan - Page [99.8-99.9] (But the forces that guide us...the impeccable life of a warrior.) Journey to Ixtlan - Page [172.1] (I felt relieved and asked him...he said in a whisper.)
SEE ALSO: *WIND, ALLIES, INORGANIC-BEINGS, SPIRITS-TYPES-THREE, SPIRITUAL-FORCES*

SPIRITS-TYPES-THREE-[THE THREE TYPES OF SPIRITS]: *(Warriors know that there are three kinds of spirits; 1) those that are silent and cannot give anything because they have nothing to give; 2) those whose only quality is to cause fear and hover around the abode of the silent type of spirit; 3) those that are true allies and givers of secrets.)*
SELECTED REFERENCES: A Separate Reality - Page [232.6-235.2] ("There are three kinds of beings...like anything one has ever touched.") Journey to Ixtlan - Page [206.4] (He warned us that there were...not have any power at all.)
SEE ALSO: *ALLIES, INORGANIC-BEINGS, SPIRITS*

SPIRITUAL-FORCES-[SPIRITUAL FORCES]: *(The warrior knows that spiritual forces is another term for spirits; forces from the second attention; inorganic beings; allies.)*
SELECTED REFERENCES: The Art of Dreaming - Page [vii.7-vii.9] (In anthropological works, shamanism is described...between the natural and supernatural realms.)
SEE ALSO: *ALLIES, INORGANIC-BEINGS, SPIRITS*

SPLIT-WARRIOR-TWO-[THE WARRIOR IS SPLIT IN TWO]: SEE : WARRIOR-SPLIT-TWO-[THE WARRIOR IS SPLIT IN TWO]

SQUARE-FOUR-CORNERS-[THE FOUR CORNERS OF THE SQUARE]: SEE: WARRIOR-FEMALE-[FEMALE WARRIOR]

STAGES-WARRIOR-FOUR-[THE FOUR STAGES OF THE WARRIOR]: SEE: WARRIOR-STAGES-FOUR-[THE FOUR STAGES OF THE WARRIOR]

STAKES-ULTIMATE-[THE ULTIMATE STAKES BEYOND LIFE AND DEATH]: *(Warriors know that everything in the sorcerers' path is a matter of life and death, but in the path of dreaming the stakes are enhanced a hundred fold; energetic currents are at stake here, energetic currents which create circumstances that are more dreadful than death.)*
SELECTED REFERENCES: The Art of Dreaming - Page [109.9-110.2] ("What happens if you fall, don...matter is enhanced a hundred fold.")
SEE ALSO: *DREAMING-ART, ENERGY*

STALKER-BREATH-[THE STALKERS' BREATH]: *(Warriors know that the stalkers' breath is the key element in the warriors' recapitulation; breath is a magical, life-giving function that restores the luminosity of the warrior.)*
SELECTED REFERENCES: The Eagle's Gift - Page [288.4-289.4] (Florinda explained that the key element...involved in the event being recollected.) The Eagle's Gift - Page [290.3-290.4] (Florinda said that her benefactor considered...important tasks a warrior can fulfill.)
SEE ALSO: *BREATHING, RECAPITULATION, STALKING-ART*

STALKER-CLASSIFICATIONS-PERSONALITY-[THE STALKERS'

*CLASSIFICATIONS OF PERSONALITY TYPES]: SEE: PEOPLE-TYPES-
[THE STALKERS' CLASSIFICATIONS OF PERSONALITY TYPES*

*STALKER-DIMENSION-[THE STALKERS' DIMENSION]: (Warriors know
that to enter the stalkers' dimension is to enter into the second attention as
stalkers do.)*
> SELECTED REFERENCES: The Eagle's Gift - Page [293.8-293.9] (I asked Florinda to
clarify the...usher me into the *stalker's* dimension.)
> SEE ALSO: *ATTENTION-SECOND, STALKING-ART*

*STALKER-EYES-MANIPULATE-[STALKERS MANIPULATE THE EYES]:
(Warriors know that the human eye is trained to focus on only the most
alien features of anything, which are known beforehand; the stalkers' art is
to create an impression by presenting the features they choose, features they
know the eyes of the onlooker are bound to notice; in this way the stalker is
able to create in the onlooker an unchallengeable conviction as to what it is
they have perceived.)*
> SELECTED REFERENCES: The Power of Silence - Page [259.8-260.2] (The nagual
Julian explained that the...to what their eyes had perceived.)
> SEE ALSO: *STALKING-ART, EYES*

*STALKER-VS-HUNTER-[STALKER VS HUNTER]: (Warriors know that a
hunter just hunts; a stalker on the other hand stalks anything, including
himself and his own weaknesses.)*
> SELECTED REFERENCES: The Second Ring of Power - Page [227.4-227.8] ("Tell me
now, what is the art...we can even stalk our own weaknesses.")
> SEE ALSO: *STALKING, STALKING-ONESELF*

*STALKER-IMPECCABLE-[THE IMPECCABLE STALKER]: (Warriors know
that they need to be impeccable stalkers with regard to their warriors'
purpose in order to enter into the other world.)*
> SELECTED REFERENCES: The Second Ring of Power - Page [229.6-230.5] ("But
stalking your weaknesses is not enough...when he thought I was indulging.)
> SEE ALSO: *WARRIOR-IMPECCABILITY, WARRIOR-PURPOSE*

*STALKER-METHOD-[THE STALKERS' METHOD]: (Warriors know that
the stalkers' method is the exercise of the warriors' strategy, a method of
using words and actions deliberately selected to cause a particular effect;
the stalkers' method fosters total realization without explanation; to get
the apprentice's full cooperation and participation is the most important
outcome of the stalkers' method)*
> SELECTED REFERENCES: The Fire From Within - Page [193.6-195.8] (Don Juan
explained that everything his...best at getting both of them.") The Power of Silence - Page
[237.4-237.5] (The nagual Elias could hardly contain...seemed to be at his command.)
> SEE ALSO: *STALKING-ART, REALIZATION, EXPLANATION, KNOWLEDGE-VS-
LANGUAGE*

*STALKER-QUEST-PRACTICALITIES-[THE STALKERS' QUEST FOR
PRACTICALITIES]: (Warriors know that stalkers are always after
practicalities; they are on an endless quest for pragmatic views and
solutions.)*
> SELECTED REFERENCES: The Power of Silence - Page [237.4-237.5] (The nagual
Elias could hardly contain...seemed to be at his command.)
> SEE ALSO: *STALKING-ART*

STALKER-RULE-THREE-PRECEPTS-[THE THREE PRECEPTS OF THE RULE FOR STALKERS]: (Warriors know that they don't have the world to cushion them, so they must have the rule; the rule of stalkers applies to everyone; the three precepts of the rule for stalkers are; 1) everything that surrounds us is an unfathomable mystery; 2) warriors must try to unravel those mysteries but without ever hoping to accomplish this; 3) warriors, aware of the unfathomable mystery around them and of their duty to try and unravel it, take their place among mysteries and regard themselves as one.)
     SELECTED REFERENCES: **The Eagle's Gift - Page [279.3-279.7]** ("Warriors don't have the world to cushion...One is equal to everything.)
     SEE ALSO: *STALKING-ART, RULE*

STALKER-TURNS-HEAD-[STALKERS TURN THEIR HEADS]: (Warriors know that the stalkers turn their heads, not to face a new direction, but to face the oncoming time.)
     SELECTED REFERENCES: **The Eagle's Gift - Page [294.3-294.7]** (When don Juan had described the...energy necessary to unravel the mystery.)
     SEE ALSO: *STALKING-ART, TIME, WARRIOR-TURNING-HEAD*

STALKER-TRUMP-CARD-[THE STALKERS' TRUMP CARD]: (Warriors know that they must use the intellectual exercise of trying to explain sorcery in cogent terms as a stalking trump card, because stalkers remain aware that perception has more possibilities than the mind can conceive.)
     SELECTED REFERENCES: **The Power of Silence - Page [243.8-244.2]** (Don Juan fixed me with his stare...possibilities than the mind can conceive.")
     SEE ALSO: *SORCERY-EXPLAINING-DESIRE, WARRIOR-DIALOGUE*

STALKING-ART-[THE ART OF STALKING]: (Warriors know that the art of stalking is a set of procedures and attitudes that enable us to get the most out of any conceivable situation; one of the three masteries of the new seers; the riddle of the heart; the art of stealth or the art of the controlled folly maker; stalking is an art applicable to everything; stalking is the art of using behavior in novel ways for specific purposes; stalking is the beginning; for sorcerers, stalking is the foundation on which everything else they do is built; before warriors can attempt anything on the warriors' path, they must learn to stalk; stalking is special behavior designed to deliver a jolt; the systematic control of the warriors' behavior is one of the two greatest accomplishments of the new seers; the art of stalking is concerned with the fixation of the assemblage point in any location to which it is displaced; stalking is based on the fact that when warriors steadily behave in ways not customary for them, the unused emanations in their cocoons begin to glow and their assemblage points shift in a mild, harmonious, barely noticeable fashion; intending is the secret to stalking; the art of stalking is learning all the quirks of your disguise and to learn them so well that no one will know you are disguised.)
     SELECTED REFERENCES: **The Second Ring of Power - Page [2.6-2.7]** (In those few days they revealed...the core of the present work.) **The Second Ring of Power - Page [205.1-205.6]** (Nestor said that they were used to...They knew the art of stalking.") **The Second Ring of Power - Page [224.1-224.3]** (That was why I interfered with...are dreamers. Your double is *dreaming.*") **The Second Ring of Power - Page [275.8-276.2]** (What don Juan struggled to vanquish...hold the images of any dream.") **The Eagle's Gift - Page [4.6-4.7]** (I expected that the three Genaros...best out of any conceivable situation.) **The Eagle's Gift - Page [15.4-15.6]** ("The Atlanteans are the nagual; they...the opposite of the front row.") **The Eagle's Gift - Page [209.5-211.5]** (A secondary issue that came up...the finality of the Eagle's dictums.) **The Eagle's Gift -**

Page [291.4-291.7] ("I hope that you have realized...have an endless capacity to improvise.") **The Fire From Within - Page [5.8-5.9]** ("After the world of the first...happened to them with power plants.) **The Fire From Within - Page [126.7-126.9]** (He assured me that no deception...their links to the nagual's party.) **The Fire From Within - Page [168.3-170.2]** (He explained that what the new...But you already know all this.") **The Fire From Within - Page [185.4-185.9]** ("One of the great maneuvers of...that may be offensive to reason.") **The Power of Silence - Page [xv.3-xv.5]** (The art of *stalking* is the...so unalterably objective and factual change.) **The Power of Silence - Page [xvi.9-xvii.2]** (A level of practical knowledge was...and *stalking,* the control of behavior.) **The Power of Silence - Page [36.2-36.4]** ("The same thing happened to me...average man and as a nagual.") **The Power of Silence - Page [65.9-66.1]** ("The art of *stalking* is learning...be ruthless, cunning, patient and sweet.") **The Power of Silence - Page [67.7-67.9]** (He made don Juan practice his...ruthlessness, cunning patience and sweetness.) **The Power of Silence - Page [68.3-68.5]** (He taught him that these four...really learn the art of *stalking.*) **The Power of Silence - Page [80.5-80.7]** (In a very low voice don Juan...move their assemblage point at will.) **The Power of Silence - Page [81.8-82.9]** (I wanted to laugh, but he...awkward to say *controlled folly maker.*") **The Power of Silence - Page [109.1-109.3]** ("When the pressure of their connecting...behavior in a ruthless, cunning way.") **The Power of Silence - Page [111.6-111.8]** ("As I hear the words...this shock of beauty is *stalking.*") **The Power of Silence - Page [165.7-165.8]** ("Sorcerers, because they are stalkers, understand human behavior to perfection," he said.) **The Power of Silence - Page [244.9-245.3]** (He smiled, his eyes shining like two...in the world of daily affairs.") **The Power of Silence - Page [264.7S-265.1]** ("What was the nagual Elias's reason...is that it can be accomplished.") **The Art of Dreaming - Page [69.4-69.6]** (Don Juan expressed his bewilderment at...location to which it is displaced.) **The Art of Dreaming - Page [77.5-77.9]** ("The art of stalking," he continued...which the old sorcerers were involved.) **The Art of Dreaming - Page [161.5-161.8]** (Don Juan said that the moment...position and you will be stalking.")

    SEE ALSO: *ASSEMBLAGE POINT-MOVING, RIDDLE-HEART, WARRIOR-MASTERIES-THREE, DREAMING-VS-STALKING, ENERGETIC-UNIFORMITY-COHESION, INTENDING, WARRIOR-DISGUISE, STALKING-(ALL)*

STALKING-ASSEMBLAGE-POINT-[STALKING THE ASSEMBLAGE POINT]: SEE: ENERGY-BODY-STALKING-[STALKING THE ENERGY BODY]

STALKING-BASES-[THE FOUR BASES OF STALKING]: SEE: STALKING-MOODS [THE FOUR MOODS OF STALKING]

STALKING-DISGUISE-[STALKING DISGUISE]: SEE: STALKING-ART-[THE ART OF STALKING]

STALKING-VS-DREAMING-[STALKING VS DREAMING]: SEE: DREAMING-VS-STALKING-[DREAMING VS STALKING]

STALKING-ELEMENTS-SIX-[THE SIX ELEMENTS OF STALKING]:
(*Warriors know that the six elements of stalking are the components of the most effective strategy worked out by the new seers; five of these elements are the attributes of warriorship, control, discipline, forbearance, timing and will; the sixth element is the petty tyrant.*)

    SELECTED REFERENCES: **The Fire From Within - Page [16.4-16.6]** (He said that the most effective...and is called the petty tyrant.)

    SEE ALSO: *WARRIOR-ATTRIBUTES, PETTY-TYRANT, CONTROL, DISCIPLINE, FORBEARANCE, TIMING, WILL*

STALKING-ENERGY-BODY-[STALKING THE ENERGY BODY]: SEE: ENERGY-BODY-STALKING-[STALKING THE ENERGY BODY]

STALKING-FOUNDATIONS-[THE FOUR FOUNDATIONS OF STALKING]: SEE: STALKING-MOODS-[THE FOUR MOODS OF STALKING]

STALKING-IDEAL-SETTING-[THE IDEAL SETTING NECESSARY FOR OPTIMUM GAINS FROM STALKING]: (Warriors know that for maximum effect in moving the assemblage point, stalking requires an ideal setting; petty tyrants in positions of total authority and power are needed; under the normal conditions of life, stalking only moves the assemblage point to a minimal degree.)
    SELECTED REFERENCES: The Fire From Within - Page [172.1-172.4] (As soon as the women left...them out became an unbearable burden.)
    SEE ALSO: STALKING-ART, PETTY-TYRANT

STALKING-INTENT-DREAMING-POSITION-[STALKING, INTENT, AND THE DREAMING POSITION]-(TOP)

STALKING-JOLT-[THE JOLT OF STALKING]: (Warriors know that the jolt of stalking is a technique which is used to stalk oneself; warriors deliver a stalkers' jolt to themselves.)
    SELECTED REFERENCES: A Separate Reality - Page [219.4] ("A warrior is aware that the...be prepared for that monumental jolt.") The Power of Silence - Page [54.5-56.7] ("The first thing a nagual does...inorganic being, a formless energy field.") The Power of Silence - Page [80.2-80.4] ("It was a way of jolting you...at the neck like a dog.") The Power of Silence - Page [109.1-109.5] ("I still don't think I understand...death to deliver that *stalking* jolt.) The Power of Silence - Page [110.6-111.8] ("I have told you that there...this shock of beauty, is *stalking*.")
    SEE ALSO: STALKING-ART, STALKING-ONESELF, BEAUTY

STALKING-JOSEPHINA-[JOSEPHINA'S STALKING]-(TOP)

STALKING-KNOWLEDGE-WITHOUT-[STALKING WITHOUT KNOWLEDGE]-(TOP)

STALKING-MANEUVER-[ONE OF THE GREAT MANEUVERS OF STALKING]: (Warriors know that one of the great maneuvers of stalking is to pit the mystery of the world against the stupidity in each of us.)
    SELECTED REFERENCES: The Fire From Within - Page [185.4] ("One of the great maneuvers of...the stupidity in each of us.")
    SEE ALSO: STALKING-ART, STUPIDITY-IGNORANCE, WORLD-MYSTERIOUS

*STALKING-MOODS-FOUR-[THE FOUR MOODS OF STALKING]: (Warriors know that the actions of the stalker are governed by four principles, four bases that are inextricably bound together; ruthlessness, cunning, patience and sweetness are four positions of the assemblage point which the warrior uses as guides; warriors utilize the four moods of stalking to induce the assemblage point to move to specific positions.)
    SELECTED REFERENCES: The Power of Silence - Page [65.9-66.1] ("The art of *stalking* is learning...be ruthless, cunning, patient and sweet.") The Power of Silence - Page [67.7-67.9] (He made don Juan practice his...ruthlessness, cunning patience and sweetness.) The Power of Silence - Page [68.2-69.7] (Don Juan said that his benefactor...not remember something that never happened.) The Power of Silence - Page [117.7-117.8] (Don Juan casually asked me if..."Ruthlessness, the opposite of self-pity?") The Power of Silence - Page [243.9-245.2] ("The sorcerers' experience is so outlandish...the possibility of buttressing themselves.)
    SEE ALSO: STALKING, RUTHLESSNESS, CUNNING, PATIENCE, SWEETNESS

STALKING-ONESELF-[STALKING ONESELF]: (Warriors know that the first precept of stalking is that we must stalk ourselves; warriors stalk themselves with the stalkers' jolt; impeccable stalkers can turn anything into prey, including their own weaknesses; stalking oneself often involves a

jolt to the warriors' connecting link with intent; warriors stalk themselves in order to break the power of their obsessions.)
    SELECTED REFERENCES: **The Second Ring of Power - Page [227.4-228.1]** ("Tell me now, what is the...up like rabbits inside a cage.") **The Power of Silence - Page [54.4-54.5]** ("I've already told you the story...he taught me to *stalk* myself.) **The Power of Silence - Page [81.8]** ("The very first principle of *stalking*...himself ruthlessly, cunningly, patiently and sweetly.") **The Power of Silence - Page [108.4-108.5]** ("Sorcerers constantly *stalk* themselves," he said...me with the sound of his voice.) **The Power of Silence - Page [109.1-109.4]** ("When the pressure of their connecting...death to deliver that *stalking* jolt.) **The Power of Silence - Page [110.5-110.7]** ("Your problem is very simple," he...and the silence delivers the jolt.") **The Power of Silence - Page [243.9-244.2]** ("The sorcerers' experience is so outlandish...possibilities than the mind can conceive.)
    SEE ALSO: *STALKING, STALKING-JOLT, OBSESSION*

STALKING-ONESELF-JUAN-[DON JUAN STALKS HIMSELF]-(TOP)

STALKING-PERCEPTION-[STALKING PERCEPTION]: SEE: PERCEPTION-STALKING-[STALKING PERCEPTION]

STALKING-PRECEPT-FIRST-[THE FIRST PRECEPT OF STALKING]:
(Warriors know that the first precept of stalking is another term for stalking oneself.)
    SELECTED REFERENCES: **The Power of Silence - Page [81.8]** ("The very first principle of *stalking*...himself ruthlessly, cunningly, patiently, and sweetly.")
    SEE ALSO: *STALKING-ONESELF*

STALKING-PRINCIPLES-SEVEN-[THE SEVEN BASIC PRINCIPLES OF STALKING]: (Warriors know that the seven basic principles of stalking are; 1) stalkers must carefully choose their battleground; 2) stalkers must discard everything that is not essential; 3) stalkers must learn to put their lives on the line with every decision; 4) stalkers must learn to relax and abandon themselves; 5) in order to regroup their resources, stalkers must enter into a new and different mood of optimism and self-confidence; 6) stalkers must learn to compress time; 7) stalkers never push themselves to the front; in order to practice the seventh principle of stalking, stalkers must apply the first six; warriors apply the seven principles of stalking to everything they do, from the most trivial acts to life and death situations; the application of the seven principles of stalking brings about the three results of stalking.)
    SELECTED REFERENCES: **The Eagle's Gift - Page [278.3-278.8]** (Florinda looked at me and smiled...giving me time to say anything.) **The Eagle's Gift - Page [280.3-281.5]** ("I've told you how the principles...Warriors don't waste an instant.") **The Eagle's Gift - Page [282.1-282.3]** (Without knowing I had used the...weak that no effort is possible.) **The Eagle's Gift - Page [290.6-291.7]** (Florinda said that her benefactor gave...have an endless capacity to improvise.")
    SEE ALSO: *STALKING-ART, STALKING-ELEMENTS-SIX, STALKING-MOODS-FOUR, STALKING-RESULTS-THREE, ABANDON*

STALKING-PURPOSES-TWO-[THE TWO PURPOSES OF STALKING]:
(Warriors know that there are two purposes of stalking; 1) the first is to move the assemblage point as steadily and safely as possible; 2) the second is to imprint its principles on such a deep level that the human inventory is bypassed.)
    SELECTED REFERENCES: **The Fire From Within - Page [185.7-185.9]** ("By not teaching it in normal awareness...that may be offensive to reason.)
    SEE ALSO: *STALKING-ART, ASSEMBLAGE-POINT-MOVING, INVENTORY*

STALKING-REASON-OFFENSIVE-[STALKING IS OFFENSIVE TO REASON]: (Warriors know that stalking practices are offensive to reason; it is therefore against everybody's best interests to discuss the principles of stalking in normal awareness; one of the purposes of stalking is to imprint its principles on such a deep level that the human inventory is bypassed, and along with it, the natural reaction of refusing or judging something that is offensive to reason.)
SELECTED REFERENCES: The Fire From Within - Page [185.4-185.9] (He explained that stalking practices are not...that may be offensive to reason.") The Fire From Within - Page [187.4-187.5] ("That's stalking," he said. "You see...Julian and you are already annoyed.")
SEE ALSO: STALKING-ART, REASON, INVENTORY

STALKING-RESULTS-THREE-[THE THREE RESULTS OF STALKING]: (Warriors know there are three results of stalking; 1) stalkers learn to never take themselves seriously, they learn to laugh at themselves; 2) stalkers learn to have endless patience, they are never in a hurry, they never fret; 3) stalkers learn to have an endless capacity to improvise.)
SELECTED REFERENCES: The Eagle's Gift - Page [291.5-291.7] ("I hope that you have realized...have an endless capacity to improvise.")
SEE ALSO: WARRIOR-HUMOR, WARRIOR-PATIENCE, IMPROVISATION, FRETTING

*STALKING-STALKER-[STALKING THE STALKERS]: (Warriors know that to stalk the stalkers means to deliberately draw energy from the inorganic beings' realm in order to perform a sorcery feat; this sorcery feat is a journey which uses awareness as a mode of travel; to break the boundaries of the normal world and enter into another using awareness as an energetic element is stalking the stalkers; this breaking and entering amounts to bypassing the influence of the inorganic beings while still using their energy.)
SELECTED REFERENCES: The Art of Dreaming - Page [184.9-185.4] ("I'm going to propose a line...to the ends of the universe.") The Art of Dreaming - Page [186.7-186.8] ("I want you to break...it still uses their energy.") The Art of Dreaming - Page [196.1-197.9] (Inexplicably and excessively out of breath...Sorcery is an endless challenge.")
SEE ALSO: STALKING-ART, INORGANIC-BEINGS, ENERGY-ASSEMBLAGE-POINT-MOVING, WARRIORSHIP-VS-SORCERY. DREAMING-GATE-THIRD, DREAMING-RATIONAL-STATE, STALKING-ULTIMATE

STALKING-TECHNIQUES-THREE-[THE THREE BASIC TECHNIQUES OF STALKING]: (Warriors know the three basic techniques of the stalker's recapitulation are; 1) the crate; 2) the list of events to be recapitulated; 3) the stalkers' breath.)
SELECTED REFERENCES: The Eagle's Gift - Page [290.3-290.5] (Florinda said that her benefactor considered...self-importance, breaking routines and so forth.)
SEE ALSO: RECAPITULATION, STALKER-BREATH, CRATE

STALKING-ULTIMATE-[THE ULTIMATE STALKING]: (Warriors know that the ultimate stalking is the stalking necessary to access the required energy from the realm of the inorganic beings without succumbing to their influence; this stalking is accomplished through the warriors' unbending intent to find freedom.)
SELECTED REFERENCES: The Art of Dreaming - Page [180.8-181.6] ("You are ready then for one final...sorcerer knows what freedom really is.")
SEE ALSO: STALKING-ART, STALKING-STALKERS, ENERGY-ASSEMBLAGE-POINT-MOVE

STALKING-WEAKNESSES-WARRIOR-[STALKING THE WARRIORS' WEAKNESSES]: SEE: STALKING-ONESELF-[STALKING ONESELF]

STANCE-WARRIOR-[THE WARRIORS' STANCE]: SEE: WARRIOR-STANCE-[THE WARRIORS' STANCE]

STAND-WARRIOR-[WARRIORS MUST MAKE THEIR STAND]: SEE: WARRIOR-STAND-[WARRIORS MUST MAKE THEIR STAND]

STAR-GAZING- [STAR GAZING]: SEE: GAZING-[GAZING]

STARS-SEEING-[SEEING STARS]: SEE: ASSEMBLAGE-POINT-MOVEMENT-INVOLUNTARY-[THE INVOLUNTARY MOVEMENT OF THE ASSEMBLAGE POINT]

STEALTH-ART-[THE ART OF STEALTH]: (Warriors know that the art of stealth is another term for the art of stalking.)
SELECTED REFERENCES: The Power of Silence - Page [82.7-82.9] ("Some sorcerers object to the term...awkward to say *controlled folly maker*.")
SEE ALSO: *STALKING-ART*

STEP-POWER-[THE FIRST STEP TO POWER]: SEE: DREAMING-SETTING-UP-[SETTING UP DREAMING]

STEPS-WARRIOR-[THE WARRIORS' STEPS]: SEE: WARRIOR-STEPS-[THE WARRIORS' STEPS]

STERNUM-[STERNUM]: SEE: ATTENTION-DREAMING-NEEDED-[THE ATTENTION NEEDED FOR DREAMING]

STOMACH-GLOW-[THE GLOW AROUND THE STOMACH]: (Warriors know that human beings have a very delicate glow around their stomachs that is always being pulled by everything around; when the pull becomes too great, the glow may become agitated, change color or fade altogether; in such instances the only thing the warrior can do is simply to throw up.)
SELECTED REFERENCES: The Second Ring of Power - Page [149.2-149.7] (It was as though she had...could do was simply to throw up.)
SEE ALSO: *AWARENESS-GLOW*

*STOPPING-WORLD-[STOPPING THE WORLD]: (Warriors know that it is our own internal talk that upholds the world, and as a result we strive to stop our talking and undo the world; the first step to "seeing" is stopping the world; stopping the world consists of introducing a dissonant element into the fabric of everyday behavior for purposes of halting the otherwise smooth flow of ordinary events, events which are normally catalogued in our minds by reason; the moment when the warriors' second attention hooks onto something is called stopping the world; stopping the world is an operational description of focusing the second attention.)
SELECTED REFERENCES: A Separate Reality - Page [218.5-219.6] ("You think and talk too much...start slowly to undo the world.") Journey to Ixtlan - Page [ix.8-ix.9] (His contention was that he was...was the first step to "seeing".) Journey to Ixtlan - Page [xi.1-xi.6] ("I mean that if your friend...one can always direct the pressure.") Journey to Ixtlan - Page [xii.5-xiv.4] (I realized then that throughout the...we have learned to call reality.") Journey to Ixtlan - Page [xiii.2-xiii.5] (In reviewing the totality of my...culminated in my "stopping the world.") Journey to Ixtlan - Page [104.7-104.9] (In a controlled fashion, without losing...know it was made to collapse.) Journey to Ixtlan - Page [136.2-136.7] (He laughed and touched my head...in order to keep on living.") Journey to Ixtlan - Page [194.4-194.5] ("*Not-doing* is very simple

but...through the technique of *not-doing*.") **Journey to Ixtlan - Page [253.3-254.3]** (Don Juan was alone in the house...have been telling us it is.") **Tales of Power - Page [13.7-13.9]** (Don Juan explained that the passageway...in your idea of the world.) **Tales of Power - Page [92.6-92.7]** ("As you know," he said...you could stop talking to yourself.) **Tales of Power - Page [236.3-236.4]** (A teacher, from the very first...technique that an apprentice can learn.) **Tales of Power - Page [243.7-243.9]** ("Did the power plants help me...especially with the devil's weed.") **The Second Ring of Power - Page 90.1-90.4]** (It started again as a ticklish...means to that suspension of judgment.) **The Second Ring of Power - Page [294.7-294.8]** (The Nagual called the moment when...that is correct, the world stops.) **The Second Ring of Power - Page [306.6-307.2]** (Don Juan had asserted time and...ourselves with our endless internal dialogue.) **The Eagle's Gift - Page [143.1-143.4]** (Both can bring the moment of...it, to make it do things.) **The Power of Silence - Page [165.4-165.6]** (He reminded me that he had...in our minds by our reason.)

SEE ALSO: *INTERNAL-DIALOGUE-STOPPING, INNER-SILENCE, STOPPING-WORLD, ATTENTION-SECOND-TRAPPING*

STOPPING-WORLD-BOY-*[STOPPING THE WORLD OF A YOUNG BOY]-(TOP)*

STOPPING-WORLD-DOING-*[STOPPING THE WORLD AND STOPPING "DOING"]: (Warriors know that to stop the world means to stop "doing".)*

SELECTED REFERENCES: **Journey to Ixtlan - Page [189.9-190.1]** ("I say that you are making this...any other thing, by *not-doing*.")

SEE ALSO: *STOPPING-WORLD, DOING*

STOPPING-WORLD-FEELING-*[THE FEELING OF STOPPING THE WORLD]: (Warriors know there is a physical sensation associated with stopping the world, a ticklish sensation at the top of the head.)*

SELECTED REFERENCES: **The Second Ring of Power - Page [58.5-58.6]** (I heard then, or perhaps I...thought that I must be dying.) **The Second Ring of Power - Page [82.8-82.9]** (I heard again, as I had...of Rosa's stick and crushed it.) **The Second Ring of Power - Page [89.1-89.2]** (I sat for a long while with the...entered dona Soledad's room awhile before.) **The Second Ring of Power - Page [89.9-91.6]** (I had a fit of anger at that point...the memory of that ticklish sensation.) **The Second Ring of Power - Page [90.3-90.4]** (Under the impact of dona Soledad...the means to that suspension of judgment.) **The Second Ring of Power - Page [109.6-109.8]** (All at once I had a monstrous...while they lay on the floor.) **The Second Ring of Power - Page [238.2-239.1]** ("How did you *see* all that...you have when you're still empty.") **The Second Ring of Power - Page [250.6-250.8]** (I had a moment of supreme uncertainty...from the trail in the darkness.)

SEE ALSO: *STOPPING-WORLD, KNOWLEDGE-SILENT*

STORIES-SORCERY-*[THE SORCERY STORIES]: SEE: SORCERY-STORIES-[THE SORCERY STORIES]*

STRANGULATION-CARLOS-*[CARLOS' STRANGULATION]-(TOP): SEE: CARLOS-STRANGULATION-[CARLOS' STRANGULATION]-(TOP)*

STRATEGIC-ELEMENTS-*[THE SIX STRATEGIC ELEMENTS]: SEE: STALKING-ELEMENTS-[THE SIX ELEMENTS OF STALKING]*

STRATEGIC-INVENTORY-*[THE WARRIORS' STRATEGIC INVENTORY]: SEE: WARRIOR-STRATEGIC-INVENTORY-[THE WARRIORS' STRATEGIC INVENTORY*

STRATEGY-DOING-*[THE DOING OF STRATEGY]: (Warriors know they must not indulge in thoughts of survival; instead they follow the "doing of strategy" when they have to act with their fellow men; in that doing there are no victories or defeats, there are only actions.)*

SELECTED REFERENCES: **Journey to Ixtlan - Page [227.4-227.9]** ("You are in a terrible bind...there to perform a specific act.)

SEE ALSO: *STRATEGY, DOING, VICTORY, DEFEAT, VICTORY-DEFEAT-EQUAL*

STRATEGY-NEW-SEER-[THE STRATEGY OF THE NEW SEERS]:
(Warriors know that the strategy of the new seers is the strategy of war for the warrior; it is a comprehensive strategy that not only rids warriors of the negative aspects of self-importance but also prepares them for the final realization that impeccability is the only thing that counts on the path of knowledge.)
    SELECTED REFERENCES: The Fire From Within - Page [16.4-16.6] (He said that the most effective strategy...and is called the petty tyrant.) **The Fire From Within - Page [18.3-18.4]** ("You haven't yet put together all...counts in the path of knowledge.)
    SEE ALSO: WARRIOR-WAR, SELF-IMPORTANCE-LOSING, WARRIOR-IMPECCABILITY, KNOWLEDGE-PATH, WARRIOR-STRATEGY, CORE-GOOD-ROTTEN

STRATEGY-WARRIOR-[THE WARRIORS' STRATEGY]: SEE: WARRIOR-STRATEGY-[THE WARRIORS' STRATEGY]

STRATEGY-WARRIOR-HIGHER-ORDER-[THE WARRIOR TAKES COVER WITH A HIGHER ORDER]: SEE: WARRIOR-STRATEGY-HIGHER-ORDER-[THE WARRIOR TAKES COVER WITH A HIGHER ORDER]

STRATEGY-WARRIOR-MAPS-[WARRIORS MAP THEIR STRATEGY]: SEE: WARRIOR-STRATEGY-MAPS-[WARRIORS MAP THEIR STRATEGY]

STRENGTH-[STRENGTH]: SEE: NORTH-[NORTHERLY WOMEN]

STRENGTH-INTERNAL-WARRIOR-[THE WARRIORS' INTERNAL STRENGTH]: SEE: WARRIOR-STRENGTH-INTERNAL-[THE WARRIORS' INTERNAL STRENGTH]

STRESS-[STRESS]: SEE: WARRIOR-DURESS-EXTREME-BENEFITS-[THE BENEFITS OF EXTREME DURESS FOR THE WARRIOR]

STRETCHING-[STRETCHING]: (Warriors know it is beneficial to stretch the body many times during the day, especially after a long period of work or rest.)
    SELECTED REFERENCES: **Journey to Ixtlan - Page [179.6-179.7]** (He did not answer. He stood...or a long period of rest.") **The Power of Silence - Page [106.1-106.2]** (Don Juan stood, stretched his arms...his muscles, making his joints crack.)
    SEE ALSO: WARRIOR-WAY, BODY-PHYSICAL

STRIFE-[STRIFE]: (Warriors know they can never succeed as paper warriors because the only way that awareness can grow is through strife and life-or-death confrontations.)
    SELECTED REFERENCES: **The Art of Dreaming - Page [101.3-101.4]** (Don Juan explained that in the...strife, through life-or-death confrontations.)
    SEE ALSO: WARRIOR-PAPER, AWARENESS, WARRIOR-CHALLENGE, WARRIOR-DURESS-EXTREME-BENEFITS, AWARENESS-GROWTH

STRUCTURAL-ANALYSIS-[THE STRUCTURAL ANALYSIS]: (An early structural analysis of nagualism by Carlos Castaneda.)
    SELECTED REFERENCES: **The Teachings of Don Juan - Page [189.3-256.6]** (The following structural scheme, abstracted from...The reality of special consensus had pragmatic value.)
    SEE ALSO: REASON

STRUGGLE-WARRIOR-[THE WARRIORS' STRUGGLE]: SEE: WARRIOR-STRUGGLE-[THE WARRIORS' STRUGGLE]

STUPIDITY-IGNORANCE-[STUPIDITY AND IGNORANCE]: (*Warriors know that man's plight is the counterpoint between his stupidity and his ignorance; warriors act to demean the stupidity of man by understanding it; it is stupidity that forces us to discard anything that does not conform to our self-reflective expectations; the average man holds tight to his self-image insured by his abysmal ignorance; the average man's stupidity is most dangerous when it prevents him from even recognizing the glimmers of his potential; the warriors' courage empowers them to be acquiescent without being stupid; it is stupidity that forces the average man to discard anything that does not conform with his self-reflective expectations and first-attention perceptions of the world.*)

SELECTED REFERENCES: **Journey to Ixtlan** - Page **[133.1-133.4]** ("You are quite cracked," he said...it, because of your own stupidity.) **Tales of Power** - Page **[191.2-191.5]** ("I've never put a ban on...are not applicable to the *nagual.*") **Tales of Power** - Page **[196.7-196.9** (As a rule of thumb, when you...are no survivors on this earth!") **The Second Ring Of Power** - Page **[189.9-190.1]** ("You said it!" he exclaimed, and...is stupidly the same to him.") **The Second Ring Of Power** - Page **[243.6-243.7]** ("If your grandfather and father would...in us. And that's what matters.) **The Second Ring Of Power** - Page **[246.8-247.1]** ("The art of sorcerers is to be...anyone of us about our attention.") **The Fire From Within** - Page **[185.2-185.4]** ("This indeed is the mystery of...the stupidity in each of us.") **The Fire From Within** - Page **[210.3-210.4]** ("You're coming of age," don Juan...Julian, except that he was brilliant.") **The Fire From Within** - Page **[228.1-228.3]** ("It's an error to isolate anything...freedom of the seers of today.) **The Power of Silence** - Page **[109.8-110.3]** ("Yes," he went on. "The idea...be ruthless without being self-important.") **The Power of Silence** - Page **[183.8-183.9]** ("Being devoured by that monster was symbolic...of being devoured by that monster now.") **The Power of Silence** - Page **[190.8-191.3]** (The farm workers continued to laugh...for the spirit to pay attention.) **The Power of Silence** - Page **[219.2-219.9]** (He said that one of the...point can be made to move.") **The Power of Silence** - Page **[228.8-228.9]** (Don Juan explained that man's predicament...between his stupidity and his ignorance.)

SEE ALSO: *MAN-PLIGHT, STALKING-ONESELF, EXPECTATION*

STUPIDITY-SELF-REFLECTION-[THE MACABRE CONNECTION BETWEEN STUPIDITY AND SELF-REFLECTION]: (*Warriors know that it is stupidity which forces us to disregard anything that does not conform to our self-reflective expectations; in essence then, stupidity is tied directly to self-reflection; when self-reflection is shattered, warriors are no longer stupid enough to deny their magical potential.*)

SELECTED REFERENCES: **The Second Ring of Power** - Page **[243.6-243.7]** ("If your grandfather and father would...in us. And that's what matters.) **The Second Ring of Power** - Page **[246.8-247.1]** ("The art of sorcerers is to...anyone of us about our attention.") **The Power of Silence** - Page **[219.2-219.9]** (He said that one of the...point can be made to move.")

SEE ALSO: *STUPIDITY-IGNORANCE, MAGIC, SELF-REFLECTION, HUMAN-ALTERNATIVES-POSSIBILITIES-POTENTIAL, WARRIOR-EXPECTATIONS*

SUBTERFUGE-[SUBTERFUGE]: SEE: ARTIFICE-SUBTERFUGE-[ARTIFICE AND SUBTERFUGE]

SUCCESS-WARRIOR-[THE WARRIORS' SUCCESS]: SEE: WARRIOR-SUCCESS-[THE WARRIORS' SUCCESS]

SUIT-JUAN-[DON JUAN'S SUIT]-(TOP)

*SULFUR-DUNES-LAND-[THE LAND OF THE SULFUR DUNES]: SEE: PARALLEL-LINES-LAND-[THE LAND BETWEEN THE PARALLEL LINES]

SUN-ENERGY-[ENERGY FROM THE SUN]: (*Warriors know that the best way to get energy is to allow the sun inside the half closed eyes, especially the left eye.*)

SELECTED REFERENCES: **The Second Ring of Power - Page [276.5-276.8]** (Maybe you could also remember *seeing*...that could shine on the eyes.) **The Second Ring of Power - Page [287.2-287.9]** (I wanted to tell her more on the...casually pushed my pad out of reach.)
SEE ALSO: *EARTH-BOOST, EYES-ENERGY-GAINING*

SUN-PIECES-[PIECES OF THE SUN]: (Warriors know that all human beings are pieces of the sun, that is why we are all luminous beings.)

SELECTED REFERENCES: **The Second Ring of Power - Page [138.3-138.9]** ("What color was it, Gorda...light," she said matter-of-factly.) **The Second Ring of Power - Page [168.5-168.7]** (The Nagual and Genaro and Eligio...the sky. I have no light.)
SEE ALSO: *LUMINOUS-BEINGS*

SUNNING-CLOTHES-[SUNNING ONE'S CLOTHES]: (Warriors know that sunning their clothes has a cleansing and recuperative effect after certain kinds of contact with the nagual.)

SELECTED REFERENCES: **The Second Ring of Power - Page [167.3-167.8]** (It was a short drive to the...and got another one for herself.)
SEE ALSO: *ALLIES-CONTACT, NAGUAL*

SUNS-TWIN-WORLD-[WORLD OF THE TWIN SUNS]-(TOP): SEE: ZULEICA-DREAMING-CELESTIAL [ZULEICA'S CELESTIAL DREAMING]-(TOP)

SUPERIORITY-FALSE-WARRIOR-[THE WARRIORS' FALSE SENSE OF SUPERIORITY]: SEE: WARRIOR-SUPERIORITY-FALSE-[THE WARRIORS' FALSE SENSE OF SUPERIORITY]

SUPERNATURAL-REALM-[THE REALM OF THE SUPERNATURAL]: (Warriors know that the supernatural realm is another term for the second attention.)

SELECTED REFERENCES: **The Art of Dreaming - Page [vii.7-vii.9]** (In anthropological works, shamanism is described...between the natural and supernatural realms.)
SEE ALSO: *ATTENTION-SECOND, NATURAL-REALM*

SURRENDER-IMPECCABILITY-WARRIOR-[THE WARRIOR SURRENDERS TO HIS IMPECCABILITY]: SEE: WARRIOR-SURRENDER-IMPECCABILITY-[THE WARRIOR SURRENDERS TO HIS IMPECCABILITY]

SURROGATE-AWARENESS-WARRIOR-[THE WARRIORS' SURROGATE AWARENESS]: SEE: AWARENESS-SURROGATE-WARRIOR-[THE WARRIORS' SURROGATE AWARENESS]

SURVIVE-WARRIOR-[ONLY WARRIORS CAN SURVIVE]: SEE: WARRIOR-SURVIVE-[ONLY WARRIORS CAN SURVIVE]

SUSPENDING-WARRIOR [SUSPENDING THE WARRIOR]: SEE: WARRIOR-SUSPENDING-[SUSPENDING THE WARRIOR]

SUSPICIOUSNESS-WARRIOR-[THE WARRIORS' SUSPICIOUSNESS]: SEE: WARRIOR-SUSPICIOUSNESS-[THE WARRIORS' SUSPICIOUSNESS]

SWEEPING-FLOOR-BELLY-[SWEEPING THE FLOOR WITH THE BELLY]-(TOP)

SWEETNESS-*[SWEETNESS]: (Warriors know that sweetness is one of the four moods of stalking; warriors learn to be sweet without being foolish; warriors are sweet but lethal.)*

    SELECTED REFERENCES: The Power of Silence - Page [68.2-68.3] (Don Juan said that his benefactor...and sweetness should not be foolishness.) **The Power of Silence - Page [68.5-68.6]** ("My benefactor used to stay to...acts this way he's being prissy.'") **The Power of Silence - Page [69.3-69.4]** ("In the past few days, I...what I taught you about them.) **The Power of Silence - Page [78.2-78.7]** ("If you hadn't indulged in being...be ruthless, cunning, patient, and sweet.") **The Power of Silence - Page [81.8]** ("The very first principle of *stalking*...himself ruthlessly, cunningly, patiently, and sweetly.")

    SEE ALSO: *STALKING-MOODS-FOUR*

SWIMMING-CARLOS-FATHER-*[CARLOS' SWIMMING STORY WITH HIS FATHER]-(TOP): SEE: CARLOS-SWIMMING-FATHER-[CARLOS' SWIMMING STORY WITH HIS FATHER]-(TOP)*

T

TABLE-WILDERNESS-[A TABLE IN THE WILDERNESS]: (*Warriors know that the table in the wilderness is a model for the tonal-nagual dichotomy.*)
SELECTED REFERENCES: The Second Ring of Power - Page [291.6-293.5] (La Gorda recounted the way don Juan...unit was the totality of oneself.)
SEE ALSO: *TONAL-NAGUAL-DICHOTOMY, ATTENTION-TONAL, ATTENTION-NAGUAL*

TAKING-CARE-WARRIOR-ANOTHER-[TAKING CARE OF ANOTHER WARRIOR]: SEE: WARRIOR-CARING-FOR-ANOTHER-[CARING FOR ANOTHER WARRIOR]

TALENT-WOMEN-[WOMEN'S TALENT]: SEE: WOMEN-TALENT-[WOMEN'S TALENT]

TALES-POWER-[TALES OF POWER]: SEE: POWER-TALES-[TALES OF POWER]

TALES-ETERNITY-[TALES OF ETERNITY]-(TOP): SEE: ETERNITY-TALES-[TALES OF ETERNITY]-(TOP)

**TALES-POWER-[TALES OF POWER]-(TOP): SEE: POWER-TALES-[TALES OF POWER]-(TOP)*

TALIA-TALES-[TALES OF TALIA]-(TOP)

TALKING-VS-ACTING-[ACTING VS TALKING]: SEE: ACTING-VS-TALKING-[ACTING VS TALKING]

TALKING-REASON-[REASON AND TALKING]: SEE: REASON-TALKING-[REASON AND TALKING]

TALKING-RECOLLECTING-[TALKING AND RECOLLECTING]:
(*Warriors know that talking is only useful in leading warriors to remember with the body; talking is not an active part of the recollection process itself.*)
SELECTED REFERENCES: The Power of Silence - Page [134.7] (Don Juan told me that there were...moved, the entire experience was relived.)
SEE ALSO: *TALKING, REMEMBERING-BODY, RECOLLECTION-SORCERER*

TASK-REMEMBERING-[THE TASK OF REMEMBERING]: SEE: REMEMBER-BODY-[REMEMBERING WITH THE BODY]

TASK-SORCERY-[SORCERY TASK]: SEE: SORCERY TASK-GRAND-[THE GRAND TASK OF SORCERY], SORCERY-TASKS-TRADITIONAL-[THE TRADITIONAL TASKS OF SORCERY]

TASK-WARRIOR-[THE WARRIORS' TASK]: SEE: WARRIOR-TASK-[THE WARRIORS' TASK]

TASK-WORLDLY-WARRIOR-[THE WARRIORS' WORLDLY TASK]: SEE: WARRIOR-TASK-WORLDLY-[THE WARRIORS' WORLDLY TASK]

TEACHER-ART-[THE ART OF THE TEACHER]: (*Warriors know the art of the teacher is to coral his apprentice and lead him to the only gate that is open.*)

SELECTED REFERENCES: The Second Ring of Power - Page [207.2-207.3] ("As far as I'm concerned, you two...the only gate that was open.)
SEE ALSO: *TEACHERS-TEACHING*

TEACHER-RECAPITULATION-[THE TEACHER'S RECAPITULATION]:
(Warriors know that at a certain point in an apprentice's training, the teacher recapitulates every step that has been taken to reorder that individual's tonal.)
SELECTED REFERENCES: Tales of Power - Page [233.4-233.6] (He said that the occasion required...me since the day we met.) Tales of Power - Page [273.7-273.9] ("I have called that cluster the...followed to arrive at that point.")
SEE ALSO: *TEACHER, TONAL-ISLAND*

TEACHER-TRAP-ARTFUL-[THE TEACHER'S ARTFUL TRAP]: SEE: TRAP-ARTFUL-TEACHER-[THE TEACHER'S ARTFUL TRAP]

TEACHERS-TEACHING-[TEACHERS AND TEACHING]:
(Those who practice the fundamental teaching method of the seers of the new cycle; a method that involves teachings for both right and left side awarenesses; a method which involves both a teacher and a benefactor; a teacher is entrusted with the care of an apprentice's tonal, while the benefactor is entrusted with showing the apprentice the nagual; this teaching method is aimed at teaching the apprentice to move and stabilize his assemblage point in its new position.)
SELECTED REFERENCES: The Teachings of Don Juan - Page [x.2-x.5] (I have described in one of...companions to conduct those teachings.) Tales of Power - Page [175.1-175.6] ("Can you tell me, don Juan...been to work with your *tonal*.") Tales of Power - Page [176.3-176.4] ("When an ordinary man is ready,...benefactor, and he becomes a sorcerer.") Tales of Power - Page [188.8-188.9] (Don Juan said that it was...not more so than the teacher.) Tales of Power - Page [230.7-230.9] ("I've already told you that I am...show how to get to it.") Tales of Power - Page [270.7-271.2] (He began to talk about Pablito and...kind teacher and a stern benefactor.) The Second Ring of Power - Page [269.5-269.9] ("You sure are dumb," she said...talk, in the other you act.") The Fire From Within - Page [x.2-x.5] (I have described in one of...their companions to conduct those teachings.) The Fire From Within - Page [xii.8-xiii.1] (The organization of his teachings for...act of jumping into an abyss.) The Fire From Within - Page [10.4-10.7] (He said that the value of the...new seers meant them to have.) The Fire From Within - Page [145.5-146.4] (Genaro turned to me and assured me...voice, or playing tricks on him.) The Fire From Within - Page [193.1-194.3] ("I really don't understand, don Juan...yanks the point from its location.) The Fire From Within - Page [266.9-267.2] (He remarked that the value of...by little at a snail's pace.) The Power of Silence - Page [xii.9-xiii.8] (Sorcerers, therefore, divided their instruction into two...awareness of one's connection with *intent*.) The Power of Silence - Page [10.8-10.9] ("For you, teaching is talking about patterns...or keeps them as they are.) The Power of Silence - Page [236.3-237.5] (He paused then asked me what...seemed to be at his command.) The Art of Dreaming - Page [viii.1-viii.2] (His role as a teacher was to...is called the art of dreaming.) The Art of Dreaming - Page [ix.3-ix.5] (In the course of his general...seek an outlet in its practices.) The Art of Dreaming - Page [17.4-17.5] (Don Juan justified the indispensability of...gives them abstract and detailed explanations.)
SEE ALSO: *BENEFACTOR, AWARENESS-RIGHT, AWARENESS-LEFT, EXPLANATIONS-ABSTRACT, WARRIOR-INSTRUCTION, BENEFACTOR, TONAL-TEACHING, AWARENESS-MASTERY-TEACHING, ASSEMBLAGE-POINT-STABILITY*

TEACHING-[TEACHING]: SEE: TEACHERS-TEACHING-[TEACHERS AND TEACHING]

TEACHING-SORCERER-[TEACHING FOR A SORCERER]:
(For warrior-sorcerers, to teach is what naguals do to their apprentices, they tap the prevailing intent of the universe and guide the consequences of that force on their apprentices.)

SELECTED REFERENCES: The Power of Silence - Page [10.8-11.2] ("For you, teaching is talking about patterns...healer, sorcerer, diviner, charlatan, or whatever.")
SEE ALSO: *INTENT, TEACHERS-TEACHING, APPRENTICESHIP-NAGUALISM*

TEACHING-VARIATIONS-TWO-[THE TWO VARIATIONS ON THE FUNDAMENTAL TEACHING METHOD OF THE NEW SEERS]: *(Warriors know there are two methods of teaching the warriors' way, one involves the extremes of talking and the other involves the extremes of stalking; the first method calls for explaining everything and letting the person know the course of action beforehand; it is a method that fosters freedom, choice and understanding; the second method is more coercive and does not allow for choice or understanding; it forces warriors to live the seers' concepts directly with no intermediary elucidation.)*

SELECTED REFERENCES: The Fire From Within - Page [193.1-194.3] ("I really don't understand, don Juan...yanks the point from its location.) The Power of Silence - Page [250.5-251.2] ("But didn't your benefactor tell you...a free movement of his assemblage point.)
SEE ALSO: *EXPLANATION, TEACHERS-TEACHING, TALKING, STALKING-ART, DOER-VS-EXPLAINER*

TEACHINGS-[THE TEACHINGS]-(TOP)

TEACHINGS-JUAN-[THE TEACHINGS OF DON JUAN]-(TOP)

TEACHINGS-NAGUALISM-[THE TEACHINGS OF NAGUALISM]: *(Warriors know that don Juan's teachings can be the only source of entry into his world; therefore warriors must let don Juan's words speak for themselves.)*

SELECTED REFERENCES: Journey to Ixtlan - Page [xiv.3-xiv.5] (My contention is that all these steps...don Juan's words speak for themselves.)
SEE ALSO: *TEACHING-VARIATIONS-TWO, NAGUALISM, KNOWLEDGE*

TEMPERAMENT-WARRIOR-[THE WARRIORS' TEMPERAMENT]: SEE: WARRIOR-TEMPERAMENT-[THE WARRIORS' TEMPERAMENT]

*TENANT-[THE TENANT]: *(Warriors know the tenant is an ancient Toltec; sometimes called the death defier, this individual is one of the last survivors of the old seers; an ancient death defier who is indistinguishable from the average man in the street; this ancient seer was nicknamed "the tenant" by the nagual Sebastian because since 1723 that ancient seer has been given energy [or lodging so to speak] and in return he has paid rent in the form of favors and knowledge; the tenant has given a gift of power to every nagual in Don Juan's lineage; the tenant has gained the ability to transform his sex from male to female and back again through the manipulation of the position of his assemblage point; the tenant also has the ability to open and close his gap at will.)*

SELECTED REFERENCES: The Fire From Within - Page [7.8-8.1] (Don Juan assured me that our...from the six who proceeded them.) The Fire From Within - Page [146.5-147.3] ("But the nagual Julian was quite...hope that you won't follow them.") The Fire From Within - Page [234.9-235.8] (It was in the early part...that knowledge was only hearsay.) The Fire From Within - Page [251.7s-255.4] (Don Juan suddenly seemed to be...as long as he possibly can.") The Power of Silence - Page [9.4-9.5] (Eagerly, I asked don Juan to tell...him to overlap into different stories.) The Power of Silence - Page [57.2-58.6] ("The nagual Julian's proficiency in moving...a classic example of an aberration.) The Art of Dreaming - Page [12.4-13.9] (Don Juan went on to explain...potentials are nothing to sneeze at.") The Art of Dreaming - Page [59.7-60.9] (I had forgotten my question about...that the two of you meet someday.) The Art of Dreaming - Page [206.8-207.9] ("You must recollect now, and repeat...over a hundred years ago.") The Art of Dreaming - Page [209.8-209.9] ("That sorcerer in there is the ...going to guide you through it.) **The Art of Dreaming - Page [211.5-211.6]** ("Your mistake is to forget that the...same forces that bind you now.") **The Art of Dreaming - Page [214.5-215.7]** (Don Juan calmly began to repeat...seen him as a man first.") **The Art of Dreaming - Page [224.5-225.7]** (As I heard her speak, I...shining like a row of pearls.) **The Art of Dreaming - Page [226.3-226.8]** (We knelt in front of a life-size...She was indeed a female.) **The Art of Dreaming - Page [234.7-234.8]** (She was thoroughly right. That was...a cleavage that ran its length.)

SEE ALSO: *DEATH-DEFIERS, TOLTECS, SEER-OLD, SORCERY-TECHNIQUES, POWER-GIFTS, GAP, TENANT-(ALL)*

TENANT-APPOINTMENT-UNAVOIDABLE-*[THE UNAVOIDABILITY OF THE APPOINTMENT WITH THE TENANT]-(TOP)*

TENANT-CARLOS-MEET-*[CARLOS MEETS THE TENANT]-(TOP): SEE: WOMAN-CHURCH-[THE WOMAN IN THE CHURCH]-(TOP)*

TENANT-COMMITMENT-*[THE TENANT'S COMMITMENT]: (Warriors know that the tenant's commitment to the naguals of don Juan's lineage was only to take a superfluous bit of energy from them in exchange for gifts of power.)*

SELECTED REFERENCES: The Fire From Within - Page **[253.4-253.7]** (Don Juan said that the nagual...look young or old at will.") The Fire From Within - Page **[255.1-255.4]** ("Why is that old seer doing...as long as he possibly can.")

SEE ALSO: *TENANT, POWER-GIFTS*

TENANT-CYCLE-*[THE TENANT'S CYCLE]: (Warriors know that the tenant is caught in a cycle which he can't break; the tenant knows that his path doesn't lead to freedom and that he's trapped in a situation of his own making; the only thing he can do is perpetuate the cycle of his ally-like existence as long as he can.)*

SELECTED REFERENCES: The Fire From Within - Page **[255.2-255.4]** ("My opinion is that he's caught...as long as he possibly can.")

SEE ALSO: *TENANT, ALLIES-PATTERN, WARRIOR-FREEDOM, INORGANIC-BEINGS-TRICKERY*

TENANT-VS-DEATH-DEFIER-*[THE TENANT VS THE OTHER DEATH DEFIERS]: (Warriors know that the tenant is an exceptional death defier because in addition to being able to pattern his emanations after the allies, he is also capable of returning his assemblage point to a position which enables him to interact with people again.)*

SELECTED REFERENCES: The Fire From Within - Page **[253.7-254.1]** (Don Juan explained that the death...as if nothing had ever happened.)

SEE ALSO: *TENANT, DEATH-DEFIER, ALLIES-PATTERN*

TENANT-ESCAPE-INORGANIC-BEINGS-*[THE ESCAPE OF THE TENANT FROM THE REALM OF THE INORGANIC BEINGS]-(TOP)*

TENANT-FORCE-DORMANT-EMANATIONS-*[THE TENANT AND THE FORCE OF THE DORMANT EMANATIONS]: (Warriors suspect that the tenant uses the force of the dormant emanations inside the donor nagual to prolong his existence; he cracks the nagual's gap and takes in through his own gap some of the energy that is released when the dormant emanations inside the nagual's cocoon become momentarily aligned.)*

SELECTED REFERENCES: The Fire From Within - Page **[253.7-255.4]** (Don Juan explained that the death...as long as he possibly can.")

SEE ALSO: *TENANT, EAGLE-EMANATIONS-DORMANT, DEATH-DEFIER*

TENANT-GIFT-*[THE TENANT'S GIFT]-(TOP)*

TENANT-JUAN-JOKE-*[DON JUAN'S JOKE ON THE TENANT]-(TOP)*

TENANT-JUAN-MEET-*[DON JUAN MEETS THE TENANT]*-*(TOP)*

TENANT-NAGUAL-LUJAN-*[THE TENANT AND THE NAGUAL LUJAN]*-*(TOP)*

TENANT-NAGUAL-SEBASTIAN-*[THE TENANT AND THE NAGUAL SEBASTIAN]*-*(TOP)*

TENANT-NAGUAL-WOMAN-MEET-*[THE NAGUAL WOMAN MEETS THE TENANT]*-*(TOP)*

TENANT-RATIONAL-DISBELIEF-*[THE PROBLEM OF RATIONAL DISBELIEF WITH REGARD TO THE TENANT]*: *(Warriors know that the problem of rational disbelief with regard to the tenant is that the shock of meeting such a being lumps several emanations together and it takes time for those emanations to separate themselves; people who have never set eyes on the tenant have less difficulty believing he is actually one of the original seers; but as the warriors' assemblage point continues to shift, a moment comes when the proper combination of emanations is struck and at that moment the proof of the existence of the tenant becomes overwhelmingly evident.)*

    SELECTED REFERENCES: **The Fire From Within - Page [252.2-252.8]** (Don Juan looked fixedly at me...would become overwhelmingly evident to me.)
    SEE ALSO: *TENANT, EAGLE-EMANATIONS, REASON*

TENANT-TALES-*[TALES OF THE TENANT]*-*(TOP)*

TENGO-SECRETOS-*[TENGO SECRETOS]*: *SEE: MAN-KNOWLEDGE-SECRETS*-*[THE SECRETS OF A MAN OF KNOWLEDGE]*

TERMINAL-PATIENT-IMPECCABLE-SPIRIT-*[THE IMPECCABLE SPIRIT OF A TERMINAL PATIENT]*-*(TOP)*

TERMS-WARRIOR-*[THE WARRIORS' TERMS]*: *SEE: WARRIOR-TERMS*-*[THE WARRIORS' TERMS]*

TERROR-VS-WONDER-*[TERROR VS WONDER]*: *(Warriors know that one of their arts is to balance the terror of being a human being with the wonder of being a human being.)*

    SELECTED REFERENCES: **Journey to Ixtlan - Page [267.6]** ("Only as a warrior can one...the wonder of being a man.") **Tales of Power - Page [91.6]** ("Good, good, " don Juan said, patting...is to balance terror and wonder.")
    SEE ALSO: *WARRIOR-ARTS, WARRIOR-BALANCE, BALANCE-HARMONY, WARRIOR-JOURNEY-DEFINITIVE, WARRIOR-CONTRADICTION-KNOWLEDGE, ETERNITY-VS HUMANNESS,EQUILIBRIUM*

TEST-FINAL-WARRIOR-*[THE WARRIORS' FINAL TEST]*: *SEE: WARRIOR-TEST-FINAL*-*[THE WARRIORS' FINAL TEST]*

TEST-GRAND-WARRIOR-*[THE WARRIORS' GRAND TEST]*: *SEE: WARRIOR-TEST-GRAND*-*[THE WARRIORS' GRAND TEST]*

THINGS-APPEAR-NOT-*[THINGS ARE NOT WHAT THEY APPEAR TO BE]*: *(Warriors know that there is more to human beings and the world than meets the eye; warriors spend a lifetime learning to perceive those differences.)*

    SELECTED REFERENCES: **The Power of Silence - Page [xi.3]** ("Everything I've put you through...to us than meets the eye.

SEE ALSO: *PERCEPTION, ATTENTION-FIRST, ATTENTION-SECOND, AWARENESS-TRUTH-FIRST*

THINKER-ABSTRACT-[ABSTRACT THINKERS]: (Warriors know that the old seers were the abstract thinkers; they built monumental edifices of abstractions proper to them and their time; the new seers on the other hand were not involved in concocting rational theories.)
SELECTED REFERENCES: The Fire From Within - Page [45.4-45.8] ("The new seers seem to have...them to construct their perceivable world.)
SEE ALSO: *THINKING, SEER-OLD, TOLTECS*

THINKER-TRUE-[A TRUE THINKER]: (Warriors know they must struggle to entice the assemblage point to the point of reason so they can be a thinker rather than merely part of an unsophisticated audience that simply loves the orderly works of reason.)
SELECTED REFERENCES: The Power of Silence - Page [240.2-240.3] (He said that the nagual Julian...loved the orderly works of reason.)
SEE ALSO: *THINKING, REASON, ASSEMBLAGE-POINT-MOVING*

THINKING-[THINKING]: (Warriors know the limitations of their thinking; warriors knows that the mysterious world does not always conform to their thoughts.)
SELECTED REFERENCES: A Separate Reality - Page [82.6-82.7] ("What you told me this afternoon...does not fit with your thoughts.") A Separate Reality - Page [91.7] ("You're thinking again," he said...he cannot encounter that possibility.) A Separate Reality - Page [180.2] ("Who are you to think...nothing about the forces you're tapping.) The Eagle's Gift - Page [307.5-307.6] (*I am already given to the power...dart past the Eagle to be free.*) The Power of Silence - [123.1-123.4] (He asserted that events difficult...you understood this sorcerers' contradiction.")
SEE ALSO: *THINKING-(ALL), DESCRIPTION-WORLD*

THINKING-VS-ASSEMBLAGE-POINT-MOVEMENT-[THINKING VS THE MOVEMENT OF THE ASSEMBLAGE POINT]: (Warriors know there are two types of memory, remembering and recollecting; remembering is dictated by day-to-day type of thinking while recollecting is dictated by the movement of the assemblage point; recollecting is also referred to as remembering with the body.)
SELECTED REFERENCES: The Power of Silence - Page [124.9] ("Remembering is dictated by the day...the movement of the assemblage point.)
SEE ALSO: *THINKING, ASSEMBLAGE-POINT-MOVING, RECOLLECTION-SORCERER, REMEMBERING-BODY*

THINKING-AVERAGE-[AVERAGE THINKING]: SEE: THINKING-TYPES-TWO-[THE TWO TYPES OF THINKING]

THINKING-CLEAR-[CLEAR THINKING]: (The warrior knows that clear thinking is another term for precise thinking or silent knowledge or "seeing".)
SELECTED REFERENCES: The Power of Silence - Page [123.8-123.9] (I want you to recall something...take over and make you recollect.")
SEE ALSO: *THINKING-TYPES-TWO, SEEING, KNOWLEDGE-SILENT*

THINKING-LOOKING-[THINKING AND LOOKING]: (Warriors know that thinking as one looks is a habit of the average man; the average man thinks as he looks and thinks as he thinks, instead of "seeing" and knowing.)
SELECTED REFERENCES: A Separate Reality - Page [84.5-85.3] (He stubbornly maintained that his preference...then whether things matter or not.)
SEE ALSO: *THINKING, LOOKING-VS-SEEING, KNOWLEDGE-SILENT*

THINKING-PRECISE-[PRECISE THINKING]: SEE: THINKING-TYPES-TWO-[THE TWO TYPES OF THINKING]

THINKING-SEEING-[THINKING VS SEEING]: SEE: SEE-THINK-[SEEING VS THINKING]

THINKING-STOPPING-[STOPPING ONE'S THINKING]: (Warriors know that the only way to think clearly is to not think at all; in order to achieve precise thinking, which requires a movement of the assemblage point, warriors must stop their average thinking processes long enough to allow the necessary movement of the assemblage point to occur; warriors must intend the movement of the assemblage point in order to stop their normal thinking.)
    SELECTED REFERENCES: **The Power of Silence - Page [123.1-124.1]** (He asserted that events difficult to explain..."*Intent* is beckoned with the eyes.")
    SEE ALSO: *THINKING, THINKING-TYPES-TWO, INTERNAL-DIALOGUE, STOPPING-WORLD, KNOWLEDGE-SILENT, SEEING*

THINKING-TALKING-ENERGY-[THE ENERGY REQUIRED FOR THINKING AND TALKING]: (Warriors know that thinking and saying exactly what we want requires untold amounts of energy; warriors realize that everything they think or say depends upon the position of the assemblage point.)
    SELECTED REFERENCES: **The Power of Silence - Page [84.5-84.7]** (The sensation I was experiencing was...to translate my feelings into thoughts.) **The Power of Silence - Page [90.2]** ("What a strange feeling: to realize...of the assemblage point," he remarked.)
    SEE ALSO: *TALKING, ATTENTION-FIRST, ENERGY, ASSEMBLAGE-POINT-POSITION*

THINKING-TYPES-TWO-[THE TWO TYPES OF THINKING]: (Warriors know there are two types of thinking; one is average thinking ruled by the normal position of the assemblage point; average thinking is very muddled and does not really answer the warriors' needs; the other type is precise thinking which is functional, economical and leaves very few things left unexplained; in order for this type of thinking to prevail, the assemblage point must move, or at least the average thinking processes must cease in order to allow for the necessary movement of the assemblage point.)
    SELECTED REFERENCES: **The Power of Silence - Page [123.1-123.9]** (He asserted that events difficult to explain...take over and make you recollect.")
    SEE ALSO: *THINKING, ASSEMBLAGE-POINT-MOVING, INTERNAL-DIALOGUE, WORLD-STOPPING*

THIRD-ENEMY-[THE THIRD ENEMY]: SEE: POWER-[POWER], WARRIOR-ENEMIES-NATURAL-[THE NATURAL ENEMIES OF THE WARRIOR]

*THIRD-POINT-[THE THIRD POINT]: SEE: POINT-THIRD-[THE THIRD POINT]

THOUGHT-IMMENSITY-[THE IMMENSITY OF THOUGHT]: (Warriors know that the immensity of thought is the sobriety of the mind; the untainted possibilities of human awareness.)
    SELECTED REFERENCES: **The Art of Dreaming - Page [2.7-2.8]** ("Do you mean, don Juan, that...I like the immensity of thought.)
    SEE ALSO: *HUMAN-ALTERNATIVES-POSSIBILITIES-POTENTIAL, WARRIOR-SOBRIETY*

THOUGHT-SOMERSAULT-*[THE SOMERSAULT OF THOUGHT INTO THE INCONCEIVABLE]*: *(Warriors know that the somersault of thought is the descent of the spirit; the act of breaking the barrier of perception; the moment in which warriors reach their perceptual limits; intent; the spirit; the act of reaching beyond our boundaries and touching the inconceivable.)*
    SELECTED REFERENCES: **The Power of Silence - Page [112.6-113.7]** ("Sorcerers defeat death and death acknowledges...what those advance runners can accomplish.") **The Power of Silence - Page [114.5]** ("I'm going to tell you something...of their thought into the inconceivable.") **The Power of Silence - Page [116.1-116.3]** (Because he can manipulate his elusive...his thought somersault into the inconceivable.") **The Power of Silence - Page [224.9]** ("The third point of reference is...our boundaries and touching the inconceivable.")
    SEE ALSO: *SPIRIT-DESCENT, PERCEPTION-BARRIER-BREAKING, SPIRIT, INTENT*

THOUGHTS-OTHERS-ENCUMBERING-*[THE ENCUMBERING THOUGHTS OF OTHERS]*: *(Warriors know that it is best to lose all personal history because it frees us from the encumbering thoughts of other people.)*
    SELECTED REFERENCES: **Journey to Ixtlan - Page [13.9-14.1]** ("It is best to erase all personal...the encumbering thoughts of other people.") **Journey to Ixtlan - Page [15.7-15.9]** ("But that's absurd," I protested...way people know you, for instance.") **The Second Ring of Power - Page [271.8]** ("It's our fate that your plugged up...at least be assured of that.")
    SEE ALSO: *PERSONAL-HISTORY-ERASING, BLACK-MAGICIANS*

THOUGHTS-QUIETING-*[QUIETING DOWN ONE'S THOUGHTS]*: *(Warriors know that quieting the thoughts is the goal of gazing and the right way of walking; warriors quiet their thoughts as part of the process of stopping the internal dialogue.)*
    SELECTED REFERENCES: **The Second Ring of Power - Page [306.1-306.4]** (From la Gorda's statements about gazing...above the line of the horizon.)
    SEE ALSO: *GAZING, WALKING-RIGHT-WAY, INTERNAL-DIALOGUE-STOPPING*

THOUGHTS-WARRIOR-*[THE WARRIORS' THOUGHTS]*: SEE: *WARRIOR-THOUGHTS-[THE WARRIORS' THOUGHTS]*

THREE-*[THE NUMBER THREE]*: *(Warriors know that the number three is a symbol of dynamics, change, movement and above all, revitalization.)*
    SELECTED REFERENCES: **The Eagle's Gift - Page [230.9-231.1]** (The three girls clustered together and...above all, a symbol of revitalization.)
    SEE ALSO: *FOUR*

THREE-PHASE-PROGRESSION-*[THE THREE PHASE PROGRESSION]*: SEE: *PROGRESSION-THREE-PHASE-[THE THREE-PHASE]*

THRESHOLD-NO-RETREAT-*[THE THRESHOLD THAT PERMITS NO RETREAT]*: *(Warriors know there is a threshold in life which is initiated by the descent of the spirit; the descent of the spirit seals a man's permanent allegiance to the abstract; this threshold is an important point of reference for warriors that reminds them of the new state of their perceptual potential; both the warrior and the average man are capable of reaching this threshold; warriors emphasize the memory of crossing this threshold as a point of reference while the average man does not cross the threshold at all and does his best to forget about ever reaching it.)*
    SELECTED REFERENCES: **The Power of Silence - Page [72.3-72.6]** (He said that heightened awareness was...from which there is no return.") **The Power of Silence - Page [89.1-

89.6] (He asked me if I remembered...his best to forget all about it.) **The Power of Silence - Page [95.1-95.4]** (As their temporary protector...would attain and cross that threshold.)
    SEE ALSO: *SPIRIT-DESCENT, WARRIOR-EMPHASIS, ABSTRACT-ALLEGIANCE*

THUNDERBOLT-SORCERER-[A THUNDERBOLT SORCERER]-(TOP): SEE: SORCERER-THUNDERBOLT-[A THUNDERBOLT SORCERER]-(TOP)

TICKLISH-SENSATION-[THE TICKLISH SENSATION ON THE TOP OF THE HEAD]: SEE: STOPPING-WORLD-FEELING-[THE FEELING OF STOPPING THE WORLD]

TIME-[TIME]:
(*Warriors know they can no longer make the world chronological; time becomes redefined for them because the glue of the description of time is no longer binding; nagual's time has nothing to do with tonal's time, the two don't jibe; time for the warrior is the essence of attention, not something measured by the movement of a clock; when warriors thinks about life in terms of hours instead of years, they realize that life is immensely long; sorcerers count their lives in terms of hours, and know that it is possible to live in one hour the equivalent in intensity of a normal life; the Eagle's emanations are made of time, and when warriors enter into any aspect of the other self, they becomes acquainted with time; there is no past or future in the universe; in the universe there is only energy, and energy has only an endless and ever-present here and now.*)
    SELECTED REFERENCES: **Tales of Power - Page [46.8-47.9]** ("A fluid warrior can no longer...time is no longer binding on him.") **Tales of Power - Page [196.7-196.9]** ("It is not as complicated as you...are no survivors on this earth!") **The Eagle's Gift - Page [305.4-306.4]** (She said that I should not...as images recede or as they approach.) **The Fire From Within - Page [293.3-294.4]** (He explained as we walked back...he had been gone only a moment.) **The Power of Silence - Page [241.8-242.3]** (Don Juan immediately noticed the change...information in the movement of the assemblage point.) **The Art of Dreaming - Page [248.1-248.3]** (I succinctly told her about my...and ever-present here and now.") **The Art of Dreaming - Page [253.3-253.5]** ("Your energy body is moving forward...In a time yet to come.")
    SEE ALSO: *TIME-DESCRIPTION, TIME-CONTINUUM, WARRIOR-FLUIDITY, ATTENTION, INTENSITY, TIME-(ALL)*

TIME-BLACK-WORLD-[TIME IN THE BLACK WORLD]: SEE: WORLD-BLACK-[THE BLACK WORLD], WORLD-BLACK-TALES-[TALES OF THE BLACK WORLD]-(TOP)

TIME-CHANGES-EVERYTHING-[TIME CHANGES EVERYTHING]:
(*Warriors know that time changes everything; every new nagual has to use new words and new ideas to describe his "seeing".*)
    SELECTED REFERENCES: **The Fire From Within - Page [49.3-49.5]** (I asked him why he had changed...said, but in a different way.")
    SEE ALSO: *TIME, WARRIOR-TERMS EXPLANATION*

TIME-COMPRESSING-[COMPRESSING TIME]:
(*Warriors know that compressing time is the sixth principle of stalking; warriors compress time, they don't waste an instant; warriors learn how to handle intensity.*)
    SELECTED REFERENCES: **The Eagle's Gift - Page [281.3-281.5]** ("You've done just that. But now...Warriors don't waste an instant.") **The Power of Silence - Page [241.9-243.7]** (If you think about life in...flow of energy is called intensity.")
    SEE ALSO: *INTENSITY, STALKING-PRINCIPLES-SEVEN, TIME*

TIME-CONTINUUM-[THE CONTINUUM OF TIME]:
(*Warriors know that the continuum of time is the linear sequence of time in the first attention.*)

SELECTED REFERENCES: **The Eagle's Gift - Page [83.4-83.5]** (Her conclusions were logical given the...lives where we could fit them.) **The Eagle's Gift - Page [312.9-313.4]** (Don Juan said then that...interruption in the continuum of my time.)
SEE ALSO: *TIME, TIME-DESCRIPTION*

TIME-DAY-WARRIOR-[THE WARRIORS' TIME OF DAY]: SEE: WARRIOR-TIME-DAY-[THE WARRIORS' TIME OF DAY]

TIME-DESCRIPTION-[THE DESCRIPTION OF TIME]: *(Warriors know that the description of time is a characteristic feature of the description of the world; our linear description of time which operates in the context of the first attention; the description of time collapses when warriors move the assemblage point beyond a specific threshold of awareness.)*

SELECTED REFERENCES: **Tales of Power - Page [47.1-47.9]** ("Can an outsider, looking at a...time is no longer binding him.")
SEE ALSO: *DESCRIPTION-WORLD, TIME, ASSEMBLAGE-POINT-MOVING, AWARENESS-THRESHOLD, ATTENTION-FIRST*

TIME-MODALITY-[THE MODALITY OF TIME]: *(Warriors know that the modality of time is the precise bundle of energy fields being perceived; time decides which precise bundle of energy fields, out of an incalculable number, are to be used; handling the modality of the time takes all of the average man's available energy, leaving him nothing that would help him use any other energy fields.)*

SELECTED REFERENCES: **The Power of Silence - Page [x.2-x.5]** ("Human beings are born with a...any of the other energy fields.")
SEE ALSO: *TIME, EAGLE-EMANATIONS, ENERGY*

TIME-NAGUAL-[NAGUAL'S TIME] *(Warriors know that for the nagual, there is no land, or air, or water, or time; the nagual glides in nagual's time, and that has nothing to do with tonal's time which is the time of the first attention.)*

SELECTED REFERENCES: **Tales of Power - Page [157.5-157.6]** ("No. I wasn't. But it's useless...with the body, not the reason.") **Tales of Power - Page [194.1-194.3]** ("No. For the nagual there is...The two things don't jibe.")
SEE ALSO: *TIME, NAGUAL, ATTENTION-FIRST*

TIME-ONCOMING-[THE ONCOMING TIME]: *(Warriors know that stalkers learn to face the oncoming time; instead of facing time as it recedes, warriors face time as it advances; from that perspective warriors do not perceive the future, but instead see time as something concrete, yet incomprehensible.)*

SELECTED REFERENCES: **The Eagle's Gift - Page [294.3-294.6s]** (When don Juan had described the...energy necessary to unravel the mystery.) **The Art of Dreaming - Page [253.3-253.5]** ("Your energy body is moving forward...In a time yet to come.")
SEE ALSO: *TIME, STALKER-TURNS-HEAD, TIME-WHEEL*

TIME-WHEEL-[THE WHEEL OF TIME]: *(Warriors know that time is the essence of attention and they strive to someday face the wheel of time; the wheel of time is like a state of heightened awareness, a part of the other self; it can physically be described as a tunnel of infinite length with reflective furrows; every furrow is infinite and there are infinite numbers of them; the force of life compels living creatures to be trapped in one furrow; warriors strive to learn to focus their will on the wheel of time in order to make it turn; warriors who succeed in turning the wheel of time can gaze into any furrow of the wheel of time and draw from it whatever they desire; to*

accomplish this means that the warrior can face images from either direction, as they recede or as they approach.)
    SELECTED REFERENCES: **The Eagle's Gift - Page [305.4-306.4]** (She said that I should not...images recede or as they approach.) **The Eagle's Gift - Page [310.5-310.6]** (The courier Juan Tuma said very...usher me into the ultimate mystery.)
    SEE ALSO: *TIME, TIME-ONCOMING*

TIMIDITY-[TIMIDITY]: *(Warriors know they must develop an appropriate perspective on death for their acts to become energized with their rightful power; when warriors accomplish this, their acts are no longer the acts of a timid human being.)*
    SELECTED REFERENCES: **Journey to Ixtlan - Page [84.8-85.3]** ("Use it. focus your attention on...and exploiting our lot as men.")
    SEE ALSO: *DEATH-ADVISER, WARRIOR-DOUBTS-REMORSE, WARRIOR-WORRY-NOT*

TIMING-[TIMING]: *(Warriors know that timing is one of the attributes of the warrior that exist in the domain of the man of knowledge.)*
    SELECTED REFERENCES: **The Second Ring of Power - Page [284.2-284.3]** ("Impeccability for me is to tell you...or it won't have any effect.") **The Second Ring of Power - Page [326.1-326.3]** (She looked at me. I had...arrival, it was alien to me.) **The Eagle's Gift - Page [59.7-59.9]** (Don Juan used to stress the need...everything we knew. She was inflexible.) **The Fire From Within - Page [23.5]** ("My benefactor developed a strategy using...control, discipline, forbearance, and timing.") **The Fire From Within - Page [24.2-24.3]** ("At that time, I was barred...them to me through his strategy.")
    SEE ALSO: *WARRIOR-ATTRIBUTES, CONTROL, DISCIPLINE, FORBEARANCE, WILL*

TIP-SCALES-[TIP THE SCALES]: SEE: SCALES-TIP-[TIP THE SCALES]

TIREDNESS-[TIREDNESS]: *(Warriors know that tiredness is the fatigue of the first attention and its self-reflection; the average man never fully overcomes his tiredness because the lull of daily affairs makes him drowsy.)*
    SELECTED REFERENCES: **The Teachings of Don Juan - Page [50.6-50.8]** (Yet you are a serious person...will come to you of itself.") **The Teachings of Don Juan - Page [87.5-87.8]** ("This is the time when a man...clarity, power, and knowledge is enough.") **A Separate Reality - Page [4.7-4.8]** ("You make it sound stupid...not complete. You have no peace.") **The Power of Silence - Page [49.1-49.2]** (He asserted that during our active...daily affairs has made us drowsy.)
    SEE ALSO: *LIFE-INTERACTIONS-DAILY, ATTENTION-FIRST, SELF-REFLECTION*

TOLTEC-[TOLTECS]: *(Warriors know that Toltec means "man of knowledge"; the Toltecs were ancient sorcerer-seers, the receivers and holders of mysteries; when a warrior receives the mysteries of stalking and dreaming he becomes a Toltec; the Toltecs were extraordinary men; powerful sorcerers, somber driven men who unraveled mysteries and fixated the awareness of others.)*
    SELECTED REFERENCES: **The Second Ring of Power - Page [184.2-185.4]** (It took two Toltecs to make us...my interest a long time ago.") **The Second Ring of Power - Page [245.9-247.1]** ("The Nagual told me that sorcerers...anyone of us about our attention.") **The Fire From Within - Page [1.8-2.4]** ("Ages before the Spaniards came to...is that awareness can be manipulated.") **The Fire From Within - Page [4.2-4.7]** (Don Juan explained then that his...lived outside the Toltecs' geographical regions.)
    SEE ALSO: *SEER-OLD, TOLTEC HISTORY, TOLTEC-(ALL), TOLTECS-(ALL)*

TOLTEC-ATTAINMENT-[THE GREATEST ATTAINMENT OF THE ANCIENT TOLTECS]: *(Warriors know that the most important achievement of the sorcerers of antiquity was the capacity to "see", to perceive the energetic essence of things.)*

SELECTED REFERENCES: **The Art of Dreaming - Page [2.9-3.2]** (Don Juan explained that the their...things, a capacity they call *seeing*.)
SEE ALSO: *SEEING, ENERGETIC-ESSENCE-PERCEIVING, TOLTECS*

TOLTEC-COMPLETENESS-[THE COMPLETENESS OF THE TOLTEC WARRIOR]: (Warriors know there are many incomplete sorcerers; to be complete is only for the Toltec warriors who have a clear purpose.)
SELECTED REFERENCES: **The Second Ring of Power - Page [240.9]** ("Not everybody has to do that...complete is only for us Toltecs.)
SEE ALSO: *WARRIOR-COMPLETENESS , TOLTECS*

TOLTEC-COURAGE-[THE TOLTECS' COURAGE]: SEE: TOLTEC-MOTIVATION-[THE MOTIVATION OF THE ANCIENT TOLTECS]

TOLTEC-DARING-[THE TOLTECS' DARING]: SEE: TOLTEC-MOTIVATION-[THE MOTIVATION OF THE ANCIENT TOLTECS]

TOLTEC-DESCENT-DEPTHS-[THE TOLTECS' DESCENT INTO THE DEPTHS]: (Warriors know that what the ancient Toltecs referred to as their "descent into the depths" was really no more than another term for the movement of the assemblage point which transported them to the realm of the inorganic beings.)
SELECTED REFERENCES: **The Fire From Within - Page [102.5-102.6]** ("Of course, by now you realize that...old seers never made that realization.") **The Fire From Within - Page [165.7-166.4]** (He added that the old seers...had to become trees to do that.")
SEE ALSO: *INORGANIC-BEINGS-REALM, TOLTECS, TOLTEC-LEVELS, ASSEMBLAGE-POINT-MOVING, OTHER-WORLDS-ASSEMBLE-TOTAL*

TOLTEC-DOMINATION-BID-[THE TOLTECS' BID TO DOMINATE]: SEE: TOLTEC-SUPREMACY-STRUGGLE-[THE TOLTECS STRUGGLE FOR SUPREMACY]

TOLTEC-DOOM-[THE DOOM OF THE ANCIENT TOLTEC SEERS]: (Warriors know that when the ancient Toltecs established one-to-one relationships with the inorganic beings, it gave them a false sense of invulnerability which eventually spelled their doom; the aberrant practices and fixations of the ancient Toltec seers lead them to their doom instead of leading them to freedom.)
SELECTED REFERENCES: **The Fire From Within - Page [2.7-3.1]** ("We are going to be talking...to freedom, but to their doom.") **The Fire From Within - Page [84.2-84.3]** (Don Juan assured me that the...of invulnerability, which spelled their doom.)
SEE ALSO: *ABERRATION-MORBIDITY, OBSESSION, INORGANIC-BEINGS-TRICKERY, TOLTECS*

*TOLTEC-GHOULS-[THE TOLTEC GHOULS]: (Warriors know there are ancient seers who have learned to prolong their lives almost indefinitely and who still roam the earth in search of victims to exploit.)
SELECTED REFERENCES: **The Eagle's Gift - Page [18.9-19.3]** ("The pyramids are harmful," Pablito went...them traps of the second attention.") **Eagle's Gift - Page [25.3-26.3]** ("I had completely forgotten about that...long after the phantoms had vanished.) **The Fire From Within - Page [71.5-72.4]** (Something got me out of my total...The mystery can only be witnessed.") **The Fire From Within - Page [103.2-103.7]** (He said that it was the...dominate, to master everybody and everything.) **The Fire From Within - Page [231.7-234.5]** ("Tonight you're going to find out some...old seers who are still alive.") **The Fire From Within - Page [289.6-289.8]** ("Where will I be don Juan...you won't be in this world.")
SEE ALSO: *TOLTECS, SEER-OLD, DEATH-DEFIERS*

TOLTEC-HISTORY-[TOLTEC HISTORY]: (Warriors know the history of the ancient Toltecs and how the cycle of the new seers began.)
SELECTED REFERENCES: **The Eagle's Gift - Page [14.5-14.8]** (I realized then that it had been...God knows how many.") **The Fire From Within - Page [1.8-10.7]** ("Ages before the Spaniards came to...new seers meant them to have.) **The Fire From Within - Page [34.3-34.7]** (Don Juan explained that the new...to separate it from the unknowable.)
SEE ALSO: *TOLTECS, SEER-OLD, SEER-NEW, CYCLE-NEW*

TOLTEC-INVULNERABILITY-FALSE-[THE TOLTECS' FALSE FEELING OF INVULNERABILITY]: SEE: TOLTEC-DOOM-[THE DOOM OF THE ANCIENT TOLTECS]

TOLTEC-KNOWLEDGE-ORIGIN-[THE ORIGIN OF THE TOLTECS' KNOWLEDGE]: (Warriors know that the Toltecs' path to knowledge originated when some of them began to eat power plants and analyze their experiences; these men were very daring but very mistaken.)
SELECTED REFERENCES: **The Fire From Within - Page [3.6-3.8]** (I asked him then about the...were very daring, but very mistaken.")
SEE ALSO: *POWER-PLANTS, KNOWLEDGE-MEN-ORIGINAL, TOLTECS*

TOLTEC-KNOWLEDGE-PRACTICES-[TOLTEC KNOWLEDGE AND PRACTICES]: (Warriors know that there is a body of aberrant knowledge and practices accumulated by the ancient Toltecs; the secret knowledge of the Toltecs that led them to total destruction; obscure formulas, incantations and ritual procedures that have to do with the handling of intent; this secret knowledge was divided into five sets of two categories each; the earth and the dark regions, fire and water, the above and the below, the loud and the silent, the moving and the stationary; the practices of the ancient Toltecs are very effective but most of the time they are deadly.)
SELECTED REFERENCES : **The Fire From Within - Page [80.3-84.7]**("The new seers were simply terrified...mysterious aspects of motion and motionlessness.) **The Fire From Within - Page [91.9-92.1]** ("But I heard a voice in my ear...of the time they are deadly.") **The Fire From Within - Page [232.7-233.7]** ("As Genaro told you, the old...the seers who practiced them are.") **The Fire From Within - Page [234.7-237.9]** (Don Juan said that the new seers...elongate those periods to cover millennia.) **The Art of Dreaming - Page [203.3-203.9]** ("For years now, I have been...or like the new ones," he said.)
SEE ALSO : *TOLTECS, ABERRATION-MORBIDITY, DEATH-DEFIERS, RITUAL*

TOLTEC-LEVELS-[THE TOLTEC LEVELS BELOW]: (Warriors know that the ancient Toltecs believed there were seven levels below; in actuality there are no depths, there are only other great bands of emanations with which the assemblage point can become aligned.)
SELECTED REFERENCES: **The Fire From Within - Page [90.2-91.3]** ("What really took place out there...that came to look us over.") **The Fire From Within - Page [93.2-93.4]** (He explained that the ancient seers...call allies do appear around waterholes.") **The Fire From Within - Page [101.9-102.6]** (He assured me that experienced seers...old seers never made that realization.") **The Fire From Within - Page [116.4-116.5]** ("Look at that flame," he said...to the depths of the unknown.") **The Fire From Within - Page [165.7-166.4]** (He added that the old seers were...to become trees to do that.") **The Fire From Within - Page [217.1-217.2]** ("Every time the old seers made...makes us perceive another total world.")
SEE ALSO: *WORLD-OTHER-LAYERS-TEN, AWARENESS-HANDLING-VS-UNDERSTANDING, TOLTEC-DESCENT-DEPTHS*

TOLTEC-LOVE-LIFE-[THE TOLTECS' LOVE OF LIFE]: SEE: TOLTEC-MOTIVATION-[THE MOTIVATION OF THE ANCIENT TOLTECS]

TOLTEC-MOOD-[THE MOOD OF THE ANCIENT TOLTECS]: SEE: SEER-OLD-MOOD-[THE MOOD OF THE OLD SEERS]

TOLTEC-MOTIVATION-[THE MOTIVATION OF THE ANCIENT TOLTECS]: (Warriors know that the ancient Toltecs were horrid creatures with completely self-serving purposes but warriors question what it was that motivated this condition; warriors suspect that the Toltecs' aberration sprang from the fact that they were never challenged and that they were spoiled like rotten children who have never had the appropriate guidance and care; warriors find it hard to believe that their accomplishments and daring could have been motivated by greed and selfishness alone; greed alone is not enough to propel a man into the vastness of the unknown; warriors suspect that in spite of their horrifying aberrations, the ancient seers were in some way motivated by love, a love for life and intrigue and mystery; the old seers had unquenchable curiosity and guts galore; their daring and courage was impeccable; warriors have no choice but to have some compassion and respect for the ancient seers for these reasons.)

SELECTED REFERENCES: **The Fire From Within - Page [249.6-250.5]** (I confessed to don Juan that...but he was laughing at it.)

SEE ALSO: *TOLTEC-GHOULS, TOLTEC-ACCOMPLISHMENTS, LOVE, ABERRATION-MORBIDITY, WARRIOR-CHALLENGE, TONAL-OVERSEER-PROTECTED, WARRIORSHIP-VS-SORCERY, TOLTECS*

TOLTEC-POWER-ARRANGEMENT-[THE TOLTEC WARRIORS' POWER ARRANGEMENT]-(TOP)

TOLTEC-POWER-PLACE-[THE TOLTEC POWER PLACE]-(TOP)

TOLTEC-RUINS-[TOLTEC RUINS]-(TOP): SEE: PYRAMIDS-[PYRAMIDS AND TOLTEC RUINS]: (TOP)

TOLTEC-SECRET-DREAMERS-FORMLESS-[SECRET OF THE FORMLESS TOLTEC DREAMERS]: (Warriors know that when the second attention has to be called upon to assemble itself, all that is needed is the motion of opening the crack between the worlds.)

SELECTED REFERENCES: **The Second Ring of Power - Page [298.3-298.9]** (I told her that once while...Toltec dreamers once they are formless.")

SEE ALSO: *CRACK-WORLDS, ATTENTION-SECOND, TOLTEC*

TOLTEC-SEER-[THE TOLTEC SEERS]: (Warriors know that the Toltec seers were the last link to a tradition and chain of knowledge that extended over thousands of years; these extraordinary men were powerful sorcerers, and were somber, driven men who victimized people through the manipulation of their awareness.)

SELECTED REFERENCES: **The Fire From Within - Page [1.9-2.4]** ("Ages before the Spaniards came to...is that awareness can be manipulated.)

SEE ALSO: *TOLTEC-TRADITION, TOLTECS, SEER-OLD, ABERRATION-MORBIDITY*

TOLTEC-SUPREMACY-STRUGGLE-[THE TOLTECS STRUGGLE FOR SUPREMACY]: (Warriors know that the ancient Toltecs are involved in a bid to dominate everything in a colossal struggle for supremacy; their bid to dominate failed, however, because they became lost in the intricacies of knowledge and the pitfalls of sorcery.)

SELECTED REFERENCES: **The Fire From Within - Page [249.4-249.6]** (He said that the tumbler's boost...and usually meant struggle for supremacy.) **The Fire From Within - [298.7-298.9]** (Don Juan said that adventurous men...the futility of self-importance.)

SEE ALSO: *SORCERY-FUTILITY-PITFALLS, WARRIORSHIP-VS-SORCERY, POWER-OBJECTS, ABERRATION-MORBIDITY, OBSESSION, ATTENTION-SECOND-FACES-TWO, KNOWLEDGE-INTRICACIES, TOLTECS*

**TOLTEC-TRADITION-*[THE TOLTEC TRADITION]: (The tradition of the ancient Toltec seers; the seers of the new cycle have scorned and deviated from this ancient tradition to a great degree, but they are inextricably linked to that old tradition in spite of their efforts to deviate from it; the knowledge of the new seers is colored with the mood of that ancient Toltec tradition because there is no escaping the fact that it was the ancient Toltecs who laid the foundation for everything the new seers know.)*

SELECTED REFERENCES: **The Fire From Within - Page [xiii.4-xiii.6]** (In this case the action at hand...the seers of a new cycle.) **The Fire From Within - Page [9.2-9.8]** ("The ancient seers were very fortunate...centuries of that kind of concentration.") **The Fire From Within - Page [167.8-167.9]** (He remarked that the mistakes the...scorn and reject their own tradition.) **The Art of Dreaming - Page [2.7-2.9]** ("Do you mean don Juan,. that...everything we know and do today.) **The Art of Dreaming - Page [79.6-81.2]** ("Do you mean, don Juan, that...price they couldn't afford to pay.)

SEE ALSO: *TOLTECS, TOLTEC-KNOWLEDGE-PRACTICES, SORCERER-ANTIQUITY-MOOD*

***TONAL-*[THE TONAL]: (Warriors know that the tonal, pronounced (toh-na'hl), is the organizer of the world; the tonal is everything we know, everything in our world, everything that meets the eye; the tonal is one of the eight points on the sorcerers' diagram; the tonal is the right side, everything the intellect can conceive of; the agreement that we are solid objects is the tonal's doing.)*

SELECTED REFERENCES: **Tales of Power - Page [96.2-96.9]** ("We mas say that every one..."dreaming" were on the right side.) **Tales of Power - Page [119.9-121.8]** ("This is my *tonal*," don Juan...it should be a broadminded guardian.") **Tales of Power - Page [122.1-126.3]** ("The *tonal* is everything we are...part of the *tonal* of our time.") **Tales of Power - Page [126.9-127.4]** (From the moment we become all...ourselves to be making perfect sense.") **Tales of Power - Page [130.2-140.9]** ("Does the *nagual* have consciousness...superb structures as you said.") **Tales of Power - Page [142.6-145.2]** (I suggested that we should go...the warrior's hour of power.") **Tales of Power - Page [155.6-156.8]** (A warrior doesn't ever leave the island...you ended up in the market.") **Tales of Power - Page [158.8-158.9]** ("But did they see me disappear...are only extraordinary for the *tonal*.) **Tales of Power - Page [191.7-191.8]** ("You know damn well that you're...use it to win an argument.") **Tales of Power - Page [193.2-193.3]** ("In order to be an average...but without endangering his being.) **The Eagle's Gift - Page [163.4-163.5]** (Don Juan had told us that...body, thus its resistance to conceptualization.)

SEE ALSO: *ATTENTION-FIRST, TONAL-ISLAND, UNITY, SORCERER-DIAGRAM, ATTENTION-TONAL, TONAL-(ALL). WORLD-SOLID-OBJECTS*

**TONAL-ACCOUNTABLE-PREDICTABLE-NOT-*[THE TONAL IS NOT ACCOUNTABLE OR PREDICTABLE]: SEE: REASON-TRICKING-[TRICKING THE REASON]*

**TONAL-BAFFLEMENT-*[THE BAFFLEMENT OF TONAL]: SEE: TONAL-BEWILDERMENT-[THE BEWILDERMENT OF THE TONAL]*

**TONAL-BEWILDERMENT-*[THE BEWILDERMENT OF THE TONAL]: (Warriors know that one of the aims of their training is to curtail the bewilderment of the tonal; this allows warriors to be so fluid that they can admit everything without admitting anything.)*

SELECTED REFERENCES: **Tales of Power - Page [179.6-179.8]** (Don Juan said that my "tonal"...could admit everything without admitting anything.)

SEE ALSO: *TONAL, TONAL-CONTROL, SELF-INDULGENCE*

TONAL-BOOSTING-[THE BOOSTING OF THE TONAL SO THE NAGUAL CAN EMERGE]: SEE: POWER-PERSONAL-[PERSONAL POWER], WARRIOR-IMPECCABILITY-[THE IMPECCABILITY OF THE WARRIOR]

TONAL-BURDEN-EASING-[EASING THE BURDEN OF THE TONAL]: (Warriors know that when facing the nagual, changing the position of the eyes always eases the burden of the tonal.)
> SELECTED REFERENCES: Tales of Power - Page [173.7-174.1] ("Another thing one should do when facing...safeguard the order of the *tonal*.)
> SEE ALSO: *NAGUAL-FACING, TONAL, EYES*

TONAL-CONTROL-[THE CONTROL OF THE TONAL]: (Warriors know they must struggle to curtail the tonal's sterile and boring insistence to have everything under its control; whenever it doesn't succeed it is baffled for a moment and then it opens itself to death because it would rather kill itself than relinquish control.)
> SELECTED REFERENCES: Tales of Power - Page [174.6-174.8] ("In your case, for instance, you...can do to change that condition.")
> SEE ALSO: *TONAL, TONAL-SUICIDE, TONAL-BEWILDERMENT*

TONAL-DAY-[THE DAY OF THE TONAL]-(TOP)

TONAL-DETHRONING-GENTLE-[GENTLY DETHRONING THE TONAL]: SEE: TONAL-OVERSEER-PROTECTED-[THE TONAL AS A PROTECTED OVERSEER], TONAL-TYRANT-[THE TONAL AS A TYRANT], SELF-IMPORTANCE-[SELF-IMPORTANCE]

TONAL-DISARRANGING-[DISARRANGING THE TONAL]: (Warriors know that encounters with power act to disarrange the tonal in ways which change it forever.)
> SELECTED REFERENCES: Tales of Power - Page [246.9-247.1] (But she's a great warrior and...acts sent you into another realm.)
> SEE ALSO: *TONAL, FACADE-TRANSFORMING*

TONAL-INDESCRIBABLE-[THE INDESCRIBABLE TONAL]: (Warriors know that reason is only a center of assemblage, a mirror that reflects something which is outside of it; reason is merely reflecting an outside order, an order which it knows nothing about; reason cannot explain that order or understand it or unravel it; reason can only witness the effects of the indescribable tonal in the same way that the will witnesses the indescribable effects of the nagual; the tonal is but a reflection of the indescribable unknown filled with order.)
SELECTED REFERENCES: Tales of Power - Page [276.8-278.3] ("To make *reason* feel safe is...of that indescribable void that contains everything.)
> SEE ALSO: *NAGUAL, WITNESSING-WE-ARE-MERELY, TONAL-REASON, SORCERER-EXPLANATION*

*TONAL-ISLAND-[THE ISLAND OF THE TONAL]: (Warriors know that the tonal is an island, an island on which we have everything; an island which is in fact, the world; warriors never leave the island of the tonal, they use it instead; the only alternative warriors have is to sweep clean the island of the tonal.)
> SELECTED REFERENCES: Tales of Power - Page [124.4-124.9] ("The *tonal* is an island," he explained...the *tonal*. See what I mean?") Tales of Power - Page [126.6-127.4] ("If the *nagual* is not any...believe ourselves to making perfect sense.) Tales of Power - Page [127.8-

127.9] ("I'm afraid I haven't asked the...the island, one finds the *nagual*.") **Tales of Power - Page [128.1]** ("But, when you call it the...to make you aware of it.") **Tales of Power - Page [130.2-130.4]** ("Does the *nagual* have consciousness...but to simply recount its effects.") **Tales of Power - Page [145.1-145.2]** ("For a *proper tonal* everything on...of course, is his bid for power.") **Tales of Power - Page [155.5-155.6]** ("Write, write," don Juan coaxed me...of the *tonal*. He uses it.") **Tales of Power - Page [174.8-174.9]** ("The island of the *tonal* has...as if there were nothing there.") **Tales of Power - Page [191.7-191.8]** ("You know damn well that you're...use it to win an argument.") **Tales of Power - Page [193.2-193.4]** ("In order to be an average...the gate for such an escape.) **Tales of Power - Page [230.7-231.2]** ("I've already told you that I...You have accomplished that task.") **Tales of Power - Page [233.4-233.6]** (He said that the occasion required...me since the day we met.) **Tales of Power - Page [242.4-243.1]** (Your self-pity is still a feature...we needed those power plants.") **Tales of Power - Page [246.4]** ("Power plants shake the *tonal*...of the whole island," he said.) **Tales of Power - Page [246.8-247.1]** ("I put you in bodily contact with her...acts sent you into another realm.) **Tales of Power - Page [253.5-253.8]** ("The delicate maneuver of leading a...that better than anyone I know.") **The Second Ring of Power - Page [291.7-293.6]** (La Gorda recounted the way don Juan...tonal, as he had called it.)

SEE ALSO: *UNITY, FACADE-TRANSFORMING, TONAL*

TONAL-NAGUAL-[THE TONAL AND THE NAGUAL]-(TOP)

TONAL-NAGUAL-DICHOTOMY-[THE TONAL NAGUAL DICHOTOMY]:
(Warriors know that the tonal-nagual dichotomy describes the true pair, the two entities, the two counterparts which become operative at the moment of birth, the tonal and the nagual; the island of the tonal and what lies beyond it; the paradox of the luminous beings; the tonal and the nagual are outside of ourselves and yet they are not; the tonal is but a reflection of the indescribable unknown filled with order, the nagual is but a reflection of that indescribable void that contains everything; the first and second rings of power; the attention of the tonal and the attention of the nagual; the attention over the table and the attention under the table.)

SELECTED REFERENCES: **Tales of Power - Page [120.1-120.7]** (He explained that every human being...until now to talk about them.) **Tales of Power - Page [126.5-127.9]** ("If the *nagual* is not any...the island, one finds the *nagual*.") **Tales of Power - Page [130.8-132.5]** ("Are the *nagual* and the *tonal*...why not, then, live with that totality?") **Tales of Power - Page [145.1-145.3]** ("For a *proper tonal* everything on...the warrior's hour of power.") **Tales of Power - Page [155.7-155.9]** ("This is your world. You can't...the harmony between *tonal* and *nagual*.) **Tales of Power - Page [158.8-158.9]** ("That is taken care of by the...are only extraordinary for the *tonal*.) **Tales of Power - Page [159.8-161.1]** ("Things like that are known to...That boosting is called personal power.") **Tales of Power - Page [172.8-174.9]** ("When one is dealing with the...as if there was nothing there.") **Tales of Power - Page [191.2-191.5]** ("I've never put a ban on talking...are not applicable to the *nagual*.") **Tales of Power - Page [192.3-194.9]** ("What about someone who doesn't...pale, absent-minded, irritable, quiet.") **Tales of Power - Page [230.7-231.7]** ("I've already told you that...the core of the sorcerers' explanation.) **Tales of Power - Page [245.5]** (One should get to the *nagual*...above all, without injuring one's body.) **Tales of Power - Page [249.1-249.4]** ("What would have happened if...all we do is to acquiesce.) **Tales of Power - Page [252.1-252.2]** ("Then it was my *tonal*," I said...cannot be lead into each other.") **Tales of Power - Page [259.7-259.8]** (Don Juan said that I had goofed...willingly and be aware of my act.) **Tales of Power - Page [271.7-278.3]** ("What Genaro wanted to show you...that indescribable void that contains everything.) **Tales of Power - Page [283.5-284.1]** ("You already know that this is...is a most unappealing affair.) **The Second Ring of Power - Page [1.6-2.2]** (Prior to that jump don Juan...say anything to clarify their nature.) **The Second Ring of Power - Page [226.2-226.9]** (I asked her then about her...to be properly called the nagual.) **The Second Ring of Power - Page [269.5-269.9]** (There was an abyss between our...talk, in the other you act.") **The Second Ring of Power - Page [274.8-275.4]** (Don Juan said that the core...impart order to the nonordinary world.) **The Second Ring of Power - Page [291.7-293.5]** (La Gorda recounted the way don Juan...unit was the totality of oneself.)

SEE ALSO: *TONAL, NAGUAL, PAIR-TRUE, LUMINOUS-BEINGS-PARADOX, POWER-RING-FIRST, POWER-RING-SECOND, ATTENTION-TONAL, ATTENTION-NAGUAL, TABLE-WILDERNESS*

TONAL-ORDER-[THE ORDER OF THE TONAL]: SEE: ATTENTION-FIRST-ORDER-[THE ORDER OF THE FIRST ATTENTION]

TONAL-OVERSEER-PROTECTED-[THE TONAL AS A PROTECTED OVERSEER]: (Warriors know that the tonal must be coaxed into relinquishing control gladly; this means that the tonal is made to give up unnecessary things like self-importance and indulging; the tonal must be protected at any cost but at the same time it must freed from the things that plunge it into boredom; the crown must be taken away from the tonal with a firm hand, but at the same time the tonal must remain as a protected overseer.)
SELECTED REFERENCES: Tales of Power - Page [156.1-156.4] ("In the beginning, one has to...anything else, a strong free *tonal*.) Tales of Power - Page [160.7-160.8] ("I had to borrow a bucket...must remain as the protected overseer.) The Power of Silence - Page [73.1-73.5] (He told me to drive across the...must work ceaselessly to dethrone it.")
SEE ALSO: *TONAL, SELF-IMPORTANCE, SELF-INDULGING*

TONAL-PERCEPTION-[THE TONAL'S PERCEPTION]: (Warriors know that the eyes guide the tonal's perception; the perception of the tonal is the perception of the first attention.)
SELECTED REFERENCES: Tales of Power - Page [258.6-258.8] (They said that I should not be...up from the ravine to the rock.)
SEE ALSO: *TONAL, DESCRIPTION-WORLD, EYES, ATTENTION-FIRST, PERCEPTION*

TONAL-PERFECT-[THE PERFECT-TONAL]: (Warriors know that to maintain order means to be a perfect tonal, and to be a perfect tonal means to be aware of everything that takes place on the island of the tonal.)
SELECTED REFERENCES: Tales of Power - Page [191.7-191.8] ("You know damn well that you're...use it to win an argument.")
SEE ALSO: *TONAL, TONAL-ISLAND*

TONAL-PERSONAL-[THE PERSONAL TONAL]: (Warriors know that every human being has a personal tonal.)
SELECTED REFERENCES: Tales of Power - Page [124.6] ("There is a personal *tonal* for...call the *tonal* of the times.") Tales of Power - Page [139.4-139.5] (After the *tonal* of the time...only thing left uncontested, the *nagual*.)
SEE ALSO: *TONAL, TONAL-TIMES*

TONAL-PREVAIL-MUST-[THE TONAL MUST PREVAIL]: (Warriors know that the tonal must prevail if they are to use the nagual the way sorcerers do; there is no way to get to the sorcerers' explanation unless one has willingly used the tonal to make sense out of one's actions in the nagual.)
SELECTED REFERENCES: Tales of Power - Page [271.7-271.8] ("What Genaro wanted to show you...the *nagual* the way sorcerers do.)
SEE ALSO: *TONAL-NAGUAL-DICHOTOMY, SORCERER-EXPLANATION, TONAL, NAGUAL*

TONAL-PROPER-[THE PROPER TONAL]: (Warriors know that a proper tonal is a tonal where its two sides are in perfect harmony and balance; for a proper tonal everything on the island of the tonal is a challenge; a proper tonal is a strong, free tonal.)
SELECTED REFERENCES: Tales of Power - Page 142.7-143.3] (I suggested that we should go...are in perfect harmony and balance.") Tales of Power - Page [145.1-145.3] ("For a *proper tonal* everything on...the warrior's hour of power.") Tales of Power - Page [156.4] That's what a sorcerer needs before anything else, a strong free tonal.)
SEE ALSO: *TONAL-SIDES-TWO, WARRIOR-CHALLENGE, BALANCE, LIFE-STRONG*

TONAL-REFUGE-NAGUAL-[THE TONAL TAKES REFUGE IN THE NAGUAL]: (Warriors know that under the conditions of utmost duress, sorcerers found themselves holding on to the only thing left uncontested, the nagual; in other words, their tonal took refuge in the nagual; this couldn't have happened had it not been for the excruciating conditions of a vanquished people; today's men of knowledge are by-products of those conditions, and as such, are the ultimate connoisseurs of the nagual since they were left there thoroughly alone.)
SELECTED REFERENCES: **Tales of Power - Page [139.4-139.6]** (After the *tonal* of the time...doesn't even have the idea it exists.)
SEE ALSO: *TONAL, NAGUAL, WARRIOR-DURESS-EXTREME-BENEFITS*

TONAL-REORDERING-[REORDERING THE TONAL]: SEE: FACADE-TRANSFORMING-[TRANSFORMING THE FACADE]

TONAL-SEEING-MAN-[SEEING A MAN AS A TONAL]: (Warriors know that to "see" a man as a tonal means to cease judging him in a moral sense, or excusing him on the grounds that he is a victim of the world of circumstance; in other words, to "see" a man as a tonal means to "see" him without thinking he is helpless or hopeless, to assess him without condemning him or forgiving him.)
SELECTED REFERENCES: **Tales of Power - Page [135.1-135.2]** ("What does it entail to see...man without condemning or forgiving him.")
SEE ALSO: *SEEING, TONAL*

*TONAL-SHRINKING-[SHRINKING THE TONAL]: (Warriors know that the tonal shrinks at given times, especially when it is frightened or embarrassed or taken by surprise; the shyness of the tonal unavoidably makes it shrink; once the tonal shrinks the nagual takes over and extraordinary things are possible, but they are only extraordinary for the tonal; the warrior struggles to shrink his tonal but at the very moment the tonal shrinks the warrior must reverse all that struggle to keep from being swept away.)
SELECTED REFERENCES: **Tales of Power - Page [156.4-156.8]** (The task then is to convince...you ended up in the market.") **Tales of Power - Page [158.9]** ("That is taken care of by...they are only extraordinary for the *tonal*.) **Tales of Power - Page [160.6-160.7]** ("Your tonal has to be convinced...your *nagual* began to take over.) **Tales of Power - Page [176.8-177.4]** ("A sudden fright always shrinks the...or he would be swept away.) **Tales of Power - Page [195.6-195.7]** ("The reason why you're afraid...away every time Genaro is around.") **The Second Ring of Power - Page [286.1-286.2]** (But when he shoved you, your...entire being went through the crack.)
SEE ALSO: *TONAL-, TONAL-NAGUAL-DICHOTOMY, WARRIOR-WORLD-COLLAPSES-REASSEMBLES, TONAL-SHRINKING*

TONAL-SIDES-TWO-[THE TWO SIDES OF THE TONAL]: (Warriors know there are two sides to every tonal; one is the outer surface of the tonal, the rugged part that's related to action and acting; the other part is the more delicate and more complex inner tonal, the softer part that deals with decision and judgment.)
SELECTED REFERENCES: **Tales of Power - Page [143.1-143.2]** ("There are, roughly speaking, two sides...softer, more delicate and more complex.)
SEE ALSO: *TONAL, TONAL-PROPER*

TONAL-SUICIDE-[THE SUICIDAL TENDENCIES OF THE TONAL]: (Warriors know that the tonal has a sterile and boring insistence on having everything under its control; whenever it doesn't succeed, there is a moment *of bafflement when the tonal opens itself to death; in some way the tonal would rather kill itself than relinquish control and there is very little warriors can do to change that condition.)*

SELECTED REFERENCES: Tales of Power - Page [10.5-10.6] (He had warned me that the...melancholy, or even a suicidal depression.) **Tales of Power - Page [157.2-157.3]** ("For a while you were all...and *nagual*, I walked you here.") **Tales of Power - Page [174.6-174.8]** (What you were doing this morning...can do to change that condition.") **Tales of Power - Page [194.8-194.9]** (Now everything depends on you...become pale, absent-minded, irritable, quiet.") **Tales of Power - Page [195.9]** (His explanation of the whole affair...taking as a suicidal plunge.) **The Fire From Within - Page [152.6-153.5]** (My experience with la Catalina delayed...to live, we couldn't help laughing.")

SEE ALSO : *TONAL, TONAL-OVERSEER-PROTECTED, WARRIOR-EVICTION-NOTICE*

TONAL-SWEEPING-ISLAND-[SWEEPING CLEAN THE ISLAND OF THE TONAL]: SEE: TONAL-ISLAND-[THE ISLAND OF THE TONAL]

TONAL-TEACHING-[TEACHING ABOUT THE TONAL]: (Warriors know that when they are being taught something about the tonal, they learn about it step by step until they understand every facet of the whole procedure.)

SELECTED REFERENCES: The Second Ring of Power - Page [269.5-269.8] ("You sure are dumb," she said...doing what he has been shown.)

SEE ALSO: *TEACHERS-TEACHING, TONAL*

TONAL-TIMES-[THE TONAL OF THE TIMES]: (Warriors know that the tonal of the times is a collective tonal for all the luminous beings existing at any given time.)

SELECTED REFERENCES: Tales of Power - Page [124.6] ("There is a personal *tonal* for...call the *tonal* of the times.") **Tales of Power - Page [139.4]** (After the *tonal* of the time...only thing left uncontested, the *nagual*.)

SEE ALSO: *TONAL, TONAL-PERSONAL*

TONAL-TOOL-[THE TONAL IS A TOOL]: (Warriors know that the perception of the tonal is a tool, the best and the only tool they've got; it is a tool to be appreciated and protected but never worshipped.)

SELECTED REFERENCES: Tales of Power - Page [272.1-272.3] ("One thing has nothing to do...but the only one we've got.)

SE ALSO: *TONAL, DESCRIPTION-WORLD*

TONAL-TYRANT-[THE TONAL AS A TYRANT]: (Warriors know that aspects of the tonal behave like tyrants or despots of sorts; the warriors' egomania for instance is a real tyrant that we must work ceaselessly to dethrone.)

SELECTED REFERENCES: The Power of Silence - Page [73.1-73.5] (He told me to drive across the...must work ceaselessly to dethrone it.")

SEE ALSO: *TONAL-OVERSEER-PROTECTED, TONAL, TYRANT, SELF-IMPORTANCE, SELF-IMAGE*

TONAL-VULNERABILITY-[THE VULNERABILITY OF THE TONAL]: (Warriors know that the tonal is vulnerable, it cannot withstand mistreatment.)

SELECTED REFERENCES: Tales of Power - Page [11.6-11.8] ("Why do I get so nervous...of all the barriers and disappointments.") **Tales of Power - Page [138.6-138.9]** ("Indians are the losers of our time...Indian it has been sheer bliss.")

SEE ALSO: *TONAL*

TONAL-WARRIOR-[THE WARRIORS' TONAL]: SEE: WARRIOR-TONAL-[THE WARRIORS' TONAL]

TONAL-WATCHING-[WATCHING THE TONAL FROM A DISTANCE]:
(Warriors know they are obligated to watch the tonal from a distance in order to have a better grasp of what is really around them.)
SELECTED REFERENCES: **The Second Ring of Power - Page [292.4-292.5]** (He told them that sorcerers were...of what was really around them.)
SEE ALSO: *TONAL*

TONAL-WEAKENING-[WEAKENING THE TONAL]: (Warriors know that human beings have learned to perfection how to make their tonals weak through self-indulging; warriors protect the tonal by avoiding self-indulgent behavior and by living the warriors' way.)
SELECTED REFERENCES: **Tales of Power - Page [136.4-136.5]** ("There is no need to treat the body...I have called that indulging.")
SEE ALSO: *TONAL, SELF-INDULGENCE, WARRIOR-WAY, WARRIOR-IMPECCABILITY, WARRIOR-PROTECT-THEMSELVES-COMMANDS, WARRIOR-PROTECT-PERSON*

TONGUE-TIED-[BEING TONGUE-TIED]: (Warriors know that sometimes the assemblage point of the average man moves without any known cause and without the individual's knowing it; this movement of the assemblage point manifests itself by leaving the individual feeling tongue-tied, confused and evasive for no apparent reason.)
SELECTED REFERENCES: **The Power of Silence - Page [81.5-81.7]** ("Sorcerers have a rule of thumb...become tongue-tied, confused and evasive.")
SEE ALSO: *ASSEMBLAGE-POINT-MOVING, KNOWLEDGE-VS-LANGUAGE, SORCERER-MUTENESS, WARRIOR-MOTOR-CONTROL-LOSS-OF*

TOTAL-BEING-[THE WARRIORS' TOTAL BEING]: (Warriors know their total being consists of two perceivable segments; the first is the physical body which anyone can perceive, and the second is the luminous cocoon which only seers can perceive; the warriors' total being is a field of energy and his second attention can transform that energy into anything suitable, anything within the boundaries of possibility.)
SELECTED REFERENCES: **The Eagle's Gift - Page [17.9-18.2]** (Don Juan had said that our...the appearance of giant luminous eggs.) **The Eagle's Gift - Page [23.5-23.7]** (He said that the second attention...of possibility is known as *will.*) **The Eagle's Gift - Page [237.4-237.6]** (Through the forced practice of journeying...is part of our total being.) **The Fire From Within - Page [53.4-53.5]** (Patiently, he explained that everything I...those other areas is to *see.*")
SEE ALSO: *BODY-PHYSICAL, LUMINOUS-COCOON*

TOTAL-FREEDOM-[TOTAL FREEDOM]: SEE: FREEDOM-TOTAL-[TOTAL FREEDOM], WARRIOR-FREEDOM-TOTAL-[WARRIORS FOR TOTAL FREEDOM]

TOTAL-QUIETNESS-[TOTAL QUIETNESS]: SEE: INNER-SILENCE-[INNER SILENCE]

TOTALITY-[TOTALITY]: (Warriors know that totality is the third attention; the tonal-nagual dichotomy; the true nature of the warrior; reaching the second attention makes it and the first attention into a single unit, and that unit is the totality of the self)
SELECTED REFERENCES: **Tales of Power - Page [4.3-4.5]** ("What matters is that a warrior...talk about the totality of oneself.) **Tales of Power - Page [8.8-8.9]** ("Do you know that you can...of yourself forever in any direction.") **Tales of Power - Page [55.7-56.2]** ("But you yourself told me...not let you go either way.") **Tales of Power - Page [97.7-97.8]** (We are an awareness; we are...we rarely emerge in our lifetime.) **Tales of Power - Page [98.7-98.8]** ("The suggestion that I want to...get to the totality of yourself.) **Tales of Power - Page [117.1-117.4]**

("My suit and all this paraphernalia..."The totality of oneself," he said.) **Tales of Power - Page [132.1-132.4]** ("I was concerned with those jolts...without the binding force of life.) **Tales of Power - Page [160.4-160.5]** ("What was going to be revealed...is a terrible way of being.) **Tales of Power - Page [244.8-245.5]** (I would say that sorcerers...arrive at the totality of oneself.) **Tales of Power - Page [272.3-272.5]** ("Last night your bubble of perception...true nature. You are a cluster.) **The Second Ring of Power - Page [84.3-84.8]** (There was no doubt left in my...human nature, he was probably right.) **The Second Ring of Power - Page [293.4-293.5]** (He said that reaching the second...that unit was the totality of the oneself.) **The Eagle's Gift - Page [23.5]** (He said that the second attention...transforms that energy into anything suitable.) **The Eagle's Gift - Page [177.5-177.8]** (The Nagual and his warriors were...seek and face their definitive journey.) **The Eagle's Gift - Page [178.9-179.1]** (His benefactor had told him that...of the totality of the body.) **The Eagle's Gift - Page [219.9-221.1]** (He then plunged them into the...a new pair of double beings.) **The Eagle's Gift - Page [299.1-299.2]** (He had helped everyone impeccably... the parallel lines in one's totality.) **The Fire From Within - Page [xiii.6-xiii.8]** (When I asked him once what...as if they never existed.) **The Fire From Within - Page [123.3-123.4]** ("The grand test that the new...called regaining the totality of oneself.")

 SEE ALSO: *ATTENTION-THIRD, TONAL-NAGUAL-DICHOTOMY, TOTALITY-(ALL)*

TOTALITY-BEING-DIE-[THE TOTALITY OF THE BEING THAT IS GOING TO DIE]: *(Warriors know they experience a particular feeling when the nagual surfaces; at those moments the tonal becomes aware of the totality of itself, the totality of the being that is going to die.)*

 SELECTED REFERENCES: Tales of Power - Page [132.1-132.2] ("I was concerned with those jolts...being that is going to die.)
 SEE ALSO: *TOTALITY, PAIR-TRUE, TONAL-NAGUAL-DICHOTOMY*

TOTALITY-CONSOLIDATING-[CONSOLIDATING THE TOTALITY OF ONESELF]: SEE: REMEMBERING-TASK-[THE TASK OF REMEMBERING]

TOTALITY-REGAINING-[REGAINING THE TOTALITY OF ONESELF]: *(Warriors know that regaining the totality of oneself is the grand test of the new seers; the retracing of the journey which the warrior-apprentice's assemblage point took under the influence of the nagual.)*

 SELECTED REFERENCES: Tales of Power - Page [92.6-92.9] ("As you know," he said...personal power that you have stored.) The Eagle's Gift - Page [220.8-220.9] (Don Juan told us that losing the...arriving at the totality of oneself.) The Eagle's Gift - Page [303.8-303.9] (As we walked back to his house...have energy to fulfill my task.) The Fire From Within - Page [123.3-123.4] ("The grand test that the new...called regaining the totality of oneself.") The Fire From Within - Page [300.2-300.3] (We know now that we were...the greater our doubts, the greater our turmoil.)
 SEE ALSO: *APPRENTICESHIP, RECOLLECTION-SORCERER, REMEMBERING-BODY, TOTALITY*

TOTALITY-WARRIOR-[THE WARRIORS' TOTALITY]: SEE: WARRIOR-TOTALITY-[THE WARRIORS" TOTALITY]

TOTALITY-WARRIOR-COMMAND-[THE WARRIORS' COMMAND OVER THE TOTALITY OF HIMSELF]: SEE: WARRIOR-TOTALITY-COMMAND-[THE WARRIORS' COMMAND OVER THE TOTALITY OF HIMSELF]

TRAINING-WARRIOR-[THE WARRIORS' TRAINING]: SEE: WARRIOR-TRAINING-[THE WARRIORS' TRAINING]

TRANSFORMATION-WARRIOR-[THE WARRIORS' TRANSFORMATION]: SEE: WARRIOR-TRANSFORMATION-[THE WARRIORS' TRANSFORMATION]

TRANSFORMING-FACADE-[TRANSFORMING THE FACADE]: SEE: FACADE-TRANSFORMING-[TRANSFORMING THE FACADE]

TRANSPORTED-FLAME-[TRANSPORTED ON THE POWER OF FLAME]- (TOP): SEE: FLAME-TRANSPORTED-[TRANSPORTED ON THE POWER OF FLAME]-(TOP)

*TRANSPORTED-WATER-[TRANSPORTED BY THE POWER OF WATER]: SEE: WATER-TRANSPORTED-[TRANSPORTED BY THE POWER OF WATER]

TRAP-ARTFUL-TEACHER-[THE TEACHER'S ARTFUL TRAP]: (Warriors know that the teacher sets an artful trap for his apprentice in order to help him overcome the unavoidable impasse; this trap involves pitting the apprentice against a worthy opponent.)
     SELECTED REFERENCES: A Separate Reality - Page [211.7-213.1] ("Whatever I have done to you today...the pressure of my irrational fear.) Journey to Ixtlan - Page [215.6-215.7] (Over a month before, I had...of a trap to ensnare me.) Tales of Power - Page [246.2-246.8] (Don Juan said that after the...long-range battle with an Indian sorceress.)
     SEE ALSO: WORTHY-OPPONENT, TEACHERS-TEACHING

TRAP-DETAIL-[THE TRAP OF DETAIL]: SEE: ENERGY-BODY- PERFECTING-[PERFECTING THE ENERGY BODY]

TRAP-INORGANIC-BEINGS-[THE TRAP OF THE INORGANIC BEINGS]: SEE: INORGANIC-BEINGS-TEACHINGS-[THE TEACHINGS OF THE INORGANIC BEINGS]

TRAPPED-WILLING-[A MAN HAS TO BE WILLING TO BE TRAPPED]: (Warriors know that in order to be trapped by unknown forces, they have to be willing to do so, they must be willing to abandon themselves to those forces.)
     SELECTED REFERENCES: A Separate Reality - Page [179.6-179.8] ("I think you must be aware...You're willing to abandon yourself.")
     SEE ALSO: INORGANIC-BEINGS-TRICKERY, ABANDON-REFUSAL

*TREES-[TREES]: (Warriors know that trees have a consciousness and purpose similar to that of the inorganic beings; that consciousness is incomprehensible to us because it is infinitely slower than ours; trees are made to stay put, they are immobile and yet they make everything move around them; like inorganic beings, trees have projections which are even less friendly to us than those of the inorganic beings; dreamers never seek them unless they have attained a state of profound amenity with trees.)
     SELECTED REFERENCES: The Eagle's Gift - Page [236.5-236.6] (Silvio Manuel told us that the...filled to the brim with it.) The Fire From Within - Page [164.9-166.4] ("This may seem like an oddity...to become trees to do that.") The Art of Dreaming - Page [86.6-87.4] ("They come in search of potential...That's why we have no friends.")
     SEE ALSO: PLANTS, INORGANIC-BEINGS

TREES-AWARENESS-[THE AWARENESS OF TREES]: (Warriors know there is no sense of strife in a tree; they draw their nourishment from the depths of the earth.)
     SELECTED REFERENCES: The Eagle's Gift - Page [236.5-236.6] (Silvio Manuel told us that the...filled to the brim with it.)
     SEE ALSO: TREES

TREES-GAZING-[TREE GAZING]: SEE: GAZING [GAZING]

TREES-INORGANIC-BEINGS-[TREES AND INORGANIC BEINGS]: (*Warriors know that the old seers believed that trees and plants have the most intense communication with the inorganic beings and used the awareness of plants to assemble the worlds of inorganic life.*)
> SELECTED REFERENCES: The Fire From Within - Page [164.9-166.4] ("This may seem like an oddity...to become trees to do that.")
> SEE ALSO: *TREES, INORGANIC-BEING*

TREES-MAN-[MAN AND TREES]: (*Warriors know that trees are closer to man than ants because they share more emanations with us.*)
> SELECTED REFERENCES: The Fire From Within - Page [164.8-165.2] (Don Juan abruptly changed the subject...much larger than the tree itself.)
> SEE ALSO: *TREES*

*TREES-WARRIOR-[WARRIOR-TREES] SEE: WARRIOR-TREE-[WARRIOR TREES]

TREMENDUM-[THE TREMENDUM]: (*Warriors know the tremendum is the limitless landscape of the second attention.*)
> SELECTED REFERENCES: The Second Ring of Power - Page [326.7-327.4] (But Eligio was stronger and his...the experience of my own journey.)
> SEE ALSO: *UNKNOWN-INTRICACIES, PERCEPTION-WINGS*

TRUE-PAIR-[THE TRUE PAIR]: SEE: PAIR-TRUE-[THE TRUE PAIR]

TRUMPETER-PEERLESS-[THE PEERLESS TRUMPETER]-(TOP)

TRUST-THEMSELVES-WARRIOR-[WARRIORS TRUST THEMSELVES]: SEE: WARRIOR-TRUST-THEMSELVES-[WARRIORS TRUST THEMSELVES]

TRUTH-[TRUTH]: (*Warriors define the truth as that which they know without words to be true; the warriors' knowledge without language, silent knowledge; a truth that requires no defense.*)
> SELECTED REFERENCES: The Fire From Within - Page [39.9-40.1] ("Those truths are not something to...that a nagual has no obsessions.") The Art of Dreaming - Page [63.2-63.3] ("How do you know he was telling...what's out there waiting for them.")
> SEE ALSO: *KNOWLEDGE-SILENT, LIFE-TRUTHFUL, AWARENESS-TRUTH-(ALL)*

TRUTH-UNDERLYING-EXPOSING-[EXPOSING THE UNDERLYING TRUTH]-(TOP)

TULIOS-FOUR-[THE FOUR TULIOS]-(TOP)

TUMBLER-[THE TUMBLER]: (*Warriors know that the tumbler is one component of the rolling force; the force that eventually breaks down mans' luminous cocoon after a lifetime of collisions and tumbles man's awareness back to the Eagle.*)
> SELECTED REFERENCES: The Fire From Within - Page [221.2-225.8] (I would have gone on seeing...result is staggering in its consequences.") The Fire From Within - Page [228.6-229.4] (Don Juan said that these new...being's gap and makes it die.") The Fire From Within - Page [233.3-233.5] (The old seers realized, don Juan...offer no ideal configuration to it.)
> SEE ALSO: *FORCE-FORCE, FORCE-CIRCULAR*

TUMBLER-BOOST-[THE TUMBLER'S BOOST]: (*Warriors know that the tumbler's boost is the force of death; the old seers discovered a way to utilize the tumbler's boost and be propelled by it; instead of succumbing to* the onslaughts of the tumbler, the old seers rode with it and let it move their assemblage points to unpredictable positions within the confines of human possibilities.)

SELECTED REFERENCES: The Fire From Within - Page [248.9-249.6] (He immediately started his explanation...and usually meant struggle for supremacy.)

SEE ALSO: *TUMBLER, DEATH-DEFIERS, SEER-OLD, EARTH-BOOST, ASSEMBLAGE-POINT-MOVING*

TUMBLING-FORCE-[THE TUMBLING FORCE]: SEE: FORCE-TUMBLING-[THE TUMBLING FORCE], TUMBLER [THE TUMBLER]

TUMBLER-HANDLING-[HANDLING THE TUMBLER]: SEE: ROLLING-FORCE-HANDLING-[HANDLING THE ROLLING FORCE]

TURNING-HEAD-WARRIOR-[TURNING THE HEAD OF THE WARRIOR]: SEE: WARRIOR-TURNING-HEAD-[TURNING THE HEAD OF THE WARRIOR]

TWIG-POWER-BREATHES-LIFE-[POWER BREATHES LIFE INTO A TWIG]-(TOP): SEE: POWER-BREATHES-LIFE-TWIG-[POWER BREATHES LIFE INTO A TWIG]-(TOP)

TWILIGHT-[TWILIGHT]: (*Warriors know that the last hour of the afternoon has special significance, it is a time of power; the warriors' hour of power.*)

SELECTED REFERENCES: The Teachings of Don Juan - Page [94.7-94.8] ("The twilight is the crack between the worlds," he said softly, without turning to me.) **The Teachings of Don Juan - Page [115.5]** (I thought of don Juan's words...there's the crack between the worlds!") **A Separate Reality - Page [209.2-209.8]** ("Sit down," he said. "The clouds...the twilight with my extended arms.) **A Separate Reality - Page [255.5-255.6]** (Don Juan explained to me that...could perform marvels at that time.) **Journey to Ixtlan - Page [64.3-64.5]** ("To believe that the world is...hard and constantly all the time.) **Journey to Ixtlan - Page [65.5-65.7]** ("Your opinions are final opinions...that power hidden in the wind.") **Journey to Ixtlan - Page [66.2-66.3]** ("If the hunter, on the other...make himself available to the wind.) **Journey to Ixtlan - Page [87.1-88.1]** (He yelled at me that the...it before the twilight was over.) **Journey to Ixtlan - Page [151.4-152.3]** (The last minutes of light, right before...the realm of the young sun.") **Journey to Ixtlan - Page [154.3-154.4]** (Don Juan's words made me shiver...a warrior's last dance of power.) **Journey to Ixtlan - Page [155.1-155.5]** ("Certainly. You are hunting personal power...to the south. To the vastness.") **Journey to Ixtlan - Page [196.4]** ("The end of the day is approaching...light to perform one last exercise.") **Journey to Ixtlan - Page [215.2]** ("We either go home now," he...use the twilight to catch her.") **Journey to Ixtlan - Page [219.3]** (Suddenly he jumped to my side...twilight was at its full power.) **Journey to Ixtlan - Page [252.5-253.2]** (Suddenly I felt that my body...but my body knew it.) **Tales of Power - Page [12.8-12.9]** ("There's only a bit of daylight left...upon before the twilight sets in.") **Tales of Power - Page [59.3-59.6]** (Don Juan made me jog on...performing those simple and idiotic movements.) **Tales of Power - Page [99.7]** (I could not catch my breath...were done only in the twilight.) **Tales of Power - Page [107.5-107.6]** ("You'll get used to it...is neither one nor the other.) **Tales of Power - Page [144.5-144.6]** (I wanted to question him further...edge of the day is an omen.) **Tales of Power - Page [161.2]** ("You must stay on this bench until twilight," he said.) **Tales of Power - Page [181.6-181.7]** (Don Juan spoke to me in a ...large insects for a long time.) **Tales of Power - Page [190.3-190.4]** ("No," he said with a serious...your case a most deadly hour,) **Tales of Power - Page [278.3-278.4]** ("Now you should sit on Genaro's place...life that binds that cluster of feelings.") **The Second Ring of Power - Page [327.9]** (She stood up and pulled me...leave before the twilight set in.) **The Eagle's Gift - Page [40.6-40.7]** (The last hour of the afternoon...have to be at that time.) **The Eagle's Gift - Page [77.6-77.8]** (I started the car and drove...mountains would never let them go.) **The Fire From Within - Page [71.2-71.3]** (It was twilight by then...moth flying around the place we sat.) **The Fire From Within - Page [204.8-205.6]** (He pointed at the mountain range...is the one that will count.) **The Fire From Within - Page [210.9-211.4]** ("Go with the boost wherever it...I were on a roller coaster.)

SEE ALSO: *CRACK-WORLDS, WARRIOR-HOUR-POWER, TWILIGHT-POWER*

TWILIGHT-POWER-[DRAWING POWER FROM THE TWILIGHT]:
(Warriors know that they can draw power from the twilight.)
SELECTED REFERENCES: **Tales of Power - Page [59.3-59.6]** (Don Juan made me jog on...performing those simple and idiotic movements.) **Tales of Power - Page [99.6-99.7]** (I could not catch my breath...were done only in the twilight.)
SEE ALSO: *TWILIGHT, WARRIOR-HOUR-POWER*

TWO-HUNDRED-TWENTY-BUTTOCKS-[TWO HUNDRED AND TWENTY BUTTOCKS]-(TOP)

TYRANNY-HELL-BLISS-[TYRANNY CAN BE HELL OR TYRANNY CAN BE
BLISS]: *(Warriors know that tyranny can be either a blessing or a curse, depending on the spirit of the warrior; tyranny can either break a man or push him relentlessly to find the only thing left uncontested, the realm of the nagual.)*
SELECTED REFERENCES: **Tales of Power - Page [138.6-139.6]** ("Indians are the losers of our time...even have the idea that it exists.")
SEE ALSO: *PETTY-TYRANT*

TYRANT-[THE TYRANT]: *(Warriors know that the tyrant is another term
for the primal source of energy, the Eagle; the one and only ruler of the universe that heads the warriors' classification of petty tyrants; the despots and authoritarians of the world are insignificant buffoons in comparison with the tyrant itself, so consequently, all these individuals were classified as petty tyrants compared to the source of everything.)*
SELECTED REFERENCES: **The Fire From Within - Page [17.2-17.4]** (The new seers, in accordance with...classified as petty tyrants, *pinches tiranos.*)
SEE ALSO: *PETTY TYRANTS, EAGLE*

U

UNAVAILABILITY-WARRIOR-[THE WARRIORS' UNAVAILABILITY]:
SEE: WARRIOR-UNAVAILABILITY-[THE WARRIORS'
UNAVAILABILITY]

UNCERTAINTY-WARRIOR-[THE WARRIORS' UNCERTAINTY]: SEE:
WARRIOR-UNCERTAINTY-[THE WARRIORS' UNCERTAINTY]

UNDECIDED-ISSUE-WARRIOR-[THE WARRIORS' UNDECIDED ISSUE]
SEE: WARRIOR-UNDECIDED-ISSUE-[THE WARRIORS' UNDECIDED
ISSUE]

UNDERSTANDING-[UNDERSTANDING]: (Warriors know the limits of
what they can understand and what is beyond any rational understanding;
warriors know that it is monstrous for them to believe that the world or
they themselves are understandable and that sometimes when they cannot
understand, they are better off than when they do understand; there are
some things the warrior "handles" without understanding; the
understanding of the average man is not the understanding of the warrior;
for the average man, understanding is an artful set of arguments and
rewards; for warriors, understanding is a trophy they bring with them on
their victorious journey of return to the spirit; warriors know there is no
way to speed up the process of true understanding; it must be carried out
little by little and at a snail's pace.)
    SELECTED REFERENCES: A Separate Reality - Page [82.6-82.7] ("What do you
want to know...way I can personally understand anything.) A Separate Reality - Page [156.5-
156.6] (I liked the idea of molding...arguments and rewards we call understanding.) A Separate
Reality - Page [257.5-257.8] ("I think I understand what don...one side of this," he said.) A
Separate Reality - Page [258.4-259.1] ("To move between these two points...been accomplished
anyway by other circumstances.") A Separate Reality - Page [260.6-262.5] ("You're chained!"
don Juan exclaimed...even turned around and saw him.") Tales of Power - Page [85.4-85.5]
(Calling the ally a moth is...is a personal matter," he said.) Tales of Power - Page [117.3-117.4]
(Now is the time to talk..."The totality of oneself," he said.) Tales of Power - Page [190.8-191.1] (I
knew that I had been...or you're beginning to become disassociated.") The Second Ring of
Power - Page [208.9-209.3] (I had been so absorbed in writing...saying that he doesn't remember
anything.") The Eagle's Gift - Page [227.9-228.1] (He told her that it is...only accept in
humbleness and awe.) The Fire From Within - Page [185.2-185.3] ("This indeed is the mystery
of awareness...apologize for either; both are needed.) The Fire From Within - Page [266.5-267.2]
(Don Juan explained that he had...by little at a snail's pace.) The Power of Silence - Page [xii.9-
xiii.9] (Don Juan stressed that this cleaning procedure...process of understanding as very
difficult.) The Power of Silence - Page [159.9-160.1] ("As I have already said to...Understanding
is one of our trophies.)
    SEE ALSO: REASON-VS-INTENT, CLARITY, EXPLANATION, ENERGY-BODY-
UNDERSTANDING, ENERGY-BODY-UNDERSTANDING, UNDERSTANDING-(ALL)

UNDERSTANDING-VS-DIRECTION-[UNDERSTANDING VS A POINT OF
DIRECTION]: (Warriors know that sometimes a piece of knowledge will
not be fully understandable, based on a lack of energetic resources to
assimilate it; in these cases, warriors do not knock themselves out trying to
understand that which at that moment is beyond understanding to them;

instead, warriors use that knowledge as a means to point out a direction for understanding to one day follow.)

SELECTED REFERENCES: Tales of Power - Page [118.5-118.6] ("Don't fret if you don't make...only to point out a direction.")

SEE ALSO: *UNDERSTANDING, KNOWLEDGE-VS-LANGUAGE*

UNDERSTANDING-PURE-[PURE UNDERSTANDING]: (Warriors know that pure understanding is the one-way bridge from reason to silent knowledge; one of the two one-way bridges between reason and silent knowledge; the recognition that reason is only one island in an endless sea of islands; pure understanding is a level of proficiency which once attained, facilitates an instantaneous shift of energy in warriors; in order to attain that instantaneous shift of energy, warriors need a clear connection with intent, and to get that clear connection, warriors need only intend it through pure understanding.)

SELECTED REFERENCES: The Power of Silence - Page [113.9-114.5] (We left the house and strolled around...and sat down on a bench.) The Power of Silence - Page [116.3-116.5] ("Because his pure understanding is an...His goal has transcended his person.") The Power of Silence - Page [240.7-240.8] (The old nagual told don Juan...in an endless sea of islands.)

SEE ALSO: *BRIDGES-TWO-ONE-WAY, CONCERN, REASON, KNOWLEDGE-SILENT, ENERGY-SHIFT-INSTANTANEOUS, WARRIOR-PROFICIENCY*

UNDERSTANDING-REVAMPING-[REVAMPING THE WARRIORS' UNDERSTANDING]: (Warriors know it is necessary at some point to revamp their understanding of the world; they must accomplish this, not just on the intellectual level but on the energetic level as well.)

SELECTED REFERENCES: The Second Ring of Power - Page [150.4-151.1] (I had never wanted to believe...order to forget his beautiful arrangement.)

SEE ALSO: *UNDERSTANDING, DESCRIPTION-WORLD, SCHOLAR-WORLD-ARRANGEMENT, CONTINUITY, WARRIOR-TRANSFORMATION*

UNDERSTANDING-SHEER-[SHEER UNDERSTANDING]: (Warriors know that sheer understanding is another term for the romance with knowledge; the drive which warriors use to know, to discover, to be bewildered.)

SELECTED REFERENCES: The Art of Dreaming - Page [75.7-75.8] ("How can I avoid all that...know, to discover, to be bewildered.") The Art of Dreaming - Page [98.6-99.1] (The unavoidable consequence for me...above all, regardless of personal convenience.)

SEE ALSO: *UNDERSTANDING*

UNEXPECTED-DOING-[DOING THE UNEXPECTED]: (Warriors know the power of doing the unexpected when encountering strange events; these unexpected actions help assure the warriors' survival and ease the strain of such encounters.)

SELECTED REFERENCES: The Second Ring of Power - Page [145.3-145.4] (Years before don Juan had told...the strain of such an encounter.)

SEE ALSO: *WARRIOR-STRATEGY*

UNIFORMITY-COHESION-[ENERGETIC UNIFORMITY AND COHESION]: SEE: ENERGETIC-UNIFORMITY-COHESION-[ENERGETIC UNIFORMITY AND COHESION]

UNIFORMITY-COHESION-REARRANGING-[REARRANGING ENERGETIC UNIFORMITY AND COHESION]: SEE: ENERGETIC-UNIFORMITY-COHESION-REARRANGING-[REARRANGING ENERGETIC UNIFORMITY AND COHESION]

UNIMPORTANCE-*[UNIMPORTANCE]*: *(Warriors know that all things are equal and by being equal they are also unimportant; once warriors have learned to "see" they "see" the same truth in everything because they know that nothing can be any more essential than anything else.)*
SELECTED REFERENCES: **A Separate Reality - Page [82.7-82.9]** ("I'm trying to think about it...by being equal they are unimportant.")
SEE ALSO: *SEEING, EQUAL-UNIMPORTANT*

UNIQUENESS-*[UNIQUENESS]*: *SEE: POWER-UNIQUENESS-[POWER AND UNIQUENESS]*

UNITY-*[UNITY]*: *(Warriors know that unity is another term for the unity of the tonal; in order to be an average tonal, a man must have his unity; his whole being must belong to the island of the tonal; warriors have to learn to disrupt that unity without endangering their being.)*
SELECTED REFERENCES: **Tales of Power - Page [193.2-193.4]** ("In order to be an average...the gate for such an escape.) **Tales of Power - Page [268.8-269.7]** (I again had the sensation of being...disintegrate and be nothing once more.) **Tales of Power - Page [270.1-270.3]** (I was speechless. The words "numb"...where my awareness was not unified.) **Tales of Power - Page [272.6-273.2]** ("This is the sorcerers 'explanation. The...as if they had never been a unit.") **The Second Ring of Power - Page [1.9]** (In my moves into the tonal...coherence. I had visions of order.) **The Art of Dreaming - Page [55.6]** ("What's the meaning of all this...in order to safeguard your unity.)
SEE ALSO: *TONAL, TONAL-ISLAND*

UNIVERSE-ENERGY-FIELDS-*[THE UNIVERSE OF INFINITE ENERGY FIELDS]*: *SEE: AWARENESS-TRUTH-FIRST-[THE FIRST TRUTH ABOUT AWARENESS], EAGLE-[THE EAGLE]*

UNIVERSE-FEMALE-*[THE FEMALE UNIVERSE]*: *SEE: FEMALE-UNIVERSE-[THE FEMALE UNIVERSE]*

UNIVERSE-PREDATORIAL-*[THE PREDATORIAL UNIVERSE]*: *(Warriors have a clear understanding that as dreamers they are always prey in the midst of a predatorial universe; the inorganic beings are the predators, bidding for the enhanced awareness of the dreamer; dreamers must be forever on their guard because they become prey the moment they venture out into the predatorial universe.)*
SELECTED REFERENCES: **The Art of Dreaming - Page [101.3-101.6]** (Don Juan explained that in the...venture out in that predatorial universe.") **The Art of Dreaming - Page [169.3-169.6]** ("Your energy body moved," he said...than admire it or examine it.") **The Art of Dreaming - Pages [170.8-170.9]** (That's the importance of the journey...as deadly as anything can be.) **The Art of Dreaming - Page [180.3-180.5]** ("There is one last issue related...for us is in that realm.")
SEE ALSO: *INORGANIC-BEINGS-REFUSING, HUNTER-SECRET*

UNKNOWABLE-*[THE UNKNOWABLE]*: *(Warriors know that the unknowable is the indescribable, the unthinkable, the unrealizable; it is something that will never be known to the warrior; and yet the unknowable is there, dazzling and at the same time horrifying in its vastness; that which is beyond the capacity of man to perceive is the unknowable; the unknowable is an eternity where the assemblage point has no way of clustering anything; the unknowable is not within human reach, therefore it should not be intruded upon foolishly or ever prudently; the new seers realized that they had to be prepared to pay the most exorbitant price for the faintest contact with it.)*

SELECTED REFERENCES: The Eagle's Gift - Page [314.1-314.3] (I knew that they were in...And then the lights were gone.) The Fire From Within - Page [19.6-19.7] (We know better now. We know...stand the pressure of the unknowable.") The Fire From Within - Page [33.6-33.7] (The unknowable, on the other hand...same time horrifying in its vastness.) The Fire From Within - Page [35.2-35.3] (Whatever is beyond our capacity to...they are confronted with the unknowable.) The Fire From Within - Page [43.3-43.5] (Only a small portion of those...the incalculable rest is the unknowable.) The Fire From Within - Page [122.7] ("Man is not the unknowable," he...one were using the eyes alone.") The Fire From Within - Page [124.2-124.3] ("One of the greatest moments the...has no way of clustering anything.") The Fire From Within - Page [206.3-207.3] ("I've been waiting for you to...is perceived and becomes the known.) The Art of Dreaming - Page [63.4] ("What's waiting for us out there..."something utterly impersonal," he said.)

SEE ALSO: *UNKNOWN, KNOWN, UNKNOWN-VS-UNKNOWABLE*

UNKNOWN-[THE UNKNOWN]: (Warriors know that the unknown and the known are on the same footing because both are within the reach of human perception; the small portion of the Eagle's emanations within the reach of human awareness is the unknown; the unknown is merely the Eagle's emanations discarded by the first attention; once the unknown is perceived, it becomes the known; the disregarded emanations within man's band are thought of as a preamble to the unknown; the unknown proper consists of the bulk of dormant emanations which are outside of man's band and which are never emphasized.)

SELECTED REFERENCES: Tales of Power - Page [245.5-245.7] ("Here is where I varied from...excursions into the *nagual*, the unknown.") The Eagle's Gift - Page [21.6-21.8] ("When you worry about what to...won't let you live in peace.") The Eagle's Gift - Page [82.7-82.9] ("Where's that spot?" "Somewhere in the...into the unknown, into another world.) The Fire From Within - Page [16.3-16.4] ("One of the first concerns of...of rechanneling that energy is impeccability.") The Fire From Within - Page [19.3-19.4] (He explained that one of the...stand the presence of the unknowable.) The Fire From Within - Page [33.2-34.1] (He told me then that before...the unknowable the results are disastrous.) The Fire From Within - Page [43.2-43.5] (Don Juan said that to see...the incalculable rest is the unknowable.) The Fire From Within - Page [66.3-66.4] ("The second attention, on the other...emanations inside man's cocoon are utilized.) The Fire From Within - Page [76.2-77.1] ("That is not quite right," don...he was not joking this time.) The Fire From Within - Page [79.5-79.7] ("The unknown is forever present," he...it or even to remember it.") The Fire From Within - Page (109.8-110.1] (The emphasized emanations compose a large...world, the unknown, the second attention.) The Fire From Within - Page [124.2-124.3] ("One of the greatest moments the...has no way of clustering anything.") The Fire From Within - Page [153.1-153.2] ("I'll tell you what the nagual...catch a glimpse of the unknown.") The Fire From Within - Page [206.3-207.3] ("I've been waiting for you to...is perceived and becomes the known.) The Fire From Within - Page [260.7-260.9] (He went back then to discussing...in an impeccable state of being.) The Fire From Within - Page [281.4] ("The only thing that soothes those...to be in the ordinary world!) The Fire From Within - Page [299.3-299.5] (He explained that the new seers...emanations inside the cocoon at once.)

SEE ALSO: *KNOWN, UNKNOWABLE, UNKNOWN-VS-THE UNKNOWABLE, EAGLE-EMANATIONS-EMPHASIZED, EAGLE-EMANATIONS-MAN-BAND, EAGLE-EMANATIONS-DORMANT, UNKNOWN-(ALL)*

UNKNOWN-ALIGNING-[ALIGNING THE UNKNOWN]: (Warriors know that the unknown is the emanations inside the cocoon that are untouched by awareness; when the glow of awareness touches them, they become active and aligned with the corresponding emanations at large; once that happens, the unknown is perceived and becomes the known.)

SELECTED REFERENCES: The Fire From Within - Page [206.8-207.3] (Don Juan restated over and over...is perceived and becomes the known.)

SEE ALSO: *UNKNOWN-ALIGNMENT, KNOWN, AWARENESS-GLOW, ASSEMBLAGE-POINT-MOVING*

UNKNOWN-BOUNDARIES-*[THE BOUNDARIES OF THE UNKNOWN]:*
(Warriors know about the boundaries between the unknown and the unknowable; the boundaries of the unknown define it as something that is veiled from man but still within his reach; within the boundaries of the unknown, the unknown becomes the known at a given time.)
SELECTED REFERENCES: The Fire From Within - Page [33.4-33.7] (He said that not to seek order...same time horrifying in its vastness.)
SEE ALSO: *UNKNOWN, UNKNOWN-VS-UNKNOWABLE, KNOWN*

UNKNOWN-ENERGY-CURRENT-*[ENERGY CURRENTS FROM THE UNKNOWN]: SEE: ENERGY-CURRENTS-UNKNOWN-[ENERGY CURRENTS FROM THE UNKNOWN]*

UNKNOWN-GRASPING-UNDERSTANDING-REMEMBERING-*[GRASPING, UNDERSTANDING AND REMEMBERING THE UNKNOWN]: (Warriors know that even though they may conserve enough energy to grasp the unknown, they still may not have enough energy to understand or remember it.)*
SELECTED REFERENCES: The Fire From Within - Page [79.5-79.7] ("The unknown is forever present...it or even to remember it.")
SEE ALSO: *UNKNOWN, REMEMBERING-BODY, ENERGY*

UNKNOWN-HIGH-ADVENTURE-*[THE HIGH ADVENTURE OF THE UNKNOWN]: (Warriors know that the high adventure of the unknown is the lure of sorcery, the lure of the inorganic beings; many sorcerers are waylaid by the high adventure of the unknown.)*
SELECTED REFERENCES: The Fire From Within - Page [143.3-143.7] ("Is she attached to your party...Catalina and you like each other.") The Fire From Within - Page [147.8-148.4] ("Be that as it may, warriors...into the unknown and love it.")
SEE ALSO: *UNKNOWN-INTRICACIES, WARRIORSHIP-VS-SORCERY, INORGANIC-BEINGS-TRAP, WARRIOR-QUEST-FREEDOM-VS-ADVENTURE-UNKNOWN*

UNKNOWN-HUMAN-*[THE HUMAN UNKNOWN]: (Warriors know that the human unknown consists of the emanations within man's band of emanations.)*
SELECTED REFERENCES: The Fire From Within - Page [124.7-124.9] ("How about the emanations that are...be hard put to describe it.")
SEE ALSO: *UNKNOWN, HUMAN-JUNKPILE*

UNKNOWN-HUMAN-VS-NON-HUMAN-*[THE HUMAN UNKNOWN VS THE NON-HUMAN UNKNOWN]: (Warriors know that the human unknown is the product of "shifts" of the assemblage point and that the non-human unknown is the product of more significant "movements" of the assemblage point; the sorcerers of antiquity were after the human unknown where they could remain, more or less, on predictable ground; they could transform themselves into anything for which they had an inventory; the new seers are after the freedom of the non-human unknown, the freedom from being human.)*
SELECTED REFERENCES: The Art of Dreaming - Page [77.9-78.7] ("What were those activities, don Juan...another person, a bird, or anything.) The Art of Dreaming - Page [79.6-81.7] ("Do you mean, don Juan, that...what it is: a mere candle.")
SEE ALSO: *UNKNOWN, ASSEMBLAGE-POINT-SHIFT-VS-MOVEMENT, UNKNOWN-HUMAN-VS-NON-HUMAN, UNKNOWN-HUMAN*

UNKNOWN-IMMEASURABLE-*[THE IMMEASURABLE UNKNOWN]:*
(Warriors know that the immeasurable unknown consists of the unused emanations outside the bounds of man's band of emanations; these emanations are perceivable but in totally indescribable ways.)
SELECTED REFERENCES: The Fire From Within - Page [124.7-124.9] ("How about the emanations that are...be hard put to describe it.") The Fire From Within - Page [156.4-156.5] (Don Juan further said that a...great band of the Eagle's emanations.)
SEE ALSO: *UNKNOWN-INTRICACIES*

UNKNOWN-INTRICACIES-*[THE INTRICACIES OF THE UNKNOWN]:*
(Warriors know that the intricacies of the unknown is another term for the intricacies of the second attention.)
SELECTED REFERENCES: The Fire From Within - Page [132.9-133.2] ("But would it be possible to encourage...being caught in the clutches of rationality.") The Fire From Within - Page [167.6-167.9] (As we walked, don Juan told...scorn and reject their own tradition.) The Art of Dreaming - Page [77.9-79.1] ("What were those activities, don Juan...as anything we know to be real.")
SE ALSO: *ATTENTION-SECOND-QUAGMIRE, KNOWLEDGE-INTRICACIES, UNKNOWN*

UNKNOWN-JOURNEY-[JOURNEY INTO THE UNKNOWN]: *(Warriors know that what they do when they journey into the unknown is very much like dying, except that their cluster of single feelings does not disintegrate but expands a bit without losing its togetherness; at the moment of death, however, the force of life leaves the body and all those single awarenesses disintegrate and sink deeply; they move independently as if they had never been a unit; in traveling into the unknown, warriors literally disassemble and then reassemble themselves through the strength of their link with intent.)*
SELECTED REFERENCES: Tales of Power - Page [272.6-273.2] ("This is the sorcerers' explanation. The nagual...as if they had never been a unit.")
SEE ALSO: *DEATH, UNKNOWN, WOMEN-TALENT*

UNKNOWN-KNOWN-*[THE UNKNOWN BECOMES THE KNOWN]: SEE:*
UNKNOWN-ALIGNING *[ALIGNING THE UNKNOWN]*

UNKNOWN-MAPPING-*[MAPPING THE UNKNOWN]:* *(Warriors know they must map the unknown through the controlled use of "seeing"; the mapping of the unknown entails making it available to our perception; warriors understand that it is possible at a given moment to leave the known and enter into the unknown.)*
SELECTED REFERENCES: The Fire From Within - Page [34.7-35.1] (The new seers did not waste...moment and enter into the unknown.)
SEE ALSO: *UNKNOWN, KNOWN, PERCEPTION*

UNKNOWN-NON-HUMAN-*[THE NON-HUMAN UNKNOWN]:* *(Warriors know that the non-human unknown is the product of significant "movements" of the assemblage point; the new seers are after the freedom of the non-human unknown, the freedom from being human.)*
SELECTED REFERENCES: The Art of Dreaming - Page [77.9-78.7] ("What were those activities, don Juan...another person, a bird, or anything.) The Art of Dreaming - Page [79.6-81.7] ("Do you mean, don Juan, that...what it is: a mere candle.")
SEE ALSO: *UNKNOWN-IMMEASURABLE, UNKNOWN-HUMAN, UNKNOWN*

UNKNOWN-PERCEIVING-[PERCEIVING THE UNKNOWN]: SEE: FIRE-WITHIN-[THE FIRE FROM WITHIN]

UNKNOWN-PREAMBLE-[THE PREAMBLE TO THE UNKNOWN]:
(Warriors know that the disregarded emanations within man's band are thought of as the preamble to the unknown; the preamble to the unknown is also known as the human junkpile; the unknown proper being the bulk of emanations which are not part of the human band.)
SELECTED REFERENCES: The Fire From Within - Page [109.8-110.1] (The emphasized emanations compose a large...world, the unknown, the second attention.)
SEE ALSO: UNKNOWN, EAGLE-EMANATIONS-EMPHASIZED, EAGLE-EMANATIONS-MAN-BAND, EAGLE-EMANATIONS-DORMANT, HUMAN-JUNKPILE

UNKNOWN-VS-UNKNOWABLE-[THE UNKNOWN VS THE UNKNOWABLE]: (Warriors know that the distinction between the unknown and unknowable is crucial, and that confusing the two puts seers at great risk whenever they confront the unknowable; the distinction between the unknown and the unknowable is the frontier between the old and the new, and the ascertation of that distinction marked the beginning of the new cycle; everything the new seers have done stems from understanding that single distinction.)
SELECTED REFERENCES: The Fire From Within - Page [33.2-35.8] (He told me then that before...awareness he was explaining to me.) The Fire From Within - Page [124.2-124.3] ("One of the greatest moments the...has no way of clustering anything.")
SEE ALSO: UNKNOWN, UNKNOWABLE, CYCLE-NEW, SEER-NEW

UNKNOWN-WHERE-[WHERE IS THE UNKNOWN]: (Warriors know that the unknown is inside the cocoon of man in the dormant emanations, and yet in a sense, it is not; warriors know that the unknown is also all around us; inside man's cocoon the unknown is the emanations untouched by awareness, but when the glow of awareness touches them they become active and aligned with the corresponding emanations at large outside the cocoon of man.)
SELECTED REFERENCES: The Fire From Within -Page [206.3-207.3] ("I've been waiting for you to...is perceived and becomes the known.)
SEE ALSO: UNKNOWN, QUESTION-ONLY-MEANINGFUL

UNOBTRUSIVENESS-ESSENCE-[THE ESSENCE OF UNOBTRUSIVENESS]-(TOP)

UNSPEAKABLE-[THE UNSPEAKABLE]: (Warriors know from their own experience that silent knowledge is indeed beyond words; the unspeakable is indeed the unspeakable.)
SELECTED REFERENCES: Tales of Power - Page [269.8-269.9] (Don Juan hugged me like a child...The unspeakable was truly the unspeakable.)
SEE ALSO: KNOWLEDGE-SILENT, LANGUAGE-VS-KNOWLEDGE

UNUSUAL-EVENTS-HAPPEN-THEMSELVES-[UNUSUAL EVENTS HAPPEN BY THEMSELVES]: (Warriors know they need not worry about procedures because the truly unusual things that happen to warriors or average men happen by themselves, with only the intervention of intent.)
SELECTED REFERENCES: The Fire From Within - Page [238.6-238.7] (After a moment's though he whispered...with only the intervention of intent.)
SEE ALSO: INTENT, AWARENESS-TRUTH-EIGHTH, INTENT-INTERVENTION

URCHIN-OPPORTUNITY-WORLD-[URCHINS IN THE STREET AND THE OPPORTUNITIES OF THE WORLD]-(TOP)

V

VAGINA-*[VAGINA]*: *(Warriors know that the extra opening between a woman's legs makes her susceptible to strange influences; strange, powerful forces possess her through that opening.)*
SELECTED REFERENCES: The Fire From Within - Page [155.2-155.9] ("Women are definitely more bizarre than...He used to do that to her.")
SEE ALSO: *WOMB, WOMEN*

VAGINA-COSMIC-*[THE COSMIC VAGINA]*: *(Warriors know that the cosmic vagina is a tongue-in-cheek term for the physical expression of the warriors' ability to move the wheel of time; the opening to the other world; the crack in between the worlds; the physical passageway to the other self.)*
SELECTED REFERENCES: The Eagle's Gift - Page [305.4-305.6] (She said that I should not...to move the "wheel of time.") The Eagle's Gift - Page [306.2-306.5] (She asserted that what warriors call...images recede or as they approach.) The Eagle's Gift - Page [312.2-312.3] (They went by me and remained...that had appeared in the room.)
SEE ALSO: *CRACK-WORLDS, SELF-OTHER, TIME-WHEEL*

VAGINA-COSMIC-THROUGH-*[THROUGH THE COSMIC VAGINA]*-*(TOP)*

VALIDATION-WARRIOR-*[THE WARRIORS' VALIDATION]*: SEE: *WARRIOR-VALIDATION*-*[THE WARRIORS' VALIDATION]*

VANITY-*[VANITY]*: *(Warriors know that vanity is an aspect of man's feelings of self-importance.)*
SELECTED REFERENCES: The Teachings of Don Juan - Page [152.8-153.3] (He said, "You think there are..."I believe that was the lesson.")
SEE ALSO: *SELF-IMPORTANCE*

VESSELS-COCOONS-*[VESSELS OR COCOONS]*: SEE: *LUMINOUS-COCOON-RECEPTACLE*-*[THE LUMINOUS COCOON AS A RECEPTACLE]*

VICENTE-GIFT-PLANTS-*[DON VICENTE'S GIFT OF PLANTS]*-*(TOP)*

VICTIM-*[VICTIM]*: *(Warriors know that the average man remains a victim because he believes he is helpless, like a leaf in the wind; but no matter how sorry for himself he feels, the average man never empowers himself beyond the boundaries of victimization; warriors, however, must assume responsibility because they know that nobody is doing anything to anybody, much less to a warrior; the idea that warriors are at the mercy of the wind is simply inadmissible.)*
SELECTED REFERENCES: A Separate Reality - Page [142.3-142.4] (There is nothing you can do...same your promise will be valid.) Journey to Ixtlan - Page [109.4-110.6] ("You feel like a leaf at...of the wind would be inadmissible.") Journey to Ixtlan - Page [120.1-120.3] (Look at yourself. Everything offends and...the best of all possible fashions.") Tales of Power - Page [135.1-135.2] ("What does it entail to see...that he is hopeless or helpless.) Tales of Power - Page [154.1-154.3] (We laughed at the image...You're not living like a warrior.) Tales of Power - Page [196.3-196.5] (I wanted to make a serious....drains his power, impeccability replenishes it.") The Fire From Within - Page [19.7-19.9] (I vociferously disagreed with him. I...retorted. "They are victims, not warriors.)
SEE ALSO: *SELF-PITY, RESPONSIBILITY-ASSUMING, WARRIOR-MOOD, VICTORY-DEFEAT-PERSECUTORS-VICTIMS, REACTIVE-STANCE, WARRIOR-PROACTIVITY*

VICTORY-[VICTORY]: (Warriors know they are in the hands of power and there is no way to fake triumph or defeat; warriors do not win victories by beating their heads against walls but by overtaking those walls instead; sorcery is a journey of return and warriors return victorious to the spirit having descended into hell; the victories of the warrior are victories of the spirit; the spirit of the warrior is not given to indulging or complaining, nor is it geared to winning or losing.)

SELECTED REFERENCES: The Teachings of Don Juan - Page [51.3-51.5] ("A man goes to knowledge as he...be no pitiful regrets over that.) The Teachings of Don Juan - Page [84.1-87.8] ("He slowly begins to learn - bit...clarity, power and knowledge is enough.") A Separate Reality - Page [88.3-88.4] ("That's not so," don Juan said...and to be defeated are equal.) A Separate Reality - Page [88.7-88.8] ("Everything is filled to the brim...my struggle was worth my while.) A Separate Reality - Page [138.3-138.6] ("You haven't been defeated yet...for reasons other than defeat itself.) A Separate Reality - Page [215.4-215.5] ("The spirit of a warrior...a warrior laughs and laughs.") Journey to Ixtlan - Page [227.6-227.7] ("What a terrible way of putting it...that *doing* there are only actions.") Tales of Power - Page [51.8-51.9] ("Certainly!" he retorted. "It's your duty...the walls; they don't demolish them.") Tales of Power - Page [55.7-56.2] ("But you yourself told me,...will not let you go either way.") Tales of Power - Page [91.7-91.8] (After I told him what I thought...if they were triumphs of the spirit.) Tales of Power - Page [284.2-284.3] ("If you choose not to return...the command over the totality of yourselves.") The Second Ring of Power - Page [51.2] (The Nagual told both of them...us wages against our old selves.) The Second Ring of Power - Page [84.3-84.8] (There was no doubt left in my...human nature, he was probably right.) The Fire From Within - Page [30.1-30.5] (I explained to don Juan that...of the petty tyrants for life.") The Fire From Within - Page [260.2-260.4] (He also said that there was...another by gripping feelings of defeat.) The Power of Silence - Page [48.9-49.5] (He said that we, as average...simple anger at having missed out.) The Power of Silence - Page [159.9] (As I have already said to...the spirit, having descended into hell.)

SEE ALSO: *ABSTRACT-RETURN, EAGLE-GIFT, DEFEAT-(ALL), VICTORY-(ALL)*

VICTORY-DEFEAT-EQUAL-[VICTORY AND DEFEAT ARE EQUAL]: (Warriors know that victory and defeat are equal because everything in the life of warriors is equal and unimportant; the spirit of the warrior is geared only for struggle and the outcome of his struggle is relatively unimportant.)

SELECTED REFERENCES: A Separate Reality - Page [88.3-88.4] ("That's not so," don Juan said...and to be defeated are equal.) A Separate Reality - Page [215.4-215.5] ("The spirit of a warrior...a warrior laughs and laughs.")

SEE ALSO: *VICTORY, DEFEAT, VICTORY-DEFEAT-EQUAL, FAILURE, EQUAL-UNIMPORTANT, WARRIOR-NOTHING-MATTERS, STRATEGY-DOING*

VICTORY-DEFEAT-PERSECUTORS-VICTIMS-[VICTORY AND DEFEAT-PERSECUTORS AND VICTIMS]: (Warriors know that men are either victorious or defeated; depending on that they either become persecutors or victims; "seeing" dispels the illusion of victory or defeat or suffering.)

SELECTED REFERENCES: A Separate Reality - Page [138.-138.5] (He explained that to be defeated...having the memory of being humiliated.)

SEE ALSO: *VICTORY, DEFEAT, VICTORY-DEFEAT-EQUAL, VICTIMS, PETTY-TYRANT, SEEING*

VICTORY-GLORY-REWARD-WITHOUT-[A VICTORY WITHOUT GLORY OR REWARD]: (Warriors know they have an ulterior purpose for their acts that has nothing to do with personal gain or profit; impeccability dictates the warriors' acts; warriors act only for the spirit.)

SELECTED REFERENCES: The Power of Silence - Page [79.4-79.9] ("Sorcerers though have an ulterior purpose...be angry or disillusioned with you.")

SEE ALSO: *VICTORY, WARRIOR-ACTING*

VICTORY-SPIRIT-[THE VICTORY OF THE SPIRIT]: SEE: VICTORY-[VICTORY]

VIDENTES-LOS-NUEVOS-[LOS NUEVOS VIDENTES-THE NEW SEERS]: **(Warriors know that los nuevos videntes is another term for the new seers.)**
SELECTED REFERENCES: The Fire From Within - Page [3.2-3.3] ("But you don't consider yourself a...The old seers were the sorcerers.)
SEE ALSO: *SEER-NEW*

VIDROS-LOS-[LOS VIDROS]-(TOP)

VIEW-WARRIOR-[THE WARRIORS' VIEW]: SEE: WARRIOR-VIEW-[THE WARRIORS' VIEW]

VIGIL-AUDITORY-WARRIOR-[THE WARRIORS' AUDITORY VIGIL]: SEE: AUDITORY-VIGIL-WARRIOR-[THE WARRIORS' AUDITORY VIGIL]

VIGIL-DYNAMIC-[DYNAMIC VIGIL]: SEE: DREAMING-STAGES-[THE FOUR STAGES OF DREAMING]

VIGIL-POSITION-WARRIOR-[THE POSITION OF SITTING "IN VIGIL"]: SEE: WARRIOR-VIGIL-POSITION-[THE WARRIORS' POSITION OF SITTING "IN VIGIL"]

VIGIL-RESTFUL-[RESTFUL VIGIL]: SEE: DREAMING-STAGES [THE FOUR STAGES OF DREAMING]

VIGOR-WARRIOR-[THE WARRIORS' VIGOR]: SEE: WARRIOR-VIGOR-[THE WARRIORS' VIGOR]

VIOLENCE-COLOR-[THE COLOR OF VIOLENCE]: **(Warriors know that the color of violence is the white color of the sun, the same color of the double.)**
SELECTED REFERENCES: The Second Ring of Power - Page [138.2-138.3] (They were lost. And you were...white, yellowish white, like the sun.")
SEE ALSO: *DOUBLE*

VIOLENCE-LIGHT-[THE LIGHT OF VIOLENCE]-(TOP)

VIOLENCE-MAN-[MAN'S VIOLENCE]: **(Warriors know that modern man has become hopelessly removed from intent and all he can do is express his despair in violent and cynical acts of self-destruction.)**
SELECTED REFERENCES: The Power of Silence - Page [149.7-150.1] (As the feeling of the individual self...peace, of satisfaction, of attainment.)
SEE ALSO: *MAN-ERROR, SELF-ORIGIN, CYNICISM, SELF-IMAGE*

VISIONS-[VISIONS]-(TOP): SEE: CARLOS-VISION-MOTHER-[CARLOS' VISION OF HIS MOTHER]-(TOP), CHURCH-VISION-[A VISION OF THE CHURCH]-(TOP), GAIT-POWER-VISION-[A VISION OF THE GAIT OF POWER]-(TOP), WORLD-APPARITIONS-[THE WORLD OF APPARITIONS]-(TOP), HELL-VISIONS-[VISIONS OF HELL]-(TOP)

VISIONS-MAN-[MAN'S VISIONS]: **(Warriors know that when man's assemblage point shifts to minute degrees it assembles worlds so close to the world of everyday life that they are in effect phantom worlds; visions of these phantom worlds are rejected by warriors because they know that they** *are products of man's inventory; these visions are of no value to the warrior for total freedom because they are produced by a lateral shift of the assemblage point.)*

SELECTED REFERENCES: **The Teachings of Don Juan - Page [173.5-173.6]** (Today I discussed this condition with...be merely the product of my fears.) **The Fire From Within - Page [134.1-134.3]** (He explained that my assemblage point...lateral shift of the assemblage point.")

SEE ALSO: *ASSEMBLAGE POINT-SHIFT-LATERAL, INVENTORY, HUMAN-JUNKPILE*

VOICE-SEEING-[THE VOICE OF SEEING]: SEE: SEEING-VOICE-[THE VOICE OF SEEING]

VOLITION-WARRIOR-[THE WARRIORS' VOLITION]: SEE: WARRIOR-VOLITION-[THE WARRIORS' VOLITION]

VOLITION-VS-EAGLE-COMMAND-WARRIOR-[THE WARRIORS' VOLITION VS THE EAGLE'S COMMANDS]: SEE: WARRIOR-VOLITION-VS-EAGLE-COMMAND-[THE WARRIORS' VOLITION VS THE EAGLE'S COMMANDS]

VOLUNTEERS-[VOLUNTEERS]: (Warriors know that volunteers are not welcome in the sorcerers' world because they have a purpose of their own which makes it hard for them to relinquish their individual selves; warriors never forget that war for the warrior is the battle to restore the power drained by the individual self.)

SELECTED REFERENCES: **The Power of Silence - Page [42.8-43.1]** (He reminded me of something he...the volunteers simply refused to change.) **The Power of Silence - Page [46.9-47.1]** (Don Juan remarked that naturally his...be volunteering for the sorcery task.)

SEE ALSO: *WARRIOR-WAR, SELF*

VOMITING-[VOMITING]: (The warrior knows that vomiting can act to relieve stress on the glow around the stomach.)

SELECTED REFERENCES: **The Second Ring of Power - Page [149.2-149.7]** (It was as though she had...could do was simply to throw up.)

SEE ALSO: *STOMACH-GLOW*

W

WAITS-WARRIOR-[THE WARRIOR WHO WAITS]: SEE: WARRIOR-WAITS-[THE WARRIOR WHO WAITS]

WALK-EYES-["MY EYES WALKED ON"]: SEE: EYES-WALK-["MY EYES WALKED ON"]

WALK-TREES-EDGE-[THE WARRIOR'S WALK TO THE EDGE OF THE TREES]-(TOP): SEE: WARRIOR-WALK-TREES-[THE WARRIOR'S WALK TO THE EDGE OF THE TREES]-(TOP)

WALK-WARRIOR-[WARRIORS WALK]: SEE: WARRIOR-WALK-[WARRIORS WALK]

WALKING-RIGHT-WAY-[THE RIGHT WAY OF WALKING]: (Warriors know that the right way of walking is a technique used by warriors to stop the internal dialogue; walking in that specific manner saturates the tonal, or floods it with information.)

SELECTED REFERENCES: Journey to Ixtlan - Page [18.9-19.7] (We walked for hours. He did...not really stupid but somehow dormant.) Journey to Ixtlan - Page [25.5-25.8] (We walked for another hour and then...my hands were pulling me forward.) Tales of Power - Page [13.1-13.5] (At the beginning of our association...said a single word to myself.) Tales of Power - Page [236.5-237.4] ("In order to stop the view...were too fleeting for normal vision.) Tales of Power - Page [243.7-243.9] ("Did the power plants help me...dialogue to come to a stop.) The Second Ring of Power - Page [306.1-306.4] (From la Gorda's statements about gazing...above the line of the horizon.) The Eagle's Gift - Page [135.8-136.2] (We thought that the essential aid...of time on one single activity.)
SEE ALSO: INTERNAL-DIALOGUE-STOPPING

WALL-DIVING-INTO-DREAMING-[DIVING INTO A WALL IN DREAMING]-(TOP)

*WALL-FOG-[THE WALL OF FOG]: SEE: FOG-WALL-[THE WALL OF FOG]

WALL-FOG-PIERCING-[PIERCING THE WALL OF FOG]: SEE: FOG-WALL-PIERCING [PIERCING THE WALL OF FOG]

WALL-FOG-SNATCHED-BEHIND-[BEING SNATCHED BEHIND THE WALL OF FOG]-(TOP): SEE: FOG-WALL-SNATCHED-BEHIND-[BEING SNATCHED BEHIND THE WALL OF FOG]-(TOP)

WALLS-OVERTAKING-WARRIOR-[WARRIORS OVERTAKE THE WALLS]: SEE: WARRIOR-WALLS-OVERTAKING-[WARRIORS OVERTAKE THE WALLS]

WANTS-WARRIOR-[THE WARRIORS' WANTS]: SEE: WARRIOR-WANTS-[THE WARRIORS' WANTS]

WAR-WARRIOR-[WAR FOR THE WARRIOR]: SEE: WARRIOR-WAR-[WAR FOR THE WARRIOR]

WAR-WARRIOR-PEACE-[WAR VS PEACE FOR WARRIORS]: SEE: WARRIOR-WAR-PEACE-[WAR VS PEACE FOR WARRIORS]

WARRIOR-[THE WARRIOR]: (One who has been lead by power to an apprenticeship in the warriors' way; it is an honor and a pleasure to be a warrior and it is the fortune of warriors to do what they must do; warriors are true thinkers and abstract sorcerers; they are individuals who have lost all self-importance and who have both one-way bridges working, they are human beings in direct contact with the spirit.)

SELECTED REFERENCES: **A Separate Reality - Page [76.6-76.7]** ("Can you bewitch him don Juan...you have a man of courage!') **Tales of Power - Page [52.3-53.4]** (There is a fourth, the correct...You have all my sympathy.") **Tales of Power - Page [144.1-144.2]** ("Is she a warrior?" I asked...Warriors come from that stock.") **Tales of Power - Page [249.8]** ("After the apprentice has been given..."He is a warrior then.) **The Second Ring of Power - Page [210.2-210.3]** ("You must take what I say seriously...to do what he has to do.) **The Eagle's Gift - Page [96.3-96.4]** (Nestor said that the Nagual Juan...with people were one-to one.)
SEE ALSO: *WARRIOR-WAY, WARRIOR-SORCERER*

WARRIOR-ABANDON-CONTROLLED-[THE WARRIORS' CONTROLLED ABANDON]: (The mood of warriors calls for them to exercise control over themselves while at the same time abandoning themselves.)

SELECTED REFERENCES: **Journey to Ixtlan - Page [111.1-112.3]** ("Self-pity doesn't jibe with power...is a difficult technique," he said.) **Journey to Ixtlan - Page [120.2-120.3]** ("A warrior, on the other hand...the best of all possible fashions.") **Journey to Ixtlan - Page [170.3-170.8]** (Don Juan came back and jogged...brought back my feelings of insecurity.) **The Fire From Within - Page [223.2-223.4]** (By reason of their activities, at...the force that makes us persons.) **The Fire From Within - Page [294.4-294.8]** ("To assemble other worlds is not...of getting stranded in inconceivable aloneness.) **The Art of Dreaming - Page [143.6-143.7]** ("Don't say anything. At the third...irrational abandon to counteract that insistence.")
SEE ALSO: *WARRIOR-MOOD, WARRIOR-BALANCE-SOBRIETY-ABANDON*

WARRIOR-ABSTRACT-CORES-CONFORMATION-[THE WARRIORS' CONFORMATION TO THE PATTERNS OF THE ABSTRACT CORES]: (Warriors strive to adjust their thoughts and actions to the patterns of the abstract cores.)

SELECTED REFERENCES: **The Power of Silence - Page [27.6-27.8]** ("Last night, I deliberately told you the...the patterns of the abstract cores.) **The Power of Silence - Page [28.4-28.6]** ("As you can see, the story...and actions to the edifices of *intent*.")
SEE ALSO: *ABSTRACT-CORES, INTENT-EDIFICE*

WARRIOR-ABSTRACT-PURPOSE-[THE WARRIORS' ABSTRACT PURPOSE]: (The warriors' abstract focus is a focus on the abstract; the warriors' intuitive guide that keeps them focused on intent and the designs of power.)

SELECTED REFERENCES: **The Power of Silence - Page [187.8-188.1]** (But the most draining pain...opposite of his own concrete needs.)
SEE ALSO: *WARRIOR-INTENT-LINK, ABSTRACT-TO, WARRIOR-INTUITION, POWER-DESIGNS*

WARRIOR-ACCEPTANCE-[THE WARRIORS' ACCEPTANCE]: (Warriors know that joyfulness comes from having accepted our fate.)

SELECTED REFERENCES: **Tales of Power - Page [289.7-289.8]** ("A warrior acknowledges his pain but...assessed what lies ahead of him.")
SEE ALSO: *WARRIOR-JOY, WARRIOR-FATE, WARRIOR-FORTUNE-GREAT*

WARRIOR-ACCESSIBILITY-[THE WARRIORS' ACCESSIBILITY]: (Warriors know they must make themselves accessible to power; the warriors' awareness of the need to abstract oneself, to make oneself available to the spirit by being aware of it.)

SELECTED REFERENCES: **Journey to Ixtlan - Page [65.4-70.8]** ("Your opinions are final opinions...moves away leaving hardly a mark.") **Journey to Ixtlan - Page [80.6-81.2]** ("You always feel compelled to explain...witnessing all the marvels of it.") **Journey to Ixtlan - Page [90.6-90.9]** ("They're weird dreams," I said...going to begin by tackling *dreaming*.") **Journey to Ixtlan - Page [93.3]** ("It's different this time," he said...how to make yourself accessible to power.") **Journey to Ixtlan - Page [104.3-104.5]** (He said that the spirit...but always with great caution.) **Journey to Ixtlan - Page [113.6]** ("You've been asking me the same...it and I'm just guiding you.") **The Power of Silence - Page [219.1-219.2]** (Every time I've had the chance...spirit by being aware of it.")

SEE ALSO: *ABSTRACT-TO, WARRIOR-AVAILABILITY*

WARRIOR-ACCOMPLISHMENT-[THE WARRIORS' ACCOMPLISHMENTS]:

(Generally speaking, warriors have two great accomplishments; the greatest accomplishment in the first attention is stalking and the greatest accomplishment in the second attention is dreaming; collectively, intending the movement of the assemblage point is the great accomplishment of warriors; warriors know that their virtuosity is to know precisely what is needed from the world of the inorganic beings; to take only what is needed from that realm is the warriors' greatest accomplishment.)

SELECTED REFERENCES: **The Eagle's Gift - Page [209.9]** (Don Juan said that, generally speaking...attention his greatest accomplishment is *stalking*.) **The Power of Silence - Page [218.5-218.6]** ("*Intending* the movement of your assemblage...the residue sorcerers look forward to.") **The Art of Dreaming - Page [109.3-109.9]** ("You have to continue your dreaming until...way of plummeting into a pitfall.")

SEE ALSO: *STALKING-ART, DREAMING-ART, WARRIOR-ATTAINMENT, STALKING-STALKERS, WARRIOR-ACCOMPLISHMENT-(ALL)*

WARRIOR-ACCOMPLISHMENT-SUPREME-[THE WARRIORS' SUPREME ACCOMPLISHMENT]:

(Warriors know that their supreme accomplishment is to move the assemblage point away from its normal position and perceive portions of the Eagle's emanations that are not ordinarily perceived.)

SELECTED REFERENCES: **The Fire From Within - Page [117.8-117.9]** ("Your assemblage point moved away from...the new seers strive to elucidate.")

SEE ALSO: *WARRIOR-ACCOMPLISHMENT, WARRIOR-ATTAINMENT, ASSEMBLAGE-POINT-MOVING, PERCEPTION, EAGLE-EMANATIONS, ASSEMBLAGE-POINT-MOVEMENT-INTENDING*

WARRIOR-ACCOMPLISHMENT-TRANSCENDENTAL- [THE WARRIORS' TRANSCENDENTAL ACCOMPLISHMENTS]:

(Warriors train themselves to do two transcendental things; 1) to conceive the existence of the assemblage point; 2) to make that assemblage point move.)

SELECTED REFERENCES: **The Power of Silence - Page [144.8-145.1]** (I mentioned to don Juan that I...to make that assemblage point move.)

SEE ALSO: *ASSEMBLAGE-POINT, ASSEMBLAGE-POINT-MOVING, WARRIOR-ACCOMPLISHMENT*

WARRIOR-ACQUIESCENCE-[THE WARRIORS' ACQUIESCENCE]:

(Warriors know the true nature of their decisions; warriors acknowledge that something beyond their understanding has set up the framework of their so-called decisions, and all warriors do is acquiesce to it; warriors acquiesce to their fate, not passively like idiots, but actively like warriors; the warriors' courage empowers them to be acquiescent without being stupid.)

SELECTED REFERENCES: **Tales of Power - Page [249.1-249.4]** ("What would have happened if I...and all we do is acquiesce.) **The Power of Silence - Page [60.1-60.3]** (Don Juan

asked Belisario to recommend...survival was to acquiesce and understand.) **The Power of Silence - Page [110.2-110.3]** ("Yes," he went on. "The idea...be ruthless without being self-important.") **The Power of Silence - Page [233.7-233.8]** (Don Juan contended that that simple...free movement of his assemblage point.) **The Art of Dreaming - Page [137.6-137.7]** ("Don't worry," he said laughing...premeditation to cut someone else's chains.")
  SEE ALSO: *WARRIOR-DECISIONS, WARRIOR-CHOICE, WARRIOR-FATE, WARRIOR-ACQUIESCENCE, STUPIDITY-IGNORANCE*

WARRIOR-ACT-AMUSE THEMSELVES-[WARRIORS NEVER ACT TO AMUSE THEMSELVES]: *(Warriors never act to amuse themselves; the warriors' actions are strategical and are dictated by need; sometimes the warriors' actions have funny consequences, but that's an entirely different matter.)*

  SELECTED REFERENCES: **The Power of Silence - Page [57.5-57.7]** ("Was there a reason for your benefactor's transformation...consequences, but that's another matter.")
  SEE ALSO: *WARRIOR-STRATEGY, JULIAN-NAGUAL-JOKES-(TOP)*

WARRIOR-ACT-IRREVOCABLE-[THE IRREVOCABILITY OF THE WARRIORS' ACTS]: *(Warriors know that acts in the sorcerers' world are irrevocable.)*

  SELECTED REFERENCES: **The Teachings of Don Juan - Page [154.5-154.6]** (I noticed that don Juan had imparted...I did not want to stop.)
  SEE ALSO: *ACT-LEARNING, WARRIOR-DEATH-COMMAND*

WARRIOR-ACT-ONLY-[THE WARRIORS' ONLY ACT]: *(Warriors know that impeccability is the only act that is free and thus the only true measure of the warriors' spirit.)*

  SELECTED REFERENCES: **Journey to Ixtlan - Page [227.5-227.6]** ("What a terrible way of putting it...that *doing* there are only actions.") **Tales of Power - Page [249.4-249.5]** ("In the life of a warrior...true measure of a warrior's spirit.")
  SEE ALSO: *WARRIOR-IMPECCABILITY, WARRIOR-SPIRIT, WARRIOR-SPIRIT-MEASURE*

WARRIOR-ACTING-[ACTING AS A WARRIOR]: *(Warriors know that the nature of their acts are unimportant as long as they act like warriors; the warriors' courage empowers them to be patient and yet take action.)*

  SELECTED REFERENCES: **Journey to Ixtlan - Page [108.6-108.7]** (He laughed and threatened to cover...as one acted as a warrior.) **The Power of Silence - Page [110.2-110.3]** ("Yes," he went on. "The idea...be ruthless without being self-important.")
  SEE ALSO: *WARRIOR, ACT-LEARNING*

WARRIOR-ADVANTAGE-[THE WARRIORS' ADVANTAGE]: *(The warriors' advantage is that they notice everything; the warriors' awareness is their advantage; the warriors' advantage is that they restrain their self-importance with the knowledge that reality is an interpretation that we make.)*

  SELECTED REFERENCES: **The Second Ring of Power - Page [209.4-209.6]** (Nestor asked me if I had noticed...Nagual said, there lies his advantage.) **The Fire From Within - Page [24.7-24.9]** (Don Juan explained that the mistake...had over the simple-minded Spaniards.)
  SEE ALSO: *AWARENESS, WARRIOR-ALERTNESS, WARRIOR-NOTICES-EVERYTHING*

WARRIOR-AFFECTION-[THE WARRIORS' AFFECTION]: *(Warriors know that their feelings of affection can impact their impeccability.)*

  SELECTED REFERENCES: **The Second Ring of Power - Page [135.1-135.3]** ("You have to refuse both, the...I had become utterly confused.) **The Power of Silence - Page [187.4-187.7]** (Don Juan said that it took about...he set out on his own.)
  SEE ALSO: *WARRIOR-IMPECCABILITY, FEELINGS*

WARRIOR-AIRBORNE-*[AIRBORNE WARRIORS]*: *(For warriors, dreaming and recapitulating go hand in hand; as warriors regurgitate their lives, they become more and more airborne.)*
SELECTED REFERENCES: **The Art of Dreaming - Page [148.3]** (Recapitulating and dreaming go hand in...we get more and more airborne.")
SEE ALSO: *RECAPITULATION, DREAMING-ART, WARRIOR-LIGHTNESS*

WARRIOR-ALERTNESS-*[THE WARRIORS' ALERTNESS]*: *(Warriors create a fog around themselves and their life situation, a life situation in which nothing is for sure; when nothing is for sure, warriors are forced to remain alert, forever on their toes; warriors are fully aware that they dream themselves in a predatorial universe.)*
SELECTED REFERENCES: **A Separate Reality - Page [256.9-257.3]** (We walked to the house in complete...nothing I could subtract from it.) **Journey to Ixtlan - Page [17.2-17.5]** ("You see," he went on...behave as if we know everything.") **Journey to Ixtlan - Page [122.1]** ("There's no plan when it comes...be in a state of readiness.) **Journey to Ixtlan - Page [234.4-235.3]** ("Chance, good luck, personal power, or...that point so I remained quiet.) **Tales of Power - Page [154.1-154.7]** (We laughed at the image...caught you with your pants down.") **The Art of Dreaming - Page [101.4-101.6]** ("The awareness of sorcerers grows when...venture out in that predatorial universe.")
SEE ALSO: *WARRIOR-PREPAREDNESS, WARRIOR-FOG-CREATE*

WARRIOR-ALONE-*[WARRIORS ARE ALONE]*: *(Warriors know they are always alone when it comes to the internalization of knowledge.)*
SELECTED REFERENCES: **A Separate Reality - Page [81.1-81.2]** ("Once a man learns to see...but folly," don Juan said cryptically.) **The Fire From Within - Page [212.4-212.5]** (We sat down. Don Juan said...much later, after years of struggle.)
SEE ALSO: *REALIZATION, KNOWLEDGE, WARRIOR*

WARRIOR-ALOOFNESS-*[THE WARRIORS' ALOOFNESS]*: *(The warriors' aloofness is a by-product of the warriors' detachment; the warriors' aloofness can be explained as an instantaneous shift of energy that automatically focuses on the warriors' connecting link with intent.)*
SELECTED REFERENCES: **Tales of Power - Page [94.4-94.5]** (Somehow you refrained from indulging in...him without any aid from me.) **The Eagle's Gift - Page [112.9-113.3]** (What I felt was not a...it; I had actually embodied it.) **The Fire From Within - Page [223.2-223.4]** (By reason of their activities, at...the force that makes us persons.) **The Power of Silence - Page [113.7-113.9]** (In the early evening, don Juan...of my shift to heightened awareness.) **The Power of Silence - Page [172.3-172.4]** (The seven women were exquisite and they...an aloofness he could never penetrate.)
SEE ALSO: *WARRIOR-DETACHMENT, ENERGY-SHIFT-INSTANTANEOUS, WARRIOR-INTENT-LINK*

WARRIOR-AMBITION-*[THE WARRIORS' AMBITION]*: *(Warriors know they must detach themselves from the ambition of their first attention agendas.)*
SELECTED REFERENCES: **The Teachings of Don Juan - Page [106.8-107.3]** (Therefore you must always keep in mind...Does this path have a heart?) **The Teachings of Don Juan - Page [160.9-161.2]** ("I have told you that to choose...you are not bidding to know.)
SEE ALSO: *WARRIOR-SOBRIETY, WARRIOR-GOAL, WARRIOR-DETACHMENT, WARRIOR-DESIRE, ATTENTION-FIRST, INVENTORY*

WARRIOR-ANGER-*[THE WARRIORS' ANGER]*: *(Warriors know it is useless to get angry and be disappointed with themselves; all that proves is that the tonal is involved in an internal struggle that is consuming a great deal of the warriors' energy; warriors avoid this wear and tear by living a tight and harmonious life; warriors have lost their self-importance and with it their capacity for anger; the acts of people are no longer important enough*

to anger them; warriors can combat their feelings of anger by rolling their
eyes; warriors know that anger is often sobering.)
    SELECTED REFERENCES: **The Teachings of Don Juan - Page [72.6-72.7]** ("No! I'm never angry at anybody...don't feel that way any longer.") **Tales of Power - Page [155.7-155.9]** ("This is your world. You can't....the harmony between *tonal* and *nagual*.) **The Eagle's Gift - Page [147.1-147.4]** (I could not believe the changes...anger had drained me of my energy.) **The Fire From Within - Page [70.9-71.2]** (Don Juan patted my back gently...had succeeded by making me rage.) **The Fire From Within - Page [260.4-260.6]** ("The new seers recommend a very simple...in lieu of true mastery of *intent*.)
    SEE ALSO: *WARRIOR-IMPECCABILITY, WARRIOR-LIVE-LIKE, WARRIOR-LIFE-TIGHT, SELF-IMPORTANCE, WARRIOR-NOTHING-MATTERS, WARRIOR-RAGE, EYES-ROLLING*

WARRIOR-ANGUISH-[THE WARRIORS' ANGUISH]: *(The warriors' anguish is an expression of a killing anxiety that surfaces when their awareness will no longer permit them to weep; the warriors' shiver; the shiver of the universe.)*
    SELECTED REFERENCES: **The Eagle's Gift - Page [311.5-311.6]** (Don Juan told me that on...of the Eagle's emanations is anguish.) **The Power of Silence - Page [48.6-48.7]** ("You used your barrier of independence...indefinite anguish perhaps not so pronounced.") **The Power of Silence - Page [49.3-49.5]** (Unfortunately, this awakening always comes hand...simple anger at having missed out.)
    SEE ALSO: *WARRIOR-SHIVER, WARRIOR-ANXIETY, DEPRESSION-MELANCHOLY, SADNESS*

WARRIOR-ANNIHILATION-FACE-[WARRIORS FACE IMMINENT ANNIHILATION]: *(Warriors know that as they follow the path of sorcery and warriorship, they face imminent annihilation every step of the way; this fact makes them keenly aware of their own death and gives them the necessary potency and concentration to transform ordinary time on earth into something magical.)*
    SELECTED REFERENCES: **A Separate Reality - Page [150.3-150.4]** ("A man who follows the paths of...ordinary time on earth into magical power.) **Journey to Ixtlan - Page [34.8-34.9]** ("You're full of crap!" he exclaimed...'I haven't touched you yet'") **The Second Ring of Power - Page [84.3-84.8]** (There was no doubt left in my...human nature, he was probably right.)
    SEE ALSO: *DEATH-INDIFFERENCE, KNOWLEDGE, DEATH-ADVISER*

WARRIOR-ANXIETY-[THE WARRIORS' ANXIETY]: *(Warriors know that any movement of the assemblage point is like dying, everything in us gets disconnected and then reconnected again to a source of much greater power; that amplification of energy is felt as a killing anxiety.)*
    SELECTED REFERENCES: **The Power of Silence - Page [50.9]** ("I think the poet senses the pressure...that realization produces," don Juan said.) **The Power of Silence - Page [148.9-149.5]** (Don Juan then started a most...know, there is no real danger.")
    SEE ALSO: *DEPRESSION-MELANCHOLY, SADNESS, WARRIOR-ANGUISH*

WARRIOR-APLOMB-[THE WARRIORS' APLOMB]: *(Warriors know that they require self-assurance and aplomb to traverse the road to knowledge; the warriors' aplomb is the warriors' sobriety.)*
    SELECTED REFERENCES: **The Art of Dreaming - Page [173.3]** (Now more than ever you need...ancient times and those of modern men.")
    SEE ALSO: *WARRIOR-ASSUREDNESS, WARRIOR-SOBRIETY*

WARRIOR-APOLOGY-[THE WARRIORS' APOLOGY]: *(Warriors know that apologies are nonsense because we have no time for regrets or looking back; the power of the warriors' decisions keep them focused on the decisions that await them.)*

SELECTED REFERENCES: Tales of Power - Page [283.4-283.5] ("Don't apologize," don Juan said to me...Be as fine as they were.") **The Fire From Within - Page [185.2-185.3]** ("This indeed is the mystery of awareness...apologize for either; both are needed.)
SEE ALSO: *WARRIOR-REGRETS, WARRIOR-DECISIONS, WARRIOR-DECISIONS-EMPOWERING*

WARRIOR-ARRANGEMENTS-[THE WARRIORS' ARRANGEMENTS]:
(The contingencies of the warrior; the arrangements which warriors make to back up their bid for power.)
SELECTED REFERENCES: Tales of Power - Page [144.6-144.8] ("What does the omen mean, don Juan...they are not arrangements at all.)
SEE ALSO : *WARRIOR-POWER-BID*

WARRIOR-ARTS-[THE WARRIORS' ARTS]: *(The many arts of the warrior; activities which warriors perform as part of the warriors' way; dreaming, stalking, controlled folly and balancing the tonal against the nagual are among the warriors' performing arts.)*
SELECTED REFERENCES: Tales of Power - Page [91.6] ("Good, good," don Juan said...is to balance terror and wonder.") **Tales of Power - Page [114.3-114.4]** ("That dying man is one of...have plucked it, but have you?") **Tales of Power - Page [160.8-161.1]** ("Any threat to the *tonal* always...That boosting is called personal power.") **Tales of Power - Page [176.8-177.1]** ("A sudden fright always shrinks the...struggle to immediately halt that shrinking.") **Tales of Power - Page [192.1]** ("It's a pity that you're so...bewilderment and miss Genaro's real art.") **The Second Ring of Power - Page [205.1-205.6]** (Nestor said that they were used to...They knew the art of stalking.") **The Second Ring of Power - Page [207.2-207.3]** ("As far as I'm concerned, you two...the only gate that was open.) **The Second Ring of Power - Page [246.8-246.9]** ("The art of sorcerers is to be...is never to waste their power.) **The Eagle's Gift - Page [143.8-143.9]** (There was a long silence. I...merely apprentices of an inexhaustible art.) **The Eagle's Gift - Page [289.7-289.8]** (Florinda emphasized that the rule defined...a recapitulation into a practical matter.) **The Power of Silence - Page [245.5-245.6]** ("Controlled folly is an art...lot of energy to exercise it.") **The Power of Silence - Page [264.9-265.1]** ("Freedom," he said. "He wanted their...is that it can be accomplished.
SEE ALSO: *DREAMING-ART, STALKING-ART, TONAL-NAGUAL-DICHOTOMY, WARRIOR-CONTROLLED-FOLLY, TERROR-VS-WONDER, SORCERER-ART*

WARRIOR-ARTS-IMPORTANCE-[THE IMPORTANCE OF THE WARRIORS' ARTS]: *(For warriors, the only thing important about an art form is that it can accomplished, whether it is the art of dreaming, the art of stalking or any other of the warriors' arts.)*
SELECTED REFERENCES : The Power of Silence - Page [264.9-265.1] ("Freedom," he said. "He wanted their ...is that it can be accomplished.")
SEE ALSO: *DREAMING-ART, STALKING-ART, WARRIOR-ARTS*

WARRIOR-ASSURANCE-[THE WARRIORS' ASSURANCE]: *(The special self-confidence and clarity of the warrior; entering into the second attention gives warriors a peculiar sense of self-assurance which requires even more sobriety on their part.)*
SELECTED REFERENCES: The Teachings of Don Juan - Page [51.3-51.4] ("A man goes to knowledge as...will live to regret his steps.") **The Art of Dreaming - Page [36.2-36.4]** (As I practiced focusing and holding...talk about it. Just do it!")
SEE ALSO: *WARRIOR-SELF-CONFIDENCE, WARRIOR-ASSUREDNESS, WARRIOR-WAR*

WARRIOR-ASSUREDNESS-[THE WARRIORS' ASSUREDNESS]:
(Warriors know they must cultivate a sense of certainty about their actions; the confidence warriors need to intelligently utilize their new continuity.)
SELECTED REFERENCES: The Power of Silence - Page [191.8-192.2] ("The sorcerers' struggle for assuredness is the most dramatic struggle...and balance the tenuousness and instability of his new continuity.") **The Power of Silence - Page [227.4-227.6]** (He described the

specific problem of...in the world of everyday life.) **The Art of Dreaming - Page [47.7-47.9]** ("Yes, but for a perfect result...is unnecessary, to say the least.") **The Art of Dreaming - Page [104.8]** ("Sorcerers' maneuvers are deadly," don Juan...having some idiotic confidence in yourself.")

SEE ALSO: *CONTINUITY, ACT-LEARNING, CLARITY, WARRIOR-ASSURANCE, SORCERER-ASSUREDNESS-STRUGGLE*

WARRIOR-ATTAINMENTS-[THE WARRIORS' ATTAINMENTS]: (The attainments of the warrior are the lack of wanting anything, joy, and total awareness .)

SELECTED REFERENCES: **The Teachings of Don Juan - Page [83.6]** (Rather, one becomes a man of...after defeating the four natural enemies.") **The Teachings of Don Juan - Page [87.7-87.8]** ("But if the man sloughs off his...clarity, power, and knowledge is enough,") **Tales of Power - Page [46.6-46.8]** (Don Juan explained that by the...them outside the bounds of prediction.) **Tales of Power - Page [57.2-57.3]** ("You're filled with tales of violence...is no such interest left in him.") **Tales of Power - Page [58.1-58.5]** ("There is no hypothetical sense when...knowledge is in control with out controlling anything.") **Tales of Power - Page [97.4-97.6]** ("What purpose are you talking about...of your life will take you.") **Tales of Power - Page [248.4]** (He said that not wanting anything was a warrior's finest attainment.) **The Eagle's Gift - Page [84.3-84.5]** (La Gorda got up; she was...don Juan's teachings to the letter.) **The Fire From Within - Page [48.8-49.3]** (After a long silence, Genaro fell...embraces everything that seers can attain.) **The Fire From Within - Page [64.5-64.9]** (He said that the danger of definitions...what we are capable of attaining.) **The Fire From Within - Page [67.5-67.9]** (He did not consider it worthwhile...the Eagle's beak to be devoured.") **The Fire From Within - Page [114.1-114.3]** ("Are those special cases, don Juan...at large, and glide into eternity.") **The Fire From Within - Page [127.7-127.9]** (Don Juan had defined the scope...only release that her spirit had.) **The Fire From Within - Page [131.5]** (He stressed over and over that...point fixed in its original position.) **The Fire From Within - Page [147.8-147.9]** ("Be that as it may, warrior...waylaid, and so was la Catalina.") **The Fire From Within - Page [271.9-272.2]** (He repeated over and over that at...accomplishments attained after years of practice.) **The Power of Silence - Page [149.8-150.1]** (Don Juan asserted that the reason...of peace, of satisfaction, of attainment.) **The Power of Silence - Page [166.6]** ("The nagual's ruthlessness has many aspects...of *intent* that the nagual attains.) **The Power of Silence - Page [226.4-226.8]** ("What you're witnessing is the result...that he was just like us.)

SEE ALSO: *AWARENESS-TOTAL, WARRIOR-JOY, WARRIOR-WANTS, WARRIOR-DESIRE*

WARRIOR-ATTENTION-PAUSE-[THE PAUSE IN THE WARRIORS' ATTENTION]: SEE: WARRIOR-PAUSE-ATTENTION-[THE PAUSE IN THE WARRIORS' ATTENTION]

WARRIOR-ATTENTION-THIRD-[WARRIORS OF THE THIRD ATTENTION]: (Warriors know the new seers sometimes refer to themselves as the warriors of the third attention.)

SELECTED REFERENCES: **The Eagle's Gift - Page [17.7-17.8]** ("The Nagual believed that the new...the fixation of the second attention.)

SEE: *WARRIOR-FREEDOM-TOTAL, SEER-NEW, ATTENTION THIRD*

WARRIOR-ATTITUDE-[THE WARRIORS' ATTITUDE]: (The attitude of the warrior is the attitude demanded by the warriors' way.)

SELECTED REFERENCES: **Tales of Power - Page [58.9-59.2]** ("Come on," he said. "A warrior...ourselves into one or the other.) **Tales of Power - Page [154.3-154.9]** (I told him that there were...into place because you're expecting nothing.") **Tales of Power - Page [249.1-249.5]** ("What would have happened if I...true measure of a warrior's spirit.") **The Second Ring of Power - Page [123.4-123.7]** ("You're wrong. A warrior doesn't seek...feeling of having lost someone irreplaceable.)

SEE ALSO: *WARRIOR-WAY*

WARRIOR-ATTRIBUTES-[THE WARRIORS' ATTRIBUTES]: (The attributes of the warrior are five of the six elements of stalking; control, discipline, forbearance, timing and will; usually only four attributes are

played by the warrior; the fifth, will, is always saved for the ultimate confrontation, when the warrior is facing the firing squad so to speak.)
SELECTED REFERENCES: The Fire From Within - Page [16.4-16.6] (He said that the most effective...and is called the petty tyrant.) The Fire From Within - Page [18.3-19.2] ("You haven't yet put together all...go out and look for one.") The Fire From Within - Page [23.6] ("My benefactor developed a strategy using...warriorship: control, discipline, forbearance, and timing.") The Fire From Within - Page [23.9-24.3] (His benefactor stressed the fact that...them to me through his strategy.") The Fire From Within - Page [26.1-29.6] ("The foreman at the house followed...is due to whoever deserves it.")
SEE ALSO: *STALKING-ELEMENTS-SIX,   CONTROL,   DISCIPLINE, FORBEARANCE, TIMING, WILL, WARRIOR-QUALITIES-TWO-BASIC*

**WARRIOR-AVAILABILITY-[THE WARRIORS' AVAILABILITY]:*
(Warriors are not willing partners; they are not available and do not involve themselves in anything unless they know what they are doing; warriors only make themselves available to power.)
SELECTED REFERENCES: A Separate Reality - Page [180.5-180.6] (Usually you behave very well...aware of what he is doing.") A Separate Reality - Page [182.1-182.6] ("All I can say to you," don...I simply will not come around.") Journey to Ixtlan - Page [66.3] ("Therein lies the secret of great...the precise turn of the road.") The Power of Silence - Page [40.9-41.1] ("This second abstract core could...the spirit knocked on the door.) The Art of Dreaming - Page [169.3-169.6] ("Your energy body moved," he said...than admire it or examine it.")
SEE ALSO: *WARRIOR-ACCESSIBILITY, ABANDON*

WARRIOR-AVAILABILITY-UNAVAILABILITY-[THE WARRIORS' AVAILABILITY AND UNAVAILABILITY]: *(Warriors know the importance of the crucial difference between hiding and showing oneself; the secret of great hunters is to learn precisely when to be available and unavailable.)*
SELECTED REFERENCES: Journey to Ixtlan - Page [66.3-67.2] ("Therein lies the secret of great...of being available and unavailable.")
SEE ALSO: *HUNTER-SECRET,   WARRIOR-AVAILABILITY,   WARRIOR-ACCESSIBILITY, WARRIOR-UNAVAILABILITY*

WARRIOR-AWARENESS-CONCEALED-[THE WARRIORS' CONCEALED AWARENESS]: *(Warriors know that there is another awareness concealed within them and that it is possible to enter into that awareness; that awareness is the second attention or the attention of the nagual.)*
SELECTED REFERENCES: The Eagle's Gift - Page [266.4-266.5] (La Gorda and I were in...had accomplished what the rule prescribed.)
SEE ALSO: *ATTENTION-SECOND, ATTENTION-NAGUAL, POWER-HIDDEN*

WARRIOR-AWARENESS-SURROGATE-[THE WARRIORS' SURROGATE AWARENESS]: SEE: AWARENESS-SURROGATE-WARRIOR-[THE WARRIORS' SURROGATE AWARENESS]

WARRIOR-BACKBONE-[THE WARRIORS' BACKBONE]: *(The backbone of warriors is their humility and efficiency; warriors act without expecting anything in return.)*
SELECTED REFERENCES : Tales of Power - Page [287.6-287.7] ("You have learned that the backbone...day, you'll need your ultimate forbearance.")
SEE ALSO: *WARRIOR-HUMBLENESS, ACT-LEARNING, WARRIOR-EFFICIENCY*

WARRIOR-BAFFLEMENT-[THE WARRIORS' BAFFLEMENT]: *(Warrior apprentices know that sometimes they are at a loss to understand the indications of power.)*
SELECTED REFERENCES: The Teachings of Don Juan - Page [48.8-49.5] ("But I don't care about seeing...are not an Indian. How baffling!") A Separate Reality - Page [261.5-261.6] (I turned around to look for don...the strain. I felt utterly disoriented.) Tales of Power - Page [192.1] ("It's a pity that you're so...bewilderment and miss Genaro's real art.") Tales of

Power - Page [196.1-196.5] (I made an involuntary gesture of...drains his power, impeccability replenishes it.") **The Second Ring of Power** - Page [41.7-41.9] ("After turning my head that first...at us. Something must have happened.)
SEE ALSO: *OMENS*

WARRIOR-BALANCE-[THE WARRIORS' BALANCE]: (The balancing art of the warrior; warriors learn to balance themselves and the forces around them in order to meet the fundamental challenges of warriorship.)

SELECTED REFERENCES: **A Separate Reality** - Page [23.4-23.5] ("Is that the way everyone...changed in that luminous egg? What?") **A Separate Reality** - Page [214.7-214.8] (To be pierced by a fellow...the strength of being a warrior.) **Separate Reality** - Page [256.9-257.3] (We walked to the house in complete...nothing I could subtract from it.) **Tales of Power** - Page [160.8-161.1] ("Any threat to the *tonal* always...That boosting is called personal power.") **The Second Ring of Power** - Page [136.7-137.4] ("Were they supposed to kill me too...the little sisters had to perform.) **The Second Ring of Power** - Page [152.7] (The Nagual taught me to be balanced and not to seek anything eagerly.) **The Second Ring of Power** - Page [250.6-250.8] (I had a moment of supreme uncertainty...from the trail in the darkness.) **The Eagle's Gift** - Page [204.9-205.1] (Don Juan said that Silvio Manuel...the silent force behind don Juan.) **The Eagle's Gift** - Page [235.8-236.1] (He said that in order to...and its vertex in the air.) **The Eagle's Gift** - Page [306.9-307.2] (Vicente came to my side next...and the unexpected, with equal efficiency.) **The Power of Silence** - Page [191.8-192.2] ("The sorcerers' struggle for assuredness is...tenuousness and instability of his new continuity.)
SEE ALSO: *WARRIOR-ARTS, WARRIOR-CHALLENGE, TERROR-VS-WONDER, SPIRIT-BALANCE, BALANCE, WARRIOR-EQUILIBRIUM, EQUILIBRIUM*

WARRIOR-BALANCE-SOBRIETY-ABANDON-[WARRIORS BALANCE SOBRIETY AND ABANDON]: (The contradictions of the warriors' path to knowledge force warriors to balance sobriety and abandon as part of their quest for freedom.)

SELECTED REFERENCES: **Journey to Ixtlan** - Page [111.1-111.2] ("Self-pity doesn't jibe with power...time it calls for abandoning himself.) **The Fire From Within** - Page [73.2-73.4] ("For example, seers have to be...him how I understood his point.) **The Power of Silence** - Page [95.1-95.3] (As their temporary protector it was...with minimal help from him.)
SEE ALSO: *WARRIOR-CONTRADICTION-KNOWLEDGE, WARRIOR-BALANCE, WARRIOR-SOBRIETY, WARRIOR-ABANDON, WARRIOR-FREEDOM, WARRIOR-MOOD, HUNTER-POWER-BECOMING, EQUILIBRIUM, SNEAKING-WORLD-MEN-WORLD-SORCERER, WARRIOR-CONTRADICTION-KNOWLEDGE, FREEDOM-TOTAL*

*WARRIOR-BATTLE-LAST-[THE WARRIORS' LAST BATTLE ON EARTH]: SEE: WARRIOR-LAST-STAND-[THE WARRIORS' LAST STAND]

WARRIOR-BATTLE-POWER-[THE WARRIORS' BATTLE OF POWER]: (The warriors' battle of power is the warriors' fundamental engagement with power itself; warriors learn to store their personal power little by little until they have enough of it to sustain them in a battle of power.)

SELECTED REFERENCES: **Journey to Ixtlan** - Page [128.3] (Don Juan whispered that the fog...engaged in a battle of power.) **Journey to Ixtlan** - Page [133.4-133.5] ("What happened to you last night...because it had not been real.) **Journey to Ixtlan** - Page [134.4-135.5] ("Did you ever see the bridge yourself...have enough power of one's own.") **Journey to Ixtlan** - Page [137.8] (He said that the battle of power...to remain trapped in those mountains.) **Journey to Ixtlan** - Page [155.3-155.4] ("And thus you will dance to your...will sit here and watch you.)
SEE ALSO: *POWER, POWER-SEAT*

WARRIOR-BATTLEFIELD-[THE WARRIORS' BATTLEFIELD]: (The second attention is the warriors' battlefield and a training ground for reaching the third attention.)

SELECTED REFERENCES: **The Teachings of Don Juan** - Page [83.9-84.3] ("When a man starts to learn...His purpose becomes a battlefield.) **The Eagle's Gift** - Page [18.8-18.9] (He added that the battlefield of...very fruitful once it was attained.)

SEE ALSO: *ATTENTION-SECOND, ATTENTION-THIRD*

WARRIOR-BEHAVIOR-[THE WARRIORS' BEHAVIOR]: (The warriors' behavior is dictated by only one thing and that is impeccability; warriors do not act for profit or reward, they act for the spirit.)
SELECTED REFERENCES: **The Power of Silence - Page [78.9-79.9]** (He stressed repeatedly that teaching...be angry or disillusioned with you.")
SEE ALSO: *WARRIOR-IMPECCABILITY, ACTING-HELL, VICTORY*

WARRIOR-BEING-THEMSELVES-[THE WARRIORS' CHALLENGE TO BE THEMSELVES WITHOUT BEING THEMSELVES]: (Warriors must train themselves to be themselves without being themselves.)
SELECTED REFERENCES: **Tales of Power - Page [230.6-230.7]** ("This is indeed a tricky maneuver...He slapped his thigh and laughed.)
SEE ALSO: *WORLD-IN-NOT-OF, EQUILIBRIUM*

WARRIOR-BEST-[WARRIORS AT THEIR BEST]: Warriors are at their best when they are facing the unknown, when they have their backs against the wall.)
SELECTED REFERENCES: **Journey to Ixtlan - Page [81.5-81.7]** ("You have never taken the responsibility...think you have plenty of time.") **Tales of Power - Page [145.5-145.6]** (You have little time left, and...wouldn't have it any other way.") **The Fire From Within -Page [33.8-33.9]** ("There is a simple rule of...in the face of the unknown.")
SEE ALSO: *UNKNOWN*

WARRIOR-BID-POWER-[THE WARRIORS' BID FOR POWER]: SEE: WARRIOR-POWER-BID [THE WARRIORS' BID FOR POWER]

WARRIOR-BONES-[THE WARRIORS' BONES]: (The bones of warriors have power in them but they will never be found in a cemetery; there is even more power in the bones of a man of knowledge, but they are practically impossible to find at all.)
SELECTED REFERENCES: **Journey to Ixtlan - Page [106.8-107.1]** ("This is not a cemetery...be practically impossible to find them.")
SEE ALSO: *CEMETERIES, WARRIOR, MAN-KNOWLEDGE*

WARRIOR-BRIDGE-[THE WARRIORS' BRIDGE]: (The warriors' bridge is the invisible span between the contradictory propositions of knowledge and power; the bridge between warriors and the people of the world; a solid bridge between the views of the sorcerers of antiquity and those of modern men.)
SELECTED REFERENCES : **The Eagle's Gift - Page [211.4-211.5]** (Don Juan said that the force...the finality of the Eagle's dictums.) **The Fire From Within - Page [73.3-73.6]** (His example left me baffled, but...affection, sobriety, love, or even kindness.") **The Power of Silence - Page [192.9-193.1]** (He wanted to explain that his...make a bridge to join sorcerers.) **The Art of Dreaming - Page [173.3]** (Now more than ever you need...ancient times and those of modern men.")
SEE ALSO : *WARRIOR-CONTRADICTIONS-KNOWLEDGE, WARRIOR-SOBRIETY, LOVE, KINDNESS, WARRIOR-CONTROLLED-FOLLY, EQUILIBRIUM*

WARRIOR-CALMNESS-[THE WARRIORS' CALMNESS]: (Warriors know that they must remain calm and collected and never lose their grip.)
SELECTED REFERENCES: **Tales of Power - Page [24.1]** ("A warrior must be calm and collected and never lose his grip.") **The Eagle's Gift - Page [260.5-260.6]** (Zuleica finally spoke to me...the second attention was calmness itself.) **The Art of Dreaming - Page [210.2-210.3]** ("Now, now," he said softly...a test. you need calmness now.)
SEE ALSO: *WARRIOR-CONTROL, CALMNESS-ATTENTION-SECOND*

WARRIOR-CARING-FOR-ANOTHER-[CARING FOR ANOTHER WARRIOR]: (Warriors know that sometimes part of their task is to look after another warrior; warriors consider it an honor to look after another warrior in this way; warriors harnesses their selfishness by extending their selfish concern to include another; the warriors' reward consists of the rare opportunity for them to give freely and impeccably in spite of their feelings.)
SELECTED REFERENCES: **Tales of Power** - Page [227.9-228.5] (Pablito laughed and told me that he...Nestor is a fine warrior.") **The Second Ring of Power** - Page [130.6-130.7] (Then the wind stopped and the...better than if they were myself.) **The Eagle's Gift** - Page [32.9-33.1] (I took Josephina to Pablito...would be in need of help.) **The Eagle's Gift** - Page [111.6-111.9] (On the surface everything seemed to be...learning English. Her progress was phenomenal.) **The Eagle's Gift** - Page [129.9-130.5] (Don Juan was telling me that...the fulfillment of my true task.) **The Eagle's Gift** - Page [131.4-131.8] (A fat Gorda asked don Juan...I be capable of harnessing my selfishness.) **The Eagle's Gift** - Page [134.6-134.8] (As far as the *dreaming* scene...don Juan's orders to the letter.) **The Eagle's Gift** - Page [183.8-184.1] (His benefactor put him under the direct...rational ballast to hold them back.) **The Eagle's Gift** - Page [203.9- 204.1] (As we drove away, don Juan...of Zoila, Zuleica, and Silvio Manuel.) **The Power of Silence** - Page [127.7-130.4] (Years before I had been both...as he peered at me.)
SEE ALSO: *SELF-IMPORTANCE-LOSING, WARRIOR-TASK, WARRIOR-REWARD, SELFISHNESS*

WARRIOR-CHALLENGE-[THE WARRIORS' CHALLENGE]: (The challenge of the warrior is the warriors' great fortune; the warriors' challenge is the bid for power; for warriors there are no blessings or curses, there are only challenges.)
SELECTED REFERENCES: **Journey to Ixtlan** - Page [81.3] (I insisted that to be bored...you are as good as dead.") **Journey to Ixtlan** - Page [82.7] ("Don't just agree with me...Take the challenge. Change.") **Tales of Power** - Page [19.2-19.3] ("You're talking nonsense," he snapped...regret but as a living challenge.) **Tales of Power** - Page [55.4-55.5] ("Have you ever asked yourself, why...the fortune of having found a challenge.") **Tales of Power** - Page [105.5] ("Only as a warrior can one...or bad. Challenges are simply challenges.") **Tales of Power** - Page [106.4-106.7] ("To wear a suit is a challenge...in favor of the warrior's way.") **Tales of Power** - Page [112.4-112.6] ("I don't like Mexico City," I...death is going to find him.) **Tales of Power** - Page [145.1-145.2] ("For a *proper tonal* everything on the...of course, is his bid for power.) **The Eagle's Gift** - Page [33.8-33.9] (She added that they had been...of what they did to me.) **The Eagle's Gift** - Page [106.7-106.8] ("The course of a warrior's destiny...destiny the breadth of one hair.") **The Eagle's Gift** - Page [298.2-298.3] (Don Juan added that it was...or blessing into a living challenge.) **The Eagle's Gift** - Page [306.9-307.3] (Vicente came to my side next...the fulfilling of a sacred trust.) **The Fire From Within** - Page [19.5-19.7] ("The average man's reaction is to...stand the pressure of the unknowable.") **The Power of Silence** - Page [82.3-82.4] ("The real challenge for those sorcerer...differentiates sorcerer seers from plain witches.") **The Power of Silence** - Page [112.1-112.6] ("Sorcerers say that death is the...go free, never to be challenged again.")
SEE ALSO : *WARRIOR-BID-POWER, DEATH*

WARRIOR-CHANCE-[THE WARRIORS' CHANCE]: (Warriors know that they always have a chance, no matter how small.)
SELECTED REFERENCES: **The Second Ring of Power** - Page [173.2-173.173.4] ("I asked the Nagual about Pablito's chances...a chance, no matter how slim.)
SEE ALSO: *WARRIOR-CHANCE-MINIMAL, POWER-PROMISE*

WARRIOR-CHANCE-ENHANCING-[ENHANCING THE WARRIORS' CHANCES]: SEE: EAGLE-MAN-[THE EAGLE AND THE FAINT REFLECTION OF MAN]

WARRIOR-CHANCE-MINIMAL-[THE WARRIORS' MINIMAL CHANCE]: (The warriors' minimal chance is the magical opportunity that power provides for warriors; the cubic centimeter of chance that pops out in front of the warriors' eyes from time to time; the gesture of the spirit; the warriors' minimal chance is not instruction, but rather consists of being made aware of the spirit.)

SELECTED REFERENCES: **Journey to Ixtlan** - Page **[234.2-234.4]** ("There is something you ought to be aware of...necessary speed, the prowess to pick it up.) **Tales of Power** - Page **[114.3-114.5]** ("That dying man is one of the cubic..."And all for you.) **Tales of Power** - Page **[156.6-156.7]** ("This morning I plucked my cubic...one must know how to *see*.) **Tales of Power** - Page **[234.1-234.2]** ("Let me begin by telling you that a...to catch his cubic centimeter of chance.) **The Second Ring of Power** - Page **[173.2-173.4]** ("I asked the Nagual about Pablito's chances...have a chance, no matter how slim.) **The Fire From Within** - Page **[176.3-176.5]** ("The conviction that the new seers have...the possibilities that seers have unraveled.") **The Power of Silence** - Page **[xiii.7-xiii.8]** (Naguals are responsible for supplying what...awareness of one's connection with *intent*.) **The Power of Silence** - Page **[158.6-158.7]** ("But there are examples of people...shatter people's mirrors of self-reflection.) **The Power of Silence** - Page **[159.3-159.5]** ("In the sorcerers' world there are only...consists of being made aware of the spirit.")
SEE ALSO: *WARRIOR-INTENT-LINK, SPIRIT-GESTURE*

WARRIOR-CHANGE-DIRECTION-[WARRIORS CHANGE DIRECTION]: (Warriors know that on the path of knowledge, they eventually change directions and learn to perceive the world in a whole new way.)

SELECTED REFERENCES: **A Separate Reality** - Page **[261.8-261.9]** ("You are going to change directions...the centers of radiation in his diagram.)
SEE ALSO: *WARRIOR-TRANSFORMATION, WARRIOR-TURNING-HEAD*

WARRIOR-CHANGE-MUST-[WARRIORS MUST CHANGE]: (Warriors know that in order to follow the path of knowledge it is necessary to change; warriors must transform themselves, they must reorder the island of the tonal, they must change their perspective regarding their individual sense of self.)

SELECTED REFERENCES: **Journey to Ixtlan** - Page **[16.8-17.2]** ("From now on," he said...to a state of irritating confusion.)
SEE ALSO: *WARRIOR-TRANSFORMATION, FACADE-TRANSFORMING, CHANGE*

WARRIOR-CHARACTER-[THE WARRIORS' CHARACTER]: SEE: WARRIOR-JOY-[THE WARRIORS' JOY], WARRIOR-BEHAVIOR-[THE WARRIORS' BEHAVIOR]

WARRIOR-CHOICE-[THE WARRIORS' CHOICE]: (Warriors know that at a specific point during their apprenticeship, they must make a critical choice; they either choose the warriors' world or choose the world of the average man; in the end warriors realize that this critical choice never really exists, because they have no real choice, they are in the hands of power; warriors must also make the sorcerers' choice; the choice between self-indulgence and sobriety, the choice between warriorship and sorcery.)

SELECTED REFERENCES: **A Separate Reality** - Page **[151.3-151.5]** ("A detached man, who knows he...him time to cling to anything.) **Tales of Power** - Page **[195.4-195.6]** ("Genaro and I have to act the...drain him and cause his demise.) **Tales of Power** - Page **[217.3-218.2]** (After more than an hour's drive...the same choice, it doesn't work.") **Tales of Power** - Page **[247.5-247.8]** ("The teacher uses the worthy opponent...decide whether or not to make it.") **Tales of Power** - Page **[249.1-249.5]** ("What would have happened if I...true measure of a warrior's spirit.") **The Second Ring of Power** - Page **[243.6-243.9]** (It takes all the time and...me than even don Genaro's acts.) **The Second Ring of Power** - Page **[280.6-280.7]** (There was a monstrous irony in...not exist. Not on this earth.") **The Eagle's Gift** - Page **[183.8-184.1]** (His benefactor put him under the direct...rational ballast to hold them back.) **The Power of Silence** - Page **[171.2-171.5]** (Your uncertainty is to be expected...victims go after a ferocious struggle.") **The Power of Silence** - Page **[201.2-201.9]** ("What can we do then...choices are dictated by silent knowledge.)

SEE ALSO: *WARRIOR-DECISIONS, WARRIOR-DECISIONS-EMPOWERING, INORGANIC-BEINGS-REFUSING, FREEDOM-INORGANIC-BEINGS, WARRIORSHIP-VS-SORCERY, WARRIOR-IMPECCABILITY, YOUTH*

WARRIOR-CHOICE-SECOND-[THE WARRIORS' SECOND CHOICE]:
(Warriors know that a second choice does not exist on this earth; warriors choose only once, to be either warriors or to be ordinary human beings.)
SELECTED REFERENCES: The Second Ring of Power - Page [280.6-280.7] (There was a monstrous irony in...not exist. Not on this earth.")
SEE ALSO: *WARRIOR-CHOICE*

WARRIOR-CHOOSES-WELL-[THE WARRIOR CHOOSES WELL]:
(Warriors know that their impeccability depends on their ability to choose wisely.)
SELECTED REFERENCES: The Second Ring of Power - Page [243.5-243.8] ("It doesn't matter what anybody says...and simplicity of a warrior's life.)
SEE ALSO: *WARRIOR-IMPECCABILITY, WARRIOR-DECISIONS, WARRIOR-PATIENCE*

WARRIOR-CHOOSING-[CHOOSING TO BE A WARRIOR]: SEE: WARRIORSHIP-CHOOSING-[CHOOSING WARRIORSHIP]

WARRIOR-CLARIFICATION-[THE WARRIORS' CLARIFICATION]:
(Warriors know that their ability to clarify things in the world of their new continuity depends solely on their personal power.)
SELECTED REFERENCES: Tales of Power - Page [85.6] ("There's no need to be confused...it's up to your personal power.")
SEE ALSO: *POWER-PERSONAL, UNDERSTANDING*

WARRIOR-COLORS-[THE WARRIORS' COLORS]: (The warriors' colors are the colors of their power and enemy spots; a warriors' favorable and unfavorable colors; colors specific to warriors that can aid in the interpretation of omens.)
SELECTED REFERENCES: The Teachings of Don Juan - Page [34.7-34.9] (He also said that the colors...was by detecting their respective colors.) Journey to Ixtlan - Page [54.6-54.7] (He reminded me that I had found...their spots at the same time.")
SEE ALSO: *ENEMY-SPOT, POWER-SPOT*

WARRIOR-COMMAND-[THE WARRIORS' COMMAND]: (Warriors know that it is possible for the Eagle's command and the warriors' command to become one and the same once they have learned the mastery of intent; the manipulation of intent begins with a command given to oneself; the command is then repeated until it becomes the Eagle's command.)
SELECTED REFERENCES: The Fire From Within - Page [297.8-298.2] ("In a moment, you're going to...the moment warriors reach inner silence.)
SEE ALSO: *EAGLE-COMMAND, INTENT, ASSEMBLAGE-POINT-POSITION-INTENDING*

WARRIOR-COMPANIONS-UNKNOWN-[THE WARRIORS' COMPANIONS IN THE IMMENSITY OF THE UNKNOWN]: (Warriors know that their allies will be their companions should they happen to get stranded in the immensity of the Eagle's emanations.)
SELECTED REFERENCES: The Fire From Within - Page [104.9-105.2] ("Are your allies useful to you...immensity that is the Eagle's emanations.") The Fire From Within - Page [294.7-294.8] (He said that for warriors the...of getting stranded in inconceivable aloneness.)
SEE ALSO: *ALLIES*

WARRIOR-COMPANY-DEAD-[THE WARRIOR AND THE COMPANY OF THE DEAD]: (*Once warriors have attained the awareness that they are dead, they only keep the company of other people or warriors who are dead in the same symbolic sense.*)

SELECTED REFERENCES: The Power of Silence - Page [194.7-194.9] ("Did you go and look for them...who are dead as I am.")

SEE ALSO: *WARRIOR-IMPECCABILITY-TICKET, WARRIOR-DEATH-SYMBOLIC*

WARRIOR-COMPASSION-[THE WARRIORS' COMPASSION]: (*Warriors have no compassion for anyone because warriors define compassion as the self-indulgent desire for someone else to be like them, and to be lent a hand for that purpose.*)

SELECTED REFERENCES: A Separate Reality - Page [20.2-23.2] (During my trip to see him...way to change anything about them.") The Second Ring of Power - Page [311.1-311.3] ("Sorcerers don't help one another like...You did that to Pablito.) The Power of Silence - Page [31.7-31.9] ("I never saw the reason for...of self-pity, self-compassion is meaningless.")

SEE ALSO: *WARRIOR-WAY, SELF-COMPASSION, WARRIOR-INTERVENTION, MANKIND-CONDITIONS*

WARRIOR-COMPLAINTS-[THE WARRIORS' COMPLAINTS]: (*Warriors know that it is meaningless to complain because life is an endless challenge.*)

SELECTED REFERENCES: A Separate Reality - Page [88.8-88.9] ("In order to become a man...to realize then that nothing matters.") A Separate Reality - Page [215.4-215.5] ("The spirit of a warrior...a warrior laughs and laughs.") Journey to Ixtlan - Page [120.8-120.9] ("If you would have been alone...or feeling offended by its acts.) Journey to Ixtlan - Page [226.7] ("It is meaningless to complain...is the strategy of your life.") Tales of Power - Page [105.4-105.5] ("Only as a warrior can one withstand...or bad. Challenges are simply challenges.")

SEE ALSO: *WARRIOR-REGRETS, WARRIOR-CHALLENGE*

WARRIOR-COMPLETENESS-[THE WARRIORS' COMPLETENESS]: (*The completeness of warriors centers on the complete integrity of their luminous cocoon, a luminous structure without holes or patches.*)

SELECTED REFERENCES: A Separate Reality - Page [4.7-4.8] ("You make it sound stupid," he said...not complete. You have no peace.") The Second Ring of Power - Page [62.4-62.8] ("Pablito is my enemy not because his eyes...power, I still have my purpose.") The Second Ring of Power - Page [118.1-119.7] ("What's the meaning of being incomplete...other people with holes like mine.") The Second Ring of Power - Page [120.1-121.8] ("The nagual patched you and me...You have welded them together.") The Second Ring of Power - Page [123.4-123.7] (Then he proceeded to smash my...feeling of having lost someone irreplaceable.) The Second Ring of Power - Page [132.5-133.1] ("An empty man uses the completeness...Genaro are now waiting for us.") The Second Ring of Power - Page [134.8-134.9] (I want to enter into the...me away from that world! Nothing!") The Second Ring of Power - Page [136.9-137.2] ("I've told you already that I'm...had three sons and one daughter.) The Second Ring of Power - Page [152.4-152.9] ("You're still incomplete," she said...whether or not to keep them.") The Second Ring of Power - Page [240.6-241.7] (I became entangled in a passionate...she said in a soft voice.) The Second Ring of Power - Page [246.6-246.7] ("The Nagual taught you and me...then that the Nagual was right.) The Second Ring of Power - Page [265.2-265.5] (La Gorda explained that power plants...be impossible for us to understand.) The Eagle's Gift - Page [63.6-63.7] ("The Nagual Juan Matus left us...she's merely riding on your back.") The Eagle's Gift - Page [143.7-143.9] ("You know what I'm talking about...merely apprentices of an inexhaustible art.) The Fire From Within - Page [xii.7-xii.8] (Don Juan had told me that...and knowledge without sobriety are useless.) The Fire From Within - Page [60.6-61.1] ("What can be done with man's natural...seen superimposed on the body itself.")

SEE ALSO: *WARRIOR-EMPTINESS, WARRIOR-EDGE*

WARRIOR-CONCEIT-[THE WARRIORS' CONCEIT]: (*Warriors know that they must develop the courage to become cunning without being conceited.*)

SELECTED REFERENCES: The Power of Silence - Page [110.2] ("Yes," he went on. "The idea...be ruthless without being self-important.")
SEE ALSO: *CUNNING, WARRIOR-COURAGE*

WARRIOR-CONCENTRATION-[THE WARRIORS' CONCENTRATION]: SEE: DREAMING-CONCENTRATION [THE CONCENTRATION NECESSARY TO DO DREAMING]

WARRIOR-CONCERN-FIRST-[THE WARRIORS' FIRST CONCERN]:
(Warriors know that one of their first concerns must be to rechannel the energy normally consumed by self-importance so that they can use it to face the unknown.)
SELECTED REFERENCES: The Fire From Within - Page [16.2-16.4] (Don Juan said then that in...of channeling that energy is impeccability.")
SEE ALSO: *WARRIOR-IMPECCABILITY, ENERGY, SELF-IMPORTANCE*

WARRIOR-CONDITION-[THE WARRIORS' CONDITION]: *(The condition of the warrior is to be aware of everything at all times.)*
SELECTED REFERENCES: Tales of Power - Page [116.8-117.3] (He unfolded his coat, and before...is no complete understanding without talking.)
SEE ALSO: *WARRIOR-PREPAREDNESS, WARRIOR-ALERTNESS*

WARRIOR-CONFIDENCE-[THE WARRIORS' CONFIDENCE]: SEE: WARRIOR-ASSUREDNESS [THE WARRIORS' ASSUREDNESS], WARRIOR-SELF-CONFIDENCE [THE WARRIORS' SELF-CONFIDENCE]

WARRIOR-CONFUSION-[THE WARRIORS' CONFUSION]: (Warriors know that their confusion is only a mood; the resolution of this confused state is a matter of the warriors' impeccability.)
SELECTED REFERENCES: Tales of Power - Page [85.5-85.6] ("There's no need to be confused...it's up to your personal power.")
SEE ALSO: *WARRIOR-IMPECCABILITY*

WARRIOR-CONSISTENCY-[THE WARRIORS' CONSISTENCY]:
(Warriors have a silent consistency to their acts that echoes their impeccability.)
SELECTED REFERENCES: A Separate Reality - Page [3.8-3.9] (Don Juan and I became friends, and...which was thoroughly baffling to me.) The Power of Silence - Page [23.7-23.9] (Don Juan commented that that was...world that admitted very few mistakes.) The Power of Silence - Page [129.3-129.5] ("If you judge me by my...myself with the most excruciating effort.") The Power of Silence - Page [237.2-237.3] (Don Juan said that because of the...consistency of the nagual Julian's actions.)
SEE ALSO: *WARRIOR-IMPECCABILITY*

WARRIOR-CONTAINMENT-[THE WARRIORS' CONTAINMENT]: SEE: WARRIOR-SOLIDITY-[THE WARRIORS' SOLIDITY]

WARRIOR-CONTRADICTION-KNOWLEDGE-[THE CONTRADICTIONS OF THE WARRIORS' QUEST FOR KNOWLEDGE]: (Warriors know that the road to knowledge is filled with contradictory propositions; warriors struggle to pit two views of the world against each other, and in the process, somehow manage to wriggle between them to find the totality of themselves; the warriors' awareness that knowledge is composed of a set of contradictory propositions.)
SELECTED REFERENCES: A Separate Reality - Page [28.6-28.7] ("I've told you already, only a...to be tricked into doing it.") Journey to Ixtlan - Page [111.2] ("Self-pity doesn't jibe with power...abandon himself at the same time?") Tales of Power - Page [8.2-8.3] ("It doesn't matter what one reveals...make a damn bit of difference.") Tales of Power - Page [52.3-52.5]

(There is a fourth, the correct one...in such a manner dissipates obsession.") **Tales of Power - Page [195.1-195.3]** ("That's a meaningless statement," he said...if your life would be different.) **Tales of Power - Page [241.5-241.6]** (Don Juan pointed out then that...the use assigned to those elements.) **Tales of Power - Page [245.3-245.4]** (I said that only if one...ordinary man or to a sorcerer.) **Tales of Power - Page [278.2-278.3]** (I once told you that those...that indescribable void that contains everything.) **The Second Ring of Power - Page [159.3]** (The Nagual told me that a...that he won't be able to.) **The Fire From Within - Page [30.4-30.6]** ("How do you measure defeat...of the petty tyrants for life.") **The Fire From Within - Page [61.2-61.4]** (I asked him if there was anything...to come, it must come of itself.") **The Fire From Within - Page [72.8-73.5]** (Don Juan said that the new...can bridge the contradictions," he said.) **The Fire From Within - Page [97.6-97.7]** (This indeed is another contradiction-how...be ready for the definitive journey.") **The Fire From Within - Page [148.1-148.3]** (He further said that to be...and has welcomed the world of boredom.) **The Fire From Within - Page [173.9]** (Don Juan said that *dreamers* have...but must be resolved in practice.) **The Power of Silence - Page [xviii.4-xviii.6]** (Until now it has been impossible...of the sorcerers of the past.) **The Power of Silence - Page [103.8-103.9]** (He emphasized that *intent* is not...said, is the essence of sorcery.) **The Power of Silence - Page [123.3-123.4]** ("Of course I insist that everyone...convinced you understood this sorcerers' contradiction.") **The Power of Silence - Page [159.3]** (In the sorcerers' world there are...In practice there are no contradictions.) **The Power of Silence - Page [162.5]** (He said that what seemed a contradiction...two sides of the same coin.) **The Power of Silence - Page [220.1]** ("This is another of the sorcerers' contradictions...the simplest thing in the world.) **The Power of Silence - Page [227.2-227.8]** (I told him I understood him...the solution. Why? No one knows.")

SEE ALSO: *WARRIOR-SOBRIETY, WARRIOR-BRIDGE, KNOWLEDGE, KNOWLEDGE-VS-LANGUAGE, SORCERER-CONTRADICTIONS-TERMS-PRACTICE, ASSEMBLAGE-POINT-MOVING-CONTRADICTION, AWARENESS-DEATH-FORESTALLS, CHANGE, DREAMING-PARADOX, ETERNITY-VS-HUMANNESS, INTENT-CONTRADICTION, PERCEPTION-REGARDING-DISREGARDING, POWER-WEIRD, RATIONALITY-EXTREMES, WARRIOR-WAY, SORCERER-CONTRADICTION-TERMS-PRACTICE, WARRIOR-WORLD-COLLAPSE-REASSEMBLE*

WARRIOR-CONTROL-[THE WARRIORS' CONTROL]: *(Warriors know they must learn to tune their spirit while someone else is trampling on them; this is the warriors' control, the first attribute of warriorship; the warriors' impeccable ability to control himself; the warriors' ability to survive in the best of all possible fashions.)*

SELECTED REFERENCES: **The Teachings of Don Juan - Page [87.2-87.4]** ("How can he defeat his third...will have defeated his third enemy.) **A Separate Reality - Page [180.9-181.7]** (Don Juan laughed until tears rolled...He would be battling to the end.) **Journey to Ixtlan - Page [111.1-111.2]** ("Self-pity doesn't jibe with...time it calls for abandoning himself.) **Journey to Ixtlan - Page [120.2-120.3]** ("A warrior, on the other hand...the best of all possible fashions.") **Tales of Power - Page [94.4-94.5]** (Somehow you refrained from indulging in...him without any aid from me.) **Tales of Power - Page [142.5]** ("One of the acts of a...a warrior has to be impeccable.") **The Eagle's Gift - Page [204.3-204.5]** (Don Juan advised me that I should...a performance staged by someone else.) **The Eagle's Gift - Page [306.9-307.3]** (Vicente came to my side next...the fulfilling of a sacred trust.) **The Fire From Within - Page [16.4-16.5]** (He said that the most effective...is fighting to lose self-importance.) **The Fire From Within - Page [23.9-24.1]** (His benefactor stressed the fact that...and continuous examination of the self.) **The Fire From Within - Page [26.1-26.4]** (But I had the proper equipment...trampling on you is called control.") **The Fire From Within - Page [30.5]** (To act in anger, without control...no forbearance, is to be defeated.") **The Fire From Within - Page [223.2-223.4]** (By reason of their activities, at...the force that makes us persons.) **The Power of Silence - Page [265.6-265.7]** (Moving the assemblage point is everything...reach the place of silent knowledge.")

SEE ALSO: *WARRIOR-ATTRIBUTES , WARRIOR-IMPECCABILITY, WARRIOR-ACCESSIBILITY*

WARRIOR-CONTROLLED-ABANDON-[THE WARRIORS' CONTROLLED ABANDON]: SEE: WARRIOR-ABANDON-CONTROLLED-[THE WARRIORS' CONTROLLED ABANDON]

WARRIOR-CONTROLLED-FOLLY-[THE WARRIORS' CONTROLLED FOLLY]: (Warriors know that controlled folly is the art of controlled deception, or the art of pretending to be thoroughly immersed in the action at hand; controlled folly is a sophisticated, artistic way of being separated from everything while remaining an integral part of everything; controlled folly is the basis for stalking as dreams are the basis for dreaming; the bridge between the folly of people and the finality of the Eagle's dictums; the warriors' application of the seven principles of stalking to everything they do, from the most trivial acts of life to life and death situations; the only way that warriors have of dealing with themselves in their state of expanded awareness and perception and with everybody and everything in the world of daily affairs; controlled folly is much like "seeing", it is something that cannot be thought about; warriors must purge and retrieve the luminous filaments of their interactions with others throughout their lifetime before they are capable of handling controlled folly because those filaments are the basis for our limitless capacity for self-importance.)

SELECTED REFERENCES: **A Separate Reality - Page [75.8-77.5]** (Lucio and Benigno had fallen asleep...That's a sorcerer's controlled folly.") **A Separate Reality - Page [78.6-81.5]** ("I wonder if you could tell...what he looks at everything becomes unimportant.") **A Separate Reality - Page [85.5-85.9]** (In other words, a man of...would also be his controlled folly.") **A Separate Reality - Page [86.4]** (Now you want me to describe...it is something you cannot think about.") **A Separate Reality - Page [91.4-91.8]** ("If I have understood you correctly...folly if I don't *see* through it?) **A Separate Reality - Page [153.5-153.6]** (The only difference between them is...from absolutely everything he knew before.") **The Eagle's Gift - Page [209.5-211.5]** (A secondary issue that came up...the finality of the Eagle's dictums.) **The Eagle's Gift - Page [248.6-249.1]** (La Gorda believed that the men...myself a master of *controlled folly*.) **The Eagle's Gift - Page [289.5-289.6]** (Unless stalkers have gone through the...be capable of laughing at oneself.) **The Eagle's Gift - Page [291.4-291.5]** ("I hope that you have realized...acts to life and death situations.) **The Power of Silence - Page [245.4-245.9]** (Don Juan had explained controlled folly...controlled folly and laugh at ourselves.")

SEE ALSO: *WORLD-IN-NOT-OF, WARRIOR-HUMOR, STALKING-ART, STALKING-PRINCIPLES-SEVEN, WARRIOR-BRIDGE, EQUILIBRIUM*

WARRIOR-CONVINCING-[CONVINCING THE WARRIOR]: (Warriors know that one of the most difficult aspects of the path of knowledge is simply convincing ourselves that we have unlimited hidden power; man tends to be dependent, we must be convinced that we can accomplish the impossible ourselves.)

SELECTED REFERENCES: **Journey to Ixtlan - Page [157.4-158.3]** ("Personal power is a feeling...even become a man of knowledge.") **Tales of Power - Page [81.5-81.9]** ("Can't don Genaro, being a sorcerer...about you, you're not ready yet.") **The Fire From Within - Page [218.9-219.1]** ("The strangest part of this mystery...And none of us wants to be.") **The Power of Silence - Page [xi.3-xi.6]** ("Everything I've put you through...hard to convince as you are.") **The Power of Silence - Page [160.2-160.5]** ("Our difficulty with this simple progression...do it ourselves? Big question, eh?") **The Art of Dreaming - Page [9.9]** ("It is obvious to me don...yourself that it can be done.) **The Art of Dreaming - Page [25.9-26.5]** ("Accept the challenge of intending," he...all the cells of your body.")

SEE ALSO: *POWER-HIDDEN, MAN-DEPENDENT, WARRIOR-IMPECCABILITY, IMPECCABLE-MAN-NO-GUIDE, SORCERY-PRACTICAL-SIDE*

WARRIOR-COUNTERPOINT-[THE WARRIORS' COUNTERPOINT]: (The warriors' counterpoint is the balance between the dictums of the rule and the behavior of warriors in the world of daily affairs; this counterpoint helps emphasize to the warrior that in the absence of self-importance, the only way to deal with the social milieu is through the warriors' controlled folly.)

SELECTED REFERENCES: **The Eagle's Gift** - Page **[210.7-211.5]** (Don Juan said that his benefactor...the finality of the Eagle's dictums.) **The Fire From Within** - Page **[83.3-83.4]** (Before I had time to say anything...the odds I was up against.)
SEE ALSO: *STALKING-ART, WARRIOR-CONTROLLED-FOLLY, RULE-, SELF-IMPORTANCE-LOSING, PERCEPTION-CHANGING-SOCIAL-BASE, EQUILIBRIUM, BALANCE*

WARRIOR-COURAGE-[THE WARRIORS' COURAGE]: (The warriors' courage is the personal capability to be crystal clear and be a person of courage; the warriors' awareness of death is the only thing that gives them true courage, the courage to be patient and yet take action, the courage to be acquiescent without being stupid, the courage to be cunning without being conceited, and above all, the courage to be ruthless without being self-important.)

SELECTED REFERENCES: **A Separate Reality** - Page **[76.6-76.7]** ("Can you bewitch him, don Juan...you have a man of courage!") **The Fire From Within** - Page **[241.7-241.9]** (Don Juan had drilled into me...no longer have anything to fear.) **The Power of Silence** - Page **[109.8-110.3]** ("Yes," he went on. "The idea...be ruthless without being self-important.")
SEE ALSO: *WARRIOR-ATTITUDE, DEATH-ADVISER, WARRIOR-ACQUIESCENCE, CUNNING, RUTHLESSNESS*

**WARRIOR-COURIER-[THE WARRIOR COURIER]:* (The warrior courier is the fourth of the male warriors; the fourth male personality; a taciturn, somber man who does very well if properly directed but who cannot stand on his own.)

SELECTED REFERENCES: **The Eagle's Gift** - Page **[174.8-175.3]** (The three male warriors and the...who cannot stand on his own.) **The Eagle's Gift** - Page **[190.5-192.1]** (Don Juan led the way to the...he passed on to the others.)
SEE ALSO: *WARRIOR-MALE*

WARRIOR-CROSSING-FREEDOM-[WARRIORS CROSS OVER TO FREEDOM]: (Warriors know that when they burn with the fire from within, they cross over to the third attention and to freedom; at the moment of that crossing the body is entirely kindled by knowledge and every cell becomes aware of itself as well as the totality of the body.)

SELECTED REFERENCES: **The Eagle's Gift** - Page **[178.8-179.1]** (Don Juan explained that the rule was...of the totality of the body.) **The Eagle's Gift** - Page **[304.7-305.2]** (La Gorda stated that not only...prepared to do it in *dreaming*.)
SEE ALSO: *FIRE-WITHIN, BODY-PHYSICAL-WITNESSING , TOTALITY, TOTAL-BEING, ATTENTION-THIRD, FREEDOM-TOTAL, WARRIOR-JOURNEY-DEFINITIVE, EAGLE-GIFT, AWARENESS-TOTAL*

WARRIOR-CRY-ANIMAL-[THE WARRIORS' ANIMAL CRY]-(TOP)

WARRIOR-CURIOSITY-[THE WARRIORS' CURIOSITY]: (The warriors' curiosity sustains them in the face of the hardships of learning.)

SELECTED REFERENCES: **The Teachings of Don Juan** - Page **[50.3-50.4]** ("All this is very easy to...in spite of yourself; that's the rule.)
SEE ALSO : *LEARNING-HARDSHIPS*

WARRIOR-CUTTING-EDGES-[THE WARRIORS' CUTTING EDGES]: *SEE: WARRIOR-DISGUISE-[THE WARRIORS' DISGUISE]*

WARRIOR-CYCLES-[THE WARRIORS' CYCLES]: (The warriors' cycles are the cycles of the nagual's party of warriors; the advent of the new nagual's party marks the beginning of a new cycle; for the new nagual's party it marks the beginning of the cycle of dreaming and for the existing nagual's

party it marks the beginning of a cycle of unequaled impeccability in their acts.)
> SELECTED REFERENCES: **The Eagle's Gift** - Page [218.7-218.9] (Don Juan and his Nagual woman...of unequaled impeccability in their acts.)
> SEE ALSO: *NAGUAL-PARTY*

WARRIOR-DANCE-LAST-POWER-[THE WARRIORS' LAST DANCE OF POWER]: *(The warriors' last dance of power is the dance of death, a movement warriors do under the influence of personal power; warriors add movements of power to their dance throughout their lives; the warriors' last dance tells of the warriors' struggle, of the battles won and lost, of the secrets and the marvels they have stored, and of the joys and bewilderments of their encounters with power.)*

> SELECTED REFERENCES: **Journey to Ixtlan** - Page [153.5-155.5] ("I will have to come with you...to the south. To the vastness.") **Journey to Ixtlan** - Page [228.3-228.4] ("So far your only defense is to...in his last stand on earth.)
> SEE ALSO: *DEATH, POWER-PERSONAL, WARRIOR-LAST-STAND, WARRIOR-FORM*

WARRIOR-DARING-[THE WARRIOR MUST BE DARING]: SEE: WARRIOR-ABANDON-[THE WARRIORS' CONTROLLED ABANDON]

WARRIOR-DEAD-AWARE-[WARRIORS ARE AWARE THAT THEY ARE DEAD]: *(Warriors know that they must be aware that they are dead; this is the grand trick of warrior-sorcerers.)*

> SELECTED REFERENCES: **The Power of Silence** - Page [195.3-195.5] ("Am I dead too," don Juan...I've kept mine in mint condition.")
> SEE ALSO: *SORCERER-TRICK, DEATH, DEATH-ADVISER*

WARRIOR-DEATH-[THE WARRIORS' DEATH]: *(Warriors know that only with warrior-sorcerers is death kind and sweet; if warriors are mortally wounded they will feel no pain; death will even hold itself in abeyance for as long as the warrior needs it to do so.)*

> SELECTED REFERENCES: **The Power of Silence** - Page [206.9-207.2] (He said that one of the most...sorcerers needed it to do so.)
> SEE ALSO: *DEATH, WARRIOR-DEATH-COMMAND, WARRIOR-LAST-DANCE-POWER, WARRIOR-DEATH-(ALL)*

WARRIOR-DEATH-CHOOSE-NOT-[WARRIORS DO NOT CHOOSE DEATH]: *(Warriors know they must choose life, not death; warriors prepare themselves to be aware and they know that to seek death is to seek nothing.)*

> SELECTED REFERENCES: **The Teachings of Don Juan** - Page [161.3-161.4] (And, the next thing, the path...seek death is to seek nothing.") **A Separate Reality** - Page [84.5-84.7] (He stubbornly maintained that his preference...spite of anything I may *see*.) **Journey to Ixtlan** - Page [108.8-108.9] (Lowering his voice to almost a whisper...overtake us regardless of anything.) **The Fire From Within** - Page [128.5-128.7] ("What are we really doing, don...are nothing do they become everything.")
> SEE ALSO: *DEATH, LIFE-CHOOSING, WARRIOR-DEATH-SEEK-NOT*

WARRIOR-DEATH-COMMAND-[WARRIORS COMMAND THEIR DEATH]: *(The warriors' attainment of the three masteries allows them to redefine the character of death; instead of being caught by death like the average man, they can choose the moment and the way of their departure from the world; the warriors' ability to "speed" enables them to avoid what might otherwise be the circumstances of a premature demise and their*

ultimate impeccability and control empower them to flow with power and burn with the fire from within when their tasks on earth are complete.)
    SELECTED REFERENCES: The Eagle's Gift - Page [103.3-103.4] (He thought that going over the...ready to disappear from this earth.) **The Fire From Within - Page** [xiii.6-xiii.8] (When I asked him once what...as if they had never existed.) **The Fire From Within - Page** [213.4-213.8] ("Is the boost from the earth...anchors; otherwise you wouldn't have returned.) **The Fire From Within - Page** [287.1-287.2] ("Who cares about sadness, he said...mysteries await us! What mysteries!") **The Fire From Within - Page** [295.2-295.3] ("I want you to bypass all...it in order to escape death.") **The Fire From Within - Page** [298.9-299.3] (One of the most fortunate decisions...the quintessence of the death defiers.) **The Power of Silence - Page** [207.2-208.4] ("The greatest difference between an average...died only when they had to.) **The Power of Silence - Page** [213.5-213.7] (I asked don Juan to explain the...fluctuate between reason and silent knowledge.)
    SEE ALSO: *FIRE-WITHIN, ATTENTION-THIRD, SPEEDING, IMMORTALITY*

WARRIOR-DEATH-VS-DECISIONS-[THE WARRIORS' DEATH VS THE WARRIORS' DECISIONS]: (In the world of everyday life, decisions can be reversed very easily and the only irrevocable thing is death; in the world of warrior-sorcerers, normal death can be countermanded, but decisions can not be changed or revised; once warriors make a decision, once they voice their intent, their decisions stand forever.)
    SELECTED REFERENCES: The Power of Silence - Page [207.4-207.5] (He then elaborated on the intricacies...had been made, they stood forever.) **The Art of Dreaming - Page** [96.9-97.1] ("Don't say anything," he advised me...is final. you'll stay there forever.")
    SEE ALSO: *DEATH, WARRIOR-DECISIONS, WARRIOR-DEATH-COMMAND, SPEED, INTENT-VOICING*

WARRIOR-DEATH-DEFIER-QUINTESSENCE-[WARRIORS BECOME THE QUINTESSENCE OF THE DEATH DEFIERS]: (Warriors resolve the dilemma of futility by choosing total awareness over the alternative of simply dying in another world; by choosing total freedom, warriors unwittingly continue the tradition of the ancient Toltecs by becoming the quintessence of the death defiers.)
    SELECTED REFERENCES: The Fire From Within - Page [298.9-299.3] (One of the most fortunate decisions...the quintessence of the death defiers.)
    SEE ALSO: *DEATH-DEFIERS, WARRIOR-DEATH-COMMAND, SPEED*

WARRIOR-DEATH-SEEK-NOT-[WARRIORS DO NOT SEEK DEATH]: (Warriors know it is no challenge to seek death.)
    SELECTED REFERENCES: The Eagle's Gift - Page [296.3-296.4] (It was then that I turned...be free is the ultimate audacity.")
    SEE ALSO: *DEATH, WARRIOR-DEATH-CHOOSE-NOT*

WARRIOR-DEATH-STOP-[THE WARRIOR STOPS DEATH]-(TOP)

WARRIOR-DEATH-SYMBOLIC-[THE WARRIORS' SYMBOLIC DEATH]: (Warriors know they must die a symbolic death; this symbolic dying is the warriors' ticket to impeccability.)
    SELECTED REFERENCES: The Power of Silence - Page [251.6-251.7] ("I was the same. For a...only really change if we die.")
    SEE ALSO: *CHANGE-DEATH-SYMBOLIC, WARRIOR-IMPECCABILITY-TICKET*

WARRIOR-DECISIONS-[THE WARRIORS' DECISIONS]: (Warriors know they must learn to empower their ability to decide and to be decisive; warriors know that deciding doesn't mean choosing an arbitrary time; deciding means that warriors have trimmed their spirit impeccably and have done everything possible to be worthy of knowledge and power; the warriors' ability to shift their decisions from the realm of the tonal to their

proper place, the realm of the nagual; the warriors' willingness to assume responsibility for all of their decisions; the power of the warriors' decisions that enables them to set their lives in a strategical manner and choose without regrets or recriminations.)

SELECTED REFERENCES : The Teachings of Don Juan - Page [106.8-107.1] (Therefore you must always keep in mind...be free of fear and ambition.) **A Separate Reality** - Page [47.5-47.7] ("Once you decided to come to...awaiting you. That's the warrior's way.") **A Separate Reality** - Page [151.3-151.6] ("A detached man, who knows he...to with gusto and lusty efficiency.) **Journey to Ixtlan** - Page [39.7-40.3] ("When a man decides to do...There is only time for decisions.") **Journey to Ixtlan** - Page [43.2-43.7] ("You are complaining," he said softly...the face of our inevitable death.") **Journey to Ixtlan** - Page [120.2-120.3] ("A warrior, on the other hand...the best of all possible fashions.") **Tales of Power** - Page [79.2-79.3] ("To decide doesn't mean to choose...be worthy of knowledge and power.) **Tales of Power** - Page [154.4] ("A rule of thumb for a warrior...him, much less drain his power.) **Tales of Power** - Page [249.1-249.5] ("What would have happened if I...true measure of a warrior's spirit.") **The Power of Silence** - Page [20.9-21.1] (Don Juan commented that it...Impostors ponder and become paralyzed.) **The Power of Silence** - Page [207.4-207.6] (He then elaborated on the intricacies...had been made, they stood forever.) **The Power of Silence** - Page [220.7-220.8] (He went on to say that...which in turn generated *unbending intent.*) **The Art of Dreaming** - Page [155.5-155.7] ("Be impeccable. I have told you...life in a helter-skelter way.")

SEE ALSO : *WARRIOR-CHOICE, RESPONSIBILITY-ASSUMING, WARRIOR-DECISIONS-(ALL), SPIRIT-DECISIONS*

WARRIOR-DECISIONS-EMPOWER-[WARRIORS EMPOWER THEIR DECISIONS]: (Warriors know the power of their decisions can be sustained only if they back them up with their impeccability from the moment they are made; warriors never look back or regret the decisions they have made; warriors assume responsibility for their decisions and humbly accept the way the that those decisions figure into the designs of the spirit.)

SELECTED REFERENCES: **A Separate Reality** - Page [47.5-47.7] ("Once you decided to come to...awaiting you. That's the warrior's way.") **A Separate Reality** - Page [151.3-151.6] ("A detached man, who knows he...to with gusto and lusty efficiency.) **Journey to Ixtlan** - Page [39.7-40.3] ("When a man decides to do...There is only time for decisions.") **Journey to Ixtlan** - Page [43.2-43.7] ("You are complaining," he said softly...the face of our inevitable death.") **Journey to Ixtlan** - Page [120.2-120.3] ("A warrior, on the other hand...the best of all possible fashions.")

SEE ALSO: *WARRIOR-DECISIONS, WARRIOR-REGRETS, WARRIOR-IMPECCABILITY, RESPONSIBILITY-ASSUMING, SPIRIT-DECISIONS, WARRIOR-HUMBLENESS, WARRIOR-DOUBTS-REMORSE*

WARRIOR-DECISIONS-FINAL-[THE FINALITY OF THE WARRIORS' DECISIONS]: (Warriors know that their dreaming decisions, the decisions they make by voicing their intent, are final and irreversible; the sorcerers' maneuvers are deadly and they must always be extraordinarily aware.)

SELECTED REFERENCES: **The Power of Silence** - Page [207.4-207.6] (He then elaborated on the intricacies...had been made, they stood forever.) **The Art of Dreaming** - Page [96.9-97.1] ("Don't say anything," he advised me...is final. You'll stay there forever.") **The Art of Dreaming** - Page [104.8] ("Sorcerers' maneuvers are deadly," don Juan...having some idiotic confidence in yourself.") **The Art of Dreaming** - Page [260.3-260.4] (I must have had an expression of...are final. Carol Tiggs is gone.")

SEE ALSO: *WARRIOR-DEATH-VS-DECISIONS, SORCERER-MANEUVER*

WARRIOR-DEDICATION-[THE WARRIORS' DEDICATION AND SINGLE-MINDEDNESS]: (Warriors know that in order to reach the crack between the worlds, they must develop an indomitable desire, a single-minded dedication; warriors must accomplish this without the help of any power or any man; warriors nourish their relationship with the spirit through their dedication and impeccability.)

SELECTED REFERENCES: **The Teachings of Don Juan - Page [185.4-185.8]** ("The particular thing to learn is how...on the other side of the boundary.) **The Eagle's Gift - Page [181.1-181.4]** (He said that there are two types...enhanced, perhaps by my own dedication.) **The Power of Silence - Page [22.8-23.1]** (The woman did not respond...it with their dedication and impeccability.) **The Power of Silence - Page [23.7-23.9]** (Don Juan commented that that was...world that admitted very few mistakes.)

SEE ALSO: *WARRIOR-STRUGGLE, WARRIOR-SPIRIT, WARRIOR-DEDICATION, WARRIOR-IMPECCABILITY, WARRIOR-INTENT-LINK, WARRIOR-INTENT-UNBENDING*

WARRIOR-DEFEAT-FEELING-COMBATING-[HOW WARRIORS CAN COMBAT THEIR FEELINGS OF DEFEAT]: (Warriors know that they can combat their feelings of defeat, impatience, despair, anger or sadness by rolling their eyes; this causes the assemblage point to move momentarily in lieu of the mastery of intent.)

SELECTED REFERENCES: **The Fire From Within - Page [260.4-260.6]** ("The new seers recommend a very simple...in lieu of true mastery of *intent*.)

SEE ALSO: *INTENT-MASTERY-IN-LIEU, INTENT-MASTERY, EYES-ROLLING, DEFEAT*

WARRIOR-DEFEND-NOTHING-[WARRIORS HAVE NO POINTS TO DEFEND]: (Warriors know that it is only reason that feels the need to defend anything; as luminous beings, warriors knows that they have nothing to defend and that even the truth requires no defense.)

SELECTED REFERENCES: **Tales of Power - Page [98.3-98.5]** ("We, the luminous beings are born...*reason* learns to accept and defend.) **The Eagle's Gift - Page [195.4-195.6]** (We walked to a restaurant a few...not protecting but merely defending myself.) **The Eagle's Gift - Page [215.8-215.9]** (His benefactor told don Juan that...impeccability, and impeccability cannot be threatened.) **The Eagle's Gift - Page [307.5-307.6]** (*I am already given to the power...dart past the Eagle to be free.*) **The Fire From Within - Page [39.5-40.1]** ("A nagual is someone flexible enough...that a nagual has no obsessions.") **The Fire From Within - Page [97.6-97.7]** ("Something is finally getting through to...be ready for the definitive journey.") **The Power of Silence - Page [123.4]** (In a loud voice I protested the obscurity...of my compulsion to defend myself.)

SEE ALSO: *OBSESSIONS, WARRIOR-IRREVERENCE*

WARRIOR-DELICACY-[THE WARRIORS' DELICACY]: (Warriors touch the world sparingly and with a delicate touch; they don't squeeze things and people until they have shriveled to nothing, especially the people they love; warriors have faith that the resources of the world will make themselves available to them and so they are never desperate.)

SELECTED REFERENCES: **Journey to Ixtlan - Page [69.7-70.8]** ("To be inaccessible means that you...moves away leaving hardly a mark.")

SEE ALSO: *WARRIOR-UNAVAILABILITY, WARRIOR-FINESSE, WARRIOR-DESPERATE-NEVER, HUNTER-ART*

WARRIOR-DESIRE-[THE WARRIORS' DESIRE]: (Warriors know they must lose their self-importance and with it their needs and desires; truly impeccable warriors are like intent itself, they have no desires of their own.)

SELECTED REFERENCES: **A Separate Reality - Page [153.4-153.5]** (I would say that this is the time...he meets them in the midst of their folly.) **The Eagle's Gift - Page [149.4-149.6]** ("I learned the *intent* of flying...the time they didn't do anything.") **The Power of Silence - Page [130.8-131.2]** ("A good hunter mesmerizes his prey...no longer interested in mesmerizing anyone.)

SEE ALSO: *INTENT, WARRIOR-NOTHING-MATTERS, EQUAL-UNIMPORTANT, DESIRE-INTERVENTION-POWER, WARRIOR-INDIFFERENCE, WARRIOR-SORCERER-SEER*

WARRIOR-DESPAIR-DETERRENT-[THE ONLY DETERRENT TO THE WARRIORS' DESPAIR]: *(Warriors know that the only true deterrent to despair is the awareness of death; that is the only thing that can give warriors the strength to withstand the pain and duress of life and the fear of the unknown; warriors know they can also combat their feelings of despair by rolling their eyes.)*
    SELECTED REFERENCES: **The Second Ring of Power - Page [234.4-234.9]** (I had an attack of profound sadness...behind the best of my feelings.) **The Fire From Within - Page [260.4-260.6]** ("The new seers recommend a very simple...in lieu of true mastery of *intent*.)
    SEE ALSO: *DEATH, FEAR, PAIN, UNKNOWN, EYES-ROLLING*

WARRIOR-DESPERATE-NEVER-[WARRIORS ARE NEVER DESPERATE]: *(Warriors are never desperate; warriors know that to worry is to become unwittingly accessible; once warriors begin to worry, they cling to anything out of desperation and that clinging exhausts them and whatever they are clinging to.)*
    SELECTED REFERENCES: **Journey to Ixtlan - Page [69.9-70.3]** ("To be unavailable means that you...or whatever you are clinging to.")
    SEE ALSO: *WARRIOR-UNAVAILABILITY, WARRIOR-FOG-CREATE, WARRIOR-WORRY-NOT, WARRIOR-DELICACY*

WARRIOR-DESTINY-[THE WARRIORS' DESTINY]: *(Warriors know that there is no destiny, only the fulfillment of power's promise.)*
    SELECTED REFERENCES: **Tales of Power - Page [145.3-145.5]** ("I still don't understand the meaning...you're about to fulfill your power.) **The Second Ring of Power - Page [283.4-284.1]** (I narrated to her the way...in my tying my shoelaces impeccably.) **The Eagle's Gift - Page [106.6-107.2]** (Don Juan had taught me to...as the petty people we were.) **The Eagle's Gift - Page [173.4-173.5]** (The Eagle, that power that governs...too insignificant to move the whole.)
    SEE ALSO : *POWER-FULFILLING-BID, POWER-PROMISE, WARRIOR-FATE*

WARRIOR-DETACHMENT-[THE WARRIORS' DETACHMENT]: *(Warriors struggle to detach themselves from everything; they use the awareness of death to detach themselves and make themselves silently lusty; only the idea of death can make warriors sufficiently detached so that they can't deny themselves anything or cling to anything; the detachment of the warrior is not born out of fear or indolence, but out of conviction.)*
    SELECTED REFERENCES: **A Separate Reality - Page [150.5-151.6]** ("Thus to be a warrior a...to with gusto and lusty efficiency.) **A Separate Reality - Page [153.4-153.8]** (Upon learning to *see* a man becomes...the most frightening waste there is.) **A Separate Reality - Page [256.9-257.3]** (We walked to the house in complete...nothing I could subtract from it.) **Journey to Ixtlan - Page [120.6-121.3]** (A warrior could be injured but...It takes power to do that.") **The Eagle's Gift - Page [112.7-113.5]** (La Gorda, upon hearing my report...to struggle unyieldingly for a lifetime.) **The Eagle's Gift - Page [125.7-125.8]** (Having lost my human form, I...including being inconsistent, and outright petty.) **The Eagle's Gift - Page [307.5-307.6]** (*I am already given to the...past the Eagle to be free.*) **The Fire From Within - Page [18.2]** ("La Gorda is in a class...she is teaching you detachment.") **The Fire From Within - Page [79.4-79.6]** (He stopped talking and solicited questions...enough energy to grasp it.) **The Fire From Within - Page [148.1-148.4]** (He further said that to be...into the unknown and love it.") **The Fire From Within - [297.9-298.1]** ("The old seers used to say that...manipulation of intent through sober commands.") **The Power of Silence - Page [23.7-23.9]** (Don Juan commented that that was...world that admitted very few mistakes.) **The Power of Silence - Page [113.7-113.9]** (In the early evening, don Juan...of my shift to heightened awareness.) **The Power of Silence - Page [169.3-169.4]** (And it was at that moment...mode of behavior from then on.) **The Power of Silence - Page [181.1-181.9]** (Everything had occurred so smoothly that...had terrorized him for so many years.) **The Power of Silence - Page [187.4-187.7]** (Don Juan said that it took...of the world of everyday life.) **The Art of Dreaming - Page [47.7-47.9]** ("Yes, but for a perfect result...is unnecessary, to say the least.") **The Art of Dreaming - Page [65.2-65.3]** ("Is this force capable of materializing...the fixation of our assemblage points.") **The Art of Dreaming - Page [80.9-81.2]** ("Where are those worlds, don Juan...price they couldn't afford to pay.) **The Art of Dreaming - Page [134.2-134.5]**

(More than two weeks went by...made their appearance in my mind.) **The Art of Dreaming -
Page [204.5-205.1]** (He did not answer me...to put aside such a gift.")
    SEE ALSO: *WARRIOR-CHOICE, DEATH-ADVISER, WARRIOR-DECISIONS,
RESPONSIBILITY-ASSUMING*

WARRIOR-DETERMINATION-[THE WARRIORS' DETERMINATION]:
*(Warriors know that determination can radically effect any human being;
the warriors' determination is unbending intent, the determination to tackle
the most arduous tasks imaginable.)*
    SELECTED REFERENCES: **The Eagle's Gift - Page [203.9-204.1]** (As we drove away,
don Juan...of Zoila, Zuleica, and Silvio Manuel.)
    SEE ALSO: *WARRIOR-INTENT-UNBENDING, SORCERY-PRACTICAL-SIDE*

WARRIOR-DEVELOPMENT-THREE-STAGES-[THE THREE STAGES OF
THE WARRIORS' DEVELOPMENT]: *(The three stages of the warriors'
development are; 1) accepting the rule as a map; 2) understanding that
human beings can gain a paramount awareness because there is such a thing;
3) entering an actual passageway into the world of concealed awareness.)*
    SELECTED REFERENCES: **The Eagle's Gift - Page [179.3-179.8]** (Don Juan said that
in the...that other concealed world of awareness.) **The Eagle's Gift - Page [204.8-205.1]** (His
proclivity to remain in a state...the silent force behind don Juan.) **The Eagle's Gift - Page [218.9-
219.7]** (His benefactor explained to don Juan...the truth contained in the rule.)
    SEE ALSO: *WARRIOR-WAY, RULE-MAP, AWARENESS-TOTAL, CRACK-
WORLDS*

WARRIOR-DIALOGUE-[THE WARRIORS' DIALOGUE OF THE NEW
SEERS]: *(Warriors carry on a warriors' dialogue to help solidify the new
position of their assemblage point; warriors know that the dialogue of the
new seers is really not a dialogue at all but the detached manipulation of
intent through sober commands; warriors feel a compelling desire to explain
sorcery in cogent, well-reasoned terms, and they must utilize this desire as
an intellectual exercise with which to stalk themselves; what makes the
assemblage point shift laterally is the nearly unavoidable desire to render
the incomprehensible in terms of what is familiar to us.)*
    SELECTED REFERENCES: **The Fire From Within - Page [153.7-153.9]** ("It's all very
simple," don Juan...get going with our warriors' dialogue.") **The Fire From Within - Page [297.9-
298.1]** ("The old seers used to say that...manipulation of intent through sober commands.)
    SEE ALSO: *ASSEMBLAGE-POINT-POSITION-NEW, WARRIOR-DIALOGUE-
SEER-OLD, INTENT, WARRIOR-COMMAND, WARRIOR-DETACHMENT, WARRIOR-
SOBRIETY, SEER-NEW, WARRIORSHIP-VS-SORCERY, SORCERY-EXPLAINING-DESIRE,
ASSEMBLAGE-POINT-SHIFT-LATERAL, WARRIOR-INTELLECTUAL-EXERCISE, INTENT-
LINK-CLEANING, STALKER-TRUMP-CARD,*

WARRIOR-DIALOGUE-SEERS-OLD-[THE WARRIORS' DIALOGUE OF
THE OLD SEERS]: *(Warriors know that the dialogue of the old seers was a
dialogue about sorcery and the enhancement of self-reflection.)*
    SELECTED REFERENCES: **The Fire From Within - Page [297.9-298.1]** ("The old
seers used to say that...manipulation of *intent* through sober commands.")
    SEE ALSO: *SORCERY, SEER-OLD, TOLTECS, WARRIORSHIP-VS-SORCERY*

WARRIOR-DIFFERENT-[WHAT MAKES THE WARRIOR DIFFERENT
FROM THE AVERAGE MAN]: *(The warriors' attainments are the only
things that differentiate them from average human beings; warriors have
succeeded in redefining themselves and their world which means they remain
in the world but they are no longer of it.)*
    SELECTED REFERENCES: **Tales of Power - Page [54.4-54.8]** (I explained to him that
my..."Of course. You yourself are changing.")

SEE ALSO: *WORLD-IN-NOT-OF, WARRIOR-ATTAINMENTS, WARRIOR-TRANSFORMATION*

WARRIOR-DIRECTION-[THE WARRIORS' DIRECTION]: *(The warriors' direction and purpose comes from the possession of the life force; without it, warriors cannot attain any of the three stages of attention.)*

SELECTED REFERENCES: **The Eagle's Gift - Page [247.6-247.9]** (He told me that I had...just before the Eagle devours it.)
SEE ALSO: *WARRIOR-PURPOSE, LIFE-FORCE, ATTENTION, WARRIOR CHANGE-DIRECTION, AWARENESS-PREREQUISITE*

WARRIOR-DIRECTION-CHANGING-[CHANGING THE DIRECTION OF THE WARRIOR]-(TOP)

WARRIOR-DISAPPEARANCE-[THE WARRIORS' DISAPPEARANCE]:
(One of the most difficult things which warriors must do is to prepare themselves to disappear in full awareness, without anger or disappointment, leaving behind the best of their feelings; preparing ourselves to disappear is even more difficult than preparing ourselves for death.)

SELECTED REFERENCES: **The Second Ring of Power - Page [234.7-234.9]** (But confronted with la Gorda's determination...behind the best of my feelings.)
SEE ALSO: *WARRIOR-DEATH, EAGLE-GIFT*

WARRIOR-DISAPPOINTMENT-[THE WARRIORS' DISAPPOINTMENT]:
(Warriors know it is useless to get angry and disappointed with themselves; all that proves is that the tonal is involved in an internal struggle that is consuming a great deal of energy; warriors avoids this wear and tear by living a tight and harmonious life .)

SELECTED REFERENCES: **Tales of Power - Page [155.7-155.9]** ("This is your world. You can't....the harmony between *tonal* and *nagual*.)
SEE ALSO: *WARRIOR-IMPECCABILITY, WARRIOR-LIVE-LIKE, WARRIOR-LIFE-TIGHT*

WARRIOR-DISASSOCIATION-[THE WARRIORS' DISASSOCIATION]:
(Warriors know that the path of knowledge causes them to appear to be "disassociated" in the eyes of the average man; but warriors also understand that this lack of rational understanding is a natural and appropriate by-product of progress on the path of knowledge.)

SELECTED REFERENCES: **Tales of Power - Page [190.8-191.2]** ("If you cannot understand, you're in...about what I had been through.)
SEE ALSO: *UNDERSTANDING, KNOWLEDGE-VS-LANGUAGE*

WARRIOR-DISCIPLINE-[THE WARRIORS' DISCIPLINE]: *(Warriors know that they must lead a disciplined life in order to become clear about themselves and their path with heart; the warriors' ability to map an adversary's strengths, weaknesses and quirks of behavior while they, the warriors, are being beaten; the second attribute of warriorship.)*

SELECTED REFERENCES: **The Teachings of Don Juan - Page [106.8-107.1]** (Therefore you must always keep in...your heart tells you to do.) **The Eagle's Gift - Page [125.8-126.1]** (The advantage of being formless is...between her actions and her purposes.) **The Fire From Within - Page [x.3-x.5]** (For years afterward I thought that...their companions to conduct those teachings.) **The Fire From Within - Page [23.5]** ("My benefactor developed a strategy using...warriorship: control, discipline, forbearance, and timing.") **The Fire From Within - Page [26.4-26.8]** (Don Juan explained that his benefactor's...is called discipline," don Juan said.) **The Fire From Within - Page [30.4-30.5]** ("Anyone who joins the petty tyrant...no forbearance, is to be defeated.") **The Fire From Within - Page [66.3-66.5]** ("The second attention, on the other...that require supreme discipline and concentration.") **The Fire From Within - Page [137.1-137.2]** ("It all depends on the warrior...recommend a twenty-three-hour vigil.") **The Art of Dreaming - Page [26.4-26.5]** ("No it isn't. Intending is much...all the cells of your body.)

SEE ALSO: *WARRIOR-ATTRIBUTES, PATH-HEART-WITH, DISCIPLINE, ENERGY-BODY-DISCIPLINE*

WARRIOR-DISCONNECTS-RECONNECTS-[WARRIORS DISCONNECT AND RECONNECT THE WORLD]: SEE: WARRIOR-WORLD-COLLAPSES-[WARRIORS COLLAPSE AND REASSEMBLE THE WORLD]

WARRIOR-DISGUISE-[THE WARRIORS' DISGUISE]: *(The warriors' task is to sharpen, yet disguise their cutting edges, so that no one would suspect their ruthlessness.)*
SELECTED REFERENCES: **The Power of Silence - Page [106.9-107.1]** (A warrior was magical and ruthless...be able to suspect his ruthlessness.)
SEE ALSO: *RUTHLESSNESS, STALKING-ART*

WARRIOR-DISPASSIONATE-[THE DISPASSIONATE WARRIOR]: *(Warriors know they must learn to become dispassionate; they have no business following the ups and downs of the world of everyday life; the warriors' formlessness and completeness facilitate the ability to remain dispassionate as they function in the world but not of it.)*
SELECTED REFERENCES: **The Second Ring of Power - Page [246.6-246.8]** ("The Nagual taught you and me...them in their ups and downs.)
SEE ALSO: *WARRIOR-FORMLESS, WARRIOR-COMPLETENESS, WORLD-IN-NOT-OF, WARRIOR-DETACHMENT*

WARRIOR-DISPOSITION-[THE WARRIORS' DISPOSITION]: *(Warriors know they must cultivate a light and amenable disposition if they are to withstand the impact of the path of knowledge.*
SELECTED REFERENCES: **A Separate Reality - Page [7.8-7.9]** (His premise was that a light...the knowledge he was teaching me.)
SEE ALSO: *WARRIOR-HUMOR, WARRIOR-JOY, WARRIOR-LIGHTNESS*

WARRIOR-DO-NOTHING-[WARRIORS DO NOTHING]: *(When warriors reach the end of their road, they no longer seek anything; they go from day to day doing nothing but waiting for freedom.)*
SELECTED REFERENCES: **The Fire From Within - Page [115.1-115.3]** ("Is that what you're doing here...We are waiting for freedom!")
SEE ALSO: *WARRIOR-FREEDOM-TOTAL, WARRIOR-DESIRE, WARRIOR-SEEKS-OTHER-SIDE-COIN, AWARENESS-MASTERY*

WARRIOR-DOING-NOT-DOING-[THE DOING AND NOT-DOING OF WARRIORS]: *(Warriors know that personal power is the only thing that matters when it comes to the doings and not-doings of life.)*
SELECTED REFERENCES: **Tales of Power - Page [105.8-105.9]** ("It depends on your personal power...should say that you're doing fine.")
SEE ALSO: *DOING, NOT-DOING, POWER-PERSONAL*

WARRIOR-DOUBTS-REMORSE-[THE WARRIORS' DOUBTS AND REMORSE]: *(Warriors must assume full responsibility for what they do; they must be clear as to why they act and then proceed with their actions without doubts or remorse; acting without doubts and remorse is the only way warriors can empower their decisions.)*
SELECTED REFERENCES: **Journey to Ixtlan - Page [39.7-40.3]** ("When a man decides to do something...There is only time for decisions.") **Journey to Ixtlan - Page [84.8-85.1]** ("Use it. Focus your attention on...the acts of a timid man.") **Journey to Ixtlan - Page [182.9-183.3]** (The soothing feeling of peace and plenitude...an unwarranted importance on the self.) **Tales of Power - Page [54.1-54.2]** ("What's wrong with me don Juan...accepts in humbleness what he is.") **Tales of Power - Page [63.5-63.8]** ("You see," don Juan said...I was very much like you.) **Tales of Power - Page [196.1-196.5]** (I made an involuntary gesture of...drains his power, impeccability replenishes it.") **The Second Ring of Power - Page [61.8-61.9]** ("But how could my

death benefit...and have second thoughts and doubts.) **The Second Ring of Power - Page [93.4-93.9]** ("Do you envy la Gorda for...the Nagual was a new life.) **The Second Ring of Power - Page [270.4-270.6]** (La Gorda came to my aid...and you pretend to be dumb.")
    SEE ALSO: *RESPONSIBILITY-ASSUMING, ACT-LEARNING, WARRIOR-DECISIONS-EMPOWER*

WARRIOR-DREAMS-[THE WARRIORS' DREAMS]: (Warriors seeking power don't refer to their dreams as dreams, they call their dreams real because that is what they are.)
    SELECTED REFERENCES: **Journey to Ixtlan - Page [91.7-92.4]** ("Become accessible to power; tackle your...you can control whatever you want.")
    SEE ALSO: *DREAMING-ART, DREAMING-VS-DREAMS*

WARRIOR-DUALISM-[THE WARRIORS' DUALISM]: (At some point in their development, warriors become aware of two distinct parts within themselves; one is extremely old, at ease and indifferent; it is heavy, dark and connected to everything; it does not care because it is equal to everything; it enjoys things with no expectation; this part of the warrior is connected to the position of silent knowledge; the other part of the warrior is light, fluffy and agitated, nervous and fast; it cares about itself because it is insecure; it does not enjoy anything because it lacks the capacity to connect itself to anything; it is alone and vulnerable; it is the part of ourselves with which we look at the world; this part of the warrior is connected to the position of reason; the awareness of this dualism is an awareness of the warriors' true pair.)
    SELECTED REFERENCES: **The Power of Silence - Page [145.6-146.9]** (I abruptly pulled over to the...knowledge that you cannot yet voice.")
    SEE ALSO: *PERCEPTUAL-DUALISM, POINT-FIRST, POINT-SECOND, POINT-THIRD, PAIR-TRUE, TONAL-NAGUAL-DICHOTOMY, KNOWLEDGE-SILENT, REASON*

WARRIOR-DUALITY-RECOLLECTION-[THE RECOLLECTION OF THE WARRIORS' DUALITY]: (When warriors are doubled, they have no notion at that moment of their duality; they actually recollect two separate single instants simultaneously, because the glue of the description of time is no longer binding them.)
    SELECTED REFERENCES: **Tales of Power - Page [47.1-47.9]** ("Can an outsider, looking at a...time is no longer binding him.")
    SEE ALSO : *RECOLLECTION, DUALISM, PERCEPTION-SPLIT, TIME-DESCRIPTION*

WARRIOR-DURESS-EXTREME-BENEFITS-[THE BENEFITS OF EXTREME DURESS FOR WARRIORS]: (Warriors know that the history of sorcery and warriorship shows that periods of the most extreme subjugation and coercion have provided warriors with the ideal circumstances to perfect their skills; oddly enough, it was the extreme rigor and duress of those periods which gave warriors the impetus to refine their new principles; strife that does not kill the warrior only makes him stronger.)
    SELECTED REFERENCES: **The Second Ring of Power - Page [224.5-224.6]** ("The nagual told me that the...kill you or to help you.") **The Fire From Within - Page [6.1-6.3]** ("The new cycle was just beginning...alone to map their findings.) **The Fire From Within - Page [29.6-29.9]** ("Do petty tyrants sometimes win, and...on discussing the mastery of awareness.)
    SEE ALSO: *TONAL-REFUGE-NAGUAL, OPPRESSED-ADVANTAGES, AWARENESS-GROWTH, WARRIOR-PAPER, STRIFE*

WARRIOR-DUTY-[THE WARRIORS' DUTY]: (Warriors have their duty as warriors and nothing else is important; the warriors' duty is the impeccable quest for freedom.)
> SELECTED REFERENCES: **The Eagle's Gift - Page [306.5-306.9]** (Don Juan called everyone to come...understood and had accepted my fate.)
> SEE ALSO: *WARRIOR-IMPECCABILITY, WARRIOR-TOTAL-FREEDOM*

WARRIOR-DYNAMISM-[THE WARRIORS' DYNAMISM]: (Warriors acquire a special dynamism as a result of living an impeccable life.)
> SELECTED REFERENCES: **The Power of Silence - Page [187.5-187.7]** (Gone was his feeling of detachment...he set out on his own.)
> SEE ALSO: *WARRIOR-IMPECCABILITY, WARRIOR-ENTERPRISE*

WARRIOR-EAT-[HOW WARRIORS EAT]: (Warriors know that it is beneficial to eat quietly and slowly, taking only four mouthfuls at a time; then a while later they eat another four mouthfuls and so on.)
> SELECTED REFERENCES: **The Second Ring of Power - Page [229.2-229.4]** ("No. I also had to learn how...another four mouthfuls and so on.) **The Power of Silence - Page [72.7-72.8]** ("Your assemblage point moved to heightened...are in mine. I drink water.")
> SEE ALSO: *WARRIOR-WAY*

WARRIOR-EDGE-[THE WARRIORS' EDGE]: (Warriors know that when one has a child, that child takes the edge of one's spirit; the loss of the warriors' edge is greatest to a child of the same sex as the warrior; warriors strive to regain their edge from their children because by so doing they regain their completeness; the edge of a person who dies goes back to the givers of that edge or the person most closely aligned by power to that individual.)
> SELECTED REFERENCES: **The Second Ring of Power - Page [121.7-121.8]** ("You love a little boy and...You have welded them together.") **The Second Ring of Power - Page [130.8-132.1]** (I began my change by taking...children all their lives, that's all.") **The Second Ring of Power - Page [133.2-135.3]** ("But how did you regain your...that I had become utterly confused.) **The Second Ring of Power - [241.1-241.5]** (The Nagual said that the edge...boost is for Soledad to die.") **The Second Ring of Power - Page [242.2]** ("The value is that we need...into that other world," she said.)
> SEE ALSO: *WARRIOR-COMPLETENESS , WARRIOR-EMPTINESS*

WARRIOR-EFFECTIVENESS-[THE WARRIORS' EFFECTIVENESS]: (Warriors know their effectiveness depends on their ability to remain detached and impeccable.)
> SELECTED REFERENCES: **The Power of Silence - Page [187.4-187.7]** (Don Juan said that it took...he set out on his own.)
> SEE ALSO: *WARRIOR-DETACHMENT, WARRIOR-IMPECCABILITY*

WARRIOR-EFFICIENCY-[THE WARRIORS' EFFICIENCY]: (Warriors strive to strike a subtle balance of positive and negative forces which will enable them to meet any conceivable situation with equal efficiency.)
> SELECTED REFERENCES: **A Separate Reality - Page [151.1-151.7]** ("Only the idea of death makes a man...a warrior and has acquired patience!") **Tales of Power - Page [94.4-94.5]** (Somehow you refrained from indulging in...him without any aid from me.) **Tales of Power - Page [287.6-287.7]** ("You have learned that the backbone...day, you'll need your ultimate forbearance.") **Tales of Power - Page [289.7-289.8]** ("A warrior acknowledges his pain but...assessed what lies ahead of him.") **The Eagle's Gift - Page [306.9-307.2]** (Vicente came to my side next...and the unexpected, with equal efficiency.)
> SEE ALSO: *WARRIOR-BALANCE, WARRIOR-PREPAREDNESS, EQUILIBRIUM, BALANCE*

WARRIOR-EMPHASIS-[THE WARRIORS' EMPHASIS]: (The warriors' emphasis is the way warriors prioritize the items on the island of the tonal; the key to the warriors' choices; warriors can make themselves miserable or they can make themselves strong; either way the amount of work is the same, so the key lies in what one emphasizes; if warriors can benefit from anything, it is not from methods but from a change of emphasis; if we become aware of the need to curtail our self-importance, then that help is real.)

SELECTED REFERENCES: Journey to Ixtlan - Page [184.1-184.2] ("The trick is in what one...amount of work is the same.") **The Power of Silence** - Page [160.1-160.5] (I told him that his sequence...do it ourselves? Big question, eh?")

SEE ALSO: *WARRIOR-CHOICE, FACADE-TRANSFORMING, ILL-BEING, WARRIOR-WELL-BEING, WARRIOR-IMPECCABILITY, SELF-IMPORTANCE*

WARRIOR-EMPTINESS-[THE WARRIORS' EMPTINESS]: *(The warriors' emptiness is written on the luminous body, it is a hole or series of holes in the luminous cocoon; the act of having children empties warriors and makes them incomplete.)*

SELECTED REFERENCES: The Second Ring of Power - Page [94.6-96.3] ("Why do you think the Nagual...closed it. She is complete again.") **The Second Ring of Power** - Page [118.1-121.8] ("What's the meaning of being incomplete...You have welded them together.") **The Second Ring of Power** - Page [123.5-123.7] (Then he proceeded to smash my...feeling of having lost someone irreplaceable.) **The Second Ring of Power** - Page [156.6-157.2] ("Why in gullies and water holes...on to what he was doing.") **The Second Ring of Power** - Page [240.4-241.7] ("Am I still shaped like an...she said in a soft voice.) **The Second Ring of Power** - Page [242.2-242.8] ("The value is that we need all...them that they can do it.") **The Second Ring of Power** - Page [246.6-246.7] ("The Nagual taught you and me...then that the Nagual was right.) **The Second Ring of Power** - Page [282.1] ("You are talking in circles, Gorda...I can't make it any clearer.) **The Eagle's Gift** - Page [45.2-45.5] (Many of those luminous eggs had...vibrant, filled with energy and whiteness.) **The Fire From Within** - Page [60.6-61.1] ("What can be done with man's...*seen* superimposed on the body itself.")

SEE ALSO: *WARRIOR-COMPLETENESS, WARRIOR-EDGE*

WARRIOR-ENEMY-FIRST-[THE FIRST ENEMY OF THE WARRIOR]: SEE: FEAR-[FEAR], WARRIOR-ENEMIES-FOUR-NATURAL-[THE FOUR NATURAL ENEMIES OF THE WARRIOR]

WARRIOR-ENEMY-FOURTH-[THE FOURTH ENEMY OF THE WARRIOR]: SEE: OLD-AGE-[OLD AGE], WARRIOR-ENEMIES-FOUR-NATURAL-[THE FOUR NATURAL ENEMIES OF THE WARRIOR]

WARRIOR-ENEMY-GREAT-[THE GREAT ENEMY OF THE WARRIOR]: *(Warriors know that one of their great enemies is not believing what is happening to them.)*

SELECTED REFERENCES: The Second Ring of Power - Page [57.9-58.4] (Don Juan had always said to me...immediately, it dallies with it instead.)

SEE ALSO: *BELIEVE-HAVING-TO*

WARRIOR-ENEMY-SECOND-[THE SECOND ENEMY OF THE WARRIOR]: SEE: CLARITY-[CLARITY], WARRIOR-ENEMIES-FOUR-NATURAL-[THE FOUR NATURAL ENEMIES OF THE WARRIOR]

WARRIOR-ENEMY-THIRD-[THE THIRD ENEMY OF THE WARRIOR]: SEE: POWER-[POWER], WARRIOR-ENEMIES-FOUR-NATURAL-[THE FOUR NATURAL ENEMIES OF THE WARRIOR]

WARRIOR-ENEMIES-FOUR-NATURAL-[THE FOUR NATURAL ENEMIES OF THE WARRIOR]: *(Warriors know they have a series of four natural enemies that they must face and conquer on the road to knowledge; the four enemies of the warrior are fear, clarity, power and old age.)*

SELECTED REFERENCES: **The Teachings of Don Juan - Page [82.6-87.8]** ("Then what must a man do...clarity, power, and knowledge is enough.") **The Teachings of Don Juan - Page [188.5]** (And, although Don Juan has not...enemy of a man of knowledge.) **The Fire From Within - Page [167.5-167.9]** (As we walked, don Juan told...scorn and reject their own tradition.)
SEE ALSO: *FEAR, CLARITY, POWER, OLD-AGE, MAN-KNOWLEDGE, INDOLENCE, WARRIOR-ENEMY-GREAT, SORCERER-ENEMY, WARRIOR-WEAKNESS-DAILY-WORLD*

WARRIOR-ENERGY-[THE WARRIORS' ENERGY: SEE: WARRIOR-IMPECCABILITY-[THE WARRIORS' IMPECCABILITY]

WARRIOR-ENERGY-INCREASED-[THE WARRIORS' INCREASED ENERGY]: (*Warriors know that when they curtail self-importance, the energy which self-importance normally consumes is no longer expended; this increased energy then becomes the springboard which launches the warriors' assemblage point on an inconceivable journey.*)
SELECTED REFERENCES: **The Power of Silence - Page [159.5-159.7]** (He explained that the specific sequence...without premeditation, into an inconceivable journey.)
SEE ALSO: *ENERGY, SELF-IMPORTANCE, SELF-REFLECTION, THOUGHT-SOMERSAULT, WARRIOR-IMPECCABILITY*

WARRIOR-ENERGY-MAXIMUM-[THE WARRIORS' MAXIMUM ENERGY LEVEL]: (*Warriors know that as they approach their time to leave the world, they attain a level of maximum energy; the completion of their task of remembering themselves sets the stage for the attainment of this maximum energy level.*)
SELECTED REFERENCES: **The Fire From Within - Page [183.9-184.1]** ("At any rate the job of...all be gone in an instant.")
SEE ALSO: *REMEMBERING-BODY, FIRE-WITHIN*

WARRIOR-ENERGY-MISER-[WARRIORS MUST BECOME MISERS WITH THEIR ENERGY]: (*Warriors know that all they need is energy in order to accept the magnificent gift of freedom which the Eagle offers to all human beings; consequently warriors become misers with all their energy.*)
SELECTED REFERENCES: **The Fire From Within - Page [299.6-299.8]** ("Is that what all of you...we must become misers of energy.")
SEE ALSO: *WARRIOR-IMPECCABILITY, ENERGY, EAGLE-GIFT*

WARRIOR-ENTERPRISE-[THE WARRIORS' ENTERPRISE]: (*Warriors know that they develop a sense of enterprise, a sense of attainment that comes through a life of impeccability.*)
SELECTED REFERENCES: **The Power of Silence - Page [187.5-187.7]** (Gone was his feeling of detachment...he set out on his own.)
SEE ALSO: *WARRIOR-IMPECCABILITY, WARRIOR-DYNAMISM*

WARRIOR-EQUALITY-AMONG-[EQUALITY AMONG WARRIORS]: (*Warriors know that there is no absolute difference between any two persons; some individuals have simply learned to follow the designs of the spirit while others have not.*)
SELECTED REFERENCES: **The Power of Silence - Page [225.8-226.8]** ("You and I are the type of...that he was just like us.")
SEE ALSO: *EQUAL-UNIMPORTANT, SPIRIT-DESIGNS*

WARRIOR-EQUILIBRIUM-[THE WARRIORS' LUMINOUS EQUILIBRIUM]: (*Warriors develop a direct knowledge of their luminous equilibrium.*)
SELECTED REFERENCES: **A Separate Reality - Page [23.4-23.6]** ("Is that the way everyone looks...changed in that luminous egg? What?) **A Separate Reality - Page [99.4]** ("Talking is not Genaro's predilection," he...you about the equilibrium of things.") **A Separate**

Reality - Page [104.3-104.5] (I laughed with embarrassment. I had...have had some inextricable, symbolic meaning.) **A Separate Reality - Page [105.5-108.6]** (He said that don Genaro, being a....knew that you had not *seen*.") **The Fire From Within - Page [178.4-178.6]** (I gently shook Genaro. He slowly...my back and restored my equilibrium.)
SEE ALSO: *BALANCE, HARMONY, ASSEMBLAGE-POINT-STABILITY, DREAMING-PARADOX, WARRIOR-CONTRADICTION-KNOWLEDGE, VICTORY, EQUILIBRIUM*

WARRIOR-ETHOS-[THE ETHOS OF WARRIORS]: (The ethos of warriors is their mood and attitude; the ethos of warriors is the courage to face anything.)
SELECTED REFERENCES: The Fire From Within - Page **[241.6-241.9]** (All of my being staggered under...no longer have anything to fear.)
SEE ALSO: *WARRIOR-MOOD, WARRIOR,-ATTITUDE, WARRIOR-COURAGE*

WARRIOR-EVICTION-NOTICE-[THE WARRIORS' EVICTION NOTICE]: (Warriors receive a metaphorical "eviction notice" when they catch a glimpse of the eternity outside the luminous cocoon; as a result of having saved enough energy, warriors disrupt the continuity of their normal perspective on the world, and issue themselves an eviction notice from their comfortable quarters in the world of everyday life; this eviction notice comes in the form of a great depression which warriors must overcome as they seek new quarters which are not as cozy but are infinitely more roomy instead.)
SELECTED REFERENCES: The Fire From Within - Page **[152.6-153.6]** (My experience with la Catalina delayed...get another pad," don Juan replied.)
SEE ALSO: *CONTINUITY, DEPRESSION-MELANCHOLY*

WARRIOR-EXAGGERATION-[THE WARRIORS' EXAGGERATION]
(Warriors must learn to avoid the tendency to exaggerate; they must learn to perceive life with sobriety; warriors must take great care not to exaggerate their encounters with power on the path of knowledge.)
SELECTED REFERENCES: The Teachings of Don Juan - Page **[48.5-48.8]** (Don Juan laughed and said,...only one who is baffled.") **The Fire From Within - Page [96.9-97.7]** (Never in my life had I...be ready for the definitive journey.") **The Power of Silence - Page [27.2-27.4]** ("You always say that your benefactor...heavily toward the aberrations of reason.")
SEE ALSO: *WARRIOR-SOBRIETY*

WARRIOR-EXALTATION-[THE WARRIORS' EXALTATION]: SEE: DEATH-PAIN-[THE PAIN OF DEATH]:

WARRIOR-EXCITATION-[THE WARRIORS' EXCITATION]: (The warriors' excitation is not contingent on the circumstances of the first attention because warriors realize that everything on the path with heart is a challenge.)
SELECTED REFERENCES: The Eagle's Gift - Page **[306.9-307.3]** (Vicente came to my side next...the fulfilling of a sacred trust.)
SEE ALSO: *WARRIOR-CHALLENGE, PATH-HEART-WITH, POWER-FULFILLING-BID*

WARRIOR-EXECUTION-SQUAD-[THE WARRIOR'S EXECUTION SQUAD]-(TOP): SEE: WARRIOR-WALK-TREE-[THE WARRIOR'S WALK TO THE EDGE OF THE TREES]-(TOP)

WARRIOR-EXPECTATION-[THE WARRIORS' EXPECTATION]:
(Warriors learn to act without expecting anything in return and without expectations of any kind; they strive to be prepared to meet any situation, expected or unexpected, with equal efficiency.)
SELECTED REFERENCES: **Tales of Power** - Page [154.7-154.9] ("Let's say that a rule of thumb...into place because you're expecting nothing.") **Tales of Power** - Page [287.6-287.7] ("You have learned that the backbone...day, you'll need your ultimate forbearance.") **The Eagle's Gift** - [112.9-113.3] (What I felt was not a...it; I had actually embodied it.) **The Eagle's Gift** - Page [306.9-307.2] (Vicente came to my side next...and the unexpected, with equal efficiency.)
SEE ALSO: *ACT-LEARNING, WARRIOR-PREPAREDNESS, WARRIOR-EFFICIENCY*

WARRIOR-EXPERIENCE-[THE EXPERIENCE OF EXPERIENCES IS BEING A WARRIOR]: *(Warriors know that the experience of experiences is being a warrior, that what counts is being alive; warriors know that life in itself is sufficient, self-explanatory and complete.)*
SELECTED REFERENCES: **Tales of Power** - Page [52.8-53.1] (You have everything needed for the...of experiences is being a warrior.")
SEE ALSO: *WARRIOR-WAY*

WARRIOR-FACES-TOLTEC-TWO-[THE TWO FACES OF THE TOLTEC WARRIOR]-(TOP)

*WARRIOR-FAREWELL-[THE WARRIORS' FAREWELL]: *(Warriors have many ways of saying farewell, the best of which may be to hold a special memory of joyfulness; that memory remains fresh and cutting for warriors as long as they live.)*
SELECTED REFERENCES: **Tales of Power** - Page [279.4-279.9] (Don Juan talked about a little...a warrior's way of saying farewell.") **Tales of Power** - Page [288.5-288.6] (I could not stand to say...to say good-by to them.) **The Second Ring of Power** - Page [114.1-115.4] ("I'm going to Mexico City," I said...alive," she said, reading my thoughts.) **The Eagle's Gift** - Page [77.6-77.8] (I started the car and drove...mountains would never let them go.)
SEE ALSO: *WARRIOR-JOY*

WARRIOR-FATE-[THE WARRIORS' FATE]: *(The warriors' joyfulness comes from having fully accepted our fate in humbleness; warriors give themselves to the power that rules their fate; warriors acquiesce to their fate, not passively like idiots, but actively like warriors; from the moment the barrier of perception is broken, man and his fate take on a different meaning for warriors; warriors know that it does not matter what their fate is, as long as they face it with ultimate abandon.)*
SELECTED REFERENCES: **The Teachings of Don Juan** - Page - [66.8-67.2] ("It was different when there were..."Perhaps," he said quietly.) **Tales of Power** - Page [287.8] ("A warrior must be always ready...in particular, but what a great fortune!") **Tales of Power** - Page [289.7-289.8] ("A warrior acknowledges his pain but...assessed what lies ahead of him.") **The Second Ring of Power** - Page [93.4-93.9] ("Do you envy la Gorda for...the Nagual was a new life.) **The Second Ring of Power** - Page [130.5-130.6] (The wind kept me there for days...and accept my fate without recrimination.) **The Second Ring of Power** - Page [223.5-223.6] (La Gorda broke the silence and...path her fate selected for her.) **The Second Ring of Power** - Page [235.2-235.6] (I told her that my sadness in leaving...of us had accepted our fate.) **The Second Ring of Power** - Page [235.9-236.3] ("The Nagual said that Pablito's good...readily than any one of us.) **The Second Ring of Power** - Page [283.4-284.1] (I narrated to her the way...in my tying my shoelaces impeccably.) **The Eagle's Gift** - Page [106.6-107.2] (Don Juan had taught me to...as the petty people we were.) **The Eagle's Gift** - Page [219.2-219.4] (Later on, sobriety took hold of his...The Eagle was welcome to it.) **The Eagle's Gift** - Page [306.5-306.9] (Don Juan called everyone to come...understood and had accepted my fate.) **The Eagle's Gift** - Page [307.5-307.6] (*I am already given to the...past the Eagle to be free.*) **The Fire From Within** - Page [295.3-295.6] (He said that breaking the barrier of...before he reaches the bottom, he dies.) **The Power of Silence** -

Page [50.9-51.2] (I think the poet senses the pressure...simplicity, that is determining our fate.")
The Power of Silence - Page [105.7-105.8] (He said that if I had to...we faced it with ultimate abandon.) **The Art of Dreaming - Page [137.6-137.7]** ("Don't worry," he said laughing...premeditation to cut someone else's chains.")
    SEE ALSO: *WARRIOR-DESTINY, WARRIOR-JOY, FORCE-RULES-LIVES, WARRIOR-FORTUNE-GREAT, PERCEPTION-BARRIER-BREAKING, POWER-PROMISE*

WARRIOR-FEAR-NOTHING-[WARRIORS HAVE NOTHING TO FEAR]: (Warriors know that once the assemblage point moves beyond a specific threshold, fear no longer exists.)
    SELECTED REFERENCES: **The Fire From Within - Page [246.2-246.3]** (He added that I had performed two...that warriors have nothing to fear.)
    SEE ALSO: *FEAR, ASSEMBLAGE-POINT-MOVING*

WARRIOR-FEAT-[THE WARRIORS' FEAT]: (Warriors know that the warriors' feat is the movement of the assemblage point to a position other than the habitual one.)
    SELECTED REFERENCES: **Tales of Power - Page [76.6-77.2]** (The Genaro of last night was...is the double who dreams the self.")
    SEE ALSO: *ASSEMBLAGE-POINT-MOVING*

WARRIOR-FEELINGS-[WARRIORS PIN THEMSELVES DOWN WITH THEIR FEELINGS]: (Warriors know that they pin themselves down with the energy of their own feelings; warriors seek freedom from such feelings by letting them go.)
    SELECTED REFERENCES: **The Second Ring of Power - Page [121.7-121.8]** ("You love a little boy and...You have welded them together.")
    SEE ALSO: *LETTING-GO, FEELINGS, RECAPITULATION, FREEDOM, BOUNDARIES-AFFECTION, WARRIOR-AFFECTION*

WARRIOR-FEMALE-[FEMALE WARRIORS]: (The four female warriors are examples of the four different female personalities that exist in the human race; they are the four moods, the four directions, the four winds, the four corners of a square; the four female warriors are called order, strength, feeling and growth.)
    SELECTED REFERENCES: **Tales of Power - Page [144.2-144.4]** (His statements aroused my curiosity...The rest is all the same.") **The Second Ring of Power - Page [31.2-31.4]** ("What do you know about...when I come through the window.") **The Second Ring of Power - Page [41.1-41.3]** ("The four winds also have personalities...they cling to their specific wind.") **The Second Ring of Power - Page [172.9-173.2]** (The Nagual and Genaro told him...if we were really his wives.) **The Second Ring of Power - Page [188.3-188.5]** ("Don't get me wrong, Maestro...help me. They wanted me dead.) **The Second Ring of Power - Page [313.6-313.9]** (She explained that the particular formation...the east, in his right hand.) **The Eagle's Gift - Page [14.9-15.3]** ("What do you think those four...highest place. See what I mean?") **The Eagle's Gift - Page [174.5-174.8]** (The female warriors are called the...shy, warm, like hot wind.) **The Eagle's Gift - Page [182.7-184.3]** (Upon reaching their house, don Juan...thoughts of gain and personal gratification.) **The Eagle's Gift - Page [185.6-186.2]** (A group composed of two sets of...lose their composure and be raving mad.) **The Eagle's Gift - Page [247.4-247.6]** (Don Juan began the task of ushering...confidence in whoever is leading them.) **The Fire From Within - Page [48.7]** (Female warriors in particular fall prey...too soon for their own good.)
    SEE ALSO: *RULE, ORDER, STRENGTH, FEELING, GROWTH, LUMINOUS-BODY-FEATURES*

WARRIOR-FIGHTING-FORM-[THE WARRIORS' FIGHTING FORM]: (Warriors know that the warriors' fighting form is a defense technique used in cases of extreme distress or danger.)
    SELECTED REFERENCES: **The Teachings of Don Juan - Page [178.1-178.5]** (Then he gave me precise instructions...simply sit cross-legged on my spot.) **A Separate Reality - Page [161.1-161.3]** (I asked what was supposed to come...cases of extreme distress or danger.) **A**

Separate Reality - Page [255.3-255.4] (I noticed a movement of his cat-like...up and went inside the house.)
   SEE ALSO: *WARRIOR-VIGIL-POSITION*

WARRIOR-FIGHTING-POSTURE-[THE WARRIORS' FIGHTING POSTURE]: SEE: WARRIOR-VIGIL-POSITION-[THE WARRIORS' POSITION OF SITTING "IN VIGIL"], WARRIOR-FIGHTING-FORM-[THE WARRIORS' FIGHTING FORM]

WARRIOR-FINESSE-[THE WARRIORS' FINESSE]: (*Warriors always act with the utmost finesse because they are aware that the worst thing one can do is to confront human beings bluntly; the warriors' reasons are simple, but their finesse is extreme.*)
   SELECTED REFERENCES: **Journey to Ixtlan - Page [x.9]** ("Your friend is not a warrior...is to confront human beings bluntly.") **The Power of Silence - Page [80.2-80.4]** ("It was a way of jolting you...at the neck like a dog.") **The Power of Silence - Page [106.9-107.1]** (A warrior was magical and ruthless...be able to suspect his ruthlessness.) **The Power of Silence - Page [130.1-130.2]** ("Warrior's reasons are very simple, but their finesse is extreme.)
   SEE ALSO: *WARRIOR-MAGIC, RUTHLESSNESS, RUTHLESSNESS-MASK, WARRIOR-DELICACY, HUNTER-ARTS*

WARRIOR-FLUIDITY-[THE WARRIORS' FLUIDITY]: (*Warriors are trained to be fluid, to be at ease in whatever situation they find themselves; when warriors burn with the fire from within they become fluid in the ultimate sense, they become what they really are, fluid, forever in motion, eternal; the warriors' fluidity enables them to glide effortlessly from the most sublime situations to the most ludicrous.*)
   SELECTED REFERENCES: **A Separate Reality - Page [7.9-8.1]** ("The reason you got scared and quit...needs to be light and fluid.") **Tales of Power - Page [46.8-46.9]** ("A fluid warrior can no longer...luminous being existing in a luminous world.) **Tales of Power - Page [107.5-107.7]** ("You'll get used to it...is neither one nor the other.) **Tales of Power - Page [114.3-114.4]** ("That dying man is one of...have plucked it, but have you?") **Tales of Power - Page [156.3-156.4]** (The whole trouble is that the...easier it is to shrink it.) **Tales of Power - Page [158.8-158.9]** ("But did they see me disappear...are only extraordinary for the *tonal.*) **Tales of Power - Page [179.3-179.8]** (Genaro always cracks me up because...could admit everything without admitting anything.) **Tales of Power - Page [182.4]** (Don Juan spoke to me...and should stop my internal dialogue.) **Tales of Power - Page [290.3]** (All of them laughed with abandon...sublime situations to utterly ludicrous ones.) **The Eagle's Gift - Page [33.8-34.1]** (She added that they had been...as fluid warrior should be.) **The Eagle's Gift - Page [80.3-80.5]** (Nestor, Pablito, and Benigno left in...entire outfit, shoes, nylons, and lingerie.) **The Fire From Within - Page [39.5-39.6]** ("A nagual is someone flexible enough...back to it over and over.") **The Fire From Within - Page [56.9-57.2]** (He said that seers maintain, naturally...are - fluid, forever in motion, eternal.) **The Art of Dreaming - Page [73.5-73.6]** (He added that what dreaming does...human domain and perceive the inconceivable.) **The Art of Dreaming - Page [78.6-78.7]** (He said that the old sorcerers...another person, a bird, or anything.) **The Art of Dreaming - Page [97.4-97.6]** (For don Juan, to revamp our...other aspects of what is real.) **The Art of Dreaming - Page [143.6-143.7]** ("Don't say anything. At the third...irrational abandon to counteract that insistence.")
   SEE ALSO: *WARRIOR-EFFICIENCY, WARRIOR-LIGHTNESS, EQUILIBRIUM*

WARRIOR-FOCUS-[THE WARRIORS' FOCUS]: (*Warriors know that the attention of male sorcerers is more difficult to train because their attention tends to remain more closed and focused on things; the focus of female warriors on the other hand, tends to be more open and unfocused, especially during their menstrual periods.*)
   SELECTED REFERENCES: **The Second Ring of Power - Page [247.1-247.7]** (Her laughter was clear and contagious...or by gazing at the clouds.)
   SEE ALSO: *ATTENTION, IMAGES-HOLDING-DREAM-WORLD, MENSTRUAL-PERIOD*

WARRIOR-FOCUS-MATERIAL-ABERRANT-[THE WARRIORS'
ABERRANT MATERIAL FOCUS]: (Warriors know that they must avoid
the aberrant fixation of the second attention; this aberrant focus of
attention produces power objects.)
> SELECTED REFERENCES: The Eagle's Gift - Page [21.7-21.8] (The recommendation for warriors is not to...won't let you live in peace.) The Eagle's Gift - Page [22.2-22.9] ("Your compulsion to possess and hold...he was protecting my *dreaming body*.")
> SEE: ALSO: *WARRIOR-FOCUS, POWER-OBJECTS, ABERRATION-MORBIDITY, ATTENTION-SECOND-FIXATION, ATTENTION-SECOND-FACES, DREAMING-BODY-PROTECTING*

WARRIOR-FOCUS-SPIRIT-[THE WARRIORS' FOCUS ON THE SPIRIT]:
(Warriors know the potential fixation of their attention and choose to focus
it on the spirit and the true flight into the unknown, rather than on trivial
material shields.)
> SELECTED REFERENCES: The Eagle's Gift - Page [21.7-21.8] (The recommendation for warriors is not to...won't let you live in peace.)
> SEE ALSO: *SPIRIT, ATTENTION-SECOND-FIXATION, WARRIOR-SHIELDS,*

WARRIOR-FOG-CREATE-[WARRIORS CREATE A FOG AROUND
THEMSELVES]: (Warriors erase their personal history and thereby create a
fog around themselves, the fog around the warrior is a very mysterious state
which even the warrior cannot predict; a technique used by warriors to
become inaccessible, to break their ties with the black magicians; the
warriors' way of not being taken for granted and not remaining too "real";
the warriors' technique of erasing themselves; the warriors' preference for
the ultimate freedom of being unknown.)
> SELECTED REFERENCES: Journey to Ixtlan - Page [14.2-15.9] ("Take yourself, for instance," he went...way people know you, for instance.") Journey to Ixtlan - Page [16.6-17.5] ("When one does not have personal...behave as if we know everything.") Journey to Ixtlan - Page [65.4-70.8] ("Your opinions are final opinions...moves away leaving hardly a mark.") The Second Ring of Power - Page [204.9-205.6] (Nestor proposed that as soon as it...They knew the art of stalking.") The Second Ring of Power - Page [246.6-246.9] ("The Nagual taught you and me...is never to waste their power.)
> SEE ALSO: *PERSONAL-HISTORY-ERASING, WARRIOR-ALERTNESS, WARRIOR-PREPAREDNESS, WARRIOR-UNAVAILABILITY*

WARRIOR-FOLLY-[THE WARRIORS' FOLLY]: (Warriors know that the
things that people do cannot possibly be more important than the world;
thus warriors treat the world as an endless mystery and what people do as
an endless folly; once a person learns to "see" they find themselves alone in
the world with nothing but folly.)
> SELECTED REFERENCES: A Separate Reality - Page [81.1-81.2] ("Once a man learns to see he...but folly," don Juan said cryptically.) A Separate Reality - Page [220.3] ("A warrior is aware of this...people do as an endless folly.") The Eagle's Gift - Page [185.1-185.2] (He warned me about a common error...all, a general ability to forget.)
> SEE ALSO: *WARRIOR-CONTROLLED-FOLLY, WARRIOR-LONELINESS*

WARRIOR-FORBEARANCE-[THE WARRIORS' FORBEARANCE]:
(Warriors know that in order to withstand the path of knowledge they must
exercise the ultimate forbearance.)
> SELECTED REFERENCES: Tales of Power - Page [287.6-287.7] ("You have learned that the backbone...day, you'll need your ultimate forbearance.")
> SEE ALSO: *ACT-LEARNING, KNOWLEDGE-PATH*

WARRIOR-FORM-[THE WARRIORS' FORM]: (*The form of the warrior is a dance, the story of a life that grows with personal power; the warriors' form is the warriors' last dance of power.*)
    SELECTED REFERENCES: Journey to Ixtlan - Page [153.4-155.5] ("I will have to come with you...to the south. To the vastness.")
    SEE ALSO: *WARRIOR-DANCE-LAST-POWER*

WARRIOR-FORMAT-LIFE-[THE FORMAT OF THE WARRIORS' LIFE]: (*The format of the warriors' life is the warriors' way, the way of the impeccable action.*)
    SELECTED REFERENCES: The Eagle's Gift - Page [31.1-31.2] (I was outraged by her callousness...let Pablito die like that.)
    SEE ALSO: *WARRIOR-IMPECCABILITY, WARRIOR-WAY*

WARRIOR-FORMLESS-[FORMLESS WARRIORS]: (*The warriors' formlessness is the condition of having lost the human form; when warriors have no form then nothing has form and yet everything is present; the advantage of being formless is that it allows warriors a moment's pause, providing they have the discipline and courage to utilize it.*)
    SELECTED REFERENCES: The Second Ring of Power - Page [160.5-160.6] (The Nagual said that everything has...see that he was absolutely right.) The Second Ring of Power - Page [246.6-246.8] ("The Nagual taught you and me...them in their ups and downs.) The Second Ring of Power - Page [271.9-272.1] (I knew that she meant it...an intriguing thing happened to me.) The Eagle's Gift - Page [80.5-80.6] (I took her for a stroll...could not get used to it.) The Eagle's Gift - Page [125.3-125.9] ("Now you are where I am...self-discipline and courage to utilize it.)
    SEE ALSO: *HUMAN-FORM-LOSING, WARRIOR-PAUSE-DETACHMENT*

WARRIOR-FORMULA-[THE WARRIORS' FORMULA] : (*The warriors' formula is an affirmation of the warriors' reality; "I am already given to the power that rules my fate. And I cling to nothing, so I will have nothing to defend. I have no thoughts so I will "see." I fear nothing so I will remember myself. Detached and at ease, I will dart past the Eagle to be free."*)
    SELECTED REFERENCES : The Eagle's Gift - Page [118.7-119.3](That night lying on my bed I...*I will dart past the Eagle to be free.*") The Eagle's Gift - Page [307.4-307.8] (Silvio Manuel came to my side...el aguila pasar a la libertad.)
    SEE ALSO : *FORCE-RULES-LIVES, SEEING, FEAR, REMEMBERING-BODY, WARRIOR-DETACHMENT, EAGLE-GIFT, SELF-FORGET-FEAR-NOTHING*

WARRIOR-FORTUNE-GREAT-[THE WARRIORS' GREAT FORTUNE]: (*Warriors appreciate the great fortune of the challenge that power has presented to them; it is the warriors' great fortune to have been tricked by the spirit and to be a prisoner of power.*)
    SELECTED REFERENCES: Journey to Ixtlan - Page [56.7-56.9] (One day I found out that if...not worth living...so I changed it.") Tales of Power - Page [287.7-287.8] ("A warrior must be always ready...in particular, but what a great fortune!") The Second Ring of Power - Page [210.2-210.3] ("You must take what I say seriously...to do what he has to do.)
    SEE ALSO: *POWER-PRISONER, ABSTRACT-CORE-THIRD, SPIRIT-TRICKERY,*

WARRIOR-FOUR-NATURAL-ENEMIES-[THE FOUR NATURAL ENEMIES OF THE WARRIOR]: SEE: WARRIOR-ENEMIES-FOUR-NATURAL-[THE FOUR NATURAL ENEMIES OF THE WARRIOR]

WARRIOR-FOUR-STAGES-[THE FOUR STAGES OF THE WARRIOR]: SEE: WARRIOR-STAGES [THE FOUR STAGES OF THE WARRIOR]

WARRIOR-FREEDOM-[THE WARRIORS' FREEDOM]: *(The only freedom warriors have is to act impeccably; the warriors' freedom is the warriors' road to power; freedom is joy, efficiency, and abandon in the face of any odds.)*

SELECTED REFERENCES: **Tales of Power - Page [20.7-21.2]** ("You're afraid of me?" he asked...time and your power fearing me.") **Tales of Power - Page [249.5]** (I once told you that the freedom...true measure of a warrior's spirit.") **Tales of Power - Page [249.2-294.3]** ("Only the love for this splendorous...That is the last lesson.) **The Second Ring of Power - Page [152.8-152.9]** ("Because they are forces and as such...choose whether or not to keep them.") **The Second Ring of Power - Page [283.1-283.2]** ("Yes, that's right," she said...warriors have is to act impeccably.") **The Eagle's Gift - Page [178.8-179.3]** (Don Juan explained that the rule...exists such an awareness at all.) **The Eagle's Gift - Page [181.2]** (An example would be to say that...man with a passageway to freedom.) **The Eagle's Gift - Page [296.4-296.5]** ("It's wrong to say that...be free is the ultimate audacity.") **The Fire From Within - Page [61.2-61.4]** (I asked him if there was anything...to come, must come of itself.") **The Fire From Within - Page [114.8-115.3]** (I've explained to you that the...for. We are waiting for freedom!) **The Fire From Within - Page [260.7-260.9]** (He went back then to discussing...in an impeccable state of being.) **The Power of Silence - Page [22.8-23.2]** (And the nagual Elias was...sorcerers along, or leave them behind.) **The Power of Silence - Page [89.8-89.9]** ("Sorcerers say that the fourth abstract...undesirable, for nobody wants to be free.") **The Power of Silence - Page [219.6-219.9]** (He added that for the rational...point can be made to move.") **The Power of Silence - Page [264.3-264.9]** (Sorcerers, however, were capable of finding...their freedom from perceptual convention.)

SEE ALSO: *WARRIOR-IMPECCABILITY, SLAVERY, WARRIOR-FREEDOM-(ALL), WARRIOR-EFFICIENCY, WARRIOR-ABANDON-CONTROLLED, WARRIOR-JOY, BIRD-FREEDOM, PERSONAL-HISTORY-ERASING, WARRIOR-QUEST-FREEDOM*

WARRIOR-FREEDOM-FIGHT-[THE WARRIORS' FIGHT FOR FREEDOM]: *(The fight for freedom is more difficult for some warriors than it is for others; warriors must resign themselves to this fact, even if they are one of those for whom the fight is difficult.)*

SELECTED REFERENCES: **The Fire From Within - Page [148.7]** ("There's no need to get so worked...for some. You are one of them.)

SEE ALSO: *WARRIOR-FREEDOM*

WARRIOR-FREEDOM-QUEST-[THE WARRIORS' QUEST FOR FREEDOM]: SEE: WARRIOR-QUEST-FREEDOM-[THE WARRIORS' QUEST FOR FREEDOM], WARRIOR-QUEST-FREEDOM-VS-ADVENTURE-UNKNOWN-[THE WARRIORS' QUEST FOR FREEDOM VS THE HIGH ADVENTURE OF THE UNKNOWN]

WARRIOR-FREEDOM-TOTAL-[WARRIORS FOR TOTAL FREEDOM]: *(The new seers characterize themselves as warriors for total freedom; as masters of awareness, stalking, and intent they are not caught by death, but choose instead the moment and the way in which they will depart from this world; the warriors for total freedom burn with the fire from within and vanish from the face of the earth as if they never existed; they are free in the ultimate sense because their impeccability allows them to dart past the Eagle to total freedom and they leave the earth as if they had never existed.)*

SELECTED REFERENCES: **The Eagle's Gift - Page [296.4-296.5]** ("It's wrong to say that...be free is the ultimate audacity.) **The Fire From Within - Page [xiii.6-xiii.8]** (When I asked him once what...as if they had never existed.) **The Fire From Within - Page [127.7-127.9]** (Don Juan had defined the scope...only release that her spirit had.) **The Fire From Within - Page [134.3-134.4]** ("Those visions are the product of...lateral shift of the assemblage point.") **The Art of Dreaming - Page [2.5-2.7]** ("And what do you call the...seers or the sorcerers in residence.") **The Art of Dreaming - Page [13.7-13.8]** ("What do you think of all...pinned down by their own machinations.)

SEE ALSO: *WARRIOR-MASTERIES-THREE, FIRE-WITHIN, EAGLE-GIFT, ATTENTION-THIRD*

WARRIOR-FULFILLMENT-[THE WARRIORS' FULFILLMENT]: (*The warriors' fulfillment is the fulfillment of a man of knowledge; the warriors' expanded perception which allows them to "see" that everything in the world is equal and that life is filled to the brim.*)

SELECTED REFERENCES: **A Separate Reality - Page [88.5-88.8]** ("And so you're afraid of the...my struggle was worth my while.)

SEE ALSO: *WARRIOR-JOY, WARRIOR-ATTAINMENT*

WARRIOR-FUTILITY-[THE WARRIORS' FUTILITY]: SEE: FUTILITY-OF-IT-ALL-[THE FUTILITY OF IT ALL]

WARRIOR-GAINS-BALANCE-[WARRIORS BALANCE THEIR EXCESSIVE GAINS]-(TOP)

WARRIOR-GATE-[THE WARRIORS' GATE]: (*The warriors' gate is the portal between the world of the tonal and the world of the nagual; that gate is intent and it closes completely behind warriors when they go through it in either direction.*)

SELECTED REFERENCES: **Tales of Power - Page [173.5-173.7]** ("How can I do that...him when he goes either way.)

SEE ALSO: *INTENT, ATTENTION-TONAL, ATTENTION-NAGUAL, NAGUAL-WIND, INTENT, DOOR-ONLY*

WARRIOR-GAZE-[THE WARRIORS' GAZE]: (*The gaze of the warrior is a forceful grabbing that is executed through the eye of the other person; in an indescribable way, warriors actually grab something that is behind the eye with their will; warriors are capable of mesmerizing their prey as they move their assemblage point; by the time warriors have really focused their eyes on intent, they have no desire to mesmerize anyone.*)

SELECTED REFERENCES: **A Separate Reality - Page [251.7-251.9]** (A warrior allows the ally to...is the master at all times.") **Tales of Power - Page [234.5-235.9]** (What I did was to grab...larger, or different in some way.") **The Power of Silence - Page [126.9-127.5]** (Don Juan stopped talking and fixed...me what I did to you.") **The Power of Silence - Page [130.3-131.4]** (His eyes were shining but without...is especially true for the naguals.")

SEE ALSO: *WILL, WILL-GRABBING , EYES*

WARRIOR-GOALS-[THE WARRIORS' GOALS]: (*The goals of the warrior are few and simple; warriors are in the world to train themselves to be unbiased witnesses and to train their tonals to not crap out when facing the nagual; the goal of the warriors' way is to dethrone self-importance so that warriors may come to understand the mystery of themselves and relish the exultation of finding out who they really are; warriors strive to sensitize their connecting link with intent until they can make it function at will; the goal of warriors is the warriors' purpose, to enter into the nagual and attain total freedom .*)

SELECTED REFERENCES: **Tales of Power - Page [174.5]** (The goal of a warrior's training...crap out. A most difficult accomplishment.) **The Second Ring of Power - Page [240.4-240.9]** ("Am I still shaped like an egg...complete is only for us Toltecs.) **The Fire From Within - Page [147.8-147.9]** ("Be that as it may, warriors are...waylaid, and so was la Catalina.") **The Power of Silence - Page [108.8-108.9]** ("That sensation of being bottled up...can make it function at will.) **The Power of Silence - Page [150.8-151.1]** (Don Juan described self-importance as...self-pity masquerading as something else.)

SEE ALSO: *WARRIOR-FREEDOM-TOTAL, TONAL-NAGUAL-DICHOTOMY, WARRIOR-INTENT-LINK*

*WARRIOR-GOURD-[THE WARRIORS' GOURD]: SEE: GOURD-SORCERER-[THE SORCERERS' GOURD]

WARRIOR-GRATITUDE-[THE WARRIORS' GRATITUDE]: (Warriors are always grateful for the favors they receive from power and for their great fortune at having found a challenge.)
SELECTED REFERENCES: Journey to Ixtlan - Page [137.5] ("You cannot leave these desolate mountains...without atoning for the favors received.")
SEE ALSO: WARRIOR-FORTUNE-GREAT, POWER

WARRIOR-GUIDE-THEMSELVES-[IMPECCABLE WARRIORS CAN GUIDE THEMSELVES]: SEE: IMPECCABLE-MAN-NO-GUIDE-[AN IMPECCABLE MAN NEEDS NO ONE TO GUIDE HIM]

WARRIOR-HAPPINESS-[THE WARRIORS' HAPPINESS]: (Warriors know they must have a sober view on their own happiness; warriors know that they must always remain alert and not allow happiness to lull them into letting their guard down; warriors know that to die with elation is still a crappy way of dying; the distinction which warriors make between happiness and joy; happiness is a sometimes disruptive emotion tied to the warriors' first attention, an emotion which must be trimmed with the rest of the warriors' tonal; joy is an expression of the warriors' connection with intent, a feeling which springs from the love for the earth and a detachment from self-reflection.)
SELECTED REFERENCES: The Teachings of Don Juan - Page [152.9-153.1] (You are a man!...there to ask about the difference.) A Separate Reality - Page [78.8-78.9] ("This is controlled folly!" he said...I care. That is controlled folly!") Journey to Ixtlan - Page [83.6-83.9] ("There are some people who are...bring your acts into that light.") Tales of Power - Page [74.8-75.3] ("Watch out!" he said. " A warrior never...elation is a crappy way of dying.") The Second Ring of Power - Page [235.7-236.2] (She said that the reason all...can feel that kind of happiness.") The Eagle's Gift - Page [142.7-142.9] (To elucidate the control of the second...the body and turn it into silence.) The Fire From Within - Page [24.4-24.6] (My benefactor was simply enjoying...of course, that one is a warrior.") The Fire From Within - Page [33.8-33.9] ("There is a simple rule of thumb...in the face of the unknown.") The Fire From Within - Page [60.1-60.2] (Their glee was always contagious....I seemed old and decrepit.) The Fire From Within - Page [152.1-152.3] (An indescribable joy possessed me,...a presence that was everything.)
SEE ALSO: WARRIOR-JOY, WARRIOR-HUMOR, ACT-POWER

WARRIOR-HAT-[THE WARRIORS' HAT]: (Warriors know that on occasion a hat can be a useful prop.)
SELECTED REFERENCES: Tales of Power - Page [233.1-233.2] (It was a mild day, a soft...may be another one of them.") Tales of Power - Page [275.5- 275.8] ("Think about your hat," he said...with an old poncho, like a turban.)
SEE ALSO: WARRIOR-PROPS

WARRIOR-HEARING-SPECIAL-[THE WARRIORS' SPECIAL SENSE OF HEARING]: (Warriors have a special sense of hearing from time to time, a range of clear auditory perception around one ear.)
SELECTED REFERENCES: Tales of Power - Page [194.3-194.8] (As don Juan spoke I felt...and become obsessed with those sensations.) Tales of Power - Page [220.8-221.1] (I had an inconceivable sensory experience...sounds which were being produced then.) The Second Ring of Power - Page [58.5-58.6] (I heard then, or perhaps I...thought that I must be dying.) The Second Ring of Power - Page [82.8-82.9] (I heard again, as I had...of Rosa's stick and crushed it.)
SEE ALSO: NAGUAL-WHISPERING, AUDITORY-VIGIL, EARS

WARRIOR-HEART-MUST-KNOW-[WARRIORS MUST KNOW THEIR HEARTS]: (*Warriors know that they must know their hearts before proceeding on the path of knowledge, because the quest for knowledge is a most serious undertaking; warriors must fortify their hearts to prevent themselves from being distorted by their encounters with power.*)
    SELECTED REFERENCES: The Teachings of Don Juan - Page [28.1-28.8] ("Would you teach me about peyote...few Indians have such a desire.") The Teachings of Don Juan - Page [55.2] ("She distorts men. She gives them...the middle of their great power.")
    SEE ALSO: *PATH-HEART-WITH, LEARNING, KNOWLEDGE, PATH-HEART-WITH, PATH-HEART-WITHOUT*

WARRIOR-HELP-NEED-NO-[WARRIORS NEED NO HELP]: (*Warriors cultivate the feeling that they need nothing; we have everything we need for the extravagant journey which is life; the only concrete help apprentices receive from their apprenticeship to nagualism is the way it attacks their self-reflection.*)
    SELECTED REFERENCES: Tales of Power - Page [52.7-52.9] ("Don't you talk with your friends...is sufficient, self-explanatory and complete.) Tales of Power - Page [53.2-53.4s] ("If a warrior needs solace," he went...You have all my sympathy.") The Power of Silence - Page [158.7-159.1] ("The only concrete help you ever...increased energy and not on instruction.")
    SEE ALSO: *WARRIOR-WANTS, WARRIOR-PRESSURE-RELIEVES, ASSEMBLAGE-POINT-MOVING, SELF-REFLECTION-MIRROR-SHATTERING, IMPECCABLE-MAN-NO-GUIDE*

WARRIOR-HELPLESS-NOT-[WARRIORS CANNOT BE HELPLESS]: (*Warriors know they cannot be helpless or bewildered of frightened; for warriors there is only impeccability because everything else drains their power.*)
    SELECTED REFERENCES: Tales of Power - Page [196.4-196.5] ("A warrior cannot be helpless...else drains his power, impeccability replenishes it.")
    SEE ALSO: *WARRIOR-IMPECCABILITY, WARRIOR-STRENGTH-INTERNAL*

WARRIOR-HOLDINGS-GIVING-UP-[WARRIORS GIVE UP THEIR HOLDINGS]: (*Every male warrior knows that at some time he must be forced by fear to give up his holdings.*)
    SELECTED REFERENCES: The Eagle's Gift - Page [157.2-157.3] ("The Nagual woman and I...has to be forced by fear.)
    SEE ALSO: *WARRIOR-LIGHTNESS, LETTING-GO, DROPPING-THINGS-LIVES*

WARRIOR-HOUR-POWER-[THE WARRIORS' HOUR OF POWER]: (*The warriors' hour of power is hour of the nagual.*)
    SELECTED REFERENCES: Journey to Ixtlan - Page [64.3-64.5] ("To believe that the world is...hard and constantly all the time.) Tales of Power - Page [112.7-112.9] ("He's dying!' don Juan said with...that man is only for us.") Tales of Power - Page [145.1-145.3] ("For a *proper tonal* everything on...approaching, the warrior's hour of power.")
    SEE ALSO: *WARRIOR-BID-POWER, WARRIOR-CHALLENGE*

WARRIOR-HUMBLENESS-[THE WARRIORS' HUMBLENESS]: (*Warriors seek impeccability in their own eyes and call that humbleness; warriors accept in humbleness both what they are and what power has in store for them; warriors are humbled by their great fortune, the good fortune of having found a challenge.*)
    SELECTED REFERENCES: A Separate Reality - Page [180.4-180.5] (You can survive in the world...treat the water with respect yesterday.) Tales of Power - Page [6.9-7.3] ("I'm afraid that you are confusing...impeccable in one's actions and feelings.") Tales of Power - Page [19.2-19.3] ("You're talking nonsense," he snapped. "A warrior...regret but as a living challenge.) Tales of Power - Page [54.1-54.2] ("You indulge." he snapped. "You feel...accepts in humbleness

what he is.") **Tales of Power - Page [154.5-154.7]** ("To be a warrior means to be...caught with your pants down.") **Tales of Power - Page [242.4-242.5]** (Your self-pity is still a...were there, without ever being used.") **Tales of Power - Page [287.6-287.7]** ("You have learned that the backbone...day, you'll need your ultimate forbearance.") **Tales of Power - Page [289.7-289.8]** ("A warrior acknowledges his pain but...assessed what lies ahead of him.") **The Eagle's Gift - Page [106.6]** (Don Juan had taught me to accept my fate in humbleness.) **The Eagle's Gift - Page [195.4-195.6]** (We walked to a restaurant a few...not protecting but merely defending myself.) **The Eagle's Gift - Page [221.8-222.2]** (Since he could not believe that his...step back and lower his head.) **The Eagle's Gift - Page [227.9-228.1]** (He told her that it is...only accept in humbleness and awe.) **The Eagle's Gift - Page [279.3-279.7]** ("Warriors don't have the world to cushion...One is equal to everything.) **The Eagle's Gift - Page [295.5-295.6]** (She said, with what I thought...and his warriors left the world.)

      SEE ALSO: *WARRIOR-SELF-CONFIDENCE, WARRIOR-IMPECCABILITY, WARRIOR-FATE, WARRIOR-CHALLENGE*

WARRIOR-HUMILITY-[THE WARRIORS' HUMILITY]: SEE: WARRIOR-HUMBLENESS-[THE WARRIORS' HUMBLENESS]

WARRIOR-HUMOR-[THE WARRIORS' HUMOR]: (*The warrior, the man of knowledge, chooses a path with heart and follows it; and then the warrior looks and rejoices and laughs; warriors are happy because they choose to look at things that make them happy and then their eyes catch the funny edge and then they laugh; the warriors' laughter is real, and yet it is also controlled folly because it is useless and it changes nothing, and yet warriors still laugh in spite of it all; warriors know that making fun is the only device that can dull the edge of the idea of death; warriors are not afraid of being fools or of laughing at themselves, they must laugh when they finally come face to face with the boring repetition of their own self-esteem; only through laughter can warriors change their condition because humor is the only means of counteracting the compulsion of human awareness to take inventories and to make cumbersome classifications; warriors know that in order to survive, they must learn to laugh at themselves because to take themselves too seriously is to engage the self-importance which they are trying so hard to lose; the warriors' sense of humor keeps them light and irreverent.*)

      SELECTED REFERENCES: **A Separate Reality - Page [7.7-7.9]** (The total mood of don Juan's teachings...the knowledge he was teaching me.) **A Separate Reality - Page [83.2-84.3]** ("For instance, we need to look...made his body feel better than crying.) **A Separate Reality - Page [89.7-89.8]** ("There is one more thing I want...Their laughter is not roaring.") **A Separate Reality - Page [197.1-197.2]** (His eyes examined me with apparently...of the idea of one's death.) **A Separate Reality - Page [215.4-215.5]** ("The spirit of a warrior...a warrior laughs and laughs.") **Tales of Power - Page [48.1-48.5]** (He moved his hand as don Juan...the agitation in my stomach muscles.) **Tales of Power - Page [50.9-51.2]** (He casually remarked that I was...the sorcerers' world was to laugh at it.) **Tales of Power - Page [219.6-219.9]** (I knew that Pablito and Nestor were..."I have no idea," Pablito said.) **The Eagle's Gift - Page [204.3-204.5]** (Don Juan advised me that I should...a performance staged by someone else.) **The Eagle's Gift - Page [289.6-289.7]** (In order to practice *controlled folly*...at the core of all human interaction.) **The Eagle's Gift - Page [291.6-291.7]** ("Applying these principles brings about...being a fool, they can fool anyone.) **The Eagle's Gift - Page [309.4-309.8]** (He examined the apprentices and concluded...with don Juan and his warriors.) **The Fire From Within - Page [16.8-17.1]** (Don Juan had a beaming smile...and to make cumbersome classifications.) **The Fire From Within - Page [17.6-17.9]** (I thought his classifications were ludicrous...the new seers were terribly irreverent.") **The Fire From Within - Page [44.3-44.7]** (He added that in his teachings...have been made half in fun.) **The Fire From Within - Page [70.5-71.1]** (Watching them laugh, I was convinced...made me respond only to anger.) **The Fire From Within - Page [97.3]** (He said that the best way...melancholy is to make fun of it.) **The Fire From Within - Page [120.7-120.8]** ("Energy! Impeccability! Impeccable warriors...their friends or with strangers.") **The Fire From Within - Page [129.1-129.3]** ("He's certainly not!"...only to make them laugh.) **The Power of Silence -**

Page [57.5-57.7] ("Was there a reason for your benefactor's...but that's another matter.") **The Power of Silence - Page [245.9]** ("By the time we come to sorcery...controlled folly and laugh at ourselves.") **The Power of Silence - Page [248.1-248.4]** (He agreed that that was exactly...himself seriously, while you still do.")

SEE ALSO: *STALKING-RESULTS-THREE, SELF-IMPORTANCE-LOSING, WARRIOR-JOY, LAUGHTER, PATH-HEART-WITH, WARRIOR-CONTROLLED-FOLLY, SELF-SERIOUSNESS, WARRIOR-LIGHTNESS, WARRIOR-IRREVERENCE*

WARRIOR-HUNTER-VS-AVERAGE-MAN-[THE WARRIOR-HUNTER VS THE AVERAGE MAN]: (Warriors know without conceit that their world of precise actions, feelings and decisions is infinitely more effective than the blunderings of the average man.)

SELECTED REFERENCES: **Journey to Ixtlan - Page [57.1-58.2]** ("But I am happy with my life...idiocy I called "my life".)

SEE ALSO: *WARRIOR-HUNTER, WARRIOR-WAY, WARRIOR-ACTING, WARRIOR-DECISIONS, WARRIOR-EFFECTIVENESS*

WARRIOR-HUNTING-GROUND-[THE WARRIORS' HUNTING GROUND]: (Warriors know they cannot escape the doing of the world so they turn their world into a hunting ground instead; warriors know the world is made to be used, so they use every bit of it and don't feel insulted when they are used and taken themselves.)

SELECTED REFERENCES: **Journey to Ixtlan - Page [214.1-214.3]** (And out there, in that world...he is used and taken himself.")

SEE ALSO: *HUNTER-POWER-BECOMING, WARRIOR-OFFENDED-NOT*

WARRIOR-IMAGINATION-[THE WARRIORS' IMAGINATION]: (Warriors know that in order to follow the path of knowledge they must be imaginative, because nothing is as clear on that path as we would like it to be.)

SELECTED REFERENCES: **The Fire From Within - Page [14.9-15.1]** ("I've said to you many times,"...clear as we'd like it to be.") **The Art of Dreaming - Page [26.4-26.5]** ("No it isn't. Intending is much...all the cells of your body.)

SEE ALSO: *KNOWLEDGE-PATH, DREAMING-IMAGINATION*

WARRIOR-IMPATIENCE-[THE WARRIORS' IMPATIENCE]: (Warriors know that when they become impatient, they should consult with death for perspective; the pettiness of being impatient cannot withstand the cold stare of the warriors' death; warriors know they can combat their feelings of impatience by rolling their eyes.)

SELECTED REFERENCES: **Journey to Ixtlan - Page [34.4-35.1]** ("The thing to do when you're...in the light of my death.) **The Fire From Within - Page [260.4-260.6]** ("The new seers recommend a very simple...in lieu of true mastery of *intent*.)

SEE ALSO: *DEATH, DEATH-ADVISER, EYES-ROLLING*

WARRIOR-IMPECCABILITY-[THE WARRIORS' IMPECCABILITY]: (Warriors know that they need energy in order to face the unknown; the action of rechanneling that energy is the warriors' impeccability; warriors redeploy, in a more intelligent manner, the energy they have and use to perceive the daily world; the only thing that stores energy for warriors is impeccability; warriors cut down any superfluous energy expenditures in life by living the warriors' way and embodying a set of behavioral choices designed to revamp life by altering their basic reactions to being alive; to be impeccable means that warriors put their lives on the line in order to back up their decisions and then do quite a lot more than their best to realize the decisions they have made; warriors must be impeccable because it takes all their energy to conquer the idiocy in themselves; impeccability is simply the best use of the warriors' energy; impeccability calls for frugality, thoughtfulness, simplicity, innocence and above all a lack of self-reflection; the fight for impeccability is waged within the warriors' being and if they succeed, that struggle will bring them vigor, youth and power; warriors have nothing but their impeccability, and impeccability cannot be threatened; the warriors' impeccability is not an investment, it produces no tangible reward, it is its own reward because impeccability in itself rejuvenates and renews warriors in an incalculable way.)

SELECTED REFERENCES: **Journey to Ixtlan - Page [168.4-168.5]** (Don Juan put his hand over my...whether it is small or enormous.") **Tales of Power - Page [196.1-196.9]** (I made an involuntary gesture of...are no survivors on this earth!") **Tales of Power - Page [249.5]** (I once told you that the...true measure of a warrior's spirit.") **Tales of Power - Page [286.9-287.4]** (You see, the warrior had run...will be for either of you.") **Tales of Power - Page [289.7-289.8]** ("A warrior acknowledges his pain but...assessed what lies ahead of him.") **The Second Ring of Power - Page [174.6-174.8]** (The Nagual told each of them that...but an impeccable warrior survives, always.") **The Second Ring of Power - Page [243.5-243.8]** ("It doesn't matter what anybody says...and simplicity of a warrior's life.) **The Second Ring of Power - Page [246.8-246.9]** ("The art of sorcerers is to be...is never to waste their power.) **The Second Ring of Power - Page [283.4-284.1]** (I narrated to her the way...in my tying my shoelaces impeccably.) **The Eagle's Gift - Page [106.7-106.8]** ("The course of a warrior's destiny is...destiny the breadth of one hair.") **The Eagle's Gift - Page [215.8-215.9]** (His benefactor told don Juan that...impeccability, and impeccability cannot be threatened.) **The Fire From Within - Page [16.2-16.4]** (Don Juan said then that in...of rechanneling that energy is impeccability.") **The Fire From Within - Page [120.7-120.8]** ("What determines whether it is one...with their friends or with strangers.") **The Fire From Within - Page [181.1]** ("So, all in all, the procedure...is impeccability in our daily life.") **The Fire From Within - Page [213.5-213.6]** ("I wouldn't recommend that you try it...be better than you are now.") **The Fire From Within - Page [260.7-260.9]** (He went back then to discussing...in an impeccable state of being.) **The Fire From Within - Page [299.5-299.6]** ("The new seers burn with the...that total freedom means total awareness.") **The Power of Silence - Page [53.3-53.4]** ("The story says that the spirit...needed to strengthen his connecting link.") **The Power of Silence - Page [128.8-129.1]** ("First of all, I'd like to...not going to understand or like.") **The Power of Silence - Page [227.6-228.3]** ("How do sorcerers resolve this problem...energy for us is impeccability.") **The Art of Dreaming - Page [9.7-9.9]** ("There is only one thing for...yourself that it can be done.) **The Art of Dreaming - Page [32.7-33.5]** (He reiterated that reaching, with deliberate...situation to fit our own configurations.") **The Art of Dreaming - Page [37.4-37.9]** (Don Juan insisted that the sorcerer'...the actual grandeur of the universe.) **The Art of Dreaming - Page [155.5-155.7]** ("Be impeccable. I have told you...life in a helter-skelter way.")

SEE ALSO: *ENERGY, WARRIOR-WAY, LIFE-WAYS-FACING-TWO, WARRIOR-REWARD, WARRIOR-SOBRIETY, VICTORY, LIFE-INTERACTIONS-DAILY, POWER-PERSONAL, VICTORY-WITHOUT-GLORY-REWARD, WARRIOR-IMPECCABILITY-(ALL), ASSEMBLAGE-POINT-SPRINGBOARD, EAGLE-MIRRORING, POWER-WASTING, SORCERY-LEARNING, WARRIOR-ENERGY-INCREASED*

WARRIOR-IMPECCABILITY-FIGHT-[THE WARRIORS' FIGHT FOR IMPECCABILITY]:
(Warriors know that they must fight for their impeccability; they must transform themselves, restraining themselves daily with the most excruciating effort.)

SELECTED REFERENCES: **The Power of Silence - Page [129.3-129.5]** ("If you judge me by my...myself with the most excruciating effort.")

SEE ALSO: *WARRIOR-IMPECCABILITY, WARRIOR-TRANSFORMATION, WARRIOR-WAR*

**WARRIOR-IMPECCABILITY-TICKET-[THE WARRIORS' TICKET TO IMPECCABILITY]*:
(The ticket to impeccability is the warriors' symbolic but final death; the warriors' ticket to freedom; the warriors' symbolic condition of being "dead", [of no longer indulging in feelings of immortality]; the warriors' grand trick of awareness, the awareness that one is already

dead; the warriors' process of invalidating their old continuity is called the ticket to impeccability.)

SELECTED REFERENCES: **The Power of Silence - Page [192.2-192.3]** ("The sorcerer seers of modern times...continuity cost me my life.") **The Power of Silence - Page [195.1-195.5]** (The nagual Julian commented that because...I've kept mine in mint condition.") **The Power of Silence - Page [249.6-250.2]** (Don Juan said that in the...he had not responded at all.)

SEE ALSO: *IMMORTALITY, DEATH, WARRIOR-IMPECCABILITY, CONTINUITY*

WARRIOR-IMPECCABILITY-TICKET-WRAPPED-AWARENESS-*[THE WARRIORS' TICKET TO IMPECCABILITY MUST BE WRAPPED IN AWARENESS]*: *(Warriors know that their ticket to impeccability must be wrapped in the awareness that they are dead.)*

SELECTED REFERENCES: **The Power of Silence - Page [195.3-195.5]** ("Am I dead too," don Juan...I've kept mine in mint condition.")

SEE ALSO: *WARRIOR-IMPECCABILITY-TICKET, WARRIOR-DEATH-SYMBOLIC*

WARRIOR-IMPECCABLE-GUIDE-THEMSELVES-*[IMPECCABLE WARRIORS CAN GUIDE THEMSELVES]: SEE: IMPECCABLE-MAN-NO-GUIDE-[AN IMPECCABLE MAN NEEDS NO ONE TO GUIDE HIM]*

WARRIOR-IMPETUS-*[THE WARRIORS' IMPETUS]: SEE: ASSEMBLAGE-POINT-SHIFT-NEED-IMPERATIVE-[THE IMPERATIVE NEED TO SHIFT THE ASSEMBLAGE POINT]*

WARRIOR-IMPROVISATION-*[THE WARRIORS' IMPROVISATION]*: *(Warriors know that improvisation is the third result of stalking; warriors learn to have an endless capacity to improvise.)*

SELECTED REFERENCES: **The Eagle's Gift - Page [291.6-291.7]** ("Applying these principles brings about three...have an endless capacity to improvise.")

SEE ALSO: *STALKING-ART, STALKING-RESULTS-THREE*

WARRIOR-INACCESSIBILITY-*[THE WARRIORS' INACCESSIBILITY]: SEE: WARRIOR-FOG-CREATE-[WARRIORS CREATE A FOG AROUND THEMSELVES], WARRIOR-UNAVAILABILITY-[THE WARRIORS' UNAVAILABILITY]*

WARRIOR-INCANTATION-*[THE WARRIORS' INCANTATION]: SEE: WARRIOR-FORMULA [THE WARRIORS' FORMULA], RITUAL*

WARRIOR-INCOMPLETE-*[THE WARRIORS' INCOMPLETENESS]: SEE: WARRIOR-COMPLETE-[THE WARRIORS' COMPLETENESS]*

WARRIOR-INDIFFERENCE-*[THE WARRIORS' INDIFFERENCE]*: *(By the time warriors have conquered dreaming and "seeing" and have a full awareness of their luminosity, they have become indifferent to their fellow men, warriors no longer have any interest in using their power to manipulate anyone or to act on them.)*

SELECTED REFERENCES: **Tales of Power - Page [57.2-57.9]** ("You're filled with tales of violence...for you, only tales of power.") **Tales of Power - Page [58.1-58.5]** ("There is no hypothetical sense when...knowledge is in control with out controlling anything.")

SEE ALSO: *WARRIORSHIP-VS-SORCERY, WARRIOR-DESIRE*

WARRIOR-INDIVIDUAL-SELF-*[THE WARRIORS' INDIVIDUAL SELF]: SEE: WARRIOR-SELF-INDIVIDUAL-[THE WARRIORS' INDIVIDUAL SELF]*

WARRIOR-INERTIA-[THE WARRIORS' INERTIA]: (*The warriors' progress on the path of knowledge can be viewed in terms of a kind of inertia; warriors tend to remain at rest if they are at rest or remain in motion if in motion if they in motion, unless they are affected by some outside force; it is the intervention of this uncontrollable outside force that is critical to the warrior.*)
SELECTED REFERENCES: A Separate Reality - Page [28.4-28.7] (I told him that perhaps it was...has to be tricked into doing it.")
SEE ALSO: *POWER, INTENT, NAGUAL, INTENT-INTERVENTION*

WARRIOR-INFORMATION-SCATTERED-[INFORMATION IS SCATTERED AMONG WARRIORS]: (*Warriors know that a party of warriors is set up in such a way that each member of the party has information that the others do not.*)
SELECTED REFERENCES: The Second Ring of Power - Page [215.5-215.7] ("Are you serious when you ask us...load had been lifted off his shoulders.)
SEE ALSO: *NAGUAL-PARTY-WARRIORS*

WARRIOR-INNER-STATE-[THE WARRIORS' INNER STATE]: (*Warriors know that control and discipline are part of their inner state; warriors are self-oriented, but not in a selfish way; the warriors' inner state revolves around their total and continuous examination of themselves; warriors are self-oriented, not in a selfish way, but in a way that allows them to rid themselves of the negative aspects of self-importance.*)
SELECTED REFERENCES: The Fire From Within - Page [23.9-24.1] (His benefactor stressed the fact that...and continuous examination of the self.)
SEE ALSO: *WARRIOR-CONTROL, WARRIOR-DISCIPLINE, WARRIOR-SELF-EXAMINATION, WARRIOR-WAR, SELF-IMPORTANCE-LOSING*

WARRIOR-INSTRUCTION-[THE WARRIORS' INSTRUCTION]: (*The warriors' instruction is the teaching which they receive from their teachers and benefactor;s the warriors' instruction in the ways of knowledge and power; warriors know there is little value in instruction; the essence of instruction is merely a means of trapping the warriors' attention; we are geared to believe that we need instruction and teaching but we don't.*)
SELECTED REFERENCES: Tales of Power - Page [155.9-156.1] ("Throughout the time I have known...way the instruction should be conducted.) Tales of Power - Page [233.4-260.9] (He said that the occasion required...comments about having saved my pants.) The Second Ring of Power - Page [269.5-269.8] ("You sure are dumb," she said...doing what he has been shown.) The Eagle's Gift - Page [245.8-246.2] (He told me that the reason he...the other half with don Juan.) The Eagle's Gift - Page [247.9-248.9] (La Gorda said that the Nagual...that he would even convince himself.) The Eagle's Gift - Page [274.6-274.9] (She told me then that to...immeasurable vastness of the other self.) The Fire From Within - Page [9.2-9.8] ("The ancient seers were very fortunate...centuries of that kind of concentration.") The Fire From Within - Page [10.4-10.7] (He said that the value of the...new seers meant them to have.) The Power of Silence - Page [vii.5-vii.8] (My books are a true account of...is as, or perhaps *more*, complex.) The Power of Silence - Page [xi.3-xi.9] ("Everything I've put you through...silent knowledge, depends on your own temperament.) The Power of Silence - Page [xii.9-xiii.9] (Don Juan stressed that this cleaning procedure...process of understanding as very difficult.) The Power of Silence - Page [xvii.4-xvii.8] (In compliance with his tradition, it was...I returned to my normal consciousness.) The Power of Silence - Page [158.7-160.5] ("The only concrete help you ever get...do it ourselves? Big question, eh?")
SEE ALSO: *TEACHERS-TEACHING, BENEFACTOR, KNOWLEDGE-PATH, KNOWLEDGE, POWER, IMPECCABLE-MAN-NO-GUIDE*

WARRIOR-INTEGRATION-MEMORIES-[THE WARRIORS' INTEGRATION OF MEMORIES]: *(Warriors know that they must move the assemblage point back to its previous positions in order to integrate memories of the left side awareness; the task of integration is the task warriors face when they have completed their training.)*
SELECTED REFERENCES: The Fire From Within - Page [284.4-284.7] (He added that the task warriors are...thing for you to integrate it.") The Fire From Within - Page [286.4-286.5] ("You still don't remember her...Her time here is short.")
SEE ALSO: *REMEMBERING-BODY, FORGET-COMMAND-TO, RECOLLECTION-SORCERER*

WARRIOR-INTELLECTUAL-EXERCISE-[THE WARRIORS' INTELLECTUAL EXERCISE]: *(Warriors know that the desire to explain sorcery in cogent, well-reasoned terms is a typical affliction among sorcerers; warriors must utilize this desire as an intellectual exercise with which to stalk themselves, all the while remembering that perception has more possibilities than the mind can conceive.)*
SELECTED REFERENCES: The Power of Silence - Page [243.8-244.2] (Don Juan fixed me with his stare...possibilities than the mind can conceive.")
SEE ALSO: *EXPLANATIONS, SORCERY, KNOWLEDGE-VS-LANGUAGE, STALKING-ONESELF, WARRIOR-DIALOGUE, SORCERY-EXPLAINING-DESIRE*

WARRIOR-INTENT-BECKON-EYES-[WARRIORS BECKON INTENT WITH THEIR EYES]: *(Warriors learn to beckon intent with their eyes; intent is intended with the eyes; the eyes summon intent with something indefinable that they have, something in their shine; intent is experienced with the eyes, not with the reason.)*
SELECTED REFERENCES: The Eagle's Gift - Page [307.9-309.2] (He told me that he was going...one's attention on the luminous shell.) The Fire From Within - Page [260.4-260.6] ("The new seers recommend a very simple...in lieu of true mastery of *intent*.) The Fire From Within - Page [273.6-273.9] (Another thing I had done that night...them as points of amber light.) The Power of Silence - Page [123.9-125.5] ("But how do I stop thinking...sorcerers let their eyes beckon it.") The Power of Silence - Page [126.1-126.3] (Ruthlessness makes sorcerers' eyes shine...specific shine associated with that spot.") The Power of Silence - Page [166.9-167.6] (He said that as soon as he...the eyes, not with the reason.") The Power of Silence - Page [243.3-243.5] ("Intensity, being an aspect of *intent*, is...But I have already explained that.")
SEE ALSO: *INTENT, EYES, EYES-ROLLING, ATTENTION-BECKONING-POWER, EYES-FUNCTION-TRUE, EYES-SHINE-INTENT-BECKON, INTENT-CALLING*

WARRIOR-INTENT-FAMILIAR-[THE WARRIORS' FAMILIARITY WITH INTENT]: *(The warriors' familiarity with the spirit is expressed in the way they handle the spirit; warriors beckon intent, entice it, become familiar with it and express it with their acts.)*
SELECTED REFERENCES: The Eagle's Gift - Page [148.6-148.7] ("He said that when we become...who was the master of it.") The Power of Silence - Page [38.5-38.7] ("For a sorcerer, the spirit is an...and expresses it with his acts.")
SEE ALSO: *INTENT, WARRIOR-INTENT-(ALL)*

WARRIOR-INTENT-LINK-[THE WARRIORS' LINK WITH INTENT]: *(The warriors' link with intent is a connection to the abstract; the warriors' luminous reality; the warriors' effort to dust off or clear the connecting link with intent; the warriors' alertness for the signs of intent; the warriors' direct link with the abstract which enables them to know things directly and intuit things accurately; intuition is the activation of the warriors' link with intent; the warriors' link with intent is something utterly real and functional; the sensation of feeling "bottled up" is a reminder of the* *warriors' connecting link with intent; when the pressure of the warriors' link with intent becomes too great, warriors relieve it by stalking themselves; after a lifetime of practice, naguals know if intent is inviting them to enter the edifice being flaunted before them because they have disciplined their connecting link with intent; as a result they are always forewarned and always know what the spirit has in store for them.)*

SELECTED REFERENCES: **The Power of Silence** - Page [xii.5-xii.9] (Then don Juan began a most...cleaning one's connecting link to *intent*.) **The Power of Silence** - Page [xiii.6-xiii.8] (Because of their extraordinary energy, naguals...awareness of one's connecting link with *intent*.) **The Power of Silence** - Page [12.4-12.5] (Don Juan explained that every act...more simply, indications or omens.) **The Power of Silence** - Page [14.3-14.7] (Then he answered my question about...knowledge is totally accurate and functional.) **The Power of Silence** - Page [42.2-42.8] ("After a lifetime of practice," he continued...his individuality. That's the difficult part.") **The Power of Silence** - Page [48.9-49.1] (He said that we, as average...us our hereditary preoccupation with fate.) **The Power of Silence** - Page [49.5-49.7] ("I like poems for many reasons...hit pretty close to it, though.") **The Power of Silence** - Page [53.3-53.4] ("The story says that the spirit...needed to strengthen his connecting link.") **The Power of Silence** - Page [104.1-105.2] (Don Juan explained that at one...of our being aware of *intent*.) **The Power of Silence** - Page [108.8-109.1] ("That sensation of being bottled up...sorcerers relieve it by *stalking* themselves.") **The Power of Silence** - Page [114.1-114.4] (He said that as the energy...to *intend* it through pure understanding.) **The Power of Silence** - Page [116.1-116.3] (Because he can manipulate his elusive...his thought somersault into the inconceivable.") **The Power of Silence** - Page [119.5-119.6] ("I've told you the nagual is...the spirit expresses itself through him.) **The Power of Silence** - Page [159.8-159.9] (Once the assemblage point has moved,...the spirit in the first place.) **The Power of Silence** - Page [226.4-226.6] ("I have described to you, in...accept the designs of the abstract.") **The Art of Dreaming** - Page [11.1-11.3] ("You may believe whatever you want...man who brings us its message.")

SEE ALSO: *INTENT, WARRIOR-INTUITION, STALKING-ONESELF, KNOWLEDGE-SILENT, OMENS, INTENT-LINK-(ALL)*

WARRIOR-INTENT-UNBENDING-[THE WARRIORS' UNBENDING

INTENT]: (The warriors' unbending intent is an unwavering concentration on the spirit; a single-mindedness that warriors exhibit; an extremely well-defined purpose not countermanded by any conflicting interests or desires; the force engendered when the assemblage point is maintained in any fixed position other than the usual one; unbending intent begins with a single act, which by the fact of being sustained breeds an unwavering focus on intent; unbending intent leads warriors to inner silence and the inner strength necessary to move the assemblage point from within; unbending intent is the catalyst which triggers the warriors' unchangeable decisions, or as the converse, the warriors' unchangeable decisions are the catalyst which propels the assemblage point to new positions, which in turn generate unbending intent.)

SELECTED REFERENCES: **The Teachings of Don Juan** - Page [35.6-35.7] ("When are you going to start...Mescalito requires a very serious intent.") **The Teachings of Don Juan** - [82.1-82.2] (Properly speaking, it is a matchless...will not let him come back.) **The Teachings of Don Juan** - Page [110.7-110.8] (I explained to him that what...he was capable of controlling them.) **The Teachings of Don Juan** - Page [188.3-188.4] (I said I could not figure...who do not have unbending intent.) **A Separate Reality** - Page [126.7-126.9] ("You really know how to talk...of things that can be explained.) **Journey to Ixtlan** - Page [36.1] (Be still. there is no need...you need the most unbending intent.) **Journey to Ixtlan** - Page [108.3] ("No, that's not a worry for a...or mountain lion could bother him.") **The Second Ring of Power** - Page [26.7-27.2] ("How is that possible," I asked...not to let her thoughts interfere.) **The Second Ring of Power** - Page [123.4-123.6] (Then he proceeded to smash my arguments...useless outburst of an empty man.) **The Second Ring of Power** - Page [134.8-134.9] (My mind was made up, my...me away from that world! Nothing!") **The Fire From Within** - Page [180.3-180.4] (Don Juan then outlined the procedure...shift in dreams to suitable positions.) **The Fire From Within** - Page [283.2-283.3] ("How does a journey like that...emanations that are inside the cocoon.") **The Power of Silence** -

Page [42.5-42.8] (He stressed that in order to...his individuality. That's the difficult part.") **The Power of Silence - Page [220.1-220.8]** ("It is," he assured me....which in turn generated *unbending intent.*) **The Art of Dreaming - Page [181.4-181.6]** ("We can't have dealings with them...sorcerer knows what freedom really is.")

SEE ALSO: *INTENT, INNER SILENCE, INTENT-(ALL), WARRIOR-DEDICATION, WARRIOR-DETERMINATION, WARRIOR-PURPOSE*

WARRIOR-INTERVENTION-[THE WARRIORS' INTERVENTION]:
(Warriors know why they must remain reluctant to intervene; the warriors' difficult task of letting others be, of trusting them to be impeccable warriors themselves; the warriors' understanding that acts of conscious intervention are nothing more than arbitrary acts guided by self-interest alone; warriors do not intervene because they do not indulge themselves in the misguided compassion of the average man, they are not so arrogant to wish that everyone be just like themselves; the impeccability of the warrior is to let others be and support them in what they are; only formless seers can afford to help anyone as they follow the indications of the spirit.)

SELECTED REFERENCES: **A Separate Reality - Page [22.6-23.2]** (Don Juan's argument gave me an uncomfortable...to change anything about them.") **The Second Ring of Power - Page [309.6-312.5]** ("You like him so much that you...for me was to let others be.)

SEE ALSO: *SELF-COMPASSION, SELF-REFLECTION, WARRIOR-COMPASSION*

WARRIOR-INTUITION-[THE WARRIORS' INTUITION]: *(The warriors' intuition is the activation of the connecting link with intent; warriors go beyond the intuitive level in order to accomplish two transcendental feats; first, to conceive the existence of the assemblage point, and second, to make that assemblage point move.)*

SELECTED REFERENCES: **Tales of Power - Page [64.7-64.8]** (He was right. I had to admit...voice tells you what's what.) **Tales of Power - Page [140.2]** ("I hear you talking," he said...on the island of the *tonal*.) **The Power of Silence - Page [14.5-14.7]** (He said that the feeling everyone...knowledge is totally accurate and functional.) **The Power of Silence - Page [47.1-47.9]** (Don Juan then said that the...invisible connection with that indefinable abstract.) **The Power of Silence - Page [49.5-49.6]** ("I like poems for many reasons...the deliberate, pragmatic way of sorcerers.) **The Power of Silence - Page [50.9-51.2]** ["I think the poet senses the...simplicity, that is determining our fate.") **The Power of Silence - Page [112.9-113.3]** ("You're not being truthful," don Juan...strong enough to surface at will.) **The Power of Silence - Page [144.6-145.1]** (He then said something which I...to make that assemblage point move.)

SEE ALSO: *WARRIOR-INTENT-LINK*

WARRIOR-INVENTORY-STRATEGIC-[THE WARRIORS' STRATEGIC INVENTORY]: *(Warriors take a strategic inventory, they make a list of everything they do in order to decide how to change those things so that they can better conserve their energy; the warriors' strategic inventory only covers behavioral patterns that are not essential to the warriors' survival and well-being.)*

SELECTED REFERENCES: **The Fire From Within - Page [15.7-15.9]** ("Warriors take strategic inventories," he said...to our survival and well-being.) **The Fire From Within - Page [16.2-16.3]** (Don Juan said then that in...hence, their effort to eradicate it.)

SEE ALSO: *INVENTORY, WARRIOR-IMPECCABILITY, FACADE-TRANSFORMING, TONAL-ISLAND*

WARRIOR-INVULNERABILITY-[THE WARRIORS' INVULNERABILITY]:
(Warriors know that without self-importance and in possession of their will, they are invulnerable.)

SELECTED REFERENCES: **A Separate Reality - Page [147.4-147.6]** ("Is the will an object...to the moon, if he wants.") **The Fire From Within - Page [12.8-12.9]** ("The new seers recommended that every...without self-importance we are invulnerable.")

SEE ALSO: *SELF-IMPORTANCE-LOSING, WARRIOR-DEATH-COMMAND, WILL*

WARRIOR-IRREVERENCE-[THE WARRIORS' IRREVERENCE]:
(Warriors know that they must not take themselves and the items of their world too seriously; there is no room for sacred cows in the world of warriors because warriors know beyond a shadow of a doubt that they have no points to defend.)
SELECTED REFERENCES: The Fire From Within - Page [44.4-44.6] ("Genaro is the one who should...certainly be made half in fun.) The Fire From Within - Page [59.4-60.1] (Genaro leaned over toward me from...he asked me in mock seriousness.)
SEE ALSO: *WARRIOR-DEFEND-NOTHING, WARRIOR-HUMOR, WARRIOR-SERIOUSNESS, WARRIOR-LIGHTNESS*

WARRIOR-JOURNEY-DEFINITIVE-[THE WARRIORS' DEFINITIVE
JOURNEY]: *(The warriors' definitive journey is another term for the journey with power to total freedom and total awareness; the warriors' journey on the path with heart; the warriors' return to the totality of themselves; the poignant counterpoint of the warriors' passion for the cozy world of the things they care for and the terribly cold immensity of the unknown; the riddle of the warriors' simultaneous awareness of all parts of themselves; the warriors' struggle to maintain the bonds of humanness while still venturing gladly into the absolute loneliness of the unknown.)*
SELECTED REFERENCES: Journey to Ixtlan - Page [266.6-267.8] (The particular one he had in...the invisible wall of a metaphor.) The Eagle's Gift - Page [177.5-177.8] (The Nagual and his warriors were...seek and face their definitive journey.) The Eagle's Gift - Page [237.6-237.8] (Silvio Manuel also said that he...reason she was supervising our work.) The Eagle's Gift - Page [303.6-303.7] (The next thing I knew...Eagle would let us go through.) The Eagle's Gift - Page [306.9-307.3] (Vicente came to my side next...the fulfilling of a sacred trust.) The Fire From Within - Page [97.6-97.7] (This indeed is another contradiction...be ready for the definitive journey.") The Fire From Within - Page [183.4-184.1] (There was a strange excitement in...all be gone in an instant.") The Fire From Within - Page [271.7-271.8] (During our long walk in the city...the unrestrainable vigor of total freedom.) The Power of Silence - Page [40.2-40.6] ("There is an interesting story about...as we discuss my definitive journey.")
SEE ALSO: *FIRE-WITHIN, LONELINESS, PATH-HEART-WITH, WARRIOR-PASSIONATE, TERROR-VS-WONDER, WARRIOR-JOURNEY-(ALL), EQUILIBRIUM*

WARRIOR-JOURNEY-EXTRAVAGANT-[THE WARRIORS'
EXTRAVAGANT JOURNEY]: *(The warriors' extravagant journey is another term for the journey of the warriors' life.)*
SELECTED REFERENCES: Tales of Power - Page [52.7-52.9] ("I never thought that you needed...is sufficient, self-explanatory and complete.)
SEE ALSO: *WARRIOR-JOURNEY-POWER*

WARRIOR-JOURNEY-JOYFUL-[THE WARRIORS' JOYFUL JOURNEY]:
(Warriors know that the path with heart will always make for a joyful journey.)
SELECTED REFERENCES: The Teachings of Don Juan - Page [107.4-107.5] (Both paths lead nowhere; but one...you strong, the other weakens you.")
SEE ALSO: *PATH-HEART-WITH, WARRIOR-JOY*

WARRIOR-JOURNEY-POWER-PATH-HEART-[THE WARRIORS'
JOURNEY WITH POWER AND THE PATH WITH HEART]: *(The warriors' journey with power is always traveled on the path with heart.)*
SELECTED REFERENCES: The Teachings of Don Juan - Page [11.3-11.4] (For me there is only the...there I travel, looking, looking, breathlessly.)
SEE ALSO: *PATH-HEART-WITH, WARRIOR-JOURNEY-JOYFUL*

WARRIOR-JOURNEY-RECOVERY-[THE WARRIORS' JOURNEY OF RECOVERY]: (*The warriors' journey of recovery is the process through which warriors conserve and rally their energy.*)
>   SELECTED REFERENCES: **The Fire From Within** - Page **[259.6-259.7]** ("To break the barrier of perception is...of recovery. Remember what you've done!")
>   SEE ALSO: *WARRIOR-IMPECCABILITY, WARRIOR-PATH, KNOWLEDGE-PATH*

WARRIOR-JOURNEY-RETURN-[THE WARRIORS' JOURNEY OF RETURN]: (*Warriorship is the warriors' journey of return to the abstract; warriors return victorious to the spirit after having descended into hell.*)
>   SELECTED REFERENCES: **The Power of Silence** - Page **[159.9-160.1]** ("As I have already said to...Understanding is one of our trophies.")
>   SEE ALSO: *ABSTRACT-RETURN, VICTORY, WARRIOR-JOURNEY-DEFINITIVE*

WARRIOR-JOURNEY-UNKNOWN-[THE WARRIORS' JOURNEY INTO THE UNKNOWN]: (*The warriors' journey into the unknown is the warriors' journey of return to the spirit; warriors must carefully monitor their journey into the unknown and not abandon their shields too quickly; as they rally their power, they must occasionally soothe themselves with the oblivion of their first attention perspective.*)
>   SELECTED REFERENCES: **Journey to Ixtlan** - Page **[135.4-135.7]** ("What's on the other side...One will only find death.") **The Fire From Within** - Page **[281.3-281.5]** (As I was telling don Juan...to be in the ordinary world!)
>   SEE ALSO: *WARRIOR-JOURNEY-POWER, WARRIOR-JOURNEY-RETURN, WARRIOR-JOURNEY-DEFINITIVE*

WARRIOR-JOY-[THE WARRIORS' JOY]: (*The mood of warriors is a mood of joy; warriors are joyful because they feel humbled by their great fortune, because they are confident of their impeccability, and above all, because they are fully aware of their efficiency; the warriors' joyfulness comes from having accepted their fate; joy is the ultimate accomplishment of warriors; warriors are joyful because their love is unalterable and their beloved earth embraces them and bestows inconceivable gifts upon them; warriors act for the spirit alone and the fact that they enjoy their acts does not count as gain; the warriors' joy is rather a condition of their character; without magic there can be no elation or joy; warriors know that they are waiting and what they are waiting for, that in itself is the great joy of warriorship.*)
>   SELECTED REFERENCES: **A Separate Reality** - Page **[64.7-65.3]** ("It is not hard, it is...drunkards. Look at my grandson here!") **Journey to Ixtlan** - Page **[155.3-155.4]** ("And thus you will dance to your...will sit here and watch you.) **Tales of Power** - Page **[219.8-219.9]** (Genaro told me that we have..."I have no idea," Pablito said.) **Tales of Power** - Page **[279.7-279.9]** (There are many ways of saying...a warrior's way of saying farewell.") **Tales of Power** - Page **[289.7-289.8]** ("A warrior acknowledges his pain but...assessed what lies ahead of him.") **Tales of Power** - Page **[292.7-292.9]** ("Only if one loves this earth...that gives shelter to their beings.") **Tales of Power** - Page **[294.2-294.4]** ("Only the love for this splendorous...Only then does it make sense.") **The Eagle's Gift** - Page **[84.4-84.6]** (La Gorda got up; she was...don Juan's teachings to the letter.) **The Fire From Within** - Page **[24.4-24.6]** (The idea of using a petty...course, that one is a warrior.") **The Fire From Within** - Page **[27.1-27.3]** ("I groveled daily," don Juan continued...is the great joy of warriorship.) **The Fire From Within** - Page **[60.1-60.2]** (Their glee was always contagious...them, I seemed old and decrepit.) **The Power of Silence** - Page **[79.4-79.6]** ("Malicious acts are performed by people...for profit but for the spirit.") **The Power of Silence** - Page **[146.2-146.3]** (The old, dark, heavy part of...to stop fretting and enjoy.) **The Power of Silence** - Page **[222.8-222.9]** ("That big cat came out of nowhere...elation, no lesson, no realizations.")
>   SEE ALSO: *WARRIOR-HUMOR, WARRIOR-FATE, WARRIOR-EFFICIENCY, WARRIOR-IMPECCABILITY, MAGIC, WARRIOR-FATE, WARRIOR-ACCOMPLISHMENT, WARRIOR-WAIT*

WARRIOR-JUDGMENT-[WARRIORS DO NOT PASS JUDGMENT]:
(Warriors know that it is not in their best interests to be judgmental; warriors know it is best to be free from self-importance so that they can celebrate the world unbiasedly.)

SELECTED REFERENCES: The Fire From Within - Page [198.9-199.8] ("He seems like a very selfish person...so that one can celebrate them unbiasedly.")

SEE ALSO: MORALITY, WARRIOR-WITNESS-UNBIASED

*WARRIOR-JUMP-[THE WARRIORS' JUMP INTO THE ABYSS]: (The warriors' jump into the abyss is the final test of warriorship; the act of breaking the barrier of perception; warriors jump from a mountaintop into an abyss while in a state of normal awareness and if they cannot break the barrier of perception and assemble another world before reaching the bottom, they die; the jump is a special method which warriors use to trap the second attention.)

SELECTED REFERENCES: The Second Ring of Power - Page [1.3-2.3] (A flat, barren mountaintop on the...did happen, that I did jump.) The Second Ring of Power - Page [43.1-43.6] (I felt like asking her if...happened, the four of you jumped.") The Second Ring of Power - Page [210.8-213.7] ("What did you do after we...But I never talk about it.") The Second Ring of Power - Page [326.6-326.9] ("Do you mean, Gorda, that we...vision, perhaps for a whole eternity.") The Eagle's Gift - Page [302.1-314.3] (At one instant, I was not...And then the lights were gone.) The Fire From Within - Page [x.1-x.3] (That apprenticeship ended with an incomprehensible...from that mountaintop into an abyss.) The Fire From Within - Page [xii.8-xiii.1] (The organization of his teachings for...act of jumping into an abyss.) The Fire From Within - Page [288.6-289.4] ("There must be no mistake about what...another world and escape this one.) The Fire From Within - Page [295.2-295.5] ("I want you to bypass all...before he reaches the bottom, he dies.)

SEE ALSO: PERCEPTION-BARRIER-BREAKING, ASSEMBLAGE-POINT-MOVING, WARRIOR-TEST-GRAND, WORLDS-OTHER-ASSEMBLE-TOTAL

WARRIOR-JUMP-PRELUDE-[THE PRELUDE TO THE WARRIORS' JUMP INTO THE ABYSS]-(TOP)

WARRIOR-KNOWLEDGE-ROAD-[THE WARRIORS' ROAD TO KNOWLEDGE]: (Warriors must not only be willing to undertake the road to knowledge, but their efforts by themselves must make them worthy of that knowledge.)

SELECTED REFERENCES: Tales of Power -Page [119.3-119.5] ("I have put on my suit...will tell you the sorcerers' explanation.")

SEE ALSO: KNOWLEDGE-PATH, WARRIOR-IMPECCABILITY, KNOWLEDGE-CLAIMING-POWER

*WARRIOR-LAST-STAND-[THE WARRIORS' LAST STAND]: (Warriors must be willing and ready to make their last stand on earth at any moment, here and now, because any battle for warriors is a battle for their lives.)

SELECTED REFERENCES: A Separate Reality - Page [215.4-215.5] ("The spirit of a warrior is...impeccable, a warrior laughs and laughs.") Journey to Ixtlan - Page [83.6-83.9] ("There are some people who are...bring your acts into that light.") Journey to Ixtlan - Page [84.4-85.1] ("Your continuity only makes you timid...the acts of a timid man.") Journey to Ixtlan - Page [85.4-85.6] ("Our death is waiting and this...dulls the edge of his fright.") Journey to Ixtlan - Page [153.4-153.9] ("I will have to come with you...there the warrior dances to his death.) Journey to Ixtlan - Page [228.3-228.4] ("What dance are you talking about...in his last stand on earth.) Tales of Power - Page [154.5-154.9] ("To be a warrior means to be...into place because you're expecting nothing.") The Eagle's Gift - Page [280.4-280.6] ("Don't complicate things," she said in...not in a helter-skelter way.")

SEE ALSO: STALKING-PRINCIPLES-SEVEN, WARRIOR-BATTLE-POWER

WARRIOR-LAST-STAND-SITE-[THE SITE OF THE WARRIORS' LAST STAND]-(TOP)

WARRIOR-LEARN-IN-SPITE-THEMSELVES-[WARRIORS LEARN IN SPITE OF THEMSELVES]: *(Warriors know that they will never be able to explain the process by which they accesses silent knowledge; they understand that knowledge comes to them in its own inexplicable way, despite fear, resistance and the warriors' shortcomings.)*
SELECTED REFERENCES: The Teachings of Don Juan - Page [50.3-50.4] ("All this is very easy to...spite of yourself; that's the rule.")
SEE ALSO: *LEARNING, WARRIOR-SHORTCOMINGS, KNOWLEDGE-SILENT*

WARRIOR-LEARNING-ASSEMBLING-[WARRIORS ASSEMBLE WHAT THEY'VE LEARNED]: *(Warriors know assembling what they have learned is part of the warriors' way; warriors assemble what they have learned without piousness or presumptuousness; they aren't wild with questions one day and wild with acceptance the next.)*
SELECTED REFERENCES: Tales of Power - Page [75.5-75.8] ("What Genaro showed you yesterday is...no one can find flaws in it.")
SEE ALSO: *LEARNING-HARDSHIPS, LEARNING, WARRIOR-QUESTIONS, PIOUS-MAN-WAY*

WARRIOR-LEARNING-TASK-[THE WARRIORS' TASK OF LEARNING]: *(Warriors know at a given point that they have been tricked into the task of learning; they are unaware of the task at first and when they become aware of it, they find knowledge to be a very frightening affair; but in the end, the warriors' curiosity sustains them in the pursuit of their task.)*
SELECTED REFERENCES: The Teachings of Don Juan - Page [49.8-50.4] (The way in which the situation...in spite of yourself; that's the rule.")
SEE ALSO: *LEARNING, LEARNING-HARDSHIPS, SPIRIT-TRICKERY, FEAR*

WARRIOR-LEDGE-[THE WARRIORS' LEDGE]: *(The warriors' ledge is a by-product of the warriors' instruction; warriors are left with a ledge to stand on because a small part of the other self is cultivated with the memories of instruction for the left side awareness; the memories of this interaction are forgotten only to resurface someday in order to serve as a rational outpost from where warriors can depart into the immeasurable vastness of the other self.)*
SELECTED REFERENCES: The Eagle's Gift - Page [274.6-274.9] (She told me then that to...the immeasurable vastness of the other self.)
SEE ALSO: *WARRIOR-INSTRUCTION, AWARENESS-LEFT, FORGET-COMMAND-TO, OTHER-SELF*

WARRIOR-LENIENCY-[LENIENCY IS NOT PERMISSIBLE FOR WARRIORS]: *(Warriors know that leniency has no place in the tight life of the warrior; warriors cannot hinge their lives on the idea that things are too much for them and that they require leniency in the first place; warriors must live like warriors in order to survive; warriors must always be prepared and alert.)*
SELECTED REFERENCES: Tales of Power - Page [154.1-154.7] (We laughed at the image...caught you with your pants down.")
SEE ALSO: *WARRIOR-LIFE-TIGHT, WARRIOR-LIVE-LIKE, WARRIOR-WAY, WARRIOR-ALERTNESS, WARRIOR-PREPAREDNESS, SELF-COMPASSION, WARRIOR-SURVIVE*

WARRIOR-LEVELS-[THE LEVELS OF THE WARRIOR]: SEE: WARRIOR-DEVELOPMENT-[THE THREE STAGES OF THE WARRIORS' DEVELOPMENT]

WARRIOR-LIFE-[THE WARRIORS' LIFE OF THE WARRIOR]: (Life for warriors is an exercise in strategy; warriors know that they have no life of their own; from the moment they understand the nature of awareness, the human condition is no longer a part of the warriors' point of view; warriors have their duty as warriors and that is sufficient; warriors can only do their impeccable best and graciously accept their fate.)
 SELECTED REFERENCES: A Separate Reality - Page [181.5-181.7] ("Life for a warrior is an...would be battling to the end.") The Eagle's Gift - Page [306.5-306.9] (Don Juan called everyone to come...understood and had accepted my fate.)
 SEE ALSO: *EXISTENCE-REASON, WARRIOR-STRATEGY, POWER-PROMISE, LIFE-STRONG, WARRIOR-FATE, HUMAN-CONDITION, LIFE-SUFFICIENT*

WARRIOR-LIFE-LUST-[THE WARRIORS' LUST FOR LIFE]: (The warriors' detachment and the power of their decisions enable them to perform everything in life with gusto and lusty efficiency.)
 A Separate Reality - Page [151.1-151.7] ("Only the idea of death makes...to with gusto and lusty efficiency.)
 SEE ALSO: *WARRIOR-DETACHMENT, WARRIOR-DECISIONS-EMPOWERING*

WARRIOR-LIFE-TIGHT-[THE WARRIORS' TIGHT LIFE]: (The apprenticeship to knowledge is long and arduous and warriors must reduce to a minimum all that is unnecessary in their lives in order to withstand the impact of their encounter with power.)
 SELECTED REFERENCES: The Teachings of Don Juan - Page [69.8] (And the man attempting to learn...by leading a hard, quiet life.) The Teachings of Don Juan - Page [105.5] ("You have to be a strong man...with deliberateness, a good, strong life.") The Teachings of Don Juan - Page [173.6-173.7] (He reminded me again that in order...to lead a strong, quiet life.) A Separate Reality - Page [43.8-43.9] (The apprenticeship was long and arduous...the impact of such an encounter.) A Separate Reality - Page [133.7-133.8] ("You're too weak," he said...to die like a goddamn fool.") A Separate Reality - Page [134.1-134.5] ("First you must live like a warrior...which of course is right for you.") Journey to Ixtlan - Page [55.2-55.3] ("Hunters must be exceptionally tight individuals...perhaps through it you will change.") Journey to Ixtlan - Page [91.8-92.2] (You must understand that a warrior...taking something for being something else.) Journey to Ixtlan - Page [99.8-99.9] ("I am not trying to make you...the impeccable life of a warrior.) Journey to Ixtlan - Page [191.4-191.5] ("Can I do that now...let the earth absorb its heaviness.") Journey to Ixtlan - Page [217.9-218.1] (We drove away and don Juan...had found for you," he said.) Journey to Ixtlan - Page [234.4-235.3] ("Chance, good luck, personal power, or...that point so I remained quiet.) Tales of Power - Page [155.7-155.9] ("This is your world. You can't...the harmony between *tonal* and *nagual*.)
 SEE ALSO: *WARRIOR-WAY, LIFE-STRONG, WARRIOR-BATTLE-POWER, POWER-ENCOUNTER, NAGUAL-FACING, WARRIOR-SIMPLICITY*

WARRIOR-LIGHTNESS-[THE WARRIORS' LIGHTNESS]: (Warriors know that they cannot take themselves too seriously; warriors must learn to balance seriousness with lightness and humor; warriors know how to laugh at themselves and behave with the confidence of someone who doesn't have a care in the world.)
 SELECTED REFERENCES: A Separate Reality - Page [7.9-8.1] (The reason you got scared and quit...needs to be light and fluid.") The Fire From Within - Page [257.9-258.2] (Don Juan had commented that that...until tears rolled down their cheeks.) The Art of Dreaming - Page [21.8-22.2] (For instance, I expressed my feelings...dreams actually be turned into dreaming.")
 SEE ALSO: *WARRIOR-HUMOR, WARRIOR-ABANDON, WARRIOR-JOY, WARRIOR-SELF-CONFIDENCE, STALKING-RESULTS-THREE, WARRIOR-DISPOSITION, WARRIOR-SERIOUSNESS, LAUGHTER, EQUILIBRIUM*

WARRIOR-LIKES-[THE WARRIORS' LIKES]: *(Warriors simply like some things, and that's all; they like whoever or whatever they want and use their controlled folly to remain unconcerned about their preferences.)*
SELECTED REFERENCES: A Separate Reality - Page [89.5-89.6] ("You're too concerned with liking people...one can do as a man.")
SEE ALSO: *WARRIOR-CONTROLLED-FOLLY, WARRIOR-DESIRE, EQUAL-UNIMPORTANT*

WARRIOR-LIMBO-[THE WARRIORS' LIMBO]: *(Warriors spend years in limbo where they are neither average human beings nor sorcerers.)*
SELECTED REFERENCES: The Power of Silence - Page [171.2-171.5] (Your uncertainty is to be expected...victims go after a ferocious struggle.")
SEE ALSO: *SELF-REFLECTION-MIRROR-SHATTERING, CONTINUITY*

WARRIOR-LIMITS-[THE WARRIORS' LIMITS]: *(Warriors know that the only limits they have are those which power itself imposes; warriors understand the boundaries they place on themselves with regard to both their actions and their perceptions of the world; warriors have one free choice, to act impeccably within their limits or to act like asses.)*
SELECTED REFERENCES: Tales of Power - Page [7.3-7.6] ("I've been trying to live in...and routines stand in your way.") Tales of Power - Page [195.3-195.5] ("Genaro and I have to act...drain him and cause his demise.) The Eagle's Gift - Page [23.6-23.8] (What channels the energy of our total being...transformed through *willing to* anything.) The Power of Silence - Page [113.5-113.6] ("A somersault of thought into the inconceivable,"...to probe our perceptual limits.)
SEE ALSO: *POWER-PRISONER, WARRIOR-IMPECCABILITY, WARRIOR-CHOICE, BOUNDARIES*

WARRIOR-LIVE-LIKE-[LIVE LIKE WARRIORS]: *(If warriors struggle impeccably for a lifetime, they know that someday they will live like warriors in spite of themselves.)*
SELECTED REFERENCES: Journey to Ixtlan - Page [136.2-136.3] ("You're really crazy," he said...*see* and to *stop the world*.") Journey to Ixtlan - Page [136.8-137.1] ("I can't tell you that." he...oneself in the world of power.") Journey to Ixtlan - Page [155.1] ("Certainly. You are hunting personal power...don't live like a warrior yet.) Journey to Ixtlan - Page [225.9] ("It would be cruel if this...warrior, one is no longer ordinary.) Tales of Power - Page [154.1-154.7] (We laughed at the image...caught you with your pants down.") The Second Ring of Power - Page [93.4-93.9] ("Do you envy la Gorda for...the Nagual was a new life.)
SEE ALSO: *WARRIOR-IMPECCABILITY, WARRIOR-STRUGGLE, LIFE-STRONG, WARRIOR-LIFE-(ALL)*

WARRIOR-LIVES-WITH-DEATH-[WARRIORS LIVE WITH DEATH]: *(Warriors know that they must live with the knowledge of death, because from that knowledge comes the courage to face anything.)*
SELECTED REFERENCES: The Fire From Within - Page [241.7-241.9] (Don Juan had drilled into me...no longer have anything to fear.)
SEE ALSO: *DEATH, DEATH-ADVISER, WARRIOR-DEATH-SYMBOLIC, WARRIOR-LIVE-LIKE, WARRIOR-COURAGE*

WARRIOR-LONELINESS-[THE WARRIORS' LONELINESS]: *(The art of warriors is to summon up and yet hold back the feelings they have for the things they know they must leave behind; the art of warriors is to balance the terror and wonder of being a man; warriors must be in touch with their loneliness without being lonely; warriors know that there is nothing more lonely than eternity.)*
SELECTED REFERENCES: A Separate Reality - Page [27.8-28.2] ("So you're afraid. There is nothing...I don't feel such a loneliness.") Journey to Ixtlan - Page [267.3-267.8] (For an instant I sensed a wave of agony...the invisible wall of a metaphor.) Tales of Power - Page [291.4-291.6] (He addressed me in particular and said...I will show you now.") The Fire From

Within - Page [97.5-97.5] (I told him that the fact remained...you'll be ready for the definitive journey.") **The Fire From Within - Page [250.3-250.4]** ("Would you venture into the unknown...your being revolted. It's embarrassing!")
    SEE ALSO: *WARRIOR-PASSIONATE, WARRIOR-LONGING, WARRIOR-SOLITUDE, WARRIOR-ARTS, ETERNITY, TERROR-VS-WONDER, WARRIOR-BALANCE, LETTING-GO, WARRIOR-HOLDINGS-GIVING-UP, EQUILIBRIUM*

WARRIOR-LONGING-[THE WARRIORS' LONGING]: *(The warriors' longing is a piercing feeling which overtakes warriors as an effect of the sudden movement of the assemblage point; the warriors' longing is for something indescribable, because deep down, warriors long for the nagual.)*

SELECTED REFERENCES: **The Second Ring of Power - Page [180.3-180.5]** ("My weakness is that I'm made to have...an ordinary man, without this awesome burden.") **The Second Ring of Power - Page [326.1-326.3]** (She looked at me. I had...arrival, it was alien to me.) **The Eagle's Gift - Page [91.9-92.1]** (My stomach was in knots...longing for something not present, unformulated.) **The Fire From Within - Page [96.9-97.1]** (Never in my life had I had such an attack...fear of their chilling solitude.) **The Power of Silence - Page [49.4-49.5]** (At this point, all there is left...and simple anger at having missed out.) **The Power of Silence - Page [110.8-111.8]** (He explained that poets unconsciously long...this shock of beauty, is *stalking*. ") **The Power of Silence - Page [125.7-125.9]** (Every time I was with don Juan,...the sudden movement of my assemblage point.)
    SEE ALSO: *WARRIOR-ANGUISH, WARRIOR-DESPAIR, WARRIOR-DESPAIR-DETERRENT, DEPRESSION-MELANCHOLY, STALKING-JOLT, POETRY, BEAUTY, ASSEMBLAGE POINT-MOVING, NAGUAL, AWARENESS-SUBLIMINAL*

WARRIOR-LOOKING-AFTER-[LOOKING AFTER A WARRIOR]: SEE: WARRIOR-CARING-FOR-ANOTHER-[CARING FOR ANOTHER WARRIOR]

WARRIOR-LOT-[THE WARRIORS' LOT]: *(Warriors accept their lot in ultimate humbleness, not as grounds for regret but as a living challenge.)*

SELECTED REFERENCES: Tales of Power - Page [19.2-19.3] (I told him that I felt unworthy...regret but as a living challenge.)
    SEE ALSO: *WARRIOR-HUMBLENESS, WARRIOR-CHALLENGE, MAN-LOT*

WARRIOR-LOVE-[THE WARRIORS' LOVE]: *(Love has many meanings for warriors; the great unconditional love of warriors is their love of this earth, this world; unconditional love is one of the bridges between the great contradictions of the warriors' world; the warriors' conditional feelings of love are part of the boundaries that feelings create around things of this world; the warriors' unconditional love grows out of a detachment from the first attention and it's agendas.)*

SELECTED REFERENCES: **Tales of Power - Page [291.5]** ("The life of a warrior cannot possibly...I will show you now.") **Tales of Power - Page [292.6-292.9]** ("This is the predilection of two warriors...that gives shelter to their beings.") **Tales of Power - Page [294.2-294.4]** ("Only the love for this splendorous...Only then does it make sense.") **The Second Ring of Power - Page [123.5-123.8]** (He said that if I would...you must forget him," he said.) **The Second Ring of Power - Page [124.9]** (I told la Gorda that my love...I would never see him again.) **The Second Ring of Power - Page [135.1-135.2]** ("You have to refuse both, the...you from entering into that realm?") **The Eagle's Gift - Page [85.1-85.4]** ("Our feelings make boundaries around anything,"...mountains the way we did," Nestor replied.) **The Fire From Within - Page [130.6-131.3]** (I was left facing the side of...we walked lazily around the patio.) **The Fire From Within - Page [159.4-160.1]** (His answer made me argue with...it is either pink, peach, or amber.) **The Fire From Within - Page [228.4-228.5]** ("Those first new seers served everybody...who were filled with morbidity.") **The Fire From Within - Page [250.1-250.4]** (I say that they were afraid...your being revolted. It's embarrassing!") **The Fire From Within - Page [269.6-270.2]** ("Are you sure you understand what...me that my promise was worthless.) **The Power of Silence - Page [28.9]** (The mere mention of my discomfort...those who were reflections of ourselves.) **The Power of Silence - Page [187.6]** (Gone was his feeling of detachment,...the

distinctive features of the world of everyday life.) **The Art of Dreaming - Page [251.2-251.6]** (I said to Carol that Immediately...Are sorcerers people in love now?")
    SEE ALSO: *WARRIOR-BRIDGE, EARTH, BOUNDARIES, WARRIOR-DETACHMENT, WARRIOR-LOVE-POWER*

WARRIOR-LOVE-POWER-[THE WARRIORS' POWER TO LOVE]:
(Warriors know that their detachment gives them the power to love.)
    SELECTED REFERENCES: **The Power of Silence - Page [187.5-187.7]** (Gone was his feeling of detachment...he set out on his own.)
    SEE ALSO: *WARRIOR-DETACHMENT, WARRIOR-LOVE*

WARRIOR-MAGIC-[THE WARRIORS' MAGIC]: *(The warriors' magic flows through their actions from the connecting link with intent.)*
    SELECTED REFERENCES: **The Power of Silence - Page [106.9-107.1]** (A warrior, he said, was on...be able to suspect his ruthlessness.)
    SEE ALSO: *RUTHLESSNESS, WARRIOR-INTENT-LINK, WARRIOR-ACTING, MAGIC*

WARRIOR-MALE-[MALE WARRIORS]: *(Warriors know there are four male personalities that exist in the human race; they are the scholar, the man of action, the organizer behind the scenes and the courier; male warriors are different from female warriors with regard to the fact that every male warrior must be forced to give up his holdings by fear.)*
    SELECTED REFERENCES: **The Eagle's Gift - Page [157.2-157.3]** ("The Nagual woman and I were...has to be forced by fear.) **The Eagle's Gift - Page [174.8-175.3]** (The three male warriors and the...who cannot stand on his own.)
    SEE ALSO: *SCHOLAR, MAN-ACTION, ORGANIZER, WARRIOR-COURIER, RULE, FEAR, WARRIOR-FEMALE, MALE-MALENESS, WARRIOR-MALE-RATIONALE*

WARRIOR-MALE-RATIONALES-[THE RATIONALES OF THE MALE WARRIOR]: *(Male warriors are unique insofar as they must be given serious reasons before they can venture safely into the unknown; female warriors are not subject to this and can go without any hesitation as long as they have complete confidence in whoever is leading them.)*
    SELECTED REFERENCES: **The Eagle's Gift - Page [247.4-247.6]** (Don Juan began the task of ushering...confidence in whoever is leading them.)
    SEE ALSO: *REASON, WARRIOR-FEMALE, LUMINOUS-BODY-FEATURES, UNKNOWN-JOURNEY*

WARRIOR-MARK-[THE WARRIORS' MARK]: *(The mark of the warrior is a controlled outburst coupled with a controlled quietness.)*
    SELECTED REFERENCES: **Journey to Ixtlan - Page [104.5-104.6]** (It involved making one's presence obvious...were the mark of a warrior.)
    SEE ALSO: *WARRIOR-WAY, WARRIOR-CONTROL, WARRIOR-BALANCE-SOBRIETY-ABANDON, MAN-MARK*

WARRIOR-MASTERY-[THE WARRIORS' MASTERY]: *(Warriors know that they are never masters, they are at best only warriors; thoughts of mastery are only the product of the warriors' inability to let go of self-reflection and self-importance; warriors have no need to dominate or master anything, because warriors have no desires to begin with.)*
    SELECTED REFERENCES: **The Teachings of Don Juan - Page [86.2-86.3]** (Power is the strongest of all enemies...because he is a master.) **A Separate Reality - Page [251.6-251.9]** ("Fright is something one can never...is the master at all times.") **Tales of Power - Page [7.8-8.1]** (I told him that I had received...don't know what a master feels like.") **The Fire From Within - Page [103.6-103.7]** ("Those old seers were terrifying men,"...to master everybody and everything.") **The Power of Silence - Page [160.2-160.4]** ("Our difficulty with this simple progression...our self-importance, that help is real.)

SEE ALSO: *SELF-REFLECTION, WARRIOR-ATTAINMENT, WARRIOR-DESIRE, SELF-REFLECTION*

WARRIOR-MASTERIES-THREE-[THE THREE MASTERIES OF THE WARRIOR]: (*The three masteries of the warrior include the mastery of three aspects of ancient knowledge based on the mastery of awareness; they are the mastery of stalking, the master of intent and the mastery of dreaming; these three areas of expertise are the three riddles that the warrior encounters in his search for knowledge, the riddle of the mind, the riddle of the heart and the riddle of the spirit; the masteries of the warrior are the crowning glory of sorcerers old and new; stalking is the beginning, so before warriors attempt anything on the warriors' path, they must first learn to stalk; next they must learn to dream and intend; only when this is accomplished can they move their assemblage points at will.*)

SELECTED REFERENCES: The Fire From Within - Page [x.6-x.8] (It was in his teachings for...seer, but also a nagual.) The Fire From Within - Page [xii.8-xiii.1] (The organization of his teachings for...act of jumping into an abyss.) The Fire From Within - Page [xiii.5-xiii.7] (When I asked him once what...free, as if they had never existed.) The Fire From Within - Page [144.6-144.7] ("What la Catalina does," don Juan interrupted,...master of *stalking*, and the master of *intent.)* The Fire From Within - Page [167.9-168.5] ("The most important thing the new...the very first day we met.) The Fire From Within - Page [170.2-171.5] (Don Juan said next that the...Silvio Manuel is the master of *intent.*) The Power of Silence - Page [xiv.9-xv.5] (These two categories allowed teachers to school...projected beyond our human condition.) The Power of Silence - Page [80.5-80.7] (In a very low voice don Juan...could they move their assemblage point at will.)

SEE ALSO: *WARRIOR-MASTERY, RIDDLE-MIND, RIDDLE-HEART, RIDDLE-SPIRIT, STALKING-ART, INTENT, DREAMING-ART, INTENDING*

WARRIOR-MATTERS-NOTHING-[NOTHING MATTERS TO WARRIORS]: SEE: WARRIOR-NOTHING-MATTERS-[NOTHING MATTERS TO WARRIORS]

WARRIOR-MATTERS-WHAT-[WHAT MATTERS TO WARRIORS]: (*The only things that matter to warriors is their impeccability and their struggle to arrive at the totality of themselves.*)

SELECTED REFERENCES: Tales of Power - Page [4.2-4.5] ("What's the thing that matters then...arriving at the totality of oneself.")

SEE ALSO: *WARRIOR-IMPECCABILITY, WARRIOR-STRUGGLE , TOTALITY-REGAINING, TOTALITY*

WARRIOR-MISER-ENERGY-[WARRIORS MUST BECOME MISERS WITH THEIR ENERGY]: SEE: WARRIOR-ENERGY-MISER-[WARRIORS MUST BECOME MISERS WITH THEIR ENERGY]

WARRIOR-MODERATION-[THE WARRIORS' MODERATION]: (*The warriors' moderation is an aspect of their sobriety and control; warriors know they must moderate their tendency to indulge themselves.*)

SELECTED REFERENCES: The Second Ring of Power - Page [301.3-301.5] ("Has my second attention been injured...but it wasn't your fate to be moderate.")

SEE ALSO: *WARRIOR-SOBRIETY, WARRIOR-CONTROL, BALANCE, SELF-INDULGENCE*

*WARRIOR-MOOD-[THE WARRIORS' MOOD: (*The warriors' mood calls for control and abandon at the same time.*)

SELECTED REFERENCES: A Separate Reality - Page [151.1-151.7] ("Only the idea of death makes...to with gusto and lusty efficiency.) Journey to Ixtlan - Page [110.4-111.4] (The hardest thing in the world...the mood of a warrior now.) Journey to Ixtlan - Page [119.1-121.3] ("The little crow pointed out that...It takes power to do that.") Journey to Ixtlan - Page [120.7-

121.4] (A warrior could be injured but...It takes power to do that.") **Journey to Ixtlan - Page** [139.3-139.4] ("This is it," he said in...shoved me gently down the slope.) **Tales of Power - Page** [289.7-289.8] ("A warrior acknowledges his pain but...assessed what lies in front of him.") **The Power of Silence - Page - [49.5]** ("I like poems for many reasons...explain what can hardly be explained.")

 SEE ALSO: *WARRIOR-CONTROL, ABANDON, WARRIOR-ABANDON-CONTROLLED, WARRIOR-PROACTIVITY, WARRIOR-CONTRADICTION-KNOWLEDGE, WARRIOR-BALANCE-SOBRIETY-ABANDON, EQUILIBRIUM*

WARRIOR-MORTALITY-RATE-[THE MORTALITY RATE OF WARRIORS]: (The figurative mortality rate of warriors is based on the number of warriors defeated by petty tyrants; although not deadly, defeat at the hands of a petty tyrant means obliteration for warriors because they will destroy themselves with their own sense of failure and unworthiness.)

 SELECTED REFERENCES: **The Fire From Within - Page [30.1-30.6]** (I explained to don Juan that...of the petty tyrants for life.")
 SEE ALSO: *PETTY-TYRANT, DEFEAT*

WARRIOR-MOTOR-CONTROL-LOSS-OF-[WARRIORS LOSE THEIR MOTOR CONTROL]: (Warriors know that encounters with the nagual can cause them to lose their motor control, their ability to speak and even their ability to think; this condition will persist until they can regain their solidity and close their gaps.)

 SELECTED REFERENCES: **The Fire From Within - Page [89.8-89.9]** (The force that had enveloped me...thawed out by tiny degrees.) **The Fire From Within - Page [276.4-276.5]** (I wanted to say something, to...of his head to join him.) **The Art of Dreaming - Page [241.7-247.1]** ("Make an effort, nagual," a woman's...began to regain my motor control.)
 SEE ALSO: *NAGUAL-FACING, WARRIOR-SPEECHLESS, WARRIOR-SEIZURE, WARRIOR-SOLIDITY, GAP, SORCERER-MUTENESS, ASSEMBLAGE-POINT-MOVEMENT-INVOLUNTARY*

WARRIOR-MYSTERIES-RECEIVE-[WARRIORS RECEIVE MYSTERIES]: (Warriors who receive mysteries must claim knowledge as power by doing what they have been shown.)

 SELECTED REFERENCES: **The Second Ring of Power - Page [269.7-269.8]** ("When the sorcerer is dealing with the nagual...doing what he has been shown.)
 SEE ALSO: *WORLD-MYSTERIOUS, KNOWLEDGE-CLAIMING-POWER*

WARRIOR-MYSTERY-ACCEPT-[WARRIORS ACCEPT THE MYSTERY OF THEMSELVES]: (Warriors accept something extremely obvious; human beings are infinitely more complex and mysterious than our wildest fantasies.")

 SELECTED REFERENCES: **The Eagle's Gift - Page [279.5-279.7]** ("The first precept of the rule...One is equal to everything.) **The Power of Silence - Page - [167.3-167.8]** ("The only way of talking about it...We are part of the mysterious.)
 SEE ALSO: *WORLD-MYSTERIOUS*

WARRIOR-NOTHING-BECOME-[WARRIORS BECOME NOTHING]: (Warriors know that once they lose the human form they become nothing.)

 SELECTED REFERENCES: **The Second Ring of Power - Page [159.1-159.5]** ("What is the point of losing your...Once it leaves, you are nothing.)
 SEE ALSO: *HUMAN-FORM-LOSING*

WARRIOR-NOTHING-DEFEND-[WARRIORS HAVE NO POINTS TO DEFEND]: SEE: WARRIOR-DEFEND-NOTHING-[WARRIORS HAVE NO POINTS TO DEFEND]

WARRIOR-NOTHING-MATTERS-[NOTHING MATTERS TO WARRIORS]: (The warriors' controlled folly and ability to "see" help them realize that nothing really matters; the warriors' understanding that all things are equal and unimportant; when warriors "see", they "see" the same truth in everything.)
> SELECTED REFERENCES: **The Teachings of Don Juan - Page [72.6-72.7]** ("No! I'm never angry at anybody...don't feel that way any longer.") **A Separate Reality - Page [79.6-81.5]** ("But it can't be true...what he looks at everything becomes unimportant.") **A Separate Reality - Page [84.4-86.2]** (At that point I suggested that...what one does is important. Nothing!) **A Separate Reality - Page [88.2-88.9]** ("If nothing really matters," I said...to realize then that nothing matters.")
> SEE ALSO: *WARRIOR-CONTROLLED-FOLLY, SEEING, EQUAL-UNIMPORTANT, LOOKING-VS-SEEING, LIFE-CHOOSING*

WARRIOR-NOTHING-PENDING-LIFE-[NOTHING IS PENDING IN THE LIVES OF WARRIORS]: (Warriors know that nothing is pending in the world; the warriors' detachment helps them understand that nothing in their lives is finished and yet nothing is unresolved.)
> SELECTED REFERENCES: **A Separate Reality - Page [209.8-209.9]** ("I still have so many things...nothing is unresolved. Go to sleep.") **Journey to Ixtlan - Page [43.7-44.1]** ("Why do you tell me all...properly have a gesture with you.")
> SEE ALSO: *WARRIOR-DETACHMENT*

WARRIOR-NOTICE-EVERYTHING-[WARRIORS NOTICE EVERYTHING]: (Warriors know that they must train themselves to notice everything, because therein lies the warriors' advantage.)
> SELECTED REFERENCES: **The Second Ring of Power - Page [209.4-209.6]** (Nestor asked me if I had noticed...Nagual said, there lies his advantage.")
> SEE ALSO: *WARRIOR-ALERTNESS, WARRIOR-ADVANTAGE, AWARENESS*

WARRIOR-OBJECT-NO-LONGER-[WARRIORS ARE NO LONGER OBJECTS]: (Fluid warriors can no longer make the world chronological because they know there is no world of solid objects; warriors are luminous beings in a luminous world.)
> SELECTED REFERENCES: **Tales of Power - Page [46.8-46.9]** ("A fluid warrior can no longer...luminous being existing in a luminous world.) **Tales of Power - Page [95.1-95.2]** ("Don't take that leap in the...conceive what I am talking about.") **Tales of Power - Page [97.6-97.8]** ("Today I have to pound the nail...which we rarely emerge in our lifetime.) **Tales of Power - Page [158.8-158.9]** ("But did they see me disappear...are only extraordinary for the *tonal*.)
> SEE ALSO: *WARRIOR-FLUIDITY, LUMINOUS-BEINGS, WARRIOR-PROACTIVITY*

WARRIOR-OBJECTIVITY-[THE WARRIORS' OBJECTIVITY]: (The warriors' objectivity is a by product of the warriors' consistency and detachment and sobriety.)
> SELECTED REFERENCES: **The Power of Silence - Page [23.7-23.9]** (Don Juan commented that that was...world that admitted very few mistakes.)
> SEE ALSO: *WARRIOR-SOBRIETY, WARRIOR-DETACHMENT, WARRIOR-CONSISTENCY*

WARRIOR-OFFENDED-NOT-[WARRIORS ARE NOT OFFENDED]: (Warriors are not offended; warriors protect themselves, or get out of the way without ever feeling morally wronged.)
> SELECTED REFERENCES: **The Teachings of Don Juan - Page [72.6-72.7]** ("No! I'm never angry at anybody...don't feel that way ant longer.") **Tales of Power - Page [142.5-142.6]** ("One of the acts of a warrior...a warrior has to be impeccable.") **Journey to Ixtlan - Page [120.1-121.3]** (There is no power in a...It takes power to do that.") **The Second Ring of Power - Page [238.1]** ("I will have to tell everybody...won't feel offended by your acts.") **The Fire From Within - Page [12.7-12.8]** ("I was provoking your self-importance...of our lives offended by someone.")

The Power of Silence - Page **[218.6-218.9]** (I thought I knew what he wanted....without feeling morally wronged.) **The Power of Silence - Page [233.5-233.7]** (The current dragged him a long distance...the river was follow its flow.)
      SEE ALSO: *WARRIOR-SOBRIETY, WARRIOR-CONTROL, WARRIOR-IMPECCABILITY, WARRIOR-PROTECT-PERSON*

WARRIOR-OPENNESS-*[THE WARRIORS' OPENNESS]:* *(Warriors define openness as receptivity to the movement of power; warriors must be paragons of sobriety while at the same time keeping themselves completely free and open to the wonders and mysteries of existence.)*
      SELECTED REFERENCES: **The Fire From Within - Page [73.2-73.3]** ("For example, seers have to be methodical...to the wonders and mysteries of existence.")
      SEE ALSO: *WARRIOR-AVAILABILITY, WORLD-MYSTERIOUS, WARRIOR-SOBRIETY, POWER-FLOW, POWER-IS-POWER-MOVES*

WARRIOR-OPTIMISM-*[THE WARRIORS' OPTIMISM]:* *(The warriors' optimism is a leaning towards the light, towards positiveness and hope; the optimism of warriors works itself harmoniously into the mystery of the darkness.)*
      SELECTED REFERENCES: **The Eagle's Gift - Page [192.5-192.6]** (However, that would have been inauspicious...they did not light their lanterns.)
      SEE ALSO: *WARRIOR-BALANCE, ENERGY-DARK*

WARRIOR-OPTIONS-ASSEMBLAGE-POINT-MOVE-*[THE TWO OPTIONS OPEN TO WARRIORS WHOSE ASSEMBLAGE POINT HAS MOVED]:* *(There are two options open to warriors whose assemblage points have shifted; 1) one is to acknowledge being ill and to behave in deranged ways; 2) the other is to remain impassive and untouched, knowing that the assemblage point always returns to its original position; it is the warriors' impeccability which makes the difference between whether they lose their minds or not.)*
      SELECTED REFERENCES: **The Fire From Within - Page [120.1-120.8]** ("What happens to the persons whose...with their friends or with strangers.")
      SEE ALSO: *INSANITY, WARRIOR-WITNESS-UNBIASED, ASSEMBLAGE-POINT-MOVING, WARRIOR-IMPECCABILITY*

WARRIOR-ORDER-*[THE WARRIORS' ORDER]:* *(Warriors understand that the order of their perception belongs exclusively to the realm of the tonal, only there do actions have a sequence; warriors understand that their sense of order is not based on any first attention agenda; the order of warriors is simply a part of their impeccable behavior.)*
      SELECTED REFERENCES: **Journey to Ixtlan - Page [167.2-167.3]** (He pointed to the darkness all...was part of his impeccable behavior.) **Tales of Power - Page [272.1-272.2]** ("One thing has nothing to do with the...best tool but the only one we've got.) **The Second Ring of Power - Page [1.8-1.9]** (In my jump my perception went through...I had visions of order.) **The Fire From Within - Page [33.3-33.5]** (He told me then that before he could...the unknowable are the same thing.)
      SEE ALSO: *TONAL, ORGANIZATION-TONAL, WARRIOR-IMPECCABILITY, ATTENTION-FIRST*

WARRIOR-ORDINARY-NO-LONGER-*[WARRIORS ARE NO LONGER ORDINARY]:* *(Warriors know that the instant they begin to live like warriors, they are no longer ordinary.)*
      SELECTED REFERENCES: **Journey to Ixtlan - Page [225.9]** ("It would be cruel if this...warrior, one is no longer ordinary.)
      SEE ALSO: *WARRIOR-WAY, WARRIOR-LIVE-LIKE A*

WARRIOR-OUTBURST-CONTROLLED-[THE WARRIORS'
CONTROLLED OUTBURST]: **(A controlled outburst is part of the mark of**
the warrior.)
  SELECTED REFERENCES: **Journey to Ixtlan - Page [104.6]** (A controlled outburst
and a controlled quietness were the mark of a warrior.)
  SEE ALSO: *WARRIOR-MARK*

WARRIOR-OVERCONFIDENCE-[THE WARRIORS'
OVERCONFIDENCE]: **(Warriors can never afford to be overconfident and**
believe that they have outwitted the mysteries of the universe; warriors
must remain humble in the face of power.)
  SELECTED REFERENCES: **The Art of Dreaming - Page [102.2-102.5]** (With practice,
my capacity to intend...confidence of a fool," he said.) **The Art of Dreaming - Page [104.7-104.8]**
(The nagual Rosendo did not mean...having some idiotic confidence in yourself.")
  SEE ALSO: *WARRIOR-HUMBLENESS, WORLD-MYSTERIOUS, POWER-*
DESIGNS

WARRIOR-PAIN-[THE WARRIORS' PAIN]: **(Warriors know that they**
must acknowledge their pain without indulging in it.)
  SELECTED REFERENCES: **A Separate Reality - Page [142.87142.9]** ("It is up to us
as...hunger and pain will destroy him.") **Tales of Power - Page [288.3-288.4]** (Nothing that I had
ever done...but only the indulging in them.) **Tales of Power - Page [289.7-289.8]** ("A warrior
acknowledges his pain but...assessed what lies ahead of him.") **The Second Ring of Power -**
Page [234.4-234.9] (I had an attack of profound sadness...behind the best of my feelings.) **The**
Eagle's Gift - Page [106.7-106.8] ("The course of a warrior's destiny is...destiny the breadth of one
hair.")
  SEE ALSO: *PAIN-AVOIDING*

WARRIOR-PAPER-[THE PAPER WARRIOR]: **(Warriors know that to be**
perfect under perfect circumstances is to be a paper warrior; warriors must
strive to meet any conceivable situation, whether it is expected or
unexpected; warriors understand that they must be more than paper
warriors because the only way awareness can grow is through strife and
life-or-death confrontations; it is no challenge for warriors to soar like
arrows by themselves; warriors must train their bodies to be at ease even in
the most trying situations by harnessing their selfishness.)
  SELECTED REFERENCES: **The Eagle's Gift - Page [129.9-130.5]** (Don Juan was
telling me that...the fulfillment of my true task.) **The Eagle's Gift - Page [131.4-131.8]** (A fat
Gorda asked don Juan...I be capable of harnessing my selfishness.) **The Eagle's Gift - Page**
[306.9-307.2] (Vicente came to my side next...was to be a paper warrior.) **The Art of Dreaming -**
Page [101.3-101.4] (Don Juan explained that in the...strife, through life-or-death confrontations.)
  SEE ALSO: *WARRIOR-CHALLENGE, WARRIOR-STRUGGLE, WARRIOR-*
CARING-FOR-ANOTHER, SELFISHNESS, WARRIOR-DURESS-EXTREME-BENEFITS,
WARRIOR-EXPECTATION

WARRIOR-PARTY-LAST-HOURS-[A WARRIOR PARTY'S LAST HOURS
ON EARTH]-(TOP)

WARRIOR-PARTY-LEADER-[THE LEADER OF THE WARRIOR'S
PARTY]-(TOP)

WARRIOR-PASSIONATE-[THE PASSIONATE WARRIOR]: **(In order to be**
warriors, human beings must be passionate; passionate men and women
have earthly belongings and things that are dear to them, if nothing else, just
the path that they walk; the warriors' passion builds like an overwhelming
tidal wave of emotion which somehow remains in check behind an invisible
wall of awareness; warriors are deeply in touch with their passion but at

the same time they stay detached from it, free to fly beyond it; in the end, warriors will always act their passion, their predilection in life.)

SELECTED REFERENCES: **Journey to Ixtlan - Page [266.5-267.8]** (He reminded me that I had...the invisible wall of a metaphor.) **Tales of Power - Page [292.7-292.9]** ("Only if one loves this earth...that gives shelter to their beings.") **The Second Ring of Power - Page [223.5-223.6]** (La Gorda broke the silence and...path the silence for her.) **The Power of Silence - Page [187.3-187.5]** (Don Juan said that it took...that made him lose his effectiveness.) **The Art of Dreaming - Page [137.6]** ("Don't worry," he said laughing...the same way I act mine.)

SEE ALSO: *FEELINGS, EARTH, POETRY, WARRIOR-MOOD, WARRIOR-SPIRIT, WARRIOR-PREDILECTION*

WARRIOR-PAST-[THE WARRIORS' PAST]: *(Warriors are vitally concerned with the past, not their personal past, but the past experience of warriors of bygone days; the average man examines the past for personal reasons, warriors examine the past to obtain a point of reference; nothing gives warriors a better view of intent than examining stories of other warriors battling to understand the same force.)*

SELECTED REFERENCES: **Journey to Ixtlan - Page [13.4-13.5]** ("I don't know how we ended up...one's past is a bunch of crap.") **Tales of Power - Page [5.6-5.7]** ("We're not going to engage ourselves...on them, but only in reference.") **The Power of Silence - Page [2.1-2.8]** ("I think its time for us...battling to understand the same force.")

SEE ALSO: *SORCERY-STORIES, ABSTRACT-CORES, PERSONAL-HISTORY-LOSING, INTENT-EXAMINE*

WARRIOR-PATH-[THE WARRIORS' PATH]: *(The warriors' path is the warriors' way; the warriors' road to power; the warriors' path with heart; warriors can intuit their silent knowledge a bit more clearly than the average man because of their involvement with the warriors' path.)*

SELECTED REFERENCES: **The Second Ring of Power - Page [223.5-223.6]** (La Gorda broke the silence and...path her fate selected for her.) **The Second Ring of Power - Page [223.9-224.1]** ("The Nagual told me that in...that would be my warrior's path.) **The Eagle's Gift - Page [106.7-106.8]** ("The course of a warrior's destiny is...destiny the breadth of one hair.") **The Fire From Within - Page [127.6-127.8]** (The thought of her gazing at...comes when they attain total awareness.) **The Fire From Within - Page [148.1-148.3]** (He further said that to be...has welcomed the world of boredom.) **The Fire From Within - Page [195.3-195.4]** ("It goes without saying that the...it is the seers' quest proper.") **The Power of Silence - Page [144.8-144.9]** (I mentioned to don Juan that I...my involvement in the warrior's path.)

SEE ALSO: *WARRIOR-WAY, WARRIOR-JOURNEY-POWER, PATH-HEART-WITH, WARRIOR-INTUITION, KNOWLEDGE-SILENT*

WARRIOR-PATH-MOST-DIFFICULT-THING-[THE MOST DIFFICULT THING ON THE WARRIORS' PATH]: *(Warriors know that the most difficult thing on the warriors' path is to make the assemblage point move.)*

SELECTED REFERENCES: **The Fire From Within - Page [195.3-195.4]** ("It goes without saying that the...it is the seers' quest proper.")

SEE ALSO: *ASSEMBLAGE-POINT-MOVING, WARRIOR-PATH*

WARRIOR-PATIENCE-[THE WARRIORS' PATIENCE]: *(Warriors are never idle and never in a hurry; warriors wait patiently because they know that they are waiting and they know what they are waiting for; warriors have only their will and their patience, and with them they build anything they want; when warriors have command over their detachment, their decisions and their choices, then they consistently choose that which is strategically the best; warriors perform everything they have to with gusto and lusty efficiency; when warriors behave in such a manner one may rightfully say that they are warriors and that they have acquired patience; the warriors' courage empowers them to take action and yet be patient.)*

SELECTED REFERENCES: **A Separate Reality - Page [142.1-142.3]** ("Can you give me any suggestions...longer have to honor your promise.) **A Separate Reality - Page [145.5-145.6]** ("A warrior has to use his...whether you like it or not.") **A Separate Reality - Page [151.5-151.7]** ("And thus with an awareness of...a warrior and has acquired patience!") **A Separate Reality - Page [191.4-191.5]** ("That ally was beckoning you...attacking a lion with your farts.") **Tales of Power - Page [286.9-287.3]** ("If you two decide to return...by the sharpshooters from the unknown.) **The Power of Silence - Page [110.2-110.3]** ("Yes," he went on. "The idea...be ruthless without being self-important.")

SEE ALSO: *WARRIOR-DETACHMENT, WARRIOR-DECISIONS, WARRIOR-CHOICE, WARRIOR-WILL, WARRIOR-WAY, EQUILIBRIUM*

WARRIOR-PAUSE-ATTENTION-[THE PAUSE IN THE WARRIORS' ATTENTION]: *(The pause in the warriors' attention is a true pause which allows knowledge to fully soak through the warrior.)*

SELECTED REFERENCES: **Tales of Power - Page [230.2-230.4]** ("Now is when I need your total...to you in an instance like this.")

SEE ALSO: *KNOWLEDGE*

WARRIOR-PAUSE-DETACHMENT-[THE PAUSE OF THE WARRIORS' DETACHMENT]: *(The warriors' detachment provides a moment's pause during which warriors can reassess situations, providing they have the self-discipline and courage to utilize it.)*

SELECTED REFERENCES: **The Eagle's Gift - Page [112.7-113.5]** (La Gorda, upon hearing my report...to struggle unyieldingly for a lifetime.) **The Eagle's Gift - Page [124.9-125.9]** (Having a sense of detachment, as...self-discipline and courage to utilize it.)

SEE ALSO: *WARRIOR-FORMLESS, HUMAN-FORM-LOSING, WARRIOR-DISCIPLINE, WARRIOR-DETACHMENT*

WARRIOR-PEACE-[PEACE FOR THE WARRIOR]: *(Peace is an anomaly for warriors; warriors find peace while they wage a never-ending war, a total struggle against the individual self that has deprived them of their power; as a result of being impeccable, warriors find peace, satisfaction and attainment in a victory without glory or reward.)*

SELECTED REFERENCES: **A Separate Reality - Page [4.8]** ("You make it sound stupid," he...not complete. You have no peace.") **Journey to Ixtlan - Page [108.4-108.7S]** (I experienced an extremely pleasant feeling...as one acted as a warrior.) **Tales of Power - Page [155.9]** (Now there is no longer a war...then the harmony between *tonal* and *nagual*.) **The Eagle's Gift - Page [112.9-113.3]** (What I felt was not a...I had actually embodied it.) **The Eagle's Gift - Page [219.2-219.4]** (Later on, sobriety took hold of his...The Eagle was welcome to it.) **The Power of Silence - Page [xiii.6-xiii.7]** (Because of their extraordinary energy, naguals...and transmit them to their companions.) **The Power of Silence - Page [149.8-150.3]** (Don Juan asserted that the reason...has deprived man of his power.")

SEE ALSO: *WARRIOR-DETACHMENT, WARRIOR-ALOOFNESS, WARRIOR-WAR-VS-PEACE, WARRIOR-SATISFACTION, WARRIOR-ATTAINMENT, VICTORY, WARRIOR-REWARD, SELF-IMPORTANCE-LOSING, EQUILIBRIUM, WARRIOR-CONTRADICTION-KNOWLEDGE, BALANCE*

WARRIOR-PENDING-NOTHING-[NOTHING IS PENDING IN THE LIVES OF WARRIORS]: SEE WARRIOR-NOTHING-PENDING-[NOTHING IS PENDING IN THE LIVES OF WARRIORS]

WARRIOR-PERSISTENCE-[THE WARRIORS' PERSISTENCE]: *(Warriors know that persistence is the active element of the warriors' training; the mind and all its defenses cannot cope with persistence and sooner or later its barriers fall, allowing for the dreaming attention to bloom: warriors know that the only way to overcome the obstacles of warriorship is to persist in acting like a warrior.)*

SELECTED REFERENCES: **Tales of Power - Page [11.7-11.8]** ("Each warrior has his own way...spite of all the barriers and disappointments.") **Tales of Power - Page [23.6-23.7]** ("All

of us go through the same...at a given moment everything changed.") **The Art of Dreaming - Page [35.9-36.2]** (I realized, almost as soon as...impact, and the dreaming attention blooms.)
SEE ALSO: *KNOWLEDGE-POWER-SECRETS-COME-THEMSELVES, WARRIOR-WAY, MIND, WARRIOR-REPETITION*

WARRIOR-PERSONALITIES-[THE PERSONALITIES OF WARRIORS]:
(The personalities of warriors range among the four female and four male personalities; the similarity of the personal likes and dislikes among people of the same group is not a matter of imitation; members of these specific blocks of people have the same input and output; the only real differences between members of the same block is the pitch of their voices and the sound of their laughter.)
SELECTED REFERENCES: **The Eagle's Gift - Page [180.6-180.8]** (He said that by the time all...their voices, the sound of their laughter.) **The Eagle's Gift - Page [186.8-187.1]** (My response to the preparations to meet...indefinite number of types of people.)
SEE ALSO: *WARRIOR-FEMALE, WARRIOR-MALE, WARRIOR-PLANETS, PEOPLE-TYPES, PLANETS-WARRIORS*

WARRIOR-PIECES-[THE WARRIOR IN PIECES]-(TOP)

WARRIOR-PLAN-[THE WARRIORS' PLAN]: *(Warriors who have stored personal power do not need a plan, they trust their personal power to guide them.)*
SELECTED REFERENCES: **Journey to Ixtlan - Page [159.3-159.7]** ("What are we going to do...don't need to have a plan.") **Journey to Ixtlan - Page [164.1-164.2]** ("You found the right place," he...without any plan on your part.") **Journey to Ixtlan - Page [168.3-168.5]** (Don Juan put his hand over my...whether it is small or enormous.")
SEE ALSO: *POWER-PERSONAL, SPIRIT-DESIGNS*

WARRIOR-POSITION-[THE WARRIORS' POSITION]: SEE: WARRIOR-VIGIL-POSITION-[THE WARRIORS' POSITION OF SITTING "IN VIGIL"]

WARRIOR-POSTURE-[THE WARRIORS' POSTURE]: SEE: WARRIOR-PROTECT-POSITION-[THE WARRIORS' PROTECTIVE POSITION], WARRIOR-FIGHTING-FORM-[THE WARRIORS' FIGHTING FORM], WARRIOR-VIGIL-POSITION-[THE WARRIORS' POSITION OF SITTING "IN VIGIL"]

WARRIOR-POWER-BID-[THE WARRIORS' BID FOR POWER]: *(The warriors' bid for power is the greatest challenge of all; the warriors' irreversible bid for power may culminate one day in the fulfillment of that same power.)*
SELECTED REFERENCES: **The Teachings of Don Juan - Page [69.2]** ("The devil's weed is for those who bid for power.) **The Teachings of Don Juan - Page [161.2-161.4]** ("The desire to learn is not ambition...seek death is to seek nothing.") **A Separate Reality - Page [95.1]** ("You fail to understand that a...*see*, he attempts to gain power.") **Tales of Power - Page [144.9-145.3]** ("What's going to happen to me, don...approaching, the warrior's hour of power.") **The Fire From Within - Page [251.2-251.4]** ("Right at this juncture is where...deep shift along the right edge.") **The Art of Dreaming - Page [47.2]** ("By going through the first two...wait for a sign from them.")
SEE ALSO: *WARRIOR-CHALLENGE, POWER-FULFILLING, POWER-PROMISE*

WARRIOR-POWER-FAVORS-[WARRIORS AND THE FAVORS OF POWER]: *(Warriors know they must never turn their backs to power without atoning for the favors which they have received.)*

SELECTED REFERENCES: Journey to Ixtlan - Page [137.4-137.5] ("You cannot leave these desolate mountains...without atoning for the favors received.")
SEE ALSO: *WARRIOR-FORTUNE-GREAT, POWER*

WARRIOR-POWER-HOUR-[THE WARRIORS' HOUR OF POWER]: SEE: WARRIOR-HOUR-POWER-[THE WARRIORS' HOUR OF POWER]

WARRIOR-POWER-RING-[THE WARRIORS' RING OF POWER]: SEE: POWER-RING-SECOND-[THE SECOND RING OF POWER]

WARRIOR-POWER-SEEKS-[WARRIORS SEEK POWER]: (Warriors actively seek power through its many avenues; warriors are on their way to power.)

SELECTED REFERENCES: Journey to Ixtlan - Page [91.3-91.8] ("A warrior, on the other hand, seeks...them dreams, he calls them real.")
SEE ALSO: *WARRIOR, POWER-AVENUES, DREAMING-ART*

WARRIOR-PRACTICE-[WARRIORS MUST PRACTICE THE PRINCIPLES OF WARRIORSHIP AND SORCERY]: (Warriors know that they must deal with the principles of warriorship and sorcery as practicing arts and not as theoretical concepts; otherwise, they can never hope to become more than just paper warriors.)

SELECTED REFERENCES: The Art of Dreaming - Page [10.1-10.2] (The marvel of sorcery is that...hope that you will practice them.")
SEE ALSO: *WARRIOR-PAPER, SORCERER-EXPERIENCE, WARRIOR-WAY, SORCERY-PRINCIPLE*

WARRIOR-PRAYER-[THE WARRIORS' PRAYER]: (Warriors know they cannot pray to, or hope for grace from, the Eagle because the human part of the Eagle is too insignificant to move the whole.)

SELECTED REFERENCES: The Eagle's Gift - Page [173.4-173.6] (The Eagle, that power that governs...too insignificant to move the whole.)
SEE ALSO: *INTENT, GOD, EAGLE, PRAYER, RELIGIOUS-BELIEF, FAITH-RELIGIOUS*

WARRIOR-PREDILECTION-[THE WARRIORS' PREDILECTION]: (The warriors' connection with the abstract is an innermost predilection; this predilection expresses itself in many ways, including the warriors' love for the earth and the fact that warriors "have to believe"; warriors have certain personal issues which press them the most; these are unbiased reactions to the warriors' lot in life; warriors realize their predilections and say, "So be it!")

SELECTED REFERENCES: A Separate Reality - Page [10.8-11.4] (Don Juan had once told me that..."Yes, that is correct.") Tales of Power - Page [66.3-66.4] ("Do you think it works better if...Genaro's knack is for *dreaming*.") Tales of Power - Page [107.6-107.9] ("The most dangerous aspect of that...believe, a warrior *has* to believe."))Tales of Power - Page [114.5-114.7] ("What an exquisite omen this is...is the predilection of my spirit.") Tales of Power - Page [115.9] (Don Juan was right. *Having to*...Without it he had nothing.) Tales of Power - Page [187.6-187.9] (I practically huddled against don Juan...the darkness would be no obstacle. Tales of Power - Page [292.6-292.7] (Don Juan squatted in front of...there can be no greater love.") The Second Ring of Power - Page [296.4-296.5] ("The Nagual said that with his...only eucalyptus tree that was around.") The Eagle's Gift - Page [104.1] (She insisted that I was fixed...because of his predilection for words.) The Art of Dreaming - Page [137.2-137.7] (Don Juan had once made a...premeditation to cut someone else's chains.")
SEE ALSO: *EARTH, WARRIOR-PASSIONATE, BELIEVE-HAVING-TO, WARRIOR-PREDILECTION-PLACE*

WARRIOR-PREDILECTION-PLACE-[THE WARRIORS' PLACE OF PREDILECTION]: (The place of a warriors' predilection is the site of the warriors' last stand; it is a place soaked with unforgettable memories, where powerful events left their mark and where the warrior has stored personal power; warriors have witnessed marvels at those places and have had secrets revealed to them there; when death taps warriors on the shoulder, warriors fly to the place of their predilection and dance to their deaths.)

SELECTED REFERENCES: **Journey to Ixtlan** - Page [153.5-153.9] ("I will have to come with you...there the warrior dances to his death.) **Journey to Ixtlan** - Page [181.9-182.2] (After a day's rest he announced...to be cleansed and restored.) **Tales of Power** - Page [230.3-230.5] (I definitely would have preferred to..."given" to me as my own.) **Tales of Power** - Page [233.1-233.2] ("You're now facing in the direction...all the props you can use.) **Tales of Power** - Page [276.7-276.8] ("Let's go back to Genaro's place of...with our backs against the rock.) **Tales of Power** - Page [278.3-278.4] ("Now you should sit on Genaro's place...life that binds that cluster of feelings.") **The Fire From Within** - Page [106.5-106.7] (Don Juan was in northern Mexico...was such a place for him.)

SEE ALSO: *WARRIOR-PREDILECTION, WARRIOR-DANCE-LAST-POWER*

WARRIOR-PREDILECTION-TWO-[THE PREDILECTION OF TWO WARRIORS]-(TOP)

WARRIOR-PREOCCUPATION-[THE WARRIORS' PREOCCUPATION]: (For warriors, to be preoccupied means that all their energetic resources are consumed, and that they have engaged their energetic resources in their totality; warriors remain aware of their level of "preoccupation" because if they are deeply preoccupied, they have no available energy and hence no possibility of dreaming.)

SELECTED REFERENCES: **The Art of Dreaming** - Page [150.1-150.4] (When I started again to recapitulate...before, you were not completely absorbed.")

SEE ALSO: *DREAMING-ART, ENERGY, WARRIOR-IMPECCABILITY*

WARRIOR-PREPARATION-[THE WARRIORS' PREPARATION]: (Warriors are prepared to back up their decisions with their lives; they are not just prepared to die, warriors are prepared to battle.)

SELECTED REFERENCES: **A Separate Reality** - Page [215.2-215.3] ("I have heard you say time...should be prepared only to battle.)

SEE ALSO: *WARRIOR-LAST-STAND, WARRIOR-BATTLEFIELD , WARRIOR-DECISIONS*

WARRIOR-PREPAREDNESS-[THE WARRIORS' PREPAREDNESS]: (Warriors prepare themselves to be aware, and in that effort they are always humble and alert; warriors never let their guard down.)

SELECTED REFERENCES: **A Separate Reality** - Page [191.4-191.5] ("That ally was beckoning you...attacking a lion with your farts.") **A Separate Reality** - Page [217.5-217.8] ("A warrior encounters those inexplicable and...your gap and make you solid.") **Journey to Ixtlan** - Page [17.5] ("When nothing is for sure we...behave as if we know everything.") **Journey to Ixtlan** - Page [122.1] ("There's no plan when it comes...be in a state of readiness.) **Tales of Power** - Page [58.9-59.2] (Don Juan gave me a long...ourselves into one or the other.) **Tales of Power** - Page [74.8-74.9] ("Watch out!' he said. "A warrior...the little power you have left.") **Tales of Power** - Page [154.3-154.7] (I told him that there were...caught with your pants down.") **Tales of Power** - Page [287.7-287.8] ("A warrior must be always ready...particular, but what a great fortune!") **The Fire From Within** - Page [128.5-128.7] ("What are we really doing, don...are nothing do they become everything.") **The Power of Silence** - Page [106.9] (A warrior, he said, was on...against the roughness of human behavior.)

SEE ALSO: *WARRIOR-ALERTNESS, WARRIOR-HUMBLENESS*

WARRIOR-PRESSURE-RELIEVES-[WARRIORS RELIEVE THEIR PRESSURE]: *(If warriors need solace, they simply relieve their pressure by talking about their turmoil with anyone at hand or through some other means; in so doing, warriors are not seeking to be understood or helped, they are simply relieving their pressure.)*

SELECTED REFERENCES: Tales of Power - Page [53.2-53.3] ("If a warrior needs solace," he went...You have all my sympathy.") The Second Ring of Power - Page [123.3-123.4] ("What do you want me to do...tone that did not admit reproach.) The Fire From Within - Page [53.6-53.7] ("I'm more confused than ever, don Juan...such, it doesn't bring one solace.)

SEE ALSO: *WARRIOR-HELP-NEED-NO*

WARRIOR-PROACTIVITY-[THE WARRIORS' PROACTIVITY]: *(The warriors' proactivity is the magical stance that positions warriors to flow with power instead of against it; warriors are proactive, they allow themselves to flow with power through their impeccable actions and attitude; warriors exchange their reactivity for proactivity; they no longer occupy their energy with their reactions to the circumstances of the first attention agendas which drain their power and keep them victims; warriors maintain a proactive stance for every single action they take, otherwise they become distorted and ugly; the warriors' proactive stance cuts through the crap and keeps them purified; warriors are not at the mercy of the wind; no one can make warriors act against themselves or their better judgment; warriors are tuned to survive and they survive in the best of all possible fashions; warriors mold their life situations by molding their awareness of being alive.)*

SELECTED REFERENCES: A Separate Reality - Page [3.8-5.4] (Don Juan and I became friends...no despair or self-pity in it.) Journey to Ixtlan - Page [110.4-111.4] (The hardest thing in the world...the mood of a warrior now.) Journey to Ixtlan - Page [119.6-120.4] ("I know that," he said smiling...the best of all possible fashions.") The Art of Dreaming - Page [33.4-33.9] ("There are two ways of facing...direction and consequences of our lives.")

SEE ALSO: *WARRIOR-IMPECCABILITY, WARRIOR-ACTING, LIFE-VS-BEING-ALIVE, VICTIM, WARRIOR-SURVIVE, REACTIVE-STANCE, WARRIOR-OBJECT-NO-LONGER*

WARRIOR-PROFICIENCY-[THE WARRIORS' PROFICIENCY]: *(Warriors know that the instantaneous shift of their energy occurs only when a certain level of proficiency has been attained; that level of proficiency is known as pure understanding.)*

SELECTED REFERENCES: The Power of Silence - Page [113.9-114.5] (We left the house and strolled around...and sat down on a bench.)

SEE ALSO: *ENERGY-SHIFT-INSTANTANEOUS, UNDERSTANDING-PURE*

WARRIOR-PROMISE-GOD-[THE WARRIORS' PROMISE TO GOD]: SEE: GOD-VS-EAGLE-EMANATIONS-[GOD VS THE EAGLE'S EMANATIONS]

WARRIOR-PROPS-[THE WARRIORS' PROPS]: *(Warriors know that props can be useful at given points in the quest for knowledge.)*

SELECTED REFERENCES: Tales of Power - Page [233.1-233.2] (It was a mild day, a soft...may be another one of them.")

SEE ALSO: *WARRIOR-PREDILECTION-PLACE, WARRIOR-HAT*

WARRIOR-PROTECT-PERSON-[THE WARRIOR PROTECTS HIS PERSON]: *(Warriors know they must protect their person without defending it; warriors must be utterly humble and carry nothing to defend; warriors must understand the nature of their luminous being and be ready to*

re-solidify themselves when their gap is opened through voluntary or involuntary means.)
    SELECTED REFERENCES: **A Separate Reality - Page [217.7-217.8s]** (To meet an ally is no party...your gap and make you solid.") **The Eagle's Gift - Page [195.4-195.6]** (We walked to a restaurant a few...not protecting but merely defending myself.)
    SEE ALSO: *WARRIOR-HUMBLENESS, WARRIOR-DEFEND-NOTHING*

WARRIOR-PROTECT-THEMSELVES-COMMANDS-[WARRIORS MUST LEARN TO PROTECT THEMSELVES FROM THEIR OWN COMMANDS]:
(Warriors know they must learn to protect themselves from their own commands; to give the skimmings of the first attention a free hand is a dire error in judgment for which warriors pay with their chance for freedom; warriors protect themselves by avoiding the ways they have learned to make the tonal weak through self-indulging.)
    SELECTED REFERENCES: **Tales of Power - Page [136.4-136.5]** ("There is no need to treat the body...I have called that indulging.") **The Fire From Within - Page [138.8-139.2]** ("The skimmings of men," don Juan...the old seers paid for theirs.")
    SEE ALSO: *EAGLE-COMMAND, MAN-PITFALL, SKIMMINGS, ATTENTION-FIRST, WARRIOR-FREEDOM, SELF-INDULGENCE, WARRIOR-SOLIDITY*

WARRIOR-PROTECTIVE-POSITION-[THE WARRIORS' PROTECTIVE POSITION]: *(A special protective posture which warriors adopt when an aspect of the nagual seems about to overwhelm them.)*
    SELECTED REFERENCES: **The Second Ring of Power - Page [144.7-145.1]** (I told her that we were...position la Gorda had just described.)
    SEE ALSO: *WARRIOR-VIGIL-POSITION, WARRIOR-FIGHTING-FORM*

WARRIOR-PURPOSE-[THE WARRIORS' PURPOSE]: *(The warriors' purpose is learning the warriors' way; warriors must have a purpose; they can stalk themselves forever but if they have no purpose it will never make a bit of difference; the warriors' transcendental purpose is to free perception and enter the other world with their total being; in order to revive the link with intent, warriors need a rigorous, fierce purpose called unbending intent; the nagual is the only being capable of supplying unbending intent.)*
    SELECTED REFERENCES: **The Teachings of Don Juan - Page [83.9-84.3]** ("When a man starts to learn...His purpose becomes a battlefield.) **The Teachings of Don Juan - Page [110.7-110.8]** (I explained to him that what...he was capable of controlling them.) **Tales of Power - Page [97.4-97.6]** ("What are you saying, don Juan...of your life will take you.") **The Second Ring of Power - Page [62.4-62.8]** ("Pablito is my enemy not because his eyes...power, I still have my purpose.") **The Second Ring of Power - Page [152.8-152.9]** ("Because they are forces and as such...choose whether or not to keep them.") **The Second Ring of Power - Page [229.6-229.7]** ("But stalking your weaknesses is not enough...stalker is to have a purpose.") **The Second Ring of Power - Page [230.3-230.5]** ("Everybody has enough personal power for...when he thought I was indulging.) **The Second Ring of Power - Page [240.4-240.9]** ("Am I still shaped like an egg...complete is only for us Toltecs.") **The Eagle's Gift - Page [247.6-247.9]** (He told me that I had...just before the Eagle devours it.) **The Fire From Within - Page [167.6-167.9]** (As we walked, don Juan told...scorn and reject their own tradition.) **The Power of Silence - Page [42.5-42.8]** (He stressed that in order to...his individuality. That's the difficult part.") **The Art of Dreaming - Page [26.4-26.5]** ("No it isn't. Intending is much...all the cells of your body.) **The Art of Dreaming - Page [78.9-79.1]** (Sorcerers, on the contrary, bring order...anything we know to be real.")
    SEE ALSO: *WARRIOR-WAY, STALKING-ONESELF, NAGUAL-MAN-WOMAN, WARRIOR-INTENT-LINK, SORCERER-PURPOSE-TRANSCENDENTAL*

WARRIOR-PURPOSE-TRANSCENDENTAL-[THE WARRIORS' TRANSCENDENTAL PURPOSE]: *(The warriors' transcendental purpose is to free perception by changing it at its social base.)*

SELECTED REFERENCES: The Art of Dreaming - Page [78.9-79.1] (Sorcerers, on the contrary, bring order...anything we know to be real.")
SEE ALSO: *WARRIOR-PURPOSE, PERCEPTION-SOCIAL-BASE, PERCEPTION-CHANGING-SOCIAL-BASE, PERCEPTION*

WARRIOR-QUALITIES-TWO-BASIC-[THE TWO BASIC QUALITIES OF WARRIORS]: *(Warriors know that the two basic qualities of warriors are sustained effort and unbending intent.)*
SELECTED REFERENCES: The Fire From Within - Page [194.7-194.8] ("With his penchant for drama," don...warriors: sustained effort and unbending intent.)
SEE ALSO: *WARRIOR-INTENT-UNBENDING, WARRIOR-PERSISTENCE, WARRIOR-ATTRIBUTES,*

WARRIOR-QUEST-[THE WARRIORS' QUEST]: SEE: WARRIORSHIP-VS-SORCERY-[WARRIORSHIP VS SORCERY]

WARRIOR-QUEST-COMPLETION-[THE COMPLETION OF THE WARRIORS' QUEST]: *(Warriors know that the movement of the assemblage point marks the completion of the warriors' quest; to go on from there is another quest, the seers' quest proper.)*
SELECTED REFERENCES: The Fire From Within - Page [195.3-195.4] ("It goes without saying that the...it is the seers' quest proper.")
SEE ALSO: *ASSEMBLAGE-POINT-MOVING, SEER-QUEST*

WARRIOR-QUEST-FREEDOM-[THE WARRIORS' QUEST FOR FREEDOM]: *(The quest of warriors is the quest for total freedom; the warriors' quest is the quest to regain their totality, the quest for the freedom to perceive, without obsession, all that is humanly possible.)*
SELECTED REFERENCES: The Teachings of Don Juan - [84.3-84.4] ("And thus he has stumbled upon...put an end to his quest.") Tales of Power - Page [11.8] ("Each warrior has his own way...of all the barriers and disappointments.") The Fire From Within - Page [143.3-143.5] ("Is she attached to your party...unknown to the quest for freedom.") The Fire From Within - Page [228.1-228.3] ("How were they wrong, don Juan...freedom of the seers of today.) The Art of Dreaming - Page [xi.9] (The definitive reason for this work...and our commitment to his quest.) The Art of Dreaming - Page [2.5-2.6] ("And what do you call the abstract...have no interest in concrete gains.)
SEE ALSO: *WARRIOR-FREEDOM-TOTAL, TOTALITY-REGAINING, HUMAN-ALTERNATIVES-POSSIBILITIES-POTENTIAL, WARRIOR-QUEST-COMPLETION, WARRIOR-FREEDOM*

WARRIOR-QUEST-FREEDOM-VS-ADVENTURE-UNKNOWN-[THE WARRIORS' QUEST FOR FREEDOM VS THE HIGH ADVENTURE OF THE UNKNOWN]: *(Warriors know that the difference between the high adventure of the unknown and the warriors' quest for freedom is the difference between sorcery and warriorship.)*
SELECTED REFERENCES: The Fire From Within - Page [143.3-143.7] ("Is she attached to your party...la Catalina like each other.") The Fire From Within - Page [147.8-128.4] ("Be that as it may, warriors...into the unknown and love it.")
SEE ALSO: *WARRIORSHIP-VS-SORCERY UNKNOWN-HIGH-ADVENTURE, FREEDOM-TOTAL, WARRIOR-FREEDOM*

WARRIOR-QUEST-KNOWLEDGE-[THE CONTRADICTIONS OF THE WARRIORS' QUEST FOR KNOWLEDGE]: SEE: WARRIOR-CONTRADICTION-KNOWLEDGE-[THE CONTRADICTIONS OF THE WARRIORS' QUEST FOR KNOWLEDGE]

WARRIOR-QUESTIONS-[THE WARRIORS' QUESTIONS]: *(Warriors question why they in particular have been selected by power to have found*

the warriors' challenge; warriors ask questions without fear and suspicion and then assemble what they have learned without presumptuousness or piousness.)

SELECTED REFERENCES: **Tales of Power - Page [55.5-55.7s]** ("All the time. I've asked you...stop the fulfillment of that design.") **Tales of Power - Page [75.5-75.8]** ("What Genaro showed you yesterday is...one can find flaws in it.")

SEE ALSO: *WARRIOR-CHALLENGE, WARRIOR-FORTUNE-GREAT, POWER-DESIGNS*

WARRIOR-QUIETNESS-CONTROLLED-[THE WARRIORS' CONTROLLED QUIETNESS]: *(Warriors know that controlled quietness is part of the mark of the warrior.)*

SELECTED REFERENCES: **Journey to Ixtlan - Page [104.6]** (A controlled outburst and a controlled quietness were the mark of a warrior.)

SEE ALSO: *WARRIOR-MARK*

WARRIOR-RAGE-[THE WARRIORS' RAGE]: *(Warriors know that as soon as they accept their true nature they will be free from rage.)*

SELECTED REFERENCES: **The Eagle's Gift - Page [147.1-147.4]** (I could not believe the changes...anger had drained me of my energy.)

SEE ALSO: *WARRIOR-ANGER*

WARRIOR-RATIONALES-[THE WARRIORS' RATIONALES]: *(The warriors' rationales are always based on the principles of warriorship.)*

SELECTED REFERENCES: **The Eagle's Gift - Page [290.5-290.9]** (Florinda said that her benefactor gave...never pushes himself to the front.)

SEE ALSO: *WARRIOR-WAY, WARRIOR-REASONS, WARRIORSHIP*

WARRIOR-REALIZATION-FINAL-[THE WARRIORS' FINAL REALIZATION]: *(The warriors' final realization is that impeccability is the only thing that matters in the path of knowledge.")*

SELECTED REFERENCES: **The Fire From Within - Page [18.3-18.4s]** ("You haven't yet put together all...counts in the path of knowledge.")

SEE ALSO: *WARRIOR-IMPECCABILITY, KNOWLEDGE-PATH*

WARRIOR-REASONS-[THE WARRIORS' REASONS]: *(The warriors' reasons are very simple but their finesse is extreme.)*

SELECTED REFERENCES: **The Power of Silence - Page [130.1-130.3]** ("I told you you were not...I am in your debt.")

SEE ALSO: *WARRIOR-FINESSE, WARRIOR-RATIONALES*

WARRIOR-RECOLLECTION-DUALITY-[THE RECOLLECTION OF THE WARRIORS' DUALITY]: SEE: WARRIOR-DUALITY-RECOLLECTION-[THE RECOLLECTION OF THE WARRIORS' DUALITY]

WARRIOR-RECOMMENDATION-[THE RECOMMENDATION FOR WARRIORS]: *(The recommendation for warriors is not to have any material things on which to focus their power, so that they can focus their power on the spirit instead, on the true flight into the unknown.)*

SELECTED REFERENCES: **The Eagle's Gift - Page [21.6-21.8]** ("When you worry about what to...won't let you live in peace.")

SEE ALSO: *WARRIOR-SHIELDS, ATTENTION-SECOND-FACES-TWO, DREAMING-BODY-PROTECTING, WARRIOR-CROSSING-FREEDOM*

WARRIOR-REGRETS-[THE WARRIORS' REGRETS]: *(Warriors know that they have no time for regrets; if they are impeccable and view life as an endless challenge, then even if they suffer a defeat they will have only lost a battle and will suffer no regrets over that.)*

SELECTED REFERENCES: The Teachings of Don Juan - Page [51.4-51.6] (I asked him why was it ...be no pitiful regrets over that.) A Separate Reality - Page [145.6-145.6] ("You have started learning the ways...whether you like it or not.") A Separate Reality - Page [151.3-151.6] (A detached man, who knows he...to with gusto and lusty efficiency.) Tales of Power - Page [105.4-105.5] ("Only as a warrior can one...Challenges are simply challenges.") The Eagle's Gift - Page [297.7-298.3]. (Don Juan expressed the feeling that...or blessing into a living challenge.)

SEE ALSO: WARRIOR-COMPLAINTS , WARRIOR-CHALLENGE, VICTORY, DEFEAT, VICTORY-DEFEAT-EQUAL

WARRIOR-REJOICE-VICTORIES-SPIRIT-[WARRIORS REJOICE IN VICTORIES OF THE SPIRIT]: (Warriors always rejoice in the true abstract victories of their fellow men.)

SELECTED REFERENCES: Tales of Power - Page [91.7-91.8] (After I told him what I thought...if they were triumphs of the spirit.)

SEE ALSO: VICTORY, WARRIOR-WISH-WARRIOR-WELL

WARRIOR-REMORSE-[THE WARRIORS' REMORSE]: SEE: WARRIOR-DOUBTS-[THE WARRIORS' DOUBTS AND REMORSE]

WARRIOR-REQUISITES-FOUR-[THE FOUR REQUISITES FOR THE WARRIOR]: SEE: KNOWLEDGE-GOING-REQUISITES-[THE FOUR REQUISITES OF GOING TO KNOWLEDGE]

WARRIOR-REPETITION-[REPETITION FOR THE WARRIOR]: (Warriors turn the concepts of warriorship into a viable way of life by a process of repetition; the concepts of warriorship must be repeated to the point of exhaustion before warriors open themselves to them.)

SELECTED REFERENCES: The Art of Dreaming - Page [33.9-34.2] (Don Juan ended our conversation about...to function in the daily world.)

SEE ALSO: WARRIOR-WAY, WARRIOR-PERSISTENCE

WARRIOR-RESERVOIR-SECRET-[THE WARRIORS' SECRET RESERVOIR]: (Warriors know they have a hidden energetic reservoir.)

SELECTED REFERENCES: Tales of Power - Page [268.8-269.7] (I again had the sensation of being...disintegrate and be nothing once more.)

SEE ALSO: TONAL-NAGUAL-DICHOTOMY, PERCEPTION-WINGS, PERCEPTION-BARRIER-BREAKING, POWER-HIDDEN

WARRIOR-RESOLUTION-[THE WARRIORS' RESOLUTION]: (Warriors know that they never resolve anything; the spirit either resolves things or it doesn't; only the warriors' impeccability counts for anything; warriors live an impeccable life and that in itself seems to beckon the resolution, but no one knows why.)

SELECTED REFERENCES: The Power of Silence - Page [227.4-227.8] (He described the specific problem of...the solution. Why? No one knows.")

SEE ALSO: WARRIOR-IMPECCABILITY, SPIRIT, SPIRIT-DESIGNS, WARRIOR-NOTHING-PENDING

WARRIOR-RESOURCEFULNESS-[THE WARRIORS' RESOURCEFULNESS]: (The warriors' attainments and acceptance of the abstract do not make warriors intrinsically different, these things only make warriors more resourceful.)

SELECTED REFERENCES: A Separate Reality - Page [88.4-88.5] "So now you're afraid of me... trust in yourself, not in me.) The Power of Silence - Page [226.5-226.7] ("I have described to you...accept the designs of the abstract.")

SEE ALSO: POWER-DESIGNS, WARRIOR-STAGES-FOUR, WARRIOR-ACCEPTANCE, WARRIOR-ATTAINMENTS, ABSTRACT-RETURN, WARRIOR-JOURNEY-RETURN

WARRIOR-RESPECT-AMONG-[RESPECT AMONG WARRIORS]: SEE: WARRIOR-INTERVENTION-[THE WARRIORS' INTERVENTION]

WARRIOR-RESPECT-AWE-LIFE-[THE WARRIORS' RESPECT AND AWE FOR LIFE]: (Warriors know that their humbleness must be reflected in the way they respect the world around them; warriors treat everything around them with respect and do not trample on anything unless they have to; warriors know that it is important to shift the assemblage point enough to realize the tremendous price that has been paid for any life; this shift gives warriors the awe and respect which their parents never felt for life in general or for being alive in particular.)

SELECTED REFERENCES: A Separate Reality - Page [180.4-180.5] (You can survive in the world...treat the water with respect yesterday.) The Fire From Within - Page [201.3-201.4] ("My benefactor told me that my...or for being alive in particular.")

SEE ALSO: *WARRIOR-HUMBLENESS, WARRIOR-DELICACY, ASSEMBLAGE-POINT-MOVING*

WARRIOR-RESPONSIBILITY-[THE WARRIORS' RESPONSIBILITY]: SEE: RESPONSIBILITY-ASSUMING-[ASSUMING RESPONSIBILITY]

WARRIOR-RESPONSIBILITY-MAN-[WARRIORS' RESPONSIBILITY TO THEIR FELLOW MEN]: SEE: SEER-RESPONSIBILITY-MAN-[SEERS' RESPONSIBILITY TO THEIR FELLOW MEN]

WARRIOR-RETREAT-[THE WARRIORS' RETREAT]: (Warriors know they have no time for retreats; they only have time to live like warriors and be impeccable.)

SELECTED REFERENCES: A Separate Reality - Page [145.6-] ("You have started learning the ways...whether you like it or not.")

SEE ALSO: *WARRIOR-IMPECCABILITY, DEFEAT, WARRIOR-REGRETS, FAILURE*

WARRIOR-RETURN-UNKNOWN-[WILL THE WARRIOR RETURN FROM THE UNKNOWN?]: (Warriors must make a decision whether or not to return from the unknown when they are finally ready to journey into it; this decision is not a decision of reason or desire, it is a decision of will, so there is no way of knowing the outcome beforehand; few warriors survive that encounter, not because it is so hard but because the nagual is enticing beyond all imagination; if warriors choose not to return they will disappear as if the earth had swallowed them; but if they do return, they must wait like true warriors do until their particular tasks are finished; once those tasks are complete they will have command over the totality of themselves.)

SELECTED REFERENCES: Tales of Power - Page [283.6-284.7] ("This will also be the last crossroad...and the freedom of your spirit.)

SEE ALSO: *UNKNOWN-JOURNEY, INORGANIC-BEINGS-TEACHINGS, INORGANIC-BEINGS-REFUSING*

WARRIOR-REWARD-[THE WARRIORS' REWARD]: (Warriors know their reward is simply the rare opportunity to be to be impeccable in spite of their basic feelings; such an opportunity to give freely and impeccably rejuvenates warriors and renews their sense of wonder.)

SELECTED REFERENCES: The Power of Silence - Page [127.7-130.3] (Years before, I had been both...mischievousness, as he peered at me.)

SEE ALSO: *WARRIOR-CHANCE-MINIMAL, VICTORY, WARRIOR-IMPECCABILITY, WARRIOR-CARING-FOR-ANOTHER, VICTORY-WITHOUT-GLORY-REWARD*

WARRIOR-RING-POWER-[THE WARRIORS' RING OF POWER]: SEE: POWER-RING-SECOND-[THE SECOND RING OF]

WARRIOR-RISK-[THE WARRIORS' RISK]: (Warriors know that they take risks as a part of life, no matter what precautions they take; there is no guarantee that life will continue beyond the moment whether we are warriors or not.)
SELECTED REFERENCES: The Power of Silence - Page [236.3-236.6] (He paused then asked me what...bush with him, no mincing words.")
SEE ALSO: *IMMORTALITY, DEATH-ADVISER*

WARRIOR-ROMANCE-KNOWLEDGE-[THE WARRIORS' ROMANCE WITH KNOWLEDGE]: SEE: UNDERSTANDING-SHEER-[SHEER UNDERSTANDING]

WARRIOR-SADNESS-[THE WARRIORS' SADNESS]: (Warriors learn to detach themselves from their sadness; warriors seek freedom, and sadness is not freedom; sadness is as powerful as terror, both can bring the moment of silence; warriors are entitled to profound states of sadness, but that sadness is there only to make them laugh; warriors know they can combat their feelings of sadness by rolling their eyes.)
SELECTED REFERENCES: Tales of Power - Page [292.7-292.9] ("Only if one loves this earth...that gives shelter to their beings.") The Eagle's Gift - Page [124.6-124.9] ("The Nagual woman is shipwrecked somewhere...We must snap out of it.") The Eagle's Gift - Page [143.1-143.2] ("The Nagual told me that for...tries for it throughout his life.") The Fire From Within - Page [xii.7-xii.8] (Don Juan had told me that...and knowledge without sobriety are useless.) The Fire From Within - Page [97.3-97.5] (He said that the best way to...focusing all its power on sadness.) The Fire From Within - Page [129.2-129.3] (When they had calmed down, don...there only to make them laugh.) The Fire From Within - Page [260.4-260.6] ("The new seers recommend a very simple...in lieu of true mastery of *intent*.) The Fire From Within - Page [287.1-287.2] ("Who cares about sadness, he said...mysteries await us! What mysteries!")
SEE ALSO: *DEPRESSION-MELANCHOLY, EYES-ROLLING, SELF-SERIOUSNESS*

WARRIOR-SATISFACTION-[THE WARRIORS' SATISFACTION]: (The warriors' satisfaction is a natural sense of peace and attainment, a feeling that grows out of the link with intent.)
SELECTED REFERENCES : Journey to Ixtlan - Page [108.4-108.87s (I experienced an extremely pleasant feeling...as one acted as a warrior.) The Power of Silence - Page [149.8s-150.1] (Don Juan asserted that the reason...of peace, of satisfaction, of attainment.)
SEE ALSO : *PEACE, WARRIOR-ATTAINMENT, WARRIOR-INTENT-LINK*

WARRIOR-SECRETS-[THE WARRIORS' SECRETS]: (Warriors learn to show people whatever they care to show them without ever telling them exactly how they've done things; warriors establish and maintain a fog around themselves.)
SELECTED REFERENCES: Journey to Ixtlan - Page [15.6-15.9] ("Begin with simple things, such as...only if you have personal history.") Journey to Ixtlan - Page [16.8-17.5] ("From now on," he said...behave as though we know everything.") The Eagle's Gift - Page [269.3-270.5] ("I beg your pardon," I said...you go around giving lectures.)
SEE ALSO: *WARRIOR-FOG-CREATE, PERSONAL-HISTORY-ERASING*

WARRIOR-SECRETIVENESS-[THE WARRIORS' SECRETIVENESS]: SEE: WARRIOR-UNAVAILABILITY-[THE WARRIORS' UNAVAILABILITY]

WARRIOR-SEEK-CHANGE-[WARRIORS SEEK CHANGE]: SEE: CHANGE-[CHANGE], WARRIOR-SEEK-OTHER-SIDE-COIN-[WARRIORS SEEK THE OTHER SIDE OF THE COIN]

WARRIOR-SEEK-DEATH-NOT-[WARRIORS DO NOT SEEK DEATH]: SEE: WARRIOR-DEATH-CHOOSE-NOT-[WARRIORS DO NOT CHOOSE DEATH]

WARRIOR-SEEK-OTHER-SIDE-COIN-[WARRIORS SEEK THE OTHER SIDE OF THE COIN]: (Warriors know that in the course of the journey with power, they must eventually seek the other side of the coin, or the alternate experience to the one they already know.)
SELECTED REFERENCES: **The Fire From Within - Page** [114.6-115.3] ("When you're here, you're always in...We are waiting for freedom!) **The Fire From Within - Page** [210.7-211.1] ("You are going to catch a boost...two sides to a coin," Genaro whispered.)
SEE ALSO: *WARRIOR-WAY*

WARRIOR-VS-SEER-[WARRIOR VS SEER]: (To "see" without first being a warrior makes a man weak, it gives him a false sense of meekness and makes him retreat; the warriors' teacher endeavors to show the warrior the inexplicable forces of the universe as sorcerers perceive them because only under that terrifying impact can human beings become warriors.)
SELECTED REFERENCES: **A Separate Reality - Page** [214.8-215.2] ("It is my commitment to teach...a warrior so you won't crumble.)
SEE ALSO: *WARRIOR, SEER, KNOWLEDGE-PATH-STEPS-FOUR*

WARRIOR-SEIZURE-[THE WARRIORS' SEIZURE]: (Warriors sometimes experience a seizure-like reaction when their bodies confront the presence of the nagual.)
SELECTED REFERENCES: **The Fire From Within - Page** [68.3-69.2] ("Just relax," he went on...straight out to your normal self.")
SEE ALSO: *NAGUAL-FACING. WARRIOR-MOTOR-CONTROL-LOSS-OF, SORCERER-MUTENESS, WARRIOR-SOLIDITY*

WARRIOR-SELF-BEGINS-ENDS-[FOR THE WARRIOR EVERYTHING BEGINS AND ENDS WITH THE SELF]: (Warriors know that everything begins and ends with the self; warriors' contact with the abstract causes them to overcome their feelings of self-importance, thereby causing their sense of self to become abstract and impersonal.)
SELECTED REFERENCES: **The Power of Silence - Page** [32.1-32.2] ("Are you saying, don Juan, that...the self becomes abstract and impersonal.)
SEE ALSO: *SELF, ABSTRACT, WARRIOR-WAR, WARRIOR-SELF-(ALL)*

WARRIOR-SELF-CONFIDENCE-[THE WARRIORS' SELF-CONFIDENCE]: (The average man seeks certainty in the eyes of the onlooker and calls that self-confidence; warriors seek impeccability in their own eyes and call that humbleness; for warriors, humbleness is self-confidence; the average man is hooked to his fellow men while warriors are hooked only to themselves; warrior aren't foolish enough to believe they can find assurance in the eyes of any other man, they know only that they must be impeccable in their actions and feelings; warriors must have self-confidence if they are ever to claim knowledge as power.)
SELECTED REFERENCES: **Tales of Power - Page** [6.8-7.3] ("You know exactly what you need...impeccable in one's actions and feelings.") **The Eagle's Gift - Page** [268.7-268.9] (I

asked her if she minded...woman can liberate you from that.) **The Art of Dreaming - Page [73.2-73.4]** (Don Juan, with extreme patience, pointed...world, of being able to predict.)
SEE ALSO: *WARRIOR-HUMBLENESS, WARRIOR-IMPECCABILITY, WARRIOR-ASSUREDNESS, WARRIOR-ASSURANCE, KNOWLEDGE-CLAIMING-POWER*

WARRIOR-SELF-EXAMINATION-[THE WARRIORS' SELF-EXAMINATION]: (Warriors are constantly observing themselves and their behavior; warriors become self-oriented, not in a selfish way, but rather in the sense of a total and continuous examination of the self; this self-examination helps warriors in their battle to transform their relationship with the individual self that has deprived them of power.)
SELECTED REFERENCES: **The Eagle's Gift - Page [186.6-186.7]** (He conceived that immersion in his...also forced a shattering self-examination.) **The Fire From Within - Page [24.1]** (A warrior is self-oriented, not...and continuous examination of the self.) **The Fire From Within - Page [114.8-115.1]** ("I've explained to you that the...the other side of the coin.") **The Art of Dreaming - Page [95.7-95.9]** (It did not take much for me...refuse to listen to my accounts.)
SEE ALSO: *WARRIOR-WAR, SELF, WARRIOR-SELF-EXAMINATION*

WARRIOR-SELF-INDIVIDUAL-[THE WARRIORS' INDIVIDUAL SELF]: (Warriors go to war with the individual self; warriors struggle to relinquish their individuality as their link with the spirit is revived.)
SELECTED REFERENCES: **The Power of Silence - Page [42.7-43.1]** ("An apprentice is someone who is...the volunteers simply refuse to change.)
SEE ALSO: *WARRIOR-WAR, SELF, VOLUNTEER, SELF-IMPORTANCE-LOSING*

WARRIOR-SELF-ORIENTATION-[THE WARRIORS' SELF-ORIENTATION]: (Warriors become self-oriented, not in a selfish way, but in the sense of a total and continuous examination of the self; this self-orientation is not designed to bolster the warriors' sense of self but to accomplish exactly the opposite; warriors have gone to war with the individual self that has deprived them of power and self-orientation is a way of monitoring their relationship with their self-reflective adversary.)
SELECTED REFERENCE: **The Fire From Within - Page [24.1]** (A warrior is self-oriented, not...and continuous examination of the self.)
SEE ALSO: *WARRIOR-WAR, SELF, WARRIOR-SELF-BEGINS-ENDS, WARRIOR-SELF-EXAMINATION*

WARRIOR-SELF-RESTRAINT-[THE WARRIORS' SELF-RESTRAINT]: (Warriors realize the importance of exercising their self-restraint, the restraint and the curtailment of the agendas of the personal self.)
SELECTED REFERENCES: **The Eagle's Gift - Page [186.3-186.8]** (Insofar as his own awakening was concerned...also forced a shattering self-examination.) **The Eagle's Gift - Page [187.1-187.6]** (The second topic was the cultural context...under the harshest conditions of suppression.)
SEE ALSO: *WARRIOR-ATTRIBUTES, WARRIOR-SOBRIETY*

WARRIOR-SENTIMENTAL-[THE WARRIOR IS NOT SENTIMENTAL]: (Warriors know that they must maintain a state of awareness that permits no sentimentality; for warriors there is only action.)
SELECTED REFERENCES: **The Fire From Within - Page [297.4-297.6]** (A couple of days later, all...in a state of total war.)
SEE ALSO: *ACTING-TALKING, SELF-COMPASSION, WARRIOR-SOBRIETY*

WARRIOR-SERENITY-[THE WARRIORS' SERENITY]: (Warriors know that they must acquire serenity and sobriety to withstand the pressure of the unknown and the unknowable; there is no better way for warriors to acquire this serenity than through the application of a construct called the three phase progression.)

SELECTED REFERENCES: The Fire From Within - Page [19.5-19.7] ("The average man's reaction is to...stand the pressure of the unknowable.")
SEE ALSO: *WARRIOR-SOBRIETY, PROGRESSION-THREE-PHASE*

WARRIOR-SERIOUSNESS-[THE WARRIORS' SERIOUSNESS]: *(Warriors know that their seriousness must remain focused on the quest to abstract themselves; the seriousness of self-reflection will only lead them to aberration and morbidity; the seriousness of the warrior is the sobriety of the warrior, nothing more and nothing less.)*

SELECTED REFERENCES: The Teachings of Don Juan - Page [50.6-50.7] ("You are the only person I...And that produces a terrible fatigue.") Tales of Power - Page [51.9-52.1] ("How can I jump over this one...sat down by my side.) The Fire From Within - Page [24.7-25.1] (Don Juan explained that the mistake...deadly seriousness while warriors do not.) The Fire From Within - Page [59.4-60.1] (Genaro leaned over toward me from...he asked me in mock seriousness.)
SEE ALSO: *WARRIOR-SOBRIETY, ABSTRACT-TO, SELF-REFLECTION, WARRIOR-LIGHTNESS, STALKING-RESULTS-THREE*

WARRIOR-SEX-[SEX FOR THE WARRIOR]: *(Warriors know that the Eagle's command concerning sex is that it be used to create life and bestow the glow of awareness; warriors also know that the only real energy they possesses is life-bestowing sexual energy; warriors also know that the bestowal of awareness leaves them incomplete; this knowledge makes warriors permanently conscious of their energetic responsibility; warriors know that if they want to learn to "see", they must become miserly with their sexual energy; impeccable warriors know that it is a mistake to recklessly waste the life-bestowing force of sex and not have children, and that it is also a mistake not to know that having children severely taxes the glow of the parent's awareness.)*

SELECTED REFERENCES: The Fire From Within - Page [59.9-61.1] (I earnestly asked don Juan what...*seen* superimposed on the body itself.")
SEE ALSO: *SEX, WARRIOR-IMPECCABILITY ENERGY, SEE, AWARENESS-BESTOWAL, AWARENESS-GLOW, WARRIOR-SEX-WEAKEST-MOMENT, SEXUAL-ENERGY-CONSERVING, WARRIOR-COMPLETE*

WARRIOR-SEX-WEAKEST-MOMENT-[SEX IS THE WARRIORS' WEAKEST MOMENT]*(Warriors know that engaging in sexual activity leads them to their weakest and most vulnerable moment.)*

SELECTED: The Second Ring of Power - Page [63.2-63.4] ("At the beginning everything worked fine...to that moment with my body.) The Second Ring of Power - Page [126.1-126.9] ("Why is the Nagual trying to...not overpower you even with that.") The Second Ring of Power - Page [135.3-135.7] ("Soledad has to take her edge...would then have come after us.) The Eagle's Gift - Page [37.9-38.2] (Their bodies are tightly sealed...to it regardless of my discomfort.) The Art of Dreaming - Page [104.3-104.6] (I asked don Juan what exactly...closet, they were no longer there.")
SEE ALSO: *SEX-LUMINOUS-REALITY, SEXUAL-ENERGY-CONSERVING*

WARRIOR-SHIELDS-[THE WARRIORS' SHIELDS]: *(Warriors deliberately select the items that make their world, for every item they choose is a shield to protect them from the onslaughts of the forces they are trying to use; as part of the warriors' change of continuity, warriors exchange the shields of the average man for the shields of the warrior; the warriors' shields give great peace and pleasure, and warriors use them to take their minds from their fright, thereby helping close their gaps and making themselves solid again after encountering the unknown.)*

SELECTED REFERENCES: **A Separate Reality - Page [216.3-218.2]** (This brings us to the last...items of a path with heart.") **A Separate Reality - Page [219.6-220.3]** ("Your problem is that you confuse...price to pay for our shields!") **A Separate Reality - Page [225.3-225.5]** (At that crucial instant a thought...I could see his entire face.) **Tales of Power - Page [74.9-75.3]** ("Watch out!" he said. "A warrior...is a crappy way of dying.") **The Second Ring of Power - Page [306.7-307.2S]** (Don Juan had also said that...ourselves with our endless internal dialogue.) **The Eagle's Gift - Page [21.6-21.8]** ("When you worry about what to...won't let you live in peace.") **The Fire From Within - Page [173.1]** ("The new seers realized that in...that suddenly become aligned in *dreaming*.") **The Fire From Within - Page [222.4-222.7]** ("What exactly is the tumbler...us a false sense of security.") **The Power of Silence - Page [47.9-48.1]** (He remarked that each of us...to disguise my complacency as independence.) **The Art of Dreaming - Page [83.5-83.7]** (He had remarked time and time...a foremost assailant of our rationality.)
SEE ALSO: *CONTINUITY, GAP, ATTENTION-FIRST, WARRIOR-SOLIDITY, PATH-HEART-WITH, GAP*

WARRIOR-SHIVER-[THE WARRIORS' SHIVER]: (The warriors' shiver is a reaction to a confrontation with the awesomeness of the unknown and the brink of the unknown abyss; on the left side there are no more tears and warriors can no longer weep, so the only expression of the warriors' anguish is a shiver that comes from the very depths of the universe; it is as if one of the Eagle's emanations is anguish; the warriors' shiver is infinite.)

SELECTED REFERENCES: **Tales of Power - Page [159.2-159.3]** (A million questions and feelings came...on blowing a cloud over it.) **The Eagle's Gift - Page [310.4]** (The setting of the poem was overpowering. I felt a shiver.) **The Eagle's Gift - Page [311.5-311.6]** (Don Juan had told me that...held me, I felt that shiver.) **The Fire From Within - Page [238.3]** (I felt a shiver run through...on talking in a hoarse whisper.) **The Fire From Within - Page [280.1-280.2]** (I felt a weird tremor that...I either fainted or fell asleep.) **The Art of Dreaming - Page [47.9-48.1]** ("I'm not clear, don Juan, about...comes from the marrow of the bones.") **The Art of Dreaming - Page [49.5-49.7]** (In my waking hours I worried...I had no fear at all.)
SEE ALSO: *WARRIOR-ANGUISH, WARRIOR-ANXIETY, UNKNOWN,*

WARRIOR-SHORTCOMINGS-[THE WARRIORS' SHORTCOMINGS]: (Warriors never know how their own shortcomings may conform to the designs of power; the warriors' shortcomings may actually represent an avenue to power, in which case warriors can't say that power would flow to them if their lives were different.)

SELECTED REFERENCES: **Tales of Power - [195.1-195.3]** ("That's a meaningless statement," he said...if your life would be different.) **The Power of Silence - Page [127.4-127.6]** ("Sometimes you are absolutely unbearable...It was a private joke.) **The Art of Dreaming - Page [42.6-42.7]** (Accepting my shortcomings seemed to give...of any item in my dreams.)
SEE ALSO: *POWER-FLOW, POWER-DESIGNS*

WARRIOR-SHOVE-[THE WARRIORS' SHOVE]: (The warriors' shove is a technique for shrinking the tonal; the shove of an impeccable warrior can cause a shift into another area of awareness; it is not the procedure that is important, the technique is only utilizable if both participants are impeccable and imbued with personal power.)

SELECTED REFERENCES: **The Teachings of Don Juan - Page [186.3]** (All he needs is a gentle shove...the ends of the other world.) **Tales of Power - Page [146.9-147.7]** (I wanted to hurry up, perhaps...and I would smash against it.) **Tales of Power - Page [156.5-156.8]** ("The *tonal* shrinks at given times...you ended up in the market.") **The Second Ring of Power - Page [286.1-286.2]** (But when he shoved you, your...entire being went through the crack.) **The Eagle's Gift - Page [56.3-56.4]** (She pointed to me and then...that a display of Indian love?") **The Eagle's Gift - Page [59.2-59.4]** (She pointed to me and pushed me...time in order to jolt you.") **The Eagle's Gift - Page [99.9-100.2]** (The following day at ten o'clock...the activities of the people there.) **The Eagle's Gift - Page [273.9-274.4]** (The Next time don Juan took...impeccable and imbued with personal power.) **The Eagle's Gift - Page [280.1-280.2]** (The next time I went to Florinda's...the wall of fog is visible.) **The Fire From Within - Page [117.7-117.9]** ("Genaro again pushed your assemblage point...the new seers strive to elucidate.")
SEE ALSO: *TONAL-SHRINKING, ASSEMBLAGE-POINT-PUSHING*

WARRIOR-SIEGE-[THE WARRIOR UNDER SIEGE]: (*Warriors are never under siege because to be under siege implies that they have personal possessions which can be blockaded; warriors have nothing in the world except their impeccability and that can never be threatened.*)
SELECTED REFERENCES: The Eagle's Gift - Page [215.8-215.9] (His benefactor told don Juan that...impeccability, and impeccability cannot be threatened.)
SEE ALSO: WARRIOR-IMPECCABILITY, WARRIOR-DEFEND-NOTHING, WARRIOR-HOLDINGS-GIVING-UP

WARRIOR-SILENCE-[THE WARRIORS' SILENCE]: (*Warriors know they must maintain silence while they allow their bodies the chance to remember; warriors are silent rather than indulging in over analysis with regard to acts of power which they have experienced.*)
SELECTED REFERENCES: The Eagle's Gift - Page [59.6-60.3] (True to her practice of waiting...we can't talk about something else.")
SEE ALSO: OVER-ANALYSIS, REMEMBERING-TASK

WARRIOR-SIMPLICITY-[THE WARRIORS' SIMPLICITY]: (*The warriors' life is simple and tight; there is nothing superfluous in the life of the warrior.*)
SELECTED REFERENCE: The Second Ring of Power - Page [243.6-243.8] ("If your grandfather and father would...and simplicity of a warrior's life.)
SEE ALSO: WARRIOR-LIFE-TIGHT, WARRIOR-WAY

WARRIOR-SINGLE-MINDEDNESS-[THE WARRIORS' DEDICATION AND SINGLE-MINDEDNESS]: SEE: WARRIOR-DEDICATION-[THE WARRIORS' DEDICATION AND SINGLE-MINDEDNESS]

WARRIOR-SOBRIETY-[THE WARRIORS' SOBRIETY]: (*The warriors' sobriety is the warriors' internal strength, a sense of equanimity, a feeling of being at ease; sobriety is a profound bent for examination and understanding; sobriety is ruthlessness, the opposite of self-pity and self-importance; sobriety is a position of the assemblage point.*)
SELECTED REFERENCES: Tales of Power - Page [239.8-239.9] ("Erasing personal history and *dreaming* should...together everything in a sorcerer's world.) Tales of Power - Page [243.1-243.3] (It had indeed taken me years...done in states of sober consciousness.) Tales of Power - Page [254.1-254.3] ("That's the side of the *tonal*...can only cover a small area.) The Second Ring of Power - Page [90.2-90.3] (My wrath disappeared and was replaced...don Juan's terms, stopped the world.) The Eagle's Gift - Page [204.5-204.6] (Silvio Manuel's case was different...everyone around him acknowledged his difference.) The Eagle's Gift - Page [219.2] (Later on, sobriety took hold of his...and the success of his party.) The Eagle's Gift - Page [261.2-261.4] (The more I practiced, the clearer...*dreamer* from excess and bizarre undertakings.) The Eagle's Gift - Page [265.1-265.3] (Zuleica took us systematically on voyages...rational causes or reasons for anything.) The Fire From Within - Page [xii.7-xii.8] (Don Juan had told me that...and knowledge without sobriety are useless.) The Fire From Within - Page [19.5-19.7] ("The average man's reaction is to...stand the pressure of the unknowable.") The Fire From Within - Page [41.6-42.8] ("This is simply the case of something...for it, a more accurate one.") The Fire From Within - Page [54.1-54.2] ("The same thing happened to the...realization, for they have realized nothing.) The Fire From Within - Page [73.2-73.6] ("For example, seers have to be...affection, sobriety, love, or even kindness.") The Fire From Within - Page [120.3-120.5] (He said that two options are...always returns to its original position.) The Fire From Within - Page [137.4-137.5] (He also said that women seers...eight women seers in his party.) The Fire From Within - Page [175.9-176.4] (With that system, the new seers...the movement of the assemblage point.) The Fire From Within - Page [181.4-181.5] (I asked him how *intent* helps...the movement of the assemblage point.) The Fire From Within - Page [216.1-216.2] (He said that the sobriety needed...the barrier of perception with impunity.) The Fire From Within - [297.9-298.1] ("The old seers used to say that...manipulation of intent through sober commands.") The Fire From Within - [298.7-298.9] (Don Juan said that adventurous men...the futility of self-importance.) The Power of Silence - Page [20.6-20.7] (The nagual then *saw* her luminosity...what misfortunes

it would cause her.) **The Power of Silence - Page [23.7-23.9]** (Don Juan commented that that was...world that admitted very few mistakes.) **The Power of Silence - Page [29.1-29.2]** (He finally commented that the nagual...training as an apprentice in sorcery.) **The Power of Silence - Page [36.5]** (He said that the nagual Elias...task of answering don Juan's questions.) **The Power of Silence - Page [58.6-58.8]** (Don Juan used to repeat every...the moving of the assemblage point.) **The Power of Silence - Page [104.2-104.3]** (Don Juan explained that at one...needed to manage all that power.) **The Power of Silence - Page [104.1-105.1]** (Don Juan explained that at one...nothing but direct contact with *intent*.) **The Power of Silence - Page [109.6-109.7]** ("The idea of death therefore is...we can protect ourselves from it.") **The Power of Silence - Page [154.4-154.6]** ("The position of self-reflection...self-importance. Ruthlessness is sobriety.") **The Power of Silence - Page [265.5-265.7]** ("Go home and think about the...reach the place of silent knowledge.") **The Art of Dreaming - Page [28.7]** ("Is it dangerous?" "And how...to be a very sober affair.) **The Art of Dreaming - Page [36.2-36.4]** (As I practiced focusing and holding...talk about it. Just do it!") **The Art of Dreaming - Page [41.6-42.2]** ("There's one problem with the second...the only safety valve for dreamers.") **The Art of Dreaming - Page [124.6-124.9]** ("I am very pleased, but very...to concreteness, a most undesirable state.") **The Art of Dreaming - Page [173.3]** (Now more than ever you need...ancient times and those of modern men.") **The Art of Dreaming - Page [203.4-203.6]** (With the fervor of someone who...they could no longer support them.)

SEE ALSO: *RUTHLESSNESS, WARRIOR-WAY, DREAMER-SAFETY VALVE, ASSEMBLAGE-POINT-POSITION, SELF-PITY, SELF-IMPORTANCE*

WARRIOR-SOBRIETY-VS-EMOTIONALITY-[THE WARRIORS' SOBRIETY VS THE WARRIORS' EMOTIONALITY]: (Warriors know that without sobriety, they have no real chance to understand anything; emotional realizations mean nothing when it comes to understanding what a warrior has "seen".)

SELECTED REFERENCES: The Fire From Within - Page [53.7-54.2] (He reiterated that my concentration had...realization, for they have realized nothing.)
SEE ALSO: *WARRIOR-SOBRIETY, REALIZATION*

WARRIOR-SOLACE-[THE WARRIORS' SOLACE]: SEE: WARRIOR-PRESSURE-[WARRIORS RELIEVE THEIR PRESSURE]

WARRIOR-SOLIDITY-[THE WARRIORS' SOLIDITY]: (Warriors know that until they have conserved enough energy to withstand the onslaughts of the nagual, encounters with the unknown weaken them and open their gaps; warriors often use immersion in water to help solidify themselves after such encounters with power; warriors can also solidify themselves using anything else which connects them to the first attention and its inventory.)

SELECTED REFERENCES: A Separate Reality - Page [217.7-217.8] (To meet an ally is no party...your gap and make you solid.") **A Separate Reality - Page [247.5-247.7]** (I asked him the meaning of my experience...you're healed and your gap is closed.") **A Separate Reality - Page [261.6-261.8]** (Don Juan stood up and made me...in his effort to help me.) **Journey to Ixtlan - Page [35.6-35.7]** ("Yes" I finally said. "Let me...he said. "You're too solid.") **Tales of Power - Page [48.6-48.8]** ("Does the double have corporealness...you feel me as being solid.") **Tales of Power - Page [72.9-73.3]** (Even though I was completely myself...out how they had done it.) **Tales of Power - Page [75.1-75.2]** ("But I don't like to be that way...That's your only shield now.) **Tales of Power - Page [89.8-90.3]** (He was commanding me to surface by...my stomach and neck, soaking me.) **Tales of Power - Page [168.8-170.4]** (Don Juan and don Genaro came...however, what they intended to do.) **Tales of Power - Page [187.6-187.9]** (I practically huddled against don Juan...the darkness would be no obstacle.) **Tales of Power - Page [270.3-270.5]** (Don Juan walked me slowly, pushing down...earth had again consolidated my form.) **The Second Ring of Power - Page [210.3-210.7]** (As you two ran toward the...wasted you precious power for nothing.") **The Second Ring of Power - Page [321.8-321.9]** ("You were like pieces of fog...on you, you became solid again.") **The Eagle's Gift - Page [48.4]** ("A talk between the two of us...must allow ourselves time to heal.") **The Fire From Within - Page [70.5-71.2]** (Watching them laugh, I was convinced...had succeeded by making me rage.) **The Fire From Within - Page [89.8-89.9]** (The force that had enveloped me...thawed out by tiny degrees.) **The Fire From Within - Page [221.9-222.2]** (Don Juan said that I had successfully...water for short periods of time.) **The Fire From Within - Page [280.6-280.7]** (Don Juan had caught up with me...no end to my self-

importance.) **The Power of Silence - Page [235.1-235.2]** (He came out on the left...off and he was whole again.) **The Power of Silence - Page [251.5-251.6]** ("Consider what happens to you," he...supreme accomplishment of magic, of *intending*.)
SEE ALSO: *NAGUAL-ASSAULT, UNKNOWN, GAP*

WARRIOR-SOLITUDE-[THE WARRIORS' SOLITUDE]: (The poignant solitude of the warrior who lives to escape to total freedom.)
SELECTED REFERENCES: **The Fire From Within - Page [127.6-128.4]** (The thought of her gazing at...*breaks loose and flows into infinity.*)
SEE ALSO: *FREEDOM-TOTAL, WARRIOR-LONELINESS, ETERNITY-VS-HUMANNESS*

WARRIOR-SORCERER-[THE WARRIOR-SORCERER]: (The warrior-sorcerer is the true abstract sorcerer.)
SELECTED REFERENCES: **The Power of Silence - Page [240.4]** (At the same time, the nagual...audience of lovers of the unknown.)
SEE ALSO: *SORCERER-ABSTRACT, WARRIORSHIP-VS-SORCERY, WARRIOR, SORCERER, SORCERER-SEER-WARRIOR*

WARRIOR-VS-SORCERER-[THE WARRIOR VS THE SORCERER]: SEE: WARRIORSHIP-VS-SORCERY-[WARRIORSHIP VS SORCERY]

WARRIOR-SORCERER-FROM-[FROM WARRIOR TO SORCERER]: (When warriors have acquired will and are capable of grabbing things with it, then it can rightfully be said that they have become sorcerers.)
SELECTED REFERENCES: **A Separate Reality - Page [152.4-152.6]** ("When the convulsions cease the warrior...and that he has acquired will.")
SEE ALSO: *WARRIOR, SORCERER, KNOWLEDGE-PATH-STEPS-FOUR, WARRIOR-SORCERER*

WARRIOR-SORCERER-SEER-[FROM WARRIOR TO SORCERER TO SEER]: (A person can become a warrior and then, through the acquisition of will, become a sorcerer; but with continued effort, the individual can go further still and learn to "see"; once warrior-sorcerers learn to "see", they no longer need to live like warriors or be sorcerers; upon learning to "see" they become everything by becoming nothing; warrior-sorcerer-seers can then get anything they desire, but they desire nothing; instead of playing with their fellow men as if they were toys, they meet them in the midst of their folly; warrior-sorcerer-seers control their folly and no longer have any active interest in their fellow men, because "seeing" has detached them from everything they knew before.)
SELECTED REFERENCES: **A Separate Reality - Page [153.3-153.6]** ("My benefactor was a sorcerer of...from absolutely everything that he knew before.")
SEE ALSO: *WARRIOR, SORCERER, WARRIOR-SORCERER, SEER, SEEING, KNOWLEDGE-PATH-STEPS-FOUR, SEEING-VS-WARRIORSHIP, WARRIOR-DESIRE, WARRIOR-WANTS, WARRIOR-FOLLY, EVERYTHING-NOTHING*

WARRIOR-SPEECHLESS-[WARRIORS ARE RENDERED SPEECHLESS]: SEE: WARRIOR-MOTOR-CONTROL-LOSS-OF-[WARRIORS LOSE THEIR MOTOR CONTROL], SORCERER-MUTENESS-[THE SORCERERS' MUTENESS]

WARRIOR-SPIRIT-[THE WARRIORS' SPIRIT OF THE WARRIOR]: (Warriors seek to repair their spirit, to purge it and make it perfect; warriors know that to seek the perfection of the spirit is the only task worthy of their efforts.)
SELECTED REFERENCES: **A Separate Reality - Page [215.2-215.5]** (I have also heard you say...impeccable, a warrior laughs and laughs.") **Journey to Ixtlan - Page [108.4-109.1]** (I

experienced an extremely pleasant feeling...only task worthy of our manhood.") **Journey to Ixtlan - Page [120.9-121.3]** ("The mood of a warrior is not...It takes power to do that.") **Journey to Ixtlan - Page [137.8]** (He said that the battle of power...to remain trapped in those mountains.) **Tales of Power - Page [133.7-133.9]** ("I said that today was going...my warrior's spirit, my warrior's *tonal.*) **Tales of Power - Page [249.5]** (I once told you that the...true measure of a warrior's spirit.") **Tales of Power - Page [294.2-294.4]** ("Only the love for this splendorous...Only then does it make sense.") **The Second Ring of Power - Page [131.8-132.1]** (I asked la Gorda what the Nagual...children all their lives, that's all.") **The Second Ring of Power - Page [189.5-189.6]** (His words plunged me into a....body and freedom to my spirit.) **The Fire From Within - Page [19.6-19.7]** (We know better now. We know...stand the pressure of the unknowable.") **The Fire From Within - Page [24.3-24.5]** ("Does this mean you couldn't...but also for enjoyment and happiness.") **The Fire From Within - Page [127.7-127.9]** (Don Juan had defined the scope...only release that her spirit had.)

 SEE ALSO: *SPIRIT, WARRIOR-IMPECCABILITY, SPIRIT-PERFECTING, WARRIOR-SPIRIT-MEASURE*

WARRIOR-SPIRIT-MEASURE-[THE TRUE MEASURE OF THE WARRIORS' SPIRIT]: (Warriors know that impeccability is the only act which is free and thus the one true measure of the warriors' spirit.)

 SELECTED REFERENCES: Tales of Power - Page [249.4-249.5] ("In the life of a warrior...true measure of a warrior's spirit.")
 SEE ALSO: *WARRIOR-IMPECCABILITY, WARRIOR-SPIRIT*

WARRIOR-SPLIT-TWO-[THE WARRIOR IS SPLIT IN TWO]: (Warriors know that they must somehow break the unity of the tonal without endangering their being; warriors spend years sweeping clean the island of the tonal so that one day they can "sneak off it" in a manner of speaking; the splitting of a human being is the gateway to that escape; the act of being split is the act of bringing forth the double.)

 SELECTED REFERENCES: Tales of Power - Page [184.1-185.9] (Don Genaro exchanged a strange look with...of the field of eucalyptus trees.) Tales of Power - Page [192.6-193.5] (I asked him about the uncharted perceptions...I felt very good for you.") The Second Ring of Power - Page [198.5-199.5] ("The reason we called him the ...why he's so screwed up now.") The Art of Dreaming - Page [51.5-51.8] (The cunningness of sorcerers, cultivated through...it all made sense to me.)
 SEE ALSO: *DREAMING-BODY, UNITY, TONAL-ISLAND, PERCEPTION-SPLIT*

WARRIOR-STAGES-FOUR-[THE FOUR STAGES OF THE WARRIOR]: (Warriors pass through four stages along the path of knowledge in terms of the connection with intent; 1) the first stage is when warriors have a rusty, untrustworthy link with intent; 2) the second is when they succeed in cleaning it; 3) the third is when they learn to manipulate it; 4) the fourth is when warriors learn to accept the designs of the abstract.)

 SELECTED REFERENCES: The Power of Silence - Page [226.5-226.7] ("I have described to you, in many...accept the designs of the abstract.")
 SEE ALSO: *KNOWLEDGE-PATH, WARRIOR-INTENT-LINK, WARRIOR-ACCEPTANCE, WILL-VS-INTENT, POWER-DESIGNS*

WARRIOR-STANCE-[THE WARRIORS' STANCE]: (Warriors know they need to adopt a special stance for wrestling with an ally.)

 SELECTED REFERENCES: Journey to Ixtlan -Page [257.9-258.8] ("I was young when I first...had the shape of a man.)
 SEE ALSO: *ALLIES, WARRIOR-STAND, ALLIES-WRESTLING*

WARRIOR-STAND-[WARRIORS MUST MAKE THEIR STAND]: (Warriors know that when they encounter an opponent that is not an ordinary human being, they must make their stand; the warriors' stand is the only thing that makes them invulnerable.)

SELECTED REFERENCES: **Journey to Ixtlan - Page [225.6-225.7]** ("What was I supposed to do...only thing that makes him invulnerable.")
SEE ALSO: *WORTHY-OPPONENT, ALLIES, WARRIOR-LAST-STAND, ALLIES-WRESTLING*

WARRIOR-STEPS-[THE WARRIORS' STEPS]: *(Warriors know the contradiction surrounding the steps that warriors take on the path of knowledge; on the one hand, warriors must follow certain steps, because in those steps they find their strength; on the other hand, warriors also know that there are no steps to anything warriors do, there is only personal power; warriors never know how power will provide for them, it may provide them with a set of specific steps or it may provide for them to circumvent those same steps in an unimaginable way.)*
SELECTED REFERENCES: **The Teachings of Don Juan - Page [158.5-158.6]** ("Is it so very difficult to...Without them we are nothing.") **A Separate Reality - Page [134.1-134.5]** ("First you must live like a warrior...which of course is right for you.") **The Eagle's Gift - Page [128.1]** ("I'm sure that if we try...And right now we have it.)
SEE ALSO: *KNOWLEDGE-PATH, POWER-PERSONAL, WARRIOR-IMPECCABILITY, WARRIOR-CONTRADICTION-KNOWLEDGE*

WARRIOR-STRATEGIC-INVENTORY-[THE WARRIORS' STRATEGIC INVENTORY]: SEE: WARRIOR-INVENTORY-STRATEGIC-[THE WARRIORS' STRATEGIC INVENTORY]

*WARRIOR-STRATEGY-[THE WARRIORS' STRATEGY]: *(Life for warriors is an exercise in strategy; warriors sets their lives strategically and battle to the very end; warriors fight self-importance as a matter of strategy.)*
SELECTED REFERENCES: **A Separate Reality - Page [151.5-151.6]** ("And thus with an awareness of...to with gusto and lusty efficiency.) **A Separate Reality - Page [181.5-181.7]** ("Life for a warrior is an...would be battling to the end.") **A Separate Reality - Page [182.3-182.6]** ("It is not possible to live...I simply will not come around.") **A Separate Reality - Page [204.2]** ("A warrior lives strategically," he said...never carries loads he cannot handle.") **Journey to Ixtlan - Page [x.9-xi.1]** ("Your friend is not a warrior..."A warrior proceeds strategically.") **Journey to Ixtlan - Page [226.7]** ("It is meaningless to complain...is the strategy of your life.") **Journey to Ixtlan - Page [227.4-227.8]** ("You are in a terrible bind...had to run away from them.") **The Eagle's Gift - Page [215.8-216.1]** (His benefactor told don Juan that...should strategically use every means available.) **The Fire From Within - Page [14.6-14.8]** ("Self-importance is not something simple...to those who have accomplished it.") **The Fire From Within - Page [15.2-15.3]** ("Warriors fight self-importance as a matter...I say in terms of morality.") **The Fire From Within - Page [16.4-16.6]** (He said that the most effective...and is called the petty tyrant.) **The Fire From Within - Page [18.3-18.4s]** ("You haven't yet put together all...counts in the path of knowledge.") **The Fire From Within - Page [24.2-24.3]** ("At that time, I was barred...them to me through his strategy.") **The Fire From Within - Page [24.7-24.9]** (Don Juan explained that the mistake...had over the simple-minded Spaniards.) **The Fire From Within - Page [26.4-26.5]** (Don Juan explained that his benefactor's...his weaknesses, his quirks of behavior.) **The Fire From Within - Page [193.6-193.7]** (Don Juan explained that everything his...they would have the necessary impact.)
SEE ALSO: *WARRIOR-WAY, WARRIOR-MOOD, STRATEGY-NEW-SEER*

WARRIOR-STRATEGY-HIGHER-ORDER-[WARRIORS TAKE COVER WITH A HIGHER ORDER]: *(Warriors know that as part of their stalking strategy they sometimes must take cover with a higher order.)*
SELECTED REFERENCES: **The Fire From Within - Page [27.3-27.5]** (He added that his benefactor's strategy...for her health and well-being.)
SEE ALSO: *WARRIOR-STRATEGY, STALKING-ART, TONAL-REFUGE-NAGUAL*

WARRIOR-STRATEGY-MAP-[WARRIORS MAP THEIR STRATEGY]:
(When warriors are under fire, they know that they must go to work mapping their strategy instead of feeling sorry for themselves.)
    SELECTED REFERENCES: **The Fire From Within - Page [26.4-26.5]** (Don Juan explained that his benefactor's...his weaknesses, his quirks of behavior.)
    SEE ALSO: *WARRIOR-STRATEGY, SELF-PITY, STALKING-ART, WARRIOR-CONTROL*

WARRIOR-STRATEGY-SHIELD-[THE SHIELD OF THE WARRIORS' STRATEGY]: SEE: WARRIOR-STRATEGY-HIGHER-ORDER-[WARRIORS TAKE COVER WITH A HIGHER ORDER]

WARRIOR-STRENGTH-INTERNAL-[THE WARRIORS' INTERNAL STRENGTH]: (The warriors' internal strength is a sense of equanimity; it is almost an indifference, a feeling of being at ease coupled with a profound bent for examination and understanding; it is the warriors' internal strength, their sobriety that enables them to live better lives; it is also the warriors' inner strength which aids the assemblage point in moving to a position which fosters understanding as opposed to a position which fosters self-importance; fortified inner strength makes the assemblage point shift into dreaming positions which are more suitable for fostering sobriety.)
    SELECTED REFERENCES: **A Separate Reality - Page [214.6s-214.8]** (To be pierced by a fellow...the strength of being a warrior.) **A Separate Reality - Page [256.1]** (At one moment don Juan stopped...should always trust my own strength.) **The Second Ring of Power - Page [234.4-234.9]** (I had an attack of profound sadness...behind the best of my feelings.) **The Fire From Within - Page [175.7-177.3]** (He said that at first the new...been the case many times before.) **The Fire From Within - Page [180.3-180.8]** (Don Juan then outlined the procedure...become more and more manageable, even orderly.) **The Art of Dreaming - Page [47.7-47.9]** ("Yes, but for a perfect result...is unnecessary, to say the least.")
    SEE ALSO: *PATH-HEART-WITH, WARRIOR-SOBRIETY, SOBRIETY-UNDERSTANDING-VS-CAPRICIOUSNESS-SELF-IMPORTANCE, DREAMING-POSITION, WARRIOR-INDIFFERENCE, WARRIOR-SELF-EXAMINATION*

WARRIOR-STRIFE-[THE WARRIORS' STRIFE]: SEE: STRIFE-[STRIFE], AWARENESS-GROWTH-[AWARENESS IS INTRINSICALLY COMPELLED TO GROW]

WARRIOR-STRUGGLE-[THE WARRIORS' STRUGGLE]: (Warriors know that in order to become men [or women] of knowledge they must struggle for a lifetime, they must be warriors, not whimpering children; it is up to warriors as single individuals to oppose the forces of their lives; as warriors wage their battles, they let their spirit flow free and clear, knowing that their spirit is impeccable, and as they struggle they laugh and laugh.)
    SELECTED REFERENCES: **A Separate Reality - Page [88.2-88.9]** ("If nothing really matters," I said...to realize then that nothing matters.") **A Separate Reality - Page [142.5-142.9]** ("I cannot truly believe that, don...hunger and pain will destroy him.") **A Separate Reality - Page [215.2-215.5]** ("I have heard you say time...impeccable, a warrior laughs and laughs.") **A Separate Reality - Page [263.3-263.6]** (Don Juan slowly walked around me...really changed in you," he said.) **Journey to Ixtlan - Page [136.9-137.1]** ("I have taught you nearly everything a warrior...oneself in the world of power.") **Journey to Ixtlan - Page [154.4-155.5]** ("Any man that hunts power has... to the south. To the vastness.") **Journey to Ixtlan - Page [199.3-199.4]** ("I don't know don Juan...one which is already following you.") **Tales of Power - Page [11.7-11.8]** ("Each warrior has his own way...of all the barriers and disappointments.") **Tales of Power - Page [23.6]** ("All of us go through the same...comes of itself and by itself.) **Tales of Power - Page [58.9-59.2]** ("Come on," he said. "A warrior...ourselves into one or the other.) **Tales of Power - Page [155.7-155.9]** ("This is your world. You can't...the harmony between *tonal* and *nagual.*) **The Eagle's Gift - Page [113.3-113.5]** (Don Juan and I had had...to struggle unyieldingly for a

lifetime.) **The Power of Silence - Page [171.2-171.5]** ("Your uncertainty is to be expected...victims go after a ferocious struggle.")
    SEE ALSO: *MAN-KNOWLEDGE, KNOWLEDGE-PATH, WARRIOR-CHALLENGE, WARRIOR-IMPECCABILITY, LAUGHTER, WARRIOR-LIGHTNESS, WARRIOR-HUMOR, WARRIOR-COMPLAINTS*

WARRIOR-SUCCESS-*[THE WARRIORS' SUCCESS]: (The true success of warriors comes only after they have begun to gain a degree of control over the world of everyday life; the success of warriors is dependent on their level of impeccability.)*
    SELECTED REFERENCES: **Tales of Power - Page [10.1-10.4]** (Don Juan's praxis of dreaming was...the world of my everyday life.)
    SEE ALSO: *WARRIOR-IMPECCABILITY, EQUILIBRIUM, VICTORY-WITHOUT-GLORY-REWARD*

WARRIOR-SUPERIORITY-FALSE-*[THE WARRIORS' FALSE SENSE OF SUPERIORITY]: (Warriors must be careful not to feel as if they are merely humoring those around them; this chintzy tactic only gives warriors a false sense of superiority and makes them feel as if they are automatically above everyone and everything; this of course cannot be, because warriors are only human beings in the midst of a mysterious world; all a sense of false security can accomplish is to cut warriors down to a crappy size.)*
    SELECTED REFERENCES: **Journey to Ixtlan - Page [179.2-179.4]** (There is something in you that...you down to a crappy size.")
    SEE ALSO: *WARRIOR-HUMBLENESS, EQUAL-UNIMPORTANT, PETTY-TYRANT, SELF-IMPORTANCE*

WARRIOR-SURRENDER-FAILURE-*[THE WARRIORS' SURRENDER TO FAILURE]: SEE: WARRIOR-SURRENDER-IMPECCABILITY-[WARRIORS SURRENDER TO THEIR IMPECCABILITY]*

WARRIOR-SURRENDER-IMPECCABILITY-*[WARRIORS SURRENDER TO THEIR IMPECCABILITY]: (Warriors surrender themselves to the impossibility of their task, and strive to reach the unattainable, even though they know they don't stand a chance; warriors live their lives by doing their ultimate best for no other reason than to be impeccable; warriors' resolve to be impeccable despite any hope for success; surrendering to the unattainable cannot be deliberately approached as a conscious strategy for success, yet by resigning themselves completely to the impossibility of their task, warriors somehow become empowered within the depths of their humility.)*
    SELECTED REFERENCES: **The Eagle's Gift - Page [218.9-219.7]** (His benefactor explained to don Juan...the truth contained in the rule.) **The Eagle's Gift - Page [221.4-222..2]** (Don Juan said that one day...step back and lower his head.)
    SEE ALSO: *WARRIOR-IMPECCABILITY, WARRIOR-CHANCE-MINIMAL, WARRIOR-HUMBLENESS, SORCERY-PRACTICAL-SIDE*

WARRIOR-SURVIVE-*[ONLY WARRIORS CAN SURVIVE]: (Only warriors can survive the path of knowledge; what helps warriors live a better life is their sobriety, the internal strength of being a warrior; warriors know there is no survival value in the state of heightened awareness.)*
    SELECTED REFERENCES: **A Separate Reality - Page [142.7-142.9]** ("It is up to us as...hunger and pain will destroy him.") **A Separate Reality - Page [149.8-149.9]** ("My benefactor said that when a...if he is going to survive.) **A Separate Reality - Page [214.6-214.7]** (To be pierced by a fellow...the strength of being a warrior.) **Journey to Ixtlan - Page [120.7-120.8]** ("The other night you were not...And that you did very well.) **Journey to Ixtlan - Page [216.1-216.3]** ("If we wouldn't be tricked, we...a lot more in order to survive.") **Tales of Power - Page**

[105.4-105.5] ("Only as a warrior can one...or bad. Challenges are simply challenges.") **Tales of Power - Page [196.1-196.9]** (I made an involuntary gesture of...are no survivors on this earth!") **The Second Ring of Power - Page [174.6-174.8]** (The Nagual told each of them that...but an impeccable warrior survives, always.") **The Fire From Within - Page [15.7-16.1]** ("Warriors take strategic inventories," he said...essential to survival and well-being.) **The Power of Silence - Page [83.2-84.1]** (I noticed that my eyes were fixed...human race would be there.)

    SEE ALSO: *KNOWLEDGE-PATH, WARRIOR-SOBRIETY, WARRIOR-STRENGTH-INTERNAL, HUNTER-POWER-BECOMING, WARRIOR-SURVIVE, WARRIOR-STRENGTH-INTERNAL*

WARRIOR-SUSPENDING-[SUSPENDING THE WARRIOR]: *(Warriors know that being suspended off the ground for long periods of time is a superb device for curing certain maladies that are not physical; the longer the individual is kept from touching the ground, suspended in midair, the better the possibilities of a true cleansing effect.)*

    SELECTED REFERENCES: **The Eagle's Gift - Page [184.1-184.4]** (Don Juan said that those women...possibilities of a true cleansing effect.) **The Eagle's Gift - Page [235.8-236.9]** (He said that in order to...perception of the world around us.) **The Eagle's Gift - Page [262.1-262.4]** (After every session of dreaming in...one I was about to undertake.) **The Eagle's Gift - Page [302.3-302.6]** (La Gorda remembered that to prepare...a device that helped them remember.)

    SEE ALSO: *STALKING-ART*

WARRIOR-SUSPICIOUSNESS-[THE WARRIORS' SUSPICIOUSNESS]: *(Warriors never let their guard down; warriors doubt everything; they are suspicious and asks questions.)*

    SELECTED REFERENCES: **Tales of Power - Page [74.8-75.2]** ("Watch out!" he said. "A warrior...That's your only shield now.)

    SEE ALSO: *WARRIOR-ALERTNESS, WARRIOR-PREPAREDNESS*

WARRIOR-TASK-[THE WARRIORS' TASK]: *(The warriors' task is to learn the warriors' way, to seek the perfection of the warriors' spirit; the task of warriors is to remember themselves in their totality; the task of warriors is to sharpen, yet disguise their cutting edges so that no one would suspect their ruthlessness.)*

    SELECTED REFERENCES: **Journey to Ixtlan - Page [108.9-109.1]** (He paused for a long time...only task worthy of our manhood.") **Tales of Power - Page [97.5-97.6]** ("Learning the warrior's way. You can't...of your life will take you.") **Tales of Power - Page [187.6-187.9]** (I practically huddled against don Juan...the darkness would be no obstacle.) **Tales of Power - Page [284.3-284.8]** ("If you choose not to return...the mountains, somewhere in that direction.") **Tales of Power - Page [286.9-287.5]** ("If you two decide to return...will be for either of you.") **The Second Ring of Power - Page [113.4-113.5]** (We were quiet for a moment...had left for them to perform.) **The Second Ring of Power - Page [126.1-126.5]** ("Why is the Nagual trying to...that was to finish you off.) **The Second Ring of Power - Page [130.6-130.7]** (Then the wind stopped and the...better than if they were myself.) **The Second Ring of Power - Page [172.4-172.5]** (She said that she had done...be in the world of people.) **The Second Ring of Power - Page [264.2-264.3]** ("Sorcerers like the Nagual and Genaro...Genaros are of the same cycle.) **The Eagle's Gift - Page [177.5-178.1]** (The Nagual and his warriors were...male warriors, and one male courier.) **The Fire From Within - Page [83.1-83.2]** ("I really don't know whether you're...of everything, as you were yesterday.") **The Fire From Within - Page [183.7-183.8]** ("It is an internal knowledge," he said...every nagual is left to do.) **The Power of Silence - Page [46.9-47.1]** (Don Juan remarked that naturally his...be volunteering for the sorcery task.) **The Power of Silence - Page [106.9-107.1]** (A warrior was magical and ruthless...be able to suspect his ruthlessness.)

    SEE ALSO: *WARRIOR-PURPOSE, WARRIOR-SPIRIT, POWER-PROMISE, WARRIOR-TASK-WORLDLY, REMEMBERING-BODY, WARRIOR-DISGUISE*

WARRIOR-TASK-WORLDLY-[THE WARRIORS' WORLDLY TASK]: *(The warriors' worldly task is to sharpen , yet disguise, their cutting edges so that no one would be able to suspect their ruthlessness.)*

    SELECTED REFERENCES: **The Power of Silence - Page [106.9-107.1]** (A warrior was magical and ruthless...be able to suspect his ruthlessness.)

SEE ALSO: *RUTHLESSNESS-MASK, WARRIOR-FINESSE, WARRIOR-MAGIC, WARRIOR-DISGUISE, STALKING-ART*

WARRIOR-TEACHER-NEEDS-ONLY-REASON-*[THE ONLY REASON WARRIORS NEEDS A TEACHER]*: (Warriors know that the only reason they need a teacher is to spur them on mercilessly.)

SELECTED REFERENCES: SELECTED REFERENCES: The Power of Silence - Page [249.3-249.5] ("I can't repeat often enough that...he was, had not spared him.)
SEE ALSO: *WARRIOR-INSTRUCTION, TEACHERS-TEACHING*

WARRIOR-TEMPERAMENT-*[THE WARRIORS' TEMPERAMENT]*: (What warriors do with their increased perception, with their silent knowledge, depends on their personal temperament; the designs of the spirit are either sublimely simple or the most complex labyrinths and the differences are discernible in the manifestations of the spirit; the more difficult the command of the spirit, the more difficult the disciple turns out to be.)

SELECTED REFERENCES: The Power of Silence - Page [xi.9] (And what any of us does with that...silent knowledge, depends on our own temperament.") The Power of Silence - Page [5.3-5.4] ("I don't feel ill at ease...something which worries me no end.") The Power of Silence - Page [8.6-8.8] (It was the luckiest thing that could...to my benefactor, the nagual Julian.") The Power of Silence - Page [43.1-43.6] ("Reviving an apprentice's link is a...the disciple turns out to be.")
SEE ALSO: *KNOWLEDGE-SILENT, POWER-PROMISE, SPIRIT-COMMANDS*

WARRIOR-TENDERNESS-*[THE WARRIORS' TENDERNESS]: SEE: WARRIOR-UNAVAILABILITY-[THE WARRIORS' UNAVAILABILITY]*

WARRIOR-TERMS-*[THE WARRIORS' TERMS]*: (Warriors know that it does not matter what terms are used in describing the truth about the universe; it only matters that those truths have been verified by "seeing"; the terms that warriors originate do not spring from reason, but originate instead from "seeing", embracing everything that seers can attain.)

SELECTED REFERENCES: The Fire From Within - Page [48.8-49.5] (After a long silence, Genaro fell...said, but in a different way.")
SEE ALSO: *SEEING, EXPLANATION, SEEING-TALKING*

WARRIOR-TEST-FINAL-*[THE WARRIORS' FINAL TEST]*: (Warriors know that the new seers use breaking the barrier of perception as a final test; the test consists of jumping from a mountaintop into an abyss in a state of normal awareness; if warriors do not succeed in assembling another world before they reaches the bottom, they die.)

SELECTED REFERENCES: The Fire From Within - Page [288.7-289.2] ("In a few days, when Genaro...pushing them to fend for themselves.) The Fire From Within - Page [295.3-295.5] (He said that breaking the barrier...before he reaches the bottom, he dies.)
SEE ALSO: *WARRIOR-JUMP-ABYSS, PERCEPTION-BARRIER-BREAKING*

WARRIOR-TEST-GRAND-*[THE WARRIORS' GRAND TEST]*: (Warriors know that the grand test for warrior-apprentices is to be able to retrace the journey that the assemblage point took under the influence of the nagual.)

SELECTED REFERENCES: The Fire From Within - Page [123.3] ("The grand test that the new seers...called regaining the totality of oneself.")
SEE ALSO: *TOTALITY-REGAINING, REMEMBERING-BODY, RECOLLECTION-SORCERER*

WARRIOR-THEMSELVES-ASSEMBLAGE-POINT-MOVE-*[WARRIORS CAN MOVE THEIR ASSEMBLAGE POINTS THEMSELVES]: SEE: IMPECCABLE-MAN-NO-GUIDE-[AN IMPECCABLE MAN NEEDS NO ONE TO GUIDE HIM]*

WARRIOR-THEMSELVES-GUIDE-[IMPECCABLE WARRIORS CAN GUIDE THEMSELVES]: SEE: IMPECCABLE-MAN-NO-GUIDE-[AN IMPECCABLE MAN NEEDS NO ONE TO GUIDE HIM]

WARRIOR-THEMSELVES-LEARN-DREAMING-[WARRIORS CAN LEARN DREAMING BY THEMSELVES]: SEE: DREAMING-LEARN [LEARNING DREAMING]

WARRIOR-THINKER-[THE WARRIOR THINKER]: SEE: THINKER-TRUE-[A TRUE THINKER]

WARRIOR-THOUGHTS-[THE WARRIORS' THOUGHTS]: (Warriors know that a man of knowledge does not think, he acts instead; warriors have no thoughts so they will "see"; warriors understand that when they do not think, everything fits into place.)
SELECTED REFERENCES: A Separate Reality - Page [82.6-82.7] ("What you told me this afternoon...does not fit with your thoughts.") A Separate Reality - Page [91.7] ("You're thinking again," he said...therefore he cannot encounter that possibility.) A Separate Reality - Page [134.1] ("How did I fail don Juan...and thus you couldn't overcome it.) A Separate Reality - Page [180.2] ("Who are you to think or...nothing about the forces you're tapping.) The Second Ring of Power - Page [173.4-173.5] (He made me see that I was...of what I knew about him.) The Eagle's Gift - Page [307.5-307.6] (*I am already given to the power...past the Eagle to be free.*) The Power of Silence - Page [123.1-123.7] (He asserted that events difficult to...was really no contradiction at all.)
SEE ALSO: *ACTING-VS-TALKING, ACTING-VS-THINKING, REASON*

WARRIOR-TIME-DAY-[THE WARRIORS' TIME OF DAY]: (The warriors' time of day is the time of day that corresponds to everything important for the warrior; the warriors' time is the time of the warriors' death or the time they leave the world.)
SELECTED REFERENCES: The Second Ring of Power - Page [286.3-286.4] (He told me that you went...leave this world around that time.)
SEE ALSO: *TIME, WARRIOR-HOUR-POWER*

WARRIOR-TONAL-[THE WARRIORS' TONAL]: (The warriors' tonal is the warriors' perfected spirit; the fluidity of the warriors' tonal allows them to admit everything without admitting anything; the goal of the warriors' training is to teach the tonal not to crap out.)
SELECTED REFERENCES: Tales of Power - Page [133.7-133.9] ("I said that today was going...my warrior's spirit, my warrior's *tonal.*) Tales of Power - Page [156.1-156.4] ("In the beginning, one has...anything else, a strong, free *tonal.*) Tales of Power - Page [174.2-174.6] ("There is nothing else I can...could even conceive witnessing the *nagual.*) Tales of Power - Page [179.6-179.8] (Don Juan said that my "tonal"...could admit everything without admitting anything.)
SEE ALSO: *WARRIOR-SPIRIT, TONAL, SPIRIT-PERFECTING, WARRIOR-CONTRADICTION-KNOWLEDGE*

WARRIOR-TOTAL-FREEDOM-[WARRIORS FOR TOTAL FREEDOM]: SEE: WARRIOR-FREEDOM-TOTAL-[WARRIORS FOR TOTAL FREEDOM]

WARRIOR-TOTALITY-[THE WARRIORS' TOTALITY]: (The warriors' totality is the totality of the warriors' being.)
SELECTED REFERENCES: Tales of Power - Page [196.1-196.5] (I made an involuntary gesture of...drains his power, impeccability replenishes it.")
SEE ALSO: *TOTALITY, BEING-DIE*

WARRIOR-TOTALITY-COMMAND-[THE WARRIORS' COMMAND OVER THE TOTALITY OF THEMSELVES]: (Warriors command the totality of themselves when they have finally encountered power; no one can tell what each warrior will do with that command, it depends on the warriors' impeccability and the freedom of their spirit.)
    SELECTED REFERENCES: Tales of Power - Page [284.2-284.7] ("If you choose not to return...impeccability and the freedom of your spirit.)
    SEE ALSO: *WARRIOR-TOTALITY, TOTALITY, WARRIOR-IMPECCABILITY, WARRIOR-TOTAL-FREEDOM, WARRIOR-RETURN, INORGANIC-BEINGS-REALM-TRANSPORTED*

WARRIOR-TOUCHES-WORLD-LIGHTLY-[WARRIORS TOUCH THE WORLD LIGHTLY]: SEE: WARRIOR-UNAVAILABILITY-[THE WARRIORS' UNAVAILABILITY], WARRIOR-DELICACY-[THE WARRIORS' DELICACY]

WARRIOR-TRAINING-[THE WARRIORS' TRAINING]: (The warriors' training guides them to perceive energy directly; warriors train themselves to do two transcendental things; 1) to conceive the existence of the assemblage point; 2) to make that assemblage point move.)
    SELECTED REFERENCES: The Power of Silence - Page [144.8-145.1] (I mentioned to don Juan that I...to make that assemblage point move.) The Art of Dreaming - Page [3.7-3.9] ("Everything is energy. The whole universe...guiding us to perceive energy directly.)
    SEE ALSO: *WARRIOR-WAY, SEEING*

WARRIOR-TRAINING-ACTIVE-ELEMENT-[THE ACTIVE ELEMENT OF THE WARRIORS' TRAINING]: SEE: WARRIOR-PERSISTENCE-[THE WARRIORS' PERSISTENCE]

WARRIOR-TRANSCENDENTAL-ACCOMPLISHMENTS-[THE WARRIORS' TRANSCENDENTAL ACCOMPLISHMENTS]: SEE: WARRIOR-ACCOMPLISHMENTS-TRANSCENDENTAL-[THE WARRIORS' TRANSCENDENTAL ACCOMPLISHMENTS]

WARRIOR-TRANSCENDENTAL-PURPOSE-[THE WARRIORS' TRANSCENDENTAL PURPOSE]: SEE: WARRIOR-PURPOSE-TRANSCENDENTAL-[THE WARRIORS' TRANSCENDENTAL PURPOSE]

WARRIOR-TRANSFORMATION-[THE WARRIORS' TRANSFORMATION]: (Warriors transform themselves from within through the technique of realization; first warriors become aware that the world they perceive is the result of the assemblage point being located on a specific spot on the luminous cocoon; once that is understood, the warriors' assemblage point can move almost at will as a result of new habits; through impeccability, the elements of the warriors' tonal undergo a drastic change, but only in terms of the use assigned to those elements.)
    SELECTED REFERENCES: A Separate Reality - Page [149.8-149.9] ("My benefactor said that when a...if he is going to survive.) Journey to Ixtlan - Page [265.4-265.7] (At any rate, in your...the things, the people he loved.) Tales of Power - Page [7.4-7.6s] ("No. You must do better than...and routines stand in your way.") Tales of Power - Page [64.6] ("You yourself know that something in...shines it, and keeps it running.") Tales of Power - Page [241.4-241.6] (Don Juan pointed out then that...the use assigned to those elements.) Tales of Power - Page [242.2-242.3] (I held onto that conviction and...done in states of sober consciousness.) Tales of Power - Page [253.5-253.8] ("The delicate maneuver of leading a...that better than anyone I know.") The Fire From Within - Page [118.7-118.9] ("How can one accomplish that change...as a consequence

of new habits.") **The Power of Silence - Page [129.3-129.5]** ("If you judge me by my...myself with the most excruciating effort.")
　　　　SEE ALSO: *FACADE-TRANSFORMING, WARRIOR-IMPECCABILITY, CHANGE, CONVENTIONS-BREAKING*

WARRIOR-TREES-[WARRIOR TREES]: (Warriors know that trees can also be warriors and that they are capable of embarking on the warriors' definitive journey.)
　　　　SELECTED REFERENCES: **The Power of Silence - Page [39.7-40.6]** (It was as cool and quiet...as we discuss my definitive journey.")
　　　　SEE ALSO: *PLANTS, WARRIOR-JOURNEY-DEFINITIVE*

WARRIOR-TRUST-THEMSELVES-[WARRIORS TRUST THEMSELVES]:
(Warriors know that they must summon the courage to trust themselves.)
　　　　SELECTED REFERENCES: **A Separate Reality - Page [88.4-88.5]** "So now you're afraid of me...trust in yourself, not in me.) **A Separate Reality - Page [256.1]** (At one moment don Juan stopped...should always trust my own strength.) **Journey to Ixtlan - Page [165.5-165.7]** ("The world is a mystery," he said...you will add one more piece.") **The Eagle's Gift - Page [310.6-310.8]** (Emilito said, as if his voice...unison that I should trust myself.)
　　　　SEE ALSO: *WARRIOR-INTUITION, WARRIOR-COURAGE, POWER-PERSONAL*

WARRIOR-TURNING-HEAD-[TURNING THE WARRIORS' HEAD]:
(Warriors turns their heads to face a new direction, or to face time in a different way; warriors face the oncoming time rather than facing time as it recedes; this means that warriors "see" time as something concrete, yet incomprehensible; facing the oncoming time does not mean that warriors see into the future.)
　　　　SELECTED REFERENCES: **The Second Ring of Power - Page [41.7-41.9]** ("After turning my head that first...at us. Something must have happened.) **The Eagle's Gift - Page [294.3-294.6]** (When don Juan had described the...energy necessary to unravel that mystery.)
　　　　SEE ALSO: *TIME-ONCOMING, WARRIOR-DIRECTION-CHANGING, STALKER-TURNS-HEAD*

WARRIOR-UNAVAILABILITY-[THE WARRIORS' UNAVAILABILITY]:
(Warriors know that to be unavailable does not mean to hide or to be secretive; for warriors, to be unavailable means to be inaccessible; being inaccessible does not mean that warriors cannot deal with people; being inaccessible means that warriors use the world sparingly and with tenderness; warriors do not squeeze the world out of shape, they tap it lightly and then swiftly move away leaving hardly a mark.)
　　　　SELECTED REFERENCES: **Journey to Ixtlan - Page [66.3-66.7]** ("Therein lies the secret of great...to take a poke at you.") **Journey to Ixtlan - Page [70.4-70.8]** (I told him that in my...moves away leaving hardly a mark.")
　　　　SEE ALSO: *WARRIOR-FOG-CREATE, WARRIOR-AVAILABILITY, WARRIOR-FINESSE, WARRIOR-DELICACY*

WARRIOR-UNCERTAINTY-[THE WARRIORS' UNCERTAINTY]:
(Warriors know they will experience feelings of uncertainty as their new continuity establishes itself; warriors spend years in limbo where they are neither average men or sorcerers.)
　　　　SELECTED REFERENCES: **The Power of Silence - Page [171.1-171.5]** (I was in a complaining mood...victims go after a ferocious struggle.")
　　　　SEE ALSO: *WARRIOR-LIMBO, CONTINUITY, WARRIOR*

WARRIOR-UNDECIDED-ISSUE-[THE WARRIORS' UNDECIDED ISSUE]:
(In the life of warriors there is only one undecided issue, how far can individual warriors go on the path of knowledge and power.)
　　　　SELECTED REFERENCES: **Tales of Power - Page [249.4-249.5]** ("In the life of a warrior...true measure of a warrior's spirit.")

SEE ALSO: *KNOWLEDGE-PATH, POWER, WARRIOR-IMPECCABILITY*

WARRIOR-VALIDATION-[THE WARRIORS' VALIDATION]: *(Warriors validate their sorcery experiences in only one way, they "see" and then they know what they have experienced is true.)*
SELECTED REFERENCES: **The Art of Dreaming - Page [9.6-9.8]** (The problem of validation always played...of self-complacency and false security.")
SEE ALSO: *SEEING*

WARRIOR-VIEW-[THE WARRIORS' VIEW]: *(Warriors avoid dwelling on explanations because that only throws them back into a view of the world which they have struggled so hard to modify.)*
SELECTED REFERENCES: **Tales of Power - Page [246.1-246.2]** ("I don't want to emphasize those...this time a much larger view.")
SEE ALSO: *EXPLANATIONS, DESCRIPTION-WORLD*

WARRIOR-VIGIL-POSITION-[THE WARRIORS' POSITION OF SITTING "IN VIGIL"]: *(The warriors' position of sitting in vigil is a sitting posture which warriors adopt when they are in need of maintaining a vigil against the unknown.)*
SELECTED REFERENCES: **A Separate Reality - Page [160.7-160.8]** (He said he was going to watch...stay there, relaxed but not " abandoned.") **A Separate Reality - Page [202.6-202.8]** (From the place where we stopped...great speed, if it were necessary.) **Journey to Ixtlan - Page [128.3]** (Don Juan whispered that the fog...engaged in a battle of power.) **Journey to Ixtlan - Page [205.2-205.6]** (Don Juan began telling them that...for the duration of his talk.) **Journey to Ixtlan - Page [207.2-207.5s]** ("I'm going to show you fellows...knees did not hurt as much.") **The Fire From Within - Page [149.2-149.9]** (We were all still laughing when...he could hardly articulate his words.)
SEE ALSO: *WARRIOR-FIGHTING-FORM*

WARRIOR-VIGIL-POSITION-RELIEVING-ONESELF-[RELIEVING ONESELF WHILE IN THE WARRIORS' POSITION OF VIGIL]-(TOP)

WARRIOR-VIGOR-[THE WARRIORS' VIGOR]: *(The warriors' vigor is the bodily energy of the warrior.)*
SELECTED REFERENCES: **The Teachings of Don Juan - Page [65.5-65.6s]** ("You see. The devil's weed is...of those who can't handle it.) **The Teachings of Don Juan - Page [107.2-107.3]** (My benefactor told me about it...Now I do understand it.) **Journey to Ixtlan - Page [160.2-160.4]** (I told him that I was simply...rather in what you don't do.") **The Second Ring of Power - Page [7.1-7.5]** (She placed her fists on her hips...rendered everyone else pale and unimportant.) **The Second Ring of Power - Page [131.8-132.1]** (I asked la Gorda what the Nagual...children all their lives, that's all.") **The Second Ring of Power - Page [189.5-189.6]** (His words plunged me into a...body and freedom to my spirit.) **The Art of Dreaming - Page [130.6-130.7]** (Florinda, although she was old, was...the eye ass youth and vigor.)
SEE ALSO: *YOUTH, ENERGY, FREEDOM-TOTAL-VIGOR*

WARRIOR-VOLITION-[THE WARRIORS' VOLITION]: *(Warriors know that their volition alone will not be the deciding factor of their fate; warriors know that the force which rules our destinies is outside of ourselves and has nothing to do with our acts or volition.)*
SELECTED REFERENCES: **The Second Ring of Power - Page [234.4-234.9]** (I had an attack of profound sadness...behind the best of my feelings.) **The Second Ring of Power - Page [283.4-283.6]** (I narrated to her the way...do with our acts or volition.) **The Eagle's Gift - Page [303.8-304.2]** (As we walked back to his house...not a matter of my volition.) **The Fire From Within - Page [89.8-89.9]** (The force that had enveloped me...thawed out by tiny degrees.)
SEE ALSO: *FORCE-RULES-LIVES, WARRIOR-DESTINY, WARRIOR-FATE, SPIRIT-DESIGNS, POWER-DESIGNS*

WARRIOR-VOLITION-VS-EAGLE-COMMAND-[THE WARRIORS' VOLITION VS THE EAGLE'S COMMANDS]: (*Warriors know that they cannot disobey the Eagle's commands, but they also know that sometimes the way out of obeying those commands is by obeying them; what warriors do with their inventory is a perfect example of this principle.*)

SELECTED REFERENCES: The Fire From Within - Page [74.1-74.4] ("I don't mean to say that human...commands us to take it, that's all.")

SEE ALSO: *WARRIOR-VOLITION, EAGLE-COMMAND, INVENTORY*

WARRIOR-WAIT-[WARRIORS WHO WAIT]: (*Warriors know that they are waiting and they know what they are waiting for; warriors are waiting for their will and for their freedom.*)

SELECTED REFERENCES: The Teachings of Don Juan - Page [35.7] ("Do I have to prepare myself...Mescalito requires a very serious intent.") A Separate Reality - Page [142.1-142.3] ("Can you give me any suggestions...longer have to honor your promise.) A Separate Reality - Page [142.7-142.9] ("It is up to us as...hunger and pain will destroy him.") A Separate Reality - Page [145.5-146.1] ("A warrior has to use his...he is waiting for his will.") A Separate Reality - Page [151.5-153.2s] ("And thus with an awareness of...dear life, holding onto his hat.) Tales of Power - Page [23.6-23.7] ("All of us go through the...at a given moment everything changed.") Tales of Power - Page [286.9-287.2] ("If you two decide to return...personal power at fulfilling your tasks.) The Eagle's Gift - Page [84.3-84.6] (La Gorda got up; she was...following don Juan's teachings to the letter.) The Fire From Within - Page [27.1-27.3] ("I groveled daily," don Juan continued...is the great joy of warriorship.) The Fire From Within - Page [115.2-115.3] ("Our case is a little bit...We are waiting for freedom!) The Fire From Within - Page [120.1-120.2] ("What happens to the persons whose...gone crazy, but they patiently wait.)

SEE ALSO: *WARRIOR-FREEDOM-TOTAL, WARRIOR-JOY*

WARRIOR-WALK-[WARRIORS WALK]: (*Warriors know it is beneficial to walk miles and miles everyday.*)

SELECTED REFERENCES: The Second Ring of Power - Page [229.4-229.5] ("A warrior also walks miles and miles...lost the fat on my buttocks.")

SEE ALSO: *WARRIOR*

WARRIOR-WALK-TREES-[THE WARRIORS' WALK TO THE EDGE OF THE TREES]-(TOP)

WARRIOR-WALLS-OVERTAKE-[WARRIORS OVERTAKE THE WALLS]: (*Warriors know they do not win their victories by beating their heads against the walls; instead, warriors overtake the walls, they jump over them rather than spending their energy trying to demolish them.*)

SELECTED REFERENCES: Tales of Power - Page [51.7-51.9] ("Should I try to find an...the walls; they don't demolish them.")

SEE ALSO: *VICTORY*

WARRIOR-WANTS-[THE WARRIORS' WANTS]: (*Not wanting anything is one of the warriors' finest attainments; warriors know that what makes them unhappy is to want; when warriors learn to cut their wants to nothing, they are free; this does not mean they do not like anything, it simply means that they are free of wants and desires.*)

SELECTED REFERENCES: A Separate Reality - Page [142.3-142.9] (There is nothing you can do...hunger and pain will destroy him.") A Separate Reality - Page [153.3-153.6] ("My benefactor was a sorcerer of great...from absolutely everything he knew before.") Tales of Power - Page [52.7-52.9] ("I never thought that you needed...is sufficient, self-explanatory and complete.) Tales of Power - Page [248.4-248.5] (Don Juan had once told me...my life was boring and empty.)

SEE ALSO: *WARRIOR-ATTAINMENT, WARRIOR-DESIRE*

WARRIOR-WAR-[WAR FOR THE WARRIOR]: (*War is the natural state for warriors; war for warriors is the total struggle against the individual self that has deprived man of his power; warriors go to knowledge as they go to war, wide-awake, with fear, with respect, and with absolute assurance.)*

SELECTED REFERENCES: **The Teachings of Don Juan - Page [51.3-51.4]** ("A man goes to knowledge as...will live to regret his steps.") **A Separate Reality - Page [88.4-88.5]** ("So now you're afraid of me...trust in yourself, not in me.) **Tales of Power - Page [155.7-155.9]** ("This is your world. You can't...the harmony between *tonal* and *nagual*.) **The Second Ring of Power - Page [51.2]** (The Nagual told both of them...us wages against our old selves.) **The Fire From Within - Page [15.2-15.3]** ("Warriors fight self-importance as a matter...my impeccability, that's all," he insisted.) **The Fire From Within - Page [15.7-15.8]** ("Warriors take strategic inventories," he said...in terms of expending their energy.") **The Fire From Within - Page [16.4-16.6]** (He said that the most effective...and is called the petty tyrant.) **The Fire From Within - Page [297.4-297.6]** (A couple of days later, all...in a state of total war.) **The Power of Silence - Page [150.1-150.3]** (I thought I had caught don...has deprived man of his power.")
SEE ALSO: *SELF, SELF-COMBAT, KNOWLEDGE, FEAR, WARRIOR-RESPECT, WARRIOR-ASSURANCE, DREAMING-WAR-ZONE, SELF-IMPORTANCE-LOSING, MAN-NEMESIS*

WARRIOR-WAR-VS-PEACE-[WAR VS PEACE FOR THE WARRIOR]:

(Peace is an anomaly for warriors; warriors lives their lives in a state of war, struggling against the individual self that has deprived them of their power; at a given moment there is no longer a war within the warrior, because the warriors' way is harmony, first the harmony between actions and decisions and then the harmony between the tonal and the nagual.)

SELECTED REFERENCES: **Tales of Power - Page [155.9]** (Now there is no longer a war...then the harmony between *tonal* and *nagual*.) **The Power of Silence - Page [149.8-150.3]** (Don Juan asserted that the reason...has deprived man of his power.")
SEE ALSO : *WAR-WARRIOR, WARRIOR-PEACE, PEACE, SELF, SELF-COMBAT, WARRIOR-CONTRADICTION-KNOWLEDGE, EQUILIBRIUM, BALANCE, HARMONY*

WARRIOR-WARRIOR-ALLOW-[WARRIORS ALLOW WARRIORS TO BE WARRIORS]: SEE: WARRIOR-INTERVENTION-[THE WARRIORS' INTERVENTION], WARRIOR-CARING-FOR-ANOTHER-[CARING FOR ANOTHER WARRIOR]

WARRIOR-WAY-[THE WARRIORS' WAY]: (The warriors' way is the way of the impeccable action, sometimes called the sorcerers' way; to be a warrior is more suitable than anything else; warriors act as if nothing had ever happened, because they don't believe in anything, yet they accept everything at its face value; warriors accept without accepting and disregard without disregarding; warriors never feel as if they know, neither do they feel as if nothing had ever happened; warriors act as if they are in control, even though they might shake in their boots; the warriors' way prepares warriors to be aware, to make their bid for power; the thrust of the warriors' way is to dethrone self-importance.)

SELECTED REFERENCES: **Teachings of Don Juan - Page [69.8]** (And the man attempting to learn...by leading a hard, quiet life.) **A Separate Reality - Page [47.5-47.7]** ("Once you decided to come to...awaiting you. That's the warrior's way.") **A Separate Reality - Page [85.2-85.8]** ("I told you once that our...no way part of his concern.") **A Separate Reality - Page [214.8-215.6]** (I am compelled by my personal...impeccable, a warrior laughs and laughs.") **Journey to Ixtlan - Page [57.9-58.6]** (He looked at me with calm...his arm and tears flooded me.) **Journey to Ixtlan - Page [177.8-178.1]**. ("But how can I store personal power...unnoticeable when it is being stored.") **Tales of Power - Page [23.7]** ("Knowledge and power. Men of knowledge...at a given moment everything changed.") **Tales of Power - Page [46.6-46.9]** (Don Juan explained that by the...being existing in a luminous world.) **Tales of Power - Page [52.3-52.5]** (There is a fourth, the correct...in such a manner dissipates obsession.") **Tales of Power - Page [75.6-75.8]** (I pointed out that he always...one can find flaws in it.") **Tales of Power - Page**

[106.5-106.6] ("The basic difference between an ordinary...scales in favor of the warrior's way.") **Tales of Power - Page [239.8-239.9]** ("What any apprentice needs to buffer...together everything in a sorcerer's world.) **The Fire From Within - Page [128.5-128.7]** ("What are we really doing, don...are nothing do they become everything.") **The Fire From Within - Page [168.5-168.8]** (He told me that he had...me a long series of explanations.) **The Fire From Within - Page [195.4-195.5]** (He repeated that in the warrior's way...position which determined what they perceived.) **The Power of Silence - Page [103.3-103.5]** (Don Juan had stated his belief...the beginning, a return to paradise.) **The Power of Silence - Page [103.9-105.2]** (Modern -day naguals, in an effort...of our being aware of *intent*.) **The Power of Silence - Page [150.8-151.1]** (Don Juan described self-importance as...self-pity masquerading as something else.) **The Art of Dreaming - Page [33.2-33.4]** (Don Juan explained that sorcerers have...our basic reactions about being alive.) **The Art of Dreaming - Page [37.4-37.9]** (Don Juan insisted that the sorcerer'...the actual grandeur of the universe.) **The Art of Dreaming - Page [250.8-251.4]** (I stretched my legs and put my...is the fear of losing the nagual.")

    SEE ALSO: *WARRIOR-IMPECCABILITY, WARRIOR-CONTROL, WARRIOR-BID-POWER, LIFE-WAYS-FACING-TWO*

WARRIOR-WAY-ASSEMBLAGE-POINT-MOVEMENT-[THE WARRIORS' WAY AND THE MOVEMENT OF THE ASSEMBLAGE POINT]: (Warriors know that with regard to the warriors' way the movement of the assemblage point is everything.)

    SELECTED REFERENCES: **The Fire From Within - Page [195.4-195.5]** (He repeated that in the warrior's way...position which determined what they perceived.)
    SEE ALSO: *WARRIOR-WAY, ASSEMBLAGE-POINT-MOVING*

WARRIOR-WEAKEST-MOMENT-[THE WARRIORS' WEAKEST MOMENT]: SEE: WARRIOR-SEX-WEAKEST-MOMENT-[SEX IS THE WARRIORS' WEAKEST MOMENT]

WARRIOR-WEAKNESS-DAILY-WORLD-[THE INTEGRAL PARTS OF THE DAILY WORLD THAT CONTRIBUTE TO THE WARRIORS' WEAKNESS]: (Warriors must be constantly on guard against the integral parts of the daily world which contribute to destroying their purpose, muddling their aims and weakening them in general; in addition to the warriors' natural enemies, those integral parts of the daily world include, indolence, laziness and self-importance.)

    SELECTED REFERENCES: **The Fire From Within - Page [167.6-167.9]** (As we walked, don Juan told...scorn and reject their own tradition.) **The Power of Silence - Page [117.1-117.6]** (I opened my backpack. The women...with his group to set me up.)
    SEE ALSO: *WARRIOR-ENEMIES-NATURAL-FOUR, INDOLENCE, SELF-IMPORTANCE*

WARRIOR-WELL-BEING-[THE WARRIORS' WELL-BEING]: (The warriors' well-being is something which they must groom, a condition which they must become acquainted with before they can seek it; the well-being of the warrior is not the well-being of the average man; the well-being of the warrior is linked to the warriors' completeness.)

    SELECTED REFERENCES: **A Separate Reality - Page [4.7-4.8]** ("You make it sound stupid," he...not complete. You have no peace.") **Journey to Ixtlan - Page [183.6-183.9]** (Before I could say anything else...of disorientation, ill-being, and confusion.) **Tales of Power - Page [74.4-74.5]** (I had a feeling of completement...because it would turn into complacency.) **The Second Ring of Power - Page [243.6-243.8]** (It takes all the time and...proper for you to choose wisely.") **The Fire From Within - Page [15.7-16.1]** ("Warriors take strategic inventories," he said...essential to survival and well-being.)
    SEE ALSO: *WARRIOR-COMPLETENESS, ILL-BEING*

WARRIOR-WISDOM-[THE WARRIORS' WISDOM]: (Warriors are aware that detachment does not automatically mean wisdom because it is still up to warriors to use the warriors' pause consistently and correctly.)

SELECTED REFERENCES: **The Eagle's Gift - Page [112.9-113.5]** (What I felt was not a...to struggle unyieldingly for a lifetime.)
SEE ALSO: *WARRIOR-DETACHMENT, WARRIOR-PAUSE*

WARRIOR-WISH-WARRIOR-WELL-[WARRIORS WISH OTHER WARRIORS WELL]: (*Warriors can afford to wish other warriors well on their journey with power.*)

SELECTED REFERENCES: **Tales of Power - Page [228.6-228.7]** ("Wish him well Carlitos," he said...can afford to wish him well.")
SEE ALSO: *WARRIOR-MOOD, WARRIOR-REJOICE-VICTORIES-SPIRIT*

WARRIOR-WITNESS-UNBIASED-[WARRIORS TRAIN THEMSELVES TO BE UNBIASED WITNESSES]: (*Warriors aim to be free, to be unbiased witnesses incapable of passing judgment; warriors train themselves to be unbiased witnesses so as to understand the mystery of themselves and relish the exultation of finding out what they really are; to become unbiased witnesses is one of the highest of the warriors' goals; warriors are clear and calm, even though they have witnessed everything; warriors are grateful for their great fortune, the fortune to witness marvels.*)

SELECTED REFERENCES: **Tales of Power - Page [27.6-27.8]** ("Don't get jumpy," he said calmly...suspect that he has witnessed everything.") **Tales of Power - Page [45.8-45.9]** ("I've told you time and time...that should be more than enough.") **Tales of Power - Page [148.6-148.8]** (Don Juan did not shake me...only for watching. Watch! Watch everything!") **The Fire From Within - Page [61.2-61.4]** (I asked him if there was...to come, must come of itself.") **The Fire From Within - Page [120.3-120.5]** (He said that two options are opened...always returns to its original position.) **The Fire From Within - Page [147.8-147.9]** ("Be that as it may, warriors...waylaid, and so was la Catalina.") **The Fire From Within - Page [148.7-148.8]** ("In order to be unbiased witnesses...witness, whatever that world might be.) **The Fire From Within - Page [199.6-199.8]** ("My great flaw at that time...so that one can celebrate them unbiasedly.")
SEE ALSO: *WITNESS, WARRIOR-FREEDOM, WARRIOR-GOAL, WARRIOR-SOBRIETY, NAGUAL-WITNESSING, WARRIOR-JUDGMENT*

WARRIOR-WOMEN-[FEMALE WARRIORS]: SEE: WARRIOR-FEMALE-[FEMALE WARRIORS]

WARRIOR-WORLD-[THE WARRIORS' WORLD]: SEE: POWER-WORLD-[THE WORLD OF POWER], WORLD-MEN-[THE WORLD OF MEN]

WARRIOR-WORLD-COLLAPSE-REASSEMBLE-[WARRIORS COLLAPSE AND REASSEMBLE THE WORLD]: (*One of the arts of warriors is their ability to collapse the world for a specific reason and then restore it again in order to keep on living.*)

SELECTED REFERENCES: **Journey to Ixtlan - Page [136.5-136.6]** ("But why would anyone wish to...in order to keep on living.") **Tales of Power - Page [176.8-177.1]** ("A sudden fright always shrinks the...struggle to immediately halt that shrinking.") **The Second Ring of Power - Page [275.8-276.1]** (What don Juan had struggled to vanquish...maintain those images, the world collapses.) **The Power of Silence - Page [149.2-149.5]** ("Any movement of the assemblage point...know, there is no real danger.")
SEE ALSO: *FIRE-WITHIN, TONAL-SHRINKING*

WARRIOR-WORLD-SELECT-[WARRIORS SELECT THE ITEMS THAT MAKE UP THEIR WORLD]: (*Warriors deliberately select the items that make up their world; every item they choose is a shield to protect themselves from the onslaught of the forces which they are striving to use.*)

SELECTED REFERENCES: **A Separate Reality - Page [216.4-218.2]** ("The other day when you saw...items of a path with heart.")
SEE ALSO: *WARRIOR-SHIELDS*

WARRIOR-WORRY-NOT-[WARRIORS DON'T WORRY]: (Warriors don't worry because they know that to worry is to become unwittingly accessible; worry is avoided by warriors because worry leads to feelings of desperation which in turn leads to clinging and exhaustion.)
    SELECTED REFERENCES: **Journey to Ixtlan - Page [70.2-70.4]** ("A hunter knows he will lure...or whatever you are clinging to.") **Journey to Ixtlan - Page [84.4-85.1]** ("Your continuity only makes you timid...the acts of a timid man.") **The Eagle's Gift - Page [299.1-299.2]** (He had helped everyone impeccably... the parallel lines in one's totality.)
    SEE ALSO: *WARRIOR-DESPERATE-NEVER, EXHAUSTION, WARRIOR-UNAVAILABILITY, WARRIOR-FOG-CREATE, FRETTING*

WARRIOR-YELL-[THE WARRIORS' YELL]: (Warriors know they can focus on their yell and use it as a vehicle.)
    SELECTED REFERENCES: **The Teachings of Don Juan - Page [178.7-179.4]** (The hurling of an object had to...had against anything that might happen.) **A Separate Reality - Page [166.7]** (I had a moment of intense panic...word don Juan had taught me.) **Journey to Ixtlan - Page [116.3-116.7]** (At that instant don Juan let out...a magnificent series of piercing yells.) **Tales of Power - Page [179.8-180.2]** (When I described don Genaro's leap...and from the tree to Genaro.) **Tales of Power - Page [182.6-182.7]** (I saw him leap to a low...had sipped him through its lines.) **Tales of Power - Page [262.5]** (The feeling that someone was holding...been, was a long chilling yell.) **The Second Ring of Power - Page [63.5-63.9]** (Then you scared my floor, yelling...but my stupid dog got excited.)
    SEE ALSO: *SORCERY-TECHNIQUES, WARRIOR-CRY-ANIMAL-(TOP)*

WARRIORSHIP-[WARRIORSHIP]: (Warriorship is the individual attempt to reestablish the link with intent and regain the use of it without succumbing to it.)
    SELECTED REFERENCES: **The Power of Silence - Page [105.1-105.2]** (Examined in this way, sorcery becomes...of our being aware of *intent*.)
    SEE ALSO: *INTENT, SORCERY, WARRIORSHIP-VS-SORCERY, POWER-PROMISE, EQUILIBRIUM*

WARRIORSHIP-ATTRIBUTES-[THE ATTRIBUTES OF WARRIORSHIP]: SEE: WARRIOR-ATTRIBUTES-[THE WARRIORS' ATTRIBUTES]

WARRIORSHIP-CHOOSING-[CHOOSING WARRIORSHIP]: (Warriors know it is not possible to "choose" warriorship; the decision as to who can be a warrior lies in the realm of the powers that guide men.)
    SELECTED REFERENCES: **Journey to Ixtlan - Page [91.4-91.5]** ("The decision as to who can be...realm of the powers that guide men.")
    SEE ALSO: *FORCE-RULES LIVES*

WARRIORSHIP-IMPETUS-[THE IMPETUS OF WARRIORSHIP]: SEE: ASSEMBLAGE-POINT-SHIFT-NEED-IMPERATIVE-[THE IMPERATIVE NEED TO SHIFT THE ASSEMBLAGE POINT]

WARRIORSHIP-JOY-GREAT-[THE GREAT JOY OF WARRIORSHIP]: (The great joy of warriorship is that warriors know that they are waiting and they know what they are waiting for.)
    SELECTED REFERENCES: **The Fire From Within - Page [27.1-27.3]** ("I groveled daily," don Juan continued...is the great joy of warriorship.)
    SEE ALSO: *WARRIOR-WAIT, WARRIOR-JOY, WARRIOR-STRATEGY*

WARRIORSHIP-PRINCIPLE-[THE FIRST PRINCIPLE OF WARRIORSHIP]: SEE: RUTHLESSNESS

WARRIORSHIP-VS-SEEING-[WARRIORSHIP VS SEEING]: SEE: WARRIOR-VS-SEER-[WARRIOR VS SEER]

WARRIORSHIP-VS-SORCERY-[WARRIORSHIP VS SORCERY]:

(Sorcerers learn to use the inexplicable forces of the world by redirecting themselves and adapting to their direction; but by opening themselves to knowledge, sorcerers fall prey to those same forces and have only their will to balance themselves; in order to accomplish this delicate balancing, sorcerers have no choice but to feel and act like warriors, for only warriors can survive on the path of knowledge; anyone who succeeds in moving the assemblage point is a sorcerer, and from that position we can do all kinds of good and bad things to our fellow men; being a sorcerer, therefore, is like being a cobbler or a baker, but the quest of warriorship is to go beyond that stand by bringing morality and beauty and a lack of self-importance to the basic position of the sorcerer; what enables the sorcerer to live a better life is the strength of being a warrior; warriorship is the attempt to reestablish the knowledge of intent and regain use of it without succumbing to it; sorcerers concentrate their dreaming on the human unknown while the warriors concentrate their dreaming on the non-human and immeasurable unknown; sorcerers are not willing to pay the price of losing their self-importance, they are driven by their attachment to the realm of human affairs and their own self image; warriors, on the other hand, are detached and struggle to lose the last vestige of their self-importance because that is the only way they can abstract themselves and finally find freedom; sorcerers come face to face with the realm of the inorganic beings and must eventually decide whether to stay in that world and remain sorcerers, or return to this world and continue their struggle as warriors; in the final analysis, warriors come to understand that they must dip into the realm of the inorganic beings for the energy necessary to complete their definitive journey; they know they can't have dealings with them but they can't stay away from them either; warriors must travel to the realm of the inorganic beings to access their energy but in the process, they must not give in to their influence; this is known as the ultimate stalking, and is accomplished through the sustaining of the warriors' unbending intent to find freedom; warriors know that only if they remain totally detached can they ever have the energy necessary to be free; eventually warrior-sorcerers face a situation where they must embrace either total detachment or total indulging; dreaming is the gateway to the light and to the darkness of the universe, and it is warrior-sorcerers' choice which they will embrace; warriors will always choose freedom.)

SELECTED REFERENCES: The Teachings of Don Juan - Page [161.8-162.4] ("Now that you know a bit...about forgetting something along the line.") **The Teachings of Don Juan - Page [184.6-185.2]** ("Do you think I could get...the paths of life is everything.) **A Separate Reality - Page [214.2-214.8]** ("The world is indeed full of...the strength of being a warrior.) **Tales of Power - Page [42.4-42.5]** ("Let go!" he commanded me dryly...Genaro, is one of those deeds.") **Tales of Power - Page [57.2-57.9]** ("You're filled with tales of violence...for you, only tales of power.") **The Fire From Within - Page [2.7-3.5]** ("We are going to be talking...like entering a dead-end street.) **The Fire From Within - Page [4.7-5.1]** (Don Juan said that after some...be obsessed with what they *saw*.) **The Fire From Within - Page [83.3-83.4]** (Before I had time to say anything...the odds I was up against.) **The Fire From Within - Page [119.5-119.8]** ("I've mentioned to you that sorcery...keeps your assemblage point rigidly fixed.) **The Fire From Within - Page [167.6-167.9]** (As we walked, don Juan told...scorn and reject their own tradition.) **The Fire From Within - Page [225.6-225.8]** ("You're such an exaggerated fellow...result is staggering in its consequences.") **The Fire From Within - Page [228.1-228.6]** ("How were they wrong, don Juan...moment in their lives was intolerable.) **The Fire From Within** - **[297.9-299.6]** ("The old seers used to say that...that total freedom means total awareness.") **The Power of Silence** - **Page [xii.7-xii.8]** (Sorcerers, or warriors, as he called...ordinary concerns of their everyday lives.) **The Power of Silence** - **Page [82.3-82.6]** ("The real challenge for those sorcerer...that, they need morality and beauty.") **The Power of Silence** - **Page [104.1-105.2]** (Don Juan explained that at one...of our being aware of *intent*.) **The Art of Dreaming** - **Page [79.5-81.7]** ("I've been saying this to you...what it is: a mere candle.") **The Art of Dreaming** - **Page [92.4-92.9]** (My dreaming ended there. I was...may add, and an ultrapersonal one.") **The Art of Dreaming** - **Page [95.7-96.7]** (It did not take much for me...dreamers have in a hostile universe.") **The Art of Dreaming** - **Page [109.3-109.9]** ("You have to continue your dreaming...way of plummeting into a pitfall.") **The Art of Dreaming** - **Page [180.3-182.3]** ("There is one last issue related...he waved good-bye to me.) **The Art of Dreaming** - **Page [203.3-203.9]** ("For years now, I have been...or like the new ones," he said.) **The Art of Dreaming** - **Page [204.5-205.1]** (He did not answer me...to put aside such a gift.") **The Art of Dreaming** - **Page [205.8-206.3]** ("As you already know, for modern...of what we don't want to be.) **The Art of Dreaming** - **Page [221.1-221.3]** (Don Juan was right in saying that...to the darkness of the universe.)

  SEE ALSO: *SORCERY, WARRIOR-WAY, DEVIL'S-WEED-VS-LITTLE-SMOKE, PATH-HEART-WITH, PATH-HEART-WITHOUT, STALKING-ULTIMATE, INORGANIC BEINGS-REALM, ENERGY-ASSEMBLAGE-POINT-MOVE, WARRIOR-JOURNEY-DEFINITIVE, WARRIOR-DETACHMENT, POWER-GIFTS, DREAMING-ART, HAUNTED-HOUSE-ANALOGY, FREEDOM, EQUILIBRIUM, SNEAKING-WORLD-MEN-WORLD-SORCERER, WARRIOR-BALANCE-SOBRIETY-ABANDON, WARRIOR-CONTRADICTION-KNOWLEDGE*

WATCH-SEE-THOSE-[THOSE WHO WANT TO WATCH AND SEE]: *(The little smoke is for those who want to watch and "see".)*

  SELECTED REFERENCES: **The Teachings of Don Juan** - **Page [69.2]** ("The devil's weed is for those...who want to watch and see.) **The Teachings of Don Juan** - **Page [82.1]** (You will smoke all the mixture...see anything you want to see.')
  SEE ALSO: *LITTLE-SMOKE, SEEING*

WATER-BODIES-[BODIES OF WATER]: SEE: ATTENTION-SECOND-ANTITHETICAL-[THINGS THAT ARE ANTITHETICAL TO THE SECOND ATTENTION]

WATER-GAZING-[WATER GAZING]: SEE: GAZING-[GAZING]

WATER-GREEN-BECOMING-[BECOMING GREEN IN THE WATER]-(TOP)

WATER-HOLE-SPIRIT-TAPPING-[TAPPING THE SPIRIT OF THE WATER HOLE]-(TOP)

WATER-SEEING-[SEEING THE WATER]-(TOP)

*WATER-TRANSPORTED-[TRANSPORTED BY THE POWER OF WATER]: *(Warriors know that water has the power to transport warriors great distances if they allow it to gather their second attention.)*

  SELECTED REFERENCES: **The Second Ring of Power** - **Page [300.9-301.1]** ("All of us are terrified of water...there is no way of stopping.)
  SEE ALSO: *ATTENTION-SECOND*

WATERFALL-GENARO-[DON GENARO SCALES THE WATERFALL]-(TOP): SEE: GENARO-WATERFALL-[DON GENARO SCALES THE WATERFALL]-(TOP)

WAY-WARRIOR-[THE WARRIORS' WAY]: SEE: WARRIOR-WAY-[THE WARRIORS' WAY]

WAY-IMPECCABLE-ACTION-[THE WAY OF THE IMPECCABLE ACTION]: SEE: WARRIOR-WAY-[THE WARRIORS' WAY]

WEAK-FACE-SECOND-ATTENTION-[THE WEAK FACE OF THE SECOND ATTENTION]: SEE: ATTENTION-SECOND-FACES-TWO-[THE TWO FACES OF THE SECOND ATTENTION]

WELL-BEING-WARRIOR-[THE WARRIORS' WELL-BEING]: SEE: WARRIOR-WELL-BEING-[THE WARRIORS' WELL-BEING]

*WEST-[WESTERLY WOMEN]: (Warriors know that the westerly woman is the third of a nagual's party of warriors; she is called feeling; she is introspective, remorseful, cunning, sly, like a cold gust of wind; westerly women are mad at times and at other times are the epitome of severity and purpose; westerly women have to be cared for because under the duress of dreaming and stalking they lose their right sides, their minds; once they lose their rational side they are peerless dreamers and stalkers since they have no rational ballast to hold them back.)

SELECTED REFERENCES: **The Eagle's Gift - Page [174.5-174.8]** (The female warriors are called the...shy, warm, like hot wind.) **The Eagle's Gift - Page [183.8-184.1]** (His benefactor put him under the direct...rational ballast to hold them back.) **The Eagle's Gift - Page [185.6-186.2]** (A group composed of two sets of...lose their composure and be raving mad.) **The Eagle's Gift - Page [204.3-204.5]** (Don Juan advised me that I should...a performance staged by someone else.)

SEE ALSO: *WARRIOR-FEMALE, WARRIOR-CARING-FOR-ANOTHER*

WHAT-WAITS-OUT-THERE-[WHAT WAITS FOR US OUT THERE?]: (Warriors know that the unknowable eternity waiting for us out there is something utterly impersonal.)

SELECTED REFERENCES: **The Art of Dreaming - Page [63.4]** ("What's waiting for us out there..."something utterly impersonal," he said.)

SEE ALSO: *UNKNOWABLE*

WHISTLE-ALLIES-[THE WHISTLE TO DISPERSE THE ALLIES]-(TOP): SEE: ALLIES-WHISTLE-[THE WHISTLE TO DISPERSE THE ALLIES]-(TOP)

WHY-[WHY]: (Warriors ask why, only in the sense that they ponder their great fortune at having found a challenge; warriors never ask why as a question that begs an answer because they know they cannot discern the designs of power.)

SELECTED REFERENCES: **Journey to Ixtlan - Page [91.4]** ("The decision as to who can...of the powers that guide men.) **Tales of Power - Page [55.4-55.7]** (Have you ever asked yourself, why...stop the fulfillment of that design.")

SEE ALSO: *WARRIOR-CHALLENGE, POWER-DESIGNS*

WILL-[WILL]: (Warriors know that will is the mysterious force that is present throughout everything there is; the new seers understand will as a blind, impersonal, ceaseless burst of energy that makes us behave in the ways we do; will is the force that keeps the Eagle's emanations separated and is not only responsible for awareness but also for everything in the universe; will is the energy of alignment; will accounts for the perception of the ordinary world and indirectly, through the force of that perception, it accounts for the placement of the assemblage point in its customary position; will is a power that has to be controlled and tuned; will can be described as the maximum control of the luminosity of the body as a field of energy, or it can be described as a level of proficiency, or a state of being that comes abruptly to warriors at a time designated by the designs of power;

will is such a complete control of the second attention that it is called the other self; will channels the energy of our total being to produce anything within the boundaries of possibility; will is another center of assemblage, through which it is possible to assess and use the extraordinary effects of the nagual; will is very quiet and unnoticeable; will belongs to the other self; will is a power within the warrior; it is not an object or a thought or a wish; will is what makes warriors invulnerable; will is what allows warriors to succeed when their thoughts tell them they are defeated; will is what sends sorcerers through a wall or to the moon if they want; it is will which assembles us; when warriors can no longer command their will, then they can no longer oppose the silent forces of their death; will is one of the eight points on the sorcerers' diagram; the power of the warriors' second attention to focus on anything they want; will is the power to select and assemble in dreaming; will is the impersonal force of alignment that keeps the assemblage point stationary.)

SELECTED REFERENCES: **A Separate Reality - Page [146.2-147.5]** ("What exactly is the will...to the moon, if he wants.") **A Separate Reality - Page [152.4-152.6]** ("When the convulsions cease the warrior...and that he has acquired will.") **A Separate Reality - Page [198.1-198.6]** (It is the area of the will...expanding fog moving beyond its limits.") **Tales of Power - Page [80.9-81.5]** ("What will his call be like...of every opposition of the reason.") **Tales of Power - Page [96.2-96.9]** ("We may say that every one..."dreaming" were on the right side.) **Tales of Power - Page [178.9-179.2]** ("Let's say that a warrior learns...the *nagual* through that single fiber.) **Tales of Power - Page [276.2-276.4]** ("Those leaps were only the beginning...although one can never explain it.) **The Second Ring of Power - Page [327.2-327.3]** (She added that the problem the...focus indefinitely on anything we wanted.) **The Eagle's Gift - Page [23.6-23.8]** (What channels the energy of our...be transformed through *will* into anything.) **The Eagle's Gift - Page [136.3-136.4]** (The energy needed in order to...the power to select, to assemble.) **The Eagle's Gift - Page [142.7-143.7]** (To elucidate the control of the...*Will* belongs to the other self.") **The Eagle's Gift - Page [144.9]** ("*Will* is such a complete control...Gorda said after a long pause.) **The Fire From Within - Page [80.7-80.8]** ("What is that mysterious force...will of the Eagle's emanations, or *intent.* ") **The Fire From Within - Page [170.7-171.4]** (At first they referred to those...of *will,* the energy of alignment.) **The Fire From Within - Page [218.7-218.9]** (He repeated, as if he were...at the service of each individual.) **The Power of Silence - Page [102.8-103.2]** (Don Juan had said that when...has with everything in the universe.)

SEE ALSO: *INTENT, ALIGNMENT, ALIGNMENT-FORCE, PERCEPTION, OTHER, ATTENTION-SECOND, SORCERER-DIAGRAM, WILL-(ALL)*

WILL-AVAILABILITY-[THE AVAILABILITY OF WILL]: (Warriors know that will does not become available until they have a great surplus of energy; until warriors gather that energy through the days of an impeccable life, they must wait for their will.)

SELECTED REFERENCES: SELECTED REFERENCES: **The Fire From Within - Page [186.3-186.4]** ("You can't remember, because *will* is...then *will* might release those memories.)

SEE ALSO: *WILL, WILL-WAIT, WARRIOR-IMPECCABILITY, ENERGY*

WILL-BECKONING-[BECKONING WITH THE WILL]: (Warriors know that they are capable of pulling things to themselves with their will, whether or not they are consciously aware of that pulling.)

SELECTED REFERENCES: **The Second Ring of Power - Page [171.1-171.4]** ("How do you know that the...he was going to see me first.)

SEE ALSO: *WILL, INTENT*

WILL-CAR-WON'T START-[WILL AND THE CAR THAT WON'T START]-(TOP): SEE: CAR-WON'T-START-WILL-[WILL AND THE CAR THAT WON'T START]-(TOP)

WILL-CONTROL-FOLLY-LIFE-[WILL CONTROLS THE FOLLY OF THE WARRIORS' LIFE]: *(Warriors know that will controls the folly of their lives; nothing matters to them except their impeccability, and they go on living because they have their will; nothing matters to them, neither their acts nor the acts of their fellow men.)*

SELECTED REFERENCES: A Separate Reality - Page [80.5-80.7s] ("Perhaps it's not possible to explain...will controls the folly of my life.")

SEE ALSO: *WILL, WARRIOR-FOLLY, WARRIOR-IMPECCABILITY, WARRIOR-NOTHING-MATTERS, EQUAL-UNIMPORTANT*

WILL-EFFECTS-[THE EFFECTS OF WILL]: *(Seers can "see" the effects of will; they can "see" that alignment is ceaselessly renewed in order to imbue perception with continuity.)*

SELECTED REFERENCES: The Fire From Within - Page [171.1-171.3] (Don Juan said that the new...rerouted to reinforce some choice alignments.)

SEE ALSO: *WILL, PERCEPTION, SEEING, ALIGNMENT, CONTINUITY*

WILL-ENGAGING-[ENGAGING THE WILL]: SEE: WILL-TAPPING-[TAPPING THE WILL]

WILL-FORCE-[THE FORCE OF WILL]: SEE: WILL-[WILL]

WILL-GRABBING-[GRABBING WITH THE WILL]: *(Warriors know they must learn to focus their will; something snaps forward from someplace below the stomach and that something has direction and can be focused on anything; warriors focus something they cannot imagine [their second attention] on their invisible connection with some indefinable abstract.)*

SELECTED REFERENCES: A Separate Reality - Page [14.2-15.3] (I wanted to explain myself and all...He stopped you with his will!") A Separate Reality - Page [134.5-134.7] (Don Juan's words distressed me profoundly...I mumbled, then stopped talking altogether.) A Separate Reality - Page [138.1-138.2] (I talked for a long time...me again and I stopped talking.) A Separate Reality - Page [152.4-152.6] ("When the convulsions cease the warrior...and that he has acquired will.") A Separate Reality - Page [251.7s-251.9] (A warrior allows the ally to...is the master at all times.") Journey to Ixtlan - Page [38.2-38.6] (I described to him the way...he had said was my death.) Tales of Power - Page [234.4-235.7] (You were left there, facing me...simply happens. No one knows how.") The Power of Silence - Page [47.6-47.9] (Don Juan said that, for instance...invisible connection with that indefinable abstract.) The Power of Silence - Page [126.9-127.5] (Don Juan stopped talking and fixed...me what I did to you.")

SEE ALSO: *WILL, WARRIOR-GAZE, ABSTRACT*

WILL-HANDLING-[HANDLING WILL]: *(Warriors know that every human being, without knowing it, learns to handle will; warriors strive to learn how to handle will in a deliberate way, they learn to will things, to intend them.)*

SELECTED REFERENCES: The Fire From Within - Page [131.8-132.2] ("This is one of the most extraordinary...*will* it, we must *intend* it.")

SEE ALSO: *WILL, AWARENESS-HANDLING, INTENDING, INTENDING-MYSTERY*

WILL-VS-INTENT-[WILL VS INTENT]: *(Warriors know that will is the aspect of alignment that keeps the assemblage point stationary and intent is the aspect of alignment that makes it shift; will is the impersonal force of alignment and somehow it changes into intent, the personalized force of alignment which is at the service of the individual; the goal of warriors is to sensitize the connecting link with intent until they can make it function at will.)*

SELECTED REFERENCES: The Fire From Within - Page [218.7-218.9] (He repeated, as if he were...at the service of each individual.) The Fire From Within - Page [299.5-299.6] ("The new seers burn with the...that total freedom means total awareness.") **The Power of Silence - Page [102.2-103.2]** (On another occasion don Juan had...has with everything in the universe.) **The Power of Silence - Page [103.7-103.9]** (In a calm voice don Juan told...of sorcerers unimaginable pain and sorrow.) **The Power of Silence - Page [108.6-108.9]** (He assured me that he had...can make it function at will.)

     SEE ALSO: *WILL, INTENT, ALIGNMENT-FORCE, ASSEMBLAGE-POINT-MOVING, ALIGNMENT-WILL-INTENT*

WILL-INTENT-MYSTERY-[THE MYSTERY OF HOW WILL CHANGES TO INTENT]: *(Warriors know that one of the world's most haunting mysteries is how will changes to intent, or how the impersonal force of alignment becomes the personalized force at the service of the warrior; the strangest part of this mystery is that the change is so easy to accomplish; it is convincing ourselves that this change is possible that presents the biggest obstacle to the realization of this change.)*

     SELECTED REFERENCES: **The Fire From Within - Page [218.7-219.1]** (He repeated, as if he were...And none of us wants to be.")

     SEE ALSO: *WILL, INTENT, WARRIOR-CONVINCE, WARRIOR-CONTRADICTION-KNOWLEDGE*

WILL-INTENT-SETTING-[WILL AND SETTING A NEW INTENT]: *(Warriors know that they must will something, they must set a new intent for something, if it is to become a command which in turn becomes the Eagle's command.)*

     SELECTED REFERENCES: **The Fire From Within - Page [131.6-132.2]** (I told him I was very...*will* it, we must *intend* it.")

     SEE ALSO: *WILL, INTENT, EAGLE-COMMAND, WARRIOR-COMMAND*

WILL-MEMORY-RELEASE-[WILL RELEASES MEMORIES]: *(Warriors know that with a life of impeccability and a great deal of surplus energy, will may eventually release the memories stored in the left side awareness.)*

     SELECTED REFERENCES: **The Fire From Within - Page [186.3-186.4]** ("You can't remember, because *will* is...then *will* might release those memories.)

     SEE ALSO: *REMEMBERING-BODY, WILL, WARRIOR-IMPECCABILITY, ENERGY, ASSEMBLAGE-POINT-MOVING, RECOLLECTION-SORCERER*

WILL-MOVING-BY-[MOVING BY THE WILL]-(TOP)

WILL-PUMA-JUAN-[DON JUAN AND THE PUMA]-(TOP)

WILL-VS-REASON-[REASON VS WILL]: SEE: REASON-WILL [REASON VS WILL]

WILL-VS-SEEING-[WILL VS SEEING]: *(Warriors know the difference between will and "seeing"; will is a force, a power while "seeing" is a way of getting through things; warriors may have a very strong will but they may not "see".)*

     SELECTED REFERENCES: **A Separate Reality - Page [148.8-148.9]** ("No. Will is a force, a power...will and also with his *seeing*.")

     SEE ALSO: *WILL, SEEING*

WILL-STOPPING-SOMEONE-[STOPPING SOMEONE WITH THE WILL]: SEE: WILL-GRABBING-[GRABBING WITH THE WILL]

WILL-TAPPING-[TAPPING THE WILL]: *(Warriors know that tapping the will is another term for using or engaging the will.)*

     SELECTED REFERENCES: **Tales of Power - Page [80.9-81.1]** ("I don't know. His call is...in order to know the call.)

     SEE ALSO: *WILL*

WILL-TUNING-[TUNING THE WILL]: *(Warriors tune their will by letting death overtake them, and when they are flat and begin to expand, their impeccable will takes over and assembles the fog into one person again.)*
    SELECTED REFERENCES: A Separate Reality - Page [198.2] (A sorcerer tunes his will by...the fog into one person again.")
    SEE ALSO: *WARRIOR-WORLD-COLLAPSE-REASSEMBLE, WILL, FIRE-WITHIN, WARRIOR-IMPECCABILITY*

WILL-WAITING-[WAITING FOR THE WILL]: *(Warriors know that they are waiting and what they are waiting for; warriors wait for their will.)*
    SELECTED REFERENCES: A Separate Reality - Page [145.5-146.1] ("A warrior has to use his will...he is waiting for his will.") A Separate Reality - Page [151.5-153.2] (And thus with an awareness of...dear life, holding onto his hat.)
    SEE ALSO: *WARRIOR WAITS, WILL*

WILL-WORLD-UPHELD-BY-[THE WORLD UPHELD BY WILL]: *(The world upheld by will makes life into an act of power, an act which warriors can "see.")*
    SELECTED REFERENCES: Tales of Power - Page [113.7-114.3] ("The world upheld by *reason* makes all...your *reason*, I with my *will*.)
    SEE ALSO: *WILL, POWER-ACT, SEEING*

*WIND-[WIND]: *(Warriors know there are four winds, four directions; the four winds each have personalities, they are like women and for that reason female warriors seek them.)*
    SELECTED REFERENCES: A Separate Reality - Page [249.3-249.5] ("What are you doing in this...to don Juan, his eyes glittering.) Journey to Ixtlan - Page [60.9-64.5] ("There it is," he said, as...hard and constantly all the time.) Journey to Ixtlan - Page [64.8-66.4] (A sudden gust of wind made...interplay between hiding and showing oneself.) Journey to Ixtlan - Page [122.1-122.2] ("You know about the wind...certain times and at certain places.) Journey to Ixtlan - Page [133.6-134.1] ("And what is real?" don Juan...by pushing you into a ravine.) The Second Ring of Power - Page [31.1-31.5] ("Now we have time," she said...the Nagual had never mentioned why.) The Second Ring of Power - Page [39.9-41.7] ("No. The wind moves inside the...because he was baffled by me.) The Eagle's Gift - Page [174.5-174.8] (The female warriors are called the...shy, warm, like a hot wind.)
    SEE ALSO: *WARRIOR-FEMALE*

WIND-NAGUAL-[THE NAGUAL WIND]: SEE: NAGUAL-WIND-[THE NAGUAL WIND]

WINDS-FOUR-[THE FOUR WINDS]: SEE: WARRIOR-FEMALE-[FEMALE WARRIORS], WIND-[WIND]

*WINGS-INTENT-FLYING-[FLYING ON THE WINGS OF INTENT]: SEE: INTENT-WINGS-FLYING-[FLYING ON THE WINGS OF INTENT]

WISDOM-[WISDOM]: *(Warriors know that true wisdom always comes painfully and in driblets.)*
    SELECTED REFERENCES: The Power of Silence - Page [59.4-59.5] (Of course I could have seen everything...to us painfully and in driblets.")
    SEE ALSO: *WARRIOR-WISDOM, KNOWLEDGE-CLAIMING-POWER*

WISDOM-WARRIOR-[THE WARRIORS' WISDOM]: SEE: WARRIOR-WISDOM-[THE WARRIORS' WISDOM]

WITCH-[WITCH]: *(Warriors know a witch is an aberrant sorcerer; a sorcerer who has not been able to resolve the issues of self-importance.)*
    SELECTED REFERENCES: A Separate Reality - Page [76.6-76.7] ("Can you bewitch him don Juan...you have a man of courage!") The Power of Silence - Page [82.3-82.4] ("The real challenge for those sorcerer...differentiates sorcerer seers from plain witches.")

SEE ALSO: *DIABLERO-DIABLERA, SELF-IMPORTANCE, SORCERER-SEER-WARRIOR, BRUJO*

WITCHCRAFT-[WITCHCRAFT]: *(Warriors know that witchcraft is a debasing term for sorcery; the average man, incapable of harnessing the energy to perceive beyond his daily limits, calls the realm of extraordinary perception sorcery, witchcraft, or the work of the devil; he shies away from it and will not examine it any further; warriors know that in reality, there is no witchcraft, or evil or devil, there is only perception.)*

SELECTED REFERENCES: **The Power of Silence - Page [ix.5-ix.7]** (At various times don Juan attempted...admitted it was not really accurate.) **The Power of Silence - Page [211.2-211.4]** (Don Juan pushed his argument further...no devil. There is only perception.")

SEE ALSO: *SORCERY, INTENT-MASTERY, NAGUALISM, TOTAL-FREEDOM, PERCEPTION, EVIL*

WITNESS-[THE WITNESS]: *(Nestor was called the witness by the nagual's party of warriors.)*

SELECTED REFERENCES: **The Second Ring of Power - Page [81.3-81.9]** ("And where's Josephina...witnessed all there is to witness.") **The Second Ring of Power - Page [205.8-205.9]** ("Nestor also jumped into the abyss...and I became the village idiot.")

SEE ALSO: *NAGUAL-PARTY-WARRIORS*

WITNESS-IMPROVISATION-[THE WITNESS' IMPROVISATION]-(TOP)

WITNESS-LAST-[THE LAST WITNESS]: *(Warriors know that death is the last witness because they "see" that it is so.)*

SELECTED REFERENCES: **Journey to Ixtlan - Page [154.1-154.3]** ("If a dying warrior has limited...until he has finished his dance.") **Journey to Ixtlan - Page [156.2-156.5]** ("It's all very simple,": he said...thus I believed I was dying.")

SEE ALSO: *DEATH, WARRIOR-DANCE-LAST-POWER*

WITNESS-NAGUAL-[WITNESSING THE NAGUAL]: *(Warriors know that the affairs of the nagual can be witnessed only with the body, not the reason; the nagual cannot be explained, it can only be witnessed by warriors at the center of the will.)*

SELECTED REFERENCES: **Tales of Power - Page [148.6-148.8]** (Don Juan did not shake me...only for watching. Watch! Watch everything!") **Tales of Power - Page [157.5-157.6]** ("But you were next to me...with the body, not the reason.") **Tales of Power - Page [191.3-191.4]** (If you remember correctly, I said...though, and that is an abomination.) **Tales of Power - Page [244.6-244.7]** (We function at the center of...therefore it is properly called the *nagual*.) **Tales of Power - Page [273.3]** ("There is no way to refer...*nagual* can only be witnessed, the *will*.) **Tales of Power - Page [277.5-277.6]** ("Sorcerers do the same thing with...it is that we are witnessing.) **The Fire From Within - Page [72.3-72.4]** ("Oh, there is the mystery," he...The mystery can only be witnessed.")

SEE ALSO: *NAGUAL, EXPLANATION, KNOWLEDGE-VS-LANGUAGE, BODY-PHYSICAL, ASSEMBLAGE-CENTERS, BODY-PHYSICAL-WITNESSING*

WITNESS-UNBIASED-WARRIOR-[WARRIORS TRAIN THEMSELVES TO BE UNBIASED WITNESSES]: SEE: WARRIOR-WITNESS-UNBIASED-[WARRIORS TRAIN THEMSELVES TO BE UNBIASED WITNESSES]

WITNESSING-PASSIVE-[PASSIVE WITNESSING]: SEE: DREAMING-STAGES-[THE FOUR STAGES OF DREAMING]

WITNESSING-TONAL-NAGUAL-[WITNESSING THE TONAL AND THE NAGUAL]-(TOP)

WITNESSING-TREE-[WITNESSING A TREE]-(TOP)

WITNESSING-WE-ARE-MERELY-[WE ARE MERELY WITNESSING]:
(Warriors know that through will they can only witness the effects of the nagual; but despite our conditioning to the contrary, warriors also realize that we are merely witnessing the effects of the tonal as well; warriors understand that in reality both the tonal and the nagual are indescribable, we have no hope ever to understand or explain what it is we are witnessing in either realm.)
SELECTED REFERENCES: **Journey to Ixtlan - Page [80.8-81.2]** ("One must assume responsibility for being...witnessing all the marvels of it.") **Tales of Power - Page [45.8-45.9]** ("I've told you time and time...that should be more than enough.") **Tales of Power - Page [277.5-277.6]** ("Sorcerers do the same thing with their will...it is that we are witnessing,)
SEE ALSO: *TONAL-INDESCRIBABLE, WITNESS-NAGUAL*

WOMAN-CHURCH-[THE WOMAN IN THE CHURCH]-(TOP)

WOMAN-WORST-THING-[THE WORST THING THAT CAN HAPPEN TO A WOMAN]-(TOP)

WOMB-[WOMB]: *(Warriors know that the womb is a magical organ for women; in a woman, the womb is the place of origin for both the attention for dreaming and the energy for dreaming; the womb is a woman's center.)*
SELECTED REFERENCES: **The Second Ring of Power - Page [39.3-40.3]** ("One day, while we were in the...I had learned to distinguish them.") **The Second Ring of Power - Page [114.9]** ("Don't you put your hands to your...They store their feelings there.") **The Second Ring of Power - Page [276.9-277.1]** (I commented that don Juan had never...over the rest of their bodies.) **The Eagle's Gift - Page [136.4-137.3]** (In a woman, both the attention...then had a most beautiful dream.)
SEE ALSO: *WOMEN, WIND, MENSTRUAL-PERIOD, ATTENTION-DREAMING, ENERGY-DREAMING, VAGINA*

WOMEN-[WOMEN]: *(Warriors appreciate the individual strengths and weaknesses of women as a gender.)*
SELECTED REFERENCES: **A Separate Reality - Page [212.2-212.3]** ("You could never touch her," he...too busy to be relentless enemies.") **Tales of Power - Page [144.2-144.5]** (His statements aroused my curiosity...The rest is the same.") **The Second Ring of Power - Page [31.3-31.6]** ("Only what the Nagual taught me...the Nagual had never mentioned why.) **The Second Ring of Power - Page [41.2-41.7]** ("The Nagual told me that the...because he was baffled by me.) **The Second Ring of Power - Page [42.1-42.3]** ("A woman, of course, is much...believed that women are unequaled, tops.) **The Second Ring of Power - Page [47.2-47.5]** (It is your fate to be...see the crack between the worlds.) **The Second Ring of Power - Page [132.5-132.6]** ("An empty man uses the completeness...had nothing to begin with.) **The Second Ring of Power - Page [171.5-172.2]** ("The men will give you very...They are dependent on men.") **The Second Ring of Power - Page [247.2s-247.7]** ("I've told you already what the...or by gazing at the clouds.) **The Second Ring of Power - Page [276.8-277.2]** (La Gorda said that the Nagual...fingers clawed in an upright position.) **The Second Ring of Power - Page [300.4-300.6]** ("By the time Benigno and Nestor...for I need to be contained.) **The Eagle's Gift - Page [15.2-15.3]** (As you yourself know, we men...highest place. See what I mean?") **The Eagle's Gift - Page [23.8-23.9]** ("The Nagual said that the *dreaming*...man's *dreaming body* is more possessive.") **The Eagle's Gift - Page [27.5-27.7]** ("There is something very wrong with...than the women," she replied dryly.) **The Eagle's Gift - Page [136.5-136.8]** ("A woman's *dreaming* has to come...needs someone else to prod her.) **The Eagle's Gift - Page [157.4-157.6]** ("Did you also have a hard...she said. "Too light, in fact.") **The Eagle's Gift - Page [174.5-174.8]** (The female warriors are called the...shy, warm, like a hot wind.) **The Eagle's Gift - Page [222.3-223.1]** (Don Juan marveled that this realization...a double man he could approach.) **The Eagle's Gift - Page [269.4-271.2]** (I answered her with a long...Nagual makes things even more difficult.") **The Fire From Within - Page [137.3-137.8]** ("Female seers have downshifts more often...woman seer, run for the hills!") **The Fire From Within - Page [155.2-155.3]** ("Women are definitely more bizarre than...way I can understand their quirks.") **The Power of Silence - Page [92.2-92.4]** (Don Juan commented that women are...and complied with the nagual's designs.) **The Art of Dreaming - Page [188.1-188.2]** ("Women in general have a natural bent...the nagual woman, has superb energy."

SEE ALSO: *WARRIOR-FEMALE, MEN, WARRIOR-MALE, WOMEN-(ALL)*

WOMEN-ACCOUNTABLE-SOCIETY-[WOMEN ARE NOT ACCOUNTABLE TO SOCIETY]:
(Warriors know that women are not accountable to society; this means that women can easily disappear; this is a splendid advantage since they are not encumbered with a man's solid history; women are not compelled to secrecy because society does not value them and count on them as it does men; a man is accountable; he cannot easily disappear; a woman is already prepared to disintegrate into thin air, in fact it is expected of her.)
SELECTED REFERENCES: The Eagle's Gift - Page [269.3-270.5] ("I beg your pardon," I said...you go around giving lectures.)
SEE ALSO: *WOMEN, MEN, PERSONAL-HISTORY-ERASING, MEN-ACCOUNTABLE-SOCIETY, WARRIOR-SECRETS, WARRIOR-UNAVAILABILITY*

WOMEN-CLOTHES-WEARING-[WEARING WOMEN'S CLOTHES]:
(Warriors know that for some men wearing women's clothes is the door into heightened awareness.)
SELECTED REFERENCES: The Power of Silence - Page [68.1-68.2] ("Of course," he replied with a grin...but are very difficult to arrange.")
SEE ALSO: *AWARENESS-HEIGHTENED*

WOMEN-FEROCITY-[WOMEN'S FEROCITY]: SEE: WOMEN-TALENT-[WOMEN'S TALENT]

WOMEN-INTENSITY-[WOMEN'S INTENSITY]: SEE: WOMEN-TALENT-[WOMEN'S TALENT]

WOMEN-RELENTLESS-ENEMY-[WOMEN ARE RELENTLESS ENEMIES]: SEE: ENEMY-RELENTLESS-WOMEN-[WOMEN ARE RELENTLESS ENEMIES]

WOMEN-STALKERS-[WOMEN ARE NATURAL STALKERS]:
(Warriors know that women are natural stalkers; they can be ruthless but charming, cunning but nice, patient but active and sweet but lethal; if a man acts this way, it is said that he is being prissy.)
SELECTED REFERENCES: The Power of Silence - Page [68.3-68.6] (He taught him that these four...acts this way he's being prissy.'")
SEE ALSO: *WOMEN, STALKING-ART*

WOMEN-TALENT-[WOMEN'S TALENT]:
(Warriors know that with regard to the journey into the unknown, it is women who have all the talent; men have sobriety and purpose but very little talent; women have the impulse to cross the immeasurable vastness of the unknown, and as a consequence have a matchless intensity and ferocity.)
SELECTED REFERENCES: The Fire From Within - Page [137.4-137.6] (He also said that women seers...flare, ease, and a matchless ferocity.)
SEE ALSO: *WOMEN, MEN, UNKNOWN-JOURNEY, WARRIOR-SOBRIETY, WARRIOR-PURPOSE, WARRIOR-CROSSING-FREEDOM*

WOMEN-WIND-FRIENDSHIP-[THE FRIENDSHIP OF WOMEN AND THE WIND]:
(Warriors know of the friendship between women and the wind.)
SELECTED REFERENCES: The Second Ring of Power - Page [39.3-40.3] ("One day, while we were in the...I had learned to distinguish them.") The Second Ring of Power - Page [41.2-41.7] ("The Nagual told me that the four...because he was baffled by me.)
SEE ALSO: *WARRIOR-FEMALE, WIND, WOMEN*

WORDS-[WORDS]: (Warriors know that to say something out loud means to set in motion energy currents that are irreversible; in days of antiquity, words were incredibly powerful, but now they are not; in the realm of the inorganic beings, words have not lost their power; words are tremendously powerful and important and are the magical property of whoever has them; the sound and meaning of words are of supreme importance to stalkers; words are used by them as the key to open anything that is closed; stalkers have to state their aim before attempting to achieve it; the problem with words is that they are never adequate to describe what can only be experienced.)

SELECTED REFERENCES: **Tales of Power** - Page **[54.9-55.2]** ("No one develops a double...that awareness such a unique challenge.") **The Second Ring of Power** - Page **[119.2-119.4]** ("The Nagual told me that you...written down and then forgotten about.) **The Eagle's Gift** - Page **[124.4-124.5]** (I wanted to start a debate...than even the fear of dying.) **The Fire From Within** - Page **[256.9]** ("Not to do this will turn everything...And words are fairly cheap.") **The Power of Silence** - Page **[80.7-81.5]** (I knew exactly what he was talking...magical property of whoever has them.) **The Power of Silence** - Page **[84.3-84.5]** (I was staring at each of them...flatten it and turn it into words.") **The Power of Silence** - Page **[220.8-221.1]** (I must have looked dumbfounded...only made them more confusing.) **The Power of Silence** - Page **[237.8-237.9]** (First, the nagual Elias explained to...aim before attempting to achieve it.) **The Art of Dreaming** - Page **[179.7-180.2]** (During our next discussion of dreaming...realm, they haven't lost their power.")

SEE ALSO: *TALKING, WARRIOR-DEATH-VS-DECISIONS, INTENT-VOICING, INTENT-WAKING-UP, WORDS-(ALL)*

WORDS-FLAW-[THE FLAW WITH WORDS]: (Warriors know that the flaw with words is that they force us to feel enlightened even though we are not; enlightenment is a result of the acquisition of true knowledge, which is a process which occurs independent of language all together.)

SELECTED REFERENCES: **Tales of Power** - Page **[24.4-24.6]** ("That's the flaw with words," he...where new acts have new reflections.")

SEE ALSO: *TALKING, REASON, KNOWLEDGE-VS-LANGUAGE, WORDS, TALKING, INTELLECT-DALLIANCE*

WORDS-IRREVOCABLE-[THE IRREVOCABILITY OF THE WARRIORS' WORDS]: SEE: WARRIOR-DEATH-DECISIONS-[THE WARRIORS' DEATH VS THE WARRIORS' DECISIONS], INTENT-VOICE-[VOICING INTENT]

WORDS-KNOWLEDGE-NO-[THERE ARE NO WORDS FOR KNOWLEDGE]: (Warriors know that there are no words for knowledge; the deeper the assemblage point moves, the more warriors have the feeling of knowledge without any words to explain it.)

SELECTED REFERENCES: **The Power of Silence** - Page **[81.5-81.7]** ("Sorcerers have a rule of thumb...become tongue-tied, confused and evasive.")

SEE ALSO: *KNOWLEDGE-SILENT, KNOWLEDGE-DIRECT, KNOWLEDGE-VS-LANGUAGE, WORDS, TALKING*

WORDS-TOSSING-[TOSSING A WORD AT SOMEONE]: (Warriors know that tossing words is another term for stopping someone with the will.)

SELECTED REFERENCES: **A Separate Reality** - Page **[14.2-15.3]** (I wanted to explain myself and all...He stopped you with his will!")

SEE ALSO: *WILL-GRABBING*

WORDS-USHER-KNOWLEDGE-[WORDS TO USHER THE APPRENTICE INTO THE REALM OF KNOWLEDGE]: SEE: KNOWLEDGE-GOING-

REQUISITES-[THE FOUR REQUISITES OF GOING TO KNOWLEDGE]

WORLD-[WORLD]: *(Warriors use the term "world" to describe everything around them; in reality though, warriors know that there is no world of solid objects, this is only a universe of the Eagle's emanations; warriors understand that the world is incomprehensible; warriors won't ever understand it so they treat the world as an endless mystery and the things that people do as an endless folly.)*
> SELECTED REFERENCES: **A Separate Reality - Page [219.9-220.4]** (The world is all that is...people do as an endless folly.") **The Fire From Within - Page [37.7-37.9]** ("I've used the term 'the world'...in motion, and yet unchanged, eternal.")
> SEE ALSO: *WORLD-SOLID-OBJECTS, EAGLE-EMANATIONS, WORLD-MYSTERIOUS, WORLD-(ALL)*

WORLD-APPARITIONS-[THE WORLD OF APPARITIONS]: *(Warriors know that the world of apparitions is an element of the tonal; a lateral shift of the assemblage point within man's band of emanations which manifests itself as a world of incomprehensible apparitions gleaming with a blinding white light; the "vision" of heaven, where everything is alive, bathed in light, a world of miraculous sights; the world of apparitions is not another total world.)*
> SELECTED REFERENCES: **The Teachings of Don Juan - Page [89.7-89.9]** ("All I want to know is if...I don't know where God is.") **Tales of Power - Page [125.5-125.7]** ("Is the *nagual* the soul?"...It is, let's say, the napkin.") **The Second Ring of Power - Page [242.2-242.4]** ("The value is that we need...nagual is the kingdom of heaven.") **The Fire From Within - Page [215.5-215.7]** (I felt a great pressure all over me...And we were walking on the clouds.) **The Fire From Within - Page [290.6-291.2]** (I recalled then that don Juan...apparitions gleaming with a blinding white light. **The Fire From Within - Page [293.1-293.3]** ("It's the easiest world to assemble...as they approach a crucial position.") **The Power of Silence - Page [96.4-96.7]** (Don Juan said it was at that instant..."You *saw* the spirit.") **The Power of Silence - Page [210.8-210.9]** (He told me that all the...memory that lasted them a lifetime.)
> SEE ALSO: *MOLD-MAN, HELL, PARALLEL-LINES-LAND*

WORLD-BLACK-[THE BLACK WORLD]: *(Warriors know that the black world is the easiest alternate world for them to assemble; a true alignment of another great band of emanations; the black world does not have the same emanations that account for time in our world, and it acts to age the physical body.)*
> SELECTED REFERENCES: **The Fire From Within - Page [292.3-292.6]** (The instant I *saw* that, I...bands of emanations: a black world.) **The Fire From Within - Page [292.9-294.2]** (I refused to think about don...strain of years of solitary struggle.) **The Fire From Within - Page [294.9-295.3]** (The inquisitive, rational part of me...it in order to escape death.")
> SEE ALSO: *WORLDS-OTHER-ASSEMBLE-TOTAL*

WORLD-BLACK-TALES-[TALES OF THE BLACK WORLD]-(TOP)

WORLD-COLLAPSE-REASSEMBLE-[WARRIORS COLLAPSE AND REASSEMBLE THE WORLD]: SEE: WARRIOR-WORLD-COLLAPSE-REASSEMBLE-[WARRIORS COLLAPSE AND REASSEMBLE THE WORLD]

WORLD-CONFORM-THOUGHT-[MAKING THE WORLD CONFORM TO OUR THOUGHTS]: *(Warriors know that the first attention has the habit of making the world conform to man's thoughts, to the description of the world.)*

SELECTED REFERENCES: Tales of Power - Page [22.1-23.7] ("How was I operating my knowledge...comes of itself and by itself.") Tales of Power - Page [83.7-84.3] ("I have no idea that I'm...the ally that night, right here.")
SEE ALSO: DESCRIPTION-WORLD, ATTENTION-FIRST, ATTENTION-TONAL

WORLD-CRACK-[THE CRACK BETWEEN THE WORLDS]: SEE: CRACK-WORLD-[THE CRACK BETWEEN THE WORLDS]

WORLD-DESCRIPTION-[THE DESCRIPTION OF THE WORLD]: SEE: DESCRIPTION-WORLD-[THE DESCRIPTION OF THE WORLD]

WORLD-DIVIDED-[THE WORLD IS DIVIDED IN TWO]: (Warriors know that the world is divided in two in a totally incomprehensible way.)
SELECTED REFERENCES: The Eagle's Gift - Page [227.8-228.3] (Don Juan began to talk to her then...from one side to the other.)
SEE ALSO: WALL-FOG, CRACK-WORLDS, TONAL-NAGUAL-DICHOTOMY

WORLD-DOMED-[THE DOMED WORLD]-(TOP): SEE: DOMED-WORLD-[THE DOMED WORLD]-(TOP)

WORLD-ERASING-[ERASING THE WORLD]: (Warriors know that if the assemblage point is displaced beyond a certain threshold, the world is simply erased, it vanishes into thin air; the stability of the perceivable world is no more than the force of alignment.)
SELECTED REFERENCES: The Fire From Within - Page [283.5-283.9] (He said that now I needed...all there is to our world.)
SEE ALSO: WARRIOR-WORLD-COLLAPSES-REASSEMBLES

WORLD-EVERYDAY-[THE WORLD OF EVERYDAY LIFE]: (Warriors know that the everyday world is only one in a cluster of consecutive worlds, and they struggle to enlarge their awareness beyond the world which they have been energetically conditioned to accept as the only possible world; without this detached awareness, warriors are left with only the distinctive features of the world of everyday life, [mundane needs, desperation, hopelessness and oblivion]; even so, warriors also know that sometimes the everyday world serves as the only shield to soothe warriors on the journey into the unknown.)
SELECTED REFERENCES: The Fire From Within - Page [281.4-281.5] (As I was telling don Juan...to be in the ordinary world!) The Power of Silence - Page [187.5-187.7] (Gone was his feeling of detachment...he set out on his own.) The Power of Silence - Page [227.4-227.6] (He described the specific problem of...in the world of everyday life.) The Art of Dreaming - Page [viii.2-viii.6] (Don Juan contended that our world...the one and only possible world.)
SEE ALSO: WARRIOR-DETACHMENT, WARRIOR-JOURNEY-UNKNOWN, OBLIVION

WORLD-FEELING-[FEELING THE WORLD]: SEE: KNOWLEDGE-DIRECT-[DIRECT KNOWLEDGE]

WORLD-IDEA-WARRIOR-[THE WARRIORS' IDEA OF THE WORLD]: SEE: CONTINUITY-[CONTINUITY]

WORLD-IN-NOT-OF-[IN THIS WORLD BUT NOT OF IT]: (Warriors are no longer in the world of daily affairs because they are no longer prey to their self-reflection; warriors are detached and dispassionate, they have no business following the ups and downs of the world of men; one of the arts of the warrior is to be outside everything and to be unnoticeable; warriors

hover between their old and new continuities; warriors know it is impossible to restore the shattered continuity of the life they once knew and they also know that the tenuousness of their new continuity will never provide them with the assuredness to function as if they were still in the world of everyday life; warriors have given up the world and yet they are still in it, they are in it and not of it; warriors practice controlled folly; in an artistic and sophisticated way, warriors separate themselves from everything while remaining an integral part of everything.)

SELECTED REFERENCES: The Second Ring of Power - Page [242.7] (I will always cheer for the...are in the midst of it.) The Second Ring of Power - Page [246.6-246.9] ("The Nagual taught you and me...is never to waste their power.) The Power of Silence - Page [90.5-91.1] ("Once our chains are cut...longer prey to their self-reflection.") The Power of Silence - Page [227.4-227.8] (He described the specific problem of...the solution. Why? No one knows.") The Power of Silence - Page [245.3-245.5] (Don Juan had explained controlled folly...remaining an integral part of everything.)

SEE ALSO: SELF-REFLECTION, WARRIOR-DETACHMENT, WARRIOR-CONTROLLED-FOLLY, CONTINUITY, WARRIOR-ASSUREDNESS, WARRIOR-FOG-CREATE, EQUILIBRIUM, SORCERER-ART, WARRIOR-DIFFERENT, WARRIOR-DISPASSIONATE

WORLD-INORGANIC-BEINGS-[THE WORLD OF THE INORGANIC BEINGS]-(TOP): SEE: INORGANIC-BEINGS-WORLD-[THE WORLD OF THE INORGANIC BEINGS]-(TOP)

WORLD-KNOWING-[KNOWING THE WORLD]: SEE: WORLD-PREDICTABILITY [THE PREDICTABILITY OF THE WORLD]

*WORLD-LUMINOUS-[THE LUMINOUS WORLD]: SEE: LUMINOUS-WORLD-[THE LUMINOUS WORLD]

WORLD-MAINTAINING-[MAINTAINING THE WORLD]: SEE: ATTENTION-FIRST-FOCUS-[THE FOCUS OF THE FIRST ATTENTION]

WORLD-MEN-[THE WORLD OF MEN]: *(Warriors know that the world of men is the warriors' world, they cannot renounce it; warriors struggle to reach a point where they are truly in the world but not of it; warriors cannot renounce the world of men but at the same time they cannot allow it to limit their possibilities either.)*

SELECTED REFERENCES: The Teachings of Don Juan - Page [152.8-153.3] (The only world available to you..."I believe that was the lesson.") Tales of Power - Page [155.5-155.9] ("Write, write," don Juan coaxed me...the harmony between *tonal* and *nagual*.) The Second Ring of Power - Page [246.7-246.8] (One day, however, you'll be complete...them in their ups and downs.) The Power of Silence - Page [187.5-187.6] (Gone was his felling of detachment...of the world of everyday life.)

SEE ALSO: WORLD-IN-NOT-OF, WORLD-EVERYDAY, LESSON-WORLDS-TWO

WORLD-MYSTERIOUS-[THE MYSTERIOUS WORLD]: *(Warriors know that the world is an unknown and marvelous place which exists far beyond the capacities of conscious reason and understanding; warriors respect the incomprehensible nature of the universe and are humble in the midst of it.)*

SELECTED REFERENCES: A Separate Reality - Page [145.7-145.8] ("I think there is no way...of using the will are astounding.) A Separate Reality - Page [219.9-220.3] (The world is incomprehensible....and what people do as an endless folly.") Journey to Ixtlan - Page [22.8] ("The world around us is very..."It doesn't yield its secrets easily.") Journey to Ixtlan - Page [25.3-25.4] ("The world around us is a mystery...she will not let us go.") Journey to Ixtlan - Page [64.3-64.5] ("To believe that the world is...hard and constantly all the time.) Journey to Ixtlan - Page [98.5] (*Dreaming* is as serious as *seeing*...thing in this awesome mysterious world.) Journey to Ixtlan - Page [99.9-100.1] (But who can tell? We are...can tell what you're capable of?")

Journey to Ixtlan - Page [135.8-135.9] ("Don't tax yourself trying to figure...in fact, that it is endless.) **Journey to Ixtlan - Page [165.5-165.7]** ("The world is a mystery," he said...you will add one more piece.") **Journey to Ixtlan - Page [167.5]** ("Trust your personal power...has in this whole mysterious world.") **Journey to Ixtlan - Page [179.3]** (You are only a man, and...the horrors of this marvelous world.) **Journey to Ixtlan - Page [182.6-182.7]** ("I can't believe that this is...the world is unknown and marvelous.) **Journey to Ixtlan - Page [216.3-216.6]** ("This is all crazy," I said...nothing about this mysterious unknown world.") **Journey to Ixtlan - Page [250.1]** (Don Juan was right...no more important than a beetle.) **Tales of Power - Page [33.2-33.4]** ("Don't waste your power on trifles,"...is petty and outright disastrous.") **Tales of Power - Page [45.8-45.9]** ("I've told you time and time...that should be more than enough.") **Tales of Power - Page [63.5-63.8]** ("You see," don Juan said...I was very much like you.) **Tales of Power - Page [84.4-84.6]** ("Those are ways of talking about mysteries for...waiting for you, everywhere and nowhere.") **Tales of Power - Page [115.8]** ("So you see, without an awareness...there is no power, no mystery.") **The Second Ring of Power - Page [184.3-184.5]** ("What do you mean that it took...mysteries and now we hold them.") **The Second Ring of Power - Page [269.7-269.8]** ("That's only if the sorcerer is teaching...as power, by doing what he has been shown.) **The Fire From Within - Page [56.9-57.2]** (He said that seers maintain...fluid, forever in motion, eternal.) **The Fire From Within - Page [59.6-59.7]** (Don Juan fought not to laugh...physical drive that one can twist at will.) **The Fire From Within - Page [147.8-147.9]** ("Be that as it may, warriors are...the highest of the new seers' goals.) **The Fire From Within - Page [148.1-148.3]** (He explained that what makes the warrior's...welcomed the world of boredom.) **The Fire From Within - Page [185.2-185.3]** ("This indeed is the mystery of awareness...stupidity of man in you by understanding it.) **The Fire From Within - Page [277.2-277.3]** (I laughed involuntarily upon seeing my...to the mystery of the world.) **The Fire From Within - Page [287.1-287.2]** ("Who cares about sadness, he said...mysteries await us! What mysteries!") **The Fire From Within - Page [290.1-290.2]** ("Los Angeles will vanish like a...it yet, and today you will.") **The Power of Silence - Page [29.5-29.6]** ("Heightened awareness is a mystery only for...immensity that surrounds us reasonable.") **The Power of Silence - Page [167.8-167.9]** ("Human beings have a very deep sense...surface, we find a sorcerer underneath.)

SEE ALSO: *MYSTERY, KNOWLEDGE-SILENT, ABSTRACT, LUMINOUS-BEINGS-MYSTERY, MYSTERY-AWARENESS*

WORLD-MYSTERY-RETURN-[RETURN TO THE MYSTERY OF THE WORLD]: (*Warriors know that the average man has turned his back on the realm of the mysterious and the unknown and welcomed the world of boredom; warriors also understand that the path of knowledge represents the exact opposite of the life situation of the average man; therefore, warriors struggle to detach themselves from the world of the functional and return to the world of mystery and foreboding.*)

SELECTED REFERENCES: **A Separate Reality - Page [219.9-220.1]** ("The world is all that is encased...as it is, a sheer mystery!) **The Eagle's Gift - Page [227.9-228.1]** (He told her that it is...only accept in humbleness and awe.) **The Eagle's Gift - Page [279.3-279.7]** ("Warriors don't have the world to cushion...One is equal to everything.) **The Fire From Within - Page [148.1-148.3]** (He explained that what makes the...has welcomed the world of boredom.)

SEE ALSO: *KNOWLEDGE-PATH, WORLD-MYSTERIOUS, WORLD-EVERYDAY, BOREDOM, WARRIOR-DETACHMENT*

WORLD-NOT-WHAT-APPEAR-[THE WORLD IS NOT WHAT IT APPEARS TO BE]: SEE: AWARENESS-TRUTH-FIRST-[THE FIRST TRUTH ABOUT AWARENESS]

WORLD-ONE-PATH-[ONE WORLD ONE PATH]: SEE: LESSON-WORLDS-TWO-[THE LESSON OF THE TWO WORLDS]

WORLD-OTHER-[THE OTHER WORLD]: (*Warriors define the other world as a new world of the warriors' vision, another world of awareness; the other worlds that warriors are capable of assembling once the assemblage point moves beyond a certain limit; the seven complete worlds that warriors can assemble [one for each great band of awareness]; two of those*

worlds [besides the world of everyday life] are relatively easy for warriors to assemble; the other five are something else, since they require warriors to make a dangerous and aberrant transformation in order to access those other great bands; the other worlds of the sorcerer represent the non-human unknown, they are mindless possibilities which are real, worlds that are wrapped one around the other like the skins of an onion; these worlds are outside the band of man and represent the side road which the new seers take; these worlds exist in positions of the assemblage point which must be arrived at by a movement of the assemblage point as opposed to a shift of the assemblage point; these worlds are total, all-inclusive worlds with endless realms outside of the human domain; these worlds can only be reached by warriors with great detachment and no self-importance whatsoever; a true change of worlds happens only when the assemblage point moves past a crucial threshold and hooks onto another of the great bands of emanations; when warriors use the force of alignment of those other great bands, they perceive other total worlds as a consequence.)

SELECTED REFERENCES: A Separate Reality - Page [153.8-154.1] ("We are men and our lot is to learn...the new worlds for our vision.") Journey to Ixtlan - Page [133.7-133.8] ("But if they were real where...they are nothing to laugh at.) Journey to Ixtlan - Page [212.1-212.2] ("You see," he continued, "every one...therefore, he can spin another world.") Journey to Ixtlan - Page [254.6] ("Do you mean, don Juan, that...They could act upon you.) Tales of Power - Page [173.4-173.5] (The point is to convince the *tonal*...or to peek into that infinity.") The Second Second Ring of Power - Page [46.6-47.7] ("Where did Eligio go...do it, but it took them years.") The Second Ring of Power - Page [62.4-62.8] ("Pablito is my enemy not because his eyes...power, I still have my purpose.") The Second Ring of Power - Page [134.8-134.9] (My mind was made up, my...me away from that world! Nothing!") The Second Ring of Power - Page [164.1-164.3] (I close my eyes and fall asleep...step through it into another world.") The Second Ring of Power - Page [322.9-323.5] ("Its very hard to get into...in the other world had been.) The Second Ring of Power - Page [324.1-324.7] ("There are no hallucinations," la Gorda...he had an awesome, fearsome side.") The Second Ring of Power - Page [327.5-327.9] (The other world, which don Juan...opened with her revelations was terrifying.) The Eagle's Gift - Page [204.7-204.9] (Due to something inexplicable in his...into that other world of awareness.) The Eagle's Gift - Page [236.9-237.6] (He then told la Gorda and me...is part of our total being.) The Fire From Within - Page [5.1-5.3] ("There were seers, however, who escaped...other worlds and never came back.) The Fire From Within - Page [125.1-125.4] ("The mystery is outside us...senses perceive in inconceivable ways.") The Fire From Within - Page [141.1-141.2] ("I've explained to you that man...entirely different from the world we know.") The Fire From Within - Page [144.7-144.8] ("But today, we are going to examine...after it moves from its original position.") The Fire From Within - Page [163.7-163.8] ("There are other complete worlds that our assemblage...the other five are something else.") The Fire From Within - Page [164.4-164.8] (He said that a true change...and consequently we perceive other worlds.") The Fire From Within - Page [209.1-209.2] (He explained that Genaro had tried...another of the great bands of emanations.) The Fire From Within - Page [216.1-216.5] (He said that the sobriety needed...will leave room for nothing else.") The Fire From Within - Page [283.6-284.2] (He said that now I needed to have one...a mirage as the old fixation.) The Fire From Within - Page [288.5-289.8] ("We've come to the end of...you won't be in this world.") The Fire From Within - Page [294.4-294.8] ("To assemble other worlds is not only...stranded in inconceivable aloneness.) The Power of Silence - Page [xvi.5-xvi.6] (7. When the assemblage point shifts, it makes...problems, or to face the unimaginable.) The Power of Silence - Page [58.4-58.8] (Don Juan used to repeat every chance...with the moving of the assemblage point.) The Art of Dreaming - Page [viii.2-viii.6] (Don Juan contended that our world...the one and only possible world.) The Art of Dreaming - Page [9.3-9.5] (Since the shifts of the assemblage...trace of human antecedents in them.) The Art of Dreaming - Page [38.8] (Let's say that there are other...energetic entities sometimes come to us.) The Art of Dreaming - Page [74.1-74.5] ("I still don't understand. What is...driven by expectations of power and gain.) The Art of Dreaming - Page [78.9-79.1] (Sorcerers, on the contrary, bring order...anything we know to be real.") The Art of Dreaming - Page [79.4-81.2] (I told him about the thought...price they couldn't afford to pay.) **The Art of Dreaming - Page [169.2-169.4]** ("This time you not only *saw*...this moment, and something attacked you.")

SEE ALSO: *AWARENESS-TRUTH-SEVENTH, WORLD-OTHER, ASSEMBLAGE-POINT-SHIFT-VS-MOVEMENT, UNKNOWN-HUMAN-VS-NON-HUMAN, EAGLE-EMANATIONS-MAN-BAND, WARRIORSHIP-VS-SORCERY*

*WORLD-OTHER-ARRANGEMENT-[THE ARRANGEMENT OF THE OTHER WORLD]: SEE: WORLD-OTHER-LAYERS-[THE TEN LAYERS OF THE OTHER WORLD]

WORLD-OTHER-CURTAIN-[THE CURTAIN OF THE OTHER WORLD]: (Warriors know that the curtain of the other world is another term for the crack in the world.)

SELECTED REFERENCES: **The Fire From Within - Page [58.6-58.9]** ("One day, without any warning at all,...getting off the subject. You always do.)

SEE ALSO: *CRACK-WORLDS*

WORLD-OTHER-LAYERS-TEN-[THE TEN LAYERS OF THE OTHER WORLD]: (There are ten layers of the other world; a master sorcerer can guide his disciple through all ten; evil or dilettante sorcerers can at best only go through three of those layers.)

SELECTED REFERENCES: **A Separate Reality - Page [98.6-99.4]** (I don't remember what prompted don...looked at me and smiled knowingly.)

SEE ALSO: *WORLD-OTHER, SORCERER-MASTER, SORCERER-LYRIC, SORCERER-EVIL, TOLTEC-LEVELS*

WORLD-OUT-OF-[OUT OF THIS WORLD]: (The most extravagant feature of sorcery is the configuration known as "out of this world"; it involves the position of the assemblage point and the particular perceptions attendant to that position.)

SELECTED REFERENCES: **The Art of Dreaming - Page [39.6-40.8]** ("You have a proclivity for behaving...He refused any further discussion.)

SEE ALSO: *ASSEMBLAGE-POINT-MOVING, WORLDS-OTHER-ASSEMBLE-TOTAL*

WORLD-PREDICTABILITY-[THE PREDICTABILITY OF THE WORLD]: (Warriors know better than to believe that they can rigidly predict the ways of the world; warriors make every effort to leave behind the stationary view of feeling that they know the world; warriors strive to destroy their sense of knowing the world by practicing dreaming and embarking on a journey of unthinkable dimensions.)

SELECTED REFERENCES: **The Art of Dreaming - Page [73.2-73.6]** (Don Juan, with extreme patience, pointed...human domain and perceive the inconceivable.)

SEE ALSO: *WARRIOR-EXPECTATION, DESCRIPTION-WORLD*

WORLD-PURPLE-[THE VIOLET-PURPLE WORLD]-(TOP)

WORLD-RED-[THE RED WORLD]: (Warriors know that there is a reddish world which resembles the traditional description of hell; this world is assembled with another of the great bands of emanations.)

SELECTED REFERENCES: **The Fire From Within - Page [208.1-209.8]** ("Don't look at Genaro," a voice...don Juan protested almost vehemently.)

SEE ALSO: *WORLD-OTHER, HELL, HELL-VISIONS-(TOP)*

WORLD-REASON-[THE WORLD OF REASON]: SEE: REASON-WORLD-[THE WORLD OF REASON]

WORLD-SELECT-WARRIOR-[WARRIORS SELECT THE ITEMS THAT MAKE UP THEIR WORLD]: SEE: WARRIOR-WORLD-SELECT-[WARRIORS SELECT THE ITEMS THAT MAKE UP THEIR WORLD]

WORLD-SHIFTING-REASON-WILL-[SHIFTING BACK AND FORTH BETWEEN THE WORLD OF REASON TO THE WORLD OF WILL]:
(Warriors know they must be fluid and shift harmoniously with the world around them, whether it is the world of reason or the world of will.)
    SELECTED REFERENCES: Tales of Power - Page [107.5-107.7] ("You'll get used to it...is neither one nor the other.) Tales of Power -Page [113.7-114.3] ("The world upheld by *reason* makes all...your *reason*, I with my *will*.)
    SEE ALSO: *REASON, WILL, EQUILIBRIUM, WARRIOR-FLUIDITY*

WORLD-SOLID-OBJECTS-[THE WORLD OF SOLID OBJECTS]:
(Warriors are aware that the world of solid objects is only a way of making our passage on earth more convenient; it is only a description that was created to help us; the solidity of the perceivable world is no more than the force of alignment; certain emanations are routinely aligned because of the fixation of the assemblage point on one specific spot and that is all there really is to our world.)
    SELECTED REFERENCES: Tales of Power - Page [97.7-97.8] (We are perceivers. We are an...we rarely emerge in a lifetime.) The Fire From Within - Page [33.1-33.2] (The first truth, he said, was...a universe of the Eagle's emanations.) The Fire From Within - Page [36.5-36.6] ("The first truth about awareness, as...world of objects and it's not.") The Fire From Within - Page [37.2-37.9] ("The first truth is that the...in motion, and yet unchanged, eternal.") The Fire From Within - Page [64.8-65.2] (Don Juan replied that human alternatives...have, therefore, nearly an inexhaustible scope.) The Fire From Within - Page [108.2] (He then began his explanation...which seers call the Eagle's emanations.) The Fire From Within - Page [283.5-283.9] (He said that now I needed...all there is to our world.) The Art of Dreaming - Page [3.5-3.6] ("What is the social base of...the world is made of concrete objects.) The Art of Dreaming - Page [4.1-4.9] (Don Juan's conception was that our...essence of everything, energy itself, directly.)
    SEE ALSO: *DESCRIPTION-WORLD, AWARENESS-TRUTH-FIRST, ATTENTION-FIRST, TONAL, ATTENTION-TONAL, PERCEPTION-SOCIAL-BASE*

WORLD-SOUNDNESS-[THE SOUNDNESS OF THE WORLD]: SEE: WORLD-STABILITY-[THE STABILITY OF THE WORLD], MIRAGE-[MIRAGE]

WORLD-SOUNDS-OF-[THE SOUNDS OF THE WORLD]: (Warriors know that they must use their ears to relieve some of the burden from their eyes; warriors listen to the sounds of the world; they listen harmoniously and with great patience as an aid to stopping the internal dialogue.)
    SELECTED REFERENCES: A Separate Reality - Page [219.1-219.3] ("First of all you must use...done harmoniously and with great patience.) A Separate Reality - Page [220.6-220.7] (I began the exercise of listening...capable of paying attention to the sounds.)
    SEE ALSO: *INTERNAL-DIALOGUE-STOPPING, EARS-RELIEVE-BURDEN-EYES, EYES, WARRIOR-HEARING*

WORLD-STABILITY-[THE STABILITY OF THE WORLD]: (Warriors know that the stability which seems to belong to the everyday world is no more than the force of alignment; certain emanations are routinely aligned because of the fixation of the assemblage point on one specific spot; that is all there is to the normal world.)
    SELECTED REFERENCES: The Fire From Within - Page [283.5-283.9] (He said that now I needed...all there is to our world.)

SEE ALSO: *WORLD-EVERYDAY, ALIGNMENT-FORCE, ASSEMBLAGE-POINT-FIXATION*

WORLD-TWIN-SUNS-[THE WORLD OF THE TWIN SUNS]-(TOP): SEE: ZULEICA-DREAMING-CELESTIAL-[ZULEICA'S CELESTIAL DREAMING]-(TOP)

WORLD-UNSEEN-[THE UNSEEN WORLD]: (Warriors know that the unseen world is also known as the other side, the other world, the realm of the supernatural, or the second attention.)
    SELECTED REFERENCES: The Art of Dreaming - Page [vii.7-viii.1] (In anthropological works, shamanism is described...the supernatural but the second attention.)
    SEE ALSO: *WORLD-OTHER, ATTENTION-SECOND, OTHER-SIDE, SUPERNATURAL REALM*

WORLD-VANISHES-[THE WORLD-VANISHES]: SEE: WORLD-ERASING-[ERASING THE WORLD]

WORLD-WEIRD-[IT IS A WEIRD WORLD]: (Warriors must assume responsibility for being in a weird world; the world is weird because it is stupendous, awesome, mysterious and unfathomable and warriors know they will only be in it for a short time.)
    SELECTED REFERENCES: **Journey to Ixtlan - Page [80.8-81.2]** ("One must assume responsibility for being...witnessing all the marvels of it.") **Journey to Ixtlan - Page [85.8]** ("I've told you, this is a...their splendor is something to witness.")
    SEE ALSO: *WORLD-MYSTERY-RETURN, WORLD-MYSTERIOUS*

WORLD-YELLOW-[THE YELLOW WORLD]: (Warriors know that the world of the inorganic beings appears to the physical body as a yellow world, a land of sulfur dunes.)
    SELECTED REFERENCES: The Art of Dreaming - Page [128.7-128.9] (I was dreaming an utterly nonsensical...was having as normal, incoherent dream.) **The Art of Dreaming - Page [133.1-133.3]** (I mentioned to don Juan that I...through sorcerers' stories, not through experience.")
    SEE ALSO: *INORGANIC-BEINGS-REALM, PARALLEL-LINES-LAND, HELL, HELL-VISIONS-(TOP)*

WORLDLY-TASK-WARRIOR-[THE WARRIORS' WORLDLY TASK]: SEE: WARRIOR-TASK-WORLDLY-[THE WARRIORS' WORLDLY TASK]

WORLDS-FIVE-[THE FIVE WORLDS THAT ARE NOT EASY FOR WARRIORS TO ASSEMBLE]: (Warriors know that five of the seven worlds available to man's awareness are extremely difficult to access; seers must undergo a dangerous transformation to do so and must tax their awareness to the limit in the process.)
    SELECTED REFERENCES: **The Fire From Within - Page [163.7-163.8]** ("There are other complete worlds that...the other five are something else.") **The Fire From Within - Page [165.7-166.4]** (He added that all the seers were...to become trees to do that.") **The Fire From Within - Page [230.5-230.6]** ("They chose to live," he repeated...of the Eagle to be devoured.")
    SEE ALSO: *WORLDS-OTHER-ASSEMBLE-TOTAL, WORLDS-SEVEN, WORLDS-THREE*

WORLDS-OTHER-ASSEMBLE-TOTAL-[ASSEMBLING OTHER TOTAL WORLDS]: (Warriors know that when the assemblage point assembles another world, that world is total; the force of alignment of the other great bands of emanations makes our normal world vanish; warriors move themselves out of this world by assembling another totally different and complete world; the assembly of another total world is the result of the profound movement of the assemblage point; to assemble other worlds is not only a matter of practice but a matter of intent; the danger of assembling other worlds is that they are as possessive as our own; assembling another total world is the most difficult accomplishment in sorcery.)

SELECTED REFERENCES: Tales of Power - Page [173.4-173.5] (The point is to convince the *tonal*...or to peek into that infinity.") The Fire From Within - Page [29.8-29.9] ("The new seers used petty tyrants...on discussing the mastery of awareness.) The Fire From Within - Page [141.1-141.2] ("I've explained to you that man...entirely different from the world we know.") The Fire From Within - Page [144.7-144.8] ("But today, we are going to examine...after it moves from its original position.") The Fire From Within - Page [163.8] ("There are other complete worlds that our assemblage...the other five are something else.") The Fire From Within - Page [216.8-217.2] ("Genaro is separated from us at...makes us perceive another total world.") The Fire From Within - Page [258.3] (Don Juan had told me then...point to gain experience in shifting.) The Fire From Within - Page [283.6-284.2] (He said that now I needed to have one...a mirage as the old fixation.) The Fire From Within - Page [288.5-289.7] ("We've come to the end of my...you won't be in this world.") The Fire From Within - Page [294.4-294.8] ("To assemble other worlds is not...of getting stranded in inconceivable aloneness.) The Fire From Within - Page [300.1-300.2] (Pablito, Nestor and I didn't die...our assemblage points and assembled other worlds.) The Power of Silence - Page [xvi.5-xvi.6] (7. When the assemblage point shifts, it makes...problems, or to face the unimaginable.) The Power of Silence - Page [58.6-58.8] (Don Juan used to repeat every chance...with the moving of the assemblage point.) The Power of Silence - Page [94.3-94.6] (The nagual Elias then shifted his...sphere of the world we know.)

SEE ALSO: ASSEMBLAGE-POINT-MOVING, EAGLE-EMANATIONS-BANDS-GREAT, WORLD-OTHER, INTENT, SORCERY-ACCOMPLISHMENT-MOST-DIFFICULT

WORLDS-OTHER-HATCH-[THE HATCH TO OTHER WORLDS]: SEE: DREAMING-VS-DREAMS-[DREAMING VS DREAMS]

WORLDS-OTHER-POSSESSIVENESS-[THE POSSESSIVENESS OF OTHER WORLDS]: (Warriors know that the danger of assembling other worlds is that they are as possessive as our own.)

SELECTED REFERENCES: The Fire From Within - Page [294.4-294.8] ("To assemble other worlds is not...of getting stranded in inconceivable aloneness.)

SEE ALSO: WORLD-OTHER, WORLDS-OTHER-ASSEMBLE-TOTAL, ASSEMBLAGE-POINT-FIXATION

WORLDS-REAL-VS-DREAM-[REAL WORLDS VS DREAM WORLDS]: (Warriors define a real world as a world that generates energy, as opposed to a world of phantom projections where nothing generates energy; in dreaming, if dreamers can "see" the energy of an item, they know they are dealing with a real world no matter how distorted that world may appear to their dreaming attention; if dreamers can't "see" the energy of an item then they know they are not in a real world; the energy body is also capable of perceiving energy from foreign sources; this energy is perceived by the energy body as sizzling energy, as in the case of the inorganic beings' realm; one of the critical issues of dreaming is the determination of the character of the items on which dreamers focus their dreaming attention; are those items energy generating, mere phantom projections or generators of foreign energy.)

SELECTED REFERENCES: The Art of Dreaming - Page [164.1-164.9] ("Dreamers have a rule of thumb...projections, or generators of foreign energy.")

SEE ALSO: DREAMING-VS-DREAMS, ENERGY

WORLDS-SEVEN-[THE SEVEN OTHER WORLDS THAT THE WARRIOR CAN ASSEMBLE]: (*Warriors know that in addition to the world of normal awareness, there are seven other worlds available to us, each one corresponding to one of the seven other great bands of emanations which produce awareness.*)

SELECTED REFERENCES: The Fire From Within - Page [179.6-180.3] (When we were back in Silvio Manuel's...the seven worlds available to man.") The Fire From Within - Page [206.4-206.7] ("The unknown is not really inside the...You never made the connection.") The Fire From Within - Page [216.8-217.2] ("Genaro is separated from us at ...makes us perceive another total world.") The Fire From Within - Page [248.1-248.5] (The ones who opted for the allies'...you can't remember it at all.) The Fire From Within - Page [256.7-256.9] ("Now, the only thing left for you...and align another great band of emanations.) The Fire From Within - Page [288.5-289.5] ("We've come to the end of my...in any of the seven worlds.")
SEE ALSO: *WORLDS-OTHER-ASSEMBLE-TOTAL, WORLDS-FIVE, WORLDS-THREE*

WORLDS-THREE-[THE THREE WORLDS THAT ARE RELATIVELY EASY FOR THE WARRIOR TO ASSEMBLE]: (*Warriors know that of the eight worlds available to us, only three of them are easy to assemble, one of those three is the world of normal awareness.*)

SELECTED REFERENCES: The Fire From Within- Page [163.7-163.8] ("There are other complete worlds that...the other five are something else.")
SEE ALSO: *WORLDS-SEVEN, WORLDS-FIVE*

WORLDS-TOTAL-ASSEMBLE-[ASSEMBLING OTHER TOTAL WORLDS]: SEE: WORLDS-OTHER-ASSEMBLE-TOTAL-[ASSEMBLING OTHER TOTAL WORLDS]

WORM-CAVORTING-WITH-[CAVORTING WITH THE GIANT WORM]- (TOP)

WORM-DEATH-GIANT-[DEATH IN THE MOUTH OF A GIANT WORM]- (TOP)

WORRY-NOT-WARRIOR-[WARRIORS DON'T WORRY]: SEE: WARRIOR-WORRY-NOT-[WARRIORS DON'T WORRY]

**WORTHY-OPPONENT-[THE WORTHY OPPONENT]:* (*Warriors know that the worthy opponent is the artful trap of the nagual; without the worthy opponent, the apprentice has no possibility of continuing on the path of knowledge; the worthy opponent is not really an enemy but a thoroughly dedicated adversary; the acts of the worthy opponent either blast apprentices to pieces or change them radically; under the pressure of the worthy opponent, apprentices either choose the world of everyday life or the world of the warrior; death is the only worthy opponent the warrior has.*)

SELECTED REFERENCES: Journey to Ixtlan - Page [179.5-179.6] ("I think I have a cure...found a worthy opponent for you.") Journey to Ixtlan - Page [199.3-199.4] ("I don't know don Juan...one which is already following you.") Journey to Ixtlan - Page [217.9-218.1] (We drove away and don Juan...had found for you," he said.) Journey to Ixtlan - Page [225.5-226.2] ("You should have known that it...You don't have any other alternative.") Journey to Ixtlan - Page [227.4-227.5] ("You are in a terrible bind...forced you to change your *doing*.") Tales of Power - Page [246.4-247.8] (Power plants shake the *tonal* and...whether or not to make it.") The Second Ring of Power - Page [263.4-263.9] (I remembered that particular decision more...a capon, feed on an onion.") The Power of Silence - Page [112.1-112.2] (Death is not our destroyer, although...about it; average men do not.")
SEE ALSO: *DEATH, WARRIOR-CHOICE, DEATH-WORTHY-OPPONENT*

WRITING-SORCERY-[WRITING AS AN EXERCISE IN SORCERY]: (The way in which Carlos Castaneda used writing as an exercise in sorcery.)

SELECTED REFERENCES: **A Separate Reality - Page [97.1-97.4]** (Don Juan looked at me, still...sorcerer by writing your way up.") **Tales of Power - Page [14.2-14.4]** (We talked until it became dark...I had nothing to do with.) **Tales of Power - Page [200.8-201.2]** ("I think he got frightened when...he be able to read it?") **The Eagle's Gift - Page [20.7-22.1]** (We had discussed this in detail...with the tip of my finger.) **The Power of Silence - Page [xiv.3-xiv.6]** (Don Juan himself set me the...but rather an exercise in sorcery.") **The Power of Silence - Page [180.3-180.8]** (There was also a mystery woman among...That, she said, was the fun part.) **The Art of Dreaming - Page [xi.6-xi.9]** (All this brings me to the...and our commitment to his quest.)

SEE ALSO: *RECOLLECTION-SORCERER'S*

Y

YELL-WARRIOR-[THE WARRIORS' YELL]: SEE: WARRIOR-YELL-[THE WARRIORS' YELL]

YELLOW-WORLD-[THE YELLOW WORLD]: SEE: WORLD-YELLOW-[THE YELLOW WORLD]

YERBERO-[YERBERO]: (Warriors know a yerbero is a person who gathers and sells medicinal herbs.)
SELECTED REFERENCES: A Separate Reality - Page [1.7-1.9] (Bill had told me that the...used by the Indians of the area.) A Separate Reality - Page [29.7-30.5] (We were talking about Oaxaca...wanted to know more about it.) The Fire From Within - Page [140.4-140.5] (Don Juan and Genaro made their yearly...used those plants to make medicines.)
SEE ALSO: PLANTS

*YOUTH-[YOUTH]: (Youth is an independent reality for warriors; warriors know that youth is in no way a barrier against the deterioration of the tonal; to be impeccable gives warriors youth and vigor and power no matter what their age.)
SELECTED REFERENCES: Journey to Ixtlan - Page [124.4-124.5] (I slowly dragged myself down the...to be extremely fit and young.) Journey to Ixtlan - Page [160.2-160.4] (I told him that I was simply...rather in what you don't do.") Tales of Power - Page [135.6-135.7] ("You know that young man's tonal...against the deterioration of the tonal.) Tales of Power - Page [218.7-218.9] (I had never seen Nestor so light...he said. "That's why he's younger.") Tales of Power - Page [228.1-228.4] ("Who has entrusted you with him...that he genuinely felt like one.) The Second Ring of Power - Page [5.7-7.1] (The house seemed deserted. The thought...in my mouth. I was afraid.) The Second Ring of Power - Page [26.3-27.2] (She observed me with a gleam in...not to let her thoughts interfere.) The Second Ring of Power - Page [243.6-243.8] ("If your grandfather and father would...proper for you to choose wisely.") The Eagle's Gift - Page [295.3-295.4] (It is nearly impossible for warriors...endless source of youth and energy.) The Art of Dreaming - Page [130.6-130.7] (Florinda, although she was old, was...the eye as youth and vigor.)
SEE ALSO: WARRIOR-IMPECCABILITY, WARRIOR-CHOICE, TONAL, VIGOR

Z

<u>*ZOILA-ZULEICA*</u>*-[ZOILA AND ZULEICA]-(TOP)*

<u>*ZULEICA-DREAMING-CELESTIAL*</u>*-[ZULEICA'S CELESTIAL DREAMING]-(TOP)*

<u>*ZULEICA-DREAMING-INSTRUCTION*</u>*-[ZULEICA'S DREAMING INSTRUCTION]-(TOP): SEE: DREAMING-INSTRUCTION-[THE WARRIORS' DREAMING INSTRUCTION]-(TOP)*

A CATALOG OF ONE THOUSAND SECRETS

Editor's Note: This subset of intuitive references is a supplement to the informational references which make up Part I of this catalog. As the author has pointed out, these intuitive references are not intended to convey analytical information. Instead, they are designed to open an intuitive doorway to the abstract order of knowledge.

In addition to individual references from all the Castaneda material, the reader will also find the individual chapters of each book and the entire books themselves listed as entries in this intuitive subset. The author has done this because he believes that in addition to the informational and intuitive references which they contain, each of these narrative passages can also be considered its own distinct "tale of power."

SUBSET II
INTUITIVE REFERENCES
(TALES OF POWER)

A

ABSTRACT-THE-[THE ABSTRACT]: (TOP)
  SELECTED REFERENCES: The Power of Silence - Page [25-39] (We returned to don Juan's house...seemed to be enjoying himself immensely.)

ABSTRACT-CORE-FIRST-[THE FIRST ABSTRACT CORE]: (TOP)
  SELECTED REFERENCES: The Power of Silence - Page [1-11] (Don Juan, whenever it was pertinent...else, until finally I fell asleep.)

ABSTRACT-MEETING-[MEETING THE ABSTRACT]: (TOP)
  SELECTED REFERENCES: The Power of Silence - Page [39.1-39.3] ("Consider this," he said. "It was...touching it or feeling its presence.")

AIRLINE-OFFICE-DOORWAY-[THE DOORWAY OF THE AIRLINE OFFICE]: (TOP)
  SELECTED REFERENCES: Tales of Power - Page [145.8-159.8] (On Wednesday morning I left my hotell...moment before a cab came along.) The Second Ring of Power - Page [285.9-286.3] (But the worst thing happened to...the morning became your new time.") The Eagle's Gift - Page [99.9-100.4] (The following day at ten o'clock....line I came from, this world.)

ALAMEDA-PARK-[DEATH FINDS A MAN IN ALAMEDA PARK]-(TOP):
SEE: DEATH-ALAMEDA-PARK-[DEATH FINDS A MAN IN ALAMEDA
PARK]-(TOP)

ALIGNMENT-MOMENT-WITNESSING-[WITNESSING THE MOMENT OF
ALIGNMENT]: (TOP)
    SELECTED REFERENCES: The Fire From Within - Page **[214.6-217.2]** ("Genaro
wants you to watch the moment...alignment makes us perceive another total world.")

ALLIES-APPOINTMENT-[THE APPOINTMENT WITH THE ALLIES]:
(TOP)
    SELECTED REFERENCES: The Second Ring of Power - Page **[125.7-126.1]** ("What is
this appointment with power...here and those things will come.")

ALLIES-CALLING-[CALLING THE ALLIES]: (TOP)
    SELECTED REFERENCES: The Second Ring of Power - Page **[164.7-165.6]** (I
laughed and told her that I...lantern and gathered up my notes.) **The Second Ring of Power -
Page [256.6-257.4]** (When I was in full control again...edge of my hand to produce it.)

ALLIES-DEATH-MERGE-[THE ALLIES TRY TO MERGE WITH THE
WARRIOR'S DEATH]: (TOP)
    SELECTED REFERENCES:: Journey to Ixtlan - Page **[174.4-176.4]** (Then a very swift
dark mass...where we had been before.) **Journey to Ixtlan - Page [178.1-178.3]** (I asked him to
explain how...that would have been your end.")

ALLIES-ENCOUNTER-[ENCOUNTER WITH THE ALLIES]: (TOP)
    SELECTED REFERENCES: A Separate Reality - Page **[234.4-235.2]** ("When a man is
facing the ally...like anything one has ever touched.")

ALLIES-FACING-[FACING THE ALLIES]: (TOP)
    SELECTED REFERENCES: Journey to Ixtlan - Page **[257.9-259.4]** ("I was young
when I first...leap forward and grab the ally.") **Journey to Ixtlan - Page [265.4-265.5]** (At any
rate, in your next...yourself live in an unknown land.) **The Art of Dreaming - Page [51.1-56.2]**
("You are stuck at a dangerous...any interference from the inorganic beings.) **The Art of
Dreaming - Page [91.8-92.3]** (The scout pushed me into a tunnel...it replied. "Energy is like
blood.")

ALLIES-GRAPPLE-HOW-TO-[HOW TO GRAPPLE WITH AN ALLY]:
(TOP)
    SELECTED REFERENCES: A Separate Reality - Page **[251.6-251.9]** ("Fright is
something one can never...is the master at all times.")

ALLIES-HURLED-AWAY-[HURLED AWAY BY THE ALLIES]: (TOP)
    SELECTED REFERENCES: The Second Ring of Power - Page **[256.7-259.9]** (When I
was in full control again...birdcall and we both started walking.) **The Second Ring of Power -
Page [270.8-271.1]** ("Now we can talk about what happened...you saw all the way through.")

ALLIES-JUAN-BOUT-[DON JUAN'S BOUT WITH THE ALLY]: (TOP)
    SELECTED REFERENCES: The Fire From Within - Page **[98.3-100.8]** ("I chose that
technique," he went...We are separated by an abyss.)

ALLIES-MESSAGE-DREAMER-[THE DREAMER'S MESSAGE FOR THE
ALLIES]: (TOP)
    SELECTED REFERENCES: The Art of Dreaming - Page **[48.6-48.8]** ("With inorganic
beings, the secret is...curious that they'll come for sure.")

ALLIES-SEEING-DREAMING-[SEEING THE ALLIES IN DREAMING]:
(TOP)
    SELECTED REFERENCES: The Second Ring of Power - Page **[75.3-75.6]** (I began to
speak but I did...behave as an innocent bystander.) **The Fire From Within - Page [245.6-245.8]**
(When I reached the group I realized...sort of wind scooped them away.) **The Fire From Within
- Page [291.4-292.2]** (Don Juan was working his glow...the allies, it was quite brilliant.) **The Fire**

SELECTED REFERENCES: The Eagle's Gift - Page [150-167] (Our discussion of was most...where had all of them gone?)

ENESS-SURVIVAL-FIRE-WITHIN-[THE SURVIVAL OF ENESS AFTER BURNING WITH THE FIRE FROM WITHIN]: (TOP)

SELECTED REFERENCES: The Fire From Within - Page [227.6-227.7] (I asked him a stions about...the other side of that force.)

From Within - Page [296.1-296.3] (I started to follow them, but...windlike force blew the world away.) The Power of Silence - Page [185.9-186.] (Very soon after I came into...nothing. I was stupid beyond belief.") The Art of Dreaming - Page [49.7-50.7] (It seemed at that time that...anguish, sadness with no apparent foundation)

ALLIES-SMOKING-[SMOKING AN ALLY]: (TOP)

SELECTED REFERENCES: A Separate Reality - Page [182.8-192.5] (My next attempt at "seeing" took place...turn against him and destroy him.")

ALLIES-SORCERER-EXCHANGE-ENERGY-[THE SORCERER'S EXCHANGE OF ENERGY WITH THE ALLIES]: (TOP)

SELECTED REFERENCES: The Art of Dreaming - Page [52.3-52.7] ("Why do you call them my friends...can foresee terrible dangers in that.") The Art of Dreaming - Page [91.8-92.3] (The scout pushed me into a tunnel...it replied. "Energy is like blood.") The Art of Dreaming - Page [123.2-123.4] ("At this level, it isn't that...with you. It knows you intimately.")

ALLIES-SPIRIT-CATCHER-[THE ALLY AND THE SPIRIT CATCHER]: (TOP)

SELECTED REFERENCES: A Separate Reality - Page [220.6-228.4] (I began the exercise of listening...after you know him very well.")

ALLIES-SUMMONING-[SUMMONING THE ALLIES]: (TOP)

SELECTED REFERENCES: The Art of Dreaming - Page [52.7-53.5] ("What do you recommend I do...tree trunks, right in front of me.)

ALLIES-TALES-[TALES OF THE ALLIES]: (TOP)

SELECTED REFERENCES: A Separate Reality - Page [43.9-44.1] (Don Juan said that his benefactor... he became one with the ally.) A Separate Reality - Page [182.8-187.3] (My next attempt at seeing took...desert shrubs became superimposed on it.) A Separate Reality - Page [228.6-247.7] (We arrived in the same valley I...healed and your gap is closed.") Journey to Ixtlan - Page [172.1-178.5] ("Powers, allies, spirits, who knows?" he... myriad of things to his aid.) Journey to Ixtlan - Page [250.1-253.9] (I wiped my eyes and as I...see the lines of the world.) Tales of Power - Page [39.1-40.4] (They sat down on either side...with my back against the wall.) Tales of Power - Page [263.6-267.2] (Don Juan spoke first; he said...could sit up by himself again.) The Second Ring of Power - Page [71.5-75.6] ("What was that?" I asked Lidia...to behave as an innocent bystander.) The Second Ring of Power - Page [140.6-141.9] (She did not let me speak...the coyote was don Juan's.) The Second Ring of Power - Page [142.9-148.4] (I tried to stop to catch...flanking us on all four sides.) The Second Ring of Power - Page [152.1-152.2] (The Nagual and Genaro could make…chicken to run inside Lidia's blouse.") Eagle's Gift - Page [68.2-68.7] (We hiked as quickly and as...steered them away from the place.) The Fire From Within - Page [71.5-72.5] (Something got me out of my...back to our explanation of awareness.") The Fire From Within - Page [76.1-77.3] ("I was explaining about the first...Juan's house in the next town.) The Fire From Within - Page [104.4-105.2] (Don Juan went on to say...immensity that is the Eagle's emanations.) The Fire From Within - Page [106.7-107.8] (On entering into heightened awareness, I...made me follow that opaque light.) The Fire From Within - Page [291.4-292.2] (Don Juan was working his glow...the allies, it was quite brilliant.)

ALLIES-TOLTEC-GHOULS-[ALLIES OF THE TOLTEC GHOULS]: (TOP)

SELECTED REFERENCES: The Fire From Within - Page [239.2-245.8] ("It's too late," Genaro said, fully...sort of wind scooped them away.) The Fire From Within - Page [246.9-248.8] ("Explain to me what happened at...and their allies as they are.)

ALLIES-TRANSPORT-DREAMER-[THE ALLIES TRANSPORT THE DREAMER]: (TOP)

SELECTED REFERENCES: The Art of Dreaming - Page [49.1-49.4] ("The novelty for us is the...to worlds beyond the human domain.")

ALLIES-VISITS-[VISITS WITH THE ALLIES]: (TOP)

SELECTED REFERENCES: The Art of Dreaming - Page [58.8-59.6] (He stared at me, smiling, and...inorganic being friends," don Juan said.)

ALLIES-WHISTLE-[THE WHISTLE TO DISPERSE THE ALLIES]: (TOP)

SELECTED REFERENCES: The Second Ring of Power - Page [250.5-250.8] (La Gorda leaned over and whispered...from the trail in the darkness.)

ALLIES-WRESTLING-[WRESTLING WITH THE ALLIES]: (TOP)
SELECTED REFERENCES: **The Fire From Within - Page [100.6-100.8]** ("What would have happened if the...We are separated by an abyss.) **The Fire From Within - Page [106.4-107.8]** (Don Juan discontinued his explanations of...crate he used as a bench.)

APPEARANCES-INTENDING-[INTENDING APPEARANCES]: (TOP)
SELECTED REFERENCES: **The Power of Silence - Page [241-265]** (Don Juan wanted us to make...reach the place of silent knowledge.")

APPEARANCES-INTENDING-[INTENDING APPEARANCES]: (TOP)
SELECTED REFERENCES: **Journey to Ixtlan - Page [206.8-210.7]** (I noticed that don Juan had...your hands," he whispered in my ear.)

APPRENTICESHIP-CARLOS-[HOW DON JUAN ENGAGED CARLOS FOR HIS APPRENTICESHIP]: (TOP)
SELECTED REFERENCES: **The Teachings of Don Juan - Page [13.2-14.9]** (In the summer of 1960, while...the training was long and arduous.) **A Separate Reality - Page [1.2-3.8]** (Ten years ago I had the...more unusual it seemed to be.) **Journey to Ixtlan - Page [2.2-3.1]** (The old man shook his head...ready I went back to Arizona.) **Tales of Power - Page [234.1-234.6]** ("Let me begin by telling you...I became obsessed with that look.)

ASSEMBLAGE POINT-[THE ASSEMBLAGE POINT]: (TOP)
SELECTED REFERENCES: **The Fire From Within - Page [106-125]** (Don Juan discontinued his explanation of...human senses perceive in inconceivable ways.")

ASSEMBLAGE-POINT-FIXATION-[THE FIXATION OF THE ASSEMBLAGE POINT]: (TOP)
SELECTED REFERENCES: **The Art of Dreaming - Page [57-81]** (Since our agreement had been to...what it is: a mere candle.")

ASSEMBLAGE-POINT-MOVEMENT-FREE-[THE FREE MOVEMENT OF THE ASSEMBLAGE-POINT]: (TOP)
SELECTED REFERENCES: **The Power of Silence - Page [233.7-236.2]** (Don Juan contended that that simple...river, and started to walk home.")

ASSEMBLAGE-POINT-MOVING-[MOVING THE ASSEMBLAGE POINT]: (TOP)
SELECTED REFERENCES: **The Power of Silence - Page [116-134]** (A couple of days later, don...called the place of no pity.)

ASSEMBLAGE-POINT-MOVING-DISPLACING-[MOVING OR DISPLACING THE ASSEMBLAGE POINT]: (TOP)
SELECTED REFERENCES: **The Power of Silence - Page [134.7-145.1]** (Don Juan told me that there...to make the assemblage point move.)

ASSEMBLAGE-POINT-MOVING-VOLITIONAL-[THE VOLITIONAL MOVEMENT OF THE ASSEMBLAGE POINT]: (TOP)
SELECTED REFERENCES: **The Power of Silence - Page [106.1-106.3]** (By the time I had reestablished...volitional movement of my assemblage point.)

ASSEMBLAGE-POINT-POSITION-[THE POSITION OF THE ASSEMBLAGE POINT]: (TOP)
SELECTED REFERENCES: **The Fire From Within - Page [126-139]** (The next time don Juan resumed...the old seers paid for theirs.")

ATLANTEANS-TALES-[TALES OF THE ATLANTEANS]: (TOP)
SELECTED REFERENCES: **The Eagle's Gift - Page [9.8-10.5]** (They wanted to know what I...going to that town scares me.") **The Eagle's Gift - Page [14.9-15.3]** ("What do you think about the...highest place. See what I mean?") **The Eagle's Gift - Page [26.4-27.4]** (I then told them that I...the Atlanteans would walk at night.)

ATTENTION-FIRST-[THE FIRST ATTENTION]: (T
SELECTED REFERENCES: **The Fire From Within - Pa** we ate breakfast...Juan's house in the next town.)

ATTENTION-SECOND-[THE SECOND ATTENTIO
SELECTED REFERENCES: **The Second Ring of Powe** to leave later on...was no limit to that vastness.)

ATTENTION-SECOND-CENTER-STROKING-[STR *OF ASSEMBLAGE FOR THE SECOND ATTENTION*
SELECTED REFERENCES: **The Eagle's Gift - Page** coincides with hundreds of...Juan Tuma, I forgot my anger.) Th **253.4]** (I disregarded Zuleica's order to enter...thought I could feel a

ATTENTION-SECOND-DENT-[THE DENT OF THE *ATTENTION]-(TOP): SEE: DENT-LUMINOUS-[TH* *(TOP)*

ATTENTION-SECOND-FIXATION-[THE FIXATION *ATTENTION]: (TOP)*
SELECTED REFERENCES: **The Eagle's Gift - Page [** when I...Genaros are in a different world.")

ATTENTION-SECOND-HANDLING-WITHOUT-PRE *[HANDLING THE SECOND ATTENTION WITHOUT* *(TOP)*
SELECTED REFERENCES: **The Eagle's Gift - Page [237.** what he...is part of our total being.)

ATTENTION-SECOND-TAKING-CONTROLS-[EXPE *SECOND ATTENTION TAKING OVER THE CONTRO*
SELECTED REFERENCES: **The Eagle's Gift - Page [251.** sessions with Zuleica's...time fully awake, aware of everything.) Th **[276.8-276.9]** (I felt a terrible discomfort, an...the people going to the n

ATTENTION-THIRD-[THE THIRD ATTENTION]: (TC
SELECTED REFERENCES: **The Eagle's Gift - Page [242.7** Manuel and Eligio seemed...and not in a figurative way.)

AWARENESS-BUNDLING-[BUNDLING AWARENESS
SELECTED REFERENCES: **The Eagle's Gift - Page [258.8** the impossibility of...and the left has gained supremacy.)

AWARENESS-GLOW-[THE GLOW OF AWARENESS]:
SELECTED REFERENCES: **The Fire From Within - Pag** Genaro, and I ...come, must come of itself.")

AWARENESS-GLOW-WORKING-[WORKING THE GI *AWARENESS]: (TOP)*
SELECTED REFERENCES: **The Fire From Within - Page** Juan, walking by...tremor, like leaves in a breeze.)

AWARENESS -HEIGHTENED-[HEIGHTENED AWARE
SELECTED REFERENCES: **The Power of Silence - P** interrupted don Juan...she entered permanently into heightened aware

AWARENESS-PLAYING-WITH-[PLAYING WITH AWA
SELECTED REFERENCES: **The Fire From Within - Page [6** to don Juan's explanation...scared and run out of them.)

AWARENESS-RIGHT-LEFT-[THE RIGHT AND THE LE *AWARENESS]: (TOP)*

dreaming

AWAR *AWAR*

lot of que

B

BARKING-DOG-SADNESS-[THE NOCTURNAL VOICE OF MAN]: (TOP)
SELECTED REFERENCES: **Tales of Power** - Page **[293.1-293.8]** (He paused. The silence around us...was over; it was already night.")

BATTLE-SOUL-[THE BATTLE FOR THE SOUL]-(TOP): SEE: SOUL-BATTLE-[THE BATTLE FOR THE SOUL]-(TOP)

BED-STRINGS-[THE BED OF STRINGS]: (TOP)
SELECTED REFERENCES: **Journey to Ixtlan** - Page **[146.7-148.2]** (After eating I felt very sleepy...bed and I fell asleep instantly.) **Journey to Ixtlan** - Page **[163.5-163.7]** (We did not speak a word...was suspended but I fell asleep.) **Journey to Ixtlan** - Page **[182.3-182.5]** (Don Juan, as he had done before..."bed" was made for that purpose.) **Journey to Ixtlan** - Page **[183.6-183.7]** (Before I could say anything else...state of peace and well-being.) **The Second Ring of Power** - Page **[78.9-79.2]** (I tried the bed and the pillow...in northern Mexico. I fell asleep.)

BEETLE-DEATH-WARRIOR-[THE BEETLE AND THE WARRIOR'S DEATH]: (TOP)
SELECTED REFERENCES: **Journey to Ixtlan** - Page **[248.6-249.9]** (The next day I ventured farther...Our death made us equal.)

BELIEVE-HAVING-TO-[HAVING TO BELIEVE]: (TOP)
SELECTED REFERENCES: **Tales of Power** - Page **[102-115]** (I walked towards downtown on the...Without it he had nothing.)

BENCH-WARRIOR-[THE BENCH OF A WARRIOR]: (TOP)
SELECTED REFERENCES: **The Eagle's Gift** - Page **[82.1-82.2]** ("We will meet at the Nagual's bench...this life will we be back.) **The Eagle's Gift** - Page **[84.6-84.7]** (In the late afternoon, before dusk...tell them about the power spot.) **The Fire From Within** - Page **[201.8-202.2]** (Don Juan rose from his favorite...and such words lose their meaning.")

BENEFACTOR-OMEN-[THE OMEN OF THE BENEFACTOR]-(TOP): SEE: OMEN-BENEFACTOR-[THE OMEN OF THE BENEFACTOR]-(TOP)

BENIGNO-EYES-PRESSES-[BENIGNO PRESSES WITH HIS EYES]: (TOP)
SELECTED REFERENCES: **The Second Ring of Power** - Page **[221.4-221.8]** (Nestor stopped talking and all of them...first to recover from his surprise.) **The Second Ring of Power** - Page **[224.1-224.3]** (That was why I interfered with what...are his true children at that.)

BENIGNO-VOICE-BOOMING-[BENIGNO'S FAVORITE VOICE]: (TOP)
SELECTED REFERENCES: **The Second Ring of Power** - Page **[198.1-198.2]** ("One of us here is a fool...then buried his face in his arms.) **The Second Ring of Power** - Page **[209.1-209.3]** ("There's nothing to understand," Nestor said...deep bass voice, making everyone laugh.) **The Second Ring of Power** - Page **[213.6-213.7]** ("He jumped with Benigno," Nestor said..."But I never talk about it.") **The Second Ring of Power** - Page **[214.3-214.9]** ("Eligio had to jump like everybody...the best one just for you.")

BLACK-DOG-[THE IRIDESCENT BLACK DOG]-(TOP): SEE: OMEN-ESCOGIDO-[THE OMEN OF THE ESCOGIDO]-(TOP)

BLACK-LAKE-[THE BLACK LAKE]: (TOP)
SELECTED REFERENCES: **The Teachings of Don Juan** - Page **[98.5-99.9]** ("Anuhctal [as I heard the word this time]...wave in reverse, until it disappeared.)

BLACK-WORLD-TALES-[TALES OF THE BLACK WORLD]-(TOP): SEE: WORLD-BLACK-TALES-[TALES OF THE BLACK WORLD]-(TOP)

BLACKNESS-HEIGHTS-ASCENDING-[ASCENDING THE HEIGHTS OF BLACKNESS]: (TOP)

SELECTED REFERENCES: The Power of Silence - Page [192.4-192.7] ("I died in that field," he said...field, covered with rocks and dirt.")

BLUE-SCOUT-[THE BLUE SCOUT]-(TOP): SEE: SCOUT-BLUE-[THE BLUE SCOUT]-(TOP)

BOOST-EARTH-[THE BOOST FROM THE EARTH]-(TOP): SEE: EARTH-BOOST-[THE BOOST FROM THE EARTH]-(TOP)

BOUNDARIES-AFFECTION-CROSSING-[CROSSING THE BOUNDARIES OF AFFECTION]: (TOP)

SELECTED REFERENCES: The Eagle's Gift - Page [66-86] ("What's happening to us, Gorda?" I ... while la Gorda and I slept.)

BOY-BUTTON-NOSED-PROMISE-[THE PROMISE TO THE BUTTON NOSED BOY]: (TOP)

SELECTED REFERENCES: A Separate Reality - Page [138.9-142.5] ("I *see* a little boy crying...hungry, or to be in pain.")

BREATHING-DREAMING-[LEARNING TO BREATHE IN DREAMING]: (TOP): SEE: DREAMING-BREATHING-[LEARNING TO BREATHE IN DREAMING]: (TOP)

BRIDGE-FOG-[THE FOG BRIDGE]: (TOP)

SELECTED REFERENCES: Journey to Ixtlan - Page [126.1-126.6] (I wanted to ask what I was...but wide enough to walk on.) Journey to Ixtlan - Page [133.6-135.5] ("And what is real?" don Juan...have enough power of one's own.") Journey to Ixtlan - Page [178.6-178.8] ("Don't tax yourself with explanations...when you have enough personal power.") The Second Ring of Power - Page [298.3-298.9] (I told her that once while...Toltec dreamers once they are formless.")

BRIDGE-TWO-ONE-WAY-[THE TWO ONE-WAY BRIDGES]: (TOP)

SELECTED REFERENCES: The Power of Silence - Page [225-241] (Don Juan and I were sitting... silently offer it to the abstract.)

BRIDGE-UNKNOWN-[THE BRIDGE TO THE UNKNOWN]: (TOP)

SELECTED REFERENCES: The Eagle's Gift - Page [90.3-91.3] (Pablito did not take us there directly...walk back to the center of town.) The Eagle's Gift - Page [94.9-99.3] (Without any verbal agreement, we left...any thoroughfare during busy hours.) The Eagle's Gift - Page [100.8-103.5] (Pablito was the first one to talk...I had devoured each other's bodies.) The Eagle's Gift - Page [241.7-244.3] (Silvio Manuel had conceived the idea...passed out in Silvio Manuel's house.) The Eagle's Gift - Page [301.1-303.7] (She had just remembered that we...Eagle would let us go through.)

BUMPKIN-OUTSMART-EVERYONE-[THE BUMPKIN WHO OUTSMARTED EVERYONE]: (TOP)

SELECTED REFERENCES: Tales of Power - Page [201.2-201.9] (Don Genaro doubled up with laughter... And the bumpkins agreed with him.")

BUSH-SPIRIT-[THE BUSH TOUCHED BY THE SPIRIT]: (TOP)

SELECTED REFERENCES: Journey to Ixtlan - Page [101.4-103.8] ("There!" he said in a whisper...that blew into that dry twig.")

C

CALIXTO-MUNI-[CALIXTO MUNI]: (TOP)
SELECTED REFERENCES: The Power of Silence - Page [114.6-116.5] (He said that some sorcerers were...His goal has transcended his person.")

CAR-DISAPPEARING-[THE DISAPPEARING CAR]: (TOP)
SELECTED REFERENCES: Journey to Ixtlan - Page [235.7-245.6] ("Genaro can do something much better...with laughter before I fell asleep.) Journey to Ixtlan - Page [255.5-255.9] (Don Juan looked at me with...and allow your body to *see*.")

CAR-WON'T-START-WILL-[WILL AND THE CAR THAT WON'T START]: (TOP)
SELECTED REFERENCES: A Separate Reality - Page [199.3-200.8] ("Sorcery is to apply one's will...had released the car. It started!) Journey to Ixtlan - Page [235.4-235.5] ("Do you remember the time when...car until he said I could.)

CARLOS-BLOND-FRIEND-[CARLOS' BLOND GIRL FRIEND]: (TOP)
SELECTED REFERENCES: Journey to Ixtlan - Page [67.6-69.7] ("Hey," he said smiling and peered...feeling that remained was boredom. True?")

CARLOS-BOY-[THE LITTLE BOY IN CARLOS' LIFE]: (TOP)
SELECTED REFERENCES: The Second Ring of Power - Page [121.7-125.1] ("You love a little boy and...to get out of that gully.) The Second Ring of Power - Page [135.1-135.2] ("You have to refuse both, the...you from entering into that realm?")

CARLOS-CHANCES-FOUR-[CARLOS' FOUR CHANCES]: (TOP)
SELECTED REFERENCES: The Second Ring of Power - Page [182.6-182.9] (The Nagual told us that one day...to find you alive and well.)

CARLOS-CROW-TRANSFORMATION-[CARLOS' TRANSFORMATION INTO A CROW]-(TOP): SEE: CROW-TRANSFORMATION-CARLOS-[CARLOS' TRANSFORMATION INTO A CROW]-(TOP)

CARLOS-DEATH-[CARLOS' DEATH]-(TOP): SEE: DEATH-CARLOS-[CARLOS DEATH]-(TOP)

CARLOS-DOUBLE-[CARLOS'-DOUBLE]-(TOP): SEE: DOUBLE-CARLOS-[THE EMERGENCE OF CARLOS' DOUBLE]-(TOP)

CARLOS-ENERGY-BLOWING-BODY-[BLOWING ENERGY INTO CARLOS' BODY]-(TOP): SEE: ENERGY-BLOWING-INTO-CARLOS-[BLOWING ENERGY INTO CARLOS' BODY]-(TOP)

CARLOS-FINDING-[HOW POWER FOUND CARLOS]-(TOP): SEE: FINDING-CARLOS-[HOW POWER FOUND CARLOS]-(TOP)

CARLOS-FLYING-[CARLOS' FLYING]-(TOP): SEE: FLYING-CARLOS-[CARLOS' FLYING]-(TOP)

CARLOS-INFANT-MEMORIES-[CARLOS MEMORIES AS AN INFANT]: (TOP)
SELECTED REFERENCES: Tales of Power - Page [203.4-206.5] (Then all of a sudden I was...turned upside down to play house.)

CARLOS-POLICEMAN-[CARLOS AND THE FLEET-FOOTED POLICEMAN]: (TOP)
SELECTED REFERENCES: The Power of Silence - Page [204.7-206.1] (He signaled me to start walking...who shattered your notion of invincibility.)

CARLOS-STRANGULATION-[CARLOS' STRANGULATION]: (TOP)

SELECTED REFERENCES: **The Second Ring of Power - Page [56.9-58.9]** (She told me to lie down...against it like a frightened child.)

CARLOS-SWIMMING-FATHER-[CARLOS' SWIMMING STORY WITH HIS FATHER]: (TOP)

SELECTED REFERENCES: **Journey to Ixtlan - Page [40.4-43.4]** (I told him the story of...were as weak as your father.)

CARLOS-VISION-MOTHER-[CARLOS' VISION OF HIS MOTHER]: (TOP)

SELECTED REFERENCES: **A Separate Reality - Page [55.1- 57.7]** (I became even more involved...on my part than being around.)

CARPENTER-METAPHOR-[THE MASTER CARPENTER METAPHOR]: (TOP)

SELECTED REFERENCES: **The Power of Silence - Page [175.3-175.9]** (The young man added that not...him in matters of manual labor.)

CATALINA-PIERCING-[PIERCING LA CATALINA]: (TOP)

SELECTED REFERENCES: **A Separate Reality - Page [204.3-211.4]** ("You know, of all the things on...take my foot off the gas pedal.)

CATALINA-TALES-[TALES OF LA CATALINA]: (TOP)

SELECTED REFERENCES: **The Teachings of Don Juan - Page [67.3-68.5]** (I didn't see don Juan sitting...I'll tell you about them someday.") **The Teachings of Don Juan - Page [183.6-184.3]** (At 11:00 A. M. don Juan came out...you caught on to her trick.") **A Separate Reality - Page [28.8-29.5]** ("I had to trick you into learning...have to be around here for that.") **A Separate Reality - Page [201.8-213.1]** (The fear traced back to years...the pressure of my irrational fear.) **Journey to Ixtlan - Page [214.8-215.8]** ("Someone is interfering with your hunting...that I became furious with him.) **Journey to Ixtlan - Page [216.7-230.2]** (I did not ask what we...of everything he had taught me.) **The Fire From Within - Page [141.4-144.9]** ("That's why there are true sorcerers...the hill and meet la Catalina.") **The Fire From Within - Page [149.2-152.5]** (We were all still laughing when...down and put on my clothes.)

CATS-STORY-[THE STORY OF THE TWO CATS]: (TOP)

SELECTED REFERENCES: **Tales of Power - Page [108.6-112.1]** ("Remember the story you once told...thought was very distressing to me.) **Tales of Power - Page [115.4-115.6]** ("We're back again to the story...ceiling of an ugly barren room.)

CAVE-SORCERER-[THE SORCERERS' CAVE OF UNDERSTANDING]: (TOP)

SELECTED REFERENCES: **The Power of Silence - Page [4.5-5.4]** ("This is the ideal place for...which worries me to no end.") **The Power of Silence - Page [12.2-12.3]** (It was very dark in the cave...the echoes of don Juan's words.) **The Power of Silence - Page [26.7-27.2]** ("You stated categorically last night that...to thought. They leaned toward action.") **The Power of Silence - Page [100.5-100.6]** (Properly speaking, I was caught between...of the sorcerers who carved it.)

CHAIR-PABLITO-[PABLITO'S CHAIR]: (TOP)

SELECTED REFERENCES: **The Second Ring of Power - Page [176.4-177.4]** (Pablito turned to me and apologized...changed completely the instant la Gorda left.) **The Second Ring of Power - Page [222.1-222.6]** (Her presence had created a strange lull...he asked me and left laughing.) **The Second Ring of Power - Page [322.4-322.9]** ("It's all right," he said...more than the rest of us.")

CHANGING-DIRECTION-WARRIOR-[CHANGING THE WARRIORS' DIRECTION]-(TOP): SEE: WARRIOR-DIRECTION-CHANGING-[CHANGING THE WARRIORS' DIRECTION]-(TOP)

CHEESE-CARLOS-LOVE-OF-[CARLOS' LOVE OF CHEESE]: (TOP)

SELECTED REFERENCES: **The Power of Silence - Page [117.1-117.6]** (I opened my backpack. The women...with his group to set me up.)

CHICKEN-LIDIA-BLOUSE-[THE CHICKEN IN LIDIA'S BLOUSE]: (TOP)
SELECTED REFERENCES: The Second Ring of Power -Page [49.50.4] (As you know the Nagual can't...with her part of the way.) The Second Ring of Power - Page [152.1-152.2] (The Nagual and Genaro could make...chicken to run inside Lidia's blouse.")

CHILDHOOD-PAIN-ESCAPING-[ESCAPING THE PAIN OF CHILDHOOD]: (TOP)
SELECTED REFERENCES: A Separate Reality - Page [45.3-46.3] (Don Juan sat quietly, looking straight...hot once the sun goes down.")

CHURCH-VISION-[A VISION OF THE CHURCH]: (TOP)
SELECTED REFERENCES: The Fire From Within - Page [130.6-131.3] (I was left facing the side of...we walked lazily around the patio.)

CHURCH-WOMAN-[THE WOMAN IN THE CHURCH]-(TOP): SEE: WOMAN-CHURCH-[THE WOMAN IN THE CHURCH]-(TOP)

CITY-UNKNOWN-DREAM-[CARLOS' DREAM OF THE UNKNOWN CITY]-(TOP): SEE: DREAM-CITY-UNKNOWN-[CARLOS' DREAM OF THE UNKNOWN CITY]-(TOP)

COFFEE-SHOP-DREAMING-JOURNEY-[CARLOS' DREAMING JOURNEY TO THE COFFEE SHOP]-(TOP): SEE: DREAMING-JOURNEY-COFFEE-SHOP-[CARLOS' DREAMING JOURNEY TO THE COFFEE SHOP]-(TOP)

CORN-MAN-PLANTS-[THE MAN WHO PLANTS CORN]: (TOP)
SELECTED REFERENCES: A Separate Reality - Page [153.7-153.8] ("You must be joking! The thing...the most frightening waste there is.)

CORN-SORCERY-[CORN SORCERY]: (TOP)
SELECTED REFERENCES: The Teachings of Don Juan - Page [22.9- 24.5] ("What power objects did you have...are like a game for children.")

COYOTE-MAGICAL-[THE MAGICAL COYOTE]-(TOP): SEE: MAGICAL-COYOTE-[THE MAGICAL COYOTE]-(TOP)

CRACKING-SOUND-NECK-[THE CRACKING SOUND AT THE BASE OF THE NECK]-(TOP): SEE: DOUBLE-SOUND-[THE SOUND OF THE DOUBLE]-(TOP)

CREATIVITY-[A DEMONSTRATION OF CREATIVITY AND THE NAGUAL]-(TOP): SEE: NAGUAL-DEMONSTRATION-[A DEMONSTRATION OF CREATIVITY AND THE NAGUAL]-(TOP)

CREATURES-OBSESSED-MOVEMENT-[THE CREATURES OBSESSED WITH MOVEMENT]: (TOP)
SELECTED REFERENCES: The Eagle's Gift - Page [191.6-191.7] (The story that impressed me most...ultimate ambition was to find quietude.)

CROSSING-EYES-[CROSSING THE EYES]-(TOP): SEE: EYES-CROSSING-[CROSSING THE EYES]-(TOP)

CROW-EMISSARY-WARRIOR-[THE EMISSARY CROWS OF ONE WARRIOR'S FATE]: (TOP)
SELECTED REFERENCES: The Teachings of Don Juan - Page [167.3-176.3] (On Thursday, March 18, I smoked...lose fear to understand what I mean.")

CROW-SEEING-[SEEING AS A CROW SEES]: (TOP)

SELECTED REFERENCES: The Teachings of Don Juan - Page [173.7-175.3] (In going over the images I...You will see it yourself.") A Separate Reality - Page [41.6-41.8] ("Can a coyote *see* an ally...They are foreboding shapes.")

CROW-TRANSFORMATION-CARLOS-[CARLOS' TRANSFORMATION INTO A CROW]: (TOP)

SELECTED REFERENCES: The Teachings of Don Juan - Page [168.3-176.3] ("You must tell me all you...lose fear to understand what I mean.") A Separate Reality - Page [199.6-200.2s] ("Watch what I do ," he said...to the best of my judgment.) The Second Ring of Power - Page [296.4-296.8] ("The Nagual said that with his...Gorda's explanation somehow had simplified everything.) The Second Ring of Power - Page [298.5-298.6] ("I know about it," she said...like a crow with that attention.) The Fire From Within - Page [136.2-136.7] (He told me then that he...which some seers find most comfortable.)

CRYSTALS-POWER-[POWER CRYSTALS]: (TOP)

SELECTED REFERENCES: The Teachings of Don Juan - Page [22.9-23.1] ("What power objects did you have..."Maiz-pinto, crystals and feathers.") The Teachings of Don Juan - Page [24.4-24.6] ("Maiz-pinto, crystals and feathers are...are like a game for children.")

D

DARKNESS-WARRIOR-[THE WARRIOR OF THE DARKNESS]: (TOP)
SELECTED REFERENCES: **The Eagle's Gift - Page [200.6-200.7]** (Don Juan spoke to the man...leader of the whole warrior's party.)

DEATH-[DEATH]: (TOP)
SELECTED REFERENCES: **Journey to Ixtlan - Page [155.8-157.1]** ("Is death a personage, don Juan...of fog, or an unknown presence.") **The Eagle's Gift - Page [74.1-74.8]** ("The nagual Juan Matus said that...idiotic tune, the same peerless trumpeter.)

DEATH-ADVISER-[DEATH AS AN ADVISER]: (TOP)
SELECTED REFERENCES: **Journey to Ixtlan - Page [26-36]** ("Would you teach me someday about... to feel its presence around you.")

DEATH-ALAMEDA-PARK-[DEATH FINDS A MAN IN ALAMEDA PARK]: (TOP)
SELECTED REFERENCES: **Tales of Power - Page [112.1-115.9]** (A mild commotion and the muffled...predilection. Without it he had nothing.) **The Fire From Within - Page [223.9-225.5]** (I asked him to clarify what he...revulsion that I'd felt that day.)

DEATH-ALLIES-MERGE-[THE ALLIES TRY TO MERGE WITH THE WARRIOR'S DEATH]-(TOP): SEE: ALLIES-DEATH-MERGE-[THE ALLIES TRY TO MERGE WITH THE WARRIOR'S DEATH]-(TOP)

DEATH-CARLOS-[CARLOS DEATH]: (TOP)
SELECTED REFERENCES: **A Separate Reality - Page [196.8-197.8]** ("Do you want to know what...of tiny crystals moving, moving away.") **Journey to Ixtlan - Page [153.4-155.6]** ("This is the place where you...to the south. To the vastness.")

DEATH-DEFIERS-[THE DEATH DEFIERS]: (TOP)
SELECTED REFERENCES: **The Fire From Within - Page [231-255]** (I arrived at Genaro's house around...as long as he possibly can.")

DEATH-DEFIERS-COURT-[THE DEATH DEFIERS AND THEIR COURT]-(TOP): SEE: TOLTEC-GHOULS-[THE TOLTEC GHOULS]-(TOP)

DEATH-EXPERIENCE-[EXPERIENCING A TRUE SENSE OF DEATH]: (TOP)
SELECTED REFERENCES: **The Eagle's Gift - Page [242.7-243.7]** (We crossed. Silvio Manuel and Eligio seemed...of awareness you ever had.")

DEATH-JUAN-[DON JUAN'S DEATH]-(TOP): SEE: JUAN-DEATH-[THE STORY OF DON JUAN'S DEATH]-(TOP)

DEATH-JUAN-PARENTS-[THE DEATH OF DON JUAN'S PARENTS]-(TOP): SEE: JUAN-PARENTS-DEATH-[THE DEATH OF DON JUAN'S PARENTS]-(TOP)

DEATH-LIGHTS-HEAD-[THE LIGHTS ON THE HEAD OF DEATH]: (TOP)
SELECTED REFERENCES: **A Separate Reality - Page [48.7-49.4]** (He asked me if there was...turns off its lights, that's all.") **A Separate Reality - Page [95.4-95.5]** (Don Juan affirmed again that a...Genaro rolled on the ground laughing.)

DEATH-PARALLEL-LINES-LAND-[DEATH IN THE LAND BETWEEN THE PARALLEL LINES]: (TOP)
SELECTED REFERENCES: **The Eagle's Gift - Page [155.1-157.3]** (On the day in question, both...has to be forced by fear.)

DEATH-REVELATION-[THE REVELATION OF DEATH]: (TOP)
SELECTED REFERENCES: Tales of Power - Page [159.2-160.5] (A million questions and feelings came...This is a terrible way of being.")

DEATH-SHADOW-[THE SHADOW OF DEATH]-(TOP): SEE: SHADOW-DEATH-[THE SHADOW OF DEATH]-(TOP)

DEATH-SULFUR-DUNES-[DEATH IN THE LAND OF THE SULFUR DUNES]-(TOP): SEE: DEATH-PARALLEL-LINES-LAND-[DEATH IN THE LAND BETWEEN THE PARALLEL LINES]-(TOP)

DEATH-WAITING-FOR-[WAITING FOR DEATH]: (TOP)
SELECTED REFERENCES: The Power of Silence - Page [189.1-189.5] (Don Juan knew that he had reached a complete...to be caught in its flow.")

DENT-LUMINOUS-FEELING-[FEELING THE LUMINOUS DENT]-(TOP): SEE: ATTENTION-SECOND-CONTROLS-[EXPERIENCING THE SECOND ATTENTION TAKING OVER THE CONTROLS]-(TOP)

DEVIL'S-WEED-TALES-[TALES OF THE DEVIL'S WEED]: (TOP)
SELECTED REFERENCES: The Teachings of Don Juan - Page [56.7-67.2] (Today, during the afternoon, don Juan..."Perhaps," he said quietly.) The Teachings of Don Juan - Page [105.7-106.8] (Don Juan inquired periodically, in a...only one of a million paths.) The Teachings of Don Juan - Page [107.6-130.7] (On Tuesday afternoon, April 16, don Juan...the rock with its heavy chain.") The Teachings of Don Juan - Page [153.5-161.4] (Don Juan seemed to want me...seek death is to seek nothing.")

DIABLEROS-TALES-[TALES OF THE DIABLEROS]: (TOP)
SELECTED REFERENCES: The Teachings of Don Juan - Page [14.9-18.2] (In describing his teacher, don Juan...was a huge pool of grease.")

DIAPHRAGM-SPASMS-[THE SPASMS OF THE DIAPHRAGM]-(TOP): SEE: ATTENTION-SECOND-CONTROLS-[EXPERIENCING THE SECOND ATTENTION TAKING OVER THE CONTROLS]-(TOP)

DIVINING-LIBRARY-THIEF-[DIVINING THE LIBRARY THIEF]: (TOP)
SELECTED REFERENCES: The Teachings of Don Juan - Page [115.8-117.5] (The paste had dried up and scaled...I was just hungry and sleepy.) The Teachings of Don Juan - Page [153.5-157.8] (Don Juan seemed to want me...into my car and fell asleep.)

DOG-BLACK-[THE IRIDESCENT BLACK DOG]-(TOP): SEE: OMEN-ESCOGIDO-[THE OMEN OF THE ESCOGIDO]-(TOP)

DOG-STOLE-CHEESE-[THE DOG WHO STOLE CHEESE]-(TOP): SEE DIABLERO-TALES-[TALES OF THE DIABLEROS]-(TOP)

DOMED-WORLD-[THE DOMED WORLD]: (TOP)
SELECTED REFERENCES: Tales of Power - Page [206.6-206.9] (I had one more coherent and...had no frame of reference for them.) The Second Ring of Power - Page [62.4-62.5] ("Pablito is my enemy not because...to destroy Pablito to do that.") The Second Ring of Power - Page [115.9-116.3] ("I've been told that you're the only...mention anything until the right moment.) The Second Ring of Power - Page [216.8-220.3] (In that particular vision I found...a long vision. Don't you see?") The Second Ring of Power - Page [324.7-327.9] (La Gorda said that the Nagual...opened with her revelations was terrifying.) The Fire From Within - Page [211.6-211.9] (The motion slowed down by degrees...was with don Juan and Genaro.)

DON-GENARO-[DON GENARO]-(TOP): SEE: GENARO-[DON GENARO]-(TOP)

DON-JUAN-[DON JUAN]-(TOP): SEE: JUAN-[DON JUAN]-(TOP)

DOUBLE-CARLOS-[THE EMERGENCE OF CARLOS' DOUBLE]: (TOP)

SELECTED REFERENCES: The Second Ring of Power - Page [58.5-58.9] (I heard then, or perhaps I...against it like a frightened child.) The Second Ring of Power - Page [82.8-83.8] (I heard again, as I had...found a way to help her.) The Second Ring of Power - Page [109.6-111.8] (All at once I had a monstrous...But somehow I was myself again.) The Second Ring of Power - Page [168.8-169.2] (With my flying I was supposed...I have no attention for it.") The Second Ring of Power - Page [284.9-285.9] ("And this brings me to the next...to it to calm it down.) The Fire From Within - Page [274.2-275.7] (Don Juan nudged me on the arm...what he wanted me to remember.)

DOUBLE-DREAMING-[DREAMING THE DOUBLE]-(TOP): SEE: DREAMING-DOUBLE-[DREAMING THE DOUBLE]-(TOP)

DOUBLE-EYES-[THE EYES OF THE DOUBLE]-(TOP): SEE: EYES-DOUBLE-[THE EYES OF THE DOUBLE]-(TOP)

DOUBLE-FACING-[FACING THE DOUBLE]: TOP)

SELECTED REFERENCES: Tales of Power - Page [62.3-63.2] ("When it first happened to me...I found myself rubbing my eyes.") Tales of Power - Page [63.8-64.6] ("But one day, a few months..."My body knew it," he replied.) Tales of Power - Page [67.7-68.4] ("Then I heard the sound of people approaching...the same ones I had seen.) Tales of Power - Page [69.2-72.7] (Don Genaro sat up straight and...the ramada of don Juan's house.) Tales of Power - Page [77.8-78.3] ("Last night Genaro guided you through..."I think he understands," don Genaro said.)

DOUBLE-MORTAL-COMBAT-[THE MORTAL COMBAT OF THE DOUBLE]: (TOP)

SELECTED REFERENCES: The Second Ring of Power - Page [57.8-59.8] (She must have felt my realization...semidarkness. He went to his corral.) The Second Ring of Power - Page [82.4-83.8] (They exchanged a coy look with... found a way to help her.) The Second Ring of Power - Page [109.2-111.8] (I experienced an unbearable anxiety. Josephina...But somehow I was myself again.)

DOUBLE-VS-NAGUAL-[THE DOUBLE VS THE NAGUAL]: (TOP)

SELECTED REFERENCES: The Second Ring of Power - Page [197.4-200.5] ("Well, how did you get out...None of us has a double.")

DOUBLE-SOUND-[THE SOUND OF THE DOUBLE]: (TOP)

SELECTED REFERENCES: The Second Ring of Power - Page [58.5-58.6] (I heard then, or perhaps I...thought that I must be dying.) The Second Ring of Power - Page [82.8-82.9] (I heard again, as I had...of Rosa's stick and crushed it.) The Second Ring of Power - Page [90.3-90.4] (Under the impact of dona Soledad...the means to that suspension of judgment.) The Second Ring of Power - Page [109.6-109.8] (All at once I had a monstrous...while they lay on the floor.) The Second Ring of Power - Page [111.4-111.5] (There were, however, two new things...out of the top of my head.) The Second Ring of Power - Page [238.9-239.6] (I asked her if she had...you with that sound," she said.) The Eagle's Gift - Page [132.5-132.6] (Then a drastic jolt in my body...I was asleep and yet thoroughly aware.) The Eagle's Gift - Page [145.3-145.4] ("What do you mean, shooting off...physical body with a loud crack.) The Eagle's Gift - Page [156.6-156.8] (I felt a powerful vibration go through me...sulfur-yellow surroundings-leaving my body.) The Eagle's Gift - Page [308.6-308.8] (I then used my eyes deliberately...the room was a luminous egg.)

DOUBLE-TRAVELS-[THE TRAVELS OF THE DOUBLE]: (TOP)

SELECTED REFERENCES: The Power of Silence - Page [32.8-33.7] (Don Juan said that the nagual Elias...his natural self be a recluse.)

DREAM-CITY-UNKNOWN-[CARLOS' DREAM OF THE UNKNOWN CITY]: (TOP)

SELECTED REFERENCES: Tales of Power - Page [10.9-11.3] (One night, quite unexpectedly, I found...street in some unknown foreign city.) The Art of Dreaming - Page [24.1-25.2] (I believed he had instantaneously put...mat, curled up on my side.) The Art of Dreaming - Page [28.5-28.6] (When I made your assemblage point shift...dream. I forced it to shift.) The Art of Dreaming - Page [39.3-40.8] (I seized the opportunity to seek...He refused any further discussion.)

DREAM-FARM-MOUNTAINS-[CARLOS' DREAM OF THE FARM AND THE MOUNTAINS]: (TOP)

SELECTED REFERENCES: The Art of Dreaming - Page [42.7-43.7] (A year went by without any...was no more scenery, just darkness.)

DREAM-HAND-[THE DREAM HAND]: (TOP)

SELECTED REFERENCES: The Second Ring of Power - Page [18.2-18.9] (I made up my mind then...her, "don't play tricks on me.") The Second Ring of Power - Page [63.6-63.7] ("You were about to leave then...that, but my power was low.) The Second Ring of Power - Page [82.8-83.8] (I heard again, as I had...found a way to help her.) The Second Ring of Power - Page [180.9-181.8] ("Let's get out of this house...have to tend to him for months.) The Second Ring of Power - Page [224.1-224..3] (That was why I interfered with what...are his true children at that.)

DREAM-IRIDIUM-WALKING-STICK-[CARLOS' DREAM OF THE IRIDIUM WALKING STICK]: (TOP)

SELECTED REFERENCES: The Art of Dreaming - Page [84.1-84.9] (The first time I noticed foreign...outstanding, although they were crystal clear.)

DREAM-SABRE-TOOTHED-TIGER-[THE DREAM OF THE SABRE-TOOTHED TIGER]: (TOP)

SELECTED REFERENCES: The Eagle's Gift - Page [53.1-53.9] (I came back once more to...that my body became more muscular.) The Eagle's Gift - Page [140.3-140.5] ("When I had learned to fly perfectly...do it while you were awake.) The Eagle's Gift - Page [159.5-161.5] (In another session of *dreaming together*...I woke up in my study.) The Eagle's Gift - Page [161.7-161.9] (Our proficiency in *dreaming together* was...most important, on forgotten past events.) The Art of Dreaming - Page [119.2-119.7] (Not only did the emissary change...it took me to the tunnels.)

DREAM-TOPAZ-[CARLOS' DREAM OF THE GLOWING TOPAZ]: (TOP)

SELECTED REFERENCES: The Art of Dreaming - Page [168.1-168.9] (As usual, he was right...swallowed me, and I woke up.)

DREAMER-ART-[THE ART OF THE DREAMER]: (TOP)

SELECTED REFERENCES: The Second Ring of Power - Page [245.2-256.6] ("Let's forget this," she said suddenly...la Gorda, breathing through their mouths.) The Second Ring of Power - Page [272.4-273.3] (And then I suddenly recalled something...recollection to the other in my mind.) The Second Ring of Power - Page [275.4-275.8] (La Gorda and the little sisters...two distinct memories of one event.) The Second Ring of Power - Page [276.2-276.3] ("We each have five other dreams...was the dream the Nagual gave us.") The Second Ring of Power - Page [277.2-277.8] ("We have been *dreaming* those dreams...do what you *saw* us doing.")

DREAMER-DREAMED-[THE DREAMER AND THE DREAMED]: (TOP)

SELECTED REFERENCES: Tales of Power - Page [50-78] (I drove to don Juan's house...think he understands," don Genaro said.)

DREAMING-ART-[THE ART OF DREAMING]: (TOP)

SELECTED REFERENCES: The Second Ring of Power - Page [223-280] (The next day I was by...not exist. Not on this earth.")

DREAMING-ART-[THE ART OF DREAMING]: (TOP)

SELECTED REFERENCES: The Eagle's Gift - Page [111-167] (A few months later, after helping...where had all of them gone?)

DREAMING-ART-[THE ART OF DREAMING]: (TOP)

SELECTED REFERENCES: The Eagle's Gift - Page [111-167] (A few months later, after helping ...where had all of them gone?)

DREAMING-BODY-[THE DREAMING BODY]: (TOP)

SELECTED REFERENCES: The Eagle's Gift - Page [140.3-14.8] ("When I had learned to fly...can fly as if I were *dreaming*.") The Fire From Within - Page [273.3-273.9] (He joked with me and horsed around...them as points of amber light.)

DREAMING-BODY-EYES-[THE EYES OF THE DREAMING BODY]: (TOP): SEE: EYES-DREAMING BODY-[THE EYES OF THE DREAMING BODY]: (TOP)

DREAMING-BODY-JOURNEY-[THE JOURNEY OF THE DREAMING BODY: (TOP)
SELECTED REFERENCES: The Fire From Within - Page [271-287] (Don Juan told me that the...mysteries must await us! What mysteries!")

DREAMING-BODY-OBSERVING-[OBSERVING THE DREAMING BODY]: (TOP)
SELECTED REFERENCES: Tales of Power - Page [69.3-72.7] (Don Genaro sat up straight and...the ramada of don Juan's house.) The Second Ring of Power - Page [168.8-169.3] (With my flying I was supposed...he had run out of time.) The Fire From Within - Page [272.7-275.4] (Over the years don Juan and...And his dancing did the trick.") The Fire From Within - Page [276.5-276.9] (My emotional distress mounted by...the people going to the market.)

DREAMING-BODY-SHOOTING-OFF-[SHOOTING OFF THE DREAMING BODY]: (TOP)
SELECTED REFERENCES: The Eagle's Gift - Page [145.1-145.5] ("Holy Jesus! We are remembering the other...dreaming body. But to no avail.")

DREAMING-BODY-TRAVELS-NAGUAL-WOMAN-[CARLOS' DREAMING BODY TRAVELS TO THE HOME OF THE NAGUAL WOMAN]-(TOP) SEE: DREAMING-BODY-JOURNEY-[THE JOURNEY OF THE DREAMING BODY]-(TOP)

DREAMING-BREATHING-[LEARNING TO BREATHE IN DREAMING]: (TOP)
SELECTED REFERENCES: The Eagle's Gift - Page [53.7-53.9] (The tiger never touched me...that my body became more muscular.) The Eagle's Gift - Page [140.3-140.5] ("When I had learned to fly perfectly...do it while you were awake.)

DREAMING-CELESTIAL-[CELESTIAL DREAMING]-(TOP): SEE: ZULEICA-CELESTIAL-DREAMING-[ZULEICA'S CELESTIAL DREAMING]-(TOP)

DREAMING-COLORS-[COLORS TO INITIATE DREAMING: (TOP)
SELECTED REFERENCES: The Eagle's Gift - Page [251.6-251.8] (Zuleica explained that a dreamer must...of the sequence of physical events.) The Eagle's Gift - Page [256.4-256.8] (La Gorda explained Josephina's and her...immersed in an orange-red coloration.)

DREAMING-DOUBLE-[DREAMING THE DOUBLE]: (TOP)
SELECTED REFERENCES: The Eagle's Gift - Page [50.2-51.9] (I related to them the events...the name of the street: Ashton.)

DREAMING-EMISSARY-VOICE-[THE VOICE OF THE DREAMING EMISSARY]: (TOP)
SELECTED REFERENCES: The Art of Dreaming - Page [63.5-64.2] (A few months later, my dreaming...add to my collection of worries.) The Art of Dreaming - Page [68.4-68.9] (In the tone of don Juan's...doing it only to appease me.) The Art of Dreaming - Page [72.8] (My gut feeling was that don...was going to be perfectly well.) The Art of Dreaming - Page [89.9-92.3] (At the instant of this realization...it replied. "Energy is like blood.") The Art of Dreaming - Page [98.2-98.5] (The area where this reconstruction of...voice giving me more complex descriptions.) The Art of Dreaming - Page [118.8-119.2] (As my anxiety grew, my body...was merely reaffirming what I felt.) The Art of Dreaming - Page [158.1-159.7] (The voice of the dreaming emissary...without any meddling from the emissary.) The Art of Dreaming - Page [212.8-213.1] (My heart began to pound so intensely...afraid it is," he admitted sheepishly.) The Art of Dreaming - Page [222.8-222.9] (I was about to talk to her...I experience a momentary agonizing anxiety.)

DREAMING-GATE-FIRST-[THE FIRST GATE OF DREAMING]: (TOP)
SELECTED REFERENCES: **The Art of Dreaming - Page [20-34]** (As a preamble to his first...awakening. Something dormant becomes suddenly functional.)

DREAMING-GATE-SECOND-[THE SECOND GATE OF]: (TOP)
SELECTED REFERENCES: **The Art of Dreaming - Page [35-56]** (I found out by means of my...any interference from the inorganic beings.)

DREAMING-GATE-THIRD-[THE THIRD GATE OF DREAMING]: (TOP)
SELECTED REFERENCES: **The Art of Dreaming - Page [141-165]** (The third gate of dreaming is reached...the simplicity and directness of sorcery.)

DREAMING-GATE-THIRD-[THE THIRD GATE OF DREAMING]: (TOP)
SELECTED REFERENCES: **The Eagle's Gift - Page [50.4-53.1]** (I *dreamed* once that I woke up...a chance to talk to him.) **The Art of Dreaming - Page [155.7-155.9]** (At the first opportunity I had...disarranged everything, and erased my view.) **The Art of Dreaming - Page [157.4-157.9]** (I engaged my best efforts to...floating, going from item to item.) **The Art of Dreaming - Page [161.9-163.2]** (To have another of my wild...observing it while I was asleep.)

DREAMING-GORDA-[LA GORDA'S DREAMING]: (TOP)
SELECTED REFERENCES: **The Second Ring of Power - Page [162.3-164.2]** ("I learned that in *dreaming*," she said...our menstrual periods *dreaming* becomes power.)

DREAMING-INSTRUCTION-[THE WARRIORS' INSTRUCTION IN DREAMING]: (TOP)
SELECTED REFERENCES: **The Eagle's Gift - Page [249.5-265.9]** (Zuleica was very effective as my...having my own tales of eternity.)

DREAMING-INTRICACIES-[THE INTRICACIES OF DREAMING]: (TOP)
SELECTED REFERENCES: **The Eagle's Gift - Page [247-265]** (Don Juan began the task of...having my own tales of eternity.)

DREAMING-JOURNEY-COFFEE-SHOP-[CARLOS' DREAMING JOURNEY TO THE COFFEE SHOP] (TOP)
SELECTED REFERENCES: **The Eagle's Gift - Page [52.1-53.1]** (Months later, when I again found...a chance to talk to him.)

DREAMING-LEARN-[LEARNING TO DO DREAMING]: (TOP)
SELECTED REFERENCES: **The Eagle's Gift - Page [136.6-137.4]** ("How long does it take you...instruction in *dreaming* should be conducted.")

DREAMING-LESSON-[A DREAMING LESSON]: (TOP)
SELECTED REFERENCES: **The Art of Dreaming - Page [205.3-260.5]** ("All I can say is that...flying on the wings of intent.")

DREAMING-MUSCULAR-[BECOMING MORE MUSCULAR THROUGH DREAMING]: (TOP)
SELECTED REFERENCES: **The Eagle's Gift - Page [53.7-53.9]** (The tiger never touched me...that my body became more muscular.)

DREAMING-SEEING-[SEEING IN DREAMING]-(TOP): SEE: SEEING-DREAMING-[SEEING IN DREAMING]-(TOP)

DREAMING-SNATCHING-ANOTHER-DREAMER-[SNATCHING ANOTHER DREAMER IN DREAMING]: (TOP)
SELECTED REFERENCES: **The Eagle's Gift - Page [58.3-58.6]** ("How did you happen to go with...being more levelheaded than I am.")

DREAMING-TALKING-IN-[TALKING IN DREAMING]: (TOP)
SELECTED REFERENCES: **The Eagle's Gift - Page [151.3-151.9]** (La Gorda quickly tried to interlock...spontaneously entered into our *dreaming* bodies.) **The Eagle's Gift - Page [159.5-159.7]** (In another session of dreaming together...movement should stem from our midsections.)

DREAMING-TOGETHER-[DREAMING TOGETHER]: (TOP)

SELECTED REFERENCES: **The Eagle's Gift - Page [57.1-57.2]** ("Did he tell all this to you...go through the rest of them.) **The Eagle's Gift - Page [127-149]** (One day, in order to alleviate...the time they didn't do anything.") **The Eagle's Gift - Page [150.7-153.1]** (In unison, we arrived then at...quite spontaneously adopted the *dreaming* position.) **The Eagle's Gift - Page [159.5-163.4]** (In another session of *dreaming together*...of what had happened to us.)

DREAMING-TREE-[THE DREAMING TREE]: (TOP)

SELECTED REFERENCES: **The Art of Dreaming - Page [70.6-72.6]** (He said then that it was time....house, in the desert in Sonora.) **The Art of Dreaming - Page [79.1-79.6]** (Don Juan then gave me a...is but one of those skins.")

DREAMING-VOICE-[A VOICE FROM DREAMING]: (TOP)

SELECTED REFERENCES: **The Eagle's Gift - Page [249.5-249.7]** (Zuleica was very effective as my guide...thought she had heard in *dreaming*.) **The Eagle's Gift - Page [262.4-262.5]** (It took many more sessions of...was merely a voice from *dreaming*.)

DRINKING-LUCIO-[DRINKING WITH LUCIO]: (TOP)

SELECTED REFERENCES: **A Separate Reality - Page [57.9-68.5]** (On September 4, 1968, I went...is drunk and Victor is asleep.")

DRUNKARDS-[THE DRUNKARDS]: (TOP)

SELECTED REFERENCES: **The Eagle's Gift - Page [230.6-230.8]** (There was another striking anomaly that...they staggered around without muscular coordination.)

E

EAGLE-EMANATIONS-[THE EAGLE'S EMANATIONS]: (TOP)
SELECTED REFERENCES: **The Fire From Within - Page [31-46]** (The next day, don Juan and...them is an eternity in itself.")

EAGLE-EMANATIONS-BANDS-GREAT-[THE GREAT BANDS OF THE EAGLE'S EMANATIONS]: (TOP)
SELECTED REFERENCES: **The Fire From Within - Page [157-166]** (Days later, in his house in...to become trees to do that.")

EAGLE-EMANATIONS-ENCOUNTER-[AN ENCOUNTER WITH THE EAGLE'S EMANATIONS]: (TOP)
SELECTED REFERENCES: **The Fire From Within - Page [221.2-222.4]** (I would have gone on *seeing*...longer it would have blasted you.")

EAGLE-EMANATIONS-MAN-SEEING-[SEEING MAN'S BAND OF EMANATIONS]: (TOP)
SELECTED REFERENCES: **The Fire From Within - Page [220.6-220.9]** (That afternoon I saw ten luminous beings...that it was the assemblage point.)

EAGLE-EMANATIONS-SEEING-[SEEING THE EAGLE'S EMANATIONS]: (TOP)
SELECTED REFERENCES: **The Fire From Within - Page [221.2-221.5]** (I would have gone on seeing...I was no longer *seeing* them.) **The Power of Silence - Page [97.5-98.9]** (By the time it became completely...vision and plunged me into darkness.)

EAGLE-GIFT-[THE EAGLE'S GIFT]: (TOP)
SELECTED REFERENCES: **The Eagle's Gift - Page [1-314]** (Although I am an anthropologist, this...And then the lights were gone.)

EAGLE-GIFT-[THE EAGLE'S GIFT]: (TOP)
SELECTED REFERENCES: **The Eagle's Gift - Page [171-314]** (Don Juan had been extremely sparing... And then the lights were gone.)

EAGLE-GLIMPSING-[GLIMPSING THE EAGLE]: (TOP)
SELECTED REFERENCES: **The Eagle's Gift - Page [241.7-243.7]** (Silvio Manuel had conceived the idea...of awareness you ever had.")

EARTH-BOOST-[THE BOOST FROM THE EARTH]: (TOP)
SELECTED REFERENCES: **The Fire From Within - Page [203-217]** ("Let's walk on the road to...makes us perceive another total world.")

EARTH-DOORS-MAGIC-KEY-[THE MAGIC KEY TO THE EARTH'S DOORS]: (TOP)
SELECTED REFERENCES: **The Fire From Within - Page [210.9-211.5]** ("Go with the boost wherever it...insignificant microbe being twisted and twirled.)

EARTH-EMBRACE-[THE EMBRACE OF THE EARTH]-(TOP) SEE: GENARO-EARTH-EMBRACES [DON GENARO EMBRACES THE EARTH]-(TOP)

EARTH-ENERGY-CRISSCROSS-[ENERGY THAT CRISSCROSSES THE EARTH]-(TOP): SEE: ENERGY-CRISSCROSS-EARTH-[ENERGY THAT CRISSCROSSES THE EARTH]-(TOP)

EARTH-PULL-[THE PULL OF THE EARTH]: (TOP)
SELECTED REFERENCES: **The Power of Silence - Page [70.1-70.3]** (It had gotten windy, but I...frightened me. I felt a chill.)

EARTH-SIGN-[THE SIGN THE EARTH MAKES WHEN WARRIORS JUMP INTO THE ABYSS]: (TOP)

SELECTED REFERENCES: The Second Ring of Power - Page [215.2-215.4] ("After Eligio and Benigno jumped," Nestor...But Eligio's side was silent.")

EAST-[EASTERLY WOMEN]: (TOP)

SELECTED REFERENCES: The Eagle's Gift - Page [192.7-195.2] (Don Juan said that the east...warrior scholar and his oldest companion.)

ELIAS-AMALIA-INORGANIC BEINGS-[THE INORGANIC BEINGS' TRAP FOR ELIAS AND AMALIA]: (TOP): SEE: INORGANIC-BEINGS-TRAP [THE TRAP OF THE INORGANIC BEINGS]: (TOP)

ELIAS-NAGUAL-DUAL-LIFE-[THE DUAL LIFE OF THE NAGUAL ELIAS]: (TOP)

SELECTED REFERENCES: The Power of Silence - Page [32.8-33.7] (Don Juan said that the nagual Elias...his natural self to be a recluse.")

ELIAS-NAGUAL-ETERNITY-OBJECTS-[THE ETERNITY OBJECTS OF THE NAGUAL ELIAS]: (TOP)

SELECTED REFERENCES: The Power of Silence - Page [34.1-34.5] (Before I could reply, he began to...were used for, or their source.)

ELIAS-NAGUAL-IMPECCABILITY-[THE IMPECCABILITY OF THE NAGUAL ELIAS]: (TOP)

SELECTED REFERENCES: The Power of Silence - Page [11-24] (I had no way of telling...he said. "Her name was Talia.")

ELIAS-NAGUAL-TALES-[TALES OF THE NAGUAL ELIAS]: (TOP)

SELECTED REFERENCES: The Power of Silence - Page [14.8-24.4] (All of a sudden he said...he said. "Her name was Talia.") The Power of Silence - Page [31.3-35.4] (He said that the difficulties I...precarious mental balance of susceptible people.)

ELIGIO-DREAMING-AVAILABILITY-[ELIGIO'S AVAILABILITY IN DREAMING]: (TOP)

SELECTED REFERENCES: The Eagle's Gift - Page [55.1-55.9] ("Josephina has something to tell you...from me to disclose Eligio's words.")

ELIGIO-MESSAGE-[ELIGIO'S MESSAGE]: (TOP)

SELECTED REFERENCES: The Eagle's Gift - Page [55.8-57.9] ("She told me," la Gorda interrupted..."No, I can't," she said after a moment.) The Eagle's Gift - Page [58.6-59.2] ("Then Eligio must have told you the...one who has to remember first.") The Eagle's Gift - Page [67.3-67.5] (La Gorda straightened herself up from...assemble everyone to go on a trip.) The Eagle's Gift - Page [83.1-83.3] (Eligio is in that other world...remember weird things now and then.")

ELIGIO-POWER-AWAY-[POWER TAKES ELIGIO AWAY]: (TOP)

SELECTED REFERENCES: The Second Ring of Power - Page [42.8-42.9] ("The Nagual had no secrets from...He knew how to let go.") The Second Ring of Power - Page [215.4-216.3] ("What do you think happened to Eligio...went to join the Nagual and Genaro.")

ELIGIO-TALES-[TALES OF ELIGIO]: (TOP)

SELECTED REFERENCES: The Eagle's Gift - Page [239.4-241.2] (Don Juan and all his warriors followed...He never spoke to me again.)

EMILITO-TALES-[TALES OF EMILITO]: (TOP)

SELECTED REFERENCES: The Eagle's Gift - Page [239.8-239.9] (I was sitting on the back porch...to whoever wanted to hear them.)

ENERGY-BLOWING-INTO-CARLOS-[BLOWING ENERGY INTO CARLOS' BODY]: (TOP)

SELECTED REFERENCES: The Eagle's Gift - Page [244.6-244.8] (La Gorda added that they did...of the Nagual Juan Matus' party.)

ENERGY-BODY-MOVING-[MOVING THE ENERGY BODY]: (TOP)

SELECTED REFERENCES: The Art of Dreaming - Page [155.7-156.7] (At the first opportunity I had...you, an area of extraordinary exploration.")

ENERGY-CRISSCROSS-EARTH-[ENERGY THAT CRISSCROSSES THE EARTH]: (TOP)

SELECTED REFERENCES: The Eagle's Gift - Page [195.9-196.1] (To me the most fascinating was...of points in the luminous body.)

ETERNITY-TALES-[TALES OF ETERNITY]: (TOP)

SELECTED REFERENCES: The Eagle's Gift - Page [191.5-192.1] (Nonetheless, she was definitely on the...he passed on to the others.). The Eagle's Gift - Page [195.8-196.4] (Then, at don Juan's request, Juan Tuma...Juan Tuma, I forgot my anger.) The Eagle's Gift - Page [265.7-265.9] (Under Zuleica's guidance during her instruction...having my own tales of eternity.)

EXPLORATION-NEW-AREA-WARRIOR-[THE NEW AREA OF EXPLORATION FOR THE WARRIOR]: (TOP)

SELECTED REFERENCES: The Art of Dreaming - Page [166-182] (Don Juan told me that in...as he waved good-bye to me.)

EYE-DOOR-OPENING-[OPENING THE EYE-DOOR]: (TOP)

SELECTED REFERENCES: The Second Ring of Power - Page [166.1-167.2] (La Gorda stood up and told...get out of here," she muttered.) The Second Ring of Power - Page [168.2-168.6] ("This was a great test for both...an orange light, like the sun.) The Second Ring of Power - Page [257.7-258.6] (I noticed that at that moment...brought them back to their senses.)

EYE-DREAMING-[THE EYE OF DREAMING]: (TOP)

SELECTED REFERENCES: The Second Ring of Power - Page [159.8-160.7] ("The Nagual told me that a...you, a bit stubborn and lazy.") The Second Ring of Power - Page [163.7-164.2] ("Then the Nagual gave me the...I just wander around in it.) The Second Ring of Power - Page [168.2-168.6] ("This was a great test for both...an orange light, like the sun.)

EYES-CROSSING-[CROSSING THE EYES]: (TOP)

SELECTED REFERENCES: Journey to Ixtlan - Page [146.7-146.8] (After eating I felt very sleepy...hilltop where I had seen the bush.)

EYES-DREAMING BODY-[THE EYES OF THE DREAMING BODY]: (TOP)

SELECTED REFERENCES: A Separate Reality - Page [254.8-255.6] (They moved away and sat in...could perform marvels at that time.) The Fire From Within - Page [178.4-178.6] (I gently shook Genaro. He slowly...my back and restored my equilibrium.) The Fire From Within - Page [273.6-273.9] (Another thing I had done that night...them as points of amber light.)

EYES-WITNESSED-ALL-[EYES THAT HAVE WITNESSED ALL THERE IS TO SEE]: (TOP)

SELECTED REFERENCES: The Eagle's Gift - Page [267.8-268.1] (Her bluntness reminded me of don Juan's...could only describe as inner life.)

F

FALCON-WHITE-[THE WHITE FALCON]: (TOP)
SELECTED REFERENCES: **Journey to Ixtlan - Page [28.6-34.2]** (He giggled like a child and...the left of the white falcon.")

FEATHER-[FEATHERS]: (TOP)
SELECTED REFERENCES: **The Teachings of Don Juan - Page [22.9-23.1]** ("What power objects did you have...Maiz-pinto, crystals and feathers.") **The Teachings of Don Juan - Page [24.4-24.6]** ("Maiz-pinto, crystals and feathers are...are like a game for children.")

FINDING-CARLOS-[HOW POWER FOUND CARLOS]: (TOP)
SELECTED REFERENCES: **The Second Ring of Power - Page [48.7-48.9]** ("A short time after he had found...said that that was your path.) **The Eagle's Gift - Page [222.7-223.7]** (After don Juan and his party...would reveal the rule to me.)

FINDING-CAROL-[HOW POWER FOUND CAROL THE NAGUAL WOMAN]-(TOP): SEE: FINDING-NAGUAL-WOMAN-[HOW POWER FOUND CAROL THE NAGUAL WOMAN AND OLINDA THE NAGUAL WOMAN]-(TOP)

FINDING-ELIGIO-[HOW POWER FOUND ELIGIO]: (TOP)
SELECTED REFERENCES: **The Second Ring of Power - Page [53.3-54.4]** ("Some years after he found la Gorda...you and that you still are.")

FINDING-GORDA-[HOW POWER FOUND GORDA]: (TOP)
SELECTED REFERENCES: **The Second Ring of Power - Page [51.4-52.1]** ("A year later Elena came...she was too weak to walk.") **The Second Ring of Power - Page [129.6-129.7]** (I was dumbfounded; I couldn't believe...seen my death circling around me.) **The Second ring of Power - Page [130.8]** (That first night he found me...no business rebelling against my fate.)

FINDING-JOSEPHINA-[HOW POWER FOUND JOSEPHINA]: (TOP)
SELECTED REFERENCES: **The Second Ring of Power - Page [49.1-49.4]** ("For three years he had only two...day she's crazier than a bat.)

FINDING-LIDIA-[HOW POWER FOUND LIDIA]: (TOP)
SELECTED REFERENCES: **The Second Ring of Power - Page [47.7-48.7]** ("How did they become apprentices...go and went with him instead.)

FINDING-NAGUAL-WOMAN-[HOW POWER FOUND CAROL THE NAGUAL WOMAN AND OLINDA THE NAGUAL WOMAN]: (TOP)
SELECTED REFERENCES: **The Eagle's Gift - Page [213.2-219.8]** (When they had all acquired a degree...had witnessed of their benefactor's world.) **The Eagle's Gift - Page [223.7-228.6]** (Almost immediately after finding me...like Silvio Manuel, she never returned.)

FINDING-OLINDA-[HOW POWER FOUND OLINDA THE NAGUAL WOMAN]-(TOP): SEE: FINDING-NAGUAL-WOMAN-[FINDING CAROL THE NAGUAL WOMAN AND OLINDA THE NAGUAL WOMAN]-(TOP)

FINDING-PABLITO-[HOW POWER FOUND PABLITO]: (TOP)
SELECTED REFERENCES: **The Second Ring of Power - Page [190.3-194.6]** (In order to start up the...be making his green stuff today.")

FINDING-ROSA-[HOW POWER FOUND ROSA]: (TOP)
SELECTED REFERENCES: **The Second Ring of Power - Page [54.8-56.1]** ("A month after he found Eligio...the most. Can you beat that?")

FIRE-TRANSPORTED-[TRANSPORTED ON THE POWER OF FLAME]-(TOP): SEE: FLAME-TRANSPORTED-[TRANSPORTED ON THE POWER OF FLAME]-(TOP)

FIRE-WITHIN-[THE FIRE FROM WITHIN]: (TOP)
SELECTED REFERENCES: **The Fire From Within - Page [ix-300]** (I have written extensive descriptive accounts...to accept the Eagle's gift ourselves.)

FIRE-WITHIN-[THE FIRE FROM WITHIN]: (TOP)
SELECTED REFERENCES: **The Fire From Within - Page [299.8-299.9]** (After that don Juan made us enter...the mind-boggling gift of freedom.)

FIRING-SQUAD-[THE WARRIOR'S FIRING SQUAD]-(TOP): SEE: WARRIOR-WALK-TREES [THE WARRIOR'S WALK TO THE EDGE OF THE TREES]-(TOP)

FISH-FACED-MAN-[THE FISH FACED MAN]: (TOP)
SELECTED REFERENCES: **The Fire From Within - Page [104.1-104.9]** ("Don't you have some allies yourself...under the spell of that fright.) **The Fire From Within - Page [191.6-192.2]** (Don Juan said that when he...made a deal with the creature.") **The Fire From Within - Page [200.4-200.5]** (Don Juan said that the nagual Julian...could adopt a grotesque human form.) **The Power of Silence - Page [55.3-55.7]** (When he had recovered enough and...inorganic being, a formless energy field.") **The Power of Silence - Page [171.7-183.9]** (He began to recount what had happened...being devoured by that monster now.")

FLAME-TRANSPORTED-[TRANSPORTED ON THE POWER OF FLAME]: (TOP)
SELECTED REFERENCES: **The Fire From Within - Page [83.4-84.1]** (He continued then with his elucidation...a quagmire with no way out.) **The Fire From Within - Page [115.9-117.5]** ("Flame is very important," he said...room with don Juan and Genaro.")

FLOOR-SOLEDAD-MAGICAL-[DONA SOLEDAD'S MAGICAL FLOOR]: (TOP)-SEE: SOLEDAD-FLOOR-MAGICAL-[DONA SOLEDAD'S MAGICAL FLOOR]-(TOP)

FLORINDA-[FLORINDA]: (TOP)
SELECTED REFERENCES: **The Eagle's Gift - Page [266-296]** (La Gorda and I were in...be free is the ultimate audacity.)

FLORINDA-[FLORINDA]: (TOP)
SELECTED REFERENCES: **The Eagle's Gift - Page [210.4-210.7]** (Don Juan explained to me at...to enter into the third attention.)

FLORINDA-LEG-[HEALING FLORINDA'S LEG]: (TOP)
SELECTED REFERENCES: **The Eagle's Gift - Page [272.3-287.3]** ("When I was fifteen," she went on...she needed absolute quiet and solitude.)

FLYING-CARLOS-[CARLOS' FLYING]: (TOP)
SELECTED REFERENCES: **The Second Ring of Power - Page [257.8-259.5]** (All of a sudden I felt the...cared less about explaining anything.)

FLYING-DEVIL'S-WEED-[FLYING WITH THE DEVIL'S WEED]: (TOP)
SELECTED REFERENCES: **The Teachings of Don Juan - Page [126.5-130.7]** (Don Juan kept staring at me...the rock with its heavy chain.")

FLYING-DREAMING-[FLYING IN DREAMING]: (TOP)
SELECTED REFERENCES: **The Eagle's Gift - Page [139.5-141.6]** (Our discussion of the second attention...it comes out of your ears.")

FLYING-GENARO-CARLOS-[DON GENARO'S FLIGHT WITH CARLOS]: (TOP)
SELECTED REFERENCES: **Tales of Power - Page [184.7-185.9]** (Don Juan told me that he...of the field of eucalyptus trees.)

FLYING-GORDA-[LA GORDA'S FLYING]: (TOP)
SELECTED REFERENCES: **The Second Ring of Power - Page [139.5-139.8]** (She squatted once again, and when...down a stairway on her belly.) **The Eagle's Gift - Page [139.6-**

141.8] ("How did you learn to fly...can fly as if I were in *dreaming*.") **The Second Ring of Power -** **Page [160.8-162.3]** ("How did you do the flying...but I really don't know how.) **The Second Ring** **of Power - Page [168.5-168.9]** (The Nagual and Genaro and Eligio...when you showed me your double.) **The Second Ring of Power - Page [166.1-167.2]** (La Gorda stood up and told...get out of here," she muttered.)

FLYING-INTENT-[THE INTENT OF FLYING]-(TOP): SEE: INTENT- *FLYING-[THE INTENT OF FLYING]-(TOP)*

FLYING-JUAN-[DON JUAN'S FLYING]: (TOP)
SELECTED REFERENCES: **The Eagle's Gift - Page [224.7-227.3]** (After three months of this, don Juan...auspicious that she had been attentive.)

FOG-CRYSTALS-[THE FOG OF CRYSTALS]: (TOP)
SELECTED REFERENCES: **A Separate Reality - Page [197.6-197.8]** ("By then you would know where...of tiny crystals moving, moving away.") **A Separate Reality - Page [198.1-198.6]** (It is the area of the will...expanding fog moving beyond its limits.") **Tales of Power -** **Page [8.8-8.9]** ("Do you know that you can...of yourself forever in any direction.")

FOG-WALL-[THE WALL OF FOG]: (TOP)
SELECTED REFERENCES: **The Eagle's Gift - Page [88.9-89.2]** ("I know what's missing!" she shouted...thought that wall was after me.") **The Eagle's Gift - Page [227.6-228.1]** (When she regained consciousness...only accept in humbleness and in awe.) **The Eagle's Gift -** **Page [237.8-241.7]** (Silvio Manuel had la Gorda and...world entails engaging our total being.) **The Eagle's Gift - Page [273.9-274.6]** (The Next time don Juan took...rather than whatever was being done.) **The Eagle's Gift - Page [278.8-278.9]** (Her account had absorbed me so...the end of our first meeting.) **The Eagle's Gift - Page [280.1-280.2]** (The next time I went to Florinda's...the wall of fog is visible.)

FOG-WALL-SNATCHED-BEHIND-[BEING SNATCHED BEHIND THE *WALL OF FOG]: (TOP)*
SELECTED REFERENCES: **The Eagle's Gift - Page [58.2-58.6]** ("I close my eyes and I...being more levelheaded than I am.")

FORCE-ROLLING-[THE ROLLING FORCE]: (TOP)
SELECTED REFERENCES: **The Fire From Within - Page [218-230]** (Don Juan was about to start...of the Eagle to be devoured.")

FORCE-ROLLING-SEEING-[SEEING THE ROLLING FORCE]: (TOP)
SELECTED REFERENCES: **The Fire From Within - Page [221.5-221.8]** (I wanted to focus my eyes...the balloons that were hitting me.)

FORCES-FOUR-[THE FOUR FORCES]: (TOP)
SELECTED REFERENCES: **The Second Ring of Power - Page [140.2-155.1]** ("I think it's time to go...do is lose your human forms.) **The Second Ring of Power - Page [249.3-250.8]** (La Gorda spoke suddenly, and the...from the trail in the darkness.) **The Eagle's Gift - Page** **[68.2-69.2]** (We hiked as quickly and as...entities at large in the world.)

FOREST-MAGICAL-TRAIL-[THE TRAIL IN THE MAGICAL FOREST]- *(TOP): SEE: MAGICAL-FOREST-TRAIL [THE TRAIL IN THE MAGICAL* *FOREST]-(TOP)*

FOUR-TULIOS-[THE FOUR TULIOS]-(TOP): SEE: TULIOS-FOUR-[THE *FOUR TULIOS]-(TOP)*

G

GAIT-POWER-*[THE GAIT OF POWER]: (TOP)*
SELECTED REFERENCES: The Fire From Within - Page [129.3-130.6] ("Genaro has something to show you...moved a few feet away from me.)

GAIT-POWER-VISION-*[A VISION OF THE GAIT OF POWER]: (TOP)*
SELECTED REFERENCES: The Fire From Within - Page [129.4-130.1] (Genaro immediately began to walk around...was taking off something stopped me.)

GATE-DREAMING-FIRST-*[THE FIRST GATE OF DREAMING]-(TOP)*: SEE: DREAMING-GATE-FIRST-*[THE FIRST GATE OF DREAMING]-(TOP)*

GATE-DREAMING-SECOND-*[THE SECOND GATE OF DREAMING]-(TOP)*: SEE: DREAMING-GATE-SECOND-*[THE SECOND GATE OF DREAMING]-(TOP)*

GATE-DREAMING-THIRD-*[THE THIRD GATE OF DREAMING]-(TOP)*: SEE: DREAMING-GATE-THIRD-*[THE THIRD GATE OF DREAMING]-(TOP)*

GAZING-*[GAZING]: (TOP)*
SELECTED REFERENCES: The Second Ring of Power - Page [288.8-289.3] (At that moment she had a sudden...That's perfect. That will give us time.")

GENARO-ALLY-MEET-*[DON GENARO MEETS HIS ALLY]: (TOP)*
SELECTED REFERENCES: Journey to Ixtlan - Page [257.9-258.3] ("I was young when I first...mean, when your neck gets hard.") Journey to Ixtlan - Page [259.8-260.2] ("What happened when you grabbed your...feeling! What a feeling it was!)

GENARO-BENCH-*[DON GENARO GETS UP OFF A BENCH WITHOUT GETTING UP]: (TOP)*
SELECTED REFERENCES: The Fire From Within - Page [275.9-276.9] (I remembered one morning, don Juan...the people going to the market.)

GENARO-BOULDER-*[DON GENARO'S DREAM BOULDER]: (TOP)*
SELECTED REFERENCES: A Separate Reality - Page [252.9-254.2] (At that very moment I heard...confusion," don Juan said very loudly.)

GENARO-CALLING-*[THE CALLING OF DON GENARO]: (TOP)*
SELECTED REFERENCES: Tales of Power - Page [36.2-38.3] ("The last person you're going to...It's the only house I've got.") Tales of Power - Page [58.6-59.7] ("Why don't you call Genaro?" don...practically danced in front of me.) Tales of Power - Page [99.3-99.6] (He commanded me to sit calmly...eyes, but my eyes were open.)

GENARO-CARLOS-MEET-*[DON GENARO MEETS CARLOS]: (TOP)*
SELECTED REFERENCES: A Separate Reality - Page [92.4-98.6] (Just as we were getting into...he was doubled over with laughter.) The Eagle's Gift - Page [205.1-207.5] (My last introductory encounter with don...had to lean against a wall.)

GENARO-DREAMING-BODY-ANTICS-*[THE ANTICS OF DON GENARO'S DREAMING BODY]: (TOP)*
SELECTED REFERENCES: A Separate Reality - Page [95.5-98.6] (Don Juan apologized to me and...he was doubled over with laughter.) A Separate Reality - Page [250.1-257.4] (They laughed loudly. Don Genaro patted...he did not let me talk.) Journey to Ixtlan - Page [231.9-233.6] (My question threw both of them...perfect that I laughed even harder.) Tales of Power - Page [40.7-41.3] (Don Genaro made some ludicrous and...eyes were shining with sheer delight.) Tales of Power - Page [43.7-43.9] (Don Juan said that I had...Don Genaro's antics were priceless.) Tales of Power - Page [44.7-45.7] (I felt an anxiety building up...gesture that

could have meant anything.) **Tales of Power - Page [48.1-48.3]** ("He's right," he said. "We're always...of my head with his knuckles.) **Tales of Power - Page [60.6-61.7]** (I fully realized that don Genaro...Juan and me practically in hysterics.) **Tales of Power - Page [99.8-100.3]** (Don Genaro yelled that it was...Genaro was hiding under my hat.") **Tales of Power - Page [214.4-215.7]** (His words were either an overpowering...and crawled into the back seat.) **The Second Ring of Power - Page [279.2-279.3]** ("Genaro was in his body of...go in and out a door.") **The Fire From Within - Page [177.9-179.6]** (Don Juan told me then, as...while I was in normal awareness.) **The Fire From Within - Page [237.4-237.5]** ("Genaro had shown you something extraordinary...more than if he were awake.") **The Fire From Within - Page [272.9-273.3]** (We had stopped for the night...performing acts that defied my reason.) **The Fire From Within - Page [275.9-276.9]** (I remembered that one morning, don...the people going to the market.)

GENARO-DREAMING-BODY-EXPERIENCES-FOUR-[DON GENARO'S FIRST FOUR EXPERIENCES WITH HIS DREAMING BODY: (TOP)

SELECTED REFERENCES: Tales of Power - Page [62.3-68.5] ("When it first happened to me...lain there. The weeds were crumpled.")

GENARO-EARTH-EMBRACES-[DON GENARO EMBRACES THE EARTH]: (TOP): (TOP)

SELECTED REFERENCES: Tales of Power - Page [291.6-292.3] (Don Genaro stood up and walked...his arms and legs spread out.)

GENARO-FLYING-CARLOS-[DON GENARO'S FLIGHT WITH CARLOS] WITH CARLOS]-(TOP): SEE: FLYING-GENARO-CARLOS-[DON GENARO'S FLIGHT WITH CARLOS] WITH CARLOS]-(TOP)

GENARO-FURRY-CROCODILE-[THE FLIGHT OF DON GENARO'S BROWN FURRY CROCODILE: (TOP)

SELECTED REFERENCES: Tales of Power - Page [182.8-183.8] (Don Genaro stayed perched on the... did not show up at all.)

GENARO-GREEN-STUFF-[DON GENARO'S GREEN STUFF]: (TOP)

SELECTED REFERENCES: The Second Ring of Power - Page [192.9-194.6] ("I was pretty miserable with the...be making his green stuff today.")

GENARO-HIDING-[DON GENARO'S TECHNIQUE FOR HIDING]: (TOP)

SELECTED REFERENCES: A Separate Reality - Page [255.6-257.4] (We were quiet for a few...he did not let me talk.)

GENARO-LEAP-[DON GERNARO'S PRODIGIOUS LEAP]: (TOP)

SELECTED REFERENCES: Tales of Power - Page [257.3-257.8] (He began to talk about an...let me ruin my clothes again.) Tales of Power - Page [41.4-41.7] ("Genaro is a man of knowledge...Genaro but his double," he said.)

GENARO-MOUNTAINS-TREMBLE-[DON GENARO MAKES THE MOUNTAINS TREMBLE]: (TOP)

SELECTED REFERENCES: A Separate Reality - Page [98.3-98.6] ("Which direction is the wind...he was doubled over with laughter. A Separate Reality - Page [252.2-254.2] (Don Genaro got up, cracked his...don Juan said very loudly.) Tales of Power - Page [229.8-229.9] (That seemed to be all he wanted to...a distant rumble, like muffled thunder.) The Eagle's Gift - Page [145.6-145.8] ("I never knew he was in his...of eating, or drinking," she replied.)

GENARO-RIDDLE-[THE RIDDLE OF DON GENARO]: (TOP)

SELECTED REFERENCES: Tales of Power - Page [79.3-87.8] ("Today, however, you must solve a...and then sat next to me.)

GENARO-SEEING-MOUNTAINS-MILES-AWAY-[SEEING DON GENARO IN THE MOUNTAINS TEN MILES AWAY]: (TOP)

SELECTED REFERENCES: A Separate Reality - Page [260.8-261.5] (At that point don Genaro stood...ten miles away the perception vanished.)

GENARO-TOUCH-CRUSHING-[DON GENARO'S CRUSHING TOUCH]: (TOP)

SELECTED REFERENCES: **A Separate Reality - Page [250.1-250.8]** (They laughed loudly. Don Genaro patted...on your shoulder," he said innocently.) **A Separate Reality - Page [254.4-254.6]** (Don Juan and don Genaro returned...trying to sleep on his lap.)

GENARO-WALK-EUCALYPTUS-TREES-[DON GENARO WALKS IN THE EUCALYPTUS TREES]: (TOP)

SELECTED REFERENCES: **Tales of Power - Page [164.5-172.4]** (I looked at my watch. It...even raised a bit of dust.)

GENARO-VANISHES-[DON GENARO VANISHES LIKE A PUFF OF AIR]: (TOP)

SELECTED REFERENCES: **The Fire From Within - Page [216.4-216.7]** ("Genaro will let his assemblage point...was gone like a puff of air.)

GENARO-WATERFALL-[DON GENARO SCALES THE WATERFALL]: (TOP)

SELECTED REFERENCES: **A Separate Reality - Page [99.4s-108.6]** ("Talking is not Genaro's predilection," he...knew that you had not *seen*.")

GENAROS-[THE GENAROS]: (TOP)

SELECTED REFERENCES: **The Second Ring of Power - Page [170-222]** (I woke up around eight in the...he asked me and left laughing.)

GIANT-TEN-FOOT-FEELING-[FEELING LIKE A TEN FOOT GIANT]: (TOP)

SELECTED REFERENCES: **The Power of Silence - Page [209.6-210.1]** ("Another maneuver silent knowledge might dictate...a shift of my assemblage point.) **The Power of Silence - Page [211.6-214.7]** ("Be gigantic," he ordered me, smiling...making so much sense to me.)

GLORY-TALES-[TALES OF GLORY]: (TOP)

SELECTED REFERENCES: **The Eagle's Gift - Page [239.4-241.2]** (Don Juan and all his warriors followed...He never spoke to me again.)

GORDA-[LA GORDA]: (TOP)

SELECTED REFERENCES: **The Second Ring of Power - Page [112-169]** (The first thing I noticed about...time to put my notes away.)

GORDA-CARING-[CARING FOR LA GORDA]: (TOP)

SELECTED REFERENCES: **The Eagle's Gift - Page [129.9-130.5]** (Don Juan was telling me that...the fulfillment of my true task.) **The Eagle's Gift - Page [131.4-131.8]** (A fat Gorda asked don Juan...I be capable of harnessing my selfishness.)

GORDA-COMPLETENESS-[LA GORDA REGAINS HER COMPLETENESS]: (TOP)

SELECTED REFERENCES: **The Second Ring of Power - Page [127.1-131.7]** ("Soledad is a woman like myself...that they have lost their edge.") **The Second Ring of Power - Page [133.2-134.9]** ("But how did you regain your completeness...me away from that world! Nothing!")

GORDA-DREAMING-[LA GORDA'S DREAMING]-(TOP): SEE: DREAMING-GORDA-[LA GORDA'S DREAMING]-(TOP)

GORDA-FLYING-[LA GORDA'S FLYING]-(TOP): SEE: FLYING-GORDA [LA GORDA'S FLYING]-(TOP)

GORDA-PETTY-TYRANT-[LA GORDA AS A PETTY TYRANT]: (TOP)

SELECTED REFERENCES: **The Fire From Within - Page [8.1-9.1]** (Don Juan must have had business...still haven't caught on to that.") **The Fire From Within - Page [11.4-13.9]** (Don Juan did not discuss the...he replied. "Realizations are always personal.")

GORDA-POWER-ROCK-[LA GORDA AND THE POWER ROCK FROM MONTE ALBAN: (TOP)

SELECTED REFERENCES: The Eagle's Gift - Page [10.6-14.1] ("Something happened to me in the...have been any fear in him.")

GORDA-PURPOSE-[LA GORDA'S PURPOSE]: (TOP)

SELECTED REFERENCES: The Second Ring of Power - Page [229.6-230.5] ("But stalking your weaknesses is not enough...when he thought I was indulging.)

GORDA-SEARCH-CARLOS-CITY-[LA GORDA SEARCHES IN THE CITY FOR CARLOS]: (TOP)

SELECTED REFERENCES: The Second Ring of Power - Page [232.4-234.3] ("Where are you going to go...Do you see what I mean?")

GORDA-SPARKS-[LA GORDA'S SPARKS]: (TOP)

SELECTED REFERENCES: The Second Ring of Power - Page [138.8-140.2] ("I'll show you my faint light...and yet I was also panting.) The Second Ring of Power - Page [143.3-144.3] (La Gorda was startled. She squatted...look of despair in her eyes.) The Second Ring of Power - Page [161.3-161.5] ("You don't believe me, do you...of energy emanating from her body.) The Second Ring of Power - Page [164.6-164.7] ("Well, it was during my periods...have learned in *dreaming* so far.")

GORDA-STORY-[LA GORDA'S STORY]: (TOP)

SELECTED REFERENCES: The Second Ring of Power - Page [127.1-131.7] ("Soledad is a woman like myself...that they have lost their edge.")

GORDA-WEAKNESS-DISASSEMBLE-[GORDA DISASSEMBLES HER WEAKNESS]: (TOP)

SELECTED REFERENCES: The Second Ring of Power - Page [228.4-229.6] (La Gorda then described how she...lost the fat on my buttocks.")

GOURD-FOOD-YOUNG-MAN-[THE GOURDS OF FOOD AND THE YOUNG MAN]: (TOP)

SELECTED REFERENCES: Journey to Ixtlan - Page [44.3-47.3] (After a couple of hours we...that that food was power too.")

GOURD-WARRIOR-[THE WARRIORS' GOURD[-(TOP) SEE: WARRIOR-GOURD-[THE WARRIORS' GOURD]-(TOP)

GUARDIAN-[THE GUARDIAN]: (TOP)

SELECTED REFERENCES: A Separate Reality - Page [113.8-121.1] (Don Juan had dropped his instructions...about it, find the guardian again.") A Separate Reality - Page [127.-133.1] (Don Juan asked me abruptly if...something you can fool around with.") A Separate Reality - Page [169.8-170.5] (The spirit of the water hole likes you...the same time, to be nothing.) The Second Ring of Power - Page [323.5-324.7] ("The Nagual told me," a Gorda...he had an awesome, fearsome side.") The Second Ring of Power - Page [325.6-325.8] (The Nagual said that you will understand...would've been strong enough to pass.)

GUAYMAS-STROKE-[A STROKE IN GUAYMAS]-(TOP): SEE: JUAN-STROKE-GUAYMAS-[DON JUAN'S STROKE IN GUAYMAS]-(TOP)

H

HAND-DREAM-[THE DREAM HAND]-(TOP): SEE: DREAM-HAND-[THE DREAM HAND]-(TOP)

HAND-JOINING-DREAMING-[JOINING HANDS IN DREAMING]: (TOP)
      SELECTED REFERENCES: **The Eagle's Gift - Page [37.8-38.1]** ("In our *dreaming*, the little sisters...for you to rally your knowledge.")

HEAVEN-VISIONS-[VISIONS OF HEAVEN]-(TOP): SEE: WORLD-APPARITIONS-[THE WORLD OF APPARITIONS]-(TOP)

HELL-VISIONS-[VISIONS OF HELL]: (TOP)
      SELECTED REFERENCES: **The Fire From Within - Page [208.1-208.3]** ("Don't look at Genaro!" a voice...moving around us, at great speed.)

HERMANITAS-BID-POWER-[LAS HERMANITAS' BID FOR POWER]: (TOP)
      SELECTED REFERENCES: **The Second Ring of Power - Page [109.1-111.8]** ("For heaven's sake, do something!" Rosa...But somehow I was myself again.) **The Second Ring of Power - Page [136.4-137.8]** ("So you see, it was all...you were about to annihilate them.") **The Second Ring of Power - Page [182.6-182.9]** (The Nagual told us that one day...to find you alive and well.) **The Second Ring of Power - Page [223.5-223.9]** (La Gorda broke the silence and...to her house and to the hills.) **The Second Ring of Power - Page [224.5-225.4]** ("The Nagual told me that the...sisters tried to take your luminosity.") **The Eagle's Gift - Page [248.9-249.3]** (La Gorda confessed that all of...been in control of my faculties.)

HERMANITAS-BOUT-[A BOUT WITH LAS HERMANITAS]: (TOP)
      SELECTED REFERENCES: **The Eagle's Gift - Page [31.9-33.1]** (The three little sisters gathered around...would be in need of help.) **The Eagle's Gift - Page [36.3-38.1]** (La Gorda said that what had happened...for you to rally your knowledge.")

HOLE-SOUND-[THE HOLES IN THE SOUNDS]: (TOP)
      SELECTED REFERENCES: **A Separate Reality - Page [221.6-226.1]** (When I had finished smoking he...would only be harmful to me.)

HOUSE-LEFT-SIDE-[THE HOUSE ON THE LEFT SIDE]: (TOP)
      SELECTED REFERENCES: **The Eagle's Gift - Page [34.4-34.9]** (We left at the crack of dawn...leaving the car to go into it.) **The Eagle's Gift - Page [49.4-49.9]** ("Can you tell us what's going on...very important that you tell us.") **The Eagle's Gift - Page [85.7-90.1]** (The force behind my explosion had...the charming lady who lived there.) **The Eagle's Gift - Page [91.4-94.9]** (After breakfast we walked to the house...from that time, from that world.") **The Eagle's Gift - Page [158.8-159.1]** ("We were in Silvio Manuel's house...he and his companions lived there.)

HOUSE-SHADOWS-[THE HOUSE OF SHADOWS]: (TOP)
      SELECTED REFERENCES: **The Fire From Within - Page [126.9-127.7]** (I protested that he had never...solitude of the warrior's endless path.)

HUMAN-FORM-[THE HUMAN FORM]: (TOP)
      SELECTED REFERENCES: **The Second Ring of Power - Page [237.5-238.1]** ("Everybody gets angry with you because...won't feel offended by your acts.") **The Second Ring of Power - Page [270.4-270.6]** (La Gorda came to my aid...and you pretend to be dumb.") **The Second Ring of Power - Page [273.9-274.1]** (She announced that she had just seen...own appearance of not knowing anything.)

HUMAN-FORM-LOSING-[LOSING THE HUMAN FORM]: (TOP)
      SELECTED REFERENCES: **The Eagle's Gift - Page [111-126]** (A few months later, after helping...still more deleterious things to us.)

HUMAN-FORM-LOSING-[LOSING THE HUMAN FORM]: (TOP)

SELECTED REFERENCES: The Eagle's Gift - Page [111.9-112.7] (Three months went by almost unnoticed...the pain and pressure had vanished.)

HUNTER-BECOMING-[BECOMING A HUNTER]: (TOP)

SELECTED REFERENCES: Journey to Ixtlan - Page [47-58] (As soon as I sat down...his arm and tears flooded me.)

HUNTING-LION-[LION HUNTING]-(TOP): SEE: LION-HUNTING-[LION HUNTING]-(TOP)

HUNTING-RATTLESNAKE-[HUNTING A RATTLESNAKE]-(TOP): SEE: RATTLESNAKE-HUNTING-[HUNTING A RATTLESNAKE]-(TOP)

I

IMPECCABILITY-NAGUAL-ELIAS-[THE IMPECCABILITY OF THE NAGUAL ELIAS]-(TOP): SEE: NAGUAL-ELIAS-IMPECCABILITY-[THE IMPECCABILITY OF THE NAGUAL ELIAS]-(TOP)

INACCESSIBLE-BEING-[BEING INACCESSIBLE]: (TOP)
  SELECTED REFERENCES: **Journey to Ixtlan - Page [59-70]** (Again don Juan, as he had...moves away leaving hardly a mark.")

INFANT-MEMORIES-[THE MEMORIES OF AN INFANT]-(TOP): SEE: CARLOS-INFANT-MEMORIES-[THE MEMORIES OF CARLOS AS AN INFANT]-(TOP)

INFINITY-JUNKYARD-[THE JUNKYARD OF INFINITY]-(TOP): SEE: NAGUAL-ELIAS-ETERNITY-OBJECTS-[THE ETERNITY OBJECTS OF THE NAGUAL ELIAS]-(TOP)

INORGANIC-BEINGS-[THE INORGANIC BEINGS]: (TOP)
  SELECTED REFERENCES: **The Fire From Within - Page [78-105]** (The next day I repeatedly asked don...immensity that is the Eagle's emanations.")

INORGANIC-BEINGS-INSIDE-[INSIDE THE INORGANIC BEINGS]: (TOP)
  SELECTED REFERENCES: **The Art of Dreaming - Page [88.1-92.4]** (At home, I tired of searching...only statement that was not true.) **The Art of Dreaming - Page [97.8-98.5]** (In dreaming the inorganic beings' realm...voice giving me more complex descriptions.)

INORGANIC-BEINGS-REALM-RESCUE-[THE RESCUE FROM THE REALM OF THE INORGANIC BEINGS]: (TOP)
  SELECTED REFERENCES: **The Eagle's Gift - Page [71.8-73.6]** (Rosa was not flustered by my outburst...one of them avoided my eyes.) **The Eagle's Gift - Page [103.4-104.2]** (Lidia faced me next. She did...to do was to talk about him.) **The Eagle's Gift - Page [244.2-245.4]** (Unfortunately, our next attempt did not...Juan Matus looked after the women.) **The Art of Dreaming - Page [128.7-128.8]** (I was dreaming an utterly nonsensical...out of a foggy, yellowish world.) **The Art of Dreaming - Page [133.1-133.9]** (I mentioned to don Juan that...into a view of what happened.") **The Art of Dreaming - Page [137.7-138.5]** (Don Juan explained that upon merging...dead, and Carol dragged you out.") **The Art of Dreaming - Page [139.5-139.7]** ("I am not flattering or humoring...I shudder at the mere thought.") **The Art of Dreaming - Page [189.6-189.8]** ("Transferring awareness is purely a matter...the trick. It'll tip the scales.")

INORGANIC-BEINGS-SEEING-NOT-[NOT BEING ABLE TO SEE THE INORGANIC BEINGS]: (TOP)
  SELECTED REFERENCES: **The Fire From Within - Page [76.3-77.3]** ("Taking an inventory makes us invulnerable...don Juan's house in the next town.)

INORGANIC-BEINGS-TRAP-[THE TRAP OF THE INORGANIC BEINGS]: (TOP)
  SELECTED REFERENCES: **The Art of Dreaming - Page [131.1-131.9]** (Finally, Florinda broke the ice...beings set for you," he answered.) **The Art of Dreaming - Page [136.9-137.2]** ("I can't even begin to assess...using your inherent aversion to chains.") **The Art of Dreaming - Page [137.9-138.1]** ("The scout is a sentient being...That's her human part now.) **The Art of Dreaming - Page [139.9]** ("You did free the scout...scout go, in exchange for you.")

INORGANIC-BEINGS-WORLD-[THE WORLD OF THE INORGANIC BEINGS]: (TOP)
  SELECTED REFERENCES: **The Art of Dreaming - Page [82-105]** (Faithful to my agreement to wait...assure you, they were very, very strange.")

INORGANIC-BEINGS-WORLD-LOST-[LOST IN THE WORLD OF THE INORGANIC BEINGS]: (TOP)

SELECTED REFERENCES: The Art of Dreaming - Page [102.3-105.2] ("Your confidence is very scary" was...assure you, they were very strange.") The Art of Dreaming - Page [137.7-137.8] (Don Juan explained that upon...remained in that world, inextricably lost.)

INTENDING-APPEARANCES-[INTENDING APPEARANCES]-(TOP): SEE: APPEARANCES-INTENDING-[INTENDING APPEARANCES]-(TOP)

INTENT-FLYING-[THE INTENT OF FLYING]: (TOP)

SELECTED REFERENCES: The Eagle's Gift - Page [149.1-149.4] ("He told me that if I...This was only one thing.)

INTENT-FLYING-WINGS-[FLYING ON THE WINGS OF INTENT]: (TOP)

SELECTED REFERENCES: The Art of Dreaming - Page [241-260] ("Make an effort, nagual," a woman's...flying on the wings of intent.")

INTENT-GIFT-[THE GIFT OF INTENT]-(TOP): SEE: TENANT-GIFT [THE TENANT'S GIFT]-(TOP)

INTENT-HANDLING-[HANDLING INTENT]: (TOP)

SELECTED REFERENCES: The Power of Silence - Page [196-265] (Don Juan often took me and...reach the place of silent knowledge.")

INTENT-REQUIREMENTS-[THE REQUIREMENTS OF INTENT]: (TOP)

SELECTED REFERENCES: The Power of Silence - Page [155-195] (We spent a night at the...I've kept mine in mint condition.")

INTENT-TRIANGLE-[THE TRIANGLE OF INTENT]: (TOP)

SELECTED REFERENCES: The Eagle's Gift - Page [235.8-236.1] (He said that in order to...and its vertex in the air.)

IRIDIUM-WALKING-STICK-[CARLOS' DREAM OF THE IRIDIUM WALKING STICK]-(TOP): SEE: DREAM-IRIDIUM-WALKING-STICK-[CARLOS' DREAM OF THE IRIDIUM WALKING STICK]-(TOP)

ITCH-OUTSIDE-BODY-[THE ITCH OUTSIDE OF THE BODY]-(TOP): SEE: ATTENTION-SECOND-CONTROLS-[EXPERIENCING THE SECOND ATTENTION TAKING OVER THE CONTROLS]-(TOP)

J

JAGUAR-CHASE-NOT-DOING-[THE NOT-DOING OF BEING CHASED BY A JAGUAR]: (TOP)
SELECTED REFERENCES: **The Power of Silence - Page [203.7-203.9]** ("It looks like we're not going to shake him off...for being chased by a jaguar.")

JAGUAR-CHOICES-MATCHING-[MATCHING THE JAGUAR'S CHOICES]-(TOP)
SELECTED REFERENCES: **The Power of Silence - Page [199.5-203.9]** (Don Juan looked at me fixedly...for being chased by a jaguar.")

JAGUAR-MAGICAL-[THE MAGICAL JAGUAR]-(TOP): SEE: POINT-THIRD [THE THIRD POINT]-(TOP)

JAPANESE-SQUIRREL-[THE JAPANESE SQUIRREL]-(TOP): SEE: NAGUAL-CREATIVITY-[THE NAGUAL AND A DEMONSTRATION OF CREATIVITY]-(TOP)

JILTED-BRIDE-PIGLET-[THE JILTED BRIDE AND HER PIGLET]: (TOP)
SELECTED REFERENCES: **The Eagle's Gift - Page [309.4-309.7]** (He examined the apprentices and concluded...laughter could we change our condition.)

JOINING-HANDS-DREAMING-[JOINING HANDS IN DREAMING] (TOP): SEE: HANDS-JOINING-DREAMING-[JOINING HANDS IN DREAMING]: (TOP)

JOSEPHINA-BABY-[JOSEPHINA'S BABY]-(TOP): SEE: JOSEPHINA-STALKING-[JOSEPHINA'S STALKING MANEUVERS]-(TOP)

JOSEPHINA-DREAMING-[JOSEPHINA'S DREAMING]: (TOP)
SELECTED REFERENCES: **The Eagle's Gift - Page [265.1-265.3]** (Zuleica took us systematically on voyages...rational causes or reasons for anything.)

JOSEPHINA-PRANKS-[JOSEPHINA'S PRANKS]: (TOP)
SELECTED REFERENCES: **The Second Ring of Power - Page [230.5-232.2]** (There was no more light for me...not their favorite, you know," she replied.) **The Second Ring of Power - Page [236.8-237.2]** ("Did they tell Josephina the same thing...get angry. They can't help themselves.")

JOSEPHINA-STALKING-[JOSEPHINA'S STALKING MANEUVERS]: (TOP)
SELECTED REFERENCES: **The Second Ring of Power - Page [97.4-109.6]** (Lidia, Rosa and I had been sitting...open and shut with nervous spasms.)

JOURNEY-IXTLAN-[JOURNEY TO IXTLAN]: (TOP)
SELECTED REFERENCES: **Journey to Ixtlan - Page [vii-268]** (On Saturday, May 22, 1971, I...it was not my time, yet.)

JOURNEY-IXTLAN-[JOURNEY TO IXTLAN]: (TOP)
SELECTED REFERENCES: **Journey to Ixtlan - Page [231-268]** (In May of 1971, I paid...it was not my time, yet.)

JOURNEY-IXTLAN-[JOURNEY TO IXTLAN]: (TOP)
SELECTED REFERENCES: **Journey to Ixtlan - Page [256-268]** (Don Genaro returned around noon and...it was not my time, yet.)

JOURNEY-IXTLAN-[JOURNEY TO IXTLAN]: (TOP)
SELECTED REFERENCES: **Journey to Ixtlan - Page [264.3-267.9]** ("What was the final outcome of...I felt euphoric. I embraced them.)

JUAN-CARLOS-MEET-[HOW CARLOS MET DON JUAN]: (TOP)
SELECTED REFERENCES: **Journey to Ixtlan - Page [1.3-9.4]** ("I understand you know a great...he said softly and waved good-bye.)

JUAN-DEATH-[THE STORY OF DON JUAN'S DEATH]: (TOP)
SELECTED REFERENCES: **The Power of Silence - Page [171.5-191.6]** (He stopped talking and seemed lost...was finally dead! I was final free!")

JUAN-DESTINY-[DON JUAN'S DESTINY]: (TOP)
SELECTED REFERENCES: **The Power of Silence - Page [185.4-185.9]** ("My benefactor knew what direction my life...worked for me, at the end.)

JUAN-DOUBLE-BEING-[DON JUAN EXPERIENCES BEING DOUBLE]: (TOP)
SELECTED REFERENCES: **The Power of Silence - Page [233.7-236.2]** (Don Juan contended that that simple...river, and started to walk home.")

JUAN-GENARO-STALKING-TEAM-[THE STALKING TEAM OF DON JUAN AND DON GENARO]: (TOP)
SELECTED REFERENCES: **The Fire From Within - Page [209.8-209.9]** (It was then that I saw...always let Genaro be the heavy.) **The Fire From Within - Page [213.9-214.3]** ("There's one thing you haven't understood...of them broke into roaring laughter.")

JUAN-HUSBAND-FATHER-[DON JUAN AS HUSBAND AND FATHER]: (TOP)
SELECTED REFERENCES: **The Power of Silence - Page [186.7-194.8]** (His superior strengths and a new...and that sorcerers never approach anyone.)

JUAN-INTUITION-[DON JUAN'S INTUITION]: (TOP)
SELECTED REFERENCES: **The Power of Silence - Page [186.4-186.6]** (Don Juan said that when he...job so he could travel north.)

JUAN-JULIAN-FINDING-[HOW THE NAGUAL JULIAN FOUND DON JUAN]: (TOP)
SELECTED REFERENCES: **The Eagle's Gift - Page [172.2-172.6]** (Don Juan said that when the rule...to the Nagual and his role.) **The Fire From Within - Page [188.8-198.5]** (Then don Juan started his story...so great that I passed out.)

JUAN-JULIAN-HOUSE-[DON JUAN'S STAY AT THE NAGUAL JULIAN'S HOUSE]: (TOP)
SELECTED REFERENCES: **The Power of Silence - Page [171.7-195.1]** (He began to recount what had happened...as if he had not left at all.) **The Power of Silence - Page [229.2-232.4]** (With no preliminaries, and without stopping...skits to the delight of all.)

JUAN-JULIAN-PARTY-MEET-[HOW DON JUAN MET THE NAGUAL JULIAN'S PARTY]: (TOP)
SELECTED REFERENCES: **The Eagle's Gift - Page [181.8-186.8]** (The instance in which that difference...also forced a shattering self-examination.)

JUAN-LEGS-LOSE-[IF DON JUAN LOST HIS LEGS]: (TOP)
SELECTED REFERENCES: **A Separate Reality - Page [181.8-181.9]** (I posed an alternative to don...hand to point all around him.)

JUAN-PARALYSIS-[DON JUAN'S PARALYSIS]: (TOP)
SELECTED REFERENCES: **The Power of Silence - Page [187.7-188.8]** (But the most draining pain was...He could hardly make ends meet.)

JUAN-PARENTS-[DON JUAN'S PARENTS]: (TOP)
SELECTED REFERENCES: **The Fire From Within - Page [200.8-201.4]** (Don Juan said that under his benefactor's...or for being alive in particular.")

JUAN-PARENTS-DEATH-[THE DEATH OF DON JUAN'S PARENTS]: *(TOP)*
> SELECTED REFERENCES: A Separate Reality - Page [136.4-137.4] ("I was a skinny child," he...child it is sometimes horror itself.") A Separate Reality - Page [143.5-143.8] ("I also made a vow once...they were, before anything else, men.")

JUAN-PIRATE-DISGUISE-[DON JUAN'S PIRATE DISGUISE]: SEE: *SHADOWS-CIRCLE-[A CIRCLE OF SHADOWS]-TOP*

JUAN-RAGE-[DON JUAN'S RAGE]: (TOP)
> SELECTED REFERENCES: The Power of Silence - Page [189.6-190.4] (One day, however, don Juan thought...until all his anger was spent.)

JUAN-RECAPITULATION-[DON JUAN'S RECAPITULATION]: (TOP)
> SELECTED REFERENCES: The Power of Silence - Page [188.8-189.3] (Another year passed. He did not...lives while they waited for death.) The Power of Silence - Page [192.4-192.6] ("I died in that field," he said...me to go back and try again.) The Power of Silence - Page [193.9-194.1] ("I did that with my feelings for...could decide the outcome of that affection.")

JUAN-RIVER-BOUT-[DON JUAN'S BOUT WITH THE RAGING RIVER]: *(TOP)*
> SELECTED REFERENCES: The Power of Silence - Page [230.7-241.3] (The rationale given for the trips...silently offer it to the abstract.)

JUAN-RUTHLESSNESS-MASK-[DON JUAN'S MASK OF *RUTHLESSNESS]: (TOP)*
> SELECTED REFERENCES: The Power of Silence - Page [163.7-164.4] (In this regard, he said, although...reach the place of no pity.")

JUAN-STROKE-GUAYMAS-[DON JUAN'S STROKE IN GUAYMAS]: *(TOP)*
> SELECTED REFERENCES: The Power of Silence - Page [134.9-144.5] (We were in the outskirts of Guaymas...as much as I have surprised you.") The Power of Silence - Page [151.8-154.4] (He then took my experience of...its customary place of self-reflection.) The Power of Silence - Page [163.7-164.4] (In this regard, he said, although...reach the place of no pity.") The Power of Silence - Page [166.6-167.2] ("The nagual's ruthlessness has many aspects...age in appearance, behavior and feeling.)

JUAN-TRANSFORMATION-[DON JUAN'S TRANSFORMATION]: (TOP)
> SELECTED REFERENCES: The Power of Silence - Page [144.1-144.5] ("Today you did just that...as much as I have surprised you.") The Power of Silence - Page [154.3-154.4] (He said that from the moment...its customary place of self-reflection.) The Power of Silence - Page - [167.6-167.8] (He refused to add anything and...best to explain away his transformation.) The Power of Silence - Page [168.2-170.6] (He remarked that that day in...began to laugh at my dismay.)
> *GUAYMAS-TOP*

JUAN-WOMAN-DISGUISE-[DON JUAN'S WOMAN DISGUISE]: (TOP)
> SELECTED REFERENCES: The Power of Silence - Page [63.1-68.9] (The next step of the plan...what being a woman is like.")

JULIAN-NAGUAL-[THE NAGUAL JULIAN]: (TOP)
> SELECTED REFERENCES: The Fire From Within - Page [183-202] (There was a strange excitement in...and such words lose their meaning.")

JULIAN-NAGUAL-AGE-[THE ABILITY OF THE NAGUAL JULIAN TO *APPEAR YOUNG OR OLD AT WILL]: (TOP)*
> SELECTED REFERENCES: The Fire From Within - Page [253.5-253.7] ("Did anybody ever get hurt in the...to look young or old at will.")

JULIAN-NAGUAL-IMPECCABILITY-[THE IMPECCABILITY OF THE NAGUAL JULIAN]: (TOP)
SELECTED REFERENCES: The Fire From Within - Page [200.5-200.8] (The nagual Julian's power was so...that he could not even walk.") The Fire From Within - Page [212.8-213.1] ("The nagual Julian did the same thing to...open the only door there is.")

JULIAN-NAGUAL-INTENT-WAKES-UP-[THE NAGUAL JULIAN WAKES UP INTENT]: (TOP)
SELECTED REFERENCES: The Power of Silence - Page [237.8-238.4] (First, the nagual Elias explained to...what he really had in mind.)

JULIAN-NAGUAL-JOKES-[THE JOKES OF THE NAGUAL JULIAN]: (TOP)
SELECTED REFERENCES: The Power of Silence - Page [55.8-56.2] (Don Juan said that he knew...when I first began my apprenticeship.") The Power of Silence - Page [181.5-181.7] (Don Juan laughed and told me...that house knew or practiced sorcery.)

JULIAN-NAGUAL-JOY-[THE JOY OF THE NAGUAL JULIAN]: (TOP)
SELECTED REFERENCES: The Fire From Within - Page [201.4-201.8] (Don Juan said that not only...of those dramas backfired on him.")

JULIAN-NAGUAL-LAST-SEDUCTION-[THE LAST SEDUCTION OF THE NAGUAL JULIAN]: (TOP)
SELECTED REFERENCES: The Power of Silence - Page [39-51] (It was as cool and quiet...simplicity, that is determining our fate.")

JULIAN-NAGUAL-MAGIC-[THE MAGIC OF THE NAGUAL JULIAN]: (TOP)
SELECTED REFERENCES: The Fire From Within - Page [200.4-200.8] (Don Juan said that the nagual Julian...that he could not even walk.") The Fire From Within - Page [201.4-201.8] (Don Juan said that not only...some of those dramas backfired on him.")

JULIAN-NAGUAL-SEX-CHANGE-[THE NAGUAL JULIAN'S SEX CHANGE]: (TOP)
SELECTED REFERENCES: The Art of Dreaming - Page [215.1-215.2] ("I mean the negative results of...like giving booze to a drunkard.")

JULIAN-NAGUAL-SPIRIT-DESCENT-[THE DESCENT OF THE SPIRIT ON THE NAGUAL JULIAN]: (TOP)
SELECTED REFERENCES: The Power of Silence - Page [91.5-96.9] (Don Juan proceeded with his story...have ever met," don Juan added.)

JULIAN-NAGUAL-STALKING-[THE STALKING OF THE NAGUAL JULIAN]: (TOP)
SELECTED REFERENCES: SELECTED REFERENCES: The Fire From Within - Page [186.1-187.3] ("I am not exaggerating when I tell...plugged nickel for any of them.") The Fire From Within - Page [193.1-201.8] ("The point is very simple," he said...some of those dramas backfired on him.")

JULIAN-NAGUAL-TALES-[TALES OF THE NAGUAL JULIAN]: (TOP)
SELECTED REFERENCES: The Fire From Within - Page [104.2-104.4] ("As you know, I have my...even take a grotesque human form.") The Fire From Within - Page [145.5-147.9 (Genaro turned to me and assured me...waylaid, and so was la Catalina.") The Power of Silence - Page [8.3-10.5] ("I had the incredible good luck...them you don't become morbidly obsessed.") The Power of Silence - Page [15.1-24.4] (Don Juan began his story...he said. "Her name was Talia.") The Power of Silence - Page [43.8-46.9] ("Everything connected with my benefactor was...he laughed until he was dead.) The Power of Silence - Page [56.6-57.4] (Soon after his first jolt, his...the keenest knowledge of human nature.") The Power of Silence - Page [58.8-68.9] (Continuing his story, don Juan said...what being a woman was like.") The Power of Silence - Page [236.3-237.5] (He paused then asked me what...seemed to be at his command.)

JULIAN-NAGUAL-TEARS-[THE TEARS OF THE NAGUAL JULIAN]: (TOP)

SELECTED REFERENCES: The Power of Silence - Page [56.1-56.2] ("If you think I laugh at you...when I first began my apprenticeship.") The Power of Silence - Page [59.8-59.9] (Belisario, aware of don Juan's fright...chores the monster wanted done daily.) The Power of Silence - Page [60.7-60.8] (Belisario exchanged looks with his wife...up until he regained his composure.) The Power of Silence - Page [61.4-61.7] (Belisario began to weep loudly and...Then he wept even more.) The Power of Silence - Page [182.7-183.6] (Filled with a strange vigor, Don Juan...filled with tears, admitted his guilt.)

JULIAN-NAGUAL-TRANSFORMATION-[THE TRANSFORMATION OF THE NAGUAL JULIAN]: (TOP)

SELECTED REFERENCES: The Power of Silence - Page [56.6-57.4] (Soon after his first jolt, his...the keenest knowledge of human nature.") The Power of Silence - Page [174.4-175.3] (After a few weeks with no change...as he felt obliged to do.)

JUMP-RAVINE-CARLOS-IN-OUT-[CARLOS JUMPS IN AND OUT OF THE RAVINE: (TOP)

SELECTED REFERENCES: Tales of Power - Page [257.8-260.9] (After I had taken my clothes...comments about having saved my pants.)

K

KING-PRONUNCIATION-[THE KING OF PRONUNCIATION]: (TOP)
SELECTED REFERENCES: Journey to Ixtlan - Page [3.6-4.9] (I wondered if it would have...artistic manner. I laughed with him.)

KNOWLEDGE-APPOINTMENT-[AN APPOINTMENT WITH KNOWLEDGE]: (TOP)
SELECTED REFERENCES: Tales of Power - Page [2-50] (I had not seen don Juan...me any time!" don Genaro shouted.)

KNOWLEDGE-SILENT-[SILENT KNOWLEDGE]: (TOP)
SELECTED REFERENCES: The Second Ring of Power - Page [89.4-89.6] (A vision of a particular ravine...need for them to stay there.) The Eagle's Gift - Page [147.5-147.6] (The thought occurred to me then...had been in charge of me.)

L

LA-CATALINA-[LA CATALINA]-(TOP): SEE: CATALINA-[LA CATALINA]-(TOP)

LA-GORDA-[LA GORDA]-(TOP): SEE: GORDA-[LA GORDA]-(TOP)

LAST-BATTLE-EARTH-WARRIOR-[THE WARRIORS' LAST BATTLE ON EARTH]-(TOP): SEE: WARRIOR-LAST-BATTLE-[THE WARRIORS' LAST BATTLE ON EARTH]-(TOP)

LAST-SEDUCTION-NAGUAL-JULIAN-[THE LAST SEDUCTION OF THE NAGUAL JULIAN]-(TOP): SEE: JULIAN-NAGUAL-LAST-SEDUCTION-[THE LAST SEDUCTION OF THE NAGUAL JULIAN]-(TOP)

LAWYER-BITTER-[A BITTER LAWYER]: (TOP)
SELECTED REFERENCES: **A Separate Reality - Page [87.4-88.1]** (To illustrate my point I told...retrieve the forty years I've lost.")

LEAF-FELL-THREE-TIMES-[THE LEAF THAT FELL THREE TIMES FROM THE SAME TREE]: (TOP)
SELECTED REFERENCES: **A Separate Reality - Page [259.3-260.7]** ("You mentioned once," don Juan began...mania always blinded me at the end.) **Tales of Power - Page [95.3-95.4]** (He had drawn a similar one years...four times from the same tree.)

LEAF-RAZOR-[THE LEAF THAT CUT LIKE A RAZOR]: (TOP)
SELECTED REFERENCES: **The Second Ring of Power - Page [50.5-51.2]** ("Josephina went off next. She was...us wages against our old selves.)

LEFT-SIDE-REMEMBERING-[REMEMBERING THE LEFT SIDE]-(TOP): SEE: REMEMBERING-LEFT-SIDE [REMEMBERING THE LEFT SIDE]-(TOP)

LIDIA-EYES-CURE-[CURING LIDIA'S EYES]: (TOP)
SELECTED REFERENCES: **The Eagle's Gift - Page [64.9-65.5]** ("Lydia also remembers something," Nestor went...as another part of me shook.)

LIDIA-RAPE-[THE ATTEMPTED RAPE OF LIDIA]: (TOP)
SELECTED REFERENCES: **The Second Ring of Power - Page [173.7-174.4]** ("How did he fail...tend to Pablito's wound for months.") **The Second Ring of Power - Page [201.8-202.6]** (In a most dramatic tone Pablito...was a bump on the head!")

LINE-MAKING-[MAKING A LINE]: (TOP)
SELECTED REFERENCES: **The Eagle's Gift - Page [37.8-38.1]** ("In our *dreaming*, the little sisters...for you to rally your knowledge.")

LINES-WORLD-[THE LINES OF THE WORLD]: (TOP)
SELECTED REFERENCES: **The Second Ring of Power - Page [272.5-273.2]** (I remembered Lidia pulling herself from...recollection to the other in my mind.) **The Fire From Within - Page [291.4-291.7]** (Don Juan was working his glow...me before the lines faded away.) **The Power of Silence - Page [97.5-98.9]** (By the time it became completely dark...vision and plunged me into darkness.)

LINES-WORLD-FEELING-[FEELING THE LINES OF THE WORLD]-(TOP): SEE: NOT-DOING-EXERCISE-[THE EXERCISE OF NOT-DOING]-(TOP)

LION-HUNTING-[HUNTING LIONS]: (TOP)
SELECTED REFERENCES: **Journey to Ixtlan - Page [114.7-121.3]** ("The only thing one can do...It takes power to do that.")

LITTLE-SISTERS-[THE LITTLE SISTERS]: (TOP)
SELECTED REFERENCES: The Second Ring of Power - Page [69-111] (Dona Soledad seemed to be explaining...But somehow I was myself again.)

LITTLE-SMOKE-TALES-[TALES OF THE LITTLE SMOKE]: (TOP)
SELECTED REFERENCES: The Teachings of Don Juan - Page [132.9-138.8] (On Thursday, December 26, I had...forth, down and down, and down.) The Teachings of Don Juan - Page [161.6-176.3] (In the month of December, 1964...fear to understand what I mean.")

LIZARD-SORCERY-[THE SORCERY OF THE LIZARDS]: (TOP)
SELECTED REFERENCES: The Teachings of Don Juan - Page [109.7-121.3] (We returned to his room where...on, then you must simply stop.") The Teachings of Don Juan - Page [153.5-159.7] (Don Juan seemed to want me...could I have seen without direction?")

LOSING-HUMAN-FORM-[LOSING THE HUMAN FORM]-(TOP): SEE: HUMAN-FORM-LOSING-[LOSING THE HUMAN FORM]-(TOP)

LOVE-LOOKING-FOR-[LOOKING FOR LOVE]: (TOP)
SELECTED REFERENCES: The Power of Silence - Page [130.4-131.2] (Don Juan began to explain what...no longer interested in mesmerizing anyone.)

LUCK-BAD-[BAD LUCK]: (TOP)
SELECTED REFERENCES: The Eagle's Gift - Page [19.3-19.9] ("What exactly did he say would...heard what we wanted to hear.)

LUMINOUS-BEINGS-SECRET-[THE SECRET OF THE LUMINOUS BEINGS]: (TOP)
SELECTED REFERENCES: Tales of Power - Page [78-100] (Don Genaro delighted me for hours...Genaro was hiding under my hat.")

LUMINOUS-BEINGS-SEEING-[SEEING THE LUMINOUS BEINGS]: (TOP)
SELECTED REFERENCES: Tales of Power - Page [31.6-36.7] (I then heard the mysterious sound...greet don Genaro?" don Juan asked.) The Eagle's Gift - Page [40.9-41.5] (My body shook with laughter and...four feet wide or even larger.) The Eagle's Gift - Page [44.3-46.1] (I began by describing to la...the luminous mass of their bodies.) The Fire From Within - Page [219.9-221.1] (I did that three times and...the thickness of the total cocoon.) The Fire From Within - Page [220.6-221.2] (That afternoon I saw ten luminous...the thickness of the total cocoon.) The Power of Silence - Page [71.9-72.3] ("What do you *see*?" I heard...about wings on a luminous cocoon?")

LUMINOUS-DENT-[THE LUMINOUS DENT]: (TOP)
SELECTED REFERENCES: The Eagle's Gift - Page [31.9-33.1] (The three little sisters gathered around...would be in need of help.) The Eagle's Gift - Page [36.4-38.1] (La Gorda said that what had happened...for you to rally your knowledge.") The Eagle's Gift - Page [253.3-254.9] (Zuleica warned me that if I...that I had nearly killed them.) The Eagle's Gift - Page [257.4-259.9] (Zuleica started then on another facet...I had other things to do.)

LUMINOUS-DENT-FEELING-[FEELING THE LUMINOUS DENT]-(TOP): SEE: ATTENTION-SECOND-CONTROLS [EXPERIENCING THE SECOND ATTENTION TAKING OVER THE CONTROLS]-(TOP)

M

MAGICAL-BEINGS-[MAGICAL BEINGS]: (TOP)

SELECTED REFERENCES: **Journey to Ixtlan - Page [76.6-78.5]** ("You like hunting; perhaps someday, in..."It's one of the darndest things.") **Journey to Ixtlan - Page [250.6-253.9]** (I moved my eyes away and...*see* the lines of the world.) **Tales of Power - Page [22.4-23.4]** ("The same thing happened with the coyote...I made the description reflect itself.) **The Second Ring of Power - Page [212.9-213.2]** (Porfirio took me to see the mold...said that he was gone forever.)

MAGICAL-COYOTE-[THE MAGICAL COYOTE]: (TOP)

SELECTED REFERENCES: **Journey to Ixtlan - Page [250.1-255.2]** (I wiped my eyes and as I...of things from his coyote brothers.") **Tales of Power - Page [5.4-5.6]** (What was most pressing on my...speech was a matter of course.) **Tales of Power - Page [22.1-22.5]** ("How was I operating my knowledge...really took place at those times.") **Tales of Power - Page [23.3-23.5]** (Our conversation engendered a most interesting...I made the description reflect itself.) **Tales of Power - Page [24.2]** ("Of course there is!" he exclaimed...that you talked with a coyote.") **The Eagle's Gift - Page [237.4]** (His contention was that a magical...second attention without having any intellect.)

MAGICAL-DEER-[THE MAGICAL DEER]: (TOP)

SELECTED REFERENCES: **Journey to Ixtlan - Page [45.5-46.1]** (Don Juan made a majestic gesture...been filled with power beyond belief.) **Journey to Ixtlan - Page [76.1-78.5]** ("There are certain animals, however, that...It's one of the darndest things.") **Tales of Power - Page [22.5-22.8]** ("When the sorcerers' explanation became clear...forced to understand it as talking.") **The Second Ring of Power - Page [145.4-145.5]** (He said that once he himself stumbled...the strain of such an encounter.) **The Eagle's Gift - Page [237.4]** (His contention was that a magical...second attention without having any intellect.)

MAGICAL-FOREST-TRAIL-[THE TRAIL IN THE MAGICAL FOREST]: (TOP)

SELECTED REFERENCES: **Journey to Ixtlan - Page [128.3-128.8]** (Don Juan whispered that the fog and...disoriented by the blackness around me.) **Journey to Ixtlan - Page [133.6-133.9]** ("And what is real?" don Juan...wind that was seeking you out.) **Journey to Ixtlan - Page [135.2-135.5]** ("What happened to you last night...have enough power of one's own.")

MAIZ-PINTO-[MAIZ PINTO]-(TOP): SEE: CORN-SORCERY-[CORN SORCERY]-(TOP)

MAN-ACTION-[THE MAN OF ACTION]: (TOP)

SELECTED REFERENCES: **The Eagle's Gift - Page [205.1-207.4]** (My last introductory encounter with don...had to lean against a wall.)

MAN-BEHIND-SCENES-[THE MAN BEHIND THE SCENES]: (TOP)

SELECTED REFERENCES: **The Eagle's Gift - Page [196.7-205.1]** (At the same time, I was...the silent force behind don Juan.)

MAN-PLANTS-CORN-[THE MAN WHO PLANTS CORN]-(TOP): SEE: CORN-MAN-PLANTS-[THE MAN WHO PLANTS CORN]-(TOP)

MANIFESTATIONS-SPIRIT-[THE MANIFESTATIONS OF THE SPIRIT]-(TOP): SEE: SPIRIT-MANIFESTATIONS [THE MANIFESTATIONS OF THE SPIRIT]-(TOP)

MAX-CAT-[MAX THE CAT]-(TOP): SEE: CATS-STORY-[THE STORY OF THE TWO CATS]-(TOP)

MERCHANTS-THREE-ASPIRING-[THE THREE ASPIRING MERCHANTS]: (TOP)

SELECTED REFERENCES: **Tales of Power - Page [137.5- 138.6]** ("Look who's coming now," he said...personally was moved by those three.)

MERGING-LUMINOSITY-[MERGING LUMINOSITY]: (TOP)

SELECTED REFERENCES: **The Eagle's Gift - Page [37.6-37.7]** (After I had kicked the two blobs...caressing the backs of my hands.)

MESCALITO-[MESCALITO]: (TOP)

SELECTED REFERENCES: **The Teachings of Don Juan - Page [36.7-50.8]** (Don Juan whispered that we were...will come to you of itself.") **The Teachings of Don Juan - [100.3-101.5]** (After a while I regained a...again and again and was gone.) **The Teachings of Don Juan - Page [143.7-153.3]** (My last encounter with Mescalito was..."I believe that was the lesson.") **A Separate Reality - Page [49.5-57.6]** (We arrived in northeastern Mexico June...on my part than being around.)

MESCALITO-ELIGIO -[ELIGIO MEETS MESCALITO]: (TOP)

SELECTED REFERENCES: **A Separate Reality - Page [72.5-77.1]** (It was nine o'clock Saturday night...I wish it had been Lucio.")

MESCALITO-ENCOUNTER-FIRST-[THE FIRST ENCOUNTER WITH MESCALITO]: (TOP)

SELECTED REFERENCES: **The Teachings of Don Juan - Page [36.7-37.3]** (Don Juan whispered that we were...one can do," don Juan said.) **The Teachings of Don Juan - Page [41.3-50.8]** (I saw the juncture of the...will come to you of itself.")

MESCALITO-ENCOUNTER-SECOND-[THE SECOND ENCOUNTER WITH MESCALITO]: (TOP)

SELECTED REFERENCES: **The Teachings of Don Juan - Page [144.2-149.5]** (During the first night of the...and then rolled away out of sight.) **The Teachings of Don Juan - Page [149.9-153.3]** (To tell don Juan about an..."I believe that was the lesson.")

MESCALITO-LIGHT-[MESCALITO'S LIGHT]: (TOP)

SELECTED REFERENCES: **A Separate Reality - Page [56.9-57.7]** (I related to don Juan the...on my part than being around.)

MESSAGE-DREAMER-ALLIES-[THE DREAMER'S MESSAGE FOR THE ALLIES]-(TOP): SEE: ALLIES-MESSAGE-DREAMER-[THE DREAMER'S MESSAGE FOR THE ALLIES]-(TOP)

MIRROR-STREAM-[THE MIRROR AND THE STREAM]: (TOP)

SELECTED REFERENCES: **The Fire From Within - Page [84.7-96.8]** (I asked him if he could...it up edgewise without any difficulty.)

MOLD-ANIMALS-[THE MOLD OF THE ANIMALS]: (TOP)

SELECTED REFERENCES: **The Second Ring of Power - Page [212.9-213.2]** (Porfirio took me this time to see...said that he was gone forever.)

MOLD-MAN-[THE MOLD OF MAN]: (TOP)

SELECTED REFERENCES: **The Fire From Within - Page [256-270]** (Right after lunch, don Juan and...me that my promise was worthless.)

MOLD-MAN-SEEING-[SEEING THE MOLD OF MAN]: (TOP)

SELECTED REFERENCES: **The Second Ring of Power - Page [155.6-156.8]** (I told her that he had sketched...scared me out of my wits.") **The Fire From Within - Page [263.8-265.6]** (What he had said put me...and I lost sight of God.) **The Fire From Within - Page [267.5-267.6]** (I remembered then that I had...of a male God became untenable.) **The Fire From Within - Page [268.2-269.3]** (Don Juan stood up then and...walked me back to the house.)

MOLD-PLANTS-[THE MOLD OF PLANTS]: (TOP)

SELECTED REFERENCES: **The Second Ring of Power - Page [212.5-212.8]** (I came back to life and I...I became a million pieces.)

MONSTROUS-MAN-[THE MONSTROUS MAN]-(TOP): SEE: FISH-FACED-MAN-[THE FISH FACED MAN]-(TOP)

MOTH-[THE MOTH]: (TOP)
SELECTED REFERENCES: Tales of Power - Page [92.9-93.6] (It started the last time you were...such a great emphasis on you.)

MOTH-CALL-[THE MOTH'S CALL]-(TOP): SEE: MOTH-SONG-[THE SONG OF THE MOTH]-(TOP)

MOTH-NIGHT-[THE NIGHT OF THE MOTH]-(TOP): SEE: KNOWLEDGE-APPOINTMENT-[AN APPOINTMENT WITH KNOWLEDGE]-(TOP)

MOTH-SONG-[THE SONG OF THE MOTH]: (TOP)
SELECTED REFERENCES: Tales of Power - Page [18.8-19.1] (Then a sudden noise interrupted his...fulfilled your appointment yet." he added) Tales of Power - Page [27.4-28.3] (I heard a strange sound at...the staccato sound of a machine gun.) Tales of Power - Page [29.2-32.2] (He said that the call of...wanted to know what had happened.) Tales of Power - Page [39.1-39.4] (At that instant I again heard...body as I had done earlier.) Tales of Power - Page [214.3-214.5] (He whispered that it was very...moving on top of the boulders.) Tales of Power - Page [220.7-221.1] (I was in the middle of a...sounds which were being produced then.)

MOTH-STEP-CARLOS-NECK-[THE MOTH STEPS ON CARLOS' NECK]: (TOP)
SELECTED REFERENCES: A Separate Reality - Page [244.2-245.2] (The muscles of my stomach were...keep from going stark, raving mad.) Tales of Power - Page [39.5-39.6] (There was a loud cracking noise...learned to perceive as an entity.) Tales of Power - Page [84.8-85.5] (Some years ago you and I...ally is a personal matter," he said.)

MOTH-TALES-[TALES OF THE MOTH]: (TOP)
SELECTED REFERENCES: Tales of Power - Page [14.4-17.7] (Don Juan asked me to sit...you still owe me six days.") Tales of Power - Page [18.8-30.1] (Then a sudden noise interrupted his...gave me the rest to drink.) The Fire From Within - Page [71.2-71.5] (It was twilight by then...every speck of dust on its wings.)

MOVING-DREAMING-[MOVING IN DREAMING]-(TOP): SEE: WILL-MOVING -[MOVING BY THE WILL]-(TOP)

MOVING-WILL-[MOVING BY THE WILL]-(TOP): SEE: WILL-MOVING-[MOVING BY THE WILL]-(TOP)

MUNI-CALIXTO-[CALIXTO MUNI]-(TOP): SEE: CALIXTO-MUNI-[CALIXTO MUNI]-(TOP)

MUSCULAR-DREAMING-[BECOMING MORE MUSCULAR THROUGH DREAMING]-(TOP): SEE: DREAMING-MUSCULAR-[BECOMING MORE MUSCULAR THROUGH DREAMING]-(TOP)

MUSEUM-OBJECTS-GAZING-[GAZING AT OBJECTS IN THE MUSEUM OF ANTHROPOLOGY AND HISTORY]: (TOP)
SELECTED REFERENCES: The Art of Dreaming - Page [143.9-145.8] (I had been normally and even excessively...the position of the assemblage point.)

N

NAGUAL-APPRENTICE-COMPLIANCE-[THE COMPLIANCE OF THE APPRENTICE NAGUAL]: (TOP)
SELECTED REFERENCES: The Power of Silence - Page [56.2-56.5] (Continuing with his story, don Juan...of labor to convince his disciple.)

NAGUAL-BLOW-[THE NAGUAL'S BLOW]: (TOP)
SELECTED REFERENCES: The Eagle's Gift - Page [218.1-218.5] (Don Juan had his wounds bandaged...There was no doubt, no hesitation.) The Eagle's Gift - Page [223.3-223.7] (That first visit to his house...would reveal the rule to me.) The Eagle's Gift - Page [227.2-228.7] (The old man helped her up and...like Silvio Manuel, she never returned.)

NAGUAL-CREATIVITY-[THE NAGUAL AND A DEMONSTRATION OF CREATIVITY] (TOP)
SELECTED REFERENCES: Tales of Power - Page [141.2-141.8] ("Creativity is this," he said and...did not remember having stood up.)

NAGUAL-ELIAS-[THE NAGUAL ELIAS[-(TOP): SEE: ELIAS-NAGUAL-[THE NAGUAL ELIAS]-(TOP)

NAGUAL-ENERGY-LOAN-[THE NAGUAL LOANS HIS ENERGY]: (TOP)
SELECTED REFERENCES: The Power of Silence - Page [72.7-72.8] ("Your assemblage point moved to heightened...are in mine. I drink water.")

NAGUAL-EYES-[THE NAGUAL'S EYES]: (TOP)
SELECTED REFERENCES: The Fire From Within - Page [210.6-210.9] (His eyes glared for an instant...the nagual's eyes again," Genaro whispered.)

NAGUAL-FACING-[FACING THE NAGUAL]: (TOP)
SELECTED REFERENCES: Tales of Power - Page [188.9-190.2] (During a short pause in our talk...and stood up and went inside.) Tales of Power - Page [199.4-200.6] (I asked Pablito about his meetings...within the sorcerers' frame of reference.)

NAGUAL-HEALING-[THE HEALING POWER OF THE NAGUAL]: (TOP)
SELECTED REFERENCES: The Second Ring of Power - Page [83.8-87.2] (Rosa walked into the room then...made me jog on the spot.)

NAGUAL-JULIAN-[THE NAGUAL JULIAN]-(TOP): SEE: JULIAN-NAGUAL-[THE NAGUAL JULIAN]-(TOP)

NAGUAL-PARTY-WARRIORS-[THE NAGUAL'S PARTY OF WARRIORS]: (TOP)
SELECTED REFERENCES: The Eagle's Gift - Page [188-211] (When don Juan judged that the...the finality of the Eagle's dictums.) The Fire From Within - Page [142.3-143.5] (Don Juan said again that la...unknown to the quest for freedom.")

NAGUAL-ROSENDO-[THE NAGUAL ROSENDO]-(TOP): SEE: ROSENDO-NAGUAL-[THE NAGUAL ROSENDO]-(TOP)

NAGUAL-RULE-[THE RULE OF THE NAGUAL]-(TOP): SEE: RULE-NAGUAL [THE RULE OF THE NAGUAL]-(TOP)

NAGUAL-RUMBLE-[THE RUMBLE OF THE NAGUAL]: (TOP)
SELECTED REFERENCES: The Fire From Within - Page [211.4-211.5] (I felt, rather than heard, a...insignificant microbe being twisted and turned.)

NAGUAL-THREE-PRONGED-[THE THREE-PRONGED NAGUAL]: (TOP)
SELECTED REFERENCES: The Eagle's Gift - Page [230.4-299.5] (Don Juan and his warriors sat...although only in a partial form.)

NAGUAL-TIME-[IN NAGUAL'S TIME]: (TOP)

SELECTED REFERENCES: **Tales of Power - Page [162-180]** (I ran up a slope in...will keep everything suspended," he said.)

NAGUAL-TONNAGE-[THE NAGUAL TONNAGE]: (TOP)

SELECTED REFERENCES: **The Power of Silence - Page [31.4-31.7]** ("What was the nagual Elias like...to call him the nagual Tonnage.)

NAGUAL-WHISPERING-[THE WHISPERING OF THE NAGUAL]: (TOP)

SELECTED REFERENCES: **Tales of Power - Page [180-196]** (As we approached the eucalyptuses I...are no survivors on this earth!")

NAGUAL-WITNESSES-FOUR-[THE FOUR WITNESSES TO THE NAGUAL]: (TOP)

SELECTED REFERENCES: **Tales of Power - Page [188.5-188.7]** (He reminded me that once, years...were the only greenhorn among them.")

NAGUAL-WITNESSES-THREE-[THREE WITNESSES TO THE NAGUAL]: (TOP)

SELECTED REFERENCES: **Tales of Power - Page [212-228]** (Upon returning home I was faced...can afford to wish him well.")

NAGUAL-WOMAN-[THE NAGUAL WOMAN]: (TOP)

SELECTED REFERENCES: **The Eagle's Gift - Page [212-229]** (Don Juan said that when he...the members of don Juan's own party.)

NAGUAL-WOMAN-[THE NAGUAL WOMAN]: (TOP)

SELECTED REFERENCES: **The Eagle's Gift - Page [71.4-71.9]** ("Of course it was him," Rosa...since I seemed to have recovered.) **The Eagle's Gift - Page [114.3-116.8]** (She wanted to know why I thought...see a white Volkswagen driving away.) **The Eagle's Gift - Page [117.2-124.9]** (La Gorda and I went through a...We must snap out of it.") **The Eagle's Gift - Page [234.6-234.8]** (Silvio Manuel was awed by the...could withstand the Nagual woman's contact.) **The Fire From Within - Page [43.9-44.2]** (Don Juan was sitting where he...from the works of Spanish-speaking poets.) **The Fire From Within - Page [277.9-281.1]** (I instantly felt the heaviness of being...had done terrible things to me.) **The Fire From Within - Page [286.4-286.5]** ("You still don't remember her...Her time here is short.")

NAGUAL-WOMAN-FINDING-[FINDING CAROL THE NAGUAL WOMAN AND OLINDA THE NAGUAL WOMAN]-(TOP): SEE: FINDING-NAGUAL-WOMAN-[HOW POWER FOUND CAROL THE NAGUAL WOMAN AND OLINDA THE NAGUAL WOMAN]-(TOP)

NAGUAL-WOMAN-LEAVING-[LEAVING THE NAGUAL WOMAN]: (TOP)

SELECTED REFERENCES: **The Eagle's Gift - Page [310.9-312.6]** (The Nagual woman came to me...not soothe me when I remembered.)

NAGUAL-WOMAN-REMEMBERING-[REMEMBERING THE NAGUAL WOMAN]: (TOP)

SELECTED REFERENCES: **The Fire From Within - Page [284.6-284.9]** ("For instance, if you would shift...How could I have forgotten her?) **The Fire From Within - Page [286.4-286.6]** ("You still don't remember her...Her time here is short.")

NAGUALS-TWO-[THE TWO NAGUALS]: (TOP)

SELECTED REFERENCES: **The Power of Silence - Page [8.3-8.8]** ("I had the incredible good luck to be...to my benefactor, the nagual Julian.") **The Power of Silence - Page [43.6-43.8]** (Don Juan explained that one of...difficult knock on his benefactor's door.)

NELIDA-[NELIDA]-(TOP): SEE: NORTH-[NORTHERLY WOMEN]-(TOP)

NESTOR-TEETH-[NESTOR'S TEETH]: (TOP)

SELECTED REFERENCES: **Tales of Power - Page [218.2-218.9]** (Nestor looked at me; he was...he said. "That's why he's younger.")

NINCOMPOOP-DIE-FRIGHT-[A NINCOMPOOP WHO COULD DIE OF FRIGHT]: (TOP)
> SELECTED REFERENCES: The Fire From Within - Page [69.9-71.2]] (Don Juan intervened and said that...had succeeded by making me rage.)

NORTH-[NORTHERLY WOMEN]: (TOP)
> SELECTED REFERENCES: The Eagle's Gift - Page [205.1-207.4] (My last introductory encounter with don...had to lean against a wall.) The Eagle's Gift - Page [208.2-208.4] (According to don Juan, his world...even had the same blood type.)

NOT-DOING-[NOT-DOING]: (TOP)
> SELECTED REFERENCES: Journey to Ixtlan - Page [181-200] (Upon returning to his house, don...the *not-doing* of the self.")

NOT-DOING-DEVICE-[THE NOT-DOING DEVICE]: (TOP)
> SELECTED REFERENCES: The Eagle's Gift - Page [137.5-137.9] (La Gorda said the don Juan told...distance, or any length of time.)

NOT-DOING-EXERCISE-[THE EXERCISE OF NOT-DOING]: (TOP)
> SELECTED REFERENCES: Journey to Ixtlan - Page [192.4-193.6] ("I was teasing you a little bit...real value in a practical situation.) The Second Ring of Power - Page [106.6-107.5] ("Sure. You can cure her and make...to attempt to move her arm.)

NOT-DOING-FEELING-[FEELING THE LINES OF THE WORLD]-(TOP): SEE: NOT-DOING-EXERCISE [THE EXERCISE OF NOT-DOING]-(TOP)

NOT-DOING-SILVIO-MANUEL-[THE NOT-DOINGS OF SILVIO MANUEL]: (TOP)
> SELECTED REFERENCES: The Eagle's Gift - Page [230-246] (Don Juan and his warriors sat...the other half with don Juan.)

NOT-DOING-SOAKING-BODY-[SOAKING THE BODY IN NOT-DOING]: (TOP)
> SELECTED REFERENCES: Journey to Ixtlan - Page [180.6-181.5] (I was shocked and began to...soaked for hours in "not-doing.")

NOT-DOING-WALKING-BACKWARD-[THE NOT-DOING OF WALKING BACKWARD]: (TOP): SEE: NOT-DOING-DEVICE-[THE NOT-DOING DEVICE]: (TOP)

NOTES-BUNDLES-WALKING-[BUNDLES OF WALKING NOTES]: (TOP)
> SELECTED REFERENCES: The Eagle's Gift - Page [22.3-22.6] (My benefactor told me that there...someone found your bundles walking around.")

NOTHING-EVERYTHING-EXPERIENCING-[EXPERIENCING NOTHING AND EVERYTHING]: (TOP)
> SELECTED REFERENCES: The Eagle's Gift - Page [242.7-243.7] (We crossed. Silvio Manuel and Eligio seemed...of awareness you ever had.)

O

OLINDA-[OLINDA]-(TOP): SEE NAGUAL-WOMAN-FINDING-[HOW
POWER FOUND CAROL THE NAGUAL WOMAN AND OLINDA THE
NAGUAL WOMAN]-(TOP)

OMEN-[OMENS]: (TOP)
    SELECTED REFERENCES: **A Separate Reality - Page [54.6-57.7]** (At a certain moment I heard...on my part than being around.) **The Second Ring of Power - Page [33.4-33.9]** ("One day the Nagual and Genaro...had pointed me out to him.") **The Second Ring of Power - Page [47.7-48.7]** ("Lidia was his first apprentice. He...go and went with him instead.") **The Second Ring of Power - Page [49.1-50.4]** ("For three years he had only...with her part of the way.") **The Second Ring of Power - Page [50.5-51.2]** ("Josephina went off next. She was...each of us wages against our old selves.") **The Second Ring of Power - Page [51.4-52.1]** ("A year later Elena came; she...she was too weak to walk.") **The Second Ring of Power - Page [299.5-300.4]** ("His first two apprentices, Benigno and Nestor...a week right in those mountains.) **The Power of Silence - Page [13.1-13.4]** (The indications the spirit gave the...less a nagual, should ever make.) **The Power of Silence - Page [14.8-16.8]** (All of a sudden he said...as if time had been suspended.)

OMEN-ACCEPTANCE-SECOND-[THE SECOND OMEN OF
ACCEPTANCE]: (TOP)-SEE: CARLOS-VISION-MOTHER [CARLOS'
VISION OF HIS MOTHER]-(TOP)

OMEN-APPRENTICE-NAGUAL-JUAN-{THE OMENS OF THE
APPRENTICE NAGUAL JUAN MATUS}: (TOP)
    SELECTED REFERENCES: **The Power of Silence - Page [13.1-13.5]** (The indications the spirit gave the...candidate to be his apprentice nagual.)

OMEN-APPRENTICE-NAGUAL-JULIAN-[THE OMENS OF THE
APPRENTICE NAGUAL JULIAN]: (TOP)
    SELECTED REFERENCES: **The Power of Silence - Page [15.1-15.4]** (Don Juan began his story...for his expensive shoes and clothes.) **The Power of Silence - Page [20.7-20.9]** (As the nagual watched the unconcern...one except the spirit as witness.)

OMEN-BENEFACTOR-[OMEN OF THE BENEFACTOR]: (TOP)
    SELECTED REFERENCES: **Tales of Power - Page [251.1-251.5]** (Don Juan said that there had...judging by the way he looked.)

OMEN-CHOLLA-[OMEN OF THE CHOLLA]-(TOP): SEE: FINDING-
ELIGIO-[HOW POWER FOUND ELIGIO]-(TOP)

OMEN-CROW-[OMEN OF THE CROW]: (TOP)
    SELECTED REFERENCES: **Journey to Ixtlan - Page [19.7-20.5]** (At that moment an enormous crow...indication about you," he replied cryptically.) **Journey to Ixtlan - Page [49.1-49.5]** ("Sometimes it is necessary to find...place to camp or to rest.") **Journey to Ixtlan - Page [106.5-106.6]** ("All you have to do is...told me not to do that.") **Journey to Ixtlan - Page [114.5-114.6]** ("This place is crawling with mountain lions...must be something special about it.") **Journey to Ixtlan - Page [118.9-119.2]** ("Well, forget about it then...in the mood of a warrior.) **Journey to Ixtlan - Page [218.2-218.3]** (Don Juan said that we had...complete circle, scanning all the surroundings.) **Tales of Power - Page [180.8-181.1]** (As we approached the eucalyptuses...until the crows had calmed down.)

OMEN-ESCOGIDO-[THE OMEN OF THE ESCOGIDO]: (TOP)
    SELECTED REFERENCES: **The Teachings of Don Juan - Page [36.7-37.3]** (Don Juan whispered that we were...one can do," don Juan said.) **The Teachings of Don Juan - Page [41.3-50.8]** (I saw the juncture of the...will come to you of itself.") **A Separate Reality - Page [56.9-57.1]** (I related to don Juan the...me his knowledge because of it.) **Journey to Ixtlan - Page [89.1-89.4]** (Two weeks before, on August 4th...of exceptionally vivid dreams and nightmares.)

OMEN-HARDNESS-TRANSFORMATION-[THE OMEN OF HARDNESS AND TRANSFORMATION]-(TOP): SEE: OMEN-WAITRESS-[THE OMEN OF THE WAITRESS]-(TOP)

OMEN-HUNT-POWER-[THE OMEN TO HUNT FOR POWER]: (TOP)
SELECTED REFERENCES: **Journey to Ixtlan - Page [139.7-146.5]** (Around ten A.M. don Juan walked...find any of them on our way.) **Journey to Ixtlan - Page [149.4-149.5]** ("Fix all this in your memory...human decision, not yours or mine.)

OMEN-LIDIA-[LIDIA'S OMEN]: (TOP)
SELECTED REFERENCES: **The Second Ring of Power - Page [47.7-48.1]** ("How did they become apprentices...and twigs and found a girl.)

OMEN-MOTH-[THE OMEN OF THE MOTH]: (TOP)
SELECTED REFERENCES: **Tales of Power - Page [92.9-93.6]** (It started the last time you...such a great emphasis on you.)

OMEN-MOTHS-CIRCLE-[THE OMEN OF LA GORDA'S CIRCLE OF MOTHS]-(TOP): SEE: FINDING-GORDA-[HOW POWER FOUND LA GORDA]-(TOP)

OMEN-POWER-SPOT-[THE OMEN OF THE POWER SPOT]: (TOP)
SELECTED REFERENCES: **The Teachings of Don Juan - Page [28.8-35.7]** (I stayed with don Juan all afternoon...Mescalito requires a very serious intent.) **The Eagle's Gift - Page [242.3]** (The power spot was on the south side, a very auspicious omen.)

OMEN-RETURN-[THE OMEN OF RETURN]: (TOP)
SELECTED REFERENCES: **The Eagle's Gift - Page [41.8-43.2]** ("Look! Look!" she yelled. "There's the...toward the east, toward her hometown.) **The Eagle's Gift - Page [63.9-64.4]** (While we were sitting on the...In the direction of this town.) **The Eagle's Gift - Page [78.4-79.9]** (When we were coming into the...all of us were going north.)

OMEN-SOLEDAD-[DONA SOLEDAD'S OMENS]: (TOP)
SELECTED REFERENCES: **The Second Ring of Power - Page [33.4-33.9]**. ("One day the Nagual and Genaro...ashamed of having refused my food.)

OMEN-SUN-[THE OMEN OF THE SUN]: (TOP)
SELECTED REFERENCES: **Journey to Ixtlan - Page [151.4-152.3]** (The last minutes of light, right before...the realm of the young sun.") **Journey to Ixtlan - Page [155.1-155.5]** ("Certainly. You are hunting personal power...to the south. To the vastness.")

OMEN-WAITRESS-[THE OMEN OF THE WAITRESS]: (TOP)
SELECTED REFERENCES: **The Power of Silence - Page [151.8-152.6]** (He then took my experience of...transformation were the indication of the spirit.")

OMEN-WARRIOR-RITUAL-[THE OMEN OF THE WARRIOR'S RITUAL]: (TOP)
SELECTED REFERENCES: **The Eagle's Gift - Page [188.7-189.4]** (Don Juan said that he had the...pomp were out of character for me.)

OTHER-SELF-[THE OTHER SELF]: (TOP)
SELECTED REFERENCES: **The Eagle's Gift - Page [9-107]** (It was mid-afternoon when I...as the petty people we were.)

P

PABLITO-ATTEMPTED-ESCAPE-[PABLITO'S ATTEMPTED ESCAPE]:
(TOP)
>SELECTED REFERENCES: The Second Ring of Power - Page [201.1-201.8] ("They've put a curse on me...let him stay on the bus.")

PABLITO-BASKET-[PABLITO'S BASKET AND HIS ENCOUNTER WITH
THE NAGUAL]: (TOP)
>SELECTED REFERENCES: Tales of Power - Page [199.4-200.4] (I asked Pablito about his meetings...stand the terror and lost consciousness.)

PABLITO-BID-NAGUAL-[PABLITO'S BID TO BE THE NAGUAL]: (TOP)
>SELECTED REFERENCES: The Second Ring of Power - Page [172.7-174.8] ("But aren't all of you supposed to...but an impeccable warrior survives, always.") The Second Ring of Power - Page [188.3-188.8] ("Don't get me wrong," Maestro...Maestro, you bring me new hope.")

PABLITO-TUG-OF-WAR-GAME-[PABLITO'S TUG OF WAR GAME]:
(TOP)
>SELECTED REFERENCES: The Eagle's Gift - Page [61.2-62.6] (I found Pablito, Nestor, and Benigno...thinks that's because her body remembers.") The Eagle's Gift - Page [302.3-302.6] (La Gorda remembered that to prepare...a device that helped them remember.)

PABLITO-MANUELITA-[PABLITO'S SWEET MANUELITA]: (TOP)
>SELECTED REFERENCES: The Second Ring of Power - Page [187.3-188.5] ("Do you hate them for what...help me. They wanted me dead.) The Second Ring of Power - Page [235.6-236.4] (La Gorda said, in a scornful...have to fight to claim her.")

PABLITO-VANISHES-[PABLITO VANISHES INTO THIN AIR]: (TOP)
>SELECTED REFERENCES: Tales of Power - Page [267.2-267.7] (Don Juan and don Genaro sat...it had vanished in thin air.)

PARALLEL-BEING-[THE PARALLEL BEING]: (TOP)
>SELECTED REFERENCES: The Eagle's Gift - Page [295.4-295.9] (Florinda stood up abruptly and took...that held no meaning for me.)

PARALLEL-LINES-[THE PARALLEL LINES]: (TOP)
>SELECTED REFERENCES: The Eagle's Gift - Page [75.8-76.9] (She peered into my eyes for...not breathe and everything went black.)

PARALLEL-LINES-JOURNEY-[JOURNEY TO THE LAND BETWEEN THE
PARALLEL LINES]: (TOP)
>SELECTED REFERENCES: The Eagle's Gift - Page [155.1-157.2] (On the day in question, both don...the ground in the everyday world.)

PARALLEL-LINES-LAND-[THE LAND BETWEEN THE PARALLEL LINE]:
(TOP)
>SELECTED REFERENCES: The Second Ring of Power - Page [325.6-325.7] (The Nagual said that you will understand...yellow sulfur world where he lives.) The Eagle's Gift - Page [152.3-153.7] (We stayed merges until something broke...barren place with our whole bodies.)

PARTY-HUNTERS-[A PARTY OF HUNTERS]: (TOP)
>SELECTED REFERENCES: A Separate Reality - Page [68.5-72.4] (Two days later, on September 6...just said isn't worth a damn.")

PERCEPTION-BARRIER-BREAKING-[BREAKING THE BARRIER OF
PERCEPTION]: (TOP)
>SELECTED REFERENCES: The Fire From Within - Page [288-296] (In the late afternoon, still in...windlike force blew the world away.)

PERCEPTION-BUBBLE-[THE BUBBLE OF PERCEPTION]: (TOP)

SELECTED REFERENCES: **Tales of Power - Page [261-278]** (I spent the day by myself...perception and fly to that infinitude.")

PERCEPTION-DOUBLE-OF-[THE PERCEPTION OF THE DOUBLE]: (TOP)

SELECTED REFERENCES: **The Second Ring of Power - Page [58.5-58.9]** (I heard then, or perhaps I...against it like a frightened child.) **The Second Ring of Power - Page [109.9-111.8]** (I then had an inconceivable feeling...But somehow I was myself again.)

PERCEPTION-DUAL-[DUAL PERCEPTION]: (TOP)

SELECTED REFERENCES: **The Eagle's Gift - Page [37.2-37.5]** (La Gorda was right. I...recall perceiving two separate scenes simultaneously.)

PERCEPTION-SPLIT-[SPLIT PERCEPTION]: (TOP)

SELECTED REFERENCES: **Tales of Power - Page [184.4-185.8]** (I could hear both of them talking...as words whispered in my ears.) **Tales of Power - Page [202.6-203.4]** (They whispered in my ears until...all capacity to differentiate my perceptions.) **The Power of Silence - Page [233.7-236.2]** (Don Juan contended that that simple...river, and started to walk home.")

PERCEPTION-WINGS-[THE WINGS OF PERCEPTION]: (TOP)

SELECTED REFERENCES: **Tales of Power - Page [197-209]** (Don Juan and I spent the...they walked me to my car.)

PERSONAL-HISTORY-ERASING-[ERASING PERSONAL HISTORY]: (TOP)

SELECTED REFERENCES: **Journey to Ixtlan - Page [9-17]** (Don Juan was sitting on the..."Be sure to come back.")

PETTY-TYRANT-[THE PETTY TYRANT]: (TOP)

SELECTED REFERENCES: **The Fire From Within - Page [11-30]** (Don Juan did not discuss the...of the petty tyrants for life.")

PETTY-TYRANT-KING-SIZE-[DON JUAN'S KING-SIZE PETTY TYRANT]: (TOP)

SELECTED REFERENCES: **The Fire From Within - Page [20.4-29.6]** ("I was lucky. A king-size...is due to whoever deserves it.")

PITY-PLACE-NO-[THE PLACE OF NO PITY]: (TOP)

SELECTED REFERENCES: **The Power of Silence - Page [134-154]** (Don Juan told me that there...or self-importance. Ruthlessness is sobriety.")

PLUMED-SERPENT-[THE PLUMED SERPENT]: (TOP)

SELECTED REFERENCES: **The Eagle's Gift - Page [297-314]** (Having accomplished every one of the...And then the lights were gone.)

POINT-THIRD-[THE THIRD POINT]: (TOP)

SELECTED REFERENCES: **The Power of Silence - Page [196-224]** (Don Juan often took me and...our boundaries and touching the inconceivable.")

POINT-THIRD-[THE THIRD POINT]: (TOP)

SELECTED REFERENCES: **The Fire From Within - Page [29.8-29.9]** ("The new seers used petty tyrants...on discussing the mastery of awareness.)

POLICEMAN-FLEET-FOOTED-[THE FLEET-FOOTED POLICEMAN]-(TOP): SEE: CARLOS-POLICEMAN-[CARLOS AND THE FLEET-FOOTED POLICEMAN]-(TOP)

POPULATIONS-LEAVE-WORLD-[POPULATIONS LEAVE THE WORLD]: (TOP)

SELECTED REFERENCES: **The Fire From Within - Page [5.1-5.3]** ("There were seers, however, who escaped...other worlds and never came back.")

PORFIRIO-[PORFIRIO]: (TOP)

SELECTED REFERENCES: The Second Ring of Power - Page [212.4-213.6] (Then, quite suddenly, the same thing...I found myself back on this earth.") The Second Ring of Power - Page [220.3-221.4] ("I didn't go beyond this world...my earth. It's my indulging perhaps.")

POWER-ACCESSIBLE-BECOMING-[BECOMING ACCESSIBLE TO POWER]: (TOP)

SELECTED REFERENCES: Journey to Ixtlan - Page [88-104] (As soon as I got out...know it was made to collapse.)

POWER-ACTS-WITNESS-[A WITNESS TO ACTS OF POWER]: (TOP)

SELECTED REFERENCES: Tales of Power - Page [2-100] (I had not seen don Juan ...Genaro was hiding under my hat.")

POWER-APPOINTMENT-[AN APPOINTMENT WITH POWER]-(TOP): SEE: DREAMER-ART-[THE ART OF THE DREAMER]-(TOP)

POWER-BATTLE-[A BATTLE OF POWER]: (TOP)

SELECTED REFERENCES: Journey to Ixtlan - Page [121-139] (We started on a journey very...shoved me gently down the slope.)

POWER-BREATHES-LIFE-TWIG-[POWER BREATHES LIFE INTO A TWIG]: (TOP)

SELECTED REFERENCES: Journey to Ixtlan - Page [101.4-104.9] ("There" he said in a whisper...know it was made to collapse.)

POWER-DANCING-[POWER DANCING]: (TOP): SEE: JUAN-FLYING-[DON JUAN'S FLYING]: (TOP)

POWER-OBJECT-[POWER OBJECTS]: (TOP)

SELECTED REFERENCES: The Teachings of Don Juan - Page [21.8-24.7] (For example, in one conversation he...of knowing things that are useless?")

POWER-PROTECTION-[THE PROTECTION OF POWER]: (TOP)

SELECTED REFERENCES: Journey to Ixtlan - Page [65.4-66.1] ("Your opinions are final opinions...I can guarantee you that.)

POWER-RING-[THE RING OF POWER]: (TOP)

SELECTED REFERENCES: Journey to Ixtlan - Page [200-214] (Don Juan felt the weight of...he is used and taken himself.)

POWER-RING-SECOND-[THE SECOND RING OF POWER]: (TOP)

SELECTED REFERENCES: The Second Ring of Power - Page [1-328] (A flat, barren mountaintop on the...was no limit to that vastness.)

POWER-RING-SORCERER-[THE SORCERERS' RING OF POWER]: (TOP)

SELECTED REFERENCES: Journey to Ixtlan - Page [231-245] (In May of 1971, I paid...with laughter before I fell asleep.)

POWER-SPOT-TALES-LOCATING-[TALES OF LOCATING POWER SPOTS]: (TOP)

SELECTED REFERENCES: The Teachings of Don Juan - Page [28.8-35.7] (I stayed with don Juan all afternoon...Mescalito requires a very serious intent.) Journey to Ixtlan - Page [48.3-48.6] (In the early evening, however, he...and the colors associated with both.) Journey to Ixtlan - Page [106.1-106.4] ("Not here, you fool," he said...one could find solutions to dilemmas.) Journey to Ixtlan - Page [158.7-164.2] ("Let's go," he said. "We have...without any plan on your part.") Tales of Power - Page [243.5-243.7] ("Why didn't you give me more time...or you wouldn't do a thing.") The Second Ring of Power - Page [297.6-297.8] (A second series in the order of...to be avoided are intensely green.) The Power of Silence - Page [155.8-156.] (Around noon, we continued on up...perceive is simply average sensory perception.")

POWER-TALES-[TALES OF POWER]: (TOP)
SELECTED REFERENCES: Tales of Power - Page [2-295] (I had not seen don Juan...jumped and then I was alone.)

POWER-WALK-FOR-[THE WALK FOR POWER]: (TOP)
SELECTED REFERENCES: Journey to Ixtlan - Page [141.5-143.4] (Don Juan tied my carrying net...finally I collapsed on the ground.)

PROMISE-BUTTON-NOSED-BOY-[THE PROMISE TO THE BUTTON-NOSED BOY]-(TOP): SEE: BOY-BUTTON-NOSED-PROMISE-[THE PROMISE TO THE BUTTON NOSED BOY]-(TOP)

PROMISE-CHILDHOOD-[THE PROMISE OF CHILDHOOD]: (TOP)
SELECTED REFERENCES: A Separate Reality - Page [134.8-143.8] ("Perhaps it's the promise," don Juan...they were, before anything else, men.")

PROMISE-WORTHLESS-SERVANT-WORTHLESS-MASTER-[THE PROMISE OF A WORTHLESS SERVANT TO A WORTHLESS MASTER]: (TOP)
SELECTED REFERENCES: The Fire From Within - Page [269.6-270.2] ("Are you sure you understand what...me that my promise was worthless.)

PSYCHIC-SURGERY-[PSYCHIC SURGERY]: (TOP)
SELECTED REFERENCES: The Power of Silence - Page [120.4-123.1] (He reminded me of an event...not think, everything fit into place.) The Power of Silence - Page [165.2-165.4] (He then compared the acts her performed...assemblage points were ready to be moved.)

PUSHING-ARM-EXERCISE-[THE EXERCISE OF PUSHING WITH THE ARM]-(TOP): SEE: NOT-DOING-EXERCISE-[THE EXERCISE OF NOT-DOING]-(TOP)

PYRAMIDS-[PYRAMID S AND TOLTEC RUINS]: (TOP)
SELECTED REFERENCES: The Eagles Gift - Page [9.3-27.4] (It was mid-afternoon when I...the Atlanteans would walk at night.)

Q

QUAIL-FIVE-[THE STORY OF THE FIVE QUAIL]: (TOP)
SELECTED REFERENCES: **Journey to Ixtlan - Page [59.4-60.2]** (Again don Juan, as he had...everything around would have pitched in.")

R

RABBIT-LAST-BATTLE-[A RABBIT'S LAST BATTLE ON EARTH]: (TOP)
SELECTED REFERENCES: Journey to Ixtlan - Page [86.3-88.6] (I was still pondering upon the...to roam in this marvelous desert.")

RATTLESNAKE-HUNTING-[HUNTING A RATTLESNAKE]: (TOP)
SELECTED REFERENCES: Journey to Ixtlan - Page [52.6-53.4] ("You have a knack for hunting...amount of information about rattlesnakes.)

RATTLESNAKE-PARTY-ARRANGEMENT-[THE ARRANGEMENT OF THE NAGUAL'S PARTY LIKE A RATTLESNAKE]: (TOP)
SELECTED REFERENCES: The Eagle's Gift - Page [66.6-67.3] (She did not finish. She came...for hours on end, Benigno and Rosa.) The Eagle's Gift - Page [67.5-68.2] (We started out before midnight, hiking...the one in front of them.) The Eagle's Gift - Page [106.5-106.6] (He added that he had laughed...last opportunity to succeed as a group.)

REAFFIRMATIONS-WORLD-[REAFFIRMATIONS FROM THE WORLD AROUND US]: (TOP)
SELECTED REFERENCES: Journey to Ixtlan - Page [1-9] ("I understand you know a great...said softly and waved good-bye.)

REALITY-SEPARATE-[A SEPARATE REALITY]: (TOP)
SELECTED REFERENCES: A Separate Reality - Page [1-263] (Ten years ago I had the...really changed in you," he said.)

REASON-ABANDONING-[ABANDONING REASON]: (TOP)
SELECTED REFERENCES: The Power of Silence - Page [211.6-212.1] ("Be gigantic," he ordered me, smiling...was feel myself breaking through it.)

REMEMBERING-BODY-[REMEMBERING WITH THE BODY]: (TOP)
SELECTED REFERENCES: The Eagle's Gift - Page [57.5-57.9] ("He told Josephina other things which..."No I can't." she said after a moment.) The Eagle's Gift - Page [58.8-58.9] ("There is no way for me to...is waiting for me in particular.") The Eagle's Gift - Page [59.9-60.3] ("We have to wait," she said...we can't talk about something else.") The Eagle's Gift - Page [62.5-63.6] ("Benigno thinks now that it is...was again in control of myself.) The Eagle's Gift - Page [64.6-65.5] (During the early hours of the evening...as another part of me shook.) The Eagle's Gift - Page [66.4-66.6] ("What's happening to us, Gorda...that you don't remember, but then...") The Eagle's Gift - Page [71.3-73.6] (Lydia avoided my eyes. She mumbled...The Nagual Juan Matus, I suppose.") The Eagle's Gift - Page [77.9-78.2] (Once we got to the lowlands...beyond the bounds of their reason.) The Eagle's Gift - Page [82.2-82.6] (La Gorda and I were alone...her face when she was fat.) The Eagle's Gift - Page [82.9-83.4] (That world and this world we...lives where we could fit them.) The Eagle's Gift - Page [83.9-84.3] ("Soledad also told me that you...why she couldn't deal with you.") The Eagle's Gift - Page [93.3-93.9] ("The Nagual Juan Matus was right...have realized what I was doing.) The Eagle's Gift - Page [117.2-124.9] (La Gorda and I went through a...We must snap out of it.") The Eagle's Gift - Page [145.3-145.5] ("What do you mean, shooting off...*dreaming body*. But to no avail.") The Eagle's Gift - Page [163.1-163.4] (La Gorda and I used *dreaming together*...of what had happened to us.) The Eagle's Gift - Page [166.3-167.3] (The task of remembering, then, was...which had been veiled by *intensity*.) The Eagle's Gift - Page [300.2-300.9] (Having made them shift levels of awareness...and I fell to the floor.) The Eagle's Gift - Page [302.1-302.2] (At one instant, I was not...of our two states of awareness.) The Fire From Within - Page [272.2-272.8] ("It is very important that you remember...I had lived that experience myself.) The Fire From Within - Page [275.7-275.9] ("I want you to realign the proper...in a state of normal awareness.) The Fire From Within - Page [284.7-285.8] (As though my recollection depended on...activities fostered serious disparities of memory.) The Power of Silence - Page [196.5-197.4] (Don Juan often took me and the...every detail of it," he warned.)

REMEMBERING-LEFT-SIDE-[REMEMBERING THE LEFT SIDE]: (TOP)
SELECTED REFERENCES: The Eagle's Gift - Page [57.2-59.6] ("What exactly has Eligio said to...tended to me with absolute kindness.)

REMEMBERING-TRACKING-HIDING-SKILLS-[REMEMBERING THE WARRIORS' TRACKING AND HIDING SKILLS]: (TOP)
> SELECTED REFERENCES: **The Eagle's Gift - Page [62.5-63.6]** ("Benigno thinks now that it is...was again in control of myself.)

RESPONSIBILITY-ASSUMING-[ASSUMING RESPONSIBILITY]: (TOP)
> SELECTED REFERENCES: **Journey to Ixtlan - Page [37-47]** (I arrived at don Juan's house...that that food was power too.")

RIVER-JUAN-SPIRIT-[DON JUAN MEETS THE SPIRIT BY BEING THROWN INTO THE RIVER]-(TOP): SEE: JUAN-RIVER-BOUT-[DON JUAN'S BOUT WITH THE RAGING RIVER]-(TOP)

ROCKS-SCENT-[THE SCENT OF ROCKS]: (TOP)
> SELECTED REFERENCES: **The Second Ring of Power - Page [297.1-297.4]** (The next step was to gaze at...because I'm guided by those scents.")

ROLLING-FORCE-[THE ROLLING FORCE]-(TOP): SEE: FORCE-ROLLING-[THE ROLLING FORCE]-(TOP)

ROLLING-FORCE-SEEING-[SEEING THE ROLLING FORCE]-(TOP): SEE: FORCE-ROLLING-SEEING-[SEEING THE ROLLING FORCE]-(TOP)

ROSENDO-NAGUAL-TALES-[TALES OF THE NAGUAL ROSENDO]: (TOP)
> SELECTED REFERENCES: **The Power of Silence - Page [32.8-32.9]** (Don Juan said that the nagual...who came from the same area.)

ROUTINES-DISRUPTING-[DISRUPTING ROUTINES]: (TOP)
> SELECTED REFERENCES: **Journey to Ixtlan - Page [71-77]** (We spent all morning watching some..."It's one of the darndest things.")

RULE-NAGUAL-[THE RULE OF THE NAGUAL]: (TOP)
> SELECTED REFERENCES: **The Eagle's Gift - Page [171-187]** (Don Juan had been extremely sparing...under the harshest conditions of suppression.)

S

SABRE-TOOTHED-TIGER-DREAM-[THE DREAM OF THE SABRE-TOOTHED TIGER]-(TOP): SEE: DREAM-SABRE-TOOTHED-TIGER-[THE DREAM OF THE SABRE-TOOTHED TIGER]-(TOP)

SACATECA-WILL-[THE WILL OF SACATECA]: (TOP)
SELECTED REFERENCES: A Separate Reality - Page [11.4-15.4] ("Take Sacateca, he's a man of...explain the event to my satisfaction.) A Separate Reality - Page [65.1-65.2] ("Valencio is not the best dancer...that's the bent of his nature.)

SCHOLAR-[THE SCHOLAR]: (TOP)
SELECTED REFERENCES: The Eagle's Gift - Page [192.7-195.2] (Don Juan said that the east...warrior scholar and his oldest companion.)

SCOUT-BLUE-[THE BLUE SCOUT]: (TOP)
SELECTED REFERENCES: The Art of Dreaming - Page [128-140] (I was dreaming an utterly nonsensical dream...inorganic beings cannot lie, you know.")

SCOUT-BLUE-[THE BLUE SCOUT]: (TOP)
SELECTED REFERENCES: The Art of Dreaming - Page [120.1-121.7] (The scout took over and made...prisoner in the organic beings' realm.) The Art of Dreaming - Page [123.8-124.4] ("I am thinking that they are...can't figure out what it is.") The Art of Dreaming - Page [125.5-127.8] (Was he right! On my next...prisoner scout and set it free.) The Art of Dreaming - Page [132.1-132.4] ("How did I end up here...me: to free the blue scout.) The Art of Dreaming - Page [134.8-140.6] (One day around noon, after a...inorganic beings cannot lie, you know.") The Art of Dreaming - Page [146.6-146.9] (Secretly, I felt somehow exonerated from...to do to liberate the blue scout.) The Art of Dreaming - Page [179.2-179.3] ("Where does the blue scout stand...a natural state in our world.)

SCOUT-ENGAGING-DREAMING-[ENGAGING A SCOUT IN DREAMING]: (TOP)
SELECTED REFERENCES: The Art of Dreaming - Page [104.3-104.5] (I asked don Juan what exactly...offer his disciples to the scout.)

SCOUT-TALES-[TALES OF THE SCOUTS]: (TOP)
SELECTED REFERENCES: The Art of Dreaming - Page [88.1-91.8] (At home, I tired of searching...was somehow darker than the others.) The Art of Dreaming - Page [119.2-119.7] (Not only did the emissary change...it took me to the tunnels.)

SEEING-[SEEING]: (TOP)
SELECTED REFERENCES: The Second Ring of Power - Page [237.3-237.4] (She was silent for awhile...the little sisters and the Genaros.") The Second Ring of Power - Page [272.4-273.3] (And then I suddenly recalled something...recollection to the other in my mind.) The Second Ring of Power - Page [288.7-289.1] (She contracted her mouth and appeared...she were delighted with the delay.) The Eagle's Gift - Page [36.3-37.7] (La Gorda said that what had happened...caressing the backs of my hands.)

SEEING-CROW-AS-[SEEING AS A CROW SEES]-(TOP): SEE: CROW-SEEING-[SEEING AS A CROW SEES]-(TOP)

SEEING-DARKNESS-IN-[SEEING IN THE DARKNESS]: (TOP)
SELECTED REFERENCES: The Teachings of Don Juan - Page [97.7-98.4] (Upon approaching the creek I noticed...audible again. My muscles stiffened.)

SEEING-DREAMING-IN-[SEEING IN DREAMING]: (TOP)
SELECTED REFERENCES: The Art of Dreaming - Page [166.8-167.2] (The first time I put into words...woke up tremendously frustrated, almost angry.)

SEEING-EAGLE-EMANATIONS-[SEEING THE EAGLE'S EMANATIONS]: (TOP)

SELECTED REFERENCES: **The Fire From Within - Page [221.2-221.8]** (I would have gone on seeing...and the balloons that were hitting me.) **The Fire From Within - Page [224.7-225.5]** (As don Juan spoke to me...revulsion that I'd felt that day.)

SEEING-FORCE-LIFE-[SEEING THE FORCE OF LIFE]: (TOP)

SELECTED REFERENCES: **The Fire From Within - Page [279.8-280.1]** (After a while she helped me...like a live furnace; it glowed.)

SEEING-PEOPLE-[SEEING PEOPLE]: (TOP)

SELECTED REFERENCES: **The Fire From Within - Page [219.6-221.2]** (He also told me not to...the thickness of the total cocoon.)

SEEING-PRELIMINARIES-[THE PRELIMINARIES OF SEEING]: (TOP)

SELECTED REFERENCES: **A Separate Reality - Page [19-108]** (Don Juan looked at me for...he knew you had not *seen*.")

SEEING-ROLLING-FORCE-[SEEING THE ROLLING FORCE]-(TOP): SEE: SEE-TUMBLER-[SEEING THE TUMBLER]-(TOP)

SEEING-SPIRIT-[SEEING THE SPIRIT]-(TOP): SEE: SPIRIT-SEEING-[SEEING THE SPIRIT]-(TOP)

SEEING-TASK-[THE TASK OF SEEING]: (TOP)

SELECTED REFERENCES: **A Separate Reality - Page [109-262]** (Don Juan was not at his...indulge too much." he said softly.)

SEEING-TOGETHER-[SEEING TOGETHER]: (TOP)

SELECTED REFERENCES: **The Eagle's Gift - Page [29-48]** (For several weeks after my return...must allow ourselves time to heal.")

SEEING-TOGETHER-[SEEING TOGETHER]: (TOP)

SELECTED REFERENCES: **The Eagle's Gift - Page [40.7-47.8]** (La Gorda put her head on my shoulder...feeling we have seen together before.")

SEEING-TUMBLER-[SEEING THE TUMBLER]: (TOP)

SELECTED REFERENCES: **The Fire From Within - Page [221.2-221.8]** (I would have gone on seeing...and the balloons that were hitting me.) **The Fire From Within - Page [224.7-225.5]** (As don Juan spoke to me...revulsion that I'd felt that day.)

SEER-NEW-[THE NEW SEERS]: (TOP)

SELECTED REFERENCES: **The Fire From Within - Page [1-10]** (I had arrived in the city...new seers meant them to have.)

SELF-IMPORTANCE-LOSING-[LOSING SELF-IMPORTANCE]: (TOP)

SELECTED REFERENCES: **Journey to Ixtlan - Page [18-25]** (I had the opportunity of discussing...but did not say a word.)

SELF-OTHER-[THE OTHER SELF]-(TOP): SEE: OTHER-SELF-[THE OTHER SELF]-(TOP)

SELF-QUASI-MEMORIES-OTHER-[QUASI MEMORIES OF THE OTHER SELF]: (TOP)

SELECTED REFERENCES: **The Eagle's Gift - Page [49-65]** ("Can you tell us what's going...as another part of me shook.)

SELF-REFLECTION-MIRROR-SHATTERING-[SHATTERING THE MIRROR OF SELF-REFLECTION]: (TOP)

SELECTED REFERENCES: **The Power of Silence - Page [155-170]** (We spent a night at the...began to laugh at my dismay.)

SHADOW-CIRCLE-[A CIRCLE OF SHADOWS]: (TOP)

SELECTED REFERENCES: **Journey to Ixtlan - Page [210.1-210.4]** (The fire was about to be extinguished...they were a circle of shadows.) **Journey to Ixtlan - Page [213.2-213.4]** (I changed the subject and asked...It would have only injured you.")

SHADOW-DEATH-[THE SHADOW OF DEATH]: (TOP)

SELECTED REFERENCES: **The Second Ring of Power - Page [129.6-129.7]** (I was dumbfounded; I couldn't believe...seen my death circling around me.) **The Power of Silence - Page [17.3-17.7]** (The nagual had to admit that...the black shadow of his death.) **The Power of Silence - Page [20.2-20.4]** (And then the nagual *saw* that...for the black shadow of death.)

SHADOW-FOLLOW-[THE SHADOW THAT FOLLOWS]: (TOP)

SELECTED REFERENCES: **Journey to Ixtlan - Page [195.4-195.7]** ("Shadows are peculiar affairs," he said...same lines, therefore both were shadows.)

SHADOW-MERGING-[MERGING SHADOWS]: (TOP)

SELECTED REFERENCES: **Journey to Ixtlan - Page [196.4-198.1]** (He led me to a place...would succeed in merging the shadows.) **Tales of Power - Page [86.5-87.3]** (I felt that I could have gone...in the world of everyday life.)

SHADOW-OBSERVING-[OBSERVING OBJECTS AND THEIR SHADOWS]: (TOP)

SELECTED REFERENCES: **Journey to Ixtlan - Page [195.7-198.3]** (He pointed to a long boulder...as a door into not-doing.")

SHADOW-WORLD-[THE SHADOWS' WORLD]: (TOP)

SELECTED REFERENCES: **The Art of Dreaming - Page [106-127]** (You must be extremely careful, for you...prisoner scout and set it free.)

SHADOW-WORLD-[THE SHADOWS' WORLD]: (TOP)

SELECTED REFERENCES: **The Art of Dreaming - Page [111.5-113.5]** (On one occasion, a scout guided...My dreaming session ended there.) **The Art of Dreaming - Page [114.1-118.3]** ("This is the shadows' world," the emissary's...was fully awake, in my bed.) **The Art of Dreaming - Page [122.7-122.9]** (For instance, I never knew about...this through the old sorcerers' stories.") **The Art of Dreaming - Page [125.5-126.7]** (Was he right! On my next...of affection for her enveloped me.) **The Art of Dreaming - Page [128.7-129.9]** (I was dreaming an utterly nonsensical...away, just like the shadow beings.)

SHIELDS-DROPPING-WARRIOR-[DROPPING THE WARRIORS' SHIELDS]-(TOP): SEE: HUMAN-FORM-LOSING-[LOSING THE HUMAN FORM]-(TOP)

SHIFT-BELOW-[THE SHIFT BELOW]: (TOP)

SELECTED REFERENCES: **The Fire From Within - Page [140-156]** (Don Juan and Genaro made their yearly...and I would need fresh concentration.)

SHOE-LACES-TIE-[A WARRIOR STOPS TO TIE THE LACES OF HIS SHOES]: (TOP)

SELECTED REFERENCES: **The Second Ring of Power - Page [283.4-284.1]** (I narrated to her the way...in my tying my shoelaces impeccably.)

SILENCE-POWER-[THE POWER OF SILENCE]: (TOP)

SELECTED REFERENCES: **The Power of Silence - Page [ix-265]** (At various times don Juan attempted...reach the place of silent knowledge.")

SILENT-KNOWLEDGE-[SILENT KNOWLEDGE]-(TOP): SEE: KNOWLEDGE-SILENT-[SILENT KNOWLEDGE]-(TOP)

SILVIO-MANUEL-BREATH-[SILVIO MANUEL'S BREATH]: (TOP)

SELECTED REFERENCES: **The Eagle's Gift - Page [103.4-103.9]** (Lydia faced me next. She did...pumped new life into my body.) **The Eagle's Gift - Page [200.6-201.3]** (Don Juan spoke to the man...his breath all over my body.) **The Eagle's Gift - Page [244.6-245.2]** (La Gorda added that they did...remembered that he was my master.)

SILVIO-MANUEL-EYES-[SILVIO MANUEL'S EYE]: (TOP)

SELECTED REFERENCES: The Eagle's Gift - Page [97.4-97.7] ("It's simplicity itself," la Gorda said...his voice - soft, like muffled coughing.") The Eagle's Gift - Page [201.3-201.5] (He then asked me to sit on...his whole face and his body.) The Eagle's Gift - Page [209.3-209.4] (His features were sharp, his aquiline...reminiscent of the eyes of a feline.)

SILVIO-MANUEL-MASTER-INTENT-[SILVIO MANUEL THE MASTER OF INTENT]: (TOP)

SELECTED REFERENCES: The Eagle's Gift - Page [146.5-149.6] ("I've got it!" she exclaimed. "The...the time they didn't do anything.")

SILVIO-MANUEL-NOT-DOING-[THE NOT-DOINGS OF SILVIO MANUEL]-(TOP) SEE: NOT-DOING-SILVIO-MANUEL-[THE NOT-DOINGS OF SILVIO MANUEL]-(TOP)

SILVIO-MANUEL-TALES-[TALES OF SILVIO MANUEL]: (TOP)

SELECTED REFERENCES: The Eagle's Gift - Page [90.6-91.1] ("Do you remember anything, Josephina...always in the darkness. Ask Rosa.") The Eagle's Gift - Page [95.1-99.1] ("Silvio Manuel is the darkness," la Gorda...have thrown her off the bridge.) The Eagle's Gift - Page [101.5-105.7] (Pablito insisted that it was important...was suddenly lifted off her shoulders.) The Eagle's Gift - Page [147.4-149.6] (I wanted to argue with her...the time they didn't do anything.") The Eagle's Gift - Page [158.8-159.1] ("We were in Silvio Manuel's house...he and his companions lived there.) The Eagle's Gift - Page [196.7-205.1] (At the same time, I was...the silent force behind don Juan.) The Eagle's Gift - Page [208.8-209.5] (But the biggest surprise to me...reminiscent of the eyes of a feline.) The Eagle's Gift - Page [241.7-243.4] (Silvio Manuel had conceived the idea...hand, ready to hurl them in.)

SNAIL-SIDEWALK-[A SNAIL ON THE SIDEWALK]: (TOP)

SELECTED REFERENCES: The Second Ring of Power - Page [311.1-312.5] ("Sorcerers don't help one another like...me was to let others be.)

SOLEDAD-BATTLE-DEATH-[A BATTLE TO THE DEATH WITH DONA SOLEDAD]-(TOP): SEE: DOUBLE-MORTAL-COMBAT-[THE MORTAL COMBAT OF THE DOUBLE]-(TOP)

SOLEDAD-BID-POWER-[DONA SOLEDAD'S BID FOR POWER]: (TOP)

SELECTED REFERENCES: The Second Ring of Power - Page [60.7-66.7] ("There is something I must tell you...more. You are the Nagual himself.") The Second Ring of Power - Page [126.1-127.2] ("Why is the Nagual trying to destroy me...life and maybe you'll understand her.) The Second Ring of Power - Page [135.3-136.7] ("Soledad has to take her edge... would try to injure their luminosity.") The Second Ring of Power - Page [182.6-182.9] (The Nagual told us that one day...to find you alive and well.) The Second Ring of Power - Page [188.3-188.8] ("Don't get me wrong," Maestro...Maestro, you bring me new hope.") The Second Ring of Power - Page [223.5-223.9] (La Gorda broke the silence and...to her house and to the hills.) The Second Ring of Power - Page [224.5-224.6] ("The nagual told me that the...kill you or to help you.") The Eagle's Gift - Page [75.9-76.9] (She broke her silence and spoke...not breathe and everything went black.) The Eagle's Gift - Page [248.9-249.3] (La Gorda confessed that all of...been in control of my faculties.)

SOLEDAD-FLOOR-MAGICAL-[THE MAGICAL FLOOR OF DONA SOLEDAD]: (TOP)

SELECTED REFERENCES: The Second Ring of Power - Page [13.2-14.9] (She jumped to her feet and...Who needs words?" she said cuttingly.) The Second Ring of Power - Page [26.3-27.2] (She observed me with a gleam in...not to let her thoughts interfere.) The Second Ring of Power - Page [31.6-32.8] ("You wanted to know who made...his fate to be so fearsome.") The Second Ring of Power - Page [63.4-63.7] (I had taken you to my room...has ever laid eyes on them.) The Second Ring of Power - Page [67.2-67.5] (I went into the kitchen and...drawers and she fell asleep instantly.) The Second Ring of Power - Page [126.1-126.9] ("Why is the Nagual trying to...not overpower you even with that.") The Second Ring of Power - Page [282.4-282.6] ("What's dona Soledad going to do...the earth where she got it.")

SOLEDAD-RECAPITULATION-[THE RECAPITULATION OF DONA SOLEDAD]: (TOP)

SELECTED REFERENCES: The Eagle's Gift - Page [291.9-292.1] (I had never been in that...She was younger and more powerful.)

SOLEDAD-TRANSFORMATION-[THE TRANSFORMATION OF DONA SOLEDAD]: (TOP)

SELECTED REFERENCES: The Second Ring of Power - Page [3-68] (I had a sudden premonition that...was surrounded by four young women.)

SOLEDAD-TRANSFORMATION-[THE TRANSFORMATION OF DONA SOLEDAD]: (TOP)

The Second Ring of Power - Page [236.4-236.7] (The time element in dona Soledad's...finding out about their true activities.) The Eagle's Gift - Page [291.9-292.1] (I had never been in that...She was younger and more powerful.)

SOMERSAULT-THOUGHT-[THE SOMERSAULT OF THOUGHT]-(TOP): SEE: THOUGHT-SOMERSAULT-[THE SOMERSAULT OF THOUGHT]-(TOP)

SORCERER-ANTIQUITY-[THE SORCERERS OF ANTIQUITY]: (TOP)

SELECTED REFERENCES: The Art of Dreaming - Page [1-19] (Don Juan stressed, time and time...systematic displacement of the assemblage point.)

SORCERER-CAVE-[THE SORCERERS' CAVE]-(TOP): SEE: CAVE-SORCERER[THE SORCERERS' CAVE OF UNDERSTANDING]-(TOP)

SORCERER-EXPLANATION-[THE SORCERER'S EXPLANATION]: (TOP)

SELECTED REFERENCES: Tales of Power - Page [212-295] (Upon returning home I was faced again...jumped and then I was alone.)

SORCERER-FACE-SEEING-[SEEING A SORCERER'S FACE]: (TOP)

SELECTED REFERENCES: A Separate Reality - Page [157.1-159.3] (At that instant I became aware..."You saw a glow, big deal.") A Separate Reality - Page [183.4-183.9] (Then very faintly I heard don...as if they were rubber fibers.) A Separate Reality - Page [185.6-186.9] (Don Juan must have turned my...and more intense and more discernible.) A Separate Reality - Page [190.4-190.6] ("What happened to me?" I asked... that out. Then you smoked an ally.")

SORCERER-FLIGHT-[A SORCERER IN FLIGHT]: (TOP)

SELECTED REFERENCES: A Separate Reality - Page [203.1-203.4] (When I asked him to explain...not mind spending the night there.)

SORCERER-HORDE-ANGRY-[A HORDE OF ANGRY SORCERERS]: (TOP)

SELECTED REFERENCES: The Eagle's Gift - Page [87-107] (We were in the town at...as the petty people we were.)

SORCERER-SEND-OFF-[A SORCERER'S SEND-OFF]: (TOP)

SELECTED REFERENCES: The Art of Dreaming - Page [200.8-260.6] (Don Juan then made one last...flying on the wings of intent.")

SORCERER-SMOKING-FACE-[SMOKING A SORCERER'S FACE]-(TOP): SEE: SORCERER-FACE-SEEING-[SEEING A SORCERER'S FACE]-(TOP)

SORCERER-SONGS-[A SORCERER'S SONGS]: (TOP)

SELECTED REFERENCES: A Separate Reality - Page [75.2-75.9] (Eligio stood up and began walking...met and that it was indeed extraordinary.)

SORCERER-STRATEGY-[THE STRATEGY OF A SORCERER]: (TOP)

SELECTED REFERENCES: Tales of Power - Page [229-260] (Don Juan was at don Genaro's...hilarious comments about having saved my pants.)

SORCERER-THUNDERBOLT-[A THUNDERBOLT SORCERER]: (TOP)

SELECTED REFERENCES: The Second Ring of Power - Page [299.5-300.4] ("Genaro was a thunderbolt sorcerer," she...a week right in those mountains.)

SOUL-BATTLE-[A BATTLE FOR THE SOUL]: (TOP)

SELECTED REFERENCES: The Teachings of Don Juan - Page [177.3-188.3] (On Thursday, September 30, 1965, I...who do not have unbending intent.)]

SOUL-LOSS-[THE LOSS OF THE SOUL]: (TOP)

SELECTED REFERENCES: The Teachings of Don Juan - Page [177.5-177.8] (Don Juan, after listening attentively to...where I had lost my soul.)

SOUTH-[THE SOUTH]: (TOP)

SELECTED REFERENCES: The Eagle's Gift - Page [189.6-191.5] (He said that the only opening to a...he called his "tales of eternity.") The Eagle's Gift - Page [201.6-204.1] (I made out the dark silhouette...of Zoila, Zuleica, and Silvio Manuel.)

SPARKS-GORDA-[LA GORDA'S SPARKS]-(TOP): SEE: GORDA-SPARKS-[LA GORDA'S SPARKS]-(TOP)

SPIRIT-AWARENESS-CAPACITY-ADJUST-[THE SPIRIT MAKES FINAL ADJUSTMENTS IN THE WARRIORS' CAPACITY FOR AWARENESS]: (TOP)

SELECTED REFERENCES: The Power of Silence - Page [33.5-34.1] (Don Juan laughed, and, since he...moment, but the moment will change.")

SPIRIT-CATCHER-[A SPIRIT CATCHER]: (TOP)

SELECTED REFERENCES: A Separate Reality - Page [160.4-163.3] (He took me to the mouth..."You will know that very soon.") A Separate Reality - Page [165.7-167.2] ("Now let us call the spirit...I got sick to my stomach.) A Separate Reality - Page [226.5-228.4] ("But all this is not important...you where to look for it.")

SPIRIT-CATCHER-SEARCH-[IN SEARCH OF A SPIRIT CATCHER]: (TOP)

SELECTED REFERENCES: A Separate Reality - Page [235.8-247.7] (Two days later, on December 17, 1969...healed and you gap is closed.")

SPIRIT-DEER-[SPIRIT DEER]-(TOP): SEE: MAGICAL-DEER-[MAGICAL DEER]-(TOP)

SPIRIT-DESCENT-[THE DESCENT OF THE SPIRIT]: (TOP)

SELECTED REFERENCES: The Power of Silence - Page [87-154] (Right after a late lunch, while...or self-importance. Ruthlessness is sobriety.")

SPIRIT-DUSTING-LINK-[DUSTING THE LINK WITH THE SPIRIT]: (TOP)

SELECTED REFERENCES: The Power of Silence - Page [52-68] (The sun had not yet risen...what being a woman was like.")

SPIRIT-KNOCK-[THE KNOCK OF THE SPIRIT]: (TOP)

SELECTED REFERENCES: The Power of Silence - Page [25-51] (We returned to don Juan's house...its simplicity, that is determining our fate.")

SPIRIT-MANIFESTATIONS-[THE MANIFESTATIONS OF THE SPIRIT]: (TOP)

SELECTED REFERENCES: The Power of Silence - Page [1-24] (Don Juan, whenever it was pertinent...he said. "Her name was Talia.")

SPIRIT-MANIFESTATIONS-[THE MANIFESTATIONS OF THE SPIRIT]: (TOP)

SELECTED REFERENCES: The Power of Silence - Page [5.5-6.4] ("The first sorcery story I am...But that is another story.") The Power of Silence - Page [11.9-12.2] (I had no way of telling how...decision either to accept or reject it.) The Power of Silence - Page [20.7-20.9] (As the nagual watched the unconcern...one except the spirit as witness.) The Power of Silence - Page [29.7-30.1] (I told him that I had been...the ulterior arrangement of the abstract.")

SPIRIT-NASTY-ENCOUNTER-[AN ENCOUNTER WITH A NASTY SPIRIT]: (TOP)
SELECTED REFERENCES: **A Separate Reality - Page [234.1-234.4]** (There were many ways in which...and bear it until the morning.)

SPIRIT-NOTHING-GIVE-ENCOUNTER-[AN ENCOUNTER WITH THE SPIRIT WITH NOTHING TO GIVE]: (TOP)
SELECTED REFERENCES: **A Separate Reality - Page [228.6-232.5]** (We arrived in the same valley...are fortunate enough to find them.")

SPIRIT-SEEING-[SEEING THE SPIRIT]: (TOP)
SELECTED REFERENCES: **The Power of Silence - Page [87-106]** (Right after a late lunch, while...to start on our way back.)

SPIRIT-SEEING-[SEEING THE SPIRIT]: (TOP)
SELECTED REFERENCES: **The Power of Silence - Page [96.2-96.9]** (The young actor, hearing his own...was quite out of the ordinary.)

SPIRIT-SHINING-[SHINING THE SPIRIT]: (TOP)
SELECTED REFERENCES: **Journey to Ixtlan - Page [42.5-43.4]** ("No, let's talk about your father...were as weak as your father.)

SPIRIT-TRICKERY-[THE TRICKERY OF THE SPIRIT]: (TOP)
SELECTED REFERENCES: **The Power of Silence - Page [52-86]** (The sun had not yet risen...to a normal state of awareness.)

SPIRIT-WATER-HOLE-[THE SPIRIT OF THE WATER HOLE]: (TOP)
SELECTED REFERENCES: **A Separate Reality - Page [160.4-163.3]** (He took me to the mouth..."You will know that very soon.") **A Separate Reality - Page [165.8-167.2]** ("Now let us call the spirit...I got sick to my stomach.) **A Separate Reality - Page [226.6-228.4]** ("But all this is not important...you where to look for it.") **The Fire From Within - Page [93.2-93.4]** (He explained that the ancient seers...call allies do appear around waterholes.")

STALKING-INTENT-DREAMING-POSITION-[STALKING, INTENT, AND THE DREAMING POSITION]: (TOP)
SELECTED REFERENCES: **The Fire From Within - Page [167-182]** (The next day, in the early...the left side, while *dreaming together*.)

STALKING-KNOWLEDGE-WITHOUT-[STALKING WITHOUT KNOWLEDGE]: (TOP)
SELECTED REFERENCES: **The Eagle's Gift - Page [248.6-248.9]** (La Gorda believed that the men...that he would even convince himself.)

STALKING-MOODS-FOUR-[THE FOUR MOODS OF STALKING]: (TOP)
SELECTED REFERENCES: **The Power of Silence - Page [69-86]** (Don Juan said that I should...to a state of normal awareness.)

STALKING-ONESELF-JUAN-[DON JUAN STALKS HIMSELF]: (TOP)
SELECTED REFERENCES: **The Power of Silence - Page [54.4-68.9]** ("I've already told you the story...what being a woman was like.")

STALKING-STALKERS-[STALKING THE STALKERS]: (TOP)
SELECTED REFERENCES: **The Art of Dreaming - Page [183-198]** (At home, I soon realized that...inanimate matter or of living beings.)

STALKING-STALKERS-[STALKING THE STALKERS]: (TOP)
SELECTED REFERENCES: **The Art of Dreaming - Page [187.1-198.3]** (We went from the restaurant to...two were already in another world.)

STOPPING-WORLD-[STOPPING THE WORLD]: (TOP)
SELECTED REFERENCES: **Journey to Ixtlan - Page [1-230]** ("I understand you know a great...of everything he had taught me.)

STOPPING-WORLD-[STOPPING THE WORLD]: (TOP)
    SELECTED REFERENCES: **Journey to Ixtlan - Page [246-256]** (The next day as soon as...is the way of a sorcerer.")

STOPPING-WORLD-BOY-[STOPPING THE WORLD OF A YOUNG BOY]: (TOP)
    SELECTED REFERENCES: **Journey to Ixtlan - Page [x.2-xii.5]** (Don Juan and I had been...never be the same for him.")

STRANGULATION-CARLOS-[CARLOS' STRANGULATION]-(TOP): CARLOS-STRANGULATION-[CARLOS' STRANGULATION]-(TOP)

SUIT-JUAN-[DON JUAN'S SUIT]: (TOP)
    SELECTED REFERENCES: **Tales of Power - Page [102.3-104.5]** (I walked towards downtown on the...quiet park a few blocks away.) **Tales of Power - Page [161.4-161.8]** (There was one more thing that...but unaffected tone and walked away.) **The Fire From Within - Page [39.2-39.6]** (Don Juan's elucidation was interrupted because...back to it over and over.")

SULFUR-DUNES-LAND-[THE LAND OF THE SULFUR DUNES]-(TOP): SEE: PARALLEL-LINES-LAND-[THE LAND BETWEEN THE PARALLEL LINE]-(TOP)

SUNS-TWIN-WORLD-[WORLD OF THE TWIN SUNS]-(TOP): SEE: ZULEICA-DREAMING-CELESTIAL [ZULEICA'S CELESTIAL DREAMING]-(TOP)

SWEEPING-FLOOR-BELLY-[SWEEPING THE FLOOR WITH THE BELLY]: (TOP)
    SELECTED REFERENCES: **The Eagle's Gift - Page [257.4-258.2]** (Zuleica started then on another facet...my body in my sitting position.) **The Eagle's Gift - Page [260.5-261.1]** (Zuleica finally spoke to me...convinced that I needed to move.)

SWIMMING-CARLOS-FATHER-[CARLOS' SWIMMING STORY WITH HIS FATHER]-(TOP): SEE: CARLOS-SWIMMING-FATHER-[CARLOS' SWIMMING STORY WITH HIS FATHER]-(TOP)

T

TALES-ETERNITY-[TALES OF ETERNITY]-(TOP): SEE: ETERNITY-TALES-[TALES OF ETERNITY]-(TOP)

TALES-POWER-[TALES OF POWER]-(TOP): SEE: POWER-TALES-[TALES OF POWER]-(TOP)

TALIA-TALES-[TALES OF TALIA]: (TOP)
    SELECTED REFERENCES: The Power of Silence - Page [24.4] ("That woman was so powerful she..."Her name was Talia."). The Power of Silence - Page [94.3-96.9] (The nagual Elias then shifted his...have ever met," don Juan added.) The Power of Silence - Page [180.3-180.8] (There was also a mystery woman among...That, she said, was the fun part.)

TEACHINGS-[THE TEACHINGS]: (TOP)
    SELECTED REFERENCES: The Teachings of Don Juan - Page [27-188] (My notes on my first session...enemy of a man of knowledge.)

TEACHINGS-JUAN-[THE TEACHINGS OF DON JUAN]: (TOP)
    SELECTED REFERENCES: The Teachings of Don Juan - Page [13-256] (In the summer of 1960, while...of special consensus had pragmatic value.)

TENANT-[THE TENANT]: (TOP)
    SELECTED REFERENCES: The Art of Dreaming - Page [199-219] (There were no more dreaming practices...that has curled up on itself.")

TENANT-APPOINTMENT-UNAVOIDABLE-[THE UNAVOIDABILITY OF THE APPOINTMENT WITH THE TENANT]: (TOP)
    SELECTED REFERENCES: The Art of Dreaming - Page [214.1-214.3] ("Don't you think that the less..."Do you understand?" he repeated.)

TENANT-CARLOS-MEET-[CARLOS MEETS THE TENANT]-(TOP): SEE: WOMAN-CHURCH-[THE WOMAN IN THE CHURCH]-(TOP)

TENANT-ESCAPE-INORGANIC-BEINGS-[THE ESCAPE OF THE TENANT FROM THE REALM OF THE INORGANIC BEINGS]: (TOP)
    SELECTED REFERENCES: The Art of Dreaming - Page [245.7-246.5] ("She took me into another facet...think it's possible to fear anything.") The Art of Dreaming - Page [258.1-258.9] (What he was saying had no meaning...of that maneuver and much more.")

TENANT-GIFT-[THE TENANT'S GIFT]: (TOP)
    SELECTED REFERENCES: The Art of Dreaming - Page [249.3-249.4] (After a long pause, during which...here-and now energy of the universe.") The Art of Dreaming - Page [253.3-253.6] ("Your energy body is moving forward...In a time yet to come.") The Art of Dreaming - Page [259.1-259.3] (He did not answer. He gazed...one day you will comprehend them.") The Art of Dreaming - Page [260.4-260.5] ("But where do you think she...flying on the wings of intent.")

TENANT-JUAN-JOKE-[DON JUAN'S JOKE ON THE TENANT]: (TOP)
    SELECTED REFERENCES: The Art of Dreaming - Page [233.8-235.1] (Still feeling absurdly bashful, I automatically...I had no more laughter in me.) The Art of Dreaming - Page [255.6-255.9] (Don Juan asked me to tell them...don't like the old sorcerers' coerciveness.")

TENANT-JUAN-MEET-[DON JUAN MEETS THE TENANT]: (TOP)
    SELECTED REFERENCES: The Art of Dreaming - Page [218.8-219.2] ("Why do I have to continue...as being not funny but ghastly.)

TENANT-NAGUAL-LUJAN-[THE TENANT AND THE NAGUAL LUJAN]: (TOP)

SELECTED REFERENCES: **The Art of Dreaming** - Page [207.7-208.1] (He shrugged his shoulders, gesturing bewilderment..."You bet!" he exclaimed.)

TENANT-NAGUAL-SEBASTIAN-[THE TENANT AND THE NAGUAL SEBASTIAN]: (TOP)

SELECTED REFERENCES: **The Fire From Within** - Page [234.9-235.9] (It was in the early part...both show you the same sample.") **The Art of Dreaming** - Page [61.1-62.9] (But, for the moment, just let...me than I could have imagined.)

TENANT-NAGUAL-WOMAN-MEET-[THE NAGUAL WOMAN MEETS THE TENANT]: (TOP)

SELECTED REFERENCES: **The Art of Dreaming** - Page [245.1-245.8] ("How can you know it?" I shouted...how she actually escaped her captors.")

TENANT-TALES-[TALES OF THE TENANT]: (TOP)

SELECTED REFERENCES: **The Fire From Within** - Page [234.9-235.7] (It was in the early part...Toltec. One of the last survivors.) **The Power of Silence** - Page 57.7-58.4] (I reminded him that I had...ward and called him "the tenant.") **The Art of Dreaming** - Page [63.1-63.3] ("How did he get to live...what's out there, waiting for them.") **The Art of Dreaming** - Page [199.7-260.5] (There were no more dreaming practices...flying on the wings of intent.) **The Art of Dreaming** - Page [215.8-216.6] (Don Juan reminded me of a time...Sebastian, and subsequently as a woman.) **The Art of Dreaming** - Page [257.6-257.9] (Don Juan's expressed concern was that he...on your offer of free energy.")

TERMINAL-PATIENT-IMPECCABLE-SPIRIT-[THE IMPECCABLE SPIRIT OF A TERMINAL PATIENT]: (TOP)

SELECTED REFERENCES: **The Second Ring of Power** - Page [106.4-107.5] (I told them that they were...to attempt to move her arm.)

THIRD-POINT-[THE THIRD POINT]-(TOP): SEE: POINT-THIRD-[THE THIRD POINT]-(TOP)

THOUGHT-SOMERSAULT-[THE SOMERSAULT OF THOUGHT]: (TOP)

SELECTED REFERENCES: **The Power of Silence** - Page [106-116] (We walked into his house around...His goal has transcended his person.")

THUNDERBOLT-SORCERER-[A THUNDERBOLT SORCERER]-(TOP): SEE: SORCERER-THUNDERBOLT-[A THUNDERBOLT SORCERER]-(TOP)

TOLTEC-GHOULS-[THE TOLTEC GHOULS]: (TOP)

SELECTED REFERENCES: **The Eagle's Gift** - Page [25.1-26.3] ("The Nagual told me that in...long after the phantoms had vanished.") **The Fire From Within** - Page [231.4-246.1] (I arrived at don Genaro's house around. "We have a long walk.") **The Fire From Within** - Page [246.6-250.5] ("What Genaro and I wanted to do...but he was laughing at it.)

TOLTEC-POWER-ARRANGEMENT-[THE TOLTEC WARRIOR'S POWER ARRANGEMENT]: (TOP)

SELECTED REFERENCES: **The Second Ring of Power** - Page [312.9-314.1] (She made us all stand up...to perform was to change directions.)

TOLTEC-POWER-PLACE-[THE TOLTEC POWER PLACE]: (TOP)

SELECTED REFERENCES: **The Fire From Within** - Page [235.9-236.3] (I wanted to talk in order to...all the power of their awareness.)

TOLTEC-RUINS-[TOLTEC RUINS]-(TOP): SEE: PYRAMIDS-[PYRAMIDS AND TOLTEC RUINS]: (TOP)

TONAL-[THE TONAL]: (TOP)

SELECTED REFERENCES: **Tales of Power** - Page [132.6-138.9] ("They're all *tonal*," he said. "I...Indian it has been sheer bliss.")

TONAL-DAY-[THE DAY OF THE TONAL]: (TOP)
> SELECTED REFERENCES: Tales of Power - Page [128-145] (As we left the restaurant I ...wouldn't have it any other way.")

TONAL-ISLAND-[THE ISLAND OF THE TONAL]: (TOP)
> SELECTED REFERENCES: Tales of Power - Page [116-128] (Don Juan and I met again the...of the true pair, the *nagual*.")

TONAL-NAGUAL-[THE TONAL AND THE NAGUAL]: (TOP)
> SELECTED REFERENCES: Tales of Power - Page [102-209[(I walked towards downtown on the...they walked me to my car.)

TONAL-SHRINKING-[SHRINKING THE TONAL]: (TOP)
> SELECTED REFERENCES: Tales of Power - Page [145-162] (On Wednesday morning I left my...the wide avenue filled with cars.)

TREES-[TREES]: (TOP)
> SELECTED REFERENCES: The Eagle's Gift - Page [236.3-236.6] (While we were suspended from the...filled to the brim with it.)

TRUMPETER-PEERLESS-[THE PEERLESS TRUMPETER]: (TOP)
> SELECTED REFERENCES: The Eagle's Gift - Page [74.1-74.8] ("The Nagual Juan Matus said that...idiotic tune, the same peerless trumpeter.)

TRUTH-UNDERLYING-EXPOSING-[EXPOSING THE UNDERLYING TRUTH]: (TOP)
> SELECTED REFERENCES: The Power of Silence - Page [127.7-130.3] (Years before, I had been both...mischievousness, as he peered at me.)

TULIOS-FOUR-[THE FOUR TULIOS]: (TOP)
> SELECTED REFERENCES: The Power of Silence - Page [251.7-262.3] (Returning to his story, don Juan...the impression of being a shadow.)

TWIG-POWER-BREATHES-LIFE-[POWER BREATHES LIFE INTO A TWIG]-(TOP): SEE: POWER-BREATHES-LIFE-TWIG-[POWER BREATHES LIFE INTO A TWIG]-(TOP)

TWO-HUNDRED-TWENTY-BUTTOCKS-[TWO HUNDRED AND TWENTY BUTTOCKS]: (TOP)
> SELECTED REFERENCES: The Second Ring of Power - Page [183.5-183.7] (But la Gorda is still what the...can't do a thing for us.)

U

UNKNOWN-JOURNEY-[JOURNEY INTO THE UNKNOWN]: (TOP)
SELECTED REFERENCES: The Fire From Within - Page [79.7-79.9 (He explained that at the site...by a legion of strange things.)

UNOBTRUSIVENESS-ESSENCE-[THE ESSENCE OF UNOBTRUSIVENESS]: (TOP)
SELECTED REFERENCES: The Power of Silence - Page [258.9-259.3] (The nagual Julian introduced each in...knew that there were four Tulios.)

URCHIN-OPPORTUNITY-WORLD-[URCHINS IN THE STREET AND THE OPPORTUNITIES OF THE WORLD]: (TOP)
SELECTED REFERENCES: A Separate Reality - Page [20.2-22.5] (During my trip to see him...eating leftovers and licking the tables.")

V

VAGINA-COSMIC-THROUGH-[THROUGH THE COSMIC VAGINA]: (TOP)

SELECTED REFERENCES: The Eagle's Gift - Page [242.7-243.4] (We crossed. Silvio Manuel and Eligio seemed...hand, ready to hurl them in.)

VICENTE-GIFT-PLANTS-[DON VICENTE'S GIFT OF PLANTS]: (TOP)

SELECTED REFERENCES: A Separate Reality - Page [30.4-36.5] ("Those concoctions were really good," don...can do to salvage your gift.") The Eagle's Gift - Page [116.8-117.1] (I mentioned one more incident involving...minutes, more than ten years before.) The Eagle's Gift - Page [133.3-133.9] (The mention of Vicente's house brought...was going to be like him.)

VIDROS-LOS-[LOS VIDROS]: (TOP)

SELECTED REFERENCES: A Separate Reality - Page [45.1-48.3] (It was late afternoon when we left...from behind, but there were none.)

VIOLENCE-LIGHT-[THE LIGHT OF VIOLENCE]: (TOP)

SELECTED REFERENCES: A Separate Reality - Page [137.7-137.8] (I was on the verge of ripping...time the violence was against myself.)

VISIONS-[VISIONS]-(TOP): SEE: CARLOS-VISION-MOTHER-[CARLOS' VISION OF HIS MOTHER]-(TOP), CHURCH-VISION-[A VISION OF THE CHURCH]-(TOP), GAIT-POWER-VISION-[A VISION OF THE GAIT OF POWER]-(TOP), WORLD-APPARITIONS-[THE WORLD OF APPARITIONS], HELL-VISIONS-[VISIONS OF HELL]-(TOP)

W

WALK-TREES-EDGE-*[THE WARRIOR'S WALK TO THE EDGE OF THE TREES]-(TOP): SEE: WARRIOR-WALK-TREE-[THE WARRIOR'S WALK TO THE EDGE OF THE TREES]-(TOP)*

WALL-DIVING-INTO-DREAMING-*[DIVING INTO A WALL IN DREAMING]: (TOP)*
      SELECTED REFERENCES: **The Art of Dreaming - Page [158.1-158.7]** (The voice of the dreaming emissary...against the wall of my room.)

WALL-FOG-*[THE WALL OF FOG]-(TOP): SEE: FOG-WALL-[THE WALL OF FOG]-(TOP)*

WALL-FOG-SNATCHED-BEHIND-*[BEING SNATCHED BEHIND THE WALL OF FOG]-(TOP): SEE: FOG-WALL-SNATCHED-BEHIND-[BEING SNATCHED BEHIND THE WALL OF FOG]-(TOP)*

WARRIOR-AVAILABLE-*[THE AVAILABLE WARRIOR]: (TOP)*
      SELECTED REFERENCES: **Journey to Ixtlan - Page [60.5-70.8]** (The wind was cold. Suddenly he...moves away leaving hardly a mark.".)

WARRIOR-BATTLE-LAST-*[THE WARRIORS' LAST BATTLE ON EARTH]: (TOP)*
      SELECTED REFERENCES: **Journey to Ixtlan - Page [78-88]** (Around mid-afternoon, after we had roamed...to roam in this marvelous desert.")

WARRIOR-COURIER-*[THE WARRIOR COURIER]: (TOP)*
      SELECTED REFERENCES: **The Eagle's Gift - Page [195.3-196.4]** (As we were leaving the plaza...Juan Tuma, I forgot my anger.)

WARRIOR-CRY-ANIMAL-*[THE WARRIORS' ANIMAL CRY]: (TOP)*
      SELECTED REFERENCES: **The Second Ring of Power - Page [211.5-211.6]** (In order to calm myself down...the warmth and protection of the earth.)

WARRIOR-DEATH-STOP-*[THE WARRIOR STOPS DEATH]: (TOP)*
      SELECTED REFERENCES: **The Power of Silence - Page [21.1-22.6]** (The nagual Elias, having made his...the impossible. He healed the young man.)

WARRIOR-DIRECTION-CHANGING-*[CHANGING THE WARRIORS' DIRECTION]: (TOP)*
      SELECTED REFERENCES: **The Second Ring of Power - Page [34.7-36.5]** ("One day I was alone in...he gave me a new direction.") **The Second Ring of Power - Page [41.7-41.9]** ("After turning my head that first...Something must have happened.) **The Second Ring of Power - Page [62.2-62.4]** ("When the Nagual changed me, he...but because he is my son.) **The Second Ring of Power - Page [129.3-129.7]** ("One day, very late in the afternoon...changed the direction of my eyes.) **The Second Ring of Power - Page [313.6-314.4]** (She explained that the particular formation...entailed putting on our second face.)

WARRIOR-EXECUTION-SQUAD-*[THE WARRIOR'S EXECUTION SQUAD]-(TOP): SEE: WARRIOR-WALK-TREE-[THE WARRIOR'S WALK TO THE EDGE OF THE TREES]-(TOP)*

WARRIOR-FACES-TOLTEC-TWO-*[THE TWO FACES OF THE TOLTEC WARRIOR]: (TOP)*
      SELECTED REFERENCES: **The Second Ring of Power - Page [312.9-321.9]** (She made us all stand up...on you, you became solid again.")

WARRIOR-FAREWELL-[THE WARRIOR'S FAREWELL: (TOP)
    SELECTED REFERENCES: **Tales of Power - Page [279.3-279.9]** (I sat quietly but my spirit...a warrior's way of saying farewell.)

WARRIOR-GAINS-BALANCE-[WARRIORS BALANCE THEIR EXCESSIVE GAINS]: (TOP)
    SELECTED REFERENCES: **The Eagle's Gift - Page [204.8-205.1]** (His proclivity to remain in a state...the silent force behind don Juan.)

WARRIOR-GAZE-[THE WARRIORS' GAZE]: (TOP)
    SELECTED REFERENCES: **Tales of Power - Page [234.6-235.9]** ("That was my quickest way of...larger, or different in some way.)

WARRIOR-GOURD-[THE WARRIORS' GOURD]: (TOP)
    SELECTED REFERENCES: **The Second Ring of Power - Page [37.4-38.5]** (In desperation, I suppose, he introduced...In both cases his gourd helped him.) **The Second Ring of Power - Page [52.1-52.3]** ("How did the girls manage to stop...two allies and makes them help him.)

WARRIOR-IMPECCABILITY-TICKET-[THE WARRIORS' TICKET TO IMPECCABILITY]: (TOP)
    SELECTED REFERENCES: **The Power of Silence - Page [170-195]** (It had gotten dark while don...I've kept mine in mint condition.")

WARRIOR-JUMP-[THE WARRIOR'S JUMP INTO THE ABYSS]: (TOP)
    SELECTED REFERENCES: **Tales of Power - Page [280.8-295.1]** (Don Genaro signaled with his hand...jumped and then I was alone.) **The Second Ring of Power - Page [1.3-2.2]** (A flat barren mountaintop on the...say anything to clarify their nature.) **The Second Ring of Power - Page [43.4-43.6]** ("The Nagual took us , me and...happened, the four of you jumped.") **The Second Ring of Power - Page [178.3-179.3]** (In a careful and deliberate manner...don't know how I got there.") **The Second Ring of Power - Page [205.8-221.4]** ("Nestor also jumped into the abyss...my earth. It's my indulging perhaps.") **The Fire From Within - Page [299.8-300.2]** (After that, don Juan made us...assemblage points and assembled other worlds.)

WARRIOR-JUMP-PRELUDE-[THE PRELUDE TO THE WARRIOR'S JUMP INTO THE ABYSS]: (TOP)
    SELECTED REFERENCES: **Tales of Power - Page [261.3-278.6]** (I spent the day by myself...perception and fly into that infinitude.")

WARRIOR-LAST-STAND-[THE WARRIORS' LAST STAND]: (TOP)
    SELECTED REFERENCES: **Journey to Ixtlan - Page [139-155]** (Around ten A.M. don Juan walked...to the south. To the vastness.)

WARRIOR-LAST-STAND-SITE-[THE SITE OF THE WARRIORS' LAST STAND]: (TOP)
    SELECTED REFERENCES: **Journey to Ixtlan - Page [148.2-150.9]** (It was late afternoon when I...of nonsense for the time being.") **Journey to Ixtlan - Page [153.4-153.9]** ("I will have to come with you...there the warrior dances to his death.)

WARRIOR-MOOD-[THE MOOD OF THE WARRIOR]: (TOP)
    SELECTED REFERENCES: **Journey to Ixtlan - Page [105-121]** (I drove up to don Juan's...It takes power to do that.")

WARRIOR-PARTY-LAST-HOURS-[A WARRIOR'S PARTY'S LAST HOURS ON EARTH]: (TOP)
    SELECTED REFERENCES: **The Eagle's Gift - Page [304.3-314.3]** (When we got to the house...And then the lights were gone.)

WARRIOR-PARTY-LEADER-[THE LEADER OF THE WARRIOR'S PARTY]: (TOP)
    SELECTED REFERENCES: **The Eagle's Gift - Page [149.6-149.7]** (In other words, Silvio Manuel could...the time they didn't do anything.") **The Eagle's Gift - Page [200.6-200.7]** (Don Juan spoke to the man...leader of the whole warrior's party.) **The Eagle's Gift - Page**

[204.5-205.1] (Silvio Manuel's case was different...the silent force behind don Juan.) **The Eagle's Gift - Page [219.9-220.1]** (The one who never forgot was...them years to accomplish both tasks.)

WARRIOR-PIECES-[THE WARRIOR IN PIECES]: (TOP)
SELECTED REFERENCES: **Tales of Power - Page [69.3-72.7]** (Don Genaro sat up straight and...the ramada of don Juan's house.)

WARRIOR-PREDILECTION-TWO-[THE PREDILECTION OF TWO WARRIORS]: (TOP)
SELECTED REFERENCES: **Tales of Power - Page [278-295]** (Don Juan woke me up at...jumped and then I was alone.)

WARRIOR-STRATEGY-[THE STRATEGY OF THE WARRIOR]: (TOP)
SELECTED REFERENCES: **A Separate Reality - Page [181.1-182.6]** (I raised the point that it...I simply will not come around.")

WARRIOR-TREES-[WARRIOR TREES]: (TOP)
SELECTED REFERENCES: **The Power of Silence - Page [39.7-40.6]** (It was as cool and quiet...as we discuss my definitive journey.)

WARRIOR-VIGIL-POSITION-RELIEVING-ONESELF-[RELIEVING ONESELF WHILE IN THE WARRIORS' POSITION OF VIGIL]: (TOP)
SELECTED REFERENCES: **The Fire From Within - Page [149.5-150.1]** ("The nagual Julian kept me once...was really there behind the bushes.)

WARRIOR-WALK-TREES-[THE WARRIOR'S WALK TO THE EDGE OF THE TREES]: (TOP)
SELECTED REFERENCES: **Tales of Power - Page [284.8-287.3]** ("Waiting to fulfill that task is...by the sharpshooters from the unknown.") **The Fire From Within - Page [18.6-18.7]** ("Usually, only four attributes are played...firing squad, so to speak.")

WATER-GREEN-BECOMING-[BECOMING GREEN IN THE WATER]: (TOP)
SELECTED REFERENCES: **A Separate Reality - Page [163.3-164.3]** (Around 11:30 A.M. we sat under...awareness of a brilliant, soothing greenness.) **A Separate Reality - Page [174.5-175.2]** (I became aware that I was...Get out of it! Out! Out!") **The Eagle's Gift - Page [179.7-180.7]** ("I think you must be aware...aware of what he is doing.") **The Second Ring of Power - Page [300.9-301.5]** ("All of us are terrified of...wasn't you fate to be moderate.")

WATER-HOLE-SPIRIT-TAPPING-[TAPPING THE SPIRIT OF THE WATER HOLE]: (TOP)
SELECTED REFERENCES: **A Separate Reality - Page [160.4-163.3]** ("Let's walk, then," he said..."You will know that very soon.") **A Separate Reality - Page [168.5-169.2]** (I realized that I had forgotten...trying to find out something else.") **A Separate Reality - Page [170.6-170.8]** ("Apparently you have no problem with water...keep your thoughts on something else.") **A Separate Reality - Page [179.8-180.3]** (I did not know what he was...it can take you any time.") **A Separate Reality - Page [213.5-214.1]** ("What you felt this morning was...to prepare yourself for the struggle.) **A Separate Reality - Page [226.9-227.9]** ("What is a spirit catcher...after pointing out the water canyon.) **Journey to Ixtlan - Page [93.5 104.9]** (He began to walk into the...know it was made to collapse.)

WATER-SEEING-[SEEING THE WATER]: (TOP)
SELECTED REFERENCES: **A Separate Reality - Page [169.5-178.9]** (Working on my notes I had...perhaps even as far as Brazil.") **Tales of Power - Page [85.7-86.5]** (He refused to say one more word...sleep and had a portentous dream.) **The Second Ring of Power - Page [300.9-301.5]** ("All of us are terrified of...wasn't you fate to be moderate.")

WATER-TRANSPORTED-[TRANSPORTED ON THE POWER OF WATER]: (TOP)
SELECTED REFERENCES: **The Fire From Within - Page [83.4-85.1]** (He continued then with his elucidation...a quagmire with no way out.) **The Fire From Within - Page [87.1-87.5]** ("Let me explain what we are...ditch behind his house in northern Mexico.) **The Fire From Within - Page [90.2-91.3]** ("What really took place out there...that came to look us over.")

*WATERFALL-GENARO-[DON GENARO SCALES THE WATERFALL]-
(TOP): SEE: GENARO-WATERFALL-[DON GENARO SCALES THE
WATERFALL]-(TOP)*

WEST-[WESTERLY WOMEN]: (TOP)
SELECTED REFERENCES: The Eagle's Gift - Page [196.5-204.5] (My next encounter with don Juan's...a performance staged by someone else.) The Eagle's Gift - Page [208.4-208.8] (For me one of the most pleasant...their outrages made me feel sad.)

*WHISTLE-ALLIES-[THE WHISTLE TO DISPERSE THE ALLIES]-(TOP):
SEE: ALLIES-WHISTLE-[THE WHISTLE TO DISPERSE THE ALLIES]-
(TOP)*

*WILL-CAR-WON'T START-[WILL AND THE CAR THAT WON'T START]-
(TOP): SEE: CAR-WON'T-START-WILL-[THE CAR THAT WON'T
START]-(TOP)*

WILL-MOVING-BY-[MOVING BY THE WILL]: (TOP)
SELECTED REFERENCES: A Separate Reality - Page [122.8-123.4] (I was very serious about that...said in a very slow monotone.) A Separate Reality - Page [126.7-127.4] ("You really know how to talk...not sure of what I did.") A Separate Reality - Page [129.3-129.4] (I saw the gnat whirling around...looking at an unbelievably enormous animal.) A Separate Reality - Page [130.9-131.2] (Suddenly the guardian appeared again at...in the middle of don Juan's room.) A Separate Reality - Page [132.5-133.1] ("Is smoking the only way to...something you can fool around with.") A Separate Reality - Page [154.8-157.1] ("You have to walk," he said..."Good, good work," he said reassuringly.) A Separate Reality - Page [158.6-158.7s] ("Don't fix your gaze on anything...We stopped by the irrigation ditch.) The Eagle's Gift - Page [50.4-53.1] (I *dreamed* once that I woke up...a chance to talk to him.) The Eagle's Gift - Page [152.6-153.1] (We began to move in unison...spontaneously adopted the *dreaming* position.) The Eagle's Gift - Page [159.7-159.9] (She was cautioning me that all...La Gorda was out of synchronization, too.) The Eagle's Gift - Page [253.7-253.8] (Zuleica's voice ordered me to stand...contracting my muscles to get up.) The Eagle's Gift - Page [257.4-258.2] (Zuleica started then on another facet...my body in my sitting position.) The Eagle's Gift - Page [260.1-261.2] (Zuleica said that first of all...was in fact a rational state.)

WILL-PUMA-JUAN-[DON JUAN AND THE PUMA]: (TOP)
SELECTED REFERENCES: A Separate Reality - Page [152.8-153.2] ("One day I was in the...dear life, holding onto his hat.)

WIND-[WIND]: (TOP)
SELECTED REFERENCES: The Second Ring of Power - Page [38.4-41.7] ("Well, the Nagual acquainted me with... because he was baffled by me.) The Second Ring of Power - Page [51.7s-52.1] ("She did fine for a while...she was too weak to walk.")

*WINGS-INTENT-FLYING-[FLYING ON THE WINGS OF INTENT]-(TOP):
SEE: INTENT-WINGS-FLYING-[FLYING ON THE WINGS OF INTENT]-
(TOP)*

WITNESS-IMPROVISATION-[THE WITNESS' IMPROVISATION]: (TOP)
SELECTED REFERENCES: Tales of Power - Page [289.9-290.3] ("Witness, please squeeze your spirit catcher...helpful in the best way he could.)

*WITNESSING-TONAL-NAGUAL-[WITNESSING THE TONAL AND THE
NAGUAL]: (TOP)*
SELECTED REFERENCES: Tales of Power - Page [202.5-209.2] (After a while they both leaned...of view of my ordinary perception.)

WITNESSING-TREE-[WITNESSING A TREE]: (TOP)
SELECTED REFERENCES: Tales of Power - Page [202.6-203.4] (They whispered in my ears until I...all capacity to differentiate my perceptions.)

WOMAN-CHURCH-[THE WOMAN IN THE CHURCH]: (TOP)
     SELECTED REFERENCES: **The Art of Dreaming - Page [220-240]** (Don Juan and I sat in silence...into a twirling descent into blackness.)

WOMAN-WORST-THING-[THE WORST THING THAT CAN HAPPEN TO A WOMAN]: (TOP)
     SELECTED REFERENCES: **The Eagle's Gift - Page [133.9-134.3]** ("Remembering Vicente makes me think about...like such an ass with you.")

WORLD-APPARITIONS-[THE WORLD OF APPARITIONS]: (TOP)
     SELECTED REFERENCES: **The Fire From Within - Page [130.8-131.2]** (I could hardly stand. My legs...people when something swished me away.) **The Fire From Within - Page [215.5-215.7]** (I felt a great pressure all...And we were walking on the clouds.) **The Power of Silence - Page [96.2-96.9]** (The young actor, hearing his own...was quite out of the ordinary.)

WORLD-BLACK-TALES-[TALES OF THE BLACK WORLD]: (TOP)
     SELECTED REFERENCES: **The Fire From Within - Page [292.3-295.3]** (The instant I saw that, I...it in order to escape death.")

WORLD-DOMED-[THE DOMED WORLD]-(TOP): SEE: DOMED-WORLD-[THE DOMED WORLD]-(TOP)

WORLD-INORGANIC-BEINGS-[THE WORLD OF THE INORGANIC BEINGS]-(TOP): SEE: INORGANIC-BEINGS-WORLD-[THE WORLD OF THE INORGANIC BEINGS]-(TOP)

WORLD-LUMINOUS-[THE LUMINOUS WORLD]: (TOP)
     SELECTED REFERENCES: **The Fire From Within - Page [215.5-215.7]** (I felt a great pressure all...And we were walking on the clouds.)

WORLD-OTHER-ARRANGEMENT-[THE ARRANGEMENT OF THE OTHER WORLD]: (TOP)
     SELECTED REFERENCES: **A Separate Reality - Page [98.6-99.4]** (I don't remember what prompted don...looked at me and smiled knowingly.

WORLD-PURPLE-[THE VIOLET-PURPLE WORLD]: (TOP)
     SELECTED REFERENCES: **The Fire From Within - Page [215.3-215.4]** (What I first detected, after *seeing*...of irregular concentric circles were everywhere.)

WORLD-TWIN-SUNS-[THE WORLD OF THE TWIN SUNS]-(TOP): SEE: SEE: ZULEICA-DREAMING-CELESTIAL-[ZULEICA'S CELESTIAL DREAMING]-(TOP)

WORM-CAVORTING-WITH-[CAVORTING WITH THE GIANT WORM]: (TOP)
     SELECTED REFERENCES: **The Fire From Within - Page [150.3-152.5]** (I did not have time to get...down and put on my clothes.)

WORM-DEATH-GIANT-[DEATH IN THE MOUTH OF A GIANT WORM]: (TOP)
     SELECTED REFERENCES: **The Second Ring of Power - Page [219.2-220.3]** (His claim was staggering to me...a long vision. Don't you see?")

WORTHY-OPPONENT-[A WORTHY OPPONENT]: (TOP)
     SELECTED REFERENCES: **Journey to Ixtlan - Page [214-230]** (My traps were perfect; the setting...of everything he had taught me.)

WRITING-EXERCISE-SORCERY-[WRITING AS AN EXERCISE IN SORCERY]: (TOP)
     SELECTED REFERENCES: **Tales of Power - Page [200.9-201.2]** ("Hey! I've got an idea," he...he be able to read it?") **The Power of Silence - Page [xiv.5-xiv.7]** ("Of course, you're not a writer...but rather an exercise in sorcery.")

Y

YOUTH-[YOUTH]: (TOP)
　　　　SELECTED REFERENCES: The Eagle's Gift - Page [267.3-267.7] (Physically she looked exactly like Nelida...girl made up to look old.) **The Eagle's Gift - Page [271.3-271.4]** (I felt obligated to defend myself...hurry in her laughter, no pressure.) **The Eagle's Gift - Page [291.9-292.1]** (I had never been in that...She was younger and more powerful.)

Z

ZOILA-ZULEICA-[ZOILA AND ZULEICA]: (TOP)
> SELECTED REFERENCES: The Eagle's Gift - Page [196.5-204.5] (My next encounter with don Juan's...a performance staged by someone else.)

ZULEICA-DREAMING-CELESTIAL-[ZULEICA'S CELESTIAL DREAMING]: (TOP)
> SELECTED REFERENCES: The Eagle's Gift - Page [262.8-265.9] (As a traveler in *dreaming* then...having my own tales of eternity.)

ZULEICA-DREAMING-INSTRUCTION-[ZULEICA'S DREAMING INSTRUCTION]-(TOP): SEE: DREAMING-INSTRUCTION-[THE WARRIORS' DREAMING INSTRUCTION]-(TOP)

AN ORGANIZATIONAL OUTLINE FOR A CATALOG OF ONE THOUSAND SECRETS

Author's Note: It is my intent that this outline be utilized in conjunction with both subsets of *A Catalog of One Thousand Secrets* to aid the reader in creating a personal overview on the thousands of terms and topics contained within the Toltec warriors' dialogue. Please remember that this outline is simply my personal attempt to reflect the organizational formats used by don Juan himself, and as such, it should not interfere with your own interpretation of this material.

I. **THE MYSTERY OF THE LUMINOUS BEINGS:** *SEE; MYSTERY-(ALL); WORLD-MYSTERIOUS-(ALL); LUMINOUS-BEINGS-(ALL); MAN-(ALL); ASSEMBLAGE-POINT-SECRETS*

   A) **THE RIDDLE OF THE MIND:** *SEE: RIDDLE-MIND*

      1) **THE EXPLANATION OF AWARENESS:** *SEE: AWARENESS-EXPLANATION; AWARENESS-TRUTHS-(ALL)*
         a) **THE EAGLE'S EMANATIONS:** *SEE: EAGLE-EMANATIONS-(ALL); LINES-WORLD-(ALL); FORCE-ROLLING*
         b) **THE EAGLE:** *SEE: EAGLE-(ALL)*
         c) **THE LUMINOUS COCOON:** *SEE: LUMINOUS-COCOON-(ALL); LUMINOUS-SHELL; GAP-(ALL); FRONT-PLATE*
         d) **THE FIXATION OF AWARENESS:** *SEE: AWARENESS-FIXATION; ASSEMBLAGE-POINT-FIXATION-(ALL); ATTENTION-FIRST-FIXATION; ATTENTION-SECOND-FIXATION; ASSEMBLAGE-POINT-IMMOVABLE*
         e) **PERCEPTION AND ALIGNMENT:** *SEE: PERCEPTION-(ALL); ALIGNMENT-(ALL); PERCEIVERS-WE-ARE; PERCEIVING-(ALL)*
         f) **THE ASSEMBLAGE POINT:** *SEE: ASSEMBLAGE-POINT-(ALL)*
         g) **MOVING THE ASSEMBLAGE POINT:** *SEE: ASSEMBLAGE-POINT-MOVE-(ALL); ASSEMBLAGE-POINT-DISPLACEMENT-TYPES; ASSEMBLAGE-POINT-SHIFT-(ALL); ASSEMBLAGE-POINT-WALKING; POWER-PLANTS; GAIT-POWER; NAGUAL-BLOW-(ALL)*
         h) **THE INTRUSION OF INTENT:** *SEE: INTENT-INTERVENTION*

i) TOTAL AWARENESS: *SEE: AWARENESS-TOTAL; FREEDOM-TOTAL; PERCEPTION-TOTAL; TOTAL-BEING; TOTALITY; TOTALITY-REGAINING; WARRIOR-FREEDOM-TOTAL; WARRIOR-TOTALITY; HUMAN-ALTERNATIVES-POSSIBILITIES-POTENTIAL*

2) THE MAGIC OF AWARENESS: *SEE: AWARENESS-(ALL); BEING-MAGIC-OF-OUR; MAGICAL-BEINGS; MAN-MAGIC-GIFT; OPENING-AWARENESS-MAGICAL-TWO; WARRIOR-MAGIC; EXISTENCE-HEIGHTENED*

3) THE ORGANIZATION OF ATTENTION: *SEE: ATTENTION-(ALL)*

   a) THE FIRST ATTENTION: *SEE: ATTENTION-FIRST-(ALL); TONAL-(ALL); KNOWN-(ALL); REASON-(ALL): THINKING-(ALL); TALKING-(ALL); POWER-RING-FIRST; BODY-PHYSICAL-(ALL); BOUNDARIES-(ALL), DOING-(ALL)*

   b) THE SECOND ATTENTION: *SEE: ATTENTION-SECOND-(ALL); UNKNOWN-(ALL); KNOWLEDGE-SILENT-(ALL); POWER-RING-SECOND; ENERGY-BODY-(ALL)*

   c) THE THIRD ATTENTION: *SEE: ATTENTION-THIRD-(ALL); UNKNOWABLE-(ALL): ETERNITY-(ALL)*

4) THE MIND: *SEE: MIND-(ALL); INVENTORY-(ALL); SANITY; INSANITY*

5) THE MOLD OF MAN: *SEE: GOD-(ALL); FAITH-RELIGIOUS; PRAYER; MORALITY; EVIL; HEAVEN; HELL*

B) THE RIDDLE OF THE HEART: *SEE: RIDDLE-HEART; AWARENESS-PERCEPTION-GIVES-RISE; AWARENESS-PERCEPTION-UNIT*

   1) THE PRINCIPLES OF STALKING: *SEE: STALKING-(ALL); STALKERS-(ALL); RECAPITULATION; CRATE*

   2) IN SUPPORT OF STALKING: *SEE: PETTY-TYRANT-(ALL); POETRY*

C) THE RIDDLE OF THE SPIRIT: *SEE: RIDDLE-SPIRIT*

   1) A RETURN TO THE ABSTRACT: *SEE: ABSTRACT-(ALL); SPIRIT-(ALL); NAGUAL-(ALL); INTENT-(ALL)*

   2) THE RULE: *SEE: RULE-(ALL)*

   3) ACQUIRING WILL: *SEE: WILL-(ALL)*

   4) FROM WILL TO INTENT: *SEE: WILL-INTENT-MYSTERY; INTENT-(ALL); INTENDING-(ALL); EYES-(ALL)*

D) THE RIDDLE OF THE DREAMER AND THE DREAMED: *SEE: RIDDLE-DREAMER-DREAMED*

1) <u>THE PRINCIPLES OF DREAMING:</u> *SEE: DREAMING-(ALL); DREAMER-(ALL); DREAMS-(ALL); HUMAN-JUNKPILE*

2) <u>THE DREAMING BODY:</u> *SEE: DREAMING-BODY-(ALL); ENERGY-BODY-(ALL); ENERGY-SHAPE; DOUBLE; OTHER-SELF; PARALLEL-BEING*

3) <u>IN SUPPORT OF DREAMING:</u> *SEE: ROUTINES-DISRUPTING; GAIT-POWER; NOT-DOING-(ALL); GAZING-(ALL)*

4) <u>THE SORCERERS' EXPLANATION:</u> *SEE: SORCERER-EXPLANATION*

II. **<u>THE PATH TO POWER'S PROMISE:</u>** *SEE: KNOWLEDGE-VS-POWER; KNOWLEDGE-PATH-(ALL); KNOWLEDGE-(ALL); POWER-(ALL); NAGUALISM; REALIZATION, POWER-PROMISE*

A) <u>THE WARRIORS' WAY:</u> *SEE: WARRIOR-WAY; WARRIOR-(ALL); WARRIORSHIP-(ALL)*

1) <u>THE WARRIORS' CHALLENGE:</u> *SEE: WARRIOR-CHALLENGE; WARRIOR-FORTUNE; BIRD-FREEDOM*
   a) <u>THE WARRIORS' ATTITUDE:</u> *SEE: WARRIOR-ATTITUDE; WARRIOR-MOOD*
      i) <u>BECOMING A HUNTER OF POWER:</u> *SEE: HUNTER-(ALL)*
      ii) <u>INTERNALIZING THE TRUTHS ABOUT AWARENESS:</u> *SEE: AWARENESS-TRUTH-(ALL)*
      iii) <u>ACCEPTING THE CONTRADICTIONS OF WARRIORSHIP:</u> *SEE: WARRIOR-CONTRADICTION-KNOWLEDGE*
      iv) <u>RECOGNIZING THE PATH WITH HEART:</u> *SEE: PATH-HEART-WITH; WARRIOR-SHIELDS; WARRIOR-JOY; WARRIOR-JOURNEY-POWER-PATH-HEART*
      v) <u>THE WARRIORS' ENEMIES:</u> *SEE: WARRIOR-ENEMIES-FOUR-NATURAL*
   b) <u>THE WARRIORS' STRATEGY:</u> *SEE: WARRIOR-STRATEGY; STRATEGY-(ALL)*
      i) <u>THE WARRIORS' ATTRIBUTES:</u> *SEE: WARRIOR-ATTRIBUTES*
      ii) <u>THE ACCESSIBILITY AND INACCESSIBILITY OF WARRIORS:</u> *SEE: WARRIOR-ACCESSIBILITY; WARRIOR-AVAILABILITY; WARRIOR-FOG-CREATE; ROUTINES-ACCESSIBILITY; WARRIOR-UNAVAILABILITY; OMENS; SPIRIT-GESTURE; INDICATIONS-SPIRIT*
      iii) <u>WARRIORS STALK THEMSELVES:</u> *SEE: STALKING-ONESELF; STALKING-JOLT; RUTHLESSNESS-(ALL)*
      iv) <u>WARRIORS TRANSFORM THEMSELVES:</u> *SEE: WARRIOR-TRANSFORMATION; FACADE-TRANSFORMING; CONTINUITY; CHANGE-(ALL)*

WARRIOR-DUALISM; PERCEPTUAL-DUALISM; CRACK-WORLDS; DOOR-ONLY; PARALLEL-LINES; BALANCE

A) <u>THE TONAL:</u> *SEE: TONAL-(ALL)*

B) <u>THE NAGUAL:</u> *SEE: NAGUAL-(ALL)*

ii) <u>THE FORCE OF PERCEPTION:</u> *SEE: PERCEPTION-FORCE*

  I) <u>BREAKING THE BARRIER OF PERCEPTION:</u> *SEE: PERCEPTION-BARRIER-BREAKING*

  II) <u>THE BUBBLE OF PERCEPTION:</u> *SEE: PERCEPTION-BUBBLE*

  III) <u>THE EARTH'S BOOST:</u> *SEE: EARTH; EARTH-BOOST*

  IV) <u>THE WINGS OF PERCEPTION:</u> *SEE: PERCEPTION-WINGS; THOUGHT-SOMERSAULT; INTENT-FLYING-WINGS; FLIGHT-UNKNOWN-INTO*

iii) <u>TOTAL FREEDOM:</u> *SEE: WARRIOR-FREEDOM-TOTAL; WARRIOR-ATTAINMENT; WARRIOR-GOAL*

  I) <u>THE FIRE FROM WITHIN:</u> *SEE: FIRE-WITHIN*

  II) <u>THE EAGLE'S GIFT:</u> *SEE: EAGLE-GIFT*

  III) <u>THE PROMISE OF POWER:</u> *SEE: POWER-PROMISE; POWER-PROMISE-FALSE*

B) <u>THE SORCERERS' WAY:</u> *SEE: SORCERER-(ALL); SORCERY-(ALL); TALES-POWER; ABSTRACT-CORES-(ALL); ALLIES-(ALL); INORGANIC-BEINGS-(ALL); TOLTECS-(ALL); ANIMAL-FORMS-ADOPTING; ATLANTEANS; BRUJO; DIABLERO-(ALL); SEER-OLD; EVIL; ABERRATION-MORBIDITY; OBSESSION; INDOLENCE; PYRAMIDS; SCOUTS; TENANT-(ALL); DEATH-DEFIERS*

C) <u>THE WARRIOR-SORCERERS' EQUILIBRIUM:</u> *SEE: WARRIORSHIP-VS-SORCERY; STALKING-STALKERS; STALKING-ULTIMATE; INORGANIC-BEINGS-REFUSING; SEER-NEW; CYCLE-NEW; SOBRIETY-UNDERSTANDING-VS-CAPRICIOUSNESS-SELF-IMPORTANCE; EQUILIBRIUM; WARRIOR-EQUILIBRIUM; BALANCE; HARMONY; VICTORY-(ALL); WARRIOR-CONTROLLED-FOLLY; WARRIOR-CONTRADICTION-KNOWLEDGE; FREEDOM; ATTENTION-THIRD-(ALL); UNKNOWABLE-(ALL)*